San Diego Christian College
2100 Greenfield Drive
El Cajon, CA 92019

CLOSER WALK®
NEW TESTAMENT
NEW INTERNATIONAL VERSION

Dr. Bruce H. Wilkinson
Executive Editor

Calvin W. Edwards
Senior Editor

Paula Kirk
Managing Editor

 Walk Thru the Bible Ministries, Inc.
Atlanta, Georgia

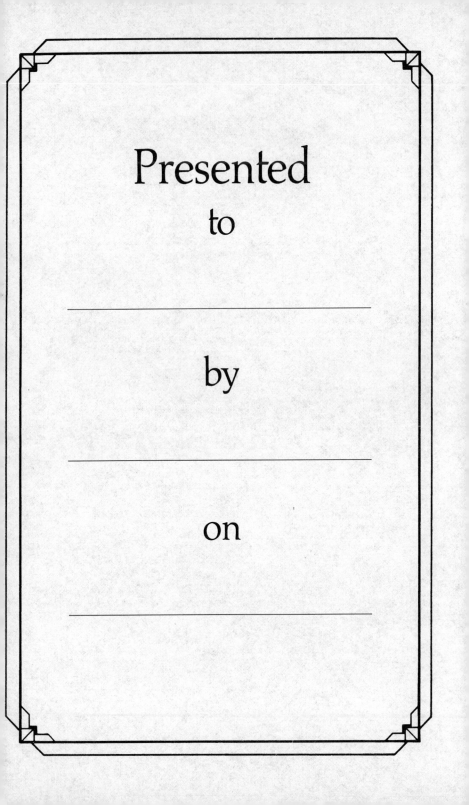

Presented
to

_____

by

_____

on

_____

Introduction

You are holding in your hands a book designed to help you in your spiritual walk. *The Closer Walk New Testament* brings together insightful devotionals from Walk Thru the Bible's *Closer Walk* reading guide and the highly readable New International Version of the Bible.

With this New Testament you can spend a fruitful time each day in God's Word by gaining practical devotional insights related to the Scripture you've read. At the end of one year you will have read the New Testament through at an easy, manageable pace. But more than that, you will find your relationship with the Lord deepening as you spend time reading and meditating on his Word.

Not only is *The Closer Walk New Testament* appropriate for personal devotions. Churches as well can use it in Bible study groups or simply to encourage congregational reading of God's Word.

As a result of using *The Closer Walk New Testament,* you will see the New Testament Scripture in a new light as you find practical answers to the perplexing problems you face each day. From great men and women of faith you will learn how to worship God in an intimate and personal way . . . how to handle your heartaches . . . how to praise God through prayer and Biblical meditation. In short, you will develop a heart for God.

We at Walk Thru the Bible Ministries are thrilled to join with Zondervan Bible Publishers to make this devotional New Testament available to you. The common purpose of our ministries is to help more Christians become grounded in Scripture.

Bruce H. Wilkinson
President and Executive Editor
Walk Thru the Bible Ministries

How to Get the Most Out of The Closer Walk New Testament

The Closer Walk New Testament is conveniently arranged for daily Bible reading 365 days of the year with each section dated with the month and the day. Each day's reading contains the following primary sections:

Scripture

Walk in the Word begins each day with a short overview of the Scripture portion you will read.

The **daily reading** from the New Testament leads you through the entire New Testament at an easy pace in one year.

Devotional

The **key verse** focuses the day's devotional on one idea from the Scripture passage.

Walk with a Christian leader provides inspiration for today from the writings of faithful Christian teachers and leaders of the past.

Walk Closer to God is a challenge to deepen your relationship with God through obedience and personal worship.

The end of each complete daily reading, which includes the Scripture and the devotional, is marked with a small ◘.

Interspersed between the daily text and the devotional copy, the "Worship from the Heart" sections provide a springboard for meditation, prayer and personal worship. From time to time a psalm related to the day's topic is printed to refresh your mind and encourage your worship. Also there is plenty of space for you to write your own worship notes, prayers and meditations. In addition, short biographies of some of the great Christian leaders of the past will give you insight into the lives of men and women whose faith and walk provide guidance and inspiration for us.

You will also find in *The Closer Walk New Testament* a helpful introductory page for the book or group of books you will read each month. A concise overview of the author's background and circumstances will help you understand his purpose for writing.

Every feature of *The Closer Walk New Testament* is designed to help you get the most out of your devotional times with the Lord. It's the tool you have been looking for to help you develop your heart for God!

Walk Thru the Bible Ministries

Walk Thru the Bible Ministries (WTB) unofficially began in the early 1970s in Portland, Oregon. A young teacher named Bruce Wilkinson developed an innovative way of teaching Old and New Testament surveys of the Bible.

From these small beginnings emerged the multifaceted Bible-teaching outreach that Dr. Wilkinson officially founded as a nonprofit ministry in 1976. WTB has grown into one of the leading Christian organizations in America with an international ministry extending to over 50 countries representing some 35 languages. International branch offices are located in Australia, Great Britain, Singapore, New Zealand, South Africa, and Ukraine.

By focusing on the central themes of Scripture and their practical application. WTB has been able to develop and maintain wide acceptance in denominations and fellowships around the world. In addition, it has carefully initiated strategic ministry alliances with over 100 Christian organizations and missions of wide diversity and background.

WTB has four major outreach ministries: seminars, publishing, leadership training, and video.

Seminars

Since it began its seminar ministry over two decades ago, WTB has instructed more than 2 million people worldwide through seminars taught by over 1,600 certified teachers. People of all ages and religious persuasions have developed a deeper understanding of the Bible through these unique Old and New Testament surveys, and many have come to know Christ in a new and more personal way.

Publishing

WTB's publishing ministry began in 1978 with the launching of *The Daily Walk* magazine. Since then, WTB Publishing has continued to develop additional publications that enable individuals and families to maintain a meaningful habit of daily devotional time in the Word of God. The publications include *Closer Walk, Family Walk, LifeWalk, Quiet Walk, Youthwalk,* and *Tapestry.*

Leadership Training

WTB's Leadership Training ministry goes into the secular marketplace as well as churches and organizations to communicate Biblical principles of leadership. There are several leadership modules available to fit the unique needs of each group. Each training module provides practical tools that make Biblical truth relevant in both personal relationships and in the marketplace.

Video Training

The newest ministry of WTB is the video training curriculum. In just a few short years, the WTB creative team has developed a number of leading video courses that have enjoyed widespread distribution. Video makes it possible to bring WTB's lifechanging Bible teaching into churches and homes throughout the world.

WTB has had a consistent history of strategic ministry from the beginning. The organization strives to help fulfill the Great Commission in obedience to the Lord's call. With this mission in mind, WTB lives out its commitment to excellence with the highest standards of ethical conduct and integrity, not only in ministry but also in its internal operational policies and procedures. No matter what the ministry, no matter where the ministry, WTB focuses on the Word of God and encourages people of all nations to grow in their knowledge of God and in unreserved obedience and service to him.

For more information about Walk Thru the Bible's publications, videos, or seminars in your area, write to Walk Thru the Bible Ministries, P.O. Box 80587, Atlanta, GA 30366 or call (770)458-9300.

Preface

T HE NEW INTERNATIONAL VERSION is a completely new translation of the Holy Bible made by over a hundred scholars working directly from the best available Hebrew, Aramaic and Greek texts. It had its beginning in 1965 when, after several years of exploratory study by committees from the Christian Reformed Church and the National Association of Evangelicals, a group of scholars met at Palos Heights, Illinois, and concurred in the need for a new translation of the Bible in contemporary English. This group, though not made up of official church representatives, was transdenominational. Its conclusion was endorsed by a large number of leaders from many denominations who met in Chicago in 1966.

Responsibility for the new version was delegated by the Palos Heights group to a self-governing body of fifteen, the Committee on Bible Translation, composed for the most part of biblical scholars from colleges, universities and seminaries. In 1967 the New York Bible Society (now the International Bible Society) generously undertook the financial sponsorship of the project—a sponsorship that made it possible to enlist the help of many distinguished scholars. The fact that participants from the United States, Great Britain, Canada, Australia and New Zealand worked together gave the project its international scope. That they were from many denominations—including Anglican, Assemblies of God, Baptist, Brethren, Christian Reformed, Church of Christ, Evangelical Free, Lutheran, Mennonite, Methodist, Nazarene, Presbyterian, Wesleyan and other churches—helped to safeguard the translation from sectarian bias.

How it was made helps to give the New International Version its distinctiveness. The translation of each book was assigned to a team of scholars. Next, one of the Intermediate Editorial Committees revised the initial translation, with constant reference to the Hebrew, Aramaic or Greek. Their work then went to one of the General Editorial Committees, which checked it in detail and made another thorough revision. This revision in turn was carefully reviewed by the Committee on Bible Translation, which made further changes and then released the final version for publication. In this way the entire Bible underwent three revisions, during each of which the translation was examined for its faithfulness to the original languages and for its English style.

All this involved many thousands of hours of research and discussion regarding the meaning of the texts and the precise way of putting them into English. It may well be that no other translation has been made by a more thorough process of review and revision from committee to committee than this one.

From the beginning of the project, the Committee on Bible Translation held to certain goals for the New International Version: that it would be an accurate translation and one that would have clarity and literary quality and so prove suitable for public and private reading, teaching, preaching, memorizing and liturgical use. The Committee also sought to preserve some measure of continuity with the long tradition of translating the Scriptures into English.

In working toward these goals, the translators were united in their commitment to the authority and infallibility of the Bible as God's Word in written form. They believe that it contains the divine answer to the deepest needs of humanity, that it sheds unique light on our path in a dark world, and that it sets forth the way to our eternal well-being.

The first concern of the translators has been the accuracy of the translation and its fidelity to the thought of the biblical writers. They have weighed the significance of the lexical and grammatical details of the Hebrew, Aramaic and Greek texts. At the same time, they have striven for more than a word-for-word translation. Because thought patterns and syntax differ from language to language, faithful communication of the meaning of the writers of the Bible demands frequent modifications in sentence structure and constant regard for the contextual meanings of words.

A sensitive feeling for style does not always accompany scholarship. Accordingly the Committee on Bible Translation submitted the developing version to a number of stylistic consultants. Two of them read every book of both Old and New Testaments twice—once before and once after the last major revision—and made invaluable suggestions. Samples of the translation were tested for clarity and ease of reading by various kinds of people—young and old, highly educated and less well educated, ministers and laymen.

Concern for clear and natural English—that the New International Version should be idiomatic but not idiosyncratic, contemporary but not dated—motivated the translators and consultants. At the same time, they tried to reflect the differing styles of the biblical writers. In view of the international use of English, the translators sought to avoid obvious Americanisms on the one hand and obvious Anglicisms on the other. A British edition reflects the comparatively few differences of significant idiom and of spelling.

As for the traditional pronouns "thou," "thee" and "thine" in reference to the Deity, the translators judged that to use these archaisms (along with the old verb forms such as "doest," "wouldest" and "hadst") would violate accuracy in translation. Neither Hebrew, Aramaic nor Greek uses special pronouns for the persons of the Godhead. A present-day translation is not enhanced by forms that in the time of the King James Version were used in everyday speech, whether referring to God or man.

For the Old Testament the standard Hebrew text, the Masoretic Text as published in the latest editions of *Biblia Hebraica*, was used throughout. The Dead Sea Scrolls contain material bearing on an earlier stage of the Hebrew text. They were consulted, as were the Samaritan Pentateuch and the ancient scribal traditions relating to textual changes. Sometimes a variant Hebrew reading in the margin of the Masoretic Text was followed instead of the text itself. Such instances, being variants within the Masoretic tradition, are not specified by footnotes. In rare cases, words in the consonantal text were divided differently from the way they appear in the Masoretic Text. Footnotes indicate this. The translators also consulted the more important early versions—the Septuagint; Aquila, Symmachus and Theodotion; the Vulgate; the Syriac Peshitta; the Targums; and for the Psalms the *Juxta Hebraica* of Jerome. Readings from these versions were occasionally followed where the Masoretic Text seemed doubtful and where accepted principles of textual criticism showed that one or more of these textual witnesses appeared to provide the correct reading. Such instances are footnoted. Sometimes vowel letters and vowel signs did not, in the judgment of the translators, represent the correct vowels for the original consonantal text. Accordingly some words were read with a different set of vowels. These instances are usually not indicated by footnotes.

The Greek text used in translating the New Testament was an eclectic one. No other piece of ancient literature has such an abundance of manuscript witnesses as does the New Testament. Where existing manuscripts differ, the translators made their choice of readings according to accepted principles of New Testament textual criticism. Footnotes call attention to places where there was uncertainty about what the original text was. The best current printed texts of the Greek New Testament were used.

There is a sense in which the work of translation is never wholly finished. This applies to all great literature and uniquely so to the Bible. In 1973 the New Testament in the New International Version was published. Since then, suggestions for corrections and revisions have been received from various sources. The Committee on Bible Translation carefully considered the suggestions and adopted a number of them. These were incorporated in the first printing of the entire Bible in 1978. Additional revisions were made by the Committee on Bible Translation in 1983 and appear in printings after that date.

Preface

As in other ancient documents, the precise meaning of the biblical texts is sometimes uncertain. This is more often the case with the Hebrew and Aramaic texts than with the Greek text. Although archaeological and linguistic discoveries in this century aid in understanding difficult passages, some uncertainties remain. The more significant of these have been called to the reader's attention in the footnotes.

In regard to the divine name *YHWH*, commonly referred to as the *Tetragrammaton*, the translators adopted the device used in most English versions of rendering that name as "Lord" in capital letters to distinguish it from *Adonai*, another Hebrew word rendered "Lord," for which small letters are used. Wherever the two names stand together in the Old Testament as a compound name of God, they are rendered "Sovereign Lord."

Because for most readers today the phrases "the Lord of hosts" and "God of hosts" have little meaning, this version renders them "the Lord Almighty" and "God Almighty." These renderings convey the sense of the Hebrew, namely, "he who is sovereign over all the 'hosts' (powers) in heaven and on earth, especially over the 'hosts' (armies) of Israel." For readers unacquainted with Hebrew this does not make clear the distinction between *Sabaoth* ("hosts" or "Almighty") and *Shaddai* (which can also be translated "Almighty"), but the latter occurs infrequently and is always footnoted. When Adonai and *YHWH Sabaoth* occur together, they are rendered "the Lord, the Lord Almighty."

As for other proper nouns, the familiar spellings of the King James Version are generally retained. Names traditionally spelled with "ch," except where it is final, are usually spelled in this translation with "k" or "c," since the biblical languages do not have the sound that "ch" frequently indicates in English—for example, in *chant*. For well-known names such as Zechariah, however, the traditional spelling has been retained. Variation in the spelling of names in the original languages has usually not been indicated. Where a person or place has two or more different names in the Hebrew, Aramaic or Greek texts, the more familiar one has generally been used, with footnotes where needed.

To achieve clarity the translators sometimes supplied words not in the original texts but required by the context. If there was uncertainty about such material, it is enclosed in brackets. Also for the sake of clarity or style, nouns, including some proper nouns, are sometimes substituted for pronouns, and vice versa. And though the Hebrew writers often shifted back and forth between first, second and third personal pronouns without change of antecedent, this translation often makes them uniform, in accordance with English style and without the use of footnotes.

Poetical passages are printed as poetry, that is, with indentation of lines with separate stanzas. These are generally designed to reflect the structure of Hebrew poetry. This poetry is normally characterized by parallelism in balanced lines. Most of the poetry in the Bible is in the Old Testament, and scholars differ regarding the scansion of Hebrew lines. The translators determined the stanza divisions for the most part by analysis of the subject matter. The stanzas therefore serve as poetic paragraphs.

As an aid to the reader, italicized sectional headings are inserted in most of the books. They are not to be regarded as part of the NIV text, are not for oral reading, and are not intended to dictate the interpretation of the sections they head.

The footnotes in this version are of several kinds, most of which need no explanation. Those giving alternative translations begin with "Or" and generally introduce the alternative with the last word preceding it in the text, except when it is a single-word alternative; in poetry quoted in a footnote a slant mark indicates a line division. Footnotes introduced by "Or" do not have uniform significance. In some cases two possible translations were considered to have about equal validity. In other cases, though the translators were convinced that the translation in the text was correct, they judged that another interpretation was possible and of sufficient importance to be represented in a footnote.

In the New Testament, footnotes that refer to uncertainty regarding the original text are introduced by "Some manuscripts" or similar expressions. In the Old Testament, evidence for the reading chosen is given first and evidence for the alternative is added after a semicolon (for example: Septuagint; Hebrew *father*). In such notes the term "Hebrew" refers to the Masoretic Text.

It should be noted that minerals, flora and fauna, architectural details, articles of clothing and jewelry, musical instruments and other articles cannot always be identified with precision. Also measures of capacity in the biblical period are particularly uncertain.

Like all translations of the Bible, made as they are by imperfect man, this one undoubtedly falls short of its goals. Yet we are grateful to God for the extent to which he has enabled us to realize these goals and for the strength he has given us and our colleagues to complete our task. We offer this version of the Bible to him in whose name and for whose glory it has been made. We pray that it will lead many into a better understanding of the Holy Scriptures and a fuller knowledge of Jesus Christ the incarnate Word, of whom the Scriptures so faithfully testify.

The Committee on Bible Translation

June 1978
(Revised August 1983)

Names of the translators and editors may be secured
from the International Bible Society,
translation sponsors of the New International Version,
1820 Jet Stream Drive, Colorado Springs, Colorado 80921-3696 U.S.A.

CLOSER WALK®
NEW TESTAMENT
NEW INTERNATIONAL VERSION

JANUARY

Discipleship: Following the Master's Footsteps

MATTHEW

Matthew presents Jesus Christ as the long-awaited Messiah ("Anointed One") of Israel. Writing to a Jewish audience, Matthew draws heavily on Old Testament prophecies to convince his readers that Jesus is the Christ, the Son of the living God.

But you needn't be Jewish to benefit from reading Matthew's Gospel. This tax-collector-turned-disciple presents some distinct impressions about Jesus of Nazareth. He was a worker of miracles, a preacher of parables, a lover of people. Everywhere he went, he taught people what right living was all about, modeling his teaching with his own life.

Jesus chose a twelve-member team of traveling companions—called disciples—who followed him everywhere and learned much from him. Their lives changed dramatically as they came in contact with the life-changing Savior. But discipleship is just as important for your own personal life. After all, you as a follower of Jesus Christ are also his disciple. Such an assignment must not be taken lightly. Jesus often spoke of the high price of being his disciple—alienation from family, self-denial, loss of earthly possessions, physical abuse, even martyrdom! Jesus knew that being his disciple would demand nothing short of a transformed life. Furthermore, before his departure from this earth, Jesus commanded his followers to "make disciples of all nations" (Matthew 28:19). Disciple-making, in other words, is a continuing responsibility; the Great Commission has been entrusted to all those who confess Christ as their Savior.

This should be an exciting month in God's Word—a month of change, of growth, of becoming more like Jesus. It will be a month to help you develop a heart for God.

JANUARY 1

Walk in the Word
Matthew 1

Matthew begins his Gospel with a genealogy of Jesus and the story of his birth. The genealogy and birth record show that Jesus is the fulfillment of Old Testament prophecies; he is Immanuel, the promised Messiah, the descendant of David.

The Genealogy of Jesus

1 A record of the genealogy of Jesus Christ the son of David, the son of Abraham:

²Abraham was the father of Isaac,
   Isaac the father of Jacob,
   Jacob the father of Judah and his brothers,
³Judah the father of Perez and Zerah, whose mother was Tamar,
   Perez the father of Hezron,
   Hezron the father of Ram,
⁴Ram the father of Amminadab,
   Amminadab the father of Nahshon,
   Nahshon the father of Salmon,
⁵Salmon the father of Boaz, whose mother was Rahab,
   Boaz the father of Obed, whose mother was Ruth,
   Obed the father of Jesse,
⁶and Jesse the father of King David.

David was the father of Solomon, whose mother had been Uriah's wife,
⁷Solomon the father of Rehoboam,
   Rehoboam the father of Abijah,
   Abijah the father of Asa,
⁸Asa the father of Jehoshaphat,
   Jehoshaphat the father of Jehoram,
   Jehoram the father of Uzziah,
⁹Uzziah the father of Jotham,
   Jotham the father of Ahaz,
   Ahaz the father of Hezekiah,
¹⁰Hezekiah the father of Manasseh,
   Manasseh the father of Amon,
   Amon the father of Josiah,
¹¹and Josiah the father of Jeconiah*ᵃ* and his brothers at the time of the exile to Babylon.

¹²After the exile to Babylon:
   Jeconiah was the father of Shealtiel,
   Shealtiel the father of Zerubbabel,
¹³Zerubbabel the father of Abiud,
   Abiud the father of Eliakim,
   Eliakim the father of Azor,

January 1

¹⁴Azor the father of Zadok,
Zadok the father of Akim,
Akim the father of Eliud,
¹⁵Eliud the father of Eleazar,
Eleazar the father of Matthan,
Matthan the father of Jacob,
¹⁶and Jacob the father of Joseph, the husband of Mary, of whom was born Jesus, who is called Christ.

¹⁷Thus there were fourteen generations in all from Abraham to David, fourteen from David to the exile to Babylon, and fourteen from the exile to the Christ.^b

The Birth of Jesus Christ

¹⁸This is how the birth of Jesus Christ came about: His mother Mary was pledged to be married to Joseph, but before they came together, she was found to be with child through the Holy Spirit. ¹⁹Because Joseph her husband was a righteous man and did not want to expose her to public disgrace, he had in mind to divorce her quietly.

²⁰But after he had considered this, an angel of the Lord appeared to him in a dream and said, "Joseph son of David, do not be afraid to take Mary home as your wife, because what is conceived in her is from the Holy Spirit. ²¹She will give birth to a son, and you are to give him the name Jesus,^c because he will save his people from their sins."

²²All this took place to fulfill what the Lord had said through the prophet: ²³"The virgin will be with child and will give birth to a son, and they will call him Immanuel"^d — which means, "God with us."

²⁴When Joseph woke up, he did what the angel of the Lord had commanded him and took Mary home as his wife. ²⁵But he had no union with her until she gave birth to a son. And he gave him the name Jesus.

---

^a11 That is, Jehoiachin; also in verse 12   ^b17 Or *Messiah.* "The Christ" (Greek) and "the Messiah" (Hebrew) both mean "the Anointed One."   ^c21 *Jesus* is the Greek form of *Joshua,* which means *the Lord saves.*   ^d23 Isaiah 7:14

The Wonderful Names of Jesus

The virgin will be with child and will give birth to a son, and they will call him Immanuel—which means, "God with us" (Matthew 1:23).

What if people wore the meaning of their names for all to see? You'd smile to meet David ("beloved"), chuckle at Mary ("stubbornness"), nod with Joanna ("God is gracious").

Matthew 1 begins with a long genealogy of more than forty names. A few are familiar, many are obscure. But all look forward to the arrival of one central figure . . . the one named Jesus ("Savior") or Immanuel ("God with us").

Charles Spurgeon was thoroughly captivated—and motivated—by the names of Jesus. What's in a name? Let's let Mr. Spurgeon explain.

Walk With Charles Spurgeon

"In these days we call children by names which have no particular meaning. But in times past names meant something. Especially is this the case in every name ascribed to the Lord Jesus.

" 'He will be called Wonderful Counselor, Mighty God, Everlasting Father, Prince of Peace' (Isaiah 9:6), because he really is all these things.

"His name is Jesus because no other name could fairly describe his great work of saving his people from their sins.

"His name is Immanuel—'God with us'—because there is no pain that tears the heart but what Jesus has been with us in it all. In the fires and in the rivers, in the cold night and under the burning sun, he cries, 'I am with you; do not be dismayed, for I am your God.' "

Walk Closer to God

You can think of Matthew 1 as a long list of names. Or you can view it as the roots of the Savior who came
—as Immanuel—to be with you.
—as Counselor—to provide wisdom.
—as Prince of Peace—to heal a relationship.

He came wearing names that truly revealed his purpose and character.

Have you come to him with your needs today?

January 2

📖 Walk in the Word
Matthew 2

Matthew tells about the wise men from other nations who come to worship Jesus as Lord and the ruthless response of the king of Judea to the news of Jesus' birth. Jesus and his parents escape to Egypt and later return to Israel and settle in Nazareth.

The Visit of the Magi

2 After Jesus was born in Bethlehem in Judea, during the time of King Herod, Magi[a] from the east came to Jerusalem [2]and asked, "Where is the one who has been born king of the Jews? We saw his star in the east[b] and have come to worship him."

[3]When King Herod heard this he was disturbed, and all Jerusalem with him. [4]When he had called together all the people's chief priests and teachers of the law, he asked them where the Christ[c] was to be born. [5]"In Bethlehem in Judea," they replied, "for this is what the prophet has written:

[6]" 'But you, Bethlehem, in the land of Judah,
 are by no means least among the rulers of Judah;
for out of you will come a ruler
 who will be the shepherd of my people Israel.'[d]"

[7]Then Herod called the Magi secretly and found out from them the exact time the star had appeared. [8]He sent them to Bethlehem and said, "Go and make a careful search for the child. As soon as you find him, report to me, so that I too may go and worship him."

[9]After they had heard the king, they went on their way, and the star they had seen in the east[e] went ahead of them until it stopped over the place where the child was. [10]When they saw the star, they were overjoyed. [11]On coming to the house, they saw the child with his mother Mary, and they bowed down and worshiped him. Then they opened their treasures and presented him with gifts of gold and of incense and of myrrh. [12]And having been warned in a dream not to go back to Herod, they returned to their country by another route.

The Escape to Egypt

[13]When they had gone, an angel of the Lord appeared to Joseph in a dream. "Get up," he said, "take the child and his mother and escape to Egypt. Stay there until I tell you, for Herod is going to search for the child to kill him."

[14]So he got up, took the child and his mother during the night and left for Egypt, [15]where he stayed until the death of Herod. And so was fulfilled what the Lord had said through the prophet: "Out of Egypt I called my son."[f]

[16]When Herod realized that he had been outwitted by the Magi, he was furious, and he gave orders to kill all the boys in Bethlehem and its vicinity who were two years old and under, in accordance with the time he had

learned from the Magi. ¹⁷Then what was said through the prophet Jeremiah was fulfilled:

> ¹⁸"A voice is heard in Ramah,
>   weeping and great mourning,
>   Rachel weeping for her children
>   and refusing to be comforted,
>   because they are no more."*ᵍ*

The Return to Nazareth

¹⁹After Herod died, an angel of the Lord appeared in a dream to Joseph in Egypt ²⁰and said, "Get up, take the child and his mother and go to the land of Israel, for those who were trying to take the child's life are dead."

²¹So he got up, took the child and his mother and went to the land of Israel. ²²But when he heard that Archelaus was reigning in Judea in place of his father Herod, he was afraid to go there. Having been warned in a dream, he withdrew to the district of Galilee, ²³and he went and lived in a town called Nazareth. So was fulfilled what was said through the prophets: "He will be called a Nazarene."

a1 Traditionally *Wise Men*   *b2* Or *star when it rose*   *c4* Or *Messiah*   *d6* Micah 5:2
e9 Or *seen when it rose*   *f15* Hosea 11:1   *g18* Jer. 31:15

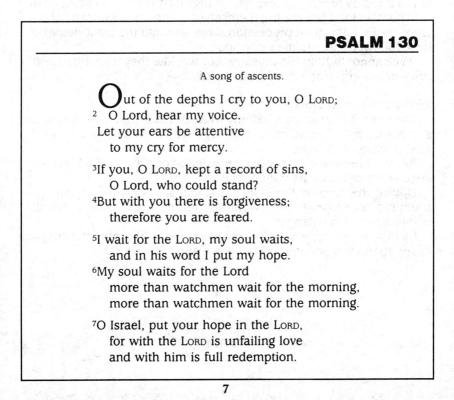

PSALM 130

A song of ascents.

Out of the depths I cry to you, O Lᴏʀᴅ;
²   O Lord, hear my voice.
Let your ears be attentive
    to my cry for mercy.

³If you, O Lᴏʀᴅ, kept a record of sins,
    O Lord, who could stand?
⁴But with you there is forgiveness;
    therefore you are feared.

⁵I wait for the Lᴏʀᴅ, my soul waits,
    and in his word I put my hope.
⁶My soul waits for the Lord
    more than watchmen wait for the morning,
    more than watchmen wait for the morning.

⁷O Israel, put your hope in the Lᴏʀᴅ,
    for with the Lᴏʀᴅ is unfailing love
    and with him is full redemption.

JANUARY 2

In the Presence of the King

Where is the one who has been born king of the Jews? (Matthew 2:2).

How far is it from St. Louis to Kansas City? About 200 miles if you're going in the right direction and about 25,000 miles if you're not!

Whether the goal is to bake a cake, put together a child's Christmas toy, or—like the wise men in Matthew 2—find the Christ child, the need is the same: good directions. And the willingness to follow them carefully.

F.B. Meyer offers this insight into the importance of hearing—and heeding—God's directions.

Walk With F.B. Meyer

"God comes to men in the spheres with which they are most familiar: to the shepherds in the fields, to the wise men by a sign in the heavens.

"God knows just where to find us, and in turn provides all we need to find and worship him.

"When we follow God's guidance, we may be sure that he will not fail to bring us to our goal. He who brings us out will also bring us in.

"The wise men prostrating themselves before the newborn babe were the first of a great procession down through the centuries who have followed them to the same spot.

"We cannot fathom the mystery, but we, like they, can adore and present our gifts, for indeed he is worthy."

Walk Closer to God

The road of life can be a baffling route indeed: smooth at times, but sometimes full of potholes . . . one day a well-marked expressway, the next a maze of detours.

But your heavenly Father has provided a road map—the Bible—to keep you moving in the right direction.

Dotting the pages of the Bible like signposts along the way are promises to encourage you, warnings to protect you and commands to detour you from danger.

By following it daily, you, like the wise men, will come safely to your destination. And you too will fall down and worship. ○

JANUARY 3

Walk in the Word
Matthew 3

Matthew records the activities and teachings of John the Baptist, as well as Jesus' baptism and the Spirit's descent to equip Jesus for his Messianic ministry.

John the Baptist Prepares the Way

3 In those days John the Baptist came, preaching in the Desert of Judea ²and saying, "Repent, for the kingdom of heaven is near." ³This is he who was spoken of through the prophet Isaiah:

"A voice of one calling in the desert,
'Prepare the way for the Lord,
    make straight paths for him.' "*a*

⁴John's clothes were made of camel's hair, and he had a leather belt around his waist. His food was locusts and wild honey. ⁵People went out to him from Jerusalem and all Judea and the whole region of the Jordan. ⁶Confessing their sins, they were baptized by him in the Jordan River.

⁷But when he saw many of the Pharisees and Sadducees coming to where he was baptizing, he said to them: "You brood of vipers! Who warned you to flee from the coming wrath? ⁸Produce fruit in keeping with repentance. ⁹And do not think you can say to yourselves, 'We have Abraham as our father.' I tell you that out of these stones God can raise up children for Abraham. ¹⁰The ax is already at the root of the trees, and every tree that does not produce good fruit will be cut down and thrown into the fire.

¹¹"I baptize you with*b* water for repentance. But after me will come one who is more powerful than I, whose sandals I am not fit to carry. He will baptize you with the Holy Spirit and with fire. ¹²His winnowing fork is in his hand, and he will clear his threshing floor, gathering his wheat into the barn and burning up the chaff with unquenchable fire."

The Baptism of Jesus

¹³Then Jesus came from Galilee to the Jordan to be baptized by John. ¹⁴But John tried to deter him, saying, "I need to be baptized by you, and do you come to me?"

¹⁵Jesus replied, "Let it be so now; it is proper for us to do this to fulfill all righteousness." Then John consented.

¹⁶As soon as Jesus was baptized, he went up out of the water. At that moment heaven was opened, and he saw the Spirit of God descending like a dove and lighting on him. ¹⁷And a voice from heaven said, "This is my Son, whom I love; with him I am well pleased."

a3 Isaiah 40:3   *b11* Or *in*

JANUARY 3

A Heritage in God's Family

This is my Son, whom I love; with him I am well pleased (Matthew 3:17).

In Matthew 3 a man named John bursts onto the scene, looking and sounding like Elijah the prophet. According to the Old Testament, that was precisely as it should have been.

Another man named Jesus came to be baptized by John. Coincidence? Or the long-awaited Messiah (Anointed One)? The audible voice of God supplied the answer.

Matthew Henry, prolific eighteenth-century Bible commentator, reveled in the Christian's privileges in Christ. If you are "in him," you enjoy a rich heritage in God's family, as Mr. Henry explains.

Walk With Matthew Henry

"Jesus is God's 'beloved Son,' not only 'with whom' but 'in whom' God is well pleased. God is pleased with all who are in Christ and are united to him by faith. Hitherto God has been displeased with the children of men; but now his anger is turned away, and he has made us 'accepted in the beloved.' Outside of Christ, God is a consuming Fire, but in Christ he is a reconciling Father.

"This is the sum of the whole gospel: God has declared by a voice from heaven that Jesus Christ is his beloved Son. With this we must by faith cheerfully concur and say that he is our beloved Savior, in whom we are well pleased."

Walk Closer to God

What is your heavenly heritage? Forgiveness. Acceptance. Salvation. Indescribable wealth in Jesus Christ, all because you are "born again" into God's family, giving you the right to call God your Father. That's your legacy. You are rich in Christ . . . but do you live as a king's heir?

You are forgiven, but do you nurture feelings of guilt? You are accepted, but do you try to "repay" God for what he has given as a free gift?

It's hard to live like a pauper when you know you're as rich as a king. And focusing on your heritage in the family of God can be exciting.

Don't be surprised if something changes when you do. And don't be content until it does. ◖▌

JANUARY 4

Walk in the Word
Matthew 4

Matthew writes about Jesus' faithfulness during temptation and testing and about the beginning of his public ministry in the area northwest of the Sea of Galilee.

The Temptation of Jesus

4 Then Jesus was led by the Spirit into the desert to be tempted by the devil. ²After fasting forty days and forty nights, he was hungry. ³The tempter came to him and said, "If you are the Son of God, tell these stones to become bread."

⁴Jesus answered, "It is written: 'Man does not live on bread alone, but on every word that comes from the mouth of God.'ᵃ"

⁵Then the devil took him to the holy city and had him stand on the highest point of the temple. ⁶"If you are the Son of God," he said, "throw yourself down. For it is written:

> " 'He will command his angels concerning you,
>   and they will lift you up in their hands,
> so that you will not strike your foot against a stone.'ᵇ"

⁷Jesus answered him, "It is also written: 'Do not put the Lord your God to the test.'ᶜ"

⁸Again, the devil took him to a very high mountain and showed him all the kingdoms of the world and their splendor. ⁹"All this I will give you," he said, "if you will bow down and worship me."

¹⁰Jesus said to him, "Away from me, Satan! For it is written: 'Worship the Lord your God, and serve him only.'ᵈ"

¹¹Then the devil left him, and angels came and attended him.

Jesus Begins to Preach

¹²When Jesus heard that John had been put in prison, he returned to Galilee. ¹³Leaving Nazareth, he went and lived in Capernaum, which was by the lake in the area of Zebulun and Naphtali — ¹⁴to fulfill what was said through the prophet Isaiah:

> ¹⁵"Land of Zebulun and land of Naphtali,
>   the way to the sea, along the Jordan,
>   Galilee of the Gentiles —
> ¹⁶the people living in darkness
>   have seen a great light;
> on those living in the land of the shadow of death
>   a light has dawned."ᵉ

¹⁷From that time on Jesus began to preach, "Repent, for the kingdom of heaven is near."

11

JANUARY 4

The Calling of the First Disciples

¹⁸As Jesus was walking beside the Sea of Galilee, he saw two brothers, Simon called Peter and his brother Andrew. They were casting a net into the lake, for they were fishermen. ¹⁹"Come, follow me," Jesus said, "and I will make you fishers of men." ²⁰At once they left their nets and followed him.

²¹Going on from there, he saw two other brothers, James son of Zebedee and his brother John. They were in a boat with their father Zebedee, preparing their nets. Jesus called them, ²²and immediately they left the boat and their father and followed him.

Jesus Heals the Sick

²³Jesus went throughout Galilee, teaching in their synagogues, preaching the good news of the kingdom, and healing every disease and sickness among the people. ²⁴News about him spread all over Syria, and people brought to him all who were ill with various diseases, those suffering severe pain, the demon-possessed, those having seizures, and the paralyzed, and he healed them. ²⁵Large crowds from Galilee, the Decapolis,ᶠ Jerusalem, Judea and the region across the Jordan followed him.

a4 Deut. 8:3   b6 Psalm 91:11,12   c7 Deut. 6:16   d10 Deut. 6:13   e16 Isaiah 9:1,2
f25 That is, the Ten Cities

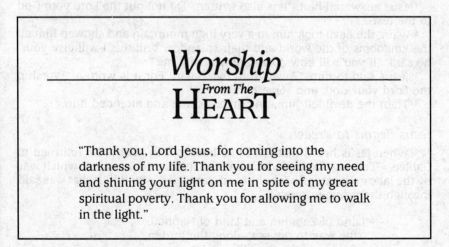

Worship
From The
HEART

"Thank you, Lord Jesus, for coming into the darkness of my life. Thank you for seeing my need and shining your light on me in spite of my great spiritual poverty. Thank you for allowing me to walk in the light."

Great Light in the Shadow of Death

The people living in darkness have seen a great light (Matthew 4:16).

___

Jesus came to bring light into a darkened world, and having been announced by John and tested by Satan, he was ready to begin his public ministry.

But where? Jerusalem, the capital of the nation? Or Samaria, hotbed of racial unrest? Maybe Nazareth, his hometown?

The answer may surprise you!

G. Campbell Morgan probes the significance of Capernaum as the place where Christ's ministry began.

Walk With G. Campbell Morgan

"When God visits his people for redemption, he comes where darkness is greatest, where the people sit in the shadow of death. Both in terms of geography and principle, Jesus did that very thing.

"Capernaum was in a despised region of the land of Palestine known as Galilee of the Gentiles. This portion of the country had been overrun more than any other by foreign invaders. Therefore, it came to be called 'the region and shadow of death.'

"That was Capernaum; and Jesus started his public ministry there.

"He did not commence where people were least likely to need it. Rather, the people who sat in darkness—in the region of the shadow of death—saw the great light."

Walk Closer to God

Shine a bright light into an already lighted room, and you have changed nothing. Shine that same light into a dark corner, and you have shattered the darkness.

For you, Capernaum may be as near as your neighborhood, school or office.

Who in your sphere of life sits in ignorance and painful darkness? Which friends or neighbors of yours are craving the light?

Where the light of the gospel needs to penetrate, there is your Capernaum. ⁋

JANUARY 5

📖 Walk in the Word
Matthew 5

Matthew records Jesus' teachings about the kind of people who experience true spiritual joy and purpose and about the kind of authentic living Jesus expects from his followers.

The Beatitudes

5 Now when he saw the crowds, he went up on a mountainside and sat down. His disciples came to him, ²and he began to teach them, saying:

³"Blessed are the poor in spirit,
for theirs is the kingdom of heaven.
⁴Blessed are those who mourn,
for they will be comforted.
⁵Blessed are the meek,
for they will inherit the earth.
⁶Blessed are those who hunger and thirst for
righteousness,
for they will be filled.
⁷Blessed are the merciful,
for they will be shown mercy.
⁸Blessed are the pure in heart,
for they will see God.
⁹Blessed are the peacemakers,
for they will be called sons of God.
¹⁰Blessed are those who are persecuted because of
righteousness,
for theirs is the kingdom of heaven.

¹¹"Blessed are you when people insult you, persecute you and falsely say all kinds of evil against you because of me. ¹²Rejoice and be glad, because great is your reward in heaven, for in the same way they persecuted the prophets who were before you.

Salt and Light

¹³"You are the salt of the earth. But if the salt loses its saltiness, how can it be made salty again? It is no longer good for anything, except to be thrown out and trampled by men.

¹⁴"You are the light of the world. A city on a hill cannot be hidden. ¹⁵Neither do people light a lamp and put it under a bowl. Instead they put it on its stand, and it gives light to everyone in the house. ¹⁶In the same way, let your light shine before men, that they may see your good deeds and praise your Father in heaven.

The Fulfillment of the Law

¹⁷"Do not think that I have come to abolish the Law or the Prophets; I have not come to abolish them but to fulfill them. ¹⁸I tell you the truth, until heaven and earth disappear, not the smallest letter, not the least

stroke of a pen, will by any means disappear from the Law until everything is accomplished. [19]Anyone who breaks one of the least of these commandments and teaches others to do the same will be called least in the kingdom of heaven, but whoever practices and teaches these commands will be called great in the kingdom of heaven. [20]For I tell you that unless your righteousness surpasses that of the Pharisees and the teachers of the law, you will certainly not enter the kingdom of heaven.

Murder

[21]"You have heard that it was said to the people long ago, 'Do not murder,[a] and anyone who murders will be subject to judgment.' [22]But I tell you that anyone who is angry with his brother[b] will be subject to judgment. Again, anyone who says to his brother, 'Raca,[c]' is answerable to the Sanhedrin. But anyone who says, 'You fool!' will be in danger of the fire of hell.

[23]"Therefore, if you are offering your gift at the altar and there remember that your brother has something against you, [24]leave your gift there in front of the altar. First go and be reconciled to your brother; then come and offer your gift.

[25]"Settle matters quickly with your adversary who is taking you to court. Do it while you are still with him on the way, or he may hand you over to the judge, and the judge may hand you over to the officer, and you may be thrown into prison. [26]I tell you the truth, you will not get out until you have paid the last penny.[d]

Adultery

[27]"You have heard that it was said, 'Do not commit adultery.'[e] [28]But I tell you that anyone who looks at a woman lustfully has already committed adultery with her in his heart. [29]If your right eye causes you to sin, gouge it out and throw it away. It is better for you to lose one part of your body than for your whole body to be thrown into hell. [30]And if your right hand causes you to sin, cut it off and throw it away. It is better for you to lose one part of your body than for your whole body to go into hell.

Divorce

[31]"It has been said, 'Anyone who divorces his wife must give her a certificate of divorce.'[f] [32]But I tell you that anyone who divorces his wife, except for marital unfaithfulness, causes her to become an adulteress, and anyone who marries the divorced woman commits adultery.

Oaths

[33]"Again, you have heard that it was said to the people long ago, 'Do not break your oath, but keep the oaths you have made to the Lord.' [34]But I tell you, Do not swear at all: either by heaven, for it is God's throne; [35]or by the earth, for it is his footstool; or by Jerusalem, for it is the city of the Great King. [36]And do not swear by your head, for you cannot make even

JANUARY 5

one hair white or black. [37]Simply let your 'Yes' be 'Yes,' and your 'No,' 'No'; anything beyond this comes from the evil one.

An Eye for an Eye

[38]"You have heard that it was said, 'Eye for eye, and tooth for tooth.'[g] [39]But I tell you, Do not resist an evil person. If someone strikes you on the right cheek, turn to him the other also. [40]And if someone wants to sue you and take your tunic, let him have your cloak as well. [41]If someone forces you to go one mile, go with him two miles. [42]Give to the one who asks you, and do not turn away from the one who wants to borrow from you.

Love for Enemies

[43]"You have heard that it was said, 'Love your neighbor[h] and hate your enemy.' [44]But I tell you: Love your enemies[i] and pray for those who persecute you, [45]that you may be sons of your Father in heaven. He causes his sun to rise on the evil and the good, and sends rain on the righteous and the unrighteous. [46]If you love those who love you, what reward will you get? Are not even the tax collectors doing that? [47]And if you greet only your brothers, what are you doing more than others? Do not even pagans do that? [48]Be perfect, therefore, as your heavenly Father is perfect.

a21 Exodus 20:13   *b22* Some manuscripts *brother without cause*   *c22* An Aramaic term of contempt   *d26* Greek *kodrantes*   *e27* Exodus 20:14   *f31* Deut. 24:1   *g38* Exodus 21:24; Lev. 24:20; Deut. 19:21   *h43* Lev. 19:18   *i44* Some late manuscripts enemies, *bless those who curse you, do good to those who hate you*

Worship
From The
HEART

Citizens of God's kingdom are merciful, pure in heart and peacemakers. That means they are different from the rest of the world. As you turn your heart to God today, examine yourself to see if you are living in the kingdom on your terms or his.

Blessed . . . in the Eyes of God

Blessed are the poor in spirit, for theirs is the kingdom of heaven (Matthew 5:3).

What is happiness? Ask twenty different people to answer that question, and you'll probably get twenty different answers.

But for the citizen of the kingdom of heaven, the path to true happiness is the path of blessedness described by Jesus in Matthew 5:1–11.

As Matthew Henry points out, until you know what true happiness really is, you will never discover God's path to find it.

Walk With Matthew Henry

"Happiness is the thing people pretend to pursue. But most form a wrong notion of it and miss the way.

"The general opinion is: Blessed are those who are rich and honorable in the world, who spend their days in mirth and their years in pleasure.

"Jesus comes to correct this fundamental error and give us quite another notion of blessedness.

"However paradoxical his teaching may appear to those in the world, to those who are saved it is a rule of eternal truth and certainty by which we must shortly be judged.

"If this, therefore, be the beginning of Christ's doctrine, the Christian's duty must be to take his measure of happiness from those maxims, and to direct his life accordingly."

Walk Closer to God

Would you consider yourself truly happy if your life were characterized by meekness . . . mercy . . . poverty in spirit . . . persecution?

You would if you had God's perspective on happiness.

Given the chance, the world will offer you a bogus substitute—a happiness dependent on money, prestige or circumstances.

Christ says true happiness consists of none of these.

But you must decide. Which notion of blessedness will you build your life on today? How do you complete the sentence:

"Happiness is . . . "

JANUARY 6

📖 Walk in the Word
Matthew 6

Matthew continues to pass on Jesus' teachings, here about three acts of righteousness — giving, praying and fasting — and about worry-free hearts fixed on God's priorities.

Giving to the Needy

6 "Be careful not to do your 'acts of righteousness' before men, to be seen by them. If you do, you will have no reward from your Father in heaven.

²"So when you give to the needy, do not announce it with trumpets, as the hypocrites do in the synagogues and on the streets, to be honored by men. I tell you the truth, they have received their reward in full. ³But when you give to the needy, do not let your left hand know what your right hand is doing, ⁴so that your giving may be in secret. Then your Father, who sees what is done in secret, will reward you.

Prayer

⁵"And when you pray, do not be like the hypocrites, for they love to pray standing in the synagogues and on the street corners to be seen by men. I tell you the truth, they have received their reward in full. ⁶But when you pray, go into your room, close the door and pray to your Father, who is unseen. Then your Father, who sees what is done in secret, will reward you. ⁷And when you pray, do not keep on babbling like pagans, for they think they will be heard because of their many words. ⁸Do not be like them, for your Father knows what you need before you ask him.

⁹"This, then, is how you should pray:

" 'Our Father in heaven,
hallowed be your name,
¹⁰your kingdom come,
your will be done
on earth as it is in heaven.
¹¹Give us today our daily bread.
¹²Forgive us our debts,
as we also have forgiven our debtors.
¹³And lead us not into temptation,
but deliver us from the evil one.ᵃ'

¹⁴For if you forgive men when they sin against you, your heavenly Father will also forgive you. ¹⁵But if you do not forgive men their sins, your Father will not forgive your sins.

Fasting

¹⁶"When you fast, do not look somber as the hypocrites do, for they disfigure their faces to show men they are fasting. I tell you the truth, they have received their reward in full. ¹⁷But when you fast, put oil on your

JANUARY 6

head and wash your face, ¹⁸so that it will not be obvious to men that you are fasting, but only to your Father, who is unseen; and your Father, who sees what is done in secret, will reward you.

Treasures in Heaven

¹⁹"Do not store up for yourselves treasures on earth, where moth and rust destroy, and where thieves break in and steal. ²⁰But store up for yourselves treasures in heaven, where moth and rust do not destroy, and where thieves do not break in and steal. ²¹For where your treasure is, there your heart will be also.

²²"The eye is the lamp of the body. If your eyes are good, your whole body will be full of light. ²³But if your eyes are bad, your whole body will be full of darkness. If then the light within you is darkness, how great is that darkness!

²⁴"No one can serve two masters. Either he will hate the one and love the other, or he will be devoted to the one and despise the other. You cannot serve both God and Money.

Do Not Worry

²⁵"Therefore I tell you, do not worry about your life, what you will eat or drink; or about your body, what you will wear. Is not life more important than food, and the body more important than clothes? ²⁶Look at the birds of the air; they do not sow or reap or store away in barns, and yet your heavenly Father feeds them. Are you not much more valuable than they? ²⁷Who of you by worrying can add a single hour to his life*b*?

²⁸"And why do you worry about clothes? See how the lilies of the field grow. They do not labor or spin. ²⁹Yet I tell you that not even Solomon in all his splendor was dressed like one of these. ³⁰If that is how God clothes the grass of the field, which is here today and tomorrow is thrown into the fire, will he not much more clothe you, O you of little faith? ³¹So do not worry, saying, 'What shall we eat?' or 'What shall we drink?' or 'What shall we wear?' ³²For the pagans run after all these things, and your heavenly Father knows that you need them. ³³But seek first his kingdom and his righteousness, and all these things will be given to you as well. ³⁴Therefore do not worry about tomorrow, for tomorrow will worry about itself. Each day has enough trouble of its own.

---

a13 Or *from evil*; some late manuscripts *one, / for yours is the kingdom and the power and the glory forever. Amen.*   *b27* Or *single cubit to his height*

JANUARY 6

A Soul Filled With Light From Heaven

The eye is the lamp of the body. If your eyes are good, your whole body will be full of light (Matthew 6:22).

Aim at nothing, and you will hit it every time. Aim at something with a whole heart and a clear sense of purpose, and you may be surprised by what you can accomplish.

In short, that's the message of Matthew 6. Call it the principle of focus: single-minded movement toward a goal.

It's what guides the basketball player as he shoots . . . the archer as he looses the arrow . . . and the disciple of Jesus Christ as he relates to others in daily life.

Pleasing God seldom happens by accident. But as John Wesley points out, it's not an impossible target to hit, provided your aim is accurate and unwavering.

Walk With John Wesley

"If your eye is single, if God is in all your thoughts, if you are constantly aiming at him who is invisible, if it is your intention in all things small and great to please God and do the will of him who sent you into the world, then the promise will certainly take place: 'Your whole body will be full of light.' Your whole soul shall be filled with the light of heaven—with the glory of the Lord resting upon you.

"In all your actions and conversation, you shall have not only the testimony of a good conscience toward God, but his Spirit will also bear witness with you that your ways are acceptable to him."

Walk Closer to God

Aiming to be godly may seem like aiming at an invisible target. But Jesus Christ came to earth to make godliness visible.

What does it mean to become godly?

It means becoming like your teacher, giving your undivided attention to his Word and your unquestioned obedience to his will.

What are your sights set on?

It's easy to tell, for where the eye of your heart is focused, your lips and feet will quickly follow. ◖◗

JANUARY 7

Walk in the Word
Matthew 7

Matthew records more of Jesus' teachings, highlighting Jesus' use of vivid imagery and picture language to teach important truths.

Judging Others

7 "Do not judge, or you too will be judged. ²For in the same way you judge others, you will be judged, and with the measure you use, it will be measured to you.

³"Why do you look at the speck of sawdust in your brother's eye and pay no attention to the plank in your own eye? ⁴How can you say to your brother, 'Let me take the speck out of your eye,' when all the time there is a plank in your own eye? ⁵You hypocrite, first take the plank out of your own eye, and then you will see clearly to remove the speck from your brother's eye.

⁶"Do not give dogs what is sacred; do not throw your pearls to pigs. If you do, they may trample them under their feet, and then turn and tear you to pieces.

Ask, Seek, Knock

⁷"Ask and it will be given to you; seek and you will find; knock and the door will be opened to you. ⁸For everyone who asks receives; he who seeks finds; and to him who knocks, the door will be opened.

⁹"Which of you, if his son asks for bread, will give him a stone? ¹⁰Or if he asks for a fish, will give him a snake? ¹¹If you, then, though you are evil, know how to give good gifts to your children, how much more will your Father in heaven give good gifts to those who ask him! ¹²So in everything, do to others what you would have them do to you, for this sums up the Law and the Prophets.

The Narrow and Wide Gates

¹³"Enter through the narrow gate. For wide is the gate and broad is the road that leads to destruction, and many enter through it. ¹⁴But small is the gate and narrow the road that leads to life, and only a few find it.

A Tree and Its Fruit

¹⁵"Watch out for false prophets. They come to you in sheep's clothing, but inwardly they are ferocious wolves. ¹⁶By their fruit you will recognize them. Do people pick grapes from thornbushes, or figs from thistles? ¹⁷Likewise every good tree bears good fruit, but a bad tree bears bad fruit. ¹⁸A good tree cannot bear bad fruit, and a bad tree cannot bear good fruit. ¹⁹Every tree that does not bear good fruit is cut down and thrown into the fire. ²⁰Thus, by their fruit you will recognize them.

²¹"Not everyone who says to me, 'Lord, Lord,' will enter the kingdom of heaven, but only he who does the will of my Father who is in heaven. ²²Many will say to me on that day, 'Lord, Lord, did we not prophesy in your

JANUARY 7

name, and in your name drive out demons and perform many miracles?' [23]Then I will tell them plainly, 'I never knew you. Away from me, you evildoers!'

The Wise and Foolish Builders

[24]"Therefore everyone who hears these words of mine and puts them into practice is like a wise man who built his house on the rock. [25]The rain came down, the streams rose, and the winds blew and beat against that house; yet it did not fall, because it had its foundation on the rock. [26]But everyone who hears these words of mine and does not put them into practice is like a foolish man who built his house on sand. [27]The rain came down, the streams rose, and the winds blew and beat against that house, and it fell with a great crash."

[28]When Jesus had finished saying these things, the crowds were amazed at his teaching, [29]because he taught as one who had authority, and not as their teachers of the law.

PSALM 6

Be merciful to me, LORD, for I am faint;
O LORD, heal me, for my bones are in agony.
[3]My soul is in anguish.
How long, O LORD, how long?

[4]Turn, O LORD, and deliver me;
save me because of your unfailing love.
[5]No one remembers you when he is dead.
Who praises you from the grave[a]?

[6]I am worn out from groaning;
all night long I flood my bed with weeping
and drench my couch with tears.
[7]My eyes grow weak with sorrow;
they fail because of all my foes.

[8]Away from me, all you who do evil,
for the LORD has heard my weeping.
[9]The LORD has heard my cry for mercy;
the LORD accepts my prayer.

[a]5 Hebrew Sheol

In Your Father's Throne Room

Ask and it will be given to you; seek and you will find; knock and the door will be opened to you (Matthew 7:7).

Nothing puts feeling into your prayers like a mighty good reason to pray. But nothing in Christianity is so rare as a praying heart.

Fifteen verses in the Sermon on the Mount concern prayer. Jesus talks about when to pray (Matthew 6:5–8), how to pray (Matthew 6:9–13), and why to pray (Matthew 7:7–11).

Why is prayer so important? The reason is simple: God gives good gifts to his children who ask him.

Augustine spoke often of the privilege of prayer, but he explains that *longing in prayer* and *long prayer* need not be synonymous.

Walk With Augustine

"It was our Lord who put an end to long-windedness, so that you would not pray as if you wanted to teach God by your many words. Piety, not verbosity, is in order when you pray, since he knows your needs.

"Now someone perhaps will say: But if he knows our needs, why should we state our requests even in a few words? Why should we pray at all? Since he knows, let him give what he deems necessary for us.

"Even so, he wants you to pray so that he may confer his gifts on one who really desires them and will not regard them lightly."

Walk Closer to God

Prayer is more than just a heavenly room service where your heart's desire is yours for the asking.

Rather, prayer is the workout room of your soul. Asking, seeking and knocking are energetic words. They show sincerity, intensity and wholeheartedness.

Have you ever asked God for great things? Things out of the ordinary? Things that your own ingenuity and energy could never provide?

If not, you've yet to discover the power of prayer. For he has told you to "ask . . . seek . . . knock," and to expect doors to open as a result. ♥

January 8

📖 Walk in the Word
Matthew 8

Matthew tells of healings and the calming of a storm, as well as Jesus' call to a radical kind of discipleship.

The Man With Leprosy

8 When he came down from the mountainside, large crowds followed him. ²A man with leprosy*a* came and knelt before him and said, "Lord, if you are willing, you can make me clean."

³Jesus reached out his hand and touched the man. "I am willing," he said. "Be clean!" Immediately he was cured*b* of his leprosy. ⁴Then Jesus said to him, "See that you don't tell anyone. But go, show yourself to the priest and offer the gift Moses commanded, as a testimony to them."

The Faith of the Centurion

⁵When Jesus had entered Capernaum, a centurion came to him, asking for help. ⁶"Lord," he said, "my servant lies at home paralyzed and in terrible suffering."

⁷Jesus said to him, "I will go and heal him."

⁸The centurion replied, "Lord, I do not deserve to have you come under my roof. But just say the word, and my servant will be healed. ⁹For I myself am a man under authority, with soldiers under me. I tell this one, 'Go,' and he goes; and that one, 'Come,' and he comes. I say to my servant, 'Do this,' and he does it."

¹⁰When Jesus heard this, he was astonished and said to those following him, "I tell you the truth, I have not found anyone in Israel with such great faith. ¹¹I say to you that many will come from the east and the west, and will take their places at the feast with Abraham, Isaac and Jacob in the kingdom of heaven. ¹²But the subjects of the kingdom will be thrown outside, into the darkness, where there will be weeping and gnashing of teeth."

¹³Then Jesus said to the centurion, "Go! It will be done just as you believed it would." And his servant was healed at that very hour.

Jesus Heals Many

¹⁴When Jesus came into Peter's house, he saw Peter's mother-in-law lying in bed with a fever. ¹⁵He touched her hand and the fever left her, and she got up and began to wait on him.

¹⁶When evening came, many who were demon-possessed were brought to him, and he drove out the spirits with a word and healed all the sick. ¹⁷This was to fulfill what was spoken through the prophet Isaiah:

> "He took up our infirmities
>   and carried our diseases."*c*

JANUARY 8

The Cost of Following Jesus

¹⁸When Jesus saw the crowd around him, he gave orders to cross to the other side of the lake. ¹⁹Then a teacher of the law came to him and said, "Teacher, I will follow you wherever you go."

²⁰Jesus replied, "Foxes have holes and birds of the air have nests, but the Son of Man has no place to lay his head."

²¹Another disciple said to him, "Lord, first let me go and bury my father."

²²But Jesus told him, "Follow me, and let the dead bury their own dead."

Jesus Calms the Storm

²³Then he got into the boat and his disciples followed him. ²⁴Without warning, a furious storm came up on the lake, so that the waves swept over the boat. But Jesus was sleeping. ²⁵The disciples went and woke him, saying, "Lord, save us! We're going to drown!"

²⁶He replied, "You of little faith, why are you so afraid?" Then he got up and rebuked the winds and the waves, and it was completely calm.

²⁷The men were amazed and asked, "What kind of man is this? Even the winds and the waves obey him!"

The Healing of Two Demon-possessed Men

²⁸When he arrived at the other side in the region of the Gadarenes,ᵈ two demon-possessed men coming from the tombs met him. They were so violent that no one could pass that way. ²⁹"What do you want with us, Son of God?" they shouted. "Have you come here to torture us before the appointed time?"

³⁰Some distance from them a large herd of pigs was feeding. ³¹The demons begged Jesus, "If you drive us out, send us into the herd of pigs."

³²He said to them, "Go!" So they came out and went into the pigs, and the whole herd rushed down the steep bank into the lake and died in the water. ³³Those tending the pigs ran off, went into the town and reported all this, including what had happened to the demon-possessed men. ³⁴Then the whole town went out to meet Jesus. And when they saw him, they pleaded with him to leave their region.

ᵃ2 The Greek word was used for various diseases affecting the skin—not necessarily leprosy. ᵇ3 Greek *made clean*   ᶜ17 Isaiah 53:4   ᵈ28 Some manuscripts *Gergesenes*; others *Gerasenes*

JANUARY 8

Panicky Prayers or Unshakable Trust

You of little faith, why are you so afraid? (Matthew 8:26).

After witnessing three powerful miracles of Jesus in the first half of Matthew 8, the disciples are dropped into the "crucible" in the Sea of Galilee. And their response in that fearful tempest shows the fickleness of their faith.

Prayers of panic . . . what child of God hasn't experienced them! Oswald Chambers explains how the way you pray reflects the character of your faith.

Walk With Oswald Chambers

"Our Lord has a right to expect that those who claim to be his should have an understanding confidence in him. But too often our trust is in God up to a certain point; then we go back to the panic prayers of those who do not know God.

"We get to our wits' end, showing that we have not the slightest confidence in him and his government of the world. He seems to be asleep, and we see nothing but breakers ahead.

'O you of little faith!'

"What a pang must have shot through the disciples. And what a pang will go through us when we suddenly realize that we might have produced downright joy in the heart of Jesus by remaining absolutely confident in Him, no matter what was ahead."

Walk Closer to God

It's hard to be a hypocrite in the vortex of a crisis.

There isn't time to paste on masks or worry about what other people think. When you're confronted by a crisis, the true character of your faith will emerge—unvarnished and unannounced.

But it's never too late to let God still the tempest in your heart and teach you to rest confidently in him. He will strengthen your faith as you rely on him.

Give yourself a simple crisis checkup by putting the words panic and pray in the following statement: When I'm facing a crisis, first I _____, then I _____. ◖

JANUARY 11

Woe on Unrepentant Cities

20Then Jesus began to denounce the cities in which most of his miracles had been performed, because they did not repent. 21"Woe to you, Korazin! Woe to you, Bethsaida! If the miracles that were performed in you had been performed in Tyre and Sidon, they would have repented long ago in sackcloth and ashes. 22But I tell you, it will be more bearable for Tyre and Sidon on the day of judgment than for you. 23And you, Capernaum, will you be lifted up to the skies? No, you will go down to the depths.d If the miracles that were performed in you had been performed in Sodom, it would have remained to this day. 24But I tell you that it will be more bearable for Sodom on the day of judgment than for you."

Rest for the Weary

25At that time Jesus said, "I praise you, Father, Lord of heaven and earth, because you have hidden these things from the wise and learned, and revealed them to little children. 26Yes, Father, for this was your good pleasure.

27"All things have been committed to me by my Father. No one knows the Son except the Father, and no one knows the Father except the Son and those to whom the Son chooses to reveal him.

28"Come to me, all you who are weary and burdened, and I will give you rest. 29Take my yoke upon you and learn from me, for I am gentle and humble in heart, and you will find rest for your souls. 30For my yoke is easy and my burden is light."

a1 Greek in their towns   b5 The Greek word was used for various diseases affecting the skin—not necessarily leprosy.   c10 Mal. 3:1   d23 Greek Hades

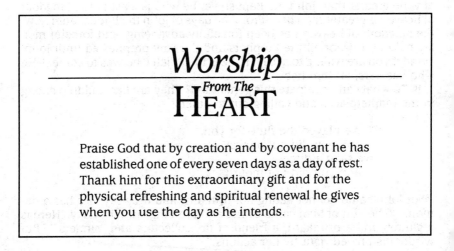

Worship
From The
HEART

Praise God that by creation and by covenant he has established one of every seven days as a day of rest. Thank him for this extraordinary gift and for the physical refreshing and spiritual renewal he gives when you use the day as he intends.

JANUARY 11

Walk in the Word
Matthew 11

Matthew reports on John the Baptist's need for reassurance, and on Jesus' denunciation of the cities that failed to repent. He presents Jesus' promise of rest for those who are weary and burdened.

Jesus and John the Baptist

11 After Jesus had finished instructing his twelve disciples, he went on from there to teach and preach in the towns of Galilee.*a*

2When John heard in prison what Christ was doing, he sent his disciples 3to ask him, "Are you the one who was to come, or should we expect someone else?"

4Jesus replied, "Go back and report to John what you hear and see: 5The blind receive sight, the lame walk, those who have leprosy*b* are cured, the deaf hear, the dead are raised, and the good news is preached to the poor. 6Blessed is the man who does not fall away on account of me."

7As John's disciples were leaving, Jesus began to speak to the crowd about John: "What did you go out into the desert to see? A reed swayed by the wind? 8If not, what did you go out to see? A man dressed in fine clothes? No, those who wear fine clothes are in kings' palaces. 9Then what did you go out to see? A prophet? Yes, I tell you, and more than a prophet. 10This is the one about whom it is written:

> " 'I will send my messenger ahead of you,
>   who will prepare your way before you.'*c*

11I tell you the truth: Among those born of women there has not risen anyone greater than John the Baptist; yet he who is least in the kingdom of heaven is greater than he. 12From the days of John the Baptist until now, the kingdom of heaven has been forcefully advancing, and forceful men lay hold of it. 13For all the Prophets and the Law prophesied until John. 14And if you are willing to accept it, he is the Elijah who was to come. 15He who has ears, let him hear.

16"To what can I compare this generation? They are like children sitting in the marketplaces and calling out to others:

> 17" 'We played the flute for you,
>   and you did not dance;
>   we sang a dirge,
>   and you did not mourn.'

18For John came neither eating nor drinking, and they say, 'He has a demon.' 19The Son of Man came eating and drinking, and they say, 'Here is a glutton and a drunkard, a friend of tax collectors and "sinners." ' But wisdom is proved right by her actions."

Answers From the Master Problem Solver

> When Jesus saw their faith, he said to the paralytic, "Take heart, son; your sins are forgiven" (Matthew 9:2).

Lingering illness. Guilt. Depression. Financial uncertainty. Loss of a loved one. It doesn't matter how big the problem is, provided you know an infinite problem solver.

The question is not one of ability, as you will see in Matthew 9, but rather one of authority—a willingness on your part to acknowledge who Jesus is as confirmed by his miracles.

Some were indifferent to his claims. Others were infuriated. But as G. Campbell Morgan explains, those who came in believing faith were met at their point of need.

Walk With G. Campbell Morgan

"To the questioning and rebellious heart Jesus proved his authority to forgive sins by an exhibition of his power to heal. The effect was instantaneous and remarkable: The multitudes feared and glorified God.

"Then in rapid succession a ruler, a woman ostracized because of her plague, two blind men, and a mute possessed with a demon crossed his path. He met their varied needs with strong, tender words and spoke to each one a message of peace and courage.

"The Pharisees, madly jealous of his power, attributed it to Satan. But the King, looking upon the crowds, was moved with compassion— the consequence of seeing them in their true condition as distressed and scattered, like sheep without a shepherd."

Walk Closer to God

God may not always give you the wisdom to solve your own problem. But you can always be assured that Jesus is strong enough to handle it . . . compassionate enough to feel it . . . loving enough to care for it . . . wise enough to deal with it.

In Matthew 9, six lives were changed after an encounter with the problem-solving Savior. Yours will be too when you stop looking at your problem and focus on the problem solver.

JANUARY 10

📖 Walk in the Word
Matthew 10

Matthew recalls the instructions given by Jesus to him and the other apostles as they are sent out to preach the message of the kingdom and to heal the hurting. He accents the promise of persecution, the call to full commitment and the assurance of God's care.

Jesus Sends Out the Twelve

10 He called his twelve disciples to him and gave them authority to drive out evil[a] spirits and to heal every disease and sickness.

2These are the names of the twelve apostles: first, Simon (who is called Peter) and his brother Andrew; James son of Zebedee, and his brother John; 3Philip and Bartholomew; Thomas and Matthew the tax collector; James son of Alphaeus, and Thaddaeus; 4Simon the Zealot and Judas Iscariot, who betrayed him.

5These twelve Jesus sent out with the following instructions: "Do not go among the Gentiles or enter any town of the Samaritans. 6Go rather to the lost sheep of Israel. 7As you go, preach this message: 'The kingdom of heaven is near.' 8Heal the sick, raise the dead, cleanse those who have leprosy,[b] drive out demons. Freely you have received, freely give. 9Do not take along any gold or silver or copper in your belts; 10take no bag for the journey, or extra tunic, or sandals or a staff; for the worker is worth his keep.

11"Whatever town or village you enter, search for some worthy person there and stay at his house until you leave. 12As you enter the home, give it your greeting. 13If the home is deserving, let your peace rest on it; if it is not, let your peace return to you. 14If anyone will not welcome you or listen to your words, shake the dust off your feet when you leave that home or town. 15I tell you the truth, it will be more bearable for Sodom and Gomorrah on the day of judgment than for that town. 16I am sending you out like sheep among wolves. Therefore be as shrewd as snakes and as innocent as doves.

17"Be on your guard against men; they will hand you over to the local councils and flog you in their synagogues. 18On my account you will be brought before governors and kings as witnesses to them and to the Gentiles. 19But when they arrest you, do not worry about what to say or how to say it. At that time you will be given what to say, 20for it will not be you speaking, but the Spirit of your Father speaking through you.

21"Brother will betray brother to death, and a father his child; children will rebel against their parents and have them put to death. 22All men will hate you because of me, but he who stands firm to the end will be saved. 23When you are persecuted in one place, flee to another. I tell you the truth, you will not finish going through the cities of Israel before the Son of Man comes.

24"A student is not above his teacher, nor a servant above his master. 25It is enough for the student to be like his teacher, and the servant like

JANUARY 10

his master. If the head of the house has been called Beelzebub,*c* how much more the members of his household!

²⁶"So do not be afraid of them. There is nothing concealed that will not be disclosed, or hidden that will not be made known. ²⁷What I tell you in the dark, speak in the daylight; what is whispered in your ear, proclaim from the roofs. ²⁸Do not be afraid of those who kill the body but cannot kill the soul. Rather, be afraid of the One who can destroy both soul and body in hell. ²⁹Are not two sparrows sold for a penny*d*? Yet not one of them will fall to the ground apart from the will of your Father. ³⁰And even the very hairs of your head are all numbered. ³¹So don't be afraid; you are worth more than many sparrows.

³²"Whoever acknowledges me before men, I will also acknowledge him before my Father in heaven. ³³But whoever disowns me before men, I will disown him before my Father in heaven.

³⁴"Do not suppose that I have come to bring peace to the earth. I did not come to bring peace, but a sword. ³⁵For I have come to turn

> " 'a man against his father,
>   a daughter against her mother,
>   a daughter-in-law against her mother-in-law—
> ³⁶   a man's enemies will be the members of his own
>   household.'*e*

³⁷"Anyone who loves his father or mother more than me is not worthy of me; anyone who loves his son or daughter more than me is not worthy of me; ³⁸and anyone who does not take his cross and follow me is not worthy of me. ³⁹Whoever finds his life will lose it, and whoever loses his life for my sake will find it.

⁴⁰"He who receives you receives me, and he who receives me receives the one who sent me. ⁴¹Anyone who receives a prophet because he is a prophet will receive a prophet's reward, and anyone who receives a righteous man because he is a righteous man will receive a righteous man's reward. ⁴²And if anyone gives even a cup of cold water to one of these little ones because he is my disciple, I tell you the truth, he will certainly not lose his reward."

---

a1 Greek *unclean*   *b8* The Greek word was used for various diseases affecting the skin— not necessarily leprosy.   *c25* Greek *Beezeboul* or *Beelzeboul*   *d29* Greek *an assarion* *e36* Micah 7:6

JANUARY 10

Sharing All With the Master

A student is not above his teacher, nor a servant above his master. It is enough for the student to be like his teacher, and the servant like his master. If the head of the house has been called Beelzebub, how much more the members of his household! (Matthew 10:24–25).

Jesus told his followers to be as shrewd as snakes, and as innocent as doves—rather unflattering similes from Matthew 10. Until you understand his point.

Being Christ's disciple demands a distinctive lifestyle. One that places you squarely in opposition to the world around you. Alexander Maclaren explains how a Christian who lives like the Master will be treated like the Master.

Walk With Alexander Maclaren

"If you are like the Master in conduct, you will be no more popular with the world than he was. As long as Christianity will be quiet, the world is content to let it alone or even to say polite things about it.

"But if Christian men and women live up to their profession, fight drunkenness, go against the lust of great cities, preach peace to a nation howling for war, or apply the golden rule to commerce and social relationships, you will soon hear a different shout.

"The disciple who is truly a disciple must share the fate of the Master."

Walk Closer to God

"God, give me the courage to be distinctive and to demonstrate my commitment as a disciple of Christ in a way that will cause others to desire a relationship with him.

"Remind me often that I am in the world but not of the world. Instead, fortify me to command the world's respect through a lifestyle of holiness and consistency, as befitting a follower of your Son. And make me aware of those areas of my life that reflect the world's ways more than yours.

"In the name of him who experienced both reception and rejection. Amen."

JANUARY 9

A Dead Girl and a Sick Woman

18While he was saying this, a ruler came and knelt before him and said, "My daughter has just died. But come and put your hand on her, and she will live." 19Jesus got up and went with him, and so did his disciples.

20Just then a woman who had been subject to bleeding for twelve years came up behind him and touched the edge of his cloak. 21She said to herself, "If I only touch his cloak, I will be healed."

22Jesus turned and saw her. "Take heart, daughter," he said, "your faith has healed you." And the woman was healed from that moment.

23When Jesus entered the ruler's house and saw the flute players and the noisy crowd, 24he said, "Go away. The girl is not dead but asleep." But they laughed at him. 25After the crowd had been put outside, he went in and took the girl by the hand, and she got up. 26News of this spread through all that region.

Jesus Heals the Blind and Mute

27As Jesus went on from there, two blind men followed him, calling out, "Have mercy on us, Son of David!"

28When he had gone indoors, the blind men came to him, and he asked them, "Do you believe that I am able to do this?"

"Yes, Lord," they replied.

29Then he touched their eyes and said, "According to your faith will it be done to you"; 30and their sight was restored. Jesus warned them sternly, "See that no one knows about this." 31But they went out and spread the news about him all over that region.

32While they were going out, a man who was demon-possessed and could not talk was brought to Jesus. 33And when the demon was driven out, the man who had been mute spoke. The crowd was amazed and said, "Nothing like this has ever been seen in Israel."

34But the Pharisees said, "It is by the prince of demons that he drives out demons."

The Workers Are Few

35Jesus went through all the towns and villages, teaching in their synagogues, preaching the good news of the kingdom and healing every disease and sickness. 36When he saw the crowds, he had compassion on them, because they were harassed and helpless, like sheep without a shepherd. 37Then he said to his disciples, "The harvest is plentiful but the workers are few. 38Ask the Lord of the harvest, therefore, to send out workers into his harvest field."

a13 Hosea 6:6

JANUARY 9

📖 Walk in the Word
Matthew 9

Matthew records his own life-changing encounter with Jesus, as well as more episodes in Jesus' ministry of teaching and preaching and healing.

Jesus Heals a Paralytic

9 Jesus stepped into a boat, crossed over and came to his own town. [2]Some men brought to him a paralytic, lying on a mat. When Jesus saw their faith, he said to the paralytic, "Take heart, son; your sins are forgiven."

[3]At this, some of the teachers of the law said to themselves, "This fellow is blaspheming!"

[4]Knowing their thoughts, Jesus said, "Why do you entertain evil thoughts in your hearts? [5]Which is easier: to say, 'Your sins are forgiven,' or to say, 'Get up and walk'? [6]But so that you may know that the Son of Man has authority on earth to forgive sins. . . ." Then he said to the paralytic, "Get up, take your mat and go home." [7]And the man got up and went home. [8]When the crowd saw this, they were filled with awe; and they praised God, who had given such authority to men.

The Calling of Matthew

[9]As Jesus went on from there, he saw a man named Matthew sitting at the tax collector's booth. "Follow me," he told him, and Matthew got up and followed him.

[10]While Jesus was having dinner at Matthew's house, many tax collectors and "sinners" came and ate with him and his disciples. [11]When the Pharisees saw this, they asked his disciples, "Why does your teacher eat with tax collectors and 'sinners'?"

[12]On hearing this, Jesus said, "It is not the healthy who need a doctor, but the sick. [13]But go and learn what this means: 'I desire mercy, not sacrifice.'[a] For I have not come to call the righteous, but sinners."

Jesus Questioned About Fasting

[14]Then John's disciples came and asked him, "How is it that we and the Pharisees fast, but your disciples do not fast?"

[15]Jesus answered, "How can the guests of the bridegroom mourn while he is with them? The time will come when the bridegroom will be taken from them; then they will fast.

[16]"No one sews a patch of unshrunk cloth on an old garment, for the patch will pull away from the garment, making the tear worse. [17]Neither do men pour new wine into old wineskins. If they do, the skins will burst, the wine will run out and the wineskins will be ruined. No, they pour new wine into new wineskins, and both are preserved."

The Place of Rest Is the Source of Strength

Come to me, all you who are weary and burdened, and I will give you rest (Matthew 11:28).

Some Christians are experts at making nothing happen . . . and doing that very slowly. Others behave as if the work of Christ were their single-handed duty. Both extremes lead to barrenness.

Every day of your life will bring a myriad of demands marked "urgent." Demands that carry the potential to change busyness into barrenness and bring spiritual and emotional burnout.

What can you do to avoid barrenness in your walk with God? J. Hudson Taylor offers wise words for those in danger of growing weary in the work of the Lord.

Walk With J. Hudson Taylor

"Never, never did Christ send an over-burdened one to work; never did he send a hungry one, a weary one, a sick or sorrowing one away on any service.

"Yet how many can tell of a time of intense distress because they felt they ought to be speaking to others about their souls, but could not?

"Oh, how different it would have been had they but first come to Jesus and found rest. Then their happy countenance would have said more than the heartfelt words were uttering. No one would then have looked at the face of the speaker and felt, 'What a dreadful religion his must be!'

"For the 'come' is not intended to exclude the 'go,' but to prepare the way for it."

Walk Closer to God

There is nothing inherently spiritual about busyness. Christ reserved some of his strongest rebukes for the Pharisees—the spiritual workaholics of his day. They were so busy working for God that they had forgotten to follow him.

Nor is there anything inherently sinful about "unproductive" moments—if they are used to refresh and energize you for renewed service. Even the Creator of the universe set aside his labors for a day of rest.

And the beauty of it all?

While you are at rest, God is at work! 〇

JANUARY 12

Walk in the Word
Matthew 12

Matthew continues his compelling portrayal of the Messiah as the loving mender of broken lives; at the same time Jesus frustrates the self-righteous and legalistic Pharisees, who find it impossible to believe that anyone with valid claims to be Messiah would speak or act as Jesus did.

Lord of the Sabbath

12 At that time Jesus went through the grainfields on the Sabbath. His disciples were hungry and began to pick some heads of grain and eat them. [2]When the Pharisees saw this, they said to him, "Look! Your disciples are doing what is unlawful on the Sabbath."

[3]He answered, "Haven't you read what David did when he and his companions were hungry? [4]He entered the house of God, and he and his companions ate the consecrated bread — which was not lawful for them to do, but only for the priests. [5]Or haven't you read in the Law that on the Sabbath the priests in the temple desecrate the day and yet are innocent? [6]I tell you that one[a] greater than the temple is here. [7]If you had known what these words mean, 'I desire mercy, not sacrifice,'[b] you would not have condemned the innocent. [8]For the Son of Man is Lord of the Sabbath."

[9]Going on from that place, he went into their synagogue, [10]and a man with a shriveled hand was there. Looking for a reason to accuse Jesus, they asked him, "Is it lawful to heal on the Sabbath?"

[11]He said to them, "If any of you has a sheep and it falls into a pit on the Sabbath, will you not take hold of it and lift it out? [12]How much more valuable is a man than a sheep! Therefore it is lawful to do good on the Sabbath."

[13]Then he said to the man, "Stretch out your hand." So he stretched it out and it was completely restored, just as sound as the other. [14]But the Pharisees went out and plotted how they might kill Jesus.

God's Chosen Servant

[15]Aware of this, Jesus withdrew from that place. Many followed him, and he healed all their sick, [16]warning them not to tell who he was. [17]This was to fulfill what was spoken through the prophet Isaiah:

> [18]"Here is my servant whom I have chosen,
> the one I love, in whom I delight;
> I will put my Spirit on him,
> and he will proclaim justice to the nations.
> [19]He will not quarrel or cry out;
> no one will hear his voice in the streets.
> [20]A bruised reed he will not break,
> and a smoldering wick he will not snuff out,
> till he leads justice to victory.
> [21] In his name the nations will put their hope."[c]

JANUARY 12

Jesus and Beelzebub

22Then they brought him a demon-possessed man who was blind and mute, and Jesus healed him, so that he could both talk and see. 23All the people were astonished and said, "Could this be the Son of David?"

24But when the Pharisees heard this, they said, "It is only by Beelzebub,*d* the prince of demons, that this fellow drives out demons."

25Jesus knew their thoughts and said to them, "Every kingdom divided against itself will be ruined, and every city or household divided against itself will not stand. 26If Satan drives out Satan, he is divided against himself. How then can his kingdom stand? 27And if I drive out demons by Beelzebub, by whom do your people drive them out? So then, they will be your judges. 28But if I drive out demons by the Spirit of God, then the kingdom of God has come upon you.

29"Or again, how can anyone enter a strong man's house and carry off his possessions unless he first ties up the strong man? Then he can rob his house.

30"He who is not with me is against me, and he who does not gather with me scatters. 31And so I tell you, every sin and blasphemy will be forgiven men, but the blasphemy against the Spirit will not be forgiven. 32Anyone who speaks a word against the Son of Man will be forgiven, but anyone who speaks against the Holy Spirit will not be forgiven, either in this age or in the age to come.

33"Make a tree good and its fruit will be good, or make a tree bad and its fruit will be bad, for a tree is recognized by its fruit. 34You brood of vipers, how can you who are evil say anything good? For out of the overflow of the heart the mouth speaks. 35The good man brings good things out of the good stored up in him, and the evil man brings evil things out of the evil stored up in him. 36But I tell you that men will have to give account on the day of judgment for every careless word they have spoken. 37For by your words you will be acquitted, and by your words you will be condemned."

The Sign of Jonah

38Then some of the Pharisees and teachers of the law said to him, "Teacher, we want to see a miraculous sign from you."

39He answered, "A wicked and adulterous generation asks for a miraculous sign! But none will be given it except the sign of the prophet Jonah. 40For as Jonah was three days and three nights in the belly of a huge fish, so the Son of Man will be three days and three nights in the heart of the earth. 41The men of Nineveh will stand up at the judgment with this generation and condemn it; for they repented at the preaching of Jonah, and now one*e* greater than Jonah is here. 42The Queen of the South will rise at the judgment with this generation and condemn it; for she came from the ends of the earth to listen to Solomon's wisdom, and now one greater than Solomon is here.

JANUARY 12

43"When an evil*f* spirit comes out of a man, it goes through arid places seeking rest and does not find it. 44Then it says, 'I will return to the house I left.' When it arrives, it finds the house unoccupied, swept clean and put in order. 45Then it goes and takes with it seven other spirits more wicked than itself, and they go in and live there. And the final condition of that man is worse than the first. That is how it will be with this wicked generation."

Jesus' Mother and Brothers

46While Jesus was still talking to the crowd, his mother and brothers stood outside, wanting to speak to him. 47Someone told him, "Your mother and brothers are standing outside, wanting to speak to you."*g*

48He replied to him, "Who is my mother, and who are my brothers?" 49Pointing to his disciples, he said, "Here are my mother and my brothers. 50For whoever does the will of my Father in heaven is my brother and sister and mother."

a6 Or *something*; also in verses 41 and 42   *b7* Hosea 6:6   *c21* Isaiah 42:1-4
d24 Greek *Beezeboul* or *Beelzeboul*; also in verse 27   *e41* Or *something*; also in verse 42
f43 Greek *unclean*   *g47* Some manuscripts do not have verse 47.

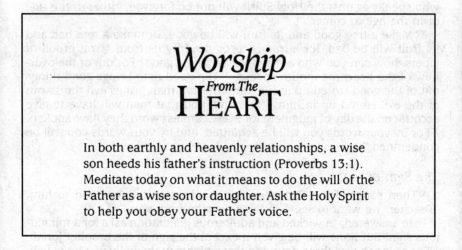

Worship
From The
HEART

In both earthly and heavenly relationships, a wise son heeds his father's instruction (Proverbs 13:1). Meditate today on what it means to do the will of the Father as a wise son or daughter. Ask the Holy Spirit to help you obey your Father's voice.

Kinship in the Family of God

For whoever does the will of my Father in heaven is my brother and sister and mother (Matthew 12:50).

Family life and acceptance are important to each of us. But true kinship does not require a blood relationship.

When Jesus spoke to the crowd in Matthew 12, he told them his disciples were his family—brothers and sisters of *faith* rather than *flesh*.

Listen as Francis of Assisi describes the richness of this family relationship.

Walk With Francis of Assisi

"We must never desire to be set above others, but to be subject to every human creature for God's sake. And all who do this shall be the brothers and mothers of our Lord Jesus Christ.

"We are his brothers when we do the will of his Father who is in heaven.

"We are his mothers when we bear him in our heart by love and a pure and sincere conscience, and bring him forth in holy deeds which must shine as an example to others.

"O, how glorious and holy and great it is to have a Father in heaven! O, how holy and delightful, pleasing and humble, peaceful and sweet, amiable and above all things to be desired it is to have a brother who laid down his life for his sheep."

Walk Closer to God

All the rags-to-riches stories ever told pale by comparison with what God has done for you in making you a full-fledged part of his family.

A son or daughter of his love.

A joint heir with Jesus of all that the Father possesses.

Comfort.

Strength.

Chastening.

Guidance.

They're all part of your family blessings in the household of God.

Think of it: Your Father in heaven cares for you as his very own . . . because that's what you are.

So welcome to the family!

JANUARY 13

📖 Walk in the Word
Matthew 13:1–52

Matthew introduces his readers to one of Jesus' favorite teaching techniques. Jesus here teaches spiritual truth through a number of stories, called parables, that are drawn from nature and ordinary human life.

The Parable of the Sower

13 That same day Jesus went out of the house and sat by the lake. ²Such large crowds gathered around him that he got into a boat and sat in it, while all the people stood on the shore. ³Then he told them many things in parables, saying: "A farmer went out to sow his seed. ⁴As he was scattering the seed, some fell along the path, and the birds came and ate it up. ⁵Some fell on rocky places, where it did not have much soil. It sprang up quickly, because the soil was shallow. ⁶But when the sun came up, the plants were scorched, and they withered because they had no root. ⁷Other seed fell among thorns, which grew up and choked the plants. ⁸Still other seed fell on good soil, where it produced a crop — a hundred, sixty or thirty times what was sown. ⁹He who has ears, let him hear."

¹⁰The disciples came to him and asked, "Why do you speak to the people in parables?"

¹¹He replied, "The knowledge of the secrets of the kingdom of heaven has been given to you, but not to them. ¹²Whoever has will be given more, and he will have an abundance. Whoever does not have, even what he has will be taken from him. ¹³This is why I speak to them in parables:

"Though seeing, they do not see;
    though hearing, they do not hear or understand.

¹⁴In them is fulfilled the prophecy of Isaiah:

" 'You will be ever hearing but never understanding;
    you will be ever seeing but never perceiving.
¹⁵For this people's heart has become calloused;
    they hardly hear with their ears,
    and they have closed their eyes.
Otherwise they might see with their eyes,
    hear with their ears,
    understand with their hearts
and turn, and I would heal them.'ᵃ

¹⁶But blessed are your eyes because they see, and your ears because they hear. ¹⁷For I tell you the truth, many prophets and righteous men longed to see what you see but did not see it, and to hear what you hear but did not hear it.

¹⁸"Listen then to what the parable of the sower means: ¹⁹When anyone hears the message about the kingdom and does not understand it, the evil one comes and snatches away what was sown in his heart. This is the seed sown along the path. ²⁰The one who received the seed that fell on rocky places is the man who hears the word and at once receives it with joy.

21But since he has no root, he lasts only a short time. When trouble or persecution comes because of the word, he quickly falls away. 22The one who received the seed that fell among the thorns is the man who hears the word, but the worries of this life and the deceitfulness of wealth choke it, making it unfruitful. 23But the one who received the seed that fell on good soil is the man who hears the word and understands it. He produces a crop, yielding a hundred, sixty or thirty times what was sown."

The Parable of the Weeds

24Jesus told them another parable: "The kingdom of heaven is like a man who sowed good seed in his field. 25But while everyone was sleeping, his enemy came and sowed weeds among the wheat, and went away. 26When the wheat sprouted and formed heads, then the weeds also appeared.

27"The owner's servants came to him and said, 'Sir, didn't you sow good seed in your field? Where then did the weeds come from?'

28" 'An enemy did this,' he replied.

"The servants asked him, 'Do you want us to go and pull them up?'

29" 'No,' he answered, 'because while you are pulling the weeds, you may root up the wheat with them. 30Let both grow together until the harvest. At that time I will tell the harvesters: First collect the weeds and tie them in bundles to be burned; then gather the wheat and bring it into my barn.' "

The Parables of the Mustard Seed and the Yeast

31He told them another parable: "The kingdom of heaven is like a mustard seed, which a man took and planted in his field. 32Though it is the smallest of all your seeds, yet when it grows, it is the largest of garden plants and becomes a tree, so that the birds of the air come and perch in its branches."

33He told them still another parable: "The kingdom of heaven is like yeast that a woman took and mixed into a large amount*b* of flour until it worked all through the dough."

34Jesus spoke all these things to the crowd in parables; he did not say anything to them without using a parable. 35So was fulfilled what was spoken through the prophet:

> "I will open my mouth in parables,
> I will utter things hidden since the creation of the
> world."*c*

The Parable of the Weeds Explained

36Then he left the crowd and went into the house. His disciples came to him and said, "Explain to us the parable of the weeds in the field."

37He answered, "The one who sowed the good seed is the Son of Man. 38The field is the world, and the good seed stands for the sons of the kingdom. The weeds are the sons of the evil one, 39and the enemy who sows them is the devil. The harvest is the end of the age, and the harvesters are angels.

41

JANUARY 13

⁴⁰"As the weeds are pulled up and burned in the fire, so it will be at the end of the age. ⁴¹The Son of Man will send out his angels, and they will weed out of his kingdom everything that causes sin and all who do evil. ⁴²They will throw them into the fiery furnace, where there will be weeping and gnashing of teeth. ⁴³Then the righteous will shine like the sun in the kingdom of their Father. He who has ears, let him hear.

The Parables of the Hidden Treasure and the Pearl

⁴⁴"The kingdom of heaven is like treasure hidden in a field. When a man found it, he hid it again, and then in his joy went and sold all he had and bought that field.

⁴⁵"Again, the kingdom of heaven is like a merchant looking for fine pearls. ⁴⁶When he found one of great value, he went away and sold everything he had and bought it.

The Parable of the Net

⁴⁷"Once again, the kingdom of heaven is like a net that was let down into the lake and caught all kinds of fish. ⁴⁸When it was full, the fishermen pulled it up on the shore. Then they sat down and collected the good fish in baskets, but threw the bad away. ⁴⁹This is how it will be at the end of the age. The angels will come and separate the wicked from the righteous ⁵⁰and throw them into the fiery furnace, where there will be weeping and gnashing of teeth.

⁵¹"Have you understood all these things?" Jesus asked.

"Yes," they replied.

⁵²He said to them, "Therefore every teacher of the law who has been instructed about the kingdom of heaven is like the owner of a house who brings out of his storeroom new treasures as well as old."

ᵃ15 Isaiah 6:9,10   ᵇ33 Greek *three satas* (probably about 1/2 bushel or 22 liters)
ᶜ35 Psalm 78:2

Glorious Jewel in the Father's Possession

> The kingdom of heaven is like . . . one [pearl] of great value (Matthew 13:45–46).

Nothing is quite as unyielding as a price tag. But if something is worth the price, you pay it anyway. After all, objects of genuine value never come cheaply.

In Matthew 13, Jesus employs seven parables to describe the incomparable value of the kingdom of heaven. And, as Matthew Henry explains, a man may gain the whole world, but unless he discovers one pearl of great value, he has failed to find true riches.

Walk With Matthew Henry

"Jesus Christ is a Pearl of great price, a Jewel of inestimable value, which will make those who have it rich, truly rich toward God.

"In having him we have enough to make us happy here and forever.

"Those who would have Christ must be willing to part with all for him, leave all to follow him. Whatever stands in opposition to Christ, or in competition with him for our love and service, we must cheerfully quit, though it is precious to us."

Walk Closer to God

Items of genuine value are always in danger of being impersonated by imitations and facsimiles.

And counterfeit Christianity—like counterfeit money—looks surprisingly like the real thing.

There is just enough truth in it to make it attractive. And just enough error to insure that it will never deliver what it promises.

Satan, the master counterfeiter, will dupe you if given the chance. His name even means "adversary" and "slanderer."

His game is simple: to offer an attractive alternative to the pearl of great value. Wealth. Education. Personal achievement. Peer acceptance.

He will sell you a "bargain." He will convince you God's kingdom is not worth seeking.

If you let him.

Counterfeit or genuine: Which pearl will you make your own? ◖

JANUARY 14

📖 Walk in the Word
Matthew 13:53 — 14:36

Matthew tells of John the Baptist's death and recalls the miraculous provision of food for five thousand people and the majestic power of Jesus over the waters.

A Prophet Without Honor

⁵³When Jesus had finished these parables, he moved on from there. ⁵⁴Coming to his hometown, he began teaching the people in their synagogue, and they were amazed. "Where did this man get this wisdom and these miraculous powers?" they asked. ⁵⁵"Isn't this the carpenter's son? Isn't his mother's name Mary, and aren't his brothers James, Joseph, Simon and Judas? ⁵⁶Aren't all his sisters with us? Where then did this man get all these things?" ⁵⁷And they took offense at him.

But Jesus said to them, "Only in his hometown and in his own house is a prophet without honor."

⁵⁸And he did not do many miracles there because of their lack of faith.

John the Baptist Beheaded

14 At that time Herod the tetrarch heard the reports about Jesus, ²and he said to his attendants, "This is John the Baptist; he has risen from the dead! That is why miraculous powers are at work in him."

³Now Herod had arrested John and bound him and put him in prison because of Herodias, his brother Philip's wife, ⁴for John had been saying to him: "It is not lawful for you to have her." ⁵Herod wanted to kill John, but he was afraid of the people, because they considered him a prophet.

⁶On Herod's birthday the daughter of Herodias danced for them and pleased Herod so much ⁷that he promised with an oath to give her whatever she asked. ⁸Prompted by her mother, she said, "Give me here on a platter the head of John the Baptist." ⁹The king was distressed, but because of his oaths and his dinner guests, he ordered that her request be granted ¹⁰and had John beheaded in the prison. ¹¹His head was brought in on a platter and given to the girl, who carried it to her mother. ¹²John's disciples came and took his body and buried it. Then they went and told Jesus.

Jesus Feeds the Five Thousand

¹³When Jesus heard what had happened, he withdrew by boat privately to a solitary place. Hearing of this, the crowds followed him on foot from the towns. ¹⁴When Jesus landed and saw a large crowd, he had compassion on them and healed their sick.

¹⁵As evening approached, the disciples came to him and said, "This is a remote place, and it's already getting late. Send the crowds away, so they can go to the villages and buy themselves some food."

¹⁶Jesus replied, "They do not need to go away. You give them something to eat."

¹⁷"We have here only five loaves of bread and two fish," they answered.

18"Bring them here to me," he said. 19And he directed the people to sit down on the grass. Taking the five loaves and the two fish and looking up to heaven, he gave thanks and broke the loaves. Then he gave them to the disciples, and the disciples gave them to the people. 20They all ate and were satisfied, and the disciples picked up twelve basketfuls of broken pieces that were left over. 21The number of those who ate was about five thousand men, besides women and children.

Jesus Walks on the Water

22Immediately Jesus made the disciples get into the boat and go on ahead of him to the other side, while he dismissed the crowd. 23After he had dismissed them, he went up on a mountainside by himself to pray. When evening came, he was there alone, 24but the boat was already a considerable distance*a* from land, buffeted by the waves because the wind was against it.

25During the fourth watch of the night Jesus went out to them, walking on the lake. 26When the disciples saw him walking on the lake, they were terrified. "It's a ghost," they said, and cried out in fear.

27But Jesus immediately said to them: "Take courage! It is I. Don't be afraid."

28"Lord, if it's you," Peter replied, "tell me to come to you on the water."

29"Come," he said.

Then Peter got down out of the boat, walked on the water and came toward Jesus. 30But when he saw the wind, he was afraid and, beginning to sink, cried out, "Lord, save me!"

31Immediately Jesus reached out his hand and caught him. "You of little faith," he said, "why did you doubt?"

32And when they climbed into the boat, the wind died down. 33Then those who were in the boat worshiped him, saying, "Truly you are the Son of God."

34When they had crossed over, they landed at Gennesaret. 35And when the men of that place recognized Jesus, they sent word to all the surrounding country. People brought all their sick to him 36and begged him to let the sick just touch the edge of his cloak, and all who touched him were healed.

a24 Greek *many stadia*

JANUARY 14

Making Prayer a Personal Priority

After he had dismissed them, he went up on a mountainside by himself to pray (Matthew 14:23).

Some people load their days with activities, clutter their calendar with appointments and fill the air with music—anything to drown out the sounds of silence. Which is too bad, really.

Because God often speaks in a still, small voice—the kind heard only in moments of silence (see 1 Kings 19:11–13).

In Matthew 14 you will discover two occasions when Jesus leaves the crowds and retires to a quiet place to pray. John Calvin comments on the importance of the Savior's search for solitude.

Walk With John Calvin

"By going to the mountain he was seeking a time of prayer free from interruption.

"We all know how easily prayer can be quenched by the least distraction.

"Although Christ did not suffer from this weakness, he warned us by his example to be careful to disengage our minds from the snares of the world, so that we may be carried up to heaven.

"The most important thing is solitude. Those who pray with God as their only witness will be more watchful, will pour forth their hearts to him, and will examine themselves more carefully.

"The freedom to pray in all places does not prevent us from praying in secret."

Walk Closer to God

Silence. How often do you experience it? What priority do you give it?

Jesus left the accolades of the crowds and climbed a mountain. There he prayed until the "fourth watch of the night"—3:00 A.M.

Jesus was committed to prayer!

God hears your hurried prayers. But he yearns for you to give him an uncluttered slice of your time, free from the distractions of a busy day.

It will seldom happen by accident. In fact, you may have to take the phone off the hook, turn off the TV, rearrange a priority. But what a small price to pay to "be still, and know" God! ◖

JANUARY 15

Walk in the Word
Matthew 15

Matthew records a conversation with the religious leaders in which Jesus penetrates to the heart of authentic living and exposes the emptiness of lip service. Matthew follows with two sensitive accounts of Jesus' compassion for the hurting.

Clean and Unclean

15 Then some Pharisees and teachers of the law came to Jesus from Jerusalem and asked, 2"Why do your disciples break the tradition of the elders? They don't wash their hands before they eat!"

3Jesus replied, "And why do you break the command of God for the sake of your tradition? 4For God said, 'Honor your father and mother'*a* and 'Anyone who curses his father or mother must be put to death.'*b* 5But you say that if a man says to his father or mother, 'Whatever help you might otherwise have received from me is a gift devoted to God,' 6he is not to 'honor his father*c*' with it. Thus you nullify the word of God for the sake of your tradition. 7You hypocrites! Isaiah was right when he prophesied about you:

8" 'These people honor me with their lips,
    but their hearts are far from me.
9They worship me in vain;
    their teachings are but rules taught by men.'*d*"

10Jesus called the crowd to him and said, "Listen and understand. 11What goes into a man's mouth does not make him 'unclean,' but what comes out of his mouth, that is what makes him 'unclean.' "

12Then the disciples came to him and asked, "Do you know that the Pharisees were offended when they heard this?"

13He replied, "Every plant that my heavenly Father has not planted will be pulled up by the roots. 14Leave them; they are blind guides.*e* If a blind man leads a blind man, both will fall into a pit."

15Peter said, "Explain the parable to us."

16"Are you still so dull?" Jesus asked them. 17"Don't you see that whatever enters the mouth goes into the stomach and then out of the body? 18But the things that come out of the mouth come from the heart, and these make a man 'unclean.' 19For out of the heart come evil thoughts, murder, adultery, sexual immorality, theft, false testimony, slander. 20These are what make a man 'unclean'; but eating with unwashed hands does not make him 'unclean.' "

The Faith of the Canaanite Woman

21Leaving that place, Jesus withdrew to the region of Tyre and Sidon. 22A Canaanite woman from that vicinity came to him, crying out, "Lord, Son of David, have mercy on me! My daughter is suffering terribly from demon-possession."

47

JANUARY 15

23Jesus did not answer a word. So his disciples came to him and urged him, "Send her away, for she keeps crying out after us."

24He answered, "I was sent only to the lost sheep of Israel."

25The woman came and knelt before him. "Lord, help me!" she said.

26He replied, "It is not right to take the children's bread and toss it to their dogs."

27"Yes, Lord," she said, "but even the dogs eat the crumbs that fall from their masters' table."

28Then Jesus answered, "Woman, you have great faith! Your request is granted." And her daughter was healed from that very hour.

Jesus Feeds the Four Thousand

29Jesus left there and went along the Sea of Galilee. Then he went up on a mountainside and sat down. 30Great crowds came to him, bringing the lame, the blind, the crippled, the mute and many others, and laid them at his feet; and he healed them. 31The people were amazed when they saw the mute speaking, the crippled made well, the lame walking and the blind seeing. And they praised the God of Israel.

32Jesus called his disciples to him and said, "I have compassion for these people; they have already been with me three days and have nothing to eat. I do not want to send them away hungry, or they may collapse on the way."

33His disciples answered, "Where could we get enough bread in this remote place to feed such a crowd?"

34"How many loaves do you have?" Jesus asked.

"Seven," they replied, "and a few small fish."

35He told the crowd to sit down on the ground. 36Then he took the seven loaves and the fish, and when he had given thanks, he broke them and gave them to the disciples, and they in turn to the people. 37They all ate and were satisfied. Afterward the disciples picked up seven basketfuls of broken pieces that were left over. 38The number of those who ate was four thousand, besides women and children. 39After Jesus had sent the crowd away, he got into the boat and went to the vicinity of Magadan.

a4 Exodus 20:12; Deut. 5:16   b4 Exodus 21:17; Lev. 20:9   c6 Some manuscripts father or his mother   d9 Isaiah 29:13   e14 Some manuscripts guides of the blind

Placing All Resources in God's Hands

> Where could we get enough bread in this remote place to feed such a crowd? (Matthew 15:33).

Seven loaves of bread and a few fish. Four thousand hungry men, plus women and children. Put them all together and you have a lot of hungry people!

But add Jesus to the scene, and you have all the ingredients for a miracle.

A world teeming with millions of unreached souls, and a few thousand missionary volunteers. Again, so little in the face of so great a need.

But as J. Hudson Taylor discovered, little is much when God is in it.

Walk With J. Hudson Taylor

"What God has given us is all we need; we require nothing more. It is not a question of large supplies—it is just a question of the presence of the Lord.

"Let us look to the Lord's methods. How were the people fed? By the united action of Christ and his disciples. He claimed their all. They gladly gave their all and unhesitatingly obeyed all his directions.

"Let us give up our work, our thoughts, our plans, ourselves, our loved ones, our influence, our all—right into his hand. And then there will be nothing left to be troubled about.

"When all is in his hand, all will be safe; all will be done and well done."

Walk Closer to God

Consecration and confidence.

Those are the responses of the disciples who took bread and fish from the Master's hands to feed the multitudes—though they could not explain the source.

With those attitudes you too can boldly share the good news of Jesus Christ with the hungry multitudes in your world. You too can have confidence in a God who is big enough . . . wise enough . . . rich enough to handle any problem when you commit your life to him.

At his table there is food to spare. It's your privilege to pass the basket. ◌

JANUARY 16

📖 Walk in the Word
Matthew 16

Matthew recalls Peter's confession that Jesus is indeed the Christ, the Son of God, and then reveals that from this point on Jesus' ministry focuses on preparing the disciples for his upcoming suffering and death.

The Demand for a Sign

16 The Pharisees and Sadducees came to Jesus and tested him by asking him to show them a sign from heaven.

[2]He replied,[a] "When evening comes, you say, 'It will be fair weather, for the sky is red,' [3]and in the morning, 'Today it will be stormy, for the sky is red and overcast.' You know how to interpret the appearance of the sky, but you cannot interpret the signs of the times. [4]A wicked and adulterous generation looks for a miraculous sign, but none will be given it except the sign of Jonah." Jesus then left them and went away.

The Yeast of the Pharisees and Sadducees

[5]When they went across the lake, the disciples forgot to take bread. [6]"Be careful," Jesus said to them. "Be on your guard against the yeast of the Pharisees and Sadducees."

[7]They discussed this among themselves and said, "It is because we didn't bring any bread."

[8]Aware of their discussion, Jesus asked, "You of little faith, why are you talking among yourselves about having no bread? [9]Do you still not understand? Don't you remember the five loaves for the five thousand, and how many basketfuls you gathered? [10]Or the seven loaves for the four thousand, and how many basketfuls you gathered? [11]How is it you don't understand that I was not talking to you about bread? But be on your guard against the yeast of the Pharisees and Sadducees." [12]Then they understood that he was not telling them to guard against the yeast used in bread, but against the teaching of the Pharisees and Sadducees.

Peter's Confession of Christ

[13]When Jesus came to the region of Caesarea Philippi, he asked his disciples, "Who do people say the Son of Man is?"

[14]They replied, "Some say John the Baptist; others say Elijah; and still others, Jeremiah or one of the prophets."

[15]"But what about you?" he asked. "Who do you say I am?"

[16]Simon Peter answered, "You are the Christ,[b] the Son of the living God."

[17]Jesus replied, "Blessed are you, Simon son of Jonah, for this was not revealed to you by man, but by my Father in heaven. [18]And I tell you that you are Peter,[c] and on this rock I will build my church, and the gates of Hades[d] will not overcome it.[e] [19]I will give you the keys of the kingdom of heaven; whatever you bind on earth will be[f] bound in heaven, and

whatever you loose on earth will beˢ loosed in heaven." ²⁰Then he warned his disciples not to tell anyone that he was the Christ.

Jesus Predicts His Death

²¹From that time on Jesus began to explain to his disciples that he must go to Jerusalem and suffer many things at the hands of the elders, chief priests and teachers of the law, and that he must be killed and on the third day be raised to life.

²²Peter took him aside and began to rebuke him. "Never, Lord!" he said. "This shall never happen to you!"

²³Jesus turned and said to Peter, "Get behind me, Satan! You are a stumbling block to me; you do not have in mind the things of God, but the things of men."

²⁴Then Jesus said to his disciples, "If anyone would come after me, he must deny himself and take up his cross and follow me. ²⁵For whoever wants to save his lifeᵍ will lose it, but whoever loses his life for me will find it. ²⁶What good will it be for a man if he gains the whole world, yet forfeits his soul? Or what can a man give in exchange for his soul? ²⁷For the Son of Man is going to come in his Father's glory with his angels, and then he will reward each person according to what he has done. ²⁸I tell you the truth, some who are standing here will not taste death before they see the Son of Man coming in his kingdom."

ᵃ2 Some early manuscripts do not have the rest of verse 2 and all of verse 3.   ᵇ16 Or Messiah; also in verse 20   ᶜ18 Peter means rock.   ᵈ18 Or hell   ᵉ18 Or not prove stronger than it   ᶠ19 Or have been   ᵍ25 The Greek word means either life or soul; also in verse 26.

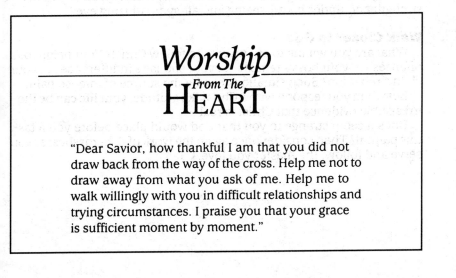

Worship
From The
Heart

"Dear Savior, how thankful I am that you did not
draw back from the way of the cross. Help me not to
draw away from what you ask of me. Help me to
walk willingly with you in difficult relationships and
trying circumstances. I praise you that your grace
is sufficient moment by moment."

JANUARY 16

Walking in the Way of the Cross

If anyone would come after me, he must deny himself and take up his cross and follow me (Matthew 16:24).

Self-denial. Suffering. Crossbearing. That's not the kind of lifestyle anyone would normally volunteer for.

But Christ put up with the shame and anguish of the cross that he might bring men and women to himself. So it shouldn't surprise you that he calls you to a similar lifestyle today.

Alexander Whyte provides a helpful insight into the disciple's role as a crossbearer.

Walk With Alexander Whyte

"There are things in all our lives that chafe and fret and crucify our hearts continually. Those you love best may even be the cause of constant and acute pain.

"There are people with whom you are compelled to stand in the closest of business relationships—people whose tempers and manners and treatment of you continually exasperate you.

"Though no mortal may ever guess you are fast sinking under the weight of such crosses as these, it is no guess with your Savior. He knows all about it.

"No one has ever understood crosses better than Jesus Christ. Be sure he is not far away.

"Every new morning, take up your cross and carry it all day in his strength and under his all-seeing and all-sympathizing eye."

Walk Closer to God

What are you willing to put up with to follow Christ? Your neighbor's offenses . . . your boss's temper . . . your spouse's indifference . . . your child's rebellion? Such situations can be the source of intense pain.

But when you respond with a Christlike attitude, your life can be the irresistible evidence that Christ is real.

Does it seem strange to you that God would place before you a task this painful? Then consider once again the work of the crossbearer you serve and follow, the master you love. ◖

JANUARY 17

Matthew writes of the awesome transfiguration scene in which Jesus appears in his glorified state, and then records Jesus' descent to the reality of a world of sickness and death.

The Transfiguration

17 After six days Jesus took with him Peter, James and John the brother of James, and led them up a high mountain by themselves. ²There he was transfigured before them. His face shone like the sun, and his clothes became as white as the light. ³Just then there appeared before them Moses and Elijah, talking with Jesus.

⁴Peter said to Jesus, "Lord, it is good for us to be here. If you wish, I will put up three shelters—one for you, one for Moses and one for Elijah."

⁵While he was still speaking, a bright cloud enveloped them, and a voice from the cloud said, "This is my Son, whom I love; with him I am well pleased. Listen to him!"

⁶When the disciples heard this, they fell facedown to the ground, terrified. ⁷But Jesus came and touched them. "Get up," he said. "Don't be afraid." ⁸When they looked up, they saw no one except Jesus.

⁹As they were coming down the mountain, Jesus instructed them, "Don't tell anyone what you have seen, until the Son of Man has been raised from the dead."

¹⁰The disciples asked him, "Why then do the teachers of the law say that Elijah must come first?"

¹¹Jesus replied, "To be sure, Elijah comes and will restore all things. ¹²But I tell you, Elijah has already come, and they did not recognize him, but have done to him everything they wished. In the same way the Son of Man is going to suffer at their hands." ¹³Then the disciples understood that he was talking to them about John the Baptist.

The Healing of a Boy With a Demon

¹⁴When they came to the crowd, a man approached Jesus and knelt before him. ¹⁵"Lord, have mercy on my son," he said. "He has seizures and is suffering greatly. He often falls into the fire or into the water. ¹⁶I brought him to your disciples, but they could not heal him."

¹⁷"O unbelieving and perverse generation," Jesus replied, "how long shall I stay with you? How long shall I put up with you? Bring the boy here to me." ¹⁸Jesus rebuked the demon, and it came out of the boy, and he was healed from that moment.

¹⁹Then the disciples came to Jesus in private and asked, "Why couldn't we drive it out?"

²⁰He replied, "Because you have so little faith. I tell you the truth, if you have faith as small as a mustard seed, you can say to this mountain, 'Move from here to there' and it will move. Nothing will be impossible for you.ᵃ"

JANUARY 17

²²When they came together in Galilee, he said to them, "The Son of Man is going to be betrayed into the hands of men. ²³They will kill him, and on the third day he will be raised to life." And the disciples were filled with grief.

The Temple Tax

²⁴After Jesus and his disciples arrived in Capernaum, the collectors of the two-drachma tax came to Peter and asked, "Doesn't your teacher pay the temple tax^b?"

²⁵"Yes, he does," he replied.

When Peter came into the house, Jesus was the first to speak. "What do you think, Simon?" he asked. "From whom do the kings of the earth collect duty and taxes — from their own sons or from others?"

²⁶"From others," Peter answered.

"Then the sons are exempt," Jesus said to him. ²⁷"But so that we may not offend them, go to the lake and throw out your line. Take the first fish you catch; open its mouth and you will find a four-drachma coin. Take it and give it to them for my tax and yours."

^a20 Some manuscripts *you.* ²¹*But this kind does not go out except by prayer and fasting.*
^b24 Greek *the two drachmas*

PSALM 16

Lord, you have assigned me my portion and my cup;
you have made my lot secure.
⁶The boundary lines have fallen for me in pleasant places;
surely I have a delightful inheritance.

⁷I will praise the LORD, who counsels me;
even at night my heart instructs me.
⁸I have set the LORD always before me.
Because he is at my right hand,
I will not be shaken.

Mustard-seed Faith in a Mighty God

If you have faith as small as a mustard seed, you can say to this mountain, "Move from here to there" and it will move. Nothing will be impossible for you (Matthew 17:20).

Atoms. Bees. Transistors. Computer chips. By anyone's standard, they're not very big. Yet a lot of little things can pack a big punch.

Take faith, for instance. According to Jesus in Matthew 17, a mustard-seed amount of faith is enough to move mountains.

Oswald Chambers probes the meaning of faith as the life attitude of the Christian.

Walk With Oswald Chambers

"Faith brings us into right relationship with God and gives God his opportunity. He frequently has to knock the bottom out of our experience to get us into contact with himself.

"God wants you to understand it is a life of faith—not a life of sentimental enjoyment of his blessings—that pleases him.

"Faith by its very nature must be tried. And the real trial of faith is not that we find it difficult to trust God, but that God's character has to be clear in our minds so that we remain true to God whatever he may do.

" 'Though he slay me,' announced Job, 'yet will I hope in him.' This is the most sublime utterance of faith in the whole Bible."

Walk Closer to God

Faith. You can't see it, hear it or touch it. But neither can you live without it.

Faith requires a commitment. It is pointless to say, "I have faith in the bank," unless you put your money there.

Likewise, it is meaningless to say, "I have faith in God," unless you trust in him.

And rest in him.

And relax.

Mustard-seed faith in a mighty God—that's how to see him move a mountain of need in your life.

And that's how to bear up under trials until he does it!

JANUARY 18

📖 Walk in the Word
Matthew 18

Matthew sets the spotlight on Jesus' loving heart through a series of object lessons centering around children and parables about restoration and about forgiveness.

The Greatest in the Kingdom of Heaven

18 At that time the disciples came to Jesus and asked, "Who is the greatest in the kingdom of heaven?"

²He called a little child and had him stand among them. ³And he said: "I tell you the truth, unless you change and become like little children, you will never enter the kingdom of heaven. ⁴Therefore, whoever humbles himself like this child is the greatest in the kingdom of heaven.

⁵"And whoever welcomes a little child like this in my name welcomes me. ⁶But if anyone causes one of these little ones who believe in me to sin, it would be better for him to have a large millstone hung around his neck and to be drowned in the depths of the sea.

⁷"Woe to the world because of the things that cause people to sin! Such things must come, but woe to the man through whom they come! ⁸If your hand or your foot causes you to sin, cut it off and throw it away. It is better for you to enter life maimed or crippled than to have two hands or two feet and be thrown into eternal fire. ⁹And if your eye causes you to sin, gouge it out and throw it away. It is better for you to enter life with one eye than to have two eyes and be thrown into the fire of hell.

The Parable of the Lost Sheep

¹⁰"See that you do not look down on one of these little ones. For I tell you that their angels in heaven always see the face of my Father in heaven.ᵃ

¹²"What do you think? If a man owns a hundred sheep, and one of them wanders away, will he not leave the ninety-nine on the hills and go to look for the one that wandered off? ¹³And if he finds it, I tell you the truth, he is happier about that one sheep than about the ninety-nine that did not wander off. ¹⁴In the same way your Father in heaven is not willing that any of these little ones should be lost.

A Brother Who Sins Against You

¹⁵"If your brother sins against you,ᵇ go and show him his fault, just between the two of you. If he listens to you, you have won your brother over. ¹⁶But if he will not listen, take one or two others along, so that 'every matter may be established by the testimony of two or three witnesses.'ᶜ ¹⁷If he refuses to listen to them, tell it to the church; and if he refuses to listen even to the church, treat him as you would a pagan or a tax collector.

¹⁸"I tell you the truth, whatever you bind on earth will beᵈ bound in heaven, and whatever you loose on earth will beᵈ loosed in heaven.

JANUARY 18

¹⁹"Again, I tell you that if two of you on earth agree about anything you ask for, it will be done for you by my Father in heaven. ²⁰For where two or three come together in my name, there am I with them."

The Parable of the Unmerciful Servant

²¹Then Peter came to Jesus and asked, "Lord, how many times shall I forgive my brother when he sins against me? Up to seven times?"

²²Jesus answered, "I tell you, not seven times, but seventy-seven times. ᵉ

²³"Therefore, the kingdom of heaven is like a king who wanted to settle accounts with his servants. ²⁴As he began the settlement, a man who owed him ten thousand talentsᶠ was brought to him. ²⁵Since he was not able to pay, the master ordered that he and his wife and his children and all that he had be sold to repay the debt.

²⁶"The servant fell on his knees before him. 'Be patient with me,' he begged, 'and I will pay back everything.' ²⁷The servant's master took pity on him, canceled the debt and let him go.

²⁸"But when that servant went out, he found one of his fellow servants who owed him a hundred denarii.ᵍ He grabbed him and began to choke him. 'Pay back what you owe me!' he demanded.

²⁹"His fellow servant fell to his knees and begged him, 'Be patient with me, and I will pay you back.'

³⁰"But he refused. Instead, he went off and had the man thrown into prison until he could pay the debt. ³¹When the other servants saw what had happened, they were greatly distressed and went and told their master everything that had happened.

³²"Then the master called the servant in. 'You wicked servant,' he said, 'I canceled all that debt of yours because you begged me to. ³³Shouldn't you have had mercy on your fellow servant just as I had on you?' ³⁴In anger his master turned him over to the jailers to be tortured, until he should pay back all he owed.

³⁵"This is how my heavenly Father will treat each of you unless you forgive your brother from your heart."

ᵃ10 Some manuscripts *heaven.* ¹¹*The Son of Man came to save what was lost.*   ᵇ15 Some manuscripts do not have *against you.*   ᶜ16 Deut. 19:15   ᵈ18 Or *have been*   ᵉ22 Or *seventy times seven*   ᶠ24 That is, millions of dollars   ᵍ28 That is, a few dollars

JANUARY 18

God Forgave My Sin in Jesus' Name

Then Peter came to Jesus and asked, "Lord, how many times shall I forgive my brother when he sins against me? Up to seven times?" Jesus answered, "I tell you, not seven times, but seventy-seven times" (Matthew 18:21–22).

Forgive and forget.

Peter was certainly comfortable with that principle. After all, hadn't Jesus taught him already that if he forgave others when they sinned against him his heavenly Father would also forgive him? And hadn't the sacrificial system he had grown up with taught him that God forgives the sins of his people?

Yes, Peter was certainly comfortable with forgiveness—seven times. But seventy-seven times?

Unfortunately, all of us since Adam are like Peter in this respect—all except one. John Flavel reminds us to imitate him who is infinite forgiveness.

Walk With John Flavel

"Imitate our pattern Christ and labor for meek forgiving spirits. I shall only propose two reasons for doing so: for the honor of Christ, and for your own peace. His glory is more than your life, and all that you enjoy in this world. Oh, do not expose it to the scorn and derision of his enemies. Let them not say, 'How is Christ a lamb, when his followers are lions? How is the church a dove, that smites and scratches like a bird of prey?'

"Consider also the quiet of your own heart. What is life worth, without the comfort of life? What comfort can you have in all that you possess in the world as long as you do not have possession of your own soul? If inside you are full of tumult and revenge, the Spirit of Christ will become a stranger to you; that dove delights in a clean and quiet heart. Oh, then imitate Christ in this excellency also!"

Walk Closer to God

The rest of the chapter is the parable of the unmerciful servant. The main character refused to forgive as he had been forgiven. Notice that he was "turned . . . over to the jailers to be tortured" (Matthew 18:34).

Are you "tortured" by an unforgiving spirit? Ephesians 4:32 has the answer: Meditate on Christ's forgiveness. There is no better way to cultivate your own. ❍

JANUARY 19

Walk in the Word
Matthew 19

Matthew follows the trick questions of the deceitful Pharisees with scenes of vulnerable little children who hold the secret to the kingdom and a pathetic rich man controlled by his wealth.

Divorce

19 When Jesus had finished saying these things, he left Galilee and went into the region of Judea to the other side of the Jordan. ²Large crowds followed him, and he healed them there.

³Some Pharisees came to him to test him. They asked, "Is it lawful for a man to divorce his wife for any and every reason?"

⁴"Haven't you read," he replied, "that at the beginning the Creator 'made them male and female,'ᵃ ⁵and said, 'For this reason a man will leave his father and mother and be united to his wife, and the two will become one flesh'ᵇ? ⁶So they are no longer two, but one. Therefore what God has joined together, let man not separate."

⁷"Why then," they asked, "did Moses command that a man give his wife a certificate of divorce and send her away?"

⁸Jesus replied, "Moses permitted you to divorce your wives because your hearts were hard. But it was not this way from the beginning. ⁹I tell you that anyone who divorces his wife, except for marital unfaithfulness, and marries another woman commits adultery."

¹⁰The disciples said to him, "If this is the situation between a husband and wife, it is better not to marry."

¹¹Jesus replied, "Not everyone can accept this word, but only those to whom it has been given. ¹²For some are eunuchs because they were born that way; others were made that way by men; and others have renounced marriageᶜ because of the kingdom of heaven. The one who can accept this should accept it."

The Little Children and Jesus

¹³Then little children were brought to Jesus for him to place his hands on them and pray for them. But the disciples rebuked those who brought them.

¹⁴Jesus said, "Let the little children come to me, and do not hinder them, for the kingdom of heaven belongs to such as these." ¹⁵When he had placed his hands on them, he went on from there.

The Rich Young Man

¹⁶Now a man came up to Jesus and asked, "Teacher, what good thing must I do to get eternal life?"

¹⁷"Why do you ask me about what is good?" Jesus replied. "There is only One who is good. If you want to enter life, obey the commandments."

¹⁸"Which ones?" the man inquired.

JANUARY 19

Jesus replied, " 'Do not murder, do not commit adultery, do not steal, do not give false testimony, ¹⁹honor your father and mother,'ᵈ and 'love your neighbor as yourself.'ᵉ "

²⁰"All these I have kept," the young man said. "What do I still lack?"

²¹Jesus answered, "If you want to be perfect, go, sell your possessions and give to the poor, and you will have treasure in heaven. Then come, follow me."

²²When the young man heard this, he went away sad, because he had great wealth.

²³Then Jesus said to his disciples, "I tell you the truth, it is hard for a rich man to enter the kingdom of heaven. ²⁴Again I tell you, it is easier for a camel to go through the eye of a needle than for a rich man to enter the kingdom of God."

²⁵When the disciples heard this, they were greatly astonished and asked, "Who then can be saved?"

²⁶Jesus looked at them and said, "With man this is impossible, but with God all things are possible."

²⁷Peter answered him, "We have left everything to follow you! What then will there be for us?"

²⁸Jesus said to them, "I tell you the truth, at the renewal of all things, when the Son of Man sits on his glorious throne, you who have followed me will also sit on twelve thrones, judging the twelve tribes of Israel. ²⁹And everyone who has left houses or brothers or sisters or father or motherᶠ or children or fields for my sake will receive a hundred times as much and will inherit eternal life. ³⁰But many who are first will be last, and many who are last will be first.

ᵃ4 Gen. 1:27   ᵇ5 Gen. 2:24   ᶜ12 Or *have made themselves eunuchs*   ᵈ19 Exodus 20:12-16; Deut. 5:16-20   ᵉ19 Lev. 19:18   ᶠ29 Some manuscripts *mother or wife*

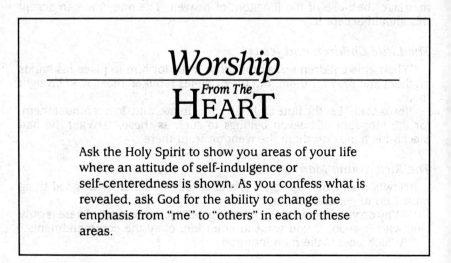

Worship
From The
HEART

Ask the Holy Spirit to show you areas of your life where an attitude of self-indulgence or self-centeredness is shown. As you confess what is revealed, ask God for the ability to change the emphasis from "me" to "others" in each of these areas.

Giving Up Your Place in Line

> But many who are first will be last, and many who are last will be first (Matthew 19:30).

Ask ten third-graders to form a straight line, and chances are good that nine of them will clamor to be first in line.

In the process, they are modeling what society has taught them: Greatness means coming in first.

In Matthew 18:4 and 19:30, Jesus addresses the subject of greatness. And clearly his concept of "coming in first" cuts across the grain with the mindset of his day.

John Calvin offers an insightful comment regarding greatness—a preoccupation not limited to the first century.

Walk With John Calvin

"The disciples were too accustomed to the common habits of men. Each one wanted the first place.

"But Christ regarded as worthy the man who forgot his superiority and humbled himself. He declares that they are greatest who abase themselves, lest we should think we lose anything when we willingly surrender all greatness.

"From this we may gather a brief definition of humility: 'He is truly humble who neither claims anything for himself over against God, nor proudly seeks superiority over his brethren, but desires only that Christ the head have preeminence.' "

Walk Closer to God

Humility.

Not a highly regarded commodity in a success-worshiping world where back-stabbing and ladder-climbing have become accepted behavior.

Listen to the world and you will hear the message, "Greatness consists of how many you lead."

Listen to God's voice and you will hear just the opposite: "Greatness consists of how many you serve."

They can't both be right.

You can push to the head of the line and receive the world's applause. Or you can give up your place in line and hear God's "well done."

The servant of God knows his place. ♥

JANUARY 20

📖 Walk in the Word
Matthew 20

Matthew recounts Jesus' dramatic parable of grace for the last and judgment for the first, then shares an incident that led to Jesus' revolutionary teaching about the key to greatness.

The Parable of the Workers in the Vineyard

20 "For the kingdom of heaven is like a landowner who went out early in the morning to hire men to work in his vineyard. ²He agreed to pay them a denarius for the day and sent them into his vineyard.

³"About the third hour he went out and saw others standing in the marketplace doing nothing. ⁴He told them, 'You also go and work in my vineyard, and I will pay you whatever is right.' ⁵So they went.

"He went out again about the sixth hour and the ninth hour and did the same thing. ⁶About the eleventh hour he went out and found still others standing around. He asked them, 'Why have you been standing here all day long doing nothing?'

⁷" 'Because no one has hired us,' they answered.

"He said to them, 'You also go and work in my vineyard.'

⁸"When evening came, the owner of the vineyard said to his foreman, 'Call the workers and pay them their wages, beginning with the last ones hired and going on to the first.'

⁹"The workers who were hired about the eleventh hour came and each received a denarius. ¹⁰So when those came who were hired first, they expected to receive more. But each one of them also received a denarius. ¹¹When they received it, they began to grumble against the landowner. ¹²'These men who were hired last worked only one hour,' they said, 'and you have made them equal to us who have borne the burden of the work and the heat of the day.'

¹³"But he answered one of them, 'Friend, I am not being unfair to you. Didn't you agree to work for a denarius? ¹⁴Take your pay and go. I want to give the man who was hired last the same as I gave you. ¹⁵Don't I have the right to do what I want with my own money? Or are you envious because I am generous?'

¹⁶"So the last will be first, and the first will be last."

Jesus Again Predicts His Death

¹⁷Now as Jesus was going up to Jerusalem, he took the twelve disciples aside and said to them, ¹⁸"We are going up to Jerusalem, and the Son of Man will be betrayed to the chief priests and the teachers of the law. They will condemn him to death ¹⁹and will turn him over to the Gentiles to be mocked and flogged and crucified. On the third day he will be raised to life!"

A Mother's Request

²⁰Then the mother of Zebedee's sons came to Jesus with her sons and, kneeling down, asked a favor of him.

²¹"What is it you want?" he asked.

She said, "Grant that one of these two sons of mine may sit at your right and the other at your left in your kingdom."

²²"You don't know what you are asking," Jesus said to them. "Can you drink the cup I am going to drink?"

"We can," they answered.

²³Jesus said to them, "You will indeed drink from my cup, but to sit at my right or left is not for me to grant. These places belong to those for whom they have been prepared by my Father."

²⁴When the ten heard about this, they were indignant with the two brothers. ²⁵Jesus called them together and said, "You know that the rulers of the Gentiles lord it over them, and their high officials exercise authority over them. ²⁶Not so with you. Instead, whoever wants to become great among you must be your servant, ²⁷and whoever wants to be first must be your slave— ²⁸just as the Son of Man did not come to be served, but to serve, and to give his life as a ransom for many."

Two Blind Men Receive Sight

²⁹As Jesus and his disciples were leaving Jericho, a large crowd followed him. ³⁰Two blind men were sitting by the roadside, and when they heard that Jesus was going by, they shouted, "Lord, Son of David, have mercy on us!"

³¹The crowd rebuked them and told them to be quiet, but they shouted all the louder, "Lord, Son of David, have mercy on us!"

³²Jesus stopped and called them. "What do you want me to do for you?" he asked.

³³"Lord," they answered, "we want our sight."

³⁴Jesus had compassion on them and touched their eyes. Immediately they received their sight and followed him.

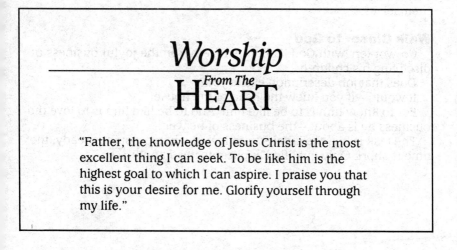

Worship
From The
HEART

"Father, the knowledge of Jesus Christ is the most excellent thing I can seek. To be like him is the highest goal to which I can aspire. I praise you that this is your desire for me. Glorify yourself through my life."

JANUARY 20

God's Glory: The Business of Heaven

For the kingdom of heaven is like a landowner who went out early in the morning to hire men to work in his vineyard (Matthew 20:1).

Ask a man his occupation, and you have learned how he pays his bills.

Ask him his preoccupation, and you have discovered his passion in life.

And if his occupation and his preoccupation are the same, you have found a worker worthy of his hire!

In Matthew 20 Jesus talks about the "business of heaven"—the labor and reward of workers in God's vineyard.

During his brief life, David Brainerd made the pursuit of God's kingdom his daily passion, as revealed by this selection from his diary.

Walk With David Brainerd

"When a soul loves God with a supreme love, he therein acts in conformity to God.

"God's interest and his become one, he longs for God to be glorified, and rejoices to think that God is unchangeably the Possessor of the highest glory and blessedness.

"Those who are totally given to God have the most complete and satisfying evidence of their being interested in all the benefits of Christ's redemption as their hearts are conformed to him.

"And these only are qualified for the employments and entertainments of God's kingdom of glory. None but these have any relish for the business of heaven, which is to give all glory to God, and not to themselves."

Walk Closer to God

Co-workers with God. Laborers together in the joyful business of discipling his children.

Does that job description excite you?

It would—if you knew the head of the house!

For to know him is to be like him. And to be like him is to love the business he is about—the business of heaven.

The task is big; the laborers are few; the harvest stands ready; the time is short. Only qualified applicants need apply. 〇

JANUARY 21

📖 Walk in the Word
Matthew 21

Matthew records Jesus' entry into Jerusalem, focusing on the temple area, where Jesus turns things upside down, both literally and figuratively, as he challenges the self-righteous Pharisees and priests.

The Triumphal Entry

21 As they approached Jerusalem and came to Bethphage on the Mount of Olives, Jesus sent two disciples, ²saying to them, "Go to the village ahead of you, and at once you will find a donkey tied there, with her colt by her. Untie them and bring them to me. ³If anyone says anything to you, tell him that the Lord needs them, and he will send them right away."

⁴This took place to fulfill what was spoken through the prophet:

⁵"Say to the Daughter of Zion,
  'See, your king comes to you,
    gentle and riding on a donkey,
      on a colt, the foal of a donkey.' "*a*

⁶The disciples went and did as Jesus had instructed them. ⁷They brought the donkey and the colt, placed their cloaks on them, and Jesus sat on them. ⁸A very large crowd spread their cloaks on the road, while others cut branches from the trees and spread them on the road. ⁹The crowds that went ahead of him and those that followed shouted,

"Hosanna*b* to the Son of David!"

"Blessed is he who comes in the name of the Lord!"*c*

"Hosanna*b* in the highest!"

¹⁰When Jesus entered Jerusalem, the whole city was stirred and asked, "Who is this?"

¹¹The crowds answered, "This is Jesus, the prophet from Nazareth in Galilee."

Jesus at the Temple

¹²Jesus entered the temple area and drove out all who were buying and selling there. He overturned the tables of the money changers and the benches of those selling doves. ¹³"It is written," he said to them, " 'My house will be called a house of prayer,'*d* but you are making it a 'den of robbers.'*e* "

¹⁴The blind and the lame came to him at the temple, and he healed them. ¹⁵But when the chief priests and the teachers of the law saw the wonderful things he did and the children shouting in the temple area, "Hosanna to the Son of David," they were indignant.

¹⁶"Do you hear what these children are saying?" they asked him.

"Yes," replied Jesus, "have you never read,

JANUARY 21

> " 'From the lips of children and infants
>   you have ordained praise'J?"

17And he left them and went out of the city to Bethany, where he spent the night.

The Fig Tree Withers

18Early in the morning, as he was on his way back to the city, he was hungry. 19Seeing a fig tree by the road, he went up to it but found nothing on it except leaves. Then he said to it, "May you never bear fruit again!" Immediately the tree withered.

20When the disciples saw this, they were amazed. "How did the fig tree wither so quickly?" they asked.

21Jesus replied, "I tell you the truth, if you have faith and do not doubt, not only can you do what was done to the fig tree, but also you can say to this mountain, 'Go, throw yourself into the sea,' and it will be done. 22If you believe, you will receive whatever you ask for in prayer."

The Authority of Jesus Questioned

23Jesus entered the temple courts, and, while he was teaching, the chief priests and the elders of the people came to him. "By what authority are you doing these things?" they asked. "And who gave you this authority?"

24Jesus replied, "I will also ask you one question. If you answer me, I will tell you by what authority I am doing these things. 25John's baptism — where did it come from? Was it from heaven, or from men?"

They discussed it among themselves and said, "If we say, 'From heaven,' he will ask, 'Then why didn't you believe him?' 26But if we say, 'From men' — we are afraid of the people, for they all hold that John was a prophet."

27So they answered Jesus, "We don't know."

Then he said, "Neither will I tell you by what authority I am doing these things.

The Parable of the Two Sons

28"What do you think? There was a man who had two sons. He went to the first and said, 'Son, go and work today in the vineyard.'

29" 'I will not,' he answered, but later he changed his mind and went.

30"Then the father went to the other son and said the same thing. He answered, 'I will, sir,' but he did not go.

31"Which of the two did what his father wanted?"

"The first," they answered.

Jesus said to them, "I tell you the truth, the tax collectors and the prostitutes are entering the kingdom of God ahead of you. 32For John came to you to show you the way of righteousness, and you did not believe him, but the tax collectors and the prostitutes did. And even after you saw this, you did not repent and believe him.

JANUARY 21

The Parable of the Tenants

33"Listen to another parable: There was a landowner who planted a vineyard. He put a wall around it, dug a winepress in it and built a watchtower. Then he rented the vineyard to some farmers and went away on a journey. 34When the harvest time approached, he sent his servants to the tenants to collect his fruit.

35"The tenants seized his servants; they beat one, killed another, and stoned a third. 36Then he sent other servants to them, more than the first time, and the tenants treated them the same way. 37Last of all, he sent his son to them. 'They will respect my son,' he said.

38"But when the tenants saw the son, they said to each other, 'This is the heir. Come, let's kill him and take his inheritance.' 39So they took him and threw him out of the vineyard and killed him.

40"Therefore, when the owner of the vineyard comes, what will he do to those tenants?"

41"He will bring those wretches to a wretched end," they replied, "and he will rent the vineyard to other tenants, who will give him his share of the crop at harvest time."

42Jesus said to them, "Have you never read in the Scriptures:

> " 'The stone the builders rejected
>   has become the capstone*g*;
>   the Lord has done this,
>   and it is marvelous in our eyes'*h*?

43"Therefore I tell you that the kingdom of God will be taken away from you and given to a people who will produce its fruit. 44He who falls on this stone will be broken to pieces, but he on whom it falls will be crushed."*i*

45When the chief priests and the Pharisees heard Jesus' parables, they knew he was talking about them. 46They looked for a way to arrest him, but they were afraid of the crowd because the people held that he was a prophet.

---

a5 Zech. 9:9   *b9* A Hebrew expression meaning "Save!" which became an exclamation of praise; also in verse 15   *c9* Psalm 118:26   *d13* Isaiah 56:7   *e13* Jer. 7:11
f16 Psalm 8:2   *g42* Or *cornerstone*   *h42* Psalm 118:22,23   *i44* Some manuscripts do not have verse 44.

JANUARY 21

Excuses: Obstacles to the Gates of Heaven

A man . . . said, "Son, go and work today in the vineyard" . . . He answered, "I will, sir," but he did not go (Matthew 21:28,30).

Ben Franklin was right. There has seldom been a man good at making excuses who was good at anything else.

Good intentions. Not enough time. Too many responsibilities. The bottom line in each case is the same: The job just doesn't get done.

The revivalist Charles Finney offers this warning about the danger of coming to God with excuses rather than repentance.

Walk With Charles Finney

"It seems to be a law of human nature that when a person is accused of wrong, either by the conscience or any other agent, he must either confess or justify.

"This is the reason why people make so many excuses and why they have so great a variety.

"But nothing can be more grievous in God's sight than excuses made by those who know they are utterly false.

"Sinners don't need their excuses. God does not ask for even one. He does not require you to justify yourself—not at all.

"I can remember the year I lived on excuses and found them to be obstacles in the way of my conversion. As soon as I let these go completely, I found the gate of God's mercy wide open.

"And so, sinner, will you."

Walk Closer to God

As you read Jesus' parables and Mr. Finney's words, do you grow uncomfortable?

That's God's way of demolishing your carefully constructed refuge of excuses in order to expose your heart to the truth.

Someday you will face up to your excuses—either in judgment or repentance. God will see to that.

But why wait? Excuses can be deadly.

"But God, you don't understand . . ."

Indeed, he does. And once you realize that, you can't ignore him any longer. ⟨⟩

JANUARY 22

Walk in the Word
Matthew 22

Matthew records more of Jesus' interaction with the religious leaders; he highlights Jesus' brilliant responses to the blatant efforts of the religious leaders to lead Jesus into verbal traps.

The Parable of the Wedding Banquet

22 Jesus spoke to them again in parables, saying: ²"The kingdom of heaven is like a king who prepared a wedding banquet for his son. ³He sent his servants to those who had been invited to the banquet to tell them to come, but they refused to come.

⁴"Then he sent some more servants and said, 'Tell those who have been invited that I have prepared my dinner: My oxen and fattened cattle have been butchered, and everything is ready. Come to the wedding banquet.'

⁵"But they paid no attention and went off—one to his field, another to his business. ⁶The rest seized his servants, mistreated them and killed them. ⁷The king was enraged. He sent his army and destroyed those murderers and burned their city.

⁸"Then he said to his servants, 'The wedding banquet is ready, but those I invited did not deserve to come. ⁹Go to the street corners and invite to the banquet anyone you find.' ¹⁰So the servants went out into the streets and gathered all the people they could find, both good and bad, and the wedding hall was filled with guests.

¹¹"But when the king came in to see the guests, he noticed a man there who was not wearing wedding clothes. ¹²'Friend,' he asked, 'how did you get in here without wedding clothes?' The man was speechless.

¹³"Then the king told the attendants, 'Tie him hand and foot, and throw him outside, into the darkness, where there will be weeping and gnashing of teeth.'

¹⁴"For many are invited, but few are chosen."

Paying Taxes to Caesar

¹⁵Then the Pharisees went out and laid plans to trap him in his words. ¹⁶They sent their disciples to him along with the Herodians. "Teacher," they said, "we know you are a man of integrity and that you teach the way of God in accordance with the truth. You aren't swayed by men, because you pay no attention to who they are. ¹⁷Tell us then, what is your opinion? Is it right to pay taxes to Caesar or not?"

¹⁸But Jesus, knowing their evil intent, said, "You hypocrites, why are you trying to trap me? ¹⁹Show me the coin used for paying the tax." They brought him a denarius, ²⁰and he asked them, "Whose portrait is this? And whose inscription?"

²¹"Caesar's," they replied.

Then he said to them, "Give to Caesar what is Caesar's, and to God what is God's."

JANUARY 22

22When they heard this, they were amazed. So they left him and went away.

Marriage at the Resurrection

23That same day the Sadducees, who say there is no resurrection, came to him with a question. 24"Teacher," they said, "Moses told us that if a man dies without having children, his brother must marry the widow and have children for him. 25Now there were seven brothers among us. The first one married and died, and since he had no children, he left his wife to his brother. 26The same thing happened to the second and third brother, right on down to the seventh. 27Finally, the woman died. 28Now then, at the resurrection, whose wife will she be of the seven, since all of them were married to her?"

29Jesus replied, "You are in error because you do not know the Scriptures or the power of God. 30At the resurrection people will neither marry nor be given in marriage; they will be like the angels in heaven. 31But about the resurrection of the dead—have you not read what God said to you, 32'I am the God of Abraham, the God of Isaac, and the God of Jacob'a? He is not the God of the dead but of the living."

33When the crowds heard this, they were astonished at his teaching.

The Greatest Commandment

34Hearing that Jesus had silenced the Sadducees, the Pharisees got together. 35One of them, an expert in the law, tested him with this question: 36"Teacher, which is the greatest commandment in the Law?"

37Jesus replied: " 'Love the Lord your God with all your heart and with all your soul and with all your mind.'b 38This is the first and greatest commandment. 39And the second is like it: 'Love your neighbor as yourself.'c 40All the Law and the Prophets hang on these two commandments."

Whose Son Is the Christ?

41While the Pharisees were gathered together, Jesus asked them, 42"What do you think about the Christd? Whose son is he?"

"The son of David," they replied.

43He said to them, "How is it then that David, speaking by the Spirit, calls him 'Lord'? For he says,

> 44" 'The Lord said to my Lord:
> "Sit at my right hand
> until I put your enemies
> under your feet." 'e

45If then David calls him 'Lord,' how can he be his son?" 46No one could say a word in reply, and from that day on no one dared to ask him any more questions.

---

a32 Exodus 3:6   b37 Deut. 6:5   c39 Lev. 19:18   d42 Or Messiah   e44 Psalm 110:1

Duty or Delight: Love Makes the Difference

Love the Lord your God with all your heart and with all your soul and with all your mind (Matthew 22:37).

The sergeant growls, "Now, do it! And that's an order!" Muttering to himself, the soldier stoops to the assigned task.

Ironic, isn't it, that the greatest command from our commander-in-chief is a command to love.

"Love the Lord your God. . . . Love your neighbor as yourself." The law of love supersedes all others. It's that "greatest commandment" of which Jesus speaks in Matthew 22 — and which became the consuming passion of Thomas à Kempis.

Walk With Thomas à Kempis

"Blessed is the man who knows what it is to love Jesus, for Jesus desires to be loved alone above all things.

"Love him and keep him for your friend, and he will stand by you when other friends depart.

"When Jesus is present, all is well and nothing seems difficult. But when love for Jesus is absent, everything becomes hard.

"How dry and hard you feel without Jesus! How foolish and empty when you seek anything apart from him!

"He is very poor who lives without Jesus; he is very rich who has him for his friend."

Walk Closer to God

Keeping the great commandment is as easy as falling in love. And love is the supreme motivation for service.

Washing windows. Cutting lawns. Bathing children. Fixing faucets. You'll seldom find these items written into a marriage contract!

Yet millions of husbands and wives do these and other chores — without being paid a cent!

Why? The law of love.

Encouraging. Nurturing. Testifying. Giving. These are just a few of your responsibilities as a disciple of Jesus Christ.

And whether you view them as a duty or a delight depends on your love for the Savior.

So how's your love life? ❍

JANUARY 23

📖 Walk in the Word
Matthew 23

Matthew relates Jesus' penetrating exposé of the hypocrisy of the Pharisees but also leaves his readers with a picture of the gentle feelings of love expressed in Jesus' sorrow for Jerusalem.

Seven Woes

23 Then Jesus said to the crowds and to his disciples: [2]"The teachers of the law and the Pharisees sit in Moses' seat. [3]So you must obey them and do everything they tell you. But do not do what they do, for they do not practice what they preach. [4]They tie up heavy loads and put them on men's shoulders, but they themselves are not willing to lift a finger to move them.

[5]"Everything they do is done for men to see: They make their phylacteries[a] wide and the tassels on their garments long; [6]they love the place of honor at banquets and the most important seats in the synagogues; [7]they love to be greeted in the marketplaces and to have men call them 'Rabbi.'

[8]"But you are not to be called 'Rabbi,' for you have only one Master and you are all brothers. [9]And do not call anyone on earth 'father,' for you have one Father, and he is in heaven. [10]Nor are you to be called 'teacher,' for you have one Teacher, the Christ.[b] [11]The greatest among you will be your servant. [12]For whoever exalts himself will be humbled, and whoever humbles himself will be exalted.

[13]"Woe to you, teachers of the law and Pharisees, you hypocrites! You shut the kingdom of heaven in men's faces. You yourselves do not enter, nor will you let those enter who are trying to.[c]

[15]"Woe to you, teachers of the law and Pharisees, you hypocrites! You travel over land and sea to win a single convert, and when he becomes one, you make him twice as much a son of hell as you are.

[16]"Woe to you, blind guides! You say, 'If anyone swears by the temple, it means nothing; but if anyone swears by the gold of the temple, he is bound by his oath.' [17]You blind fools! Which is greater: the gold, or the temple that makes the gold sacred? [18]You also say, 'If anyone swears by the altar, it means nothing; but if anyone swears by the gift on it, he is bound by his oath.' [19]You blind men! Which is greater: the gift, or the altar that makes the gift sacred? [20]Therefore, he who swears by the altar swears by it and by everything on it. [21]And he who swears by the temple swears by it and by the one who dwells in it. [22]And he who swears by heaven swears by God's throne and by the one who sits on it.

[23]"Woe to you, teachers of the law and Pharisees, you hypocrites! You give a tenth of your spices — mint, dill and cummin. But you have neglected the more important matters of the law — justice, mercy and faithfulness. You should have practiced the latter, without neglecting the former. [24]You blind guides! You strain out a gnat but swallow a camel.

[25]"Woe to you, teachers of the law and Pharisees, you hypocrites! You clean the outside of the cup and dish, but inside they are full of greed and

self-indulgence. ²⁶Blind Pharisee! First clean the inside of the cup and dish, and then the outside also will be clean.

²⁷"Woe to you, teachers of the law and Pharisees, you hypocrites! You are like whitewashed tombs, which look beautiful on the outside but on the inside are full of dead men's bones and everything unclean. ²⁸In the same way, on the outside you appear to people as righteous but on the inside you are full of hypocrisy and wickedness.

²⁹"Woe to you, teachers of the law and Pharisees, you hypocrites! You build tombs for the prophets and decorate the graves of the righteous. ³⁰And you say, 'If we had lived in the days of our forefathers, we would not have taken part with them in shedding the blood of the prophets.' ³¹So you testify against yourselves that you are the descendants of those who murdered the prophets. ³²Fill up, then, the measure of the sin of your forefathers!

³³"You snakes! You brood of vipers! How will you escape being condemned to hell? ³⁴Therefore I am sending you prophets and wise men and teachers. Some of them you will kill and crucify; others you will flog in your synagogues and pursue from town to town. ³⁵And so upon you will come all the righteous blood that has been shed on earth, from the blood of righteous Abel to the blood of Zechariah son of Berekiah, whom you murdered between the temple and the altar. ³⁶I tell you the truth, all this will come upon this generation.

³⁷"O Jerusalem, Jerusalem, you who kill the prophets and stone those sent to you, how often I have longed to gather your children together, as a hen gathers her chicks under her wings, but you were not willing. ³⁸Look, your house is left to you desolate. ³⁹For I tell you, you will not see me again until you say, 'Blessed is he who comes in the name of the Lord.'ᵈ"

ᵃ5 That is, boxes containing Scripture verses, worn on forehead and arm   ᵇ10 Or Messiah
ᶜ13 Some manuscripts to. ¹⁴Woe to you, teachers of the law and Pharisees, you hypocrites!
You devour widows' houses and for a show make lengthy prayers. Therefore you will be
punished more severely.   ᵈ39 Psalm 118:26

JANUARY 23

Healer of the Brokenhearted

O Jerusalem, Jerusalem . . . how often I have longed to gather your children together . . . but you were not willing (Matthew 23:37).

Wonder adhesives. Miracle glues. With all of our twentieth-century know-how, you'd think we could fix anything. But science has yet to discover a product strong enough to mend a broken heart.

For that you'll have to go to the Savior who specializes in such matters.

He's the one who, in the final days of his life on earth, surveyed the city of Jerusalem . . . and what he saw made him weep.

Evangelist Dwight L. Moody offers some thoughts about the Savior's tears.

Walk With Dwight L. Moody

"From Adam's day to ours, tears have been shed, and a wail has gone up from the brokenhearted.

"And it is a mystery to me how all those broken hearts can keep away from him who has come to heal them.

"Jesus often looked up to heaven and sighed. I believe it was because of so much suffering around him.

"It was on his right and on his left—everywhere on earth. And the thought that he had come to relieve the people of their burdens, yet so few would accept him, made him sorrowful.

"Do you think there is a heart so broken that it can't be healed by him? He can heal them all. But the great trouble is that people won't come."

Walk Closer to God

Jesus wept over a city. Not for its buildings, but for its people. People like you—with broken hearts and broken spirits. People in need of repentance and repair.

Though he wept, he can tenderly wipe the tears from your eyes. For he is the mighty physician, capable of healing every wounded heart brought to him. But you must be willing to put yourself under his care.

He has so much to give. But so few are willing to receive. Let the few include you. ❍

JANUARY 24

Walk in the Word
Matthew 24

Matthew writes Jesus' response to the disciples' question about the end times and the signs of Jesus' coming.

Signs of the End of the Age

24 Jesus left the temple and was walking away when his disciples came up to him to call his attention to its buildings. ²"Do you see all these things?" he asked. "I tell you the truth, not one stone here will be left on another; every one will be thrown down."

³As Jesus was sitting on the Mount of Olives, the disciples came to him privately. "Tell us," they said, "when will this happen, and what will be the sign of your coming and of the end of the age?"

⁴Jesus answered: "Watch out that no one deceives you. ⁵For many will come in my name, claiming, 'I am the Christ,ᵃ' and will deceive many. ⁶You will hear of wars and rumors of wars, but see to it that you are not alarmed. Such things must happen, but the end is still to come. ⁷Nation will rise against nation, and kingdom against kingdom. There will be famines and earthquakes in various places. ⁸All these are the beginning of birth pains.

⁹"Then you will be handed over to be persecuted and put to death, and you will be hated by all nations because of me. ¹⁰At that time many will turn away from the faith and will betray and hate each other, ¹¹and many false prophets will appear and deceive many people. ¹²Because of the increase of wickedness, the love of most will grow cold, ¹³but he who stands firm to the end will be saved. ¹⁴And this gospel of the kingdom will be preached in the whole world as a testimony to all nations, and then the end will come.

¹⁵"So when you see standing in the holy place 'the abomination that causes desolation,'ᵇ spoken of through the prophet Daniel — let the reader understand — ¹⁶then let those who are in Judea flee to the mountains. ¹⁷Let no one on the roof of his house go down to take anything out of the house. ¹⁸Let no one in the field go back to get his cloak. ¹⁹How dreadful it will be in those days for pregnant women and nursing mothers! ²⁰Pray that your flight will not take place in winter or on the Sabbath. ²¹For then there will be great distress, unequaled from the beginning of the world until now — and never to be equaled again. ²²If those days had not been cut short, no one would survive, but for the sake of the elect those days will be shortened. ²³At that time if anyone says to you, 'Look, here is the Christ!' or, 'There he is!' do not believe it. ²⁴For false Christs and false prophets will appear and perform great signs and miracles to deceive even the elect — if that were possible. ²⁵See, I have told you ahead of time.

²⁶"So if anyone tells you, 'There he is, out in the desert,' do not go out; or, 'Here he is, in the inner rooms,' do not believe it. ²⁷For as lightning that comes from the east is visible even in the west, so will be the coming of the Son of Man. ²⁸Wherever there is a carcass, there the vultures will gather.

JANUARY 24

29"Immediately after the distress of those days

" 'the sun will be darkened,
    and the moon will not give its light;
the stars will fall from the sky,
    and the heavenly bodies will be shaken.'c

30"At that time the sign of the Son of Man will appear in the sky, and all the nations of the earth will mourn. They will see the Son of Man coming on the clouds of the sky, with power and great glory. 31And he will send his angels with a loud trumpet call, and they will gather his elect from the four winds, from one end of the heavens to the other.

32"Now learn this lesson from the fig tree: As soon as its twigs get tender and its leaves come out, you know that summer is near. 33Even so, when you see all these things, you know that itd is near, right at the door. 34I tell you the truth, this generatione will certainly not pass away until all these things have happened. 35Heaven and earth will pass away, but my words will never pass away.

The Day and Hour Unknown

36"No one knows about that day or hour, not even the angels in heaven, nor the Son,f but only the Father. 37As it was in the days of Noah, so it will be at the coming of the Son of Man. 38For in the days before the flood, people were eating and drinking, marrying and giving in marriage, up to the day Noah entered the ark; 39and they knew nothing about what would happen until the flood came and took them all away. That is how it will be at the coming of the Son of Man. 40Two men will be in the field; one will be taken and the other left. 41Two women will be grinding with a hand mill; one will be taken and the other left.

42"Therefore keep watch, because you do not know on what day your Lord will come. 43But understand this: If the owner of the house had known at what time of night the thief was coming, he would have kept watch and would not have let his house be broken into. 44So you also must be ready, because the Son of Man will come at an hour when you do not expect him.

45"Who then is the faithful and wise servant, whom the master has put in charge of the servants in his household to give them their food at the proper time? 46It will be good for that servant whose master finds him doing so when he returns. 47I tell you the truth, he will put him in charge of all his possessions. 48But suppose that servant is wicked and says to himself, 'My master is staying away a long time,' 49and he then begins to beat his fellow servants and to eat and drink with drunkards. 50The master of that servant will come on a day when he does not expect him and at an hour he is not aware of. 51He will cut him to pieces and assign him a place with the hypocrites, where there will be weeping and gnashing of teeth.

a5 Or Messiah; also in verse 23   b15 Daniel 9:27; 11:31; 12:11   c29 Isaiah 13:10; 34:4
d33 Or he   e34 Or race   f36 Some manuscripts do not have nor the Son.

Someday Will Be the Last Day

And this gospel of the kingdom will be preached in the whole world as a testimony to all nations, and then the end will come (Matthew 24:14).

The End. Those words often mark the last page, the last scene, the conclusion. Like the referee's gun when time has expired, they remind us of how finite life is.

Tomorrow will not always be a continuation of today. Some day will mark the last day of life as we now know it—"and then the end will come."

Just before his own earthly life ended, Jesus described "the end" and the events preceding it. F.B. Meyer shows how contemporary these two-thousand-year-old warnings are.

Walk With F.B. Meyer

"The signs of the times in our own day are much as they were then.

"People still love pleasure rather than God. Those who want to live a godly life must still be prepared to suffer persecution.

"The forms of hatred and dislike of the gospel change, but the hatred of the cross is as deep-rooted as ever.

"There are abroad today the seeds of hurtful and false doctrine. Propagated by the spoken word and written page, they produce unrest in the young and unstable.

"We must judge these damaging teachings, not by their pleasant and innocent appearance, but by their effect on heart and character."

Walk Closer to God

Wars. Rumors of war. Famine. Epidemics. Earthquakes. False prophets. Lukewarm love.

Jesus was right: The outlook wouldn't be too comforting just before the end.

But the uplook? Still as bright as the promises of God! And there is good news to share with a dying world.

As a child of God, you have the privilege of introducing others to Jesus. It's as simple as telling someone what you know to be true about him.

But don't put it off. "The End" has a way of coming when you least expect it. ◖

AUGUSTINE

(354–430) TEACHER, AUTHOR, STUDENT OF GOD'S WORD

A Life of Balance

Augustine grew up in Tagaste, North Africa, in the fourth century A.D., the son of a non-Christian father and a devout Christian mother. His mother faithfully taught him about Christianity.

When he began attending school away from home, he rejected Christianity and began a long investigation of various philosophies and lifestyles. Finally, at age thirty-two, he found that the Christian faith offered what he had been searching for. He wrote vividly of his pilgrimage and quest for truth in his *Confessions*.

Returning to Tagaste, Augustine longed to retire to a life of meditation and Bible study. But the spiritually needy church in North Africa was crying out for leadership, so he reluctantly began to serve as a pastor and teacher, working tirelessly to help others grow in the faith. His background had made him acutely sensitive to the false doctrines and vain philosophies of his day, and he frequently debated those issues.

Numerous works came from his pen: treatises on theology, commentaries, manuals on the Christian life, and above all, *The City of God*, a defense against those who blamed the fall of Rome on Christianity. In it Augustine showed the superiority and benefits of Christianity over anything the world might offer.

Augustine is probably the most important figure in church history between the apostle Paul and Martin Luther. Yet he faced the same daily challenge you face: to balance the demands of responsibility with the need for time to reflect on God and his Word. The secret, he found, is proper priorities. Feeding on the Word of God is as essential for your spiritual vitality as feeding on nourishing food is for your physical vitality.

A LESSON FROM THE LIFE OF AUGUSTINE

I need to balance my time between helping others and spending time with God and his Word.

JANUARY 25

Walk in the Word
Matthew 25:1–30

Matthew retells Jesus' parables about the ten virgins and about the talents, calling for a response of readiness and faithfulness.

The Parable of the Ten Virgins

25 "At that time the kingdom of heaven will be like ten virgins who took their lamps and went out to meet the bridegroom. ²Five of them were foolish and five were wise. ³The foolish ones took their lamps but did not take any oil with them. ⁴The wise, however, took oil in jars along with their lamps. ⁵The bridegroom was a long time in coming, and they all became drowsy and fell asleep.

⁶"At midnight the cry rang out: 'Here's the bridegroom! Come out to meet him!'

⁷"Then all the virgins woke up and trimmed their lamps. ⁸The foolish ones said to the wise, 'Give us some of your oil; our lamps are going out.'

⁹" 'No,' they replied, 'there may not be enough for both us and you. Instead, go to those who sell oil and buy some for yourselves.'

¹⁰"But while they were on their way to buy the oil, the bridegroom arrived. The virgins who were ready went in with him to the wedding banquet. And the door was shut.

¹¹"Later the others also came. 'Sir! Sir!' they said. 'Open the door for us!'

¹²"But he replied, 'I tell you the truth, I don't know you.'

¹³"Therefore keep watch, because you do not know the day or the hour.

The Parable of the Talents

¹⁴"Again, it will be like a man going on a journey, who called his servants and entrusted his property to them. ¹⁵To one he gave five talents*ᵃ* of money, to another two talents, and to another one talent, each according to his ability. Then he went on his journey. ¹⁶The man who had received the five talents went at once and put his money to work and gained five more. ¹⁷So also, the one with the two talents gained two more. ¹⁸But the man who had received the one talent went off, dug a hole in the ground and hid his master's money.

¹⁹"After a long time the master of those servants returned and settled accounts with them. ²⁰The man who had received the five talents brought the other five. 'Master,' he said, 'you entrusted me with five talents. See, I have gained five more.'

²¹"His master replied, 'Well done, good and faithful servant! You have been faithful with a few things; I will put you in charge of many things. Come and share your master's happiness!'

²²"The man with the two talents also came. 'Master,' he said, 'you entrusted me with two talents; see, I have gained two more.'

²³"His master replied, 'Well done, good and faithful servant! You have been faithful with a few things; I will put you in charge of many things. Come and share your master's happiness!'

January 25

24"Then the man who had received the one talent came. 'Master,' he said, 'I knew that you are a hard man, harvesting where you have not sown and gathering where you have not scattered seed. 25So I was afraid and went out and hid your talent in the ground. See, here is what belongs to you.'

26"His master replied, 'You wicked, lazy servant! So you knew that I harvest where I have not sown and gather where I have not scattered seed? 27Well then, you should have put my money on deposit with the bankers, so that when I returned I would have received it back with interest.

28" 'Take the talent from him and give it to the one who has the ten talents. 29For everyone who has will be given more, and he will have an abundance. Whoever does not have, even what he has will be taken from him. 30And throw that worthless servant outside, into the darkness, where there will be weeping and gnashing of teeth.'

a15 A talent was worth more than a thousand dollars.

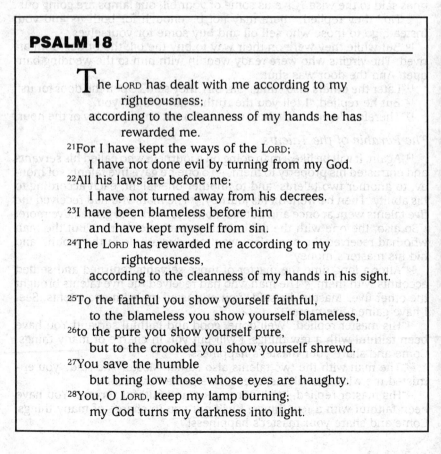

PSALM 18

The LORD has dealt with me according to my
        righteousness;
    according to the cleanness of my hands he has
        rewarded me.
21For I have kept the ways of the LORD;
    I have not done evil by turning from my God.
22All his laws are before me;
    I have not turned away from his decrees.
23I have been blameless before him
    and have kept myself from sin.
24The LORD has rewarded me according to my
        righteousness,
    according to the cleanness of my hands in his sight.

25To the faithful you show yourself faithful,
    to the blameless you show yourself blameless,
26to the pure you show yourself pure,
    but to the crooked you show yourself shrewd.
27You save the humble
    but bring low those whose eyes are haughty.
28You, O LORD, keep my lamp burning;
    my God turns my darkness into light.

A Gloriously Difficult Life

Therefore keep watch, because you do not know the day or the hour (Matthew 25:13).

Christianity is not a rest stop on the way to heaven. Instead, the New Testament pictures it as a walk of perseverance. A race of endurance. A battle of spiritual forces.

In the concluding paragraphs of the Olivet discourse, Jesus underscores the challenging demands of discipleship—the necessity of being watchful in conduct and fervent in service.

Oswald Chambers describes these pursuits as those which demand your "utmost for his highest."

Walk With Oswald Chambers

"The Christian life is gloriously difficult. But the difficulty of it does not make us faint and cave in; it rouses us to overcome. Do we so appreciate the marvelous salvation of Jesus Christ that we give our utmost for his highest?

"Thank God he does give us difficult things to do! His salvation is a glad thing, but it also tests us for all we are worth.

"Jesus is bringing many sons and daughters unto glory, and God will not shield us from the requirements of being his child.

"God's grace turns out men and women with a strong family likeness to Jesus Christ."

Walk Closer to God

God is working in you to produce a strong family likeness to Jesus Christ. But are you helping or hindering the process?

Construction projects take time. Are you frequently irritated with God's timetable?

Construction projects involve heat and pressure. Are you instead seeking the easy way out, stubbornly resisting God's efforts to shape your attitudes and actions?

Construction projects are costly. Are you willing to pay the price following Christ may involve?

Your utmost for his highest may sound like a tall order. But considering what God has invested in your life, it's a fitting way to say, "Thank you!"

JANUARY 26

Walk in the Word
Matthew 25:31–46

Matthew captures the poignancy of Jesus' picturesque story about the judgment, underscoring the Lord's magnanimous grace, the joy of the compassionate who are assigned to eternal life and the tragedy of the hardhearted who are assigned to eternal punishment.

The Sheep and the Goats

31"When the Son of Man comes in his glory, and all the angels with him, he will sit on his throne in heavenly glory. 32All the nations will be gathered before him, and he will separate the people one from another as a shepherd separates the sheep from the goats. 33He will put the sheep on his right and the goats on his left.

34"Then the King will say to those on his right, 'Come, you who are blessed by my Father; take your inheritance, the kingdom prepared for you since the creation of the world. 35For I was hungry and you gave me something to eat, I was thirsty and you gave me something to drink, I was a stranger and you invited me in, 36I needed clothes and you clothed me, I was sick and you looked after me, I was in prison and you came to visit me.'

37"Then the righteous will answer him, 'Lord, when did we see you hungry and feed you, or thirsty and give you something to drink? 38When did we see you a stranger and invite you in, or needing clothes and clothe you? 39When did we see you sick or in prison and go to visit you?'

40"The King will reply, 'I tell you the truth, whatever you did for one of the least of these brothers of mine, you did for me.'

41"Then he will say to those on his left, 'Depart from me, you who are cursed, into the eternal fire prepared for the devil and his angels. 42For I was hungry and you gave me nothing to eat, I was thirsty and you gave me nothing to drink, 43I was a stranger and you did not invite me in, I needed clothes and you did not clothe me, I was sick and in prison and you did not look after me.'

44"They also will answer, 'Lord, when did we see you hungry or thirsty or a stranger or needing clothes or sick or in prison, and did not help you?'

45"He will reply, 'I tell you the truth, whatever you did not do for one of the least of these, you did not do for me.'

46"Then they will go away to eternal punishment, but the righteous to eternal life."

The Choice That Determines the Course of Life

Then they will go away to eternal punishment, but the righteous to eternal life (Matthew 25:46).

Everlasting punishment is the penalty for failing to do what is right in the sight of God. It is the result of—not the remedy for—falling short of God's glory.

But God has provided a path to peace through personal faith in his Son, Jesus Christ. But only you can choose that path, as Jonathan Edwards explains.

Walk With Jonathan Edwards

"That you may escape the dreadful and eternal torments, you must embrace him who came into the world for the purpose of saving sinners from such torments. He alone has paid the whole debt due to the divine law, and has exhausted eternal sufferings.

"What great encouragement it is that you are exposed to eternal punishment, that there is a Savior provided who offers to save you from that punishment, and that he will do it in a way which is perfectly in keeping with the glory of God. In fact it is more to the glory of God than it would be if you should suffer the eternal punishment of hell.

"Those who are sent to hell will never pay the whole of the debt which they owe to God. Justice can never be actually satisfied in their damnation; but it is satisfied in Christ. Therefore he is accepted of the Father, and all who believe are accepted and justified in him."

Walk Closer to God

The course of your life is determined by the choice you make in life—a choice centering around the person of Jesus Christ.

You can ignore him, or embrace him. But you cannot avoid him . . . or the consequences of your choice.

Jonathan Edwards preached eloquently of the horrors of hell because he realized what was at stake in the lives of his listeners.

If you haven't as yet realized what is at stake in your own life, "be entreated to flee and embrace him."

JANUARY 27

Walk in the Word
Matthew 26:1–46

Matthew begins now to relate the events leading up to Jesus' death, from the plot of the religious leaders to the betrayal offer of Judas, the Passover meal and the Gethsemane experience.

The Plot Against Jesus

26 When Jesus had finished saying all these things, he said to his disciples, ²"As you know, the Passover is two days away — and the Son of Man will be handed over to be crucified."

³Then the chief priests and the elders of the people assembled in the palace of the high priest, whose name was Caiaphas, ⁴and they plotted to arrest Jesus in some sly way and kill him. ⁵"But not during the Feast," they said, "or there may be a riot among the people."

Jesus Anointed at Bethany

⁶While Jesus was in Bethany in the home of a man known as Simon the Leper, ⁷a woman came to him with an alabaster jar of very expensive perfume, which she poured on his head as he was reclining at the table.

⁸When the disciples saw this, they were indignant. "Why this waste?" they asked. ⁹"This perfume could have been sold at a high price and the money given to the poor."

¹⁰Aware of this, Jesus said to them, "Why are you bothering this woman? She has done a beautiful thing to me. ¹¹The poor you will always have with you, but you will not always have me. ¹²When she poured this perfume on my body, she did it to prepare me for burial. ¹³I tell you the truth, wherever this gospel is preached throughout the world, what she has done will also be told, in memory of her."

Judas Agrees to Betray Jesus

¹⁴Then one of the Twelve — the one called Judas Iscariot — went to the chief priests ¹⁵and asked, "What are you willing to give me if I hand him over to you?" So they counted out for him thirty silver coins. ¹⁶From then on Judas watched for an opportunity to hand him over.

The Lord's Supper

¹⁷On the first day of the Feast of Unleavened Bread, the disciples came to Jesus and asked, "Where do you want us to make preparations for you to eat the Passover?"

¹⁸He replied, "Go into the city to a certain man and tell him, 'The Teacher says: My appointed time is near. I am going to celebrate the Passover with my disciples at your house.' " ¹⁹So the disciples did as Jesus had directed them and prepared the Passover.

²⁰When evening came, Jesus was reclining at the table with the Twelve. ²¹And while they were eating, he said, "I tell you the truth, one of you will betray me."

22They were very sad and began to say to him one after the other, "Surely not I, Lord?"

23Jesus replied, "The one who has dipped his hand into the bowl with me will betray me. 24The Son of Man will go just as it is written about him. But woe to that man who betrays the Son of Man! It would be better for him if he had not been born."

25Then Judas, the one who would betray him, said, "Surely not I, Rabbi?" Jesus answered, "Yes, it is you."*a*

26While they were eating, Jesus took bread, gave thanks and broke it, and gave it to his disciples, saying, "Take and eat; this is my body."

27Then he took the cup, gave thanks and offered it to them, saying, "Drink from it, all of you. 28This is my blood of the*b* covenant, which is poured out for many for the forgiveness of sins. 29I tell you, I will not drink of this fruit of the vine from now on until that day when I drink it anew with you in my Father's kingdom."

30When they had sung a hymn, they went out to the Mount of Olives.

Jesus Predicts Peter's Denial

31Then Jesus told them, "This very night you will all fall away on account of me, for it is written:

> " 'I will strike the shepherd,
>   and the sheep of the flock will be scattered.'*c*

32But after I have risen, I will go ahead of you into Galilee."

33Peter replied, "Even if all fall away on account of you, I never will."

34"I tell you the truth," Jesus answered, "this very night, before the rooster crows, you will disown me three times."

35But Peter declared, "Even if I have to die with you, I will never disown you." And all the other disciples said the same.

Gethsemane

36Then Jesus went with his disciples to a place called Gethsemane, and he said to them, "Sit here while I go over there and pray." 37He took Peter and the two sons of Zebedee along with him, and he began to be sorrowful and troubled. 38Then he said to them, "My soul is overwhelmed with sorrow to the point of death. Stay here and keep watch with me."

39Going a little farther, he fell with his face to the ground and prayed, "My Father, if it is possible, may this cup be taken from me. Yet not as I will, but as you will."

40Then he returned to his disciples and found them sleeping. "Could you men not keep watch with me for one hour?" he asked Peter. 41"Watch and pray so that you will not fall into temptation. The spirit is willing, but the body is weak."

42He went away a second time and prayed, "My Father, if it is not possible for this cup to be taken away unless I drink it, may your will be done."

JANUARY 27

⁴³When he came back, he again found them sleeping, because their eyes were heavy. ⁴⁴So he left them and went away once more and prayed the third time, saying the same thing.

⁴⁵Then he returned to the disciples and said to them, "Are you still sleeping and resting? Look, the hour is near, and the Son of Man is betrayed into the hands of sinners. ⁴⁶Rise, let us go! Here comes my betrayer!"

a25 Or *"You yourself have said it"*   *b28* Some manuscripts *the new*   *c31* Zech. 13:7

PSALM 41

For the director of music. A psalm of David.

Blessed is he who has regard for the weak;
the LORD delivers him in times of trouble.
²The LORD will protect him and preserve his life;
he will bless him in the land
and not surrender him to the desire of his foes.
³The LORD will sustain him on his sickbed
and restore him from his bed of illness.

⁴I said, "O LORD, have mercy on me;
heal me, for I have sinned against you."
⁵My enemies say of me in malice,
"When will he die and his name perish?"
⁶Whenever one comes to see me,
he speaks falsely, while his heart gathers slander;
then he goes out and spreads it abroad.

⁷All my enemies whisper together against me;
they imagine the worst for me, saying,
⁸"A vile disease has beset him;
he will never get up from the place where he lies."
⁹Even my close friend, whom I trusted,
he who shared my bread,
has lifted up his heel against me.

¹⁰But you, O LORD, have mercy on me;
raise me up, that I may repay them.
¹¹I know that you are pleased with me,
for my enemy does not triumph over me.
¹²In my integrity you uphold me
and set me in your presence forever.

Sharing the Burden of Another's Soul

My Father, if it is possible, may this cup be taken from me. Yet not as I will, but as you will (Matthew 26:39).

Never be afraid to do what God tells you to do—it's always good. But be certain your will is in neutral first so that God can shift it.

After enjoying a last meal with his disciples, Jesus made his way to the Garden of Gethsemane. He went, not to relax, but to wrestle in prayer. Not to while away the moments, but to urge his disciples to watch with him in prayer.

Alfred Edersheim provides insight into the struggles of the Savior just before his death.

Walk With Alfred Edersheim

"Alone, as in his first conflict with the evil one in the wilderness, the Savior entered into the last contest.

"On his knees, prostrate on the ground, his agony began. His prayer was that—if it were possible—the hour might pass away from him.

"Fallen man is born with the taste of death in his soul. Not so Christ. It was he who had no experience of it. His going into death was his final conflict with Satan for man, and on man's behalf.

"At the close of that hour his sweat—mingled with blood—fell in great drops on the ground. And while he lay in prayer, the disciples lay in sleep."

Walk Closer to God

Christ yearned for support in prayer during his darkest hour.

It's possible—even probable—that someone near you is wrestling in prayer to discover God's will or overcome the enemy. That person knows the way ahead may be painful, yet he yearns to do God's will. But the battle for his will is raging and the issue is undecided.

You can slumber indifferently, like the disciples. Or you can kneel at that person's side and share his or her burden. That's one of the privileges—and responsibilities—of being a brother or a sister in Christ.

JANUARY 28

Walk in the Word
Matthew 26:47–75

Matthew continues to move his report toward its dramatic end, here recalling Jesus' arrest and the first stage of his trial, as well as Peter's failure to stand alongside his Lord.

Jesus Arrested

47While he was still speaking, Judas, one of the Twelve, arrived. With him was a large crowd armed with swords and clubs, sent from the chief priests and the elders of the people. 48Now the betrayer had arranged a signal with them: "The one I kiss is the man; arrest him." 49Going at once to Jesus, Judas said, "Greetings, Rabbi!" and kissed him.

50Jesus replied, "Friend, do what you came for."*a*

Then the men stepped forward, seized Jesus and arrested him. 51With that, one of Jesus' companions reached for his sword, drew it out and struck the servant of the high priest, cutting off his ear.

52"Put your sword back in its place," Jesus said to him, "for all who draw the sword will die by the sword. 53Do you think I cannot call on my Father, and he will at once put at my disposal more than twelve legions of angels? 54But how then would the Scriptures be fulfilled that say it must happen in this way?"

55At that time Jesus said to the crowd, "Am I leading a rebellion, that you have come out with swords and clubs to capture me? Every day I sat in the temple courts teaching, and you did not arrest me. 56But this has all taken place that the writings of the prophets might be fulfilled." Then all the disciples deserted him and fled.

Before the Sanhedrin

57Those who had arrested Jesus took him to Caiaphas, the high priest, where the teachers of the law and the elders had assembled. 58But Peter followed him at a distance, right up to the courtyard of the high priest. He entered and sat down with the guards to see the outcome.

59The chief priests and the whole Sanhedrin were looking for false evidence against Jesus so that they could put him to death. 60But they did not find any, though many false witnesses came forward.

Finally two came forward 61and declared, "This fellow said, 'I am able to destroy the temple of God and rebuild it in three days.'"

62Then the high priest stood up and said to Jesus, "Are you not going to answer? What is this testimony that these men are bringing against you?" 63But Jesus remained silent.

The high priest said to him, "I charge you under oath by the living God: Tell us if you are the Christ,*b* the Son of God."

64"Yes, it is as you say," Jesus replied. "But I say to all of you: In the future you will see the Son of Man sitting at the right hand of the Mighty One and coming on the clouds of heaven."

65Then the high priest tore his clothes and said, "He has spoken blasphemy! Why do we need any more witnesses? Look, now you have heard the blasphemy. ⁶⁶What do you think?"

"He is worthy of death," they answered.

⁶⁷Then they spit in his face and struck him with their fists. Others slapped him ⁶⁸and said, "Prophesy to us, Christ. Who hit you?"

Peter Disowns Jesus

⁶⁹Now Peter was sitting out in the courtyard, and a servant girl came to him. "You also were with Jesus of Galilee," she said.

⁷⁰But he denied it before them all. "I don't know what you're talking about," he said.

⁷¹Then he went out to the gateway, where another girl saw him and said to the people there, "This fellow was with Jesus of Nazareth."

⁷²He denied it again, with an oath: "I don't know the man!"

⁷³After a little while, those standing there went up to Peter and said, "Surely you are one of them, for your accent gives you away."

⁷⁴Then he began to call down curses on himself and he swore to them, "I don't know the man!"

Immediately a rooster crowed. ⁷⁵Then Peter remembered the word Jesus had spoken: "Before the rooster crows, you will disown me three times." And he went outside and wept bitterly.

a50 Or "Friend, why have you come?"   *b63 Or Messiah; also in verse 68*

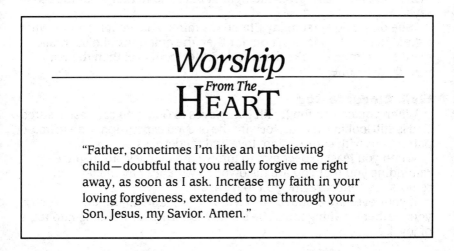

Worship
H*From The*EART

"Father, sometimes I'm like an unbelieving child—doubtful that you really forgive me right away, as soon as I ask. Increase my faith in your loving forgiveness, extended to me through your Son, Jesus, my Savior. Amen."

JANUARY 28

Turning Tears of Guilt Into Tears of Joy

Then Peter remembered the word Jesus had spoken: "Before the rooster crows, you will disown me three times." And he went outside and wept bitterly (Matthew 26:75).

You have failed someone who was counting on you. Guilt is written all over your face. You lower your head in shame and remorse.

Guilty! That's the unspoken verdict for many individuals who have faced failure in the service of the Lord. But as the apostle Peter discovered and Hannah Whitall Smith describes, God's forgiveness is as near as a prayer.

Walk With Hannah Whitall Smith

"A little girl once asked if the Lord Jesus always forgave us for our sins as soon as we asked him, and I had said, 'Yes, of course he does.'

" '*Just* as soon?' she repeated doubtfully. 'Yes,' I replied, 'the minute we ask, he forgives us.'

" 'Well, I cannot believe that,' she replied deliberately. 'I should think he would make us feel sorry for two or three days first. And then I think he would make us ask him a great many times, and not just in common talk. And I believe that is the way he does, and you need not try to make me think he forgives me right at once, no matter what the Bible says.'

"She only said what many Christians think, and what is worse, what a great many Christians act on, for then the emotions of discouragement and remorse make them feel further from God than their sin would have done."

Walk Closer to God

When you can no longer lift guilty eyes to God, you can rest assured God is still looking at you. Not with the peeved expression of an irritated parent, but with compassion, love and tenderness.

When you least expect him to forgive, he reaches out in grace—reminding you that you are his own . . . wiping away the tears of remorse . . . encouraging you to try again.

If your eyes are clouded with tears of guilt and failure today, run to your Father's waiting arms. He's ready to turn your weeping into tears of joy. ◖

JANUARY 29

📖 Walk in the Word
Matthew 27:1–31

Matthew skillfully profiles a determined high court, a remorseful Judas, a perplexed Pilate, and a suffering Jesus led away to be crucified.

Judas Hangs Himself

27 Early in the morning, all the chief priests and the elders of the people came to the decision to put Jesus to death. ²They bound him, led him away and handed him over to Pilate, the governor.

³When Judas, who had betrayed him, saw that Jesus was condemned, he was seized with remorse and returned the thirty silver coins to the chief priests and the elders. ⁴"I have sinned," he said, "for I have betrayed innocent blood."

"What is that to us?" they replied. "That's your responsibility."

⁵So Judas threw the money into the temple and left. Then he went away and hanged himself.

⁶The chief priests picked up the coins and said, "It is against the law to put this into the treasury, since it is blood money." ⁷So they decided to use the money to buy the potter's field as a burial place for foreigners. ⁸That is why it has been called the Field of Blood to this day. ⁹Then what was spoken by Jeremiah the prophet was fulfilled: "They took the thirty silver coins, the price set on him by the people of Israel, ¹⁰and they used them to buy the potter's field, as the Lord commanded me."*a*

Jesus Before Pilate

¹¹Meanwhile Jesus stood before the governor, and the governor asked him, "Are you the king of the Jews?"

"Yes, it is as you say," Jesus replied.

¹²When he was accused by the chief priests and the elders, he gave no answer. ¹³Then Pilate asked him, "Don't you hear the testimony they are bringing against you?" ¹⁴But Jesus made no reply, not even to a single charge—to the great amazement of the governor.

¹⁵Now it was the governor's custom at the Feast to release a prisoner chosen by the crowd. ¹⁶At that time they had a notorious prisoner, called Barabbas. ¹⁷So when the crowd had gathered, Pilate asked them, "Which one do you want me to release to you: Barabbas, or Jesus who is called Christ?" ¹⁸For he knew it was out of envy that they had handed Jesus over to him.

¹⁹While Pilate was sitting on the judge's seat, his wife sent him this message: "Don't have anything to do with that innocent man, for I have suffered a great deal today in a dream because of him."

²⁰But the chief priests and the elders persuaded the crowd to ask for Barabbas and to have Jesus executed.

²¹"Which of the two do you want me to release to you?" asked the governor.

"Barabbas," they answered.

²²"What shall I do, then, with Jesus who is called Christ?" Pilate asked.

January 29

They all answered, "Crucify him!"
23"Why? What crime has he committed?" asked Pilate.
But they shouted all the louder, "Crucify him!"

24When Pilate saw that he was getting nowhere, but that instead an uproar was starting, he took water and washed his hands in front of the crowd. "I am innocent of this man's blood," he said. "It is your responsibility!"

25All the people answered, "Let his blood be on us and on our children!"

26Then he released Barabbas to them. But he had Jesus flogged, and handed him over to be crucified.

The Soldiers Mock Jesus

27Then the governor's soldiers took Jesus into the Praetorium and gathered the whole company of soldiers around him. 28They stripped him and put a scarlet robe on him, 29and then twisted together a crown of thorns and set it on his head. They put a staff in his right hand and knelt in front of him and mocked him. "Hail, king of the Jews!" they said. 30They spit on him, and took the staff and struck him on the head again and again. 31After they had mocked him, they took off the robe and put his own clothes on him. Then they led him away to crucify him.

a10 See Zech. 11:12,13; Jer. 19:1-13; 32:6-9.

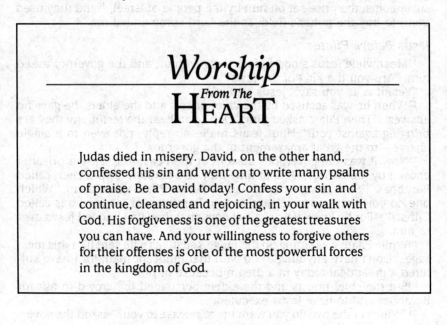

Worship From The HEART

Judas died in misery. David, on the other hand, confessed his sin and went on to write many psalms of praise. Be a David today! Confess your sin and continue, cleansed and rejoicing, in your walk with God. His forgiveness is one of the greatest treasures you can have. And your willingness to forgive others for their offenses is one of the most powerful forces in the kingdom of God.

Forgiveness: Yours for the Asking

"I have sinned," [Judas] said, "for I have betrayed innocent blood". . . So Judas threw the money into the temple and left. Then he went away and hanged himself (Matthew 27:3–5).

After a particularly embarrassing moment, the thought might cross your mind: "I wish I could just die."

It's a thought you really don't mean. But for Judas, knowing that he had betrayed the Lord so filled him with remorse that he sought escape through death. Rather than seek forgiveness and a new start, Judas decided to give up and end his own life.

The special circumstances of Judas's life and death provide lessons you can profit from. Alexander Maclaren shares his thoughts on the nature of sin and forgiveness.

Walk With Alexander Maclaren

"I do not suppose that Judas was lost because he betrayed Jesus Christ, but because, having betrayed Jesus Christ, he never asked to be forgiven.

"I pray you to learn this lesson: You cannot think too blackly of your own sins, but you may think too exclusively of them; and if you do, they will drive you to madness or despair.

"My dear friend, there is no remorse which is deep enough for the smallest transgression; but there is no transgression which is so great but that forgiveness for it may come. And we may have it for the asking, if we will go to that dear Christ who died for us.

"If Judas died without hope and pardon, it was not because his crime was too great for forgiveness, but because the forgiveness had never been asked."

Walk Closer to God

Judas could not forgive himself. But God could. "[God] does not treat us as our sins deserve or repay us according to our iniquities . . . as far as the east is from the west, so far has he removed our transgressions from us" (Psalm 103:10,12).

Forgiveness is yours for the asking when you take God at his Word. ⊙

MARTIN LUTHER

(1483–1546) CHAMPION OF SALVATION

Boldly Declaring the Truth

On October 31, 1517, a professor in Wittenberg, Germany, nailed several sheets of paper to the door of the town church, hoping to open debate on some theological problems he had with official church positions. This is often viewed as the start of the Protestant Reformation.

Born in 1483, Luther's early training and education prepared him to become a lawyer. But a terrifying experience in a thunderstorm caused him to seek spiritual comfort by becoming a priest. He received formal theological training and began lecturing on the Bible, all the while wrestling with his own spiritual condition. How could he be saved? Despite centuries of tradition to the contrary, the answer came with ringing clarity from the Bible: God saves those who look to Christ alone for their salvation.

Luther was called to stand trial for his beliefs before church and secular courts. His reply was strong and sure: "Here I stand; I can do no other." And in order that the message of salvation would continue to pierce hearts, he translated the Bible into German, wrote various pamphlets, developed worship services and preached the Word of God.

The Protestant Reformation affected family life, politics, the arts, and education—all because one man boldly declared the true meaning of salvation in Jesus Christ. By the time of his death in 1546, Luther had made a powerful impact on society. Every generation needs its Martin Luthers—Christians of commitment and courage who know what they believe and can defend those beliefs by word and deed. Determining to believe and obey God's Word and walk closer to him, regardless of popular opinion, is the first requirement. Expose yourself daily to the Bible and the truth it contains.

A LESSON FROM THE LIFE OF MARTIN LUTHER

When I am sure of what I believe, I will have the courage to stand against error.

JANUARY 30

Walk in the Word
Matthew 27:32–66

Matthew tells the story of Jesus' last hours: the walk to the crucifixion site, the insults, the death, the burial, the securing of the tomb.

The Crucifixion

[32]As they were going out, they met a man from Cyrene, named Simon, and they forced him to carry the cross. [33]They came to a place called Golgotha (which means The Place of the Skull). [34]There they offered Jesus wine to drink, mixed with gall; but after tasting it, he refused to drink it. [35]When they had crucified him, they divided up his clothes by casting lots.[a] [36]And sitting down, they kept watch over him there. [37]Above his head they placed the written charge against him: THIS IS JESUS, THE KING OF THE JEWS. [38]Two robbers were crucified with him, one on his right and one on his left. [39]Those who passed by hurled insults at him, shaking their heads [40]and saying, "You who are going to destroy the temple and build it in three days, save yourself! Come down from the cross, if you are the Son of God!"

[41]In the same way the chief priests, the teachers of the law and the elders mocked him. [42]"He saved others," they said, "but he can't save himself! He's the King of Israel! Let him come down now from the cross, and we will believe in him. [43]He trusts in God. Let God rescue him now if he wants him, for he said, 'I am the Son of God.'" [44]In the same way the robbers who were crucified with him also heaped insults on him.

The Death of Jesus

[45]From the sixth hour until the ninth hour darkness came over all the land. [46]About the ninth hour Jesus cried out in a loud voice, *"Eloi, Eloi,[b] lama sabachthani?"* — which means, "My God, my God, why have you forsaken me?"[c]

[47]When some of those standing there heard this, they said, "He's calling Elijah."

[48]Immediately one of them ran and got a sponge. He filled it with wine vinegar, put it on a stick, and offered it to Jesus to drink. [49]The rest said, "Now leave him alone. Let's see if Elijah comes to save him."

[50]And when Jesus had cried out again in a loud voice, he gave up his spirit.

[51]At that moment the curtain of the temple was torn in two from top to bottom. The earth shook and the rocks split. [52]The tombs broke open and the bodies of many holy people who had died were raised to life. [53]They came out of the tombs, and after Jesus' resurrection they went into the holy city and appeared to many people.

[54]When the centurion and those with him who were guarding Jesus saw the earthquake and all that had happened, they were terrified, and exclaimed, "Surely he was the Son[d] of God!"

[55]Many women were there, watching from a distance. They had fol-

JANUARY 30

lowed Jesus from Galilee to care for his needs. ⁵⁶Among them were Mary Magdalene, Mary the mother of James and Joses, and the mother of Zebedee's sons.

The Burial of Jesus

⁵⁷As evening approached, there came a rich man from Arimathea, named Joseph, who had himself become a disciple of Jesus. ⁵⁸Going to Pilate, he asked for Jesus' body, and Pilate ordered that it be given to him. ⁵⁹Joseph took the body, wrapped it in a clean linen cloth, ⁶⁰and placed it in his own new tomb that he had cut out of the rock. He rolled a big stone in front of the entrance to the tomb and went away. ⁶¹Mary Magdalene and the other Mary were sitting there opposite the tomb.

The Guard at the Tomb

⁶²The next day, the one after Preparation Day, the chief priests and the Pharisees went to Pilate. ⁶³"Sir," they said, "we remember that while he was still alive that deceiver said, 'After three days I will rise again.' ⁶⁴So give the order for the tomb to be made secure until the third day. Otherwise, his disciples may come and steal the body and tell the people that he has been raised from the dead. This last deception will be worse than the first."

⁶⁵"Take a guard," Pilate answered. "Go, make the tomb as secure as you know how." ⁶⁶So they went and made the tomb secure by putting a seal on the stone and posting the guard.

ᵃ35 A few late manuscripts *lots that the word spoken by the prophet might be fulfilled: "They divided my garments among themselves and cast lots for my clothing"* (Psalm 22:18)
ᵇ46 Some manuscripts *Eli, Eli*   ᶜ46 Psalm 22:1   ᵈ54 Or *a son*

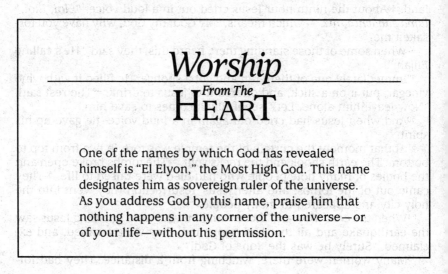

Worship
From The
HEART

One of the names by which God has revealed himself is "El Elyon," the Most High God. This name designates him as sovereign ruler of the universe. As you address God by this name, praise him that nothing happens in any corner of the universe—or of your life—without his permission.

Pride: The Thief of Faith

The chief priests, the teachers of the law, and the elders mocked him. "He saved others," they said, "but he can't save himself!" (Matthew 27:41–42).

Pride. It is a deadly weed that grows rampant on the earth. It is one of the seven things God hates.

The pride of men nailed Jesus to the cross.

Pride hurled abuses as he suffered and died.

Pride watched with curious detachment as he uttered his final words.

Martin Luther, outspoken critic of the pride and self-righteousness which infected his own day, comments on the cause and condemnation of pride.

Walk With Martin Luther

"Pride is really the haughtiness of Satan against the name and word of God.

"People who claim to be wise in matters of faith pompously exalt themselves, regarding God himself as nothing and all others in comparison to themselves as mere fools. When this happens there is no humility and no fear of God.

"At present there are many such haughty people. They have discovered that they are learned or are otherwise esteemed by the people in points on which they take pride. In fact, they are destitute.

"Such people are enemies of God and must be overthrown, for they have excluded themselves from the kingdom and grace of God."

Walk Closer to God

Those who called for Jesus' death were the religious leaders of his day. They were content with the spiritual status quo, proud of their spiritual heritage and blind to their spiritual need.

Pride will cause you to say with the chief priests, "He saved others, but he can't save himself."

Only by abandoning pride can you say with the centurion, "Surely he was the Son of God."

Are you too proud to admit you are lost in your sins? Then beware — you are too proud to see the kingdom of heaven.

Is your pride really worth that? ❍

JANUARY 31

📖 Walk in the Word
Matthew 28

Matthew concludes his book with a thunderbolt ending: the account of Jesus' resurrection, the devious plot to bury the truth, and Jesus' words of challenge and comfort.

The Resurrection

28 After the Sabbath, at dawn on the first day of the week, Mary Magdalene and the other Mary went to look at the tomb.

²There was a violent earthquake, for an angel of the Lord came down from heaven and, going to the tomb, rolled back the stone and sat on it. ³His appearance was like lightning, and his clothes were white as snow. ⁴The guards were so afraid of him that they shook and became like dead men.

⁵The angel said to the women, "Do not be afraid, for I know that you are looking for Jesus, who was crucified. ⁶He is not here; he has risen, just as he said. Come and see the place where he lay. ⁷Then go quickly and tell his disciples: 'He has risen from the dead and is going ahead of you into Galilee. There you will see him.' Now I have told you."

⁸So the women hurried away from the tomb, afraid yet filled with joy, and ran to tell his disciples. ⁹Suddenly Jesus met them. "Greetings," he said. They came to him, clasped his feet and worshiped him. ¹⁰Then Jesus said to them, "Do not be afraid. Go and tell my brothers to go to Galilee; there they will see me."

The Guards' Report

¹¹While the women were on their way, some of the guards went into the city and reported to the chief priests everything that had happened. ¹²When the chief priests had met with the elders and devised a plan, they gave the soldiers a large sum of money, ¹³telling them, "You are to say, 'His disciples came during the night and stole him away while we were asleep.' ¹⁴If this report gets to the governor, we will satisfy him and keep you out of trouble." ¹⁵So the soldiers took the money and did as they were instructed. And this story has been widely circulated among the Jews to this very day.

The Great Commission

¹⁶Then the eleven disciples went to Galilee, to the mountain where Jesus had told them to go. ¹⁷When they saw him, they worshiped him; but some doubted. ¹⁸Then Jesus came to them and said, "All authority in heaven and on earth has been given to me. ¹⁹Therefore go and make disciples of all nations, baptizing them in^a the name of the Father and of the Son and of the Holy Spirit, ²⁰and teaching them to obey everything I have commanded you. And surely I am with you always, to the very end of the age."

---

a19 Or *into*; see Acts 8:16; 19:5; Romans 6:3; 1 Cor. 1:13; 10:2 and Gal. 3:27.

Practicing the Presence of God by Faith

And surely I am with you always, to the very end of the age (Matthew 28:20).

Did you ever play hide-and-seek as a child? Sometimes someone hid so well that you never did find him. Or sometimes you just weren't looking in the right place.

When Jesus said he'd always be with us, he wasn't playing games. And he didn't mean maybe or sometimes. If you are a child of God, Jesus is always with you.

Frances Havergal explores why some Christians seem to have trouble with this concept.

Walk With Frances Havergal

"Some of us think and say a good deal about a sense of his presence. Sometimes we rejoice in it; sometimes we mourn because we don't seem to have it. We pray for it and measure our own position and that of others by it.

"One moment we are on the heights, then in the depths. We have gloom instead of glow because we are turning our attention upon the sense of his presence instead of the reality of it!

"All our disappointment vanishes in the simple faith that grasps his presence. For if Jesus says simply and absolutely, 'I am with you always,' what have we to do with feeling or sense about it? We have only to believe it and to recollect it. And it is only by thus believing and recollecting that we can realize his presence."

Walk Closer to God

Jesus doesn't play hide-and-seek with us. He is always available — even when we don't feel that he is. And when you practice his presence by faith, you'll find that feeling will follow.

Do you expect Jesus to go with you everywhere you go? Do you think about whether or not he'll be comfortable everywhere you take him?

Jesus is not someone who lives in a box that you can take out on Sundays and put in storage the rest of the week.

If you've invited him into your heart, he's there! He goes where you go! And that's something to think about. ❍

FEBRUARY

In the Savior's School of Servanthood

Mark, the shortest and simplest of the four Gospels, provides a vivid, action-packed account of the life of Jesus Christ. Names and places change rapidly, and Mark keeps the account brisk by using words like "immediately" and "at once" more than forty times. Just when you think you've caught up with the Savior, he moves on again.

Writing to a Roman audience, Mark presents Jesus primarily as a servant, who ministers first as a servant to the crowds (Mark 1–7), then as a servant to the disciples (Mark 8–10), and finally as a servant to all humanity by giving his life as a ransom (Mark 11–16; see especially 10:45). In the final analysis, however, Jesus was a servant of his heavenly Father, sent forth to do his will.

The call to service is rarely a call to convenience, and Jesus' life of servanthood was not easy. Note how Isaiah describes the role of the Servant-Messiah centuries before Jesus' birth (Isaiah 52:13–53:12). Mark frequently describes the difficult life of the servant. You'll see Jesus interrupted as he spends time in prayer. You'll feel the eager crowds pressing in to tap his power. You'll sense his compassion for those in need and his anger at those using traditions as an excuse to avoid serving others. And you'll sense his resolute commitment to face the cross in spite of its agony and shame. Truly Jesus is the supreme model of servanthood.

Your call as a disciple is likewise a call to servanthood. Do you place your Master's will ahead of your own? Does your heart respond with compassion at the sight of needy people? Do your actions speak louder than words? Active, compassionate, obedient service to the Master—that's your joyful privilege today and every day. Are you ready to enter the Savior's school of servanthood?

FEBRUARY 1

Walk in the Word
Mark 1:1–20

Mark begins his story of Jesus Christ with a brief summary of the ministry of the messenger called John the Baptist, as well as sketches of Jesus' baptism and temptation, an account of the first call to discipleship and the first miracles.

John the Baptist Prepares the Way

1 The beginning of the gospel about Jesus Christ, the Son of God.*a*

²It is written in Isaiah the prophet:

"I will send my messenger ahead of you,
who will prepare your way"*b* —
³"a voice of one calling in the desert,
'Prepare the way for the Lord,
make straight paths for him.' "*c*

⁴And so John came, baptizing in the desert region and preaching a baptism of repentance for the forgiveness of sins. ⁵The whole Judean countryside and all the people of Jerusalem went out to him. Confessing their sins, they were baptized by him in the Jordan River. ⁶John wore clothing made of camel's hair, with a leather belt around his waist, and he ate locusts and wild honey. ⁷And this was his message: "After me will come one more powerful than I, the thongs of whose sandals I am not worthy to stoop down and untie. ⁸I baptize you with*d* water, but he will baptize you with the Holy Spirit."

The Baptism and Temptation of Jesus

⁹At that time Jesus came from Nazareth in Galilee and was baptized by John in the Jordan. ¹⁰As Jesus was coming up out of the water, he saw heaven being torn open and the Spirit descending on him like a dove. ¹¹And a voice came from heaven: "You are my Son, whom I love; with you I am well pleased."

¹²At once the Spirit sent him out into the desert, ¹³and he was in the desert forty days, being tempted by Satan. He was with the wild animals, and angels attended him.

The Calling of the First Disciples

¹⁴After John was put in prison, Jesus went into Galilee, proclaiming the good news of God. ¹⁵"The time has come," he said. "The kingdom of God is near. Repent and believe the good news!"

¹⁶As Jesus walked beside the Sea of Galilee, he saw Simon and his brother Andrew casting a net into the lake, for they were fishermen. ¹⁷"Come, follow me," Jesus said, "and I will make you fishers of men." ¹⁸At once they left their nets and followed him.

101

FEBRUARY 1

[19]When he had gone a little farther, he saw James son of Zebedee and his brother John in a boat, preparing their nets. [20]Without delay he called them, and they left their father Zebedee in the boat with the hired men and followed him.

[a1] Some manuscripts do not have *the Son of God.*   [b2] Mal. 3:1   [c3] Isaiah 40:3
[d8] Or *in*

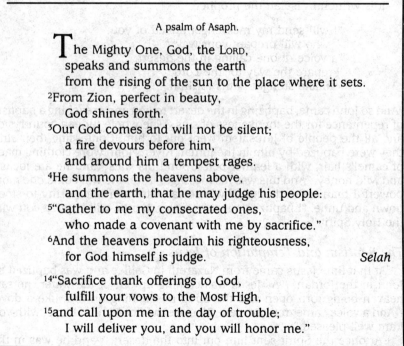

PSALM 50

A psalm of Asaph.

The Mighty One, God, the LORD,
  speaks and summons the earth
  from the rising of the sun to the place where it sets.
[2]From Zion, perfect in beauty,
  God shines forth.
[3]Our God comes and will not be silent;
  a fire devours before him,
  and around him a tempest rages.
[4]He summons the heavens above,
  and the earth, that he may judge his people:
[5]"Gather to me my consecrated ones,
  who made a covenant with me by sacrifice."
[6]And the heavens proclaim his righteousness,
  for God himself is judge.   *Selah*

[14]"Sacrifice thank offerings to God,
  fulfill your vows to the Most High,
[15]and call upon me in the day of trouble;
  I will deliver you, and you will honor me."

Called to Obey Without Delay

At once they left their nets and followed him (Mark 1:18).

Procrastination. It's a thief of time and the grave of opportunity.

Two fishermen in Mark 1 were confronted with a command from the Savior: "Follow me."

It was not a particularly convenient command, what with nets to mend, fish to catch, business to tend and families to care for. But there was no time to procrastinate. This was a clear statement of the Master's will for them.

Charles Spurgeon, whose preaching prompted thousands to follow Christ, explains the danger of "later" in the life of a disciple.

Walk With Charles Spurgeon

"When they heard the call of Jesus, Simon and Andrew obeyed without delay. If we would always, punctually and with determination, immediately put into practice what we hear, it could not fail to enrich us spiritually.

"A person will not lose his loaf once he has eaten it; neither will a believer be deprived of doctrine once he or she has acted on it.

"Most readers and hearers are moved to the point of deciding to amend; but, alas! No fruit comes of it. They wait, they waver, and then they forget.

"That fatal 'tomorrow' is blood-red with the murder of good resolutions. The practice of truth is the most profitable reading of it."

Walk Closer to God

Even today, Jesus' call to obedience doesn't always come at a convenient moment. Obedience is often inconvenient; it costs.

When we hear a command of Christ, we often hear within us two conflicting voices: one a call to delay, the other a call to obey. You can't answer both calls, for each excludes the other. But you must respond to one of them.

It's not an easy decision; the appeal of both is strong. But remember, for some people, later has a way of meaning never. Disciples obey without delay. ❍

FEBRUARY 2

📖 Walk in the Word
Mark 1:21–45

Mark highlights Jesus' power in teaching and healing, undergirded by Jesus' fellowship with the Father in prayer.

Jesus Drives Out an Evil Spirit

²¹They went to Capernaum, and when the Sabbath came, Jesus went into the synagogue and began to teach. ²²The people were amazed at his teaching, because he taught them as one who had authority, not as the teachers of the law. ²³Just then a man in their synagogue who was possessed by an evil*a* spirit cried out, ²⁴"What do you want with us, Jesus of Nazareth? Have you come to destroy us? I know who you are—the Holy One of God!"

²⁵"Be quiet!" said Jesus sternly. "Come out of him!" ²⁶The evil spirit shook the man violently and came out of him with a shriek.

²⁷The people were all so amazed that they asked each other, "What is this? A new teaching—and with authority! He even gives orders to evil spirits and they obey him." ²⁸News about him spread quickly over the whole region of Galilee.

Jesus Heals Many

²⁹As soon as they left the synagogue, they went with James and John to the home of Simon and Andrew. ³⁰Simon's mother-in-law was in bed with a fever, and they told Jesus about her. ³¹So he went to her, took her hand and helped her up. The fever left her and she began to wait on them.

³²That evening after sunset the people brought to Jesus all the sick and demon-possessed. ³³The whole town gathered at the door, ³⁴and Jesus healed many who had various diseases. He also drove out many demons, but he would not let the demons speak because they knew who he was.

Jesus Prays in a Solitary Place

³⁵Very early in the morning, while it was still dark, Jesus got up, left the house and went off to a solitary place, where he prayed. ³⁶Simon and his companions went to look for him, ³⁷and when they found him, they exclaimed: "Everyone is looking for you!"

³⁸Jesus replied, "Let us go somewhere else—to the nearby villages—so I can preach there also. That is why I have come." ³⁹So he traveled throughout Galilee, preaching in their synagogues and driving out demons.

A Man With Leprosy

⁴⁰A man with leprosy*b* came to him and begged him on his knees, "If you are willing, you can make me clean."

⁴¹Filled with compassion, Jesus reached out his hand and touched the man. "I am willing," he said. "Be clean!" ⁴²Immediately the leprosy left him and he was cured.

February 2

43Jesus sent him away at once with a strong warning: 44"See that you don't tell this to anyone. But go, show yourself to the priest and offer the sacrifices that Moses commanded for your cleansing, as a testimony to them." 45Instead he went out and began to talk freely, spreading the news. As a result, Jesus could no longer enter a town openly but stayed outside in lonely places. Yet the people still came to him from everywhere.

a23 Greek *unclean;* also in verses 26 and 27   *b40* The Greek word was used for various diseases affecting the skin—not necessarily leprosy.

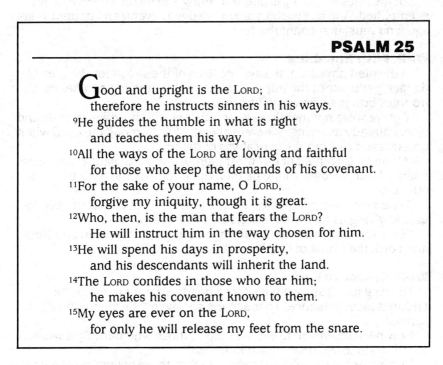

PSALM 25

Good and upright is the Lord;
    therefore he instructs sinners in his ways.
9He guides the humble in what is right
    and teaches them his way.
10All the ways of the Lord are loving and faithful
    for those who keep the demands of his covenant.
11For the sake of your name, O Lord,
    forgive my iniquity, though it is great.
12Who, then, is the man that fears the Lord?
    He will instruct him in the way chosen for him.
13He will spend his days in prosperity,
    and his descendants will inherit the land.
14The Lord confides in those who fear him;
    he makes his covenant known to them.
15My eyes are ever on the Lord,
    for only he will release my feet from the snare.

FEBRUARY 2

Lifegiver, Lightbearer, Great Physician

News about him spread quickly over the whole region of Galilee (Mark 1:28).

Good news has a way of getting around. If you were to begin a ministry to hurting people, word would spread and you—like Jesus—would never lack an audience.

But the price of serving is often suffering and inconvenience, as Jesus exemplified. And as Eusebius acknowledged seventeen hundred years ago, you must first count the cost.

Walk With Eusebius

"A devoted physician, to save the lives of the sick, sees the horrible danger, yet touches the infected place, and in treating another man's troubles brings suffering on himself.

"But we were not merely sick, or afflicted with horrible wounds and ulcers already festering. We were actually lying among the dead when Christ saved us from the very abyss of death.

"Alone he took hold of our most painful perishing nature. Alone he endured our sorrows. Alone he took upon himself the retribution for our sins.

"When we were lying in tombs and graves, he raised us up, saving us and giving us his Father's blessings without measure.

"He is the Lifegiver, the Lightbringer, our great Physician and King and Lord, the Christ of God."

Walk Closer to God

To bring life, Jesus willingly faced death. To offer comfort, he endured inconvenience. To touch the sorrowing, he shared their sorrow.

Now he calls on you to extend help to those who hurt. By a word. A touch. A smile. An unexpected kindness.

Hurting people aren't hard to find. In fact, those willing to search will find them all around.

Widows and orphans . . . the sick and bereaved . . . the lonely and neglected. All need to hear the good news that there is a Great Physician.

But let the word get out that you are looking for those who hurt, and you—like Jesus—may find yourself permanently popular!

So how will you help the hurting today? ❍

FEBRUARY 3

▶ **Walk in the Word**
Mark 2

Mark records Jesus' revelation of himself as the Son of Man who has power to forgive sins and depicts him offering healing for those who hurt and new life for sinners.

Jesus Heals a Paralytic

2 A few days later, when Jesus again entered Capernaum, the people heard that he had come home. ²So many gathered that there was no room left, not even outside the door, and he preached the word to them. ³Some men came, bringing to him a paralytic, carried by four of them. ⁴Since they could not get him to Jesus because of the crowd, they made an opening in the roof above Jesus and, after digging through it, lowered the mat the paralyzed man was lying on. ⁵When Jesus saw their faith, he said to the paralytic, "Son, your sins are forgiven."

⁶Now some teachers of the law were sitting there, thinking to themselves, ⁷"Why does this fellow talk like that? He's blaspheming! Who can forgive sins but God alone?"

⁸Immediately Jesus knew in his spirit that this was what they were thinking in their hearts, and he said to them, "Why are you thinking these things? ⁹Which is easier: to say to the paralytic, 'Your sins are forgiven,' or to say, 'Get up, take your mat and walk'? ¹⁰But that you may know that the Son of Man has authority on earth to forgive sins . . . ." He said to the paralytic, ¹¹"I tell you, get up, take your mat and go home." ¹²He got up, took his mat and walked out in full view of them all. This amazed everyone and they praised God, saying, "We have never seen anything like this!"

The Calling of Levi

¹³Once again Jesus went out beside the lake. A large crowd came to him, and he began to teach them. ¹⁴As he walked along, he saw Levi son of Alphaeus sitting at the tax collector's booth. "Follow me," Jesus told him, and Levi got up and followed him.

¹⁵While Jesus was having dinner at Levi's house, many tax collectors and "sinners" were eating with him and his disciples, for there were many who followed him. ¹⁶When the teachers of the law who were Pharisees saw him eating with the "sinners" and tax collectors, they asked his disciples: "Why does he eat with tax collectors and 'sinners'?"

¹⁷On hearing this, Jesus said to them, "It is not the healthy who need a doctor, but the sick. I have not come to call the righteous, but sinners."

Jesus Questioned About Fasting

¹⁸Now John's disciples and the Pharisees were fasting. Some people came and asked Jesus, "How is it that John's disciples and the disciples of the Pharisees are fasting, but yours are not?"

¹⁹Jesus answered, "How can the guests of the bridegroom fast while he is with them? They cannot, so long as they have him with them. ²⁰But the

FEBRUARY 3

time will come when the bridegroom will be taken from them, and on that day they will fast.

²¹"No one sews a patch of unshrunk cloth on an old garment. If he does, the new piece will pull away from the old, making the tear worse. ²²And no one pours new wine into old wineskins. If he does, the wine will burst the skins, and both the wine and the wineskins will be ruined. No, he pours new wine into new wineskins."

Lord of the Sabbath

²³One Sabbath Jesus was going through the grainfields, and as his disciples walked along, they began to pick some heads of grain. ²⁴The Pharisees said to him, "Look, why are they doing what is unlawful on the Sabbath?"

²⁵He answered, "Have you never read what David did when he and his companions were hungry and in need? ²⁶In the days of Abiathar the high priest, he entered the house of God and ate the consecrated bread, which is lawful only for priests to eat. And he also gave some to his companions."

²⁷Then he said to them, "The Sabbath was made for man, not man for the Sabbath. ²⁸So the Son of Man is Lord even of the Sabbath."

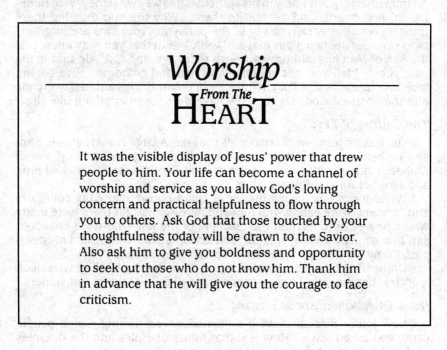

Worship
From The
HEART

It was the visible display of Jesus' power that drew people to him. Your life can become a channel of worship and service as you allow God's loving concern and practical helpfulness to flow through you to others. Ask God that those touched by your thoughtfulness today will be drawn to the Savior. Also ask him to give you boldness and opportunity to seek out those who do not know him. Thank him in advance that he will give you the courage to face criticism.

Running a Risk to Offer a Cure

The . . . Pharisees . . . asked his disciples: "Why does he eat with tax collectors and 'sinners'?" (Mark 2:16).

A child hovers between life and death as anxious parents wait. The physician is called, but refuses to come. "I'm sorry," he explains, "but I don't make house calls."

Ridiculous? Perhaps. But consider this. What if the Great Physician had been unwilling to make a "house call" to planet earth?

His life calls you to minister to people who may never have visited your church, and possibly never will.

His example calls you to rub shoulders with people who are lost . . . sick . . . without hope.

G. Campbell Morgan presses home the importance of making "house calls."

Walk With G. Campbell Morgan

"I believe one of the reasons for the condition of the church is the aloofness of Christians from sinning men and women.

"We still build our sanctuaries, set up our standards, make our arrangements, and say to the sinning ones: 'If you come to us, we will help you!'

"But the way of the Lord is to go and sit where they sit, without looking down on them.

"We may run great risks if we will dare to do it because someone will say that we are consorting with sinning men, and that we are in moral and spiritual peril. I am afraid, however, that the church is not often criticized for this."

Walk Closer to God

A doctor takes personal risks when he tends the sick. But they need his help.

You have what the world needs—the good news of sins forgiven.

But it's good news to them only if they've heard it. It's the cure only if they know they are terminally ill.

House calls may be a thing of the past for family doctors. But in God's program they are never out of date.

Make one, and you'll find out why! ⟦⟧

February 4

Walk in the Word
Mark 3:1–19

Mark demonstrates that Jesus is Lord over all, including deformities and diseases and demons.

3 Another time he went into the synagogue, and a man with a shriveled hand was there. ²Some of them were looking for a reason to accuse Jesus, so they watched him closely to see if he would heal him on the Sabbath. ³Jesus said to the man with the shriveled hand, "Stand up in front of everyone."

⁴Then Jesus asked them, "Which is lawful on the Sabbath: to do good or to do evil, to save life or to kill?" But they remained silent.

⁵He looked around at them in anger and, deeply distressed at their stubborn hearts, said to the man, "Stretch out your hand." He stretched it out, and his hand was completely restored. ⁶Then the Pharisees went out and began to plot with the Herodians how they might kill Jesus.

Crowds Follow Jesus

⁷Jesus withdrew with his disciples to the lake, and a large crowd from Galilee followed. ⁸When they heard all he was doing, many people came to him from Judea, Jerusalem, Idumea, and the regions across the Jordan and around Tyre and Sidon. ⁹Because of the crowd he told his disciples to have a small boat ready for him, to keep the people from crowding him. ¹⁰For he had healed many, so that those with diseases were pushing forward to touch him. ¹¹Whenever the evil*ᵃ* spirits saw him, they fell down before him and cried out, "You are the Son of God." ¹²But he gave them strict orders not to tell who he was.

The Appointing of the Twelve Apostles

¹³Jesus went up on a mountainside and called to him those he wanted, and they came to him. ¹⁴He appointed twelve—designating them apostles*ᵇ*—that they might be with him and that he might send them out to preach ¹⁵and to have authority to drive out demons. ¹⁶These are the twelve he appointed: Simon (to whom he gave the name Peter); ¹⁷James son of Zebedee and his brother John (to them he gave the name Boanerges, which means Sons of Thunder); ¹⁸Andrew, Philip, Bartholomew, Matthew, Thomas, James son of Alphaeus, Thaddaeus, Simon the Zealot ¹⁹and Judas Iscariot, who betrayed him.

ᵃ11 Greek *unclean*; also in verse 30   *ᵇ14* Some manuscripts do not have *designating them apostles.*

Living in the Spotlight of High Visibility

Some of them were looking for a reason to accuse Jesus, so they watched him closely to see if he would heal him on the Sabbath (Mark 3:2).

It's an uneasy feeling . . . the feeling of being watched. And evaluated. And talked about.

But it's a feeling Jesus was familiar with. For he had attracted the attention of many in Jerusalem . . . including the Jewish authorities.

Just like Christ, his followers are also on center stage. And as J.C. Ryle comments, that kind of visibility can either move you to action — or immobilize you.

Walk With J.C. Ryle

"Christ's people must not expect to fare better than their Master.

"They are always watched by the world. Their conduct is scrutinized. Their ways are noted and diligently observed. They can do nothing without the world noticing it. Their dress, their expenditures, their use of time, their conduct in all areas of life — all are closely observed.

"The thought should make us exercise a holy jealousy over all our conduct.

"It should make us diligent to avoid even the appearance of evil.

"Above all, it should make us pray to be kept pure in our attitudes, speech, and daily conduct.

"That Savior, who himself was watched, knows how to sympathize with his people, and to supply grace to help in time of need."

Walk Closer to God

As a servant of Christ you have a life of high visibility. Others are watching your life and evaluating the person you claim to follow.

Like it or not, you may be the best Christian someone knows. Or the worst.

Someone near you may one day say yes to Christ because he or she saw him living in you.

Christian, you have no choice about whether you will be in the spotlight or not. But you do have a choice about what that spotlight will reveal to those who watch.

You're on! 〇

FEBRUARY 5

📖 Walk in the Word
Mark 3:20–35

Mark records a strong reaction to Jesus' ministry that centers on accusations of madness and demon-possession; while Jesus' family members puzzle over his behavior, Jesus declares that obedience to God's will puts one within Jesus' family.

Jesus and Beelzebub

20Then Jesus entered a house, and again a crowd gathered, so that he and his disciples were not even able to eat. 21When his family heard about this, they went to take charge of him, for they said, "He is out of his mind."

22And the teachers of the law who came down from Jerusalem said, "He is possessed by Beelzebub*a*! By the prince of demons he is driving out demons."

23So Jesus called them and spoke to them in parables: "How can Satan drive out Satan? 24If a kingdom is divided against itself, that kingdom cannot stand. 25If a house is divided against itself, that house cannot stand. 26And if Satan opposes himself and is divided, he cannot stand; his end has come. 27In fact, no one can enter a strong man's house and carry off his possessions unless he first ties up the strong man. Then he can rob his house. 28I tell you the truth, all the sins and blasphemies of men will be forgiven them. 29But whoever blasphemes against the Holy Spirit will never be forgiven; he is guilty of an eternal sin."

30He said this because they were saying, "He has an evil spirit."

Jesus' Mother and Brothers

31Then Jesus' mother and brothers arrived. Standing outside, they sent someone in to call him. 32A crowd was sitting around him, and they told him, "Your mother and brothers are outside looking for you."

33"Who are my mother and my brothers?" he asked.

34Then he looked at those seated in a circle around him and said, "Here are my mother and my brothers! 35Whoever does God's will is my brother and sister and mother."

a22 Greek Beezeboul or Beelzeboul

A Passionate Devotion to the Will of God

His family . . . went to take charge of him, for they said, "He is out of his mind" (Mark 3:21).

Fanatic! That's a word which evokes the image of a wild-eyed, sign-toting, religious zealot.

And that is unfortunate, really, since fanatic literally means "inspired by God."

Jesus' popularity with the common people and his zeal for the business of heaven prompted even his friends and family to conclude that he was beside himself, a fanatic.

But for the Christian there can be no higher compliment, as G. Campbell Morgan explains.

Walk With G. Campbell Morgan

"People today never seem to think that passionate and sacrificial devotion suggests madness in any realm except the spiritual.

"No one suggests that the athlete, who gives himself totally to his sport and sacrifices all for the sake of physical prowess, is beside himself.

"No one imagines that the businessman, who is so devoted to amassing wealth that he shortens his life, is beside himself.

"No! This suggestion is retained only for those whose service for the souls of men and women is sacrificial.

"Let all such servants be comforted. They are in holy comradeship! At the same time, let them determine to be among those who have the highest resemblance to the Son of Man, because they are devoted to the will of God."

Walk Closer to God

"Lord, show me areas of my life in which—because of my fear of being labeled a fanatic—I have ceased to be excited and moved and compelled by you.

"May I always be a fanatic more of heavenly endeavors than of earthly pursuits.

"A zealot more for holiness than for hobbies.

"An enthusiast more of lost sinners than of sports.

"A lover more of Christ than of personal goals.

"I pray this in the name of the one whose zeal for his Father's house consumed him. Amen." ⟨⟩

FEBRUARY 6

📖 Walk in the Word
Mark 4:1–20

Mark retells the parable of the sower, a parable also remembered and recorded by Matthew and Luke.

The Parable of the Sower

4 Again Jesus began to teach by the lake. The crowd that gathered around him was so large that he got into a boat and sat in it out on the lake, while all the people were along the shore at the water's edge. ²He taught them many things by parables, and in his teaching said: ³"Listen! A farmer went out to sow his seed. ⁴As he was scattering the seed, some fell along the path, and the birds came and ate it up. ⁵Some fell on rocky places, where it did not have much soil. It sprang up quickly, because the soil was shallow. ⁶But when the sun came up, the plants were scorched, and they withered because they had no root. ⁷Other seed fell among thorns, which grew up and choked the plants, so that they did not bear grain. ⁸Still other seed fell on good soil. It came up, grew and produced a crop, multiplying thirty, sixty, or even a hundred times."

⁹Then Jesus said, "He who has ears to hear, let him hear."

¹⁰When he was alone, the Twelve and the others around him asked him about the parables. ¹¹He told them, "The secret of the kingdom of God has been given to you. But to those on the outside everything is said in parables ¹²so that,

> " 'they may be ever seeing but never perceiving,
>   and ever hearing but never understanding;
>   otherwise they might turn and be forgiven!'ᵃ "

¹³Then Jesus said to them, "Don't you understand this parable? How then will you understand any parable? ¹⁴The farmer sows the word. ¹⁵Some people are like seed along the path, where the word is sown. As soon as they hear it, Satan comes and takes away the word that was sown in them. ¹⁶Others, like seed sown on rocky places, hear the word and at once receive it with joy. ¹⁷But since they have no root, they last only a short time. When trouble or persecution comes because of the word, they quickly fall away. ¹⁸Still others, like seed sown among thorns, hear the word; ¹⁹but the worries of this life, the deceitfulness of wealth and the desires for other things come in and choke the word, making it unfruitful. ²⁰Others, like seed sown on good soil, hear the word, accept it, and produce a crop—thirty, sixty or even a hundred times what was sown."

ᵃ12 Isaiah 6:9,10

A Soil Analysis of the Human Heart

Others, like seed sown on good soil, hear the word, accept it, and produce a crop—thirty, sixty or even a hundred times what was sown (Mark 4:20).

You can't sow thistles and expect to reap roses. Nor will oak trees grow in rock-strewn deserts.

What is sown, and where, are both crucial elements in producing a harvest.

The divine seed, God's Word, falls on all kinds of ground and produces fruit—little, much, or none at all, depending on the condition of the soil.

Alexander Maclaren provides this soil analysis of the human heart.

Walk With Alexander Maclaren

"No one is obliged, either by his temperament or circumstances, to be 'wayside,' or 'stony,' or 'thorny' ground.

"The true acceptance of the Word requires that we do not let it lie only on the surface of our minds, nor be satisfied only to have it penetrate a little deeper and take root in our emotions, or let competing desires grow up unchecked. Instead, we must cherish the word of truth in our deepest hearts, guard it against foes, let it rule there, and mold our conduct to its principles.

"The psalmist said, 'I have hidden your word in my heart.' If we do that we shall be fruitful, because his Word will bear fruit in us.

"There will be increase wherever a heart opens to receive the gospel and keeps it steadfastly.

"Not in equal measure in all, but in each according to faithfulness and diligence."

Walk Closer to God

Fruitbearing requires three things: seed, sower and soil. The first two have already been provided. The perfect seed is the living Word of God. The patient sower is the life-giving Son of God. But as the parable of the sower points out, even that is not enough to guarantee a harvest.

Only you can provide that. And come harvest-time, you'll be mighty glad you did!

Barren, rocky, thorny or good. Pick your soil carefully; it could make a hundredfold difference in your life.

FEBRUARY 7

📖 Walk in the Word
Mark 4:21–41

In skillful teaching Jesus reveals more about the kingdom of God; when he calms the storm he reveals his authority over creation.

A Lamp on a Stand

²¹He said to them, "Do you bring in a lamp to put it under a bowl or a bed? Instead, don't you put it on its stand? ²²For whatever is hidden is meant to be disclosed, and whatever is concealed is meant to be brought out into the open. ²³If anyone has ears to hear, let him hear."

²⁴"Consider carefully what you hear," he continued. "With the measure you use, it will be measured to you — and even more. ²⁵Whoever has will be given more; whoever does not have, even what he has will be taken from him."

The Parable of the Growing Seed

²⁶He also said, "This is what the kingdom of God is like. A man scatters seed on the ground. ²⁷Night and day, whether he sleeps or gets up, the seed sprouts and grows, though he does not know how. ²⁸All by itself the soil produces grain — first the stalk, then the head, then the full kernel in the head. ²⁹As soon as the grain is ripe, he puts the sickle to it, because the harvest has come."

The Parable of the Mustard Seed

³⁰Again he said, "What shall we say the kingdom of God is like, or what parable shall we use to describe it? ³¹It is like a mustard seed, which is the smallest seed you plant in the ground. ³²Yet when planted, it grows and becomes the largest of all garden plants, with such big branches that the birds of the air can perch in its shade."

³³With many similar parables Jesus spoke the word to them, as much as they could understand. ³⁴He did not say anything to them without using a parable. But when he was alone with his own disciples, he explained everything.

Jesus Calms the Storm

³⁵That day when evening came, he said to his disciples, "Let us go over to the other side." ³⁶Leaving the crowd behind, they took him along, just as he was, in the boat. There were also other boats with him. ³⁷A furious squall came up, and the waves broke over the boat, so that it was nearly swamped. ³⁸Jesus was in the stern, sleeping on a cushion. The disciples woke him and said to him, "Teacher, don't you care if we drown?"

³⁹He got up, rebuked the wind and said to the waves, "Quiet! Be still!" Then the wind died down and it was completely calm.

⁴⁰He said to his disciples, "Why are you so afraid? Do you still have no faith?"

⁴¹They were terrified and asked each other, "Who is this? Even the wind and the waves obey him!"

Lessons Learned in the Gale of Affliction

They were terrified and asked each other, "Who is this? Even the wind and the waves obey him!" (Mark 4:41).

Some things are certain. Like death—and taxes—and taxing situations!

Count on it: There will be storms and difficulties in every human life.

You—like the disciples in Mark 4—may sometimes wonder, "Teacher, don't you care if we drown?"

Yes, he does care. Infinitely. Christ is faithful to see you through difficulties. J.C. Ryle offers some reassuring words for stormy times.

Walk With J.C. Ryle

"Here were the twelve disciples in the path of duty. They were obediently following Jesus wherever he went.

"Yet here we see these men in trouble, tossed by a tempest and in danger of being drowned.

"Mark well this lesson. Being in Christ's service does not exempt his servants from storms.

"It will not be strange if we have to endure sickness, losses, and disappointments just like other people. Our Savior has never promised that we shall have no afflictions. He loves us too well to promise that.

"By affliction he teaches us many precious lessons, which otherwise we would never learn. By affliction he shows us our emptiness and weakness, draws us to the throne of grace, purifies our affections, weans us from the world, and makes us long for heaven."

Walk Closer to God

It's easy to breathe a prayer of thanks when a storm is over.

But what about when the waves are breaking? When there's water in the boat? When the noise of your circumstances threatens to drown out the prayer on your lips?

If faith in God works, it had better work then!

Rest assured, it works.

But—as the disciples learned—there's nothing like a good gale to add zest to your prayers! 〇

117

FEBRUARY 8

📖 Walk in the Word
Mark 5:1–20

In bold strokes Mark paints a portrait of a tragically tormented man who was transformed when he came face to face with the compassionate, powerful Messiah.

The Healing of a Demon-possessed Man

5 They went across the lake to the region of the Gerasenes.*a* ²When Jesus got out of the boat, a man with an evil*b* spirit came from the tombs to meet him. ³This man lived in the tombs, and no one could bind him any more, not even with a chain. ⁴For he had often been chained hand and foot, but he tore the chains apart and broke the irons on his feet. No one was strong enough to subdue him. ⁵Night and day among the tombs and in the hills he would cry out and cut himself with stones.

⁶When he saw Jesus from a distance, he ran and fell on his knees in front of him. ⁷He shouted at the top of his voice, "What do you want with me, Jesus, Son of the Most High God? Swear to God that you won't torture me!" ⁸For Jesus had said to him, "Come out of this man, you evil spirit!"

⁹Then Jesus asked him, "What is your name?"

"My name is Legion," he replied, "for we are many." ¹⁰And he begged Jesus again and again not to send them out of the area.

¹¹A large herd of pigs was feeding on the nearby hillside. ¹²The demons begged Jesus, "Send us among the pigs; allow us to go into them." ¹³He gave them permission, and the evil spirits came out and went into the pigs. The herd, about two thousand in number, rushed down the steep bank into the lake and were drowned.

¹⁴Those tending the pigs ran off and reported this in the town and countryside, and the people went out to see what had happened. ¹⁵When they came to Jesus, they saw the man who had been possessed by the legion of demons, sitting there, dressed and in his right mind; and they were afraid. ¹⁶Those who had seen it told the people what had happened to the demon-possessed man—and told about the pigs as well. ¹⁷Then the people began to plead with Jesus to leave their region.

¹⁸As Jesus was getting into the boat, the man who had been demon-possessed begged to go with him. ¹⁹Jesus did not let him, but said, "Go home to your family and tell them how much the Lord has done for you, and how he has had mercy on you." ²⁰So the man went away and began to tell in the Decapolis*c* how much Jesus had done for him. And all the people were amazed.

a1 Some manuscripts *Gadarenes*; other manuscripts *Gergesenes*   *b2* Greek *unclean*; also in verses 8 and 13   *c20* That is, the Ten Cities

The Best Place to Be Is the Place God Chooses

Jesus . . . said, "Go home to your family and tell them how much the Lord has done for you" (Mark 5:19).

Children and busy roads don't mix. Why? Because children, if unattended, often play in the road, heedless of danger. So until a child reaches maturity, the parent takes responsibility for the child's protection, guidance and nurture.

Christian, do you sometimes think you know better than your heavenly Father which road is best for you? Listen as J.C. Ryle explains that "Father knows best."

Walk With J.C. Ryle

"The place where Christians wish to be is not always the best place for their souls. There are none who need this lesson so much as believers newly converted to God.

"Seeing everything in a new light, yet knowing little of the depths of Satan and the weakness of their own hearts, they are in the greatest danger of making mistakes. With the best intentions they may fall into mistakes about their plans, their choices, or their professions. They forget that what we like best is not always best for our souls.

"Let us pray that God would guide us in all our ways after conversion, and not allow us to err. It may not be quite what we like. But if Christ by his providence has placed us in it, let us not be in a hurry to leave it."

Walk Closer to God

Elijah supposed he was the only man left in Israel who worshiped God.

Moses was an obscure shepherd for forty years before he led God's people out of Egypt.

John lived out his life in exile on a desolate island while he wrote the book of Revelation.

That's because God's best sometimes comes wrapped in unpleasant circumstances and unexpected changes of plan.

Like the man from Gadara in Mark 5, don't hesitate to submit your plans to God's providence. Great things can happen when God's best becomes yours.

FEBRUARY 9

📖 Walk in the Word
Mark 5:21–43

A synagogue ruler, a dying twelve-year-old girl and a chronically ill woman are the objects of Jesus' compassion and healing power in this report.

A Dead Girl and a Sick Woman

21When Jesus had again crossed over by boat to the other side of the lake, a large crowd gathered around him while he was by the lake. 22Then one of the synagogue rulers, named Jairus, came there. Seeing Jesus, he fell at his feet 23and pleaded earnestly with him, "My little daughter is dying. Please come and put your hands on her so that she will be healed and live." 24So Jesus went with him.

A large crowd followed and pressed around him. 25And a woman was there who had been subject to bleeding for twelve years. 26She had suffered a great deal under the care of many doctors and had spent all she had, yet instead of getting better she grew worse. 27When she heard about Jesus, she came up behind him in the crowd and touched his cloak, 28because she thought, "If I just touch his clothes, I will be healed." 29Immediately her bleeding stopped and she felt in her body that she was freed from her suffering.

30At once Jesus realized that power had gone out from him. He turned around in the crowd and asked, "Who touched my clothes?"

31"You see the people crowding against you," his disciples answered, "and yet you can ask, 'Who touched me?'"

32But Jesus kept looking around to see who had done it. 33Then the woman, knowing what had happened to her, came and fell at his feet and, trembling with fear, told him the whole truth. 34He said to her, "Daughter, your faith has healed you. Go in peace and be freed from your suffering."

35While Jesus was still speaking, some men came from the house of Jairus, the synagogue ruler. "Your daughter is dead," they said. "Why bother the teacher any more?"

36Ignoring what they said, Jesus told the synagogue ruler, "Don't be afraid; just believe."

37He did not let anyone follow him except Peter, James and John the brother of James. 38When they came to the home of the synagogue ruler, Jesus saw a commotion, with people crying and wailing loudly. 39He went in and said to them, "Why all this commotion and wailing? The child is not dead but asleep." 40But they laughed at him.

After he put them all out, he took the child's father and mother and the disciples who were with him, and went in where the child was. 41He took her by the hand and said to her, *"Talitha koum!"* (which means, "Little girl, I say to you, get up!"). 42Immediately the girl stood up and walked around (she was twelve years old). At this they were completely astonished. 43He gave strict orders not to let anyone know about this, and told them to give her something to eat.

Tapping the Reservoir of God's Power

He said to her, "Daughter, your faith has healed you. Go in peace" (Mark 5:34).

Jesus felt at home in Jerusalem. Among the crush of people surrounding him, he never forgot his mission. He never lost sight of the lost men and women . . . the busy, distracted crowds . . . . the lonely, hurting people jostling for space around him.

In Mark 5, an unnamed woman is immortalized. F.B. Meyer explains that she had learned how little it takes to get the Savior's attention when faith is your motive.

Walk With F.B. Meyer

"Let those who are conscious of the ravages of evil in their hearts—which is destroying their strength—establish a connection with Christ as slight as the finger's touch of the garment hem, and instantly his power will enter and heal their inward disorder.

"His power is always going forth, and faith receives as much as it desires.

"The reservoir of power is always full, but very few have learned the secret of tapping it! Crowds throng him, but only one touches.

"Proximity to Christ does not necessarily imply the appropriation of Christ. But where there is the faintest touch of faith, there is an instantaneous response.

"There may be great weakness. The fingers may be too nerveless to grasp; they can only touch. But the slightest degree of faith saves, because it is the channel by which Christ enters."

Walk Closer to God

You cannot experience the Savior's power by standing on the sidelines. For that power, a personal step of commitment is needed . . . a personal touch of faith.

Faith for salvation. Faith for service. Faith for strength.

Simple faith in a great God. It's not something you'll learn by watching the crowd.

But then, praying in faith has never been a spectator sport. ⟦⟧

FEBRUARY 10

📖 Walk in the Word
Mark 6:1–29

Mark zeroes in on the reaction of amazement—in Nazarenes, who stared at Jesus in rejection and disbelief, and in Jesus, who was astonished by their unbelief; Jesus broadens his ministry by sending out the twelve apostles. Mark also records the execution of John the Baptist.

A Prophet Without Honor

6 Jesus left there and went to his hometown, accompanied by his disciples. ²When the Sabbath came, he began to teach in the synagogue, and many who heard him were amazed.

"Where did this man get these things?" they asked. "What's this wisdom that has been given him, that he even does miracles! ³Isn't this the carpenter? Isn't this Mary's son and the brother of James, Joseph,*ᵃ* Judas and Simon? Aren't his sisters here with us?" And they took offense at him.

⁴Jesus said to them, "Only in his hometown, among his relatives and in his own house is a prophet without honor." ⁵He could not do any miracles there, except lay his hands on a few sick people and heal them. ⁶And he was amazed at their lack of faith.

Jesus Sends Out the Twelve

Then Jesus went around teaching from village to village. ⁷Calling the Twelve to him, he sent them out two by two and gave them authority over evil*ᵇ* spirits.

⁸These were his instructions: "Take nothing for the journey except a staff—no bread, no bag, no money in your belts. ⁹Wear sandals but not an extra tunic. ¹⁰Whenever you enter a house, stay there until you leave that town. ¹¹And if any place will not welcome you or listen to you, shake the dust off your feet when you leave, as a testimony against them."

¹²They went out and preached that people should repent. ¹³They drove out many demons and anointed many sick people with oil and healed them.

John the Baptist Beheaded

¹⁴King Herod heard about this, for Jesus' name had become well known. Some were saying,*ᶜ* "John the Baptist has been raised from the dead, and that is why miraculous powers are at work in him."

¹⁵Others said, "He is Elijah."

And still others claimed, "He is a prophet, like one of the prophets of long ago."

¹⁶But when Herod heard this, he said, "John, the man I beheaded, has been raised from the dead!"

¹⁷For Herod himself had given orders to have John arrested, and he had him bound and put in prison. He did this because of Herodias, his brother Philip's wife, whom he had married. ¹⁸For John had been saying to Herod, "It is not lawful for you to have your brother's wife." ¹⁹So Herodias nursed

a grudge against John and wanted to kill him. But she was not able to, [20]because Herod feared John and protected him, knowing him to be a righteous and holy man. When Herod heard John, he was greatly puzzled[d]; yet he liked to listen to him.

[21]Finally the opportune time came. On his birthday Herod gave a banquet for his high officials and military commanders and the leading men of Galilee. [22]When the daughter of Herodias came in and danced, she pleased Herod and his dinner guests.

The king said to the girl, "Ask me for anything you want, and I'll give it to you." [23]And he promised her with an oath, "Whatever you ask I will give you, up to half my kingdom."

[24]She went out and said to her mother, "What shall I ask for?"

"The head of John the Baptist," she answered.

[25]At once the girl hurried in to the king with the request: "I want you to give me right now the head of John the Baptist on a platter."

[26]The king was greatly distressed, but because of his oaths and his dinner guests, he did not want to refuse her. [27]So he immediately sent an executioner with orders to bring John's head. The man went, beheaded John in the prison, [28]and brought back his head on a platter. He presented it to the girl, and she gave it to her mother. [29]On hearing of this, John's disciples came and took his body and laid it in a tomb.

[a]3 Greek *Joses*, a variant of *Joseph*   [b]7 Greek *unclean*   [c]14 Some early manuscripts *He was saying*   [d]20 Some early manuscripts *he did many things*

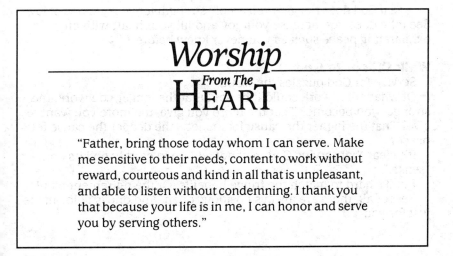

Worship
From The
HEART

"Father, bring those today whom I can serve. Make me sensitive to their needs, content to work without reward, courteous and kind in all that is unpleasant, and able to listen without condemning. I thank you that because your life is in me, I can honor and serve you by serving others."

FEBRUARY 10

The Service of Love in Every Situation

Only in his hometown . . . is a prophet without honor (Mark 6:4).

No glory. No recognition. No thanks. That's why very few people make a career of being a servant. But servanthood is the calling of every true disciple of Christ.

In chapter 6, Jesus meets rejection in Nazareth. There is no honor or welcome for the Savior in his own hometown.

And yet, his motivation to serve did not spring from a desire for human recognition.

Abraham Kuyper speaks of the proper motive for service.

Walk With Abraham Kuyper

"Let your life be one continuous service of love, a service which never grows irksome, a service which will ennoble even the smallest task.

"Do not seek the external, the visible, that which the world chooses as its goal. Seek instead that which is invisible—the hidden power behind the things we see.

"In short, seek the kingdom of God, where God is enthroned and self is denied.

"Seek these things not only in seasons of prayer and worship, but always—in every situation, in every daily task.

"See if God does not give you ample strength for your service of love. See if he does not increase your joy and fill your heart with an exhilarating peace such as you never knew before."

Walk Closer to God

Service for God puzzles the world.

Of what other work could it be said that the longer you work, the stronger you become? That the more you give, the more you want to give? That the higher the cause for anxiety, the deeper the cause for peace?

It's clear that serving God may not add up in earthly dollars and "sense."

But it's hard to match the fringe benefits. Or the retirement plan!

Best of all, there are always positions open. And one is tailor-made just for you. ◖

FEBRUARY 11

Walk in the Word
Mark 6:30-56

Mark gives his account of the miraculous feeding of five thousand men as well as Jesus' walking on water and his calming the waves.

Jesus Feeds the Five Thousand

³⁰The apostles gathered around Jesus and reported to him all they had done and taught. ³¹Then, because so many people were coming and going that they did not even have a chance to eat, he said to them, "Come with me by yourselves to a quiet place and get some rest."

³²So they went away by themselves in a boat to a solitary place. ³³But many who saw them leaving recognized them and ran on foot from all the towns and got there ahead of them. ³⁴When Jesus landed and saw a large crowd, he had compassion on them, because they were like sheep without a shepherd. So he began teaching them many things.

³⁵By this time it was late in the day, so his disciples came to him. "This is a remote place," they said, "and it's already very late. ³⁶Send the people away so they can go to the surrounding countryside and villages and buy themselves something to eat."

³⁷But he answered, "You give them something to eat."

They said to him, "That would take eight months of a man's wages[a]! Are we to go and spend that much on bread and give it to them to eat?"

³⁸"How many loaves do you have?" he asked. "Go and see."

When they found out, they said, "Five—and two fish."

³⁹Then Jesus directed them to have all the people sit down in groups on the green grass. ⁴⁰So they sat down in groups of hundreds and fifties. ⁴¹Taking the five loaves and the two fish and looking up to heaven, he gave thanks and broke the loaves. Then he gave them to his disciples to set before the people. He also divided the two fish among them all. ⁴²They all ate and were satisfied, ⁴³and the disciples picked up twelve basketfuls of broken pieces of bread and fish. ⁴⁴The number of the men who had eaten was five thousand.

Jesus Walks on the Water

⁴⁵Immediately Jesus made his disciples get into the boat and go on ahead of him to Bethsaida, while he dismissed the crowd. ⁴⁶After leaving them, he went up on a mountainside to pray.

⁴⁷When evening came, the boat was in the middle of the lake, and he was alone on land. ⁴⁸He saw the disciples straining at the oars, because the wind was against them. About the fourth watch of the night he went out to them, walking on the lake. He was about to pass by them, ⁴⁹but when they saw him walking on the lake, they thought he was a ghost. They cried out, ⁵⁰because they all saw him and were terrified.

Immediately he spoke to them and said, "Take courage! It is I. Don't be afraid." ⁵¹Then he climbed into the boat with them, and the wind died down. They were completely amazed, ⁵²for they had not understood about the loaves; their hearts were hardened.

FEBRUARY 11

⁵³When they had crossed over, they landed at Gennesaret and anchored there. ⁵⁴As soon as they got out of the boat, people recognized Jesus. ⁵⁵They ran throughout that whole region and carried the sick on mats to wherever they heard he was. ⁵⁶And wherever he went—into villages, towns or countryside—they placed the sick in the marketplaces. They begged him to let them touch even the edge of his cloak, and all who touched him were healed.

ᵃ37 Greek *take two hundred denarii*

PSALM 34

Of David. When he pretended to be insane before Abimelech, who drove him away, and he left.

I will extol the LORD at all times;
　his praise will always be on my lips.
²My soul will boast in the LORD;
　let the afflicted hear and rejoice.
³Glorify the LORD with me;
　let us exalt his name together.

⁴I sought the LORD, and he answered me;
　he delivered me from all my fears.
⁵Those who look to him are radiant;
　their faces are never covered with shame.
⁶This poor man called, and the LORD heard him;
　he saved him out of all his troubles.
⁷The angel of the LORD encamps around those who fear
　　him,
　and he delivers them.

⁸Taste and see that the LORD is good;
　blessed is the man who takes refuge in him.
⁹Fear the LORD, you his saints,
　for those who fear him lack nothing.
¹⁰The lions may grow weak and hungry,
　but those who seek the LORD lack no good thing.

FEBRUARY 11

Standing by Faith in the Crucible of Crisis

[Jesus] said, "Take courage! It is I. Don't be afraid" (Mark 6:50).

It's not really unusual when someone drops in unannounced for a meal. But when that "someone" turns out to be five thousand hungry guests, then you're facing a crisis.

Twice in chapter 6 the disciples faced overwhelming challenges. Once beside the sea, and later on the sea, they ran out of resources long before they ran out of problems.

George Müller, who often tested the resources of God, probes the inconsistency of worry in the life of the believer.

Walk With George Müller

"Ponder these words of Jesus: 'Only believe.'

"As long as we are able to trust in God—holding fast in our heart the knowledge that he is able and willing to help those who rest on the Lord Jesus for salvation, in all matters which are for his glory and their good—the heart remains calm and peaceful.

"It is when we let go of faith in his power or his love that we lose our peace and become troubled.

"This very day I am in great trial in connection with my work; yet my soul was calmed and quieted by the remembrance of God's power and love, and the result was peace of soul.

"The very time for faith to work is when sight ceases. The greater the difficulties, the easier for faith."

Walk Closer to God

Everything about the disciples' circumstances encouraged them to give up. Yet Jesus wanted them to "take courage" even as hungry stomachs growled and angry winds blew. That's faith . . . standing strong in the crucible of crisis.

Where faith begins, anxiety ends. It won't make sense to others around you that you can maintain your peace and composure when everyone else is losing theirs.

Perhaps it will make them curious enough to ask you how you do it. What will you tell them? ⟨⟩

127

JOHN CALVIN

(1509–1564) REFORMER AND THEOLOGIAN

An Influence for God

In 1536 a twenty-seven-year-old Swiss published *The Institutes of the Christian Religion*, a book now called "one of the ten books that shook the world." The author, John Calvin, guided the emerging Protestant Reformation with his valuable teaching and scholarship.

Born in 1509 at Noyon, France, Calvin planned to enter the service of the Roman Catholic Church. But after the death of his father, he decided to study law instead. Soon after that he had a conversion experience to Christ as Lord.

Forced to leave Paris because he had helped on a speech that sounded too "Protestant," Calvin made his way to Basel, Switzerland, where he wrote *The Institutes*. In this work he summarized and systematized the Protestant faith, demonstrating how far the church had drifted from historical, Biblical Christianity.

From Basel, Calvin was invited to come to Geneva, where he spent the rest of his life. Calvin found this city in political, moral and spiritual chaos. Riots were common; prostitution was rampant; Christianity was nominal. Calvin began to preach virtually every day and became involved in civic affairs. He emphasized the importance of Christian and secular education for everyone; and he sought, with limited success, to make Biblical principles the basis for Geneva's government and business affairs.

Calvin died in 1564, having influenced many to apply the Word of God in every area of life. Your life too can be an influence for God. But that takes time in the Word of God—time to read, to study and to meditate on what God has said, and time to translate that truth into action.

A LESSON FROM THE LIFE OF JOHN CALVIN

My Christianity can make a difference in others' lives if I allow it to be the ruling force in my life.

FEBRUARY 12

Walk in the Word
Mark 7:1–23

Mark records Jesus' strong condemnation of the religious leaders for their hypocritical habit of living by legalism.

Clean and Unclean

7 The Pharisees and some of the teachers of the law who had come from Jerusalem gathered around Jesus and ²saw some of his disciples eating food with hands that were "unclean," that is, unwashed. ³(The Pharisees and all the Jews do not eat unless they give their hands a ceremonial washing, holding to the tradition of the elders. ⁴When they come from the marketplace they do not eat unless they wash. And they observe many other traditions, such as the washing of cups, pitchers and kettles. *a*)

⁵So the Pharisees and teachers of the law asked Jesus, "Why don't your disciples live according to the tradition of the elders instead of eating their food with 'unclean' hands?"

⁶He replied, "Isaiah was right when he prophesied about you hypocrites; as it is written:

> " 'These people honor me with their lips,
>   but their hearts are far from me.
> ⁷They worship me in vain;
>   their teachings are but rules taught by men.' *b*

⁸You have let go of the commands of God and are holding on to the traditions of men."

⁹And he said to them: "You have a fine way of setting aside the commands of God in order to observe *c* your own traditions! ¹⁰For Moses said, 'Honor your father and your mother,' *d* and, 'Anyone who curses his father or mother must be put to death.' *e* ¹¹But you say that if a man says to his father or mother: 'Whatever help you might otherwise have received from me is Corban' (that is, a gift devoted to God), ¹²then you no longer let him do anything for his father or mother. ¹³Thus you nullify the word of God by your tradition that you have handed down. And you do many things like that."

¹⁴Again Jesus called the crowd to him and said, "Listen to me, everyone, and understand this. ¹⁵Nothing outside a man can make him 'unclean' by going into him. Rather, it is what comes out of a man that makes him 'unclean.' *f*"

¹⁷After he had left the crowd and entered the house, his disciples asked him about this parable. ¹⁸"Are you so dull?" he asked. "Don't you see that nothing that enters a man from the outside can make him 'unclean'? ¹⁹For it doesn't go into his heart but into his stomach, and then out of his body." (In saying this, Jesus declared all foods "clean.")

²⁰He went on: "What comes out of a man is what makes him 'unclean.' ²¹For from within, out of men's hearts, come evil thoughts, sexual immo-

FEBRUARY 12

rality, theft, murder, adultery, ²²greed, malice, deceit, lewdness, envy, slander, arrogance and folly. ²³All these evils come from inside and make a man 'unclean.' "

a4 Some early manuscripts *pitchers, kettles and dining couches*   *b6,7* Isaiah 29:13
c9 Some manuscripts *set up*   *d10* Exodus 20:12; Deut. 5:16   *e10* Exodus 21:17; Lev.
20:9   *f15* Some early manuscripts *'unclean.'* ¹⁶*If anyone has ears to hear, let him hear.*

PSALM 37

Turn from evil and do good;
    then you will dwell in the land forever.
²⁸For the LORD loves the just
    and will not forsake his faithful ones.

They will be protected forever,
    but the offspring of the wicked will be cut off;
²⁹the righteous will inherit the land
    and dwell in it forever.

³⁰The mouth of the righteous man utters wisdom,
    and his tongue speaks what is just.
³¹The law of his God is in his heart;
    his feet do not slip.

³²The wicked lie in wait for the righteous,
    seeking their very lives;
³³but the LORD will not leave them in their power
    or let them be condemned when brought to trial.

³⁴Wait for the LORD
    and keep his way.
He will exalt you to inherit the land;
    when the wicked are cut off, you will see it.

The Strong Beat of a Pure Heart

These people honor me with their lips, but their hearts are far from me (Mark 7:6).

A coat of paint can conceal many a jagged crack. And, as the saying goes, you can't judge a book by its cover.

Similarly, the way people act does not necessarily explain the motives behind their actions.

Jesus had a way of penetrating to the heart of things, of tearing off the mask to see the motive. As a result, he came into growing conflict with the hypocritical religious leaders of his day.

F.B. Meyer analyzes the heart condition at the root of the Pharisees' problem.

Walk With F.B. Meyer

"It is a natural tendency of the human heart to reduce its religious life to an outward and literal obedience, while its thoughts continue unhampered.

"In the life of true holiness, everything depends on the control of the thoughts. 'For as he thinks in his heart, so is he.'

"And Jesus put evil thoughts first in the black category of the contents of the evil heart.

"That the hands should be often washed, that household vessels should be kept cleansed, that there should be decorum and neatness in the outward life—all these customs are good.

"But you should ask yourself whether you are not more eager for the outward than the inward cleanliness.

" 'Create in me a pure heart' should be your constant prayer."

Walk Closer to God

It's easier to maintain clean hands than a pure heart. And because the mind is a private domain, no one may notice whether your thought life is pure or polluted.

No one, that is, except God.

Listen to your heart; what do you hear?

A clean, strong heartbeat of devotion? Or the confused rhythm of a heart far from God?

Right now might be a good time for some cleansing prayer. ◖◗

FEBRUARY 13

📖 Walk in the Word
Mark 7:24–37

Mark turns the spotlight on a woman's faith and on Jesus' powerful word of healing for her daughter; a deaf and mute man experiences Jesus' heartfelt compassion.

The Faith of a Syrophoenician Woman

²⁴Jesus left that place and went to the vicinity of Tyre.ᵃ He entered a house and did not want anyone to know it; yet he could not keep his presence secret. ²⁵In fact, as soon as she heard about him, a woman whose little daughter was possessed by an evilᵇ spirit came and fell at his feet. ²⁶The woman was a Greek, born in Syrian Phoenicia. She begged Jesus to drive the demon out of her daughter.

²⁷"First let the children eat all they want," he told her, "for it is not right to take the children's bread and toss it to their dogs."

²⁸"Yes, Lord," she replied, "but even the dogs under the table eat the children's crumbs."

²⁹Then he told her, "For such a reply, you may go; the demon has left your daughter."

³⁰She went home and found her child lying on the bed, and the demon gone.

The Healing of a Deaf and Mute Man

³¹Then Jesus left the vicinity of Tyre and went through Sidon, down to the Sea of Galilee and into the region of the Decapolis.ᶜ ³²There some people brought to him a man who was deaf and could hardly talk, and they begged him to place his hand on the man.

³³After he took him aside, away from the crowd, Jesus put his fingers into the man's ears. Then he spit and touched the man's tongue. ³⁴He looked up to heaven and with a deep sigh said to him, *"Ephphatha!"* (which means, "Be opened!"). ³⁵At this, the man's ears were opened, his tongue was loosened and he began to speak plainly.

³⁶Jesus commanded them not to tell anyone. But the more he did so, the more they kept talking about it. ³⁷People were overwhelmed with amazement. "He has done everything well," they said. "He even makes the deaf hear and the mute speak."

ᵃ24 Many early manuscripts *Tyre and Sidon*   ᵇ25 Greek *unclean*   ᶜ31 That is, the Ten Cities

132

Sighs That Speak of Sympathy and Power

He looked up to heaven . . . with a deep sigh (Mark 7:34).

Deeply moved by the needs all around him, Jesus responded in the best way possible—not with fine-sounding words, but with a sigh of compassion followed by meaningful action.

A man who could neither hear nor speak . . . a multitude who had followed Jesus without eating for three days—each experienced his unspoken, yet unmistakable love.

Jesus sighed. Yet it was no mere sigh of resignation or frustration, as F.B. Meyer makes clear.

Walk With F.B. Meyer

"In this passage, along with Mark 8:12, Mark twice calls attention to the Lord's sighs. A sigh is one of the most touching and significant tokens of excessive grief. When our natures are too disturbed to remember to take a normal breath and must compensate for this omission by one deep-drawn breath, we sigh deeply in our spirit.

" 'He looked up to heaven . . . with a deep sigh.' As the deaf-mute stood before him—an image of all the closed hearts around him, of all the inarticulate unexpressed desires, of all the sin and sorrow of mankind—Jesus' sensitive heart responded with a deep-drawn sigh.

"But there was simultaneously a heavenward look which mingled infinite hope in it. If the sigh spoke of his tender sympathy, the look declared his close union with God, by virtue of which he was competent to meet the direst need.

"Jesus, in doing good, would look to heaven and sigh; but his sighs were followed by the touch and word of power. Let us not be content with a sigh of sympathy and regret."

Walk Closer to God

You, like Jesus, can couple a heartfelt sigh with effective action, looking to God for the power to correct that which made you sigh in the first place.

There's a sighing, dying world waiting for someone like you to take compassionate action. What will be your answer: A sigh or a shrug? Or a sigh and service? ◯

FEBRUARY 14

Walk in the Word
Mark 8:1–13

Hungry people eat their fill in yet another account of a "feeding" miracle recorded by Mark.

Jesus Feeds the Four Thousand

8 During those days another large crowd gathered. Since they had nothing to eat, Jesus called his disciples to him and said, 2"I have compassion for these people; they have already been with me three days and have nothing to eat. 3If I send them home hungry, they will collapse on the way, because some of them have come a long distance."

4His disciples answered, "But where in this remote place can anyone get enough bread to feed them?"

5"How many loaves do you have?" Jesus asked.

"Seven," they replied.

6He told the crowd to sit down on the ground. When he had taken the seven loaves and given thanks, he broke them and gave them to his disciples to set before the people, and they did so. 7They had a few small fish as well; he gave thanks for them also and told the disciples to distribute them. 8The people ate and were satisfied. Afterward the disciples picked up seven basketfuls of broken pieces that were left over. 9About four thousand men were present. And having sent them away, 10he got into the boat with his disciples and went to the region of Dalmanutha.

11The Pharisees came and began to question Jesus. To test him, they asked him for a sign from heaven. 12He sighed deeply and said, "Why does this generation ask for a miraculous sign? I tell you the truth, no sign will be given to it." 13Then he left them, got back into the boat and crossed to the other side.

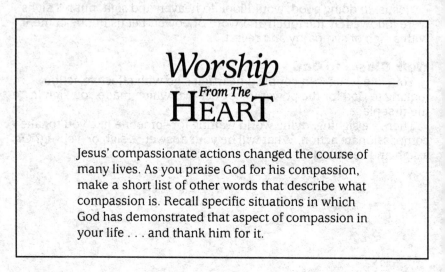

Worship
From The
HEART

Jesus' compassionate actions changed the course of many lives. As you praise God for his compassion, make a short list of other words that describe what compassion is. Recall specific situations in which God has demonstrated that aspect of compassion in your life . . . and thank him for it.

A Feeling, Healing Compassion

Jesus called his disciples to him and said, "I have compassion for these people" (Mark 8:1–2).

Have you ever happened upon a scene of misfortune that caused you to pity the poor victim?

Weep over the victim's plight?

Exchange places with the sufferer?

Mark 8 describes a scene in which pity was plentiful, but only compassionate action could meet the needs.

English clergyman John Henry Jowett contrasts pity—which tends to be passive—with compassion—which is active and often costly.

Walk With John Henry Jowett

"Jesus' compassion was part of his passion. It culminated upon Calvary, but it was bleeding all along the road.

"It was a fellow-feeling with all the pangs and sorrows of the race. Only a pity that bleeds is a pity that heals.

"As in Jesus' day, the multitude is around us still.

"There is the multitude of misfortune, the children of disadvantage. There is the multitude of outcasts, the vast army of modern-day publicans and sinners. There are the bewildering multitudes who have nothing to eat.

"How do I share the compassion of the Lord?

"Do I exercise a sensitive and sanctified imagination, and enter somehow into the pangs of their cravings?

"I must. For my Lord calls me to help."

Walk Closer to God

Pity looks and says, "How awful." Compassion weeps and says, "I'll help."

Pity looks on from afar. Compassion rolls up its sleeves and pitches in to help.

Pity waits for a convenient time. Compassion knows no office hours.

Pity is cheap and plentiful. Compassion is rare and priceless and costly.

Jesus said, "I have compassion." What do you have? 〇

FEBRUARY 15

📖 Walk in the Word
Mark 8:14 — 9:1

Mark juxtaposes the disciples' spiritual blindness and lack of understanding with Jesus' healing of a man's physical blindness and with Peter's key confession that Jesus is the Christ, the Messiah.

The Yeast of the Pharisees and Herod

[14]The disciples had forgotten to bring bread, except for one loaf they had with them in the boat. [15]"Be careful," Jesus warned them. "Watch out for the yeast of the Pharisees and that of Herod."

[16]They discussed this with one another and said, "It is because we have no bread."

[17]Aware of their discussion, Jesus asked them: "Why are you talking about having no bread? Do you still not see or understand? Are your hearts hardened? [18]Do you have eyes but fail to see, and ears but fail to hear? And don't you remember? [19]When I broke the five loaves for the five thousand, how many basketfuls of pieces did you pick up?"

"Twelve," they replied.

[20]"And when I broke the seven loaves for the four thousand, how many basketfuls of pieces did you pick up?"

They answered, "Seven."

[21]He said to them, "Do you still not understand?"

The Healing of a Blind Man at Bethsaida

[22]They came to Bethsaida, and some people brought a blind man and begged Jesus to touch him. [23]He took the blind man by the hand and led him outside the village. When he had spit on the man's eyes and put his hands on him, Jesus asked, "Do you see anything?"

[24]He looked up and said, "I see people; they look like trees walking around."

[25]Once more Jesus put his hands on the man's eyes. Then his eyes were opened, his sight was restored, and he saw everything clearly. [26]Jesus sent him home, saying, "Don't go into the village.*a*"

Peter's Confession of Christ

[27]Jesus and his disciples went on to the villages around Caesarea Philippi. On the way he asked them, "Who do people say I am?"

[28]They replied, "Some say John the Baptist; others say Elijah; and still others, one of the prophets."

[29]"But what about you?" he asked. "Who do you say I am?"

Peter answered, "You are the Christ.*b*"

[30]Jesus warned them not to tell anyone about him.

Jesus Predicts His Death

[31]He then began to teach them that the Son of Man must suffer many things and be rejected by the elders, chief priests and teachers of the law,

and that he must be killed and after three days rise again. ³²He spoke plainly about this, and Peter took him aside and began to rebuke him.

³³But when Jesus turned and looked at his disciples, he rebuked Peter. "Get behind me, Satan!" he said. "You do not have in mind the things of God, but the things of men."

³⁴Then he called the crowd to him along with his disciples and said: "If anyone would come after me, he must deny himself and take up his cross and follow me. ³⁵For whoever wants to save his life*c* will lose it, but whoever loses his life for me and for the gospel will save it. ³⁶What good is it for a man to gain the whole world, yet forfeit his soul? ³⁷Or what can a man give in exchange for his soul? ³⁸If anyone is ashamed of me and my words in this adulterous and sinful generation, the Son of Man will be ashamed of him when he comes in his Father's glory with the holy angels."

9 And he said to them, "I tell you the truth, some who are standing here will not taste death before they see the kingdom of God come with power."

a26 Some manuscripts *Don't go and tell anyone in the village*   *b29* Or *Messiah.* "The Christ" (Greek) and "the Messiah" (Hebrew) both mean "the Anointed One."
c35 The Greek word means either *life* or *soul;* also in verse 36.

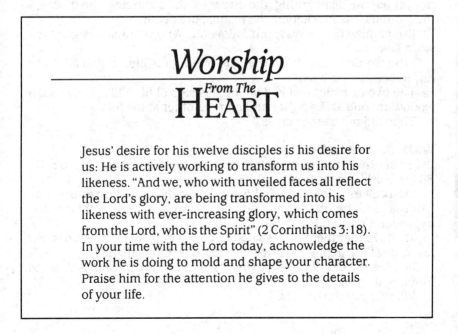

Worship
HEART From The

Jesus' desire for his twelve disciples is his desire for us: He is actively working to transform us into his likeness. "And we, who with unveiled faces all reflect the Lord's glory, are being transformed into his likeness with ever-increasing glory, which comes from the Lord, who is the Spirit" (2 Corinthians 3:18). In your time with the Lord today, acknowledge the work he is doing to mold and shape your character. Praise him for the attention he gives to the details of your life.

FEBRUARY 15

What Way Are We to Follow?

If anyone would come after me, he must deny himself and take up his cross and follow me (Mark 8:34).

When Jesus spoke to his own about the demands of discipleship, the words were strong and foreboding.

"Deny . . . take up your cross . . . follow." Those are the words of Jesus.

"Pamper yourself . . . indulge . . . grab the gusto." Those are the words of the world.

Augustine reminds all Christians that servanthood involves both a privilege . . . and a price.

Walk With Augustine

"It is good to follow Christ. But we must see by what way we are to follow.

"For when the Lord spoke the words of Mark 8, he had not already risen from the dead. He had not yet suffered, not yet come to the cross, not yet felt the dishonoring, the outrages, the scourging, the thorns, the wounds, the mockeries, the insults, the death.

"Rough may be the way, but follow on. Where Christ has gone is worn smooth.

"Who would not wish to be exalted? Honor is pleasing to all. But humility is the path to it.

"The two disciples disliked taking this step of humility. They sought exaltation, one at the right hand and the other at the left.

"They did not see the cross."

Walk Closer to God

Christ's invitation to discipleship is an invitation to die. Die to self. To the world. To personal ambition.

It is a call to follow Jesus in his life. In his death. In his resurrection.

It is a reminder that exaltation and elevation in God's sight are the byproducts of humility.

Small wonder there is so seldom a crowd gathered at the cross. For few are willing to pay the price that discipleship demands.

But it's a price well worth paying, for a life of discipleship is the most fulfilling life of all.

Will you pay the price?

FEBRUARY 16

Walk in the Word
Mark 9:2–32

Elijah and Moses talk with Jesus on a mountain and a voice rings out from a cloud in this, Mark's account of the transfiguration. The painful reality of physical and spiritual struggles confronts Jesus as he descends the mountain.

The Transfiguration

²After six days Jesus took Peter, James and John with him and led them up a high mountain, where they were all alone. There he was transfigured before them. ³His clothes became dazzling white, whiter than anyone in the world could bleach them. ⁴And there appeared before them Elijah and Moses, who were talking with Jesus.

⁵Peter said to Jesus, "Rabbi, it is good for us to be here. Let us put up three shelters — one for you, one for Moses and one for Elijah." ⁶(He did not know what to say, they were so frightened.)

⁷Then a cloud appeared and enveloped them, and a voice came from the cloud: "This is my Son, whom I love. Listen to him!"

⁸Suddenly, when they looked around, they no longer saw anyone with them except Jesus.

⁹As they were coming down the mountain, Jesus gave them orders not to tell anyone what they had seen until the Son of Man had risen from the dead. ¹⁰They kept the matter to themselves, discussing what "rising from the dead" meant.

¹¹And they asked him, "Why do the teachers of the law say that Elijah must come first?"

¹²Jesus replied, "To be sure, Elijah does come first, and restores all things. Why then is it written that the Son of Man must suffer much and be rejected? ¹³But I tell you, Elijah has come, and they have done to him everything they wished, just as it is written about him."

The Healing of a Boy With an Evil Spirit

¹⁴When they came to the other disciples, they saw a large crowd around them and the teachers of the law arguing with them. ¹⁵As soon as all the people saw Jesus, they were overwhelmed with wonder and ran to greet him.

¹⁶"What are you arguing with them about?" he asked.

¹⁷A man in the crowd answered, "Teacher, I brought you my son, who is possessed by a spirit that has robbed him of speech. ¹⁸Whenever it seizes him, it throws him to the ground. He foams at the mouth, gnashes his teeth and becomes rigid. I asked your disciples to drive out the spirit, but they could not."

¹⁹"O unbelieving generation," Jesus replied, "how long shall I stay with you? How long shall I put up with you? Bring the boy to me."

²⁰So they brought him. When the spirit saw Jesus, it immediately threw

FEBRUARY 16

the boy into a convulsion. He fell to the ground and rolled around, foaming at the mouth.

21Jesus asked the boy's father, "How long has he been like this?"

"From childhood," he answered. 22"It has often thrown him into fire or water to kill him. But if you can do anything, take pity on us and help us."

23"'If you can'?" said Jesus. "Everything is possible for him who believes."

24Immediately the boy's father exclaimed, "I do believe; help me overcome my unbelief!"

25When Jesus saw that a crowd was running to the scene, he rebuked the evila spirit. "You deaf and mute spirit," he said, "I command you, come out of him and never enter him again."

26The spirit shrieked, convulsed him violently and came out. The boy looked so much like a corpse that many said, "He's dead." 27But Jesus took him by the hand and lifted him to his feet, and he stood up.

28After Jesus had gone indoors, his disciples asked him privately, "Why couldn't we drive it out?"

29He replied, "This kind can come out only by prayer.b"

30They left that place and passed through Galilee. Jesus did not want anyone to know where they were, 31because he was teaching his disciples. He said to them, "The Son of Man is going to be betrayed into the hands of men. They will kill him, and after three days he will rise." 32But they did not understand what he meant and were afraid to ask him about it.

a25 Greek *unclean*   b29 Some manuscripts *prayer and fasting*

Worship
From The HEART

God had promised Abraham descendants as numerous as the stars (Genesis 15:5). Abraham wondered how this could be, yet he knew that somehow God would do it, and his faith was eventually rewarded. By the time their son Isaac was born, Abraham and Sarah had learned the answer to the question, "Is anything too hard for the Lord?" Think of the "impossibilities" in your own life and worship God today by praising him for his faithfulness.

The Power to Do, to Dare, and to Suffer

Jesus [said], "Everything is possible for him who believes" (Mark 9:23).

The father's heart was cracking with grief and his mind was wrestling with doubt as his son writhed on the ground in the grip of an evil spirit. "Lord, I do believe," he cried, "help me overcome my unbelief!"

If you find yourself discouraged by doubt, remember this father's honest prayer—and these encouraging words from Charles Spurgeon.

Walk With Charles Spurgeon

"The father said to Jesus, 'If you can do anything, take pity on us and help us.'

"Now there was an *if* in the question. But the poor, trembling father had put the *if* in the wrong place. Christ, without commanding him to retract the *if*, kindly puts it in its legitimate position.

"He seemed to say, 'There should be no *if* about my power, nor concerning my willingness; the *if* lies elsewhere. If you can believe, everything is possible for him who believes.'

"We, like this man, often see that there is an *if* somewhere, but we are perpetually blundering by putting it in the wrong place.

"Faith stands in God's power and is robed in God's majesty; it wears the royal apparel and rides on the King's horse, for it is the grace which the King delights to honor. Girding itself with the glorious might of the all-working Spirit, faith becomes, in the omnipotence of God, power to do, to dare, and to suffer. All things, without limit, are possible to the one who believes."

Walk Closer to God

Jesus later reminds his disciples that "all things are possible with God" (Mark 10:27).

Even his closest followers were prone to forget the power they saw him exercise time after time. Like Abraham, they needed to be "fully persuaded that God had power to do what he had promised" (Romans 4:21).

God's Word gives numerous examples of God's power at work in response to man's faith. So when doubts assail you, remember this: With God, the possibilities are limitless!

FEBRUARY 17

📖 Walk in the Word
Mark 9:33 — 10:16

Vignettes from Jesus' life illustrate Jesus' incomparable teaching style;
Mark intersperses teachings about discipleship and divorce with teachings
about children and greatness in Jesus' kingdom.

Who Is the Greatest?

[33]They came to Capernaum. When he was in the house, he asked them, "What were you arguing about on the road?" [34]But they kept quiet because on the way they had argued about who was the greatest.

[35]Sitting down, Jesus called the Twelve and said, "If anyone wants to be first, he must be the very last, and the servant of all."

[36]He took a little child and had him stand among them. Taking him in his arms, he said to them, [37]"Whoever welcomes one of these little children in my name welcomes me; and whoever welcomes me does not welcome me but the one who sent me."

Whoever Is Not Against Us Is for Us

[38]"Teacher," said John, "we saw a man driving out demons in your name and we told him to stop, because he was not one of us."

[39]"Do not stop him," Jesus said. "No one who does a miracle in my name can in the next moment say anything bad about me, [40]for whoever is not against us is for us. [41]I tell you the truth, anyone who gives you a cup of water in my name because you belong to Christ will certainly not lose his reward.

Causing to Sin

[42]"And if anyone causes one of these little ones who believe in me to sin, it would be better for him to be thrown into the sea with a large millstone tied around his neck. [43]If your hand causes you to sin, cut it off. It is better for you to enter life maimed than with two hands to go into hell, where the fire never goes out.[a] [45]And if your foot causes you to sin, cut it off. It is better for you to enter life crippled than to have two feet and be thrown into hell.[b] [47]And if your eye causes you to sin, pluck it out. It is better for you to enter the kingdom of God with one eye than to have two eyes and be thrown into hell, [48]where

> " 'their worm does not die,
>   and the fire is not quenched.'[c]

[49]Everyone will be salted with fire.

[50]"Salt is good, but if it loses its saltiness, how can you make it salty again? Have salt in yourselves, and be at peace with each other."

Divorce

10 Jesus then left that place and went into the region of Judea and across the Jordan. Again crowds of people came to him, and as was his custom, he taught them.

²Some Pharisees came and tested him by asking, "Is it lawful for a man to divorce his wife?"

³"What did Moses command you?" he replied.

⁴They said, "Moses permitted a man to write a certificate of divorce and send her away."

⁵"It was because your hearts were hard that Moses wrote you this law," Jesus replied. ⁶"But at the beginning of creation God 'made them male and female.'ᵈ ⁷"For this reason a man will leave his father and mother and be united to his wife,ᵉ ⁸and the two will become one flesh.'ᶠ So they are no longer two, but one. ⁹Therefore what God has joined together, let man not separate."

¹⁰When they were in the house again, the disciples asked Jesus about this. ¹¹He answered, "Anyone who divorces his wife and marries another woman commits adultery against her. ¹²And if she divorces her husband and marries another man, she commits adultery."

The Little Children and Jesus

¹³People were bringing little children to Jesus to have him touch them, but the disciples rebuked them. ¹⁴When Jesus saw this, he was indignant. He said to them, "Let the little children come to me, and do not hinder them, for the kingdom of God belongs to such as these. ¹⁵I tell you the truth, anyone who will not receive the kingdom of God like a little child will never enter it." ¹⁶And he took the children in his arms, put his hands on them and blessed them.

ᵃ43 Some manuscripts out, *⁴⁴where / " 'their worm does not die, / and the fire is not quenched.'* *ᵇ45 Some manuscripts* hell, *⁴⁶where / " 'their worm does not die, / and the fire is not quenched.'* *ᶜ48 Isaiah 66:24* *ᵈ6 Gen. 1:27* *ᵉ7 Some early manuscripts do not have* and be united to his wife. *ᶠ8 Gen. 2:24*

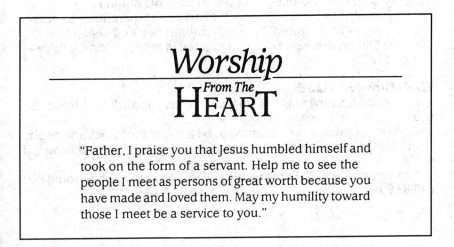

Worship
From The
HEART

"Father, I praise you that Jesus humbled himself and took on the form of a servant. Help me to see the people I meet as persons of great worth because you have made and loved them. May my humility toward those I meet be a service to you."

FEBRUARY 17

Humility That Leads to Healing

If anyone wants to be first, he must be the very last, and the servant of all (Mark 9:35).

Imagine that in your favorite store, you are waiting to be "waited upon"—when someone mistakes you for an employee.

Are you flattered or embarrassed? Do you laugh, or are you offended?

Being mistaken for a sales clerk can be humorous. It might also be highly revealing!

In Mark 9 and 10, Christ had more to say about serving than he did about being served.

Dwight L. Moody, whose ministry often placed him in prominent positions, shares two examples of the stature of the servant.

Walk With Dwight L. Moody

"There is a story told of William Carey, the great missionary, who was at a party attended by the governor-general of India. Also present were some military officers who looked down upon the missionaries with contempt.

"One of those officers said at the table: 'I believe that Carey was a shoemaker, wasn't he, before he took up the profession of a missionary?'

"Mr. Carey spoke up and said: 'Oh, no, I was only a cobbler. I could mend shoes, and wasn't ashamed of it.'

"The one prominent virtue of Christ, next to his obedience, was his humility. And even his obedience grew out of his humility.

"In his lowly birth, his submission to his earthly parents, his contact with the poor and despised, his entire submission and dependence upon his Father, this virtue—consummated in his death on the cross— shines out."

Walk Closer to God

Isn't it strange how many vie to be first when, according to Jesus, the prize goes to the one who is last!

William Carey was not ashamed to be a mender of soles and heels, if only by that he might find opportunity to be a mender and healer of souls.

"Only a servant . . . " Some would call that an insult. What would you call it? ♥

FEBRUARY 18

📖 Walk in the Word
Mark 10:17–52

By recounting more stories about encounters with Jesus, Mark accents the cost of discipleship — the necessity of removing whatever keeps someone from following Jesus and committing to a life of humble and loving service.

The Rich Young Man

¹⁷As Jesus started on his way, a man ran up to him and fell on his knees before him. "Good teacher," he asked, "what must I do to inherit eternal life?"

¹⁸"Why do you call me good?" Jesus answered. "No one is good — except God alone. ¹⁹You know the commandments: 'Do not murder, do not commit adultery, do not steal, do not give false testimony, do not defraud, honor your father and mother.'ᵃ"

²⁰"Teacher," he declared, "all these I have kept since I was a boy."

²¹Jesus looked at him and loved him. "One thing you lack," he said. "Go, sell everything you have and give to the poor, and you will have treasure in heaven. Then come, follow me."

²²At this the man's face fell. He went away sad, because he had great wealth.

²³Jesus looked around and said to his disciples, "How hard it is for the rich to enter the kingdom of God!"

²⁴The disciples were amazed at his words. But Jesus said again, "Children, how hard it isᵇ to enter the kingdom of God! ²⁵It is easier for a camel to go through the eye of a needle than for a rich man to enter the kingdom of God."

²⁶The disciples were even more amazed, and said to each other, "Who then can be saved?"

²⁷Jesus looked at them and said, "With man this is impossible, but not with God; all things are possible with God."

²⁸Peter said to him, "We have left everything to follow you!"

²⁹"I tell you the truth," Jesus replied, "no one who has left home or brothers or sisters or mother or father or children or fields for me and the gospel ³⁰will fail to receive a hundred times as much in this present age (homes, brothers, sisters, mothers, children and fields — and with them, persecutions) and in the age to come, eternal life. ³¹But many who are first will be last, and the last first."

Jesus Again Predicts His Death

³²They were on their way up to Jerusalem, with Jesus leading the way, and the disciples were astonished, while those who followed were afraid. Again he took the Twelve aside and told them what was going to happen to him. ³³"We are going up to Jerusalem," he said, "and the Son of Man will be betrayed to the chief priests and teachers of the law. They will condemn him to death and will hand him over to the Gentiles, ³⁴who will mock him and spit on him, flog him and kill him. Three days later he will rise."

February 18

The Request of James and John

35Then James and John, the sons of Zebedee, came to him. "Teacher," they said, "we want you to do for us whatever we ask."

36"What do you want me to do for you?" he asked.

37They replied, "Let one of us sit at your right and the other at your left in your glory."

38"You don't know what you are asking," Jesus said. "Can you drink the cup I drink or be baptized with the baptism I am baptized with?"

39"We can," they answered.

Jesus said to them, "You will drink the cup I drink and be baptized with the baptism I am baptized with, 40but to sit at my right or left is not for me to grant. These places belong to those for whom they have been prepared."

41When the ten heard about this, they became indignant with James and John. 42Jesus called them together and said, "You know that those who are regarded as rulers of the Gentiles lord it over them, and their high officials exercise authority over them. 43Not so with you. Instead, whoever wants to become great among you must be your servant, 44and whoever wants to be first must be slave of all. 45For even the Son of Man did not come to be served, but to serve, and to give his life as a ransom for many."

Blind Bartimaeus Receives His Sight

46Then they came to Jericho. As Jesus and his disciples, together with a large crowd, were leaving the city, a blind man, Bartimaeus (that is, the Son of Timaeus), was sitting by the roadside begging. 47When he heard that it was Jesus of Nazareth, he began to shout, "Jesus, Son of David, have mercy on me!"

48Many rebuked him and told him to be quiet, but he shouted all the more, "Son of David, have mercy on me!"

49Jesus stopped and said, "Call him."

So they called to the blind man, "Cheer up! On your feet! He's calling you." 50Throwing his cloak aside, he jumped to his feet and came to Jesus.

51"What do you want me to do for you?" Jesus asked him.

The blind man said, "Rabbi, I want to see."

52"Go," said Jesus, "your faith has healed you." Immediately he received his sight and followed Jesus along the road.

a19 Exodus 20:12-16; Deut. 5:16-20   b24 Some manuscripts *is for those who trust in riches*

146

FEBRUARY 18

A Personal Preference for Jesus Christ

Peter said to him, "We have left everything to follow you!" (Mark 10:28).

Bargaining with God is a favorite pastime for many of us: "Lord, I'll follow you if . . . " "I'll put you first, God, when . . . "

In Mark 10, Peter reminded Jesus of the personal sacrifice involved in being his disciple: "We have left everything."

Implied is Peter's unspoken concern: "What will we get in return?"

Commitment with strings attached is not new. But as Oswald Chambers points out, it's really not commitment at all.

Walk With Oswald Chambers

"We have become so commercialized that we only go to God for something from him, and not for himself.

"If we only give up something to God because we want more back, there is nothing of the Holy Spirit in our abandonment. It is miserable commercial self-interest.

"That we gain heaven, that we are delivered from sin, that we are made useful to God—these things never enter as considerations into real abandonment, which is a personal sovereign preference for Jesus Christ himself.

"Beware of stopping short of abandonment to God, for most of us know abandonment in word only."

Walk Closer to God

Unconditional surrender allows no exceptions.

You cannot be totally available to God *if* . . .

You cannot surrender to God's will *when* . . .

You cannot leave all and follow, *provided* . . .

It just doesn't work that way.

There are many ways to express your level of commitment to Jesus Christ:

"I'm not willing to put you first."

"I'll put you first if . . . "

"I'll put you first, regardless."

On this commitment scale, where would you place the apostle Peter in Mark 10? And where would you place yourself?

FEBRUARY 19

Walk in the Word
Mark 11:1–19

Mark begins his narration of Jesus' last days on earth with the triumphal entry into Jerusalem and the temple cleansing.

The Triumphal Entry

11 As they approached Jerusalem and came to Bethphage and Bethany at the Mount of Olives, Jesus sent two of his disciples, ²saying to them, "Go to the village ahead of you, and just as you enter it, you will find a colt tied there, which no one has ever ridden. Untie it and bring it here. ³If anyone asks you, 'Why are you doing this?' tell him, 'The Lord needs it and will send it back here shortly.' "

⁴They went and found a colt outside in the street, tied at a doorway. As they untied it, ⁵some people standing there asked, "What are you doing, untying that colt?" ⁶They answered as Jesus had told them to, and the people let them go. ⁷When they brought the colt to Jesus and threw their cloaks over it, he sat on it. ⁸Many people spread their cloaks on the road, while others spread branches they had cut in the fields. ⁹Those who went ahead and those who followed shouted,

"Hosanna!ᵃ"

"Blessed is he who comes in the name of the Lord!"ᵇ

¹⁰"Blessed is the coming kingdom of our father David!"

"Hosanna in the highest!"

¹¹Jesus entered Jerusalem and went to the temple. He looked around at everything, but since it was already late, he went out to Bethany with the Twelve.

Jesus Clears the Temple

¹²The next day as they were leaving Bethany, Jesus was hungry. ¹³Seeing in the distance a fig tree in leaf, he went to find out if it had any fruit. When he reached it, he found nothing but leaves, because it was not the season for figs. ¹⁴Then he said to the tree, "May no one ever eat fruit from you again." And his disciples heard him say it.

¹⁵On reaching Jerusalem, Jesus entered the temple area and began driving out those who were buying and selling there. He overturned the tables of the money changers and the benches of those selling doves, ¹⁶and would not allow anyone to carry merchandise through the temple courts. ¹⁷And as he taught them, he said, "Is it not written:

" 'My house will be called
  a house of prayer for all nations'ᶜ?

But you have made it 'a den of robbers.'ᵈ "

FEBRUARY 19

¹⁸The chief priests and the teachers of the law heard this and began looking for a way to kill him, for they feared him, because the whole crowd was amazed at his teaching.

¹⁹When evening came, they*ᵉ* went out of the city.

a9 A Hebrew expression meaning "Save!" which became an exclamation of praise; also in verse 10   b9 Psalm 118:25,26   c17 Isaiah 56:7   d17 Jer. 7:11   e19 Some early manuscripts he

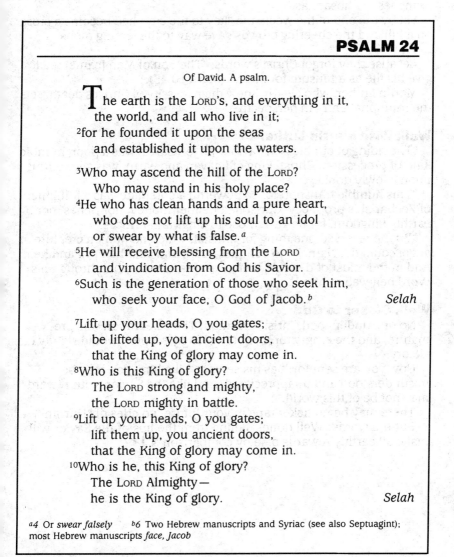

PSALM 24

Of David. A psalm.

The earth is the LORD's, and everything in it,
    the world, and all who live in it;
²for he founded it upon the seas
    and established it upon the waters.

³Who may ascend the hill of the LORD?
    Who may stand in his holy place?
⁴He who has clean hands and a pure heart,
    who does not lift up his soul to an idol
    or swear by what is false.*ᵃ*
⁵He will receive blessing from the LORD
    and vindication from God his Savior.
⁶Such is the generation of those who seek him,
    who seek your face, O God of Jacob.*ᵇ*   *Selah*

⁷Lift up your heads, O you gates;
    be lifted up, you ancient doors,
    that the King of glory may come in.
⁸Who is this King of glory?
    The LORD strong and mighty,
    the LORD mighty in battle.
⁹Lift up your heads, O you gates;
    lift them up, you ancient doors,
    that the King of glory may come in.
¹⁰Who is he, this King of glory?
    The LORD Almighty—
    he is the King of glory.   *Selah*

a4 Or swear falsely   b6 Two Hebrew manuscripts and Syriac (see also Septuagint); most Hebrew manuscripts face, Jacob

FEBRUARY 19

Earthly Service in Heavenly Perspective

Those who went ahead and those who followed shouted, "Hosanna!" "Blessed is he who comes in the name of the Lord!" (Mark 11:9).

The last week of Christ's life began with a hero's welcome . . . palm branches . . . hosannas.

Yet by the end of the week, the "key to the city" had become a cross on a hill and the cheering crowds gave way to the jeering mobs. Why?

Because they forgot Christ's words: "The Son of Man [came] . . . to give his life as a ransom for many" (Mark 10:45).

Martin Luther, who clearly knew the necessity of Christ's death, sets the triumphal entry in perspective.

Walk With Martin Luther

"The riding of our blessed Savior into Jerusalem was a poor, humble kind of procession. Christ, king of heaven and earth, was seen sitting upon a lowly donkey.

"This humble transport for so powerful a potentate was a fulfillment of Zechariah's prophecy. Christ had neither money, nor riches, nor earthly kingdom, for he gave those to kings and princes.

"But he reserved one thing for himself, which no human creature or angel could do. Namely, to conquer death and sin, the devil and hell. And in the midst of death to deliver and save those that through his Word believed in him."

Walk Closer to God

No one understood Christ's triumph. The celebration was premature, and the empty tomb, not the kingly scepter, would signify his victory.

Now you are sent forth as his servant. Like him, you may be misunderstood and unappreciated. And like the Savior, your reward may not be of this world.

There may be no ticker tape in your future, no cries of "Hurrah!"

But the words "Well done!" falling from the lips of the Savior will make all earthly rewards pale by comparison. ◖

FEBRUARY 20

Walk in the Word
Mark 11:20 — 12:12

Mark shows Jesus skillfully weaving the themes of faith and judgment into an object lesson about a fig tree and a parable about vineyard tenants.

The Withered Fig Tree

20In the morning, as they went along, they saw the fig tree withered from the roots. 21Peter remembered and said to Jesus, "Rabbi, look! The fig tree you cursed has withered!"

22"Have *a* faith in God," Jesus answered. 23"I tell you the truth, if anyone says to this mountain, 'Go, throw yourself into the sea,' and does not doubt in his heart but believes that what he says will happen, it will be done for him. 24Therefore I tell you, whatever you ask for in prayer, believe that you have received it, and it will be yours. 25And when you stand praying, if you hold anything against anyone, forgive him, so that your Father in heaven may forgive you your sins. *b* "

The Authority of Jesus Questioned

27They arrived again in Jerusalem, and while Jesus was walking in the temple courts, the chief priests, the teachers of the law and the elders came to him. 28"By what authority are you doing these things?" they asked. "And who gave you authority to do this?"

29Jesus replied, "I will ask you one question. Answer me, and I will tell you by what authority I am doing these things. 30John's baptism — was it from heaven, or from men? Tell me!"

31They discussed it among themselves and said, "If we say, 'From heaven,' he will ask, 'Then why didn't you believe him?' 32But if we say, 'From men'. . . ." (They feared the people, for everyone held that John really was a prophet.)

33So they answered Jesus, "We don't know."

Jesus said, "Neither will I tell you by what authority I am doing these things."

The Parable of the Tenants

12 He then began to speak to them in parables: "A man planted a vineyard. He put a wall around it, dug a pit for the winepress and built a watchtower. Then he rented the vineyard to some farmers and went away on a journey. 2At harvest time he sent a servant to the tenants to collect from them some of the fruit of the vineyard. 3But they seized him, beat him and sent him away empty-handed. 4Then he sent another servant to them; they struck this man on the head and treated him shamefully. 5He sent still another, and that one they killed. He sent many others; some of them they beat, others they killed.

6"He had one left to send, a son, whom he loved. He sent him last of all, saying, 'They will respect my son.'

151

FEBRUARY 20

⁷"But the tenants said to one another, 'This is the heir. Come, let's kill him, and the inheritance will be ours.' ⁸So they took him and killed him, and threw him out of the vineyard.

⁹"What then will the owner of the vineyard do? He will come and kill those tenants and give the vineyard to others. ¹⁰Haven't you read this scripture:

> " 'The stone the builders rejected
>   has become the capstone*c*;
> ¹¹the Lord has done this,
>   and it is marvelous in our eyes'*d*?"

¹²Then they looked for a way to arrest him because they knew he had spoken the parable against them. But they were afraid of the crowd; so they left him and went away.

a22 Some early manuscripts *If you have*   *b25* Some manuscripts *sins.* ²⁶*But if you do not forgive, neither will your Father who is in heaven forgive your sins.*   *c10* Or *cornerstone* *d11* Psalm 118:22,23

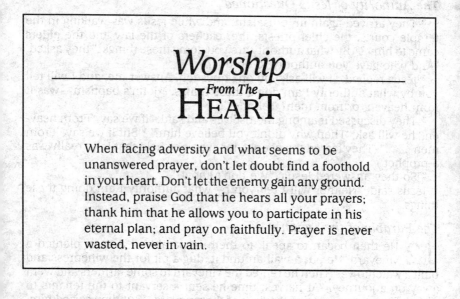

Worship
From The
HEART

When facing adversity and what seems to be unanswered prayer, don't let doubt find a foothold in your heart. Don't let the enemy gain any ground. Instead, praise God that he hears all your prayers; thank him that he allows you to participate in his eternal plan; and pray on faithfully. Prayer is never wasted, never in vain.

Faith in the Faithful One

"Have faith in God," Jesus answered (Mark 11:22).

Faith works no miracles. It never has. But God does. And always will.

God is the provider of power; faith is simply the channel through which his power is released.

In Mark 11 Jesus used the withered fig tree as an object lesson to teach the importance of well-placed faith—faith that is in God, the faithful one.

J. Hudson Taylor, pioneer missionary to China, knew firsthand a lifestyle of faith in a great and faithful God.

Walk With J. Hudson Taylor

"We should bring every care for temporal things to him and then be anxious for nothing.

"Is our path dark? He is our sun. Are we in danger? He is our shield.

"If we trust him we shall not be put to shame. But if our faith should fail, *his* will not—'If we are faithless, he remains faithful.'

"As the light which shines from the dark waters of the lake is the reflection of the sun's rays, so a person's faith is the impress and reflection of God's faith.

"The one who holds God's faith will not be reckless or foolhardy but will be ready for every emergency.

"The person who holds God's faith will dare to obey him."

Walk Closer to God

Do you have a friend who has proved faithful in the past? Then you will have little trouble trusting that friend in the future.

So it is with faith in God—faithfulness begets faith. You trust your trustworthy supplier, not yourself or your feelings.

The living, loving God of creation—the one who made the mountains and therefore has no trouble removing them at the proper time—generates a faith that will not shrink when washed in the waters of affliction . . . a faith against which mountains of adversity don't stand a chance! ◖

FEBRUARY 21

📖 Walk in the Word
Mark 12:13–44

Jesus exposes the deceit of the religious leaders who pull out all the stops in their efforts to destroy Jesus; Mark cites Jesus' responses to questions about taxes, marriage and the commandments.

Paying Taxes to Caesar

¹³Later they sent some of the Pharisees and Herodians to Jesus to catch him in his words. ¹⁴They came to him and said, "Teacher, we know you are a man of integrity. You aren't swayed by men, because you pay no attention to who they are; but you teach the way of God in accordance with the truth. Is it right to pay taxes to Caesar or not? ¹⁵Should we pay or shouldn't we?"

But Jesus knew their hypocrisy. "Why are you trying to trap me?" he asked. "Bring me a denarius and let me look at it." ¹⁶They brought the coin, and he asked them, "Whose portrait is this? And whose inscription?"

"Caesar's," they replied.

¹⁷Then Jesus said to them, "Give to Caesar what is Caesar's and to God what is God's."

And they were amazed at him.

Marriage at the Resurrection

¹⁸Then the Sadducees, who say there is no resurrection, came to him with a question. ¹⁹"Teacher," they said, "Moses wrote for us that if a man's brother dies and leaves a wife but no children, the man must marry the widow and have children for his brother. ²⁰Now there were seven brothers. The first one married and died without leaving any children. ²¹The second one married the widow, but he also died, leaving no child. It was the same with the third. ²²In fact, none of the seven left any children. Last of all, the woman died too. ²³At the resurrection*a* whose wife will she be, since the seven were married to her?"

²⁴Jesus replied, "Are you not in error because you do not know the Scriptures or the power of God? ²⁵When the dead rise, they will neither marry nor be given in marriage; they will be like the angels in heaven. ²⁶Now about the dead rising—have you not read in the book of Moses, in the account of the bush, how God said to him, 'I am the God of Abraham, the God of Isaac, and the God of Jacob'*b*? ²⁷He is not the God of the dead, but of the living. You are badly mistaken!"

The Greatest Commandment

²⁸One of the teachers of the law came and heard them debating. Noticing that Jesus had given them a good answer, he asked him, "Of all the commandments, which is the most important?"

²⁹"The most important one," answered Jesus, "is this: 'Hear, O Israel, the Lord our God, the Lord is one.*c* ³⁰Love the Lord your God with all your heart and with all your soul and with all your mind and with all your

strength.'[d] [31]The second is this: 'Love your neighbor as yourself.'[e] There is no commandment greater than these."

[32]"Well said, teacher," the man replied. "You are right in saying that God is one and there is no other but him. [33]To love him with all your heart, with all your understanding and with all your strength, and to love your neighbor as yourself is more important than all burnt offerings and sacrifices."

[34]When Jesus saw that he had answered wisely, he said to him, "You are not far from the kingdom of God." And from then on no one dared ask him any more questions.

Whose Son Is the Christ?

[35]While Jesus was teaching in the temple courts, he asked, "How is it that the teachers of the law say that the Christ[f] is the son of David? [36]David himself, speaking by the Holy Spirit, declared:

> " 'The Lord said to my Lord:
> "Sit at my right hand
> until I put your enemies
> under your feet." '[g]

[37]David himself calls him 'Lord.' How then can he be his son?"

The large crowd listened to him with delight.

[38]As he taught, Jesus said, "Watch out for the teachers of the law. They like to walk around in flowing robes and be greeted in the marketplaces, [39]and have the most important seats in the synagogues and the places of honor at banquets. [40]They devour widows' houses and for a show make lengthy prayers. Such men will be punished most severely."

The Widow's Offering

[41]Jesus sat down opposite the place where the offerings were put and watched the crowd putting their money into the temple treasury. Many rich people threw in large amounts. [42]But a poor widow came and put in two very small copper coins,[h] worth only a fraction of a penny.[i]

[43]Calling his disciples to him, Jesus said, "I tell you the truth, this poor widow has put more into the treasury than all the others. [44]They all gave out of their wealth; but she, out of her poverty, put in everything—all she had to live on."

---

[a]23 Some manuscripts *resurrection, when men rise from the dead,*   [b]26 Exodus 3:6
[c]29 Or *the Lord our God is one Lord*   [d]30 Deut. 6:4,5   [e]31 Lev. 19:18   [f]35 Or *Messiah*   [g]36 Psalm 110:1   [h]42 Greek *two lepta*   [i]42 Greek *kodrantes*

FEBRUARY 21

Making So Much Out of So Little

Jesus sat down opposite the place where the offerings were put and watched the crowd putting their money into the temple treasury (Mark 12:41).

The Bible has much to say about money matters because, in God's eyes, money matters!

In Mark 12, many rich people were giving huge sums out of their bloated bank accounts. But their "much" seemed as nothing to Jesus when compared with the "all" that the poor widow gave out of her poverty.

Adam Clarke explains how a widow's two small copper coins could add up to more than a rich man's millions.

Walk With Adam Clarke

"Christ observes all people and all things. All our actions are before his eyes. What we do in public and what we do in private are equally known to him.

"His eye was upon the abundance of the rich who had given much; and he was well acquainted with the poverty and desolate state of the widow who had given her all, though that was only a little in itself.

"Christ sees all the motives which lead people to perform their good deeds. He knows whether they act through vanity, self-love, ambition, hypocrisy . . . or through love, charity, zeal for his glory, and a hearty desire to please him.

"He observes the motivations which accompany our actions—whether we act with care or negligence, with a ready mind or with reluctance."

Walk Closer to God

There are many who are willing to give God credit . . . but few willing to give him cash!

Many willing to give him some—even much—but few willing to give him all.

Many willing to give a tithe or offering . . . but few willing to admit that the balance also belongs to him.

If God rewarded your giving on the basis of motive, not amount, would he make little ado about much, or much ado about little?

How you give, not *how much*. That's where a servant's heart is revealed. ◖◗

FEBRUARY 22

📖 Walk in the Word
Mark 13:1–31

With keen insight into the danger of deception faced by the disciples, Jesus reveals the signs of the end of the age in this account recorded by Mark.

Signs of the End of the Age

13 As he was leaving the temple, one of his disciples said to him, "Look, Teacher! What massive stones! What magnificent buildings!"

²"Do you see all these great buildings?" replied Jesus. "Not one stone here will be left on another; every one will be thrown down."

³As Jesus was sitting on the Mount of Olives opposite the temple, Peter, James, John and Andrew asked him privately, ⁴"Tell us, when will these things happen? And what will be the sign that they are all about to be fulfilled?"

⁵Jesus said to them: "Watch out that no one deceives you. ⁶Many will come in my name, claiming, 'I am he,' and will deceive many. ⁷When you hear of wars and rumors of wars, do not be alarmed. Such things must happen, but the end is still to come. ⁸Nation will rise against nation, and kingdom against kingdom. There will be earthquakes in various places, and famines. These are the beginning of birth pains.

⁹"You must be on your guard. You will be handed over to the local councils and flogged in the synagogues. On account of me you will stand before governors and kings as witnesses to them. ¹⁰And the gospel must first be preached to all nations. ¹¹Whenever you are arrested and brought to trial, do not worry beforehand about what to say. Just say whatever is given you at the time, for it is not you speaking, but the Holy Spirit.

¹²"Brother will betray brother to death, and a father his child. Children will rebel against their parents and have them put to death. ¹³All men will hate you because of me, but he who stands firm to the end will be saved.

¹⁴"When you see 'the abomination that causes desolation'ᵃ standing where itᵇ does not belong—let the reader understand—then let those who are in Judea flee to the mountains. ¹⁵Let no one on the roof of his house go down or enter the house to take anything out. ¹⁶Let no one in the field go back to get his cloak. ¹⁷How dreadful it will be in those days for pregnant women and nursing mothers! ¹⁸Pray that this will not take place in winter, ¹⁹because those will be days of distress unequaled from the beginning, when God created the world, until now—and never to be equaled again. ²⁰If the Lord had not cut short those days, no one would survive. But for the sake of the elect, whom he has chosen, he has shortened them. ²¹At that time if anyone says to you, 'Look, here is the Christᶜ!' or, 'Look, there he is!' do not believe it. ²²For false Christs and false prophets will appear and perform signs and miracles to deceive the elect—if that were possible. ²³So be on your guard; I have told you everything ahead of time.

157

FEBRUARY 22

24"But in those days, following that distress,

" 'the sun will be darkened,
   and the moon will not give its light;
25the stars will fall from the sky,
   and the heavenly bodies will be shaken.'*d*

26"At that time men will see the Son of Man coming in clouds with great power and glory. 27And he will send his angels and gather his elect from the four winds, from the ends of the earth to the ends of the heavens.

28"Now learn this lesson from the fig tree: As soon as its twigs get tender and its leaves come out, you know that summer is near. 29Even so, when you see these things happening, you know that it is near, right at the door. 30I tell you the truth, this generation*e* will certainly not pass away until all these things have happened. 31Heaven and earth will pass away, but my words will never pass away.

a14 Daniel 9:27; 11:31; 12:11   *b14* Or *he*; also in verse 29   *c21* Or *Messiah*
d25 Isaiah 13:10; 34:4   *e30* Or *race*

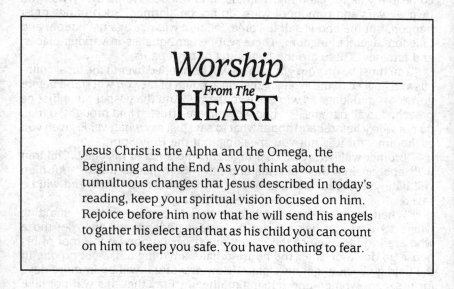

Worship
From The
HEART

Jesus Christ is the Alpha and the Omega, the Beginning and the End. As you think about the tumultuous changes that Jesus described in today's reading, keep your spiritual vision focused on him. Rejoice before him now that he will send his angels to gather his elect and that as his child you can count on him to keep you safe. You have nothing to fear.

Commotion, Change, and Consummation in His Plan

> When you hear of wars and rumors of wars, do not be alarmed. Such things must happen, but the end is still to come . . . These are the beginning of birth pains (Mark 13:7–8).

Birth pangs are a bittersweet experience. On the one hand they signal a long-awaited event. On the other, the beginning of hours of intense labor.

So it is with the signs of the times in Mark 13 — signs which mark the urgency of the hour.

Though the tendency in every age has been to mistake the birth pangs for the actual moment of birth, J.A. Alexander offers this helpful insight. (And keep in mind that he penned these words more than a century ago!)

Walk With J.A. Alexander

"Do not be troubled or filled with concern, as if these commotions necessarily imply some great catastrophe or the final consummation.

"The necessity of this caution — given not only to the first disciples but also to their successors — is abundantly apparent.

"Pious people in every age have concluded that national commotions and collisions were decisive proof that the world was near its end.

"There are no doubt true Christians at this moment drawing such conclusions from the mutiny in India and the war in China, in direct opposition to our Lord's command. The meaning of his words is not that such changes may not be immediately followed by the greatest change of all, but only that they do not guarantee it."

Walk Closer to God

The disciples were asking for a sign. Jesus concentrated on the assignment.

Nations will rise and fall, wars will rage, earthquakes will rock, famines will ravage.

But in the midst of it all, there's a job to be done: "The gospel must first be preached to all nations" (Mark 13:10).

Only the servant of God, with his task clearly in view, will be able to watch and pray — and faithfully engage in fruitful service — even as the birth pangs grow. Are you such a servant? ()

FEBRUARY 23

📖 Walk in the Word
Mark 13:32—14:11

Various attitudes toward Jesus are juxtaposed here, ranging from the bitter hatred of the religious leaders to the loving devotion of a woman with a jar of ointment and concluding with the opportunistic attitude of Judas Iscariot.

The Day and Hour Unknown

³²"No one knows about that day or hour, not even the angels in heaven, nor the Son, but only the Father. ³³Be on guard! Be alert[a]! You do not know when that time will come. ³⁴It's like a man going away: He leaves his house and puts his servants in charge, each with his assigned task, and tells the one at the door to keep watch.

³⁵"Therefore keep watch because you do not know when the owner of the house will come back—whether in the evening, or at midnight, or when the rooster crows, or at dawn. ³⁶If he comes suddenly, do not let him find you sleeping. ³⁷What I say to you, I say to everyone: 'Watch!' "

Jesus Anointed at Bethany

14 Now the Passover and the Feast of Unleavened Bread were only two days away, and the chief priests and the teachers of the law were looking for some sly way to arrest Jesus and kill him. ²"But not during the Feast," they said, "or the people may riot."

³While he was in Bethany, reclining at the table in the home of a man known as Simon the Leper, a woman came with an alabaster jar of very expensive perfume, made of pure nard. She broke the jar and poured the perfume on his head.

⁴Some of those present were saying indignantly to one another, "Why this waste of perfume? ⁵It could have been sold for more than a year's wages[b] and the money given to the poor." And they rebuked her harshly.

⁶"Leave her alone," said Jesus. "Why are you bothering her? She has done a beautiful thing to me. ⁷The poor you will always have with you, and you can help them any time you want. But you will not always have me. ⁸She did what she could. She poured perfume on my body beforehand to prepare for my burial. ⁹I tell you the truth, wherever the gospel is preached throughout the world, what she has done will also be told, in memory of her."

¹⁰Then Judas Iscariot, one of the Twelve, went to the chief priests to betray Jesus to them. ¹¹They were delighted to hear this and promised to give him money. So he watched for an opportunity to hand him over.

ᵃ33 Some manuscripts *alert and pray*   ᵇ5 Greek *than three hundred denarii*

Filling the Room With the Aroma of Praise

"She did what she could. She poured perfume on my body beforehand to prepare for my burial" (Mark 14:8).

Whether in words or by actions, true love cannot be contained. It always finds a means of expression.

But you don't always have to talk about love, as Mark 14 illustrates. There a nameless woman expressed her love for the Lord, apparently without uttering a single word.

Scottish minister Robert Murray McCheyne speaks of the woman's act of loving adoration in anointing her precious Savior with a very costly and precious perfume.

Walk With Robert Murray McCheyne

"If we have been saved by Christ, we should pour out our best affections on him.

"It is good to love his disciples, good to love his ministers, good to love his poor. But it is best to love him.

"We cannot now reach his blessed head, nor anoint his holy feet. But we can fall down at his footstool and pour out our affections toward him.

"It was not the ointment Jesus desired, for what does the King of Glory care for a little ointment?

"But it is the loving heart poured out upon his feet; it is the adoration, praise, love, and prayers of a believer's broken heart that Christ cares for.

"The new heart is the alabaster box that Jesus loves—broken and filling the room with the aroma of praise."

Walk Closer to God

It's easy to become preoccupied with the work of the Lord . . . and overlook the Lord of the work. To concentrate on the people of God or the business of God . . . and ignore the person of God.

Activity is vital in the life of a servant. But so too is bringing your alabaster box to Jesus . . . breaking it . . . pouring out your heart . . . and allowing the sweet fragrance of praise to say as nothing else can, "I love you, Lord."

You need not be eloquent to do that, for God hears the sincere sentiments of his children's hearts.

FEBRUARY 24

📖 Walk in the Word
Mark 14:12–42

Mark gives his account of the Lord's Supper, the prediction of Peter's denial, and the agonizing prayer scene in Gethsemane.

The Lord's Supper

¹²On the first day of the Feast of Unleavened Bread, when it was customary to sacrifice the Passover lamb, Jesus' disciples asked him, "Where do you want us to go and make preparations for you to eat the Passover?"

¹³So he sent two of his disciples, telling them, "Go into the city, and a man carrying a jar of water will meet you. Follow him. ¹⁴Say to the owner of the house he enters, 'The Teacher asks: Where is my guest room, where I may eat the Passover with my disciples?' ¹⁵He will show you a large upper room, furnished and ready. Make preparations for us there."

¹⁶The disciples left, went into the city and found things just as Jesus had told them. So they prepared the Passover.

¹⁷When evening came, Jesus arrived with the Twelve. ¹⁸While they were reclining at the table eating, he said, "I tell you the truth, one of you will betray me—one who is eating with me."

¹⁹They were saddened, and one by one they said to him, "Surely not I?"

²⁰"It is one of the Twelve," he replied, "one who dips bread into the bowl with me. ²¹The Son of Man will go just as it is written about him. But woe to that man who betrays the Son of Man! It would be better for him if he had not been born."

²²While they were eating, Jesus took bread, gave thanks and broke it, and gave it to his disciples, saying, "Take it; this is my body."

²³Then he took the cup, gave thanks and offered it to them, and they all drank from it.

²⁴"This is my blood of the[a] covenant, which is poured out for many," he said to them. ²⁵"I tell you the truth, I will not drink again of the fruit of the vine until that day when I drink it anew in the kingdom of God."

²⁶When they had sung a hymn, they went out to the Mount of Olives.

Jesus Predicts Peter's Denial

²⁷"You will all fall away," Jesus told them, "for it is written:

> " 'I will strike the shepherd,
>   and the sheep will be scattered.'[b]

²⁸But after I have risen, I will go ahead of you into Galilee."

²⁹Peter declared, "Even if all fall away, I will not."

³⁰"I tell you the truth," Jesus answered, "today—yes, tonight—before the rooster crows twice[c] you yourself will disown me three times."

³¹But Peter insisted emphatically, "Even if I have to die with you, I will never disown you." And all the others said the same.

162

Gethsemane

³²They went to a place called Gethsemane, and Jesus said to his disciples, "Sit here while I pray." ³³He took Peter, James and John along with him, and he began to be deeply distressed and troubled. ³⁴"My soul is overwhelmed with sorrow to the point of death," he said to them. "Stay here and keep watch."

³⁵Going a little farther, he fell to the ground and prayed that if possible the hour might pass from him. ³⁶"*Abba*,ᵈ Father," he said, "everything is possible for you. Take this cup from me. Yet not what I will, but what you will."

³⁷Then he returned to his disciples and found them sleeping. "Simon," he said to Peter, "are you asleep? Could you not keep watch for one hour? ³⁸Watch and pray so that you will not fall into temptation. The spirit is willing, but the body is weak."

³⁹Once more he went away and prayed the same thing. ⁴⁰When he came back, he again found them sleeping, because their eyes were heavy. They did not know what to say to him.

⁴¹Returning the third time, he said to them, "Are you still sleeping and resting? Enough! The hour has come. Look, the Son of Man is betrayed into the hands of sinners. ⁴²Rise! Let us go! Here comes my betrayer!"

ᵃ24 Some manuscripts *the new*   ᵇ27 Zech. 13:7   ᶜ30 Some early manuscripts do not have *twice*.   ᵈ36 Aramaic for *Father*

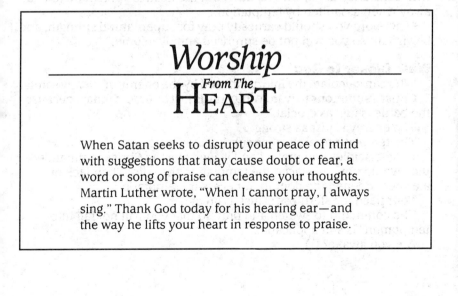

Worship
From The
Heart

When Satan seeks to disrupt your peace of mind
with suggestions that may cause doubt or fear, a
word or song of praise can cleanse your thoughts.
Martin Luther wrote, "When I cannot pray, I always
sing." Thank God today for his hearing ear—and
the way he lifts your heart in response to praise.

February 24

Strong Enemy, Sleepy Saints, and the Master's Summons

Watch and pray so that you will not fall into temptation. The spirit is willing, but the body is weak (Mark 14:38).

Peter, James, and John were involved in serious spiritual combat. But they didn't know it.

Their commander had told them to "watch and pray" so they would not fall victim to the enemy. Instead they slept, giving in to the very temptation they had been warned to avoid.

Temptation is more than something to be met and conquered. As Matthew Poole explains, it is also something to be avoided.

Walk With Matthew Poole

"Here Jesus calls his disciples to a greater watching—spiritual watching—that they might not fall under temptation.

"By exhorting them to watch, he directed them to use such means as were within their power to use. By adding prayer, he let them know that it was not in their power to stand without God's help and assistance, and which—upon their praying—would not be denied.

"The spirit is willing, but the body is weak. The spirit is resolved with constancy to perform its duty, but the flesh is apt to faint and fall away when assaulted by temptation.

"Therefore you should earnestly pray for supernatural strength, and be vigilant so you will not be surprised and overcome."

Walk Closer to God

Who can calculate the injury inflicted by the enemy on sleepy saints?

Christ's summons to watch and pray is just as urgent today, because the battle is just as crucial.

The enemy is just as strong.

The temptations are just as subtle.

If the disciples had prayed and stayed alert as Christ commanded, they would not have faced the temptation they did. Their lack of alertness opened the door to unnecessary temptation.

Your need for alertness is just as great.

The command to "watch and pray so that you will not fall into temptation" is still applicable.

Are you awake? ❑

FEBRUARY 25

📖 Walk in the Word
Mark 14:43–72

Jesus' arrest, the first stage of his Jewish trial, and the denial by Peter are highlighted by Mark.

Jesus Arrested

⁴³Just as he was speaking, Judas, one of the Twelve, appeared. With him was a crowd armed with swords and clubs, sent from the chief priests, the teachers of the law, and the elders.

⁴⁴Now the betrayer had arranged a signal with them: "The one I kiss is the man; arrest him and lead him away under guard." ⁴⁵Going at once to Jesus, Judas said, "Rabbi!" and kissed him. ⁴⁶The men seized Jesus and arrested him. ⁴⁷Then one of those standing near drew his sword and struck the servant of the high priest, cutting off his ear.

⁴⁸"Am I leading a rebellion," said Jesus, "that you have come out with swords and clubs to capture me? ⁴⁹Every day I was with you, teaching in the temple courts, and you did not arrest me. But the Scriptures must be fulfilled." ⁵⁰Then everyone deserted him and fled.

⁵¹A young man, wearing nothing but a linen garment, was following Jesus. When they seized him, ⁵²he fled naked, leaving his garment behind.

Before the Sanhedrin

⁵³They took Jesus to the high priest, and all the chief priests, elders and teachers of the law came together. ⁵⁴Peter followed him at a distance, right into the courtyard of the high priest. There he sat with the guards and warmed himself at the fire.

⁵⁵The chief priests and the whole Sanhedrin were looking for evidence against Jesus so that they could put him to death, but they did not find any. ⁵⁶Many testified falsely against him, but their statements did not agree.

⁵⁷Then some stood up and gave this false testimony against him: ⁵⁸"We heard him say, 'I will destroy this man-made temple and in three days will build another, not made by man.' " ⁵⁹Yet even then their testimony did not agree.

⁶⁰Then the high priest stood up before them and asked Jesus, "Are you not going to answer? What is this testimony that these men are bringing against you?" ⁶¹But Jesus remained silent and gave no answer.

Again the high priest asked him, "Are you the Christ,ᵃ the Son of the Blessed One?"

⁶²"I am," said Jesus. "And you will see the Son of Man sitting at the right hand of the Mighty One and coming on the clouds of heaven."

⁶³The high priest tore his clothes. "Why do we need any more witnesses?" he asked. ⁶⁴"You have heard the blasphemy. What do you think?"

They all condemned him as worthy of death. ⁶⁵Then some began to spit at him; they blindfolded him, struck him with their fists, and said, "Prophesy!" And the guards took him and beat him.

FEBRUARY 25

Peter Disowns Jesus

⁶⁶While Peter was below in the courtyard, one of the servant girls of the high priest came by. ⁶⁷When she saw Peter warming himself, she looked closely at him.

"You also were with that Nazarene, Jesus," she said.

⁶⁸But he denied it. "I don't know or understand what you're talking about," he said, and went out into the entryway.ᵇ

⁶⁹When the servant girl saw him there, she said again to those standing around, "This fellow is one of them." ⁷⁰Again he denied it.

After a little while, those standing near said to Peter, "Surely you are one of them, for you are a Galilean."

⁷¹He began to call down curses on himself, and he swore to them, "I don't know this man you're talking about."

⁷²Immediately the rooster crowed the second time.ᶜ Then Peter remembered the word Jesus had spoken to him: "Before the rooster crows twiceᵈ you will disown me three times." And he broke down and wept.

ᵃ61 Or *Messiah*   ᵇ68 Some early manuscripts *entryway and the rooster crowed*   ᶜ72 Some early manuscripts do not have *the second time.*   ᵈ72 Some early manuscripts do not have *twice.*

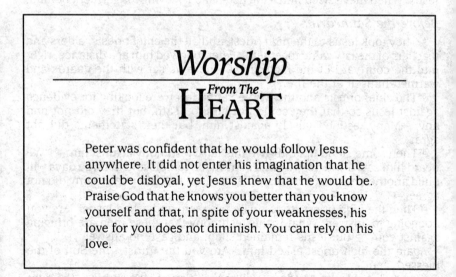

Worship
From The HEART

Peter was confident that he would follow Jesus anywhere. It did not enter his imagination that he could be disloyal, yet Jesus knew that he would be. Praise God that he knows you better than you know yourself and that, in spite of your weaknesses, his love for you does not diminish. You can rely on his love.

The Heat of the Battle or the Warmth of the Fire

Peter followed him at a distance. . . . There he sat with the guards and warmed himself at the fire (Mark 14:54).

Peter: a servant at last. Unfortunately, he picked the wrong time, the wrong place, and the wrong master!

Christ's call to serve involves a willingness to face persecution. But fear became Peter's master in the face of danger. He chose the guise of a servant in order to escape the hardships of being identified with Christ.

Matthew Henry, one of God's committed servants, suggests where Peter went wrong.

Walk With Matthew Henry

"He followed Christ, but it was afar off. Fear and concern for his own safety prevailed.

"It looks bad, and bodes worse, when those who are willing to be Christ's disciples are not willing to be known as such.

"Here begins Peter's denial: For to follow Jesus afar off is to turn away little by little.

"Peter should have gone back up to the court and appeared for his Master. But he went in where there was a good fire and sat with the servants. Not to silence their reproaches, but to screen himself.

"He followed him, led more by his curiosity than by his conscience. He attended as an idle spectator, rather than as a disciple."

Walk Closer to God

There is something inconsistent about a servant in the shadows.

A servant more concerned about his own welfare than his master's.

A servant more intent on being comfortable than on being a comforter.

Times of crisis should be the showcase for God's servants. After all, that's what he has uniquely equipped you to handle.

But when the choice falls between the heat of the battle and the warmth of the fire, only you can decide whether you will sit with the servants . . . or stand with the Savior. ❍

FEBRUARY 26

📖 Walk in the Word
Mark 15:1–20

Mark fixes the readers' eyes on the path to the cross, here taking us step by step from the trial before Pilate to the merciless floggings and mockings.

Jesus Before Pilate

15 Very early in the morning, the chief priests, with the elders, the teachers of the law and the whole Sanhedrin, reached a decision. They bound Jesus, led him away and handed him over to Pilate.

²"Are you the king of the Jews?" asked Pilate.

"Yes, it is as you say," Jesus replied.

³The chief priests accused him of many things. ⁴So again Pilate asked him, "Aren't you going to answer? See how many things they are accusing you of."

⁵But Jesus still made no reply, and Pilate was amazed.

⁶Now it was the custom at the Feast to release a prisoner whom the people requested. ⁷A man called Barabbas was in prison with the insurrectionists who had committed murder in the uprising. ⁸The crowd came up and asked Pilate to do for them what he usually did.

⁹"Do you want me to release to you the king of the Jews?" asked Pilate, ¹⁰knowing it was out of envy that the chief priests had handed Jesus over to him. ¹¹But the chief priests stirred up the crowd to have Pilate release Barabbas instead.

¹²"What shall I do, then, with the one you call the king of the Jews?" Pilate asked them.

¹³"Crucify him!" they shouted.

¹⁴"Why? What crime has he committed?" asked Pilate.

But they shouted all the louder, "Crucify him!"

¹⁵Wanting to satisfy the crowd, Pilate released Barabbas to them. He had Jesus flogged, and handed him over to be crucified.

The Soldiers Mock Jesus

¹⁶The soldiers led Jesus away into the palace (that is, the Praetorium) and called together the whole company of soldiers. ¹⁷They put a purple robe on him, then twisted together a crown of thorns and set it on him. ¹⁸And they began to call out to him, "Hail, king of the Jews!" ¹⁹Again and again they struck him on the head with a staff and spit on him. Falling on their knees, they paid homage to him. ²⁰And when they had mocked him, they took off the purple robe and put his own clothes on him. Then they led him out to crucify him.

The Heavenly Strength of Patient Endurance

"What crime has he committed?" asked Pilate. But they shouted all the louder, "Crucify him!" (Mark 15:14).

It's nice to get more than you deserve. But for all the good Jesus did, he received a cross.

Servanthood is often like that. In exchange for selflessness and sacrifice, you may receive misunderstanding . . . jeers . . . persecution . . . hatred . . . perhaps even death.

Abraham Kuyper offers this insight into Christ's greatest act of service for sinful humanity.

Walk With Abraham Kuyper

"That heavenly strength which overcame every effort to thrust the Holy One out of the world is endurance.

"This patience is displayed in Jesus' spiritual struggles against Satan. First in the wilderness, then in Pilate's judgment hall, and finally upon the cross, he was steadfast. He endured.

"Satan left nothing untried in his efforts to destroy that glorious, holy, divine life. But the holiness of Jesus was neither marred nor even slightly soiled.

"The full glory of Jesus' endurance is revealed when, on the third morning, he arises from the grave. He endured that last enemy and overcame it—death!

"There is nothing more that Satan can do now against the Christ. And it is Christ who works that same strength in those who are his."

Walk Closer to God

Heat and pressure have a way of revealing and proving the quality of a product.

In the same way, the truest test of commitment comes not on the days when everything goes well, but on the days when everything goes wrong . . . when you are misunderstood . . . ill-treated . . . wrongly accused.

But the strength that enabled Jesus to endure is available for you as you follow daily in his steps. Draw on it.

And don't be surprised if you prove to be just as durable. ◖◗

A Life Spent in Service

Matthew Henry, the second son of prominent minister Phillip Henry, grew up in the warm nurture of a Christian home. Born in 1662 during a time of political unrest in England, Henry's childhood was marked by frequent ailments. His mind, however, was sharp. Always a thinker and notetaker, he began reading and commenting on the Bible at the age of three, and he responded personally to the claims of Christ at the age of eleven.

Young Henry never wavered from his intention to follow in his father's footsteps. Unstable times forced him temporarily to switch to a study of law, but when he was about twenty-five, he was able to resume his original course. He began his ministry by serving a church in Chester, where he remained for the next twenty-five years.

The final two years of his life were spent at a church in London. He died at the age of fifty-one while on a preaching tour. His dying words form a fitting epitaph to his life: "A life spent in the service of God is the most comfortable and pleasant life that one can live in the present world."

Matthew Henry left behind more than a legacy of faithful church ministry; his commentary on the entire Bible is one of the most popular commentaries in use yet today, more than 270 years after it was originally published. Notable for its rich devotional insights, Henry's commentary is the product of one mind and heart devoted to mining the truths of God's Word.

Perhaps this month would be a good time to add his commentary to your own library of Bible-study tools. Henry's commentary can be your guide in discovering new riches from the pages of Scripture.

A LESSON FROM THE LIFE OF MATTHEW HENRY

I can have a close relationship with God as I study his Word.

FEBRUARY 27

Walk in the Word
Mark 15:21–47

Mark captures the darkness of history's turning point — the brutal cruelty of human beings, the ignominious and lonely death of God's Son for the sins of all people, and the hasty, unceremonious burial of Jesus by his friends.

The Crucifixion

21A certain man from Cyrene, Simon, the father of Alexander and Rufus, was passing by on his way in from the country, and they forced him to carry the cross. 22They brought Jesus to the place called Golgotha (which means The Place of the Skull). 23Then they offered him wine mixed with myrrh, but he did not take it. 24And they crucified him. Dividing up his clothes, they cast lots to see what each would get.

25It was the third hour when they crucified him. 26The written notice of the charge against him read: THE KING OF THE JEWS. 27They crucified two robbers with him, one on his right and one on his left.*a* 29Those who passed by hurled insults at him, shaking their heads and saying, "So! You who are going to destroy the temple and build it in three days, 30come down from the cross and save yourself!"

31In the same way the chief priests and the teachers of the law mocked him among themselves. "He saved others," they said, "but he can't save himself! 32Let this Christ,*b* this King of Israel, come down now from the cross, that we may see and believe." Those crucified with him also heaped insults on him.

The Death of Jesus

33At the sixth hour darkness came over the whole land until the ninth hour. 34And at the ninth hour Jesus cried out in a loud voice, *"Eloi, Eloi, lama sabachthani?"* — which means, "My God, my God, why have you forsaken me?"*c*

35When some of those standing near heard this, they said, "Listen, he's calling Elijah."

36One man ran, filled a sponge with wine vinegar, put it on a stick, and offered it to Jesus to drink. "Now leave him alone. Let's see if Elijah comes to take him down," he said.

37With a loud cry, Jesus breathed his last.

38The curtain of the temple was torn in two from top to bottom. 39And when the centurion, who stood there in front of Jesus, heard his cry and*d* saw how he died, he said, "Surely this man was the Son*e* of God!"

40Some women were watching from a distance. Among them were Mary Magdalene, Mary the mother of James the younger and of Joses, and Salome. 41In Galilee these women had followed him and cared for his needs. Many other women who had come up with him to Jerusalem were also there.

FEBRUARY 27

The Burial of Jesus

⁴²It was Preparation Day (that is, the day before the Sabbath). So as evening approached, ⁴³Joseph of Arimathea, a prominent member of the Council, who was himself waiting for the kingdom of God, went boldly to Pilate and asked for Jesus' body. ⁴⁴Pilate was surprised to hear that he was already dead. Summoning the centurion, he asked him if Jesus had already died. ⁴⁵When he learned from the centurion that it was so, he gave the body to Joseph. ⁴⁶So Joseph bought some linen cloth, took down the body, wrapped it in the linen, and placed it in a tomb cut out of rock. Then he rolled a stone against the entrance of the tomb. ⁴⁷Mary Magdalene and Mary the mother of Joses saw where he was laid.

ᵃ27 Some manuscripts left, ²⁸and the scripture was fulfilled which says, "He was counted with the lawless ones" (Isaiah 53:12)   ᵇ32 Or Messiah   ᶜ34 Psalm 22:1   ᵈ39 Some manuscripts do not have *heard his cry and*   ᵉ39 Or *a son*

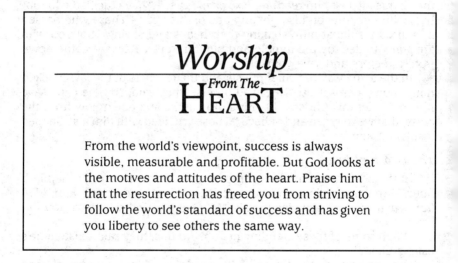

Worship
H^{From The}EART

From the world's viewpoint, success is always visible, measurable and profitable. But God looks at the motives and attitudes of the heart. Praise him that the resurrection has freed you from striving to follow the world's standard of success and has given you liberty to see others the same way.

Tragedy Transformed Into Eternal Triumph

And when the centurion, who stood there in front of Jesus, heard his cry and saw how he died, he said, "Surely this man was the Son of God!" (Mark 15:39).

Mark's account of Jesus' death is an agonizing record of what seems to be a total failure. A mock trial . . . brutal crucifixion . . . cruel taunts . . . hurried burial.

And for three days hope died in the disciples' hearts.

A.W. Tozer explains how failure in the eyes of the world may be success in God's eyes.

Walk With A.W. Tozer

"The current mania of people seeking to succeed in the world is a good thing perverted.

"The desire to fulfill the purpose for which we were created is, of course, a gift from God. But sin has twisted this impulse about and turned it into a selfish lust for first place and top honors.

"When we come to Christ, we enter a different realm, one infinitely higher than and altogether contrary to that of the world.

"Our Lord died an apparent failure, discredited by the leaders of established religion, rejected by society, and forsaken by his friends. It took the resurrection to demonstrate how gloriously Christ had triumphed and how tragically the world had failed.

"The resurrection demonstrated once and for all who won and who lost."

Walk Closer to God

There is no greater success story than the resurrection when apparent tragedy was transformed into eternal triumph.

That would be good news enough. But there's more! Christ's resurrection makes a similar success story possible in the lives of Christians who know the truth of this verse: "I have been crucified with Christ and I no longer live, but Christ lives in me" (Galatians 2:20).

That's a success story with new chapters being written every day. One of those chapters is reserved just for you.

How will today's page read? ❍

FEBRUARY 28

📖 Walk in the Word
Mark 16

From the darkness of the tomb explodes the light of victory over death; Jesus' story ends not in death and defeat, but in life and power, as Mark makes clear in his succinct record of the resurrection.

The Resurrection

16 When the Sabbath was over, Mary Magdalene, Mary the mother of James, and Salome bought spices so that they might go to anoint Jesus' body. ²Very early on the first day of the week, just after sunrise, they were on their way to the tomb ³and they asked each other, "Who will roll the stone away from the entrance of the tomb?"

⁴But when they looked up, they saw that the stone, which was very large, had been rolled away. ⁵As they entered the tomb, they saw a young man dressed in a white robe sitting on the right side, and they were alarmed.

⁶"Don't be alarmed," he said. "You are looking for Jesus the Nazarene, who was crucified. He has risen! He is not here. See the place where they laid him. ⁷But go, tell his disciples and Peter, 'He is going ahead of you into Galilee. There you will see him, just as he told you.' "

⁸Trembling and bewildered, the women went out and fled from the tomb. They said nothing to anyone, because they were afraid.

[The earliest manuscripts and some other ancient witnesses do not have Mark 16:9–20.]

⁹When Jesus rose early on the first day of the week, he appeared first to Mary Magdalene, out of whom he had driven seven demons. ¹⁰She went and told those who had been with him and who were mourning and weeping. ¹¹When they heard that Jesus was alive and that she had seen him, they did not believe it.

¹²Afterward Jesus appeared in a different form to two of them while they were walking in the country. ¹³These returned and reported it to the rest; but they did not believe them either.

¹⁴Later Jesus appeared to the Eleven as they were eating; he rebuked them for their lack of faith and their stubborn refusal to believe those who had seen him after he had risen.

¹⁵He said to them, "Go into all the world and preach the good news to all creation. ¹⁶Whoever believes and is baptized will be saved, but whoever does not believe will be condemned. ¹⁷And these signs will accompany those who believe: In my name they will drive out demons; they will speak in new tongues; ¹⁸they will pick up snakes with their hands; and when they drink deadly poison, it will not hurt them at all; they will place their hands on sick people, and they will get well."

FEBRUARY 28

¹⁹After the Lord Jesus had spoken to them, he was taken up into heaven and he sat at the right hand of God. ²⁰Then the disciples went out and preached everywhere, and the Lord worked with them and confirmed his word by the signs that accompanied it.

PSALM 146

Praise the LORD.ᵃ

Praise the LORD, O my soul.
2 I will praise the LORD all my life;
   I will sing praise to my God as long as I live.

³Do not put your trust in princes,
   in mortal men, who cannot save.
⁴When their spirit departs, they return to the ground;
   on that very day their plans come to nothing.

⁵Blessed is he whose help is the God of Jacob,
   whose hope is in the LORD his God,
⁶the Maker of heaven and earth,
   the sea, and everything in them—
   the LORD, who remains faithful forever.
⁷He upholds the cause of the oppressed
   and gives food to the hungry.
   The LORD sets prisoners free,
8   the LORD gives sight to the blind,
   the LORD lifts up those who are bowed down,
   the LORD loves the righteous.
⁹The LORD watches over the alien
   and sustains the fatherless and the widow,
   but he frustrates the ways of the wicked.

¹⁰The LORD reigns forever,
   your God, O Zion, for all generations.

Praise the LORD.

ᵃ1 Hebrew *Hallelu Yah*; also in verse 10

February 28

His Power, His Presence, His People

Then the disciples went out and preached everywhere, and the Lord worked with them (Mark 16:20).

When an experienced orator delivers a moving address, no one is surprised. But when fishermen begin to make stirring speeches, that's news.

The resurrection of Christ in Mark 16 transformed the disciples from timid men into bold witnesses.

John Calvin examines the transformation of these fugitives-turned-preachers.

Walk With John Calvin

"Every person would have thought that, by his death on the cross, Christ would either be altogether annihilated or so completely overwhelmed that he would never again be mentioned except with shame and loathing.

"The apostles, whom he had chosen to be his witnesses, had deserted him. And such was the contempt in which they were held that they hardly ventured to utter a word in public.

"There is great emphasis therefore in the words, 'They went out and preached everywhere.'

"For it was impossible that so sudden a change should be accomplished in a moment by human power.

"Therefore Mark adds, 'The Lord worked with them,' by which he means that this was truly a divine work."

Walk Closer to God

A servant's life isn't difficult. Without the right motivation, it's impossible!

Eleven men were entrusted with the good news of a risen Christ—a worldwide assignment that was humanly impossible.

That was by design.

For without the power and presence of Christ, their efforts were doomed from the start.

Even today, God is looking for servants through whom he can do a divine work, men and women willing to exchange their weakness and timidity for his strength and boldness.

Men and women . . . like you. ◖◗

MARCH

Jesus: Seeing, Seeking, Saving

LUKE

After your brisk walk with Jesus in the Gospel of Mark, it's time to take a slower-paced journey through the Gospel of Luke, the longest book in the New Testament. Drawing on carefully investigated details and eyewitness accounts, Luke writes "an orderly account" (Luke 1:3) of the life of Christ. As a divinely inspired investigative reporter, Luke unveils the indisputable facts about the man from Galilee.

Luke's unique portrait of Jesus presents him as God's Son who "came to seek and to save what was lost" (Luke 19:10). From the opening verses, Jesus emerges as the one who came to lead lost men and women out of their darkness and confusion.

Human interest stories abound in Luke's account, for he was interested in people—their hurts, fears, hopes and joys. Throughout the book you'll meet individuals whose lives were touched by the power of God in Roman-occupied Palestine: the priest Zechariah, Elizabeth and Mary, an unnamed widow at Nain, diminutive Zacchaeus, two disciples on the road to Emmaus. Jesus interacted with all manner of people: young and old, men and women, infamous and religious, poor and rich. Some came with physical needs, and he healed them with a touch. Others came with notorious reputations and found they were within the reach of his saving love. Some were called to be his disciples, and gladly left all to follow him. Others came asking to become disciples and departed in dejection because of their unwillingness to pay the price that discipleship demanded.

This month, accompany Jesus on his mission to seek and to save lost people and learn how to read the needs of people. Let his example of sensitivity inspire you to reach out to others in the strength of his Spirit. When you do, Luke's purpose for writing will have been fulfilled in your life. So let's get started!

MARCH 1

📖 Walk in the Word
Luke 1:1–38

After a brief preface, Luke sets the stage for his story of the life of Jesus by recounting Gabriel's mission first to Zechariah and then to Mary.

Introduction

1 Many have undertaken to draw up an account of the things that have been fulfilled[a] among us, ²just as they were handed down to us by those who from the first were eyewitnesses and servants of the word. ³Therefore, since I myself have carefully investigated everything from the beginning, it seemed good also to me to write an orderly account for you, most excellent Theophilus, ⁴so that you may know the certainty of the things you have been taught.

The Birth of John the Baptist Foretold

⁵In the time of Herod king of Judea there was a priest named Zechariah, who belonged to the priestly division of Abijah; his wife Elizabeth was also a descendant of Aaron. ⁶Both of them were upright in the sight of God, observing all the Lord's commandments and regulations blamelessly. ⁷But they had no children, because Elizabeth was barren; and they were both well along in years.

⁸Once when Zechariah's division was on duty and he was serving as priest before God, ⁹he was chosen by lot, according to the custom of the priesthood, to go into the temple of the Lord and burn incense. ¹⁰And when the time for the burning of incense came, all the assembled worshipers were praying outside.

¹¹Then an angel of the Lord appeared to him, standing at the right side of the altar of incense. ¹²When Zechariah saw him, he was startled and was gripped with fear. ¹³But the angel said to him: "Do not be afraid, Zechariah; your prayer has been heard. Your wife Elizabeth will bear you a son, and you are to give him the name John. ¹⁴He will be a joy and delight to you, and many will rejoice because of his birth, ¹⁵for he will be great in the sight of the Lord. He is never to take wine or other fermented drink, and he will be filled with the Holy Spirit even from birth.[b] ¹⁶Many of the people of Israel will he bring back to the Lord their God. ¹⁷And he will go on before the Lord, in the spirit and power of Elijah, to turn the hearts of the fathers to their children and the disobedient to the wisdom of the righteous—to make ready a people prepared for the Lord."

¹⁸Zechariah asked the angel, "How can I be sure of this? I am an old man and my wife is well along in years."

¹⁹The angel answered, "I am Gabriel. I stand in the presence of God, and I have been sent to speak to you and to tell you this good news. ²⁰And now you will be silent and not able to speak until the day this happens, because you did not believe my words, which will come true at their proper time."

²¹Meanwhile, the people were waiting for Zechariah and wondering why he stayed so long in the temple. ²²When he came out, he could not

speak to them. They realized he had seen a vision in the temple, for he kept making signs to them but remained unable to speak.

²³When his time of service was completed, he returned home. ²⁴After this his wife Elizabeth became pregnant and for five months remained in seclusion. ²⁵"The Lord has done this for me," she said. "In these days he has shown his favor and taken away my disgrace among the people."

The Birth of Jesus Foretold

²⁶In the sixth month, God sent the angel Gabriel to Nazareth, a town in Galilee, ²⁷to a virgin pledged to be married to a man named Joseph, a descendant of David. The virgin's name was Mary. ²⁸The angel went to her and said, "Greetings, you who are highly favored! The Lord is with you."

²⁹Mary was greatly troubled at his words and wondered what kind of greeting this might be. ³⁰But the angel said to her, "Do not be afraid, Mary, you have found favor with God. ³¹You will be with child and give birth to a son, and you are to give him the name Jesus. ³²He will be great and will be called the Son of the Most High. The Lord God will give him the throne of his father David, ³³and he will reign over the house of Jacob forever; his kingdom will never end."

³⁴"How will this be," Mary asked the angel, "since I am a virgin?"

³⁵The angel answered, "The Holy Spirit will come upon you, and the power of the Most High will overshadow you. So the holy one to be born will be called^c the Son of God. ³⁶Even Elizabeth your relative is going to have a child in her old age, and she who was said to be barren is in her sixth month. ³⁷For nothing is impossible with God."

³⁸"I am the Lord's servant," Mary answered. "May it be to me as you have said." Then the angel left her.

---

¹ Or been surely believed   *ᵇ15 Or from his mother's womb*   *ᶜ35 Or So the child to be born will be called holy,*

Worship
From The
HEART

"Father, help me measure greatness by your standards and not by the world's. Help me apply your definition of greatness in my life and use your standards of measure when I look at others. Teach me, Lord, what true greatness is. Amen."

MARCH 1

Greatness From God's Point of View

For he will be great in the sight of the Lord (Luke 1:15).

John the Baptist obviously never read Dalius Carnegius's book, *How to Win Jews and Influence Greeks*. He didn't fit in with the crowd. Instead everything about him seemed to smack of the peculiar.

His clothes were made of camel skins. His diet was strictly organic. And his behavior was decidedly antisocial. But the impact of John's ministry is undeniable.

You'll discover a clue to John's greatness in the words Matthew Poole wrote over three hundred years ago.

Walk With Matthew Poole

"We have a natural ambition to be great in the sight of men. But true greatness is to be great in the sight of God.

"In God's sight, a great man is one of whom God makes great use, especially in turning many souls to himself.

"Consider John. His father was an ordinary priest. He had no palace, no stately habitation. Nature was his cook. Yet Christ said of him, 'Among those born of women there is no one greater than John.'

"Where was his greatness but in this: He was a great and faithful preacher of God's message, and God blessed his labors to convert souls.

"They are great who do much of the work for which God has sent them into the world, and do much good in their generation."

Walk Closer to God

The world views greatness as rising above the crowd, but God's perspective is just the opposite. In his eyes greatness is stooping to serve the crowd and daring at all times to obey God. That's a greatness all can achieve, if they choose to.

Your determination to do God's will may not be understood by the people around you. The things you do and say . . . the company you keep . . . your zeal for the things of God—none of these will fit the status quo.

But take comfort from the fact that you—like John—won't get lost in the crowd.

MARCH 2

Walk in the Word
Luke 1:39–56

Luke depicts the joy welling up within Elizabeth, within the baby in her womb and within Mary as Elizabeth and Mary share their delight over the news that Gabriel brings; Mary's joy spills over in a hymn of praise to the Lord.

Mary Visits Elizabeth

³⁹At that time Mary got ready and hurried to a town in the hill country of Judea, ⁴⁰where she entered Zechariah's home and greeted Elizabeth. ⁴¹When Elizabeth heard Mary's greeting, the baby leaped in her womb, and Elizabeth was filled with the Holy Spirit. ⁴²In a loud voice she exclaimed: "Blessed are you among women, and blessed is the child you will bear! ⁴³But why am I so favored, that the mother of my Lord should come to me? ⁴⁴As soon as the sound of your greeting reached my ears, the baby in my womb leaped for joy. ⁴⁵Blessed is she who has believed that what the Lord has said to her will be accomplished!"

Mary's Song

⁴⁶And Mary said:

> "My soul glorifies the Lord
> ⁴⁷   and my spirit rejoices in God my Savior,
> ⁴⁸for he has been mindful
>   of the humble state of his servant.
> From now on all generations will call me blessed,
> ⁴⁹   for the Mighty One has done great things for me —
>   holy is his name.
> ⁵⁰His mercy extends to those who fear him,
>   from generation to generation.
> ⁵¹He has performed mighty deeds with his arm;
>   he has scattered those who are proud in their inmost
>   thoughts.
> ⁵²He has brought down rulers from their thrones
>   but has lifted up the humble.
> ⁵³He has filled the hungry with good things
>   but has sent the rich away empty.
> ⁵⁴He has helped his servant Israel,
>   remembering to be merciful
> ⁵⁵to Abraham and his descendants forever,
>   even as he said to our fathers."

⁵⁶Mary stayed with Elizabeth for about three months and then returned home.

March 2

God's Ways With the Proud and the Lowly

[God] has brought down rulers from their thrones but has lifted up the humble (Luke 1:52).

Mary learned firsthand the unpredictable character of God's gracious dealings. A young girl of humble means, she seemed an unlikely choice for the momentous role she would soon play in giving birth to the Son of God.

In her hymn of praise, Mary acknowledges the greatness of her God and the marvelous—yet mysterious—ways of his goodness. As Matthew Henry notes, he is the God of life-changing, world-shaking surprises.

Walk With Matthew Henry

"Proud people expect to carry all before them, to have their way and their will. But God scatters them in the imagination of their hearts, breaks their measures, blasts their projects, and brings them low, by those very counsels with which they thought to advance and establish themselves.

"The mighty think to secure themselves by might, but he puts them down. On the other hand, those of low degree, who despaired of ever advancing themselves, and thought no other than of being ever low, are wonderfully exalted.

"God takes pleasure in disappointing the expectations of those who promise themselves great things in the world, and in outdoing the expectations of those who promise themselves but a little.

"As a righteous God, it is his glory to abase those who exalt themselves, and strike terror on the secure. And as a good God, it is his glory to exalt those who fear him."

Walk Closer to God

Reread Matthew Henry's last two paragraphs carefully. Which kind of expectations do you hold?

Promise yourself success as a result of your own efforts, and you are sure to be disappointed. Humbly entrust your way to God, and he may surprise you today in a way you least expect.

Great expectations in God—that's one good way to ensure the surprises coming your way are the kind you'll welcome with open arms! ◖

MARCH 3

Walk in the Word
Luke 1:57–80

Luke records John's birth to Elizabeth and Zechariah and the ecstatic response of Zechariah, who breaks out in a joyous hymn of prophecy.

The Birth of John the Baptist

57When it was time for Elizabeth to have her baby, she gave birth to a son. 58Her neighbors and relatives heard that the Lord had shown her great mercy, and they shared her joy.

59On the eighth day they came to circumcise the child, and they were going to name him after his father Zechariah, 60but his mother spoke up and said, "No! He is to be called John."

61They said to her, "There is no one among your relatives who has that name."

62Then they made signs to his father, to find out what he would like to name the child. 63He asked for a writing tablet, and to everyone's astonishment he wrote, "His name is John." 64Immediately his mouth was opened and his tongue was loosed, and he began to speak, praising God. 65The neighbors were all filled with awe, and throughout the hill country of Judea people were talking about all these things. 66Everyone who heard this wondered about it, asking, "What then is this child going to be?" For the Lord's hand was with him.

Zechariah's Song

67His father Zechariah was filled with the Holy Spirit and prophesied:

68"Praise be to the Lord, the God of Israel,
　　because he has come and has redeemed his people.
69He has raised up a horn*a* of salvation for us
　　in the house of his servant David
70(as he said through his holy prophets of long ago),
71salvation from our enemies
　　and from the hand of all who hate us—
72to show mercy to our fathers
　　and to remember his holy covenant,
73　the oath he swore to our father Abraham:
74to rescue us from the hand of our enemies,
　　and to enable us to serve him without fear
75　in holiness and righteousness before him all our days.

76And you, my child, will be called a prophet of the Most
　　High;
　　for you will go on before the Lord to prepare the way for
　　　him,
77to give his people the knowledge of salvation
　　through the forgiveness of their sins,

183

March 3

⁷⁸because of the tender mercy of our God,
    by which the rising sun will come to us from heaven
⁷⁹to shine on those living in darkness
    and in the shadow of death,
    to guide our feet into the path of peace."

⁸⁰And the child grew and became strong in spirit; and he lived in the desert until he appeared publicly to Israel.

^a69 *Horn* here symbolizes strength.

PSALM 57

For the director of music. To the tune of, "Do Not Destroy." Of David. A *miktam.* ^a When he had fled from Saul into the cave.

Have mercy on me, O God, have mercy on me,
    for in you my soul takes refuge.
I will take refuge in the shadow of your wings
    until the disaster has passed.

²I cry out to God Most High,
    to God, who fulfills his purpose for me.
³He sends from heaven and saves me,
    rebuking those who hotly pursue me;   *Selah*
God sends his love and his faithfulness.

⁴I am in the midst of lions;
    I lie among ravenous beasts—
men whose teeth are spears and arrows,
    whose tongues are sharp swords.

⁹I will praise you, O Lord, among the nations;
    I will sing of you among the peoples.
¹⁰For great is your love, reaching to the heavens;
    your faithfulness reaches to the skies.

¹¹Be exalted, O God, above the heavens;
    let your glory be over all the earth.

^aTitle: Probably a literary or musical term

Mercy: Not Receiving What You Deserve

" . . . to give his people the knowledge of salvation through the forgiveness of their sins, because of the tender mercy of our God" (Luke 1:76–77).

Mercy. Everyone wants it when he or she least deserves it. Yet most hesitate to give it when another asks for it.

In Luke 1 mercy is mentioned five times. The one giving it is God; those who don't deserve it are men. And this mercy consists of God's becoming a man—the gift of Christ to sinners.

John Flavel explains that believers have the mercy of God in Jesus Christ.

Walk With John Flavel

"Jesus Christ is an incomparable and matchless mercy. You will find none in heaven or on earth to equal him.

"He is more than all externals, as the light of the sun is more than that of a candle. He is more than life, as the cause is more than the effect. More than all peace, all joy, as the tree is more than the fruit.

"When you compare Christ with things eternal, you will find him better than they. For what is heaven without Christ?

"If Christ should say to the saints, 'Take heaven among you, but I will withdraw from you,' the saints would weep, even in heaven itself, and say, 'Lord, heaven will not be heaven unless you are there, for you yourself are the joy of heaven!' "

Walk Closer to God

Justice is receiving what you deserve. Mercy is not receiving what you deserve. Grace is receiving what you do not deserve.

All three come true in Jesus Christ (Luke 1:68,69,77). His life and death provide redemption (that's justice—the price fully paid), remission (that's mercy—the guilt fully removed), and salvation (that's grace—eternal life freely given).

Giving others what's coming to them—that's only natural. Treating others with the mercy they don't deserve—that's supernatural.

Perhaps that's why Shakespeare wrote, "Earthly power doth show like God's when mercy seasons justice." Does that supernatural seasoning flow through your life to others? ❏

MARCH 4

📖 Walk in the Word
Luke 2

Luke turns his literary skills to the early years of Jesus' life, from birth to the age of twelve, capturing reactions to Jesus ranging from the joy of the angels and the shepherds to the gratitude of Simeon and Anna and the amazement of the teachers in the temple.

The Birth of Jesus

2 In those days Caesar Augustus issued a decree that a census should be taken of the entire Roman world. ²(This was the first census that took place while Quirinius was governor of Syria.) ³And everyone went to his own town to register.

⁴So Joseph also went up from the town of Nazareth in Galilee to Judea, to Bethlehem the town of David, because he belonged to the house and line of David. ⁵He went there to register with Mary, who was pledged to be married to him and was expecting a child. ⁶While they were there, the time came for the baby to be born, ⁷and she gave birth to her firstborn, a son. She wrapped him in cloths and placed him in a manger, because there was no room for them in the inn.

The Shepherds and the Angels

⁸And there were shepherds living out in the fields nearby, keeping watch over their flocks at night. ⁹An angel of the Lord appeared to them, and the glory of the Lord shone around them, and they were terrified. ¹⁰But the angel said to them, "Do not be afraid. I bring you good news of great joy that will be for all the people. ¹¹Today in the town of David a Savior has been born to you; he is Christ*ᵃ* the Lord. ¹²This will be a sign to you: You will find a baby wrapped in cloths and lying in a manger."

¹³Suddenly a great company of the heavenly host appeared with the angel, praising God and saying,

> ¹⁴"Glory to God in the highest,
>   and on earth peace to men on whom his favor rests."

¹⁵When the angels had left them and gone into heaven, the shepherds said to one another, "Let's go to Bethlehem and see this thing that has happened, which the Lord has told us about."

¹⁶So they hurried off and found Mary and Joseph, and the baby, who was lying in the manger. ¹⁷When they had seen him, they spread the word concerning what had been told them about this child, ¹⁸and all who heard it were amazed at what the shepherds said to them. ¹⁹But Mary treasured up all these things and pondered them in her heart. ²⁰The shepherds returned, glorifying and praising God for all the things they had heard and seen, which were just as they had been told.

Jesus Presented in the Temple

²¹On the eighth day, when it was time to circumcise him, he was named Jesus, the name the angel had given him before he had been conceived.

22When the time of their purification according to the Law of Moses had been completed, Joseph and Mary took him to Jerusalem to present him to the Lord 23(as it is written in the Law of the Lord, "Every firstborn male is to be consecrated to the Lord"b), 24and to offer a sacrifice in keeping with what is said in the Law of the Lord: "a pair of doves or two young pigeons."c

25Now there was a man in Jerusalem called Simeon, who was righteous and devout. He was waiting for the consolation of Israel, and the Holy Spirit was upon him. 26It had been revealed to him by the Holy Spirit that he would not die before he had seen the Lord's Christ. 27Moved by the Spirit, he went into the temple courts. When the parents brought in the child Jesus to do for him what the custom of the Law required, 28Simeon took him in his arms and praised God, saying:

> 29"Sovereign Lord, as you have promised,
>   you now dismissd your servant in peace.
> 30For my eyes have seen your salvation,
> 31   which you have prepared in the sight of all people,
> 32a light for revelation to the Gentiles
>   and for glory to your people Israel."

33The child's father and mother marveled at what was said about him. 34Then Simeon blessed them and said to Mary, his mother: "This child is destined to cause the falling and rising of many in Israel, and to be a sign that will be spoken against, 35so that the thoughts of many hearts will be revealed. And a sword will pierce your own soul too."

36There was also a prophetess, Anna, the daughter of Phanuel, of the tribe of Asher. She was very old; she had lived with her husband seven years after her marriage, 37and then was a widow until she was eighty-four.e She never left the temple but worshiped night and day, fasting and praying. 38Coming up to them at that very moment, she gave thanks to God and spoke about the child to all who were looking forward to the redemption of Jerusalem.

39When Joseph and Mary had done everything required by the Law of the Lord, they returned to Galilee to their own town of Nazareth. 40And the child grew and became strong; he was filled with wisdom, and the grace of God was upon him.

The Boy Jesus at the Temple

41Every year his parents went to Jerusalem for the Feast of the Passover. 42When he was twelve years old, they went up to the Feast, according to the custom. 43After the Feast was over, while his parents were returning home, the boy Jesus stayed behind in Jerusalem, but they were unaware of it. 44Thinking he was in their company, they traveled on for a day. Then they began looking for him among their relatives and friends. 45When they did not find him, they went back to Jerusalem to look for him. 46After three days they found him in the temple courts, sitting among the teachers,

March 4

listening to them and asking them questions. ⁴⁷Everyone who heard him was amazed at his understanding and his answers. ⁴⁸When his parents saw him, they were astonished. His mother said to him, "Son, why have you treated us like this? Your father and I have been anxiously searching for you."

⁴⁹"Why were you searching for me?" he asked. "Didn't you know I had to be in my Father's house?" ⁵⁰But they did not understand what he was saying to them.

⁵¹Then he went down to Nazareth with them and was obedient to them. But his mother treasured all these things in her heart. ⁵²And Jesus grew in wisdom and stature, and in favor with God and men.

a11 Or *Messiah.* "The Christ" (Greek) and "the Messiah" (Hebrew) both mean "the Anointed One"; also in verse 26.   *b23* Exodus 13:2,12   *c24* Lev. 12:8   *d29* Or *promised, / now dismiss*   *e37* Or *widow for eighty-four years*

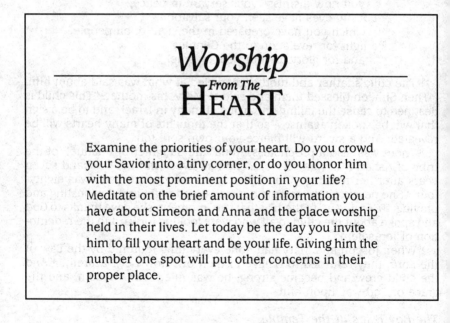

Worship
From The HEART

Examine the priorities of your heart. Do you crowd your Savior into a tiny corner, or do you honor him with the most prominent position in your life? Meditate on the brief amount of information you have about Simeon and Anna and the place worship held in their lives. Let today be the day you invite him to fill your heart and be your life. Giving him the number one spot will put other concerns in their proper place.

Success or Failure—This Is the Test

And she gave birth to her firstborn, a son. She . . . placed him in a manger, because there was no room for them in the inn (Luke 2:7).

The "No Vacancy" sign was prominently displayed that night in Bethlehem. And nearly two thousand years later it still hangs in many lives.

Normally, a woman in Mary's condition might expect the simple courtesy of a place to stay. But those were not normal times.

James Hastings paints a word picture of that crowded night in Bethlehem.

Walk With James Hastings

"It was a time when every available accommodation was called for, and the people of the inn were too busy to recognize that here was a claim which, in their less occupied moments, they never would have denied. And so Christ was simply crowded out. There was no room.

"Without doubt it is the same today. Every chamber of the soul is so filled with human interests that there is little room for Christ. There is little—if any—time for him.

"And this is true because a thousand other things demand our time. Our interest is drawn off in other directions. Our life is crowded with possessions and pleasures until, strange though it seems, there is no room for the Savior . . . except in the stable.

"If we are so preoccupied as to have no room for Christ in our life, then our life is a failure. This is the test of everything: room for Christ."

Walk Closer to God

There is a way to discover the passions of your life. Simply check your schedule. Find out what consumes your hours.

You'll quickly discover that if something—or someone—is important enough, you'll never allow it—or him—to be crowded out by other interests.

If the innkeeper on that Christmas Eve had known who would be born in his stable, surely the "No Vacancy" sign would have come down.

Can there be any good reason to leave it hanging in your life?

MARCH 5

📖 Walk in the Word
Luke 3

John the Baptist is spotlighted here as the one who prepared the way for Jesus and his ministry.

John the Baptist Prepares the Way

3 In the fifteenth year of the reign of Tiberius Caesar—when Pontius Pilate was governor of Judea, Herod tetrarch of Galilee, his brother Philip tetrarch of Iturea and Traconitis, and Lysanias tetrarch of Abilene— ²during the high priesthood of Annas and Caiaphas, the word of God came to John son of Zechariah in the desert. ³He went into all the country around the Jordan, preaching a baptism of repentance for the forgiveness of sins. ⁴As is written in the book of the words of Isaiah the prophet:

> "A voice of one calling in the desert,
> 'Prepare the way for the Lord,
>   make straight paths for him.
> ⁵Every valley shall be filled in,
>   every mountain and hill made low.
> The crooked roads shall become straight,
>   the rough ways smooth.
> ⁶And all mankind will see God's salvation.' "*a*

⁷John said to the crowds coming out to be baptized by him, "You brood of vipers! Who warned you to flee from the coming wrath? ⁸Produce fruit in keeping with repentance. And do not begin to say to yourselves, 'We have Abraham as our father.' For I tell you that out of these stones God can raise up children for Abraham. ⁹The ax is already at the root of the trees, and every tree that does not produce good fruit will be cut down and thrown into the fire."

¹⁰"What should we do then?" the crowd asked.

¹¹John answered, "The man with two tunics should share with him who has none, and the one who has food should do the same."

¹²Tax collectors also came to be baptized. "Teacher," they asked, "what should we do?"

¹³"Don't collect any more than you are required to," he told them.

¹⁴Then some soldiers asked him, "And what should we do?"

He replied, "Don't extort money and don't accuse people falsely—be content with your pay."

¹⁵The people were waiting expectantly and were all wondering in their hearts if John might possibly be the Christ.*b* ¹⁶John answered them all, "I baptize you with*c* water. But one more powerful than I will come, the thongs of whose sandals I am not worthy to untie. He will baptize you with the Holy Spirit and with fire. ¹⁷His winnowing fork is in his hand to clear his threshing floor and to gather the wheat into his barn, but he will burn up the chaff with unquenchable fire." ¹⁸And with many other words John exhorted the people and preached the good news to them.

MARCH 5

¹⁹But when John rebuked Herod the tetrarch because of Herodias, his brother's wife, and all the other evil things he had done, ²⁰Herod added this to them all: He locked John up in prison.

The Baptism and Genealogy of Jesus

²¹When all the people were being baptized, Jesus was baptized too. And as he was praying, heaven was opened ²²and the Holy Spirit descended on him in bodily form like a dove. And a voice came from heaven: "You are my Son, whom I love; with you I am well pleased."

²³Now Jesus himself was about thirty years old when he began his ministry. He was the son, so it was thought, of Joseph,

the son of Heli, ²⁴the son of Matthat,
the son of Levi, the son of Melki,
the son of Jannai, the son of Joseph,
²⁵the son of Mattathias, the son of Amos,
the son of Nahum, the son of Esli,
the son of Naggai, ²⁶the son of Maath,
the son of Mattathias, the son of Semein,
the son of Josech, the son of Joda,
²⁷the son of Joanan, the son of Rhesa,
the son of Zerubbabel, the son of Shealtiel,
the son of Neri, ²⁸the son of Melki,
the son of Addi, the son of Cosam,
the son of Elmadam, the son of Er,
²⁹the son of Joshua, the son of Eliezer,
the son of Jorim, the son of Matthat,
the son of Levi, ³⁰the son of Simeon,
the son of Judah, the son of Joseph,
the son of Jonam, the son of Eliakim,
³¹the son of Melea, the son of Menna,
the son of Mattatha, the son of Nathan,
the son of David, ³²the son of Jesse,
the son of Obed, the son of Boaz,
the son of Salmon,ᵈ the son of Nahshon,
³³the son of Amminadab, the son of Ram,ᵉ
the son of Hezron, the son of Perez,
the son of Judah, ³⁴the son of Jacob,
the son of Isaac, the son of Abraham,
the son of Terah, the son of Nahor,
³⁵the son of Serug, the son of Reu,
the son of Peleg, the son of Eber,
the son of Shelah, ³⁶the son of Cainan,
the son of Arphaxad, the son of Shem,
the son of Noah, the son of Lamech,

March 5

37the son of Methuselah, the son of Enoch,
  the son of Jared, the son of Mahalalel,
  the son of Kenan, 38the son of Enosh,
  the son of Seth, the son of Adam,
  the son of God.

a6 Isaiah 40:3-5   b15 Or *Messiah*   c16 Or *in*   d32 Some early manuscripts *Sala*
e33 Some manuscripts *Amminadab, the son of Admin, the son of Arni*; other manuscripts
vary widely.

PSALM 32

Of David. A *maskil.* a

Blessed is he
  whose transgressions are forgiven,
  whose sins are covered.
2Blessed is the man
  whose sin the LORD does not count against him
  and in whose spirit is no deceit.

3When I kept silent,
  my bones wasted away
  through my groaning all day long.
4For day and night
  your hand was heavy upon me;
  my strength was sapped
  as in the heat of summer.   *Selah*
5Then I acknowledged my sin to you
  and did not cover up my iniquity.
I said, "I will confess
  my transgressions to the LORD"—
  and you forgave
  the guilt of my sin.   *Selah*

aTitle: Probably a literary or musical term

Repentance Is More Than Sorrow for Sin

Produce fruit in keeping with repentence (Luke 3:8).

Fruit trees without fruit soon end up as firewood. Their blossoms may be pretty and fragrant, but they provide no nourishment, no seeds, no means of reproduction.

You can tell a tree—and a true Christian—by the fruit you see. Alexander Maclaren provides insight into John's call for the fruit of repentance from his listeners along the Jordan.

Walk With Alexander Maclaren

"John demanded not only repentance, but its fruits. For there is no value in a repentance which does not change the life, even if such a thing were possible.

"Repentance is more than sorrow for sin. Many people have that, yet they rush again into the old mire. To change the mind and the will is not enough; real change is certified by corresponding deeds.

"So John preached the true nature of repentance when he called for its fruits. And he preached the greatest motive he knew when he pressed home on the sluggish consciences of his listeners the close approach of a judgment for which everything was ready, with the axe already lying at the root of the tree."

Walk Closer to God

Repentance is more than saying I'm sorry.

Repentance is changing your mind about your actions.

It is seeing that what you did was wrong, not just risky.

It is turning around in God's strength and moving in a new direction . . . God's direction.

True repentance bears visible fruit: compassion, fairness, wholesome speech, contentment (Luke 3:10–14).

Take away the fruit, and whatever you have left is not genuine repentance.

But it is cause for alarm.

And a change of mind.

And a change of direction.

Before the axe falls and the root disappears with the fruit. ◖◗

MARCH 6

📖 Walk in the Word
Luke 4

Luke's account of the beginning of Jesus' ministry is preceded by the story of Satan's devious efforts to tempt Jesus to turn his back on his mission to carry out his Father's will.

The Temptation of Jesus

4 Jesus, full of the Holy Spirit, returned from the Jordan and was led by the Spirit in the desert, ²where for forty days he was tempted by the devil. He ate nothing during those days, and at the end of them he was hungry.

³The devil said to him, "If you are the Son of God, tell this stone to become bread."

⁴Jesus answered, "It is written: 'Man does not live on bread alone.'ᵃ"

⁵The devil led him up to a high place and showed him in an instant all the kingdoms of the world. ⁶And he said to him, "I will give you all their authority and splendor, for it has been given to me, and I can give it to anyone I want to. ⁷So if you worship me, it will all be yours."

⁸Jesus answered, "It is written: 'Worship the Lord your God and serve him only.'ᵇ"

⁹The devil led him to Jerusalem and had him stand on the highest point of the temple. "If you are the Son of God," he said, "throw yourself down from here. ¹⁰For it is written:

" 'He will command his angels concerning you
    to guard you carefully;
¹¹they will lift you up in their hands,
    so that you will not strike your foot against a stone.'ᶜ"

¹²Jesus answered, "It says: 'Do not put the Lord your God to the test.'ᵈ"
¹³When the devil had finished all this tempting, he left him until an opportune time.

Jesus Rejected at Nazareth

¹⁴Jesus returned to Galilee in the power of the Spirit, and news about him spread through the whole countryside. ¹⁵He taught in their synagogues, and everyone praised him.

¹⁶He went to Nazareth, where he had been brought up, and on the Sabbath day he went into the synagogue, as was his custom. And he stood up to read. ¹⁷The scroll of the prophet Isaiah was handed to him. Unrolling it, he found the place where it is written:

¹⁸"The Spirit of the Lord is on me,
    because he has anointed me
    to preach good news to the poor.
He has sent me to proclaim freedom for the prisoners
    and recovery of sight for the blind,

to release the oppressed,
19 to proclaim the year of the Lord's favor."*e*

²⁰Then he rolled up the scroll, gave it back to the attendant and sat down. The eyes of everyone in the synagogue were fastened on him, ²¹and he began by saying to them, "Today this scripture is fulfilled in your hearing."

²²All spoke well of him and were amazed at the gracious words that came from his lips. "Isn't this Joseph's son?" they asked.

²³Jesus said to them, "Surely you will quote this proverb to me: 'Physician, heal yourself! Do here in your hometown what we have heard that you did in Capernaum.'"

²⁴"I tell you the truth," he continued, "no prophet is accepted in his hometown. ²⁵I assure you that there were many widows in Israel in Elijah's time, when the sky was shut for three and a half years and there was a severe famine throughout the land. ²⁶Yet Elijah was not sent to any of them, but to a widow in Zarephath in the region of Sidon. ²⁷And there were many in Israel with leprosy*f* in the time of Elisha the prophet, yet not one of them was cleansed—only Naaman the Syrian."

²⁸All the people in the synagogue were furious when they heard this. ²⁹They got up, drove him out of the town, and took him to the brow of the hill on which the town was built, in order to throw him down the cliff. ³⁰But he walked right through the crowd and went on his way.

Jesus Drives Out an Evil Spirit

³¹Then he went down to Capernaum, a town in Galilee, and on the Sabbath began to teach the people. ³²They were amazed at his teaching, because his message had authority.

³³In the synagogue there was a man possessed by a demon, an evil*g* spirit. He cried out at the top of his voice, ³⁴"Ha! What do you want with us, Jesus of Nazareth? Have you come to destroy us? I know who you are—the Holy One of God!"

³⁵"Be quiet!" Jesus said sternly. "Come out of him!" Then the demon threw the man down before them all and came out without injuring him.

³⁶All the people were amazed and said to each other, "What is this teaching? With authority and power he gives orders to evil spirits and they come out!" ³⁷And the news about him spread throughout the surrounding area.

Jesus Heals Many

³⁸Jesus left the synagogue and went to the home of Simon. Now Simon's mother-in-law was suffering from a high fever, and they asked Jesus to help her. ³⁹So he bent over her and rebuked the fever, and it left her. She got up at once and began to wait on them.

⁴⁰When the sun was setting, the people brought to Jesus all who had various kinds of sickness, and laying his hands on each one, he healed them. ⁴¹Moreover, demons came out of many people, shouting, "You are the Son of God!" But he rebuked them and would not allow them to speak, because they knew he was the Christ.*h*

March 6

⁴²At daybreak Jesus went out to a solitary place. The people were looking for him and when they came to where he was, they tried to keep him from leaving them. ⁴³But he said, "I must preach the good news of the kingdom of God to the other towns also, because that is why I was sent." ⁴⁴And he kept on preaching in the synagogues of Judea.[i]

a4 Deut. 8:3 b8 Deut. 6:13 c11 Psalm 91:11,12 d12 Deut. 6:16 e19 Isaiah 61:1,2
f27 The Greek word was used for various diseases affecting the skin—not necessarily leprosy.
g33 Greek unclean; also in verse 36 h41 Or Messiah i44 Or the land of the Jews; some
manuscripts Galilee

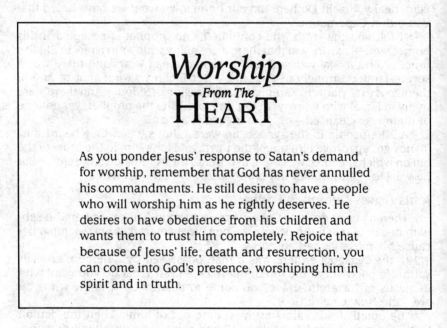

Worship
From The
Heart

As you ponder Jesus' response to Satan's demand for worship, remember that God has never annulled his commandments. He still desires to have a people who will worship him as he rightly deserves. He desires to have obedience from his children and wants them to trust him completely. Rejoice that because of Jesus' life, death and resurrection, you can come into God's presence, worshiping him in spirit and in truth.

Your Sure Defense When Satan Comes Calling

[Jesus] was hungry. The devil said to him, "If you are the Son of God, tell this stone to become bread." Jesus answered, "It is written: 'Man does not live on bread alone' " (Luke 4:1–2,4).

Eve lived in a garden filled with good things to eat. Jesus had been in a desert forty days without food. Yet, when the temptation to eat came, the one who needed it most resisted it best.

Under attack, Eve disobeyed God's Word not to eat; Jesus used God's Word to defend himself.

The Word is still a sure defense against the wily schemes of Satan, as Martin Luther proclaims.

Walk With Martin Luther

"In every temptation simply close your eyes and follow the Word. Outside the Word there is nothing but tribulation and affliction. Through temptations and afflictions God proves the strength and virtue of his Word.

"Satan constantly tempts the heart. Therefore we must overcome the feeling of the flesh and adhere to the Word; for God does not forsake us but, like a mother, lovingly cherishes and carries us. Go to Christ, who is the sacrifice for our sins. In him the Devil, sin, and death have been crucified.

"One way to conquer is to despise the thoughts suggested by Satan. The more you dwell on those thoughts in your mind, the more they oppress you. Once you lose sight of the Word, the ways and means of help are no more. But as soon as you lay hold of some saying of Scripture and rely on it as a holy anchor, the temptations are driven away."

Walk Closer to God

The Word of God is a sword with which you can defend yourself (Ephesians 6:17). But only if you carry it with you.

That doesn't mean wearing a sheath with your Bible at your side. But it does suggest the need to know the Word of God intimately in your heart and mind.

His Sword is your sure defense when Satan comes calling. Don't leave home without it. ⟁

MARCH 7

📖 Walk in the Word
Luke 5

Luke sketches brief word pictures of struggling, "sick" people drawn to Jesus, and self-righteous, "healthy" people offended by him.

The Calling of the First Disciples

5 One day as Jesus was standing by the Lake of Gennesaret,*a* with the people crowding around him and listening to the word of God, ²he saw at the water's edge two boats, left there by the fishermen, who were washing their nets. ³He got into one of the boats, the one belonging to Simon, and asked him to put out a little from shore. Then he sat down and taught the people from the boat.

⁴When he had finished speaking, he said to Simon, "Put out into deep water, and let down*b* the nets for a catch."

⁵Simon answered, "Master, we've worked hard all night and haven't caught anything. But because you say so, I will let down the nets."

⁶When they had done so, they caught such a large number of fish that their nets began to break. ⁷So they signaled their partners in the other boat to come and help them, and they came and filled both boats so full that they began to sink.

⁸When Simon Peter saw this, he fell at Jesus' knees and said, "Go away from me, Lord; I am a sinful man!" ⁹For he and all his companions were astonished at the catch of fish they had taken, ¹⁰and so were James and John, the sons of Zebedee, Simon's partners.

Then Jesus said to Simon, "Don't be afraid; from now on you will catch men." ¹¹So they pulled their boats up on shore, left everything and followed him.

The Man With Leprosy

¹²While Jesus was in one of the towns, a man came along who was covered with leprosy.*c* When he saw Jesus, he fell with his face to the ground and begged him, "Lord, if you are willing, you can make me clean."

¹³Jesus reached out his hand and touched the man. "I am willing," he said. "Be clean!" And immediately the leprosy left him.

¹⁴Then Jesus ordered him, "Don't tell anyone, but go, show yourself to the priest and offer the sacrifices that Moses commanded for your cleansing, as a testimony to them."

¹⁵Yet the news about him spread all the more, so that crowds of people came to hear him and to be healed of their sicknesses. ¹⁶But Jesus often withdrew to lonely places and prayed.

Jesus Heals a Paralytic

¹⁷One day as he was teaching, Pharisees and teachers of the law, who had come from every village of Galilee and from Judea and Jerusalem, were sitting there. And the power of the Lord was present for him to heal the sick. ¹⁸Some men came carrying a paralytic on a mat and tried to take him into the house to lay him before Jesus. ¹⁹When they could not find

a way to do this because of the crowd, they went up on the roof and lowered him on his mat through the tiles into the middle of the crowd, right in front of Jesus.

20When Jesus saw their faith, he said, "Friend, your sins are forgiven."

21The Pharisees and the teachers of the law began thinking to themselves, "Who is this fellow who speaks blasphemy? Who can forgive sins but God alone?"

22Jesus knew what they were thinking and asked, "Why are you thinking these things in your hearts? 23Which is easier: to say, 'Your sins are forgiven,' or to say, 'Get up and walk'? 24But that you may know that the Son of Man has authority on earth to forgive sins. . . ." He said to the paralyzed man, "I tell you, get up, take your mat and go home." 25Immediately he stood up in front of them, took what he had been lying on and went home praising God. 26Everyone was amazed and gave praise to God. They were filled with awe and said, "We have seen remarkable things today."

The Calling of Levi

27After this, Jesus went out and saw a tax collector by the name of Levi sitting at his tax booth. "Follow me," Jesus said to him, 28and Levi got up, left everything and followed him.

29Then Levi held a great banquet for Jesus at his house, and a large crowd of tax collectors and others were eating with them. 30But the Pharisees and the teachers of the law who belonged to their sect complained to his disciples, "Why do you eat and drink with tax collectors and 'sinners'?"

31Jesus answered them, "It is not the healthy who need a doctor, but the sick. 32I have not come to call the righteous, but sinners to repentance."

Jesus Questioned About Fasting

33They said to him, "John's disciples often fast and pray, and so do the disciples of the Pharisees, but yours go on eating and drinking."

34Jesus answered, "Can you make the guests of the bridegroom fast while he is with them? 35But the time will come when the bridegroom will be taken from them; in those days they will fast."

36He told them this parable: "No one tears a patch from a new garment and sews it on an old one. If he does, he will have torn the new garment, and the patch from the new will not match the old. 37And no one pours new wine into old wineskins. If he does, the new wine will burst the skins, the wine will run out and the wineskins will be ruined. 38No, new wine must be poured into new wineskins. 39And no one after drinking old wine wants the new, for he says, 'The old is better.' "

a1 That is, Sea of Galilee   b4 The Greek verb is plural.   c12 The Greek word was used for various diseases affecting the skin—not necessarily leprosy.

MARCH 7

Jesus—High Above Us, Yet Bending Over Us

A man . . . who was covered with leprosy . . . saw Jesus . . . and begged him, "Lord, if you are willing, you can make me clean." Jesus reached out his hand and touched the man. "I am willing," he said. "Be clean!" (Luke 5:12–13).

Leprosy! Unclean! Unclean! Virtually incurable in Bible times, this dreaded disease meant that the sufferer became an outcast from family, friends, society—in fact, from everyone except other lepers . . . and the Savior!

In Luke 5 Jesus heals a leper with a touch. His act of compassion changes the man's life and, with it, the course of Jesus' public ministry (Luke 5:15).

Alexander Maclaren reflects on the touch of the Man from Galilee.

Walk With Alexander Maclaren

"All true sympathy involves a touch.

"Jesus reaches the leper with the touch of a universal love and pity which disregards all that is repellent and overflows every barrier.

"He is high above us and yet bending over us. He stretches his hand from the throne as truly as he put it out when here on earth. And he is ready to take us all to his heart—in spite of our weakness and shortcomings, the leprosy of our many corruptions, and the depth of our sins—and to hold us ever in the strong, gentle clasp of his divine, omnipotent, and tender hand.

"This Christ lays hold on us because he loves us, and will not be turned from his compassion by our most loathsome foulness."

Walk Closer to God

Like a leper, you may feel unworthy of God's forgiveness, love and cleansing. And you are.

You may sense that God is grieved by your sin. And he is.

You may feel that your conduct has placed you beyond his reach. But that's where you're wrong!

No sin is too great for him to forgive. No life is too damaged for him to redeem.

Is it possible that the only thing standing between you and the Savior's words, "Be clean," is your own self-pity?

MARCH 8

📖 Walk in the Word
Luke 6:1-26

Here in Luke's narrative Jesus overrules laws concerning the Sabbath and calls twelve men to be his apostles.

Lord of the Sabbath

6 One Sabbath Jesus was going through the grainfields, and his disciples began to pick some heads of grain, rub them in their hands and eat the kernels. ²Some of the Pharisees asked, "Why are you doing what is unlawful on the Sabbath?"

³Jesus answered them, "Have you never read what David did when he and his companions were hungry? ⁴He entered the house of God, and taking the consecrated bread, he ate what is lawful only for priests to eat. And he also gave some to his companions." ⁵Then Jesus said to them, "The Son of Man is Lord of the Sabbath."

⁶On another Sabbath he went into the synagogue and was teaching, and a man was there whose right hand was shriveled. ⁷The Pharisees and the teachers of the law were looking for a reason to accuse Jesus, so they watched him closely to see if he would heal on the Sabbath. ⁸But Jesus knew what they were thinking and said to the man with the shriveled hand, "Get up and stand in front of everyone." So he got up and stood there.

⁹Then Jesus said to them, "I ask you, which is lawful on the Sabbath: to do good or to do evil, to save life or to destroy it?"

¹⁰He looked around at them all, and then said to the man, "Stretch out your hand." He did so, and his hand was completely restored. ¹¹But they were furious and began to discuss with one another what they might do to Jesus.

The Twelve Apostles

¹²One of those days Jesus went out to a mountainside to pray, and spent the night praying to God. ¹³When morning came, he called his disciples to him and chose twelve of them, whom he also designated apostles: ¹⁴Simon (whom he named Peter), his brother Andrew, James, John, Philip, Bartholomew, ¹⁵Matthew, Thomas, James son of Alphaeus, Simon who was called the Zealot, ¹⁶Judas son of James, and Judas Iscariot, who became a traitor.

Blessings and Woes

¹⁷He went down with them and stood on a level place. A large crowd of his disciples was there and a great number of people from all over Judea, from Jerusalem, and from the coast of Tyre and Sidon, ¹⁸who had come to hear him and to be healed of their diseases. Those troubled by evil*a* spirits were cured, ¹⁹and the people all tried to touch him, because power was coming from him and healing them all.

MARCH 8

²⁰Looking at his disciples, he said:

"Blessed are you who are poor,
for yours is the kingdom of God.
²¹Blessed are you who hunger now,
for you will be satisfied.
Blessed are you who weep now,
for you will laugh.
²²Blessed are you when men hate you,
when they exclude you and insult you
and reject your name as evil,
because of the Son of Man.

²³"Rejoice in that day and leap for joy, because great is your reward in heaven. For that is how their fathers treated the prophets.

²⁴"But woe to you who are rich,
for you have already received your comfort.
²⁵Woe to you who are well fed now,
for you will go hungry.
Woe to you who laugh now,
for you will mourn and weep.
²⁶Woe to you when all men speak well of you,
for that is how their fathers treated the false prophets.

a18 Greek *unclean*

Worship From The HEART

Reexamine the fact that God has set aside a day—"the Sabbath"—for you to come apart from the routine tasks of life, a day for you to fellowship with him in a deep and intimate way through worship and rest. Do your best to keep that day holy by pausing in your routine work, worshiping with other believers, and having a special time of personal meditation or prayer. This day of rest is a time of refreshment for body and soul. Say thank you for your Father's design.

The Refreshing Nature of Prayer

Jesus went out to the mountainside to pray, and spent the night praying to God (Luke 6:12).

The end of a hectic day. A rocky mountainside. Undisturbed moments alone. For Jesus it was the perfect time and place to pass the entire night in prayer with his Father.

Charles Spurgeon points out the significance of the time, place, persistence and occasion for this all-night prayer vigil.

Walk With Charles Spurgeon

"If ever one born of woman might have lived without prayer, it was our perfect Lord. And yet none was ever so much in supplication as he!

"The time he chose was the hour of silence when the crowd would not disturb him and when all but he had ceased to labor. While others found rest in sleep, he refreshed himself with prayer.

"The place was also well selected. He was alone where none would intrude, where none could observe.

"The persistence of his pleadings is remarkable: The long watches were not too long; the cold wind did not chill his devotions; the grim darkness did not darken his faith, or loneliness check his importunity.

"The occasion for this prayer is notable; it was after his enemies had been enraged—prayer was his refuge and solace; it was before he sent for the twelve apostles—prayer was the gate of his enterprise, the herald of his new work.

"The fact of this eminent prayerfulness of Jesus is a lesson for us— he has given us an example that we may follow in his steps."

Walk Closer to God

Students of prayer should find it no different. When big decisions confront you, when commitments need to be strengthened, there is no better place to begin than with a quiet time and place for prayer.

As one commentator has wisely observed, "You can do more than pray after you have prayed. But you can do no more than pray until you have prayed." ◖

MARCH 9

📖 Walk in the Word
Luke 6:27–49

The secret to purposeful living is taught by Jesus to a large crowd in this "Sermon on the Plain."

Love for Enemies

27"But I tell you who hear me: Love your enemies, do good to those who hate you, 28bless those who curse you, pray for those who mistreat you. 29If someone strikes you on one cheek, turn to him the other also. If someone takes your cloak, do not stop him from taking your tunic. 30Give to everyone who asks you, and if anyone takes what belongs to you, do not demand it back. 31Do to others as you would have them do to you.

32"If you love those who love you, what credit is that to you? Even 'sinners' love those who love them. 33And if you do good to those who are good to you, what credit is that to you? Even 'sinners' do that. 34And if you lend to those from whom you expect repayment, what credit is that to you? Even 'sinners' lend to 'sinners,' expecting to be repaid in full. 35But love your enemies, do good to them, and lend to them without expecting to get anything back. Then your reward will be great, and you will be sons of the Most High, because he is kind to the ungrateful and wicked. 36Be merciful, just as your Father is merciful.

Judging Others

37"Do not judge, and you will not be judged. Do not condemn, and you will not be condemned. Forgive, and you will be forgiven. 38Give, and it will be given to you. A good measure, pressed down, shaken together and running over, will be poured into your lap. For with the measure you use, it will be measured to you."

39He also told them this parable: "Can a blind man lead a blind man? Will they not both fall into a pit? 40A student is not above his teacher, but everyone who is fully trained will be like his teacher.

41"Why do you look at the speck of sawdust in your brother's eye and pay no attention to the plank in your own eye? 42How can you say to your brother, 'Brother, let me take the speck out of your eye,' when you yourself fail to see the plank in your own eye? You hypocrite, first take the plank out of your eye, and then you will see clearly to remove the speck from your brother's eye.

A Tree and Its Fruit

43"No good tree bears bad fruit, nor does a bad tree bear good fruit. 44Each tree is recognized by its own fruit. People do not pick figs from thornbushes, or grapes from briers. 45The good man brings good things out of the good stored up in his heart, and the evil man brings evil things out of the evil stored up in his heart. For out of the overflow of his heart his mouth speaks.

The Wise and Foolish Builders

⁴⁶"Why do you call me, 'Lord, Lord,' and do not do what I say? ⁴⁷I will show you what he is like who comes to me and hears my words and puts them into practice. ⁴⁸He is like a man building a house, who dug down deep and laid the foundation on rock. When a flood came, the torrent struck that house but could not shake it, because it was well built. ⁴⁹But the one who hears my words and does not put them into practice is like a man who built a house on the ground without a foundation. The moment the torrent struck that house, it collapsed and its destruction was complete."

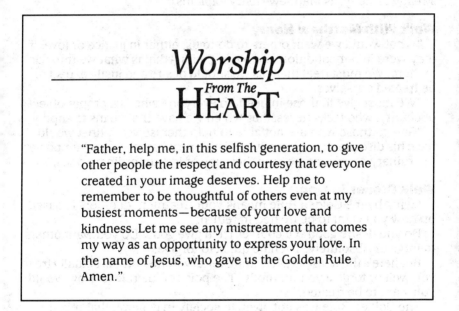

Worship From The HEART

"Father, help me, in this selfish generation, to give other people the respect and courtesy that everyone created in your image deserves. Help me to remember to be thoughtful of others even at my busiest moments—because of your love and kindness. Let me see any mistreatment that comes my way as an opportunity to express your love. In the name of Jesus, who gave us the Golden Rule. Amen."

MARCH 9

Freely Giving What You Can Supply

Do to others as you would have them do to you (Luke 6:31).

Today's popular version of the Golden Rule might go something like this: "Do unto others before they undo you!"—a sure sign of a society preoccupied with itself.

Focusing on the needs of others. That's fairly difficult when you're wrapped up in yourself. But for the Christian, the Golden Rule provides a ready remedy, as Matthew Henry explains.

Walk With Matthew Henry

"What would we want others to do to us, either in justice or love, if they were in our condition and we in theirs—that is what we must do to them. We must treat them as we should desire and justly expect to be treated ourselves.

"We must give to those in need, to everyone who is a proper object of charity, who lacks necessities which we have the means to supply.

"Give to those who are not able to help themselves. Christ would have his disciples always ready to distribute what is within their power in ordinary cases, and beyond their power in extraordinary ones."

Walk Closer to God

Living by the Golden Rule means your treatment of others is based on how you want to be treated in return.

Do you desire good? Of course! Then give good. Do you want others to forgive? Absolutely! Then be quick to forgive.

But here's the hard part: It is immaterial whether others actually treat you well or forgive you promptly. The point of the rule is: How would you want to be treated?

The Golden Rule was not given to society in general; that might explain its rather tarnished image. Rather, it was issued to the only group of people empowered to keep it—the people of God!

Who do you know that needs a golden touch today? He or she may be surprised to learn that someone remembers the original rule, which is untarnished and still shines. ◖◗

March 10

Walk in the Word
Luke 7:1–35

Jesus heals a man who is on his deathbed, restores life to a widow's son, and reassures John the Baptist that Jesus is in fact the promised Messiah. Luke also reports that Jesus speaks to the crowd about the Pharisees and their rejection of both John's ministry and Jesus' ministry.

The Faith of the Centurion

7 When Jesus had finished saying all this in the hearing of the people, he entered Capernaum. ²There a centurion's servant, whom his master valued highly, was sick and about to die. ³The centurion heard of Jesus and sent some elders of the Jews to him, asking him to come and heal his servant. ⁴When they came to Jesus, they pleaded earnestly with him, "This man deserves to have you do this, ⁵because he loves our nation and has built our synagogue." ⁶So Jesus went with them.

He was not far from the house when the centurion sent friends to say to him: "Lord, don't trouble yourself, for I do not deserve to have you come under my roof. ⁷That is why I did not even consider myself worthy to come to you. But say the word, and my servant will be healed. ⁸For I myself am a man under authority, with soldiers under me. I tell this one, 'Go,' and he goes; and that one, 'Come,' and he comes. I say to my servant, 'Do this,' and he does it."

⁹When Jesus heard this, he was amazed at him, and turning to the crowd following him, he said, "I tell you, I have not found such great faith even in Israel." ¹⁰Then the men who had been sent returned to the house and found the servant well.

Jesus Raises a Widow's Son

¹¹Soon afterward, Jesus went to a town called Nain, and his disciples and a large crowd went along with him. ¹²As he approached the town gate, a dead person was being carried out—the only son of his mother, and she was a widow. And a large crowd from the town was with her. ¹³When the Lord saw her, his heart went out to her and he said, "Don't cry."

¹⁴Then he went up and touched the coffin, and those carrying it stood still. He said, "Young man, I say to you, get up!" ¹⁵The dead man sat up and began to talk, and Jesus gave him back to his mother.

¹⁶They were all filled with awe and praised God. "A great prophet has appeared among us," they said. "God has come to help his people." ¹⁷This news about Jesus spread throughout Judea*ᵃ* and the surrounding country.

Jesus and John the Baptist

¹⁸John's disciples told him about all these things. Calling two of them, ¹⁹he sent them to the Lord to ask, "Are you the one who was to come, or should we expect someone else?"

²⁰When the men came to Jesus, they said, "John the Baptist sent us to you to ask, 'Are you the one who was to come, or should we expect someone else?' "

MARCH 10

²¹At that very time Jesus cured many who had diseases, sicknesses and evil spirits, and gave sight to many who were blind. ²²So he replied to the messengers, "Go back and report to John what you have seen and heard: The blind receive sight, the lame walk, those who have leprosy*b* are cured, the deaf hear, the dead are raised, and the good news is preached to the poor. ²³Blessed is the man who does not fall away on account of me."

²⁴After John's messengers left, Jesus began to speak to the crowd about John: "What did you go out into the desert to see? A reed swayed by the wind? ²⁵If not, what did you go out to see? A man dressed in fine clothes? No, those who wear expensive clothes and indulge in luxury are in palaces. ²⁶But what did you go out to see? A prophet? Yes, I tell you, and more than a prophet. ²⁷This is the one about whom it is written:

> " 'I will send my messenger ahead of you,
>   who will prepare your way before you.'*c*

²⁸I tell you, among those born of women there is no one greater than John; yet the one who is least in the kingdom of God is greater than he."

²⁹(All the people, even the tax collectors, when they heard Jesus' words, acknowledged that God's way was right, because they had been baptized by John. ³⁰But the Pharisees and experts in the law rejected God's purpose for themselves, because they had not been baptized by John.)

³¹"To what, then, can I compare the people of this generation? What are they like? ³²They are like children sitting in the marketplace and calling out to each other:

> " 'We played the flute for you,
>   and you did not dance;
> we sang a dirge,
>   and you did not cry.'

³³For John the Baptist came neither eating bread nor drinking wine, and you say, 'He has a demon.' ³⁴The Son of Man came eating and drinking, and you say, 'Here is a glutton and a drunkard, a friend of tax collectors and "sinners." ' ³⁵But wisdom is proved right by all her children."

a17 Or *the land of the Jews*   *b22* The Greek word was used for various diseases affecting the skin—not necessarily leprosy.   *c27* Mal. 3:1

Believing Faith Makes the Difference

When Jesus heard this, he was amazed at him, and turning to the crowd following him, he said, "I tell you, I have not found such great faith even in Israel" (Luke 7:9).

Faith is a concept more easily demonstrated than defined. You exercise faith when you fly in an airplane or visit a doctor. Chances are good that you couldn't land the airplane or diagnose your illness. Yet you rely on the strength and skill of someone who can. And that's faith!

In Luke 7 Jesus commends the great faith of a Roman officer—a commodity so scarce as to amaze even Jesus!

George Whitefield highlights the necessity of believing faith.

Walk With George Whitefield

"I am not against going to church, nor against the creed, the Lord's prayer, or the commandments. But believing is something more than those. It is coming to Jesus, receiving him, rolling ourselves on him, trusting in him.

"I do not know of any one single thing more often repeated in Scriptures than believing. It is described as a coming, trusting, receiving, and relying, under a felt conviction that we are lost, undone, and condemned without him.

"As a good old Puritan observed, we never come to Jesus Christ—the sinner's only hope—until we feel we cannot do without him."

Walk Closer to God

Faith in Jesus Christ sets Christianity apart from religion.

Religion is based on what you do for God; Christianity is what God has done for you.

Religion is man's attempt to work his way to heaven; Christianity is God's good news that heaven is a free gift.

Religion involves trying; Christianity is relying.

Have you come to the point of realizing you can no longer do without the Savior? He's patiently waiting for you to come . . . receive . . . trust. He's waiting for you to put your faith in him. ❍

MARCH 11

📖 Walk in the Word
Luke 7:36–50

A sinful woman overcome by love and gratitude, a self-righteous Pharisee and a grace-dispensing Savior are the key actors in this dramatic story told by Luke.

Jesus Anointed by a Sinful Woman

36Now one of the Pharisees invited Jesus to have dinner with him, so he went to the Pharisee's house and reclined at the table. 37When a woman who had lived a sinful life in that town learned that Jesus was eating at the Pharisee's house, she brought an alabaster jar of perfume, 38and as she stood behind him at his feet weeping, she began to wet his feet with her tears. Then she wiped them with her hair, kissed them and poured perfume on them.

39When the Pharisee who had invited him saw this, he said to himself, "If this man were a prophet, he would know who is touching him and what kind of woman she is—that she is a sinner."

40Jesus answered him, "Simon, I have something to tell you."

"Tell me, teacher," he said.

41"Two men owed money to a certain moneylender. One owed him five hundred denarii,ª and the other fifty. 42Neither of them had the money to pay him back, so he canceled the debts of both. Now which of them will love him more?"

43Simon replied, "I suppose the one who had the bigger debt canceled."

"You have judged correctly," Jesus said.

44Then he turned toward the woman and said to Simon, "Do you see this woman? I came into your house. You did not give me any water for my feet, but she wet my feet with her tears and wiped them with her hair. 45You did not give me a kiss, but this woman, from the time I entered, has not stopped kissing my feet. 46You did not put oil on my head, but she has poured perfume on my feet. 47Therefore, I tell you, her many sins have been forgiven—for she loved much. But he who has been forgiven little loves little."

48Then Jesus said to her, "Your sins are forgiven."

49The other guests began to say among themselves, "Who is this who even forgives sins?"

50Jesus said to the woman, "Your faith has saved you; go in peace."

ª41 A denarius was a coin worth about a day's wages.

MARCH 11

The Freeing Power of Forgiveness

Neither of them had the money to pay him back, so he canceled the debts of both. (Luke 7:42).

In Luke 7 Jesus likens the forgiveness of sins to the forgiveness of a large debt. A large debt freely canceled prompts the debtor's great gratitude for the creditor's great kindness.

Jesus' parables of the two forgiven debtors points to every person's need of forgiveness, as Albert Barnes explains.

Walk With Albert Barnes

"If it was a mere debt which we owed to God, he might forgive—as this creditor did—without any equivalent. But it is a crime he forgives.

"So our sins against God are called 'debts' figuratively. God cannot forgive us without maintaining his word, the honor of his government, and law—that is, without an atonement.

"It is clear that by the creditor here our Savior meant God, and by the debtors, sinners and the woman present. Simon, whose life had been comparatively upright, was denoted by the one owing fifty denarii; the woman, who had been a shameless sinner, was represented by the one owing five hundred. Yet neither could pay. Both must be forgiven or perish.

"So, however much difference there is among people, all need the pardoning mercy of God, and all, without that, must perish."

Walk Closer to God

Imagine the heartache of the one who owes an enormous debt he can never hope to repay but that may come due at any moment. Such is the fate of every individual without the forgiveness offered by Christ.

Who could refuse the offer of one to pay such a debt? Jesus' parable makes clear the freeing power of forgiveness, and the only proper response: love.

The apostle Paul would later give this instruction: "Let no debt remain outstanding, except the continuing debt to love one another" (Romans 13:8). If you are in Christ, then you are freely forgiven. Will you follow yet further by owing only a debt of loving service? ❏

MARCH 12

📖 Walk in the Word
Luke 8

Luke records Jesus' parable about the sower and the Word, following up with stories of Jesus' active power over nature and disease and death.

The Parable of the Sower

8 After this, Jesus traveled about from one town and village to another, proclaiming the good news of the kingdom of God. The Twelve were with him, ²and also some women who had been cured of evil spirits and diseases: Mary (called Magdalene) from whom seven demons had come out; ³Joanna the wife of Cuza, the manager of Herod's household; Susanna; and many others. These women were helping to support them out of their own means.

⁴While a large crowd was gathering and people were coming to Jesus from town after town, he told this parable: ⁵"A farmer went out to sow his seed. As he was scattering the seed, some fell along the path; it was trampled on, and the birds of the air ate it up. ⁶Some fell on rock, and when it came up, the plants withered because they had no moisture. ⁷Other seed fell among thorns, which grew up with it and choked the plants. ⁸Still other seed fell on good soil. It came up and yielded a crop, a hundred times more than was sown."

When he said this, he called out, "He who has ears to hear, let him hear."

⁹His disciples asked him what this parable meant. ¹⁰He said, "The knowledge of the secrets of the kingdom of God has been given to you, but to others I speak in parables, so that,

" 'though seeing, they may not see;
though hearing, they may not understand.'ᵃ

¹¹"This is the meaning of the parable: The seed is the word of God. ¹²Those along the path are the ones who hear, and then the devil comes and takes away the word from their hearts, so that they may not believe and be saved. ¹³Those on the rock are the ones who receive the word with joy when they hear it, but they have no root. They believe for a while, but in the time of testing they fall away. ¹⁴The seed that fell among thorns stands for those who hear, but as they go on their way they are choked by life's worries, riches and pleasures, and they do not mature. ¹⁵But the seed on good soil stands for those with a noble and good heart, who hear the word, retain it, and by persevering produce a crop.

A Lamp on a Stand

¹⁶"No one lights a lamp and hides it in a jar or puts it under a bed. Instead, he puts it on a stand, so that those who come in can see the light. ¹⁷For there is nothing hidden that will not be disclosed, and nothing concealed that will not be known or brought out into the open. ¹⁸Therefore consider carefully how you listen. Whoever has will be given more; whoever does not have, even what he thinks he has will be taken from him."

MARCH 12

Jesus' Mother and Brothers

[19]Now Jesus' mother and brothers came to see him, but they were not able to get near him because of the crowd. [20]Someone told him, "Your mother and brothers are standing outside, wanting to see you."

[21]He replied, "My mother and brothers are those who hear God's word and put it into practice."

Jesus Calms the Storm

[22]One day Jesus said to his disciples, "Let's go over to the other side of the lake." So they got into a boat and set out. [23]As they sailed, he fell asleep. A squall came down on the lake, so that the boat was being swamped, and they were in great danger.

[24]The disciples went and woke him, saying, "Master, Master, we're going to drown!"

He got up and rebuked the wind and the raging waters; the storm subsided, and all was calm. [25]"Where is your faith?" he asked his disciples.

In fear and amazement they asked one another, "Who is this? He commands even the winds and the water, and they obey him."

The Healing of a Demon-possessed Man

[26]They sailed to the region of the Gerasenes,[b] which is across the lake from Galilee. [27]When Jesus stepped ashore, he was met by a demon-possessed man from the town. For a long time this man had not worn clothes or lived in a house, but had lived in the tombs. [28]When he saw Jesus, he cried out and fell at his feet, shouting at the top of his voice, "What do you want with me, Jesus, Son of the Most High God? I beg you, don't torture me!" [29]For Jesus had commanded the evil[c] spirit to come out of the man. Many times it had seized him, and though he was chained hand and foot and kept under guard, he had broken his chains and had been driven by the demon into solitary places.

[30]Jesus asked him, "What is your name?"

"Legion," he replied, because many demons had gone into him. [31]And they begged him repeatedly not to order them to go into the Abyss.

[32]A large herd of pigs was feeding there on the hillside. The demons begged Jesus to let them go into them, and he gave them permission. [33]When the demons came out of the man, they went into the pigs, and the herd rushed down the steep bank into the lake and was drowned.

[34]When those tending the pigs saw what had happened, they ran off and reported this in the town and countryside, [35]and the people went out to see what had happened. When they came to Jesus, they found the man from whom the demons had gone out, sitting at Jesus' feet, dressed and in his right mind; and they were afraid. [36]Those who had seen it told the people how the demon-possessed man had been cured. [37]Then all the people of the region of the Gerasenes asked Jesus to leave them, because they were overcome with fear. So he got into the boat and left.

MARCH 12

38The man from whom the demons had gone out begged to go with him, but Jesus sent him away, saying, 39"Return home and tell how much God has done for you." So the man went away and told all over town how much Jesus had done for him.

A Dead Girl and a Sick Woman

40Now when Jesus returned, a crowd welcomed him, for they were all expecting him. 41Then a man named Jairus, a ruler of the synagogue, came and fell at Jesus' feet, pleading with him to come to his house 42because his only daughter, a girl of about twelve, was dying.

As Jesus was on his way, the crowds almost crushed him. 43And a woman was there who had been subject to bleeding for twelve years,d but no one could heal her. 44She came up behind him and touched the edge of his cloak, and immediately her bleeding stopped.

45"Who touched me?" Jesus asked.

When they all denied it, Peter said, "Master, the people are crowding and pressing against you."

46But Jesus said, "Someone touched me; I know that power has gone out from me."

47Then the woman, seeing that she could not go unnoticed, came trembling and fell at his feet. In the presence of all the people, she told why she had touched him and how she had been instantly healed. 48Then he said to her, "Daughter, your faith has healed you. Go in peace."

49While Jesus was still speaking, someone came from the house of Jairus, the synagogue ruler. "Your daughter is dead," he said. "Don't bother the teacher any more."

50Hearing this, Jesus said to Jairus, "Don't be afraid; just believe, and she will be healed."

51When he arrived at the house of Jairus, he did not let anyone go in with him except Peter, John and James, and the child's father and mother. 52Meanwhile, all the people were wailing and mourning for her. "Stop wailing," Jesus said. "She is not dead but asleep."

53They laughed at him, knowing that she was dead. 54But he took her by the hand and said, "My child, get up!" 55Her spirit returned, and at once she stood up. Then Jesus told them to give her something to eat. 56Her parents were astonished, but he ordered them not to tell anyone what had happened.

a10 Isaiah 6:9   b26 Some manuscripts *Gadarenes*; other manuscripts *Gergesenes*; also in verse 37   c29 Greek *unclean*   d43 Many manuscripts *years, and she had spent all she had on doctors*

Personal Attention From the Great Physician

As Jesus was on his way, the crowds almost crushed him. And a woman . . . came up behind him and touched the edge of his cloak (Luke 8:42–44).

A doctor's waiting room. A crowded street. The doctor's office admits people one by one. Each is a person . . . with a face . . . a medical history . . . and a reason for being there.

By contrast the street can be an impersonal place. People are just as needy, but no one is concerned enough to do anything about those needs.

Jesus was often surrounded by throngs of people, but as Charles Spurgeon explains, Jesus never viewed his audience as a mass of faceless figures.

Walk With Charles Spurgeon

"Jesus is passing through the crowd to the house of Jairus, to raise the ruler's dead daughter. But he has so much power and goodness that he works another miracle while on the road.

"It is enough for us, if we have one need set before us, straightway to relieve it; it might even seem unwise to expend our energies by the way.

"Hastening to rescue one, we cannot afford to exhaust our strength upon another in like danger.

"But our Master knows no limit of power or boundary of mission.

"What delightful encouragement this truth gives us!

"If our Lord is so ready to heal the sick and bless the needy, be not slow to put yourself in his way, that he may smile upon you!"

Walk Closer to God

Cares. The universal experience of those on planet earth.

Some cares are as persistent as the woman's twelve-year illness. Others are as heartbreaking as Jairus's dying daughter. But all are within the scope of the Great Physician's strength and skill.

Touching the hem of his garment in faithful prayer may be the only thing you have strength left to do.

But as the woman in Luke 8 discovered, it's a touch that won't go unnoticed. ◖

MARCH 13

📖 Walk in the Word
Luke 9:1–36

The apostles are sent to preach and heal, hungry people are miraculously fed and filled, Peter announces the truth about Jesus' identity, and three disciples receive a glimpse at the glory of a transfigured Jesus in this part of Luke's narrative.

Jesus Sends Out the Twelve

9 When Jesus had called the Twelve together, he gave them power and authority to drive out all demons and to cure diseases, ²and he sent them out to preach the kingdom of God and to heal the sick. ³He told them: "Take nothing for the journey—no staff, no bag, no bread, no money, no extra tunic. ⁴Whatever house you enter, stay there until you leave that town. ⁵If people do not welcome you, shake the dust off your feet when you leave their town, as a testimony against them." ⁶So they set out and went from village to village, preaching the gospel and healing people everywhere.

⁷Now Herod the tetrarch heard about all that was going on. And he was perplexed, because some were saying that John had been raised from the dead, ⁸others that Elijah had appeared, and still others that one of the prophets of long ago had come back to life. ⁹But Herod said, "I beheaded John. Who, then, is this I hear such things about?" And he tried to see him.

Jesus Feeds the Five Thousand

¹⁰When the apostles returned, they reported to Jesus what they had done. Then he took them with him and they withdrew by themselves to a town called Bethsaida, ¹¹but the crowds learned about it and followed him. He welcomed them and spoke to them about the kingdom of God, and healed those who needed healing.

¹²Late in the afternoon the Twelve came to him and said, "Send the crowd away so they can go to the surrounding villages and countryside and find food and lodging, because we are in a remote place here."

¹³He replied, "You give them something to eat."

They answered, "We have only five loaves of bread and two fish—unless we go and buy food for all this crowd." ¹⁴(About five thousand men were there.)

But he said to his disciples, "Have them sit down in groups of about fifty each." ¹⁵The disciples did so, and everybody sat down. ¹⁶Taking the five loaves and the two fish and looking up to heaven, he gave thanks and broke them. Then he gave them to the disciples to set before the people. ¹⁷They all ate and were satisfied, and the disciples picked up twelve basketfuls of broken pieces that were left over.

Peter's Confession of Christ

¹⁸Once when Jesus was praying in private and his disciples were with him, he asked them, "Who do the crowds say I am?"

19They replied, "Some say John the Baptist; others say Elijah; and still others, that one of the prophets of long ago has come back to life."

20"But what about you?" he asked. "Who do you say I am?"

Peter answered, "The Christ*a* of God."

21Jesus strictly warned them not to tell this to anyone. 22And he said, "The Son of Man must suffer many things and be rejected by the elders, chief priests and teachers of the law, and he must be killed and on the third day be raised to life."

23Then he said to them all: "If anyone would come after me, he must deny himself and take up his cross daily and follow me. 24For whoever wants to save his life will lose it, but whoever loses his life for me will save it. 25What good is it for a man to gain the whole world, and yet lose or forfeit his very self? 26If anyone is ashamed of me and my words, the Son of Man will be ashamed of him when he comes in his glory and in the glory of the Father and of the holy angels. 27I tell you the truth, some who are standing here will not taste death before they see the kingdom of God."

The Transfiguration

28About eight days after Jesus said this, he took Peter, John and James with him and went up onto a mountain to pray. 29As he was praying, the appearance of his face changed, and his clothes became as bright as a flash of lightning. 30Two men, Moses and Elijah, 31appeared in glorious splendor, talking with Jesus. They spoke about his departure, which he was about to bring to fulfillment at Jerusalem. 32Peter and his companions were very sleepy, but when they became fully awake, they saw his glory and the two men standing with him. 33As the men were leaving Jesus, Peter said to him, "Master, it is good for us to be here. Let us put up three shelters — one for you, one for Moses and one for Elijah." (He did not know what he was saying.)

34While he was speaking, a cloud appeared and enveloped them, and they were afraid as they entered the cloud. 35A voice came from the cloud, saying, "This is my Son, whom I have chosen; listen to him." 36When the voice had spoken, they found that Jesus was alone. The disciples kept this to themselves, and told no one at that time what they had seen.

a20 Or *Messiah*

MARCH 13

Getting to the Source of Life

He replied, "You give them something to eat" (Luke 9:13).

What if you were close friends with an author whose works you admired? Would you prize his books over his friendship? Of course not.

The disciples were so concerned about finding food for the crowd that they forgot they were in the presence of the bread of life.

Mary Ann Lathbury wrote of our need for daily spiritual food from the Word of God, which reveals the living word who is the bread of life.

Walk With Mary Ann Lathbury

Break Thou the bread of life,
    Dear Lord, to me,
As Thou didst break the loaves
    Beside the sea:
Beyond the sacred page
    I seek Thee, Lord;
My spirit pants for Thee, O living Word.
Bless Thou the truth, dear Lord,
    To me—to me,
As Thou didst bless the bread
    By Galilee:
Then shall all bondage cease,
    All fetters fall,
And I shall find my peace, My all in all.
Thou art the bread of life,
    O Lord, to me;
Thy holy Word the truth
    That saveth me:
Give me to eat and live
    With Thee above;
Teach me to love Thy truth, For Thou art Love.

Walk Closer to God

You wouldn't throw away a book just because you knew the author. In fact, you would probably strive to know him better by reading his works!

So as you read and meditate on God's Word, expect to get closer to your Lord. And the next time you see a loaf of bread, let it be a reminder of your relationship with the one who is the bread of life. ◗

MARCH 14

Walk in the Word
Luke 9:37–62

Luke records Jesus' encounters with people and forces that oppose him and relates further teachings about the cost of discipleship.

The Healing of a Boy With an Evil Spirit

[37]The next day, when they came down from the mountain, a large crowd met him. [38]A man in the crowd called out, "Teacher, I beg you to look at my son, for he is my only child. [39]A spirit seizes him and he suddenly screams; it throws him into convulsions so that he foams at the mouth. It scarcely ever leaves him and is destroying him. [40]I begged your disciples to drive it out, but they could not."

[41]"O unbelieving and perverse generation," Jesus replied, "how long shall I stay with you and put up with you? Bring your son here."

[42]Even while the boy was coming, the demon threw him to the ground in a convulsion. But Jesus rebuked the evil[a] spirit, healed the boy and gave him back to his father. [43]And they were all amazed at the greatness of God.

While everyone was marveling at all that Jesus did, he said to his disciples, [44]"Listen carefully to what I am about to tell you: The Son of Man is going to be betrayed into the hands of men." [45]But they did not understand what this meant. It was hidden from them, so that they did not grasp it, and they were afraid to ask him about it.

Who Will Be the Greatest?

[46]An argument started among the disciples as to which of them would be the greatest. [47]Jesus, knowing their thoughts, took a little child and had him stand beside him. [48]Then he said to them, "Whoever welcomes this little child in my name welcomes me; and whoever welcomes me welcomes the one who sent me. For he who is least among you all—he is the greatest."

[49]"Master," said John, "we saw a man driving out demons in your name and we tried to stop him, because he is not one of us."

[50]"Do not stop him," Jesus said, "for whoever is not against you is for you."

Samaritan Opposition

[51]As the time approached for him to be taken up to heaven, Jesus resolutely set out for Jerusalem. [52]And he sent messengers on ahead, who went into a Samaritan village to get things ready for him; [53]but the people there did not welcome him, because he was heading for Jerusalem. [54]When the disciples James and John saw this, they asked, "Lord, do you want us to call fire down from heaven to destroy them[b]?" [55]But Jesus turned and rebuked them, [56]and[c] they went to another village.

The Cost of Following Jesus

[57]As they were walking along the road, a man said to him, "I will follow you wherever you go."

MARCH 14

⁵⁸Jesus replied, "Foxes have holes and birds of the air have nests, but the Son of Man has no place to lay his head."

⁵⁹He said to another man, "Follow me."

But the man replied, "Lord, first let me go and bury my father."

⁶⁰Jesus said to him, "Let the dead bury their own dead, but you go and proclaim the kingdom of God."

⁶¹Still another said, "I will follow you, Lord; but first let me go back and say good-by to my family."

⁶²Jesus replied, "No one who puts his hand to the plow and looks back is fit for service in the kingdom of God."

ᵃ42 Greek *unclean*   ᵇ54 Some manuscripts *them, even as Elijah did*   ᶜ55,56 Some manuscripts *them. And he said, "You do not know what kind of spirit you are of, for the Son of Man did not come to destroy men's lives, but to save them." 56And*

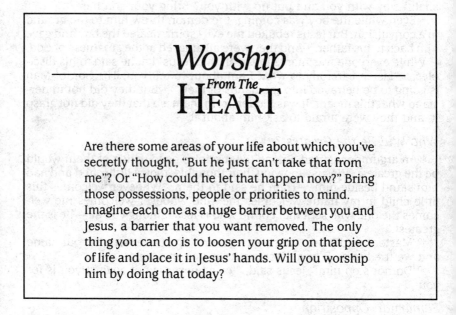

Worship
From The
HEART

Are there some areas of your life about which you've secretly thought, "But he just can't take that from me"? Or "How could he let that happen now?" Bring those possessions, people or priorities to mind. Imagine each one as a huge barrier between you and Jesus, a barrier that you want removed. The only thing you can do is to loosen your grip on that piece of life and place it in Jesus' hands. Will you worship him by doing that today?

The Rigors of Following Jesus

Jesus said to him, "Let the dead bury their own dead, but you go and proclaim the kingdom of God" (Luke 9:60).

In Luke 9:23 Jesus made it clear that becoming his disciple involves self-denial—taking up your cross every day and following him.

He never guaranteed five-star accommodations. Sometimes he asked his followers to oppose social customs and traditions. He expected undivided allegiance.

The three men Jesus talked with in Luke 9 all needed to learn that comfort, social acceptance and even family ties become secondary when Jesus is supreme. Matthew Henry explains.

Walk With Matthew Henry

"Our religion teaches us to show piety at home and to honor our parents. But we must not make these an excuse from our duty to God.

"If the nearest and dearest relation we have in the world stands in our way to keep us from Christ, it is necessary that we have a zeal that will make us forget that one.

"The disciple is called to be a minister, and therefore must not entangle himself with the affairs of this world (2 Timothy 2:4). And it is a rule that, whenever Christ calls us to any duty, we must not consult with flesh and blood (Galatians 1:15–16).

"No excuses must be admitted against a present obedience to the call of Christ."

Walk Closer to God

Physical fitness dominates the activities of many today. But spiritual fitness is far more crucial to the life of the Christian, for when Christ calls you to become his disciple, he summons you to a life of labor, not of leisure.

Discipleship is likened to the rigors of being a soldier, an athlete and a hardworking farmer (2 Timothy 2:3–6). That means being free from distractions, fit for action and steadfast in your labors.

If flabbiness rather than fitness characterizes your Christian life, perhaps you need to exchange a few excuses for some exercise in the service of your Lord. ◖

MARCH 15

📖 Walk in the Word
Luke 10

Luke presents three more vignettes from Jesus' ministry: the sending out of kingdom workers, the dramatic parable of the Good Samaritan, and the scene at the home of Mary and Martha.

Jesus Sends Out the Seventy-two

10 After this the Lord appointed seventy-two[a] others and sent them two by two ahead of him to every town and place where he was about to go. ²He told them, "The harvest is plentiful, but the workers are few. Ask the Lord of the harvest, therefore, to send out workers into his harvest field. ³Go! I am sending you out like lambs among wolves. ⁴Do not take a purse or bag or sandals; and do not greet anyone on the road.

⁵"When you enter a house, first say, 'Peace to this house.' ⁶If a man of peace is there, your peace will rest on him; if not, it will return to you. ⁷Stay in that house, eating and drinking whatever they give you, for the worker deserves his wages. Do not move around from house to house.

⁸"When you enter a town and are welcomed, eat what is set before you. ⁹Heal the sick who are there and tell them, 'The kingdom of God is near you.' ¹⁰But when you enter a town and are not welcomed, go into its streets and say, ¹¹'Even the dust of your town that sticks to our feet we wipe off against you. Yet be sure of this: The kingdom of God is near.' ¹²I tell you, it will be more bearable on that day for Sodom than for that town.

¹³"Woe to you, Korazin! Woe to you, Bethsaida! For if the miracles that were performed in you had been performed in Tyre and Sidon, they would have repented long ago, sitting in sackcloth and ashes. ¹⁴But it will be more bearable for Tyre and Sidon at the judgment than for you. ¹⁵And you, Capernaum, will you be lifted up to the skies? No, you will go down to the depths.[b]

¹⁶"He who listens to you listens to me; he who rejects you rejects me; but he who rejects me rejects him who sent me."

¹⁷The seventy-two returned with joy and said, "Lord, even the demons submit to us in your name."

¹⁸He replied, "I saw Satan fall like lightning from heaven. ¹⁹I have given you authority to trample on snakes and scorpions and to overcome all the power of the enemy; nothing will harm you. ²⁰However, do not rejoice that the spirits submit to you, but rejoice that your names are written in heaven."

²¹At that time Jesus, full of joy through the Holy Spirit, said, "I praise you, Father, Lord of heaven and earth, because you have hidden these things from the wise and learned, and revealed them to little children. Yes, Father, for this was your good pleasure.

²²"All things have been committed to me by my Father. No one knows who the Son is except the Father, and no one knows who the Father is except the Son and those to whom the Son chooses to reveal him."

²³Then he turned to his disciples and said privately, "Blessed are the eyes that see what you see. ²⁴For I tell you that many prophets and kings

wanted to see what you see but did not see it, and to hear what you hear but did not hear it."

The Parable of the Good Samaritan

25On one occasion an expert in the law stood up to test Jesus. "Teacher," he asked, "what must I do to inherit eternal life?"

26"What is written in the Law?" he replied. "How do you read it?"

27He answered: "'Love the Lord your God with all your heart and with all your soul and with all your strength and with all your mind'*c*; and, 'Love your neighbor as yourself.'*d*"

28"You have answered correctly," Jesus replied. "Do this and you will live."

29But he wanted to justify himself, so he asked Jesus, "And who is my neighbor?"

30In reply Jesus said: "A man was going down from Jerusalem to Jericho, when he fell into the hands of robbers. They stripped him of his clothes, beat him and went away, leaving him half dead. 31A priest happened to be going down the same road, and when he saw the man, he passed by on the other side. 32So too, a Levite, when he came to the place and saw him, passed by on the other side. 33But a Samaritan, as he traveled, came where the man was; and when he saw him, he took pity on him. 34He went to him and bandaged his wounds, pouring on oil and wine. Then he put the man on his own donkey, took him to an inn and took care of him. 35The next day he took out two silver coins*e* and gave them to the innkeeper. 'Look after him,' he said, 'and when I return, I will reimburse you for any extra expense you may have.'

36"Which of these three do you think was a neighbor to the man who fell into the hands of robbers?"

37The expert in the law replied, "The one who had mercy on him." Jesus told him, "Go and do likewise."

At the Home of Martha and Mary

38As Jesus and his disciples were on their way, he came to a village where a woman named Martha opened her home to him. 39She had a sister called Mary, who sat at the Lord's feet listening to what he said. 40But Martha was distracted by all the preparations that had to be made. She came to him and asked, "Lord, don't you care that my sister has left me to do the work by myself? Tell her to help me!"

41"Martha, Martha," the Lord answered, "you are worried and upset about many things, 42but only one thing is needed.*f* Mary has chosen what is better, and it will not be taken away from her."

a1 Some manuscripts *seventy*; also in verse 17   *b15* Greek *Hades*   *c27* Deut. 6:5
d27 Lev. 19:18   *e35* Greek *two denarii*   *f42* Some manuscripts *but few things are needed—or only one*

MARCH 15

Discovering the One Necessary Thing

But only one thing is needed. Mary has chosen what is better, and it will not be taken away from her (Luke 10:42).

How do you show God that you love him? You might answer that question by listing the number of times you went to church. Or attended a Bible study. Or taught a class. Or gave an offering.

But in the final analysis, your activities for God aren't the best barometer of your adoration. Your attitude is! A.W. Tozer explains that God wants more than just your output.

Walk With A.W. Tozer

"Some Christians feel it is a mark of spirituality to attend banquets, seminars, workshops, and conferences week after week.

"This brings up a lesson concerning Martha and Mary. I think it is plain that Martha loved Jesus, but her concept of devotion was activity.

"Mary also loved Jesus but with a different attitude in her devotion. She was fervently occupied in spirit with her love for him.

"Our Lord marked the distinction then, and he marks the distinction today.

"Jesus commended Mary for knowing that one thing is necessary— that God should be loved and praised above all other business which may occupy us bodily, mentally, or spiritually.

"He wants first an inner experience of the heart, and from that will grow the profound and divine activities which are necessary."

Walk Closer to God

"Slow me down, Lord.

"Keep me from becoming so engrossed in working for you that I fail to nurture my personal relationship with you.

"I have often felt the exhaustion of activity. Let me today experience a bit of the joy Mary felt—the joy of adoration.

"Teach me how to say, 'I love you, Lord,' while standing still. In the name of him who first demonstrated what the service of worship is all about. Amen." ◐

MARCH 16

Walk in the Word
Luke 11

Jesus teaches about prayer and the struggle between the kingdom of darkness and the kingdom of light; he pronounces six woes on the Pharisees and the teachers of the law, condemning them for their spiritual blindness.

Jesus' Teaching on Prayer

11 One day Jesus was praying in a certain place. When he finished, one of his disciples said to him, "Lord, teach us to pray, just as John taught his disciples."

²He said to them, "When you pray, say:

" 'Father,*a*
hallowed be your name,
your kingdom come. *b*
³Give us each day our daily bread.
⁴Forgive us our sins,
    for we also forgive everyone who sins against us. *c*
And lead us not into temptation. *d* ' "

⁵Then he said to them, "Suppose one of you has a friend, and he goes to him at midnight and says, 'Friend, lend me three loaves of bread, ⁶because a friend of mine on a journey has come to me, and I have nothing to set before him.'

⁷"Then the one inside answers, 'Don't bother me. The door is already locked, and my children are with me in bed. I can't get up and give you anything.' ⁸I tell you, though he will not get up and give him the bread because he is his friend, yet because of the man's boldness*e* he will get up and give him as much as he needs.

⁹"So I say to you: Ask and it will be given to you; seek and you will find; knock and the door will be opened to you. ¹⁰For everyone who asks receives; he who seeks finds; and to him who knocks, the door will be opened.

¹¹"Which of you fathers, if your son asks for*f* a fish, will give him a snake instead? ¹²Or if he asks for an egg, will give him a scorpion? ¹³If you then, though you are evil, know how to give good gifts to your children, how much more will your Father in heaven give the Holy Spirit to those who ask him!"

Jesus and Beelzebub

¹⁴Jesus was driving out a demon that was mute. When the demon left, the man who had been mute spoke, and the crowd was amazed. ¹⁵But some of them said, "By Beelzebub,*g* the prince of demons, he is driving out demons." ¹⁶Others tested him by asking for a sign from heaven.

¹⁷Jesus knew their thoughts and said to them: "Any kingdom divided against itself will be ruined, and a house divided against itself will fall. ¹⁸If Satan is divided against himself, how can his kingdom stand? I say this because you claim that I drive out demons by Beelzebub. ¹⁹Now if I drive

MARCH 16

out demons by Beelzebub, by whom do your followers drive them out? So then, they will be your judges. ²⁰But if I drive out demons by the finger of God, then the kingdom of God has come to you.

²¹"When a strong man, fully armed, guards his own house, his possessions are safe. ²²But when someone stronger attacks and overpowers him, he takes away the armor in which the man trusted and divides up the spoils.

²³"He who is not with me is against me, and he who does not gather with me, scatters.

²⁴"When an evil ʰ spirit comes out of a man, it goes through arid places seeking rest and does not find it. Then it says, 'I will return to the house I left.' ²⁵When it arrives, it finds the house swept clean and put in order. ²⁶Then it goes and takes seven other spirits more wicked than itself, and they go in and live there. And the final condition of that man is worse than the first."

²⁷As Jesus was saying these things, a woman in the crowd called out, "Blessed is the mother who gave you birth and nursed you."

²⁸He replied, "Blessed rather are those who hear the word of God and obey it."

The Sign of Jonah

²⁹As the crowds increased, Jesus said, "This is a wicked generation. It asks for a miraculous sign, but none will be given it except the sign of Jonah. ³⁰For as Jonah was a sign to the Ninevites, so also will the Son of Man be to this generation. ³¹The Queen of the South will rise at the judgment with the men of this generation and condemn them; for she came from the ends of the earth to listen to Solomon's wisdom, and now one ⁱ greater than Solomon is here. ³²The men of Nineveh will stand up at the judgment with this generation and condemn it; for they repented at the preaching of Jonah, and now one greater than Jonah is here.

The Lamp of the Body

³³"No one lights a lamp and puts it in a place where it will be hidden, or under a bowl. Instead he puts it on its stand, so that those who come in may see the light. ³⁴Your eye is the lamp of your body. When your eyes are good, your whole body also is full of light. But when they are bad, your body also is full of darkness. ³⁵See to it, then, that the light within you is not darkness. ³⁶Therefore, if your whole body is full of light, and no part of it dark, it will be completely lighted, as when the light of a lamp shines on you."

Six Woes

³⁷When Jesus had finished speaking, a Pharisee invited him to eat with him; so he went in and reclined at the table. ³⁸But the Pharisee, noticing that Jesus did not first wash before the meal, was surprised.

MARCH 16

³⁹Then the Lord said to him, "Now then, you Pharisees clean the outside of the cup and dish, but inside you are full of greed and wickedness. ⁴⁰You foolish people! Did not the one who made the outside make the inside also? ⁴¹But give what is inside ⌊the dish⌋^j to the poor, and everything will be clean for you.

⁴²"Woe to you Pharisees, because you give God a tenth of your mint, rue and all other kinds of garden herbs, but you neglect justice and the love of God. You should have practiced the latter without leaving the former undone.

⁴³"Woe to you Pharisees, because you love the most important seats in the synagogues and greetings in the marketplaces.

⁴⁴"Woe to you, because you are like unmarked graves, which men walk over without knowing it."

⁴⁵One of the experts in the law answered him, "Teacher, when you say these things, you insult us also."

⁴⁶Jesus replied, "And you experts in the law, woe to you, because you load people down with burdens they can hardly carry, and you yourselves will not lift one finger to help them.

⁴⁷"Woe to you, because you build tombs for the prophets, and it was your forefathers who killed them. ⁴⁸So you testify that you approve of what your forefathers did; they killed the prophets, and you build their tombs. ⁴⁹Because of this, God in his wisdom said, 'I will send them prophets and apostles, some of whom they will kill and others they will persecute.' ⁵⁰Therefore this generation will be held responsible for the blood of all the prophets that has been shed since the beginning of the world, ⁵¹from the blood of Abel to the blood of Zechariah, who was killed between the altar and the sanctuary. Yes, I tell you, this generation will be held responsible for it all.

⁵²"Woe to you experts in the law, because you have taken away the key to knowledge. You yourselves have not entered, and you have hindered those who were entering."

⁵³When Jesus left there, the Pharisees and the teachers of the law began to oppose him fiercely and to besiege him with questions, ⁵⁴waiting to catch him in something he might say.

---

^a2 Some manuscripts *Our Father in heaven*   ^b2 Some manuscripts *come. May your will be done on earth as it is in heaven.*   ^c4 Greek *everyone who is indebted to us*   ^d4 Some manuscripts *temptation but deliver us from the evil one*   ^e8 Or *persistence*   ^f11 Some manuscripts *for bread, will give him a stone; or if he asks for*   ^g15 Greek *Beezeboul* or *Beelzeboul*; also in verses 18 and 19   ^h24 Greek *unclean*   ⁱ31 Or *something*; also in verse 32   ^j41 Or *what you have*

MARCH 16

The Danger of Light Becoming Darkness

See to it, then, that the light within you is not darkness (Luke 11:35).

Fear of the dark ranks right up there with snakes, heights and loud noises among common childhood fears. And adults are not immune to them either.

You may take some comfort in the fact that common sense dictates that in life-and-death situations, you need all the light you can get. Anything less is foolhardy.

However, the Pharisees were in the dark about Jesus. G. Campbell Morgan sheds some light on the causes of their spiritual blindness.

Walk With G. Campbell Morgan

"Is it possible for a lighted lamp to be darkness? Yes, it is.

"That lighted lamp is darkness when it is put out of sight, in the cellar or under a bushel. That lighted lamp is light when it is placed on a stand, so that people may see the light.

"Light then is only of value when it is kept shining, and the steps are guided by it.

"Light hidden is darkness. Truth disobeyed is valueless. Knowledge unyielded to is ignorance.

"How often the light within us is darkness!

"The will of the Lord, clearly revealed to us, is apprehended intellectually, but not carried out in practice; then the light is darkness.

"The Word of the Lord, studied and interpreted by the Spirit, is retained in the intellect, but not permitted to be the guiding principle of the will. Then too the light is darkness."

Walk Closer to God

The Pharisees responded to Jesus by closing their eyes to the truth. They preferred the comfort of the darkness to the brightness of God's light.

The status quo, after all, is best maintained in the dark. But if you are eager to know God's will—and do it—there's no need to be in the dark.

The Word of God is a source which will shed light on every subject. Let it always be a lamp to your feet and a light for your path (Psalm 119:105). Don't allow it to go unheeded. ❍

MARCH 17

📖 Walk in the Word
Luke 12

Luke records various teachings of Jesus about the necessity of trust, the danger of riches, the importance of watchfulness, and the inevitability of division and conflict.

Warnings and Encouragements

12 Meanwhile, when a crowd of many thousands had gathered, so that they were trampling on one another, Jesus began to speak first to his disciples, saying: "Be on your guard against the yeast of the Pharisees, which is hypocrisy. ²There is nothing concealed that will not be disclosed, or hidden that will not be made known. ³What you have said in the dark will be heard in the daylight, and what you have whispered in the ear in the inner rooms will be proclaimed from the roofs.

⁴"I tell you, my friends, do not be afraid of those who kill the body and after that can do no more. ⁵But I will show you whom you should fear: Fear him who, after the killing of the body, has power to throw you into hell. Yes, I tell you, fear him. ⁶Are not five sparrows sold for two pennies*a*? Yet not one of them is forgotten by God. ⁷Indeed, the very hairs of your head are all numbered. Don't be afraid; you are worth more than many sparrows.

⁸"I tell you, whoever acknowledges me before men, the Son of Man will also acknowledge him before the angels of God. ⁹But he who disowns me before men will be disowned before the angels of God. ¹⁰And everyone who speaks a word against the Son of Man will be forgiven, but anyone who blasphemes against the Holy Spirit will not be forgiven.

¹¹"When you are brought before synagogues, rulers and authorities, do not worry about how you will defend yourselves or what you will say, ¹²for the Holy Spirit will teach you at that time what you should say."

The Parable of the Rich Fool

¹³Someone in the crowd said to him, "Teacher, tell my brother to divide the inheritance with me."

¹⁴Jesus replied, "Man, who appointed me a judge or an arbiter between you?" ¹⁵Then he said to them, "Watch out! Be on your guard against all kinds of greed; a man's life does not consist in the abundance of his possessions."

¹⁶And he told them this parable: "The ground of a certain rich man produced a good crop. ¹⁷He thought to himself, 'What shall I do? I have no place to store my crops.'

¹⁸"Then he said, 'This is what I'll do. I will tear down my barns and build bigger ones, and there I will store all my grain and my goods. ¹⁹And I'll say to myself, "You have plenty of good things laid up for many years. Take life easy; eat, drink and be merry."'

²⁰"But God said to him, 'You fool! This very night your life will be demanded from you. Then who will get what you have prepared for yourself?'

MARCH 17

21"This is how it will be with anyone who stores up things for himself but is not rich toward God."

Do Not Worry

22Then Jesus said to his disciples: "Therefore I tell you, do not worry about your life, what you will eat; or about your body, what you will wear. 23Life is more than food, and the body more than clothes. 24Consider the ravens: They do not sow or reap, they have no storeroom or barn; yet God feeds them. And how much more valuable you are than birds! 25Who of you by worrying can add a single hour to his life*b*? 26Since you cannot do this very little thing, why do you worry about the rest?

27"Consider how the lilies grow. They do not labor or spin. Yet I tell you, not even Solomon in all his splendor was dressed like one of these. 28If that is how God clothes the grass of the field, which is here today, and tomorrow is thrown into the fire, how much more will he clothe you, O you of little faith! 29And do not set your heart on what you will eat or drink; do not worry about it. 30For the pagan world runs after all such things, and your Father knows that you need them. 31But seek his kingdom, and these things will be given to you as well.

32"Do not be afraid, little flock, for your Father has been pleased to give you the kingdom. 33Sell your possessions and give to the poor. Provide purses for yourselves that will not wear out, a treasure in heaven that will not be exhausted, where no thief comes near and no moth destroys. 34For where your treasure is, there your heart will be also.

Watchfulness

35"Be dressed ready for service and keep your lamps burning, 36like men waiting for their master to return from a wedding banquet, so that when he comes and knocks they can immediately open the door for him. 37It will be good for those servants whose master finds them watching when he comes. I tell you the truth, he will dress himself to serve, will have them recline at the table and will come and wait on them. 38It will be good for those servants whose master finds them ready, even if he comes in the second or third watch of the night. 39But understand this: If the owner of the house had known at what hour the thief was coming, he would not have let his house be broken into. 40You also must be ready, because the Son of Man will come at an hour when you do not expect him."

41Peter asked, "Lord, are you telling this parable to us, or to everyone?"

42The Lord answered, "Who then is the faithful and wise manager, whom the master puts in charge of his servants to give them their food allowance at the proper time? 43It will be good for that servant whom the master finds doing so when he returns. 44I tell you the truth, he will put him in charge of all his possessions. 45But suppose the servant says to himself, 'My master is taking a long time in coming,' and he then begins to beat the menservants and maidservants and to eat and drink and get drunk. 46The master of that servant will come on a day when he does not expect him and at an hour he is not aware of. He will cut him to pieces and assign him a place with the unbelievers.

47"That servant who knows his master's will and does not get ready or does not do what his master wants will be beaten with many blows. 48But the one who does not know and does things deserving punishment will be beaten with few blows. From everyone who has been given much, much will be demanded; and from the one who has been entrusted with much, much more will be asked.

Not Peace but Division

49"I have come to bring fire on the earth, and how I wish it were already kindled! 50But I have a baptism to undergo, and how distressed I am until it is completed! 51Do you think I came to bring peace on earth? No, I tell you, but division. 52From now on there will be five in one family divided against each other, three against two and two against three. 53They will be divided, father against son and son against father, mother against daughter and daughter against mother, mother-in-law against daughter-in-law and daughter-in-law against mother-in-law."

Interpreting the Times

54He said to the crowd: "When you see a cloud rising in the west, immediately you say, 'It's going to rain,' and it does. 55And when the south wind blows, you say, 'It's going to be hot,' and it is. 56Hypocrites! You know how to interpret the appearance of the earth and the sky. How is it that you don't know how to interpret this present time?

57"Why don't you judge for yourselves what is right? 58As you are going with your adversary to the magistrate, try hard to be reconciled to him on the way, or he may drag you off to the judge, and the judge turn you over to the officer, and the officer throw you into prison. 59I tell you, you will not get out until you have paid the last penny.c"

a6 Greek *two assaria*   b25 Or *single cubit to his height*   c59 Greek *lepton*

MARCH 17

Making Secure Investments in an Uncertain World

But seek his kingdom, and these things will be given to you as well (Luke 12:31).

Would you be willing to invest in a venture if you knew part of the dividends would be paid, not to you, but to your brother or sister?

Of course you would—if you're a member of God's family!

God has promised to meet the needs of his children. And frequently the way he does it is by blessing one in order to benefit another.

The twelfth-century saint, Bernard of Clairvaux, clarifies the way in which God helps those who help their neighbors.

Walk With Bernard of Clairvaux

"What if, by giving to our neighbor, we find ourselves in want?

"What should we do except go confidently to God, 'who gives to all liberally,' and opening his hand fills all things living.

"Without a doubt he who gives most men more than they need will not deny us bare necessities.

"Has he not told us, 'Seek first his kingdom . . . and all these things will be given to you as well'?

"He has bound himself to give all things needful to those people who discipline themselves and love their neighbors.

"Moreover, it is but justice that we should share the blessings of this life with others."

Walk Closer to God

Earthly investments are often iffy at best. There are just too many factors that you cannot control.

That's why God's heavenly investment portfolio looks better than ever. Consider this prospectus:

Your investment is secure, untouchable by thief, worm or rust.

Interest is compounded eternally. Where your treasure is, there will your heart be also.

Best of all, you have the joy of seeing God meet the needs of others out of the overflow of your own life.

Seeking the kingdom of God. When you add it up, there's no better way to invest your life! ◖

MARCH 18

Walk in the Word
Luke 13

Jesus continues to teach about the kingdom, demonstrating his power in word and deed as he convicts the unrepentant and heals the hurting.

Repent or Perish

13 Now there were some present at that time who told Jesus about the Galileans whose blood Pilate had mixed with their sacrifices. [2]Jesus answered, "Do you think that these Galileans were worse sinners than all the other Galileans because they suffered this way? [3]I tell you, no! But unless you repent, you too will all perish. [4]Or those eighteen who died when the tower in Siloam fell on them—do you think they were more guilty than all the others living in Jerusalem? [5]I tell you, no! But unless you repent, you too will all perish."

[6]Then he told this parable: "A man had a fig tree, planted in his vineyard, and he went to look for fruit on it, but did not find any. [7]So he said to the man who took care of the vineyard, 'For three years now I've been coming to look for fruit on this fig tree and haven't found any. Cut it down! Why should it use up the soil?'

[8]"'Sir,' the man replied, 'leave it alone for one more year, and I'll dig around it and fertilize it. [9]If it bears fruit next year, fine! If not, then cut it down.'"

A Crippled Woman Healed on the Sabbath

[10]On a Sabbath Jesus was teaching in one of the synagogues, [11]and a woman was there who had been crippled by a spirit for eighteen years. She was bent over and could not straighten up at all. [12]When Jesus saw her, he called her forward and said to her, "Woman, you are set free from your infirmity." [13]Then he put his hands on her, and immediately she straightened up and praised God.

[14]Indignant because Jesus had healed on the Sabbath, the synagogue ruler said to the people, "There are six days for work. So come and be healed on those days, not on the Sabbath."

[15]The Lord answered him, "You hypocrites! Doesn't each of you on the Sabbath untie his ox or donkey from the stall and lead it out to give it water? [16]Then should not this woman, a daughter of Abraham, whom Satan has kept bound for eighteen long years, be set free on the Sabbath day from what bound her?"

[17]When he said this, all his opponents were humiliated, but the people were delighted with all the wonderful things he was doing.

The Parables of the Mustard Seed and the Yeast

[18]Then Jesus asked, "What is the kingdom of God like? What shall I compare it to? [19]It is like a mustard seed, which a man took and planted in his garden. It grew and became a tree, and the birds of the air perched in its branches."

MARCH 18

²⁰Again he asked, "What shall I compare the kingdom of God to? ²¹It is like yeast that a woman took and mixed into a large amount*a* of flour until it worked all through the dough."

The Narrow Door

²²Then Jesus went through the towns and villages, teaching as he made his way to Jerusalem. ²³Someone asked him, "Lord, are only a few people going to be saved?"

He said to them, ²⁴"Make every effort to enter through the narrow door, because many, I tell you, will try to enter and will not be able to. ²⁵Once the owner of the house gets up and closes the door, you will stand outside knocking and pleading, 'Sir, open the door for us.'

"But he will answer, 'I don't know you or where you come from.'

²⁶"Then you will say, 'We ate and drank with you, and you taught in our streets.'

²⁷"But he will reply, 'I don't know you or where you come from. Away from me, all you evildoers!'

²⁸"There will be weeping there, and gnashing of teeth, when you see Abraham, Isaac and Jacob and all the prophets in the kingdom of God, but you yourselves thrown out. ²⁹People will come from east and west and north and south, and will take their places at the feast in the kingdom of God. ³⁰Indeed there are those who are last who will be first, and first who will be last."

Jesus' Sorrow for Jerusalem

³¹At that time some Pharisees came to Jesus and said to him, "Leave this place and go somewhere else. Herod wants to kill you."

³²He replied, "Go tell that fox, 'I will drive out demons and heal people today and tomorrow, and on the third day I will reach my goal.' ³³In any case, I must keep going today and tomorrow and the next day — for surely no prophet can die outside Jerusalem!

³⁴"O Jerusalem, Jerusalem, you who kill the prophets and stone those sent to you, how often I have longed to gather your children together, as a hen gathers her chicks under her wings, but you were not willing! ³⁵Look, your house is left to you desolate. I tell you, you will not see me again until you say, 'Blessed is he who comes in the name of the Lord.'*b*"

a21 Greek *three satas* (probably about 1/2 bushel or 22 liters)   *b35* Psalm 118:26

Sticking to the Straight and Narrow

Make every effort to enter through the narrow door, because many, I tell you, will try to enter and will not be able to (Luke 13:24).

Narrow-mindedness is seldom considered a virtue. Yet it's dangerous to be tolerant when the issues are life and death.

Take salvation, for instance. Jesus was narrow-minded about it: "I am the way."

Peter was equally narrow: "Salvation is found in no one else."

And Paul made it clear that the gift of God is eternal life through Jesus Christ our Lord.

John Calvin offers these straight words of warning about broad paths and those who would seek to travel on them.

Walk With John Calvin

"Christ urges his men to enter in by the narrow door. By these words he intended to move his folk away from that foolish curiosity which hinders and complicates.

"Many look around to see whether others are joining them, as if they could only gain salvation in a crowd. But the faithful will not be curious about the crowd of stragglers.

"In this way we avoid our empty hopes letting us down, as if we had imagined that a crowd of companions would help us enter in.

"Many seek for an easy access to life, and constantly indulge themselves. Christ would have his people shake off such soft behavior, for he warns that those will be shut out who devote themselves to any other supposed entrance to life."

Walk Closer to God

Jesus took no public opinion poll to determine the crowd's preference in the matter of salvation.

Rather, he proclaimed the way to God. A narrow way. A way few are finding. A way that allows no alternate routes.

Salvation through Jesus Christ. It may sound like a narrow path. And it is. But when a life is at stake, who could deny that it's better to stick to the straight and narrow path?

So who can you lead to that path today? ⟨⟩

March 19

📖 Walk in the Word
Luke 14

*A dining room table in the home of a Pharisee is the setting for Jesus'
teachings about humility and the danger of missing the Messianic banquet
that is to come.*

Jesus at a Pharisee's House

14 One Sabbath, when Jesus went to eat in the house of a prominent Pharisee, he was being carefully watched. ²There in front of him was a man suffering from dropsy. ³Jesus asked the Pharisees and experts in the law, "Is it lawful to heal on the Sabbath or not?" ⁴But they remained silent. So taking hold of the man, he healed him and sent him away.

⁵Then he asked them, "If one of you has a son*ᵃ* or an ox that falls into a well on the Sabbath day, will you not immediately pull him out?" ⁶And they had nothing to say.

⁷When he noticed how the guests picked the places of honor at the table, he told them this parable: ⁸"When someone invites you to a wedding feast, do not take the place of honor, for a person more distinguished than you may have been invited. ⁹If so, the host who invited both of you will come and say to you, 'Give this man your seat.' Then, humiliated, you will have to take the least important place. ¹⁰But when you are invited, take the lowest place, so that when your host comes, he will say to you, 'Friend, move up to a better place.' Then you will be honored in the presence of all your fellow guests. ¹¹For everyone who exalts himself will be humbled, and he who humbles himself will be exalted."

¹²Then Jesus said to his host, "When you give a luncheon or dinner, do not invite your friends, your brothers or relatives, or your rich neighbors; if you do, they may invite you back and so you will be repaid. ¹³But when you give a banquet, invite the poor, the crippled, the lame, the blind, ¹⁴and you will be blessed. Although they cannot repay you, you will be repaid at the resurrection of the righteous."

The Parable of the Great Banquet

¹⁵When one of those at the table with him heard this, he said to Jesus, "Blessed is the man who will eat at the feast in the kingdom of God."

¹⁶Jesus replied: "A certain man was preparing a great banquet and invited many guests. ¹⁷At the time of the banquet he sent his servant to tell those who had been invited, 'Come, for everything is now ready.'

¹⁸"But they all alike began to make excuses. The first said, 'I have just bought a field, and I must go and see it. Please excuse me.'

¹⁹"Another said, 'I have just bought five yoke of oxen, and I'm on my way to try them out. Please excuse me.'

²⁰"Still another said, 'I just got married, so I can't come.'

²¹"The servant came back and reported this to his master. Then the owner of the house became angry and ordered his servant, 'Go out quickly into the streets and alleys of the town and bring in the poor, the crippled, the blind and the lame.'

MARCH 19

²²" 'Sir,' the servant said, 'what you ordered has been done, but there is still room.'

²³"Then the master told his servant, 'Go out to the roads and country lanes and make them come in, so that my house will be full. ²⁴I tell you, not one of those men who were invited will get a taste of my banquet.' "

The Cost of Being a Disciple

²⁵Large crowds were traveling with Jesus, and turning to them he said: ²⁶"If anyone comes to me and does not hate his father and mother, his wife and children, his brothers and sisters—yes, even his own life—he cannot be my disciple. ²⁷And anyone who does not carry his cross and follow me cannot be my disciple.

²⁸"Suppose one of you wants to build a tower. Will he not first sit down and estimate the cost to see if he has enough money to complete it? ²⁹For if he lays the foundation and is not able to finish it, everyone who sees it will ridicule him, ³⁰saying, 'This fellow began to build and was not able to finish.'

³¹"Or suppose a king is about to go to war against another king. Will he not first sit down and consider whether he is able with ten thousand men to oppose the one coming against him with twenty thousand? ³²If he is not able, he will send a delegation while the other is still a long way off and will ask for terms of peace. ³³In the same way, any of you who does not give up everything he has cannot be my disciple.

³⁴"Salt is good, but if it loses its saltiness, how can it be made salty again? ³⁵It is fit neither for the soil nor for the manure pile; it is thrown out.

"He who has ears to hear, let him hear."

ᵃ5 Some manuscripts donkey

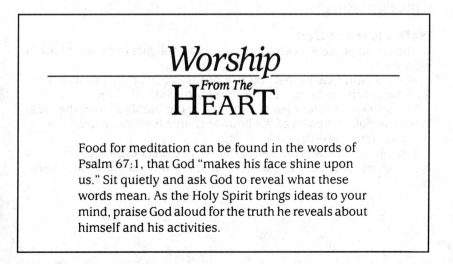

Worship
From The
HEART

Food for meditation can be found in the words of Psalm 67:1, that God "makes his face shine upon us." Sit quietly and ask God to reveal what these words mean. As the Holy Spirit brings ideas to your mind, praise God aloud for the truth he reveals about himself and his activities.

MARCH 19

The Path to Nowhere in the Kingdom of God

For everyone who exalts himself will be humbled, and he who humbles himself will be exalted (Luke 14:11).

Can you imagine an awards presentation honoring the "Servant of the Year" . . . sponsored by the one receiving the award?

Humility and horn blowing. They simply don't mix, according to Jesus in Luke 14.

The servant who seeks to shine the spotlight of recognition on his own achievements has forgotten an important truth.

Promotion in the business of heaven is based on sacrifice for others—not superiority over others, as A.W. Tozer explains.

Walk With A.W. Tozer

"Watch out for the danger of arrogance in assuming that you are somebody indeed.

"The Lord will remind you of his own example, and will rebuke and chasten you in his own way.

"The Lord had no hired servants. He bossed no one around, and he never took a tyrannical attitude toward anyone. He never allowed any success or temporary honor to lead him astray.

"I think it is very good spiritual advice that we should never tie ourselves up to public opinion and never consider any honors we may receive as being due us because of our superior gifts.

"Early church fathers wrote that if a man feels he is getting somewhere in the kingdom of God, that's pride. And until that dies, he is getting nowhere!"

Walk Closer to God

The world applauds celebrities; but God delights in exalting faithful servants.

Self-acclaim may propel you to a position of worldly prominence— for a time. But the honor it brings is short-lived.

By contrast, consider Jesus' example in the humiliation of the cross. What the public viewed as his hour of shame became instead the occasion for his exaltation.

It might not make good earthly sense to expect exaltation to follow humiliation. But in the kingdom of God, the way up has always been down! ◖

MARCH 20

📖 Walk in the Word
Luke 15

Luke's version of three important parables spotlights God's joy at receiving back what was lost, in contrast to the exclusive attitude of the Pharisees.

The Parable of the Lost Sheep

15 Now the tax collectors and "sinners" were all gathering around to hear him. ²But the Pharisees and the teachers of the law muttered, "This man welcomes sinners and eats with them."

³Then Jesus told them this parable: ⁴"Suppose one of you has a hundred sheep and loses one of them. Does he not leave the ninety-nine in the open country and go after the lost sheep until he finds it? ⁵And when he finds it, he joyfully puts it on his shoulders ⁶and goes home. Then he calls his friends and neighbors together and says, 'Rejoice with me; I have found my lost sheep.' ⁷I tell you that in the same way there will be more rejoicing in heaven over one sinner who repents than over ninety-nine righteous persons who do not need to repent.

The Parable of the Lost Coin

⁸"Or suppose a woman has ten silver coins*a* and loses one. Does she not light a lamp, sweep the house and search carefully until she finds it? ⁹And when she finds it, she calls her friends and neighbors together and says, 'Rejoice with me; I have found my lost coin.' ¹⁰In the same way, I tell you, there is rejoicing in the presence of the angels of God over one sinner who repents."

The Parable of the Lost Son

¹¹Jesus continued: "There was a man who had two sons. ¹²The younger one said to his father, 'Father, give me my share of the estate.' So he divided his property between them.

¹³"Not long after that, the younger son got together all he had, set off for a distant country and there squandered his wealth in wild living. ¹⁴After he had spent everything, there was a severe famine in that whole country, and he began to be in need. ¹⁵So he went and hired himself out to a citizen of that country, who sent him to his fields to feed pigs. ¹⁶He longed to fill his stomach with the pods that the pigs were eating, but no one gave him anything.

¹⁷"When he came to his senses, he said, 'How many of my father's hired men have food to spare, and here I am starving to death! ¹⁸I will set out and go back to my father and say to him: Father, I have sinned against heaven and against you. ¹⁹I am no longer worthy to be called your son; make me like one of your hired men.' ²⁰So he got up and went to his father.

"But while he was still a long way off, his father saw him and was filled with compassion for him; he ran to his son, threw his arms around him and kissed him.

²¹"The son said to him, 'Father, I have sinned against heaven and against you. I am no longer worthy to be called your son.*b*'

239

March 20

²²"But the father said to his servants, 'Quick! Bring the best robe and put it on him. Put a ring on his finger and sandals on his feet. ²³Bring the fattened calf and kill it. Let's have a feast and celebrate. ²⁴For this son of mine was dead and is alive again; he was lost and is found.' So they began to celebrate.

²⁵"Meanwhile, the older son was in the field. When he came near the house, he heard music and dancing. ²⁶So he called one of the servants and asked him what was going on. ²⁷'Your brother has come,' he replied, 'and your father has killed the fattened calf because he has him back safe and sound.'

²⁸"The older brother became angry and refused to go in. So his father went out and pleaded with him. ²⁹But he answered his father, 'Look! All these years I've been slaving for you and never disobeyed your orders. Yet you never gave me even a young goat so I could celebrate with my friends. ³⁰But when this son of yours who has squandered your property with prostitutes comes home, you kill the fattened calf for him!'

³¹" 'My son,' the father said, 'you are always with me, and everything I have is yours. ³²But we had to celebrate and be glad, because this brother of yours was dead and is alive again; he was lost and is found.' "

a8 Greek ten drachmas, each worth about a day's wages   b21 Some early manuscripts son. Make me like one of your hired men.

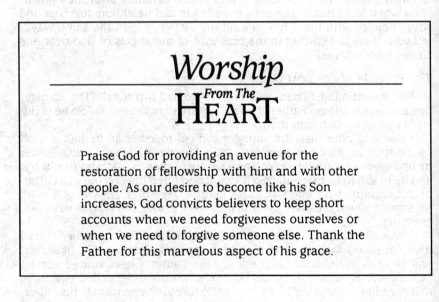

Worship
From The
Heart

Praise God for providing an avenue for the restoration of fellowship with him and with other people. As our desire to become like his Son increases, God convicts believers to keep short accounts when we need forgiveness ourselves or when we need to forgive someone else. Thank the Father for this marvelous aspect of his grace.

Finding Forgiveness in the Father's Heart

> I will set out and go back to my father and say to him: Father, I have sinned against heaven and against you (Luke 15:18).

Confession. Forgiveness. Inseparable halves of the same cleansing transaction. But it takes two willing hearts, as the lost son discovered.

Mired in the pigpen, he came to his senses and began the long trip home to his waiting father—a father only too willing to forgive.

Confession. It's good for the soul and a whole lot more, as Charles Spurgeon notes.

Walk With Charles Spurgeon

"The grace of God in the heart teaches us that we, as Christians, own the duty of confession to our heavenly Father. We daily offend, and ought not to rest without daily pardon.

"If I have not sought forgiveness and been washed from the offenses against my Father, I shall feel like the prodigal, who, though still a child, was yet far off from his father.

"But if I go to him with a child's sorrow at offending so gracious and loving a parent, and tell him all, and do not rest until I realize that I am forgiven, then I shall feel a holy love for my Father. I shall enjoy peace with God through Jesus Christ my Lord.

"There is a wide distinction between confessing sin as a culprit and confessing sin as a child. The Father's bosom is the place for sorrowful confessions and for cleansing from the daily defilement of our daily walk."

Walk Closer to God

The lost son must have wondered what reception awaited him:

"I told you so . . . Get out and stay out . . . You're no longer my son."

But his fears were unfounded.

While the son was still far off, his father ran to embrace him.

Nothing is as tragic as a son or daughter unwilling to confess . . . unless it is a parent unwilling to forgive. But the child of God never needs to fear what coming home to the heavenly Father will bring. ◖

March 21

📖 Walk in the Word
Luke 16

Jesus continues teaching in parables, here making his point with stories about a shrewd manager and about a rich man and a beggar.

The Parable of the Shrewd Manager

16 Jesus told his disciples: "There was a rich man whose manager was accused of wasting his possessions. ²So he called him in and asked him, 'What is this I hear about you? Give an account of your management, because you cannot be manager any longer.'

³"The manager said to himself, 'What shall I do now? My master is taking away my job. I'm not strong enough to dig, and I'm ashamed to beg— ⁴I know what I'll do so that, when I lose my job here, people will welcome me into their houses.'

⁵"So he called in each one of his master's debtors. He asked the first, 'How much do you owe my master?'

⁶" 'Eight hundred gallons*a* of olive oil,' he replied.

"The manager told him, 'Take your bill, sit down quickly, and make it four hundred.'

⁷"Then he asked the second, 'And how much do you owe?'

" 'A thousand bushels*b* of wheat,' he replied.

"He told him, 'Take your bill and make it eight hundred.'

⁸"The master commended the dishonest manager because he had acted shrewdly. For the people of this world are more shrewd in dealing with their own kind than are the people of the light. ⁹I tell you, use worldly wealth to gain friends for yourselves, so that when it is gone, you will be welcomed into eternal dwellings.

¹⁰"Whoever can be trusted with very little can also be trusted with much, and whoever is dishonest with very little will also be dishonest with much. ¹¹So if you have not been trustworthy in handling worldly wealth, who will trust you with true riches? ¹²And if you have not been trustworthy with someone else's property, who will give you property of your own?

¹³"No servant can serve two masters. Either he will hate the one and love the other, or he will be devoted to the one and despise the other. You cannot serve both God and Money."

¹⁴The Pharisees, who loved money, heard all this and were sneering at Jesus. ¹⁵He said to them, "You are the ones who justify yourselves in the eyes of men, but God knows your hearts. What is highly valued among men is detestable in God's sight.

Additional Teachings

¹⁶"The Law and the Prophets were proclaimed until John. Since that time, the good news of the kingdom of God is being preached, and everyone is forcing his way into it. ¹⁷It is easier for heaven and earth to disappear than for the least stroke of a pen to drop out of the Law.

¹⁸"Anyone who divorces his wife and marries another woman commits adultery, and the man who marries a divorced woman commits adultery.

MARCH 21

The Rich Man and Lazarus

¹⁹"There was a rich man who was dressed in purple and fine linen and lived in luxury every day. ²⁰At his gate was laid a beggar named Lazarus, covered with sores ²¹and longing to eat what fell from the rich man's table. Even the dogs came and licked his sores.

²²"The time came when the beggar died and the angels carried him to Abraham's side. The rich man also died and was buried. ²³In hell,ᶜ where he was in torment, he looked up and saw Abraham far away, with Lazarus by his side. ²⁴So he called to him, 'Father Abraham, have pity on me and send Lazarus to dip the tip of his finger in water and cool my tongue, because I am in agony in this fire.'

²⁵"But Abraham replied, 'Son, remember that in your lifetime you received your good things, while Lazarus received bad things, but now he is comforted here and you are in agony. ²⁶And besides all this, between us and you a great chasm has been fixed, so that those who want to go from here to you cannot, nor can anyone cross over from there to us.'

²⁷"He answered, 'Then I beg you, father, send Lazarus to my father's house, ²⁸for I have five brothers. Let him warn them, so that they will not also come to this place of torment.'

²⁹"Abraham replied, 'They have Moses and the Prophets; let them listen to them.'

³⁰" 'No, father Abraham,' he said, 'but if someone from the dead goes to them, they will repent.'

³¹"He said to him, 'If they do not listen to Moses and the Prophets, they will not be convinced even if someone rises from the dead.' "

ᵃ6 Greek *one hundred batous* (probably about 3 kiloliters)   ᵇ7 Greek *one hundred korous* (probably about 35 kiloliters)   ᶜ23 Greek *Hades*

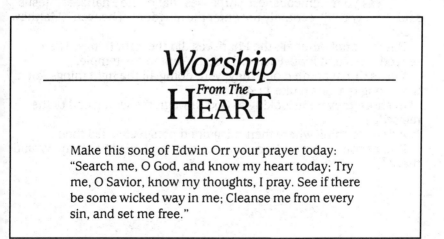

Worship
H<small>From The</small>EART

Make this song of Edwin Orr your prayer today: "Search me, O God, and know my heart today; Try me, O Savior, know my thoughts, I pray. See if there be some wicked way in me; Cleanse me from every sin, and set me free."

MARCH 21

Working Hard at Doing Nothing

The Pharisees, who loved money . . . were sneering at Jesus. He said to them, "You are the ones who justify yourselves in the eyes of men, but God knows your hearts" (Luke 16:14–15).

A telescope is helpful for studying the moon—if you look through the right end. But turn it around and the perspective becomes distorted.

In Luke 16 Jesus challenges the perspective of the Pharisees in their relationship with God. Charles Finney analyzes their wrong-ended perspective on righteous living.

Walk With Charles Finney

"Many professing Christians judge themselves falsely because they judge by a false standard.

"Like the Pharisees, they employ a merely negative standard.

"Suppose someone lets a house burn down and makes no effort to save it or its occupants. They hope not to be judged harshly, since they did not set the house on fire. They only let it alone.

"All they did was do nothing.

"That is all many persons plead as their religious duty. They do nothing to pluck sinners out of the fire, and they seem to think theirs is a very commendable religion.

"Such was the religion of the Pharisees.

"But was this the religion of Jesus or Paul?"

Walk Closer to God

"Unless your righteousness surpasses that of the Pharisees," Jesus said, ". . . you will certainly not enter the kingdom of heaven" (Matthew 5:20).

Harsh words. After all, the Pharisees did the right things. They prayed often and long. Fasted. Tithed. Went to the temple.

But as Christ pointed out, they were doing all the right things, for all the wrong reasons (Luke 11:42).

In short, they were looking at God through the wrong end of the telescope.

It's sad to think where their misguided perspective led them.

But, of course, no one would make that fatal mistake today. Would they?

MARCH 22

📖 Walk in the Word
Luke 17

Luke places his account of the healing of ten men with leprosy between Jesus' teachings about kingdom standards and prophecies.

Sin, Faith, Duty

17 Jesus said to his disciples: "Things that cause people to sin are bound to come, but woe to that person through whom they come. ²It would be better for him to be thrown into the sea with a millstone tied around his neck than for him to cause one of these little ones to sin. ³So watch yourselves.

"If your brother sins, rebuke him, and if he repents, forgive him. ⁴If he sins against you seven times in a day, and seven times comes back to you and says, 'I repent,' forgive him."

⁵The apostles said to the Lord, "Increase our faith!"

⁶He replied, "If you have faith as small as a mustard seed, you can say to this mulberry tree, 'Be uprooted and planted in the sea,' and it will obey you.

⁷"Suppose one of you had a servant plowing or looking after the sheep. Would he say to the servant when he comes in from the field, 'Come along now and sit down to eat'? ⁸Would he not rather say, 'Prepare my supper, get yourself ready and wait on me while I eat and drink; after that you may eat and drink'? ⁹Would he thank the servant because he did what he was told to do? ¹⁰So you also, when you have done everything you were told to do, should say, 'We are unworthy servants; we have only done our duty.' "

Ten Healed of Leprosy

¹¹Now on his way to Jerusalem, Jesus traveled along the border between Samaria and Galilee. ¹²As he was going into a village, ten men who had leprosy*a* met him. They stood at a distance ¹³and called out in a loud voice, "Jesus, Master, have pity on us!"

¹⁴When he saw them, he said, "Go, show yourselves to the priests." And as they went, they were cleansed.

¹⁵One of them, when he saw he was healed, came back, praising God in a loud voice. ¹⁶He threw himself at Jesus' feet and thanked him — and he was a Samaritan.

¹⁷Jesus asked, "Were not all ten cleansed? Where are the other nine? ¹⁸Was no one found to return and give praise to God except this foreigner?" ¹⁹Then he said to him, "Rise and go; your faith has made you well."

The Coming of the Kingdom of God

²⁰Once, having been asked by the Pharisees when the kingdom of God would come, Jesus replied, "The kingdom of God does not come with your careful observation, ²¹nor will people say, 'Here it is,' or 'There it is,' because the kingdom of God is within*b* you."

²²Then he said to his disciples, "The time is coming when you will long

March 22

to see one of the days of the Son of Man, but you will not see it. ²³Men will tell you, 'There he is!' or 'Here he is!' Do not go running off after them. ²⁴For the Son of Man in his day*c* will be like the lightning, which flashes and lights up the sky from one end to the other. ²⁵But first he must suffer many things and be rejected by this generation.

²⁶"Just as it was in the days of Noah, so also will it be in the days of the Son of Man. ²⁷People were eating, drinking, marrying and being given in marriage up to the day Noah entered the ark. Then the flood came and destroyed them all.

²⁸"It was the same in the days of Lot. People were eating and drinking, buying and selling, planting and building. ²⁹But the day Lot left Sodom, fire and sulfur rained down from heaven and destroyed them all.

³⁰"It will be just like this on the day the Son of Man is revealed. ³¹On that day no one who is on the roof of his house, with his goods inside, should go down to get them. Likewise, no one in the field should go back for anything. ³²Remember Lot's wife! ³³Whoever tries to keep his life will lose it, and whoever loses his life will preserve it. ³⁴I tell you, on that night two people will be in one bed; one will be taken and the other left. ³⁵Two women will be grinding grain together; one will be taken and the other left.*d*"

³⁷"Where, Lord?" they asked.

He replied, "Where there is a dead body, there the vultures will gather."

a12 The Greek word was used for various diseases affecting the skin—not necessarily leprosy. b21 Or among   c24 Some manuscripts do not have in his day.   d35 Some manuscripts left. 36Two men will be in the field; one will be taken and the other left.

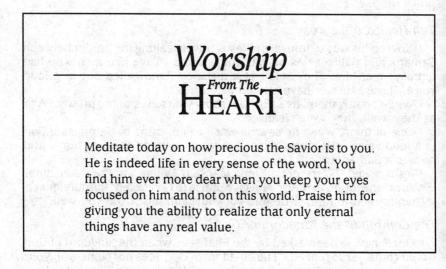

Worship
From The
Heart

Meditate today on how precious the Savior is to you.
He is indeed life in every sense of the word. You
find him ever more dear when you keep your eyes
focused on him and not on this world. Praise him for
giving you the ability to realize that only eternal
things have any real value.

The Message of a Monumental Mistake

Remember Lot's wife! Whoever tries to keep his life will lose it, and whoever loses his life will preserve it (Luke 17:32–33).

Nostalgia. It's usually a harmless pastime of fond reflection on the good old days.

But for Lot's wife, the old way of life cost her more than she bargained for and turned out to be dearer than life itself.

In chapter 17 Jesus strongly rebuked those who, after coming to him, looked back fondly on their former way of life.

Jonathan Edwards probes Mrs. Lot's attraction to Sodom's lifestyle . . . and its tragic consequences.

Walk With Jonathan Edwards

"All the enjoyments of Sodom will soon be burned. As it is with all the enjoyments of sin, they are all appointed to the fire. And surely it is not worthwhile to look back upon the things that are perishing.

"Lot's wife looked back because she remembered the pleasant things she left in Sodom.

"So it is very often with some Christians. But when they look back, they put themselves under vast disadvantages. They dreadfully harden their own hearts and stupefy their souls by quenching the Spirit of God.

"They make way for discouragements. They give Satan great advantage to ruin them. Their souls presently become hard like the body of Lot's wife.

"And though they live long after, they never get much further."

Walk Closer to God

The call to discipleship is a call to new life. Looking back means something in your old life is of greater value to you than your new life in Jesus Christ. Looking back allows momentary pleasures to compete with the eternal Savior.

God desires your undivided attention and devotion—a truth Lot's wife learned the hard way, and too late.

Don't miss the message of her disastrous and monumental mistake. Looking back can be hazardous to your health!

MARCH 23

Walk in the Word
Luke 18

After retelling two more of Jesus' parables, Luke describes scenes of Jesus and little children, Jesus and a rich ruler, Jesus and his disciples, and Jesus and a blind beggar.

The Parable of the Persistent Widow

18 Then Jesus told his disciples a parable to show them that they should always pray and not give up. ²He said: "In a certain town there was a judge who neither feared God nor cared about men. ³And there was a widow in that town who kept coming to him with the plea, 'Grant me justice against my adversary.'

⁴"For some time he refused. But finally he said to himself, 'Even though I don't fear God or care about men, ⁵yet because this widow keeps bothering me, I will see that she gets justice, so that she won't eventually wear me out with her coming!' "

⁶And the Lord said, "Listen to what the unjust judge says. ⁷And will not God bring about justice for his chosen ones, who cry out to him day and night? Will he keep putting them off? ⁸I tell you, he will see that they get justice, and quickly. However, when the Son of Man comes, will he find faith on the earth?"

The Parable of the Pharisee and the Tax Collector

⁹To some who were confident of their own righteousness and looked down on everybody else, Jesus told this parable: ¹⁰"Two men went up to the temple to pray, one a Pharisee and the other a tax collector. ¹¹The Pharisee stood up and prayed about*ᵃ* himself: 'God, I thank you that I am not like other men — robbers, evildoers, adulterers — or even like this tax collector. ¹²I fast twice a week and give a tenth of all I get.'

¹³"But the tax collector stood at a distance. He would not even look up to heaven, but beat his breast and said, 'God, have mercy on me, a sinner.'

¹⁴"I tell you that this man, rather than the other, went home justified before God. For everyone who exalts himself will be humbled, and he who humbles himself will be exalted."

The Little Children and Jesus

¹⁵People were also bringing babies to Jesus to have him touch them. When the disciples saw this, they rebuked them. ¹⁶But Jesus called the children to him and said, "Let the little children come to me, and do not hinder them, for the kingdom of God belongs to such as these. ¹⁷I tell you the truth, anyone who will not receive the kingdom of God like a little child will never enter it."

The Rich Ruler

¹⁸A certain ruler asked him, "Good teacher, what must I do to inherit eternal life?"

19"Why do you call me good?" Jesus answered. "No one is good — except God alone. 20You know the commandments: 'Do not commit adultery, do not murder, do not steal, do not give false testimony, honor your father and mother.'*b*"

21"All these I have kept since I was a boy," he said.

22When Jesus heard this, he said to him, "You still lack one thing. Sell everything you have and give to the poor, and you will have treasure in heaven. Then come, follow me."

23When he heard this, he became very sad, because he was a man of great wealth. 24Jesus looked at him and said, "How hard it is for the rich to enter the kingdom of God! 25Indeed, it is easier for a camel to go through the eye of a needle than for a rich man to enter the kingdom of God."

26Those who heard this asked, "Who then can be saved?"

27Jesus replied, "What is impossible with men is possible with God."

28Peter said to him, "We have left all we had to follow you!"

29"I tell you the truth," Jesus said to them, "no one who has left home or wife or brothers or parents or children for the sake of the kingdom of God 30will fail to receive many times as much in this age and, in the age to come, eternal life."

Jesus Again Predicts His Death

31Jesus took the Twelve aside and told them, "We are going up to Jerusalem, and everything that is written by the prophets about the Son of Man will be fulfilled. 32He will be handed over to the Gentiles. They will mock him, insult him, spit on him, flog him and kill him. 33On the third day he will rise again."

34The disciples did not understand any of this. Its meaning was hidden from them, and they did not know what he was talking about.

A Blind Beggar Receives His Sight

35As Jesus approached Jericho, a blind man was sitting by the roadside begging. 36When he heard the crowd going by, he asked what was happening. 37They told him, "Jesus of Nazareth is passing by."

38He called out, "Jesus, Son of David, have mercy on me!"

39Those who led the way rebuked him and told him to be quiet, but he shouted all the more, "Son of David, have mercy on me!"

40Jesus stopped and ordered the man to be brought to him. When he came near, Jesus asked him, 41"What do you want me to do for you?"

"Lord, I want to see," he replied.

42Jesus said to him, "Receive your sight; your faith has healed you." 43Immediately he received his sight and followed Jesus, praising God. When all the people saw it, they also praised God.

a11 Or *to*   *b20* Exodus 20:12-16; Deut. 5:16-20

249

MARCH 23

A Heart in Tune With the Heartbeat of God

Then Jesus told his disciples a parable to show them that they should always pray and not give up (Luke 18:1).

Doctors can learn a lot about their patients by listening to their heartbeats. It's an important barometer of health, even when everything else appears normal.

The same could be said of the spiritual health of the Christian. Outwardly, things may seem fine. But the health of the inner life is crucial. The heartbeat must be strong to know God.

Physically weak, David Brainerd possessed a vibrant spiritual health. The words of his diary reveal the powerful, prayerful beating of a heart strong for God.

Walk With David Brainerd

"I withdrew to my usual place of retirement, in great tranquility. I knew only to breathe out my desire for a perfect conformity to him in all things.

"God was so precious that the world with all its enjoyments seemed infinitely vile. I had no more desire for the favor of men than for pebbles.

"At noon I had the most ardent longings after God which I ever felt in my life.

"In my secret retirement, I could do nothing but tell my dear Lord in a sweet calmness that he knew I desired nothing but him, nothing but holiness, that he had given me these desires and he only could give the thing desired.

"I never seemed to be so unhinged from myself, and to be so wholly devoted to God.

"My heart was swallowed up in God most of the day."

Walk Closer to God

"Father, make my heart strong to know you.

"Where my heartbeat is faint, fortify it with your Word.

"Where it is erratic, stabilize it with your faithful promises.

"Great Physician, give me a heart like David Brainerd's. A heart that will not rest till it finds its rest in you. Amen."

MARCH 24

Walk in the Word
Luke 19

A tax collector meets Jesus in a life-changing encounter, a parable about faithfulness is recounted, and Jesus' entry into Jerusalem is recorded in Luke's ongoing story of the life of Jesus.

Zacchaeus the Tax Collector

19 Jesus entered Jericho and was passing through. ²A man was there by the name of Zacchaeus; he was a chief tax collector and was wealthy. ³He wanted to see who Jesus was, but being a short man he could not, because of the crowd. ⁴So he ran ahead and climbed a sycamore-fig tree to see him, since Jesus was coming that way.

⁵When Jesus reached the spot, he looked up and said to him, "Zacchaeus, come down immediately. I must stay at your house today." ⁶So he came down at once and welcomed him gladly.

⁷All the people saw this and began to mutter, "He has gone to be the guest of a 'sinner.' "

⁸But Zacchaeus stood up and said to the Lord, "Look, Lord! Here and now I give half of my possessions to the poor, and if I have cheated anybody out of anything, I will pay back four times the amount."

⁹Jesus said to him, "Today salvation has come to this house, because this man, too, is a son of Abraham. ¹⁰For the Son of Man came to seek and to save what was lost."

The Parable of the Ten Minas

¹¹While they were listening to this, he went on to tell them a parable, because he was near Jerusalem and the people thought that the kingdom of God was going to appear at once. ¹²He said: "A man of noble birth went to a distant country to have himself appointed king and then to return. ¹³So he called ten of his servants and gave them ten minas.ª 'Put this money to work,' he said, 'until I come back.'

¹⁴"But his subjects hated him and sent a delegation after him to say, 'We don't want this man to be our king.'

¹⁵"He was made king, however, and returned home. Then he sent for the servants to whom he had given the money, in order to find out what they had gained with it.

¹⁶"The first one came and said, 'Sir, your mina has earned ten more.'

¹⁷" 'Well done, my good servant!' his master replied. 'Because you have been trustworthy in a very small matter, take charge of ten cities.'

¹⁸"The second came and said, 'Sir, your mina has earned five more.'

¹⁹"His master answered, 'You take charge of five cities.'

²⁰"Then another servant came and said, 'Sir, here is your mina; I have kept it laid away in a piece of cloth. ²¹I was afraid of you, because you are a hard man. You take out what you did not put in and reap what you did not sow.'

²²"His master replied, 'I will judge you by your own words, you wicked servant! You knew, did you, that I am a hard man, taking out what I did

MARCH 24

not put in, and reaping what I did not sow? 23Why then didn't you put my money on deposit, so that when I came back, I could have collected it with interest?'

24"Then he said to those standing by, 'Take his mina away from him and give it to the one who has ten minas.'

25" 'Sir,' they said, 'he already has ten!'

26"He replied, 'I tell you that to everyone who has, more will be given, but as for the one who has nothing, even what he has will be taken away. 27But those enemies of mine who did not want me to be king over them— bring them here and kill them in front of me.' "

The Triumphal Entry

28After Jesus had said this, he went on ahead, going up to Jerusalem. 29As he approached Bethphage and Bethany at the hill called the Mount of Olives, he sent two of his disciples, saying to them, 30"Go to the village ahead of you, and as you enter it, you will find a colt tied there, which no one has ever ridden. Untie it and bring it here. 31If anyone asks you, 'Why are you untying it?' tell him, 'The Lord needs it.' "

32Those who were sent ahead went and found it just as he had told them. 33As they were untying the colt, its owners asked them, "Why are you untying the colt?"

34They replied, "The Lord needs it."

35They brought it to Jesus, threw their cloaks on the colt and put Jesus on it. 36As he went along, people spread their cloaks on the road.

37When he came near the place where the road goes down the Mount of Olives, the whole crowd of disciples began joyfully to praise God in loud voices for all the miracles they had seen:

> 38"Blessed is the king who comes in the name of the
> Lord!"b
>
> "Peace in heaven and glory in the highest!"

39Some of the Pharisees in the crowd said to Jesus, "Teacher, rebuke your disciples!"

40"I tell you," he replied, "if they keep quiet, the stones will cry out."

41As he approached Jerusalem and saw the city, he wept over it 42and said, "If you, even you, had only known on this day what would bring you peace—but now it is hidden from your eyes. 43The days will come upon you when your enemies will build an embankment against you and encircle you and hem you in on every side. 44They will dash you to the ground, you and the children within your walls. They will not leave one stone on another, because you did not recognize the time of God's coming to you."

Jesus at the Temple

45Then he entered the temple area and began driving out those who were selling. 46"It is written," he said to them, " 'My house will be a house of prayer'c; but you have made it 'a den of robbers.'d "

252

MARCH 24

⁴⁷Every day he was teaching at the temple. But the chief priests, the teachers of the law and the leaders among the people were trying to kill him. ⁴⁸Yet they could not find any way to do it, because all the people hung on his words.

ª13 A mina was about three months' wages.   *ᵇ38* Psalm 118:26   *ᶜ46* Isaiah 56:7
ᵈ46 Jer. 7:11

PSALM 72

Of Solomon.

Endow the king with your justice, O God,
   the royal son with your righteousness.
²He will*ª* judge your people in righteousness,
   your afflicted ones with justice.
³The mountains will bring prosperity to the people,
   the hills the fruit of righteousness.
⁴He will defend the afflicted among the people
   and save the children of the needy;
   he will crush the oppressor.

⁵He will endure*ᵇ* as long as the sun,
   as long as the moon, through all generations.
⁶He will be like rain falling on a mown field,
   like showers watering the earth.
⁷In his days the righteous will flourish;
   prosperity will abound till the moon is no more.

ª2 Or *May he*; similarly in verses 3-11 and 17   *ᵇ5* Septuagint; Hebrew *You will be feared*

MARCH 24

Small Beginnings, Eternal Endings

For the Son of Man came to seek and to save what was lost (Luke 19:10).

Tax collectors have never been popular. In Jesus' day, the publicans were Jews who collected taxes for the Roman government. Their countrymen thought them traitorous and corrupt.

Zaccheus was one such publican, small in physical stature, and smaller in the eyes of his countrymen because of his loathsome job.

However, Jesus saw in Zaccheus what other people missed: a curiosity for the things of God.

And as J.C. Ryle comments, God often works in small ways to accomplish great things.

Walk With J.C. Ryle

"The ways by which the Holy Spirit leads men and women to Christ are wonderful and mysterious. He is often beginning in a heart a work which shall stand for eternity, when an onlooker observes nothing remarkable.

"In every work there must be a beginning, and in spiritual work that beginning is often very small.

"Do we see a careless brother coming to church and listening to the gospel after a long indifference? When we see such things, let us remember Zaccheus.

"Let us not look coldly on such a person because his motives are at present very poor and questionable. It is far better to hear the gospel out of curiosity than not to hear it at all.

"Our brother is with Zaccheus in the tree! Who can tell but that he may one day receive Christ as joyfully?"

Walk Closer to God

It may be difficult to see how salvation can result from a man climbing a tree.

That's because you see a man in a tree, but God sees a man lost and searching.

Before you write off a Zaccheus near you, take another look—this time through the eyes of the Son of Man.

Those whom the world would label "little" have a way of appearing much larger when seen from the perspective of the seeking Savior. ◯

MARCH 25

📖 Walk in the Word
Luke 20

Luke skillfully captures the emotion of a long day of controversy during Jesus' last week as the religious leaders turn up the heat in an all-out effort to trap Jesus.

The Authority of Jesus Questioned

20 One day as he was teaching the people in the temple courts and preaching the gospel, the chief priests and the teachers of the law, together with the elders, came up to him. ²"Tell us by what authority you are doing these things," they said. "Who gave you this authority?"

³He replied, "I will also ask you a question. Tell me, ⁴John's baptism — was it from heaven, or from men?"

⁵They discussed it among themselves and said, "If we say, 'From heaven,' he will ask, 'Why didn't you believe him?' ⁶But if we say, 'From men,' all the people will stone us, because they are persuaded that John was a prophet."

⁷So they answered, "We don't know where it was from."

⁸Jesus said, "Neither will I tell you by what authority I am doing these things."

The Parable of the Tenants

⁹He went on to tell the people this parable: "A man planted a vineyard, rented it to some farmers and went away for a long time. ¹⁰At harvest time he sent a servant to the tenants so they would give him some of the fruit of the vineyard. But the tenants beat him and sent him away empty-handed. ¹¹He sent another servant, but that one also they beat and treated shamefully and sent away empty-handed. ¹²He sent still a third, and they wounded him and threw him out.

¹³"Then the owner of the vineyard said, 'What shall I do? I will send my son, whom I love; perhaps they will respect him.'

¹⁴"But when the tenants saw him, they talked the matter over. 'This is the heir,' they said. 'Let's kill him, and the inheritance will be ours.' ¹⁵So they threw him out of the vineyard and killed him.

"What then will the owner of the vineyard do to them? ¹⁶He will come and kill those tenants and give the vineyard to others."

When the people heard this, they said, "May this never be!"

¹⁷Jesus looked directly at them and asked, "Then what is the meaning of that which is written:

> " 'The stone the builders rejected
> has become the capstone[a]'[b]?

¹⁸Everyone who falls on that stone will be broken to pieces, but he on whom it falls will be crushed."

¹⁹The teachers of the law and the chief priests looked for a way to arrest him immediately, because they knew he had spoken this parable against them. But they were afraid of the people.

MARCH 25

Paying Taxes to Caesar

[20]Keeping a close watch on him, they sent spies, who pretended to be honest. They hoped to catch Jesus in something he said so that they might hand him over to the power and authority of the governor. [21]So the spies questioned him: "Teacher, we know that you speak and teach what is right, and that you do not show partiality but teach the way of God in accordance with the truth. [22]Is it right for us to pay taxes to Caesar or not?"

[23]He saw through their duplicity and said to them, [24]"Show me a denarius. Whose portrait and inscription are on it?"

[25]"Caesar's," they replied.

He said to them, "Then give to Caesar what is Caesar's, and to God what is God's."

[26]They were unable to trap him in what he had said there in public. And astonished by his answer, they became silent.

The Resurrection and Marriage

[27]Some of the Sadducees, who say there is no resurrection, came to Jesus with a question. [28]"Teacher," they said, "Moses wrote for us that if a man's brother dies and leaves a wife but no children, the man must marry the widow and have children for his brother. [29]Now there were seven brothers. The first one married a woman and died childless. [30]The second [31]and then the third married her, and in the same way the seven died, leaving no children. [32]Finally, the woman died too. [33]Now then, at the resurrection whose wife will she be, since the seven were married to her?"

[34]Jesus replied, "The people of this age marry and are given in marriage. [35]But those who are considered worthy of taking part in that age and in the resurrection from the dead will neither marry nor be given in marriage, [36]and they can no longer die; for they are like the angels. They are God's children, since they are children of the resurrection. [37]But in the account of the bush, even Moses showed that the dead rise, for he calls the Lord 'the God of Abraham, and the God of Isaac, and the God of Jacob.'[c] [38]He is not the God of the dead, but of the living, for to him all are alive."

[39]Some of the teachers of the law responded, "Well said, teacher!" [40]And no one dared to ask him any more questions.

Whose Son Is the Christ?

[41]Then Jesus said to them, "How is it that they say the Christ[d] is the Son of David? [42]David himself declares in the Book of Psalms:

> " 'The Lord said to my Lord:
> "Sit at my right hand
> [43]until I make your enemies
> a footstool for your feet." '[e]

[44]David calls him 'Lord.' How then can he be his son?"

[45]While all the people were listening, Jesus said to his disciples, [46]"Beware of the teachers of the law. They like to walk around in flowing robes

and love to be greeted in the marketplaces and have the most important seats in the synagogues and the places of honor at banquets. 47They devour widows' houses and for a show make lengthy prayers. Such men will be punished most severely."

a17 Or *cornerstone*   *b17* Psalm 118:22   *c37* Exodus 3:6   *d41* Or *Messiah*
e43 Psalm 110:1

PSALM 71

But as for me, I will always have hope;
　　I will praise you more and more.
15My mouth will tell of your righteousness,
　　of your salvation all day long,
　　though I know not its measure.
16I will come and proclaim your mighty acts, O Sovereign
　　Lord;
　　I will proclaim your righteousness, yours alone.
17Since my youth, O God, you have taught me,
　　and to this day I declare your marvelous deeds.
18Even when I am old and gray,
　　do not forsake me, O God,
　till I declare your power to the next generation,
　　your might to all who are to come.

19Your righteousness reaches to the skies, O God,
　　you who have done great things.
　　Who, O God, is like you?
20Though you have made me see troubles, many and
　　　bitter,
　　you will restore my life again;
　from the depths of the earth
　　you will again bring me up.
21You will increase my honor
　　and comfort me once again.

MARCH 25

What Do You Think of Jesus?

"The stone the builders rejected has become the capstone" (Luke 20:17).

It may surprise you to learn that the opposite of love is not hate.

Hate at least acknowledges the other person's presence. The opposite of love is something much colder, much crueler. It is indifference.

There was little apathy toward Jesus during his years on earth. He inspired sacrificial devotion, openmouthed wonder, and even sinister opposition. "What do you think about the Christ?" was seldom answered with just a shrug.

Yet today's indifference betrays a lack of contact with the Son of God. James Hastings describes this present-day malady.

Walk With James Hastings

"It may be that our attitude toward Christ is not that of scorn and insulting rejection. It may be that we just treat the Son of God with indifference.

"We may hear his name, but it awakens no interest. We would not cross the street to hear it again. He does not enter into our lives. He is not a partner in our affairs. It is altogether to us as if he had never come into the world.

"We do not invest in him at all. We do not put anything into his enterprises. We do not mix his stock with our financial concerns.

"Multitudes of men and women will not give him even five minutes. 'The Son of God is come, but they kill him with indifference.' "

Walk Closer to God

Those who have made a difference for Christ down through the centuries were consumed by the thought of Christ.

They were men and women of action, not apathy.

They did more than talk about prayer; they prayed. They did more than yearn to know Christ; they learned.

And that brings up a crucial question: "What do you think of Jesus?"

MARCH 26

Walk in the Word
Luke 21

After relating the story of the widow's offering, Luke records Jesus' teachings about the signs of the end of the age.

The Widow's Offering

21 As he looked up, Jesus saw the rich putting their gifts into the temple treasury. ²He also saw a poor widow put in two very small copper coins. ᵃ ³"I tell you the truth," he said, "this poor widow has put in more than all the others. ⁴All these people gave their gifts out of their wealth; but she out of her poverty put in all she had to live on."

Signs of the End of the Age

⁵Some of his disciples were remarking about how the temple was adorned with beautiful stones and with gifts dedicated to God. But Jesus said, ⁶"As for what you see here, the time will come when not one stone will be left on another; every one of them will be thrown down."

⁷"Teacher," they asked, "when will these things happen? And what will be the sign that they are about to take place?"

⁸He replied: "Watch out that you are not deceived. For many will come in my name, claiming, 'I am he,' and, 'The time is near.' Do not follow them. ⁹When you hear of wars and revolutions, do not be frightened. These things must happen first, but the end will not come right away."

¹⁰Then he said to them: "Nation will rise against nation, and kingdom against kingdom. ¹¹There will be great earthquakes, famines and pestilences in various places, and fearful events and great signs from heaven.

¹²"But before all this, they will lay hands on you and persecute you. They will deliver you to synagogues and prisons, and you will be brought before kings and governors, and all on account of my name. ¹³This will result in your being witnesses to them. ¹⁴But make up your mind not to worry beforehand how you will defend yourselves. ¹⁵For I will give you words and wisdom that none of your adversaries will be able to resist or contradict. ¹⁶You will be betrayed even by parents, brothers, relatives and friends, and they will put some of you to death. ¹⁷All men will hate you because of me. ¹⁸But not a hair of your head will perish. ¹⁹By standing firm you will gain life.

²⁰"When you see Jerusalem being surrounded by armies, you will know that its desolation is near. ²¹Then let those who are in Judea flee to the mountains, let those in the city get out, and let those in the country not enter the city. ²²For this is the time of punishment in fulfillment of all that has been written. ²³How dreadful it will be in those days for pregnant women and nursing mothers! There will be great distress in the land and wrath against this people. ²⁴They will fall by the sword and will be taken as prisoners to all the nations. Jerusalem will be trampled on by the Gentiles until the times of the Gentiles are fulfilled.

²⁵"There will be signs in the sun, moon and stars. On the earth, nations will be in anguish and perplexity at the roaring and tossing of the sea.

MARCH 26

²⁶Men will faint from terror, apprehensive of what is coming on the world, for the heavenly bodies will be shaken. ²⁷At that time they will see the Son of Man coming in a cloud with power and great glory. ²⁸When these things begin to take place, stand up and lift up your heads, because your redemption is drawing near."

²⁹He told them this parable: "Look at the fig tree and all the trees. ³⁰When they sprout leaves, you can see for yourselves and know that summer is near. ³¹Even so, when you see these things happening, you know that the kingdom of God is near.

³²"I tell you the truth, this generation^b will certainly not pass away until all these things have happened. ³³Heaven and earth will pass away, but my words will never pass away.

³⁴"Be careful, or your hearts will be weighed down with dissipation, drunkenness and the anxieties of life, and that day will close on you unexpectedly like a trap. ³⁵For it will come upon all those who live on the face of the whole earth. ³⁶Be always on the watch, and pray that you may be able to escape all that is about to happen, and that you may be able to stand before the Son of Man."

³⁷Each day Jesus was teaching at the temple, and each evening he went out to spend the night on the hill called the Mount of Olives, ³⁸and all the people came early in the morning to hear him at the temple.

^a2 Greek *two lepta*   ^b32 Or *race*

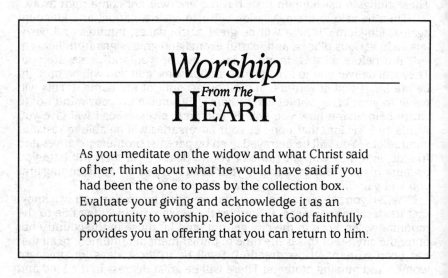

Worship
From The HEART

As you meditate on the widow and what Christ said of her, think about what he would have said if you had been the one to pass by the collection box. Evaluate your giving and acknowledge it as an opportunity to worship. Rejoice that God faithfully provides you an offering that you can return to him.

When Small Gifts Become Great Treasures

"I tell you the truth," he said, "this poor widow has put in more than all the others" (Luke 21:3).

How is it possible to add together the offerings of countless rich men, and declare the total less than the two small copper coins of a poor widow? How is it possible for so little to amount to so much?

Jesus' arithmetic is not hard to comprehend when you understand as he did that the secret of giving is not in the amount that was given, but rather what was given up.

Attitude—not abundance—is the key. Bishop Ambrose discusses the kind of giving that really adds up.

Walk With Bishop Ambrose

"Liberality is determined not by the amount of our possessions but by the disposition of our giving.

"For by the voice of the Lord, a widow is preferred above all, of whom it was said: 'She has put in more than all.'

"The Lord teaches that none should be held back from giving through shame of their own poverty, nor should the rich flatter themselves that they seem to give more than the poor.

"The piece of money out of a small stock is richer than treasures out of abundance, because it is not the amount that is given but the amount that remains which is considered.

"No one gives more than she who has nothing left for herself."

Walk Closer to God

Giving is not a function of cold numbers, but the result of a warm heart.

A small gift humbly given is of greater value than a vast sum given out of pride, compulsion or guilt.

The amount of your gifts may vary with your resources. But the attitude of your gift should remain constant—and commendable—even if you are a poor widow on a two-coin pension.

Peter Marshall said it well: "Help us to give according to our incomes, lest thou, O God, make our incomes according to our gifts." ◖◗

MARCH 27

📖 Walk in the Word
Luke 22:1–38

Moment by moment Jesus moves inexorably toward his death, as Luke records Judas's betrayal plot and the sharing of the Passover meal with the disciples.

Judas Agrees to Betray Jesus

22 Now the Feast of Unleavened Bread, called the Passover, was approaching, ²and the chief priests and the teachers of the law were looking for some way to get rid of Jesus, for they were afraid of the people. ³Then Satan entered Judas, called Iscariot, one of the Twelve. ⁴And Judas went to the chief priests and the officers of the temple guard and discussed with them how he might betray Jesus. ⁵They were delighted and agreed to give him money. ⁶He consented, and watched for an opportunity to hand Jesus over to them when no crowd was present.

The Last Supper

⁷Then came the day of Unleavened Bread on which the Passover lamb had to be sacrificed. ⁸Jesus sent Peter and John, saying, "Go and make preparations for us to eat the Passover."

⁹"Where do you want us to prepare for it?" they asked.

¹⁰He replied, "As you enter the city, a man carrying a jar of water will meet you. Follow him to the house that he enters, ¹¹and say to the owner of the house, 'The Teacher asks: Where is the guest room, where I may eat the Passover with my disciples?' ¹²He will show you a large upper room, all furnished. Make preparations there."

¹³They left and found things just as Jesus had told them. So they prepared the Passover.

¹⁴When the hour came, Jesus and his apostles reclined at the table. ¹⁵And he said to them, "I have eagerly desired to eat this Passover with you before I suffer. ¹⁶For I tell you, I will not eat it again until it finds fulfillment in the kingdom of God."

¹⁷After taking the cup, he gave thanks and said, "Take this and divide it among you. ¹⁸For I tell you I will not drink again of the fruit of the vine until the kingdom of God comes."

¹⁹And he took bread, gave thanks and broke it, and gave it to them, saying, "This is my body given for you; do this in remembrance of me."

²⁰In the same way, after the supper he took the cup, saying, "This cup is the new covenant in my blood, which is poured out for you. ²¹But the hand of him who is going to betray me is with mine on the table. ²²The Son of Man will go as it has been decreed, but woe to that man who betrays him." ²³They began to question among themselves which of them it might be who would do this.

²⁴Also a dispute arose among them as to which of them was considered to be greatest. ²⁵Jesus said to them, "The kings of the Gentiles lord it over them; and those who exercise authority over them call themselves Bene-

factors. ²⁶But you are not to be like that. Instead, the greatest among you should be like the youngest, and the one who rules like the one who serves. ²⁷For who is greater, the one who is at the table or the one who serves? Is it not the one who is at the table? But I am among you as one who serves. ²⁸You are those who have stood by me in my trials. ²⁹And I confer on you a kingdom, just as my Father conferred one on me, ³⁰so that you may eat and drink at my table in my kingdom and sit on thrones, judging the twelve tribes of Israel.

³¹"Simon, Simon, Satan has asked to sift you*ᵃ* as wheat. ³²But I have prayed for you, Simon, that your faith may not fail. And when you have turned back, strengthen your brothers."

³³But he replied, "Lord, I am ready to go with you to prison and to death."

³⁴Jesus answered, "I tell you, Peter, before the rooster crows today, you will deny three times that you know me."

³⁵Then Jesus asked them, "When I sent you without purse, bag or sandals, did you lack anything?"

"Nothing," they answered.

³⁶He said to them, "But now if you have a purse, take it, and also a bag; and if you don't have a sword, sell your cloak and buy one. ³⁷It is written: 'And he was numbered with the transgressors'ᵇ; and I tell you that this must be fulfilled in me. Yes, what is written about me is reaching its fulfillment."

³⁸The disciples said, "See, Lord, here are two swords."

"That is enough," he replied.

ᵃ31 The Greek is plural.   *ᵇ37* Isaiah 53:12

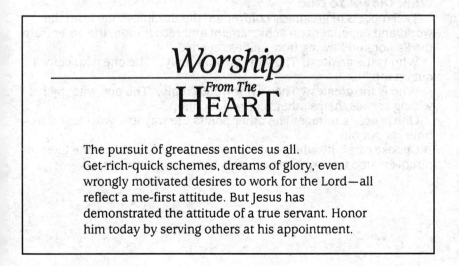

Worship
From The
HEART

The pursuit of greatness entices us all. Get-rich-quick schemes, dreams of glory, even wrongly motivated desires to work for the Lord—all reflect a me-first attitude. But Jesus has demonstrated the attitude of a true servant. Honor him today by serving others at his appointment.

MARCH 27

Coming Out on Top: Meaning or Mirage?

The greatest among you should be like the youngest, and the one who rules like the one who serves. . . . I am among you as one who serves (Luke 22:26–27).

Things are not always as they appear.

The man who struggles across the barren desert may see water on the horizon, yet never reach it. That's called a mirage.

In Luke 22 the disciples argued with each other over who deserved the title of "Tops Among the Twelve."

But as Christ pointed out, they were striving after a mirage. W.H. Griffith Thomas explains that true greatness lies in another direction.

Walk With W.H. Griffith Thomas

"Our Lord's claim upon us presses us at every point, and the world and the church wait to see something of the infinite possibilities of the life of the true Christian.

"Four great words of the New Testament surely sum up our responsibility. Be it ours to realize them in all their fullness of meaning. 'I should'; 'I ought'; 'I must'; 'I will.'

"That is, I am inclined to respond; I am impelled to respond; I am compelled to respond; I am determined to respond.

"It is ours to say what David's followers said to their master: 'We are your servants, ready to do whatever my lord the king commands.' "

Walk Closer to God

Two models of greatness confronted the disciples: one from the world and dependent on achievement and recognition, the other from the Savior and flowing from selfless service.

Who is the greatest? The world would reply, "The one who comes out on top."

Who is the greatest? The Savior would reply, "The one who, by his willing service, helps others come out on top."

One is only a mirage. The other points the way to a greatness that time cannot dim.

Choose carefully which course you follow. After all, no one likes to discover—too late—that he or she was chasing a mirage. ❍

MARCH 28

📖 Walk in the Word
Luke 22:39-71

Luke highlights other scenes from Jesus' last days, including his anguished prayer time on the Mount of Olives, his arrest, and Peter's low moment of denial.

Jesus Prays on the Mount of Olives

39Jesus went out as usual to the Mount of Olives, and his disciples followed him. 40On reaching the place, he said to them, "Pray that you will not fall into temptation." 41He withdrew about a stone's throw beyond them, knelt down and prayed, 42"Father, if you are willing, take this cup from me; yet not my will, but yours be done." 43An angel from heaven appeared to him and strengthened him. 44And being in anguish, he prayed more earnestly, and his sweat was like drops of blood falling to the ground. *a*

45When he rose from prayer and went back to the disciples, he found them asleep, exhausted from sorrow. 46"Why are you sleeping?" he asked them. "Get up and pray so that you will not fall into temptation."

Jesus Arrested

47While he was still speaking a crowd came up, and the man who was called Judas, one of the Twelve, was leading them. He approached Jesus to kiss him, 48but Jesus asked him, "Judas, are you betraying the Son of Man with a kiss?"

49When Jesus' followers saw what was going to happen, they said, "Lord, should we strike with our swords?" 50And one of them struck the servant of the high priest, cutting off his right ear.

51But Jesus answered, "No more of this!" And he touched the man's ear and healed him.

52Then Jesus said to the chief priests, the officers of the temple guard, and the elders, who had come for him, "Am I leading a rebellion, that you have come with swords and clubs? 53Every day I was with you in the temple courts, and you did not lay a hand on me. But this is your hour—when darkness reigns."

Peter Disowns Jesus

54Then seizing him, they led him away and took him into the house of the high priest. Peter followed at a distance. 55But when they had kindled a fire in the middle of the courtyard and had sat down together, Peter sat down with them. 56A servant girl saw him seated there in the firelight. She looked closely at him and said, "This man was with him."

57But he denied it. "Woman, I don't know him," he said.

58A little later someone else saw him and said, "You also are one of them."

"Man, I am not!" Peter replied.

59About an hour later another asserted, "Certainly this fellow was with him, for he is a Galilean."

MARCH 28

⁶⁰Peter replied, "Man, I don't know what you're talking about!" Just as he was speaking, the rooster crowed. ⁶¹The Lord turned and looked straight at Peter. Then Peter remembered the word the Lord had spoken to him: "Before the rooster crows today, you will disown me three times." ⁶²And he went outside and wept bitterly.

The Guards Mock Jesus

⁶³The men who were guarding Jesus began mocking and beating him. ⁶⁴They blindfolded him and demanded, "Prophesy! Who hit you?" ⁶⁵And they said many other insulting things to him.

Jesus Before Pilate and Herod

⁶⁶At daybreak the council of the elders of the people, both the chief priests and teachers of the law, met together, and Jesus was led before them. ⁶⁷"If you are the Christ,ᵇ" they said, "tell us."

Jesus answered, "If I tell you, you will not believe me, ⁶⁸and if I asked you, you would not answer. ⁶⁹But from now on, the Son of Man will be seated at the right hand of the mighty God."

⁷⁰They all asked, "Are you then the Son of God?"

He replied, "You are right in saying I am."

⁷¹Then they said, "Why do we need any more testimony? We have heard it from his own lips."

ᵃ44 Some early manuscripts do not have verses 43 and 44.   ᵇ67 Or Messiah

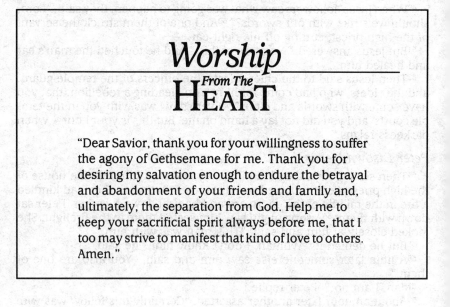

Worship
From The
HEART

"Dear Savior, thank you for your willingness to suffer the agony of Gethsemane for me. Thank you for desiring my salvation enough to endure the betrayal and abandonment of your friends and family and, ultimately, the separation from God. Help me to keep your sacrificial spirit always before me, that I too may strive to manifest that kind of love to others. Amen."

To Take the Cup and Drink It

And being in anguish, he prayed more earnestly, and his sweat was like drops of blood falling to the ground (Luke 22:44).

Aside from the crucifixion itself, Gethsemane was the darkest hour of Christ's life.

Friends misunderstood him; armed soldiers came to arrest him; one of his own followers betrayed him; he agonized in the garden alone.

And while three of his trusted disciples slept, he went to his Father in prayer.

Jonathan Edwards describes the prayer that showed the full extent of Jesus' love.

Walk With Jonathan Edwards

"When the dreadful cup was before Christ, he did not say 'Why should I go to plunge myself into such torments for worthless, wretched worms that deserve to be hated by me?

" 'Why should I who have been living from all eternity in the enjoyment of the Father's love, cast myself into such a furnace for those who never can pay me for it?

" 'Why should I yield myself to be crushed by the divine wrath for those who have no love for me, and are my enemies? They do not deserve any union with me, and never did, and never will.'

"Such, however, was not the language of Christ's heart in these circumstances.

"On the contrary, he resolved even then, in the midst of his agony, to yield himself up to the will of God, and to take the cup and drink it."

Walk Closer to God

A real battle was fought and won in the agony of Gethsemane.

If anyone had the right to sidestep undeserved suffering, Jesus had that right.

Yet he prayed above all for God's will to be done.

To die an undeserved death for undeserving men and women — no one can fully comprehend such love.

But any grateful heart can respond in praise and adoration. A heart, for example, like yours. ❒

March 29

📖 Walk in the Word
Luke 23:1–25

After recording Jesus' appearance before the Sanhedrin, Luke tells of Jesus' trial before Pilate and Herod.

---

23 Then the whole assembly rose and led him off to Pilate. ²And they began to accuse him, saying, "We have found this man subverting our nation. He opposes payment of taxes to Caesar and claims to be Christ,ᵃ a king."

³So Pilate asked Jesus, "Are you the king of the Jews?"

"Yes, it is as you say," Jesus replied.

⁴Then Pilate announced to the chief priests and the crowd, "I find no basis for a charge against this man."

⁵But they insisted, "He stirs up the people all over Judeaᵇ by his teaching. He started in Galilee and has come all the way here."

⁶On hearing this, Pilate asked if the man was a Galilean. ⁷When he learned that Jesus was under Herod's jurisdiction, he sent him to Herod, who was also in Jerusalem at that time.

⁸When Herod saw Jesus, he was greatly pleased, because for a long time he had been wanting to see him. From what he had heard about him, he hoped to see him perform some miracle. ⁹He plied him with many questions, but Jesus gave him no answer. ¹⁰The chief priests and the teachers of the law were standing there, vehemently accusing him. ¹¹Then Herod and his soldiers ridiculed and mocked him. Dressing him in an elegant robe, they sent him back to Pilate. ¹²That day Herod and Pilate became friends—before this they had been enemies.

¹³Pilate called together the chief priests, the rulers and the people, ¹⁴and said to them, "You brought me this man as one who was inciting the people to rebellion. I have examined him in your presence and have found no basis for your charges against him. ¹⁵Neither has Herod, for he sent him back to us; as you can see, he has done nothing to deserve death. ¹⁶Therefore, I will punish him and then release him.ᶜ"

¹⁸With one voice they cried out, "Away with this man! Release Barabbas to us!" ¹⁹(Barabbas had been thrown into prison for an insurrection in the city, and for murder.)

²⁰Wanting to release Jesus, Pilate appealed to them again. ²¹But they kept shouting, "Crucify him! Crucify him!"

²²For the third time he spoke to them: "Why? What crime has this man committed? I have found in him no grounds for the death penalty. Therefore I will have him punished and then release him."

²³But with loud shouts they insistently demanded that he be crucified, and their shouts prevailed. ²⁴So Pilate decided to grant their demand. ²⁵He released the man who had been thrown into prison for insurrection and murder, the one they asked for, and surrendered Jesus to their will.

ᵃ2 Or *Messiah*; also in verses 35 and 39   ᵇ5 Or *over the land of the Jews*   ᶜ16 Some manuscripts *him." ¹⁷Now he was obliged to release one man to them at the Feast.*

Viewing the Greatest Victory of All Time

With one voice they cried out, "Away with this man! Release Barabbas to us!" (Luke 23:18).

At first glance it appears the raucous shouts of a bloodthirsty crowd caused Pilate to send Jesus to his death. But in fact, an unseen higher will was at work in and through the human actors in this moving drama.

Alexander Maclaren shares this fascinating sketch of the criminal Barabbas.

Walk With Alexander Maclaren

"This coarse desperado was the people's favorite because he embodied their notions and aspirations, and had been bold enough to do what every one of them would have done if he had dared. He had headed one of the many small riots against Rome. There had been bloodshed in which he had himself taken part.

"Jesus had taught what the people did not care to hear, given blessings which even the recipients soon forgot, and lived a life whose 'beauty of holiness' rebuked the common life of all.

"What chance did truth, kindness and purity have against the sort of bravery that slashes with a sword and is not elevated above the mob by beauty of thought or character? Even now, after nineteen centuries, are the popular 'heroes' of Christian nations saints or teachers or humanitarians, whose Christlikeness is the thing venerated?

"The vote for Barabbas and against Jesus is an instructive commentary on human nature."

Walk Closer to God

Popularity is often a fleeting illusion. Today's bestsellers soon sit on the shelf unnoticed. Superstars endure only for a few brief seasons.

Society exalts winners and ignores losers. The world saw only a pitiful loss when Jesus went to the cross. In fact, they were viewing the greatest victory of all time.

When you think about it, who would remember Barabbas today if Jesus had not died and been raised?

"Better to be condemned with Jesus than accepted with Barabbas." Wouldn't you agree? ◖

MARCH 30

📖 Walk in the Word
Luke 23:26–56

Luke preserves several of Jesus' poignant sayings as Jesus is led away and nailed to the cross, where he dies and then is taken down and placed in a tomb.

The Crucifixion

²⁶As they led him away, they seized Simon from Cyrene, who was on his way in from the country, and put the cross on him and made him carry it behind Jesus. ²⁷A large number of people followed him, including women who mourned and wailed for him. ²⁸Jesus turned and said to them, "Daughters of Jerusalem, do not weep for me; weep for yourselves and for your children. ²⁹For the time will come when you will say, 'Blessed are the barren women, the wombs that never bore and the breasts that never nursed!' ³⁰Then

> " 'they will say to the mountains, "Fall on us!"
> and to the hills, "Cover us!" ' ᵃ

³¹For if men do these things when the tree is green, what will happen when it is dry?"

³²Two other men, both criminals, were also led out with him to be executed. ³³When they came to the place called the Skull, there they crucified him, along with the criminals — one on his right, the other on his left. ³⁴Jesus said, "Father, forgive them, for they do not know what they are doing."ᵇ And they divided up his clothes by casting lots.

³⁵The people stood watching, and the rulers even sneered at him. They said, "He saved others; let him save himself if he is the Christ of God, the Chosen One."

³⁶The soldiers also came up and mocked him. They offered him wine vinegar ³⁷and said, "If you are the king of the Jews, save yourself."

³⁸There was a written notice above him, which read: THIS IS THE KING OF THE JEWS.

³⁹One of the criminals who hung there hurled insults at him: "Aren't you the Christ? Save yourself and us!"

⁴⁰But the other criminal rebuked him. "Don't you fear God," he said, "since you are under the same sentence? ⁴¹We are punished justly, for we are getting what our deeds deserve. But this man has done nothing wrong."

⁴²Then he said, "Jesus, remember me when you come into your kingdom.ᶜ"

⁴³Jesus answered him, "I tell you the truth, today you will be with me in paradise."

Jesus' Death

⁴⁴It was now about the sixth hour, and darkness came over the whole land until the ninth hour, ⁴⁵for the sun stopped shining. And the curtain of the temple was torn in two. ⁴⁶Jesus called out with a loud voice, "Father,

into your hands I commit my spirit." When he had said this, he breathed his last.

⁴⁷The centurion, seeing what had happened, praised God and said, "Surely this was a righteous man." ⁴⁸When all the people who had gathered to witness this sight saw what took place, they beat their breasts and went away. ⁴⁹But all those who knew him, including the women who had followed him from Galilee, stood at a distance, watching these things.

Jesus' Burial

⁵⁰Now there was a man named Joseph, a member of the Council, a good and upright man, ⁵¹who had not consented to their decision and action. He came from the Judean town of Arimathea and he was waiting for the kingdom of God. ⁵²Going to Pilate, he asked for Jesus' body. ⁵³Then he took it down, wrapped it in linen cloth and placed it in a tomb cut in the rock, one in which no one had yet been laid. ⁵⁴It was Preparation Day, and the Sabbath was about to begin.

⁵⁵The women who had come with Jesus from Galilee followed Joseph and saw the tomb and how his body was laid in it. ⁵⁶Then they went home and prepared spices and perfumes. But they rested on the Sabbath in obedience to the commandment.

a30 Hosea 10:8   *b34* Some early manuscripts do not have this sentence.   *c42* Some manuscripts *come with your kingly power*

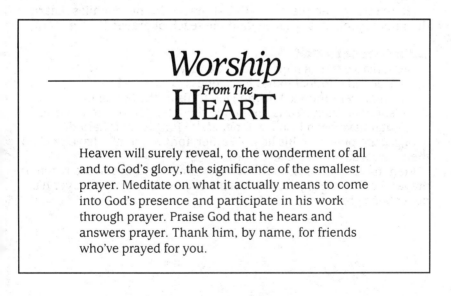

Worship
From The
HEART

Heaven will surely reveal, to the wonderment of all and to God's glory, the significance of the smallest prayer. Meditate on what it actually means to come into God's presence and participate in his work through prayer. Praise God that he hears and answers prayer. Thank him, by name, for friends who've prayed for you.

MARCH 30

No One Beyond the Reach of Prayer

Jesus said, "Father, forgive them, for they do not know what they are doing" (Luke 23:34).

When you are suffering from pain and thirst, it's hard to see beyond your own needs.

Yet from the agony of the cross, Jesus looked out . . . saw his tormentors . . . and forgave them.

To pray for help in the midst of suffering would be understandable; to pray for those causing the agony surpasses human comprehension.

A.W. Pink sees in Christ's example a parable on prayer—the kind that reaches into hearts considered untouchable.

Walk With A.W. Pink

"In praying for his enemies, not only did Christ set before us a perfect example of how we should treat those who wrong and hate us, but he also taught us never to regard anyone as beyond the reach of prayer.

"Christian reader, never lose hope. Does it seem a waste of time for you to continue praying for that man, that woman, that wayward child of yours? Does their case seem to become more hopeless every day? Does it look as though they have gotten beyond the reach of divine mercy?

"Remember then the cross. Christ prayed for his enemies. Learn then not to look on any as beyond the reach of prayer."

Walk Closer to God

Remarkable things happened at Calvary.

A hardened criminal found forgiveness.

A Roman centurion acknowledged Jesus as the Son of God. Why? What softened their hearts and made them tender toward the truth?

Might it have been Jesus' willingness to forgive their hatred?

Might the prayer on his lips—"Father, forgive them"—have pricked their hearts as nothing else could?

Men may run far from God. But they are never beyond the reach of prayer. Look around you. The need for fervent, forgiving prayer has never been greater. ○

MARCH 31

📖 Walk in the Word
Luke 24

Luke's account of Jesus' resurrection highlights Jesus' appearances to two travelers on the road to Emmaus and to his disciples behind locked doors; Luke concludes his Gospel with a brief account of Jesus' ascension.

The Resurrection

24 On the first day of the week, very early in the morning, the women took the spices they had prepared and went to the tomb. 2They found the stone rolled away from the tomb, 3but when they entered, they did not find the body of the Lord Jesus. 4While they were wondering about this, suddenly two men in clothes that gleamed like lightning stood beside them. 5In their fright the women bowed down with their faces to the ground, but the men said to them, "Why do you look for the living among the dead? 6He is not here; he has risen! Remember how he told you, while he was still with you in Galilee: 7'The Son of Man must be delivered into the hands of sinful men, be crucified and on the third day be raised again.'" 8Then they remembered his words.

9When they came back from the tomb, they told all these things to the Eleven and to all the others. 10It was Mary Magdalene, Joanna, Mary the mother of James, and the others with them who told this to the apostles. 11But they did not believe the women, because their words seemed to them like nonsense. 12Peter, however, got up and ran to the tomb. Bending over, he saw the strips of linen lying by themselves, and he went away, wondering to himself what had happened.

On the Road to Emmaus

13Now that same day two of them were going to a village called Emmaus, about seven miles*a* from Jerusalem. 14They were talking with each other about everything that had happened. 15As they talked and discussed these things with each other, Jesus himself came up and walked along with them; 16but they were kept from recognizing him.

17He asked them, "What are you discussing together as you walk along?"

They stood still, their faces downcast. 18One of them, named Cleopas, asked him, "Are you only a visitor to Jerusalem and do not know the things that have happened there in these days?"

19"What things?" he asked.

"About Jesus of Nazareth," they replied. "He was a prophet, powerful in word and deed before God and all the people. 20The chief priests and our rulers handed him over to be sentenced to death, and they crucified him; 21but we had hoped that he was the one who was going to redeem Israel. And what is more, it is the third day since all this took place. 22In addition, some of our women amazed us. They went to the tomb early this morning 23but didn't find his body. They came and told us that they had seen a

MARCH 31

vision of angels, who said he was alive. ²⁴Then some of our companions
went to the tomb and found it just as the women had said, but him they
did not see."

²⁵He said to them, "How foolish you are, and how slow of heart to be-
lieve all that the prophets have spoken! ²⁶Did not the Christ^b have to suffer
these things and then enter his glory?" ²⁷And beginning with Moses and
all the Prophets, he explained to them what was said in all the Scriptures
concerning himself.

²⁸As they approached the village to which they were going, Jesus acted
as if he were going farther. ²⁹But they urged him strongly, "Stay with us,
for it is nearly evening; the day is almost over." So he went in to stay with
them.

³⁰When he was at the table with them, he took bread, gave thanks, broke
it and began to give it to them. ³¹Then their eyes were opened and they
recognized him, and he disappeared from their sight. ³²They asked each
other, "Were not our hearts burning within us while he talked with us on
the road and opened the Scriptures to us?"

³³They got up and returned at once to Jerusalem. There they found the
Eleven and those with them, assembled together ³⁴and saying, "It is true!
The Lord has risen and has appeared to Simon." ³⁵Then the two told what
had happened on the way, and how Jesus was recognized by them when
he broke the bread.

Jesus Appears to the Disciples

³⁶While they were still talking about this, Jesus himself stood among
them and said to them, "Peace be with you."

³⁷They were startled and frightened, thinking they saw a ghost. ³⁸He said
to them, "Why are you troubled, and why do doubts rise in your minds?
³⁹Look at my hands and my feet. It is I myself! Touch me and see; a ghost
does not have flesh and bones, as you see I have."

⁴⁰When he had said this, he showed them his hands and feet. ⁴¹And
while they still did not believe it because of joy and amazement, he asked
them, "Do you have anything here to eat?" ⁴²They gave him a piece of
broiled fish, ⁴³and he took it and ate it in their presence.

⁴⁴He said to them, "This is what I told you while I was still with you:
Everything must be fulfilled that is written about me in the Law of Moses,
the Prophets and the Psalms."

⁴⁵Then he opened their minds so they could understand the Scriptures.
⁴⁶He told them, "This is what is written: The Christ will suffer and rise from
the dead on the third day, ⁴⁷and repentance and forgiveness of sins will
be preached in his name to all nations, beginning at Jerusalem. ⁴⁸You are
witnesses of these things. ⁴⁹I am going to send you what my Father has
promised; but stay in the city until you have been clothed with power from
on high."

MARCH 31

The Ascension

⁵⁰When he had led them out to the vicinity of Bethany, he lifted up his hands and blessed them. ⁵¹While he was blessing them, he left them and was taken up into heaven. ⁵²Then they worshiped him and returned to Jerusalem with great joy. ⁵³And they stayed continually at the temple, praising God.

a13 Greek *sixty stadia* (about 11 kilometers)   *b26* Or *Messiah*; also in verse 46

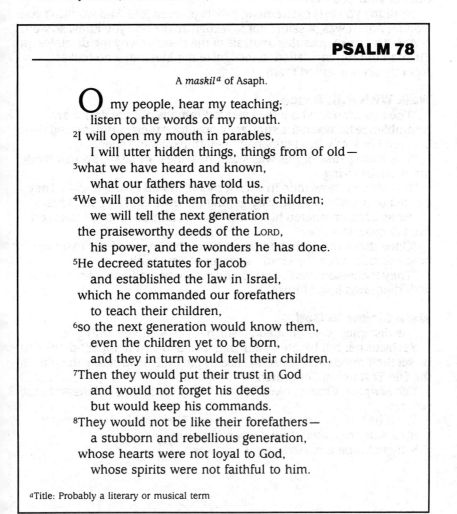

PSALM 78

A *maskil*ᵃ of Asaph.

O my people, hear my teaching;
    listen to the words of my mouth.
²I will open my mouth in parables,
    I will utter hidden things, things from of old—
³what we have heard and known,
    what our fathers have told us.
⁴We will not hide them from their children;
    we will tell the next generation
the praiseworthy deeds of the LORD,
    his power, and the wonders he has done.
⁵He decreed statutes for Jacob
    and established the law in Israel,
which he commanded our forefathers
    to teach their children,
⁶so the next generation would know them,
    even the children yet to be born,
    and they in turn would tell their children.
⁷Then they would put their trust in God
    and would not forget his deeds
    but would keep his commands.
⁸They would not be like their forefathers—
    a stubborn and rebellious generation,
whose hearts were not loyal to God,
    whose spirits were not faithful to him.

*a*Title: Probably a literary or musical term

MARCH 31

Eyes Open to the Savior

Then their eyes were opened and they recognized him (Luke 24:31).

What if you learned that the stranger you sat beside today—the one with whom you shared small talk and pleasantries—was in fact the ruler of your country!

Wouldn't you feel excitement, privilege, even joy? And wouldn't you wonder how it was possible not to recognize the one you know so well?

A.B. Bruce provides this analysis of the reasons why the disciples on the road to Emmaus failed to recognize the Messiah who had so recently accompanied them.

Walk With A.B. Bruce

"The two friends who journeyed to Emmaus did not notice any resemblance between the stranger who joined their company and their beloved Lord, of whom they had been thinking and speaking.

"The main cause of this was sheer heaviness of heart. Sorrow made them unobserving.

"It is obvious how men in such a mood should be dealt with. They can get outward vision only by getting the inward eye opened first.

"Jesus accommodated himself to their condition, and led them on from despair to hope.

"Once these thoughts had taken hold, the hearts of the two men began to burn with the kindling power of new truth.

"They looked outward, and lo, the man who had been discoursing with them was Jesus himself!"

Walk Closer to God

The disciples were blinded by sorrow, preoccupied with grief.

Yet Jesus neither berated them, nor called for a stiff upper lip. Instead he set their minds and hearts at ease by patiently instructing them from the Old Testament Scriptures.

The Scriptures that spoke of a Savior who could lift burdens and ease sorrows.

What began as sorrow ended with joy: The Lord is risen indeed!

It's a story repeated thousands of times each day.

Why not repeat it to someone you know?

APRIL

Eternity Invading Time

JOHN

Having read Matthew, Mark and Luke, you will find that the Gospel of John requires a mental "shifting of gears." The first three Gospels emphasize Jesus' actions and events, with occasional parables and sermons interspersed. But in John's account, the works of Jesus take a back seat to his words. Only John, for example, captures the intimate conversation in the upper room just hours before Jesus' death, in which Jesus promises his disciples a divine Counselor, heavenly peace and his abiding presence.

From the opening verses, John writes of One who was more than just a man. He was God, the Creator of all things, the source of light and the giver of life (John 1:1,3–4,9). He was the Word who became flesh (John 1:14); God had become a man. John continues this theme throughout the book. Those who came in contact with Jesus—John the Baptist, Nicodemus, the Samaritan woman, the man blind from birth, Mary, Martha, Peter, Thomas—all came to the same inescapable conclusion: God had visited the human race! At least eight times Jesus ascribes to himself the name "I AM," the name God used to identify himself to his people in Egypt (Exodus 3:14–15). Jesus said, "I am the bread . . . the light . . . the good shepherd . . . the door . . . the resurrection . . . the way and the truth and the life . . . the vine . . ." and simply "I am."

Jesus' claims are authenticated by his miracles (called "signs"); his deeds prove his words. Only John describes the miracle of the man born blind receiving his sight; who but God can give sight to the sightless? Only John records the raising of Lazarus; who but God can give life to the lifeless?

This month you will listen to Jesus make startling claims to the gathered crowds, and then confirm those claims with a dramatic demonstration of his power. You will be confronted with the same question they faced: "Who is Jesus of Nazareth?" You will develop a bigger, brighter picture of God's Son—Jesus Christ. Are you ready to meet him?

APRIL 1

📖 Walk in the Word
John 1:1–34

After introducing his Gospel with a prologue that affirms the deity of Jesus Christ, John omits all birth narratives, beginning his record of Jesus' life with a brief account of John the Baptist's ministry.

The Word Became Flesh

1 In the beginning was the Word, and the Word was with God, and the Word was God. ²He was with God in the beginning.

³Through him all things were made; without him nothing was made that has been made. ⁴In him was life, and that life was the light of men. ⁵The light shines in the darkness, but the darkness has not understood*a* it.

⁶There came a man who was sent from God; his name was John. ⁷He came as a witness to testify concerning that light, so that through him all men might believe. ⁸He himself was not the light; he came only as a witness to the light. ⁹The true light that gives light to every man was coming into the world.*b*

¹⁰He was in the world, and though the world was made through him, the world did not recognize him. ¹¹He came to that which was his own, but his own did not receive him. ¹²Yet to all who received him, to those who believed in his name, he gave the right to become children of God— ¹³children born not of natural descent,*c* nor of human decision or a husband's will, but born of God.

¹⁴The Word became flesh and made his dwelling among us. We have seen his glory, the glory of the One and Only,*d* who came from the Father, full of grace and truth.

¹⁵John testifies concerning him. He cries out, saying, "This was he of whom I said, 'He who comes after me has surpassed me because he was before me.'" ¹⁶From the fullness of his grace we have all received one blessing after another. ¹⁷For the law was given through Moses; grace and truth came through Jesus Christ. ¹⁸No one has ever seen God, but God the One and Only,*d,e* who is at the Father's side, has made him known.

John the Baptist Denies Being the Christ

¹⁹Now this was John's testimony when the Jews of Jerusalem sent priests and Levites to ask him who he was. ²⁰He did not fail to confess, but confessed freely, "I am not the Christ.*f*"

²¹They asked him, "Then who are you? Are you Elijah?"

He said, "I am not."

"Are you the Prophet?"

He answered, "No."

²²Finally they said, "Who are you? Give us an answer to take back to those who sent us. What do you say about yourself?"

²³John replied in the words of Isaiah the prophet, "I am the voice of one calling in the desert, 'Make straight the way for the Lord.'"*g*

24Now some Pharisees who had been sent 25questioned him, "Why then do you baptize if you are not the Christ, nor Elijah, nor the Prophet?"

26"I baptize with ʰ water," John replied, "but among you stands one you do not know. 27He is the one who comes after me, the thongs of whose sandals I am not worthy to untie."

28This all happened at Bethany on the other side of the Jordan, where John was baptizing.

Jesus the Lamb of God

29The next day John saw Jesus coming toward him and said, "Look, the Lamb of God, who takes away the sin of the world! 30This is the one I meant when I said, 'A man who comes after me has surpassed me because he was before me.' 31I myself did not know him, but the reason I came baptizing with water was that he might be revealed to Israel."

32Then John gave this testimony: "I saw the Spirit come down from heaven as a dove and remain on him. 33I would not have known him, except that the one who sent me to baptize with water told me, 'The man on whom you see the Spirit come down and remain is he who will baptize with the Holy Spirit.' 34I have seen and I testify that this is the Son of God."

ᵃ5 Or *darkness, and the darkness has not overcome*   ᵇ9 Or *This was the true light that gives light to every man who comes into the world*   ᶜ13 Greek *of bloods*   ᵈ14,18 Or *the Only Begotten*   ᵉ18 Some manuscripts *but the only* (or *only begotten*) *Son*   ᶠ20 Or *Messiah.* "The Christ" (Greek) and "the Messiah" (Hebrew) both mean "the Anointed One"; also in verse 25.   ᵍ23 Isaiah 40:3   ʰ26 Or *in*; also in verses 31 and 33

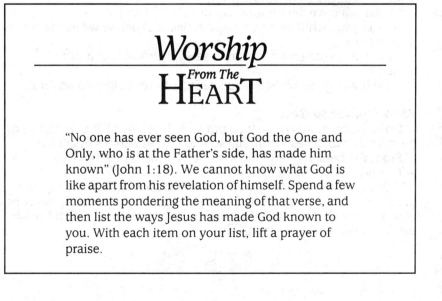

Worship
From The
HEART

"No one has ever seen God, but God the One and Only, who is at the Father's side, has made him known" (John 1:18). We cannot know what God is like apart from his revelation of himself. Spend a few moments pondering the meaning of that verse, and then list the ways Jesus has made God known to you. With each item on your list, lift a prayer of praise.

APRIL 1

Great Grace Deserves Great Gratitude

The Word became flesh and made his dwelling among us . . . full of grace and truth (John 1:14).

John 1 describes a transformation that's more amazing than any metamorphosis in the animal kingdom . . . and infinitely more significant. There you'll read about the incarnation—God coming to earth in human form.

Why would he do that?

Jonathan Edwards probes the meaning of the incarnation and God's matchless, marvelous grace.

Walk With Jonathan Edwards

"It was total grace that God gave us his only begotten Son.

"The grace is great because of the excellency of what is given. The gift was infinitely precious because it was a person of infinite glory, one infinitely near and dear to God, one infinitely worthy.

"The grace is great in proportion to the benefit we have in him: deliverance from an infinite, eternal misery, and enjoyment of eternal joy and glory.

"The grace is great in proportion to our unworthiness; instead of deserving such a gift, we merited infinite ill from God's hands.

"The grace in bestowing this gift is most free. It was what God was under no obligation to bestow.

"It was what we did nothing to merit.

"It was given while we were yet enemies, and before we had so much as repented.

"It was from the love of God that saw no excellency in us to attract it.

"And it was given without expectation of ever being repaid for it."

Walk Closer to God

Grace is something more than prayer before a meal. It is God sending his only Son to die as a criminal so that God's enemies might live.

From the perspective of most human beings, grace is a free gift—undeserved and unearned.

From God's perspective, grace is a priceless sacrifice—costly and precious. Such great grace deserves great gratitude. You may never be able to thank God adequately for what he has done for you in Christ. But it's never too late to start. ❍

APRIL 2

Walk in the Word
John 1:35–51

John briefly states how some of the disciples first became acquainted with Jesus.

Jesus' First Disciples

[35]The next day John was there again with two of his disciples. [36]When he saw Jesus passing by, he said, "Look, the Lamb of God!"

[37]When the two disciples heard him say this, they followed Jesus. [38]Turning around, Jesus saw them following and asked, "What do you want?"

They said, "Rabbi" (which means Teacher), "where are you staying?"

[39]"Come," he replied, "and you will see."

So they went and saw where he was staying, and spent that day with him. It was about the tenth hour.

[40]Andrew, Simon Peter's brother, was one of the two who heard what John had said and who had followed Jesus. [41]The first thing Andrew did was to find his brother Simon and tell him, "We have found the Messiah" (that is, the Christ). [42]And he brought him to Jesus.

Jesus looked at him and said, "You are Simon son of John. You will be called Cephas" (which, when translated, is Peter[a]).

Jesus Calls Philip and Nathanael

[43]The next day Jesus decided to leave for Galilee. Finding Philip, he said to him, "Follow me."

[44]Philip, like Andrew and Peter, was from the town of Bethsaida. [45]Philip found Nathanael and told him, "We have found the one Moses wrote about in the Law, and about whom the prophets also wrote—Jesus of Nazareth, the son of Joseph."

[46]"Nazareth! Can anything good come from there?" Nathanael asked.

"Come and see," said Philip.

[47]When Jesus saw Nathanael approaching, he said of him, "Here is a true Israelite, in whom there is nothing false."

[48]"How do you know me?" Nathanael asked.

Jesus answered, "I saw you while you were still under the fig tree before Philip called you."

[49]Then Nathanael declared, "Rabbi, you are the Son of God; you are the King of Israel."

[50]Jesus said, "You believe[b] because I told you I saw you under the fig tree. You shall see greater things than that." [51]He then added, "I tell you[c] the truth, you[c] shall see heaven open, and the angels of God ascending and descending on the Son of Man."

---

[a]42 Both *Cephas* (Aramaic) and *Peter* (Greek) mean *rock.*   [b]50 Or *Do you believe . . . ?*
[c]51 The Greek is plural.

APRIL 2

The Change That Comes Through Contact With Jesus

The first thing Andrew did was to find his brother Simon and tell him, "We have found the Messiah." . . . And he brought him to Jesus (John 1:41–42).

You can't force other people to read a book you enjoyed or try a tasty new recipe you discovered. Once you've shared the good news, they must respond for themselves.

In John 1 Andrew encounters the Messiah . . . and immediately thinks of his brother Simon.

But bringing Simon to the Savior and having Simon trust him for salvation are two different things—as Andrew discovers, and as B.H. Carroll explains.

Walk With B.H. Carroll

"We cannot convert a person. That is not a part of our duty. We have reached our limit of responsibility when we have brought another to Jesus. He will attend to his part of it.

"Yet how many believers have tried to do God's work—attempting to make Christians out of other people, and giving formulas for it.

"Our limit is reached when we have brought that person to Jesus; and the sooner we find that out, the better.

"God alone can forgive sins. It is blasphemy for any man to claim that power.

"Andrew brought Simon to Jesus and stopped. That is the limit of our work."

Walk Closer to God

It will take more than your own persuasive powers to convince others that Jesus is the Savior.

And that's where Jesus comes in.

His life, his words, his death and resurrection are far more convincing than any human argument.

In order for others to be changed by Christ, they must first come in contact with him.

And that's where you come in!

Get excited enough about something—or someone—and others will show an interest.

Have you accepted your responsibility to bring your neighbor, co-worker or relative to Jesus?

Be an Andrew to some Simon today, and see what happens in that person's life—and your own. ◖

APRIL 3

 Walk in the Word
John 2

John recounts Jesus' first miracle and gives an account of a cleansing of the temple in Jerusalem.

Jesus Changes Water to Wine

2 On the third day a wedding took place at Cana in Galilee. Jesus' mother was there, ²and Jesus and his disciples had also been invited to the wedding. ³When the wine was gone, Jesus' mother said to him, "They have no more wine."

⁴"Dear woman, why do you involve me?" Jesus replied. "My time has not yet come."

⁵His mother said to the servants, "Do whatever he tells you."

⁶Nearby stood six stone water jars, the kind used by the Jews for ceremonial washing, each holding from twenty to thirty gallons.ᵃ

⁷Jesus said to the servants, "Fill the jars with water"; so they filled them to the brim.

⁸Then he told them, "Now draw some out and take it to the master of the banquet."

They did so, ⁹and the master of the banquet tasted the water that had been turned into wine. He did not realize where it had come from, though the servants who had drawn the water knew. Then he called the bridegroom aside ¹⁰and said, "Everyone brings out the choice wine first and then the cheaper wine after the guests have had too much to drink; but you have saved the best till now."

¹¹This, the first of his miraculous signs, Jesus performed at Cana in Galilee. He thus revealed his glory, and his disciples put their faith in him.

Jesus Clears the Temple

¹²After this he went down to Capernaum with his mother and brothers and his disciples. There they stayed for a few days.

¹³When it was almost time for the Jewish Passover, Jesus went up to Jerusalem. ¹⁴In the temple courts he found men selling cattle, sheep and doves, and others sitting at tables exchanging money. ¹⁵So he made a whip out of cords, and drove all from the temple area, both sheep and cattle; he scattered the coins of the money changers and overturned their tables. ¹⁶To those who sold doves he said, "Get these out of here! How dare you turn my Father's house into a market!"

¹⁷His disciples remembered that it is written: "Zeal for your house will consume me."ᵇ

¹⁸Then the Jews demanded of him, "What miraculous sign can you show us to prove your authority to do all this?"

¹⁹Jesus answered them, "Destroy this temple, and I will raise it again in three days."

²⁰The Jews replied, "It has taken forty-six years to build this temple, and you are going to raise it in three days?" ²¹But the temple he had spoken

APRIL 3

of was his body. ²²After he was raised from the dead, his disciples recalled what he had said. Then they believed the Scripture and the words that Jesus had spoken.

²³Now while he was in Jerusalem at the Passover Feast, many people saw the miraculous signs he was doing and believed in his name.^c ²⁴But Jesus would not entrust himself to them, for he knew all men. ²⁵He did not need man's testimony about man, for he knew what was in a man.

^a6 Greek *two to three metretes* (probably about 75 to 115 liters)   ^b17 Psalm 69:9
^c23 Or *and believed in him*

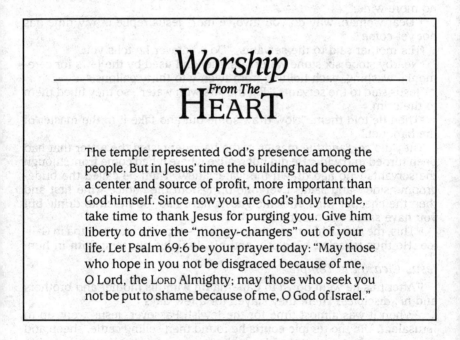

Worship
From The
HEART

The temple represented God's presence among the people. But in Jesus' time the building had become a center and source of profit, more important than God himself. Since now you are God's holy temple, take time to thank Jesus for purging you. Give him liberty to drive the "money-changers" out of your life. Let Psalm 69:6 be your prayer today: "May those who hope in you not be disgraced because of me, O Lord, the LORD Almighty; may those who seek you not be put to shame because of me, O God of Israel."

Leaving the "When" and "How" to God

His mother said to the servants, "Do whatever he tells you" (John 2:5).

A formal dinner served on paper plates and folding tables would be an affront to the guests and a disgrace to the host.

John 2 records the story of a wedding at which the host faced a disgraceful lack of provisions. Suddenly, there was no more wine.

But Jesus was there. And as Mary knew, he was all that was needed to correct the situation.

Ole Hallesby spotlights Mary's restful faith in her miracle-working son.

Walk with Ole Hallesby

"The mother of Jesus reveals herself as a tried and true woman of prayer.

"She goes to the right place with the need she has become acquainted with. She goes to Jesus and tells him everything.

"Let us notice that she did nothing more.

"She knew that she did not have to help him by suggesting what he should do.

"She knew also that she did not have to influence him or persuade him to give these friends a helping hand. No one is so willing to help as he is!

"Jesus' mother had learned a secret of successful prayer: We should not interfere in our prayers but should leave the when and the how concerning the fulfillment of those prayers entirely to God.

"Most of us have a great deal to learn in this connection."

Walk Closer to God

The door of prayer is always open. Therefore, come confidently to "ask . . . seek . . . knock," expecting an answer in return.

But in your asking, be careful that you do not tell God how to answer—and how soon.

Mary brought the need to her Son, and Jesus did the answering—in a way that caused wonder and faith.

Let your prayers today be revitalized with the knowledge that God gives the very best to those who leave the choice with him. ◯

APRIL 4

📖 Walk in the Word
John 3

Nicodemus meets Jesus and receives far more than he expected when Jesus engages him in dialogue; John the Baptist testifies that Jesus is the one sent by God.

Jesus Teaches Nicodemus

3 Now there was a man of the Pharisees named Nicodemus, a member of the Jewish ruling council. ²He came to Jesus at night and said, "Rabbi, we know you are a teacher who has come from God. For no one could perform the miraculous signs you are doing if God were not with him."

³In reply Jesus declared, "I tell you the truth, no one can see the kingdom of God unless he is born again.*ᵃ*"

⁴"How can a man be born when he is old?" Nicodemus asked. "Surely he cannot enter a second time into his mother's womb to be born!"

⁵Jesus answered, "I tell you the truth, no one can enter the kingdom of God unless he is born of water and the Spirit. ⁶Flesh gives birth to flesh, but the Spiritᵇ gives birth to spirit. ⁷You should not be surprised at my saying, 'Youᶜ must be born again.' ⁸The wind blows wherever it pleases. You hear its sound, but you cannot tell where it comes from or where it is going. So it is with everyone born of the Spirit."

⁹"How can this be?" Nicodemus asked.

¹⁰"You are Israel's teacher," said Jesus, "and do you not understand these things? ¹¹I tell you the truth, we speak of what we know, and we testify to what we have seen, but still you people do not accept our testimony. ¹²I have spoken to you of earthly things and you do not believe; how then will you believe if I speak of heavenly things? ¹³No one has ever gone into heaven except the one who came from heaven—the Son of Man.ᵈ ¹⁴Just as Moses lifted up the snake in the desert, so the Son of Man must be lifted up, ¹⁵that everyone who believes in him may have eternal life.ᵉ

¹⁶"For God so loved the world that he gave his one and only Son,ᶠ that whoever believes in him shall not perish but have eternal life. ¹⁷For God did not send his Son into the world to condemn the world, but to save the world through him. ¹⁸Whoever believes in him is not condemned, but whoever does not believe stands condemned already because he has not believed in the name of God's one and only Son.ᵍ ¹⁹This is the verdict: Light has come into the world, but men loved darkness instead of light because their deeds were evil. ²⁰Everyone who does evil hates the light, and will not come into the light for fear that his deeds will be exposed. ²¹But whoever lives by the truth comes into the light, so that it may be seen plainly that what he has done has been done through God."ʰ

John the Baptist's Testimony About Jesus

²²After this, Jesus and his disciples went out into the Judean countryside, where he spent some time with them, and baptized. ²³Now John also was baptizing at Aenon near Salim, because there was plenty of water, and

people were constantly coming to be baptized. ²⁴(This was before John was put in prison.) ²⁵An argument developed between some of John's disciples and a certain Jew*i* over the matter of ceremonial washing. ²⁶They came to John and said to him, "Rabbi, that man who was with you on the other side of the Jordan — the one you testified about — well, he is baptizing, and everyone is going to him."

²⁷To this John replied, "A man can receive only what is given him from heaven. ²⁸You yourselves can testify that I said, 'I am not the Christ*j* but am sent ahead of him.' ²⁹The bride belongs to the bridegroom. The friend who attends the bridegroom waits and listens for him, and is full of joy when he hears the bridegroom's voice. That joy is mine, and it is now complete. ³⁰He must become greater; I must become less.

³¹"The one who comes from above is above all; the one who is from the earth belongs to the earth, and speaks as one from the earth. The one who comes from heaven is above all. ³²He testifies to what he has seen and heard, but no one accepts his testimony. ³³The man who has accepted it has certified that God is truthful. ³⁴For the one whom God has sent speaks the words of God, for God*k* gives the Spirit without limit. ³⁵The Father loves the Son and has placed everything in his hands. ³⁶Whoever believes in the Son has eternal life, but whoever rejects the Son will not see life, for God's wrath remains on him."*l*

a3 Or *born from above*; also in verse 7   *b6* Or *but spirit*   *c7* The Greek is plural.
d13 Some manuscripts *Man, who is in heaven*   *e15* Or *believes may have eternal life in him*   *f16* Or *his only begotten Son*   *g18* Or *God's only begotten Son*   *h21* Some interpreters end the quotation after verse 15.   *i25* Some manuscripts *and certain Jews*
j28 Or *Messiah*   *k34* Greek *he*   *l36* Some interpreters end the quotation after verse 30.

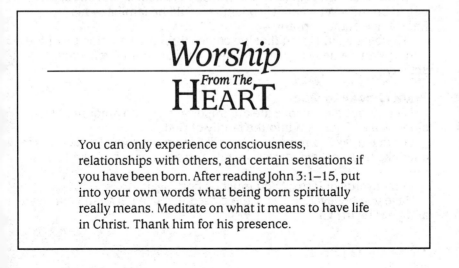

Worship
From The
HEART

You can only experience consciousness, relationships with others, and certain sensations if you have been born. After reading John 3:1–15, put into your own words what being born spiritually really means. Meditate on what it means to have life in Christ. Thank him for his presence.

APRIL 4

Closing the Gap Between Head and Heart

No one can see the kingdom of God unless he is born again (John 3:3).

Many people are in danger of missing heaven by eighteen inches. That's roughly the distance from your head to your heart. And it marks the difference between believing about Jesus Christ, and believing in Jesus.

Nicodemus was a religious leader of his day who had head knowledge rather than heart knowledge about God. Yet he had religious questions he could not answer.

But the answers Nicodemus received when he questioned Jesus demanded more than an intellectual nod, as G. Campbell Morgan explains.

Walk With G. Campbell Morgan

"We often hear it said today that there are many excellent people in the world who make no profession of Christianity.

"Nicodemus was that kind of man, particularly on the intellectual side. And it was to him that Christ first declared the necessity of the new birth.

"Nicodemus was a Pharisee, a ruler of the Jews. Narrow, dogmatic, educated and patriotic, he stood high in public position and prestige.

"But he was in danger of missing the kingdom of God.

"Jesus, looking at Nicodemus with all his intellect and strength, began on the level where Nicodemus would be familiar—his knowledge of the Scriptures.

"There he would learn that life comes through the lifting up of the Son of Man—a heavenly fact demanding more than intellectual activity."

Walk Closer to God

Facts about the Savior's life are important. But no amount of facts alone will ever get you into the family of God.

For that it takes a miracle of rebirth. You must come to the cross in childlike faith, believing in Jesus rather than simply believing about him.

In the words of Jesus, "You must be born again."

Have you believed in Jesus and closed that gap between your head and your heart? ❍

APRIL 5

📖 Walk in the Word
John 4:1–26

A Samaritan woman is the recipient of Jesus' revolutionary accepting love in this startling story retold by John.

Jesus Talks With a Samaritan Woman

4 The Pharisees heard that Jesus was gaining and baptizing more disciples than John, [2]although in fact it was not Jesus who baptized, but his disciples. [3]When the Lord learned of this, he left Judea and went back once more to Galilee.

[4]Now he had to go through Samaria. [5]So he came to a town in Samaria called Sychar, near the plot of ground Jacob had given to his son Joseph. [6]Jacob's well was there, and Jesus, tired as he was from the journey, sat down by the well. It was about the sixth hour.

[7]When a Samaritan woman came to draw water, Jesus said to her, "Will you give me a drink?" [8](His disciples had gone into the town to buy food.)

[9]The Samaritan woman said to him, "You are a Jew and I am a Samaritan woman. How can you ask me for a drink?" (For Jews do not associate with Samaritans. [a])

[10]Jesus answered her, "If you knew the gift of God and who it is that asks you for a drink, you would have asked him and he would have given you living water."

[11]"Sir," the woman said, "you have nothing to draw with and the well is deep. Where can you get this living water? [12]Are you greater than our father Jacob, who gave us the well and drank from it himself, as did also his sons and his flocks and herds?"

[13]Jesus answered, "Everyone who drinks this water will be thirsty again, [14]but whoever drinks the water I give him will never thirst. Indeed, the water I give him will become in him a spring of water welling up to eternal life."

[15]The woman said to him, "Sir, give me this water so that I won't get thirsty and have to keep coming here to draw water."

[16]He told her, "Go, call your husband and come back."

[17]"I have no husband," she replied.

Jesus said to her, "You are right when you say you have no husband. [18]The fact is, you have had five husbands, and the man you now have is not your husband. What you have just said is quite true."

[19]"Sir," the woman said, "I can see that you are a prophet. [20]Our fathers worshiped on this mountain, but you Jews claim that the place where we must worship is in Jerusalem."

[21]Jesus declared, "Believe me, woman, a time is coming when you will worship the Father neither on this mountain nor in Jerusalem. [22]You Samaritans worship what you do not know; we worship what we do know, for salvation is from the Jews. [23]Yet a time is coming and has now come when the true worshipers will worship the Father in spirit and truth, for

APRIL 5

they are the kind of worshipers the Father seeks. ²⁴God is spirit, and his worshipers must worship in spirit and in truth."

²⁵The woman said, "I know that Messiah" (called Christ) "is coming. When he comes, he will explain everything to us."

²⁶Then Jesus declared, "I who speak to you am he."

a9 Or do not use dishes Samaritans have used

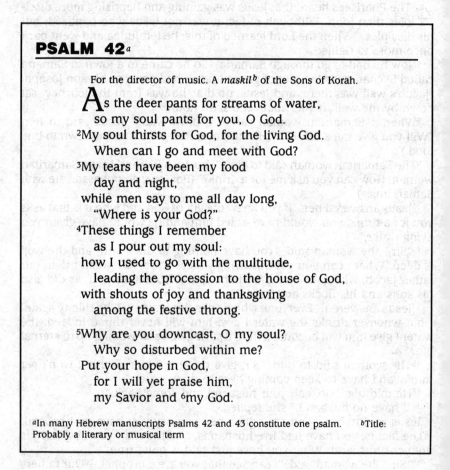

PSALM 42ᵃ

For the director of music. A *maskil*ᵇ of the Sons of Korah.

As the deer pants for streams of water,
    so my soul pants for you, O God.
²My soul thirsts for God, for the living God.
    When can I go and meet with God?
³My tears have been my food
    day and night,
while men say to me all day long,
    "Where is your God?"
⁴These things I remember
    as I pour out my soul:
how I used to go with the multitude,
    leading the procession to the house of God,
with shouts of joy and thanksgiving
    among the festive throng.

⁵Why are you downcast, O my soul?
    Why so disturbed within me?
Put your hope in God,
    for I will yet praise him,
    my Savior and ⁶my God.

aIn many Hebrew manuscripts Psalms 42 and 43 constitute one psalm.   *bTitle: Probably a literary or musical term*

Lavish Rivers of Irrepressible Life

> The water I give him will become in him a spring of water welling up to eternal life (John 4:14).

"Give me a drink." Was that just a casual request of a thirsty traveler . . . or something more?

The Samaritan woman in John 4 came to satisfy her physical thirst, but Jesus saw in her life a more dangerous condition: spiritual drought that only he could relieve.

The well of spiritual life is Jesus himself. Oswald Chambers examines the source of water that eternally satisfies.

Walk with Oswald Chambers

"The picture our Lord gives is not that of a channel, but a fountain.

"Be filled, and the sweetness of a vital relationship to Jesus will flow out of the saint as lavishly as it is imparted to him.

"Keep right at the Source, and out of you will flow rivers of living life — irrepressible life.

"We are to be centers through which Jesus can flow as rivers of living water blessing everyone.

"As surely as we receive from him, he will pour out through us.

'Keep at the Source, guard well your belief in Jesus Christ and your relationship to him, and there will be a steady flow for other lives — no dryness and no deadness."

Walk Closer to God

It is a simple matter to satisfy physical thirst . . . for a time. Drink deeply and your thirst will be quenched . . . temporarily. But again and again the yearning for water will return.

But in the spiritual realm, Jesus offers a fountain that never stops flowing . . . a river of life that never runs dry . . . a drink to quench the most desperate longing.

The woman at the well took Jesus at his word and found eternal satisfaction, as he promised. And the overflow of that fountain within her life reached many of those around her.

"Keep at the Source," and through you the fountain of life will satisfy those around you.

Drink deeply. See for yourself. ⟨⟩

APRIL 6

📖 Walk in the Word
John 4:27–54

John records the reactions of the disciples, the Samaritan woman herself, and the townspeople; John tells the story of another miracle at Cana in Galilee.

The Disciples Rejoin Jesus

²⁷Just then his disciples returned and were surprised to find him talking with a woman. But no one asked, "What do you want?" or "Why are you talking with her?"

²⁸Then, leaving her water jar, the woman went back to the town and said to the people, ²⁹"Come, see a man who told me everything I ever did. Could this be the Christ*a*?" ³⁰They came out of the town and made their way toward him.

³¹Meanwhile his disciples urged him, "Rabbi, eat something."

³²But he said to them, "I have food to eat that you know nothing about."

³³Then his disciples said to each other, "Could someone have brought him food?"

³⁴"My food," said Jesus, "is to do the will of him who sent me and to finish his work. ³⁵Do you not say, 'Four months more and then the harvest'? I tell you, open your eyes and look at the fields! They are ripe for harvest. ³⁶Even now the reaper draws his wages, even now he harvests the crop for eternal life, so that the sower and the reaper may be glad together. ³⁷Thus the saying 'One sows and another reaps' is true. ³⁸I sent you to reap what you have not worked for. Others have done the hard work, and you have reaped the benefits of their labor."

Many Samaritans Believe

³⁹Many of the Samaritans from that town believed in him because of the woman's testimony, "He told me everything I ever did." ⁴⁰So when the Samaritans came to him, they urged him to stay with them, and he stayed two days. ⁴¹And because of his words many more became believers.

⁴²They said to the woman, "We no longer believe just because of what you said; now we have heard for ourselves, and we know that this man really is the Savior of the world."

Jesus Heals the Official's Son

⁴³After the two days he left for Galilee. ⁴⁴(Now Jesus himself had pointed out that a prophet has no honor in his own country.) ⁴⁵When he arrived in Galilee, the Galileans welcomed him. They had seen all that he had done in Jerusalem at the Passover Feast, for they also had been there.

⁴⁶Once more he visited Cana in Galilee, where he had turned the water into wine. And there was a certain royal official whose son lay sick at Capernaum. ⁴⁷When this man heard that Jesus had arrived in Galilee from Judea, he went to him and begged him to come and heal his son, who was close to death.

⁴⁸"Unless you people see miraculous signs and wonders," Jesus told him, "you will never believe."

⁴⁹The royal official said, "Sir, come down before my child dies."

⁵⁰Jesus replied, "You may go. Your son will live."

The man took Jesus at his word and departed. ⁵¹While he was still on the way, his servants met him with the news that his boy was living. ⁵²When he inquired as to the time when his son got better, they said to him, "The fever left him yesterday at the seventh hour."

⁵³Then the father realized that this was the exact time at which Jesus had said to him, "Your son will live." So he and all his household believed.

⁵⁴This was the second miraculous sign that Jesus performed, having come from Judea to Galilee.

a29 Or *Messiah*

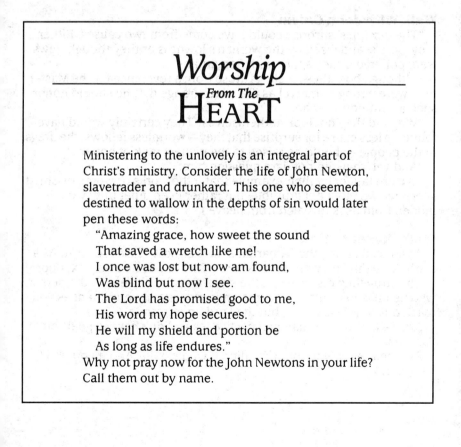

Worshipᵣᵣₒₘ ₜₕₑ
HEART

Ministering to the unlovely is an integral part of Christ's ministry. Consider the life of John Newton, slavetrader and drunkard. This one who seemed destined to wallow in the depths of sin would later pen these words:

"Amazing grace, how sweet the sound
That saved a wretch like me!
I once was lost but now am found,
Was blind but now I see.
The Lord has promised good to me,
His word my hope secures.
He will my shield and portion be
As long as life endures."

Why not pray now for the John Newtons in your life? Call them out by name.

APRIL 6

When the Work of Christ Shocks Us

His disciples . . . were surprised to find him talking with a woman (John 4:27).

Jesus cut right through the cultural prejudices of his day. But he was more interested in the salvation of a woman than in avoiding special stigma.

Unfortunately, his disciples misunderstood both his action and his motives.

Try demonstrating sensitivity toward a castoff of society, and you can expect to become the target of verbal abuse—perhaps even from your own side. John Calvin explains why.

Walk With John Calvin

"The disciples' surprise could have come from two causes. Either they were scandalized by the woman's lowness or they thought Jews were polluted if they spoke with Samaritans.

"Although both these feelings arose from a reverence for the Master, they were wrong to marvel as if it were strange that he should honor such a common woman.

"Why did they not look at themselves? They certainly would have found no less cause for surprise that they—worthless fellows, the dregs of the people—should be raised to the highest rank of honor.

"And yet, they did not dare question him.

"We are taught by their example that if the works or words of Christ shock us, we must not grumble; but rather keep quiet until what is hidden from us is revealed from heaven."

Walk Closer to God

As a racial entity, the Samaritans have almost ceased to exist. As a spiritual reality, they are everywhere—perhaps as near as next door.

The struggling divorcee . . . the shut-in senior citizen . . . the person who belongs to a cult. Others may misunderstand your intent as you reach out with Jesus' love, but the Lord understands.

After all, from a human perspective Jesus didn't have to go through Samaria.

And neither do you. But if he didn't, who would? And if you don't, who will? ◖

APRIL 7

📖 Walk in the Word
John 5:1–15

A longtime invalid is the object of Jesus' healing power in this dramatic account recorded by John.

The Healing at the Pool

5 Some time later, Jesus went up to Jerusalem for a feast of the Jews. ²Now there is in Jerusalem near the Sheep Gate a pool, which in Aramaic is called Bethesda*ᵃ* and which is surrounded by five covered colonnades. ³Here a great number of disabled people used to lie — the blind, the lame, the paralyzed. *ᵇ* ⁵One who was there had been an invalid for thirty-eight years. ⁶When Jesus saw him lying there and learned that he had been in this condition for a long time, he asked him, "Do you want to get well?"

⁷"Sir," the invalid replied, "I have no one to help me into the pool when the water is stirred. While I am trying to get in, someone else goes down ahead of me."

⁸Then Jesus said to him, "Get up! Pick up your mat and walk." ⁹At once the man was cured; he picked up his mat and walked.

The day on which this took place was a Sabbath, ¹⁰and so the Jews said to the man who had been healed, "It is the Sabbath; the law forbids you to carry your mat."

¹¹But he replied, "The man who made me well said to me, 'Pick up your mat and walk.'"

¹²So they asked him, "Who is this fellow who told you to pick it up and walk?"

¹³The man who was healed had no idea who it was, for Jesus had slipped away into the crowd that was there.

¹⁴Later Jesus found him at the temple and said to him, "See, you are well again. Stop sinning or something worse may happen to you." ¹⁵The man went away and told the Jews that it was Jesus who had made him well.

ᵃ2 Some manuscripts *Bethzatha*; other manuscripts *Bethsaida*   *ᵇ3* Some less important manuscripts *paralyzed—and they waited for the moving of the waters. ⁴From time to time an angel of the Lord would come down and stir up the waters. The first one into the pool after each such disturbance would be cured of whatever disease he had.*

APRIL 7

Waiting in the Strength of Hope

Here [a pool called Bethesda] a great number of disabled people used to lie—the blind, the lame, the paralyzed (John 5:3).

There are two types of waiting: waiting because you have to and waiting because you want to.

The people around the pool at Bethesda waited because they had to; they needed to bathe in the healing waters. One man had waited years to be healed.

But when approached by Jesus, the man found himself being asked, "Do you want to be made well?"

Joseph Parker probes these two ways of waiting.

Walk With Joseph Parker

"The world is a hospital. The person who is in the most robust health today may be struck before the setting of the sun with a fatal disease. In the midst of life we are in death.

"Life is a perpetual crisis; it can be snapped at any moment.

"Blessed is that servant who shall be found waiting, watching, and working when his Lord comes.

"These folk were all waiting, groaning, sighing. A sigh was a prayer, a groan was an entreaty, a cry of distress was a supplication.

"All the people in the porches were waiting. Are we not all doing the same thing?

"We are waiting for help, waiting till our ship comes in, waiting for sympathy, waiting for a friend without whose presence there seems to be nobody on the face of the earth. Waiting.

"One method of waiting means patience, hope, contentment, assurance that God will redeem his promises and make the heart strong; the other method of waiting is fretfulness, impatience, distrust and complaining—and that kind of waiting wears out the soul."

Walk Closer to God

"Father, teach me what it means to wait on you for my every need.

"You have promised to provide in your time. Guard my heart from fretfulness and complaining, and make my heart strong to hope." ❍

APRIL 8

Walk in the Word
John 5:16–47

John recounts Jesus' teachings in response to hostile Jews.

Life Through the Son

[16]So, because Jesus was doing these things on the Sabbath, the Jews persecuted him. [17]Jesus said to them, "My Father is always at his work to this very day, and I, too, am working." [18]For this reason the Jews tried all the harder to kill him; not only was he breaking the Sabbath, but he was even calling God his own Father, making himself equal with God.

[19]Jesus gave them this answer: "I tell you the truth, the Son can do nothing by himself; he can do only what he sees his Father doing, because whatever the Father does the Son also does. [20]For the Father loves the Son and shows him all he does. Yes, to your amazement he will show him even greater things than these. [21]For just as the Father raises the dead and gives them life, even so the Son gives life to whom he is pleased to give it. [22]Moreover, the Father judges no one, but has entrusted all judgment to the Son, [23]that all may honor the Son just as they honor the Father. He who does not honor the Son does not honor the Father, who sent him.

[24]"I tell you the truth, whoever hears my word and believes him who sent me has eternal life and will not be condemned; he has crossed over from death to life. [25]I tell you the truth, a time is coming and has now come when the dead will hear the voice of the Son of God and those who hear will live. [26]For as the Father has life in himself, so he has granted the Son to have life in himself. [27]And he has given him authority to judge because he is the Son of Man.

[28]"Do not be amazed at this, for a time is coming when all who are in their graves will hear his voice [29]and come out—those who have done good will rise to live, and those who have done evil will rise to be condemned. [30]By myself I can do nothing; I judge only as I hear, and my judgment is just, for I seek not to please myself but him who sent me.

Testimonies About Jesus

[31]"If I testify about myself, my testimony is not valid. [32]There is another who testifies in my favor, and I know that his testimony about me is valid.

[33]"You have sent to John and he has testified to the truth. [34]Not that I accept human testimony; but I mention it that you may be saved. [35]John was a lamp that burned and gave light, and you chose for a time to enjoy his light.

[36]"I have testimony weightier than that of John. For the very work that the Father has given me to finish, and which I am doing, testifies that the Father has sent me. [37]And the Father who sent me has himself testified concerning me. You have never heard his voice nor seen his form, [38]nor does his word dwell in you, for you do not believe the one he sent. [39]You diligently study[a] the Scriptures because you think that by them you possess eternal life. These are the Scriptures that testify about me, [40]yet you refuse to come to me to have life.

APRIL 8

⁴¹"I do not accept praise from men, ⁴²but I know you. I know that you do not have the love of God in your hearts. ⁴³I have come in my Father's name, and you do not accept me; but if someone else comes in his own name, you will accept him. ⁴⁴How can you believe if you accept praise from one another, yet make no effort to obtain the praise that comes from the only God ᵇ?

⁴⁵"But do not think I will accuse you before the Father. Your accuser is Moses, on whom your hopes are set. ⁴⁶If you believed Moses, you would believe me, for he wrote about me. ⁴⁷But since you do not believe what he wrote, how are you going to believe what I say?"

ᵃ39 Or *Study diligently* (the imperative)   ᵇ44 Some early manuscripts *the Only One*

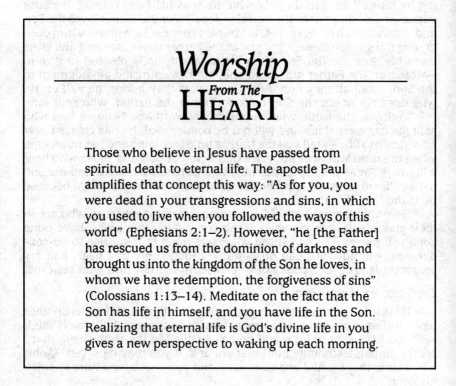

Worship
From The
HEART

Those who believe in Jesus have passed from spiritual death to eternal life. The apostle Paul amplifies that concept this way: "As for you, you were dead in your transgressions and sins, in which you used to live when you followed the ways of this world" (Ephesians 2:1–2). However, "he [the Father] has rescued us from the dominion of darkness and brought us into the kingdom of the Son he loves, in whom we have redemption, the forgiveness of sins" (Colossians 1:13–14). Meditate on the fact that the Son has life in himself, and you have life in the Son. Realizing that eternal life is God's divine life in you gives a new perspective to waking up each morning.

Words Resounding With the Testimony of Truth

You diligently study the Scriptures because you think that by them you possess eternal life. These are the Scriptures that testify about me (John 5:39).

In John 5 the Jews had a problem. While clinging zealously to their Old Testament Scriptures, they refused to embrace the person of whom those Scriptures spoke so eloquently . . . and frequently.

J.C. Ryle, who devoted his life to preaching the clear, insistent truths of God's Word, comments on the message of the Old Testament.

Walk With J.C. Ryle

"The 'Scriptures' of which our Lord speaks are, of course, the Old Testament.

"And his words show the important truth which too many are likely to overlook: that every part of the Bible is meant to teach us about Christ.

"Christ is not merely in the Gospels and the Epistles. Christ is to be found directly and indirectly in the Law, the Psalms, and the Prophets.

"In the promises to Adam, Abraham, Moses, and David . . . in the pictures and emblems of the ceremonial law . . . in the predictions of Isaiah and the other prophets . . . Jesus, the Messiah, is everywhere to be found in the Old Testament.

"How is it that men see these things so little?

"The plain truth is that the chief seat of unbelief is the heart. Many do not wish to believe, and therefore remain unbelievers. To talk of lacking evidence is childish folly."

Walk Closer to God

Searching is more than merely seeing. Many in Jesus' day saw with their eyes what they were unwilling to believe with their hearts.

They knew the Scriptures but refused to acknowledge the Messiah of whom those Scriptures spoke. The Messiah whom John the Baptist proclaimed. The big picture of Christ is there in the Old Testament for those willing to see it. And it's difficult—and dangerous—to ignore such compelling evidence.

The psalmist would describe it another way.

Foolish! ☐

April 9

Walk in the Word
John 6:1–24

John sets the stage for Jesus' testimony that he is the bread of life by recording the feeding of the five thousand.

Jesus Feeds the Five Thousand

6 Some time after this, Jesus crossed to the far shore of the Sea of Galilee (that is, the Sea of Tiberias), ²and a great crowd of people followed him because they saw the miraculous signs he had performed on the sick. ³Then Jesus went up on a mountainside and sat down with his disciples. ⁴The Jewish Passover Feast was near.

⁵When Jesus looked up and saw a great crowd coming toward him, he said to Philip, "Where shall we buy bread for these people to eat?" ⁶He asked this only to test him, for he already had in mind what he was going to do.

⁷Philip answered him, "Eight months' wages*a* would not buy enough bread for each one to have a bite!"

⁸Another of his disciples, Andrew, Simon Peter's brother, spoke up, ⁹"Here is a boy with five small barley loaves and two small fish, but how far will they go among so many?"

¹⁰Jesus said, "Have the people sit down." There was plenty of grass in that place, and the men sat down, about five thousand of them. ¹¹Jesus then took the loaves, gave thanks, and distributed to those who were seated as much as they wanted. He did the same with the fish.

¹²When they had all had enough to eat, he said to his disciples, "Gather the pieces that are left over. Let nothing be wasted." ¹³So they gathered them and filled twelve baskets with the pieces of the five barley loaves left over by those who had eaten.

¹⁴After the people saw the miraculous sign that Jesus did, they began to say, "Surely this is the Prophet who is to come into the world." ¹⁵Jesus, knowing that they intended to come and make him king by force, withdrew again to a mountain by himself.

Jesus Walks on the Water

¹⁶When evening came, his disciples went down to the lake, ¹⁷where they got into a boat and set off across the lake for Capernaum. By now it was dark, and Jesus had not yet joined them. ¹⁸A strong wind was blowing and the waters grew rough. ¹⁹When they had rowed three or three and a half miles,*b* they saw Jesus approaching the boat, walking on the water; and they were terrified. ²⁰But he said to them, "It is I; don't be afraid." ²¹Then they were willing to take him into the boat, and immediately the boat reached the shore where they were heading.

²²The next day the crowd that had stayed on the opposite shore of the lake realized that only one boat had been there, and that Jesus had not

entered it with his disciples, but that they had gone away alone. ²³Then some boats from Tiberias landed near the place where the people had eaten the bread after the Lord had given thanks. ²⁴Once the crowd realized that neither Jesus nor his disciples were there, they got into the boats and went to Capernaum in search of Jesus.

a7 Greek *two hundred denarii*   *b19* Greek *rowed twenty-five or thirty stadia* (about 5 or 6 kilometers)

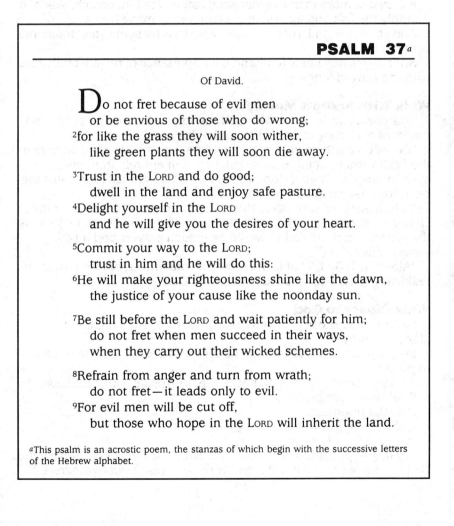

PSALM 37*a*

Of David.

Do not fret because of evil men
  or be envious of those who do wrong;
²for like the grass they will soon wither,
  like green plants they will soon die away.

³Trust in the LORD and do good;
  dwell in the land and enjoy safe pasture.
⁴Delight yourself in the LORD
  and he will give you the desires of your heart.

⁵Commit your way to the LORD;
  trust in him and he will do this:
⁶He will make your righteousness shine like the dawn,
  the justice of your cause like the noonday sun.

⁷Be still before the LORD and wait patiently for him;
  do not fret when men succeed in their ways,
  when they carry out their wicked schemes.

⁸Refrain from anger and turn from wrath;
  do not fret—it leads only to evil.
⁹For evil men will be cut off,
  but those who hope in the LORD will inherit the land.

*a*This psalm is an acrostic poem, the stanzas of which begin with the successive letters of the Hebrew alphabet.

April 9

The Priority of Being in His Presence

> Jesus, knowing that they intended to come and make him king by force, withdrew again to a mountain by himself (John 6:15).

John 6 describes one of Jesus' busiest days—a day filled with sermons and miracles.

A crowd of more than five thousand listened to him preach, saw him multiply the fish and loaves, then clamored to make him king.

And yet, in the midst of it all, Jesus withdrew for some quiet moments with the Father.

Andrew Murray knew firsthand the importance of private audiences with the King of kings.

Walk With Andrew Murray

"Man needs to be alone with God, to sense again the presence and power of his holiness, of his life, and of his love.

"Christ on earth needed it. He could not live the life of a Son here in the flesh without at times separating himself entirely from his surroundings and being alone with God. And how much more must this be indispensable to us!

"When our Lord Jesus gave the blessed command to enter our inner chamber, to shut the door and pray to our Father in secret, he gave us the promise that the Father would hear such prayers and mightily answer them.

"Alone with God. That is the secret of true prayer, of true power, of real living in face-to-face fellowship with God."

Walk Closer to God

Before Jesus chose his twelve disciples, he spent a night— alone—in prayer.

Before Jesus went to the cross, he agonized in Gethsemane—alone— in prayer.

Solitary prayer. There's no better way to wrestle with a decision.

Deal with a temptation.

Refocus priorities.

Cultivate your love for God.

Worship your Lord and Savior.

Try it, and you'll soon discover how habit-forming being alone with God can be. And how it will empower you to reach out to others. ◖◗

APRIL 10

Walk in the Word
John 6:25–59

Jesus uses his miracle of providing for the hungry with physical bread as a springboard for teaching that he is the bread that sustains spiritual life.

Jesus the Bread of Life

²⁵When they found him on the other side of the lake, they asked him, "Rabbi, when did you get here?"

²⁶Jesus answered, "I tell you the truth, you are looking for me, not because you saw miraculous signs but because you ate the loaves and had your fill. ²⁷Do not work for food that spoils, but for food that endures to eternal life, which the Son of Man will give you. On him God the Father has placed his seal of approval."

²⁸Then they asked him, "What must we do to do the works God requires?"

²⁹Jesus answered, "The work of God is this: to believe in the one he has sent."

³⁰So they asked him, "What miraculous sign then will you give that we may see it and believe you? What will you do? ³¹Our forefathers ate the manna in the desert; as it is written: 'He gave them bread from heaven to eat.'ᵃ"

³²Jesus said to them, "I tell you the truth, it is not Moses who has given you the bread from heaven, but it is my Father who gives you the true bread from heaven. ³³For the bread of God is he who comes down from heaven and gives life to the world."

³⁴"Sir," they said, "from now on give us this bread."

³⁵Then Jesus declared, "I am the bread of life. He who comes to me will never go hungry, and he who believes in me will never be thirsty. ³⁶But as I told you, you have seen me and still you do not believe. ³⁷All that the Father gives me will come to me, and whoever comes to me I will never drive away. ³⁸For I have come down from heaven not to do my will but to do the will of him who sent me. ³⁹And this is the will of him who sent me, that I shall lose none of all that he has given me, but raise them up at the last day. ⁴⁰For my Father's will is that everyone who looks to the Son and believes in him shall have eternal life, and I will raise him up at the last day."

⁴¹At this the Jews began to grumble about him because he said, "I am the bread that came down from heaven." ⁴²They said, "Is this not Jesus, the son of Joseph, whose father and mother we know? How can he now say, 'I came down from heaven'?"

⁴³"Stop grumbling among yourselves," Jesus answered. ⁴⁴"No one can come to me unless the Father who sent me draws him, and I will raise him up at the last day. ⁴⁵It is written in the Prophets: 'They will all be taught by God.'ᵇ Everyone who listens to the Father and learns from him comes to me. ⁴⁶No one has seen the Father except the one who is from God; only he has seen the Father. ⁴⁷I tell you the truth, he who believes has everlast-

303

APRIL 10

ing life. ⁴⁸I am the bread of life. ⁴⁹Your forefathers ate the manna in the desert, yet they died. ⁵⁰But here is the bread that comes down from heaven, which a man may eat and not die. ⁵¹I am the living bread that came down from heaven. If anyone eats of this bread, he will live forever. This bread is my flesh, which I will give for the life of the world."

⁵²Then the Jews began to argue sharply among themselves, "How can this man give us his flesh to eat?"

⁵³Jesus said to them, "I tell you the truth, unless you eat the flesh of the Son of Man and drink his blood, you have no life in you. ⁵⁴Whoever eats my flesh and drinks my blood has eternal life, and I will raise him up at the last day. ⁵⁵For my flesh is real food and my blood is real drink. ⁵⁶Whoever eats my flesh and drinks my blood remains in me, and I in him. ⁵⁷Just as the living Father sent me and I live because of the Father, so the one who feeds on me will live because of me. ⁵⁸This is the bread that came down from heaven. Your forefathers ate manna and died, but he who feeds on this bread will live forever." ⁵⁹He said this while teaching in the synagogue in Capernaum.

ᵃ31 Exodus 16:4; Neh. 9:15; Psalm 78:24,25   ᵇ45 Isaiah 54:13

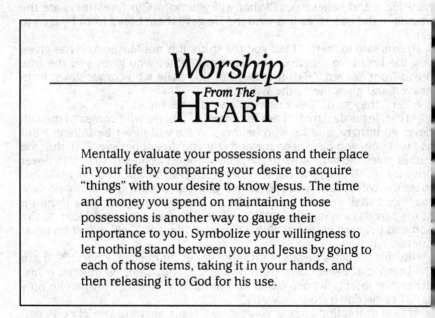

Worship
From The
HEART

Mentally evaluate your possessions and their place in your life by comparing your desire to acquire "things" with your desire to know Jesus. The time and money you spend on maintaining those possessions is another way to gauge their importance to you. Symbolize your willingness to let nothing stand between you and Jesus by going to each of those items, taking it in your hands, and then releasing it to God for his use.

Seeking God for Who He Is, Not What He Provides

I tell you the truth, you are looking for me, not because you saw miraculous signs but because you ate the loaves and had your fill (John 6:26).

Life in Christ. It's not the promise of a chicken in every pot and two cars in every garage.

But in Jesus' day—and still today—many have viewed religion from the perspective, "What's in it for me?"

But Jesus rebuked such self-seeking individuals in John 6. And the result of this hard-hitting sermon? Many turned back and no longer followed him.

Albert Barnes examines the motives that would cause people to be such fair-weather followers.

Walk With Albert Barnes

"To seek him because they had seen miracles and were convinced by them that he was the Messiah would have been proper. But to follow him simply because their wants were supplied was mere selfishness—and selfishness of a gross kind.

"And yet, many seek religion from no better motive than this. They suppose it will add to their earthly happiness. Or they seek heaven only as a place of happiness, and regard religion as valuable only for this. All this is mere selfishness.

"Religion does not forbid regarding our own happiness, or seeking it in any proper way. But when this is the prevailing motive, it is evidence that we have never yet sought God aright.

"If so, we are aiming at the loaves and fishes, and not at the honor of God and the good of his kingdom."

Walk Closer to God

It's true that in Christ you have ample reason to be happy. After all, you've received "every spiritual blessing" (Ephesians 1:3) . . . and many material ones as well (James 1:17).

Like the fish-filled crowd, you might be tempted to seek him for the supply he provides. But what if there were no feast tomorrow? Would you still pledge allegiance to the living bread?

The psalmist said it well: "Earth has nothing I desire besides you" (Psalm 73:25).

What do you say? ☾

APRIL 11

Walk in the Word
John 6:60–71

The cost of discipleship and the radical nature of Jesus' teachings lead many followers to turn away from Jesus, but Peter speaks for the Twelve in choosing to remain.

Many Disciples Desert Jesus

⁶⁰On hearing it, many of his disciples said, "This is a hard teaching. Who can accept it?"

⁶¹Aware that his disciples were grumbling about this, Jesus said to them, "Does this offend you? ⁶²What if you see the Son of Man ascend to where he was before! ⁶³The Spirit gives life; the flesh counts for nothing. The words I have spoken to you are spirit*a* and they are life. ⁶⁴Yet there are some of you who do not believe." For Jesus had known from the beginning which of them did not believe and who would betray him. ⁶⁵He went on to say, "This is why I told you that no one can come to me unless the Father has enabled him."

⁶⁶From this time many of his disciples turned back and no longer followed him.

⁶⁷"You do not want to leave too, do you?" Jesus asked the Twelve.

⁶⁸Simon Peter answered him, "Lord, to whom shall we go? You have the words of eternal life. ⁶⁹We believe and know that you are the Holy One of God."

⁷⁰Then Jesus replied, "Have I not chosen you, the Twelve? Yet one of you is a devil!" ⁷¹(He meant Judas, the son of Simon Iscariot, who, though one of the Twelve, was later to betray him.)

a63 Or Spirit

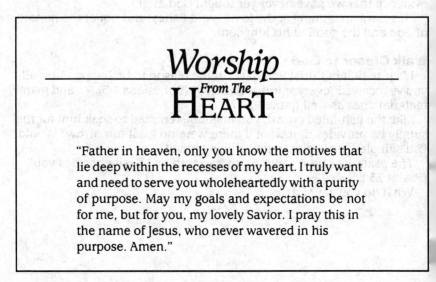

Worship
From The
HEART

"Father in heaven, only you know the motives that
lie deep within the recesses of my heart. I truly want
and need to serve you wholeheartedly with a purity
of purpose. May my goals and expectations be not
for me, but for you, my lovely Savior. I pray this in
the name of Jesus, who never wavered in his
purpose. Amen."

Following Christ for the Right Reasons

From this time many of his disciples turned back and no longer followed him (John 6:66).

Hard sayings have a way of quickly thinning the ranks of lukewarm followers. In John 6 Jesus cut straight to the heart of the matter: "You are looking for me, not because you saw miraculous signs but because you ate the loaves and had your fill" (John 6:26).

Is it because of what you think he can do for you that you call him "Lord"—or because of who he is?

As James Stalker comments, wrong motives for following Christ often flow from faulty expectations about Christ.

Walk With James Stalker

"Jesus had heard of the tragic death of John the Baptist and immediately hurried to a desert place with his disciples to talk over the event.

"When moved by compassion for the helpless multitude, Jesus performed the stupendous miracle of feeding five thousand. The effect was overwhelming.

"The crowd became instantaneously convinced that this was none other than the Messiah. Having only one conception of what that meant, they endeavored to take him by force and make him a king, that is, force him to be the leader of a messianic revolt.

"It seemed the crowning hour of success. But to Jesus himself it was an hour of sadness and shame.

"This was all his work had come to? This was the conception they had of him? Were they to try to determine the course of his future action instead of humbly asking what he would have them do?

"They were looking for a 'bread king' who would give them idleness and plenty, mountains of loaves, rivers of milk, every comfort without labor. What he had to give was eternal life."

Walk Closer to God

"No one can come to me unless the Father . . . draws him, and I will raise him up at the last day" (John 6:44).

"Lord, draw me to you, that I too may know the one who is the resurrection and the life. I find my satisfaction in you, the bread of life."

April 12

Walk in the Word
John 7

John records Jesus' journey to the Feast of Tabernacles, as well as Jesus' teachings during the Feast and the strong reaction they provoked.

Jesus Goes to the Feast of Tabernacles

7 After this, Jesus went around in Galilee, purposely staying away from Judea because the Jews there were waiting to take his life. ²But when the Jewish Feast of Tabernacles was near, ³Jesus' brothers said to him, "You ought to leave here and go to Judea, so that your disciples may see the miracles you do. ⁴No one who wants to become a public figure acts in secret. Since you are doing these things, show yourself to the world." ⁵For even his own brothers did not believe in him.

⁶Therefore Jesus told them, "The right time for me has not yet come; for you any time is right. ⁷The world cannot hate you, but it hates me because I testify that what it does is evil. ⁸You go to the Feast. I am not yet[a] going up to this Feast, because for me the right time has not yet come." ⁹Having said this, he stayed in Galilee.

¹⁰However, after his brothers had left for the Feast, he went also, not publicly, but in secret. ¹¹Now at the Feast the Jews were watching for him and asking, "Where is that man?"

¹²Among the crowds there was widespread whispering about him. Some said, "He is a good man."

Others replied, "No, he deceives the people." ¹³But no one would say anything publicly about him for fear of the Jews.

Jesus Teaches at the Feast

¹⁴Not until halfway through the Feast did Jesus go up to the temple courts and begin to teach. ¹⁵The Jews were amazed and asked, "How did this man get such learning without having studied?"

¹⁶Jesus answered, "My teaching is not my own. It comes from him who sent me. ¹⁷If anyone chooses to do God's will, he will find out whether my teaching comes from God or whether I speak on my own. ¹⁸He who speaks on his own does so to gain honor for himself, but he who works for the honor of the one who sent him is a man of truth; there is nothing false about him. ¹⁹Has not Moses given you the law? Yet not one of you keeps the law. Why are you trying to kill me?"

²⁰"You are demon-possessed," the crowd answered. "Who is trying to kill you?"

²¹Jesus said to them, "I did one miracle, and you are all astonished. ²²Yet, because Moses gave you circumcision (though actually it did not come from Moses, but from the patriarchs), you circumcise a child on the Sabbath. ²³Now if a child can be circumcised on the Sabbath so that the law of Moses may not be broken, why are you angry with me for healing the whole man on the Sabbath? ²⁴Stop judging by mere appearances, and make a right judgment."

APRIL 13

📖 Walk in the Word
John 8:1–30

John captures the spirited dialogue between Jesus and the Pharisees centering around whether Jesus really was who he claimed to be.

8 But Jesus went to the Mount of Olives. ²At dawn he appeared again in the temple courts, where all the people gathered around him, and he sat down to teach them. ³The teachers of the law and the Pharisees brought in a woman caught in adultery. They made her stand before the group ⁴and said to Jesus, "Teacher, this woman was caught in the act of adultery. ⁵In the Law Moses commanded us to stone such women. Now what do you say?" ⁶They were using this question as a trap, in order to have a basis for accusing him.

But Jesus bent down and started to write on the ground with his finger. ⁷When they kept on questioning him, he straightened up and said to them, "If any one of you is without sin, let him be the first to throw a stone at her." ⁸Again he stooped down and wrote on the ground.

⁹At this, those who heard began to go away one at a time, the older ones first, until only Jesus was left, with the woman still standing there. ¹⁰Jesus straightened up and asked her, "Woman, where are they? Has no one condemned you?"

¹¹"No one, sir," she said.

"Then neither do I condemn you," Jesus declared. "Go now and leave your life of sin."

The Validity of Jesus' Testimony

¹²When Jesus spoke again to the people, he said, "I am the light of the world. Whoever follows me will never walk in darkness, but will have the light of life."

¹³The Pharisees challenged him, "Here you are, appearing as your own witness; your testimony is not valid."

¹⁴Jesus answered, "Even if I testify on my own behalf, my testimony is valid, for I know where I came from and where I am going. But you have no idea where I come from or where I am going. ¹⁵You judge by human standards; I pass judgment on no one. ¹⁶But if I do judge, my decisions are right, because I am not alone. I stand with the Father, who sent me. ¹⁷In your own Law it is written that the testimony of two men is valid. ¹⁸I am one who testifies for myself; my other witness is the Father, who sent me."

¹⁹Then they asked him, "Where is your father?"

"You do not know me or my Father," Jesus replied. "If you knew me, you would know my Father also." ²⁰He spoke these words while teaching in the temple area near the place where the offerings were put. Yet no one seized him, because his time had not yet come.

Fountain of Life for Thirsty Hearts

If anyone is thirsty, let him come to me and drink. Whoever believes in me, as the Scripture has said, streams of living water will flow from within him (John 7:37–38).

Bread. Light. Water. Vine. Door.

Jesus described himself and his heavenly powers in unusual ways.

Some were difficult for his audience to understand—no doubt because his words carried significance far beyond that of the object he used.

Bernard of Clairvaux composed this hymn of praise to the Christ who is the fountain of life—and much more.

Walk With Bernard of Clairvaux

Jesus, Thou joy of loving hearts,
    Thou fount of life, Thou light of men,
From the best bliss that earth imparts
    We turn unfilled to Thee again.
Thy truth unchanged hath ever stood;
    Thou savest those that on Thee call;
To them that seek Thee, Thou art good;
    To them that find Thee, all in all.
We taste Thee, O Thou living Bread,
    And long to feast upon Thee still;
We drink of Thee, the Fountainhead,
    And thirst our souls from Thee to fill.
Our restless spirits yearn for Thee,
    Where'er our changeful lot is cast,
Glad when Thy gracious smile we see,
    Blest when our faith can hold Thee fast.

Walk Closer to God

"I am the light of the world."

"If anyone is thirsty, let him come to me and drink."

"I am the bread of life."

Light. Water. Bread. The essentials of spiritual life. All to be found in the person of Jesus Christ.

Are you hungry to know God? In the dark about God's will? Thirsting to find life in all its fullness?

Those who seek will find that Jesus is truly "all in all."

APRIL 12

⁵⁰Nicodemus, who had gone to Jesus earlier and who was one of their own number, asked, ⁵¹"Does our law condemn anyone without first hearing him to find out what he is doing?"

⁵²They replied, "Are you from Galilee, too? Look into it, and you will find that a prophet*e* does not come out of Galilee."

[The earliest manuscripts and many other ancient witnesses do not have John 7:53–8:11.]

⁵³Then each went to his own home.

a8 Some early manuscripts do not have *yet.*   *b26* Or *Messiah*; also in verses 27, 31, 41 and 42   *c37,38* Or / *If anyone is thirsty, let him come to me.* / *And let him drink,* *38who believes in me.* / *As*   *d42* Greek *seed*   *e52* Two early manuscripts *the Prophet*

Worship From The HEART

Jesus described the effect of his presence in a person's life as a river of living water flowing from within him. Contrast a flowing, living stream with a stagnant pool, and then use this picture to gauge the vitality of your spiritual life. Praise God for specific ways the living water works in you—nourishing, cleansing, refreshing, soothing, satisfying. And praise him for the opportunities you have to let that stream overflow into the lives of other people.

APRIL 12

Is Jesus the Christ?

25At that point some of the people of Jerusalem began to ask, "Isn't this the man they are trying to kill? 26Here he is, speaking publicly, and they are not saying a word to him. Have the authorities really concluded that he is the Christ*b*? 27But we know where this man is from; when the Christ comes, no one will know where he is from."

28Then Jesus, still teaching in the temple courts, cried out, "Yes, you know me, and you know where I am from. I am not here on my own, but he who sent me is true. You do not know him, 29but I know him because I am from him and he sent me."

30At this they tried to seize him, but no one laid a hand on him, because his time had not yet come. 31Still, many in the crowd put their faith in him. They said, "When the Christ comes, will he do more miraculous signs than this man?"

32The Pharisees heard the crowd whispering such things about him. Then the chief priests and the Pharisees sent temple guards to arrest him.

33Jesus said, "I am with you for only a short time, and then I go to the one who sent me. 34You will look for me, but you will not find me; and where I am, you cannot come."

35The Jews said to one another, "Where does this man intend to go that we cannot find him? Will he go where our people live scattered among the Greeks, and teach the Greeks? 36What did he mean when he said, 'You will look for me, but you will not find me,' and 'Where I am, you cannot come'?"

37On the last and greatest day of the Feast, Jesus stood and said in a loud voice, "If anyone is thirsty, let him come to me and drink. 38Whoever believes in me, as*c* the Scripture has said, streams of living water will flow from within him." 39By this he meant the Spirit, whom those who believed in him were later to receive. Up to that time the Spirit had not been given, since Jesus had not yet been glorified.

40On hearing his words, some of the people said, "Surely this man is the Prophet."

41Others said, "He is the Christ."

Still others asked, "How can the Christ come from Galilee? 42Does not the Scripture say that the Christ will come from David's family*d* and from Bethlehem, the town where David lived?" 43Thus the people were divided because of Jesus. 44Some wanted to seize him, but no one laid a hand on him.

Unbelief of the Jewish Leaders

45Finally the temple guards went back to the chief priests and Pharisees, who asked them, "Why didn't you bring him in?"

46"No one ever spoke the way this man does," the guards declared.

47"You mean he has deceived you also?" the Pharisees retorted. 48"Has any of the rulers or of the Pharisees believed in him? 49No! But this mob that knows nothing of the law—there is a curse on them."

APRIL 15

📖 Walk in the Word
John 9:1–12

The eyes of a man born blind are opened in John's account of a dramatic encounter with Jesus.

Jesus Heals a Man Born Blind

9 As he went along, he saw a man blind from birth. ²His disciples asked him, "Rabbi, who sinned, this man or his parents, that he was born blind?"

³"Neither this man nor his parents sinned," said Jesus, "but this happened so that the work of God might be displayed in his life. ⁴As long as it is day, we must do the work of him who sent me. Night is coming, when no one can work. ⁵While I am in the world, I am the light of the world."

⁶Having said this, he spit on the ground, made some mud with the saliva, and put it on the man's eyes. ⁷"Go," he told him, "wash in the Pool of Siloam" (this word means Sent). So the man went and washed, and came home seeing.

⁸His neighbors and those who had formerly seen him begging asked, "Isn't this the same man who used to sit and beg?" ⁹Some claimed that he was.

Others said, "No, he only looks like him."

But he himself insisted, "I am the man."

¹⁰"How then were your eyes opened?" they demanded.

¹¹He replied, "The man they call Jesus made some mud and put it on my eyes. He told me to go to Siloam and wash. So I went and washed, and then I could see."

¹²"Where is this man?" they asked him.

"I don't know," he said.

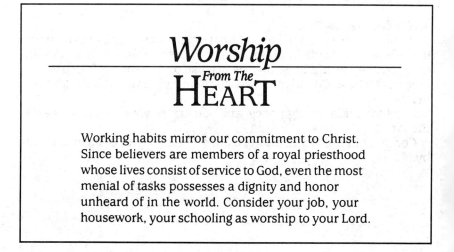

Worship
H*From The*EART

Working habits mirror our commitment to Christ. Since believers are members of a royal priesthood whose lives consist of service to God, even the most menial of tasks possesses a dignity and honor unheard of in the world. Consider your job, your housework, your schooling as worship to your Lord.

Faith—A Relationship, Not a Formula

Jesus said, "If you hold to my teaching, you are really my disciples" (John 8:31).

You can find a formula for doing just about anything. For example:
Physics: $E = mc^2$
Politics: "If you can't convince the voters, confuse them."
Finances: "Live within your income, even if you have to borrow to do it."

But the life of faith cannot be reduced to a formula. It is more than just plugging numbers into an equation and getting the right answer.

In John 8, Jesus revealed that faith is a way of life. As Alexander Maclaren explains, faith goes far deeper than mere mental acknowledgment.

Walk With Alexander Maclaren

"The notion that a man who does not contradict the teaching of the New Testament is thereby a Christian is a very old and very dangerous idea.

"There are many who have no better claim to be called Christians than the fact that they never denied anything that Jesus Christ said.

"This kind of faith hardens into mere formalism, or liquefies into mere careless indifference as to the very truth that it professes to believe.

"There is nothing more impotent than creeds which lie dormant in our brains and have no influence on our lives.

"See to it that all your convictions be translated into practice, and all your practice be informed by your convictions."

Walk Closer to God

In John 8 those who believed Christ's claims were called to continue in his Word . . . abide in his teaching . . . be "at home" in his truth. In that way they would be known as his disciples—learner-friends—followers whose Christianity was no mere formula, but faith on the march.

Read the Bible through once, and you are on your way to mastering the Word.

Continue in the Word, and you are on your way to being mastered by it! ❍

APRIL 14

⁵²At this the Jews exclaimed, "Now we know that you are demon-possessed! Abraham died and so did the prophets, yet you say that if anyone keeps your word, he will never taste death. ⁵³Are you greater than our father Abraham? He died, and so did the prophets. Who do you think you are?"

⁵⁴Jesus replied, "If I glorify myself, my glory means nothing. My Father, whom you claim as your God, is the one who glorifies me. ⁵⁵Though you do not know him, I know him. If I said I did not, I would be a liar like you, but I do know him and keep his word. ⁵⁶Your father Abraham rejoiced at the thought of seeing my day; he saw it and was glad."

⁵⁷"You are not yet fifty years old," the Jews said to him, "and you have seen Abraham!"

⁵⁸"I tell you the truth," Jesus answered, "before Abraham was born, I am!" ⁵⁹At this, they picked up stones to stone him, but Jesus hid himself, slipping away from the temple grounds.

ᵃ33 Greek seed; also in verse 37   ᵇ38 Or presence. Therefore do what you have heard from the Father.   ᶜ39 Some early manuscripts "If you are Abraham's children," said Jesus, "then

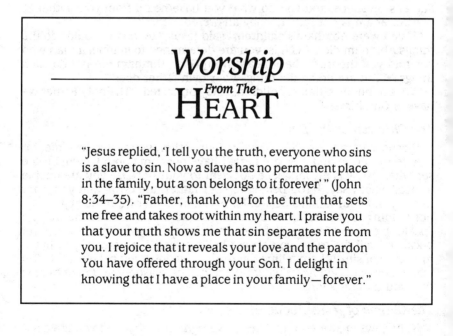

Worship
From The
HEART

"Jesus replied, 'I tell you the truth, everyone who sins is a slave to sin. Now a slave has no permanent place in the family, but a son belongs to it forever' " (John 8:34–35). "Father, thank you for the truth that sets me free and takes root within my heart. I praise you that your truth shows me that sin separates me from you. I rejoice that it reveals your love and the pardon You have offered through your Son. I delight in knowing that I have a place in your family—forever."

APRIL 14

Walk in the Word
John 8:31–59

Jesus tests the genuineness of the Jews who had responded positively to his teachings; they soon reveal their lack of allegiance as they exhibit hostility and lack of understanding.

The Children of Abraham

³¹To the Jews who had believed him, Jesus said, "If you hold to my teaching, you are really my disciples. ³²Then you will know the truth, and the truth will set you free."

³³They answered him, "We are Abraham's descendants*ᵃ* and have never been slaves of anyone. How can you say that we shall be set free?"

³⁴Jesus replied, "I tell you the truth, everyone who sins is a slave to sin. ³⁵Now a slave has no permanent place in the family, but a son belongs to it forever. ³⁶So if the Son sets you free, you will be free indeed. ³⁷I know you are Abraham's descendants. Yet you are ready to kill me, because you have no room for my word. ³⁸I am telling you what I have seen in the Father's presence, and you do what you have heard from your father.*ᵇ*"

³⁹"Abraham is our father," they answered.

"If you were Abraham's children," said Jesus, "then you would*ᶜ* do the things Abraham did. ⁴⁰As it is, you are determined to kill me, a man who has told you the truth that I heard from God. Abraham did not do such things. ⁴¹You are doing the things your own father does."

"We are not illegitimate children," they protested. "The only Father we have is God himself."

The Children of the Devil

⁴²Jesus said to them, "If God were your Father, you would love me, for I came from God and now am here. I have not come on my own; but he sent me. ⁴³Why is my language not clear to you? Because you are unable to hear what I say. ⁴⁴You belong to your father, the devil, and you want to carry out your father's desire. He was a murderer from the beginning, not holding to the truth, for there is no truth in him. When he lies, he speaks his native language, for he is a liar and the father of lies. ⁴⁵Yet because I tell the truth, you do not believe me! ⁴⁶Can any of you prove me guilty of sin? If I am telling the truth, why don't you believe me? ⁴⁷He who belongs to God hears what God says. The reason you do not hear is that you do not belong to God."

The Claims of Jesus About Himself

⁴⁸The Jews answered him, "Aren't we right in saying that you are a Samaritan and demon-possessed?"

⁴⁹"I am not possessed by a demon," said Jesus, "but I honor my Father and you dishonor me. ⁵⁰I am not seeking glory for myself; but there is one who seeks it, and he is the judge. ⁵¹I tell you the truth, if anyone keeps my word, he will never see death."

Working Faithfully on the Task at Hand

> As long as it is day, we must do the work of him who sent me.
> Night is coming, when no one can work (John 9:4).

To become a diligent worker, but not a workaholic—that is the challenge of every Christian.

Jesus was a model worker in more ways than one. Tirelessly he went about his Father's business. He first learned good work habits at Joseph's workbench, and later called hardworking fishermen as some of his first followers. And always the focus of his life was to "do the work of him who sent me."

Listen as James Hastings provides this sound advice on putting all you have into God's work.

Walk With James Hastings

"A sure method of finding out what God wishes us to do is to work faithfully and conscientiously at the task that falls to our hand, watching ever for the guidance that God will surely send us.

"We shall never miss God's call as long as we are in the path of duty.

"We may not know where God is leading us, but we can be sure that doing our present work as well and as thoroughly as lies within our power is the best possible training for anything the future may hold for us.

"The work that we are doing may seem to us to be useless and unimportant. It is remarkable, however, how things which at the time seemed to be of no importance turn out to be useful, and how the training we have received, unconscious of its value though we were, bears fruit."

Walk Closer to God

The church of Jesus Christ today is full of willing people: a few willing to work, the rest willing to let them.

When zest departs in the work of the Lord, labor becomes drudgery.

Don't allow busyness to turn to barrenness. After all, it's not so much how busy you are, but why you are busy. The bee is praised; the mosquito is swatted. Ask God's blessing on your job, and then do it willingly, joyfully and faithfully. ❍

APRIL 16

Walk in the Word
John 9:13–41

John spotlights the spiritual blindness of the Pharisees in his account of the Jew's investigation into the healing of the man born blind.

The Pharisees Investigate the Healing

13They brought to the Pharisees the man who had been blind. 14Now the day on which Jesus had made the mud and opened the man's eyes was a Sabbath. 15Therefore the Pharisees also asked him how he had received his sight. "He put mud on my eyes," the man replied, "and I washed, and now I see."

16Some of the Pharisees said, "This man is not from God, for he does not keep the Sabbath."

But others asked, "How can a sinner do such miraculous signs?" So they were divided.

17Finally they turned again to the blind man, "What have you to say about him? It was your eyes he opened."

The man replied, "He is a prophet."

18The Jews still did not believe that he had been blind and had received his sight until they sent for the man's parents. 19"Is this your son?" they asked. "Is this the one you say was born blind? How is it that now he can see?"

20"We know he is our son," the parents answered, "and we know he was born blind. 21But how he can see now, or who opened his eyes, we don't know. Ask him. He is of age; he will speak for himself." 22His parents said this because they were afraid of the Jews, for already the Jews had decided that anyone who acknowledged that Jesus was the Christ*a* would be put out of the synagogue. 23That was why his parents said, "He is of age; ask him."

24A second time they summoned the man who had been blind. "Give glory to God,*b*" they said. "We know this man is a sinner."

25He replied, "Whether he is a sinner or not, I don't know. One thing I do know. I was blind but now I see!"

26Then they asked him, "What did he do to you? How did he open your eyes?"

27He answered, "I have told you already and you did not listen. Why do you want to hear it again? Do you want to become his disciples, too?"

28Then they hurled insults at him and said, "You are this fellow's disciple! We are disciples of Moses! 29We know that God spoke to Moses, but as for this fellow, we don't even know where he comes from."

30The man answered, "Now that is remarkable! You don't know where he comes from, yet he opened my eyes. 31We know that God does not listen to sinners. He listens to the godly man who does his will. 32Nobody has ever heard of opening the eyes of a man born blind. 33If this man were not from God, he could do nothing."

34To this they replied, "You were steeped in sin at birth; how dare you lecture us!" And they threw him out.

APRIL 16

Spiritual Blindness

³⁵Jesus heard that they had thrown him out, and when he found him, he said, "Do you believe in the Son of Man?"

³⁶"Who is he, sir?" the man asked. "Tell me so that I may believe in him."

³⁷Jesus said, "You have now seen him; in fact, he is the one speaking with you."

³⁸Then the man said, "Lord, I believe," and he worshiped him.

³⁹Jesus said, "For judgment I have come into this world, so that the blind will see and those who see will become blind."

⁴⁰Some Pharisees who were with him heard him say this and asked, "What? Are we blind too?"

⁴¹Jesus said, "If you were blind, you would not be guilty of sin; but now that you claim you can see, your guilt remains.

a22 Or *Messiah*   *b24* A solemn charge to tell the truth (see Joshua 7:19)

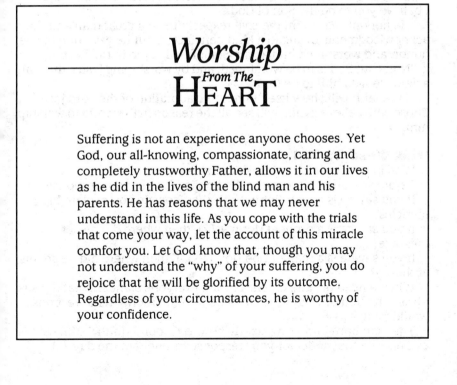

Worship From The HEART

Suffering is not an experience anyone chooses. Yet God, our all-knowing, compassionate, caring and completely trustworthy Father, allows it in our lives as he did in the lives of the blind man and his parents. He has reasons that we may never understand in this life. As you cope with the trials that come your way, let the account of this miracle comfort you. Let God know that, though you may not understand the "why" of your suffering, you do rejoice that he will be glorified by its outcome. Regardless of your circumstances, he is worthy of your confidence.

APRIL 16

All the Reason in the World to Worship

Then the man said, "Lord, I believe," and he worshiped him (John 9:38).

John 9 describes a story of front-page significance. A man born blind received his sight—a miracle duplicated nowhere in the Old Testament. A miracle that the Pharisees found disturbing.

For the more they investigated, the more they were faced with a decision regarding the sight-giver.

They were unwilling to admit in their unbelief what the man born blind was only too willing to acknowledge, as Matthew Henry describes.

Walk With Matthew Henry

"Believing with the heart, the man professed his faith in Christ: 'Lord, I believe you to be the Son of God.'

"He not only gave him the civil respect due to a great man and the acknowledgments owing to a kind benefactor, but he gave him divine honor, and worshiped him as the Son of God come in the flesh.

"None but God is to be worshiped, and by worshiping Jesus, the man acknowledged him to be God.

"True faith will show itself in humble adoration of the Lord Jesus. Those who believe in him will see all the reason in the world to worship him."

Walk Closer to God

Who in your opinion is Jesus of Nazareth?

Before you answer, consider the implications of your response.

If you say he is a man (John 9:11), then how do you explain his miracles?

If you say he is a prophet (John 9:17), then where did he get his message?

If you say he is a man of God (John 9:33), then where did he get his authority?

When a head of state enters a room, everyone stands. What if Jesus Christ, the Son of God, were to come into the room? What response would he deserve?

The man born blind saw clearly how to respond (John 9:38). Let his example be the model for your response throughout the day. ◖

APRIL 17

Walk in the Word
John 10

Jesus uses the Old Testament imagery of "shepherd" to describe his relationship to those who belong to him, and John tells of mixed reaction to the words and deeds of Jesus.

The Shepherd and His Flock

10 "I tell you the truth, the man who does not enter the sheep pen by the gate, but climbs in by some other way, is a thief and a robber. ²The man who enters by the gate is the shepherd of his sheep. ³The watchman opens the gate for him, and the sheep listen to his voice. He calls his own sheep by name and leads them out. ⁴When he has brought out all his own, he goes on ahead of them, and his sheep follow him because they know his voice. ⁵But they will never follow a stranger; in fact, they will run away from him because they do not recognize a stranger's voice." ⁶Jesus used this figure of speech, but they did not understand what he was telling them.

⁷Therefore Jesus said again, "I tell you the truth, I am the gate for the sheep. ⁸All who ever came before me were thieves and robbers, but the sheep did not listen to them. ⁹I am the gate; whoever enters through me will be saved.ᵃ He will come in and go out, and find pasture. ¹⁰The thief comes only to steal and kill and destroy; I have come that they may have life, and have it to the full.

¹¹"I am the good shepherd. The good shepherd lays down his life for the sheep. ¹²The hired hand is not the shepherd who owns the sheep. So when he sees the wolf coming, he abandons the sheep and runs away. Then the wolf attacks the flock and scatters it. ¹³The man runs away because he is a hired hand and cares nothing for the sheep.

¹⁴"I am the good shepherd; I know my sheep and my sheep know me— ¹⁵just as the Father knows me and I know the Father—and I lay down my life for the sheep. ¹⁶I have other sheep that are not of this sheep pen. I must bring them also. They too will listen to my voice, and there shall be one flock and one shepherd. ¹⁷The reason my Father loves me is that I lay down my life—only to take it up again. ¹⁸No one takes it from me, but I lay it down of my own accord. I have authority to lay it down and authority to take it up again. This command I received from my Father."

¹⁹At these words the Jews were again divided. ²⁰Many of them said, "He is demon-possessed and raving mad. Why listen to him?"

²¹But others said, "These are not the sayings of a man possessed by a demon. Can a demon open the eyes of the blind?"

The Unbelief of the Jews

²²Then came the Feast of Dedicationᵇ at Jerusalem. It was winter, ²³and Jesus was in the temple area walking in Solomon's Colonnade. ²⁴The Jews gathered around him, saying, "How long will you keep us in suspense? If you are the Christ,ᶜ tell us plainly."

APRIL 17

²⁵Jesus answered, "I did tell you, but you do not believe. The miracles I do in my Father's name speak for me, ²⁶but you do not believe because you are not my sheep. ²⁷My sheep listen to my voice; I know them, and they follow me. ²⁸I give them eternal life, and they shall never perish; no one can snatch them out of my hand. ²⁹My Father, who has given them to me, is greater than all*ᵈ*; no one can snatch them out of my Father's hand. ³⁰I and the Father are one."

³¹Again the Jews picked up stones to stone him, ³²but Jesus said to them, "I have shown you many great miracles from the Father. For which of these do you stone me?"

³³"We are not stoning you for any of these," replied the Jews, "but for blasphemy, because you, a mere man, claim to be God."

³⁴Jesus answered them, "Is it not written in your Law, 'I have said you are gods'ᵉ? ³⁵If he called them 'gods,' to whom the word of God came — and the Scripture cannot be broken— ³⁶what about the one whom the Father set apart as his very own and sent into the world? Why then do you accuse me of blasphemy because I said, 'I am God's Son'? ³⁷Do not believe me unless I do what my Father does. ³⁸But if I do it, even though you do not believe me, believe the miracles, that you may know and understand that the Father is in me, and I in the Father." ³⁹Again they tried to seize him, but he escaped their grasp.

⁴⁰Then Jesus went back across the Jordan to the place where John had been baptizing in the early days. Here he stayed ⁴¹and many people came to him. They said, "Though John never performed a miraculous sign, all that John said about this man was true." ⁴²And in that place many believed in Jesus.

ᵃ9 Or kept safe   ᵇ22 That is, Hanukkah   ᶜ24 Or Messiah   ᵈ29 Many early manuscripts What my Father has given me is greater than all   ᵉ34 Psalm 82:6

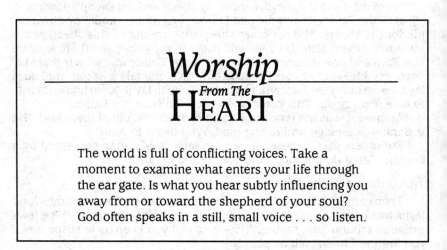

Worship
From The
HEART

The world is full of conflicting voices. Take a moment to examine what enters your life through the ear gate. Is what you hear subtly influencing you away from or toward the shepherd of your soul? God often speaks in a still, small voice . . . so listen.

We Know With Whom We Go

My sheep listen to my voice; I know them, and they follow me (John 10:27).

A musician who ignores the conductor.
A soldier who disobeys his commander.
A reporter who covers his eyes and ears.

Such situations are hard to imagine. But no one has any trouble at all thinking about a sheep who fails to follow its shepherd. Everybody knows sheep might be just that dumb.

Charles Spurgeon points out why Christ's use of the shepherd/sheep imagery in John 10 is both appropriate and compelling.

Walk With Charles Spurgeon

"We should follow our Lord as unhesitatingly as sheep follow their shepherd, for he has a right to lead us wherever he pleases.

"We are not our own; we are bought with a price. Let us recognize the rights of the redeeming blood.

"The soldier follows his captain, the servant his master. Much more must we follow our Redeemer, to whom we are a purchased possession.

"We are not true to our profession of being Christians if we question the bidding of our leader and commander. Submission is our duty; making excuses is not.

"Wherever Jesus may lead us, he goes before us. If we do not know where we go, we know with whom we go. With such a companion, who will dread the perils of the road?"

Walk Closer to God

Think back to the familiar phrases of Psalm 23. What does the Good Shepherd whom you follow do for you?

"He makes me lie down in green pastures"—provision!
"He restores my soul"—refreshment!
"He guides me in paths of righteousness"—leadership!

Following the Shepherd is not a chore, but the way to an abundant life.

When the shepherd calls, be quick to follow. After all, you are his!

APRIL 18

📖 Walk in the Word
John 11

John exposes the powerful emotion surrounding the death of Jesus' friend Lazarus, climaxing in the raising of Lazarus and the intensification of the plot to kill Jesus.

The Death of Lazarus

11 Now a man named Lazarus was sick. He was from Bethany, the village of Mary and her sister Martha. ²This Mary, whose brother Lazarus now lay sick, was the same one who poured perfume on the Lord and wiped his feet with her hair. ³So the sisters sent word to Jesus, "Lord, the one you love is sick."

⁴When he heard this, Jesus said, "This sickness will not end in death. No, it is for God's glory so that God's Son may be glorified through it." ⁵Jesus loved Martha and her sister and Lazarus. ⁶Yet when he heard that Lazarus was sick, he stayed where he was two more days.

⁷Then he said to his disciples, "Let us go back to Judea."

⁸"But Rabbi," they said, "a short while ago the Jews tried to stone you, and yet you are going back there?"

⁹Jesus answered, "Are there not twelve hours of daylight? A man who walks by day will not stumble, for he sees by this world's light. ¹⁰It is when he walks by night that he stumbles, for he has no light."

¹¹After he had said this, he went on to tell them, "Our friend Lazarus has fallen asleep; but I am going there to wake him up."

¹²His disciples replied, "Lord, if he sleeps, he will get better." ¹³Jesus had been speaking of his death, but his disciples thought he meant natural sleep.

¹⁴So then he told them plainly, "Lazarus is dead, ¹⁵and for your sake I am glad I was not there, so that you may believe. But let us go to him."

¹⁶Then Thomas (called Didymus) said to the rest of the disciples, "Let us also go, that we may die with him."

Jesus Comforts the Sisters

¹⁷On his arrival, Jesus found that Lazarus had already been in the tomb for four days. ¹⁸Bethany was less than two miles*a* from Jerusalem, ¹⁹and many Jews had come to Martha and Mary to comfort them in the loss of their brother. ²⁰When Martha heard that Jesus was coming, she went out to meet him, but Mary stayed at home.

²¹"Lord," Martha said to Jesus, "if you had been here, my brother would not have died. ²²But I know that even now God will give you whatever you ask."

²³Jesus said to her, "Your brother will rise again."

²⁴Martha answered, "I know he will rise again in the resurrection at the last day."

²⁵Jesus said to her, "I am the resurrection and the life. He who believes in me will live, even though he dies; ²⁶and whoever lives and believes in me will never die. Do you believe this?"

APRIL 18

²⁷"Yes, Lord," she told him, "I believe that you are the Christ,^b the Son of God, who was to come into the world."

²⁸And after she had said this, she went back and called her sister Mary aside. "The Teacher is here," she said, "and is asking for you." ²⁹When Mary heard this, she got up quickly and went to him. ³⁰Now Jesus had not yet entered the village, but was still at the place where Martha had met him. ³¹When the Jews who had been with Mary in the house, comforting her, noticed how quickly she got up and went out, they followed her, supposing she was going to the tomb to mourn there.

³²When Mary reached the place where Jesus was and saw him, she fell at his feet and said, "Lord, if you had been here, my brother would not have died."

³³When Jesus saw her weeping, and the Jews who had come along with her also weeping, he was deeply moved in spirit and troubled. ³⁴"Where have you laid him?" he asked.

"Come and see, Lord," they replied.

³⁵Jesus wept.

³⁶Then the Jews said, "See how he loved him!"

³⁷But some of them said, "Could not he who opened the eyes of the blind man have kept this man from dying?"

Jesus Raises Lazarus From the Dead

³⁸Jesus, once more deeply moved, came to the tomb. It was a cave with a stone laid across the entrance. ³⁹"Take away the stone," he said.

"But, Lord," said Martha, the sister of the dead man, "by this time there is a bad odor, for he has been there four days."

⁴⁰Then Jesus said, "Did I not tell you that if you believed, you would see the glory of God?"

⁴¹So they took away the stone. Then Jesus looked up and said, "Father, I thank you that you have heard me. ⁴²I knew that you always hear me, but I said this for the benefit of the people standing here, that they may believe that you sent me."

⁴³When he had said this, Jesus called in a loud voice, "Lazarus, come out!" ⁴⁴The dead man came out, his hands and feet wrapped with strips of linen, and a cloth around his face.

Jesus said to them, "Take off the grave clothes and let him go."

The Plot to Kill Jesus

⁴⁵Therefore many of the Jews who had come to visit Mary, and had seen what Jesus did, put their faith in him. ⁴⁶But some of them went to the Pharisees and told them what Jesus had done. ⁴⁷Then the chief priests and the Pharisees called a meeting of the Sanhedrin.

"What are we accomplishing?" they asked. "Here is this man performing many miraculous signs. ⁴⁸If we let him go on like this, everyone will believe in him, and then the Romans will come and take away both our place^c and our nation."

APRIL 18

⁴⁹Then one of them, named Caiaphas, who was high priest that year, spoke up, "You know nothing at all! ⁵⁰You do not realize that it is better for you that one man die for the people than that the whole nation perish."

⁵¹He did not say this on his own, but as high priest that year he prophesied that Jesus would die for the Jewish nation, ⁵²and not only for that nation but also for the scattered children of God, to bring them together and make them one. ⁵³So from that day on they plotted to take his life.

⁵⁴Therefore Jesus no longer moved about publicly among the Jews. Instead he withdrew to a region near the desert, to a village called Ephraim, where he stayed with his disciples.

⁵⁵When it was almost time for the Jewish Passover, many went up from the country to Jerusalem for their ceremonial cleansing before the Passover. ⁵⁶They kept looking for Jesus, and as they stood in the temple area they asked one another, "What do you think? Isn't he coming to the Feast at all?" ⁵⁷But the chief priests and Pharisees had given orders that if anyone found out where Jesus was, he should report it so that they might arrest him.

a18 Greek *fifteen stadia* (about 3 kilometers)   *b27* Or *Messiah*   *c48* Or *temple*

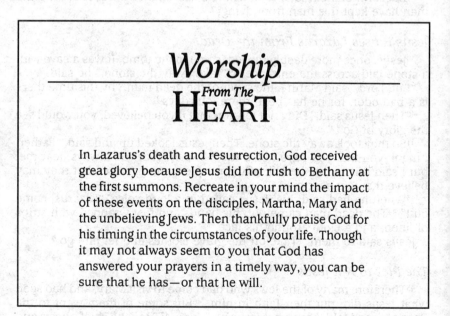

Worship
From The
HEART

In Lazarus's death and resurrection, God received great glory because Jesus did not rush to Bethany at the first summons. Recreate in your mind the impact of these events on the disciples, Martha, Mary and the unbelieving Jews. Then thankfully praise God for his timing in the circumstances of your life. Though it may not always seem to you that God has answered your prayers in a timely way, you can be sure that he has—or that he will.

APRIL 18

Discipline, Disappointment and the Delays of Love

Jesus loved Martha and her sister and Lazarus. Yet when he heard that Lazarus was sick, he stayed where he was two more days (John 11:5–6).

When news reaches Jesus that his friend Lazarus is critically ill, everyone expects him to rush to Lazarus's side.

Instead, Jesus waits—an act of love misunderstood by many of his disciples.

But the pain was purposeful: that God might be glorified through it all. Alexander Maclaren offers these comforting words concerning the love of Christ.

Walk With Alexander Maclaren

"Christ's delays are the delays of love. If we could once get that conviction into our hearts, how quietly we should go about our work!

"What patience we would have if we recognized that the only reason which moves God in his choice of when to fulfill our desires and lift away burdens is our own good!

"Nothing but the purest, simplest love sways him in all that he does.

"Why should it be difficult for us to believe this?

"If we were more akin to looking at life—with all its often unwelcome duty, and its arrows of pain and sorrow—as a discipline, and were to think less about the unpleasantness and more about the purpose of what befalls us, we should find far less difficulty in understanding that his delay is born of love, and is a token of his tender care."

Walk Closer to God

God loves his children too much to give them less than his best. His love is evident in different ways. He disciplines. He delays. He disappoints.

Not to dishearten us, but to show us that even in the moments of waiting, he is at work.

Can we pierce through our own circumstances to see that truth? In a day when everything from coffee to cameras is "instant," learning to wait on the Lord may prove to be a challenging assignment.

But then, isn't it worth it all when you know that the best is yet to come?

APRIL 19

📖 Walk in the Word
John 12:1–19

*Before relating the story of Jesus' triumphal entry into Jerusalem, John tells
of a dinner where Lazarus's sister Mary anoints Jesus.*

Jesus Anointed at Bethany

12 Six days before the Passover, Jesus arrived at Bethany, where Lazarus lived, whom Jesus had raised from the dead. ²Here a dinner was
given in Jesus' honor. Martha served, while Lazarus was among those reclining at the table with him. ³Then Mary took about a pint*a* of pure nard,
an expensive perfume; she poured it on Jesus' feet and wiped his feet with
her hair. And the house was filled with the fragrance of the perfume.

⁴But one of his disciples, Judas Iscariot, who was later to betray him,
objected, ⁵"Why wasn't this perfume sold and the money given to the
poor? It was worth a year's wages.*b*" ⁶He did not say this because he cared
about the poor but because he was a thief; as keeper of the money bag,
he used to help himself to what was put into it.

⁷"Leave her alone," Jesus replied. "It was intended that she should save
this perfume for the day of my burial. ⁸You will always have the poor
among you, but you will not always have me."

⁹Meanwhile a large crowd of Jews found out that Jesus was there and
came, not only because of him but also to see Lazarus, whom he had
raised from the dead. ¹⁰So the chief priests made plans to kill Lazarus as
well, ¹¹for on account of him many of the Jews were going over to Jesus
and putting their faith in him.

The Triumphal Entry

¹²The next day the great crowd that had come for the Feast heard that
Jesus was on his way to Jerusalem. ¹³They took palm branches and went
out to meet him, shouting,

> "Hosanna!*c*"
>
> "Blessed is he who comes in the name of the Lord!"*d*
>
> "Blessed is the King of Israel!"

¹⁴Jesus found a young donkey and sat upon it, as it is written,

> ¹⁵"Do not be afraid, O Daughter of Zion;
>   see, your king is coming,
>   seated on a donkey's colt."*e*

¹⁶At first his disciples did not understand all this. Only after Jesus was
glorified did they realize that these things had been written about him and
that they had done these things to him.

APRIL 19

¹⁷Now the crowd that was with him when he called Lazarus from the tomb and raised him from the dead continued to spread the word. ¹⁸Many people, because they had heard that he had given this miraculous sign, went out to meet him. ¹⁹So the Pharisees said to one another, "See, this is getting us nowhere. Look how the whole world has gone after him!"

a3 Greek *a litra* (probably about 0.5 liter)   *b5* Greek *three hundred denarii*   *c13* A Hebrew expression meaning "Save!" which became an exclamation of praise   *d13* Psalm 118:25, 26   *e15* Zech. 9:9

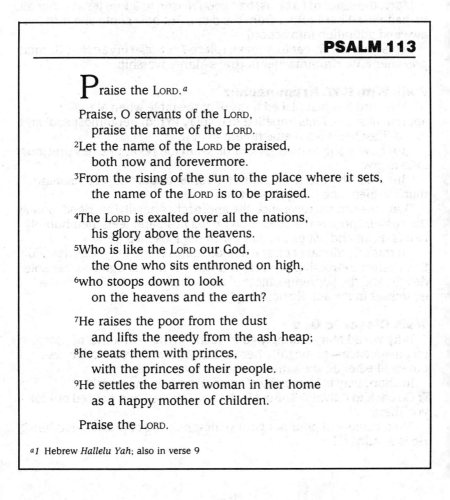

PSALM 113

Praise the LORD.^a

Praise, O servants of the LORD,
    praise the name of the LORD.
²Let the name of the LORD be praised,
    both now and forevermore.
³From the rising of the sun to the place where it sets,
    the name of the LORD is to be praised.

⁴The LORD is exalted over all the nations,
    his glory above the heavens.
⁵Who is like the LORD our God,
    the One who sits enthroned on high,
⁶who stoops down to look
    on the heavens and the earth?

⁷He raises the poor from the dust
    and lifts the needy from the ash heap;
⁸he seats them with princes,
    with the princes of their people.
⁹He settles the barren woman in her home
    as a happy mother of children.

Praise the LORD.

a1 Hebrew *Hallelu Yah*; also in verse 9

APRIL 19

Worship: Act of Awe and Adoration

Then Mary took about a pint of pure nard, an expensive perfume; she poured it on Jesus' feet and wiped his feet with her hair (John 12:3).

Worship: The act of centering one's attention on another worthy to receive it.

Mary, the sister of Lazarus, had good reason to adore Jesus. After all, he had raised her brother from the dead. But how could she turn her awe and adoration into action?

In his nineteenth-century masterpiece *The Suffering Savior,* German preacher F.W. Krummacher portrays Mary's worship.

Walk With F.W. Krummacher

"The Lord has just placed himself at the table when Mary approaches. She feels impelled to display to him her inmost soul and to manifest her devout attachment to him.

"But how is she to do this? Words seem too poor. She has precious little to give.

"But what she has is an alabaster vessel of pure oil of spikenard, much valued. She brings it with her.

"With the utmost reverence she approaches her divine friend, breaks the vessel, spreads the spikenard on his head and feet, then humbly bends down and wipes the latter with her loosened tresses.

"In this affectionate act, she demonstrates a rare degree of devotion. She desires to worship him. He is always in her thoughts as her sole delight and the supreme object of her affections—all of which she expresses in the act of anointing."

Walk Closer to God

Why would Mary willingly go to such lengths—in terms of cost and inconvenience—to magnify her Savior? And why would countless others like her do the same?

In short, why is he worthy of your reverence and worship?

Go back to Calvary. Think of what was broken and poured out for you there.

Then come and pour out your richest offering of praise upon him. He is worthy! ◖

APRIL 20

Walk in the Word
John 12:20–50

John chronicles the dramatic words spoken by Jesus in prediction of his death, as well as the thunderous voice from heaven; John then focuses on various responses to Jesus' revelation and his appeal for belief.

Jesus Predicts His Death

20Now there were some Greeks among those who went up to worship at the Feast. 21They came to Philip, who was from Bethsaida in Galilee, with a request. "Sir," they said, "we would like to see Jesus." 22Philip went to tell Andrew; Andrew and Philip in turn told Jesus.

23Jesus replied, "The hour has come for the Son of Man to be glorified. 24I tell you the truth, unless a kernel of wheat falls to the ground and dies, it remains only a single seed. But if it dies, it produces many seeds. 25The man who loves his life will lose it, while the man who hates his life in this world will keep it for eternal life. 26Whoever serves me must follow me; and where I am, my servant also will be. My Father will honor the one who serves me.

27"Now my heart is troubled, and what shall I say? 'Father, save me from this hour'? No, it was for this very reason I came to this hour. 28Father, glorify your name!"

Then a voice came from heaven, "I have glorified it, and will glorify it again." 29The crowd that was there and heard it said it had thundered; others said an angel had spoken to him.

30Jesus said, "This voice was for your benefit, not mine. 31Now is the time for judgment on this world; now the prince of this world will be driven out. 32But I, when I am lifted up from the earth, will draw all men to myself." 33He said this to show the kind of death he was going to die.

34The crowd spoke up, "We have heard from the Law that the Christ[a] will remain forever, so how can you say, 'The Son of Man must be lifted up'? Who is this 'Son of Man'?"

35Then Jesus told them, "You are going to have the light just a little while longer. Walk while you have the light, before darkness overtakes you. The man who walks in the dark does not know where he is going. 36Put your trust in the light while you have it, so that you may become sons of light." When he had finished speaking, Jesus left and hid himself from them.

The Jews Continue in Their Unbelief

37Even after Jesus had done all these miraculous signs in their presence, they still would not believe in him. 38This was to fulfill the word of Isaiah the prophet:

> "Lord, who has believed our message
>   and to whom has the arm of the Lord been revealed?"[b]

39For this reason they could not believe, because, as Isaiah says elsewhere:

APRIL 20

⁴⁰"He has blinded their eyes
    and deadened their hearts,
  so they can neither see with their eyes,
    nor understand with their hearts,
    nor turn — and I would heal them."*c*

⁴¹Isaiah said this because he saw Jesus' glory and spoke about him.

⁴²Yet at the same time many even among the leaders believed in him. But because of the Pharisees they would not confess their faith for fear they would be put out of the synagogue; ⁴³for they loved praise from men more than praise from God.

⁴⁴Then Jesus cried out, "When a man believes in me, he does not believe in me only, but in the one who sent me. ⁴⁵When he looks at me, he sees the one who sent me. ⁴⁶I have come into the world as a light, so that no one who believes in me should stay in darkness.

⁴⁷"As for the person who hears my words but does not keep them, I do not judge him. For I did not come to judge the world, but to save it. ⁴⁸There is a judge for the one who rejects me and does not accept my words; that very word which I spoke will condemn him at the last day. ⁴⁹For I did not speak of my own accord, but the Father who sent me commanded me what to say and how to say it. ⁵⁰I know that his command leads to eternal life. So whatever I say is just what the Father has told me to say."

a34 Or *Messiah*   *b38* Isaiah 53:1   *c40* Isaiah 6:10

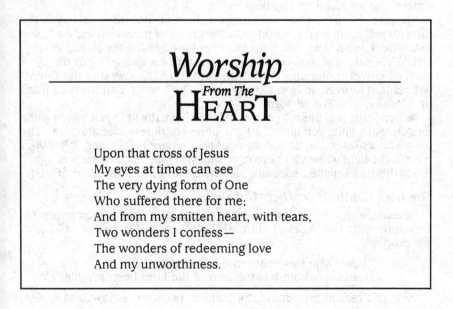

Worship From The HEART

Upon that cross of Jesus
My eyes at times can see
The very dying form of One
Who suffered there for me;
And from my smitten heart, with tears,
Two wonders I confess—
The wonders of redeeming love
And my unworthiness.

Death and the "Law of Increase"

Unless a kernel of wheat falls to the ground and dies, it remains only a single seed. But if it dies, it produces many seeds (John 12:24).

Take one barren field, bury a handful of seed, add a little water and the care of the farmer, and what do you have?

At first, you still have only a barren field.

But after a few months, the field will produce an abundant harvest.

In John 12 we read how Jesus uses the simple illustration of a dying seed to explain to his followers the reason behind his death.

And A.B. Bruce provides this timely explanation of the "law of increase"—a law that Jesus' death portrays.

Walk With A.B. Bruce

"Jesus' purpose is to make it clear to his disciples that death and increase may go together.

"Such is true in the case of grain; and the law of increase is equally true in his own case.

"He might have explained it this way: 'A grain of wheat, by dying, becomes fruitful; so I must die in order to become, on a large scale, an object of faith and source of life.

" 'During my lifetime I have had little visible success. Few have believed, many have disbelieved; and they are about to crown their unbelief by putting me to death.

" 'But my death, far from being—as they fancy—my defeat and destruction, will be but the beginning of my glorification.' "

Walk Closer to God

The Good News of the gospel began with the bad news of a tragic, unjust execution. It began with death.

A grain of wheat . . . dead and buried . . . lifeless . . . fruitless . . . or so it would seem.

But three days later, all that changed.

From death sprang eternal life.

The seemingly fruitless became the firstfruits of a mighty harvest that is still bearing fruit today.

Thank God right now for the harvest the death of his Son has accomplished in your life. ◖

APRIL 21

📖 Walk in the Word
John 13

The evening in the upper room is vividly recounted by John, who begins by telling how Jesus washes the disciples' feet and predicts his betrayal by Judas and his denial by Peter.

Jesus Washes His Disciples' Feet

13 It was just before the Passover Feast. Jesus knew that the time had come for him to leave this world and go to the Father. Having loved his own who were in the world, he now showed them the full extent of his love. [a]

²The evening meal was being served, and the devil had already prompted Judas Iscariot, son of Simon, to betray Jesus. ³Jesus knew that the Father had put all things under his power, and that he had come from God and was returning to God; ⁴so he got up from the meal, took off his outer clothing, and wrapped a towel around his waist. ⁵After that, he poured water into a basin and began to wash his disciples' feet, drying them with the towel that was wrapped around him.

⁶He came to Simon Peter, who said to him, "Lord, are you going to wash my feet?"

⁷Jesus replied, "You do not realize now what I am doing, but later you will understand."

⁸"No," said Peter, "you shall never wash my feet."

Jesus answered, "Unless I wash you, you have no part with me."

⁹"Then, Lord," Simon Peter replied, "not just my feet but my hands and my head as well!"

¹⁰Jesus answered, "A person who has had a bath needs only to wash his feet; his whole body is clean. And you are clean, though not every one of you." ¹¹For he knew who was going to betray him, and that was why he said not every one was clean.

¹²When he had finished washing their feet, he put on his clothes and returned to his place. "Do you understand what I have done for you?" he asked them. ¹³"You call me 'Teacher' and 'Lord,' and rightly so, for that is what I am. ¹⁴Now that I, your Lord and Teacher, have washed your feet, you also should wash one another's feet. ¹⁵I have set you an example that you should do as I have done for you. ¹⁶I tell you the truth, no servant is greater than his master, nor is a messenger greater than the one who sent him. ¹⁷Now that you know these things, you will be blessed if you do them.

Jesus Predicts His Betrayal

¹⁸"I am not referring to all of you; I know those I have chosen. But this is to fulfill the scripture: 'He who shares my bread has lifted up his heel against me.' [b]

¹⁹"I am telling you now before it happens, so that when it does happen you will believe that I am He. ²⁰I tell you the truth, whoever accepts anyone I send accepts me; and whoever accepts me accepts the one who sent me."

APRIL 21

²¹After he had said this, Jesus was troubled in spirit and testified, "I tell you the truth, one of you is going to betray me."

²²His disciples stared at one another, at a loss to know which of them he meant. ²³One of them, the disciple whom Jesus loved, was reclining next to him. ²⁴Simon Peter motioned to this disciple and said, "Ask him which one he means."

²⁵Leaning back against Jesus, he asked him, "Lord, who is it?"

²⁶Jesus answered, "It is the one to whom I will give this piece of bread when I have dipped it in the dish." Then, dipping the piece of bread, he gave it to Judas Iscariot, son of Simon. ²⁷As soon as Judas took the bread, Satan entered into him.

"What you are about to do, do quickly," Jesus told him, ²⁸but no one at the meal understood why Jesus said this to him. ²⁹Since Judas had charge of the money, some thought Jesus was telling him to buy what was needed for the Feast, or to give something to the poor. ³⁰As soon as Judas had taken the bread, he went out. And it was night.

Jesus Predicts Peter's Denial

³¹When he was gone, Jesus said, "Now is the Son of Man glorified and God is glorified in him. ³²If God is glorified in him,ᶜ God will glorify the Son in himself, and will glorify him at once.

³³"My children, I will be with you only a little longer. You will look for me, and just as I told the Jews, so I tell you now: Where I am going, you cannot come.

³⁴"A new command I give you: Love one another. As I have loved you, so you must love one another. ³⁵By this all men will know that you are my disciples, if you love one another."

³⁶Simon Peter asked him, "Lord, where are you going?"

Jesus replied, "Where I am going, you cannot follow now, but you will follow later."

³⁷Peter asked, "Lord, why can't I follow you now? I will lay down my life for you."

³⁸Then Jesus answered, "Will you really lay down your life for me? I tell you the truth, before the rooster crows, you will disown me three times!

ᵃ1 Or *he loved them to the last*   ᵇ18 Psalm 41:9   ᶜ32 Many early manuscripts do not have *If God is glorified in him.*

APRIL 21

Dressing as the King in a Servant's Towel

Jesus knew that the Father had put all things under his power
. . . so he got up from the meal . . . wrapped a towel around his
waist . . . and began to wash his disciples' feet (John 13:3–5).

Presidents, kings, queens and ambassadors.
They're called VIPs. Ordinary people they're not!
So try to imagine an ambassador washing a taxi driver's car. And a
queen collecting garbage. And a king mopping the floor for the janitor.
That will give you an inkling of what Christ stooped to do, and why
his model of servanthood made such an impact on his followers.
John Henry Jowett describes the scene we find in John 13.

Walk With John Henry Jowett
"We might have assumed that divinity would have moved only in
planetary orbits, and would have overlooked the petty streets and ways
of men.
"But here the Lord of Glory girds himself with the apron of the slave
and does menial service.
"That is the test of a growing servant's heart.
"We may be sure that we are growing smaller when we begin to
degrade humble services. We are growing larger when we love
ministries that never cry or lift their voices in the streets.
"When a man begins to despise the 'towel,' he has forgotten the
words of the King who was not ashamed to wear it: 'I have set you an
example that you should do as I have done for you.' "

Walk Closer to God
You are a child of the King. That makes you part of a royal family.
And the tendency is to want to live like royalty, when in fact you have
been called to live like Christ.
Jesus had every right to demand the attentions of his men. Instead,
he took up a servant's towel and assumed a servant's role.
It's a humbling experience to follow his example. Especially in a day
when humility is already in short supply.
Even so, the Servant-King's command to his followers still stands:
"I have set you an example that you should do as I have done . . . "(John
13:15).

APRIL 22

Walk in the Word
John 14

Jesus addresses the turmoil in the disciples' hearts with words of comfort and promise in this upper room conversation with his disciples.

Jesus Comforts His Disciples

14 "Do not let your hearts be troubled. Trust in God*a*; trust also in me. [2]In my Father's house are many rooms; if it were not so, I would have told you. I am going there to prepare a place for you. [3]And if I go and prepare a place for you, I will come back and take you to be with me that you also may be where I am. [4]You know the way to the place where I am going."

Jesus the Way to the Father

[5]Thomas said to him, "Lord, we don't know where you are going, so how can we know the way?"

[6]Jesus answered, "I am the way and the truth and the life. No one comes to the Father except through me. [7]If you really knew me, you would know*b* my Father as well. From now on, you do know him and have seen him."

[8]Philip said, "Lord, show us the Father and that will be enough for us."

[9]Jesus answered: "Don't you know me, Philip, even after I have been among you such a long time? Anyone who has seen me has seen the Father. How can you say, 'Show us the Father'? [10]Don't you believe that I am in the Father, and that the Father is in me? The words I say to you are not just my own. Rather, it is the Father, living in me, who is doing his work. [11]Believe me when I say that I am in the Father and the Father is in me; or at least believe on the evidence of the miracles themselves. [12]I tell you the truth, anyone who has faith in me will do what I have been doing. He will do even greater things than these, because I am going to the Father. [13]And I will do whatever you ask in my name, so that the Son may bring glory to the Father. [14]You may ask me for anything in my name, and I will do it.

Jesus Promises the Holy Spirit

[15]"If you love me, you will obey what I command. [16]And I will ask the Father, and he will give you another Counselor to be with you forever— [17]the Spirit of truth. The world cannot accept him, because it neither sees him nor knows him. But you know him, for he lives with you and will be*c* in you. [18]I will not leave you as orphans; I will come to you. [19]Before long, the world will not see me anymore, but you will see me. Because I live, you also will live. [20]On that day you will realize that I am in my Father, and you are in me, and I am in you. [21]Whoever has my commands and obeys them, he is the one who loves me. He who loves me will be loved by my Father, and I too will love him and show myself to him."

[22]Then Judas (not Judas Iscariot) said, "But, Lord, why do you intend to show yourself to us and not to the world?"

APRIL 22

²³Jesus replied, "If anyone loves me, he will obey my teaching. My Father will love him, and we will come to him and make our home with him. ²⁴He who does not love me will not obey my teaching. These words you hear are not my own; they belong to the Father who sent me.

²⁵"All this I have spoken while still with you. ²⁶But the Counselor, the Holy Spirit, whom the Father will send in my name, will teach you all things and will remind you of everything I have said to you. ²⁷Peace I leave with you; my peace I give you. I do not give to you as the world gives. Do not let your hearts be troubled and do not be afraid.

²⁸"You heard me say, 'I am going away and I am coming back to you.' If you loved me, you would be glad that I am going to the Father, for the Father is greater than I. ²⁹I have told you now before it happens, so that when it does happen you will believe. ³⁰I will not speak with you much longer, for the prince of this world is coming. He has no hold on me, ³¹but the world must learn that I love the Father and that I do exactly what my Father has commanded me.

"Come now; let us leave.

^a1 Or *You trust in God*   ^b7 Some early manuscripts *If you really have known me, you will know*   ^c17 Some early manuscripts *and is*

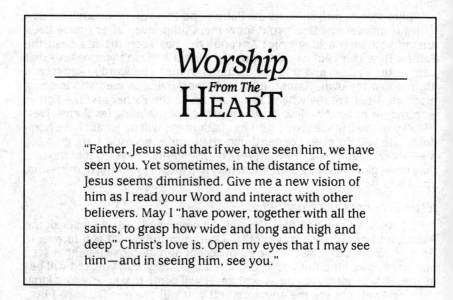

Worship
From The
HEART

"Father, Jesus said that if we have seen him, we have seen you. Yet sometimes, in the distance of time, Jesus seems diminished. Give me a new vision of him as I read your Word and interact with other believers. May I "have power, together with all the saints, to grasp how wide and long and high and deep" Christ's love is. Open my eyes that I may see him—and in seeing him, see you."

One Way, His Way—The Only Way

> I am the way and the truth and the life. No one comes to the Father except through me (John 14:6).

Christianity claims to offer the only way of salvation, to the exclusion of others. There are not any number of doors into heaven.

Nor are there any alternate routes into the family of God. Not if you take Jesus at his word (John 14).

And that excludes many who are sincere . . . but sincerely wrong, as J.C. Ryle explains.

Walk With J.C. Ryle

"It avails nothing that a man is clever, learned, highly gifted, amiable, charitable, kindhearted, and zealous about some sort of religion.

"All this will not save his soul if he does not draw near to God by Christ's atonement and make use of God's own Son as his Mediator and Savior.

"God is so holy that all men are guilty and debtors in his sight. Sin is so sinful that no mortal man can make satisfaction for it. There must be a mediator, a ransom-payer, a redeemer, between us and God, or else we never can be saved.

"There is only one door, one bridge, one ladder, between earth and heaven: the crucified Son of God. Whosoever will enter in by that door may be saved; but to him who refuses, the Bible holds out no hope at all. Earnestness will never take one to heaven."

Walk Closer to God

The Jews thought they could attain salvation by keeping the law. Many others, before and since, have worked out their own procedures to gain salvation.

But procedures don't save. Only one person does.

Jesus is the only way to God. Any other imagined approach can only lead to a dead end . . . literally.

Someone near you needs to know that—someone who has tried many of those dead-end streets.

You won't always be popular for pointing the way. But then, if one person finds the path of life because you cared enough to show it, will it really matter what others may say? ☽

APRIL 23

📖 Walk in the Word
John 15:1 — 16:4

John recalls Jesus' memorable analogy of the vineyard and the branches, his command to love and his warning that the disciples would be hated and persecuted by the world.

The Vine and the Branches

15 "I am the true vine, and my Father is the gardener. ²He cuts off every branch in me that bears no fruit, while every branch that does bear fruit he prunes*ᵃ* so that it will be even more fruitful. ³You are already clean because of the word I have spoken to you. ⁴Remain in me, and I will remain in you. No branch can bear fruit by itself; it must remain in the vine. Neither can you bear fruit unless you remain in me.

⁵"I am the vine; you are the branches. If a man remains in me and I in him, he will bear much fruit; apart from me you can do nothing. ⁶If anyone does not remain in me, he is like a branch that is thrown away and withers; such branches are picked up, thrown into the fire and burned. ⁷If you remain in me and my words remain in you, ask whatever you wish, and it will be given you. ⁸This is to my Father's glory, that you bear much fruit, showing yourselves to be my disciples.

⁹"As the Father has loved me, so have I loved you. Now remain in my love. ¹⁰If you obey my commands, you will remain in my love, just as I have obeyed my Father's commands and remain in his love. ¹¹I have told you this so that my joy may be in you and that your joy may be complete. ¹²My command is this: Love each other as I have loved you. ¹³Greater love has no one than this, that he lay down his life for his friends. ¹⁴You are my friends if you do what I command. ¹⁵I no longer call you servants, because a servant does not know his master's business. Instead, I have called you friends, for everything that I learned from my Father I have made known to you. ¹⁶You did not choose me, but I chose you and appointed you to go and bear fruit—fruit that will last. Then the Father will give you whatever you ask in my name. ¹⁷This is my command: Love each other.

The World Hates the Disciples

¹⁸"If the world hates you, keep in mind that it hated me first. ¹⁹If you belonged to the world, it would love you as its own. As it is, you do not belong to the world, but I have chosen you out of the world. That is why the world hates you. ²⁰Remember the words I spoke to you: 'No servant is greater than his master.'*ᵇ* If they persecuted me, they will persecute you also. If they obeyed my teaching, they will obey yours also. ²¹They will treat you this way because of my name, for they do not know the One who sent me. ²²If I had not come and spoken to them, they would not be guilty of sin. Now, however, they have no excuse for their sin. ²³He who hates me hates my Father as well. ²⁴If I had not done among them what no one else did, they would not be guilty of sin. But now they have seen these miracles, and yet they have hated both me and my Father. ²⁵But this is

to fulfill what is written in their Law: 'They hated me without reason.'[c]

[26]"When the Counselor comes, whom I will send to you from the Father, the Spirit of truth who goes out from the Father, he will testify about me. [27]And you also must testify, for you have been with me from the beginning.

16 "All this I have told you so that you will not go astray. [2]They will put you out of the synagogue; in fact, a time is coming when anyone who kills you will think he is offering a service to God. [3]They will do such things because they have not known the Father or me. [4]I have told you this, so that when the time comes you will remember that I warned you. I did not tell you this at first because I was with you.

[a]2 The Greek for *prunes* also means *cleans*.   [b]20 John 13:16   [c]25 Psalms 35:19; 69:4

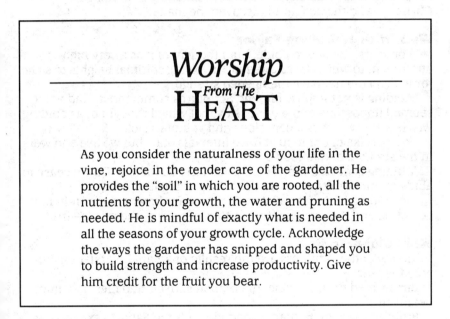

Worship From The HEART

As you consider the naturalness of your life in the vine, rejoice in the tender care of the gardener. He provides the "soil" in which you are rooted, all the nutrients for your growth, the water and pruning as needed. He is mindful of exactly what is needed in all the seasons of your growth cycle. Acknowledge the ways the gardener has snipped and shaped you to build strength and increase productivity. Give him credit for the fruit you bear.

APRIL 23

Vine-life Is the Only Life

Remain in me, and I will remain in you. No branch can bear fruit by itself; it must remain in the vine. Neither can you bear fruit unless you remain in me (John 15:4).

The only part of a vine that bears fruit is the branch. But an unattached branch can never bear fruit.

In capsule form, that is the lesson of John 15. There Christ describes the process by which the true vine produces fruit through Christians. J. Hudson Taylor brought forth much spiritual fruit during his missionary career in China. He shares this personal insight regarding his struggles to understand the life of remaining or abiding in Christ . . . and the delightful discovery he made.

Walk With J. Hudson Taylor

"For years I longed to abide, but I thought of it as a very high attainment to which I was unequal, involving spiritual heights to scale for which I did not have the needed strength.

"Abiding is not impossible; the Scriptures command it. And yet it seemed impossible to me until I saw that what I thought of as abiding was feeding, which is a conscious and voluntary act.

"We partake of our food at fixed intervals only, but we live and work in the strength of that food continuously.

"Abiding is not a thing of consciousness, but of fact. Do we cease to abide in our homes when we are asleep at night?

"So abiding in Christ is a state which commitment to Christ in faith achieves, and the reality of that faith is proved by the result—fruit."

Walk Closer to God

Vitality and fruitfulness are the results of an abiding relationship with the vine.

But severed from the vine, the branch shrivels and dies. It cannot bear fruit.

Fruitfulness is more than a good idea. It's the Father's expectation for you as one of his children.

And after all, who should know more about turning barren lives into fruitful branches than the Gardener? ◯

APRIL 24

Walk in the Word
John 16:5–33

Jesus encourages his grieving disciples with the promise of the Spirit's presence and power and the promise that their grief will turn to joy.

The Work of the Holy Spirit

⁵"Now I am going to him who sent me, yet none of you asks me, 'Where are you going?' ⁶Because I have said these things, you are filled with grief. ⁷But I tell you the truth: It is for your good that I am going away. Unless I go away, the Counselor will not come to you; but if I go, I will send him to you. ⁸When he comes, he will convict the world of guilt*a* in regard to sin and righteousness and judgment: ⁹in regard to sin, because men do not believe in me; ¹⁰in regard to righteousness, because I am going to the Father, where you can see me no longer; ¹¹and in regard to judgment, because the prince of this world now stands condemned.

¹²"I have much more to say to you, more than you can now bear. ¹³But when he, the Spirit of truth, comes, he will guide you into all truth. He will not speak on his own; he will speak only what he hears, and he will tell you what is yet to come. ¹⁴He will bring glory to me by taking from what is mine and making it known to you. ¹⁵All that belongs to the Father is mine. That is why I said the Spirit will take from what is mine and make it known to you.

¹⁶"In a little while you will see me no more, and then after a little while you will see me."

The Disciples' Grief Will Turn to Joy

¹⁷Some of his disciples said to one another, "What does he mean by saying, 'In a little while you will see me no more, and then after a little while you will see me,' and 'Because I am going to the Father'?" ¹⁸They kept asking, "What does he mean by 'a little while'? We don't understand what he is saying."

¹⁹Jesus saw that they wanted to ask him about this, so he said to them, "Are you asking one another what I meant when I said, 'In a little while you will see me no more, and then after a little while you will see me'? ²⁰I tell you the truth, you will weep and mourn while the world rejoices. You will grieve, but your grief will turn to joy. ²¹A woman giving birth to a child has pain because her time has come; but when her baby is born she forgets the anguish because of her joy that a child is born into the world. ²²So with you: Now is your time of grief, but I will see you again and you will rejoice, and no one will take away your joy. ²³In that day you will no longer ask me anything. I tell you the truth, my Father will give you whatever you ask in my name. ²⁴Until now you have not asked for anything in my name. Ask and you will receive, and your joy will be complete.

²⁵"Though I have been speaking figuratively, a time is coming when I will no longer use this kind of language but will tell you plainly about my Father. ²⁶In that day you will ask in my name. I am not saying that I will

APRIL 24

ask the Father on your behalf. ²⁷No, the Father himself loves you because you have loved me and have believed that I came from God. ²⁸I came from the Father and entered the world; now I am leaving the world and going back to the Father."

²⁹Then Jesus' disciples said, "Now you are speaking clearly and without figures of speech. ³⁰Now we can see that you know all things and that you do not even need to have anyone ask you questions. This makes us believe that you came from God."

³¹"You believe at last!"ᵇ Jesus answered. ³²"But a time is coming, and has come, when you will be scattered, each to his own home. You will leave me all alone. Yet I am not alone, for my Father is with me.

³³"I have told you these things, so that in me you may have peace. In this world you will have trouble. But take heart! I have overcome the world."

ᵃ8 Or *will expose the guilt of the world*   ᵇ31 Or *"Do you now believe?"*

Worship
From The
HEART

As our teacher, the Holy Spirit unveils Jesus Christ in the written Word of God. Yet he is not content to stop there. His work is also to reproduce the life of Christ in every believer. Thank God for revealing himself in you through the presence of the Holy Spirit. Rejoice in his patience and the circumstances he uses to make you more like Jesus. Meditate on the fruit of the Spirit as it is described in Galatians 5:22–23: "love, joy, peace, patience, kindness, goodness, faithfulness, gentleness and self-control." Ponder how those qualities manifest themselves in your life.

Coming From Glory to Dwell in Our Hearts

But I tell you the truth: It is for your good that I am going away. Unless I go away, the Counselor will not come to you; but if I go, I will send him to you (John 16:7).

It's easy to be confused about something—or someone—you cannot see.

In order to make the unseen clear, Jesus devoted much of his last discourse to the subject of the Holy Spirit . . . the helper . . . the third person of the Trinity.

R.A. Torrey explains who the Holy Spirit is and why his coming would be a source of comfort for Jesus' followers.

Walk With R.A. Torrey

"If we think of the Holy Spirit only as an impersonal power or influence, then our thought will constantly be, 'How can I get hold of and use the Holy Spirit?'

"But if we think of him in the Biblical way as a divine person—infinitely wise, infinitely holy, infinitely tender—then our thought will constantly be, 'How can the Holy Spirit get hold of and use me?'

"If we think of the Holy Spirit merely as a divine power or influence, there will be the temptation to feel as if we belong to a superior order of Christians.

"But if we think of the Holy Spirit in the Biblical way as a divine being of infinite majesty, coming down from glory to dwell in our hearts and take possession of our lives, it will put us in the dust, and make us walk very softly before God."

Walk Closer to God

Christ knew it would be advantageous for his disciples if he returned to the Father, for his departure meant that the helper was coming!

Not an "it" but a "he."

Not an impersonal force, but a personal teacher, guide, consoler, and counselor.

Reread Mr. Torrey's final paragraph above. Then come to God today with soft steps and a grateful heart for the work of the Holy Spirit in your life. ❍

April 25

Walk in the Word
John 17

John pens Jesus' prayer to the Father, a prayer that is a fitting benediction on the time together in the upper room.

Jesus Prays for Himself

17 After Jesus said this, he looked toward heaven and prayed:

"Father, the time has come. Glorify your Son, that your Son may glorify you. ²For you granted him authority over all people that he might give eternal life to all those you have given him. ³Now this is eternal life: that they may know you, the only true God, and Jesus Christ, whom you have sent. ⁴I have brought you glory on earth by completing the work you gave me to do. ⁵And now, Father, glorify me in your presence with the glory I had with you before the world began.

Jesus Prays for His Disciples

⁶"I have revealed you*a* to those whom you gave me out of the world. They were yours; you gave them to me and they have obeyed your word. ⁷Now they know that everything you have given me comes from you. ⁸For I gave them the words you gave me and they accepted them. They knew with certainty that I came from you, and they believed that you sent me. ⁹I pray for them. I am not praying for the world, but for those you have given me, for they are yours. ¹⁰All I have is yours, and all you have is mine. And glory has come to me through them. ¹¹I will remain in the world no longer, but they are still in the world, and I am coming to you. Holy Father, protect them by the power of your name — the name you gave me — so that they may be one as we are one. ¹²While I was with them, I protected them and kept them safe by that name you gave me. None has been lost except the one doomed to destruction so that Scripture would be fulfilled.

¹³"I am coming to you now, but I say these things while I am still in the world, so that they may have the full measure of my joy within them. ¹⁴I have given them your word and the world has hated them, for they are not of the world any more than I am of the world. ¹⁵My prayer is not that you take them out of the world but that you protect them from the evil one. ¹⁶They are not of the world, even as I am not of it. ¹⁷Sanctify*b* them by the truth; your word is truth. ¹⁸As you sent me into the world, I have sent them into the world. ¹⁹For them I sanctify myself, that they too may be truly sanctified.

Jesus Prays for All Believers

²⁰"My prayer is not for them alone. I pray also for those who

will believe in me through their message, ²¹that all of them may be one, Father, just as you are in me and I am in you. May they also be in us so that the world may believe that you have sent me. ²²I have given them the glory that you gave me, that they may be one as we are one: ²³I in them and you in me. May they be brought to complete unity to let the world know that you sent me and have loved them even as you have loved me.

²⁴"Father, I want those you have given me to be with me where I am, and to see my glory, the glory you have given me because you loved me before the creation of the world.

²⁵"Righteous Father, though the world does not know you, I know you, and they know that you have sent me. ²⁶I have made you known to them, and will continue to make you known in order that the love you have for me may be in them and that I myself may be in them."

ᵃ6 Greek *your name*; also in verse 26   ᵇ17 Greek *hagiazo (set apart for sacred use* or *make holy)*; also in verse 19

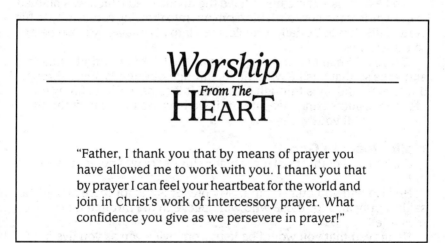

Worship
From The
Heart

"Father, I thank you that by means of prayer you have allowed me to work with you. I thank you that by prayer I can feel your heartbeat for the world and join in Christ's work of intercessory prayer. What confidence you give as we persevere in prayer!"

APRIL 25

He Is Praying for You

I have made you known to them, and will continue to make you known in order that the love you have for me may be in them and that I myself may be in them (John 17:26).

"If I could hear Christ praying for me in the next room,' declared Robert Murray McCheyne, "I would not fear a million enemies. Yet distance makes no difference; he is praying for me."

In John 17 we learn exactly what Jesus' desires for his followers are, as Ruth Paxson explains.

Walk With Ruth Paxson

"Have you ever pondered the last words of this prayer: ' . . . that I myself may be in them.' These simple but significant words breathe for the deepest desire of Christ's heart in relationship to his own. It is his consuming desire to reincarnate himself in the Christian.

"To be a Christian means to have the divine seed which was planted in our spirit at the new birth blossom out into growing conformity to his perfect life. It is to be daily 'transformed into his image.' Are you being so transformed?

"To be a Christian is to have Christ as the life of our minds, hearts, and wills so that it is he who thinks through our minds, loves through our hearts, and wills through our wills. It is to have Christ filling our life in ever-increasing measure until we have no life apart from him. Does he so fill you?"

Walk Closer to God

Christ's prayer that final night before his death was not for the eleven only.

He also had you on his mind. "My prayer is not for them alone," he said. "I pray also for those who will believe in me through their message."

He prayed that you would be kept from evil, even as you live in an evil world.

He prayed that you would experience his love, even while the world hates you.

He prayed for your unity with other believers in a world marked by strife.

You may not audibly hear his voice. But you can face each day with confidence.

He is praying for you! ❍

APRIL 26

📖 Walk in the Word
John 18

Beginning with Jesus' arrest, John recalls the events leading up to Jesus' sentence: his appearances before Annas, Caiaphas and Pilate, and Peter's three denials.

Jesus Arrested

18 When he had finished praying, Jesus left with his disciples and crossed the Kidron Valley. On the other side there was an olive grove, and he and his disciples went into it.

²Now Judas, who betrayed him, knew the place, because Jesus had often met there with his disciples. ³So Judas came to the grove, guiding a detachment of soldiers and some officials from the chief priests and Pharisees. They were carrying torches, lanterns and weapons.

⁴Jesus, knowing all that was going to happen to him, went out and asked them, "Who is it you want?"

⁵"Jesus of Nazareth," they replied.

"I am he," Jesus said. (And Judas the traitor was standing there with them.) ⁶When Jesus said, "I am he," they drew back and fell to the ground.

⁷Again he asked them, "Who is it you want?"

And they said, "Jesus of Nazareth."

⁸"I told you that I am he," Jesus answered. "If you are looking for me, then let these men go." ⁹This happened so that the words he had spoken would be fulfilled: "I have not lost one of those you gave me."*ᵃ*

¹⁰Then Simon Peter, who had a sword, drew it and struck the high priest's servant, cutting off his right ear. (The servant's name was Malchus.)

¹¹Jesus commanded Peter, "Put your sword away! Shall I not drink the cup the Father has given me?"

Jesus Taken to Annas

¹²Then the detachment of soldiers with its commander and the Jewish officials arrested Jesus. They bound him ¹³and brought him first to Annas, who was the father-in-law of Caiaphas, the high priest that year. ¹⁴Caiaphas was the one who had advised the Jews that it would be good if one man died for the people.

Peter's First Denial

¹⁵Simon Peter and another disciple were following Jesus. Because this disciple was known to the high priest, he went with Jesus into the high priest's courtyard, ¹⁶but Peter had to wait outside at the door. The other disciple, who was known to the high priest, came back, spoke to the girl on duty there and brought Peter in.

¹⁷"You are not one of his disciples, are you?" the girl at the door asked Peter.

He replied, "I am not."

APRIL 26

¹⁸It was cold, and the servants and officials stood around a fire they had made to keep warm. Peter also was standing with them, warming himself.

The High Priest Questions Jesus

¹⁹Meanwhile, the high priest questioned Jesus about his disciples and his teaching.

²⁰"I have spoken openly to the world," Jesus replied. "I always taught in synagogues or at the temple, where all the Jews come together. I said nothing in secret. ²¹Why question me? Ask those who heard me. Surely they know what I said."

²²When Jesus said this, one of the officials nearby struck him in the face. "Is this the way you answer the high priest?" he demanded.

²³"If I said something wrong," Jesus replied, "testify as to what is wrong. But if I spoke the truth, why did you strike me?" ²⁴Then Annas sent him, still bound, to Caiaphas the high priest. ᵇ

Peter's Second and Third Denials

²⁵As Simon Peter stood warming himself, he was asked, "You are not one of his disciples, are you?"

He denied it, saying, "I am not."

²⁶One of the high priest's servants, a relative of the man whose ear Peter had cut off, challenged him, "Didn't I see you with him in the olive grove?" ²⁷Again Peter denied it, and at that moment a rooster began to crow.

Jesus Before Pilate

²⁸Then the Jews led Jesus from Caiaphas to the palace of the Roman governor. By now it was early morning, and to avoid ceremonial uncleanness the Jews did not enter the palace; they wanted to be able to eat the Passover. ²⁹So Pilate came out to them and asked, "What charges are you bringing against this man?"

³⁰"If he were not a criminal," they replied, "we would not have handed him over to you."

³¹Pilate said, "Take him yourselves and judge him by your own law."

"But we have no right to execute anyone," the Jews objected. ³²This happened so that the words Jesus had spoken indicating the kind of death he was going to die would be fulfilled.

³³Pilate then went back inside the palace, summoned Jesus and asked him, "Are you the king of the Jews?"

³⁴"Is that your own idea," Jesus asked, "or did others talk to you about me?"

³⁵"Am I a Jew?" Pilate replied. "It was your people and your chief priests who handed you over to me. What is it you have done?"

³⁶Jesus said, "My kingdom is not of this world. If it were, my servants would fight to prevent my arrest by the Jews. But now my kingdom is from another place."

³⁷"You are a king, then!" said Pilate.

Jesus answered, "You are right in saying I am a king. In fact, for this

APRIL 26

reason I was born, and for this I came into the world, to testify to the truth. Everyone on the side of truth listens to me."

³⁸"What is truth?" Pilate asked. With this he went out again to the Jews and said, "I find no basis for a charge against him. ³⁹But it is your custom for me to release to you one prisoner at the time of the Passover. Do you want me to release 'the king of the Jews'?"

⁴⁰They shouted back, "No, not him! Give us Barabbas!" Now Barabbas had taken part in a rebellion.

ᵃ9 John 6:39   ᵇ24 Or *(Now Annas had sent him, still bound, to Caiaphas the high priest.)*

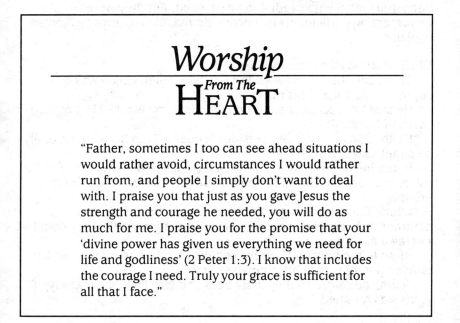

Worship
From The
HEART

"Father, sometimes I too can see ahead situations I would rather avoid, circumstances I would rather run from, and people I simply don't want to deal with. I praise you that just as you gave Jesus the strength and courage he needed, you will do as much for me. I praise you for the promise that your 'divine power has given us everything we need for life and godliness' (2 Peter 1:3). I know that includes the courage I need. Truly your grace is sufficient for all that I face."

APRIL 26

Tragedy at Gethsemane

Jesus . . . asked them, "Who is it you want?" "Jesus of Nazareth," they replied. "I am he," Jesus said. [And] . . . they drew back and fell to the ground (John 18:4–6).

"Jesus, knowing all that was going to happen to him, went out" (John 18:4).

He—and he alone—knew every step on the road to the cross.

The soldiers coming to seize him thought he was no more than a dangerous rebel who needed to be silenced. But they were unsuspecting participants in a divine drama, as G. Campbell Morgan explains.

Walk With G. Campbell Morgan

"There and then a remarkable thing happened, which was a supreme evidence of his majesty.

"He faced the soldiers and said, 'Who is it you want?' They replied, 'Jesus of Nazareth.'

"He then said, 'I am.' Our versions render it 'I am he.' Quite literally he simply said, 'I am.'

"When he did so, a cohort of Roman soldiers, the temple police, the rulers themselves, and Judas guiding them, drew back and fell to the ground.

"I think that something in the bearing of Jesus as he stood confronting his enemies caused their shrinking and fall. They could not lay a hand on him.

"Right to the very end he revealed the fact that no man could lay hands upon him until his hour was come.

" 'I am,' he said, and they drew back and fell. Thus the majesty of Jesus was revealed."

Walk Closer to God

Sovereign.

It's a big word to describe a majestic God. The God who knows the end from the beginning.

Human perception could see only tragedy in Gethsemane. Yet the plan of God was unfolding in all its perfection.

The soldiers came to Jesus to arrest him. Instead, his "I am" drove them to fall on their faces.

Let the thought of his "I am" cause you to fall before him as well.

APRIL 27

📖 Walk in the Word
John 19:1—27

John profiles a confused and unsettled Pilate, who finally gives in to the crowd and hands Jesus over to be crucified.

Jesus Sentenced to be Crucified

19 Then Pilate took Jesus and had him flogged. ²The soldiers twisted together a crown of thorns and put it on his head. They clothed him in a purple robe ³and went up to him again and again, saying, "Hail, king of the Jews!" And they struck him in the face.

⁴Once more Pilate came out and said to the Jews, "Look, I am bringing him out to you to let you know that I find no basis for a charge against him." ⁵When Jesus came out wearing the crown of thorns and the purple robe, Pilate said to them, "Here is the man!"

⁶As soon as the chief priests and their officials saw him, they shouted, "Crucify! Crucify!"

But Pilate answered, "You take him and crucify him. As for me, I find no basis for a charge against him."

⁷The Jews insisted, "We have a law, and according to that law he must die, because he claimed to be the Son of God."

⁸When Pilate heard this, he was even more afraid, ⁹and he went back inside the palace. "Where do you come from?" he asked Jesus, but Jesus gave him no answer. ¹⁰"Do you refuse to speak to me?" Pilate said. "Don't you realize I have power either to free you or to crucify you?"

¹¹Jesus answered, "You would have no power over me if it were not given to you from above. Therefore the one who handed me over to you is guilty of a greater sin."

¹²From then on, Pilate tried to set Jesus free, but the Jews kept shouting, "If you let this man go, you are no friend of Caesar. Anyone who claims to be a king opposes Caesar."

¹³When Pilate heard this, he brought Jesus out and sat down on the judge's seat at a place known as the Stone Pavement (which in Aramaic is Gabbatha). ¹⁴It was the day of Preparation of Passover Week, about the sixth hour.

"Here is your king," Pilate said to the Jews.

¹⁵But they shouted, "Take him away! Take him away! Crucify him!"

"Shall I crucify your king?" Pilate asked.

"We have no king but Caesar," the chief priests answered.

¹⁶Finally Pilate handed him over to them to be crucified.

The Crucifixion

So the soldiers took charge of Jesus. ¹⁷Carrying his own cross, he went out to the place of the Skull (which in Aramaic is called Golgotha). ¹⁸Here they crucified him, and with him two others — one on each side and Jesus in the middle.

¹⁹Pilate had a notice prepared and fastened to the cross. It read: JESUS

APRIL 27

OF NAZARETH, THE KING OF THE JEWS. ²⁰Many of the Jews read this sign, for the place where Jesus was crucified was near the city, and the sign was written in Aramaic, Latin and Greek. ²¹The chief priests of the Jews protested to Pilate, "Do not write 'The King of the Jews,' but that this man claimed to be king of the Jews."

²²Pilate answered, "What I have written, I have written."

²³When the soldiers crucified Jesus, they took his clothes, dividing them into four shares, one for each of them, with the undergarment remaining. This garment was seamless, woven in one piece from top to bottom.

²⁴"Let's not tear it," they said to one another. "Let's decide by lot who will get it."

This happened that the scripture might be fulfilled which said,

> "They divided my garments among them
>   and cast lots for my clothing."^a

So this is what the soldiers did.

²⁵Near the cross of Jesus stood his mother, his mother's sister, Mary the wife of Clopas, and Mary Magdalene. ²⁶When Jesus saw his mother there, and the disciple whom he loved standing nearby, he said to his mother, "Dear woman, here is your son," ²⁷and to the disciple, "Here is your mother." From that time on, this disciple took her into his home.

^a24 Psalm 22:18

Worship
From The
HEART

For a moment, imagine that you are Pilate trying to maintain control in a country seething with religious and political rivalries. Where on earth could you look for guidance? Ask God to give you insight into the spiritual reality behind the contemporary political and social events that you see. Praise him that he won the victory over the evil forces of this world.

A Deadly Decision, Yet Part of God's Plan

The Jews insisted, "We have a law, and according to that law he must die, because he claimed to be the Son of God" (John 19:7).

Pontius Pilate's otherwise obscure career will forever be remembered because of a decision he made: He condemned the Son of God to death.

Yet his deadly decision fulfilled God's will. As Jesus told him, "You would have no power over me if it were not given to you from above."

Martin Luther reflects on the purpose of God as revealed in the crucifixion of his Son.

Walk With Martin Luther

"The greatest wonder on earth is that the Son of God should die the shameful death of the cross.

"It is astonishing that the Father should say to his only Son, who by nature is God: 'Go, let them hang you on the gallows.'

"The love of the everlasting Father was immeasurably greater towards his only begotten Son than the love of Abraham toward Isaac.

"Yet the Son was cast away like a worm, a scorn of men, an outcast of the people.

"At this the understanding of man stumbles, saying, 'How does he deal so unmercifully with him? He showed himself more kind to Caiaphas, Herod, and Pilate, than towards his only Son.'

"But to true Christians it is the greatest comfort; for we recognize that the merciful Father so loved the world, that he spared not his only begotten Son, but gave him up for us all, that whoever believes in him should not perish but have everlasting life."

Walk Closer to God

From the perspective of earth, Pilate condemned an innocent man to death. From the perspective of heaven, "God so loved . . . that he gave . . . ."

In spite of the worst that human beings could do, God still brought forth the best. His loving purposes could not be undone.

Divine love is like that—never failing, always pursuing, always prevailing. And think of it—you're part of his plan! ⟨⟩

APRIL 28

📖 Walk in the Word
John 19:28–42

John gives his version of the death and burial of Jesus, highlighting Old Testament fulfillment in some of the details of Jesus' crucifixion and death.

The Death of Jesus

28Later, knowing that all was now completed, and so that the Scripture would be fulfilled, Jesus said, "I am thirsty." 29A jar of wine vinegar was there, so they soaked a sponge in it, put the sponge on a stalk of the hyssop plant, and lifted it to Jesus' lips. 30When he had received the drink, Jesus said, "It is finished." With that, he bowed his head and gave up his spirit.

31Now it was the day of Preparation, and the next day was to be a special Sabbath. Because the Jews did not want the bodies left on the crosses during the Sabbath, they asked Pilate to have the legs broken and the bodies taken down. 32The soldiers therefore came and broke the legs of the first man who had been crucified with Jesus, and then those of the other. 33But when they came to Jesus and found that he was already dead, they did not break his legs. 34Instead, one of the soldiers pierced Jesus' side with a spear, bringing a sudden flow of blood and water. 35The man who saw it has given testimony, and his testimony is true. He knows that he tells the truth, and he testifies so that you also may believe. 36These things happened so that the scripture would be fulfilled: "Not one of his bones will be broken,"*a* 37and, as another scripture says, "They will look on the one they have pierced."*b*

The Burial of Jesus

38Later, Joseph of Arimathea asked Pilate for the body of Jesus. Now Joseph was a disciple of Jesus, but secretly because he feared the Jews. With Pilate's permission, he came and took the body away. 39He was accompanied by Nicodemus, the man who earlier had visited Jesus at night. Nicodemus brought a mixture of myrrh and aloes, about seventy-five pounds.*c* 40Taking Jesus' body, the two of them wrapped it, with the spices, in strips of linen. This was in accordance with Jewish burial customs. 41At the place where Jesus was crucified, there was a garden, and in the garden a new tomb, in which no one had ever been laid. 42Because it was the Jewish day of Preparation and since the tomb was nearby, they laid Jesus there.

---

*a*36 Exodus 12:46; Num. 9:12; Psalm 34:20   *b*37 Zech. 12:10   *c*39 Greek *a hundred litrai* (about 34 kilograms)

No Need for Additions

Jesus said, "It is finished." With that, he bowed his head and gave up his spirit (John 19:30).

Most Christians begin well; but finishing well—or even at all—is another matter entirely.

Jesus was a finisher. He completed the work of redemption that he came to accomplish. He left nothing undone.

In the closing hours of his life he could pray to his Father, "I have brought you glory on earth by completing the work you gave me to do" (John 17:4).

John Flavel shares this thought on the completed work of Christ.

Walk With John Flavel

"Did Christ finish his work? How dangerous it is to join anything of our own to the righteousness of Christ, in pursuit of justification before God! Jesus Christ will never endure this; it reflects upon his work dishonorably. He will be all, or none, in our justification.

"If he has finished the work, what need is there of our additions? And if not, to what purpose are they? Can we finish that which Christ himself could not complete?

"Did he finish the work, and will he ever divide the glory and praise of it with us? No, no; Christ is no half-Savior.

"It is a hard thing to bring proud hearts to rest upon Christ for righteousness. God humbles the proud by calling sinners wholly from their own righteousness to Christ for their justification."

Walk Closer to God

If these thoughts from the apostle Paul are the expression of your heart, pray them back to God

"I want to know Christ and the power of his resurrection and the fellowship of sharing in his sufferings, becoming like him in his death . . . Brothers, I do not consider myself yet to have taken hold of it. But one thing I do: Forgetting what is behind and straining toward what is ahead, I press on toward the goal to win the prize for which God has called me heavenward in Christ Jesus" (Philippians 3:10,13–14).

APRIL 29

📖 Walk in the Word
John 20

John captures the powerful emotions surrounding the resurrection of Jesus, including the distress of Mary Magdalene, the puzzlement and fear of the disciples, and the hardheaded skepticism of Thomas.

The Empty Tomb

20 Early on the first day of the week, while it was still dark, Mary Magdalene went to the tomb and saw that the stone had been removed from the entrance. ²So she came running to Simon Peter and the other disciple, the one Jesus loved, and said, "They have taken the Lord out of the tomb, and we don't know where they have put him!"

³So Peter and the other disciple started for the tomb. ⁴Both were running, but the other disciple outran Peter and reached the tomb first. ⁵He bent over and looked in at the strips of linen lying there but did not go in. ⁶Then Simon Peter, who was behind him, arrived and went into the tomb. He saw the strips of linen lying there, ⁷as well as the burial cloth that had been around Jesus' head. The cloth was folded up by itself, separate from the linen. ⁸Finally the other disciple, who had reached the tomb first, also went inside. He saw and believed. ⁹(They still did not understand from Scripture that Jesus had to rise from the dead.)

Jesus Appears to Mary Magdalene

¹⁰Then the disciples went back to their homes, ¹¹but Mary stood outside the tomb crying. As she wept, she bent over to look into the tomb ¹²and saw two angels in white, seated where Jesus' body had been, one at the head and the other at the foot.

¹³They asked her, "Woman, why are you crying?"

"They have taken my Lord away," she said, "and I don't know where they have put him." ¹⁴At this, she turned around and saw Jesus standing there, but she did not realize that it was Jesus.

¹⁵"Woman," he said, "why are you crying? Who is it you are looking for?"

Thinking he was the gardener, she said, "Sir, if you have carried him away, tell me where you have put him, and I will get him."

¹⁶Jesus said to her, "Mary."

She turned toward him and cried out in Aramaic, "Rabboni!" (which means Teacher).

¹⁷Jesus said, "Do not hold on to me, for I have not yet returned to the Father. Go instead to my brothers and tell them, 'I am returning to my Father and your Father, to my God and your God.' "

¹⁸Mary Magdalene went to the disciples with the news: "I have seen the Lord!" And she told them that he had said these things to her.

Jesus Appears to His Disciples

¹⁹On the evening of that first day of the week, when the disciples were together, with the doors locked for fear of the Jews, Jesus came and stood

among them and said, "Peace be with you!" ²⁰After he said this, he showed them his hands and side. The disciples were overjoyed when they saw the Lord.

²¹Again Jesus said, "Peace be with you! As the Father has sent me, I am sending you." ²²And with that he breathed on them and said, "Receive the Holy Spirit. ²³If you forgive anyone his sins, they are forgiven; if you do not forgive them, they are not forgiven."

Jesus Appears to Thomas

²⁴Now Thomas (called Didymus), one of the Twelve, was not with the disciples when Jesus came. ²⁵So the other disciples told him, "We have seen the Lord!"

But he said to them, "Unless I see the nail marks in his hands and put my finger where the nails were, and put my hand into his side, I will not believe it."

²⁶A week later his disciples were in the house again, and Thomas was with them. Though the doors were locked, Jesus came and stood among them and said, "Peace be with you!" ²⁷Then he said to Thomas, "Put your finger here; see my hands. Reach out your hand and put it into my side. Stop doubting and believe."

²⁸Thomas said to him, "My Lord and my God!"

²⁹Then Jesus told him, "Because you have seen me, you have believed; blessed are those who have not seen and yet have believed."

³⁰Jesus did many other miraculous signs in the presence of his disciples, which are not recorded in this book. ³¹But these are written that you may[a] believe that Jesus is the Christ, the Son of God, and that by believing you may have life in his name.

^a31 Some manuscripts *may continue to*

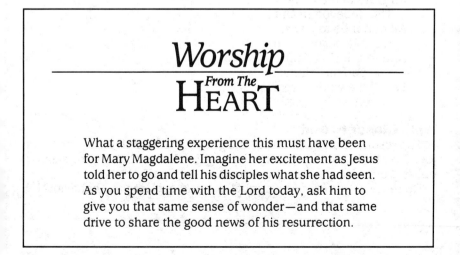

Worship
From The
HEART

What a staggering experience this must have been for Mary Magdalene. Imagine her excitement as Jesus told her to go and tell his disciples what she had seen. As you spend time with the Lord today, ask him to give you that same sense of wonder—and that same drive to share the good news of his resurrection.

APRIL 29

Basing Behavior on Your Belief

Mary Magdalene went to the disciples with the news: "I have seen the Lord!" (John 20:18).

Heedless of his reminders that his death would not be permanent, the disciples mourned Jesus for three long days. When Sunday morning dawned, their attitude was no different, until . . .

Columba, an Irish missionary nearly fifteen hundred years ago, gives praise to God in this celebration of the first Easter.

Walk With Columba

Christ is the Great Redeemer,
The lover of the pure,
The fount of heavenly wisdom,
Our trust and hope secure;
The armor of His soldiers,
The Lord of earth and sky;
Our health while we are living,
Our life when we shall die.
Down in the realm of darkness
He lay a captive bound,
But at the hour appointed
He rose, a victor crowned;
And now, to heaven ascended,
He sits upon the throne,
In glorious dominion,
His Father's and His own.
All glory to the Father,
The unbegotten One;
All honor be to Jesus,
His sole begotten Son;
And to the Holy Spirit—
The perfect Trinity.
Let all the world give answer,
'Amen, so let it be.'

Walk Closer to God

The resurrection transformed the grief of the disciples into hope and joy. They had seen the Lord! He lived again! Even Thomas—the skeptic of the group—responded, "My Lord and my God!"

Do these words express your belief—and explain your behavior? ♡

Committed to the Study of God's Word

Jonathan Edwards, although usually viewed as a cold, unbending Puritan preacher of gloom and doom, was in fact one of the outstanding minds of early America. Born in 1703, Jonathan was the son and grandson of ministers, enjoying the stability of a family that loved the Lord. He received his early education at home, learning Latin at the age of six and Greek and Hebrew by age thirteen, whereupon he entered Yale.

At Yale, Edwards exchanged an intellectual knowledge of the Christian life for a life-changing commitment to the Savior. Moving to Northhampton, Massachusetts, he became co-pastor with his grandfather and, within two years, the sole pastor. As Edwards spent long hours in study and prayer, God used his keen mind and potent pen to bring revival—first to his church and eventually throughout New England.

The Great Awakening in America saw the return of vital, life-changing Christianity. Edwards' fire-and-brimstone message, "Sinners in the Hands of an Angry God," was really a powerful plea for calloused churchgoers to reconsider God's love and mercy. His ministry transformed thousands of lives during that great revival. His own deep faith is evident in his correspondence with his wife and children. Edwards was eventually appointed as president of the College of New Jersey (today known as Princeton University). A month later, however, he died of smallpox at the age of fifty-five.

Edwards was committed to the study of God's Word, spending as many as thirteen hours a day in Bible study and sermon preparation. Thirteen hours in God's Word may be more than you can devote today! But any time spent reading and reflecting on Scripture will bring benefit to you—and those around you.

A LESSON FROM THE LIFE OF JONATHAN EDWARDS

The time I spend in Bible study both glorifies God and enriches my own life.

APRIL 30

Walk in the Word
John 21

John concludes his eyewitness account of Jesus' life with an account of Peter's renewed fellowship with Jesus.

Jesus and the Miraculous Catch of Fish

21 Afterward Jesus appeared again to his disciples, by the Sea of Tiberias.*a* It happened this way: **2**Simon Peter, Thomas (called Didymus), Nathanael from Cana in Galilee, the sons of Zebedee, and two other disciples were together. **3**"I'm going out to fish," Simon Peter told them, and they said, "We'll go with you." So they went out and got into the boat, but that night they caught nothing.

4Early in the morning, Jesus stood on the shore, but the disciples did not realize that it was Jesus.

5He called out to them, "Friends, haven't you any fish?"

"No," they answered.

6He said, "Throw your net on the right side of the boat and you will find some." When they did, they were unable to haul the net in because of the large number of fish.

7Then the disciple whom Jesus loved said to Peter, "It is the Lord!" As soon as Simon Peter heard him say, "It is the Lord," he wrapped his outer garment around him (for he had taken it off) and jumped into the water. **8**The other disciples followed in the boat, towing the net full of fish, for they were not far from shore, about a hundred yards.*b* **9**When they landed, they saw a fire of burning coals there with fish on it, and some bread.

10Jesus said to them, "Bring some of the fish you have just caught."

11Simon Peter climbed aboard and dragged the net ashore. It was full of large fish, 153, but even with so many the net was not torn. **12**Jesus said to them, "Come and have breakfast." None of the disciples dared ask him, "Who are you?" They knew it was the Lord. **13**Jesus came, took the bread and gave it to them, and did the same with the fish. **14**This was now the third time Jesus appeared to his disciples after he was raised from the dead.

Jesus Reinstates Peter

15When they had finished eating, Jesus said to Simon Peter, "Simon son of John, do you truly love me more than these?"

"Yes, Lord," he said, "you know that I love you."

Jesus said, "Feed my lambs."

16Again Jesus said, "Simon son of John, do you truly love me?"

He answered, "Yes, Lord, you know that I love you."

Jesus said, "Take care of my sheep."

17The third time he said to him, "Simon son of John, do you love me?"

Peter was hurt because Jesus asked him the third time, "Do you love me?" He said, "Lord, you know all things; you know that I love you."

Jesus said, "Feed my sheep. **18**I tell you the truth, when you were younger you dressed yourself and went where you wanted; but when you are

364

old you will stretch out your hands, and someone else will dress you and lead you where you do not want to go." ¹⁹Jesus said this to indicate the kind of death by which Peter would glorify God. Then he said to him, "Follow me!"

²⁰Peter turned and saw that the disciple whom Jesus loved was following them. (This was the one who had leaned back against Jesus at the supper and had said, "Lord, who is going to betray you?") ²¹When Peter saw him, he asked, "Lord, what about him?"

²²Jesus answered, "If I want him to remain alive until I return, what is that to you? You must follow me." ²³Because of this, the rumor spread among the brothers that this disciple would not die. But Jesus did not say that he would not die; he only said, "If I want him to remain alive until I return, what is that to you?"

²⁴This is the disciple who testifies to these things and who wrote them down. We know that his testimony is true.

²⁵Jesus did many other things as well. If every one of them were written down, I suppose that even the whole world would not have room for the books that would be written.

---

a1 That is, Sea of Galilee   *b8* Greek *about two hundred cubits* (about 90 meters)

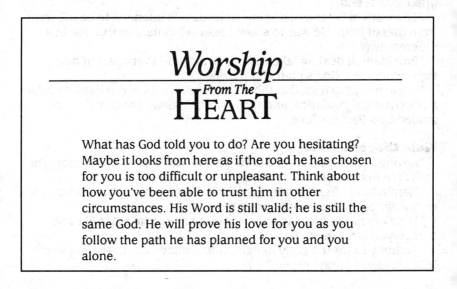

Worship
From The
HEART

What has God told you to do? Are you hesitating? Maybe it looks from here as if the road he has chosen for you is too difficult or unpleasant. Think about how you've been able to trust him in other circumstances. His Word is still valid; he is still the same God. He will prove his love for you as you follow the path he has planned for you and you alone.

APRIL 30

Guarded and Guided by the Father's Love

Jesus answered, "If I want him to remain alive until I return, what is that to you? You must follow me" (John 21:22).

Peter was unique among the twelve. He had unique potential. Unique problems. Unique personality.

But in John 21, Peter compares himself with another disciple, wondering if the future course of their lives will be similar.

The Lord's reply is a simple "Follow me."

Timothy Dwight offers this insight on the danger of comparing one Christian's lot in life with another's.

Walk With Timothy Dwight

"How often we find that we never escape certain difficulties. We hope to escape them; we wonder why we do not.

"The Lord's reasoning is clear: We were made for the accomplishment of a special divine purpose—for the showing forth of a divinely formed character and life—and all allotments of experience are wisely fitted to that end.

"The work of Peter as a disciple of Jesus was intended to be different from that of John. He was to show the development of true life in a different way.

"Providential dealing takes all our living, and every part of our experience, into God's plan and purpose.

"It teaches us to trust that the natural movement of our lives is under a supernatural guidance, and that in all things we are guarded and guided by a Father's love."

Walk Closer to God

"Loving Father, you are the Lord over all, my Creator, my Savior. You know me better than I know myself.

"Remind me often that my life is still under construction as you use my particular abilities for your glory.

"Help me to see trials as opportunities to become more like the person you want me to be.

"Thank you for the daily delight of following you. In the name of Jesus my Lord I pray. Amen." ◖

MAY

Life and Death in the Arena of Faith

ACTS

The book of Acts has all the makings of a best-selling novel. Plenty of action. Tense confrontation. Martyrdom. Controversy. Gripping dialogue. Travel. Courtroom drama. Even humorous situations. And undergirding all is a sense that in the end everything will turn out as the Author intended.

The main character in Acts is not Peter, Paul, nor any human figure, but rather the Holy Spirit. In the opening verses, Jesus commands his followers to wait in Jerusalem until "the Holy Spirit comes on you; and you will be my witnesses in Jerusalem, and in all Judea and Samaria, and to the ends of the earth" (Acts 1:8). The rest of the book recounts how those words of Jesus began to be fulfilled. Acts 1–7 presents the early days of the New Testament church in Jerusalem. Peter preaches Spirit-inspired sermons that pierce the hearts of thousands. Others begin to speak out as the influence of the gospel multiplies, until Stephen's martyrdom ushers in a period of intense persecution. Acts 8–12 chronicles the spread of the gospel into the regions surrounding Jerusalem. Paul's transformation from antagonist to apostle of Christ and the conversion of the Roman centurion Cornelius set the stage for the good news to be carried to "the ends of the earth." Acts 13–28 begins in Antioch, the first great missionary center of the church, and ends in Rome, the capital of the then-known world. Paul and his various companions spread the good news of the resurrected Christ everywhere they travel.

The book of Acts closes with chapter 28, but the story of Acts continues today as disciples of Jesus Christ take the gospel to their Jerusalem, Judea, Samaria and the ends of the earth. Think of Acts as your training manual on "How to Be an Effective Witness." Jesus Christ has provided the plan; the Holy Spirit provides the power. All that is needed is a person through whom God can work. God wants you to take the good news of salvation to your neighborhood, your school and your office. It's an exciting assignment!

MAY 1

📖 Walk in the Word
Acts 1

Luke begins his second volume with a brief summary of his first work and a statement of this book's theme as recorded in Jesus' words to his disciples just prior to his ascension.

Jesus Taken Up Into Heaven

1 In my former book, Theophilus, I wrote about all that Jesus began to do and to teach ²until the day he was taken up to heaven, after giving instructions through the Holy Spirit to the apostles he had chosen. ³After his suffering, he showed himself to these men and gave many convincing proofs that he was alive. He appeared to them over a period of forty days and spoke about the kingdom of God. ⁴On one occasion, while he was eating with them, he gave them this command: "Do not leave Jerusalem, but wait for the gift my Father promised, which you have heard me speak about. ⁵For John baptized with*ᵃ* water, but in a few days you will be baptized with the Holy Spirit."

⁶So when they met together, they asked him, "Lord, are you at this time going to restore the kingdom to Israel?"

⁷He said to them: "It is not for you to know the times or dates the Father has set by his own authority. ⁸But you will receive power when the Holy Spirit comes on you; and you will be my witnesses in Jerusalem, and in all Judea and Samaria, and to the ends of the earth."

⁹After he said this, he was taken up before their very eyes, and a cloud hid him from their sight.

¹⁰They were looking intently up into the sky as he was going, when suddenly two men dressed in white stood beside them. ¹¹"Men of Galilee," they said, "why do you stand here looking into the sky? This same Jesus, who has been taken from you into heaven, will come back in the same way you have seen him go into heaven."

Matthias Chosen to Replace Judas

¹²Then they returned to Jerusalem from the hill called the Mount of Olives, a Sabbath day's walk*ᵇ* from the city. ¹³When they arrived, they went upstairs to the room where they were staying. Those present were Peter, John, James and Andrew; Philip and Thomas, Bartholomew and Matthew; James son of Alphaeus and Simon the Zealot, and Judas son of James. ¹⁴They all joined together constantly in prayer, along with the women and Mary the mother of Jesus, and with his brothers.

¹⁵In those days Peter stood up among the believers*ᶜ* (a group numbering about a hundred and twenty) ¹⁶and said, "Brothers, the Scripture had to be fulfilled which the Holy Spirit spoke long ago through the mouth of David concerning Judas, who served as guide for those who arrested Jesus— ¹⁷he was one of our number and shared in this ministry."

¹⁸(With the reward he got for his wickedness, Judas bought a field; there he fell headlong, his body burst open and all his intestines spilled out.

¹⁹Everyone in Jerusalem heard about this, so they called that field in their language Akeldama, that is, Field of Blood.)

²⁰"For," said Peter, "it is written in the book of Psalms,

> " 'May his place be deserted;
> let there be no one to dwell in it,'ᵈ

and,

> " 'May another take his place of leadership.'ᵉ

²¹Therefore it is necessary to choose one of the men who have been with us the whole time the Lord Jesus went in and out among us, ²²beginning from John's baptism to the time when Jesus was taken up from us. For one of these must become a witness with us of his resurrection."

²³So they proposed two men: Joseph called Barsabbas (also known as Justus) and Matthias. ²⁴Then they prayed, "Lord, you know everyone's heart. Show us which of these two you have chosen ²⁵to take over this apostolic ministry, which Judas left to go where he belongs." ²⁶Then they cast lots, and the lot fell to Matthias; so he was added to the eleven apostles.

ᵃ5 Or *in*   ᵇ12 That is, about 3/4 mile (about 1,100 meters)   ᶜ15 Greek *brothers*
ᵈ20 Psalm 69:25   ᵉ20 Psalm 109:8

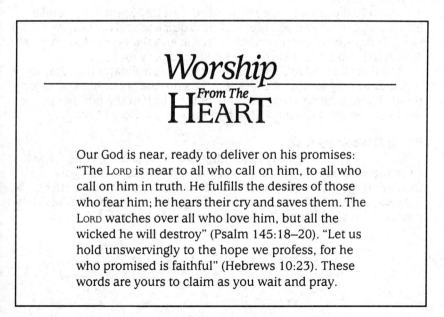

Worship
From The
HEART

Our God is near, ready to deliver on his promises: "The LORD is near to all who call on him, to all who call on him in truth. He fulfills the desires of those who fear him; he hears their cry and saves them. The LORD watches over all who love him, but all the wicked he will destroy" (Psalm 145:18–20). "Let us hold unswervingly to the hope we profess, for he who promised is faithful" (Hebrews 10:23). These words are yours to claim as you wait and pray.

May 1

Waiting on the Promises

When they arrived, they went upstairs to the room . . . They all joined together constantly in prayer (Acts 1:13–14).

A man appears alive to many after his execution, then disappears into the clouds before a group of his closest friends.

Could you keep quiet if you had been part of that group of privileged observers?

Jesus' disciples did keep quiet until the proper time to unleash the Good News. Jesus told them to wait for the Holy Spirit before beginning the missionary enterprise he had committed to them.

Matthew Henry describes how they prayerfully obeyed.

Walk With Matthew Henry

"It was now a time of trouble and danger with the disciples of Christ; they were as sheep in the middle of wolves. They had new work, and before they entered into it, they were continuously in prayer to God for his presence with them in it.

"They are in the best frame to receive spiritual blessings who are in a praying frame.

"Christ had promised shortly to send the Holy Spirit—a promise intended not to supersede prayer, but to quicken and encourage it. God will be enquired of for promised mercies, and the nearer the promise seems to be, the more earnestly we should pray for it.

"The disciples did this with one accord. This intimates that they were together in holy love, and that there was no quarrel or discord among them. Those who so keep the unity of the Spirit in the bond of peace are best prepared to receive the comforts of the Holy Ghost."

Walk Closer to God

For the disciples, hastily beginning the work of the gospel—apart from the Holy Spirit—might have caused more harm than good. Instead, they prayed and waited for God's timetable to take effect.

Walking with God, rather than running ahead of him. That's still the best way to "work" the will of God in your life today. ◯

May 2

📖 Walk in the Word
Acts 2

Luke tells the gripping story of the coming of the Holy Spirit and records Peter's message to the crowd and the positive response of many who heard the message and saw the power of the early church.

The Holy Spirit Comes at Pentecost

2 When the day of Pentecost came, they were all together in one place. ²Suddenly a sound like the blowing of a violent wind came from heaven and filled the whole house where they were sitting. ³They saw what seemed to be tongues of fire that separated and came to rest on each of them. ⁴All of them were filled with the Holy Spirit and began to speak in other tongues*ᵃ* as the Spirit enabled them.

⁵Now there were staying in Jerusalem God-fearing Jews from every nation under heaven. ⁶When they heard this sound, a crowd came together in bewilderment, because each one heard them speaking in his own language. ⁷Utterly amazed, they asked: "Are not all these men who are speaking Galileans? ⁸Then how is it that each of us hears them in his own native language? ⁹Parthians, Medes and Elamites; residents of Mesopotamia, Judea and Cappadocia, Pontus and Asia, ¹⁰Phrygia and Pamphylia, Egypt and the parts of Libya near Cyrene; visitors from Rome ¹¹(both Jews and converts to Judaism); Cretans and Arabs—we hear them declaring the wonders of God in our own tongues!" ¹²Amazed and perplexed, they asked one another, "What does this mean?"

¹³Some, however, made fun of them and said, "They have had too much wine.*ᵇ*"

Peter Addresses the Crowd

¹⁴Then Peter stood up with the Eleven, raised his voice and addressed the crowd: "Fellow Jews and all of you who live in Jerusalem, let me explain this to you; listen carefully to what I say. ¹⁵These men are not drunk, as you suppose. It's only nine in the morning! ¹⁶No, this is what was spoken by the prophet Joel:

¹⁷" 'In the last days, God says,
  I will pour out my Spirit on all people.
Your sons and daughters will prophesy,
  your young men will see visions,
  your old men will dream dreams.
¹⁸Even on my servants, both men and women,
  I will pour out my Spirit in those days,
  and they will prophesy.
¹⁹I will show wonders in the heaven above
  and signs on the earth below,
  blood and fire and billows of smoke.

May 2

20The sun will be turned to darkness
and the moon to blood
before the coming of the great and glorious day of the
Lord.
21And everyone who calls
on the name of the Lord will be saved.'c

22"Men of Israel, listen to this: Jesus of Nazareth was a man accredited by God to you by miracles, wonders and signs, which God did among you through him, as you yourselves know. 23This man was handed over to you by God's set purpose and foreknowledge; and you, with the help of wicked men,d put him to death by nailing him to the cross. 24But God raised him from the dead, freeing him from the agony of death, because it was impossible for death to keep its hold on him. 25David said about him:

" 'I saw the Lord always before me.
Because he is at my right hand,
I will not be shaken.
26Therefore my heart is glad and my tongue rejoices;
my body also will live in hope,
27because you will not abandon me to the grave,
nor will you let your Holy One see decay.
28You have made known to me the paths of life;
you will fill me with joy in your presence.'e

29"Brothers, I can tell you confidently that the patriarch David died and was buried, and his tomb is here to this day. 30But he was a prophet and knew that God had promised him on oath that he would place one of his descendants on his throne. 31Seeing what was ahead, he spoke of the resurrection of the Christ,f that he was not abandoned to the grave, nor did his body see decay. 32God has raised this Jesus to life, and we are all witnesses of the fact. 33Exalted to the right hand of God, he has received from the Father the promised Holy Spirit and has poured out what you now see and hear. 34For David did not ascend to heaven, and yet he said,

" 'The Lord said to my Lord:
"Sit at my right hand
35until I make your enemies
a footstool for your feet." 'g

36"Therefore let all Israel be assured of this: God has made this Jesus, whom you crucified, both Lord and Christ."
37When the people heard this, they were cut to the heart and said to Peter and the other apostles, "Brothers, what shall we do?"
38Peter replied, "Repent and be baptized, every one of you, in the name of Jesus Christ for the forgiveness of your sins. And you will receive the gift of the Holy Spirit. 39The promise is for you and your children and for all who are far off—for all whom the Lord our God will call."
40With many other words he warned them; and he pleaded with them,

MAY 2

"Save yourselves from this corrupt generation." ⁴¹Those who accepted his message were baptized, and about three thousand were added to their number that day.

The Fellowship of the Believers

⁴²They devoted themselves to the apostles' teaching and to the fellowship, to the breaking of bread and to prayer. ⁴³Everyone was filled with awe, and many wonders and miraculous signs were done by the apostles. ⁴⁴All the believers were together and had everything in common. ⁴⁵Selling their possessions and goods, they gave to anyone as he had need. ⁴⁶Every day they continued to meet together in the temple courts. They broke bread in their homes and ate together with glad and sincere hearts, ⁴⁷praising God and enjoying the favor of all the people. And the Lord added to their number daily those who were being saved.

a4 Or *languages*; also in verse 11   *b13* Or *sweet wine*   *c21* Joel 2:28-32   *d23* Or *of those not having the law* (that is, Gentiles)   *e28* Psalm 16:8-11   *f31* Or *Messiah.* "The Christ" (Greek) and "the Messiah" (Hebrew) both mean "the Anointed One"; also in verse 36.   *g35* Psalm 110:1

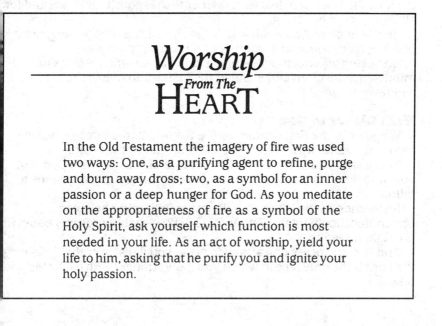

Worship
From The HEART

In the Old Testament the imagery of fire was used two ways: One, as a purifying agent to refine, purge and burn away dross; two, as a symbol for an inner passion or a deep hunger for God. As you meditate on the appropriateness of fire as a symbol of the Holy Spirit, ask yourself which function is most needed in your life. As an act of worship, yield your life to him, asking that he purify you and ignite your holy passion.

MAY 2

Not a Destination, But a Beginning

They devoted themselves to the apostles' teaching and to the fellowship, to the breaking of bread and to prayer (Acts 2:42).

Perhaps you thought you had "arrived" when you became a Christian. And in a sense, you had!

You arrived at the starting line of a race—a race that required devotion, as the first converts to Christianity learned (Acts 2:42).

A.W. Tozer echoes this theme in his insightful look at conversion—an event which the Bible portrays more as a place to start than to finish.

Walk With A.W. Tozer

"Conversion for the early Christians was not a destination; it was the beginning of a journey.

"And right there is often where the Biblical emphasis differs from our own.

"In our eagerness to make converts, we allow our hearers to absorb the idea that they can deal with their entire responsibility once and for all by an act of believing.

"In the Book of Acts, faith was for each believer a beginning, not a bed in which to lie while waiting for the Lord's triumph.

"Believing was not a once-done act. It was an attitude of heart and mind which inspired and enabled the believer to follow the Lord wherever he went."

Walk Closer to God

Whether in the first century or the twentieth, the hope of heaven comes the same way—through believing faith in the Savior.

That's step one in the lifelong adventure of walking with God. But one step does not make a journey. Indeed, there are many steps to follow.

Instruction in the Word . . . fellowship with other believers . . . communication with the Father (Acts 2:42)—each represents a step in the right direction.

And in the process of learning to walk, you'll discover that following the Lord is the only race in which you grow stronger with each step you take. ◖

MAY 3

Walk in the Word
Acts 3

Luke recounts the healing of a crippled beggar; Peter uses the occasion to once again tell the story of Jesus and call for repentance into life and blessing in Jesus.

Peter Heals the Crippled Beggar

3 One day Peter and John were going up to the temple at the time of prayer — at three in the afternoon. ²Now a man crippled from birth was being carried to the temple gate called Beautiful, where he was put every day to beg from those going into the temple courts. ³When he saw Peter and John about to enter, he asked them for money. ⁴Peter looked straight at him, as did John. Then Peter said, "Look at us!" ⁵So the man gave them his attention, expecting to get something from them.

⁶Then Peter said, "Silver or gold I do not have, but what I have I give you. In the name of Jesus Christ of Nazareth, walk." ⁷Taking him by the right hand, he helped him up, and instantly the man's feet and ankles became strong. ⁸He jumped to his feet and began to walk. Then he went with them into the temple courts, walking and jumping, and praising God. ⁹When all the people saw him walking and praising God, ¹⁰they recognized him as the same man who used to sit begging at the temple gate called Beautiful, and they were filled with wonder and amazement at what had happened to him.

Peter Speaks to the Onlookers

¹¹While the beggar held on to Peter and John, all the people were astonished and came running to them in the place called Solomon's Colonnade. ¹²When Peter saw this, he said to them: "Men of Israel, why does this surprise you? Why do you stare at us as if by our own power or godliness we had made this man walk? ¹³The God of Abraham, Isaac and Jacob, the God of our fathers, has glorified his servant Jesus. You handed him over to be killed, and you disowned him before Pilate, though he had decided to let him go. ¹⁴You disowned the Holy and Righteous One and asked that a murderer be released to you. ¹⁵You killed the author of life, but God raised him from the dead. We are witnesses of this. ¹⁶By faith in the name of Jesus, this man whom you see and know was made strong. It is Jesus' name and the faith that comes through him that has given this complete healing to him, as you can all see.

¹⁷"Now, brothers, I know that you acted in ignorance, as did your leaders. ¹⁸But this is how God fulfilled what he had foretold through all the prophets, saying that his Christ*a* would suffer. ¹⁹Repent, then, and turn to God, so that your sins may be wiped out, that times of refreshing may come from the Lord, ²⁰and that he may send the Christ, who has been appointed for you — even Jesus. ²¹He must remain in heaven until the time comes for God to restore everything, as he promised long ago through his holy prophets. ²²For Moses said, 'The Lord your God will raise up for you a prophet like me from among your own people; you must listen to every-

May 3

thing he tells you. ²³Anyone who does not listen to him will be completely cut off from among his people.'ᵇ

²⁴"Indeed, all the prophets from Samuel on, as many as have spoken, have foretold these days. ²⁵And you are heirs of the prophets and of the covenant God made with your fathers. He said to Abraham, 'Through your offspring all peoples on earth will be blessed.'ᶜ ²⁶When God raised up his servant, he sent him first to you to bless you by turning each of you from your wicked ways."

ᵃ18 Or *Messiah*; also in verse 20   ᵇ23 Deut. 18:15,18,19   ᶜ25 Gen. 22:18; 26:4

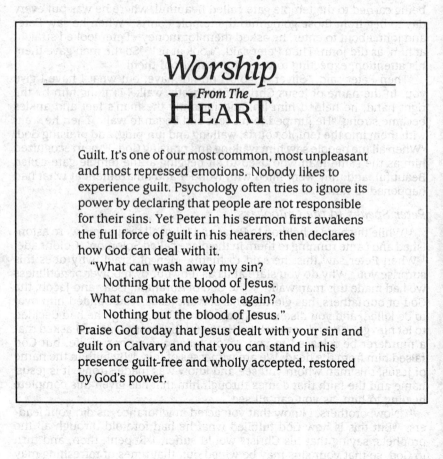

Worship
From The HEART

Guilt. It's one of our most common, most unpleasant and most repressed emotions. Nobody likes to experience guilt. Psychology often tries to ignore its power by declaring that people are not responsible for their sins. Yet Peter in his sermon first awakens the full force of guilt in his hearers, then declares how God can deal with it.

"What can wash away my sin?
   Nothing but the blood of Jesus.
What can make me whole again?
   Nothing but the blood of Jesus."

Praise God today that Jesus dealt with your sin and guilt on Calvary and that you can stand in his presence guilt-free and wholly accepted, restored by God's power.

The Greater Blessedness of Giving

Then Peter said, "Silver or gold I do not have, but what I have I give you. In the name of Jesus Christ of Nazareth, walk" (Acts 3:6).

There are still some things money can't buy. Like salvation, for instance. And the power of God at work in a life.

The lame man in Acts 3 learned that lesson.

When Peter and John passed by, he begged for alms . . . but instead received legs. A miraculous testimony to the God whose power cannot be bought or sold!

Alexander Maclaren examines Peter's words, and the message they convey to servants of God.

Walk With Alexander Maclaren

"Peter did not say 'what I have,' as if what he was offering was inferior to money. Instead he intended a very different tone.

"The expression eloquently magnifies the power which he possessed as far more precious than wealth.

"God gives us all our possessions and spiritual riches as well, not only that we may enjoy them ourselves, but that we may impart them, and so experience the greater blessedness of giving over receiving.

"How often it has been true that a poor church has been a miracle-working church.

"But when a church could not say 'Silver or gold I do not have,' it has also had no power to say 'In the name of Jesus Christ of Nazareth, walk.' "

Walk Closer to God

Peter did not have what the lame man expected. But he did have what the lame man needed: the power of God. The same power that transformed Peter from a denier to a declarer of the Savior. Perhaps you hesitate to share your Savior with someone because of what you don't possess: money, status, ability with words.

If so, consider this liberating thought: Even without a coin in your pocket or purse, you possess something that is more precious than gold, and more powerful than dynamite. ◖◗

MAY 4

📖 Walk in the Word
Acts 4

Luke accents the boldness and power of Jesus' followers in scenes featuring Peter and John before the Sanhedrin, believers in prayer and believers engaged in sharing with one another.

Peter and John Before the Sanhedrin

4 The priests and the captain of the temple guard and the Sadducees came up to Peter and John while they were speaking to the people. ²They were greatly disturbed because the apostles were teaching the people and proclaiming in Jesus the resurrection of the dead. ³They seized Peter and John, and because it was evening, they put them in jail until the next day. ⁴But many who heard the message believed, and the number of men grew to about five thousand.

⁵The next day the rulers, elders and teachers of the law met in Jerusalem. ⁶Annas the high priest was there, and so were Caiaphas, John, Alexander and the other men of the high priest's family. ⁷They had Peter and John brought before them and began to question them: "By what power or what name did you do this?"

⁸Then Peter, filled with the Holy Spirit, said to them: "Rulers and elders of the people! ⁹If we are being called to account today for an act of kindness shown to a cripple and are asked how he was healed, ¹⁰then know this, you and all the people of Israel: It is by the name of Jesus Christ of Nazareth, whom you crucified but whom God raised from the dead, that this man stands before you healed. ¹¹He is

" 'the stone you builders rejected,
   which has become the capstone.*ᵃ*'*ᵇ*

¹²Salvation is found in no one else, for there is no other name under heaven given to men by which we must be saved."

¹³When they saw the courage of Peter and John and realized that they were unschooled, ordinary men, they were astonished and they took note that these men had been with Jesus. ¹⁴But since they could see the man who had been healed standing there with them, there was nothing they could say. ¹⁵So they ordered them to withdraw from the Sanhedrin and then conferred together. ¹⁶"What are we going to do with these men?" they asked. "Everybody living in Jerusalem knows they have done an outstanding miracle, and we cannot deny it. ¹⁷But to stop this thing from spreading any further among the people, we must warn these men to speak no longer to anyone in this name."

¹⁸Then they called them in again and commanded them not to speak or teach at all in the name of Jesus. ¹⁹But Peter and John replied, "Judge for yourselves whether it is right in God's sight to obey you rather than God. ²⁰For we cannot help speaking about what we have seen and heard."

²¹After further threats they let them go. They could not decide how to punish them, because all the people were praising God for what had hap-

MAY 4

pened. [22]For the man who was miraculously healed was over forty years old.

The Believers' Prayer

[23]On their release, Peter and John went back to their own people and reported all that the chief priests and elders had said to them. [24]When they heard this, they raised their voices together in prayer to God. "Sovereign Lord," they said, "you made the heaven and the earth and the sea, and everything in them. [25]You spoke by the Holy Spirit through the mouth of your servant, our father David:

> " 'Why do the nations rage
> and the peoples plot in vain?
> [26]The kings of the earth take their stand
> and the rulers gather together
> against the Lord
> and against his Anointed One.[c'd]

[27]Indeed Herod and Pontius Pilate met together with the Gentiles and the people[e] of Israel in this city to conspire against your holy servant Jesus, whom you anointed. [28]They did what your power and will had decided beforehand should happen. [29]Now, Lord, consider their threats and enable your servants to speak your word with great boldness. [30]Stretch out your hand to heal and perform miraculous signs and wonders through the name of your holy servant Jesus."

[31]After they prayed, the place where they were meeting was shaken. And they were all filled with the Holy Spirit and spoke the word of God boldly.

The Believers Share Their Possessions

[32]All the believers were one in heart and mind. No one claimed that any of his possessions was his own, but they shared everything they had. [33]With great power the apostles continued to testify to the resurrection of the Lord Jesus, and much grace was upon them all. [34]There were no needy persons among them. For from time to time those who owned lands or houses sold them, brought the money from the sales [35]and put it at the apostles' feet, and it was distributed to anyone as he had need.

[36]Joseph, a Levite from Cyprus, whom the apostles called Barnabas (which means Son of Encouragement), [37]sold a field he owned and brought the money and put it at the apostles' feet.

[a]11 Or cornerstone   [b]11 Psalm 118:22   [c]26 That is, Christ or Messiah   [d]26 Psalm 2:1,2   [e]27 The Greek is plural.

MAY 4

Making the Life of Christ Visible

When they saw the courage of Peter and John . . . they were astonished and they took note that these men had been with Jesus (Acts 4:13).

Peter and John were men of meager means and lowly reputation, men who were at home on the sea and out of place before the educated Jewish leaders of the Sanhedrin.

They had every reason to stand in awe of their accusers. Instead, the Sanhedrin marveled at the boldness of these unlearned men.

Joseph Parker comments on the encounter that transformed these rough fishermen into robust spokesmen for the gospel.

Walk With Joseph Parker

"We cannot have personal contact with Christ without people knowing it.

"Once there were some very poor, unlettered men—men who might have been taken from the fishing boat, from the plow, or from some ordinary job.

"And they went before some very great magistrates who did not do manual labor. And these magistrates looked at them and said, 'How ordinary these men are! What disadvantages they must have undergone! And yet there is something about them that makes them special. There is a kind of radiance on all that roughness of exterior.'

"To be with Jesus is an education; to be closeted with Christ is a refining process.

"We ask no other distinction, we long for no greater fame, than to be taken knowledge of that we have been with Jesus."

Walk Closer to God

Peter and John impressed the Sanhedrin with their bold stand for the Savior. They had taken Christ's words to heart: "Let your light shine before men, that they may see your good deeds and praise your Father in heaven" (Matthew 5:16).

They reflected the light of Christ to the Sanhedrin; and, true to his word, God was praised.

It's seldom hard for others to detect when you have been with the Savior. And that's a nice reflection on him!

MAY 5

Walk in the Word
Acts 5

Luke explores some painful and powerful realities as he tells of the sin and deceit of Ananias and Sapphira, numerous healings and conversions, and persecutions directed against the apostles.

Ananias and Sapphira

5 Now a man named Ananias, together with his wife Sapphira, also sold a piece of property. [2]With his wife's full knowledge he kept back part of the money for himself, but brought the rest and put it at the apostles' feet.

[3]Then Peter said, "Ananias, how is it that Satan has so filled your heart that you have lied to the Holy Spirit and have kept for yourself some of the money you received for the land? [4]Didn't it belong to you before it was sold? And after it was sold, wasn't the money at your disposal? What made you think of doing such a thing? You have not lied to men but to God."

[5]When Ananias heard this, he fell down and died. And great fear seized all who heard what had happened. [6]Then the young men came forward, wrapped up his body, and carried him out and buried him.

[7]About three hours later his wife came in, not knowing what had happened. [8]Peter asked her, "Tell me, is this the price you and Ananias got for the land?"

"Yes," she said, "that is the price."

[9]Peter said to her, "How could you agree to test the Spirit of the Lord? Look! The feet of the men who buried your husband are at the door, and they will carry you out also."

[10]At that moment she fell down at his feet and died. Then the young men came in and, finding her dead, carried her out and buried her beside her husband. [11]Great fear seized the whole church and all who heard about these events.

The Apostles Heal Many

[12]The apostles performed many miraculous signs and wonders among the people. And all the believers used to meet together in Solomon's Colonnade. [13]No one else dared join them, even though they were highly regarded by the people. [14]Nevertheless, more and more men and women believed in the Lord and were added to their number. [15]As a result, people brought the sick into the streets and laid them on beds and mats so that at least Peter's shadow might fall on some of them as he passed by. [16]Crowds gathered also from the towns around Jerusalem, bringing their sick and those tormented by evil[a] spirits, and all of them were healed.

The Apostles Persecuted

[17]Then the high priest and all his associates, who were members of the party of the Sadducees, were filled with jealousy. [18]They arrested the apostles and put them in the public jail. [19]But during the night an angel of the Lord opened the doors of the jail and brought them out. [20]"Go, stand

May 5

in the temple courts," he said, "and tell the people the full message of this new life."

²¹At daybreak they entered the temple courts, as they had been told, and began to teach the people.

When the high priest and his associates arrived, they called together the Sanhedrin—the full assembly of the elders of Israel—and sent to the jail for the apostles. ²²But on arriving at the jail, the officers did not find them there. So they went back and reported, ²³"We found the jail securely locked, with the guards standing at the doors; but when we opened them, we found no one inside." ²⁴On hearing this report, the captain of the temple guard and the chief priests were puzzled, wondering what would come of this.

²⁵Then someone came and said, "Look! The men you put in jail are standing in the temple courts teaching the people." ²⁶At that, the captain went with his officers and brought the apostles. They did not use force, because they feared that the people would stone them.

²⁷Having brought the apostles, they made them appear before the Sanhedrin to be questioned by the high priest. ²⁸"We gave you strict orders not to teach in this name," he said. "Yet you have filled Jerusalem with your teaching and are determined to make us guilty of this man's blood."

²⁹Peter and the other apostles replied: "We must obey God rather than men! ³⁰The God of our fathers raised Jesus from the dead—whom you had killed by hanging him on a tree. ³¹God exalted him to his own right hand as Prince and Savior that he might give repentance and forgiveness of sins to Israel. ³²We are witnesses of these things, and so is the Holy Spirit, whom God has given to those who obey him."

³³When they heard this, they were furious and wanted to put them to death. ³⁴But a Pharisee named Gamaliel, a teacher of the law, who was honored by all the people, stood up in the Sanhedrin and ordered that the men be put outside for a little while. ³⁵Then he addressed them: "Men of Israel, consider carefully what you intend to do to these men. ³⁶Some time ago Theudas appeared, claiming to be somebody, and about four hundred men rallied to him. He was killed, all his followers were dispersed, and it all came to nothing. ³⁷After him, Judas the Galilean appeared in the days of the census and led a band of people in revolt. He too was killed, and all his followers were scattered. ³⁸Therefore, in the present case I advise you: Leave these men alone! Let them go! For if their purpose or activity is of human origin, it will fail. ³⁹But if it is from God, you will not be able to stop these men; you will only find yourselves fighting against God."

⁴⁰His speech persuaded them. They called the apostles in and had them flogged. Then they ordered them not to speak in the name of Jesus, and let them go.

⁴¹The apostles left the Sanhedrin, rejoicing because they had been counted worthy of suffering disgrace for the Name. ⁴²Day after day, in the temple courts and from house to house, they never stopped teaching and proclaiming the good news that Jesus is the Christ.ᵇ

ᵃ16 Greek *unclean*   ᵇ42 Or *Messiah*

The High Price for a Precious Message

The apostles left the Sanhedrin, rejoicing because they had been counted worthy of suffering disgrace for the Name (Acts 5:41).

At times, the bearer of good news may be in for a rude awakening! Not everyone will receive it as such.

In Acts 5 the apostles were on trial for declaring the gospel of a risen Savior. The threat of personal injury was real. Was the Good News urgent enough to risk even that?

Martin Luther probes the attitude of the disciples—men who were willing to pay a high price to carry a precious message.

Walk With Martin Luther

"See to it when you suffer persecution that you have a genuine divine cause for which you suffer and you are truly convinced of it.

"Then you can have the confidence to say: 'This cause does not belong to me but to Christ, my Lord. At his word I will take the risk of doing and forsaking whatever I should.

" 'Who cares if a foolish emperor fumes in his rage and threatens as long as I am right with God in heaven?' He who comforts you and takes pleasure in you is almighty and eternal. When it is all over, he will still be with you.

"Be grateful and happy in your heart that you are worthy of suffering, like the apostles who went forth leaping for joy over the fact that they were disgraced and beaten."

Walk Closer to God

The disciples feared no earthly tyrant because they answered to the God of heaven.

Suffering could not daunt them.

Threats could not deter them.

On the contrary, they rejoiced to suffer shame for the one who suffered for them.

Have your attempts at sharing the Good News of Christ resulted in ridicule or rejection? Then you are in good company!

Remember whose cause it is—and whose comfort you are promised—when your "Good News" for others turns into "bad news" for you. ◖

MAY 6

Walk in the Word
Acts 6

Seven men are chosen and commissioned to care for the needy in a ministry of mercy; one of those men, Stephen, is falsely charged and brought before the Sanhedrin.

The Choosing of the Seven

6 In those days when the number of disciples was increasing, the Grecian Jews among them complained against the Hebraic Jews because their widows were being overlooked in the daily distribution of food. 2So the Twelve gathered all the disciples together and said, "It would not be right for us to neglect the ministry of the word of God in order to wait on tables. 3Brothers, choose seven men from among you who are known to be full of the Spirit and wisdom. We will turn this responsibility over to them 4and will give our attention to prayer and the ministry of the word."

5This proposal pleased the whole group. They chose Stephen, a man full of faith and of the Holy Spirit; also Philip, Procorus, Nicanor, Timon, Parmenas, and Nicolas from Antioch, a convert to Judaism. 6They presented these men to the apostles, who prayed and laid their hands on them.

7So the word of God spread. The number of disciples in Jerusalem increased rapidly, and a large number of priests became obedient to the faith.

Stephen Seized

8Now Stephen, a man full of God's grace and power, did great wonders and miraculous signs among the people. 9Opposition arose, however, from members of the Synagogue of the Freedmen (as it was called) — Jews of Cyrene and Alexandria as well as the provinces of Cilicia and Asia. These men began to argue with Stephen, 10but they could not stand up against his wisdom or the Spirit by whom he spoke.

11Then they secretly persuaded some men to say, "We have heard Stephen speak words of blasphemy against Moses and against God."

12So they stirred up the people and the elders and the teachers of the law. They seized Stephen and brought him before the Sanhedrin. 13They produced false witnesses, who testified, "This fellow never stops speaking against this holy place and against the law. 14For we have heard him say that this Jesus of Nazareth will destroy this place and change the customs Moses handed down to us."

15All who were sitting in the Sanhedrin looked intently at Stephen, and they saw that his face was like the face of an angel.

The Message of Power in a Manner of Meekness

> Now Stephen, a man full of God's grace and power, did great wonders and miraculous signs among the people (Acts 6:8).

Acts 6 introduces you to Stephen, a man "full of God's grace and power." A man with an irresistible message.

And yet, when called on to defend the faith with his life, Stephen responded with Christlike humility.

Though his message was full of power, his demeanor was full of meekness—a contrast that Jonathan Edwards helps to explain.

Walk With Jonathan Edwards

"The truly humble Christian is clothed with lowliness, mildness, meekness, gentleness of spirit and behavior. These things are just like garments to him.

"Christian humility has no such thing as roughness, or contempt, or fierceness, or bitterness in its nature. It makes a person like a little child, harmless and innocent, that no one needs to fear; or like a lamb, free of all bitterness, wrath, anger, and clamor.

"Yet in searching and awakening the conscience, he should be a son of thunder. He should do it without judging individuals, leaving it to conscience and the Spirit of God to make the particular application.

"But all his conversation should reflect lowliness and good will, love and pity to all mankind.

"He should be like a lion to guilty consciences, but like a lamb to men and women."

Walk Closer to God

Gentle as a lamb and powerful as a lion. A seeming contradiction—until you know the Lamb of God who is also the Lion of Judah. Jesus Christ, the one who possesses all power, yet dealt tenderly with those he came to serve, points the way to a witness that is more powerful than words alone.

A witness that is both tender and tough. That speaks the truth in love, and clothes strength in humility.

A witness that others around you need to hear and experience today. ◌

May 7

📖 Walk in the Word
Acts 7:1—8:3

Luke memorializes Stephen's impassioned speech to the Sanhedrin, which so offended the hearers that they stoned Stephen to death.

Stephen's Speech to the Sanhedrin

7 Then the high priest asked him, "Are these charges true?" [2]To this he replied: "Brothers and fathers, listen to me! The God of glory appeared to our father Abraham while he was still in Mesopotamia, before he lived in Haran. [3]'Leave your country and your people,' God said, 'and go to the land I will show you.'[a]

[4]"So he left the land of the Chaldeans and settled in Haran. After the death of his father, God sent him to this land where you are now living. [5]He gave him no inheritance here, not even a foot of ground. But God promised him that he and his descendants after him would possess the land, even though at that time Abraham had no child. [6]God spoke to him in this way: 'Your descendants will be strangers in a country not their own, and they will be enslaved and mistreated four hundred years. [7]But I will punish the nation they serve as slaves,' God said, 'and afterward they will come out of that country and worship me in this place.'[b] [8]Then he gave Abraham the covenant of circumcision. And Abraham became the father of Isaac and circumcised him eight days after his birth. Later Isaac became the father of Jacob, and Jacob became the father of the twelve patriarchs.

[9]"Because the patriarchs were jealous of Joseph, they sold him as a slave into Egypt. But God was with him [10]and rescued him from all his troubles. He gave Joseph wisdom and enabled him to gain the goodwill of Pharaoh king of Egypt; so he made him ruler over Egypt and all his palace.

[11]"Then a famine struck all Egypt and Canaan, bringing great suffering, and our fathers could not find food. [12]When Jacob heard that there was grain in Egypt, he sent our fathers on their first visit. [13]On their second visit, Joseph told his brothers who he was, and Pharaoh learned about Joseph's family. [14]After this, Joseph sent for his father Jacob and his whole family, seventy-five in all. [15]Then Jacob went down to Egypt, where he and our fathers died. [16]Their bodies were brought back to Shechem and placed in the tomb that Abraham had bought from the sons of Hamor at Shechem for a certain sum of money.

[17]"As the time drew near for God to fulfill his promise to Abraham, the number of our people in Egypt greatly increased. [18]Then another king, who knew nothing about Joseph, became ruler of Egypt. [19]He dealt treacherously with our people and oppressed our forefathers by forcing them to throw out their newborn babies so that they would die.

[20]"At that time Moses was born, and he was no ordinary child.[c] For three months he was cared for in his father's house. [21]When he was placed outside, Pharaoh's daughter took him and brought him up as her own son. [22]Moses was educated in all the wisdom of the Egyptians and was powerful in speech and action.

[23]"When Moses was forty years old, he decided to visit his fellow Israel-

ites. ²⁴He saw one of them being mistreated by an Egyptian, so he went to his defense and avenged him by killing the Egyptian. ²⁵Moses thought that his own people would realize that God was using him to rescue them, but they did not. ²⁶The next day Moses came upon two Israelites who were fighting. He tried to reconcile them by saying, 'Men, you are brothers; why do you want to hurt each other?'

²⁷"But the man who was mistreating the other pushed Moses aside and said, 'Who made you ruler and judge over us? ²⁸Do you want to kill me as you killed the Egyptian yesterday?'ᵈ ²⁹When Moses heard this, he fled to Midian, where he settled as a foreigner and had two sons.

³⁰"After forty years had passed, an angel appeared to Moses in the flames of a burning bush in the desert near Mount Sinai. ³¹When he saw this, he was amazed at the sight. As he went over to look more closely, he heard the Lord's voice: ³²'I am the God of your fathers, the God of Abraham, Isaac and Jacob.'ᵉ Moses trembled with fear and did not dare to look.

³³"Then the Lord said to him, 'Take off your sandals; the place where you are standing is holy ground. ³⁴I have indeed seen the oppression of my people in Egypt. I have heard their groaning and have come down to set them free. Now come, I will send you back to Egypt.'ᶠ

³⁵"This is the same Moses whom they had rejected with the words, 'Who made you ruler and judge?' He was sent to be their ruler and deliverer by God himself, through the angel who appeared to him in the bush. ³⁶He led them out of Egypt and did wonders and miraculous signs in Egypt, at the Red Seaᵍ and for forty years in the desert.

³⁷"This is that Moses who told the Israelites, 'God will send you a prophet like me from your own people.'ʰ ³⁸He was in the assembly in the desert, with the angel who spoke to him on Mount Sinai, and with our fathers; and he received living words to pass on to us.

³⁹"But our fathers refused to obey him. Instead, they rejected him and in their hearts turned back to Egypt. ⁴⁰They told Aaron, 'Make us gods who will go before us. As for this fellow Moses who led us out of Egypt—we don't know what has happened to him!'ⁱ ⁴¹That was the time they made an idol in the form of a calf. They brought sacrifices to it and held a celebration in honor of what their hands had made. ⁴²But God turned away and gave them over to the worship of the heavenly bodies. This agrees with what is written in the book of the prophets:

> " 'Did you bring me sacrifices and offerings
>   forty years in the desert, O house of Israel?
> ⁴³You have lifted up the shrine of Molech
>   and the star of your god Rephan,
>   the idols you made to worship.
> Therefore I will send you into exile'ʲ beyond Babylon.

⁴⁴"Our forefathers had the tabernacle of the Testimony with them in the desert. It had been made as God directed Moses, according to the pattern he had seen. ⁴⁵Having received the tabernacle, our fathers under Joshua brought it with them when they took the land from the nations God drove

May 7

out before them. It remained in the land until the time of David, [46]who enjoyed God's favor and asked that he might provide a dwelling place for the God of Jacob.[k] [47]But it was Solomon who built the house for him.

[48]"However, the Most High does not live in houses made by men. As the prophet says:

> [49]" 'Heaven is my throne,
>   and the earth is my footstool.
> What kind of house will you build for me?
>
> says the Lord.
>
> Or where will my resting place be?
>   [50]Has not my hand made all these things?'[l]

[51]"You stiff-necked people, with uncircumcised hearts and ears! You are just like your fathers: You always resist the Holy Spirit! [52]Was there ever a prophet your fathers did not persecute? They even killed those who predicted the coming of the Righteous One. And now you have betrayed and murdered him — [53]you who have received the law that was put into effect through angels but have not obeyed it."

The Stoning of Stephen

[54]When they heard this, they were furious and gnashed their teeth at him. [55]But Stephen, full of the Holy Spirit, looked up to heaven and saw the glory of God, and Jesus standing at the right hand of God. [56]"Look," he said, "I see heaven open and the Son of Man standing at the right hand of God."

[57]At this they covered their ears and, yelling at the top of their voices, they all rushed at him, [58]dragged him out of the city and began to stone him. Meanwhile, the witnesses laid their clothes at the feet of a young man named Saul.

[59]While they were stoning him, Stephen prayed, "Lord Jesus, receive my spirit." [60]Then he fell on his knees and cried out, "Lord, do not hold this sin against them." When he had said this, he fell asleep.

8 And Saul was there, giving approval to his death.

The Church Persecuted and Scattered

On that day a great persecution broke out against the church at Jerusalem, and all except the apostles were scattered throughout Judea and Samaria. [2]Godly men buried Stephen and mourned deeply for him. [3]But Saul began to destroy the church. Going from house to house, he dragged off men and women and put them in prison.

---

[a]3 Gen. 12:1   [b]7 Gen. 15:13,14   [c]20 Or *was fair in the sight of God*   [d]28 Exodus 2:14
[e]32 Exodus 3:6   [f]34 Exodus 3:5,7,8,10   [g]36 That is, Sea of Reeds   [h]37 Deut. 18:15
[i]40 Exodus 32:1   [j]43 Amos 5:25-27   [k]46 Some early manuscripts *the house of Jacob*
[l]50 Isaiah 66:1,2

Gazing Into Heaven's Window

But Stephen, full of the Holy Spirit, looked up to heaven and saw the glory of God, and Jesus standing at the right hand of God (Acts 7:55).

Stephen's last message provides a moving portrayal of God's dealings on behalf of his people.

The priests and rabbis, no doubt impressed with Stephen's grasp of the Old Testament, were not at all impressed with his application of that truth to their lives:

"You are just like your fathers: You always resist the Holy Spirit!" (Acts 7:51).

Blood boiled. Stones flew. And Stephen's death became a turning point in the history of the New Testament church.

Matthew Henry looks at the significance of Stephen's life to Christians today.

Walk With Matthew Henry

"The heavens were opened to give Stephen a view of the happiness he was going to so that he might, in prospect of it, go cheerfully through death.

"Would we by faith look up, we might see the heavens opened.

"Heaven is opened for the settling of a correspondence between God and humans, that his favors and blessings may come down to us, and our prayers and praises may go up to him.

"We may also see the glory of God, as far as he has revealed it in his Word, and the sight of this will carry us through all the terrors of suffering and death."

Walk Closer to God

At the moment of his death, Stephen's gaze was fixed in the right place. He looked directly up into heaven and saw Jesus standing at God's right hand. He saw beyond the torment, cursing and physical abuse he suffered to the heavenly reunion awaiting him with his Savior.

"Look, I see heaven open." It's really not that difficult a sight to see even today—if God's Word is your compass, and God's Son is your guide! ◖

MAY 8

📖 Walk in the Word
Acts 8:4–40

After noting that Stephen's death precipitates a great persecution, Luke relates how the gospel spread through Judea and Samaria, highlighting Philip's ministry in Samaria and his encounter with an Ethiopian.

Philip in Samaria

4Those who had been scattered preached the word wherever they went. 5Philip went down to a city in Samaria and proclaimed the Christ[a] there. 6When the crowds heard Philip and saw the miraculous signs he did, they all paid close attention to what he said. 7With shrieks, evil[b] spirits came out of many, and many paralytics and cripples were healed. 8So there was great joy in that city.

Simon the Sorcerer

9Now for some time a man named Simon had practiced sorcery in the city and amazed all the people of Samaria. He boasted that he was someone great, 10and all the people, both high and low, gave him their attention and exclaimed, "This man is the divine power known as the Great Power." 11They followed him because he had amazed them for a long time with his magic. 12But when they believed Philip as he preached the good news of the kingdom of God and the name of Jesus Christ, they were baptized, both men and women. 13Simon himself believed and was baptized. And he followed Philip everywhere, astonished by the great signs and miracles he saw.

14When the apostles in Jerusalem heard that Samaria had accepted the word of God, they sent Peter and John to them. 15When they arrived, they prayed for them that they might receive the Holy Spirit, 16because the Holy Spirit had not yet come upon any of them; they had simply been baptized into[c] the name of the Lord Jesus. 17Then Peter and John placed their hands on them, and they received the Holy Spirit.

18When Simon saw that the Spirit was given at the laying on of the apostles' hands, he offered them money 19and said, "Give me also this ability so that everyone on whom I lay my hands may receive the Holy Spirit."

20Peter answered: "May your money perish with you, because you thought you could buy the gift of God with money! 21You have no part or share in this ministry, because your heart is not right before God. 22Repent of this wickedness and pray to the Lord. Perhaps he will forgive you for having such a thought in your heart. 23For I see that you are full of bitterness and captive to sin."

24Then Simon answered, "Pray to the Lord for me so that nothing you have said may happen to me."

25When they had testified and proclaimed the word of the Lord, Peter and John returned to Jerusalem, preaching the gospel in many Samaritan villages.

MAY 8

Philip and the Ethiopian

26Now an angel of the Lord said to Philip, "Go south to the road — the desert road — that goes down from Jerusalem to Gaza." 27So he started out, and on his way he met an Ethiopian*d* eunuch, an important official in charge of all the treasury of Candace, queen of the Ethiopians. This man had gone to Jerusalem to worship, 28and on his way home was sitting in his chariot reading the book of Isaiah the prophet. 29The Spirit told Philip, "Go to that chariot and stay near it."

30Then Philip ran up to the chariot and heard the man reading Isaiah the prophet. "Do you understand what you are reading?" Philip asked.

31"How can I," he said, "unless someone explains it to me?" So he invited Philip to come up and sit with him.

32The eunuch was reading this passage of Scripture:

> "He was led like a sheep to the slaughter,
>   and as a lamb before the shearer is silent,
>   so he did not open his mouth.
> 33In his humiliation he was deprived of justice.
>   Who can speak of his descendants?
>   For his life was taken from the earth."*e*

34The eunuch asked Philip, "Tell me, please, who is the prophet talking about, himself or someone else?" 35Then Philip began with that very passage of Scripture and told him the good news about Jesus.

36As they traveled along the road, they came to some water and the eunuch said, "Look, here is water. Why shouldn't I be baptized?"*f* 38And he gave orders to stop the chariot. Then both Philip and the eunuch went down into the water and Philip baptized him. 39When they came up out of the water, the Spirit of the Lord suddenly took Philip away, and the eunuch did not see him again, but went on his way rejoicing. 40Philip, however, appeared at Azotus and traveled about, preaching the gospel in all the towns until he reached Caesarea.

*a*5 Or *Messiah*   *b*7 Greek *unclean*   *c*16 Or *in*   *d*27 That is, from the upper Nile region   *e*33 Isaiah 53:7,8   *f*36 Some late manuscripts *baptized?" 37Philip said, "If you believe with all your heart, you may." The eunuch answered, "I believe that Jesus Christ is the Son of God."*

MAY 8

Something Money Can't Buy

When Simon saw that the Spirit was given . . . he offered them money and said, "Give me also this ability" (Acts 8:18–19).

Simon the magician.

He was known in Samaria as "the Great Power." Yet he sought to buy what no amount of money could buy. He tried to buy the power of the Holy Spirit.

Misunderstanding about the Holy Spirit—who he is and why he came—lay at the root of Simon's problem. Gregory of Nazianzus, the fourth-century church father, offers this helpful insight.

Walk With Gregory of Nazianzus

"The deity of the Holy Spirit ought to be clearly recognized in Scripture.

"Look at these facts: Christ is born; the Spirit is his forerunner. Christ is baptized; the Spirit bears witness. Christ is tempted; the Spirit leads him up. Christ ascends; the Spirit takes his place.

"What great things are there in the character of God which are not found in the Spirit? What titles which belong to God are not also applied to him?

"He is called the Spirit of God, the Spirit of Christ, the mind of Christ, the Spirit of the Lord, the Spirit of adoption, of truth, of liberty; the Spirit of wisdom, of understanding, of counsel, of might, of knowledge, of godliness, of the fear of God.

"This only begins to show how unlimited he is."

Walk Closer to God

The Holy Spirit is more than a power to be reckoned with. He is a person to indwell you.

A Comforter to console you.

A Counselor to advise you.

An Advocate to defend you.

An Intercessor to pray for you.

A Guide to direct you.

As you continue your journey through the book of Acts, don't be surprised if you encounter the Holy Spirit frequently.

All the resources of God were available to the New Testament believers in the person of the Holy Spirit. The disciples depended daily on his power and leading. And that power is available to you today!

MAY 9

📖 Walk in the Word
Acts 9

Saul comes to know the resurrected Lord in a most dramatic way in this record of Saul's conversion and his subsequent preaching of the gospel.

Saul's Conversion

9 Meanwhile, Saul was still breathing out murderous threats against the Lord's disciples. He went to the high priest ²and asked him for letters to the synagogues in Damascus, so that if he found any there who belonged to the Way, whether men or women, he might take them as prisoners to Jerusalem. ³As he neared Damascus on his journey, suddenly a light from heaven flashed around him. ⁴He fell to the ground and heard a voice say to him, "Saul, Saul, why do you persecute me?"

⁵"Who are you, Lord?" Saul asked.

"I am Jesus, whom you are persecuting," he replied. ⁶"Now get up and go into the city, and you will be told what you must do."

⁷The men traveling with Saul stood there speechless; they heard the sound but did not see anyone. ⁸Saul got up from the ground, but when he opened his eyes he could see nothing. So they led him by the hand into Damascus. ⁹For three days he was blind, and did not eat or drink anything.

¹⁰In Damascus there was a disciple named Ananias. The Lord called to him in a vision, "Ananias!"

"Yes, Lord," he answered.

¹¹The Lord told him, "Go to the house of Judas on Straight Street and ask for a man from Tarsus named Saul, for he is praying. ¹²In a vision he has seen a man named Ananias come and place his hands on him to restore his sight."

¹³"Lord," Ananias answered, "I have heard many reports about this man and all the harm he has done to your saints in Jerusalem. ¹⁴And he has come here with authority from the chief priests to arrest all who call on your name."

¹⁵But the Lord said to Ananias, "Go! This man is my chosen instrument to carry my name before the Gentiles and their kings and before the people of Israel. ¹⁶I will show him how much he must suffer for my name."

¹⁷Then Ananias went to the house and entered it. Placing his hands on Saul, he said, "Brother Saul, the Lord—Jesus, who appeared to you on the road as you were coming here—has sent me so that you may see again and be filled with the Holy Spirit." ¹⁸Immediately, something like scales fell from Saul's eyes, and he could see again. He got up and was baptized, ¹⁹and after taking some food, he regained his strength.

Saul in Damascus and Jerusalem

Saul spent several days with the disciples in Damascus. ²⁰At once he began to preach in the synagogues that Jesus is the Son of God. ²¹All those who heard him were astonished and asked, "Isn't he the man who raised

May 9

havoc in Jerusalem among those who call on this name? And hasn't he come here to take them as prisoners to the chief priests?" [22]Yet Saul grew more and more powerful and baffled the Jews living in Damascus by proving that Jesus is the Christ.[a]

[23]After many days had gone by, the Jews conspired to kill him, [24]but Saul learned of their plan. Day and night they kept close watch on the city gates in order to kill him. [25]But his followers took him by night and lowered him in a basket through an opening in the wall.

[26]When he came to Jerusalem, he tried to join the disciples, but they were all afraid of him, not believing that he really was a disciple. [27]But Barnabas took him and brought him to the apostles. He told them how Saul on his journey had seen the Lord and that the Lord had spoken to him, and how in Damascus he had preached fearlessly in the name of Jesus. [28]So Saul stayed with them and moved about freely in Jerusalem, speaking boldly in the name of the Lord. [29]He talked and debated with the Grecian Jews, but they tried to kill him. [30]When the brothers learned of this, they took him down to Caesarea and sent him off to Tarsus.

[31]Then the church throughout Judea, Galilee and Samaria enjoyed a time of peace. It was strengthened; and encouraged by the Holy Spirit, it grew in numbers, living in the fear of the Lord.

Aeneas and Dorcas

[32]As Peter traveled about the country, he went to visit the saints in Lydda. [33]There he found a man named Aeneas, a paralytic who had been bedridden for eight years. [34]"Aeneas," Peter said to him, "Jesus Christ heals you. Get up and take care of your mat." Immediately Aeneas got up. [35]All those who lived in Lydda and Sharon saw him and turned to the Lord.

[36]In Joppa there was a disciple named Tabitha (which, when translated, is Dorcas[b]), who was always doing good and helping the poor. [37]About that time she became sick and died, and her body was washed and placed in an upstairs room. [38]Lydda was near Joppa; so when the disciples heard that Peter was in Lydda, they sent two men to him and urged him, "Please come at once!"

[39]Peter went with them, and when he arrived he was taken upstairs to the room. All the widows stood around him, crying and showing him the robes and other clothing that Dorcas had made while she was still with them.

[40]Peter sent them all out of the room; then he got down on his knees and prayed. Turning toward the dead woman, he said, "Tabitha, get up." She opened her eyes, and seeing Peter she sat up. [41]He took her by the hand and helped her to her feet. Then he called the believers and the widows and presented her to them alive. [42]This became known all over Joppa, and many people believed in the Lord. [43]Peter stayed in Joppa for some time with a tanner named Simon.

[a]22 Or *Messiah*   [b]36 Both *Tabitha* (Aramaic) and *Dorcas* (Greek) mean *gazelle*.

The Transforming Power of Forgiveness

He [Saul] . . . tried to join the disciples, but they were all afraid of him (Acts 9:26).

Saul of Tarsus, public enemy number one of the church!

Yet God had plans for Saul to become his chosen vessel . . . to bear his name before the Gentiles . . . to spread his truth far and wide.

At first the church had grave doubts about Saul. H.A. Ironside shares this illustration of the response only God can produce toward an enemy-turned-brother.

Walk With H.A. Ironside

"On the Lord's Day a group of missionaries and believers in New Guinea were gathered together to observe the Lord's Supper.

"After one young man sat down, a missionary recognized that a sudden tremor had passed through the young man's body that indicated he was under a great nervous strain. Then in a moment all was quiet again.

"The missionary whispered, 'What was it that troubled you?'

" 'Ah,' he said, 'But the man who just came in killed and ate the body of my father. And now he has come in to remember the Lord with us.

" 'At first I didn't know whether I could endure it. But it is all right now. He is washed in the same precious blood.'

"And so together they had Communion. It is a marvelous thing, the work of the Holy Spirit of God. Does the world know anything of this?"

Walk Closer to God

Is it really possible to truly forgive a former enemy who is now your Christian brother or sister?

Consider:

From the cross, Jesus forgave those responsible for putting him there.

The Jerusalem believers forgave the man who formerly sought to destroy them.

A young man in New Guinea found strength to forgive his father's murderer.

Indeed, does the world know anything of this? Do you know anything of this?

MAY 10

📖 Walk in the Word
Acts 10

Luke records the prejudice-shattering experience of Peter, who preaches a powerful sermon on the Lord's acceptance of all who come to Jesus.

Cornelius Calls for Peter

10 At Caesarea there was a man named Cornelius, a centurion in what was known as the Italian Regiment. ²He and all his family were devout and God-fearing; he gave generously to those in need and prayed to God regularly. ³One day at about three in the afternoon he had a vision. He distinctly saw an angel of God, who came to him and said, "Cornelius!"

⁴Cornelius stared at him in fear. "What is it, Lord?" he asked.

The angel answered, "Your prayers and gifts to the poor have come up as a memorial offering before God. ⁵Now send men to Joppa to bring back a man named Simon who is called Peter. ⁶He is staying with Simon the tanner, whose house is by the sea."

⁷When the angel who spoke to him had gone, Cornelius called two of his servants and a devout soldier who was one of his attendants. ⁸He told them everything that had happened and sent them to Joppa.

Peter's Vision

⁹About noon the following day as they were on their journey and approaching the city, Peter went up on the roof to pray. ¹⁰He became hungry and wanted something to eat, and while the meal was being prepared, he fell into a trance. ¹¹He saw heaven opened and something like a large sheet being let down to earth by its four corners. ¹²It contained all kinds of four-footed animals, as well as reptiles of the earth and birds of the air. ¹³Then a voice told him, "Get up, Peter. Kill and eat."

¹⁴"Surely not, Lord!" Peter replied. "I have never eaten anything impure or unclean."

¹⁵The voice spoke to him a second time, "Do not call anything impure that God has made clean."

¹⁶This happened three times, and immediately the sheet was taken back to heaven.

¹⁷While Peter was wondering about the meaning of the vision, the men sent by Cornelius found out where Simon's house was and stopped at the gate. ¹⁸They called out, asking if Simon who was known as Peter was staying there.

¹⁹While Peter was still thinking about the vision, the Spirit said to him, "Simon, three*ᵃ* men are looking for you. ²⁰So get up and go downstairs. Do not hesitate to go with them, for I have sent them."

²¹Peter went down and said to the men, "I'm the one you're looking for. Why have you come?"

²²The men replied, "We have come from Cornelius the centurion. He is a righteous and God-fearing man, who is respected by all the Jewish peo-

MAY 10

ple. A holy angel told him to have you come to his house so that he could hear what you have to say." 23Then Peter invited the men into the house to be his guests.

Peter at Cornelius' House

The next day Peter started out with them, and some of the brothers from Joppa went along. 24The following day he arrived in Caesarea. Cornelius was expecting them and had called together his relatives and close friends. 25As Peter entered the house, Cornelius met him and fell at his feet in reverence. 26But Peter made him get up. "Stand up," he said, "I am only a man myself."

27Talking with him, Peter went inside and found a large gathering of people. 28He said to them: "You are well aware that it is against our law for a Jew to associate with a Gentile or visit him. But God has shown me that I should not call any man impure or unclean. 29So when I was sent for, I came without raising any objection. May I ask why you sent for me?"

30Cornelius answered: "Four days ago I was in my house praying at this hour, at three in the afternoon. Suddenly a man in shining clothes stood before me 31and said, 'Cornelius, God has heard your prayer and remembered your gifts to the poor. 32Send to Joppa for Simon who is called Peter. He is a guest in the home of Simon the tanner, who lives by the sea.' 33So I sent for you immediately, and it was good of you to come. Now we are all here in the presence of God to listen to everything the Lord has commanded you to tell us."

34Then Peter began to speak: "I now realize how true it is that God does not show favoritism 35but accepts men from every nation who fear him and do what is right. 36You know the message God sent to the people of Israel, telling the good news of peace through Jesus Christ, who is Lord of all. 37You know what has happened throughout Judea, beginning in Galilee after the baptism that John preached— 38how God anointed Jesus of Nazareth with the Holy Spirit and power, and how he went around doing good and healing all who were under the power of the devil, because God was with him.

39"We are witnesses of everything he did in the country of the Jews and in Jerusalem. They killed him by hanging him on a tree, 40but God raised him from the dead on the third day and caused him to be seen. 41He was not seen by all the people, but by witnesses whom God had already chosen—by us who ate and drank with him after he rose from the dead. 42He commanded us to preach to the people and to testify that he is the one whom God appointed as judge of the living and the dead. 43All the prophets testify about him that everyone who believes in him receives forgiveness of sins through his name."

44While Peter was still speaking these words, the Holy Spirit came on all who heard the message. 45The circumcised believers who had come with Peter were astonished that the gift of the Holy Spirit had been poured

MAY 10

out even on the Gentiles. [46]For they heard them speaking in tongues[b] and praising God.

Then Peter said, [47]"Can anyone keep these people from being baptized with water? They have received the Holy Spirit just as we have." [48]So he ordered that they be baptized in the name of Jesus Christ. Then they asked Peter to stay with them for a few days.

[a]19 One early manuscript *two*; other manuscripts do not have the number.
[b]46 Or *other languages*

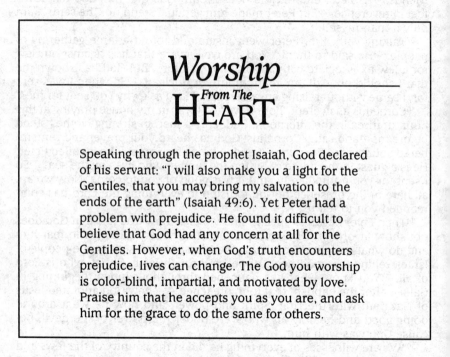

Worship
From The
HEART

Speaking through the prophet Isaiah, God declared of his servant: "I will also make you a light for the Gentiles, that you may bring my salvation to the ends of the earth" (Isaiah 49:6). Yet Peter had a problem with prejudice. He found it difficult to believe that God had any concern at all for the Gentiles. However, when God's truth encounters prejudice, lives can change. The God you worship is color-blind, impartial, and motivated by love. Praise him that he accepts you as you are, and ask him for the grace to do the same for others.

To Hear Is to Obey

While Peter was still thinking about the vision, the Spirit said to him . . . "Get up and go downstairs. Do not hesitate to go with them, for I have sent them" (Acts 10:19–20).

Peter could have written a book entitled *The Pitfalls of Disobedience,* for he surely stumbled into many of them! When it was time to think, Peter would talk. When it was time to stand, Peter would run. And when it was time to "get up and go," Peter would stop and ponder.

Even when God chose Peter to take the gospel to the Gentiles, it took three times for his reticent apostle finally to get the message!

John Calvin explains the importance of prompt obedience to the Lord's commands.

Walk With John Calvin

"We must not follow God with a doubting and vacillating mind, but with one that is composed and firm.

"The Lord wishes us to defer to him so much that, when we have heard him, we will have no argument about what we need to do, but will decide without any question that what he commands must be done.

"Certainly his will is worthy to show us the way, when all the doubts have been scattered, and to bring our minds into ready obedience.

"Peter is not permitted to pass judgment on the question, because God is the originator of the business.

"What it amounts to is that we ought to be content merely with God's say-so, so that we may obey his command."

Walk Closer to God

There is a time to wait on the Lord and a time to act on his will. God's part is to make his will clear; your part is to do his will promptly.

Disobedience—thinking when you should be doing or questioning when you should be trusting—can only result in delay and disappointment.

To obey or not to obey. Child of God, that's a decision you shouldn't have to think about for very long!

MAY 11

📖 Walk in the Word
Acts 11

Peter retells the story of his encounter with Cornelius to some Jewish Christians who had heard that Peter had eaten with Gentiles; the gospel begins to spread among Gentiles in Antioch.

Peter Explains His Actions

11 The apostles and the brothers throughout Judea heard that the Gentiles also had received the word of God. ²So when Peter went up to Jerusalem, the circumcised believers criticized him ³and said, "You went into the house of uncircumcised men and ate with them."

⁴Peter began and explained everything to them precisely as it had happened: ⁵"I was in the city of Joppa praying, and in a trance I saw a vision. I saw something like a large sheet being let down from heaven by its four corners, and it came down to where I was. ⁶I looked into it and saw four-footed animals of the earth, wild beasts, reptiles, and birds of the air. ⁷Then I heard a voice telling me, 'Get up, Peter. Kill and eat.'

⁸"I replied, 'Surely not, Lord! Nothing impure or unclean has ever entered my mouth.'

⁹"The voice spoke from heaven a second time, 'Do not call anything impure that God has made clean.' ¹⁰This happened three times, and then it was all pulled up to heaven again.

¹¹"Right then three men who had been sent to me from Caesarea stopped at the house where I was staying. ¹²The Spirit told me to have no hesitation about going with them. These six brothers also went with me, and we entered the man's house. ¹³He told us how he had seen an angel appear in his house and say, 'Send to Joppa for Simon who is called Peter. ¹⁴He will bring you a message through which you and all your household will be saved.'

¹⁵"As I began to speak, the Holy Spirit came on them as he had come on us at the beginning. ¹⁶Then I remembered what the Lord had said: 'John baptized with*ª* water, but you will be baptized with the Holy Spirit.' ¹⁷So if God gave them the same gift as he gave us, who believed in the Lord Jesus Christ, who was I to think that I could oppose God?"

¹⁸When they heard this, they had no further objections and praised God, saying, "So then, God has granted even the Gentiles repentance unto life."

The Church in Antioch

¹⁹Now those who had been scattered by the persecution in connection with Stephen traveled as far as Phoenicia, Cyprus and Antioch, telling the message only to Jews. ²⁰Some of them, however, men from Cyprus and Cyrene, went to Antioch and began to speak to Greeks also, telling them the good news about the Lord Jesus. ²¹The Lord's hand was with them, and a great number of people believed and turned to the Lord.

²²News of this reached the ears of the church at Jerusalem, and they sent Barnabas to Antioch. ²³When he arrived and saw the evidence of the grace of God, he was glad and encouraged them all to remain true to the Lord

with all their hearts. ²⁴He was a good man, full of the Holy Spirit and faith, and a great number of people were brought to the Lord.

²⁵Then Barnabas went to Tarsus to look for Saul, ²⁶and when he found him, he brought him to Antioch. So for a whole year Barnabas and Saul met with the church and taught great numbers of people. The disciples were called Christians first at Antioch.

²⁷During this time some prophets came down from Jerusalem to Antioch. ²⁸One of them, named Agabus, stood up and through the Spirit predicted that a severe famine would spread over the entire Roman world. (This happened during the reign of Claudius.) ²⁹The disciples, each according to his ability, decided to provide help for the brothers living in Judea. ³⁰This they did, sending their gift to the elders by Barnabas and Saul.

ª16 Or *in*

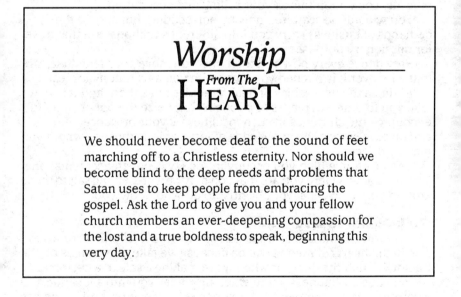

Worship From The HEART

We should never become deaf to the sound of feet marching off to a Christless eternity. Nor should we become blind to the deep needs and problems that Satan uses to keep people from embracing the gospel. Ask the Lord to give you and your fellow church members an ever-deepening compassion for the lost and a true boldness to speak, beginning this very day.

MAY 11

Carrying Christ With You

The Lord's hand was with them, and a great number of people believed and turned to the Lord (Acts 11:21).

The disciples must have seemed out of place in the bustling commercial atmosphere of Antioch. But sensing they were there by divine appointment, they dedicated themselves to share their faith. And the result? A secular city turned upside down.

Regardless of your employment situation, the Lord has placed you where you are for a purpose: to introduce others to the Savior. Charles Spurgeon wisely challenges you to use every opportunity.

Walk With Charles Spurgeon

"Wherever you are called to go, you should make known the gospel of Jesus. Look upon this as your calling and occupation.

"You will not be scattered now by persecution, but should the demands of business carry you into different situations, use that travel for missionary purposes.

"Providence every now and then bids you move your tent; take care that wherever it is pitched you carry with you a testimony for Jesus.

"At times the necessities of health require relaxation, and this may take you to different places of public resort. Seize the opportunity to encourage the churches in such localities by your presence, and endeavor to spread the knowledge of Jesus among those to whom you may be directed.

"The position which you occupy in society is not an accidental one. You are placed where you are that you may be a preserving salt to those around you, a sweet savor of Christ to all who know you."

Walk Closer to God

One writer summarizes the challenge this way: "If Christ comes to rule in the hearts of men, it will be because we take him with us on the tractor, behind the desk, or when we're making a sale to a customer."

God knows what he is about when he guides you into a location and a vocation. All that remains is for you to seize the opportunities he has placed within your reach. ◗

MAY 12

Walk in the Word
Acts 12

James's death at Herod's order, Peter's arrest and imprisonment and escape, and Herod's death are spotlighted here by Luke.

Peter's Miraculous Escape From Prison

12 It was about this time that King Herod arrested some who belonged to the church, intending to persecute them. ²He had James, the brother of John, put to death with the sword. ³When he saw that this pleased the Jews, he proceeded to seize Peter also. This happened during the Feast of Unleavened Bread. ⁴After arresting him, he put him in prison, handing him over to be guarded by four squads of four soldiers each. Herod intended to bring him out for public trial after the Passover.

⁵So Peter was kept in prison, but the church was earnestly praying to God for him.

⁶The night before Herod was to bring him to trial, Peter was sleeping between two soldiers, bound with two chains, and sentries stood guard at the entrance. ⁷Suddenly an angel of the Lord appeared and a light shone in the cell. He struck Peter on the side and woke him up. "Quick, get up!" he said, and the chains fell off Peter's wrists.

⁸Then the angel said to him, "Put on your clothes and sandals." And Peter did so. "Wrap your cloak around you and follow me," the angel told him. ⁹Peter followed him out of the prison, but he had no idea that what the angel was doing was really happening; he thought he was seeing a vision. ¹⁰They passed the first and second guards and came to the iron gate leading to the city. It opened for them by itself, and they went through it. When they had walked the length of one street, suddenly the angel left him.

¹¹Then Peter came to himself and said, "Now I know without a doubt that the Lord sent his angel and rescued me from Herod's clutches and from everything the Jewish people were anticipating."

¹²When this had dawned on him, he went to the house of Mary the mother of John, also called Mark, where many people had gathered and were praying. ¹³Peter knocked at the outer entrance, and a servant girl named Rhoda came to answer the door. ¹⁴When she recognized Peter's voice, she was so overjoyed she ran back without opening it and exclaimed, "Peter is at the door!"

¹⁵"You're out of your mind," they told her. When she kept insisting that it was so, they said, "It must be his angel."

¹⁶But Peter kept on knocking, and when they opened the door and saw him, they were astonished. ¹⁷Peter motioned with his hand for them to be quiet and described how the Lord had brought him out of prison. "Tell James and the brothers about this," he said, and then he left for another place.

¹⁸In the morning, there was no small commotion among the soldiers as to what had become of Peter. ¹⁹After Herod had a thorough search made

MAY 12

for him and did not find him, he cross-examined the guards and ordered that they be executed.

Herod's Death

Then Herod went from Judea to Caesarea and stayed there a while. [20]He had been quarreling with the people of Tyre and Sidon; they now joined together and sought an audience with him. Having secured the support of Blastus, a trusted personal servant of the king, they asked for peace, because they depended on the king's country for their food supply.

[21]On the appointed day Herod, wearing his royal robes, sat on his throne and delivered a public address to the people. [22]They shouted, "This is the voice of a god, not of a man." [23]Immediately, because Herod did not give praise to God, an angel of the Lord struck him down, and he was eaten by worms and died.

[24]But the word of God continued to increase and spread.

[25]When Barnabas and Saul had finished their mission, they returned from[a] Jerusalem, taking with them John, also called Mark.

[a]25 Some manuscripts *to*

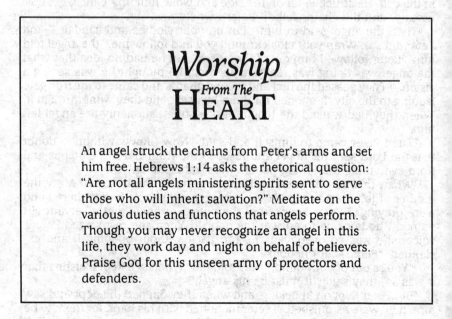

Worship
From The
HEART

An angel struck the chains from Peter's arms and set him free. Hebrews 1:14 asks the rhetorical question: "Are not all angels ministering spirits sent to serve those who will inherit salvation?" Meditate on the various duties and functions that angels perform. Though you may never recognize an angel in this life, they work day and night on behalf of believers. Praise God for this unseen army of protectors and defenders.

Seeing Is Not Always Believing

Peter was kept in prison, but the church was earnestly praying to God for him (Acts 12:5).

If the opponents of the church had known better, they would have left it alone.

Persecution only poured oil on the fire, spreading the gospel all the more. Killing James and imprisoning Peter drove the church to its knees—not in submission, but in prayer.

Yet even the church was surprised by God's miraculous power! A.B. Simpson reflects on the awesome power of prayer.

Walk With A.B. Simpson

"Prayer is the link that connects us with God. It is the bridge that spans every gulf and bears us over every abyss of danger or need.

"How significant is this picture of the New Testament church: Peter in prison, the Jews triumphant, Herod supreme, the arena of martyrdom awaiting the dawning of the morning.

" 'But the church was earnestly praying to God for him.'

"And what is the sequel?

"The prison open, the apostle free, the Jews baffled, the wicked king divinely smitten, and the Word of God rolling on in greater victory.

"Do we know the power of our supernatural weapon? Do we dare to use it with the authority of a faith that commands as well as asks? God grant us holy audacity and divine confidence.

"He is not wanting great men and women, but he is wanting people who will dare to prove the greatness of their God."

Walk Closer to God

Which motto summarizes your habits in prayer?

"When all else fails, pray."

"Before doing anything, pray."

The first views prayer as the place of last resort when human abilities have run out. The second realizes that unless God empowers and directs, human strength and wisdom will never suffice.

Are you tired of trying to stand on your own?

Dropping to your knees gives God the opportunity to prove his greatness in your life. ⬭

MAY 13

📖 Walk in the Word
Acts 13

Barnabas and Saul (Paul) are commissioned by the church to preach the gospel on the island of Cyprus and in Pisidian Antioch.

Barnabas and Saul Sent Off

13 In the church at Antioch there were prophets and teachers: Barnabas, Simeon called Niger, Lucius of Cyrene, Manaen (who had been brought up with Herod the tetrarch) and Saul. ²While they were worshiping the Lord and fasting, the Holy Spirit said, "Set apart for me Barnabas and Saul for the work to which I have called them." ³So after they had fasted and prayed, they placed their hands on them and sent them off.

On Cyprus

⁴The two of them, sent on their way by the Holy Spirit, went down to Seleucia and sailed from there to Cyprus. ⁵When they arrived at Salamis, they proclaimed the word of God in the Jewish synagogues. John was with them as their helper.

⁶They traveled through the whole island until they came to Paphos. There they met a Jewish sorcerer and false prophet named Bar-Jesus, ⁷who was an attendant of the proconsul, Sergius Paulus. The proconsul, an intelligent man, sent for Barnabas and Saul because he wanted to hear the word of God. ⁸But Elymas the sorcerer (for that is what his name means) opposed them and tried to turn the proconsul from the faith. ⁹Then Saul, who was also called Paul, filled with the Holy Spirit, looked straight at Elymas and said, ¹⁰"You are a child of the devil and an enemy of everything that is right! You are full of all kinds of deceit and trickery. Will you never stop perverting the right ways of the Lord? ¹¹Now the hand of the Lord is against you. You are going to be blind, and for a time you will be unable to see the light of the sun."

Immediately mist and darkness came over him, and he groped about, seeking someone to lead him by the hand. ¹²When the proconsul saw what had happened, he believed, for he was amazed at the teaching about the Lord.

In Pisidian Antioch

¹³From Paphos, Paul and his companions sailed to Perga in Pamphylia, where John left them to return to Jerusalem. ¹⁴From Perga they went on to Pisidian Antioch. On the Sabbath they entered the synagogue and sat down. ¹⁵After the reading from the Law and the Prophets, the synagogue rulers sent word to them, saying, "Brothers, if you have a message of encouragement for the people, please speak."

¹⁶Standing up, Paul motioned with his hand and said: "Men of Israel and you Gentiles who worship God, listen to me! ¹⁷The God of the people of Israel chose our fathers; he made the people prosper during their stay in Egypt, with mighty power he led them out of that country, ¹⁸he endured

their conduct*a* for about forty years in the desert, ¹⁹he overthrew seven nations in Canaan and gave their land to his people as their inheritance. ²⁰All this took about 450 years.

"After this, God gave them judges until the time of Samuel the prophet. ²¹Then the people asked for a king, and he gave them Saul son of Kish, of the tribe of Benjamin, who ruled forty years. ²²After removing Saul, he made David their king. He testified concerning him: 'I have found David son of Jesse a man after my own heart; he will do everything I want him to do.'

²³"From this man's descendants God has brought to Israel the Savior Jesus, as he promised. ²⁴Before the coming of Jesus, John preached repentance and baptism to all the people of Israel. ²⁵As John was completing his work, he said: 'Who do you think I am? I am not that one. No, but he is coming after me, whose sandals I am not worthy to untie.'

²⁶"Brothers, children of Abraham, and you God-fearing Gentiles, it is to us that this message of salvation has been sent. ²⁷The people of Jerusalem and their rulers did not recognize Jesus, yet in condemning him they fulfilled the words of the prophets that are read every Sabbath. ²⁸Though they found no proper ground for a death sentence, they asked Pilate to have him executed. ²⁹When they had carried out all that was written about him, they took him down from the tree and laid him in a tomb. ³⁰But God raised him from the dead, ³¹and for many days he was seen by those who had traveled with him from Galilee to Jerusalem. They are now his witnesses to our people.

³²"We tell you the good news: What God promised our fathers ³³he has fulfilled for us, their children, by raising up Jesus. As it is written in the second Psalm:

" 'You are my Son;
     today I have become your Father.'*b*'*c*

³⁴The fact that God raised him from the dead, never to decay, is stated in these words:

" 'I will give you the holy and sure blessings promised to
     David.'*d*

³⁵So it is stated elsewhere:

" 'You will not let your Holy One see decay.'*e*

³⁶"For when David had served God's purpose in his own generation, he fell asleep; he was buried with his fathers and his body decayed. ³⁷But the one whom God raised from the dead did not see decay.

³⁸"Therefore, my brothers, I want you to know that through Jesus the forgiveness of sins is proclaimed to you. ³⁹Through him everyone who believes is justified from everything you could not be justified from by the law of Moses. ⁴⁰Take care that what the prophets have said does not happen to you:

MAY 13

⁴¹" 'Look, you scoffers,
    wonder and perish,
for I am going to do something in your days
    that you would never believe,
    even if someone told you.'*f*"

⁴²As Paul and Barnabas were leaving the synagogue, the people invited them to speak further about these things on the next Sabbath. ⁴³When the congregation was dismissed, many of the Jews and devout converts to Judaism followed Paul and Barnabas, who talked with them and urged them to continue in the grace of God.

⁴⁴On the next Sabbath almost the whole city gathered to hear the word of the Lord. ⁴⁵When the Jews saw the crowds, they were filled with jealousy and talked abusively against what Paul was saying.

⁴⁶Then Paul and Barnabas answered them boldly: "We had to speak the word of God to you first. Since you reject it and do not consider yourselves worthy of eternal life, we now turn to the Gentiles. ⁴⁷For this is what the Lord has commanded us:

" 'I have made you*g* a light for the Gentiles,
    that you*g* may bring salvation to the ends of the earth.'*h*"

⁴⁸When the Gentiles heard this, they were glad and honored the word of the Lord; and all who were appointed for eternal life believed.

⁴⁹The word of the Lord spread through the whole region. ⁵⁰But the Jews incited the God-fearing women of high standing and the leading men of the city. They stirred up persecution against Paul and Barnabas, and expelled them from their region. ⁵¹So they shook the dust from their feet in protest against them and went to Iconium. ⁵²And the disciples were filled with joy and with the Holy Spirit.

a18 Some manuscripts *and cared for them*   *b33* Or *have begotten you*   *c33* Psalm 2:7
d34 Isaiah 55:3   *e35* Psalm 16:10   *f41* Hab. 1:5   *g47* The Greek is singular.
h47 Isaiah 49:6

Known by Name and Reputation

> Then Saul, who was also called Paul, filled with the Holy Spirit, looked straight at [him] (Acts 13:9).

It may surprise you to learn that the apostle Paul is better known by his humble nickname Paul (which means "little one") than by his kingly given name Saul (which means "asked of God").

But as one scholar described it, the day soon came in the Roman Empire when men would call their dogs Nero and their sons Paul!

Alexander Maclaren probes the significance of Paul's change of name and his change of direction and attitude.

Walk With Alexander Maclaren

"From the change of the apostle's name, we may learn that the only way to help people is to get to their level.

"If you want to bless people, you must identify yourself with them. It is no use standing on a pedestal above them, and patronizingly talking down to them. You cannot scold, or bully, or lecture men and women into the acceptance of religious truth if you take a position of superiority.

"The motivation which led to the apostle's change of name from Saul—with its memories of royal dignity—to the Roman name Paul, is this: 'I have become all things to all men, so that by all possible means I might save some.'

"The principle demonstrated in this comparatively little matter is the same principle that influenced the Master in the mightiest of all events."

Walk Closer to God

No matter what name you answer to, humility must be your "calling card" when you present the gospel.

Even the Son of God "made himself nothing, taking the very nature of a servant, being made in human likeness" (Philippians 2:7), that he might bring men and women to himself.

If your reputation or title gets in the way of another's response to the claims of Christ, it's time for a change . . . in you!

After all, the only names that really count are the ones written in the book of life. ⟡

MAY 14

📖 Walk in the Word
Acts 14

Luke relates the mixed reaction to Barnabas's and Paul's preaching and miracles of healing as they go from Iconium to Lystra and Derbe and eventually back to Antioch in Syria.

In Iconium

14 At Iconium Paul and Barnabas went as usual into the Jewish synagogue. There they spoke so effectively that a great number of Jews and Gentiles believed. ²But the Jews who refused to believe stirred up the Gentiles and poisoned their minds against the brothers. ³So Paul and Barnabas spent considerable time there, speaking boldly for the Lord, who confirmed the message of his grace by enabling them to do miraculous signs and wonders. ⁴The people of the city were divided; some sided with the Jews, others with the apostles. ⁵There was a plot afoot among the Gentiles and Jews, together with their leaders, to mistreat them and stone them. ⁶But they found out about it and fled to the Lycaonian cities of Lystra and Derbe and to the surrounding country, ⁷where they continued to preach the good news.

In Lystra and Derbe

⁸In Lystra there sat a man crippled in his feet, who was lame from birth and had never walked. ⁹He listened to Paul as he was speaking. Paul looked directly at him, saw that he had faith to be healed ¹⁰and called out, "Stand up on your feet!" At that, the man jumped up and began to walk.

¹¹When the crowd saw what Paul had done, they shouted in the Lycaonian language, "The gods have come down to us in human form!" ¹²Barnabas they called Zeus, and Paul they called Hermes because he was the chief speaker. ¹³The priest of Zeus, whose temple was just outside the city, brought bulls and wreaths to the city gates because he and the crowd wanted to offer sacrifices to them.

¹⁴But when the apostles Barnabas and Paul heard of this, they tore their clothes and rushed out into the crowd, shouting: ¹⁵"Men, why are you doing this? We too are only men, human like you. We are bringing you good news, telling you to turn from these worthless things to the living God, who made heaven and earth and sea and everything in them. ¹⁶In the past, he let all nations go their own way. ¹⁷Yet he has not left himself without testimony: He has shown kindness by giving you rain from heaven and crops in their seasons; he provides you with plenty of food and fills your hearts with joy." ¹⁸Even with these words, they had difficulty keeping the crowd from sacrificing to them.

¹⁹Then some Jews came from Antioch and Iconium and won the crowd over. They stoned Paul and dragged him outside the city, thinking he was dead. ²⁰But after the disciples had gathered around him, he got up and went back into the city. The next day he and Barnabas left for Derbe.

The Return to Antioch in Syria

²¹They preached the good news in that city and won a large number of disciples. Then they returned to Lystra, Iconium and Antioch, ²²strengthening the disciples and encouraging them to remain true to the faith. "We must go through many hardships to enter the kingdom of God," they said. ²³Paul and Barnabas appointed elders*ᵃ* for them in each church and, with prayer and fasting, committed them to the Lord, in whom they had put their trust. ²⁴After going through Pisidia, they came into Pamphylia, ²⁵and when they had preached the word in Perga, they went down to Attalia.

²⁶From Attalia they sailed back to Antioch, where they had been committed to the grace of God for the work they had now completed. ²⁷On arriving there, they gathered the church together and reported all that God had done through them and how he had opened the door of faith to the Gentiles. ²⁸And they stayed there a long time with the disciples.

ᵃ23 Or *Barnabas ordained elders*; or *Barnabas had elders elected*

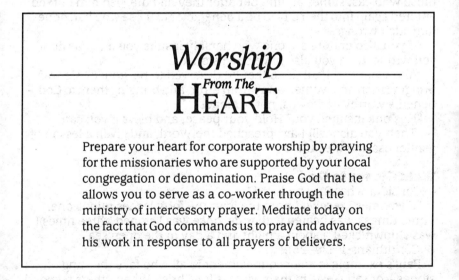

Worship
From The HEART

Prepare your heart for corporate worship by praying for the missionaries who are supported by your local congregation or denomination. Praise God that he allows you to serve as a co-worker through the ministry of intercessory prayer. Meditate today on the fact that God commands us to pray and advances his work in response to all prayers of believers.

MAY 14

Responding to Words That Wound

> Then some Jews . . . won the crowd over. They stoned Paul and dragged him outside the city, thinking he was dead (Acts 14:19).

There is plenty in the gospel for people to find upsetting. The fact of sin. The ugly specter of the cross. The need for repentance.

So it shouldn't surprise you when your witness produces a "rocky" response.

John Chrysostom, a fourth-century preacher, offers this timeless insight on how to respond to sticks, stones and words.

Walk With John Chrysostom

"Paul's enemies wounded him with stones; there is a wounding with words even worse than stones.

"What then must we do? The same thing Paul did. He did not hate those who cast stones at him; but after they had dragged him out, he entered again into their city to be a benefactor to those who had done him such wrongs.

"If you also endure anyone who harshly insults you and has done you wrong, then you also have been stoned.

"And what had Paul done that he deserved to be stoned? He was bringing men and women away from error, and bringing them to God—benefits worthy of crowns, not of stones.

"Has one insulted you? Hold your peace, and bless if you can.

"Then you also will have preached the Word, and given a lesson of gentleness and meekness."

Walk Closer to God

Consider what Paul endured:

"Five times I received from the Jews the forty lashes minus one. Three times I was beaten with rods, once was I stoned, three times I was shipwrecked, I spent a night and a day in the open sea" (2 Corinthians 11:24–25).

Paul's example is an encouragement to all who face the sting of stones—or rebukes—in their witness for Christ. When others respond by striking back, rejoice that at least a seed has been planted. And leave it to God that someday a crown will follow!

MAY 15

📖 Walk in the Word
Acts 15:1–21

The council at Jerusalem is convened to settle a dispute over what was required of Gentiles before they could become Christians; Barnabas and Paul give their account of God's work among the Gentiles, Peter speaks a word in favor of the "yoke" of grace, and James offers a solution.

The Council at Jerusalem

15 Some men came down from Judea to Antioch and were teaching the brothers: "Unless you are circumcised, according to the custom taught by Moses, you cannot be saved." ²This brought Paul and Barnabas into sharp dispute and debate with them. So Paul and Barnabas were appointed, along with some other believers, to go up to Jerusalem to see the apostles and elders about this question. ³The church sent them on their way, and as they traveled through Phoenicia and Samaria, they told how the Gentiles had been converted. This news made all the brothers very glad. ⁴When they came to Jerusalem, they were welcomed by the church and the apostles and elders, to whom they reported everything God had done through them.

⁵Then some of the believers who belonged to the party of the Pharisees stood up and said, "The Gentiles must be circumcised and required to obey the law of Moses."

⁶The apostles and elders met to consider this question. ⁷After much discussion, Peter got up and addressed them: "Brothers, you know that some time ago God made a choice among you that the Gentiles might hear from my lips the message of the gospel and believe. ⁸God, who knows the heart, showed that he accepted them by giving the Holy Spirit to them, just as he did to us. ⁹He made no distinction between us and them, for he purified their hearts by faith. ¹⁰Now then, why do you try to test God by putting on the necks of the disciples a yoke that neither we nor our fathers have been able to bear? ¹¹No! We believe it is through the grace of our Lord Jesus that we are saved, just as they are."

¹²The whole assembly became silent as they listened to Barnabas and Paul telling about the miraculous signs and wonders God had done among the Gentiles through them. ¹³When they finished, James spoke up: "Brothers, listen to me. ¹⁴Simon*ᵃ* has described to us how God at first showed his concern by taking from the Gentiles a people for himself. ¹⁵The words of the prophets are in agreement with this, as it is written:

> ¹⁶" 'After this I will return
> and rebuild David's fallen tent.
> Its ruins I will rebuild,
> and I will restore it,
> ¹⁷that the remnant of men may seek the Lord,
> and all the Gentiles who bear my name,
> says the Lord, who does these things'ᵇ
> ¹⁸ that have been known for ages.ᶜ

MAY 15

¹⁹"It is my judgment, therefore, that we should not make it difficult for the Gentiles who are turning to God. ²⁰Instead we should write to them, telling them to abstain from food polluted by idols, from sexual immorality, from the meat of strangled animals and from blood. ²¹For Moses has been preached in every city from the earliest times and is read in the synagogues on every Sabbath."

a14 Greek *Simeon*, a variant of *Simon*; that is, Peter   *b17* Amos 9:11,12
c17,18 Some manuscripts *things'—* / *18known to the Lord for ages is his work*

PSALM 111 *a*

Praise the LORD. *b*

I will extol the LORD with all my heart
  in the council of the upright and in the assembly.

²Great are the works of the LORD;
  they are pondered by all who delight in them.
³Glorious and majestic are his deeds,
  and his righteousness endures forever.
⁴He has caused his wonders to be remembered;
  the LORD is gracious and compassionate.
⁵He provides food for those who fear him;
  he remembers his covenant forever.
⁶He has shown his people the power of his works,
  giving them the lands of other nations.
⁷The works of his hands are faithful and just;
  all his precepts are trustworthy.
⁸They are steadfast for ever and ever,
  done in faithfulness and uprightness.
⁹He provided redemption for his people;
  he ordained his covenant forever—
  holy and awesome is his name.

¹⁰The fear of the LORD is the beginning of wisdom;
  all who follow his precepts have good understanding.
  To him belongs eternal praise.

aThis psalm is an acrostic poem, the lines of which begin with the successive letters of the Hebrew alphabet.   b1 Hebrew Hallelu Yah

Standing Fast for Our Freedom in Christ

Then some of the believers who belonged to the party of the Pharisees stood up and said, "The Gentiles must be circumcised and required to obey the law of Moses" (Acts 15:5).

Prejudice is a dirty word. But prejudice is not limited to race. The first church council was called because of the prejudice of one group of Christians. The newly converted Pharisees wanted the Gentiles to participate in ceremonies that foreshadowed the sacrifice of Christ.

But Paul would have none of it. Once Jesus shed his blood, God required no more blood to be shed. And if God no longer required it, how could the Pharisees? Paul's thought is echoed by Charles Hodge.

Walk With Charles Hodge

"It is a great error in morals, and a great practical evil, to make that sinful which is in fact innocent. Christian love never requires this or any other sacrifice of truth. Paul would not consent, even for the sake of avoiding offense, that eating food offered to idols should be made a sin; he strenuously maintained the reverse. He represents those who thought differently as weak in faith, as being under an error from which more knowledge and piety would free them.

"We should stand fast in the freedom for which Christ has set us free, and not allow our consciences to be burdened by a yoke of slavery to human opinions. There is a strong tendency to treat as matters of conscience things which God has never enjoined.

"It is often necessary to assert our Christian liberty at the expense of incurring censure in order to preserve right principles. Our Savior consented to be regarded as a Sabbath-breaker, a drunkard, and a friend of tax collectors and 'sinners'; but wisdom was proved right by her actions."

Walk Closer to God

In a way, we are in a better position to settle such issues than those in Paul's time. We may not have an infallible council, but we have his infallible counsel—the completed Bible. Praise God that in his Word we have a trustworthy standard to distinguish duty from freedom.

Judgment by the standard of the Bible is required (2 Timothy 3:16). But judgment by an arbitrary standard is forbidden (Matthew 7:1). Have you held some personal traditions and opinions so dear that you have judged others by them?

MAY 16

📖 Walk in the Word
Acts 15:22–41

The decision of the Jerusalem council is conveyed to the Gentile believers via a letter and a visit from church leaders; Paul and Barnabas disagree over John Mark's traveling with them.

The Council's Letter to Gentile Believers

²²Then the apostles and elders, with the whole church, decided to choose some of their own men and send them to Antioch with Paul and Barnabas. They chose Judas (called Barsabbas) and Silas, two men who were leaders among the brothers. ²³With them they sent the following letter:

The apostles and elders, your brothers,

To the Gentile believers in Antioch, Syria and Cilicia:

Greetings.

²⁴We have heard that some went out from us without our authorization and disturbed you, troubling your minds by what they said. ²⁵So we all agreed to choose some men and send them to you with our dear friends Barnabas and Paul— ²⁶men who have risked their lives for the name of our Lord Jesus Christ. ²⁷Therefore we are sending Judas and Silas to confirm by word of mouth what we are writing. ²⁸It seemed good to the Holy Spirit and to us not to burden you with anything beyond the following requirements: ²⁹You are to abstain from food sacrificed to idols, from blood, from the meat of strangled animals and from sexual immorality. You will do well to avoid these things.

Farewell.

³⁰The men were sent off and went down to Antioch, where they gathered the church together and delivered the letter. ³¹The people read it and were glad for its encouraging message. ³²Judas and Silas, who themselves were prophets, said much to encourage and strengthen the brothers. ³³After spending some time there, they were sent off by the brothers with the blessing of peace to return to those who had sent them. *ᵃ* ³⁵But Paul and Barnabas remained in Antioch, where they and many others taught and preached the word of the Lord.

Disagreement Between Paul and Barnabas

³⁶Some time later Paul said to Barnabas, "Let us go back and visit the brothers in all the towns where we preached the word of the Lord and see how they are doing." ³⁷Barnabas wanted to take John, also called Mark, with them, ³⁸but Paul did not think it wise to take him, because he had

deserted them in Pamphylia and had not continued with them in the work. ³⁹They had such a sharp disagreement that they parted company. Barnabas took Mark and sailed for Cyprus, ⁴⁰but Paul chose Silas and left, commended by the brothers to the grace of the Lord. ⁴¹He went through Syria and Cilicia, strengthening the churches.

a33 Some manuscripts *them, 34but Silas decided to remain there*

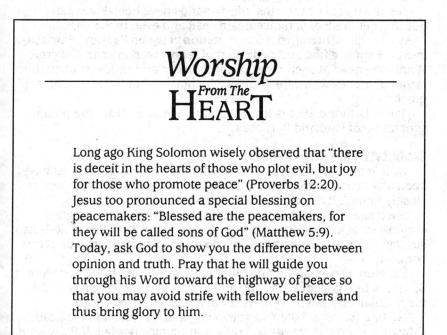

Worship From The HEART

Long ago King Solomon wisely observed that "there is deceit in the hearts of those who plot evil, but joy for those who promote peace" (Proverbs 12:20). Jesus too pronounced a special blessing on peacemakers: "Blessed are the peacemakers, for they will be called sons of God" (Matthew 5:9). Today, ask God to show you the difference between opinion and truth. Pray that he will guide you through his Word toward the highway of peace so that you may avoid strife with fellow believers and thus bring glory to him.

MAY 16

Painful Partings and Struggling Saints

They had such a sharp disagreement that they parted company (Acts 15:39).

Contrary to what you may have heard, missionaries are neither "supermen" nor "wonder women."

Like the rest of us humans, missionaries have been known to quarrel, get tired, experience heartbreak and even make mistakes.

As you will learn from the confrontation between Paul and Barnabas, even the most gifted and dedicated of fellow workers can disagree. What they need at such times is not criticism and condemnation, but rather churches who care, friends who pray and individuals who are quick to forgive.

Martin Luther explores the lesson to be learned from the painful separation of Paul and Barnabas.

Walk With Martin Luther

"Here it appears either Paul or Barnabas went too far. It must have been a violent disagreement to separate two associates who were so closely united. Indeed, the text indicates as much.

"Such examples are written for our consolation: for it is a great comfort to us to hear that great saints, who have the Spirit of God, also struggle. Those who say that saints do not sin would deprive us of this comfort.

"Samson, David, and many other celebrated men full of the Holy Spirit fell into grievous sins. Job and Jeremiah cursed the day of their birth; Elijah and Jonah were weary of life and desired death.

"No one has ever fallen so grievously that he may not rise again. Conversely, no one stands so firmly that he may not fall. If Peter (and Paul and Barnabas) fell, I too may fall. If they rose again, I too may rise again."

Walk Closer to God

"God is not a man, that he should lie, nor a son of man, that he should change his mind. Does he speak and then not act? Does he promise and not fulfill?" (Numbers 23:19).

Fix your gaze upon him, and regardless of who stumbles and falls around you, you can rest assured—he stands eternally!

MAY 17

📖 Walk in the Word
Acts 16:1–15

Silas accompanies Paul on another missionary journey, and Timothy joins them in Lystra; Luke himself joins the group at Troas, and the missionary endeavor expands to Macedonia.

Timothy Joins Paul and Silas

16 He came to Derbe and then to Lystra, where a disciple named Timothy lived, whose mother was a Jewess and a believer, but whose father was a Greek. 2The brothers at Lystra and Iconium spoke well of him. 3Paul wanted to take him along on the journey, so he circumcised him because of the Jews who lived in that area, for they all knew that his father was a Greek. 4As they traveled from town to town, they delivered the decisions reached by the apostles and elders in Jerusalem for the people to obey. 5So the churches were strengthened in the faith and grew daily in numbers.

Paul's Vision of the Man of Macedonia

6Paul and his companions traveled throughout the region of Phrygia and Galatia, having been kept by the Holy Spirit from preaching the word in the province of Asia. 7When they came to the border of Mysia, they tried to enter Bithynia, but the Spirit of Jesus would not allow them to. 8So they passed by Mysia and went down to Troas. 9During the night Paul had a vision of a man of Macedonia standing and begging him, "Come over to Macedonia and help us." 10After Paul had seen the vision, we got ready at once to leave for Macedonia, concluding that God had called us to preach the gospel to them.

Lydia's Conversion in Philippi

11From Troas we put out to sea and sailed straight for Samothrace, and the next day on to Neapolis. 12From there we traveled to Philippi, a Roman colony and the leading city of that district of Macedonia. And we stayed there several days.

13On the Sabbath we went outside the city gate to the river, where we expected to find a place of prayer. We sat down and began to speak to the women who had gathered there. 14One of those listening was a woman named Lydia, a dealer in purple cloth from the city of Thyatira, who was a worshiper of God. The Lord opened her heart to respond to Paul's message. 15When she and the members of her household were baptized, she invited us to her home. "If you consider me a believer in the Lord," she said, "come and stay at my house." And she persuaded us.

MAY 17

How Wise His Way, How Strong His Will

Having been kept by the Holy Spirit from preaching the word in the province of Asia . . . they tried to enter Bithynia, but the Spirit of Jesus would not allow them to (Acts 16:6–7).

Paul's ambition was right, but his timing was wrong. He had a good idea: evangelize Asia. But God had a better idea: evangelize Europe!

And once God's will was clear, Paul wasted no time in obeying.

G. Campbell Morgan provides this helpful analysis of how to respond when the what of God's will is clear, but the why is not.

Walk With G. Campbell Morgan

"Obedience to the Spirit's guidance when we cannot understand the reason—that experience is not so rare.

"Over and over again in the path of true service a great opportunity is open right before us, and we are not permitted to avail ourselves of it.

"Or we are in the midst of work which is full of real success, and we are called to abandon it. We should never hesitate to do so.

"This wonderful page of apostolic history teaches us that God's outlook is greater and grander than our own. We may always leave the issue to him, and presently we shall learn how wise his way, how strong his will."

Walk Closer to God

From Paul's perspective, the closed doors to Bithynia and Asia must have seemed puzzling. But from the perspective of hindsight—a perspective God enjoys from the start—consider what happened:

Paul traveled throughout Greece, preaching and establishing churches. Afterward, he returned to Ephesus, the heart of the province of Asia, and preached until "all the Jews and Greeks who lived in the province of Asia heard the word of the Lord" (Acts 19:10).

And Bithynia? Paul may not have returned there personally; but Peter did address his first letter to the Christians "in Bithynia." It's a truth you cannot learn too well: Understanding God's plan can wait; obeying God's will cannot. 〇

420

MAY 18

📖 Walk in the Word
Acts 16:16–40

Luke recalls an encounter with a slave girl, which resulted in imprisonment for Paul and Silas and salvation for the Philippian jailer who responded to the gospel proclamation.

Paul and Silas in Prison

[16]Once when we were going to the place of prayer, we were met by a slave girl who had a spirit by which she predicted the future. She earned a great deal of money for her owners by fortune-telling. [17]This girl followed Paul and the rest of us, shouting, "These men are servants of the Most High God, who are telling you the way to be saved." [18]She kept this up for many days. Finally Paul became so troubled that he turned around and said to the spirit, "In the name of Jesus Christ I command you to come out of her!" At that moment the spirit left her.

[19]When the owners of the slave girl realized that their hope of making money was gone, they seized Paul and Silas and dragged them into the marketplace to face the authorities. [20]They brought them before the magistrates and said, "These men are Jews, and are throwing our city into an uproar [21]by advocating customs unlawful for us Romans to accept or practice."

[22]The crowd joined in the attack against Paul and Silas, and the magistrates ordered them to be stripped and beaten. [23]After they had been severely flogged, they were thrown into prison, and the jailer was commanded to guard them carefully. [24]Upon receiving such orders, he put them in the inner cell and fastened their feet in the stocks.

[25]About midnight Paul and Silas were praying and singing hymns to God, and the other prisoners were listening to them. [26]Suddenly there was such a violent earthquake that the foundations of the prison were shaken. At once all the prison doors flew open, and everybody's chains came loose. [27]The jailer woke up, and when he saw the prison doors open, he drew his sword and was about to kill himself because he thought the prisoners had escaped. [28]But Paul shouted, "Don't harm yourself! We are all here!"

[29]The jailer called for lights, rushed in and fell trembling before Paul and Silas. [30]He then brought them out and asked, "Sirs, what must I do to be saved?"

[31]They replied, "Believe in the Lord Jesus, and you will be saved—you and your household." [32]Then they spoke the word of the Lord to him and to all the others in his house. [33]At that hour of the night the jailer took them and washed their wounds; then immediately he and all his family were baptized. [34]The jailer brought them into his house and set a meal before them; he was filled with joy because he had come to believe in God—he and his whole family.

[35]When it was daylight, the magistrates sent their officers to the jailer with the order: "Release those men." [36]The jailer told Paul, "The magis-

MAY 18

trates have ordered that you and Silas be released. Now you can leave. Go in peace."

37But Paul said to the officers: "They beat us publicly without a trial, even though we are Roman citizens, and threw us into prison. And now do they want to get rid of us quietly? No! Let them come themselves and escort us out."

38The officers reported this to the magistrates, and when they heard that Paul and Silas were Roman citizens, they were alarmed. 39They came to appease them and escorted them from the prison, requesting them to leave the city. 40After Paul and Silas came out of the prison, they went to Lydia's house, where they met with the brothers and encouraged them. Then they left.

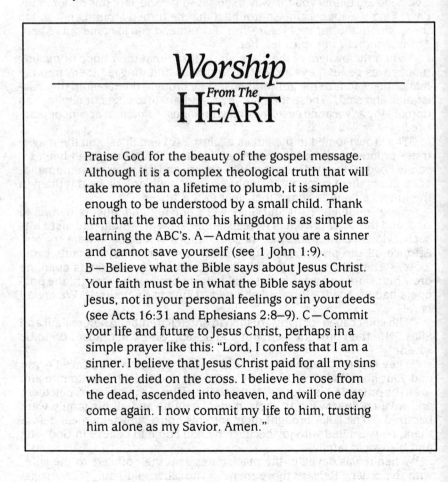

Worship
From The
HEART

Praise God for the beauty of the gospel message. Although it is a complex theological truth that will take more than a lifetime to plumb, it is simple enough to be understood by a small child. Thank him that the road into his kingdom is as simple as learning the ABC's. A—Admit that you are a sinner and cannot save yourself (see 1 John 1:9). B—Believe what the Bible says about Jesus Christ. Your faith must be in what the Bible says about Jesus, not in your personal feelings or in your deeds (see Acts 16:31 and Ephesians 2:8–9). C—Commit your life and future to Jesus Christ, perhaps in a simple prayer like this: "Lord, I confess that I am a sinner. I believe that Jesus Christ paid for all my sins when he died on the cross. I believe he rose from the dead, ascended into heaven, and will one day come again. I now commit my life to him, trusting him alone as my Savior. Amen."

Keeping the Simple Truth Simple

"Sirs, what must I do to be saved?" They replied, "Believe in the Lord Jesus, and you will be saved" (Acts 16:30–31).

Two notorious "outlaws" in the prison at Philippi . . . locked in solitary confinement . . . singing hymns at midnight. Suddenly, without warning, a violent earthquake . . . every prisoner's chains loosed . . . every door opened.

Imagine the dismay of the Philippian jailer. For a man in his position the escape of even one prisoner meant certain death. Yet in his midnight moment of crisis, the jailer discovered someone who specializes in giving life. J. Wilbur Chapman provides this timely comment on the jailer's newfound life.

Walk With J. Wilbur Chapman

"God makes it clear that there can be no real life until there is a step taken first of all by faith.

"To make it very clear, the best answer is the one given to the Philippian jailer: 'Believe in the Lord Jesus, and you will be saved.'

"There is something very significant in the way the names of Jesus Christ are used. When he is called Lord, it is to emphasize his kingly office, his reigning power; and what can the meaning be but this, when we are told to believe on him as Lord?

"We must reach the place where we are willing to let him rule and reign in our lives.

"Can you submit to this? He will never make a failure of it.

"Give him absolute control; never take a step without his guidance—this is the secret of grace and joy."

Walk Closer to God

The Philippian jailer didn't need a lecture on theology. He just needed a simple, one-sentence sermon: "Believe in the Lord Jesus, and you will be saved—you and your household."

When the heart is prepared, the odds are good you won't need oratory or arguments to lead another to the Savior.

So keep it short. Clear. Sincere. And when the door swings ajar, be ready to enter!

MAY 19

📖 Walk in the Word
Acts 17

Luke documents some of the missionary efforts in Thessalonica, Berea and Athens.

In Thessalonica

17 When they had passed through Amphipolis and Apollonia, they came to Thessalonica, where there was a Jewish synagogue. ²As his custom was, Paul went into the synagogue, and on three Sabbath days he reasoned with them from the Scriptures, ³explaining and proving that the Christ*ᵃ* had to suffer and rise from the dead. "This Jesus I am proclaiming to you is the Christ,*ᵃ*" he said. ⁴Some of the Jews were persuaded and joined Paul and Silas, as did a large number of God-fearing Greeks and not a few prominent women.

⁵But the Jews were jealous; so they rounded up some bad characters from the marketplace, formed a mob and started a riot in the city. They rushed to Jason's house in search of Paul and Silas in order to bring them out to the crowd.*ᵇ* ⁶But when they did not find them, they dragged Jason and some other brothers before the city officials, shouting: "These men who have caused trouble all over the world have now come here, ⁷and Jason has welcomed them into his house. They are all defying Caesar's decrees, saying that there is another king, one called Jesus." ⁸When they heard this, the crowd and the city officials were thrown into turmoil. ⁹Then they made Jason and the others post bond and let them go.

In Berea

¹⁰As soon as it was night, the brothers sent Paul and Silas away to Berea. On arriving there, they went to the Jewish synagogue. ¹¹Now the Bereans were of more noble character than the Thessalonians, for they received the message with great eagerness and examined the Scriptures every day to see if what Paul said was true. ¹²Many of the Jews believed, as did also a number of prominent Greek women and many Greek men.

¹³When the Jews in Thessalonica learned that Paul was preaching the word of God at Berea, they went there too, agitating the crowds and stirring them up. ¹⁴The brothers immediately sent Paul to the coast, but Silas and Timothy stayed at Berea. ¹⁵The men who escorted Paul brought him to Athens and then left with instructions for Silas and Timothy to join him as soon as possible.

In Athens

¹⁶While Paul was waiting for them in Athens, he was greatly distressed to see that the city was full of idols. ¹⁷So he reasoned in the synagogue with the Jews and the God-fearing Greeks, as well as in the marketplace day by day with those who happened to be there. ¹⁸A group of Epicurean and Stoic philosophers began to dispute with him. Some of them asked, "What is this babbler trying to say?" Others remarked, "He seems to be advocating foreign gods." They said this because Paul was preaching the

good news about Jesus and the resurrection. ¹⁹Then they took him and brought him to a meeting of the Areopagus, where they said to him, "May we know what this new teaching is that you are presenting? ²⁰You are bringing some strange ideas to our ears, and we want to know what they mean." ²¹(All the Athenians and the foreigners who lived there spent their time doing nothing but talking about and listening to the latest ideas.)

²²Paul then stood up in the meeting of the Areopagus and said: "Men of Athens! I see that in every way you are very religious. ²³For as I walked around and looked carefully at your objects of worship, I even found an altar with this inscription: TO AN UNKNOWN GOD. Now what you worship as something unknown I am going to proclaim to you.

²⁴"The God who made the world and everything in it is the Lord of heaven and earth and does not live in temples built by hands. ²⁵And he is not served by human hands, as if he needed anything, because he himself gives all men life and breath and everything else. ²⁶From one man he made every nation of men, that they should inhabit the whole earth; and he determined the times set for them and the exact places where they should live. ²⁷God did this so that men would seek him and perhaps reach out for him and find him, though he is not far from each one of us. ²⁸'For in him we live and move and have our being.' As some of your own poets have said, 'We are his offspring.'

²⁹"Therefore since we are God's offspring, we should not think that the divine being is like gold or silver or stone—an image made by man's design and skill. ³⁰In the past God overlooked such ignorance, but now he commands all people everywhere to repent. ³¹For he has set a day when he will judge the world with justice by the man he has appointed. He has given proof of this to all men by raising him from the dead."

³²When they heard about the resurrection of the dead, some of them sneered, but others said, "We want to hear you again on this subject." ³³At that, Paul left the Council. ³⁴A few men became followers of Paul and believed. Among them was Dionysius, a member of the Areopagus, also a woman named Damaris, and a number of others.

a3 Or Messiah   b5 Or the assembly of the people

MAY 19

Inquiring Minds and Searching Hearts

The Bereans were of more noble character than the Thessalonians, for they received the message with great eagerness and examined the Scriptures every day to see if what Paul said was true (Acts 17:11).

Envy in Thessalonica.
Mocking in Athens.
Intimidation in Corinth.
But in Berea? A breath of fresh air.

The Bereans were "of more noble character" than the other groups Paul encountered.

More responsive. More serious about the claims of Christ on their lives.

More inquisitive about the implications of what they were hearing.

Johann Peter Lange expands on the attitude that set the Bereans apart.

Walk With Johann Peter Lange

"Christian nobility of soul exhibits two features: readiness to receive truth and eagerness to examine the evidence.

"True faith is not blind acceptance. It does not dispense with reason, evidence, and argument.

"It is, on the contrary, ready to prove all things with sincerity, to investigate earnestly, to institute a thorough search.

"The people of Berea did not blindly accept Paul's words, but first searched whether he taught the truth.

"They are not criticized for this, but instead are commended for the noble spirit which motivated them."

Walk Closer to God

Apart from one verse in Acts 20, the Bereans are not mentioned again in the Bible. But their testimony lives on in the noble character they displayed.

The same character you can demonstrate today in your attitude toward God's Word.

The character you can pray for in the lives of those who hear your witness.

The character you can develop, involving a ready mind and a searching heart.

Does God's truth deserve anything less? ◖◗

MAY 20

📖 Walk in the Word
Acts 18

Luke's felicitous meeting with Aquila and Priscilla in Corinth and their brief stopover in Ephesus before Paul traveled on to Antioch concludes the second missionary jouney.

In Corinth

18 After this, Paul left Athens and went to Corinth. ²There he met a Jew named Aquila, a native of Pontus, who had recently come from Italy with his wife Priscilla, because Claudius had ordered all the Jews to leave Rome. Paul went to see them, ³and because he was a tentmaker as they were, he stayed and worked with them. ⁴Every Sabbath he reasoned in the synagogue, trying to persuade Jews and Greeks.

⁵When Silas and Timothy came from Macedonia, Paul devoted himself exclusively to preaching, testifying to the Jews that Jesus was the Christ. *ᵃ* ⁶But when the Jews opposed Paul and became abusive, he shook out his clothes in protest and said to them, "Your blood be on your own heads! I am clear of my responsibility. From now on I will go to the Gentiles."

⁷Then Paul left the synagogue and went next door to the house of Titius Justus, a worshiper of God. ⁸Crispus, the synagogue ruler, and his entire household believed in the Lord; and many of the Corinthians who heard him believed and were baptized.

⁹One night the Lord spoke to Paul in a vision: "Do not be afraid; keep on speaking, do not be silent. ¹⁰For I am with you, and no one is going to attack and harm you, because I have many people in this city." ¹¹So Paul stayed for a year and a half, teaching them the word of God.

¹²While Gallio was proconsul of Achaia, the Jews made a united attack on Paul and brought him into court. ¹³"This man," they charged, "is persuading the people to worship God in ways contrary to the law."

¹⁴Just as Paul was about to speak, Gallio said to the Jews, "If you Jews were making a complaint about some misdemeanor or serious crime, it would be reasonable for me to listen to you. ¹⁵But since it involves questions about words and names and your own law—settle the matter yourselves. I will not be a judge of such things." ¹⁶So he had them ejected from the court. ¹⁷Then they all turned on Sosthenes the synagogue ruler and beat him in front of the court. But Gallio showed no concern whatever.

Priscilla, Aquila and Apollos

¹⁸Paul stayed on in Corinth for some time. Then he left the brothers and sailed for Syria, accompanied by Priscilla and Aquila. Before he sailed, he had his hair cut off at Cenchrea because of a vow he had taken. ¹⁹They arrived at Ephesus, where Paul left Priscilla and Aquila. He himself went into the synagogue and reasoned with the Jews. ²⁰When they asked him to spend more time with them, he declined. ²¹But as he left, he promised, "I will come back if it is God's will." Then he set sail from Ephesus. ²²When he landed at Caesarea, he went up and greeted the church and then went down to Antioch.

May 20

²³After spending some time in Antioch, Paul set out from there and traveled from place to place throughout the region of Galatia and Phrygia, strengthening all the disciples.

²⁴Meanwhile a Jew named Apollos, a native of Alexandria, came to Ephesus. He was a learned man, with a thorough knowledge of the Scriptures. ²⁵He had been instructed in the way of the Lord, and he spoke with great fervor[b] and taught about Jesus accurately, though he knew only the baptism of John. ²⁶He began to speak boldly in the synagogue. When Priscilla and Aquila heard him, they invited him to their home and explained to him the way of God more adequately.

²⁷When Apollos wanted to go to Achaia, the brothers encouraged him and wrote to the disciples there to welcome him. On arriving, he was a great help to those who by grace had believed. ²⁸For he vigorously refuted the Jews in public debate, proving from the Scriptures that Jesus was the Christ.

[a]5 Or *Messiah;* also in verse 28   [b]25 Or *with fervor in the Spirit*

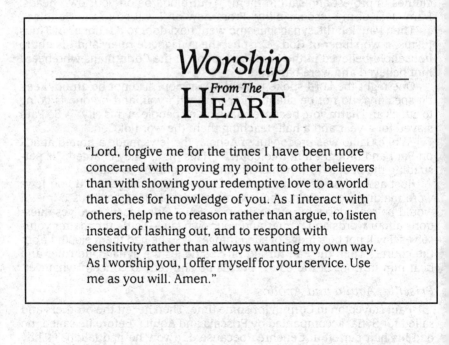

Worship
From The
HEART

"Lord, forgive me for the times I have been more concerned with proving my point to other believers than with showing your redemptive love to a world that aches for knowledge of you. As I interact with others, help me to reason rather than argue, to listen instead of lashing out, and to respond with sensitivity rather than always wanting my own way. As I worship you, I offer myself for your service. Use me as you will. Amen."

The Danger Is Real

While Gallio was proconsul of Achaia, the Jews made a united attack on Paul . . . But Gallio showed no concern whatever (Acts 18:12,17).

Apathy suffocates the church of Jesus Christ and paralyzes the work of truth. All that is necessary for evil to prevail is for good people to do nothing. And nothing is precisely what indifference breeds.

What happens when unconcerned listeners encounter uncompromising truth? The apathetic person comes out the loser every time. H.A. Ironside elaborates.

Walk With H.A. Ironside

"Gallio the Indifferent! History tells us that he was the brother of Seneca the philosopher, who exclaimed, 'Few men are so agreeable about anything as my brother Gallio is about everything!'

"Yet this amiable man lost a marvelous opportunity to hear the gospel from the lips of Paul, and perhaps lost his soul as well, just because he did not consider eternal things worthy of his attention.

"To him the whole matter was beneath contempt, consisting only, as he supposed, of a quarrel about words and names and Jewish ceremonial observances. So he turned scornfully away without hearing that glad message which God was sending out in grace to a needy world.

"His attitude stands out as a warning to others not to treat lightly the privileges God gives, lest the day of doom find them still in their sins."

Walk Closer to God

If someone announced in words both clear and plain, "The building is on fire!" would you respond with a yawn and a shrug? Of course not! Life-threatening situations demand life-saving steps. If the warning is true, then the danger is real. And only prompt action can avert certain disaster.

Think of the gospel as just such a call to action. The danger is real; the penalty for sin is sure; but the lifeboat is standing by in the person of Jesus Christ, the Savior. Good news indeed for all who take shelter in him. But not for those who—like Gallio—greet him with a yawn and a shrug.

MAY 21

📖 Walk in the Word
Acts 19:1–22

After spending some time in the region of Galatia and Phrygia, Paul returns to a powerful ministry of preaching and healing in Ephesus.

Paul in Ephesus

19 While Apollos was at Corinth, Paul took the road through the interior and arrived at Ephesus. There he found some disciples ²and asked them, "Did you receive the Holy Spirit when*a* you believed?"

They answered, "No, we have not even heard that there is a Holy Spirit."

³So Paul asked, "Then what baptism did you receive?"

"John's baptism," they replied.

⁴Paul said, "John's baptism was a baptism of repentance. He told the people to believe in the one coming after him, that is, in Jesus." ⁵On hearing this, they were baptized into*b* the name of the Lord Jesus. ⁶When Paul placed his hands on them, the Holy Spirit came on them, and they spoke in tongues*c* and prophesied. ⁷There were about twelve men in all.

⁸Paul entered the synagogue and spoke boldly there for three months, arguing persuasively about the kingdom of God. ⁹But some of them became obstinate; they refused to believe and publicly maligned the Way. So Paul left them. He took the disciples with him and had discussions daily in the lecture hall of Tyrannus. ¹⁰This went on for two years, so that all the Jews and Greeks who lived in the province of Asia heard the word of the Lord.

¹¹God did extraordinary miracles through Paul, ¹²so that even handkerchiefs and aprons that had touched him were taken to the sick, and their illnesses were cured and the evil spirits left them.

¹³Some Jews who went around driving out evil spirits tried to invoke the name of the Lord Jesus over those who were demon-possessed. They would say, "In the name of Jesus, whom Paul preaches, I command you to come out." ¹⁴Seven sons of Sceva, a Jewish chief priest, were doing this. ¹⁵One day, the evil spirit answered them, "Jesus I know, and I know about Paul, but who are you?" ¹⁶Then the man who had the evil spirit jumped on them and overpowered them all. He gave them such a beating that they ran out of the house naked and bleeding.

¹⁷When this became known to the Jews and Greeks living in Ephesus, they were all seized with fear, and the name of the Lord Jesus was held in high honor. ¹⁸Many of those who believed now came and openly confessed their evil deeds. ¹⁹A number who had practiced sorcery brought their scrolls together and burned them publicly. When they calculated the value of the scrolls, the total came to fifty thousand drachmas.*d* ²⁰In this way the word of the Lord spread widely and grew in power.

²¹After all this had happened, Paul decided to go to Jerusalem, passing through Macedonia and Achaia. "After I have been there," he said, "I must visit Rome also." ²²He sent two of his helpers, Timothy and Erastus, to Macedonia, while he stayed in the province of Asia a little longer.

a2 Or *after*   *b5* Or *in*   *c6* Or *other languages*   *d19* A drachma was a silver coin worth about a day's wages.

Burning Books and Bridges

A number who had practiced sorcery brought their scrolls together and burned them publicly (Acts 19:19).

Would you build a bonfire using $350,000 worth of kindling?

That's approximately what "fifty thousand drachmas" in Roman times would be worth in today's currency!

The book-burning in Ephesus was expensive, and Luke records how the gospel brought about economic disruption in the idolatrous city of Ephesus. But such changes are often necessary when God is at work, as Albert Barnes explains.

Walk With Albert Barnes

"The Word of God had power in this wicked city, and the power must have been mighty which would make them willing to destroy their property.

"From this instructive passage we may learn that: 1. True religion has the power to break the hold of sinners on unjust and dishonest means of living. 2. Those who have been engaged in an un-Christian and dishonorable practice will abandon it when they become Christians. 3. Their abhorrence of their former course ought to be expressed as publicly as was the offence. 4. The evil practice will be abandoned at any sacrifice, however great. The question is 'what is right?' Not 'what will it cost?'

"If what they did when they were converted was right—and who can doubt it?—it sets forth a great principle on which new converts should act."

Walk Closer to God

Cherished dreams. Ingrained habits. Goals for advancement in a career. Previously unquestioned ethics. Sorcery in its many subtle forms. Each may take on a new appearance when seen in the light of God's Word.

Albert Barnes' remarks provide helpful guidelines to show believers how the Word of God prevails in our daily life to replace un-Christlike conduct with Christian convictions. ⟡

MAY 22

📖 Walk in the Word
Acts 19:23-41

Luke tells of the riot in Ephesus provoked by craftsmen anticipating a decrease in revenue because of Paul's preaching about the one true God.

The Riot in Ephesus

²³About that time there arose a great disturbance about the Way. ²⁴A silversmith named Demetrius, who made silver shrines of Artemis, brought in no little business for the craftsmen. ²⁵He called them together, along with the workmen in related trades, and said: "Men, you know we receive a good income from this business. ²⁶And you see and hear how this fellow Paul has convinced and led astray large numbers of people here in Ephesus and in practically the whole province of Asia. He says that man-made gods are no gods at all. ²⁷There is danger not only that our trade will lose its good name, but also that the temple of the great goddess Artemis will be discredited, and the goddess herself, who is worshiped throughout the province of Asia and the world, will be robbed of her divine majesty."

²⁸When they heard this, they were furious and began shouting: "Great is Artemis of the Ephesians!" ²⁹Soon the whole city was in an uproar. The people seized Gaius and Aristarchus, Paul's traveling companions from Macedonia, and rushed as one man into the theater. ³⁰Paul wanted to appear before the crowd, but the disciples would not let him. ³¹Even some of the officials of the province, friends of Paul, sent him a message begging him not to venture into the theater.

³²The assembly was in confusion: Some were shouting one thing, some another. Most of the people did not even know why they were there. ³³The Jews pushed Alexander to the front, and some of the crowd shouted instructions to him. He motioned for silence in order to make a defense before the people. ³⁴But when they realized he was a Jew, they all shouted in unison for about two hours: "Great is Artemis of the Ephesians!"

³⁵The city clerk quieted the crowd and said: "Men of Ephesus, doesn't all the world know that the city of Ephesus is the guardian of the temple of the great Artemis and of her image, which fell from heaven? ³⁶Therefore, since these facts are undeniable, you ought to be quiet and not do anything rash. ³⁷You have brought these men here, though they have neither robbed temples nor blasphemed our goddess. ³⁸If, then, Demetrius and his fellow craftsmen have a grievance against anybody, the courts are open and there are proconsuls. They can press charges. ³⁹If there is anything further you want to bring up, it must be settled in a legal assembly. ⁴⁰As it is, we are in danger of being charged with rioting because of today's events. In that case we would not be able to account for this commotion, since there is no reason for it." ⁴¹After he had said this, he dismissed the assembly.

We Take Captive Every Thought

"Men, you know we receive a good income from this business. And you see and hear how this fellow Paul has convinced and led astray large numbers of people here in Ephesus and in practically the whole province of Asia. He says that man-made gods are no gods at all" (Acts 19:25–26).

"Christianity is just a crutch."

Has anyone ever summarily dismissed your faith with those words? To such a critic, Christianity is made foolish because the Christian has a vested interest in believing in God. But according to Matthew Henry, Christians are not the only ones bringing vested interests to the claims of Christ.

Walk With Matthew Henry

"It is natural for men to jealously guard, whether right or wrong, the means by which they get their wealth. Many have, for this reason alone, set themselves against the gospel of Christ, because it calls men off from those crafts which are unlawful, however much wealth is to be obtained by them.

"There are those who will haggle for that which is most grossly absurd and unreasonable, and which carries along with it its own conviction of falsehood, if it has but human laws and worldly interests on its side."

Walk Closer to God

Is our critic's criticism legitimate? In a word, no. A "vested interest" critic is wielding a two-edged sword. His decision not to believe is not without its motives. Since he rejects Christ because of his own vested interest, his criticism of us is hypocrisy.

Be prepared to give an answer for the hope that you have. God commands us to "answer a fool according to his folly, or he will be wise in his own eyes" (Proverbs 26:5).

MAY 23

Walk in the Word
Acts 20

The raising of a young man at Troas and Paul's poignant farewell address to the Ephesian elders are spotlighted by Luke.

Through Macedonia and Greece

20 When the uproar had ended, Paul sent for the disciples and, after encouraging them, said good-by and set out for Macedonia. ²He traveled through that area, speaking many words of encouragement to the people, and finally arrived in Greece, ³where he stayed three months. Because the Jews made a plot against him just as he was about to sail for Syria, he decided to go back through Macedonia. ⁴He was accompanied by Sopater son of Pyrrhus from Berea, Aristarchus and Secundus from Thessalonica, Gaius from Derbe, Timothy also, and Tychicus and Trophimus from the province of Asia. ⁵These men went on ahead and waited for us at Troas. ⁶But we sailed from Philippi after the Feast of Unleavened Bread, and five days later joined the others at Troas, where we stayed seven days.

Eutychus Raised From the Dead at Troas

⁷On the first day of the week we came together to break bread. Paul spoke to the people and, because he intended to leave the next day, kept on talking until midnight. ⁸There were many lamps in the upstairs room where we were meeting. ⁹Seated in a window was a young man named Eutychus, who was sinking into a deep sleep as Paul talked on and on. When he was sound asleep, he fell to the ground from the third story and was picked up dead. ¹⁰Paul went down, threw himself on the young man and put his arms around him. "Don't be alarmed," he said. "He's alive!" ¹¹Then he went upstairs again and broke bread and ate. After talking until daylight, he left. ¹²The people took the young man home alive and were greatly comforted.

Paul's Farewell to the Ephesian Elders

¹³We went on ahead to the ship and sailed for Assos, where we were going to take Paul aboard. He had made this arrangement because he was going there on foot. ¹⁴When he met us at Assos, we took him aboard and went on to Mitylene. ¹⁵The next day we set sail from there and arrived off Kios. The day after that we crossed over to Samos, and on the following day arrived at Miletus. ¹⁶Paul had decided to sail past Ephesus to avoid spending time in the province of Asia, for he was in a hurry to reach Jerusalem, if possible, by the day of Pentecost.

¹⁷From Miletus, Paul sent to Ephesus for the elders of the church. ¹⁸When they arrived, he said to them: "You know how I lived the whole time I was with you, from the first day I came into the province of Asia. ¹⁹I served the Lord with great humility and with tears, although I was severely tested by the plots of the Jews. ²⁰You know that I have not hesitated

MAY 23

to preach anything that would be helpful to you but have taught you publicly and from house to house. ²¹I have declared to both Jews and Greeks that they must turn to God in repentance and have faith in our Lord Jesus.

²²"And now, compelled by the Spirit, I am going to Jerusalem, not knowing what will happen to me there. ²³I only know that in every city the Holy Spirit warns me that prison and hardships are facing me. ²⁴However, I consider my life worth nothing to me, if only I may finish the race and complete the task the Lord Jesus has given me—the task of testifying to the gospel of God's grace.

²⁵"Now I know that none of you among whom I have gone about preaching the kingdom will ever see me again. ²⁶Therefore, I declare to you today that I am innocent of the blood of all men. ²⁷For I have not hesitated to proclaim to you the whole will of God. ²⁸Keep watch over yourselves and all the flock of which the Holy Spirit has made you overseers.ᵃ Be shepherds of the church of God,ᵇ which he bought with his own blood. ²⁹I know that after I leave, savage wolves will come in among you and will not spare the flock. ³⁰Even from your own number men will arise and distort the truth in order to draw away disciples after them. ³¹So be on your guard! Remember that for three years I never stopped warning each of you night and day with tears.

³²"Now I commit you to God and to the word of his grace, which can build you up and give you an inheritance among all those who are sanctified. ³³I have not coveted anyone's silver or gold or clothing. ³⁴You yourselves know that these hands of mine have supplied my own needs and the needs of my companions. ³⁵In everything I did, I showed you that by this kind of hard work we must help the weak, remembering the words the Lord Jesus himself said: 'It is more blessed to give than to receive.' "

³⁶When he had said this, he knelt down with all of them and prayed. ³⁷They all wept as they embraced him and kissed him. ³⁸What grieved them most was his statement that they would never see his face again. Then they accompanied him to the ship.

ᵃ28 Traditionally *bishops*   ᵇ28 Many manuscripts *of the Lord*

MAY 23

Functioning in a Sphere of Divine Design

"I consider my life worth nothing to me, if only I may finish the race and complete the task the Lord Jesus has given me—the task of testifying to the gospel of God's grace" (Acts 20:24).

What things can you think of that just might be worth dying for? Your family. Perhaps a few close friends. Your country.

What about a group of people you've never met?

In effect, that's what Paul told the Ephesian elders. He was prepared to die in order to take the gospel to those who hadn't heard.

What's more, he didn't call such sacrifice a burden, but a joy. Let Oswald Chambers probe the basis of Paul's unusual joy.

Walk With Oswald Chambers

"Joy means the perfect fulfillment of that for which I was created and saved.

"The joy of our Lord came in doing what the Father sent him to do. And now he says: 'As the Father has sent me, I am sending you.'

"Have I received a ministry from the Lord?

"If so, I have to be loyal to it, to count my life precious only for the fulfilling of that ministry.

"Think of the satisfaction it will be to hear Jesus say, 'Well done, good and faithful servant'; to know that you have done what he sent you to do.

"We all have to find our niche in life, and spiritually we find it when we receive our ministry from the Lord.

"In order to do this we must be in close fellowship with Jesus; we must know him as personal Savior—and more."

Walk Closer to God

Like a ship out of water or a train off the tracks, you'll find that you don't function well outside the sphere of God's will for your life.

That is by design—his design! A design that promises joy as the by-product of walking in his will.

Joy in serving Jesus.

There's no better way to know you have done what he sent you to do! ◖

Walk in the Word
Acts 21:1–36

Luke paints a portrait of a determined Paul, who heads for Jerusalem, where he reports to the elders and later is taken into custody by Roman troops to protect him from a rioting mob.

On to Jerusalem

21 After we had torn ourselves away from them, we put out to sea and sailed straight to Cos. The next day we went to Rhodes and from there to Patara. ²We found a ship crossing over to Phoenicia, went on board and set sail. ³After sighting Cyprus and passing to the south of it, we sailed on to Syria. We landed at Tyre, where our ship was to unload its cargo. ⁴Finding the disciples there, we stayed with them seven days. Through the Spirit they urged Paul not to go on to Jerusalem. ⁵But when our time was up, we left and continued on our way. All the disciples and their wives and children accompanied us out of the city, and there on the beach we knelt to pray. ⁶After saying good-by to each other, we went aboard the ship, and they returned home.

⁷We continued our voyage from Tyre and landed at Ptolemais, where we greeted the brothers and stayed with them for a day. ⁸Leaving the next day, we reached Caesarea and stayed at the house of Philip the evangelist, one of the Seven. ⁹He had four unmarried daughters who prophesied.

¹⁰After we had been there a number of days, a prophet named Agabus came down from Judea. ¹¹Coming over to us, he took Paul's belt, tied his own hands and feet with it and said, "The Holy Spirit says, 'In this way the Jews of Jerusalem will bind the owner of this belt and will hand him over to the Gentiles.' "

¹²When we heard this, we and the people there pleaded with Paul not to go up to Jerusalem. ¹³Then Paul answered, "Why are you weeping and breaking my heart? I am ready not only to be bound, but also to die in Jerusalem for the name of the Lord Jesus." ¹⁴When he would not be dissuaded, we gave up and said, "The Lord's will be done."

¹⁵After this, we got ready and went up to Jerusalem. ¹⁶Some of the disciples from Caesarea accompanied us and brought us to the home of Mnason, where we were to stay. He was a man from Cyprus and one of the early disciples.

Paul's Arrival at Jerusalem

¹⁷When we arrived at Jerusalem, the brothers received us warmly. ¹⁸The next day Paul and the rest of us went to see James, and all the elders were present. ¹⁹Paul greeted them and reported in detail what God had done among the Gentiles through his ministry.

²⁰When they heard this, they praised God. Then they said to Paul: "You see, brother, how many thousands of Jews have believed, and all of them are zealous for the law. ²¹They have been informed that you teach all the Jews who live among the Gentiles to turn away from Moses, telling them

May 24

not to circumcise their children or live according to our customs. ²²What shall we do? They will certainly hear that you have come, ²³so do what we tell you. There are four men with us who have made a vow. ²⁴Take these men, join in their purification rites and pay their expenses, so that they can have their heads shaved. Then everybody will know there is no truth in these reports about you, but that you yourself are living in obedience to the law. ²⁵As for the Gentile believers, we have written to them our decision that they should abstain from food sacrificed to idols, from blood, from the meat of strangled animals and from sexual immorality."

²⁶The next day Paul took the men and purified himself along with them. Then he went to the temple to give notice of the date when the days of purification would end and the offering would be made for each of them.

Paul Arrested

²⁷When the seven days were nearly over, some Jews from the province of Asia saw Paul at the temple. They stirred up the whole crowd and seized him, ²⁸shouting, "Men of Israel, help us! This is the man who teaches all men everywhere against our people and our law and this place. And besides, he has brought Greeks into the temple area and defiled this holy place." ²⁹(They had previously seen Trophimus the Ephesian in the city with Paul and assumed that Paul had brought him into the temple area.)

³⁰The whole city was aroused, and the people came running from all directions. Seizing Paul, they dragged him from the temple, and immediately the gates were shut. ³¹While they were trying to kill him, news reached the commander of the Roman troops that the whole city of Jerusalem was in an uproar. ³²He at once took some officers and soldiers and ran down to the crowd. When the rioters saw the commander and his soldiers, they stopped beating Paul.

³³The commander came up and arrested him and ordered him to be bound with two chains. Then he asked who he was and what he had done. ³⁴Some in the crowd shouted one thing and some another, and since the commander could not get at the truth because of the uproar, he ordered that Paul be taken into the barracks. ³⁵When Paul reached the steps, the violence of the mob was so great he had to be carried by the soldiers. ³⁶The crowd that followed kept shouting, "Away with him!"

MAY 24

The Privilege of Paying a Debt

"I am ready not only to be bound, but also to die in Jerusalem for the name of the Lord Jesus" (Acts 21:13).

In spite of rumors to the contrary, missionaries are only human. They aren't ten-feet tall physically . . . or spiritually.

Like other Christians, they struggle with illness, attitudes and rebellious children. And their "job description" is basically the same as that of every other Christian: to proclaim the gospel.

David Livingstone describes the attitude that is essential for successful service for the Lord—whether at home or abroad.

Walk With David Livingstone

"People talk of the sacrifice I have made in spending so much of my life in Africa.

"Can that be called a sacrifice which is simply acknowledging a great debt we owe to our God, which we can never repay?

"Is that a sacrifice which brings its own reward in healthful activity, the consciousness of doing good, peace of mind, and a bright hope of a glorious destiny? It is emphatically no sacrifice. Rather it is a privilege.

"Anxiety, sickness, suffering, danger, foregoing the common conveniences of life—these may make us pause, and cause the spirit to waver, and the soul to sink; but let this only be for a moment.

"All these are nothing compared with the glory which shall later be revealed in and through us.

"I never made a sacrifice. Of this we ought not to talk, when we remember the great sacrifice which he made who left his Father's throne on high to give himself for us."

Walk Closer to God

Christ gave his life gladly, not considering it too great a sacrifice to die for sinners.

Why then should it be too great a sacrifice to invest your life in spreading his love today?

You don't have to cross an ocean to do that. Your mission field may be as near as your neighbor.

A neighbor who needs to hear the news that God has only one Son. A Son he sent as a missionary to all the world.

MAY 25

📖 Walk in the Word
Acts 21:37 — 22:29

Luke records Paul's personal testimony, spoken to a hostile crowd who erupted in disapproval; Paul averts a beating by disclosing his Roman citizenship.

Paul Speaks to the Crowd

³⁷As the soldiers were about to take Paul into the barracks, he asked the commander, "May I say something to you?"

"Do you speak Greek?" he replied. ³⁸"Aren't you the Egyptian who started a revolt and led four thousand terrorists out into the desert some time ago?"

³⁹Paul answered, "I am a Jew, from Tarsus in Cilicia, a citizen of no ordinary city. Please let me speak to the people."

⁴⁰Having received the commander's permission, Paul stood on the steps and motioned to the crowd. When they were all silent, he said to them
22 in Aramaicᵃ: ¹"Brothers and fathers, listen now to my defense." ²When they heard him speak to them in Aramaic, they became very quiet.

Then Paul said: ³"I am a Jew, born in Tarsus of Cilicia, but brought up in this city. Under Gamaliel I was thoroughly trained in the law of our fathers and was just as zealous for God as any of you are today. ⁴I persecuted the followers of this Way to their death, arresting both men and women and throwing them into prison, ⁵as also the high priest and all the Council can testify. I even obtained letters from them to their brothers in Damascus, and went there to bring these people as prisoners to Jerusalem to be punished.

⁶"About noon as I came near Damascus, suddenly a bright light from heaven flashed around me. ⁷I fell to the ground and heard a voice say to me, 'Saul! Saul! Why do you persecute me?'

⁸ 'Who are you, Lord?' I asked.

" 'I am Jesus of Nazareth, whom you are persecuting,' he replied. ⁹My companions saw the light, but they did not understand the voice of him who was speaking to me.

¹⁰" 'What shall I do, Lord?' I asked.

" 'Get up,' the Lord said, 'and go into Damascus. There you will be told all that you have been assigned to do.' ¹¹My companions led me by the hand into Damascus, because the brilliance of the light had blinded me.

¹²"A man named Ananias came to see me. He was a devout observer of the law and highly respected by all the Jews living there. ¹³He stood beside me and said, 'Brother Saul, receive your sight!' And at that very moment I was able to see him.

¹⁴"Then he said: 'The God of our fathers has chosen you to know his will and to see the Righteous One and to hear words from his mouth. ¹⁵You will be his witness to all men of what you have seen and heard. ¹⁶And now what are you waiting for? Get up, be baptized and wash your sins away, calling on his name.'

¹⁷"When I returned to Jerusalem and was praying at the temple, I fell into a trance ¹⁸and saw the Lord speaking. 'Quick!' he said to me. 'Leave Jerusalem immediately, because they will not accept your testimony about me.'

¹⁹" 'Lord,' I replied, 'these men know that I went from one synagogue to another to imprison and beat those who believe in you. ²⁰And when the blood of your martyr[b] Stephen was shed, I stood there giving my approval and guarding the clothes of those who were killing him.'

²¹"Then the Lord said to me, 'Go; I will send you far away to the Gentiles.' "

Paul the Roman Citizen

²²The crowd listened to Paul until he said this. Then they raised their voices and shouted, "Rid the earth of him! He's not fit to live!"

²³As they were shouting and throwing off their cloaks and flinging dust into the air, ²⁴the commander ordered Paul to be taken into the barracks. He directed that he be flogged and questioned in order to find out why the people were shouting at him like this. ²⁵As they stretched him out to flog him, Paul said to the centurion standing there, "Is it legal for you to flog a Roman citizen who hasn't even been found guilty?"

²⁶When the centurion heard this, he went to the commander and reported it. "What are you going to do?" he asked. "This man is a Roman citizen."

²⁷The commander went to Paul and asked, "Tell me, are you a Roman citizen?"

"Yes, I am," he answered.

²⁸Then the commander said, "I had to pay a big price for my citizenship."

"But I was born a citizen," Paul replied.

²⁹Those who were about to question him withdrew immediately. The commander himself was alarmed when he realized that he had put Paul, a Roman citizen, in chains.

ᵃ40 Or possibly *Hebrew*; also in 22:2   ᵇ20 Or *witness*

MAY 25

Willingly Led by the Savior's Hand

"What shall I do Lord?" I asked. "Get up," the Lord said, "and go into Damascus. There you will be told" (Acts 22:10).

On the road to Damascus, Paul was the zealous leader of a "hunting party."

His prey: followers of Christ.

His license: letters from the high priest.

His intent: death and imprisonment of believers—the destruction of the church.

But before he reached his objective, Paul had joined forces with those he had sought to destroy.

Andrew Murray analyzes how Paul the persecutor became Paul the proclaimer of the gospel.

Walk With Andrew Murray

"Many have asked what could be the secret of the amazing devotion and power in the life of Paul. The above verse suggests one answer.

"At the time of his conversion, as soon as he knew who it was that called him, he surrendered himself to the will of the Lord. 'What shall I do, Lord?'

"His life was so wonderfully fruitful because he remained true to those words.

"The Lord has a will for each of us, a plan by which he wants us to live. He wants to make his will known to each one.

"He wants us to ask him to reveal his will.

"Such a request sincerely made implies willingness to give oneself to his will and service.

"We may be sure he will answer such prayer. He will lead the child who wants to be led."

Walk Closer to God

The Damascus road was more than the place of Paul's conversion. It also marked the place where his will was conquered.

His life was no longer his own; he now lived to serve the one who had saved him.

And what was the result? Near the end of his life Paul could say triumphantly, "There is . . . the crown of righteousness, which the Lord . . . will award to me" (2 Timothy 4:8). God had led him well.

He will do the same in your life when you ask, "What shall I do, Lord?"

MAY 26

Walk in the Word
Acts 22:30—23:35

Paul boldly denounces the Sanhedrin; his opponents vow to kill him, which in turn provokes the Roman commander to order Paul's transfer to Governor Felix in Caesarea.

Before the Sanhedrin

³⁰The next day, since the commander wanted to find out exactly why Paul was being accused by the Jews, he released him and ordered the chief priests and all the Sanhedrin to assemble. Then he brought Paul and had him stand before them.

23 Paul looked straight at the Sanhedrin and said, "My brothers, I have fulfilled my duty to God in all good conscience to this day." ²At this the high priest Ananias ordered those standing near Paul to strike him on the mouth. ³Then Paul said to him, "God will strike you, you whitewashed wall! You sit there to judge me according to the law, yet you yourself violate the law by commanding that I be struck!"

⁴Those who were standing near Paul said, "You dare to insult God's high priest?"

⁵Paul replied, "Brothers, I did not realize that he was the high priest; for it is written: 'Do not speak evil about the ruler of your people.'ᵃ"

⁶Then Paul, knowing that some of them were Sadducees and the others Pharisees, called out in the Sanhedrin, "My brothers, I am a Pharisee, the son of a Pharisee. I stand on trial because of my hope in the resurrection of the dead." ⁷When he said this, a dispute broke out between the Pharisees and the Sadducees, and the assembly was divided. ⁸(The Sadducees say that there is no resurrection, and that there are neither angels nor spirits, but the Pharisees acknowledge them all.)

⁹There was a great uproar, and some of the teachers of the law who were Pharisees stood up and argued vigorously. "We find nothing wrong with this man," they said. "What if a spirit or an angel has spoken to him?" ¹⁰The dispute became so violent that the commander was afraid Paul would be torn to pieces by them. He ordered the troops to go down and take him away from them by force and bring him into the barracks.

¹¹The following night the Lord stood near Paul and said, "Take courage! As you have testified about me in Jerusalem, so you must also testify in Rome."

The Plot to Kill Paul

¹²The next morning the Jews formed a conspiracy and bound themselves with an oath not to eat or drink until they had killed Paul. ¹³More than forty men were involved in this plot. ¹⁴They went to the chief priests and elders and said, "We have taken a solemn oath not to eat anything until we have killed Paul. ¹⁵Now then, you and the Sanhedrin petition the commander to bring him before you on the pretext of wanting more accurate information about his case. We are ready to kill him before he gets here."

MAY 26

16But when the son of Paul's sister heard of this plot, he went into the barracks and told Paul.

17Then Paul called one of the centurions and said, "Take this young man to the commander; he has something to tell him." 18So he took him to the commander.

The centurion said, "Paul, the prisoner, sent for me and asked me to bring this young man to you because he has something to tell you."

19The commander took the young man by the hand, drew him aside and asked, "What is it you want to tell me?"

20He said: "The Jews have agreed to ask you to bring Paul before the Sanhedrin tomorrow on the pretext of wanting more accurate information about him. 21Don't give in to them, because more than forty of them are waiting in ambush for him. They have taken an oath not to eat or drink until they have killed him. They are ready now, waiting for your consent to their request."

22The commander dismissed the young man and cautioned him, "Don't tell anyone that you have reported this to me."

Paul Transferred to Caesarea

23Then he called two of his centurions and ordered them, "Get ready a detachment of two hundred soldiers, seventy horsemen and two hundred spearmenᵇ to go to Caesarea at nine tonight. 24Provide mounts for Paul so that he may be taken safely to Governor Felix."

25He wrote a letter as follows:

26Claudius Lysias,

To His Excellency, Governor Felix:

Greetings.

27This man was seized by the Jews and they were about to kill him, but I came with my troops and rescued him, for I had learned that he is a Roman citizen. 28I wanted to know why they were accusing him, so I brought him to their Sanhedrin. 29I found that the accusation had to do with questions about their law, but there was no charge against him that deserved death or imprisonment. 30When I was informed of a plot to be carried out against the man, I sent him to you at once. I also ordered his accusers to present to you their case against him.

31So the soldiers, carrying out their orders, took Paul with them during the night and brought him as far as Antipatris. 32The next day they let the cavalry go on with him, while they returned to the barracks. 33When the cavalry arrived in Caesarea, they delivered the letter to the governor and handed Paul over to him. 34The governor read the letter and asked what

province he was from. Learning that he was from Cilicia, ³⁵he said, "I will hear your case when your accusers get here." Then he ordered that Paul be kept under guard in Herod's palace.

^a5 Exodus 22:28   ^b23 The meaning of the Greek for this word is uncertain.

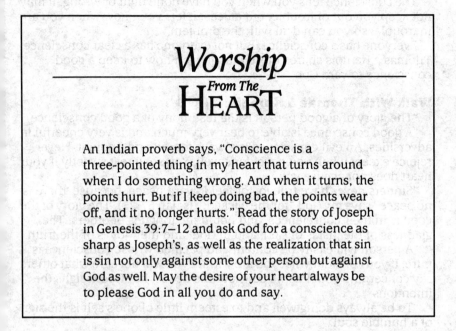

Worship From The HEART

An Indian proverb says, "Conscience is a three-pointed thing in my heart that turns around when I do something wrong. And when it turns, the points hurt. But if I keep doing bad, the points wear off, and it no longer hurts." Read the story of Joseph in Genesis 39:7–12 and ask God for a conscience as sharp as Joseph's, as well as the realization that sin is sin not only against some other person but against God as well. May the desire of your heart always be to please God in all you do and say.

MAY 26

A Conscience Touched by God

Paul . . . said, "My brothers, I have fulfilled my duty to God in all good conscience to this day" (Acts 23:1).

The conscience tells you when you have done right or wrong. It may not keep you out of trouble, but at least it lets you know when you are in trouble, so you can deal with the problem.

Everyone has a conscience. But not everyone has a clear conscience. Thomas à Kempis shares these thoughts on how to keep a good conscience toward God.

Walk With Thomas à Kempis

"The glory of a good person is the testimony of a good conscience.

"A good conscience is able to bear very much and is very cheerful in adversities. An evil conscience is always fearful and unquiet. Never rejoice except when you have done well. You shall rest sweetly if your heart does not accuse you.

"Sinners never have true joy or feel inward peace, because 'there is no peace,' says my God, 'for the wicked,' (Isaiah 57:21). The glory of the good is in their consciences, and not in the tongues of others. The gladness of the just is of God, and in God; and their joy is of the truth.

"A person will easily be content and pacified whose conscience is pure. If you consider what you are within, you will not care what others say concerning you. People consider the deeds, but God weighs the intentions.

"To be always doing well and to esteem little of one's self is the sign of a humble soul.

" 'For it is not the one who commends himself who is approved, but the one whom the Lord commends,' says Paul (2 Corinthians 10:18). To walk inwardly with God, and not to be kept abroad by any outward affection, is the state of a spiritual person."

Walk Closer to God

All it takes to maintain a bad conscience is to do nothing. Ignore the tugging of the Spirit and the still, small voice of God. By contrast, a good conscience is a Christ-cleansed conscience. And that is only a heartfelt prayer away!

MAY 27

Walk in the Word
Acts 24

Luke skillfully captures the hypocrisy of those bringing charges against Paul and the integrity of Paul's defense before Felix.

The Trial Before Felix

24 Five days later the high priest Ananias went down to Caesarea with some of the elders and a lawyer named Tertullus, and they brought their charges against Paul before the governor. ²When Paul was called in, Tertullus presented his case before Felix: "We have enjoyed a long period of peace under you, and your foresight has brought about reforms in this nation. ³Everywhere and in every way, most excellent Felix, we acknowledge this with profound gratitude. ⁴But in order not to weary you further, I would request that you be kind enough to hear us briefly.

⁵"We have found this man to be a troublemaker, stirring up riots among the Jews all over the world. He is a ringleader of the Nazarene sect ⁶and even tried to desecrate the temple; so we seized him. ⁸By*ᵃ* examining him yourself you will be able to learn the truth about all these charges we are bringing against him."

⁹The Jews joined in the accusation, asserting that these things were true.

¹⁰When the governor motioned for him to speak, Paul replied: "I know that for a number of years you have been a judge over this nation; so I gladly make my defense. ¹¹You can easily verify that no more than twelve days ago I went up to Jerusalem to worship. ¹²My accusers did not find me arguing with anyone at the temple, or stirring up a crowd in the synagogues or anywhere else in the city. ¹³And they cannot prove to you the charges they are now making against me. ¹⁴However, I admit that I worship the God of our fathers as a follower of the Way, which they call a sect. I believe everything that agrees with the Law and that is written in the Prophets, ¹⁵and I have the same hope in God as these men, that there will be a resurrection of both the righteous and the wicked. ¹⁶So I strive always to keep my conscience clear before God and man.

¹⁷"After an absence of several years, I came to Jerusalem to bring my people gifts for the poor and to present offerings. ¹⁸I was ceremonially clean when they found me in the temple courts doing this. There was no crowd with me, nor was I involved in any disturbance. ¹⁹But there are some Jews from the province of Asia, who ought to be here before you and bring charges if they have anything against me. ²⁰Or these who are here should state what crime they found in me when I stood before the Sanhedrin— ²¹unless it was this one thing I shouted as I stood in their presence: 'It is concerning the resurrection of the dead that I am on trial before you today.'"

²²Then Felix, who was well acquainted with the Way, adjourned the proceedings. "When Lysias the commander comes," he said, "I will decide your case." ²³He ordered the centurion to keep Paul under guard but to give him some freedom and permit his friends to take care of his needs.

²⁴Several days later Felix came with his wife Drusilla, who was a Jewess.

MAY 27

He sent for Paul and listened to him as he spoke about faith in Christ Jesus. [25]As Paul discoursed on righteousness, self-control and the judgment to come, Felix was afraid and said, "That's enough for now! You may leave. When I find it convenient, I will send for you." [26]At the same time he was hoping that Paul would offer him a bribe, so he sent for him frequently and talked with him.

[27]When two years had passed, Felix was succeeded by Porcius Festus, but because Felix wanted to grant a favor to the Jews, he left Paul in prison.

[a]6-8 Some manuscripts *him and wanted to judge him according to our law.* [7]*But the commander, Lysias, came and with the use of much force snatched him from our hands* [8]*and ordered his accusers to come before you. By*

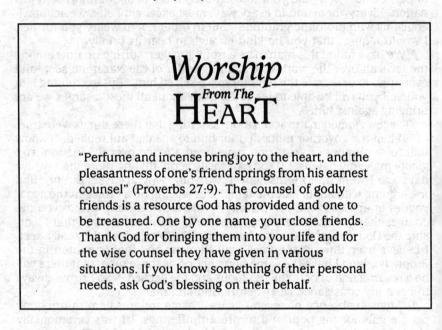

Worship From The HEART

"Perfume and incense bring joy to the heart, and the pleasantness of one's friend springs from his earnest counsel" (Proverbs 27:9). The counsel of godly friends is a resource God has provided and one to be treasured. One by one name your close friends. Thank God for bringing them into your life and for the wise counsel they have given in various situations. If you know something of their personal needs, ask God's blessing on their behalf.

God's Law: A Diagnostic Tool

Therefore no one will be declared righteous in his sight by observing the law; rather, through the law we become conscious of sin (Romans 3:20).

A patient with hypertension who dutifully checks his blood pressure morning and evening might still die of a stroke. For simply taking his blood pressure would not solve the problem; it would only reveal a situation in need of treatment.

The Jews made a similar mistake in thinking that the law was the means of their salvation, when in fact it was designed by God to show their need for salvation.

Martin Luther clarifies the issue.

Walk With Martin Luther

"The first understanding of the law should be that we see the inability of human nature to keep it.

"You may do good works outwardly; but God is not satisfied unless they are performed from the heart and out of love, which is not possible unless a man is born anew through the Holy Spirit.

"God, then, wants to achieve no more with the law than getting us to recognize our inability, our frailty, our sickness—to recognize that, so far as we are concerned, we cannot keep one letter of the law. When you feel that, the law has done its work.

"This is what Paul means when he says to the Romans: 'Through the law we become conscious of sin.' "

Walk Closer to God

A wall may appear straight—until you hold a plumb line against it. A garment may look white—until you lay it next to a whiter one. In each case, you need a standard against which all other objects can be compared.

In the realm of righteousness, the standard is God's law. It is there you discover how far you have drifted from God's holiness, how soiled you are with sin. It is there you see an accurate diagnosis of your problem.

It is there you come to realize that you are powerless to save yourself.

Are you ready to acknowledge your predicament? Then you are also ready to receive God's provision. ◖

JUNE 6

📖 Walk in the Word
Romans 3:21–31

Paul begins to reveal the divine answer to humanity's sin and unrighteousness — the canceling of guilt and the crediting of righteousness to those who believe in Christ as Savior.

Righteousness Through Faith

21But now a righteousness from God, apart from law, has been made known, to which the Law and the Prophets testify. 22This righteousness from God comes through faith in Jesus Christ to all who believe. There is no difference, 23for all have sinned and fall short of the glory of God, 24and are justified freely by his grace through the redemption that came by Christ Jesus. 25God presented him as a sacrifice of atonement,*a* through faith in his blood. He did this to demonstrate his justice, because in his forbearance he had left the sins committed beforehand unpunished — 26he did it to demonstrate his justice at the present time, so as to be just and the one who justifies those who have faith in Jesus.

27Where, then, is boasting? It is excluded. On what principle? On that of observing the law? No, but on that of faith. 28For we maintain that a man is justified by faith apart from observing the law. 29Is God the God of Jews only? Is he not the God of Gentiles too? Yes, of Gentiles too, 30since there is only one God, who will justify the circumcised by faith and the uncircumcised through that same faith. 31Do we, then, nullify the law by this faith? Not at all! Rather, we uphold the law.

a25 Or as the one who would turn aside his wrath, taking away sin

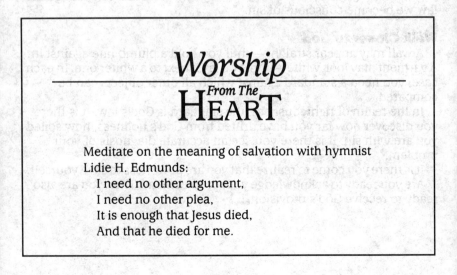

Worship
From The HEART

Meditate on the meaning of salvation with hymnist
Lidie H. Edmunds:
    I need no other argument,
    I need no other plea,
    It is enough that Jesus died,
    And that he died for me.

No Hope—Except in Christ

He did it to demonstrate his justice at the present time, so as to be just and the one who justifies those who have faith in Jesus (Romans 3:26).

The gospel is so simple that little children can understand it. And yet it is so complex that the Bible uses a word like justification to describe one of its many facets.

Boil it all down and you can simplify the complex into just two words: Jesus Christ. In him all the big words come together to explain the significance of your salvation. Take justification, for example. Charles Spurgeon provides this analysis of its meaning and importance.

Walk With Charles Spurgeon

"If God is just, then I a sinner—alone and without a substitute—must be punished.

"But Jesus stands in my place and is punished for me. So now, if God is just, then I a sinner—standing in Christ—can never be punished. Jesus has taken the place of the believer and received the full penalty of divine wrath.

"My hope lives not because I am sinless, but because I am a sinner for whom Christ died. My trust is not that I am holy, but that, since I am unholy, he is my righteousness.

"My faith rests not upon what I am, or shall be, or feel, or know, but in what Christ is, in what he has done, and in what he is now doing for me."

Walk Closer to God

If you died and awoke at the gates of heaven, and there God confronted you with the question, "Why should I allow you into my heaven?"—what would you say?

"I did my best" . . . "I'm better than most" . . . "I was sincere in my beliefs"?

All have sinned. God is just in punishing those who have broken his law. And either Jesus Christ becomes your substitute . . . or you feel the force of God's wrath yourself.

"Justified freely by his grace" through Christ Jesus. With that as your passport, you need never fear the reception you'll get in heaven! ◖

JUNE 7

📖 Walk in the Word
Romans 4:1–12

Abraham serves as a glorious example of righteousness by faith, not by works, as Paul defends the way of faith as the way to acceptance by God.

Abraham Justified by Faith

4 What then shall we say that Abraham, our forefather, discovered in this matter? [2]If, in fact, Abraham was justified by works, he had something to boast about—but not before God. [3]What does the Scripture say? "Abraham believed God, and it was credited to him as righteousness."[a]

[4]Now when a man works, his wages are not credited to him as a gift, but as an obligation. [5]However, to the man who does not work but trusts God who justifies the wicked, his faith is credited as righteousness. [6]David says the same thing when he speaks of the blessedness of the man to whom God credits righteousness apart from works:

> [7]"Blessed are they
>   whose transgressions are forgiven,
>   whose sins are covered.
> [8]Blessed is the man
>   whose sin the Lord will never count against him."[b]

[9]Is this blessedness only for the circumcised, or also for the uncircumcised? We have been saying that Abraham's faith was credited to him as righteousness. [10]Under what circumstances was it credited? Was it after he was circumcised, or before? It was not after, but before! [11]And he received the sign of circumcision, a seal of the righteousness that he had by faith while he was still uncircumcised. So then, he is the father of all who believe but have not been circumcised, in order that righteousness might be credited to them. [12]And he is also the father of the circumcised who not only are circumcised but who also walk in the footsteps of the faith that our father Abraham had before he was circumcised.

[a]3 Gen. 15:6; also in verse 22   [b]8 Psalm 32:1,2

The Overflow of God's Love

David says the same thing when he speaks of the blessedness of the man to whom God credits righteousness apart from works: "Blessed are they whose transgressions are forgiven" (Romans 4:6–7).

Imagine you owe a vast sum of money . . . but then the debt is totally forgiven. How do you react?

Imagine you face a death-row execution . . . but then you receive a full pardon. How do you feel?

Joyful. Happy. Relieved beyond measure. A future previously fearful now brims with expectancy.

Getting right with God is cause for unspeakable joy—a joy that David extols in Psalm 32 when he writes of forgiveness.

C.S. Lewis, who wrote often of his own joyful conversion, provides this analysis of the gift that seems too good to be true.

Walk With C.S. Lewis

"The man who has experienced conversion feels like one who has awakened from nightmare into ecstasy.

"He feels that he has done nothing, and never could have done anything, to deserve such astonishing happiness.

"All the initiative has been on God's side; all has been free, unbounded grace.

"His own puny efforts would be as helpless to retain the joy as they would have been to attain it in the first place. Fortunately, they need not. Bliss is not for sale; it cannot be earned.

"Works have no merit, though of course faith inevitably flows out into works of love. He is not saved because he does works of love; he does works of love because he is saved.

"It is faith alone that has saved him: faith bestowed as the sheer gift of God."

Walk Closer to God

Joy—the by-product of God's inexpressible gift.

Joy—the overflow of God's inexhaustible love.

Have you experienced God's grace at work in your life? If so, no one needs to tell you that "the God of hope [can] fill you with all joy" (Romans 15:13).

JUNE 8

📖 Walk in the Word
Romans 4:13–25

Paul continues to spotlight Abraham's faith in God's promises, illustrating God's marvelous provision of grace for the undeserving as his way of dealing with humanity.

---

¹³It was not through law that Abraham and his offspring received the promise that he would be heir of the world, but through the righteousness that comes by faith. ¹⁴For if those who live by law are heirs, faith has no value and the promise is worthless, ¹⁵because law brings wrath. And where there is no law there is no transgression.

¹⁶Therefore, the promise comes by faith, so that it may be by grace and may be guaranteed to all Abraham's offspring — not only to those who are of the law but also to those who are of the faith of Abraham. He is the father of us all. ¹⁷As it is written: "I have made you a father of many nations."ᵃ He is our father in the sight of God, in whom he believed — the God who gives life to the dead and calls things that are not as though they were.

¹⁸Against all hope, Abraham in hope believed and so became the father of many nations, just as it had been said to him, "So shall your offspring be."ᵇ ¹⁹Without weakening in his faith, he faced the fact that his body was as good as dead — since he was about a hundred years old — and that Sarah's womb was also dead. ²⁰Yet he did not waver through unbelief regarding the promise of God, but was strengthened in his faith and gave glory to God, ²¹being fully persuaded that God had power to do what he had promised. ²²This is why "it was credited to him as righteousness." ²³The words "it was credited to him" were written not for him alone, ²⁴but also for us, to whom God will credit righteousness — for us who believe in him who raised Jesus our Lord from the dead. ²⁵He was delivered over to death for our sins and was raised to life for our justification.

ᵃ17 Gen. 17:5   ᵇ18 Gen. 15:5

A Passing Grade in the School of Righteousness

For if those who live by law are heirs, faith has no value and the promise is worthless, because law brings wrath (Romans 4:14–15).

According to some views, God will grade "on the curve," looking at your life in comparison with others. If the good outweighs the bad, you pass the test of life and get into heaven. However, a passing grade in God's school of righteousness has always been 100 percent. Anything less, and you fail.

Donald Barnhouse provides this insightful look at the folly of trying to "make the grade" on the basis of good works rather than on God's work.

Walk With Donald Barnhouse

"We can see where an argument about salvation by works would lead us.

"Suppose a man has made certain sacrifices in his giving to worthy causes. Has he made sacrifices enough? Is there a percentage that may be established?

"If that is so, what about a poor man and a rich man? A poor man may have five children and fifty dollars a week. Is he supposed to give five dollars a week to good Christian causes? And if another man has a thousand dollars a week and only a wife and one child, can he get by with God by giving a hundred dollars a week?

"The absurdities of the comparisons become evident the further we push them to logical conclusions."

Walk Closer to God

You may be smarter than most, more generous than many, more honest than some. But when the comparison is made between sinful man and holy God, your best efforts resemble "filthy rags" (Isaiah 64:6).

God knew that. So he sent his Son to pass the test for you. By placing your confidence in him, his grade becomes yours.

And when the choice is between a perfect score or failure, with eternal consequences, wouldn't you prefer having Christ's grade to your own? ◯

JUNE 9

📖 Walk in the Word
Romans 5:1–11

Paul explores the implications of acceptance by God, accenting the new relationship believers enjoy with God — a relationship that gives peace and joy and hope.

Peace and Joy

5 Therefore, since we have been justified through faith, we[a] have peace with God through our Lord Jesus Christ, ²through whom we have gained access by faith into this grace in which we now stand. And we[a] rejoice in the hope of the glory of God. ³Not only so, but we[a] also rejoice in our sufferings, because we know that suffering produces perseverance; ⁴perseverance, character; and character, hope. ⁵And hope does not disappoint us, because God has poured out his love into our hearts by the Holy Spirit, whom he has given us.

⁶You see, at just the right time, when we were still powerless, Christ died for the ungodly. ⁷Very rarely will anyone die for a righteous man, though for a good man someone might possibly dare to die. ⁸But God demonstrates his own love for us in this: While we were still sinners, Christ died for us.

⁹Since we have now been justified by his blood, how much more shall we be saved from God's wrath through him! ¹⁰For if, when we were God's enemies, we were reconciled to him through the death of his Son, how much more, having been reconciled, shall we be saved through his life! ¹¹Not only is this so, but we also rejoice in God through our Lord Jesus Christ, through whom we have now received reconciliation.

a1,2,3 Or *let us*

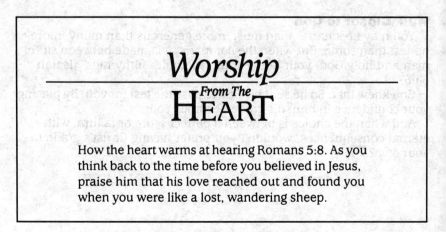

Worship
From The
HEART

How the heart warms at hearing Romans 5:8. As you think back to the time before you believed in Jesus, praise him that his love reached out and found you when you were like a lost, wandering sheep.

Precious Products of Tribulation

We also rejoice in our sufferings, because we know that suffering produces perseverance; perseverance, character; and character, hope (Romans 5:3–4).

The Christian life is not a parade but a battle in which the opposition is intense and the enemy tenacious. But you can neither be defeated nor disheartened . . . as long as you remember the one with whom you are at war and the one with whom you are at peace!

Abraham Kuyper probes the power and purpose behind victorious spiritual warfare.

Walk With Abraham Kuyper

"When we are attacked, when our opponent takes hold and attempts to throw us, only then does our strength appear.

"Each fierce attack inspires more determined resistance, and we put forth all our strength to remain standing. And thus endurance is born.

"Tribulation and struggle call forth strength to endure; endurance produces the confidence of proven character; and with that new confidence, hope waxes stronger—the hope of never being overcome by an assailant, the hope of winning the crown.

"Thus the child of God, struggling against the forces of evil in and around him, discovers within himself a God-given strength which enables him to endure all assault triumphantly."

Walk Closer to God

When called upon to stand, the believer knows where his strength lies.

Paul explains it this way: "I can do everything through him who gives me strength" (Philippians 4:13).

Each "round" with the enemy, each conflict successfully met in the strength of the Lord, only serves to make you stronger for the next.

More patient. More experienced.

More enduring. More hopeful.

More like Christ.

There is no more glorious way to live in this world than to "rejoice in our sufferings."

JUNE 10

📖 Walk in the Word
Romans 5:12–21

By the striking contrast between Adam and Christ, Paul demonstrates humanity's dire situation of sin and guilt through Adam and divinity's great provision of the way out through Christ.

Death Through Adam, Life Through Christ

¹²Therefore, just as sin entered the world through one man, and death through sin, and in this way death came to all men, because all sinned—¹³for before the law was given, sin was in the world. But sin is not taken into account when there is no law. ¹⁴Nevertheless, death reigned from the time of Adam to the time of Moses, even over those who did not sin by breaking a command, as did Adam, who was a pattern of the one to come.

¹⁵But the gift is not like the trespass. For if the many died by the trespass of the one man, how much more did God's grace and the gift that came by the grace of the one man, Jesus Christ, overflow to the many! ¹⁶Again, the gift of God is not like the result of the one man's sin: The judgment followed one sin and brought condemnation, but the gift followed many trespasses and brought justification. ¹⁷For if, by the trespass of the one man, death reigned through that one man, how much more will those who receive God's abundant provision of grace and of the gift of righteousness reign in life through the one man, Jesus Christ.

¹⁸Consequently, just as the result of one trespass was condemnation for all men, so also the result of one act of righteousness was justification that brings life for all men. ¹⁹For just as through the disobedience of the one man the many were made sinners, so also through the obedience of the one man the many will be made righteous.

²⁰The law was added so that the trespass might increase. But where sin increased, grace increased all the more, ²¹so that, just as sin reigned in death, so also grace might reign through righteousness to bring eternal life through Jesus Christ our Lord.

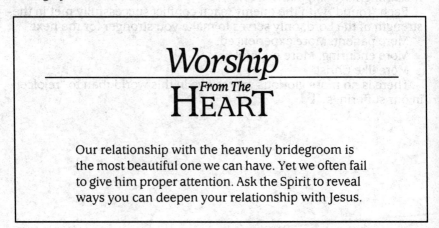

Worship
From The
HEART

Our relationship with the heavenly bridegroom is the most beautiful one we can have. Yet we often fail to give him proper attention. Ask the Spirit to reveal ways you can deepen your relationship with Jesus.

JUNE 10

We Must Go to Jesus Christ

Grace . . . reign[s] through righteousness to bring eternal life through Jesus Christ our Lord (Romans 5:21).

The church is packed. The organist plays reverently. The smiling groom awaits his bride.

And here she comes down the aisle—dress tattered and torn, face streaked with grime—anything but the picture of beauty.

Yet the groom lovingly cleans her up and then receives her. That's the picture of Christ—who is both groom and groomer—and his church.

The same gift of grace that saves is a gift of righteousness that purifies, as Anne Ross Cousin explains.

Walk With Anne Ross Cousin

Oh! I am my Beloved's,
    And my Beloved is mine!
He brings a poor vile sinner
    Into His "House of wine."
I stand upon His merit,
    I know no other stand
Not e'en where glory dwelleth
    In Immanuel's land.

The Bride eyes not her garment,
    But her dear Bridegroom's face;
I will not gaze at glory,
    But on my King of Grace -
Not at the crown He giveth,
    But on His pierced hand:
The Lamb is all the glory
    Of Immanuel's land.

Walk Closer to God

The church is the bride of Christ (Ephesians 5:25–32). And in Christ the bride becomes beautiful with a purity acceptable to God. The dirt of sin and the curse of death cannot be removed in any other way.

Christ is preparing for himself a bride that is cleansed, spotless, holy and without blemish.

Grace leading to righteousness. Unmerited favor leading to upright behavior. They go hand in hand for the one eagerly preparing to meet the Lord. ♡

JUNE 11

📖 Walk in the Word
Romans 6:1–14

Anticipating a charge of being soft on obedience, Paul shows that believers die to the consuming grip of sin and become alive to Christ and the power that he provides to live a new kind of life.

Dead to Sin, Alive in Christ

6 What shall we say, then? Shall we go on sinning so that grace may increase? ²By no means! We died to sin; how can we live in it any longer? ³Or don't you know that all of us who were baptized into Christ Jesus were baptized into his death? ⁴We were therefore buried with him through baptism into death in order that, just as Christ was raised from the dead through the glory of the Father, we too may live a new life.

⁵If we have been united with him like this in his death, we will certainly also be united with him in his resurrection. ⁶For we know that our old self was crucified with him so that the body of sin might be done away with,ᵃ that we should no longer be slaves to sin— ⁷because anyone who has died has been freed from sin.

⁸Now if we died with Christ, we believe that we will also live with him. ⁹For we know that since Christ was raised from the dead, he cannot die again; death no longer has mastery over him. ¹⁰The death he died, he died to sin once for all; but the life he lives, he lives to God.

¹¹In the same way, count yourselves dead to sin but alive to God in Christ Jesus. ¹²Therefore do not let sin reign in your mortal body so that you obey its evil desires. ¹³Do not offer the parts of your body to sin, as instruments of wickedness, but rather offer yourselves to God, as those who have been brought from death to life; and offer the parts of your body to him as instruments of righteousness. ¹⁴For sin shall not be your master, because you are not under law, but under grace.

ᵃ6 Or *be rendered powerless*

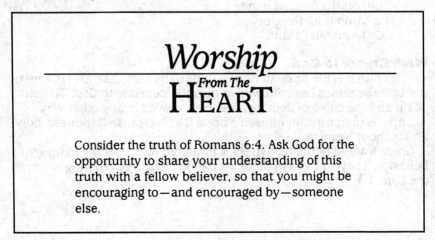

Worship From The HEART

Consider the truth of Romans 6:4. Ask God for the opportunity to share your understanding of this truth with a fellow believer, so that you might be encouraging to—and encouraged by—someone else.

Sin That Crucifies the Lord Again

For we know that our old self was crucified with him so that the body of sin might be done away with, that we should no longer be slaves to sin (Romans 6:6).

In Romans 6, Paul addresses the issue of sin and its relation to the Christian. In Christ you have been set free from the penalty of sin, but you are still in the presence of sin and its deadly influence.

But even though sin continues to beckon, you no longer have to listen, as Charles Spurgeon teaches in this helpful insight.

Walk With Charles Spurgeon

"All sin is contrary to the designs of eternal love, which has an eye to your purity and holiness. Do not run counter to the purposes of the Lord.

"Be free, and let the remembrance of your past bondage forbid you to enter the net again.

"Christians can never sin cheaply; they pay a heavy price for iniquity.

"Each time you 'serve sin,' you have crucified the Lord afresh, and put him to an open shame. Can you bear that thought?

"Turn to Jesus anew; he has not forgotten his love to you; his grace is still the same. With weeping and repentance, come into his presence and there you shall stand firm."

Walk Closer to God

Equipped with new life in Jesus Christ, you no longer have to give in to sin.

But that doesn't mean you'll never have to face sin. For God has called you to represent him in a sin-filled world.

Old relationships may lure you. Sinful pleasures may invite you. But in Christ you have the power to say no.

And it's important that you do precisely that, for while sin doesn't pay, you will if you fail to draw on his strength.

You'll pay by bearing the effects of sin. You'll pay in the loss of fellowship with him. You'll pay by receiving God's loving but firm discipline. You'll pay with a life that's joyless and empty.

Is it worth all that? ◖

June 12

Walk in the Word
Romans 6:15–23

Paul uses the imagery of slavery to hammer home the truth that believers can and must live holy lives; we are gloriously free in Christ, yet at one and the same time slaves to righteousness.

Slaves to Righteousness

¹⁵What then? Shall we sin because we are not under law but under grace? By no means! ¹⁶Don't you know that when you offer yourselves to someone to obey him as slaves, you are slaves to the one whom you obey—whether you are slaves to sin, which leads to death, or to obedience, which leads to righteousness? ¹⁷But thanks be to God that, though you used to be slaves to sin, you wholeheartedly obeyed the form of teaching to which you were entrusted. ¹⁸You have been set free from sin and have become slaves to righteousness.

¹⁹I put this in human terms because you are weak in your natural selves. Just as you used to offer the parts of your body in slavery to impurity and to ever-increasing wickedness, so now offer them in slavery to righteousness leading to holiness. ²⁰When you were slaves to sin, you were free from the control of righteousness. ²¹What benefit did you reap at that time from the things you are now ashamed of? Those things result in death! ²²But now that you have been set free from sin and have become slaves to God, the benefit you reap leads to holiness, and the result is eternal life. ²³For the wages of sin is death, but the gift of God is eternal life in*ᵃ* Christ Jesus our Lord.

ᵃ23 Or through

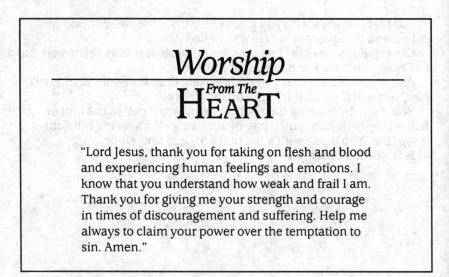

Worship From The HEART

"Lord Jesus, thank you for taking on flesh and blood
and experiencing human feelings and emotions. I
know that you understand how weak and frail I am.
Thank you for giving me your strength and courage
in times of discouragement and suffering. Help me
always to claim your power over the temptation to
sin. Amen."

Christel: The Defender of Your Liberty

You have been set free from sin and have become slaves to righteousness (Romans 6:18).

The battle for your soul may be over, but the battle for your allegiance still rages. But Jesus Christ has conquered the power of sin, and you are free! Free to say no to sin and yes to God.

As John Calvin affirms, that can be very comforting for anyone tired of struggling against sin.

Walk With John Calvin

"The apostle is comforting and strengthening believers, lest they should falter in their zeal and desire for holiness, because they feel their own weakness.

"To prevent discouragement arising from a consciousness of this weakness, he reminds believers that their works are not judged according to the rigid demands of the law.

"The stings of sin continue to harass us, yet they cannot bring us under their power, because we are rendered superior to them by the work of Christ. We are also freed from the rigid demand of the law, because we are in his grace. On this account, believers must fly to Christ and implore his assistance as a defender of their liberty, which he is always ready to do."

Walk Closer to God

By his death, Christ broke the power of sin and death. Captives have been liberated. Slaves to sin have been set free to serve a new Master.

Hebrews describes it this way: Christ "shared in their humanity so that by his death he might destroy him who holds the power of death—that is, the devil—and free those who all their lives were held in slavery by their fear of death" (Hebrews 2:14–15).

No longer afraid of death. No longer bound to sin. No longer giving in to uncleanness. But instead, giving in to God.

Never have you enjoyed anything as free . . . or as costly.

JUNE 13

📖 Walk in the Word
Romans 7:1-6

Paul teaches that the believer is dead to the old way of living under law and alive to the new way of the Spirit.

An Illustration From Marriage

7 Do you not know, brothers—for I am speaking to men who know the law—that the law has authority over a man only as long as he lives? [2]For example, by law a married woman is bound to her husband as long as he is alive, but if her husband dies, she is released from the law of marriage. [3]So then, if she marries another man while her husband is still alive, she is called an adulteress. But if her husband dies, she is released from that law and is not an adulteress, even though she marries another man.

[4]So, my brothers, you also died to the law through the body of Christ, that you might belong to another, to him who was raised from the dead, in order that we might bear fruit to God. [5]For when we were controlled by the sinful nature,[a] the sinful passions aroused by the law were at work in our bodies, so that we bore fruit for death. [6]But now, by dying to what once bound us, we have been released from the law so that we serve in the new way of the Spirit, and not in the old way of the written code.

[a]5 Or *the flesh*; also in verse 25

Worship
From The
HEART

"My heart is Christ's home." Meditate on the metaphor of your heart, or inner being, as the dwelling place of Christ. Have you simply tried to "clean up a few rooms for company," or are all the rooms of your life available for his use? In a prayer of commitment, give him the key to all the rooms of your heart and invite him to make the changes he feels necessary.

My Heart, Christ's Home

For when we were controlled by the sinful nature, the sinful passions aroused by the law were at work in our bodies, so that we bore fruit for death. But now . . . we have been released from the law (Romans 7:5–6).

An X-ray reveals a serious break in your leg. Do you blame the X-ray for the problem? Or would you blame your doctor for informing you of a life-threatening situation? Of course not!

In the same way, the law was designed by God to diagnose the sinful condition of the human race—to make men and women aware of their need for a Savior.

In *The Pilgrim's Progress*, John Bunyan gives this illustration of the relationship of the law to the gospel of grace, as spoken through the interpreter.

Walk With John Bunyan

"This parlor is the heart of a man who was never cleansed by the sweet grace of the gospel; that dust is his inward corruption that has defiled the whole man.

"He who began to sweep at first is the law, but she who brought the water and did sprinkle it is the gospel.

"Now, so soon as the first began to sweep, the dust did so fly about that you were almost choked therewith. This is to show you that the law, instead of cleansing the heart from sin, does revive, put strength into, and increase it, for it does not give the power to subdue.

"Again, the damsel sprinkling the room with water is to show you what happens when the gospel comes in.

"As the damsel settled the dust by sprinkling the floor with water, sin is vanquished and subdued, and the soul made clean through faith; and consequently made fit for the King of Glory to inhabit."

Walk Closer to God

The law merely reveals the soiled condition of the human heart.

What the law of God stirs up, only the grace of God can clean up.

It's enough to make even twentieth-century pilgrims respond in grateful praise!

JUNE 14

📖 Walk in the Word
Romans 7:7–25

Sin and law and their operation within the human heart is openly discussed by Paul in a continuation of his discourse about freedom from the law's condemnation.

Struggling With Sin

⁷What shall we say, then? Is the law sin? Certainly not! Indeed I would not have known what sin was except through the law. For I would not have known what coveting really was if the law had not said, "Do not covet."ᵃ ⁸But sin, seizing the opportunity afforded by the commandment, produced in me every kind of covetous desire. For apart from law, sin is dead. ⁹Once I was alive apart from law; but when the commandment came, sin sprang to life and I died. ¹⁰I found that the very commandment that was intended to bring life actually brought death. ¹¹For sin, seizing the opportunity afforded by the commandment, deceived me, and through the commandment put me to death. ¹²So then, the law is holy, and the commandment is holy, righteous and good.

¹³Did that which is good, then, become death to me? By no means! But in order that sin might be recognized as sin, it produced death in me through what was good, so that through the commandment sin might become utterly sinful.

¹⁴We know that the law is spiritual; but I am unspiritual, sold as a slave to sin. ¹⁵I do not understand what I do. For what I want to do I do not do, but what I hate I do. ¹⁶And if I do what I do not want to do, I agree that the law is good. ¹⁷As it is, it is no longer I myself who do it, but it is sin living in me. ¹⁸I know that nothing good lives in me, that is, in my sinful nature.ᵇ For I have the desire to do what is good, but I cannot carry it out. ¹⁹For what I do is not the good I want to do; no, the evil I do not want to do—this I keep on doing. ²⁰Now if I do what I do not want to do, it is no longer I who do it, but it is sin living in me that does it.

²¹So I find this law at work: When I want to do good, evil is right there with me. ²²For in my inner being I delight in God's law; ²³but I see another law at work in the members of my body, waging war against the law of my mind and making me a prisoner of the law of sin at work within my members. ²⁴What a wretched man I am! Who will rescue me from this body of death? ²⁵Thanks be to God—through Jesus Christ our Lord!

So then, I myself in my mind am a slave to God's law, but in the sinful nature a slave to the law of sin.

ᵃ7 Exodus 20:17; Deut. 5:21   ᵇ18 Or *my flesh*

Battling in a War That's Already Won

What a wretched man I am! Who will rescue me from this body of death? Thanks be to God—through Jesus Christ our Lord! (Romans 7:24–25).

Without benefit of bullets or bombs, the world, the flesh and the devil have mounted an all-out attack aimed at crippling "everyone who wants to live a godly life in Christ Jesus" (2 Timothy 3:12).

Paul describes this "guerrilla warfare" in Romans 7. And as Thomas à Kempis notes, this is one battle that is best fought on your knees.

Walk With Thomas à Kempis

"I confess my own unrighteousness; I confess my weakness unto thee, O Lord.

"Often it is a small matter that makes me sad and dejected. I resolve that I will act with courage, but when even a small temptation comes, I am at once in great distress. It is sometimes a tiny trifle that sparks a great temptation.

"And though I do not altogether consent, yet their continued assaults are troublesome and grievous to me; and it is exceedingly irksome to live thus daily in conflict.

"O Lord, strengthen me with heavenly courage, lest the flesh prevail and get the upper hand."

Walk Closer to God

When David met Goliath, he knew God would be victorious, for David knew the battle was indeed the Lord's. Believers face battles daily too. But they're spiritual battles, against the giants of Satan and self.

The best defense against the warring flesh is a good offense—a confidence that Satan and his allies are already defeated. The ultimate outcome has already been determined . . . the cross of Christ has seen to that!

Now you, like Paul, can respond to the question, "Who will rescue me from this body of death?" with the ringing affirmation, "Jesus Christ our Lord!"

After all, there's nothing like knowing that someone has already won the war to give you strength to face each daily skirmish! ◖

JUNE 15

📖 Walk in the Word
Romans 8:1–11

Paul gives a compelling picture of life lived as children of God in the power of the Spirit.

Life Through the Spirit

8 Therefore, there is now no condemnation for those who are in Christ Jesus,*a* ²because through Christ Jesus the law of the Spirit of life set me free from the law of sin and death. ³For what the law was powerless to do in that it was weakened by the sinful nature,*b* God did by sending his own Son in the likeness of sinful man to be a sin offering.*c* And so he condemned sin in sinful man,*d* ⁴in order that the righteous requirements of the law might be fully met in us, who do not live according to the sinful nature but according to the Spirit.

⁵Those who live according to the sinful nature have their minds set on what that nature desires; but those who live in accordance with the Spirit have their minds set on what the Spirit desires. ⁶The mind of sinful man*e* is death, but the mind controlled by the Spirit is life and peace; ⁷the sinful mind*f* is hostile to God. It does not submit to God's law, nor can it do so. ⁸Those controlled by the sinful nature cannot please God.

⁹You, however, are controlled not by the sinful nature but by the Spirit, if the Spirit of God lives in you. And if anyone does not have the Spirit of Christ, he does not belong to Christ. ¹⁰But if Christ is in you, your body is dead because of sin, yet your spirit is alive because of righteousness. ¹¹And if the Spirit of him who raised Jesus from the dead is living in you, he who raised Christ from the dead will also give life to your mortal bodies through his Spirit, who lives in you.

a1 Some later manuscripts *Jesus, who do not live according to the sinful nature but according to the Spirit,* *b3* Or *the flesh*; also in verses 4, 5, 8, 9, 12 and 13 *c3* Or *man, for sin* *d3* Or *in the flesh* *e6* Or *mind set on the flesh* *f7* Or *the mind set on the flesh*

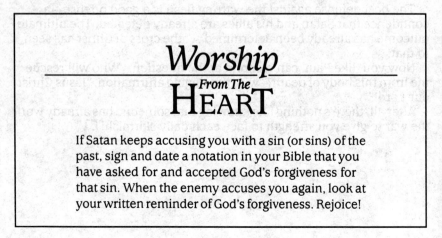

Worship
From The HEART

If Satan keeps accusing you with a sin (or sins) of the past, sign and date a notation in your Bible that you have asked for and accepted God's forgiveness for that sin. When the enemy accuses you again, look at your written reminder of God's forgiveness. Rejoice!

Delighting Yourself in Peace and Freedom

> Therefore, there is now no condemnation for those who are in Christ Jesus (Romans 8:1).

Before you believed in Jesus Christ, you were on death row—condemned by God, deserving of his wrath and judgment.

But now, set free by Christ's death in your place, you are serving a life sentence instead—eternal life in his service.

Read thankfully these words spoken by Thomas Chalmers from a Scottish pulpit more than a hundred years ago.

Walk With Thomas Chalmers

"When a sinner comes to Christ, God reconciles him to himself and remembers his sins no more. They are among the things that are left behind and which ought to be forgotten.

"The believer should feel his conscience relieved from the guilt and dread of his sins. He can look on the account as closed between him and God.

"It is wrong in a believer to live beneath his privileges. How will the spirit of bondage ever be done away with or the joy of the gospel ever be made to spring up in the heart if the believer tries to hang the forgiveness of his sins on anything other than the blood of Jesus?

"Look to Christ lifted up for the offenses of sinners and be encouraged in this thought: Christ has made full payment, and with it God is satisfied.

"If so, you too may be satisfied—delighting yourself greatly in the abundance of peace, and going forth in the light and liberty of this comforting knowledge."

Walk Closer to God

"Father, often I find myself remembering what you have forgotten and condemning myself for what you have erased.

"Teach me never to forget your forgiveness.

"Because only then will I be at peace with myself—when I remember that I am at peace with you.

"I pray in the name of Christ, my deliverer from condemnation. Amen."

JUNE 16

📖 Walk in the Word
Romans 8:12–39

Paul's words are intended to bring comfort and hope to believers who share in the reality of suffering but who have the promise of the Spirit's help and God's never-failing love.

¹²Therefore, brothers, we have an obligation — but it is not to the sinful nature, to live according to it. ¹³For if you live according to the sinful nature, you will die; but if by the Spirit you put to death the misdeeds of the body, you will live, ¹⁴because those who are led by the Spirit of God are sons of God. ¹⁵For you did not receive a spirit that makes you a slave again to fear, but you received the Spirit of sonship.ᵃ And by him we cry, "*Abba,*ᵇ Father." ¹⁶The Spirit himself testifies with our spirit that we are God's children. ¹⁷Now if we are children, then we are heirs — heirs of God and co-heirs with Christ, if indeed we share in his sufferings in order that we may also share in his glory.

Future Glory

¹⁸I consider that our present sufferings are not worth comparing with the glory that will be revealed in us. ¹⁹The creation waits in eager expectation for the sons of God to be revealed. ²⁰For the creation was subjected to frustration, not by its own choice, but by the will of the one who subjected it, in hope ²¹thatᶜ the creation itself will be liberated from its bondage to decay and brought into the glorious freedom of the children of God. ²²We know that the whole creation has been groaning as in the pains of childbirth right up to the present time. ²³Not only so, but we ourselves, who have the firstfruits of the Spirit, groan inwardly as we wait eagerly for our adoption as sons, the redemption of our bodies. ²⁴For in this hope we were saved. But hope that is seen is no hope at all. Who hopes for what he already has? ²⁵But if we hope for what we do not yet have, we wait for it patiently.

²⁶In the same way, the Spirit helps us in our weakness. We do not know what we ought to pray for, but the Spirit himself intercedes for us with groans that words cannot express. ²⁷And he who searches our hearts knows the mind of the Spirit, because the Spirit intercedes for the saints in accordance with God's will.

More Than Conquerors

²⁸And we know that in all things God works for the good of those who love him,ᵈ whoᵉ have been called according to his purpose. ²⁹For those God foreknew he also predestined to be conformed to the likeness of his Son, that he might be the firstborn among many brothers. ³⁰And those he predestined, he also called; those he called, he also justified; those he justified, he also glorified.

³¹What, then, shall we say in response to this? If God is for us, who can be against us? ³²He who did not spare his own Son, but gave him up for us all — how will he not also, along with him, graciously give us all things?

³³Who will bring any charge against those whom God has chosen? It is God who justifies. ³⁴Who is he that condemns? Christ Jesus, who died — more than that, who was raised to life — is at the right hand of God and is also interceding for us. ³⁵Who shall separate us from the love of Christ? Shall trouble or hardship or persecution or famine or nakedness or danger or sword? ³⁶As it is written:

> "For your sake we face death all day long;
>   we are considered as sheep to be slaughtered."ᶠ

³⁷No, in all these things we are more than conquerors through him who loved us. ³⁸For I am convinced that neither death nor life, neither angels nor demons,ᵍ neither the present nor the future, nor any powers, ³⁹neither height nor depth, nor anything else in all creation, will be able to separate us from the love of God that is in Christ Jesus our Lord.

ᵃ15 Or *adoption*   ᵇ15 Aramaic for *Father*   ᶜ20,21 Or *subjected it in hope.* ²¹*For*
ᵈ28 Some manuscripts *And we know that all things work together for good to those who love God*   ᵉ28 Or *works together with those who love him to bring about what is good—with those who*   ᶠ36 Psalm 44:22   ᵍ38 Or *nor heavenly rulers*

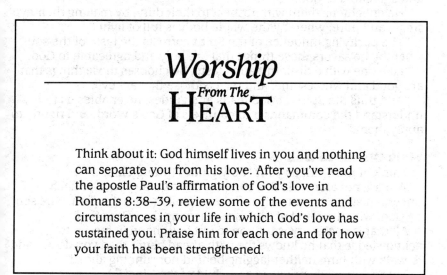

Worship From The HEART

Think about it: God himself lives in you and nothing can separate you from his love. After you've read the apostle Paul's affirmation of God's love in Romans 8:38–39, review some of the events and circumstances in your life in which God's love has sustained you. Praise him for each one and for how your faith has been strengthened.

JUNE 16

The Way in Which His Spirit Leads

Those who are led by the Spirit of God are sons of God (Romans 8:14).

Romans 8 highlights the many facets of life in the Spirit. God has not called you to live for him in a vacuum.

Rather, in the person of the Holy Spirit, he has provided all you need to enjoy daily victory and vitality in your walk with him.

Through the words of Jonathan Edwards, focus today on the importance of the Holy Spirit as your leader.

Walk With Jonathan Edwards

"The Spirit leads the children of God by inclining them to do the will of God from a holy, heavenly disposition which the Spirit of God gives them.

"The Spirit inclines and leads them to those things that are excellent and agreeable to God.

"He enlightens them with respect to their duty, by making their eye single and pure, whereby the whole body is full of light.

"The purifying influence of the Spirit corrects the taste of the soul, whereby he savors those things that are holy and agreeable to God.

"Like one with a discriminating taste, he chooses those things that are good and wholesome, and rejects those that are evil.

"And thus the Spirit of God leads and guides; he enables us to understand the commands and counsels of God's Word, and rightly to apply them."

Walk Closer to God

Think of the Spirit as your "holy guide" through life.

You are not alone. He is a companion to guide you over each uncertain step. One already infinitely familiar with the path. One sent by God, with the mind of God, and knowing the will of God.

All that is necessary is for you to put your hand in his . . . to acknowledge that he knows the path ahead better than you do . . . and to walk with him, neither lagging behind nor running ahead.

That's your daily privilege as a child of the King!

JUNE 17

Walk in the Word
Romans 9:1–29

Paul defends God's justice in his dealings with the nation of Israel, highlighting God's sovereign freedom in dealing with humanity.

God's Sovereign Choice

9 I speak the truth in Christ—I am not lying, my conscience confirms it in the Holy Spirit— 2I have great sorrow and unceasing anguish in my heart. 3For I could wish that I myself were cursed and cut off from Christ for the sake of my brothers, those of my own race, 4the people of Israel. Theirs is the adoption as sons; theirs the divine glory, the covenants, the receiving of the law, the temple worship and the promises. 5Theirs are the patriarchs, and from them is traced the human ancestry of Christ, who is God over all, forever praised!*a* Amen.

6It is not as though God's word had failed. For not all who are descended from Israel are Israel. 7Nor because they are his descendants are they all Abraham's children. On the contrary, "It is through Isaac that your offspring will be reckoned."*b* 8In other words, it is not the natural children who are God's children, but it is the children of the promise who are regarded as Abraham's offspring. 9For this was how the promise was stated: "At the appointed time I will return, and Sarah will have a son."*c*

10Not only that, but Rebekah's children had one and the same father, our father Isaac. 11Yet, before the twins were born or had done anything good or bad—in order that God's purpose in election might stand: 12not by works but by him who calls—she was told, "The older will serve the younger."*d* 13Just as it is written: "Jacob I loved, but Esau I hated."*e*

14What then shall we say? Is God unjust? Not at all! 15For he says to Moses,

> "I will have mercy on whom I have mercy,
> and I will have compassion on whom I have
> compassion."*f*

16It does not, therefore, depend on man's desire or effort, but on God's mercy. 17For the Scripture says to Pharaoh: "I raised you up for this very purpose, that I might display my power in you and that my name might be proclaimed in all the earth."*g* 18Therefore God has mercy on whom he wants to have mercy, and he hardens whom he wants to harden.

19One of you will say to me: "Then why does God still blame us? For who resists his will?" 20But who are you, O man, to talk back to God? "Shall what is formed say to him who formed it, 'Why did you make me like this?' "*h* 21Does not the potter have the right to make out of the same lump of clay some pottery for noble purposes and some for common use?

22What if God, choosing to show his wrath and make his power known, bore with great patience the objects of his wrath—prepared for destruction? 23What if he did this to make the riches of his glory known to the objects of his mercy, whom he prepared in advance for glory— 24even us, whom he also called, not only from the Jews but also from the Gentiles?

JUNE 17

25As he says in Hosea:

> "I will call them 'my people' who are not my people;
>   and I will call her 'my loved one' who is not my loved
>   one,"*i*

26and,

> "It will happen that in the very place where it was said to
>   them,
>   'You are not my people,'
> they will be called 'sons of the living God.' "*j*

27Isaiah cries out concerning Israel:

> "Though the number of the Israelites be like the sand by
>   the sea,
>   only the remnant will be saved.
> 28For the Lord will carry out
>   his sentence on earth with speed and finality."*k*

29It is just as Isaiah said previously:

> "Unless the Lord Almighty
>   had left us descendants,
> we would have become like Sodom,
>   we would have been like Gomorrah."*l*

a5 Or *Christ, who is over all. God be forever praised!* Or *Christ. God who is over all be forever praised!*   *b7* Gen. 21:12   *c9* Gen. 18:10,14   *d12* Gen. 25:23   *e13* Mal. 1:2,3   *f15* Exodus 33:19   *g17* Exodus 9:16   *h20* Isaiah 29:16; 45:9   *i25* Hosea 2:23   *j26* Hosea 1:10   *k28* Isaiah 10:22,23   *l29* Isaiah 1:9

Worship
From The
HEART

When you worship with God's people, pray for those
in the congregation who have never believed God's
message of life. Thank God for his never-failing
compassion that made him pay the great price for
your salvation, and ask him for compassion that
would make you willing to pay a price that others
might be saved.

JUNE 17

No Price Too High for Salvation

For I could wish that I myself were cursed and cut off from Christ for the sake of my brothers (Romans 9:3).

If you heard that a friend was critically ill in the hospital, would you go out of your way to visit and help?

Of course you would. Compassion often causes detours around previously arranged plans.

Paul carried just such a burden of compassion for his "brothers"—but it was not unique to him. J. Hudson Taylor shares his own burden for Christless men and women.

Walk With J. Hudson Taylor

"We are not exempt from trials, and some of them are very painful and difficult to bear.

"But I shall feel amply repaid if one soul only is, by my witness, rescued from the powers of darkness and brought into the fold of Christ.

"And I trust that not one only, but many, will be turned to righteousness by the Word of God ministered by me.

"Were it at the expense of every source of earthly enjoyment; were health and peace, and comfort and happiness, and even life itself to be sacrificed that we might communicate the blessings of Christianity to others, we ought gladly to make it.

"But there is no surer way of finding happiness than by heartily engaging in the work of the Lord, no more certain way of increasing our own blessings than by endeavoring to communicate them to others."

Walk Closer to God

A fellow worker. A family member. A neighbor.

What would you be willing to endure for the privilege of seeing one of these respond to the Good News of sins forgiven?

J. Hudson Taylor gladly faced a foreign culture—and the misunderstandings of many of his fellow Britishers—to share the Good News with China.

Paul was willing to be "cursed" if by that his "brothers" would accept the gospel of Christ.

What price are you willing to pay that a lost soul might hear God's message of life? ◖

ALBERT BARNES

(1798–1870) STUDENT OF GOD'S WORD

Practical Application of the Truth

For centuries the Bible has been by far the best of the best sellers. Additional works designed to aid the student of the Scriptures are numberless. Many of these have a short life; a few remain, however, guiding each new generation of readers through God's Word year after year. One such work is Albert Barnes' *Notes on the Old and New Testaments*. For well over a century, students and teachers have benefited from the author's insights into every "jot and tittle" of the Bible.

Albert Barnes was born on December 1, 1798, in Rome, New York. At age seventeen he decided to go to school to become a lawyer. While there, he seriously committed his life to Jesus. Although he had lived an outwardly moral life, he had not inwardly acknowledged the truth of Christianity. Upon graduation, rather than going to law school, he entered Princeton Seminary, where Charles Hodge had just begun to teach. In 1825 he began pastoring a church in New Jersey, and moved to a large Presbyterian church in Philadelphia five years later. He remained there until shortly before his death in 1870.

Throughout his pastorates he wrote his famous *Notes*, primarily to help Sunday school teachers with their classes. He covered the entire Bible verse by verse, offering practical application of the truths it contained. In addition, he addressed the heated issues of his day, such as fighting against the abuse of alcohol and working for the abolition of slavery.

You may not have the opportunity to write a best-selling set of Bible notes. But don't let that keep you from making God's Word your noteworthy study project today—and every day.

A LESSON FROM THE LIFE OF ALBERT BARNES

When my entire life is committed to God, it may have far-reaching effects that I cannot even imagine.

JUNE 18

Walk in the Word
Romans 9:30—10:21

Paul liberally quotes the Old Testament to demonstrate Israel's responsibility for failing to meet God's requirement of faith.

Israel's Unbelief

30What then shall we say? That the Gentiles, who did not pursue righteousness, have obtained it, a righteousness that is by faith; 31but Israel, who pursued a law of righteousness, has not attained it. 32Why not? Because they pursued it not by faith but as if it were by works. They stumbled over the "stumbling stone." 33As it is written:

> "See, I lay in Zion a stone that causes men to stumble
>   and a rock that makes them fall,
>   and the one who trusts in him will never be put to
>   shame."*a*

10 Brothers, my heart's desire and prayer to God for the Israelites is that they may be saved. 2For I can testify about them that they are zealous for God, but their zeal is not based on knowledge. 3Since they did not know the righteousness that comes from God and sought to establish their own, they did not submit to God's righteousness. 4Christ is the end of the law so that there may be righteousness for everyone who believes. 5Moses describes in this way the righteousness that is by the law: "The man who does these things will live by them."*b* 6But the righteousness that is by faith says: "Do not say in your heart, 'Who will ascend into heaven?'*c*" (that is, to bring Christ down) 7"or 'Who will descend into the deep?'*d*" (that is, to bring Christ up from the dead). 8But what does it say? "The word is near you; it is in your mouth and in your heart,"*e* that is, the word of faith we are proclaiming: 9That if you confess with your mouth, "Jesus is Lord," and believe in your heart that God raised him from the dead, you will be saved. 10For it is with your heart that you believe and are justified, and it is with your mouth that you confess and are saved. 11As the Scripture says, "Anyone who trusts in him will never be put to shame."*f* 12For there is no difference between Jew and Gentile—the same Lord is Lord of all and richly blesses all who call on him, 13for, "Everyone who calls on the name of the Lord will be saved."*g*

14How, then, can they call on the one they have not believed in? And how can they believe in the one of whom they have not heard? And how can they hear without someone preaching to them? 15And how can they preach unless they are sent? As it is written, "How beautiful are the feet of those who bring good news!"*h*

16But not all the Israelites accepted the good news. For Isaiah says, "Lord, who has believed our message?"*i* 17Consequently, faith comes from hearing the message, and the message is heard through the word of Christ. 18But I ask: Did they not hear? Of course they did:

> "Their voice has gone out into all the earth,
>   their words to the ends of the world."*j*

JUNE 18

¹⁹Again I ask: Did Israel not understand? First, Moses says,

"I will make you envious by those who are not a nation;
I will make you angry by a nation that has no
understanding."ᵏ

²⁰And Isaiah boldly says,

"I was found by those who did not seek me;
I revealed myself to those who did not ask for me."ˡ

²¹But concerning Israel he says,

"All day long I have held out my hands
to a disobedient and obstinate people."ᵐ

a33 Isaiah 8:14; 28:16   b5 Lev. 18:5   c6 Deut. 30:12   d7 Deut. 30:13
e8 Deut. 30:14   f11 Isaiah 28:16   g13 Joel 2:32   h15 Isaiah 52:7   i16 Isaiah 53:1
j18 Psalm 19:4   k19 Deut. 32:21   l20 Isaiah 65:1   m21 Isaiah 65:2

Worship
From The
HEART

"Little ones to him belong; They are weak, but he is
strong." We are his "little ones"; he did not call us
because he saw strength in us, but because he loved
us with all of his strength. When you offer yourself
to him as a living sacrifice of worship, he can use
you in ways you never imagined.

God Loves to Use the Weakest Saint

And how can they preach unless they are sent? As it is written, "How beautiful are the feet of those who bring good news!" (Romans 10:15).

When God calls for volunteers, do you respond? It may surprise you to learn that God is not looking for the most capable candidates to do his work, but for the most faithful.

He doesn't need your talent as much as he does your trustworthiness. He can supply you with everything you need to do all he calls you to do.

Oswald Chambers analyzes the qualifications of God's "sent ones"—qualifications that help to insure that God gets the credit for whatever is accomplished.

Walk With Oswald Chambers

"The Christian must be sent; he must not merely elect to go. How am I to know I have been sent of God? By the realization that I am utterly weak and powerless, and if I am to be of any use to God, God must do it all the time.

"Is this the humbling certainty of my soul?

"The only way to be sent is to let God lift us right out of any sense of fitness in ourselves and place us where he will.

"The man whose work tells for God is the one who not only realizes what God has done for him but who realizes his own utter unfitness and overwhelming unsuitability—the impossibility of God ever calling him."

Walk Closer to God

Of those who were called, "Not many were wise" —so that the wisdom might come from him. "Not many were influential"—so that he might prove to be the source of strength. "Not many were of noble birth"—so that the glory might be wholly his.

Moses, Gideon, Jeremiah and Isaiah considered themselves totally inadequate to do anything of lasting significance for God. But in their weakness, his glorious strength could be clearly seen.

When God has a job to do, only weak people need apply. Weak people who are willing to say, "Here am I. Send me!" (Isaiah 6:8).

JUNE 19

📖 Walk in the Word
Romans 11:1–10

Paul spotlights God's work of grace in preserving a remnant who followed the way of faith.

The Remnant of Israel

11 I ask then: Did God reject his people? By no means! I am an Israelite myself, a descendant of Abraham, from the tribe of Benjamin. ²God did not reject his people, whom he foreknew. Don't you know what the Scripture says in the passage about Elijah—how he appealed to God against Israel: ³"Lord, they have killed your prophets and torn down your altars; I am the only one left, and they are trying to kill me"*ᵃ*? ⁴And what was God's answer to him? "I have reserved for myself seven thousand who have not bowed the knee to Baal."*ᵇ* ⁵So too, at the present time there is a remnant chosen by grace. ⁶And if by grace, then it is no longer by works; if it were, grace would no longer be grace.*ᶜ*

⁷What then? What Israel sought so earnestly it did not obtain, but the elect did. The others were hardened, ⁸as it is written:

> "God gave them a spirit of stupor,
> > eyes so that they could not see
> > and ears so that they could not hear,
> to this very day."*ᵈ*

⁹And David says:

> "May their table become a snare and a trap,
> > a stumbling block and a retribution for them.
> ¹⁰May their eyes be darkened so they cannot see,
> > and their backs be bent forever."*ᵉ*

ᵃ3 1 Kings 19:10,14   *ᵇ4* 1 Kings 19:18   *ᶜ6* Some manuscripts *by grace. But if by works, then it is no longer grace; if it were, work would no longer be work.*   *ᵈ8* Deut. 29:4; Isaiah 29:10   *ᵉ10* Psalm 69:22,23

JUNE 19

One Is a Majority With God

God did not reject his people, whom he foreknew . . . What was God's answer to him [Elijah]? "I have reserved for myself seven thousand" (Romans 11:2,4).

Perhaps you have experienced that sinking feeling that it's you against the world. And frankly, the world seems to have you badly outnumbered.

But an amazing transformation takes place when you realize it's not simply you, but you . . . and God . . . and the remnant God has promised never to be without.

W.H. Griffith Thomas points out how Paul uses the life of Elijah to encourage both his countrymen and his fellow believers that God always has a remnant of believers who remain loyal to him.

Walk With W.H. Griffith Thomas

"To support his contention that God has not cast away his people, Paul points out that the same state of affairs existed in the time of Elijah.

"Appearances are not always the same as reality, and there is still a godly remnant, though disregarded by the entire nation.

"When Elijah on Mt. Horeb brought an accusation against his countrymen of such unfaithfulness to God that he alone was left, the divine response quickly showed him that there was a kernel of loyalty.

"In exactly the same way in Paul's day, the mass of people were unfaithful, but there was a remnant of loyal Israelites who had accepted thankfully the divine righteousness by faith.

"Like the quiet group that welcomed the birth of Jesus at Bethlehem, there were many in this remnant who 'waited for the salvation of Israel.' "

Walk Closer to God

It's never easy to stand alone for what you believe. But learn a lesson from Elijah:

When hostility comes, when you feel like it's you against the world, look up.

It may surprise you to see how many others are standing with you. You, like Elijah, are part of an entire army of faith!

JUNE 20

📖 Walk in the Word
Romans 11:11-24

Paul reveals his heart of compassion for the Jews as he reminds his readers that God's rejection of the Jews is not final.

Ingrafted Branches

11Again I ask: Did they stumble so as to fall beyond recovery? Not at all! Rather, because of their transgression, salvation has come to the Gentiles to make Israel envious. 12But if their transgression means riches for the world, and their loss means riches for the Gentiles, how much greater riches will their fullness bring!

13I am talking to you Gentiles. Inasmuch as I am the apostle to the Gentiles, I make much of my ministry 14in the hope that I may somehow arouse my own people to envy and save some of them. 15For if their rejection is the reconciliation of the world, what will their acceptance be but life from the dead? 16If the part of the dough offered as firstfruits is holy, then the whole batch is holy; if the root is holy, so are the branches.

17If some of the branches have been broken off, and you, though a wild olive shoot, have been grafted in among the others and now share in the nourishing sap from the olive root, 18do not boast over those branches. If you do, consider this: You do not support the root, but the root supports you. 19You will say then, "Branches were broken off so that I could be grafted in." 20Granted. But they were broken off because of unbelief, and you stand by faith. Do not be arrogant, but be afraid. 21For if God did not spare the natural branches, he will not spare you either.

22Consider therefore the kindness and sternness of God: sternness to those who fell, but kindness to you, provided that you continue in his kindness. Otherwise, you also will be cut off. 23And if they do not persist in unbelief, they will be grafted in, for God is able to graft them in again. 24After all, if you were cut out of an olive tree that is wild by nature, and contrary to nature were grafted into a cultivated olive tree, how much more readily will these, the natural branches, be grafted into their own olive tree!

Standing by God's Grace Alone

Consider therefore the kindness and sternness of God: sternness to those who fell, but kindness to you, provided that you continue in his kindness (Romans 11:22).

Longevity is no guarantee of legitimacy. Tradition alone is no safeguard of the truth. Over a period of time, what is right and true can easily become perverted and powerless.

It happens in the Christian life with surprising regularity. The revolutionary claims of the gospel become routine; holiness becomes humdrum. And when that happens, it's time for God to snap his children out of their spiritual stupor, as Matthew Henry explains.

Walk With Matthew Henry

"God is most severe toward those who, in their profession, have been nearest to him, if they rebel against him. Patience and abused privilege turn to the greatest wrath.

"It is possible for churches that have long stood by faith to fall into such a state of infidelity as to be their ruin. Their unbelief not only provoked God to cut them off, but by this they cut themselves off.

"You do not stand in any strength of your own. You are no more than the grace of God makes you.

"Continue in his goodness, in a dependence upon and compliance with the free grace of God. Be careful to keep up your interest in God's favor by being continually careful to please him and equally fearful of offending him. The sum of your duty, the condition of your happiness, is to keep yourself in the love of God. 'Come trembling to the LORD and to his blessings' (Hosea 3:5)."

Walk Closer to God

Serving God should be the pattern of your existence. But in the process, never let it become routine—ordinary, stale, monotonous. Greet each new day as a fresh challenge to display the goodness of God to a waiting world.

Just as there was no stale manna for Israel in the wilderness, so keep your faith fresh through daily feeding on the bread of life. Then you, as Mr. Henry suggests, will be "continually careful to please [God] and equally fearful of offending him."

JUNE 21

Walk in the Word
Romans 11:25–36

After revealing God's merciful plan of salvation for both Jew and Gentile, Paul responds in an outpouring of praise to God.

All Israel Will Be Saved

25I do not want you to be ignorant of this mystery, brothers, so that you may not be conceited: Israel has experienced a hardening in part until the full number of the Gentiles has come in. 26And so all Israel will be saved, as it is written:

> "The deliverer will come from Zion;
>   he will turn godlessness away from Jacob.
> 27And this is*a* my covenant with them
>   when I take away their sins."*b*

28As far as the gospel is concerned, they are enemies on your account; but as far as election is concerned, they are loved on account of the patriarchs, 29for God's gifts and his call are irrevocable. 30Just as you who were at one time disobedient to God have now received mercy as a result of their disobedience, 31so they too have now become disobedient in order that they too may now*c* receive mercy as a result of God's mercy to you. 32For God has bound all men over to disobedience so that he may have mercy on them all.

Doxology

> 33Oh, the depth of the riches of the wisdom and*d*
>   knowledge of God!
> How unsearchable his judgments,
>   and his paths beyond tracing out!
> 34"Who has known the mind of the Lord?
>   Or who has been his counselor?"*e*
> 35"Who has ever given to God,
>   that God should repay him?"*f*
> 36For from him and through him and to him are all things.
>   To him be the glory forever! Amen.

a27 Or *will be*   *b27* Isaiah 59:20,21; 27:9; Jer. 31:33,34   *c31* Some manuscripts do not have *now*.   *d33* Or *riches and the wisdom and the*   *e34* Isaiah 40:13   *f35* Job 41:11

The Rich and Unsearchable Wisdom of God

Oh, the depth of the riches of the wisdom and knowledge of God! How unsearchable his judgments, and his paths beyond tracing out! (Romans 11:33).

As Paul explains God's plan for the Jews and Gentiles, many questions surface. Questions for which God has answers, but which his children sometimes lack the understanding to grasp.

In such cases, often the best answer God can supply is "Father knows best."

And the proper response of his children? Allow Martin Luther to answer.

Walk With Martin Luther

"God's ways are what he intends to do, and that cannot be discovered by human reason or thought.

"Therefore, people had better not dictate to God in the presumption of what is right or wrong, or how a divine act ought to be performed.

"On the contrary, people should humble themselves before God and confess that they know nothing of these matters, and can neither advise nor teach anything concerning them.

"They should glorify God by acknowledging that, as their God and Creator, he knows and understands better what he is about and how he ought to govern than do we as his creatures."

Walk Closer to God

Who knows better what makes watches "tick" than the watchmaker himself?

Who understands better the business of heaven and earth than the Creator of both?

God is in control. He knows what he is doing and how best to accomplish his purposes.

Moses, who talked with God face to face for forty years, discovered that "the secret things belong to the LORD our God, but the things revealed belong to us and to our children forever, that we may follow all the words of this law" (Deuteronomy 29:29).

That means God is not looking for your opinion, but rather for your obedience.

And obedience is something you should never have any question about. ❍

JUNE 22

Walk in the Word
Romans 12:1–8

The great revelation of freedom in Christ demands a response of committed lives, as Paul makes clear in his instructions about living lives of integrity.

Living Sacrifices

12 Therefore, I urge you, brothers, in view of God's mercy, to offer your bodies as living sacrifices, holy and pleasing to God — this is your spiritual[a] act of worship. [2]Do not conform any longer to the pattern of this world, but be transformed by the renewing of your mind. Then you will be able to test and approve what God's will is — his good, pleasing and perfect will.

[3]For by the grace given me I say to every one of you: Do not think of yourself more highly than you ought, but rather think of yourself with sober judgment, in accordance with the measure of faith God has given you. [4]Just as each of us has one body with many members, and these members do not all have the same function, [5]so in Christ we who are many form one body, and each member belongs to all the others. [6]We have different gifts, according to the grace given us. If a man's gift is prophesying, let him use it in proportion to his[b] faith. [7]If it is serving, let him serve; if it is teaching, let him teach; [8]if it is encouraging, let him encourage; if it is contributing to the needs of others, let him give generously; if it is leadership, let him govern diligently; if it is showing mercy, let him do it cheerfully.

[a]1 Or *reasonable*   [b]6 Or *in agreement with the*

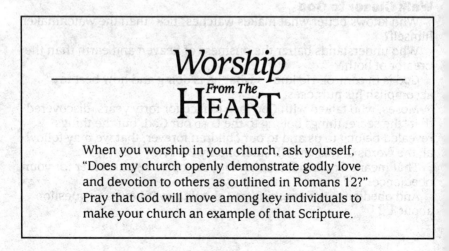

Worship
From The
HEART

When you worship in your church, ask yourself,
"Does my church openly demonstrate godly love
and devotion to others as outlined in Romans 12?"
Pray that God will move among key individuals to
make your church an example of that Scripture.

JUNE 22

The Sacrifice That Lives and Breathes

Therefore, I urge you, brothers, in view of God's mercy, to offer your bodies as living sacrifices, holy and pleasing to God—this is your spiritual act of worship (Romans 12:1).

Today it's considered a "sacrifice" to forego a second dessert or give a dollar to charity.

Contrast that with an Old Testament sacrifice, which was precious, personal and costly.

There is nothing cheap about the sacrifice Paul calls for in Romans 12. Far more than a dead animal or a hard-earned buck, it involves your very life.

Listen as John Henry Jowett explains.

Walk With John Henry Jowett

"The Lord wants my body. He needs its members as ministers of righteousness. He works in the world through my brain, and eyes, and ears, and lips, and hands, and feet. And the Lord wants my body as a 'living sacrifice.' He asks for it when it is thoroughly alive!

"We so often deny the Lord our bodies until they are infirm and sickly, and sometimes we do not offer them to him until they are quite worn out. It is best to offer our bodies to the Lord when they are strong and vigorous and serviceable, and when they can be used in the strenuous places of the field.

"And so let me have a daily consecration service, and let me every morning present my body a living sacrifice to God. Let me regard it as a most holy possession, and let me keep it clean. Let me recoil from all abuse of it. Let me look upon my body as a temple, and let the service of consecration continue all day long."

Walk Closer to God

When God required a sacrifice from His people, he asked for the cream of the crop. In the same way, God is looking for living sacrifices today that can serve him in prime condition and energetic consecration.

Are you ready to give him that? Remember, your body is the temple in which his Spirit resides (1 Corinthians 6:19).

JUNE 23

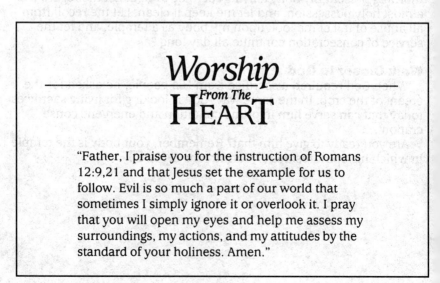 Walk in the Word
Romans 12:9–21

Paul accents the need for love within the believer's relationships, particularly in relationships within the family of God.

Love

⁹Love must be sincere. Hate what is evil; cling to what is good. ¹⁰Be devoted to one another in brotherly love. Honor one another above yourselves. ¹¹Never be lacking in zeal, but keep your spiritual fervor, serving the Lord. ¹²Be joyful in hope, patient in affliction, faithful in prayer. ¹³Share with God's people who are in need. Practice hospitality.

¹⁴Bless those who persecute you; bless and do not curse. ¹⁵Rejoice with those who rejoice; mourn with those who mourn. ¹⁶Live in harmony with one another. Do not be proud, but be willing to associate with people of low position.ᵃ Do not be conceited.

¹⁷Do not repay anyone evil for evil. Be careful to do what is right in the eyes of everybody. ¹⁸If it is possible, as far as it depends on you, live at peace with everyone. ¹⁹Do not take revenge, my friends, but leave room for God's wrath, for it is written: "It is mine to avenge; I will repay,"ᵇ says the Lord. ²⁰On the contrary:

> "If your enemy is hungry, feed him;
>   if he is thirsty, give him something to drink.
> In doing this, you will heap burning coals on his head."ᶜ

²¹Do not be overcome by evil, but overcome evil with good.

ᵃ16 Or *willing to do menial work*   ᵇ19 Deut. 32:35   ᶜ20 Prov. 25:21,22

Worship
From The
HEART

"Father, I praise you for the instruction of Romans 12:9,21 and that Jesus set the example for us to follow. Evil is so much a part of our world that sometimes I simply ignore it or overlook it. I pray that you will open my eyes and help me assess my surroundings, my actions, and my attitudes by the standard of your holiness. Amen."

Overcoming Evil With Good

Do not be overcome by evil, but overcome evil with good (Romans 12:21).

Being familiar with the book of Romans is one thing. Putting its teaching to work in your life is something else again.

Beginning with chapter 12, Paul focuses his thoughts on the practical side of Christian living.

Home and government, church and community—each should reflect the dynamic nature of the doctrine you believe, as John Henry Jowett describes.

Walk With John Henry Jowett

"How can we cast out evil?

"The surgeon cannot cut out the disease if his instruments are defiled; while he removes one ill growth, he sows the seeds of another.

"It must be health which fights disease.

"And therefore I must cultivate a virtue if I would eradicate a vice. If there is some immoral habit in my life, the best way to destroy it would be to cultivate a good one.

"Take the mind away from the evil one. Deprive it of thought food. Give the thought to the nobler mood, and the ignoble will die.

"And this also applies to the faults and vices of my brother. I must fight them with their opposites. If he is harsh and cruel, I must be considerate and gentle. If he is grasping, I must be generous. If he is acting devilish, I must act Christlike.

"This is the warfare which tells upon the empire of sin. I can overcome evil with good."

Walk Closer to God

As darkness is the absence of light, evil is the absence of good.

And all that is necessary for evil to prevail is for good men to do nothing . . . to take their light and hide it under a bushel basket . . . to "leave well enough alone."

Overcome. A word that demands an active response if what you believe is truly going to affect how you behave. ◖

JUNE 24

📖 Walk in the Word
Romans 13:1–7

Paul teaches how believers should act with respect to the world, particularly in our attitude toward the governing authorities.

Submission to the Authorities

13 Everyone must submit himself to the governing authorities, for there is no authority except that which God has established. The authorities that exist have been established by God. ²Consequently, he who rebels against the authority is rebelling against what God has instituted, and those who do so will bring judgment on themselves. ³For rulers hold no terror for those who do right, but for those who do wrong. Do you want to be free from fear of the one in authority? Then do what is right and he will commend you. ⁴For he is God's servant to do you good. But if you do wrong, be afraid, for he does not bear the sword for nothing. He is God's servant, an agent of wrath to bring punishment on the wrongdoer. ⁵Therefore, it is necessary to submit to the authorities, not only because of possible punishment but also because of conscience.

⁶This is also why you pay taxes, for the authorities are God's servants, who give their full time to governing. ⁷Give everyone what you owe him: If you owe taxes, pay taxes; if revenue, then revenue; if respect, then respect; if honor, then honor.

PSALM 18

For the director of music. Of David the servant of the LORD. He sang to the LORD the words of this song when the LORD delivered him from the hand of all his enemies and from the hand of Saul. He said:

I love you, O LORD, my strength.

²The LORD is my rock, my fortress and my deliverer;
　　my God is my rock, in whom I take refuge.
　　He is my shield and the horn*ᵃ* of my salvation, my
　　　　stronghold.
³I call to the LORD, who is worthy of praise,
　　and I am saved from my enemies.

⁵The cords of the grave*ᵇ* coiled around me;
　　the snares of death confronted me.
⁶In my distress I called to the LORD;
　　I cried to my God for help.
　From his temple he heard my voice;
　　my cry came before him, into his ears.

ᵃ2 Horn here symbolizes strength.　ᵇ5 Hebrew Sheol

The Blessing of Civil Government

Everyone must submit himself to the governing authorities, for there is no authority except that which God has established. The authorities that exist have been established by God (Romans 13:1).

"Those whom God hath joined together let no man put asunder." In a traditional wedding, those words are the last ones heard before the couple is pronounced man and wife. The idea is that mere mortals do not have the right to "tear apart" an institution God established.

Just as God established marriage, he established civil government. To arbitrarily rebel against what he established is to rebel against him. On the other hand, to govern without regard to the one who established government is equally rebellious. In one brilliant stroke Paul forbids anarchy and tyranny.

What does this mean in our time? W.H. Griffith Thomas gives helpful application.

Walk With W.H. Griffith Thomas

"(1) *How beautifully applicable this teaching is to every form of government.* Whatever country may be ours these great principles apply. The institution of civil authority is according to the will and plan of God, but no particular type is necessarily expressive of the divine will.

"(2) *How clearly the apostle insists on the Christian's fulfillment of his duties to the state.* They are as truly an obligation as the most spiritual of our church functions. Paying taxes is just as Christian as praying at a meeting. Of course, we are not to do at the bidding of the state that which is morally wrong, but, short of this, submission, not resistance, is the Christian law.

"(3) *How entirely independent of the moral character of the civil government is this fulfillment of our duty.* Questions as to the state's precise moral character do not touch our duty, so long as the demand does not entrench on the domain of the conscience.

"(4) *How agreeable it would be to the progress and welfare of Christianity if such loyalty and submission were always practiced.* If our duties as citizens were fully realized, it would constitute a splendid witness for God."

Walk Closer to God

Paul wrote this at a time when the civil rulers were unbelievers. Yet he still called for submission to God's institution.

In our time, we are both the governed and the government. Since we have the privilege to play a role in placing our leaders in their positions, we share responsibility for how they lead. Have you considered ways that you can be faithful in this stewardship God has providentially given you? ❍

JUNE 25

📖 Walk in the Word
Romans 13:8–14

In light of the end times, Paul urges his readers to live with a sense of urgency—relating to others in love and holy living.

Love, for the Day Is Near

⁸Let no debt remain outstanding, except the continuing debt to love one another, for he who loves his fellowman has fulfilled the law. ⁹The commandments, "Do not commit adultery," "Do not murder," "Do not steal," "Do not covet,"ᵃ and whatever other commandment there may be, are summed up in this one rule: "Love your neighbor as yourself."ᵇ ¹⁰Love does no harm to its neighbor. Therefore love is the fulfillment of the law.

¹¹And do this, understanding the present time. The hour has come for you to wake up from your slumber, because our salvation is nearer now than when we first believed. ¹²The night is nearly over; the day is almost here. So let us put aside the deeds of darkness and put on the armor of light. ¹³Let us behave decently, as in the daytime, not in orgies and drunkenness, not in sexual immorality and debauchery, not in dissension and jealousy. ¹⁴Rather, clothe yourselves with the Lord Jesus Christ, and do not think about how to gratify the desires of the sinful nature.ᶜ

ᵃ9 Exodus 20:13-15,17; Deut. 5:17-19,21   ᵇ9 Lev. 19:18   ᶜ14 Or *the flesh*

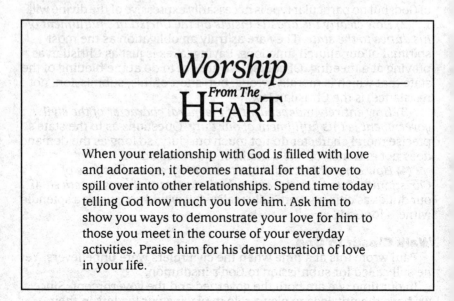

Worship
From The HEART

When your relationship with God is filled with love and adoration, it becomes natural for that love to spill over into other relationships. Spend time today telling God how much you love him. Ask him to show you ways to demonstrate your love for him to those you meet in the course of your everyday activities. Praise him for his demonstration of love in your life.

Love: The Fulfillment of the Law

Let no debt remain outstanding, except the continuing debt to love one another . . . Love does no harm to its neighbor. Therefore love is the fulfillment of the law (Romans 13:8,10).

Love and law.

Seemingly incompatible. Until you recall that the two greatest commands in the Bible are commands to love!

"Love the Lord your God. . . . Love your neighbor as yourself" (Matthew 22:37,39).

How do you fulfill the law of God? Not by gritting your teeth and trying harder, but by loving God and neighbor.

Augustine provides this helpful illustration of the permeating effect of love in life's relationships.

Walk With Augustine

"If a man loves a certain actor and enjoys his art as a great good, he loves all those who share his love for the actor—not on their own account, but on account of him whom they love together.

"And the more fervent is his love for the actor, the more he will behave in every way possible so that the actor will be loved by many.

"Does not this pattern of behavior fit the action of us who are united in the brotherhood of the love of God?

"Thus it is that we also love our enemies. For we do not fear them, since they cannot take away that which we love. Rather, we are sorry for them.

"If they were to turn to him and love him as the source of blessedness, they would necessarily love us also as companions in a great good."

Walk Closer to God

Augustine elsewhere summarizes the demands of the Christian life this way: "Love God, and do as you please."

That is, when your vertical relationship with God is right, then your horizontal relationships with others will be right.

When your goal is to please the Father, it's remarkable how well you will get along with your brothers and sisters in the family of God.

Try it—and see how fulfilling love can be. ❍

JUNE 26

📖 Walk in the Word
Romans 14:1–12

Paul asks believers to focus on their relationship to the Lord—how that comes to expression in holy living and godly service—and not on the nonessential matters that often divide believers.

The Weak and the Strong

14 Accept him whose faith is weak, without passing judgment on disputable matters. [2]One man's faith allows him to eat everything, but another man, whose faith is weak, eats only vegetables. [3]The man who eats everything must not look down on him who does not, and the man who does not eat everything must not condemn the man who does, for God has accepted him. [4]Who are you to judge someone else's servant? To his own master he stands or falls. And he will stand, for the Lord is able to make him stand.

[5]One man considers one day more sacred than another; another man considers every day alike. Each one should be fully convinced in his own mind. [6]He who regards one day as special, does so to the Lord. He who eats meat, eats to the Lord, for he gives thanks to God; and he who abstains, does so to the Lord and gives thanks to God. [7]For none of us lives to himself alone and none of us dies to himself alone. [8]If we live, we live to the Lord; and if we die, we die to the Lord. So, whether we live or die, we belong to the Lord.

[9]For this very reason, Christ died and returned to life so that he might be the Lord of both the dead and the living. [10]You, then, why do you judge your brother? Or why do you look down on your brother? For we will all stand before God's judgment seat. [11]It is written:

> " 'As surely as I live,' says the Lord,
> 'every knee will bow before me;
>   every tongue will confess to God.' "[a]

[12]So then, each of us will give an account of himself to God.

[a]11 Isaiah 45:23

Under the Scrutiny of the Lord

For this very reason, Christ died and returned to life so that he might be the Lord of both the dead and the living . . . So then, each of us will give an account of himself to God (Romans 14:9,12).

Aspiring politicians dread the thought of skeletons in the closet coming to light. But even the most anonymous John or Jane Doe will one day stand before the light of God's judgment. And then, no secrets will be safe.

"Everything is uncovered and laid bare before the eyes of him to whom we must give account" (Hebrews 4:13). The God who knows even the thoughts and intentions of the heart will one day judge all.

Donald Barnhouse advises the Christian how to live in the light of that knowledge.

Walk With Donald Barnhouse

"We must understand that 'whatever a man sows' must be taken in its widest meaning, and that every thought and intent of the heart will come under the scrutiny of our Lord at his coming.

"We can be sure that at the judgment seat of Christ there will be a marked difference between the Christian who has lived his life before the Lord, clearly discerning what was for the glory of God, and another Christian who was saved in a rescue mission at the tag end of a depraved and vicious life, or a nominal Christian saved on his deathbed after a life of self-pride, self-righteousness, self-love, and self-sufficiency.

"All will be in heaven, but the differences will be eternal. We may be sure that the consequences of our character will survive the grave and that we shall face those consequences at the judgment seat of Christ."

Walk Closer to God

Although the penalty of sin is removed for the Christian, the consequences of sin continue to operate in a fallen world. Murder always means the loss of life; adultery, the destruction of a home; lying, the loss of integrity—for Christian and non-Christian alike.

This is ample reason to keep on your toes and stay on your knees in your walk with the Lord. ◖

JUNE 27

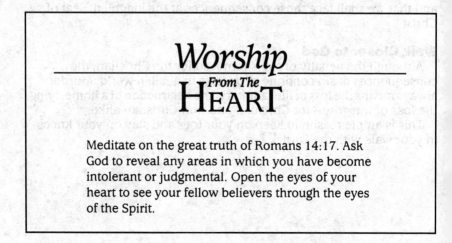 Walk in the Word
Romans 14:13–23

Paul encourages those who are strong to act in love and humility by promoting peace and spiritual growth within individuals and within the church.

---

¹³Therefore let us stop passing judgment on one another. Instead, make up your mind not to put any stumbling block or obstacle in your brother's way. ¹⁴As one who is in the Lord Jesus, I am fully convinced that no food*a* is unclean in itself. But if anyone regards something as unclean, then for him it is unclean. ¹⁵If your brother is distressed because of what you eat, you are no longer acting in love. Do not by your eating destroy your brother for whom Christ died. ¹⁶Do not allow what you consider good to be spoken of as evil. ¹⁷For the kingdom of God is not a matter of eating and drinking, but of righteousness, peace and joy in the Holy Spirit, ¹⁸because anyone who serves Christ in this way is pleasing to God and approved by men.

¹⁹Let us therefore make every effort to do what leads to peace and to mutual edification. ²⁰Do not destroy the work of God for the sake of food. All food is clean, but it is wrong for a man to eat anything that causes someone else to stumble. ²¹It is better not to eat meat or drink wine or to do anything else that will cause your brother to fall.

²²So whatever you believe about these things keep between yourself and God. Blessed is the man who does not condemn himself by what he approves. ²³But the man who has doubts is condemned if he eats, because his eating is not from faith; and everything that does not come from faith is sin.

a14 Or *that nothing*

Worship
H<small>EART</small> *From The*

Meditate on the great truth of Romans 14:17. Ask God to reveal any areas in which you have become intolerant or judgmental. Open the eyes of your heart to see your fellow believers through the eyes of the Spirit.

The Gentle Calmness of True Strength

Let us therefore make every effort to do what leads to peace and to mutual edification (Romans 14:19).

Consider the irony of freedom.

Define it as "the right to do as you please," and you will never be truly free.

Define it as "the right to do as you ought," and you will have discovered the essence of true freedom.

In Romans 14 Paul describes the use—and abuse—of Christian liberty, as H.C.G. Moule explains.

Walk With H.C.G. Moule

"In principle, Paul's own convictions lay with 'the strong,' those who 'knew that nothing was unclean.'

"He knew that the Lord was not grieved, but pleased, by the moderate and thankful use of his natural bounties.

"But though the strong may be right in principle concerning certain activities, this leaves untouched the still more stringent overruling principle, to 'walk in love'; to live for the benefit of others.

"The strong are not to be ashamed of their liberty. But they are to be ashamed of one hour's unloving conduct.

"Their 'strength' in Christ is never to be ungentle. It is to be shown, first and most, by patience. It is to take the form of the calm, strong readiness to understand another's point of view."

Walk Closer to God

When it comes to the exercise of Christian liberty, God is looking for men and women who are strong in the Lord, yet tender toward those who are weak in the faith; he is looking for believers who temper their liberty with love.

When you encounter a "gray area" in your walk with God . . . when you're not sure of the right course of action . . . when the Scriptures are silent on a particular activity . . . what then?

Then, put Paul's principle to work: "When in doubt, love!"

JUNE 28

📖 Walk in the Word
Romans 15:1–13

Paul continues his discussion of the weak and the strong by pleading for an attitude of acceptance and unity that will bring glory to God and hope to believers and seekers.

15 We who are strong ought to bear with the failings of the weak and not to please ourselves. ²Each of us should please his neighbor for his good, to build him up. ³For even Christ did not please himself but, as it is written: "The insults of those who insult you have fallen on me."ᵃ ⁴For everything that was written in the past was written to teach us, so that through endurance and the encouragement of the Scriptures we might have hope.

⁵May the God who gives endurance and encouragement give you a spirit of unity among yourselves as you follow Christ Jesus, ⁶so that with one heart and mouth you may glorify the God and Father of our Lord Jesus Christ.

⁷Accept one another, then, just as Christ accepted you, in order to bring praise to God. ⁸For I tell you that Christ has become a servant of the Jewsᵇ on behalf of God's truth, to confirm the promises made to the patriarchs ⁹so that the Gentiles may glorify God for his mercy, as it is written:

"Therefore I will praise you among the Gentiles;
I will sing hymns to your name."ᶜ

¹⁰Again, it says,

"Rejoice, O Gentiles, with his people."ᵈ

¹¹And again,

"Praise the Lord, all you Gentiles,
and sing praises to him, all you peoples."ᵉ

¹²And again, Isaiah says,

"The Root of Jesse will spring up,
one who will arise to rule over the nations;
the Gentiles will hope in him."ᶠ

¹³May the God of hope fill you with all joy and peace as you trust in him, so that you may overflow with hope by the power of the Holy Spirit.

ᵃ3 Psalm 69:9   ᵇ8 Greek *circumcision*   ᶜ9 2 Samuel 22:50; Psalm 18:49
ᵈ10 Deut. 32:43   ᵉ11 Psalm 117:1   ᶠ12 Isaiah 11:10

The Ever-Relevant Word of God

For everything that was written in the past was written to teach us, so that through endurance and the encouragement of the Scriptures we might have hope (Romans 15:4).

Thousands of years separate you from the events of Scripture. But even though life today seems very different, those inspired words remain your instruction manual from the Creator of the world.

No matter what your age—or distance from the Scripture's writing— God's truth is never out of date.

John Calvin, lifelong student of the Scriptures, has this to say about God's eternally relevant Word.

Walk With John Calvin

"There is no part of the Scriptures which cannot contribute to our instruction and to the forming of our life and manners.

"The Word of God contains nothing vain or unprofitable. Diligent study and reading of these records of unchanging wisdom cannot help but contribute to our holiness of life.

"Let us, therefore, labor diligently to learn the contents of the Book of God, and never forget it is the only writing in which the Creator of heaven and earth condescends to converse with mankind.

"The Scriptures are chiefly devoted to the object of forming in us patience—of strengthening and confirming our faith—of raising us to the hope of eternal life—and of keeping our meditation and contemplation fixed on that glorious kingdom of God."

Walk Closer to God

Patience. Comfort. Strength.

Just a few of the dividends you'll receive from mastering God's Word . . . and allowing it to master you.

Study. Diligence. Meditation.

This is the investment you must make to achieve that end.

God has placed all that you need to know about him between the covers of the Bible.

But only you can open its pages to discover what he is saying to you. ⟡

JUNE 29

Walk in the Word
Romans 15:14–33

After summarizing his God-given ambition to work among the Gentiles, Paul writes of his need for prayer and his desire to visit the Roman Christians.

Paul the Minister to the Gentiles

[14]I myself am convinced, my brothers, that you yourselves are full of goodness, complete in knowledge and competent to instruct one another. [15]I have written you quite boldly on some points, as if to remind you of them again, because of the grace God gave me [16]to be a minister of Christ Jesus to the Gentiles with the priestly duty of proclaiming the gospel of God, so that the Gentiles might become an offering acceptable to God, sanctified by the Holy Spirit.

[17]Therefore I glory in Christ Jesus in my service to God. [18]I will not venture to speak of anything except what Christ has accomplished through me in leading the Gentiles to obey God by what I have said and done— [19]by the power of signs and miracles, through the power of the Spirit. So from Jerusalem all the way around to Illyricum, I have fully proclaimed the gospel of Christ. [20]It has always been my ambition to preach the gospel where Christ was not known, so that I would not be building on someone else's foundation. [21]Rather, as it is written:

> "Those who were not told about him will see,
> and those who have not heard will understand."[a]

[22]This is why I have often been hindered from coming to you.

Paul's Plan to Visit Rome

[23]But now that there is no more place for me to work in these regions, and since I have been longing for many years to see you, [24]I plan to do so when I go to Spain. I hope to visit you while passing through and to have you assist me on my journey there, after I have enjoyed your company for a while. [25]Now, however, I am on my way to Jerusalem in the service of the saints there. [26]For Macedonia and Achaia were pleased to make a contribution for the poor among the saints in Jerusalem. [27]They were pleased to do it, and indeed they owe it to them. For if the Gentiles have shared in the Jews' spiritual blessings, they owe it to the Jews to share with them their material blessings. [28]So after I have completed this task and have made sure that they have received this fruit, I will go to Spain and visit you on the way. [29]I know that when I come to you, I will come in the full measure of the blessing of Christ.

[30]I urge you, brothers, by our Lord Jesus Christ and by the love of the Spirit, to join me in my struggle by praying to God for me. [31]Pray that I may be rescued from the unbelievers in Judea and that my service in Jeru-

salem may be acceptable to the saints there, [32]so that by God's will I may come to you with joy and together with you be refreshed. [33]The God of peace be with you all. Amen.

a21 Isaiah 52:15

PSALM 119

ד   Daleth

I am laid low in the dust;
   preserve my life according to your word.
[26]I recounted my ways and you answered me;
   teach me your decrees.
[27]Let me understand the teaching of your precepts;
   then I will meditate on your wonders.
[28]My soul is weary with sorrow;
   strengthen me according to your word.
[29]Keep me from deceitful ways;
   be gracious to me through your law.
[30]I have chosen the way of truth;
   I have set my heart on your laws.
[31]I hold fast to your statutes, O LORD;
   do not let me be put to shame.
[32]I run in the path of your commands,
   for you have set my heart free.

JUNE 29

Praising God With the Angels

Therefore I glory in Christ Jesus in my service to God (Romans 15:17).

You may know the heart of the gospel—salvation in Jesus Christ. But do you have a heart for the gospel—a passion to proclaim it?

After presenting the contents of his message, Paul shares the burden he carries for communicating that message to others. Motivated by a desire to glorify God, he wants to go where no other messenger of the gospel has gone before.

David Brainerd, another of God's choice servants, was equally compelled to reach others for God's glory. Even a few weeks before his death, he wrote of his desire to serve God.

Walk With David Brainerd

"I do not go to heaven to be advanced, but to give honor to God. It is no matter where I shall be stationed in heaven; to love, and please, and glorify God is all.

"Had I a thousand souls, if they were worth anything, I would give them all to God; but I have nothing to give, when all is done.

"I long to be in heaven, praising and glorifying God with all the holy angels. All my desire is to glorify God.

"There is nothing in the world worth living for but doing good and finishing God's work, doing the work that Christ did.

"I see nothing else in the world that can yield any satisfaction besides living to God, pleasing him, and doing his whole will."

Walk Closer to God

David Brainerd. The apostle Paul. Both shared burdens for the glory of God and the souls of men.

They experienced the comfort of the gospel. But beyond that, they felt the compulsion of the gospel—the restless dissatisfaction of knowing that others had not yet heard.

You enjoy the same gospel of life that transformed David Brainerd and Paul. Ask God to give you the same burden that ignited their lives to his glory. ◖

JUNE 30

📖 Walk in the Word
Romans 16

Paul concludes his letter with a long list of people to whom he sends greetings, a warning to avoid divisive people, the passing on of greetings from some of his companions, and a concluding doxology.

Personal Greetings

16 I commend to you our sister Phoebe, a servant*a* of the church in Cenchrea. ²I ask you to receive her in the Lord in a way worthy of the saints and to give her any help she may need from you, for she has been a great help to many people, including me.

³Greet Priscilla*b* and Aquila, my fellow workers in Christ Jesus. ⁴They risked their lives for me. Not only I but all the churches of the Gentiles are grateful to them.
⁵Greet also the church that meets at their house.
  Greet my dear friend Epenetus, who was the first convert to Christ in the province of Asia.
⁶Greet Mary, who worked very hard for you.
⁷Greet Andronicus and Junias, my relatives who have been in prison with me. They are outstanding among the apostles, and they were in Christ before I was.
⁸Greet Ampliatus, whom I love in the Lord.
⁹Greet Urbanus, our fellow worker in Christ, and my dear friend Stachys.
¹⁰Greet Apelles, tested and approved in Christ.
  Greet those who belong to the household of Aristobulus.
¹¹Greet Herodion, my relative.
  Greet those in the household of Narcissus who are in the Lord.
¹²Greet Tryphena and Tryphosa, those women who work hard in the Lord.
  Greet my dear friend Persis, another woman who has worked very hard in the Lord.
¹³Greet Rufus, chosen in the Lord, and his mother, who has been a mother to me, too.
¹⁴Greet Asyncritus, Phlegon, Hermes, Patrobas, Hermas and the brothers with them.
¹⁵Greet Philologus, Julia, Nereus and his sister, and Olympas and all the saints with them.
¹⁶Greet one another with a holy kiss.
  All the churches of Christ send greetings.

¹⁷I urge you, brothers, to watch out for those who cause divisions and put obstacles in your way that are contrary to the teaching you have learned. Keep away from them. ¹⁸For such people are not serving our Lord Christ, but their own appetites. By smooth talk and flattery they deceive the minds of naive people. ¹⁹Everyone has heard about your obedience, so I am full of joy over you; but I want you to be wise about what is good, and innocent about what is evil.
²⁰The God of peace will soon crush Satan under your feet.

June 30

The grace of our Lord Jesus be with you.

21Timothy, my fellow worker, sends his greetings to you, as do Lucius, Jason and Sosipater, my relatives.

22I, Tertius, who wrote down this letter, greet you in the Lord.

23Gaius, whose hospitality I and the whole church here enjoy, sends you his greetings.

Erastus, who is the city's director of public works, and our brother Quartus send you their greetings.c

25Now to him who is able to establish you by my gospel and the proclamation of Jesus Christ, according to the revelation of the mystery hidden for long ages past, 26but now revealed and made known through the prophetic writings by the command of the eternal God, so that all nations might believe and obey him— 27to the only wise God be glory forever through Jesus Christ! Amen.

a1 Or deaconess   b3 Greek Prisca, a variant of Priscilla   c23 Some manuscripts their greetings. 24May the grace of our Lord Jesus Christ be with all of you. Amen.

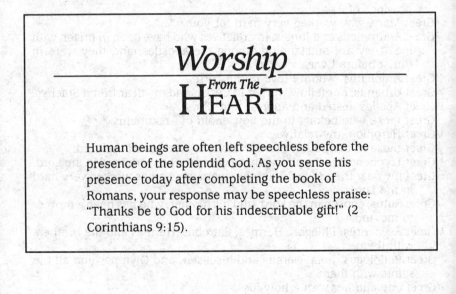

Worship
From The
HEART

Human beings are often left speechless before the presence of the splendid God. As you sense his presence today after completing the book of Romans, your response may be speechless praise: "Thanks be to God for his indescribable gift!" (2 Corinthians 9:15).

Doxology for the Revealed Mystery

Now to him who is able to establish you by my gospel and the proclamation of Jesus Christ, according to the revelation of the mystery . . . (Romans 16:25).

According to Paul, the Good News was a mystery for many years. But the final page fell open with the coming of Jesus Christ. And Paul's response in Romans 16—after explaining the mystery of Christ and the gospel—is praise.

Columba, one the earliest missionaries to Scotland, provides this fitting doxology of praise.

Walk With Columba

God, Thou art the Father
Of all that have believed:
From whom all hosts of angels
Have life and power received.
O God, Thou art the Maker
Of all created things,
The righteous Judge of judges,
The almighty King of Kings.

High in the heavenly Zion
Thou reignest God adored;
And in the coming glory
Thou shalt be Sovereign Lord.
Beyond our view Thou shinest,
The everlasting Light;
Ineffable in loving,
Unthinkable in might.

Thou to the meek and lowly
Thy secrets dost unfold;
O God, Thou doest all things,
All things both new and old.
I walk secure and blessed
In every clime or coast,
In name of God the Father,
And Son, and Holy Ghost.

Walk Closer to God

Remember, what is the Good News to you may still be a mystery to others around you—others who will gladly join in your chorus of praise once they have heard and responded. ◖

July

Christian Living at the Practical Level

1 AND 2 CORINTHIANS

"All roads lead to Rome." If that saying was true in Paul's day, then it was equally true that most of those roads led through Corinth. A crossroads of commerce and trade, Corinth was a prosperous, bustling city whose influence—both good and bad—stretched far beyond the city limits. It became a key center for the ministry of the apostle Paul. Chased out of Thessalonica and Berea by Jewish troublemakers and confronted by indifference in Athens, Paul probably arrived in Corinth in low spirits. There he stayed for the next eighteen months, preaching the good news and seeing fruit from his ministry. His message was refreshing good news in a city like Corinth!

Paul's two letters to the Corinthians deal with growing pains in the Christian life. Living in the center of a corrupt society, the Corinthian church had mighty potential . . . and many problems. Paul's first letter responds to questions raised by the Corinthians on a variety of topics, both personal and corporate. He expresses concern over divisions and factions, immorality, abuse of Christian liberty, misunderstandings about the resurrection, disorderly church worship and improper use of spiritual gifts. In his second letter, the apostle opens his heart to show his fatherly concern for those who have come to Christ through his ministry. It resembles a miniature autobiography in which he sets forth his calling, credentials, message and struggles on behalf of the Corinthian believers. He seeks to silence any who question his motives and his authority as an apostle of Christ.

From time to time you may find that Paul's words produce an uncomfortable "pinching" sensation in your Christian life. That's God's way of showing you where you need to grow in him or where you need to work on your relationships with others. With the guidance of God's Word and the insight of godly people, you can do just that this month. So take a trip to Corinth. With the influence of the Scriptures and through the Spirit, you'll come back a changed person.

JULY 1

Walk in the Word
1 Corinthians 1

Paul greets the Corinthian Christians and gives thanks to God for them.
He then chides them for creating divisions within their church and shows
them how the cross of Christ is the answer to their difficulties.

1 Paul, called to be an apostle of Christ Jesus by the will of God, and
our brother Sosthenes,

²To the church of God in Corinth, to those sanctified in Christ Jesus and
called to be holy, together with all those everywhere who call on the name
of our Lord Jesus Christ — their Lord and ours:

³Grace and peace to you from God our Father and the Lord Jesus Christ.

Thanksgiving

⁴I always thank God for you because of his grace given you in Christ
Jesus. ⁵For in him you have been enriched in every way — in all your
speaking and in all your knowledge — ⁶because our testimony about
Christ was confirmed in you. ⁷Therefore you do not lack any spiritual gift
as you eagerly wait for our Lord Jesus Christ to be revealed. ⁸He will keep
you strong to the end, so that you will be blameless on the day of our Lord
Jesus Christ. ⁹God, who has called you into fellowship with his Son Jesus
Christ our Lord, is faithful.

Divisions in the Church

¹⁰I appeal to you, brothers, in the name of our Lord Jesus Christ, that
all of you agree with one another so that there may be no divisions among
you and that you may be perfectly united in mind and thought. ¹¹My
brothers, some from Chloe's household have informed me that there are
quarrels among you. ¹²What I mean is this: One of you says, "I follow
Paul"; another, "I follow Apollos"; another, "I follow Cephas*a*"; still another, "I follow Christ."

¹³Is Christ divided? Was Paul crucified for you? Were you baptized into*b*
the name of Paul? ¹⁴I am thankful that I did not baptize any of you except
Crispus and Gaius, ¹⁵so no one can say that you were baptized into my
name. ¹⁶(Yes, I also baptized the household of Stephanas; beyond that, I
don't remember if I baptized anyone else.) ¹⁷For Christ did not send me
to baptize, but to preach the gospel — not with words of human wisdom,
lest the cross of Christ be emptied of its power.

Christ the Wisdom and Power of God

¹⁸For the message of the cross is foolishness to those who are perishing,
but to us who are being saved it is the power of God. ¹⁹For it is written:

"I will destroy the wisdom of the wise;
the intelligence of the intelligent I will frustrate."*c*

JULY 1

20Where is the wise man? Where is the scholar? Where is the philosopher of this age? Has not God made foolish the wisdom of the world? 21For since in the wisdom of God the world through its wisdom did not know him, God was pleased through the foolishness of what was preached to save those who believe. 22Jews demand miraculous signs and Greeks look for wisdom, 23but we preach Christ crucified: a stumbling block to Jews and foolishness to Gentiles, 24but to those whom God has called, both Jews and Greeks, Christ the power of God and the wisdom of God. 25For the foolishness of God is wiser than man's wisdom, and the weakness of God is stronger than man's strength.

26Brothers, think of what you were when you were called. Not many of you were wise by human standards; not many were influential; not many were of noble birth. 27But God chose the foolish things of the world to shame the wise; God chose the weak things of the world to shame the strong. 28He chose the lowly things of this world and the despised things — and the things that are not — to nullify the things that are, 29so that no one may boast before him. 30It is because of him that you are in Christ Jesus, who has become for us wisdom from God — that is, our righteousness, holiness and redemption. 31Therefore, as it is written: "Let him who boasts boast in the Lord."d

a12 That is, Peter   b13 Or in; also in verse 15   c19 Isaiah 29:14   d31 Jer. 9:24

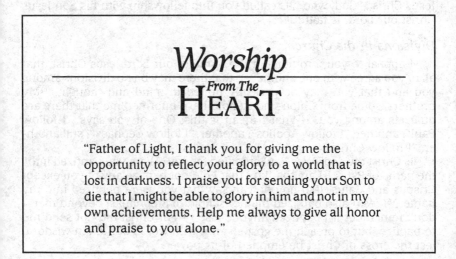

Worship
From The
HEART

"Father of Light, I thank you for giving me the opportunity to reflect your glory to a world that is lost in darkness. I praise you for sending your Son to die that I might be able to glory in him and not in my own achievements. Help me always to give all honor and praise to you alone."

I Will Glory in the Lord

Because of him . . . you are in Christ Jesus . . . Therefore, as it is written: "Let him who boasts boast in the Lord" (1 Corinthians 1:30–31).

Prestige and pride. They often go together. The city of Corinth provides a case in point.

A crossroads of trade and transportation, Corinth became a first-century boomtown. Gold was abundant—and with it came a kind of "fool's-gold" glory based on human wisdom and material prosperity.

Jonathan Edwards comments on Paul's first letter to the Corinthians and the problem of misplaced pride.

Walk With Jonathan Edwards

"Let us exalt God alone and ascribe to him all the glory of redemption.

"Man is naturally prone to exalt himself and depend on his own power or goodness. But this chapter should teach us to exalt God alone, not only by trust and reliance, but also by praise: 'Let him who boasts boast in the Lord.'

"Do you have hope that you are converted, that your sins are forgiven, and that you have been received into God's favor and are his child, an heir of eternal life? Then give God the glory!

"If you excel in holiness, take no glory to yourself, but ascribe it to him whose workmanship you are."

Walk Closer to God

From a human perspective, the Corinthians had much to brag about.

But God sent his Son not to save those who gloried in their achievements, but those who willingly acknowledged they were "foolish . . . weak . . . lowly . . . despised . . . that no one may boast before him" (1 Corinthians 1:27–29).

What a glorious thought!

God saved you—"foolish" sinner that you were—that you might become a trophy of his love, a mirror of his glory.

You can reflect his glory back to him right now by giving thanks for his grace on your behalf. ❍

JULY 2

📖 Walk in the Word
1 Corinthians 2

Paul explains how true wisdom comes to us from God through the Spirit, a wisdom that is not available to the world.

2 When I came to you, brothers, I did not come with eloquence or superior wisdom as I proclaimed to you the testimony about God.*a* ²For I resolved to know nothing while I was with you except Jesus Christ and him crucified. ³I came to you in weakness and fear, and with much trembling. ⁴My message and my preaching were not with wise and persuasive words, but with a demonstration of the Spirit's power, ⁵so that your faith might not rest on men's wisdom, but on God's power.

Wisdom From the Spirit

⁶We do, however, speak a message of wisdom among the mature, but not the wisdom of this age or of the rulers of this age, who are coming to nothing. ⁷No, we speak of God's secret wisdom, a wisdom that has been hidden and that God destined for our glory before time began. ⁸None of the rulers of this age understood it, for if they had, they would not have crucified the Lord of glory. ⁹However, as it is written:

> "No eye has seen,
>   no ear has heard,
> no mind has conceived
>   what God has prepared for those who love him"*b* —

¹⁰but God has revealed it to us by his Spirit.

The Spirit searches all things, even the deep things of God. ¹¹For who among men knows the thoughts of a man except the man's spirit within him? In the same way no one knows the thoughts of God except the Spirit of God. ¹²We have not received the spirit of the world but the Spirit who is from God, that we may understand what God has freely given us. ¹³This is what we speak, not in words taught us by human wisdom but in words taught by the Spirit, expressing spiritual truths in spiritual words.*c* ¹⁴The man without the Spirit does not accept the things that come from the Spirit of God, for they are foolishness to him, and he cannot understand them, because they are spiritually discerned. ¹⁵The spiritual man makes judgments about all things, but he himself is not subject to any man's judgment:

> ¹⁶"For who has known the mind of the Lord
>   that he may instruct him?"*d*

But we have the mind of Christ.

a1 Some manuscripts *as I proclaimed to you God's mystery*   *b9* Isaiah 64:4   *c13* Or *Spirit, interpreting spiritual truths to spiritual men*   *d16* Isaiah 40:13

The Soul Turned Toward God in Obedient Faith

In the same way no one knows the thoughts of God except the Spirit of God. We have not received the spirit of the world but the Spirit who is from God, that we may understand what God has freely given us (1 Corinthians 2:11–12).

At birth you received five senses with which to perceive the physical world around you.

Coming to Christ, you received a "sixth sense" in the person of the Holy Spirit who opens up a world of spiritual reality.

Read carefully as F.B. Meyer examines the work of God's "sixth sense" in the lives of men and women.

Walk With F.B. Meyer

"When we turn toward God in obedient faith, we are lifted through faith into union with the heavenly man, the Lord Jesus Christ, and rise above the natural level.

"Then we walk in a new world; then we become aware of the unseen and eternal; then the spiritual senses are as quick to discern good and evil as our physical is to distinguish light from dark.

"The spirit is our capacity for God. When it is brought to life, we move on to new levels of experience; we touch reality.

"When a channel is formed between the Spirit of God and the spirit of man, there is an instant communication of grace and power which finds its way into every avenue of the soul, enlightening the mind and imparting a divine enthusiasm."

Walk Closer to God

Jesus said, "When he, the Spirit of truth, comes, he will guide you into all truth . . . .and he will tell you what is yet to come" (John 16:13).

The Spirit was given to help you understand the world as it really is—the world as God sees it.

Do you need guidance to choose the right path? Wisdom to order your priorities aright?

Then look to the Spirit of God. He will guide you, through prayer and the pages of Scripture, into a realm of insight about which the world knows nothing.

JULY 3

📖 Walk in the Word
1 Corinthians 3

Paul stresses that all those who work in God's kingdom should see themselves as fellow workers, building on the one foundation, Christ.

On Divisions in the Church

3 Brothers, I could not address you as spiritual but as worldly — mere infants in Christ. [2]I gave you milk, not solid food, for you were not yet ready for it. Indeed, you are still not ready. [3]You are still worldly. For since there is jealousy and quarreling among you, are you not worldly? Are you not acting like mere men? [4]For when one says, "I follow Paul," and another, "I follow Apollos," are you not mere men?

[5]What, after all, is Apollos? And what is Paul? Only servants, through whom you came to believe — as the Lord has assigned to each his task. [6]I planted the seed, Apollos watered it, but God made it grow. [7]So neither he who plants nor he who waters is anything, but only God, who makes things grow. [8]The man who plants and the man who waters have one purpose, and each will be rewarded according to his own labor. [9]For we are God's fellow workers; you are God's field, God's building.

[10]By the grace God has given me, I laid a foundation as an expert builder, and someone else is building on it. But each one should be careful how he builds. [11]For no one can lay any foundation other than the one already laid, which is Jesus Christ. [12]If any man builds on this foundation using gold, silver, costly stones, wood, hay or straw, [13]his work will be shown for what it is, because the Day will bring it to light. It will be revealed with fire, and the fire will test the quality of each man's work. [14]If what he has built survives, he will receive his reward. [15]If it is burned up, he will suffer loss; he himself will be saved, but only as one escaping through the flames.

[16]Don't you know that you yourselves are God's temple and that God's Spirit lives in you? [17]If anyone destroys God's temple, God will destroy him; for God's temple is sacred, and you are that temple.

[18]Do not deceive yourselves. If any one of you thinks he is wise by the standards of this age, he should become a "fool" so that he may become wise. [19]For the wisdom of this world is foolishness in God's sight. As it is written: "He catches the wise in their craftiness"[a]; [20]and again, "The Lord knows that the thoughts of the wise are futile."[b] [21]So then, no more boasting about men! All things are yours, [22]whether Paul or Apollos or Cephas[c] or the world or life or death or the present or the future — all are yours, [23]and you are of Christ, and Christ is of God.

[a]19 Job 5:13   [b]20 Psalm 94:11   [c]22 That is, Peter

Being Wise in God's Eyes

If any one of you thinks he is wise by the standards of this age, he should become a "fool" so that he may become wise. For the wisdom of this world is foolishness in God's sight (1 Corinthians 3:18–19).

Suppose a renowned scientist reported the conclusion that there is no God.

What would you conclude about his conclusion?

If you are wise, you would respond with the words of the psalmist: "The fool says in his heart, 'There is no God' " (Psalm 14:1).

John Calvin provides a helpful insight into this issue of human foolishness.

Walk With John Calvin

"Paul does not require that we should altogether renounce the wisdom that is implanted in us by nature but simply that we subject it to the service of God.

"The 'wisdom of the world' is that which assumes to itself authority, and does not allow itself to be regulated by the Word of God. We become a fool in this world when we give way to God and embrace with fear and reverence everything he teaches us, rather than follow what seems plausible.

"It is necessary for our wisdom to vanish in this way in order that God may have authority over us, and that we be emptied of our own understanding and be filled with the wisdom of God.

"Until an individual acknowledges that he knows nothing but what he has learned from God, he is wise in the world's account, but he is foolish in the estimation of God."

Walk Closer to God

The Christian acknowledges that God exists. The world thinks it is wise to try to live without him.

What do you think?

The Christian knows there is a God—and is labeled a "fool" by the world for believing so.

The world denies there is a God—and is labeled a "fool" by God's Word for believing so.

In the final analysis, whose "fool" would you rather be? ◖

JULY 4

📖 Walk in the Word
1 Corinthians 4

After showing how Apollos and he are both humble servants of Christ, Paul becomes angry at the Corinthians for their spiritual pride.

Apostles of Christ

4 So then, men ought to regard us as servants of Christ and as those entrusted with the secret things of God. ²Now it is required that those who have been given a trust must prove faithful. ³I care very little if I am judged by you or by any human court; indeed, I do not even judge myself. ⁴My conscience is clear, but that does not make me innocent. It is the Lord who judges me. ⁵Therefore judge nothing before the appointed time; wait till the Lord comes. He will bring to light what is hidden in darkness and will expose the motives of men's hearts. At that time each will receive his praise from God.

⁶Now, brothers, I have applied these things to myself and Apollos for your benefit, so that you may learn from us the meaning of the saying, "Do not go beyond what is written." Then you will not take pride in one man over against another. ⁷For who makes you different from anyone else? What do you have that you did not receive? And if you did receive it, why do you boast as though you did not?

⁸Already you have all you want! Already you have become rich! You have become kings—and that without us! How I wish that you really had become kings so that we might be kings with you! ⁹For it seems to me that God has put us apostles on display at the end of the procession, like men condemned to die in the arena. We have been made a spectacle to the whole universe, to angels as well as to men. ¹⁰We are fools for Christ, but you are so wise in Christ! We are weak, but you are strong! You are honored, we are dishonored! ¹¹To this very hour we go hungry and thirsty, we are in rags, we are brutally treated, we are homeless. ¹²We work hard with our own hands. When we are cursed, we bless; when we are persecuted, we endure it; ¹³when we are slandered, we answer kindly. Up to this moment we have become the scum of the earth, the refuse of the world.

¹⁴I am not writing this to shame you, but to warn you, as my dear children. ¹⁵Even though you have ten thousand guardians in Christ, you do not have many fathers, for in Christ Jesus I became your father through the gospel. ¹⁶Therefore I urge you to imitate me. ¹⁷For this reason I am sending to you Timothy, my son whom I love, who is faithful in the Lord. He will remind you of my way of life in Christ Jesus, which agrees with what I teach everywhere in every church.

¹⁸Some of you have become arrogant, as if I were not coming to you. ¹⁹But I will come to you very soon, if the Lord is willing, and then I will find out not only how these arrogant people are talking, but what power they have. ²⁰For the kingdom of God is not a matter of talk but of power. ²¹What do you prefer? Shall I come to you with a whip, or in love and with a gentle spirit?

To Make Known the Treasures of His Love

So then, men ought to regard us as servants of Christ and as those entrusted with the secret things of God. Now it is required that those who have been given a trust must prove faithful (1 Corinthians 4:1–2).

It may surprise you to learn that your responsibilities as a steward extend far beyond your financial resources.

You are also commanded to be a steward of God's grace (1 Peter 4:10) . . . of your words (Matthew 12:36) . . . of your time (Psalm 90:12) . . . in short, of yourself (Romans 14:12).

Andrew Murray explains your role as a steward of money . . . and much more.

Walk With Andrew Murray

"A steward is the one to whom the master entrusts his treasures or goods, to divide among those who have a right to them.

"God in heaven is looking for men and women on earth to make known the treasures of his love by giving them to those who have need.

"A steward must be a faithful person, fully devoted to his life task. And the messenger of the gospel must be faithful in living each day in the love and fellowship of God. God's messenger must be faithful also to others, ready to recommend God's love and to share it with others.

"Child of God, seek to have a deeper insight into what it means to be a steward of the wonderful love of God to sinners."

Walk Closer to God

Paul underscores the attitude of a steward this way: "What do you have that you did not receive?" (1 Corinthians 4:7).

Nothing! And you are responsible for everything you have received — to do with as God wills.

The twelve disciples were the first trustees of the message of life. If they had proven unfaithful in the task, where might you be today?

Now the responsibility is yours. You can give so that others might receive the gift of life.

It's a stewardship of something far more precious than money. Are you handling it that way? ◖◗

July 5

📖 Walk in the Word
1 Corinthians 5

Paul instructs the Corinthian church on how to deal with a moral problem in their midst—a man was having sexual relations with his stepmother.

Expel the Immoral Brother!

5 It is actually reported that there is sexual immorality among you, and of a kind that does not occur even among pagans: A man has his father's wife. [2]And you are proud! Shouldn't you rather have been filled with grief and have put out of your fellowship the man who did this? [3]Even though I am not physically present, I am with you in spirit. And I have already passed judgment on the one who did this, just as if I were present. [4]When you are assembled in the name of our Lord Jesus and I am with you in spirit, and the power of our Lord Jesus is present, [5]hand this man over to Satan, so that the sinful nature[a] may be destroyed and his spirit saved on the day of the Lord.

[6]Your boasting is not good. Don't you know that a little yeast works through the whole batch of dough? [7]Get rid of the old yeast that you may be a new batch without yeast—as you really are. For Christ, our Passover lamb, has been sacrificed. [8]Therefore let us keep the Festival, not with the old yeast, the yeast of malice and wickedness, but with bread without yeast, the bread of sincerity and truth.

[9]I have written you in my letter not to associate with sexually immoral people— [10]not at all meaning the people of this world who are immoral, or the greedy and swindlers, or idolaters. In that case you would have to leave this world. [11]But now I am writing you that you must not associate with anyone who calls himself a brother but is sexually immoral or greedy, an idolater or a slanderer, a drunkard or a swindler. With such a man do not even eat.

[12]What business is it of mine to judge those outside the church? Are you not to judge those inside? [13]God will judge those outside. "Expel the wicked man from among you."[b]

[a]5 Or *that his body*; or *that the flesh*   [b]13 Deut. 17:7; 19:19; 21:21; 22:21,24; 24:7

A Truly Unleavened Lump

Don't you know that a little yeast works through the whole batch of dough? Get rid of the old yeast that you may be a new batch without yeast—as you really are (1 Corinthians 5:6–7).

The Corinthian church was suffering from a serious condition . . . and didn't realize it.

Moral laxness, like yeast in a batch of dough, was threatening to permeate the entire assembly—a radical condition calling for an equally radical solution, as G. Campbell Morgan explains.

Walk With G. Campbell Morgan

"The whole body of Christ is affected by the sin of one member.

"The church's life is weaker if one in the fellowship continues in sin. The church's testimony to those outside is weakened by that fact.

"Thus, we have no right to refuse to exercise the discipline of love in the case of anyone who, to our knowledge, has flagrantly sinned.

"The law which the apostle states here is that the leaven [yeast] is to be purged. Leaven communicates itself, spreads its own corrupting force wherever it goes.

"A little leaven—one man sinning and permitted to remain within the fellowship of the church—will spread, first unconsciously and insidiously, but most surely throughout the whole church.

"There is no more difficult or delicate thing awaiting us in our church fellowship than the matter of discipline.

"May God give us of his Spirit that we may dare to deal with sin and refuse to give it harbor or refuge within our fellowship."

Walk Closer to God

Surgery is never pleasant.

But when the choice is between difficult, delicate discipline and a body whose strength is sapped by sin, which course would you choose?

Better yet, don't wait until surgery is called for. Deal with sin promptly . . . personally . . . Biblically (Matthew 18:15–17). It's much less painful than surgery for all involved. ❍

July 6

Walk in the Word
1 Corinthians 6

Paul orders the Christians in Corinth to cease instigating lawsuits against each other and to refrain from prostitution and other sexual sins; after all, they belong to Christ.

Lawsuits Among Believers

6 If any of you has a dispute with another, dare he take it before the ungodly for judgment instead of before the saints? [2]Do you not know that the saints will judge the world? And if you are to judge the world, are you not competent to judge trivial cases? [3]Do you not know that we will judge angels? How much more the things of this life! [4]Therefore, if you have disputes about such matters, appoint as judges even men of little account in the church![a] [5]I say this to shame you. Is it possible that there is nobody among you wise enough to judge a dispute between believers? [6]But instead, one brother goes to law against another—and this in front of unbelievers!

[7]The very fact that you have lawsuits among you means you have been completely defeated already. Why not rather be wronged? Why not rather be cheated? [8]Instead, you yourselves cheat and do wrong, and you do this to your brothers.

[9]Do you not know that the wicked will not inherit the kingdom of God? Do not be deceived: Neither the sexually immoral nor idolaters nor adulterers nor male prostitutes nor homosexual offenders [10]nor thieves nor the greedy nor drunkards nor slanderers nor swindlers will inherit the kingdom of God. [11]And that is what some of you were. But you were washed, you were sanctified, you were justified in the name of the Lord Jesus Christ and by the Spirit of our God.

Sexual Immorality

[12]"Everything is permissible for me"—but not everything is beneficial. "Everything is permissible for me"—but I will not be mastered by anything. [13]"Food for the stomach and the stomach for food"—but God will destroy them both. The body is not meant for sexual immorality, but for the Lord, and the Lord for the body. [14]By his power God raised the Lord from the dead, and he will raise us also. [15]Do you not know that your bodies are members of Christ himself? Shall I then take the members of Christ and unite them with a prostitute? Never! [16]Do you not know that he who unites himself with a prostitute is one with her in body? For it is said, "The two will become one flesh."[b] [17]But he who unites himself with the Lord is one with him in spirit.

[18]Flee from sexual immorality. All other sins a man commits are outside his body, but he who sins sexually sins against his own body. [19]Do you not know that your body is a temple of the Holy Spirit, who

JULY 6

is in you, whom you have received from God? You are not your own; ²⁰you were bought at a price. Therefore honor God with your body.

ᵃ4 Or matters, do you appoint as judges men of little account in the church?
ᵇ16 Gen. 2:24

PSALM 99

The LORD reigns,
    let the nations tremble;
he sits enthroned between the cherubim,
    let the earth shake.
²Great is the LORD in Zion;
    he is exalted over all the nations.
³Let them praise your great and awesome name —
    he is holy.

⁴The King is mighty, he loves justice —
    you have established equity;
 in Jacob you have done
    what is just and right.
⁵Exalt the LORD our God
    and worship at his footstool;
    he is holy.

⁶Moses and Aaron were among his priests,
    Samuel was among those who called on his name;
 they called on the LORD
    and he answered them.
⁷He spoke to them from the pillar of cloud;
    they kept his statutes and the decrees he gave them.

⁸O LORD our God,
    you answered them;
 you were to Israelᵃ a forgiving God,
    though you punished their misdeeds. ᵇ
⁹Exalt the LORD our God
    and worship at his holy mountain,
    for the LORD our God is holy.

ᵃ8 Hebrew them   ᵇ8 Or / an avenger of the wrongs done to them

JULY 6

Giving All, Gaining All

Do you not know that your body is a temple of the Holy Spirit, who is in you, whom you have received from God? You are not your own (1 Corinthians 6:19).

"Haven't you heard?"

It's a question often asked when a piece of news—good or bad—is assumed to be common knowledge.

In chapters five and six, Paul uses a similar question to jog the memories of the church members at Corinth. Seven times he challenges them by asking, "Do you not know?" (1 Corinthians 5:6; 6:2-3,9,15-16,19).

Listen as A.B. Simpson expounds on how you belong to God.

Walk With A.B. Simpson

"What a privilege that we may consecrate ourselves! What rest and comfort lie hidden in those words, 'not my own.'

"I am not responsible for my salvation, not burdened by my cares, not obliged to live for my interest, but I am altogether his. I am redeemed, owned, saved, loved, and kept in his strong, unchanging arms.

"Oh, the rest from sin and self and anxiety-producing care which true consecration brings. To be able to give him our poor weak life, with its awful possibilities and its utter helplessness. To know he will accept it, and take a joy and pride in making out of it the utmost possibilities of blessing, power, and usefulness. To give all, and find in so doing that we have gained all. To be so yielded to him in entire self-surrender that he is bound to care for us as for himself.

"We are putting ourselves in the hands of a loving Father, more solicitous for our good than we can be, and only wanting us to be fully submitted to him that he may be more free to bless us."

Walk Closer to God

God owns you because he bought you at a staggering price. Your salvation—though a free gift to you—was no "cheap grace" from God. Rather, it cost him "the precious blood of Christ, a lamb without blemish" (1 Peter 1:19).

What—haven't you heard?

JULY 7

📖 Walk in the Word
1 Corinthians 7

Paul responds to a letter from the Corinthian church, asking for advice concerning marriage and the single life.

Marriage

7 Now for the matters you wrote about: It is good for a man not to marry.[a] [2]But since there is so much immorality, each man should have his own wife, and each woman her own husband. [3]The husband should fulfill his marital duty to his wife, and likewise the wife to her husband. [4]The wife's body does not belong to her alone but also to her husband. In the same way, the husband's body does not belong to him alone but also to his wife. [5]Do not deprive each other except by mutual consent and for a time, so that you may devote yourselves to prayer. Then come together again so that Satan will not tempt you because of your lack of self-control. [6]I say this as a concession, not as a command. [7]I wish that all men were as I am. But each man has his own gift from God; one has this gift, another has that.

[8]Now to the unmarried and the widows I say: It is good for them to stay unmarried, as I am. [9]But if they cannot control themselves, they should marry, for it is better to marry than to burn with passion.

[10]To the married I give this command (not I, but the Lord): A wife must not separate from her husband. [11]But if she does, she must remain unmarried or else be reconciled to her husband. And a husband must not divorce his wife.

[12]To the rest I say this (I, not the Lord): If any brother has a wife who is not a believer and she is willing to live with him, he must not divorce her. [13]And if a woman has a husband who is not a believer and he is willing to live with her, she must not divorce him. [14]For the unbelieving husband has been sanctified through his wife, and the unbelieving wife has been sanctified through her believing husband. Otherwise your children would be unclean, but as it is, they are holy.

[15]But if the unbeliever leaves, let him do so. A believing man or woman is not bound in such circumstances; God has called us to live in peace. [16]How do you know, wife, whether you will save your husband? Or, how do you know, husband, whether you will save your wife?

[17]Nevertheless, each one should retain the place in life that the Lord assigned to him and to which God has called him. This is the rule I lay down in all the churches. [18]Was a man already circumcised when he was called? He should not become uncircumcised. Was a man uncircumcised when he was called? He should not be circumcised. [19]Circumcision is nothing and uncircumcision is nothing. Keeping God's commands is what counts. [20]Each one should remain in the situation which he was in when God called him. [21]Were you a slave when you were called? Don't let it trouble you — although if you can gain your freedom, do so. [22]For he who was a slave when he was called by the Lord is the Lord's freedman; similarly, he who was a free man when he was called is Christ's slave. [23]You were

JULY 7

bought at a price; do not become slaves of men. 24Brothers, each man, as responsible to God, should remain in the situation God called him to.

25Now about virgins: I have no command from the Lord, but I give a judgment as one who by the Lord's mercy is trustworthy. 26Because of the present crisis, I think that it is good for you to remain as you are. 27Are you married? Do not seek a divorce. Are you unmarried? Do not look for a wife. 28But if you do marry, you have not sinned; and if a virgin marries, she has not sinned. But those who marry will face many troubles in this life, and I want to spare you this.

29What I mean, brothers, is that the time is short. From now on those who have wives should live as if they had none; 30those who mourn, as if they did not; those who are happy, as if they were not; those who buy something, as if it were not theirs to keep; 31those who use the things of the world, as if not engrossed in them. For this world in its present form is passing away.

32I would like you to be free from concern. An unmarried man is concerned about the Lord's affairs—how he can please the Lord. 33But a married man is concerned about the affairs of this world—how he can please his wife— 34and his interests are divided. An unmarried woman or virgin is concerned about the Lord's affairs: Her aim is to be devoted to the Lord in both body and spirit. But a married woman is concerned about the affairs of this world—how she can please her husband. 35I am saying this for your own good, not to restrict you, but that you may live in a right way in undivided devotion to the Lord.

36If anyone thinks he is acting improperly toward the virgin he is engaged to, and if she is getting along in years and he feels he ought to marry, he should do as he wants. He is not sinning. They should get married. 37But the man who has settled the matter in his own mind, who is under no compulsion but has control over his own will, and who has made up his mind not to marry the virgin—this man also does the right thing. 38So then, he who marries the virgin does right, but he who does not marry her does even better. b

39A woman is bound to her husband as long as he lives. But if her husband dies, she is free to marry anyone she wishes, but he must belong to the Lord. 40In my judgment, she is happier if she stays as she is—and I think that I too have the Spirit of God.

a1 Or "It is good for a man not to have sexual relations with a woman."   b36-38 Or 36If anyone thinks he is not treating his daughter properly, and if she is getting along in years, and he feels she ought to marry, he should do as he wants. He is not sinning. He should let her get married. 37But the man who has settled the matter in his own mind, who is under no compulsion but has control over his own will, and who has made up his mind to keep the virgin unmarried—this man also does the right thing. 38So then, he who gives his virgin in marriage does right, but he who does not give her in marriage does even better.

Two Plus One Equals One

The husband should fulfill his marital duty to his wife, and likewise the wife to her husband (1 Corinthians 7:3).

No other institution has been pushed, pulled, probed and prodded over the centuries like the institution of marriage. And yet it has never grown obsolete, because it is not merely a good idea—it is God's idea.

Martin Luther, husband and the father of six, considered marriage to be a school of character building. Listen as he extols the high calling of holy matrimony:

Walk With Martin Luther

"Married life is no jest or to be taken lightly, but it is an excellent thing and a matter of divine seriousness.

"For it is of the highest importance to God that people be raised who may serve the Lord and promote knowledge of him through godly living and virtue, in order to fight against wickedness and the devil.

"I have always taught that marriage should not be despised, but that it be regarded according to God's Word, by which it is adorned and sanctified.

"Therefore it is not a peculiar estate [condition], but the most common and noblest estate, which pervades all Christendom, and even extends through all the world."

Walk Closer to God

For two to become truly one, there must be a third: God—the one who designed marriage in the first place.

And he has authored the most successful marriage manual of all time.

Of course, that "manual" is—the Bible. But do you know what it says in such important chapters as 1 Corinthians 7, Ephesians 5, 1 Peter 3, and Deuteronomy 6? If not, it's time to find out.

After all, who should know more about helping your marriage to succeed than the one who performed the first wedding—and blessed it with his benediction (Genesis 1:28)!

July 8

📖 Walk in the Word
1 Corinthians 8

In dealing with the issue of whether Christians may eat meat sacrificed to idols, Paul emphasizes a balance between Christian freedom and Christian love.

Food Sacrificed to Idols

8 Now about food sacrificed to idols: We know that we all possess knowledge.[a] Knowledge puffs up, but love builds up. [2]The man who thinks he knows something does not yet know as he ought to know. [3]But the man who loves God is known by God.

[4]So then, about eating food sacrificed to idols: We know that an idol is nothing at all in the world and that there is no God but one. [5]For even if there are so-called gods, whether in heaven or on earth (as indeed there are many "gods" and many "lords"), [6]yet for us there is but one God, the Father, from whom all things came and for whom we live; and there is but one Lord, Jesus Christ, through whom all things came and through whom we live.

[7]But not everyone knows this. Some people are still so accustomed to idols that when they eat such food they think of it as having been sacrificed to an idol, and since their conscience is weak, it is defiled. [8]But food does not bring us near to God; we are no worse if we do not eat, and no better if we do.

[9]Be careful, however, that the exercise of your freedom does not become a stumbling block to the weak. [10]For if anyone with a weak conscience sees you who have this knowledge eating in an idol's temple, won't he be emboldened to eat what has been sacrificed to idols? [11]So this weak brother, for whom Christ died, is destroyed by your knowledge. [12]When you sin against your brothers in this way and wound their weak conscience, you sin against Christ. [13]Therefore, if what I eat causes my brother to fall into sin, I will never eat meat again, so that I will not cause him to fall.

[a]1 Or *"We all possess knowledge,"* as you say

Lord of All Grand Designs and Daily Details

Yet for us there is but . . . one Lord, Jesus Christ, through whom all things came, and through whom we live (1 Corinthians 8:6).

Jesus had no less than forty names! Names such as Son of God, Alpha and Omega, Good Shepherd. Names that describe who he is, what he is like, what he does and will do.

But one word summarizes them all: Lord.

It's a designation the Corinthians had lost sight of, causing them to abuse their Christian freedom and ignore their Christian obligations.

Allow Cyril of Jerusalem to explain why "Lord" is a summary of who Jesus is.

Walk With Cyril of Jerusalem

"It is for the good of each individual that the Savior comes in many characters.

"He stands as the Door before those who should be entering. Before those who have prayers to pray, he stands as their mediating High Priest. He is the Lamb, to those with sins upon them, to be slain for those sins.

"He 'becomes all things to all men,' and yet never changes from his own proper nature. He adapts himself to our infirmities as the kindest of physicians or as an understanding teacher.

"He really is Lord, not because he worked at achieving it, but because he possesses by nature the dignity of being Lord. He is not called Lord out of courtesy but because he is Lord in sheer fact.

"He is the Maker of all things; thus, he is Lord of all things."

Walk Closer to God

"By him all things were created . . . . He is before all things, and in him all things hold together" (Colossians 1:16–18).

That means he has owner's rights to the universe. And that includes you.

He owns you because he made you. And he loved you enough to die for you. No wonder he deserves to be called Lord of your life. ❍

July 9

📖 Walk in the Word
1 Corinthians 9

Paul presents himself as an example of someone who has the freedom to engage in various activities but refrains from doing so in order that the cause of Christ may be advanced in the lives of others.

The Rights of an Apostle

9 Am I not free? Am I not an apostle? Have I not seen Jesus our Lord? Are you not the result of my work in the Lord? ²Even though I may not be an apostle to others, surely I am to you! For you are the seal of my apostleship in the Lord.

³This is my defense to those who sit in judgment on me. ⁴Don't we have the right to food and drink? ⁵Don't we have the right to take a believing wife along with us, as do the other apostles and the Lord's brothers and Cephas*a*? ⁶Or is it only I and Barnabas who must work for a living?

⁷Who serves as a soldier at his own expense? Who plants a vineyard and does not eat of its grapes? Who tends a flock and does not drink of the milk? ⁸Do I say this merely from a human point of view? Doesn't the Law say the same thing? ⁹For it is written in the Law of Moses: "Do not muzzle an ox while it is treading out the grain."*b* Is it about oxen that God is concerned? ¹⁰Surely he says this for us, doesn't he? Yes, this was written for us, because when the plowman plows and the thresher threshes, they ought to do so in the hope of sharing in the harvest. ¹¹If we have sown spiritual seed among you, is it too much if we reap a material harvest from you? ¹²If others have this right of support from you, shouldn't we have it all the more?

But we did not use this right. On the contrary, we put up with anything rather than hinder the gospel of Christ. ¹³Don't you know that those who work in the temple get their food from the temple, and those who serve at the altar share in what is offered on the altar? ¹⁴In the same way, the Lord has commanded that those who preach the gospel should receive their living from the gospel.

¹⁵But I have not used any of these rights. And I am not writing this in the hope that you will do such things for me. I would rather die than have anyone deprive me of this boast. ¹⁶Yet when I preach the gospel, I cannot boast, for I am compelled to preach. Woe to me if I do not preach the gospel! ¹⁷If I preach voluntarily, I have a reward; if not voluntarily, I am simply discharging the trust committed to me. ¹⁸What then is my reward? Just this: that in preaching the gospel I may offer it free of charge, and so not make use of my rights in preaching it.

¹⁹Though I am free and belong to no man, I make myself a slave to everyone, to win as many as possible. ²⁰To the Jews I became like a Jew, to win the Jews. To those under the law I became like one under the law (though I myself am not under the law), so as to win those under the law. ²¹To those not having the law I became like one not having the law (though I am not free from God's law but am under Christ's law), so as to win those not having the law. ²²To the weak I became weak, to win the weak. I have

become all things to all men so that by all possible means I might save some. ²³I do all this for the sake of the gospel, that I may share in its blessings.

²⁴Do you not know that in a race all the runners run, but only one gets the prize? Run in such a way as to get the prize. ²⁵Everyone who competes in the games goes into strict training. They do it to get a crown that will not last; but we do it to get a crown that will last forever. ²⁶Therefore I do not run like a man running aimlessly; I do not fight like a man beating the air. ²⁷No, I beat my body and make it my slave so that after I have preached to others, I myself will not be disqualified for the prize.

a5 That is, Peter   *b9* Deut. 25:4

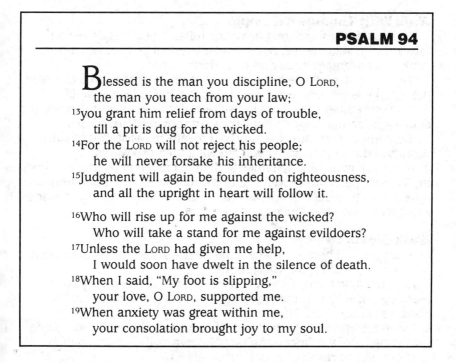

PSALM 94

Blessed is the man you discipline, O LORD,
   the man you teach from your law;
¹³you grant him relief from days of trouble,
   till a pit is dug for the wicked.
¹⁴For the LORD will not reject his people;
   he will never forsake his inheritance.
¹⁵Judgment will again be founded on righteousness,
   and all the upright in heart will follow it.

¹⁶Who will rise up for me against the wicked?
   Who will take a stand for me against evildoers?
¹⁷Unless the LORD had given me help,
   I would soon have dwelt in the silence of death.
¹⁸When I said, "My foot is slipping,"
   your love, O LORD, supported me.
¹⁹When anxiety was great within me,
   your consolation brought joy to my soul.

July 9

Mastering the Self, Conquering the Flesh

Everyone who competes in the game goes into strict training . . . I beat my body and make it my slave (1 Corinthians 9:25,27).

The Corinthians had much to learn about moderation and self-control—lessons Paul was eager to teach them.

In ancient times athletes disciplined their minds and bodies just to win a fragile wreath of laurel. How much more those who "compete in the games" with eternal, indestructible rewards in view!

More than five hundred years ago, Thomas à Kempis gave this counsel about the problem of self-control.

Walk With Thomas à Kempis

"Various desires and longings often inflame you and drive you forward with vehemence. But consider whether you are not moved for your own advantage rather than for God's honor.

"Not every desire which seems good is immediately to be followed; nor again is every unpleasant desire at the first to be avoided.

"It is sometimes expedient to use restraint even in good desires and endeavors, so that they do not become annoying distractions.

"Sometimes you must use physical means to resist valiantly the desires of the senses, and disregard what the flesh wants.

"The flesh must be disciplined and forced to remain under servitude until it is prepared for everything, and until you learn to be content with little and to be pleased with plain and simple things, not murmuring against any inconvenience."

Walk Closer to God

"Compete . . . beat . . . make it my slave." Those words demand a willful resolve and an active response.

How much you eat, sleep, exercise, relax—all these are part of learning self-mastery, that you might be strong and ready for the Master's service.

Many are unwilling to pay the price and are therefore unprepared for the rigors of the "marathon race" known as the Christian life.

How will you resolve . . . and respond?

JULY 10

📖 Walk in the Word
1 Corinthians 10:1 — 11:1

Paul warns the Corinthians against associating too closely with idol gods and then summarizes this section on Christian freedom by insisting that everything a Christian does should be done to the glory of God.

Warnings From Israel's History

10 For I do not want you to be ignorant of the fact, brothers, that our forefathers were all under the cloud and that they all passed through the sea. ²They were all baptized into Moses in the cloud and in the sea. ³They all ate the same spiritual food ⁴and drank the same spiritual drink; for they drank from the spiritual rock that accompanied them, and that rock was Christ. ⁵Nevertheless, God was not pleased with most of them; their bodies were scattered over the desert.

⁶Now these things occurred as examples*a* to keep us from setting our hearts on evil things as they did. ⁷Do not be idolaters, as some of them were; as it is written: "The people sat down to eat and drink and got up to indulge in pagan revelry."*b* ⁸We should not commit sexual immorality, as some of them did — and in one day twenty-three thousand of them died. ⁹We should not test the Lord, as some of them did — and were killed by snakes. ¹⁰And do not grumble, as some of them did — and were killed by the destroying angel.

¹¹These things happened to them as examples and were written down as warnings for us, on whom the fulfillment of the ages has come. ¹²So, if you think you are standing firm, be careful that you don't fall! ¹³No temptation has seized you except what is common to man. And God is faithful; he will not let you be tempted beyond what you can bear. But when you are tempted, he will also provide a way out so that you can stand up under it.

Idol Feasts and the Lord's Supper

¹⁴Therefore, my dear friends, flee from idolatry. ¹⁵I speak to sensible people; judge for yourselves what I say. ¹⁶Is not the cup of thanksgiving for which we give thanks a participation in the blood of Christ? And is not the bread that we break a participation in the body of Christ? ¹⁷Because there is one loaf, we, who are many, are one body, for we all partake of the one loaf.

¹⁸Consider the people of Israel: Do not those who eat the sacrifices participate in the altar? ¹⁹Do I mean then that a sacrifice offered to an idol is anything, or that an idol is anything? ²⁰No, but the sacrifices of pagans are offered to demons, not to God, and I do not want you to be participants with demons. ²¹You cannot drink the cup of the Lord and the cup of demons too; you cannot have a part in both the Lord's table and the table of demons. ²²Are we trying to arouse the Lord's jealousy? Are we stronger than he?

July 10

The Believer's Freedom

23"Everything is permissible"—but not everything is beneficial. "Everything is permissible"—but not everything is constructive. 24Nobody should seek his own good, but the good of others.

25Eat anything sold in the meat market without raising questions of conscience, 26for, "The earth is the Lord's, and everything in it."c

27If some unbeliever invites you to a meal and you want to go, eat whatever is put before you without raising questions of conscience. 28But if anyone says to you, "This has been offered in sacrifice," then do not eat it, both for the sake of the man who told you and for conscience' saked— 29the other man's conscience, I mean, not yours. For why should my freedom be judged by another's conscience? 30If I take part in the meal with thankfulness, why am I denounced because of something I thank God for?

31So whether you eat or drink or whatever you do, do it all for the glory of God. 32Do not cause anyone to stumble, whether Jews, Greeks or the church of God— 33even as I try to please everybody in every way. For I am not seeking my own good but the good of many, so that they may be saved. 1Follow my example, as I follow the example of Christ.

a6 Or types; also in verse 11   b7 Exodus 32:6   c26 Psalm 24:1   d28 Some manuscripts conscience' sake, for "the earth is the Lord's and everything in it"

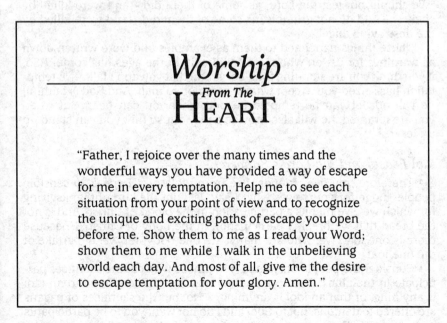

Worship
From The
Heart

"Father, I rejoice over the many times and the wonderful ways you have provided a way of escape for me in every temptation. Help me to see each situation from your point of view and to recognize the unique and exciting paths of escape you open before me. Show them to me as I read your Word; show them to me while I walk in the unbelieving world each day. And most of all, give me the desire to escape temptation for your glory. Amen."

In Days of Danger, Seeing the Paths of Safety

God is faithful; he will not let you be tempted beyond what you can bear. But when you are tempted, he will also provide a way out so that you can stand up under it (1 Corinthians 10:13).

Thomas à Kempis was right when he said, "Temptations discover what we are."

Daily confrontation with temptation is part of the price of being human.

But while you have no say in the matter of whether you will be tempted (you will be!), you do have much to say about the outcome. There will always be a way out.

John Calvin highlights this important but infrequently applied truth.

Walk With John Calvin

"Paul exhorts us to look to the Lord, because even the slightest temptation will overcome us if we rely on our own strength.

"He speaks of the Lord as faithful and true to his promises, as though he had said, 'The Lord is the sure guardian of his people, under whose protection you are safe. For he never leaves his people destitute.'

"When you are under his protection, you have no cause to fear, provided you depend entirely upon him.

"Now God helps us in two ways so that we may not be overcome by the temptation: he supplies us with strength, and he sets limits to the temptation. He knows the measure of our power, which he has conferred. According to that he regulates our temptations."

Walk Closer to God

If God has promised a way out when temptation strikes, then the real issue is not, "Can I emerge victorious?"

You can!

Rather, the questions are: "Lord, am I willing to look for your way out? When I find it, am I willing to use it? And once I've used it, am I willing to resist the urge to leave a forwarding address?"

Where there's a *willingness*, there's a way! ○

July 11

Walk in the Word
1 Corinthians 11:2–34

Paul deals with two further issues that were troubling the Corinthians: whether women should pray with their heads covered and how believers could express love for one another in their celebration of the Lord's Supper.

Propriety in Worship

²I praise you for remembering me in everything and for holding to the teachings,[a] just as I passed them on to you.

³Now I want you to realize that the head of every man is Christ, and the head of the woman is man, and the head of Christ is God. ⁴Every man who prays or prophesies with his head covered dishonors his head. ⁵And every woman who prays or prophesies with her head uncovered dishonors her head—it is just as though her head were shaved. ⁶If a woman does not cover her head, she should have her hair cut off; and if it is a disgrace for a woman to have her hair cut or shaved off, she should cover her head. ⁷A man ought not to cover his head,[b] since he is the image and glory of God; but the woman is the glory of man. ⁸For man did not come from woman, but woman from man; ⁹neither was man created for woman, but woman for man. ¹⁰For this reason, and because of the angels, the woman ought to have a sign of authority on her head.

¹¹In the Lord, however, woman is not independent of man, nor is man independent of woman. ¹²For as woman came from man, so also man is born of woman. But everything comes from God. ¹³Judge for yourselves: Is it proper for a woman to pray to God with her head uncovered? ¹⁴Does not the very nature of things teach you that if a man has long hair, it is a disgrace to him, ¹⁵but that if a woman has long hair, it is her glory? For long hair is given to her as a covering. ¹⁶If anyone wants to be contentious about this, we have no other practice—nor do the churches of God.

The Lord's Supper

¹⁷In the following directives I have no praise for you, for your meetings do more harm than good. ¹⁸In the first place, I hear that when you come together as a church, there are divisions among you, and to some extent I believe it. ¹⁹No doubt there have to be differences among you to show which of you have God's approval. ²⁰When you come together, it is not the Lord's Supper you eat, ²¹for as you eat, each of you goes ahead without waiting for anybody else. One remains hungry, another gets drunk. ²²Don't you have homes to eat and drink in? Or do you despise the church of God and humiliate those who have nothing? What shall I say to you? Shall I praise you for this? Certainly not!

²³For I received from the Lord what I also passed on to you: The Lord Jesus, on the night he was betrayed, took bread, ²⁴and when he had given thanks, he broke it and said, "This is my body, which is for you; do this in remembrance of me." ²⁵In the same way, after supper he took the cup, saying, "This cup is the new covenant in my blood; do this, whenever you

drink it, in remembrance of me." 26For whenever you eat this bread and drink this cup, you proclaim the Lord's death until he comes.

27Therefore, whoever eats the bread or drinks the cup of the Lord in an unworthy manner will be guilty of sinning against the body and blood of the Lord. 28A man ought to examine himself before he eats of the bread and drinks of the cup. 29For anyone who eats and drinks without recognizing the body of the Lord eats and drinks judgment on himself. 30That is why many among you are weak and sick, and a number of you have fallen asleep. 31But if we judged ourselves, we would not come under judgment. 32When we are judged by the Lord, we are being disciplined so that we will not be condemned with the world.

33So then, my brothers, when you come together to eat, wait for each other. 34If anyone is hungry, he should eat at home, so that when you meet together it may not result in judgment.

And when I come I will give further directions.

a2 Or traditions   b4-7 Or 4Every man who prays or prophesies with long hair dishonors his head. 5And every woman who prays or prophesies with no covering ,of hair, on her head dishonors her head—she is just like one of the "shorn women." 6If a woman has no covering, let her be for now with short hair, but since it is a disgrace for a woman to have her hair shorn or shaved, she should grow it again. 7A man ought not to have long hair

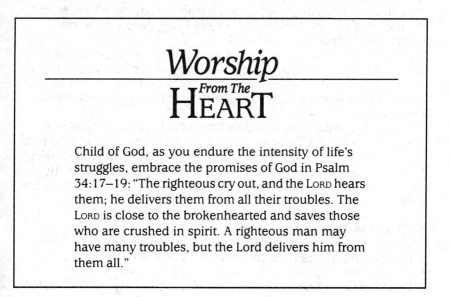

Worship
From The
HEART

Child of God, as you endure the intensity of life's struggles, embrace the promises of God in Psalm 34:17–19: "The righteous cry out, and the LORD hears them; he delivers them from all their troubles. The LORD is close to the brokenhearted and saves those who are crushed in spirit. A righteous man may have many troubles, but the Lord delivers him from them all."

July 11

God's Presence in Troubled Times

When we are judged by the Lord, we are being disciplined so that we will not be condemned with the world (1 Corinthians 11:32).

Joseph in the pit. Job among the ashes. Jeremiah in the dungeon. Paul in the Philippian jail.

Individuals God forgot about? Quite the contrary! Individuals in close communication with their Creator. Each learned that a child of God need never be alarmed at the presence of trouble when God is an ever-present companion.

Martin Luther underscores this truth.

Walk With Martin Luther

"Reason holds that if God had a watchful eye on us and loved us, he would prevent all evil and not let us suffer. But now, since all sorts of calamities come to us, we conclude: 'Either God has forgotten me, or God is hostile to me and does not want me.'

"Against such thoughts, which we harbor by nature, we must arm ourselves with God's Word. We must not judge according to our opinion but according to the Word.

"First Corinthians 11 tells us that God disciplines those whom he intends to keep and preserve for eternal life—that he cannot be hostile to them, but that they must nonetheless suffer all sorts of trouble, crosses, and temptations. We should cling to such passages in times of temptation.

"Suppose a person has a trouble from which he would gladly be relieved. If he thinks: 'See here! If I did not have this affliction, I would fall into this or that mischief; God is acting in my best interests, to keep me in his fear and drive me to the Word and prayer.' It will clearly appear that God does not discipline us because he is hostile to us, but to show us his love."

Walk Closer to God

"Father, I confess how frequently I view my problems as evidence that you have forgotten me, rather than as tokens of your constant watch and care over me.

"When troubles and trials cause me to doubt your goodness, help me instead to cling to your Word."

JULY 12

Walk in the Word
1 Corinthians 12:1–31a

Since the church in Corinth was being fragmented over the matter of spiritual gifts, Paul stresses how everything we have received from God should be used to benefit the church as a whole.

Spiritual Gifts

12 Now about spiritual gifts, brothers, I do not want you to be ignorant. ²You know that when you were pagans, somehow or other you were influenced and led astray to mute idols. ³Therefore I tell you that no one who is speaking by the Spirit of God says, "Jesus be cursed," and no one can say, "Jesus is Lord," except by the Holy Spirit.

⁴There are different kinds of gifts, but the same Spirit. ⁵There are different kinds of service, but the same Lord. ⁶There are different kinds of working, but the same God works all of them in all men.

⁷Now to each one the manifestation of the Spirit is given for the common good. ⁸To one there is given through the Spirit the message of wisdom, to another the message of knowledge by means of the same Spirit, ⁹to another faith by the same Spirit, to another gifts of healing by that one Spirit, ¹⁰to another miraculous powers, to another prophecy, to another distinguishing between spirits, to another speaking in different kinds of tongues,ᵃ and to still another the interpretation of tongues.ᵃ ¹¹All these are the work of one and the same Spirit, and he gives them to each one, just as he determines.

One Body, Many Parts

¹²The body is a unit, though it is made up of many parts; and though all its parts are many, they form one body. So it is with Christ. ¹³For we were all baptized byᵇ one Spirit into one body—whether Jews or Greeks, slave or free—and we were all given the one Spirit to drink.

¹⁴Now the body is not made up of one part but of many. ¹⁵If the foot should say, "Because I am not a hand, I do not belong to the body," it would not for that reason cease to be part of the body. ¹⁶And if the ear should say, "Because I am not an eye, I do not belong to the body," it would not for that reason cease to be part of the body. ¹⁷If the whole body were an eye, where would the sense of hearing be? If the whole body were an ear, where would the sense of smell be? ¹⁸But in fact God has arranged the parts in the body, every one of them, just as he wanted them to be. ¹⁹If they were all one part, where would the body be? ²⁰As it is, there are many parts, but one body.

²¹The eye cannot say to the hand, "I don't need you!" And the head cannot say to the feet, "I don't need you!" ²²On the contrary, those parts of the body that seem to be weaker are indispensable, ²³and the parts that we think are less honorable we treat with special honor. And the parts that are unpresentable are treated with special modesty, ²⁴while our presentable parts need no special treatment. But God has combined the members of the body and has given greater honor to the parts that lacked it, ²⁵so

JULY 12

that there should be no division in the body, but that its parts should have equal concern for each other. ²⁶If one part suffers, every part suffers with it; if one part is honored, every part rejoices with it.

²⁷Now you are the body of Christ, and each one of you is a part of it. ²⁸And in the church God has appointed first of all apostles, second prophets, third teachers, then workers of miracles, also those having gifts of healing, those able to help others, those with gifts of administration, and those speaking in different kinds of tongues. ²⁹Are all apostles? Are all prophets? Are all teachers? Do all work miracles? ³⁰Do all have gifts of healing? Do all speak in tonguesᶜ? Do all interpret? ³¹But eagerly desireᵈ the greater gifts.

*a10 Or languages; also in verse 28   b13 Or with; or in   c30 Or other languages
d31 Or But you are eagerly desiring*

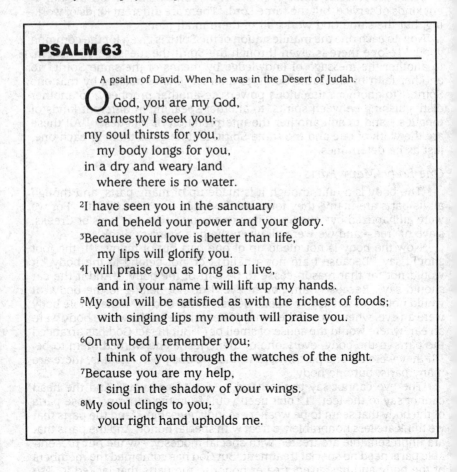

PSALM 63

A psalm of David. When he was in the Desert of Judah.

O God, you are my God,
   earnestly I seek you;
my soul thirsts for you,
   my body longs for you,
in a dry and weary land
   where there is no water.

²I have seen you in the sanctuary
   and beheld your power and your glory.
³Because your love is better than life,
   my lips will glorify you.
⁴I will praise you as long as I live,
   and in your name I will lift up my hands.
⁵My soul will be satisfied as with the richest of foods;
   with singing lips my mouth will praise you.

⁶On my bed I remember you;
   I think of you through the watches of the night.
⁷Because you are my help,
   I sing in the shadow of your wings.
⁸My soul clings to you;
   your right hand upholds me.

The Body—Where All the Bits Fit

There are different kinds of gifts, but the same Spirit
(1 Corinthians 12:4).

Chances are good you've never seen your stapes or sternum, your spleen or scapula. But look up those words in a medical dictionary, and you'll be glad they're on the job!

Each part of your anatomy differs from all the others, but all parts work together harmoniously, enabling you to live, breathe, walk and talk. Each member of Christ's body depends on all the other members for life, health and growth.

This interdependence leads John Henry Jowett to remind us to concentrate on making our unique contribution to the life of the body.

Walk With John Henry Jowett

"Our gifts will be manifold, and we must not allow the difference to breed a spirit of suspicion. Because my brother's gift is not mine, I must not suspect his calling. To one is given a trumpet, to another a lamp, to another a spade. All are holy gifts of grace.

"And thus the gifts are manifold in order that everyone may find his completeness in his brother. One person is like an eye—he is a seer of visions! Another is like a hand—he has the genius of practicality. He is a 'handy-man'! One is the architect, the other is the builder. And each requires the other, if either is to be perfected.

"And so, by God's gracious Spirit, the individual is only a bit, a portion, and he is intended to fit into the other bits, and so make the complete body of Christ."

Walk Closer to God

Are you a trumpeter for the Lord? Then blow your horn!

Does your lamp brighten another's darkness? Keep it burning!

Do you have the voice of an angel? Then let your tongue sing God's praises!

Someone else in the body needs your ministry. Only you can perform a particular act of service. Don't neglect that responsibility, for God counts on your *response to his ability*! ◖

July 13

Walk in the Word
1 Corinthians 12:31b—13:13

In this hymnlike chapter, Paul establishes that walking in love is the most important quality that a Christian should exercise.

Love

And now I will show you the most excellent way.

13 If I speak in the tongues[a] of men and of angels, but have not love, I am only a resounding gong or a clanging cymbal. ²If I have the gift of prophecy and can fathom all mysteries and all knowledge, and if I have a faith that can move mountains, but have not love, I am nothing. ³If I give all I possess to the poor and surrender my body to the flames,[b] but have not love, I gain nothing.

⁴Love is patient, love is kind. It does not envy, it does not boast, it is not proud. ⁵It is not rude, it is not self-seeking, it is not easily angered, it keeps no record of wrongs. ⁶Love does not delight in evil but rejoices with the truth. ⁷It always protects, always trusts, always hopes, always perseveres.

⁸Love never fails. But where there are prophecies, they will cease; where there are tongues, they will be stilled; where there is knowledge, it will pass away. ⁹For we know in part and we prophesy in part, ¹⁰but when perfection comes, the imperfect disappears. ¹¹When I was a child, I talked like a child, I thought like a child, I reasoned like a child. When I became a man, I put childish ways behind me. ¹²Now we see but a poor reflection as in a mirror; then we shall see face to face. Now I know in part; then I shall know fully, even as I am fully known.

¹³And now these three remain: faith, hope and love. But the greatest of these is love.

a1 Or languages *b3 Some early manuscripts body that I may boast*

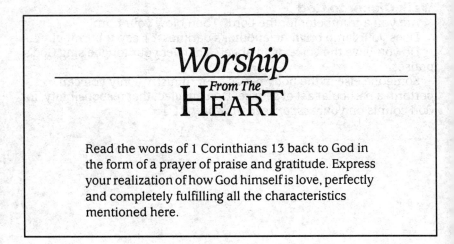

Worship
From The
Heart

Read the words of 1 Corinthians 13 back to God in the form of a prayer of praise and gratitude. Express your realization of how God himself is love, perfectly and completely fulfilling all the characteristics mentioned here.

The Last Word on Love

And now these three remain: faith, hope and love. But the greatest of these is love (1 Corinthians 13:13).

Love means giving yourself. It is patterned on the example of God himself.

God gave his only Son to individuals deserving far less. Now, in words of beauty and depth, Paul calls on grateful believers to love in return.

Jonathan Edwards probes the Bible's greatest chapter on love.

Walk With Jonathan Edwards

"A true respect for either God or man consists in love. If a man sincerely loves God, it will lead him to show all proper respect to him; and men need no other motivation to show each other all the respect that is due than the motivation of love.

"Love for God will lead a man to honor him, worship and adore him, and heartily acknowledge his greatness, glory, and dominion.

"And so it will lead to acts of obedience to God; for the servant that loves his master—like the citizen that loves his ruler—will be inclined to proper subjection.

"Love will lead us to praise God for the mercies we receive from him. Love will incline our hearts to submit to the will of God, for we are more willing that the will of those we love should be done than the will of others.

"True affection for God will lead us to acknowledge God's right and worthiness to govern.

"The true Christian is willing to admit that God is worthy of this, and it is with delight that he casts himself before the Most High, because of his sincere love for him."

Walk Closer to God

Today "I love" often means "I want" or "I desire." A fallen world has twisted the meaning of love 180 degrees.

As both Jonathan Edwards and Paul suggest, love is what you give, not what you get.

Loving God means giving yourself to God.

When was the last time you told your heavenly Father, "I love you"? ◯

July 14

📖 Walk in the Word
1 Corinthians 14:1–25

Paul points out to the Christians in Corinth that the gift of prophecy far surpasses the gift of speaking in tongues, since those who use it build up the entire church.

Gifts of Prophecy and Tongues

14 Follow the way of love and eagerly desire spiritual gifts, especially the gift of prophecy. ²For anyone who speaks in a tongue*a* does not speak to men but to God. Indeed, no one understands him; he utters mysteries with his spirit. *b* ³But everyone who prophesies speaks to men for their strengthening, encouragement and comfort. ⁴He who speaks in a tongue edifies himself, but he who prophesies edifies the church. ⁵I would like every one of you to speak in tongues,*c* but I would rather have you prophesy. He who prophesies is greater than one who speaks in tongues,*c* unless he interprets, so that the church may be edified.

⁶Now, brothers, if I come to you and speak in tongues, what good will I be to you, unless I bring you some revelation or knowledge or prophecy or word of instruction? ⁷Even in the case of lifeless things that make sounds, such as the flute or harp, how will anyone know what tune is being played unless there is a distinction in the notes? ⁸Again, if the trumpet does not sound a clear call, who will get ready for battle? ⁹So it is with you. Unless you speak intelligible words with your tongue, how will anyone know what you are saying? You will just be speaking into the air. ¹⁰Undoubtedly there are all sorts of languages in the world, yet none of them is without meaning. ¹¹If then I do not grasp the meaning of what someone is saying, I am a foreigner to the speaker, and he is a foreigner to me. ¹²So it is with you. Since you are eager to have spiritual gifts, try to excel in gifts that build up the church.

¹³For this reason anyone who speaks in a tongue should pray that he may interpret what he says. ¹⁴For if I pray in a tongue, my spirit prays, but my mind is unfruitful. ¹⁵So what shall I do? I will pray with my spirit, but I will also pray with my mind; I will sing with my spirit, but I will also sing with my mind. ¹⁶If you are praising God with your spirit, how can one who finds himself among those who do not understand*d* say "Amen" to your thanksgiving, since he does not know what you are saying? ¹⁷You may be giving thanks well enough, but the other man is not edified.

¹⁸I thank God that I speak in tongues more than all of you. ¹⁹But in the church I would rather speak five intelligible words to instruct others than ten thousand words in a tongue.

²⁰Brothers, stop thinking like children. In regard to evil be infants, but in your thinking be adults. ²¹In the Law it is written:

> "Through men of strange tongues
> and through the lips of foreigners

JULY 14

> I will speak to this people,
>> but even then they will not listen to me,"[e]
> says the Lord.

[22]Tongues, then, are a sign, not for believers but for unbelievers; prophecy, however, is for believers, not for unbelievers. [23]So if the whole church comes together and everyone speaks in tongues, and some who do not understand[f] or some unbelievers come in, will they not say that you are out of your mind? [24]But if an unbeliever or someone who does not understand[g] comes in while everybody is prophesying, he will be convinced by all that he is a sinner and will be judged by all, [25]and the secrets of his heart will be laid bare. So he will fall down and worship God, exclaiming, "God is really among you!"

a2 Or *another language*; also in verses 4, 13, 14, 19, 26 and 27   b2 Or *by the Spirit*
c5 Or *other languages*; also in verses 6, 18, 22, 23 and 39   d16 Or *among the inquirers*
e21 Isaiah 28:11,12   f23 Or *some inquirers*   g24 Or *or some inquirer*

PSALM 95

Come, let us sing for joy to the Lord;
> let us shout aloud to the Rock of our salvation.
[2]Let us come before him with thanksgiving
> and extol him with music and song.

[3]For the Lord is the great God,
> the great King above all gods.
[4]In his hand are the depths of the earth,
> and the mountain peaks belong to him.
[5]The sea is his, for he made it,
> and his hands formed the dry land.

[6]Come, let us bow down in worship,
> let us kneel before the Lord our Maker;
[7]for he is our God
> and we are the people of his pasture,
> the flock under his care.

JULY 14

Spirit of Worship, Spirit of God

I will pray with my spirit, but I will also pray with my mind; I will sing with my spirit, but I will also sing with my mind (1 Corinthians 14:15).

In one church, the piano is out of tune, the sound system buzzes, the hymnals are dog-eared, and few in the congregation can sing on key.

In another church, the building is a historic treasure, the choir is resplendently robed, singing is accompanied by organ and orchestra, and the service moves with flawless precision.

Question: In which church is worship taking place?

Answer: Either . . . or neither . . . or both. It all depends on who is leading the service. Confused?

Listen as Johann Peter Lange helps to unravel the mystery.

Walk With Johann Peter Lange

"In all true worship that is honorable to God and beneficial to his children, the Holy Spirit is the reason that it is so.

"It is only so far as he helps our infirmities and teaches us how to pray, only so far as he gives us an insight and understanding into divine truth, only so far as he inspires our songs and praises, that our worship is truly spiritual and edifying.

"So what is most needed in preparation for worship is to seek his presence and aid.

"No amount of learning, natural gifts, acquired skills, or refinements of art can compensate for that anointing of the Holy One which is promised to the believer to teach him all things."

Walk Closer to God

With the Holy Spirit, you can worship in spirit and truth, regardless of the "technical problems."

Without the Holy Spirit, you can create an elaborate production that pleases people—without worshiping God.

You needn't wait till Sunday to worship the Lord. Even now, the Spirit can lead you to declare his greatness and goodness in adoring praise.

Whether you're on key or off, the Spirit can tune your worship to please God.

JULY 15

📖 Walk in the Word
1 Corinthians 14:26–40

Paul attempts to guide the worship of the Corinthian congregation by giving several pointed rules of orderly conduct.

Orderly Worship

26What then shall we say, brothers? When you come together, everyone has a hymn, or a word of instruction, a revelation, a tongue or an interpretation. All of these must be done for the strengthening of the church. 27If anyone speaks in a tongue, two — or at the most three — should speak, one at a time, and someone must interpret. 28If there is no interpreter, the speaker should keep quiet in the church and speak to himself and God.

29Two or three prophets should speak, and the others should weigh carefully what is said. 30And if a revelation comes to someone who is sitting down, the first speaker should stop. 31For you can all prophesy in turn so that everyone may be instructed and encouraged. 32The spirits of prophets are subject to the control of prophets. 33For God is not a God of disorder but of peace.

As in all the congregations of the saints, 34women should remain silent in the churches. They are not allowed to speak, but must be in submission, as the Law says. 35If they want to inquire about something, they should ask their own husbands at home; for it is disgraceful for a woman to speak in the church.

36Did the word of God originate with you? Or are you the only people it has reached? 37If anybody thinks he is a prophet or spiritually gifted, let him acknowledge that what I am writing to you is the Lord's command. 38If he ignores this, he himself will be ignored. *a*

39Therefore, my brothers, be eager to prophesy, and do not forbid speaking in tongues. 40But everything should be done in a fitting and orderly way.

a38 Some manuscripts If he is ignorant of this, let him be ignorant

JULY 15

Peace: A Priority for Worship

For God is not a God of disorder but of peace (1 Corinthians 14:33).

The pastor was leading a group of young children from his church in a spelling bee. "All right," he turned to the next child, "your word to spell is worship."

"Warship. W-A-R-S-H-I-P. Am I right?" the child asked. With a deep sigh, the pastor replied, "Yes, unfortunately, much of the time you are!"

In the Corinthian church, confusion and strife were marking the worship services. John Calvin points to the importance of peace and order as priorities in corporate worship.

Walk With John Calvin

"We do not serve God unless we are in any case lovers of peace and are eager to promote it. Whenever there is a disposition to quarrel, there you can be certain God does not reign.

"Yet many people fly into a rage about nothing, or they trouble the church from a desire that they may somehow ride into view and seem to be someone.

"Let us therefore bear in mind that, as servants of Christ, this mark must be kept in view—to aim at peace and concord, conduct ourselves peaceably, and avoid contentions to the utmost of our power.

"For if we are called to contend against wicked doctrines, we must persevere in the contest. We must make it our aim that the truth of God may maintain its ground without contention."

Walk Closer to God

Interruptions and distractions, disorder and discord—not a pretty scene under any circumstances but particularly inappropriate in the church of Jesus Christ.

Why? Because God has called his people to worship him in a way that draws attention to the object of worship, not the worshipers themselves. Worship that is in spirit . . . in truth . . . in peace . . . in order.

As John Calvin has commented, "How easy it is to *say* this!" But what will you do about it?

JULY 16

Walk in the Word
1 Corinthians 15:1–34

As some in Corinth were denying that there would ever be a day of resurrection, Paul points out their faulty teaching by centering his thoughts on the resurrection of Christ.

The Resurrection of Christ

15 Now, brothers, I want to remind you of the gospel I preached to you, which you received and on which you have taken your stand. ²By this gospel you are saved, if you hold firmly to the word I preached to you. Otherwise, you have believed in vain.

³For what I received I passed on to you as of first importance[a]: that Christ died for our sins according to the Scriptures, ⁴that he was buried, that he was raised on the third day according to the Scriptures, ⁵and that he appeared to Peter,[b] and then to the Twelve. ⁶After that, he appeared to more than five hundred of the brothers at the same time, most of whom are still living, though some have fallen asleep. ⁷Then he appeared to James, then to all the apostles, ⁸and last of all he appeared to me also, as to one abnormally born.

⁹For I am the least of the apostles and do not even deserve to be called an apostle, because I persecuted the church of God. ¹⁰But by the grace of God I am what I am, and his grace to me was not without effect. No, I worked harder than all of them—yet not I, but the grace of God that was with me. ¹¹Whether, then, it was I or they, this is what we preach, and this is what you believed.

The Resurrection of the Dead

¹²But if it is preached that Christ has been raised from the dead, how can some of you say that there is no resurrection of the dead? ¹³If there is no resurrection of the dead, then not even Christ has been raised. ¹⁴And if Christ has not been raised, our preaching is useless and so is your faith. ¹⁵More than that, we are then found to be false witnesses about God, for we have testified about God that he raised Christ from the dead. But he did not raise him if in fact the dead are not raised. ¹⁶For if the dead are not raised, then Christ has not been raised either. ¹⁷And if Christ has not been raised, your faith is futile; you are still in your sins. ¹⁸Then those also who have fallen asleep in Christ are lost. ¹⁹If only for this life we have hope in Christ, we are to be pitied more than all men.

²⁰But Christ has indeed been raised from the dead, the firstfruits of those who have fallen asleep. ²¹For since death came through a man, the resurrection of the dead comes also through a man. ²²For as in Adam all die, so in Christ all will be made alive. ²³But each in his own turn: Christ, the firstfruits; then, when he comes, those who belong to him. ²⁴Then the end will come, when he hands over the kingdom to God the Father after he has destroyed all dominion, authority and power. ²⁵For he must reign until he has put all his enemies under his feet. ²⁶The last enemy to be destroyed is death. ²⁷For he "has put everything under his feet."[c] Now when it says

July 16

that "everything" has been put under him, it is clear that this does not include God himself, who put everything under Christ. 28When he has done this, then the Son himself will be made subject to him who put everything under him, so that God may be all in all.

29Now if there is no resurrection, what will those do who are baptized for the dead? If the dead are not raised at all, why are people baptized for them? 30And as for us, why do we endanger ourselves every hour? 31I die every day—I mean that, brothers—just as surely as I glory over you in Christ Jesus our Lord. 32If I fought wild beasts in Ephesus for merely human reasons, what have I gained? If the dead are not raised,

> "Let us eat and drink,
>   for tomorrow we die."d

33Do not be misled: "Bad company corrupts good character." 34Come back to your senses as you ought, and stop sinning; for there are some who are ignorant of God—I say this to your shame.

a3 Or *you at the first*   b5 Greek *Cephas*   c27 Psalm 8:6   d32 Isaiah 22:13

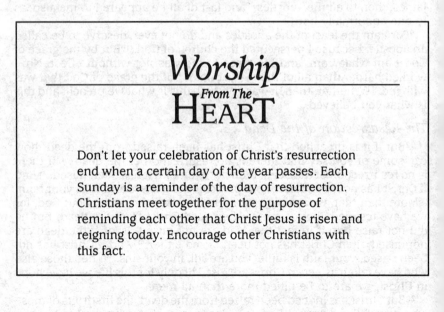

Worship
From The
Heart

Don't let your celebration of Christ's resurrection end when a certain day of the year passes. Each Sunday is a reminder of the day of resurrection. Christians meet together for the purpose of reminding each other that Christ Jesus is risen and reigning today. Encourage other Christians with this fact.

Silver Thread of the Resurrection

And if Christ has not been raised, your faith is futile; you are still in your sins. . . . But Christ has indeed been raised from the dead, the firstfruits of those who have fallen asleep (1 Corinthians 15:17,20).

Resurrection, the grand theme of 1 Corinthians 15, is the heart of the Christian faith. Expose it as a fraud, and all else becomes meaningless.

Yet, the resurrection is no mere illusion. It is a fact of history, confirmed by hundreds of eyewitnesses and abundant evidence.

Charles Spurgeon expands these thoughts.

Walk With Charles Spurgeon

"Christianity rests upon the fact that 'Christ is risen from the dead.' The deity of Christ finds its surest proof in his resurrection, since he was 'declared to be the Son of God with power . . . by the resurrection from the dead.' It would be reasonable to doubt his deity if he had not risen.

"Moreover, Christ's sovereignty depends upon his resurrection, 'for to this end Christ died and rose and lived again, that he might be Lord of both the dead and the living.'

"Our justification is linked with Christ's triumphant victory over death and the grave; for he 'was delivered up because of our offenses, and was raised because of our justification.'

"And most certainly our ultimate resurrection rests here; for 'he who raised up Christ from the dead will also give life to your mortal bodies through his Spirit who dwells in you.'

"The silver thread of resurrection runs through all the believer's blessings, from his regeneration to his eternal glory, binding them together."

Walk Closer to God

Many have scoffed at the resurrection, only to find themselves later bowing in submission to the risen Christ. The Athenians responded with mocking and ridicule (Acts 17:32); the Bereans, with careful investigation and belief (Acts 17:11–12).

And you? What will you do with the compelling evidence for the resurrection—evidence only a scoffer would ignore?

July 17

Walk in the Word
1 Corinthians 15:35–58

Paul continues his discussion of the resurrection by giving various details of the glorified body and of the order of events on the day of resurrection.

The Resurrection Body

[35]But someone may ask, "How are the dead raised? With what kind of body will they come?" [36]How foolish! What you sow does not come to life unless it dies. [37]When you sow, you do not plant the body that will be, but just a seed, perhaps of wheat or of something else. [38]But God gives it a body as he has determined, and to each kind of seed he gives its own body. [39]All flesh is not the same: Men have one kind of flesh, animals have another, birds another and fish another. [40]There are also heavenly bodies and there are earthly bodies; but the splendor of the heavenly bodies is one kind, and the splendor of the earthly bodies is another. [41]The sun has one kind of splendor, the moon another and the stars another; and star differs from star in splendor.

[42]So will it be with the resurrection of the dead. The body that is sown is perishable, it is raised imperishable; [43]it is sown in dishonor, it is raised in glory; it is sown in weakness, it is raised in power; [44]it is sown a natural body, it is raised a spiritual body.

If there is a natural body, there is also a spiritual body. [45]So it is written: "The first man Adam became a living being"[a]; the last Adam, a life-giving spirit. [46]The spiritual did not come first, but the natural, and after that the spiritual. [47]The first man was of the dust of the earth, the second man from heaven. [48]As was the earthly man, so are those who are of the earth; and as is the man from heaven, so also are those who are of heaven. [49]And just as we have borne the likeness of the earthly man, so shall we[b] bear the likeness of the man from heaven.

[50]I declare to you, brothers, that flesh and blood cannot inherit the kingdom of God, nor does the perishable inherit the imperishable. [51]Listen, I tell you a mystery: We will not all sleep, but we will all be changed— [52]in a flash, in the twinkling of an eye, at the last trumpet. For the trumpet will sound, the dead will be raised imperishable, and we will be changed. [53]For the perishable must clothe itself with the imperishable, and the mortal with immortality. [54]When the perishable has been clothed with the imperishable, and the mortal with immortality, then the saying that is written will come true: "Death has been swallowed up in victory."[c]

[55]"Where, O death, is your victory?
Where, O death, is your sting?"[d]

[56]The sting of death is sin, and the power of sin is the law. [57]But thanks be to God! He gives us the victory through our Lord Jesus Christ.

[58]Therefore, my dear brothers, stand firm. Let nothing move you. Always give yourselves fully to the work of the Lord, because you know that your labor in the Lord is not in vain.

[a]45 Gen. 2:7   [b]49 Some early manuscripts *so let us*   [c]54 Isaiah 25:8   [d]55 Hosea 13:14

The Believer's Sure Victory—in Jesus

"Where, O death, is your victory? Where, O death, is your sting?". . . But thanks be to God! He gives us the victory through our Lord Jesus Christ (1 Corinthians 15:55,57).

An eternity with God and away from the presence of corruption and sin. For the Christian, that's the glory that lies beyond the doorway of death.

That's a thought that prompts Paul to break forth in thanks and praise.

Matthew Henry adds his own postscript of praise—a word written not long before his death.

Walk With Matthew Henry

"What can be more joyous in itself than the saints' triumph over death, when they shall rise again?

"Those who remain under the power of death can have no heart to praise. But such triumphs tune the tongues of the saints to thankfulness and praise for the victory and for the means by which it is obtained.

"That victory is not obtained by our power, but by God's power; not given because we are worthy, but because Christ is worthy.

"How many springs of joy to the saints and thanksgiving to God are opened by the death and resurrection, the suffering and conquest, of our Redeemer! With what acclamations will saints rising from the dead applaud him! How the heavens will resound with his praises forever!

" 'Thanks be to God' will be the theme of their song, and angels will join the chorus and declare their consent with a loud 'Amen. Hallelujah!' "

Walk Closer to God

Those without Christ face a hopeless end; those with Christ look forward to an endless hope.

Those under the power of death can have no heart to praise.

But you have a message of life to share with those living in the fear of death.

What grander chorus of praise could you sing to God—or share with others—than that of victory in Jesus! You'll never tire of singing it eternally. ◖

A Blind Writer of Hymns

Though blinded as an infant by faulty medical care, Fanny Crosby chose not to live as an invalid. Relying on friends to write as she dictated, she wrote hymns that continue to convict sinners and call Christians to action.

Born in New York in 1823, Miss Crosby entered the New York Institute for the Blind at age eleven, remaining there for twenty-three years as pupil and teacher. It was there she began writing poetry, and in 1858 she married a blind musician, Alexander Van Alstype; together they produced a number of hymns. By the time of her death in 1915, she had written more than two thousand songs and hymns, of which sixty are still commonly sung today.

Some of Fanny's themes were suggested by pastors; others were inspired by tunes presented to her; still others originated with her own experiences as she interacted with other Christians. The hymn "Nearer My God to Thee," for example, came to her while sitting on the porch of Dr. William Doane. The family described for her the beautiful sunset, and they began marvelling together about the Creator of that sunset. Suddenly Fanny asked Dr. Doane if he would write down a verse that had come to her mind during that discussion. She then dictated the hymn in perfect form, and he set it to music.

Singing is one of the most powerful expressions of the Christian faith and one of the ways in which God wants us to bring praise to him. Why not let Fanny Crosby's life of service to God and his people inspire you to sing his praises as you continue your study of God's Word?

A LESSON FROM THE LIFE OF FANNY CROSBY

I shall know him, I shall know him, And redeemed by his side I shall stand. I shall know him, I shall know him, By the print of the nails in his hands.

JULY 18

📖 Walk in the Word
1 Corinthians 16

Paul draws this first letter to the Corinthians to a close by discussing his future plans and urging them to remain steadfast in their Christian walk of life.

The Collection for God's People

16 Now about the collection for God's people: Do what I told the Galatian churches to do. [2]On the first day of every week, each one of you should set aside a sum of money in keeping with his income, saving it up, so that when I come no collections will have to be made. [3]Then, when I arrive, I will give letters of introduction to the men you approve and send them with your gift to Jerusalem. [4]If it seems advisable for me to go also, they will accompany me.

Personal Requests

[5]After I go through Macedonia, I will come to you — for I will be going through Macedonia. [6]Perhaps I will stay with you awhile, or even spend the winter, so that you can help me on my journey, wherever I go. [7]I do not want to see you now and make only a passing visit; I hope to spend some time with you, if the Lord permits. [8]But I will stay on at Ephesus until Pentecost, [9]because a great door for effective work has opened to me, and there are many who oppose me.

[10]If Timothy comes, see to it that he has nothing to fear while he is with you, for he is carrying on the work of the Lord, just as I am. [11]No one, then, should refuse to accept him. Send him on his way in peace so that he may return to me. I am expecting him along with the brothers.

[12]Now about our brother Apollos: I strongly urged him to go to you with the brothers. He was quite unwilling to go now, but he will go when he has the opportunity.

[13]Be on your guard; stand firm in the faith; be men of courage; be strong. [14]Do everything in love.

[15]You know that the household of Stephanas were the first converts in Achaia, and they have devoted themselves to the service of the saints. I urge you, brothers, [16]to submit to such as these and to everyone who joins in the work, and labors at it. [17]I was glad when Stephanas, Fortunatus and Achaicus arrived, because they have supplied what was lacking from you. [18]For they refreshed my spirit and yours also. Such men deserve recognition.

Final Greetings

[19]The churches in the province of Asia send you greetings. Aquila and Priscilla[a] greet you warmly in the Lord, and so does the church that meets at their house. [20]All the brothers here send you greetings. Greet one another with a holy kiss.

July 18

²¹I, Paul, write this greeting in my own hand.
²²If anyone does not love the Lord—a curse be on him. Come, O Lord[b]!
²³The grace of the Lord Jesus be with you.
²⁴My love to all of you in Christ Jesus. Amen.[c]

[a]19 Greek *Prisca*, a variant of *Priscilla*   [b]22 In Aramaic the expression *Come, O Lord* is *Marana tha*.   [c]24 Some manuscripts do not have *Amen*.

PSALM 116

I love the LORD, for he heard my voice;
  he heard my cry for mercy.
²Because he turned his ear to me,
  I will call on him as long as I live.

³The cords of death entangled me,
  the anguish of the grave[a] came upon me;
  I was overcome by trouble and sorrow.
⁴Then I called on the name of the LORD:
  "O LORD, save me!"

⁵The LORD is gracious and righteous;
  our God is full of compassion.
⁶The LORD protects the simplehearted;
  when I was in great need, he saved me.

⁷Be at rest once more, O my soul,
  for the LORD has been good to you.

¹²How can I repay the LORD
  for all his goodness to me?
¹³I will lift up the cup of salvation
  and call on the name of the LORD.
¹⁴I will fulfill my vows to the LORD
  in the presence of all his people.

[a]3 Hebrew *Sheol*

The Test of Our Love

If anyone does not love the Lord—a curse be on him. Come, O Lord! (1 Corinthians 16:22).

Here in the last chapter, Paul poses the "final examination question" on which all others hinge: Do you love the Lord Jesus Christ?

No matter how impressive your record of service, how extensive the credentials or expertise you bring to the Lord or offer to his people, you must honestly answer that basic question. If you love the Lord with the same kind of love that a child shows a parent, you will pass life's final exam—and all the others in between—as Charles Hodge explains.

Walk With Charles Hodge

"If we love Christ, we shall be zealous for his glory. Any neglect or irreverence shown the Savior will wound our hearts. Any honor rendered him will give us delight.

"We will love those who love and honor him, and avoid those who neglect and abuse him.

"The son who loves his father desires to please him, to do his will, obey his command, observe his counsel, always and in all places. So those who love Christ keep his commandments. This is the test of love for Christ: not emotion, not excited feelings, but obedience.

"What say you? Do you love the Lord Jesus Christ? On this question depends eternity.

"Here on earth those who love and those who do not love form distinct classes, though intermingled. Hereafter they will be separated. Do you desire to love? It is love only if it leads to a constant endeavor to do his will and to associate with his people."

Walk Closer to God

Jesus lovingly came to bring God's love to earth. He lovingly served all who acknowledged their need. He lovingly sacrificed his life that sins might be forgiven.

Now he waits for you to return that love in simple gratitude, in loving obedience to him, in loving service to others, in loving fellowship with those who call him Lord. ◖

JULY 19

📖 Walk in the Word
2 Corinthians 1:1 — 2:11

Paul opens his second letter to Corinth with some personal matters: how difficult his ministry in Ephesus has been, why he had to change his travel plans, and how badly he feels about a harsh letter that he wrote to them.

1 Paul, an apostle of Christ Jesus by the will of God, and Timothy our brother,

To the church of God in Corinth, together with all the saints throughout Achaia:

²Grace and peace to you from God our Father and the Lord Jesus Christ.

The God of All Comfort

³Praise be to the God and Father of our Lord Jesus Christ, the Father of compassion and the God of all comfort, ⁴who comforts us in all our troubles, so that we can comfort those in any trouble with the comfort we ourselves have received from God. ⁵For just as the sufferings of Christ flow over into our lives, so also through Christ our comfort overflows. ⁶If we are distressed, it is for your comfort and salvation; if we are comforted, it is for your comfort, which produces in you patient endurance of the same sufferings we suffer. ⁷And our hope for you is firm, because we know that just as you share in our sufferings, so also you share in our comfort.

⁸We do not want you to be uninformed, brothers, about the hardships we suffered in the province of Asia. We were under great pressure, far beyond our ability to endure, so that we despaired even of life. ⁹Indeed, in our hearts we felt the sentence of death. But this happened that we might not rely on ourselves but on God, who raises the dead. ¹⁰He has delivered us from such a deadly peril, and he will deliver us. On him we have set our hope that he will continue to deliver us, ¹¹as you help us by your prayers. Then many will give thanks on our*ᵃ* behalf for the gracious favor granted us in answer to the prayers of many.

Paul's Change of Plans

¹²Now this is our boast: Our conscience testifies that we have conducted ourselves in the world, and especially in our relations with you, in the holiness and sincerity that are from God. We have done so not according to worldly wisdom but according to God's grace. ¹³For we do not write you anything you cannot read or understand. And I hope that, ¹⁴as you have understood us in part, you will come to understand fully that you can boast of us just as we will boast of you in the day of the Lord Jesus.

¹⁵Because I was confident of this, I planned to visit you first so that you might benefit twice. ¹⁶I planned to visit you on my way to Macedonia and to come back to you from Macedonia, and then to have you send me on my way to Judea. ¹⁷When I planned this, did I do it lightly? Or do I make my plans in a worldly manner so that in the same breath I say, "Yes, yes" and "No, no"?

[18]But as surely as God is faithful, our message to you is not "Yes" and "No." [19]For the Son of God, Jesus Christ, who was preached among you by me and Silas[b] and Timothy, was not "Yes" and "No," but in him it has always been "Yes." [20]For no matter how many promises God has made, they are "Yes" in Christ. And so through him the "Amen" is spoken by us to the glory of God. [21]Now it is God who makes both us and you stand firm in Christ. He anointed us, [22]set his seal of ownership on us, and put his Spirit in our hearts as a deposit, guaranteeing what is to come.

[23]I call God as my witness that it was in order to spare you that I did not return to Corinth. [24]Not that we lord it over your faith, but we work with you for your joy, because it is by faith you stand firm. [1]So I made up my mind that I would not make another painful visit to you. [2]For if I grieve you, who is left to make me glad but you whom I have grieved? [3]I wrote as I did so that when I came I should not be distressed by those who ought to make me rejoice. I had confidence in all of you, that you would all share my joy. [4]For I wrote you out of great distress and anguish of heart and with many tears, not to grieve you but to let you know the depth of my love for you.

Forgiveness for the Sinner

[5]If anyone has caused grief, he has not so much grieved me as he has grieved all of you, to some extent — not to put it too severely. [6]The punishment inflicted on him by the majority is sufficient for him. [7]Now instead, you ought to forgive and comfort him, so that he will not be overwhelmed by excessive sorrow. [8]I urge you, therefore, to reaffirm your love for him. [9]The reason I wrote you was to see if you would stand the test and be obedient in everything. [10]If you forgive anyone, I also forgive him. And what I have forgiven — if there was anything to forgive — I have forgiven in the sight of Christ for your sake, [11]in order that Satan might not outwit us. For we are not unaware of his schemes.

a11 Many manuscripts your   *b19 Greek Silvanus, a variant of Silas*

JULY 19

Trouble: Sign of an Active Soul

> For just as the sufferings of Christ flow over into our lives, so also through Christ our comfort overflows (2 Corinthians 1:5).

When Christ gives peace, he says, "I have told you these things, so that in me you may have peace. In this world you will have trouble. But take heart! I have overcome the world" (John 16:33).

He is a peace that conquers and comforts.

In the opening words of the second letter to the Corinthians, Paul speaks of the comfort of Christ.

But, as John Henry Jowett points out, it is peace that comes to aid in the struggle, not to avoid it.

Walk With John Henry Jowett

"It is possible to evade a multitude of sorrows by the cultivation of an insignificant life.

"Indeed, if a man's ambition is to avoid the troubles of life, the recipe is simple: Shed your ambitions in every direction, cut the wings of every soaring purpose, and seek a little life with the fewest contacts and relations.

"If you want to get through the world with the smallest trouble, you must reduce yourself to the smallest compass. Tiny souls can dodge through life; bigger souls are blocked on every side.

"As soon as a man begins to enlarge his life, his resistances are multiplied. Let a man remove his petty selfish purposes and enthrone Christ, and his sufferings will be increased on every side.

"So it was with the Savior. His all-absorbing, redemptive purpose was bound to introduce him to endless suffering."

Walk Closer to God

Who is better qualified to work for peace than those who have experienced God's peace firsthand?

You have been comforted by Christ—not to make you comfortable but to make you a comforter, a dispenser of peace.

But it begins with a life at peace with God . . . forgiven . . . cleansed . . . comforted.

Is that you?

It can be if you make 2 Corinthians 1:3–5 the prayer of your heart . . . right now. ○

JULY 20

📖 Walk in the Word
2 Corinthians 2:12 – 3:18

Paul excitedly shows how the new covenant in Jesus Christ is so much greater than the old covenant that came through Moses.

Ministers of the New Covenant

¹²Now when I went to Troas to preach the gospel of Christ and found that the Lord had opened a door for me, ¹³I still had no peace of mind, because I did not find my brother Titus there. So I said good-by to them and went on to Macedonia.

¹⁴But thanks be to God, who always leads us in triumphal procession in Christ and through us spreads everywhere the fragrance of the knowledge of him. ¹⁵For we are to God the aroma of Christ among those who are being saved and those who are perishing. ¹⁶To the one we are the smell of death; to the other, the fragrance of life. And who is equal to such a task? ¹⁷Unlike so many, we do not peddle the word of God for profit. On the contrary, in Christ we speak before God with sincerity, like men sent from God.

3 Are we beginning to commend ourselves again? Or do we need, like some people, letters of recommendation to you or from you? ²You yourselves are our letter, written on our hearts, known and read by everybody. ³You show that you are a letter from Christ, the result of our ministry, written not with ink but with the Spirit of the living God, not on tablets of stone but on tablets of human hearts.

⁴Such confidence as this is ours through Christ before God. ⁵Not that we are competent in ourselves to claim anything for ourselves, but our competence comes from God. ⁶He has made us competent as ministers of a new covenant—not of the letter but of the Spirit; for the letter kills, but the Spirit gives life.

The Glory of the New Covenant

⁷Now if the ministry that brought death, which was engraved in letters on stone, came with glory, so that the Israelites could not look steadily at the face of Moses because of its glory, fading though it was, ⁸will not the ministry of the Spirit be even more glorious? ⁹If the ministry that condemns men is glorious, how much more glorious is the ministry that brings righteousness! ¹⁰For what was glorious has no glory now in comparison with the surpassing glory. ¹¹And if what was fading away came with glory, how much greater is the glory of that which lasts!

¹²Therefore, since we have such a hope, we are very bold. ¹³We are not like Moses, who would put a veil over his face to keep the Israelites from gazing at it while the radiance was fading away. ¹⁴But their minds were made dull, for to this day the same veil remains when the old covenant is read. It has not been removed, because only in Christ is it taken away. ¹⁵Even to this day when Moses is read, a veil covers their hearts. ¹⁶But whenever anyone turns to the Lord, the veil is taken away. ¹⁷Now the Lord is the Spirit, and where the Spirit of the Lord is, there is freedom. ¹⁸And

July 20

we, who with unveiled faces all reflect[a] the Lord's glory, are being transformed into his likeness with ever-increasing glory, which comes from the Lord, who is the Spirit.

[a]18 Or *contemplate*

PSALM 1

Blessed is the man
  who does not walk in the counsel of the wicked
or stand in the way of sinners
  or sit in the seat of mockers.
2But his delight is in the law of the LORD,
  and on his law he meditates day and night.
3He is like a tree planted by streams of water,
  which yields its fruit in season
and whose leaf does not wither.
  Whatever he does prospers.

4Not so the wicked!
  They are like chaff
  that the wind blows away.
5Therefore the wicked will not stand in the judgment,
  nor sinners in the assembly of the righteous.

6For the LORD watches over the way of the righteous,
  but the way of the wicked will perish.

A Letter to the World

You yourselves are our letter, written on our hearts, known and read by everybody . . . written not with ink but with the Spirit of the living God (2 Corinthians 3:2–3).

In this passage, Paul likens the Christian to a literary production ("letter") of Christ—a letter others can read.

It's as if he were asking the reader: "Would the message of your life demonstrate the personality and character of Christ . . . or something else?"

H.A. Ironside itemizes what some of those telltale markings of Christ in your life might be.

Walk With H.A. Ironside

"Do people see something of the patience of Christ, the meekness of Christ, the purity of Christ, the love of Christ, and the tender compassion of Christ in me?

"As I mingle with others in my daily employment, those with whom I have the most to do should see a difference.

"Do they say, 'Well, so-and-so may be a Christian; if he is, I do not think much of Christianity'?

"Or are we so living Christ that others looking upon us say, 'Well, if that is Christianity, I wish I knew something of it in my own life'?

"Long for someone to say to you: 'I cannot help but believe in the reality of the message you preach because of the effect it has on the people I have seen who believe it.'

"This is what Paul means when he says that we are the letter of Christ."

Walk Closer to God

When you are truly a letter of Christ, no one will be able to deny the fact.

The markings will be there: Patience. Kindness. Goodness. Love. Self-control . . . in essence, all the fruit of the Spirit (Galatians 5:22–23).

Your life can be an open book for all to see the life of Christ in you—a love letter to a lost world.

The "letter" of one life is worth a thousand words. But only you can determine the content of that letter and what it will reveal to those who take the time to read it.

July 21

Walk in the Word
2 Corinthians 4

Even though life on this earth can be difficult at times, Paul stresses how easy it is to persevere when we see the glory of Jesus Christ and his gospel.

Treasures in Jars of Clay

4 Therefore, since through God's mercy we have this ministry, we do not lose heart. [2]Rather, we have renounced secret and shameful ways; we do not use deception, nor do we distort the word of God. On the contrary, by setting forth the truth plainly we commend ourselves to every man's conscience in the sight of God. [3]And even if our gospel is veiled, it is veiled to those who are perishing. [4]The god of this age has blinded the minds of unbelievers, so that they cannot see the light of the gospel of the glory of Christ, who is the image of God. [5]For we do not preach ourselves, but Jesus Christ as Lord, and ourselves as your servants for Jesus' sake. [6]For God, who said, "Let light shine out of darkness,"[a] made his light shine in our hearts to give us the light of the knowledge of the glory of God in the face of Christ.

[7]But we have this treasure in jars of clay to show that this all-surpassing power is from God and not from us. [8]We are hard pressed on every side, but not crushed; perplexed, but not in despair; [9]persecuted, but not abandoned; struck down, but not destroyed. [10]We always carry around in our body the death of Jesus, so that the life of Jesus may also be revealed in our body. [11]For we who are alive are always being given over to death for Jesus' sake, so that his life may be revealed in our mortal body. [12]So then, death is at work in us, but life is at work in you.

[13]It is written: "I believed; therefore I have spoken."[b] With that same spirit of faith we also believe and therefore speak, [14]because we know that the one who raised the Lord Jesus from the dead will also raise us with Jesus and present us with you in his presence. [15]All this is for your benefit, so that the grace that is reaching more and more people may cause thanksgiving to overflow to the glory of God.

[16]Therefore we do not lose heart. Though outwardly we are wasting away, yet inwardly we are being renewed day by day. [17]For our light and momentary troubles are achieving for us an eternal glory that far outweighs them all. [18]So we fix our eyes not on what is seen, but on what is unseen. For what is seen is temporary, but what is unseen is eternal.

[a]6 Gen. 1:3   [b]13 Psalm 116:10

JULY 21

Focusing on the Future Is a Glorious Way to Live

For our light and momentary troubles are achieving for us an eternal glory that far outweighs them all (2 Corinthians 4:17).

Anticipation is the delight of looking forward to not-yet-experienced events: graduation, Christmas, birthdays, reunions, summer.

And for the Christian, life after death and a home in heaven.

When the present is unpleasant, take the advice of Charles Spurgeon and try focusing instead on the future.

Walk With Charles Spurgeon

"In our Christian pilgrimage, it is good to be looking forward.

"Whether it be for hope or joy, for consolation or for the inspiring of our love, the future must, after all, be the grand object of the eye of faith.

"Looking into the future, we see sin cast out, the body of sin and death destroyed, the soul made perfect and fit to be a partaker of the saints in light.

"Looking further yet, the believer's enlightened eye can see death's river passed and the celestial city standing ahead.

"He sees himself enter the gates, hailed as more than conqueror, embraced in the arms of Jesus, glorified, and made to sit together with him.

"The thought of this future may well relieve the darkness of the past and the gloom of the present.

"The joys of heaven will surely compensate for the sorrows of earth."

Walk Closer to God

Struggles with sin.

Pressures at work.

Relationships that have soured.

It's for certain the "light and momentary troubles" Paul speaks about weren't reserved for only the first-century believers!

But when the outlook is bleak, try the uplook.

You have an eternity with the Father to look forward to. Dwelling on the past may cause you to groan. But focusing on the future is a glorious way to live!

July 22

Walk in the Word
2 Corinthians 5:1–10

*Paul assures the Corinthians of what is in store for them when they die —
they go to the heavenly dwelling place that the Lord is preparing.*

Our Heavenly Dwelling

5 Now we know that if the earthly tent we live in is destroyed, we have a building from God, an eternal house in heaven, not built by human hands. ²Meanwhile we groan, longing to be clothed with our heavenly dwelling, ³because when we are clothed, we will not be found naked. ⁴For while we are in this tent, we groan and are burdened, because we do not wish to be unclothed but to be clothed with our heavenly dwelling, so that what is mortal may be swallowed up by life. ⁵Now it is God who has made us for this very purpose and has given us the Spirit as a deposit, guaranteeing what is to come.

⁶Therefore we are always confident and know that as long as we are at home in the body we are away from the Lord. ⁷We live by faith, not by sight. ⁸We are confident, I say, and would prefer to be away from the body and at home with the Lord. ⁹So we make it our goal to please him, whether we are at home in the body or away from it. ¹⁰For we must all appear before the judgment seat of Christ, that each one may receive what is due him for the things done while in the body, whether good or bad.

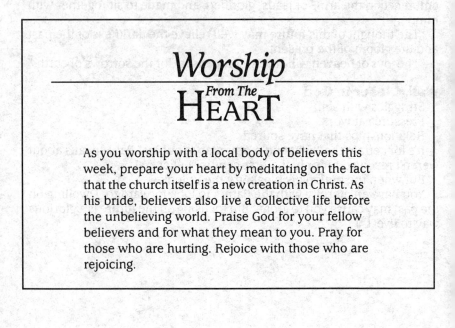

Worship
From The
HEART

As you worship with a local body of believers this week, prepare your heart by meditating on the fact that the church itself is a new creation in Christ. As his bride, believers also live a collective life before the unbelieving world. Praise God for your fellow believers and for what they mean to you. Pray for those who are hurting. Rejoice with those who are rejoicing.

Bringing Delight to the Heart of God

For we must all appear before the judgment seat of Christ, that each one may receive what is due him for the things done while in the body, whether good or bad (2 Corinthians 5:10).

People want approval and acceptance and will do any number of things to achieve it.

It is one thing to seek the fleeting approval of a parent, spouse or employer. It is something infinitely more significant to seek—and experience—the approval of almighty God, as C.S. Lewis explains.

Walk With C.S. Lewis

"How God thinks of us is infinitely more important than how we think of God. Indeed, how we think of him is only of importance in so far as it is related to how he thinks of us.

"In the end that face which is the delight or the terror of the universe must be turned upon each of us either with one expression or the other, either conferring glory inexpressible or inflicting shame that can never be cured or disguised.

"It is written that we shall 'stand before' him, shall appear, shall be inspected. The promise of glory is the promise—only possible by the work of Christ—that some of us shall find approval with God.

"To please God, to be a real ingredient in the divine happiness, to be loved by God, not merely pitied, but delighted in as an artist delights in his work or a father in his son—it seems impossible, a weight or burden of glory which our thoughts can hardly sustain. But so it is."

Walk Closer to God

Perhaps without knowing it, you have been bringing delight to the heart of God. The satisfaction of an artist gazing at his masterpiece, the joy of a Father well pleased with his child.

Put the two together, and they spell "approval"—approval that will one day be expressed and rewarded at the judgment seat of Christ.

It's an "eternal glory" (2 Corinthians 4:17) that can lift your thoughts in praise to the one who made it possible.

JULY 23

Walk in the Word
2 Corinthians 5:11—6:2

Paul has been preaching how humans can be reconciled with God through Christ; he encourages all the Corinthians to make sure that they have been reconciled with God and then to proclaim that same message of salvation to others.

The Ministry of Reconciliation

11Since, then, we know what it is to fear the Lord, we try to persuade men. What we are is plain to God, and I hope it is also plain to your conscience. 12We are not trying to commend ourselves to you again, but are giving you an opportunity to take pride in us, so that you can answer those who take pride in what is seen rather than in what is in the heart. 13If we are out of our mind, it is for the sake of God; if we are in our right mind, it is for you. 14For Christ's love compels us, because we are convinced that one died for all, and therefore all died. 15And he died for all, that those who live should no longer live for themselves but for him who died for them and was raised again.

16So from now on we regard no one from a worldly point of view. Though we once regarded Christ in this way, we do so no longer. 17Therefore, if anyone is in Christ, he is a new creation; the old has gone, the new has come! 18All this is from God, who reconciled us to himself through Christ and gave us the ministry of reconciliation: 19that God was reconciling the world to himself in Christ, not counting men's sins against them. And he has committed to us the message of reconciliation. 20We are therefore Christ's ambassadors, as though God were making his appeal through us. We implore you on Christ's behalf: Be reconciled to God. 21God made him who had no sin to be sin*a* for us, so that in him we might become the righteousness of God.

6 As God's fellow workers we urge you not to receive God's grace in vain. 2For he says,

> "In the time of my favor I heard you,
>   and in the day of salvation I helped you."*b*

I tell you, now is the time of God's favor, now is the day of salvation.

a21 Or be a sin offering   *b2 Isaiah 49:8*

Our Arbitrator, Counselor, and Mediator

All this is from God, who reconciled us to himself through Christ and gave us the ministry of reconciliation (2 Corinthians 5:18).

Two companies working on a contract experience irreconcilable differences. Two teams during a game disagree on the interpretation of a particular rule. A husband and wife have problems that threaten to break up their marriage.

In each case the need is the same: an arbitrator, umpire, counselor, mediator—someone to reconcile the alienated parties. In a similar way sin has caused a breach in our relationship with God. But it is not an "irreconcilable difference." Matthew Henry explains.

Walk With Matthew Henry

"Sin has broken the friendship between God and humanity. The heart of the sinner is filled with enmity against God, and God is justly offended by the sinner. Yet there may be a reconciliation; the offended Majesty of heaven is willing to be reconciled. He has appointed the Mediator of reconciliation, Jesus Christ.

"As God is willing to be reconciled to us, we ought to be reconciled to God. And it is the great end and design of the gospel, the word of reconciliation, to prevail upon sinners to lay aside their enmity against God.

"Wonderful condescension! God can be no loser by the quarrel, nor gainer by the peace. Yet by his ministers he beseeches sinners to lay aside their enmity and accept the terms he offers, that they would be reconciled to him, to believe in the Mediator, to accept the atonement, and comply with his gospel."

Walk Closer to God

Ambassadors represent their native lands in foreign countries. They provide the crucial link between homeland and host land.

Your privilege as a Christian on planet earth is similar: to represent the Mediator and his "native land." To be involved in the "ministry of reconciliation" by sharing the word of reconciliation with sinners alienated from God. ◖

JULY 24

Walk in the Word
2 Corinthians 6:3—7:1

As he has done before, Paul first discusses the many hardships he has suffered for Christ. Then he instructs Christians to remain separate from the world.

Paul's Hardships

[3]We put no stumbling block in anyone's path, so that our ministry will not be discredited. [4]Rather, as servants of God we commend ourselves in every way: in great endurance; in troubles, hardships and distresses; [5]in beatings, imprisonments and riots; in hard work, sleepless nights and hunger; [6]in purity, understanding, patience and kindness; in the Holy Spirit and in sincere love; [7]in truthful speech and in the power of God; with weapons of righteousness in the right hand and in the left; [8]through glory and dishonor, bad report and good report; genuine, yet regarded as impostors; [9]known, yet regarded as unknown; dying, and yet we live on; beaten, and yet not killed; [10]sorrowful, yet always rejoicing; poor, yet making many rich; having nothing, and yet possessing everything.

[11]We have spoken freely to you, Corinthians, and opened wide our hearts to you. [12]We are not withholding our affection from you, but you are withholding yours from us. [13]As a fair exchange—I speak as to my children—open wide your hearts also.

Do Not Be Yoked With Unbelievers

[14]Do not be yoked together with unbelievers. For what do righteousness and wickedness have in common? Or what fellowship can light have with darkness? [15]What harmony is there between Christ and Belial[a]? What does a believer have in common with an unbeliever? [16]What agreement is there between the temple of God and idols? For we are the temple of the living God. As God has said: "I will live with them and walk among them, and I will be their God, and they will be my people."[b]

[17]"Therefore come out from them
and be separate,

says the Lord.

Touch no unclean thing,
and I will receive you."[c]
[18]"I will be a Father to you,
and you will be my sons and daughters,

says the Lord Almighty."[d]

7 Since we have these promises, dear friends, let us purify ourselves from everything that contaminates body and spirit, perfecting holiness out of reverence for God.

---

[a]15 Greek *Beliar*, a variant of *Belial*   [b]16 Lev. 26:12; Jer. 32:38; Ezek. 37:27
[c]17 Isaiah 52:11; Ezek. 20:34,41   [d]18 2 Samuel 7:14; 7:8

A Dwelling in Which God Lives

We are the temple of the living God. As God has said: "I will live with them and walk among them, and I will be their God, and they will be my people" (2 Corinthians 6:16).

Temples don't mean much to 20th-century Christians. Most of us worship God in places that have little in common with the temples of antiquity.

To understand more fully what Paul's temple metaphor means, we need to be "time-travelers"—we need to put ourselves in the historical context of Paul and his audience.

Travel back in time with Alfred Edersheim as he shows us how one old temple ceremony perfectly pictured the new temple made up of Christ and those on whom he has poured living water.

Walk With Alfred Edersheim

"When the water was being poured out, the temple music began. When the choir sang 'Hosanna, Lord,' all the worshipers shook their palms towards the altar. One year, on the last day of the feast (after the priest had poured out the water and the interest of the worshipers had been raised to its highest pitch), a voice resounded through the temple from amidst the mass of people chanting and shaking a forest of leafy branches. It was Jesus, who stood and cried, 'If anyone is thirsty, let him come to me and drink . . . . Streams of living water will flow from within him.' The effect was instantaneous. Suddenly roused by being face to face with him in whom every type and prophecy is fulfilled, many said, 'Surely this man is the Prophet.'

"When the crowd from Jerusalem took palm branches and went out to meet him shouting, 'Hosanna to the Son of David,' they applied to Christ one of the chief ceremonies of the feast. They were praying that God through the Son of David would now send the salvation which was symbolized by the pouring out of water."

Walk Closer to God

In the Old Testament, the glory of the Lord filled the temple through the cloud. In the New Testament, God the Son fills the Church—the new temple—through God the Holy Spirit. Paul expects that to energize the Corinthians to greater holiness. Wouldn't he expect it to do the same for us?

July 25

📖 Walk in the Word
2 Corinthians 7:2–16

Paul expresses his excitement and joy over the fact that the Corinthians have repented of some specific sins that he had warned them about in an earlier letter.

Paul's Joy

²Make room for us in your hearts. We have wronged no one, we have corrupted no one, we have exploited no one. ³I do not say this to condemn you; I have said before that you have such a place in our hearts that we would live or die with you. ⁴I have great confidence in you; I take great pride in you. I am greatly encouraged; in all our troubles my joy knows no bounds.

⁵For when we came into Macedonia, this body of ours had no rest, but we were harassed at every turn—conflicts on the outside, fears within. ⁶But God, who comforts the downcast, comforted us by the coming of Titus, ⁷and not only by his coming but also by the comfort you had given him. He told us about your longing for me, your deep sorrow, your ardent concern for me, so that my joy was greater than ever.

⁸Even if I caused you sorrow by my letter, I do not regret it. Though I did regret it—I see that my letter hurt you, but only for a little while—⁹yet now I am happy, not because you were made sorry, but because your sorrow led you to repentance. For you became sorrowful as God intended and so were not harmed in any way by us. ¹⁰Godly sorrow brings repentance that leads to salvation and leaves no regret, but worldly sorrow brings death. ¹¹See what this godly sorrow has produced in you: what earnestness, what eagerness to clear yourselves, what indignation, what alarm, what longing, what concern, what readiness to see justice done. At every point you have proved yourselves to be innocent in this matter. ¹²So even though I wrote to you, it was not on account of the one who did the wrong or of the injured party, but rather that before God you could see for yourselves how devoted to us you are. ¹³By all this we are encouraged.

In addition to our own encouragement, we were especially delighted to see how happy Titus was, because his spirit has been refreshed by all of you. ¹⁴I had boasted to him about you, and you have not embarrassed me. But just as everything we said to you was true, so our boasting about you to Titus has proved to be true as well. ¹⁵And his affection for you is all the greater when he remembers that you were all obedient, receiving him with fear and trembling. ¹⁶I am glad I can have complete confidence in you.

His All-Sufficient Strength

When we came into Macedonia, this body of ours had no rest, but we were harassed at every turn—conflicts on the outside, fears within (2 Corinthians 7:5).

Burnout.

A space-age term that refers to the point at which a missile's fuel is completely expended. It's often used today to describe the symptoms of extreme stress. Paul's words in 2 Corinthians 7:5—conflicts on the outside, fears on the inside—capture the feelings of a person who is emotionally and physically spent . . . burned out.

A.B. Simpson comments on why God would allow pressure like that to attack life.

Walk With A.B. Simpson

"Why should God have to lead us thus, and allow the pressure to be so hard and constant? In the first place, it shows his all-sufficient strength and grace much better than if we were exempt from pressure and trial.

"It makes us more conscious of our dependence upon him. God is constantly trying to teach us our dependence, and to hold us absolutely in his hand and hanging upon his care. This was the place where Jesus himself stood and where he wants us to stand, not with a self-constituted strength, but with a hand ever leaning upon his, and a trust that dares not take one step alone. It teaches us trust. There is no way of learning faith except by trial. It is God's school of faith, and it is far better for us to learn to trust God than to enjoy life.

"The lesson of faith, once learned, is an everlasting acquisition and an eternal fortune made; and without trust even riches will leave us poor."

Walk Closer to God

God may want to use you in the life of a burned-out brother or sister in Christ today. As a minister of encouragement, a bringer of refreshment. And that means you can't afford to be burned out yourself.

Ministering strength to others demands that you be experiencing strength yourself—strength that comes from depending on God.

"Fuel" for thought, wouldn't you agree?

July 26

📖 Walk in the Word
2 Corinthians 8

Paul attempts to motivate the Christians in Corinth to give generously for the poor Christians in Jerusalem; then he assures them that the money they give will be carried to Jerusalem by respected Christian leaders.

Generosity Encouraged

8 And now, brothers, we want you to know about the grace that God has given the Macedonian churches. [2]Out of the most severe trial, their overflowing joy and their extreme poverty welled up in rich generosity. [3]For I testify that they gave as much as they were able, and even beyond their ability. Entirely on their own, [4]they urgently pleaded with us for the privilege of sharing in this service to the saints. [5]And they did not do as we expected, but they gave themselves first to the Lord and then to us in keeping with God's will. [6]So we urged Titus, since he had earlier made a beginning, to bring also to completion this act of grace on your part. [7]But just as you excel in everything—in faith, in speech, in knowledge, in complete earnestness and in your love for us[a]—see that you also excel in this grace of giving.

[8]I am not commanding you, but I want to test the sincerity of your love by comparing it with the earnestness of others. [9]For you know the grace of our Lord Jesus Christ, that though he was rich, yet for your sakes he became poor, so that you through his poverty might become rich.

[10]And here is my advice about what is best for you in this matter: Last year you were the first not only to give but also to have the desire to do so. [11]Now finish the work, so that your eager willingness to do it may be matched by your completion of it, according to your means. [12]For if the willingness is there, the gift is acceptable according to what one has, not according to what he does not have.

[13]Our desire is not that others might be relieved while you are hard pressed, but that there might be equality. [14]At the present time your plenty will supply what they need, so that in turn their plenty will supply what you need. Then there will be equality, [15]as it is written: "He who gathered much did not have too much, and he who gathered little did not have too little."[b]

Titus Sent to Corinth

[16]I thank God, who put into the heart of Titus the same concern I have for you. [17]For Titus not only welcomed our appeal, but he is coming to you with much enthusiasm and on his own initiative. [18]And we are sending along with him the brother who is praised by all the churches for his service to the gospel. [19]What is more, he was chosen by the churches to accompany us as we carry the offering, which we administer in order to honor the Lord himself and to show our eagerness to help. [20]We want to avoid any criticism of the way we administer this liberal gift. [21]For we

are taking pains to do what is right, not only in the eyes of the Lord but also in the eyes of men. ²²In addition, we are sending with them our brother who has often proved to us in many ways that he is zealous, and now even more so because of his great confidence in you. ²³As for Titus, he is my partner and fellow worker among you; as for our brothers, they are representatives of the churches and an honor to Christ. ²⁴Therefore show these men the proof of your love and the reason for our pride in you, so that the churches can see it.

a7 Some manuscripts *in our love for you*   *b15* Exodus 16:18

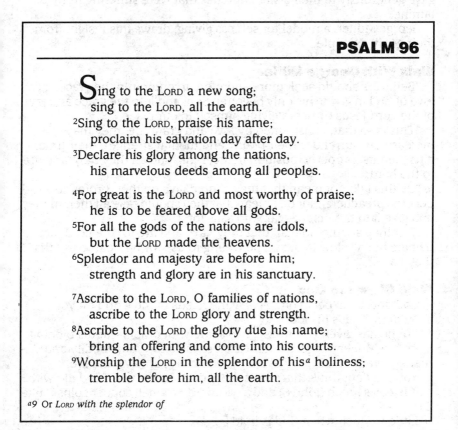

PSALM 96

Sing to the Lord a new song;
  sing to the Lord, all the earth.
²Sing to the Lord, praise his name;
  proclaim his salvation day after day.
³Declare his glory among the nations,
  his marvelous deeds among all peoples.

⁴For great is the Lord and most worthy of praise;
  he is to be feared above all gods.
⁵For all the gods of the nations are idols,
  but the Lord made the heavens.
⁶Splendor and majesty are before him;
  strength and glory are in his sanctuary.

⁷Ascribe to the Lord, O families of nations,
  ascribe to the Lord glory and strength.
⁸Ascribe to the Lord the glory due his name;
  bring an offering and come into his courts.
⁹Worship the Lord in the splendor of his*a* holiness;
  tremble before him, all the earth.

a9 Or *Lord with the splendor of*

JULY 26

Little Is Much When God Is in It!

For you know the grace of our Lord Jesus Christ, that though he was rich, yet for your sakes he became poor, so that you through his poverty might become rich (2 Corinthians 8:9).

Have you ever wondered what you would do with a million dollars? Here is one way to tell.

Look at what you're doing with the money you have already.

The Macedonian believers could scarcely be called rich. And yet they gave generously to their sister churches that were suffering from famine.

George Müller, a model for selfless giving, draws this insight from their godly example.

Walk With George Müller

"Believers should seek more and more to enter into the grace and love of God in giving his only begotten Son, and into the grace and love of the Lord Jesus Christ in giving himself in our place.

"This is so that, constrained by love and gratitude, they may increasingly surrender their bodily and mental strength, their time, gifts, talents, property, position in life, rank, and all they have and are to the Lord.

"By this I do not mean that they should give up their profession and become preachers. Nor do I mean that they should take all their money and give it to the first beggar who asks for it.

"But they should hold all that they have and are for the Lord, not as owners but as stewards, and be willing to use for him part or all that they have."

Walk Closer to God

God doesn't expect you to carry the needs of the world on your shoulders. That's his job.

But he has given you treasure to share with others—at his bidding.

As Mr. Muller suggests, that treasure includes your "bodily and mental strength, time, gifts, talents, . . . all [you] have and are."

You may not think that's much. But don't forget what God did with a little boy's lunch (John 6) and a widow's two small copper coins (Luke 21).

Little is much when God is in it! ◖◗

JULY 27

Walk in the Word
2 Corinthians 9

Paul completes his appeal to the church at Corinth to give generously for the poor Christians in Jerusalem.

---

9 There is no need for me to write to you about this service to the saints. ²For I know your eagerness to help, and I have been boasting about it to the Macedonians, telling them that since last year you in Achaia were ready to give; and your enthusiasm has stirred most of them to action. ³But I am sending the brothers in order that our boasting about you in this matter should not prove hollow, but that you may be ready, as I said you would be. ⁴For if any Macedonians come with me and find you unprepared, we — not to say anything about you — would be ashamed of having been so confident. ⁵So I thought it necessary to urge the brothers to visit you in advance and finish the arrangements for the generous gift you had promised. Then it will be ready as a generous gift, not as one grudgingly given.

Sowing Generously

⁶Remember this: Whoever sows sparingly will also reap sparingly, and whoever sows generously will also reap generously. ⁷Each man should give what he has decided in his heart to give, not reluctantly or under compulsion, for God loves a cheerful giver. ⁸And God is able to make all grace abound to you, so that in all things at all times, having all that you need, you will abound in every good work. ⁹As it is written:

> "He has scattered abroad his gifts to the poor;
> his righteousness endures forever."[a]

¹⁰Now he who supplies seed to the sower and bread for food will also supply and increase your store of seed and will enlarge the harvest of your righteousness. ¹¹You will be made rich in every way so that you can be generous on every occasion, and through us your generosity will result in thanksgiving to God.

¹²This service that you perform is not only supplying the needs of God's people but is also overflowing in many expressions of thanks to God. ¹³Because of the service by which you have proved yourselves, men will praise God for the obedience that accompanies your confession of the gospel of Christ, and for your generosity in sharing with them and with everyone else. ¹⁴And in their prayers for you their hearts will go out to you, because of the surpassing grace God has given you. ¹⁵Thanks be to God for his indescribable gift!

---

[a]9 Psalm 112:9

The Giving That Shows Gratitude

And God is able to make all grace abound to you, so that in all things at all times, having all that you need, you will abound in every good work (2 Corinthians 9:8).

The truth of Paul's message is clear: God gives, that you in turn might give. God causes your life to overflow, that other lives might be touched by his love as well.

We love . . . because he first loved us. We give . . . because God first gave the gift of his Son.

Albert Barnes explains that such a response is as appropriate—and desperately needed—as ever.

Walk with Albert Barnes

"There is no less occasion for Christian liberality now than there was in the time of Paul. There are still multitudes of poor who need the kind and efficient aid of Christians.

"Happy are they who are influenced by the gospel to do good to all people!

"Let us remember that it was because Jesus Christ came that there is any possibility of benefiting a dying world; and that all who profess to love him are bound to imitate his example and show their sense of obligation to God for giving a Savior.

"How poor and worthless are all our gifts compared with the great gift of God; how slight our expressions of compassion for others, compared with the compassion which he has shown for us!

"When God has given his Son to die for us, what should we not be willing to give that we may show our gratitude!"

Walk Closer to God

The gift of Christ is "the gift that keeps on giving"—through you!

It can happen each day as you share the gospel . . . share your possessions . . . share your life.

No doubt you thank God often for what you receive.

But when was the last time you thanked him for what he has privileged you to give?

After all, when a world is dying around you, that's not the time to hoard the gift of eternal life.

JULY 28

Walk in the Word
2 Corinthians 10

Paul becomes angry at certain members of the church in Corinth who have refused to acknowledge him as the leader and pastor of that church, warning them that he may have to deal with them severely.

Paul's Defense of His Ministry

10 By the meekness and gentleness of Christ, I appeal to you — I, Paul, who am "timid" when face to face with you, but "bold" when away! [2]I beg you that when I come I may not have to be as bold as I expect to be toward some people who think that we live by the standards of this world. [3]For though we live in the world, we do not wage war as the world does. [4]The weapons we fight with are not the weapons of the world. On the contrary, they have divine power to demolish strongholds. [5]We demolish arguments and every pretension that sets itself up against the knowledge of God, and we take captive every thought to make it obedient to Christ. [6]And we will be ready to punish every act of disobedience, once your obedience is complete.

[7]You are looking only on the surface of things.[a] If anyone is confident that he belongs to Christ, he should consider again that we belong to Christ just as much as he. [8]For even if I boast somewhat freely about the authority the Lord gave us for building you up rather than pulling you down, I will not be ashamed of it. [9]I do not want to seem to be trying to frighten you with my letters. [10]For some say, "His letters are weighty and forceful, but in person he is unimpressive and his speaking amounts to nothing." [11]Such people should realize that what we are in our letters when we are absent, we will be in our actions when we are present.

[12]We do not dare to classify or compare ourselves with some who commend themselves. When they measure themselves by themselves and compare themselves with themselves, they are not wise. [13]We, however, will not boast beyond proper limits, but will confine our boasting to the field God has assigned to us, a field that reaches even to you. [14]We are not going too far in our boasting, as would be the case if we had not come to you, for we did get as far as you with the gospel of Christ. [15]Neither do we go beyond our limits by boasting of work done by others.[b] Our hope is that, as your faith continues to grow, our area of activity among you will greatly expand, [16]so that we can preach the gospel in the regions beyond you. For we do not want to boast about work already done in another man's territory. [17]But, "Let him who boasts boast in the Lord."[c] [18]For it is not the one who commends himself who is approved, but the one whom the Lord commends.

---

[a]7 Or *Look at the obvious facts* [b]13-15 Or *[13]We, however, will not boast about things that cannot be measured, but we will boast according to the standard of measurement that the God of measure has assigned us—a measurement that relates even to you. [14] . . . . [15]Neither do we boast about things that cannot be measured in regard to the work done by others.* [c]17 Jer. 9:24

JULY 28

Greatness That Comes Through Total Surrender

For it is not the one who commends himself who is approved, but the one whom the Lord commends (2 Corinthians 10:18).

When it came to credentials, the apostle Paul didn't have to apologize. He had traveled thousands of miles, preached countless sermons, faced criticism and persecution, all for the sake of the gospel.

Yet some people accused Paul of selfish motives and self-serving methods.

Paul's defense was to boast—not about his accomplishments, but about his Lord.

As G. Campbell Morgan points out, letting the Lord work through him made Paul great.

Walk With G. Campbell Morgan

"The apostle's greatness was created in the first place by the absoluteness of his surrender to Jesus. On the way to Damascus—surprised, startled, and stricken to the earth by the revelation of the living Christ—he in one brief and simple question handed over his whole life to Jesus. 'What shall I do, Lord?' (Acts 22:10).

"The greatness of Paul as an apostle is further to be accounted for by his attitude toward all the things of his former life. 'But whatever was to my profit I now consider loss for the sake of Christ' (Philippians 3:7).

"Finally, his greatness is to be accounted for by the resulting experience which he crystallized into one brief sentence, 'To me, to live is Christ' (Philippians 1:21).

"Truly this was the great apostle, the great pattern for all time for those who would desire to be messengers of the cross of Christ."

Walk Closer to God

Paul served Christ. Paul sacrificed for Christ. Paul lived for Christ.

Once you have met a truly great man like Paul—a Christlike man who could not care less for money or fame—you will know how poor you really are . . . until you respond as he did. By seeking the commendation of God, not man.

By counting all things as loss for the sake of your Lord. By living only for his glory. ◖◗

JULY 29

Walk in the Word
2 Corinthians 11:1–15

Paul continues his defense against those who resist his authority, particularly those who criticize him for not accepting a salary for preaching the gospel to them.

Paul and the False Apostles

11 I hope you will put up with a little of my foolishness; but you are already doing that. ²I am jealous for you with a godly jealousy. I promised you to one husband, to Christ, so that I might present you as a pure virgin to him. ³But I am afraid that just as Eve was deceived by the serpent's cunning, your minds may somehow be led astray from your sincere and pure devotion to Christ. ⁴For if someone comes to you and preaches a Jesus other than the Jesus we preached, or if you receive a different spirit from the one you received, or a different gospel from the one you accepted, you put up with it easily enough. ⁵But I do not think I am in the least inferior to those "super-apostles." ⁶I may not be a trained speaker, but I do have knowledge. We have made this perfectly clear to you in every way.

⁷Was it a sin for me to lower myself in order to elevate you by preaching the gospel of God to you free of charge? ⁸I robbed other churches by receiving support from them so as to serve you. ⁹And when I was with you and needed something, I was not a burden to anyone, for the brothers who came from Macedonia supplied what I needed. I have kept myself from being a burden to you in any way, and will continue to do so. ¹⁰As surely as the truth of Christ is in me, nobody in the regions of Achaia will stop this boasting of mine. ¹¹Why? Because I do not love you? God knows I do! ¹²And I will keep on doing what I am doing in order to cut the ground from under those who want an opportunity to be considered equal with us in the things they boast about.

¹³For such men are false apostles, deceitful workmen, masquerading as apostles of Christ. ¹⁴And no wonder, for Satan himself masquerades as an angel of light. ¹⁵It is not surprising, then, if his servants masquerade as servants of righteousness. Their end will be what their actions deserve.

JULY 29

Standing Firm Against Satan's Schemes

And no wonder, for Satan himself masquerades as an angel of light (2 Corinthians 11:14).

If you had the task of devising clever schemes to deceive people about the person and program of God, what dirty tricks would you suggest?

Perhaps you would start a "God Can't Be Trusted" campaign . . . or you'd encourage people to procrastinate with their souls . . . or you'd spread the lie that Christians don't enjoy life. Sadly, all of these schemes—and countless others—have been used by the father of lies and his demons.

The need has never been greater for Christians who can stand tall against Satan's deceitful attacks, as Martin Luther points out.

Walk With Martin Luther

"The person who takes to heart the lesson that Christ hurts when the heart of a Christian is sad or frightened has won half the battle. For when I get to know the enemy who wants to frighten and depress me, I already have solid ground on which I can stand against him.

"The devil disguises himself as an angel of light. But this is a sign by which we may recognize him: He creates a timid, frightened, troubled conscience.

"False teachers cannot comfort or make happy a timid conscience; they only make hearts confused, sad, and melancholy so that people are gloomy and act sad. This, however, is nothing but the deception of the devil, who delights to make hearts fearful, cowardly, and timid.

"To be sure, a Christian leads a life that has much suffering and many temptations on the outside. Nevertheless, he can have a confident, happy heart toward God and can expect the best from him."

Walk Closer to God

For the first half of his life, Luther lived like the very people he describes: afraid of God, dismayed by life. But once he understood the grace of God, Luther's fears gave way to a contagious exuberance that God would use to transform a continent.

Don't be deceived by an angel of light. Instead, fall at the feet of the light of the world, and discover anew that life is worth the living. ◖

JULY 30

📖 Walk in the Word
2 Corinthians 11:16—12:10

Paul boasts about how much he has had to suffer for the Lord Jesus Christ, going on to explain that he would rather boast about his weaknesses (his thorn in the flesh), because those weaknesses remind him how much he needs to depend on Christ.

Paul Boasts About His Sufferings

[16]I repeat: Let no one take me for a fool. But if you do, then receive me just as you would a fool, so that I may do a little boasting. [17]In this self-confident boasting I am not talking as the Lord would, but as a fool. [18]Since many are boasting in the way the world does, I too will boast. [19]You gladly put up with fools since you are so wise! [20]In fact, you even put up with anyone who enslaves you or exploits you or takes advantage of you or pushes himself forward or slaps you in the face. [21]To my shame I admit that we were too weak for that!

What anyone else dares to boast about—I am speaking as a fool—I also dare to boast about. [22]Are they Hebrews? So am I. Are they Israelites? So am I. Are they Abraham's descendants? So am I. [23]Are they servants of Christ? (I am out of my mind to talk like this.) I am more. I have worked much harder, been in prison more frequently, been flogged more severely, and been exposed to death again and again. [24]Five times I received from the Jews the forty lashes minus one. [25]Three times I was beaten with rods, once I was stoned, three times I was shipwrecked, I spent a night and a day in the open sea, [26]I have been constantly on the move. I have been in danger from rivers, in danger from bandits, in danger from my own countrymen, in danger from Gentiles; in danger in the city, in danger in the country, in danger at sea; and in danger from false brothers. [27]I have labored and toiled and have often gone without sleep; I have known hunger and thirst and have often gone without food; I have been cold and naked. [28]Besides everything else, I face daily the pressure of my concern for all the churches. [29]Who is weak, and I do not feel weak? Who is led into sin, and I do not inwardly burn?

[30]If I must boast, I will boast of the things that show my weakness. [31]The God and Father of the Lord Jesus, who is to be praised forever, knows that I am not lying. [32]In Damascus the governor under King Aretas had the city of the Damascenes guarded in order to arrest me. [33]But I was lowered in a basket from a window in the wall and slipped through his hands.

Paul's Vision and His Thorn

12 I must go on boasting. Although there is nothing to be gained, I will go on to visions and revelations from the Lord. [2]I know a man in Christ who fourteen years ago was caught up to the third heaven. Whether it was in the body or out of the body I do not know—God knows. [3]And I know that this man—whether in the body or apart from the body I do not know, but God knows— [4]was caught up to paradise. He heard inexpressible things, things that man is not permitted to tell. [5]I will boast about

July 30

a man like that, but I will not boast about myself, except about my weaknesses. ⁶Even if I should choose to boast, I would not be a fool, because I would be speaking the truth. But I refrain, so no one will think more of me than is warranted by what I do or say.

⁷To keep me from becoming conceited because of these surpassingly great revelations, there was given me a thorn in my flesh, a messenger of Satan, to torment me. ⁸Three times I pleaded with the Lord to take it away from me. ⁹But he said to me, "My grace is sufficient for you, for my power is made perfect in weakness." Therefore I will boast all the more gladly about my weaknesses, so that Christ's power may rest on me. ¹⁰That is why, for Christ's sake, I delight in weaknesses, in insults, in hardships, in persecutions, in difficulties. For when I am weak, then I am strong.

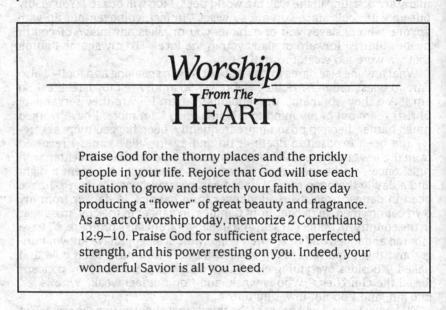

Worship
From The
HEART

Praise God for the thorny places and the prickly people in your life. Rejoice that God will use each situation to grow and stretch your faith, one day producing a "flower" of great beauty and fragrance. As an act of worship today, memorize 2 Corinthians 12:9–10. Praise God for sufficient grace, perfected strength, and his power resting on you. Indeed, your wonderful Savior is all you need.

Never a Burden That He Cannot Bear

Three times I pleaded with the Lord to take it away from me. But he said to me, "My grace is sufficient for you, for my power is made perfect in weakness" (2 Corinthians 12:8–9).

Few verses on prayer are quoted as frequently as James 4:2—"You do not have, because you do not ask God."

And few are quoted as rarely as James 4:3—"When you ask, you do not receive, because you ask with wrong motives."

For the Christian, there is no such thing as an unanswered prayer. God's answer may be "no," or "not yet." But the requests of his children never go unheeded—even the misguided ones.

J. Hudson Taylor has this to say about God's wise answers to his children's prayers.

Walk With J. Hudson Taylor

"Paul was distressed by a burden which he had not strength to bear, and asked that the burden might be removed.

"God answered the prayer not by taking it away, but by showing him the power and grace to bear it joyfully.

"Thus, that which had been the cause of sorrow and regret became the occasion of rejoicing and triumph.

"And wasn't this really a better answer to Paul's prayer than the mere removing of the thorn?

"The latter course would have left him open to the same trouble when the next distress came; but God's method at once delivered him from all the oppression of the present and of all future similar trials.

"God's answer to Paul is a lesson to all. Let none fear to step out in glad obedience to the Master's command."

Walk Closer to God

God may have sent you something quite different—like more problems!

Don't be hesitant to pray. But don't be surprised if God answers in ways you never expected in order to show you—as he did Paul—that his grace is sufficient. ❍

JULY 31

Walk in the Word
2 Corinthians 12:11 — 13:14

Paul wraps up this second letter to the Corinthians both by expressing his deep love for them and by warning them that he may still have to deal harshly with them if they do not listen to what he has to say.

Paul's Concern for the Corinthians

[11]I have made a fool of myself, but you drove me to it. I ought to have been commended by you, for I am not in the least inferior to the "super-apostles," even though I am nothing. [12]The things that mark an apostle — signs, wonders and miracles — were done among you with great perseverance. [13]How were you inferior to the other churches, except that I was never a burden to you? Forgive me this wrong!

[14]Now I am ready to visit you for the third time, and I will not be a burden to you, because what I want is not your possessions but you. After all, children should not have to save up for their parents, but parents for their children. [15]So I will very gladly spend for you everything I have and expend myself as well. If I love you more, will you love me less? [16]Be that as it may, I have not been a burden to you. Yet, crafty fellow that I am, I caught you by trickery! [17]Did I exploit you through any of the men I sent you? [18]I urged Titus to go to you and I sent our brother with him. Titus did not exploit you, did he? Did we not act in the same spirit and follow the same course?

[19]Have you been thinking all along that we have been defending ourselves to you? We have been speaking in the sight of God as those in Christ; and everything we do, dear friends, is for your strengthening. [20]For I am afraid that when I come I may not find you as I want you to be, and you may not find me as you want me to be. I fear that there may be quarreling, jealousy, outbursts of anger, factions, slander, gossip, arrogance and disorder. [21]I am afraid that when I come again my God will humble me before you, and I will be grieved over many who have sinned earlier and have not repented of the impurity, sexual sin and debauchery in which they have indulged.

Final Warnings

13 This will be my third visit to you. "Every matter must be established by the testimony of two or three witnesses."[a] [2]I already gave you a warning when I was with you the second time. I now repeat it while absent: On my return I will not spare those who sinned earlier or any of the others, [3]since you are demanding proof that Christ is speaking through me. He is not weak in dealing with you, but is powerful among you. [4]For to be sure, he was crucified in weakness, yet he lives by God's power. Likewise, we are weak in him, yet by God's power we will live with him to serve you.

[5]Examine yourselves to see whether you are in the faith; test yourselves. Do you not realize that Christ Jesus is in you — unless, of course, you fail the test? [6]And I trust that you will discover that we have not failed the test.

7Now we pray to God that you will not do anything wrong. Not that people will see that we have stood the test but that you will do what is right even though we may seem to have failed. 8For we cannot do anything against the truth, but only for the truth. 9We are glad whenever we are weak but you are strong; and our prayer is for your perfection. 10This is why I write these things when I am absent, that when I come I may not have to be harsh in my use of authority — the authority the Lord gave me for building you up, not for tearing you down.

Final Greetings

11Finally, brothers, good-by. Aim for perfection, listen to my appeal, be of one mind, live in peace. And the God of love and peace will be with you. 12Greet one another with a holy kiss. 13All the saints send their greetings.

14May the grace of the Lord Jesus Christ, and the love of God, and the fellowship of the Holy Spirit be with you all.

a1 Deut. 19:15

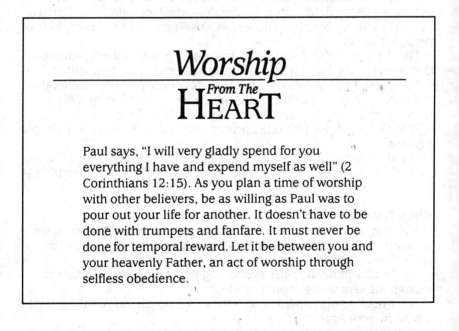

Worship
From The
HEART

Paul says, "I will very gladly spend for you everything I have and expend myself as well" (2 Corinthians 12:15). As you plan a time of worship with other believers, be as willing as Paul was to pour out your life for another. It doesn't have to be done with trumpets and fanfare. It must never be done for temporal reward. Let it be between you and your heavenly Father, an act of worship through selfless obedience.

JULY 31

Deliberate Love That Plays for Keeps

So I will very gladly spend for you everthing I have and expend myself as well. If I love you more, will you love me less? (2 Corinthians 12:15).

Paul didn't know when to quit loving people.

They might stop loving him, but he would never stop loving them.

The Corinthians found this out. Paul loved them enough to reprimand them and set them straight.

And when they protested by criticizing him, he didn't turn away. After all, they didn't ask him to love them; God did!

God's love is like that—seeking even those who spurn it, as Oswald Chambers describes.

Walk With Oswald Chambers

"When the Spirit of God has shed abroad the love of God in our hearts, we begin deliberately to identify ourselves with Jesus Christ's interests in other people—and Jesus Christ is interested in every kind of person there is.

"We have no right in Christian work to be guided by our affinities; this is one of the biggest tests in your relationship to Jesus Christ.

"The delight of sacrifice is that I lay down my life for my Friend—not fling it away, but deliberately lay my life out for him and his interests in other people, not for a cause.

"Paul spent himself for one purpose only—that he might win people to Jesus Christ.

"Paul attracted others to Jesus all the time, never to himself. 'I make myself a slave to everyone, to win as many as possible' (1 Corinthians 9:19)."

Walk Closer to God

You may not like the people you are called to love. But you have someone to fall back on when you find it difficult to respond with smiles and warm feelings.

Paul was willing to spend everything he had for the Corinthians, though his love was seldom returned.

After reading his two inspired letters this month, do you think it was a wise investment?

And who are you investing your life in—a day at a time? ◖

AUGUST

The Believer's Lifelong Challenge

**GALATIANS
EPHESIANS
PHILIPPIANS
COLOSSIANS**

Galatia. Ephesus. Philippi. Colosse. You won't find them on a modern map. Once important religious and commercial centers, all that remain now are archaeological ruins and historical records. But though nineteen centuries have swept over their memory, they are still vitally important to you today because of four letters written in the first century by Paul.

Many books written today offer struggling Christians the "secret" to living the Christian life. But the best way to confront that issue is to focus on what the apostle writes in these books: "I have been crucified with Christ and I no longer live, but Christ lives in me. The life I live in the body, I live by faith in the Son of God, who loved me and gave himself for me" (Galatians 2:20); "that Christ may dwell in your hearts through faith . . . that you may be filled to the measure of all the fullness of God" (Ephesians 3:17–19); "filled with the fruit of righteousness that comes through Jesus Christ—to the glory and praise of God" (Philippians 1:11); "So then, just as you received Christ Jesus as Lord, continue to live in him" (Colossians 2:6). In other words, the Christian life is life in Christ. You cannot study it or live it without him.

Christ is the focal point of these four letters. In them, Paul explains who Christ is, what he is like and what he has done. In Galatians, Paul reminds forgetful Christians of the wonderful salvation they enjoy. In Ephesians, he breaks forth in praise for the riches of life that God's children enjoy through Jesus Christ. In Philippians, the apostle writes to encourage a church to improve in Christlikeness. And in Colossians, Paul addresses a congregation he has never met face to face, reminding them of the incomparable greatness of Christ as Lord and Savior.

There is no greater challenge—or privilege—for the one who has "received Christ Jesus as Lord" than to "live in him." At the end of this month, you should be many steps closer to resembling the one you call "Lord."

August 1

Walk in the Word
Galatians 1

Because certain people were criticizing Paul's message of salvation by faith alone, Paul stresses that he was called directly by God to be an apostle and that he received his message from the Lord.

1 Paul, an apostle — sent not from men nor by man, but by Jesus Christ and God the Father, who raised him from the dead — [2]and all the brothers with me,

To the churches in Galatia:

[3]Grace and peace to you from God our Father and the Lord Jesus Christ, [4]who gave himself for our sins to rescue us from the present evil age, according to the will of our God and Father, [5]to whom be glory for ever and ever. Amen.

No Other Gospel

[6]I am astonished that you are so quickly deserting the one who called you by the grace of Christ and are turning to a different gospel — [7]which is really no gospel at all. Evidently some people are throwing you into confusion and are trying to pervert the gospel of Christ. [8]But even if we or an angel from heaven should preach a gospel other than the one we preached to you, let him be eternally condemned! [9]As we have already said, so now I say again: If anybody is preaching to you a gospel other than what you accepted, let him be eternally condemned!

[10]Am I now trying to win the approval of men, or of God? Or am I trying to please men? If I were still trying to please men, I would not be a servant of Christ.

Paul Called by God

[11]I want you to know, brothers, that the gospel I preached is not something that man made up. [12]I did not receive it from any man, nor was I taught it; rather, I received it by revelation from Jesus Christ.

[13]For you have heard of my previous way of life in Judaism, how intensely I persecuted the church of God and tried to destroy it. [14]I was advancing in Judaism beyond many Jews of my own age and was extremely zealous for the traditions of my fathers. [15]But when God, who set me apart from birth[a] and called me by his grace, was pleased [16]to reveal his Son in me so that I might preach him among the Gentiles, I did not consult any man, [17]nor did I go up to Jerusalem to see those who were apostles before I was, but I went immediately into Arabia and later returned to Damascus.

[18]Then after three years, I went up to Jerusalem to get acquainted with Peter[b] and stayed with him fifteen days. [19]I saw none of the other apostles — only James, the Lord's brother. [20]I assure you before God that what I am writing you is no lie. [21]Later I went to Syria and Cilicia. [22]I was person-

ally unknown to the churches of Judea that are in Christ. [23]They only heard the report: "The man who formerly persecuted us is now preaching the faith he once tried to destroy." [24]And they praised God because of me.

[a]15 Or *from my mother's womb*   [b]18 Greek *Cephas*

PSALM 51

For the director of music. A psalm of David. When the prophet Nathan came to him after David had committed adultery with Bathsheba.

Have mercy on me, O God,
    according to your unfailing love;
according to your great compassion
    blot out my transgressions.
[2]Wash away all my iniquity
    and cleanse me from my sin.

[3]For I know my transgressions,
    and my sin is always before me.
[4]Against you, you only, have I sinned
    and done what is evil in your sight,
so that you are proved right when you speak
    and justified when you judge.
[5]Surely I was sinful at birth,
    sinful from the time my mother conceived me.
[6]Surely you desire truth in the inner parts[a];
    you teach[b] me wisdom in the inmost place.

[7]Cleanse me with hyssop, and I will be clean;
    wash me, and I will be whiter than snow.
[8]Let me hear joy and gladness;
    let the bones you have crushed rejoice.
[9]Hide your face from my sins
    and blot out all my iniquity.

[10]Create in me a pure heart, O God,
    and renew a steadfast spirit within me.
[11]Do not cast me from your presence
    or take your Holy Spirit from me.

[a]6 The meaning of the Hebrew for this phrase is uncertain.   [b]6 Or *you desired . . . ; / you taught*

AUGUST 1

Finding the Path From Prison to Peace

The Lord Jesus Christ . . . gave himself for our sins to rescue us from the present evil age (Galatians 1:3–4).

Nearly five hundred years ago, a young monk wrestled with the question of his relationship to God. He had done all he knew to do but still had found no peace in his soul. It seemed that everything he tried fell short of heaven's demands.

Though at times he despaired of ever getting right with God, he one day found the forgiveness he had sought "through Jesus Christ our Lord."

What acts of piety alone could not give, Martin Luther experienced in Christ—and you can too!

Walk With Martin Luther

"Say with confidence: 'Christ, the Son of God, was given not for the righteous, but for sinners!' If I had no sin I should not need Christ.

"My sins are not imaginary transgressions, but sins against God: unbelief, doubt, despair, contempt, hatred, ingratitude, ignorance of God, misuse of his name, neglect of his Word; and sins against others: dishonor of parents, disobedience of government, coveting another's possessions.

"Even if I have not committed murder, adultery, theft, or similar sins in deed, nevertheless I have committed them in the heart, and therefore I am a transgressor of all the commandments of God.

"Because my transgressions are multiplied and my own efforts at self-justification more a hindrance than a furtherance, therefore Christ the Son of God gave himself unto death for my sins.

"To believe this is to have eternal life."

Walk Closer to God

Luther staggered under a load of sin and guilt that no amount of penance could fit. Finally, leaving that burden at the cross, he experienced the peace that only God can give.

Have you, like Luther, been trying to live the Christian life without knowing the giver of life?

The first step is to receive gratefully the gift of God's Son. Only then can you rise up in joyful service for your Lord and Savior. ❍

AUGUST 2

Walk in the Word
Galatians 2

Paul records how his message of salvation by faith apart from observing the law was supported by a council of Christian leaders that met in Jerusalem.

Paul Accepted by the Apostles

2 Fourteen years later I went up again to Jerusalem, this time with Barnabas. I took Titus along also. [2] I went in response to a revelation and set before them the gospel that I preach among the Gentiles. But I did this privately to those who seemed to be leaders, for fear that I was running or had run my race in vain. [3] Yet not even Titus, who was with me, was compelled to be circumcised, even though he was a Greek. [4] This matter arose, because some false brothers had infiltrated our ranks to spy on the freedom we have in Christ Jesus and to make us slaves. [5] We did not give in to them for a moment, so that the truth of the gospel might remain with you.

[6] As for those who seemed to be important—whatever they were makes no difference to me; God does not judge by external appearance—those men added nothing to my message. [7] On the contrary, they saw that I had been entrusted with the task of preaching the gospel to the Gentiles, [a] just as Peter had been to the Jews. [b] [8] For God, who was at work in the ministry of Peter as an apostle to the Jews, was also at work in my ministry as an apostle to the Gentiles. [9] James, Peter [c] and John, those reputed to be pillars, gave me and Barnabas the right hand of fellowship when they recognized the grace given to me. They agreed that we should go to the Gentiles, and they to the Jews. [10] All they asked was that we should continue to remember the poor, the very thing I was eager to do.

Paul Opposes Peter

[11] When Peter came to Antioch, I opposed him to his face, because he was clearly in the wrong. [12] Before certain men came from James, he used to eat with the Gentiles. But when they arrived, he began to draw back and separate himself from the Gentiles because he was afraid of those who belonged to the circumcision group. [13] The other Jews joined him in his hypocrisy, so that by their hypocrisy even Barnabas was led astray.

[14] When I saw that they were not acting in line with the truth of the gospel, I said to Peter in front of them all, "You are a Jew, yet you live like a Gentile and not like a Jew. How is it, then, that you force Gentiles to follow Jewish customs?

[15] "We who are Jews by birth and not 'Gentile sinners' [16] know that a man is not justified by observing the law, but by faith in Jesus Christ. So we, too, have put our faith in Christ Jesus that we may be justified by faith in Christ and not by observing the law, because by observing the law no one will be justified.

[17] "If, while we seek to be justified in Christ, it becomes evident that we ourselves are sinners, does that mean that Christ promotes sin? Absolutely

AUGUST 2

not! [18]If I rebuild what I destroyed, I prove that I am a lawbreaker. [19]For through the law I died to the law so that I might live for God. [20]I have been crucified with Christ and I no longer live, but Christ lives in me. The life I live in the body, I live by faith in the Son of God, who loved me and gave himself for me. [21]I do not set aside the grace of God, for if righteousness could be gained through the law, Christ died for nothing!"[d]

[a]7 Greek *uncircumcised*   [b]7 Greek *circumcised*; also in verses 8 and 9   [c]9 Greek *Cephas*; also in verses 11 and 14   [d]21 Some interpreters end the quotation after verse 14.

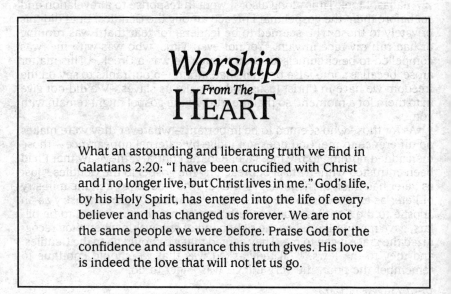

Worship From The HEART

What an astounding and liberating truth we find in Galatians 2:20: "I have been crucified with Christ and I no longer live, but Christ lives in me." God's life, by his Holy Spirit, has entered into the life of every believer and has changed us forever. We are not the same people we were before. Praise God for the confidence and assurance this truth gives. His love is indeed the love that will not let us go.

August 2

Becoming Like Him in Death—and in Life

I have been crucified with Christ and I no longer live, but Christ lives in me (Galatians 2:20).

To the Roman mind, the cross marked a place of execution, not a haven for life.

And yet that cruelest of deaths would one day become a mark of distinction. Paul would later rejoice to proclaim, "I have been crucified with Christ."

Confused? Listen as Andrew Murray probes the significance of the cross in Jesus' day . . . and in yours.

Walk with Andrew Murray

"All his life Christ bore his cross—the death sentence that he should die for the world.

"And each Christian must bear his cross, acknowledging that he is worthy of death, and believing that he is crucified with Christ, and that the Crucified One lives in him.

"When we have accepted the life of the cross, we will be able to say with Paul: 'May I never boast except in the cross of our Lord Jesus Christ' (Galatians 6:14).

"Let the disposition of Christ on the cross, his humility, his sacrifice of all worldly honor, his spirit of self-denial, take possession of you.

"The power of his death will work in you, and you will become like him in his death; you will know him and the power of his resurrection."

Walk Closer to God

Christ died an ignoble death that he might rise to glorious life. Now he invites you to "live by faith in the Son of God" (Galatians 2:20).

You are crucified with Christ that you might experience the life of Christ.

Let the words of Isaac Watts lift your heart in praise for the life-bringing cross of Christ:

Alas! and did my Savior bleed?
    And did my Sov'reign die?
Would He devote that sacred head
    For such a worm as I?
But drops of grief can ne'er repay
    The debt of love I owe:
Here, Lord, I give myself away,
    'Tis all that I can do! ◖

AUGUST 3

Walk in the Word
Galatians 3:1–14

After chiding the Galatians for departing from the message he preached to them, Paul proves from the Old Testament law that the gospel is true.

Faith or Observance of the Law

3 You foolish Galatians! Who has bewitched you? Before your very eyes Jesus Christ was clearly portrayed as crucified. ²I would like to learn just one thing from you: Did you receive the Spirit by observing the law, or by believing what you heard? ³Are you so foolish? After beginning with the Spirit, are you now trying to attain your goal by human effort? ⁴Have you suffered so much for nothing—if it really was for nothing? ⁵Does God give you his Spirit and work miracles among you because you observe the law, or because you believe what you heard?

⁶Consider Abraham: "He believed God, and it was credited to him as righteousness."ᵃ ⁷Understand, then, that those who believe are children of Abraham. ⁸The Scripture foresaw that God would justify the Gentiles by faith, and announced the gospel in advance to Abraham: "All nations will be blessed through you."ᵇ ⁹So those who have faith are blessed along with Abraham, the man of faith.

¹⁰All who rely on observing the law are under a curse, for it is written: "Cursed is everyone who does not continue to do everything written in the Book of the Law."ᶜ ¹¹Clearly no one is justified before God by the law, because, "The righteous will live by faith."ᵈ ¹²The law is not based on faith; on the contrary, "The man who does these things will live by them."ᵉ ¹³Christ redeemed us from the curse of the law by becoming a curse for us, for it is written: "Cursed is everyone who is hung on a tree."ᶠ ¹⁴He redeemed us in order that the blessing given to Abraham might come to the Gentiles through Christ Jesus, so that by faith we might receive the promise of the Spirit.

ᵃ6 Gen. 15:6   ᵇ8 Gen. 12:3; 18:18; 22:18   ᶜ10 Deut. 27:26   ᵈ11 Hab. 2:4   ᵉ12 Lev. 18:5   ᶠ13 Deut. 21:23

Open Your Hands to Receive What Christ Gives

Understand, then, that those who believe are children of
Abraham (Galatians 3:7).

Abraham lived long before camera crews could follow his every step.
But Abraham's name is enshrined in Scripture as one of the great
examples of a person who took God at his word.

"Abraham believed God, and it was credited to him as righteousness"
(Romans 4:3). Faith was the sole basis of Abraham's right standing with
God.

Does that seem hard to believe? It did to the Galatians! So Paul
reminds them in chapter three of the sufficiency of faith—the same
truth underscored by F.B. Meyer in this insight.

Walk With F.B. Meyer

"The strong tendency of the Galatian Christians to depend on
ceremonies or legal obedience in addition to their faith in Christ, brings
about in this chapter a magnificent demonstration of the sufficiency
of faith alone.

"Faith had marked the beginning of the [Galatians'] Christian lives.
They had found peace with God through faith.

"Faith had been the means, too, of Abraham's acceptance with God.
Long before he had become a Jew by the initial rite of Judaism, he had
been a humble believer in God's promise, on the basis of which he was
reckoned righteous.

"Simple faith was the only condition that he had fulfilled. Surely
what was sufficient for the father of the faithful is good enough for his
children!

"Let each reader see to it that he does not merely believe about
Christ, but believes in him."

Walk Closer to God

Abraham was "fully persuaded that God had power to do what he
had promised" (Romans 4:21).

Abraham had not earned salvation (Galatians 3:6) or deserved it
(Galatians 3:22). His responsibility had been simply to receive it by
believing what he heard (Galatians 3:2,5).

Incredible? Unbelievable? Too good to be true?

You'll never know until you open your empty hands to receive what
Christ alone can give. ◯

AUGUST 4

Walk in the Word
Galatians 3:15–25

Paul shows why God gave his law in the Old Testament — to make people realize that they cannot get right with God by keeping the law and so to prepare the way for the coming of Christ.

The Law and the Promise

¹⁵Brothers, let me take an example from everyday life. Just as no one can set aside or add to a human covenant that has been duly established, so it is in this case. ¹⁶The promises were spoken to Abraham and to his seed. The Scripture does not say "and to seeds," meaning many people, but "and to your seed,"ᵃ meaning one person, who is Christ. ¹⁷What I mean is this: The law, introduced 430 years later, does not set aside the covenant previously established by God and thus do away with the promise. ¹⁸For if the inheritance depends on the law, then it no longer depends on a promise; but God in his grace gave it to Abraham through a promise.

¹⁹What, then, was the purpose of the law? It was added because of transgressions until the Seed to whom the promise referred had come. The law was put into effect through angels by a mediator. ²⁰A mediator, however, does not represent just one party; but God is one.

²¹Is the law, therefore, opposed to the promises of God? Absolutely not! For if a law had been given that could impart life, then righteousness would certainly have come by the law. ²²But the Scripture declares that the whole world is a prisoner of sin, so that what was promised, being given through faith in Jesus Christ, might be given to those who believe.

²³Before this faith came, we were held prisoners by the law, locked up until faith should be revealed. ²⁴So the law was put in charge to lead us to Christᵇ that we might be justified by faith. ²⁵Now that faith has come, we are no longer under the supervision of the law.

ᵃ16 Gen. 12:7; 13:15; 24:7   ᵇ24 Or *charge until Christ came*

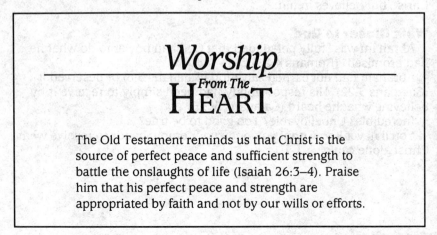

Worship
From The HEART

The Old Testament reminds us that Christ is the source of perfect peace and sufficient strength to battle the onslaughts of life (Isaiah 26:3–4). Praise him that his perfect peace and strength are appropriated by faith and not by our wills or efforts.

Living by Faith in the Son

So the law was put in charge to lead us to Christ that we might be justified by faith (Galatians 3:24).

Although the Galatians had graduated from "law school," they were living like undergraduates. But the law's work as their schoolmaster was finished. Since they had received salvation through faith in Christ, they didn't need to return to their "alma mater." Paul reminds them how the law's chief purpose was to point men and women to faith in Christ.

Now, as Christians, the Galatians were guilty of making the law's demands their path to perfection. As John Calvin relates, the Christian life is walking in the light of God's revealed Word.

Walk With John Calvin

"Faith denotes the full revelation of those things which, during the darkness of the shadows of the law, were dimly seen; for Paul does not intend to say that the fathers, who lived under the law, did not possess faith. Those who were under the law were partakers of the same faith as New Testament believers.

"The Old Testament might be said to foreshadow Christ, but to us he is represented as actually being present. They had only the mirror; we have the substance.

"Whatever might be the amount of darkness under the law, the fathers were not ignorant of the road in which they ought to walk. Though the dawn is not equal to the splendor of noon, yet, as far as a trip is concerned, travelers do not wait till the sun is fully risen. Their portion of light resembled the dawn, which was enough to preserve them from all error and guide them to everlasting blessedness."

Walk Closer to God

If the Old Testament saints' portion of light resembled the dawn, you enjoy the full blaze of the noontime sun.

If they were able to live by faith with only a glimpse of the coming Savior, you can surely live by faith, thanks to the full portrait of his appearing, which you possess in the Word of God. □

AUGUST 5

📖 Walk in the Word
Galatians 3:26—4:20

Once again Paul emphasizes how anyone can become a child of God through faith in Christ. He goes on to express his deep regret that so many of the Christians in Galatia have been turning their backs on this message.

Sons of God

26You are all sons of God through faith in Christ Jesus, 27for all of you who were baptized into Christ have clothed yourselves with Christ. 28There is neither Jew nor Greek, slave nor free, male nor female, for you are all one in Christ Jesus. 29If you belong to Christ, then you are Abraham's seed, and heirs according to the promise.

4 What I am saying is that as long as the heir is a child, he is no different from a slave, although he owns the whole estate. 2He is subject to guardians and trustees until the time set by his father. 3So also, when we were children, we were in slavery under the basic principles of the world. 4But when the time had fully come, God sent his Son, born of a woman, born under law, 5to redeem those under law, that we might receive the full rights of sons. 6Because you are sons, God sent the Spirit of his Son into our hearts, the Spirit who calls out, *"Abba,a* Father." 7So you are no longer a slave, but a son; and since you are a son, God has made you also an heir.

Paul's Concern for the Galatians

8Formerly, when you did not know God, you were slaves to those who by nature are not gods. 9But now that you know God—or rather are known by God—how is it that you are turning back to those weak and miserable principles? Do you wish to be enslaved by them all over again? 10You are observing special days and months and seasons and years! 11I fear for you, that somehow I have wasted my efforts on you.

12I plead with you, brothers, become like me, for I became like you. You have done me no wrong. 13As you know, it was because of an illness that I first preached the gospel to you. 14Even though my illness was a trial to you, you did not treat me with contempt or scorn. Instead, you welcomed me as if I were an angel of God, as if I were Christ Jesus himself. 15What has happened to all your joy? I can testify that, if you could have done so, you would have torn out your eyes and given them to me. 16Have I now become your enemy by telling you the truth?

17Those people are zealous to win you over, but for no good. What they want is to alienate you ⸢from us⸣, so that you may be zealous for them. 18It is fine to be zealous, provided the purpose is good, and to be so always and not just when I am with you. 19My dear children, for whom I am again in the pains of childbirth until Christ is formed in you, 20how I wish I could be with you now and change my tone, because I am perplexed about you!

a6 Aramaic for *Father*

Grace—The Great Expense

You are all sons of God through faith in Christ Jesus (Galatians 3:26).

Paul knew both the agonies and the ecstasies of spiritual parenthood. He was like a mother, nurse, tutor, father, and friend. He longed for each of the Galatians to reach maturity in Christ. He reminded them that every Christian is a member of God's own family, a son or daughter of the Lord.

Martin Luther discusses Paul's writings in relation to the costly grace of God. You are a child of God, Luther observes, because God was willing to pay the terrible price to redeem you.

Walk With Martin Luther

"Above all things, Christ must be kept in this matter of salvation.

"It certainly is truth that, as David says (Psalm 32:2) and Paul writes (Romans 4:8): 'Blessed is the man whose sin the Lord will never count against him.' Paul shows that this divine imputation comes only to him who believes in Christ and not because of good works.

"Although out of pure grace God does not impute our sins to us, he nonetheless did not want to do this until complete and ample satisfaction of his law and his righteousness had been made. Since this was impossible for us, God ordained for us, in our place, one who took upon himself all the punishment we deserve.

"He fulfilled the law for us. He averted the judgment of God from us and appeased God's wrath. Grace, therefore, costs us nothing, but it cost Another much to get it for us. Grace was purchased with an incalculable, infinite treasure, the Son of God himself."

Walk Closer to God

Because both Paul and Luther studied the Scriptures intently, they were able to proclaim clearly the necessity of faith in Christ. Both men remind Christ's forgetful followers of the high price of God's grace.

Think of it as the family secret of the faithful—a secret God never intended for you to keep to yourself! ◖

ALEXANDER MACLAREN

(1826–1910) THE PRIORITY OF PREACHING

Spending Time in the Word

For Alexander Maclaren, the minister's greatest priority is preaching the Word. His own preaching, exuding clarity, originality and power, has been preserved in his *Expositions of Holy Scripture*, one of the first collections of sermons ever compiled.

Born in 1826 to godly parents in Glasgow, Scotland, Maclaren became a Christian at age fourteen. His father wanted him to enter the ministry, but the young man seemed to lack the necessary aptitude. Nevertheless, he pursued this career in college, where his hard-working nature propelled him to the head of his class. After graduation, he took a position as the pastor of Portland Chapel, a small church teetering on the brink of collapse. Over a period of a dozen years, Maclaren built the church into a thriving congregation. His obvious abilities caught the attention of Union Chapel of Manchester, England, where, beginning in 1858, he served as pastor for forty-five years.

His reputation soon spread to other cities and counties. Speaking tours resulted, bringing thousands to hear this devoted study of the Scriptures. Even after retirement he continued to travel and speak.

What enabled this preacher of God's Word to excel? First and foremost, he let nothing interfere with his time of study and preparation in the Bible. He refused all social activities or speaking engagements if it meant forsaking time in God's Word. He would spend as much as sixty hours preparing one sermon, in which he took a passage of Scripture, explained its meaning, and then applied its truth to himself and to his hearers. You face the same challenge with the Bible: find the meaning of the Word and then apply it to your life.

A LESSON FROM THE LIFE OF ALEXANDER MACLAREN

The priority of time spent in the Scriptures will ensure the primacy of God's rule in my life.

AUGUST 6

Walk in the Word
Galatians 4:21 — 5:15

Paul concludes his argument that Christians are free from observing the law as a necessary ingredient for salvation; but this does not mean that they can do whatever they want, for their freedom is only in order to serve Christ and others in love.

Hagar and Sarah

[21]Tell me, you who want to be under the law, are you not aware of what the law says? [22]For it is written that Abraham had two sons, one by the slave woman and the other by the free woman. [23]His son by the slave woman was born in the ordinary way; but his son by the free woman was born as the result of a promise.

[24]These things may be taken figuratively, for the women represent two covenants. One covenant is from Mount Sinai and bears children who are to be slaves: This is Hagar. [25]Now Hagar stands for Mount Sinai in Arabia and corresponds to the present city of Jerusalem, because she is in slavery with her children. [26]But the Jerusalem that is above is free, and she is our mother. [27]For it is written:

> "Be glad, O barren woman,
> who bears no children;
> break forth and cry aloud,
> you who have no labor pains;
> because more are the children of the desolate woman
> than of her who has a husband."[a]

[28]Now you, brothers, like Isaac, are children of promise. [29]At that time the son born in the ordinary way persecuted the son born by the power of the Spirit. It is the same now. [30]But what does the Scripture say? "Get rid of the slave woman and her son, for the slave woman's son will never share in the inheritance with the free woman's son."[b] [31]Therefore, brothers, we are not children of the slave woman, but of the free woman.

Freedom in Christ

5 It is for freedom that Christ has set us free. Stand firm, then, and do not let yourselves be burdened again by a yoke of slavery.

[2]Mark my words! I, Paul, tell you that if you let yourselves be circumcised, Christ will be of no value to you at all. [3]Again I declare to every man who lets himself be circumcised that he is obligated to obey the whole law. [4]You who are trying to be justified by law have been alienated from Christ; you have fallen away from grace. [5]But by faith we eagerly await through the Spirit the righteousness for which we hope. [6]For in Christ Jesus neither circumcision nor uncircumcision has any value. The only thing that counts is faith expressing itself through love.

[7]You were running a good race. Who cut in on you and kept you from obeying the truth? [8]That kind of persuasion does not come from the one who calls you. [9]"A little yeast works through the whole batch of dough."

August 6

¹⁰I am confident in the Lord that you will take no other view. The one who is throwing you into confusion will pay the penalty, whoever he may be. ¹¹Brothers, if I am still preaching circumcision, why am I still being persecuted? In that case the offense of the cross has been abolished. ¹²As for those agitators, I wish they would go the whole way and emasculate themselves!

¹³You, my brothers, were called to be free. But do not use your freedom to indulge the sinful nature*c*; rather, serve one another in love. ¹⁴The entire law is summed up in a single command: "Love your neighbor as yourself."*d* ¹⁵If you keep on biting and devouring each other, watch out or you will be destroyed by each other.

a27 Isaiah 54:1   *b30* Gen. 21:10   *c13* Or *the flesh*; also in verses 16, 17, 19 and 24
d14 Lev. 19:18

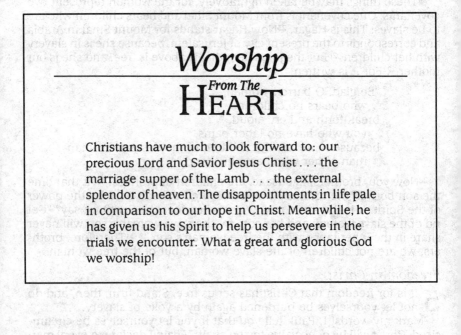

Worship
From The
HEART

Christians have much to look forward to: our precious Lord and Savior Jesus Christ . . . the marriage supper of the Lamb . . . the external splendor of heaven. The disappointments in life pale in comparison to our hope in Christ. Meanwhile, he has given us his Spirit to help us persevere in the trials we encounter. What a great and glorious God we worship!

The Object of Our Hope

But by faith we eagerly await through the Spirit the righteousness for which we hope (Galatians 5:5).

Waiting room. The very words conjure up images of unpleasant times in the doctor's or dentist's office. For the Christian, waiting on God is a way of life.

Paul spent much of his early Christian life alone in the desert—learning to wait. In Galatians 5:5, he shares one of the keys he discovered about waiting on God: waiting by faith.

Matthew Henry explains why waiting is an essential discipline.

Walk With Matthew Henry

"Here we observe what Christians are waiting for—the hope of righteousness, the happiness of the other world. This is called the hope of Christians, the great object of their hope, which they desire and pursue above everything else.

"Though a life of righteousness leads to this happiness, yet it is the righteousness of Christ alone which has procured it for us.

"We also learn how Christians hope to obtain this happiness by faith in Jesus Christ, not by the works of the law, or anything they can do to deserve it, but only by faith, receiving and relying on him as the Lord, our righteousness. We also see how Christians are waiting for the hope of righteousness—through the Spirit.

"They act under the direction and influence of the Holy Spirit. Under his conduct and by his assistance, they are both persuaded and enabled to believe on Christ, and to look for the hope of righteousness through him."

Walk Closer to God

A long wait is often helped by having someone to wait with you. You have been given such a companion—the Holy Spirit. His presence can help you view disappointments as divine appointments.

Commit your waiting moments to him. Ask for insight in knowing how to use each postponement and delay for eternal purposes. And while you wait, meditate on the hope of righteousness—eternal life with Jesus Christ.

AUGUST 7

Walk in the Word
Galatians 5:16–26

Paul indicates the struggle that Christians must go through as they fight against the sinful nature and live out of the full power of the Holy Spirit.

Life by the Spirit

¹⁶So I say, live by the Spirit, and you will not gratify the desires of the sinful nature. ¹⁷For the sinful nature desires what is contrary to the Spirit, and the Spirit what is contrary to the sinful nature. They are in conflict with each other, so that you do not do what you want. ¹⁸But if you are led by the Spirit, you are not under law.

¹⁹The acts of the sinful nature are obvious: sexual immorality, impurity and debauchery; ²⁰idolatry and witchcraft; hatred, discord, jealousy, fits of rage, selfish ambition, dissensions, factions ²¹and envy; drunkenness, orgies, and the like. I warn you, as I did before, that those who live like this will not inherit the kingdom of God.

²²But the fruit of the Spirit is love, joy, peace, patience, kindness, goodness, faithfulness, ²³gentleness and self-control. Against such things there is no law. ²⁴Those who belong to Christ Jesus have crucified the sinful nature with its passions and desires. ²⁵Since we live by the Spirit, let us keep in step with the Spirit. ²⁶Let us not become conceited, provoking and envying each other.

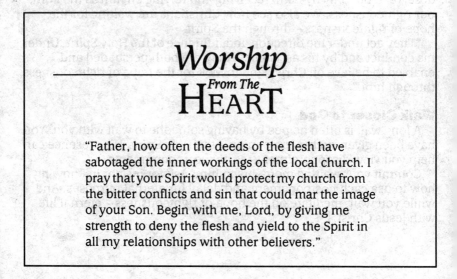

Worship
From The
HEART

"Father, how often the deeds of the flesh have sabotaged the inner workings of the local church. I pray that your Spirit would protect my church from the bitter conflicts and sin that could mar the image of your Son. Begin with me, Lord, by giving me strength to deny the flesh and yield to the Spirit in all my relationships with other believers."

A Conflict of Interests

Those who belong to Christ Jesus have crucified the sinful nature with its passions and desires (Galatians 5:24).

Two wrestlers grapple in the ring, each striving to master the other. Their names: "Flesh" (or your "sinful nature") and "Spirit." The ring in which they struggle is the arena of your life.

The "Flesh" keeps trying to lure you away from the things of God. The "Spirit" continues to woo you with the love of Christ. And the one to whom you yield your life will dominate your life, as Johann Peter Lange explains.

Walk With Johann Peter Lange

"Paul's meaning is not that the flesh, with its affections and lusts, is no longer present at all with those that have become Christians, but that a walk in the flesh should not any longer exist in the case of Christians. A walk in the Spirit might be rightly expected of believers. This is only possible for those who have crucified the flesh. The word is not slain, but crucified. It is a task of the Christian to be accomplished only by continual effort (Colossians 3:5).

"In 'crucified,' however, the simple slaying is not the main idea, but the condemning, giving sentence, surrendering to infamous death. This has necessarily taken place in becoming Christ's. Fellowship with Christ involves a crucifixion of the flesh for the very reason that it is fellowship with Christ's death on the cross.

"Christ indeed has only suffered what people have deserved on account of their sinful flesh. Whoever appropriates to himself Christ's death upon the cross regards the flesh in himself no longer. For him, in Christ's death, the flesh has been crucified."

Walk Closer to God

Have you identified the forces wrestling for control in your life? Paul contrasts the works of the flesh with the works of the Spirit. He reminds you of your twofold responsibility—to crucify the flesh, and to cultivate the fruit of the Spirit. Flesh or Spirit. Which one will you yield to right now? ◯

AUGUST 8

📖 Walk in the Word
Galatians 6

Paul concludes this letter by giving some practical instructions on how to live in relationship with other people, both Christian and non-Christian.

Doing Good to All

6 Brothers, if someone is caught in a sin, you who are spiritual should restore him gently. But watch yourself, or you also may be tempted. ²Carry each other's burdens, and in this way you will fulfill the law of Christ. ³If anyone thinks he is something when he is nothing, he deceives himself. ⁴Each one should test his own actions. Then he can take pride in himself, without comparing himself to somebody else, ⁵for each one should carry his own load.

⁶Anyone who receives instruction in the word must share all good things with his instructor.

⁷Do not be deceived: God cannot be mocked. A man reaps what he sows. ⁸The one who sows to please his sinful nature, from that nature^a will reap destruction; the one who sows to please the Spirit, from the Spirit will reap eternal life. ⁹Let us not become weary in doing good, for at the proper time we will reap a harvest if we do not give up. ¹⁰Therefore, as we have opportunity, let us do good to all people, especially to those who belong to the family of believers.

Not Circumcision but a New Creation

¹¹See what large letters I use as I write to you with my own hand!

¹²Those who want to make a good impression outwardly are trying to compel you to be circumcised. The only reason they do this is to avoid being persecuted for the cross of Christ. ¹³Not even those who are circumcised obey the law, yet they want you to be circumcised that they may boast about your flesh. ¹⁴May I never boast except in the cross of our Lord Jesus Christ, through which^b the world has been crucified to me, and I to the world. ¹⁵Neither circumcision nor uncircumcision means anything; what counts is a new creation. ¹⁶Peace and mercy to all who follow this rule, even to the Israel of God.

¹⁷Finally, let no one cause me trouble, for I bear on my body the marks of Jesus.

¹⁸The grace of our Lord Jesus Christ be with your spirit, brothers. Amen.

a8 Or his flesh, from the flesh   b14 Or whom

Leaving a Legacy That Will Not Be Forgotten

Therefore, as we have opportunity, let us do good to all people, especially to those who belong to the family of believers (Galatians 6:10).

Charity was never an "extra-curricular activity" with Jesus; it was a Spirit-empowered way of life.

As Jesus went about doing good, that goodness marked the lives of those he touched. According to Thomas Chalmers, there's no better way to leave a lasting legacy.

Walk with Thomas Chalmers

"Thousands of Christians breathe, move and live, pass off the stage of life, and are heard no more—why?

"They did not partake of good, and none in the world were blessed by them. None could point to them as the guide to their redemption. They wrote nothing, and nothing they said could be recalled. And so they passed on, remembered no more than insects of yesterday.

"Will you live and die this way, O man immortal? Live for something. Do good, and leave behind a monument of virtue. Write your name in kindness, love, and mercy on the hearts of all you come in contact with; you will never be forgotten.

"No, your name, your deeds will be as legible on the hearts you leave behind as the stars on the brow of evening. Good deeds will shine as the stars of heaven."

Walk Closer to God

The *good* life. For some, it's defined as *getting* all you can *out of* life. For the Christian, it's *giving* all you can *to* life.

Jesus put it this way: "Let your light shine before men, that they may see your good deeds and praise your Father in heaven" (Matthew 5:16).

The possibilities are endless.

Brightening someone's day with a kindness. Returning good for evil in the office, the classroom or on the highway. Sharing someone's grief.

The person you help may never know your name. But God will never forget the good you did in his name. ⟨⟩

AUGUST 9

📖 Walk in the Word
Ephesians 1:1–14

Paul explains the wonderful spiritual blessings that we as Christians have in Christ, especially the knowledge that we have been chosen by him before the creation of the world.

1 Paul, an apostle of Christ Jesus by the will of God,

To the saints in Ephesus,*a* the faithful*b* in Christ Jesus:

²Grace and peace to you from God our Father and the Lord Jesus Christ.

Spiritual Blessings in Christ

³Praise be to the God and Father of our Lord Jesus Christ, who has blessed us in the heavenly realms with every spiritual blessing in Christ. ⁴For he chose us in him before the creation of the world to be holy and blameless in his sight. In love ⁵he*c* predestined us to be adopted as his sons through Jesus Christ, in accordance with his pleasure and will— ⁶to the praise of his glorious grace, which he has freely given us in the One he loves. ⁷In him we have redemption through his blood, the forgiveness of sins, in accordance with the riches of God's grace ⁸that he lavished on us with all wisdom and understanding. ⁹And he*d* made known to us the mystery of his will according to his good pleasure, which he purposed in Christ, ¹⁰to be put into effect when the times will have reached their fulfillment—to bring all things in heaven and on earth together under one head, even Christ.

¹¹In him we were also chosen,*e* having been predestined according to the plan of him who works out everything in conformity with the purpose of his will, ¹²in order that we, who were the first to hope in Christ, might be for the praise of his glory. ¹³And you also were included in Christ when you heard the word of truth, the gospel of your salvation. Having believed, you were marked in him with a seal, the promised Holy Spirit, ¹⁴who is a deposit guaranteeing our inheritance until the redemption of those who are God's possession—to the praise of his glory.

---

a1 Some early manuscripts do not have *in Ephesus.*   *b1* Or *believers who are*   *c4,5* Or *sight in love.* ⁵*He*   *d8,9* Or *us. With all wisdom and understanding,* ⁹*he*   *e11* Or *were made heirs*

AUGUST 9

Spiritual Treasures All Believers Possess

Praise be to the God and Father of our Lord Jesus Christ, who has blessed us in the heavenly realms with every spiritual blessing in Christ (Ephesians 1:3).

Words cascade when something excites the heart.

In the original Greek text, Ephesians 1:3–14 is one continuous sentence of praise to God for benefits and blessings which are all "connected" in the person of Christ.

Don't be surprised if you find Paul's attitude contagious as you read A.W. Tozer's description of these riches in Christ—past, present, and future.

Walk with A.W. Tozer

"The spiritual blessings which are ours in Christ may be divided into three types:

"The first are those which come to us immediately upon our believing unto salvation, such as forgiveness, justification, sonship in the family of God. In Christ we possess these even before we know they are ours!

"The second are those riches which we cannot enjoy in actuality until our Lord returns. These include ultimate mental and moral perfection, the glorification of our bodies, and the maturing of the divine image in our redeemed personalities. These treasures are as surely ours as if we possessed them now!

"The third consists of spiritual treasures which only come as we make a determined effort to possess them. These include deliverance from the sins of the flesh, victory over self, fruitfulness in service, awareness of God's presence, growth in grace, and an unbroken spirit of worship. These come as our faith and courage mount."

Walk Closer to God

As you read that catalog of blessings, perhaps you found yourself getting excited.

Excited about what God has already done—in Christ. Confident about what he has promised to do—in Christ. Committed to claim his resources for today—in Christ.

Past. Present. Future. His blessings encompass your entire life—in Christ. ◖◗

AUGUST 10

📖 Walk in the Word
Ephesians 1:15–23

Paul prays that Christians may come to know the glorious inheritance we have in Christ and the full spiritual power that is available to us in him.

Thanksgiving and Prayer

¹⁵For this reason, ever since I heard about your faith in the Lord Jesus and your love for all the saints, ¹⁶I have not stopped giving thanks for you, remembering you in my prayers. ¹⁷I keep asking that the God of our Lord Jesus Christ, the glorious Father, may give you the Spirit[a] of wisdom and revelation, so that you may know him better. ¹⁸I pray also that the eyes of your heart may be enlightened in order that you may know the hope to which he has called you, the riches of his glorious inheritance in the saints, ¹⁹and his incomparably great power for us who believe. That power is like the working of his mighty strength, ²⁰which he exerted in Christ when he raised him from the dead and seated him at his right hand in the heavenly realms, ²¹far above all rule and authority, power and dominion, and every title that can be given, not only in the present age but also in the one to come. ²²And God placed all things under his feet and appointed him to be head over everything for the church, ²³which is his body, the fullness of him who fills everything in every way.

a17 Or a spirit

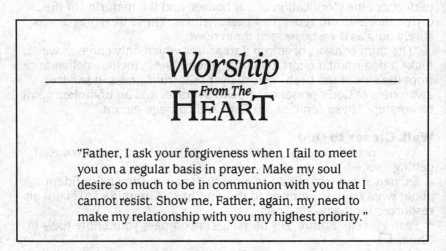

Worship
From The HEART

"Father, I ask your forgiveness when I fail to meet you on a regular basis in prayer. Make my soul desire so much to be in communion with you that I cannot resist. Show me, Father, again, my need to make my relationship with you my highest priority."

AUGUST 10

Taking Time for Prayer

For this reason, ever since I heard about your faith in the Lord Jesus and your love for all the saints, I have not stopped giving thanks for you, remembering you in my prayers (Ephesians 1:15–16).

"I can't believe it. I absolutely promised myself (more important, I promised God!) that I would pray for at least thirty minutes this morning. Instead, I pushed the snooze button on the alarm so many times that I didn't have time to pray at all. The worst of it is that I haven't had a decent quiet time now for four days in a row! What in the world is wrong with me?"

Sound familiar? Many of us have feeble prayer lives. In contrast, Paul prayed constantly and instructed us to do the same. Our world is a busy world, and God understands that. But it remains true that a prayerless Christian is unheard of in Scripture . . . yet not unheard of in our day.

Alexander Whyte encourages us to work at prayer (rather than just pray at work).

Walk With Alexander Whyte

"I am certain that the secret of much mischief to our own souls and to the souls of others lies in the way that we starve our prayers by hurrying over them. Prayer that God will call true prayer takes far more time than one-in-a-thousand thinks. After all that the Holy Spirit has done to make true prayer independent of times, and of places, and of all kinds of instruments and assistances—as long as we remain in this unspiritual and undevotional world—we shall not succeed in prayer without such times, and places, and other assistances.

"Take good care lest you take your salvation far too cheaply. If you find your life of prayer to be always so short, and so easy, and so spiritual, as to be without strain and sweat to you, you may depend upon it, you have not yet begun to pray. As sure as you sit there, it is just in this matter of *time* in prayer that so many of us are making shipwrecks of our souls and of the souls of others."

Walk Closer to God

"The Spirit helps us in our weakness. We do not know what we ought to pray for, but the Spirit himself intercedes for us with groans that words cannot express" (Romans 8:26). Keep that in mind and you will struggle *in* prayer rather than *with* prayer. ◖

AUGUST 11

Walk in the Word
Ephesians 2:1–10

Paul stresses the wonder of God's grace that has made us alive in Christ and now enables us to live a life of good works.

Made Alive in Christ

2 As for you, you were dead in your transgressions and sins, ²in which you used to live when you followed the ways of this world and of the ruler of the kingdom of the air, the spirit who is now at work in those who are disobedient. ³All of us also lived among them at one time, gratifying the cravings of our sinful nature*a* and following its desires and thoughts. Like the rest, we were by nature objects of wrath. ⁴But because of his great love for us, God, who is rich in mercy, ⁵made us alive with Christ even when we were dead in transgressions — it is by grace you have been saved. ⁶And God raised us up with Christ and seated us with him in the heavenly realms in Christ Jesus, ⁷in order that in the coming ages he might show the incomparable riches of his grace, expressed in his kindness to us in Christ Jesus. ⁸For it is by grace you have been saved, through faith — and this not from yourselves, it is the gift of God — ⁹not by works, so that no one can boast. ¹⁰For we are God's workmanship, created in Christ Jesus to do good works, which God prepared in advance for us to do.

a3 Or our flesh

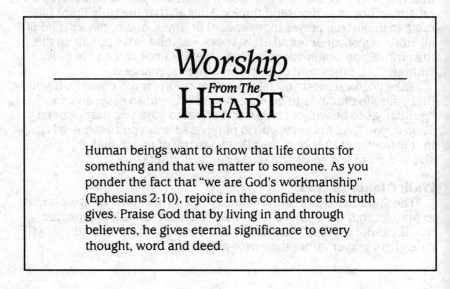

Worship
From The
HEART

Human beings want to know that life counts for something and that we matter to someone. As you ponder the fact that "we are God's workmanship" (Ephesians 2:10), rejoice in the confidence this truth gives. Praise God that by living in and through believers, he gives eternal significance to every thought, word and deed.

AUGUST 11

Adding Up the Facts About Faith

For it is by grace you have been saved, through faith—and this not from yourselves, it is the gift of God—not by works, so that no one can boast (Ephesians 2:8–9).

In Romans 1:21 Paul speaks of people who, "although they knew God, they neither glorified him as God nor gave thanks to him" (Romans 1:21).

Though the fact of God's existence was before them, they closed their eyes to the truth of it.

Faith that saves is more than acquired facts about Christianity.

Philip Melanchthon helps set the facts straight about faith. Read his words slowly and prayerfully.

Walk With Philip Melanchthon

"That faith which justifies is not merely an acknowledgment of facts, but it is a recognition of the promise of God in which, for Christ's sake, the remission of sins and justification are freely offered.

"It is regarding with my whole heart the promises of God as certain and true, through which there are offered me, without my merit, the forgiveness of sins, grace, and salvation through Christ the Mediator.

"Faith means that my whole heart takes to itself this treasure. It is not my doing, not my presenting or giving, not my work of preparation.

"Rather, my heart comforts itself, and is perfectly confident with respect to this, namely, that God sheds upon me as a gift every treasure of grace in Christ."

Walk Closer to God

Fact: Christ died for sins.

Fact: Christ was buried.

Fact: Christ rose the third day.

Fact: Christ is the only way to God.

The evidence is ample to confirm these facts (1 Corinthians 15:1–8; John 14:6).

And you may agree with all that has been said so far.

But, according to Paul, true faith is something more. It is recognizing that these facts apply to you.

Fact: Eternal life can be yours—right now.

That's a fact everyone needs to take to heart by reaching out by faith to receive Jesus as Savior. ◐

AUGUST 12

Walk in the Word
Ephesians 2:11-22

Paul shows how all divisions that we as humans make between one another have been broken down in Christ; in the church we should be one unified body.

One in Christ

[11]Therefore, remember that formerly you who are Gentiles by birth and called "uncircumcised" by those who call themselves "the circumcision" (that done in the body by the hands of men) — [12]remember that at that time you were separate from Christ, excluded from citizenship in Israel and foreigners to the covenants of the promise, without hope and without God in the world. [13]But now in Christ Jesus you who once were far away have been brought near through the blood of Christ.

[14]For he himself is our peace, who has made the two one and has destroyed the barrier, the dividing wall of hostility, [15]by abolishing in his flesh the law with its commandments and regulations. His purpose was to create in himself one new man out of the two, thus making peace, [16]and in this one body to reconcile both of them to God through the cross, by which he put to death their hostility. [17]He came and preached peace to you who were far away and peace to those who were near. [18]For through him we both have access to the Father by one Spirit.

[19]Consequently, you are no longer foreigners and aliens, but fellow citizens with God's people and members of God's household, [20]built on the foundation of the apostles and prophets, with Christ Jesus himself as the chief cornerstone. [21]In him the whole building is joined together and rises to become a holy temple in the Lord. [22]And in him you too are being built together to become a dwelling in which God lives by his Spirit.

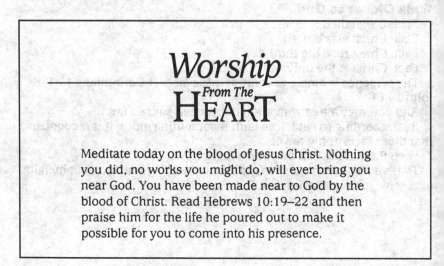

Worship
From The
HEART

Meditate today on the blood of Jesus Christ. Nothing you did, no works you might do, will ever bring you near God. You have been made near to God by the blood of Christ. Read Hebrews 10:19-22 and then praise him for the life he poured out to make it possible for you to come into his presence.

AUGUST 12

Peace With God and With Others

For he himself [Jesus Christ] is our peace, who has made the two [Jew and Gentile] one and has destroyed the barrier, the dividing wall of hostility (Ephesians 2:14).

Class struggle . . . generation gap . . . racial tension. None of these problems is unique to our century.

Consider the Jews and Gentiles of Paul's day. Their prejudice ran so deep that it was not uncommon for a Jew to pray, "I thank you, God, that you have not seen fit to make me a Gentile."

Yet healed relationships can result when both sides see their need for the same Savior. Only Jesus Christ can bring peace that overcomes prejudice, as Albert Barnes relates.

Walk With Albert Barnes

"Formerly Jews and Gentiles were alienated and separate. The Jews regarded the Gentiles with hatred; the Gentiles regarded the Jews with scorn.

"Now, says the apostle, they are at peace. They worship the same God. They have the same Savior.

"They depend upon the same atonement. Reconciliation has not only taken place with God, but with each other.

"The best way to produce peace between alienated minds is to bring them to the same Savior. The love of Christ is so absorbing, and the dependence on his blood so entire, they will lay aside these alienations and cease their contentions.

"The work of the atonement is thus designed not only to produce peace with God, but peace between alienated and belligerent minds."

Walk Closer to God

In the last 3,500 years of recorded history, less than 300 have been warless. In that same period of time, more than 8,000 treaties have been made . . . and broken.

Why? Because parties alienated from God cannot help but be alienated from one another.

Christ came to provide peace with God (Romans 5:1) and peace with others (Ephesians 2:14) — permanently.

Where else but in Jesus Christ could that kind of peace be found? ❏

AUGUST 13

📖 Walk in the Word
Ephesians 3

As the one whom God called to preach the Good News of salvation to the Gentiles, Paul prays fervently that every one of us will realize the full magnitude of the love of Christ, who dwells in us.

Paul the Preacher to the Gentiles

3 For this reason I, Paul, the prisoner of Christ Jesus for the sake of you Gentiles —

²Surely you have heard about the administration of God's grace that was given to me for you, ³that is, the mystery made known to me by revelation, as I have already written briefly. ⁴In reading this, then, you will be able to understand my insight into the mystery of Christ, ⁵which was not made known to men in other generations as it has now been revealed by the Spirit to God's holy apostles and prophets. ⁶This mystery is that through the gospel the Gentiles are heirs together with Israel, members together of one body, and sharers together in the promise in Christ Jesus.

⁷I became a servant of this gospel by the gift of God's grace given me through the working of his power. ⁸Although I am less than the least of all God's people, this grace was given me: to preach to the Gentiles the unsearchable riches of Christ, ⁹and to make plain to everyone the administration of this mystery, which for ages past was kept hidden in God, who created all things. ¹⁰His intent was that now, through the church, the manifold wisdom of God should be made known to the rulers and authorities in the heavenly realms, ¹¹according to his eternal purpose which he accomplished in Christ Jesus our Lord. ¹²In him and through faith in him we may approach God with freedom and confidence. ¹³I ask you, therefore, not to be discouraged because of my sufferings for you, which are your glory.

A Prayer for the Ephesians

¹⁴For this reason I kneel before the Father, ¹⁵from whom his whole family*ᵃ* in heaven and on earth derives its name. ¹⁶I pray that out of his glorious riches he may strengthen you with power through his Spirit in your inner being, ¹⁷so that Christ may dwell in your hearts through faith. And I pray that you, being rooted and established in love, ¹⁸may have power, together with all the saints, to grasp how wide and long and high and deep is the love of Christ, ¹⁹and to know this love that surpasses knowledge — that you may be filled to the measure of all the fullness of God.

²⁰Now to him who is able to do immeasurably more than all we ask or imagine, according to his power that is at work within us, ²¹to him be glory in the church and in Christ Jesus throughout all generations, for ever and ever! Amen.

ᵃ15 Or whom all fatherhood

Exalting the Savior Worthy of Praise

That Christ may dwell in your hearts through faith. And I pray that you, being rooted and established in love, may . . . know this love that surpasses knowledge (Ephesians 3:17–19).

Awe is an appropriate response to glorious sights of nature: sunrise over the Grand Canyon . . . Niagara Falls . . . the Milky Way. But how do you respond to the wonder of salvation?

After nearly three chapters of explanation regarding life in Christ, Paul breaks forth in spontaneous exaltation of his praiseworthy Christ.

A few centuries later Bernard of Clairvaux captured his emotions at the thought of his Lord this way.

Walk With Bernard of Clairvaux

Jesus, the very thought of thee
  With sweetness fills my breast;
But sweeter far thy face to see,
  And in thy presence rest.

O Hope of every contrite heart,
  O Joy of all the meek,
To those who fall, how kind thou art!
  How good to those who seek!

But what to those who find? Ah, this
  Nor tongue nor pen can show,
The love of Jesus, what it is
  None but his loved ones know.

Jesus, our only joy be thou,
  As thou our prize wilt be;
Jesus, be thou our glory now,
  And through eternity.

Walk Closer to God

Paul challenged the Ephesians to comprehend "how wide and long and high and deep is the love of Christ" and ended by saying, "To him be glory in the church and in Christ Jesus throughout all generations, for ever and ever! Amen."

Reread Paul's prayer in chapter three.

Then voice your own praises to the one who enabled you to become his "loved one" eternally. ◑

AUGUST 14

📖 Walk in the Word
Ephesians 4:1–16

Paul instructs everyone in the church to work toward complete unity and to become mature in their Christian faith.

Unity in the Body of Christ

4 As a prisoner for the Lord, then, I urge you to live a life worthy of the calling you have received. [2]Be completely humble and gentle; be patient, bearing with one another in love. [3]Make every effort to keep the unity of the Spirit through the bond of peace. [4]There is one body and one Spirit— just as you were called to one hope when you were called— [5]one Lord, one faith, one baptism; [6]one God and Father of all, who is over all and through all and in all.

[7]But to each one of us grace has been given as Christ apportioned it. [8]This is why it[a] says:

> "When he ascended on high,
>   he led captives in his train
>   and gave gifts to men."[b]

[9](What does "he ascended" mean except that he also descended to the lower, earthly regions[c]? [10]He who descended is the very one who ascended higher than all the heavens, in order to fill the whole universe.) [11]It was he who gave some to be apostles, some to be prophets, some to be evangelists, and some to be pastors and teachers, [12]to prepare God's people for works of service, so that the body of Christ may be built up [13]until we all reach unity in the faith and in the knowledge of the Son of God and become mature, attaining to the whole measure of the fullness of Christ.

[14]Then we will no longer be infants, tossed back and forth by the waves, and blown here and there by every wind of teaching and by the cunning and craftiness of men in their deceitful scheming. [15]Instead, speaking the truth in love, we will in all things grow up into him who is the Head, that is, Christ. [16]From him the whole body, joined and held together by every supporting ligament, grows and builds itself up in love, as each part does its work.

[a]8 Or *God*   [b]8 Psalm 68:18   [c]9 Or *the depths of the earth*

AUGUST 14

The Best Way to Promote Unity

Live a life worthy of the calling you have received. . . . Make every effort to keep the unity of the Spirit through the bond of peace (Ephesians 4:1,3).

Paul's concern in chapter four is for one body—the body of Christ—and the unity needed to encourage its healthy growth.

To do this, Paul emphasizes the "ones" of the faith and the responsibilities of the body's members one to another.

Charles Spurgeon adds these thoughts on promoting soundness and oneness in the body of Christ.

Walk With Charles Spurgeon

"Let us cultivate everything that would tend to unity. Are any sick? Let us care for them. Are any suffering? Let us weep with them. Do we perceive faults in a brother? Let us admonish him in love and affection.

"Let us remember that we cannot keep the unity of the Spirit unless we all believe the truth of God.

"Let us search our Bibles, therefore, and conform our views to the teaching of God's Word.

"Let us live near to Christ, for this is the best way of promoting unity. Divisions in churches never begin with those full of love for the Savior. Cold hearts, unholy lives, inconsistent actions—these are the seeds which sow schisms in the body.

"But he who lives near to Jesus, wears his likeness and copies his example, will be, wherever he goes, a holy link to bind the church more closely than ever together."

Walk Closer to God

Paul exhorted his readers to unity in Christ; Jesus spent his last evening before the crucifixion praying for the same thing.

"I in them and you in me. May they be brought to complete unity to let the world know that you sent me" (John 17:23).

The nearer you draw to the Lord Jesus Christ, the stronger will grow your love for others in his body.

And the closer will you move to the oneness of heart and purpose for which Christ prayed. ◖

AUGUST 15

📖 Walk in the Word
Ephesians 4:17–32

Paul gives some specific pointers on how Christians can live as children of light in the midst of a world of darkness.

Living as Children of Light

[17]So I tell you this, and insist on it in the Lord, that you must no longer live as the Gentiles do, in the futility of their thinking. [18]They are darkened in their understanding and separated from the life of God because of the ignorance that is in them due to the hardening of their hearts. [19]Having lost all sensitivity, they have given themselves over to sensuality so as to indulge in every kind of impurity, with a continual lust for more.

[20]You, however, did not come to know Christ that way. [21]Surely you heard of him and were taught in him in accordance with the truth that is in Jesus. [22]You were taught, with regard to your former way of life, to put off your old self, which is being corrupted by its deceitful desires; [23]to be made new in the attitude of your minds; [24]and to put on the new self, created to be like God in true righteousness and holiness.

[25]Therefore each of you must put off falsehood and speak truthfully to his neighbor, for we are all members of one body. [26]"In your anger do not sin"[a]: Do not let the sun go down while you are still angry, [27]and do not give the devil a foothold. [28]He who has been stealing must steal no longer, but must work, doing something useful with his own hands, that he may have something to share with those in need.

[29]Do not let any unwholesome talk come out of your mouths, but only what is helpful for building others up according to their needs, that it may benefit those who listen. [30]And do not grieve the Holy Spirit of God, with whom you were sealed for the day of redemption. [31]Get rid of all bitterness, rage and anger, brawling and slander, along with every form of malice. [32]Be kind and compassionate to one another, forgiving each other, just as in Christ God forgave you.

[a]26 Psalm 4:4

The Mind Is a Tool in the Hand of God

You must no longer live as the Gentiles do, in the futility of their thinking. They are darkened in their understanding . . . because of the ignorance that is in them due to the hardening of their hearts (Ephesians 4:17–18).

You may not understand how one death nearly two thousand years ago can bring forgiveness of sins today, but you still believe it.

And building on that belief, your understanding begins to grow as you learn to lean on God, rather than on your own understanding.

Reliance on human wisdom can keep you from God. But once enlightened by faith, your mind can also become a keen tool for God. Read as Martin Luther describes the wise use of human wisdom.

Walk With Martin Luther

"The natural wisdom of a human creature in matters of faith, until he is born anew, is altogether darkness. But in a person who is regenerated by the Holy Spirit through the Word, the mind is a glorious instrument and work of God: for all God's gifts are wholesome to the good and godly.

"The understanding, through faith, receives life from faith; that which was dead is made alive again.

"Just as our bodies in broad daylight are likely to rise, move, and walk more readily and safely than they would in the dead of night, so it is with dark reason, which, when enlightened, does not strive against faith but rather advances it."

Walk Closer to God

Without faith it is impossible to please God (Hebrews 11:6). Without faith, a person is in the dark concerning the things of God (Romans 1:22).

Wisdom to understand God's ways must come from a heavenly source. Therefore, "if any of you lacks wisdom, he should ask God" (James 1:5).

Wait until you understand all about God before you come to him, and you will wait for eternity.

On the other hand, come to him today to learn from him, and you'll discover that you can both know and do his will.

AUGUST 16

Walk in the Word
Ephesians 5:1–21

In this section Paul continues his instructions on how God's children should live in the light and avoid the deeds of darkness.

5 Be imitators of God, therefore, as dearly loved children ²and live a life of love, just as Christ loved us and gave himself up for us as a fragrant offering and sacrifice to God.

³But among you there must not be even a hint of sexual immorality, or of any kind of impurity, or of greed, because these are improper for God's holy people. ⁴Nor should there be obscenity, foolish talk or coarse joking, which are out of place, but rather thanksgiving. ⁵For of this you can be sure: No immoral, impure or greedy person—such a man is an idolater—has any inheritance in the kingdom of Christ and of God.[a] ⁶Let no one deceive you with empty words, for because of such things God's wrath comes on those who are disobedient. ⁷Therefore do not be partners with them.

⁸For you were once darkness, but now you are light in the Lord. Live as children of light ⁹(for the fruit of the light consists in all goodness, righteousness and truth) ¹⁰and find out what pleases the Lord. ¹¹Have nothing to do with the fruitless deeds of darkness, but rather expose them. ¹²For it is shameful even to mention what the disobedient do in secret. ¹³But everything exposed by the light becomes visible, ¹⁴for it is light that makes everything visible. This is why it is said:

> "Wake up, O sleeper,
>   rise from the dead,
>   and Christ will shine on you."

¹⁵Be very careful, then, how you live—not as unwise but as wise, ¹⁶making the most of every opportunity, because the days are evil. ¹⁷Therefore do not be foolish, but understand what the Lord's will is. ¹⁸Do not get drunk on wine, which leads to debauchery. Instead, be filled with the Spirit. ¹⁹Speak to one another with psalms, hymns and spiritual songs. Sing and make music in your heart to the Lord, ²⁰always giving thanks to God the Father for everything, in the name of our Lord Jesus Christ.

²¹Submit to one another out of reverence for Christ.

a5 Or kingdom of the Christ and God

The Concrete Form of Goodness

Live as children of light . . . find out what pleases the Lord. . . . "and Christ will shine on you" (Ephesians 5:8,10,14).

The question of how to live like Jesus Christ is easy to ask, yet hard to answer—and even harder to achieve.

And yet, Christlikeness is a theme that dominates the writings of Paul (Romans 8:29), Peter (2 Peter 1:4) and John (1 John 3:2).

Alexander Maclaren offers this helpful explanation of what Christlikeness is, and how God expects us to achieve it.

Walk With Alexander Maclaren

"What is it that pleases Jesus Christ? His own likeness.

"Jesus Christ desires most that we be like him. That we are to bear his image is a comprehensive and at the same time specific way of defining Christian duty.

"And what is the likeness of Jesus Christ which is thus our supreme obligation to bear? We can put it all into two thoughts: suppression of the self-will and continual consciousness of obedience to the divine will.

"The life of Jesus Christ is the great example of these two qualities. His life contains within its narrow compass adequate direction for human life.

"The man or woman who has in his heart these thoughts—that the definition of virtue is pleasing Jesus Christ, that the concrete form of goodness is likeness to him in denying self and obeying God—needs no other goal to fill his life."

Walk Closer to God

Is it really possible to live a godly life in an ungodly world? Absolutely!

Jesus modeled it for his disciples, then commanded, "Do as I have done" (John 13:15).

Paul modeled it for his churches, then exhorted, "Live as children of light" (Ephesians 5:8).

Let your steps be guided today by the prayer that Jesus prayed in the garden of Gethsemane: "Not as I will, but as you will" (Matthew 26:39). ◖

AUGUST 17

📖 Walk in the Word
Ephesians 5:22–33

Paul now turns to relationships in the home, beginning with an extended discussion on the beauty of marriage and on the responsibilities of husbands and wives.

Wives and Husbands

[22]Wives, submit to your husbands as to the Lord. [23]For the husband is the head of the wife as Christ is the head of the church, his body, of which he is the Savior. [24]Now as the church submits to Christ, so also wives should submit to their husbands in everything.

[25]Husbands, love your wives, just as Christ loved the church and gave himself up for her [26]to make her holy, cleansing[a] her by the washing with water through the word, [27]and to present her to himself as a radiant church, without stain or wrinkle or any other blemish, but holy and blameless. [28]In this same way, husbands ought to love their wives as their own bodies. He who loves his wife loves himself. [29]After all, no one ever hated his own body, but he feeds and cares for it, just as Christ does the church— [30]for we are members of his body. [31]"For this reason a man will leave his father and mother and be united to his wife, and the two will become one flesh."[b] [32]This is a profound mystery—but I am talking about Christ and the church. [33]However, each one of you also must love his wife as he loves himself, and the wife must respect her husband.

[a]26 Or *having cleansed*   [b]31 Gen. 2:24

Worship
From The
HEART

The body of Christ is a complex, living organism that encompasses people from every race, color, economic position and walk of life. Why not pray for members of the body who are far removed from your neighborhood? From your church's literature or from various mission organizations, you can find the names of believers from other countries. Thank God for the privilege of praying for brothers and sisters you will meet in eternity.

Unity and Diversity in the Body

> For we are members of his body (Ephesians 5:30).

Every cell in the human body is alike in some ways to every other. But different cells perform different functions in the body—an analogy C.S. Lewis draws on and applies to your role in the body of Christ.

Walk With C.S. Lewis
"The society into which the Christian is called is not a collective but a body. It is in fact that body of which the family unit is an image on the natural level.

"If anyone came to it with the misconception that the church was a massing together of persons as if they were pennies or chips, he would be corrected at the threshold by the discovery that the Head of this body is utterly unlike its inferior members—they share no divinity with him except by analogy.

"We are summoned at the outset to combine as creatures with our Creator, as mortals with immortal, as redeemed sinners with sinless Redeemer.

"His presence, the interaction between him and us, must always be the overwhelmingly dominant factor in the life we are to lead within the body; and any conception of Christian fellowship which does not mean primarily fellowship with him is out of order."*

Walk Closer to God
You are a cell in the body of Christ—like millions of other Christians. But are you a . . .
. . . nerve cell (to feel)?
. . . blood cell (to nourish)?
. . . brain cell (to direct)?
. . . muscle cell (to strengthen)?
. . . bone cell (to support)?
Cells all alike, yet all different. And each is crucial to the effective functioning of the body. The nucleus of all these cells is Christ himself. Without the nucleus, the cell dies. Unity is found only in Christ; diversity of function in his body.

*From *Transposition and Other Addresses*; used by permission of William Collins Sons and Co., Ltd.

August 18

📖 Walk in the Word
Ephesians 6:1–9

Paul continues his discussion on relationships by discussing the responsibilities of parents and children, servants and masters.

Children and Parents

6 Children, obey your parents in the Lord, for this is right. [2]"Honor your father and mother" — which is the first commandment with a promise — [3]"that it may go well with you and that you may enjoy long life on the earth."[a]

[4]Fathers, do not exasperate your children; instead, bring them up in the training and instruction of the Lord.

Slaves and Masters

[5]Slaves, obey your earthly masters with respect and fear, and with sincerity of heart, just as you would obey Christ. [6]Obey them not only to win their favor when their eye is on you, but like slaves of Christ, doing the will of God from your heart. [7]Serve wholeheartedly, as if you were serving the Lord, not men, [8]because you know that the Lord will reward everyone for whatever good he does, whether he is slave or free.

[9]And masters, treat your slaves in the same way. Do not threaten them, since you know that he who is both their Master and yours is in heaven, and there is no favoritism with him.

[a]3 Deut. 5:16

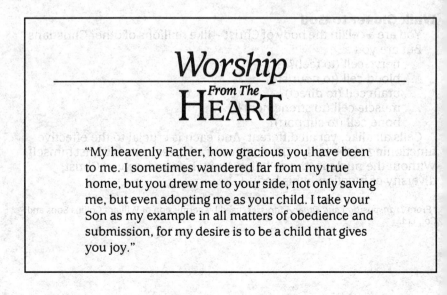

Worship From The HEART

"My heavenly Father, how gracious you have been to me. I sometimes wandered far from my true home, but you drew me to your side, not only saving me, but even adopting me as your child. I take your Son as my example in all matters of obedience and submission, for my desire is to be a child that gives you joy."

AUGUST 18

Family Life at its Finest

Children, obey your parents in the Lord, for this is right. "Honor your father and mother"—which is the first commandment with a promise (Ephesians 6:1–2).

Paul quotes the words of Moses to show that obedient children enjoy life "well . . . and . . . long . . . on the earth" (Ephesians 6:3). And obedient children develop best when rooted "in the training and instruction of the Lord" (Ephesians 6:4).

John and Charles Wesley, great eighteenth-century revival leaders in England, were taught to obey as Jesus did. Their mother, Susannah Wesley, gave this description of their upbringing.

Walk With Susannah Wesley

"I insisted on conquering a child's will, for when this is thoroughly done a child can be governed by the reason and piety of his parents until its own understanding comes into maturity, and the principles of religion have taken root in its mind.

"Self-will is the root of all sin and misery. Whatever promotes this in children ensures their wretchedness; whatever checks it increases their future happiness. The parent who indulges the child's self-will does the devil's work: makes religion impracticable, salvation unattainable, and is working to damn his child's soul forever.

"Without renouncing the world no one can follow my method. Very few would devote more than twenty years of their life to save the souls of their children which they think may be saved without so much ado. Yet that was my intention, however unskillfully and unsuccessfully managed."

Walk Closer to God

Young person, if God's own Son willingly submitted to earthly parents, is he asking too much for you to do the same? Parents, if your children see you as "standing in the place of God," what needs to change in order for the picture to be accurate and consistent?

Obedient children . . . honored parents . . . God-honoring lives. That's family life at its finest—in the family of God!

AUGUST 19

📖 Walk in the Word
Ephesians 6:10–24

Paul concludes his letter to the Ephesians with this section on how we can gain victory over the devil by using the spiritual armor God has provided us in Christ.

The Armor of God

¹⁰Finally, be strong in the Lord and in his mighty power. ¹¹Put on the full armor of God so that you can take your stand against the devil's schemes. ¹²For our struggle is not against flesh and blood, but against the rulers, against the authorities, against the powers of this dark world and against the spiritual forces of evil in the heavenly realms. ¹³Therefore put on the full armor of God, so that when the day of evil comes, you may be able to stand your ground, and after you have done everything, to stand. ¹⁴Stand firm then, with the belt of truth buckled around your waist, with the breastplate of righteousness in place, ¹⁵and with your feet fitted with the readiness that comes from the gospel of peace. ¹⁶In addition to all this, take up the shield of faith, with which you can extinguish all the flaming arrows of the evil one. ¹⁷Take the helmet of salvation and the sword of the Spirit, which is the word of God. ¹⁸And pray in the Spirit on all occasions with all kinds of prayers and requests. With this in mind, be alert and always keep on praying for all the saints.

¹⁹Pray also for me, that whenever I open my mouth, words may be given me so that I will fearlessly make known the mystery of the gospel, ²⁰for which I am an ambassador in chains. Pray that I may declare it fearlessly, as I should.

Final Greetings

²¹Tychicus, the dear brother and faithful servant in the Lord, will tell you everything, so that you also may know how I am and what I am doing. ²²I am sending him to you for this very purpose, that you may know how we are, and that he may encourage you.

²³Peace to the brothers, and love with faith from God the Father and the Lord Jesus Christ. ²⁴Grace to all who love our Lord Jesus Christ with an undying love.

AUGUST 19

Better a Conqueror Than a Casualty

Therefore put on the full armor of God, so that . . . you may be able to stand your ground, and after you have done everything, to stand (Ephesians 6:13).

The Christian is confronted daily with an all-too familiar struggle— the struggle against the world, the flesh and the devil.

And without proper protection, he would quickly find himself a casualty, rather than a conqueror.

In Ephesians 6:10–17, Paul provides a checklist of spiritual armor. Check to see that yours is in place as H.C.G. Moule itemizes each piece.

Walk With H.C.G. Moule

"The soldier of faith appears before us made strong for a victory which is impossible, except by his relation to his Lord.

"He is safe because he is spiritually right with Christ in God-given truth and righteousness; because he is sure of Christ beneath his feet as the equipment of the gospel of peace for his own soul; because he finds Christ the mighty shield against the fiery volley when he follows him in faith; because he covers his head in the day of battle with Christ as his salvation; because Christ speaks through the Word of God, and so makes himself his servant's sword to cut the accuser down; because prayer in the Spirit grasps him and holds him fast.

"Yes, here, to the last hour of our conflict and our siege—and here only—lies our victory.

"It is Christ himself, not the armor alone. It is the all-sufficient Lord whom the believer stands safely behind."

Walk Closer to God

It's dangerous to be ineffective because of faulty or missing equipment. Now would be a good time for an inspection of your spiritual armor.

Have you put on the full armor of God?

Is every piece in place?

Are you covered from head to toe?

If not, consult your omnipotent supplier and general. He has everything you need for spiritual victory.

In fact, he is everything you need! ◖

A Testimony of God's Faithfulness

During the nineteenth century, the great revivals that swept Britain and America sparked interest in sharing the good news of Christ with those who had never heard it. William Carey went to India, David Livingstone to Africa, Adoniram Judson to Burma, J. Hudson Taylor to China—all pioneers of modern missions.

Born in 1832 to godly parents, Hudson grew up telling others, "When I am a man, I plan to be a missionary and go to China." Discussions of Christianity around the family table nurtured this early ambition.

First, however, he had to come face to face with his own need of a Savior. One day in his seventeenth year, Taylor came across the phrase, "the finished work of Christ." Seizing the importance of that phrase in his own life, he fell to his knees and expressed his faith in the finished work of Christ on his behalf.

After several years of preparation, Taylor sailed for China. From the outset, he preferred to imitate the Chinese in dress and lifestyle rather than live by his Western cultural patterns. He concentrated extensively on the interior regions of China rather than the more accessible coastal regions. Twelve years later he began his own mission organization, the China Inland Mission. By the time of his death in China in 1905, this organization had sent out more than 800 missionaries and had seen more than 125,000 Chinese come to Christ.

The struggles and victories of this tender man of vision testified to the faithfulness of God on behalf of his servants. But God's faithfulness is not limited to missionaries in faraway places. Perhaps today you are troubled by a nagging concern or worry—leave it in the hands of your faithful God. Take the time to talk to him about it right now. He can be trusted!

A LESSON FROM THE LIFE OF J. HUDSON TAYLOR

I can count on God to supply what I need to accomplish the work he has given me to do.

AUGUST 20

📖 Walk in the Word
Philippians 1

From prison Paul writes a joyful letter to encourage the Christians in Philippi. Though being bound in chains is difficult, he has been able to use even this experience as an opportunity to preach the gospel.

1 Paul and Timothy, servants of Christ Jesus,

To all the saints in Christ Jesus at Philippi, together with the overseers[a] and deacons:

2Grace and peace to you from God our Father and the Lord Jesus Christ.

Thanksgiving and Prayer
3I thank my God every time I remember you. 4In all my prayers for all of you, I always pray with joy 5because of your partnership in the gospel from the first day until now, 6being confident of this, that he who began a good work in you will carry it on to completion until the day of Christ Jesus.

7It is right for me to feel this way about all of you, since I have you in my heart; for whether I am in chains or defending and confirming the gospel, all of you share in God's grace with me. 8God can testify how I long for all of you with the affection of Christ Jesus.

9And this is my prayer: that your love may abound more and more in knowledge and depth of insight, 10so that you may be able to discern what is best and may be pure and blameless until the day of Christ, 11filled with the fruit of righteousness that comes through Jesus Christ—to the glory and praise of God.

Paul's Chains Advance the Gospel
12Now I want you to know, brothers, that what has happened to me has really served to advance the gospel. 13As a result, it has become clear throughout the whole palace guard[b] and to everyone else that I am in chains for Christ. 14Because of my chains, most of the brothers in the Lord have been encouraged to speak the word of God more courageously and fearlessly.

15It is true that some preach Christ out of envy and rivalry, but others out of goodwill. 16The latter do so in love, knowing that I am put here for the defense of the gospel. 17The former preach Christ out of selfish ambition, not sincerely, supposing that they can stir up trouble for me while I am in chains.[c] 18But what does it matter? The important thing is that in every way, whether from false motives or true, Christ is preached. And because of this I rejoice.

Yes, and I will continue to rejoice, 19for I know that through your prayers and the help given by the Spirit of Jesus Christ, what has happened to me will turn out for my deliverance.[d] 20I eagerly expect and hope that I will in no way be ashamed, but will have sufficient courage so that now as always Christ will be exalted in my body, whether by life or by death. 21For

August 20

to me, to live is Christ and to die is gain. ²²If I am to go on living in the body, this will mean fruitful labor for me. Yet what shall I choose? I do not know! ²³I am torn between the two: I desire to depart and be with Christ, which is better by far; ²⁴but it is more necessary for you that I remain in the body. ²⁵Convinced of this, I know that I will remain, and I will continue with all of you for your progress and joy in the faith, ²⁶so that through my being with you again your joy in Christ Jesus will overflow on account of me.

²⁷Whatever happens, conduct yourselves in a manner worthy of the gospel of Christ. Then, whether I come and see you or only hear about you in my absence, I will know that you stand firm in one spirit, contending as one man for the faith of the gospel ²⁸without being frightened in any way by those who oppose you. This is a sign to them that they will be destroyed, but that you will be saved—and that by God. ²⁹For it has been granted to you on behalf of Christ not only to believe on him, but also to suffer for him, ³⁰since you are going through the same struggle you saw I had, and now hear that I still have.

a1 Traditionally *bishops* *b13* Or *whole palace* *c16,17* Some late manuscripts have verses 16 and 17 in reverse order. *d19* Or *salvation*

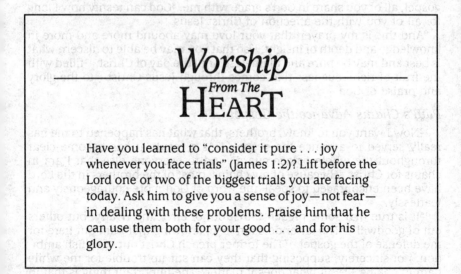

Worship From The HEART

Have you learned to "consider it pure . . . joy whenever you face trials" (James 1:2)? Lift before the Lord one or two of the biggest trials you are facing today. Ask him to give you a sense of joy—not fear—in dealing with these problems. Praise him that he can use them both for your good . . . and for his glory.

Suffering: An Honor Conferred Rather Than a Burden Endured

Now I want you to know, brothers, that what has happened to me has really served to advance the gospel (Philippians 1:12).

Chains could not chill Paul's zeal for the gospel. On the contrary, he saw his imprisonment as an opportunity for the gospel to penetrate where no preacher had gone before.

If Christ could be magnified more from a dungeon than from a pulpit, so be it!

G. Campbell Morgan explains how Paul considered his calling to be of greater concern than his circumstances.

Walk With G. Campbell Morgan

"Paul's situation is an example of how life in fellowship with Christ triumphs over all adverse circumstances. It is a recognition of the fact that all apparently adverse conditions are made allies in victory under the Lord's dominion.

" 'What has happened to me has really served to advance the gospel,' exclaimed the apostle. His very bonds opened the door of opportunity throughout the Praetorian guard.

"Suffering on behalf of Christ is referred to as an honor conferred, rather than a burden endured. It is something granted to the Christian as a privilege, the very granting of which is a gift of grace. To this concept all will agree who have ever really known what it is to suffer on behalf of Christ.

"They are not callous; the suffering is very real, very acute. But it brings a sense of joy which finds no equal in human experience."

Walk Closer to God

A man dives into an icy river to save a drowning child and later comments that he never felt the cold. His mind was on something more important.

For Paul, being in prison didn't matter when there was preaching to be done; he considered himself privileged to be there.

What do you focus on—the circumstances that confront you or your calling that surmounts any circumstances? ⟨⟩

AUGUST 21

Walk in the Word
Philippians 2:1-11

In order to instruct the Philippian Christians on living in humble service to each other, Paul outlines the example of Christ's willing sacrifice.

Imitating Christ's Humility

2 If you have any encouragement from being united with Christ, if any comfort from his love, if any fellowship with the Spirit, if any tenderness and compassion, ²then make my joy complete by being like-minded, having the same love, being one in spirit and purpose. ³Do nothing out of selfish ambition or vain conceit, but in humility consider others better than yourselves. ⁴Each of you should look not only to your own interests, but also to the interests of others.

⁵Your attitude should be the same as that of Christ Jesus:

⁶Who, being in very nature*a* God,
   did not consider equality with God something to be
      grasped,
⁷but made himself nothing,
   taking the very nature*b* of a servant,
   being made in human likeness.
⁸And being found in appearance as a man,
   he humbled himself
   and became obedient to death—
      even death on a cross!
⁹Therefore God exalted him to the highest place
   and gave him the name that is above every name,
¹⁰that at the name of Jesus every knee should bow,
   in heaven and on earth and under the earth,
¹¹and every tongue confess that Jesus Christ is Lord,
   to the glory of God the Father.

a6 Or in the form of   b7 Or the form

What Trifling Sacrifices He Asks of Us

Christ Jesus . . . being in very nature God . . . made himself nothing, taking the very nature of a servant, being made in human likeness (Philippians 2:5–7).

At your annual job review, your employer praises you for your outstanding work, but instead of the promotion you had hoped for, he demotes you so that others might receive promotions. How do you react?

Jesus, seated at the right hand of the Father, willingly "demoted" himself to take a servant's role—God condescending to become a man so that sinners might be "promoted" to heaven.

With J. Hudson Taylor, consider the humility of Christ.

Walk With J. Hudson Taylor

"Let us reflect on what he gave up on leaving heaven's throne to be cradled in a manger.

"Having filled all things and wielded omnipotence, he became a feeble infant and was wrapped in swaddling clothes. Being the Loved One of the Father, never unappreciated, never misunderstood, and always receiving the ceaseless adoration of the hierarchies of heaven, he became a despised Nazarene, misunderstood even by his followers, suspected by those whom he came to bless, rejected by those who owed him their very being, and whose salvation he had come to seek.

"Finally, he was mocked and spit upon, crucified and slain, with thieves and outlaws.

"Will any brother or sister in Christ reflect on this, and yet hesitate to make the trifling sacrifices he asks us to make?"

Walk Closer to God

Being like Christ means thinking like Christ (Philippians 2:5). But when he came from heaven, he wasn't thinking of himself; he was thinking of others.

Loss of privilege and setting aside of power meant little, if by that he might save the objects of his love.

Would you be willing to volunteer for a similar demotion?

Think carefully before you respond; he may take you at your word. ○

AUGUST 22

Walk in the Word
Philippians 2:12–18

Paul wants all Christians to do their very best for Christ, even though it may at times be difficult in a sinful world.

Shining as Stars

¹²Therefore, my dear friends, as you have always obeyed — not only in my presence, but now much more in my absence — continue to work out your salvation with fear and trembling, ¹³for it is God who works in you to will and to act according to his good purpose.

¹⁴Do everything without complaining or arguing, ¹⁵so that you may become blameless and pure, children of God without fault in a crooked and depraved generation, in which you shine like stars in the universe ¹⁶as you hold out[a] the word of life — in order that I may boast on the day of Christ that I did not run or labor for nothing. ¹⁷But even if I am being poured out like a drink offering on the sacrifice and service coming from your faith, I am glad and rejoice with all of you. ¹⁸So you too should be glad and rejoice with me.

[a]16 Or *hold on to*

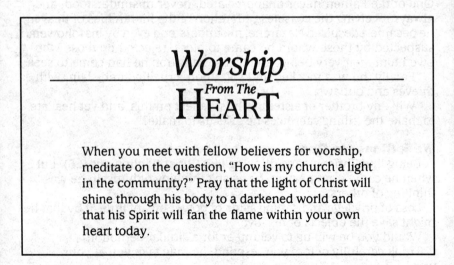

Worship From The HEART

When you meet with fellow believers for worship, meditate on the question, "How is my church a light in the community?" Pray that the light of Christ will shine through his body to a darkened world and that his Spirit will fan the flame within your own heart today.

An Accurate Reflection of the Light Within

That you may become blameless and pure, children of God without fault in a crooked and depraved generation, in which you shine like stars in the universe (Philippians 2:15).

Reflections in a dirty mirror aren't very flattering, are they? Neither is it flattering when Christ is reflected in the mirror of an unclean life.

Paul describes Christlikeness as reflecting in a mirror the glory of the Lord (2 Corinthians 3:18)—Christ shining through you to a world in darkness.

Here's how Albert Barnes describes the radiant Christian life.

Walk With Albert Barnes

"Christians should let their light shine. God has called them into his kingdom so that they may illustrate in their lives the nature of the gospel and show its value in purifying the soul and in sustaining it in the time of trial.

"The world is dependent upon Christians for a correct view of religion, and every day that a Christian lives he either honors or dishonors the gospel.

"Every word that is spoken, every expression of the eye, every cloud or beam of sunshine on his brow, will have some effect in doing this.

"A believer cannot live without making some impression upon the world around him, either favorable or unfavorable to the cause of his Redeemer."

Walk Closer to God

Take a bright, clear light, reflect it off a surface, and what do you see?

If the surface is dirty, the reflection will be dull. If the surface is uneven, the reflection will be fuzzy.

And therein lies a parable of the Christian life. You are called to be a light for the world, providing an accurate reflection of the light that is within you.

Light that is clean (1 John 1:9) . . . consistent (Ephesians 5:8) . . . inviting (Luke 8:16).

If you cannot live a day without making an impression on those around you, then what needs to change for your life to become a clear reflection of the Savior you serve?

AUGUST 23

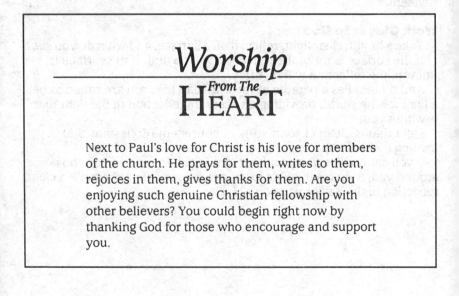

Walk in the Word
Philippians 2:19–30

Paul gives thanks for two of his fellow workers — Timothy, whom he hopes to send to Philippi, and Epaphroditus, whom the Philippians had sent to minister to Paul in prison.

Timothy and Epaphroditus

[19]I hope in the Lord Jesus to send Timothy to you soon, that I also may be cheered when I receive news about you. [20]I have no one else like him, who takes a genuine interest in your welfare. [21]For everyone looks out for his own interests, not those of Jesus Christ. [22]But you know that Timothy has proved himself, because as a son with his father he has served with me in the work of the gospel. [23]I hope, therefore, to send him as soon as I see how things go with me. [24]And I am confident in the Lord that I myself will come soon.

[25]But I think it is necessary to send back to you Epaphroditus, my brother, fellow worker and fellow soldier, who is also your messenger, whom you sent to take care of my needs. [26]For he longs for all of you and is distressed because you heard he was ill. [27]Indeed he was ill, and almost died. But God had mercy on him, and not on him only but also on me, to spare me sorrow upon sorrow. [28]Therefore I am all the more eager to send him, so that when you see him again you may be glad and I may have less anxiety. [29]Welcome him in the Lord with great joy, and honor men like him, [30]because he almost died for the work of Christ, risking his life to make up for the help you could not give me.

Worship
From The
HEART

Next to Paul's love for Christ is his love for members of the church. He prays for them, writes to them, rejoices in them, gives thanks for them. Are you enjoying such genuine Christian fellowship with other believers? You could begin right now by thanking God for those who encourage and support you.

God's Will: Your Willingness

For everyone looks out for his own interests, not those of Jesus Christ (Philippians 2:21).

WANTED: Understudy for well-traveled, soon-to-retire missionary. Must be able to suffer hardship; to teach and be taught; to evangelize, organize and perform a variety of vital church functions. Low pay, long hours, intense opposition. Interested applicants contact Paul the apostle.

That ad is fictitious, but the position was real. It was filled by a young man named Timothy.

Timothy was like a spiritual son to Paul, so when Paul needed someone to check on the Philippians' spiritual growth, he knew he could count on Timothy. Albert Barnes discusses Timothy's commitment to Paul and to the ministry of Christ at Philippi.

Walk With Albert Barnes

"How many professing Christians in our cities and towns are there now who would be willing to leave their comfortable homes and go on embassy duty to Philippi as Timothy did?

"How many are there who would not seek some excuse, and thus show that they 'looked out for their own interests' rather than the things which pertained to the kingdom of Jesus Christ?

"Paul implies here that it is the duty of those who profess faith to seek the things which pertain to the kingdom of the Redeemer, to make that the great and leading object of their lives.

"There are few Christians who deny themselves much to promote the kingdom of the Redeemer. People live for their own ease, for their families, for their businesses—as if a Christian could have anything which he has a right to pursue, and without regard to God's will and glory."

Walk Closer to God

The foremost qualification for the job of disciple in Timothy's day—and yours—is willingness. Willingness to learn, to obey, to serve. Timothy demonstrated this willingness to do God's will at the sacrifice of his own will. You can do the same today.

So what will you do? ⟡

AUGUST 24

Walk in the Word
Philippians 3:1–11

Paul warns the Philippians to watch out for those who claim to be Christians but who believe that we can earn our way into God's favor.

No Confidence in the Flesh

3 Finally, my brothers, rejoice in the Lord! It is no trouble for me to write the same things to you again, and it is a safeguard for you.

²Watch out for those dogs, those men who do evil, those mutilators of the flesh. ³For it is we who are the circumcision, we who worship by the Spirit of God, who glory in Christ Jesus, and who put no confidence in the flesh— ⁴though I myself have reasons for such confidence.

If anyone else thinks he has reasons to put confidence in the flesh, I have more: ⁵circumcised on the eighth day, of the people of Israel, of the tribe of Benjamin, a Hebrew of Hebrews; in regard to the law, a Pharisee; ⁶as for zeal, persecuting the church; as for legalistic righteousness, faultless.

⁷But whatever was to my profit I now consider loss for the sake of Christ. ⁸What is more, I consider everything a loss compared to the surpassing greatness of knowing Christ Jesus my Lord, for whose sake I have lost all things. I consider them rubbish, that I may gain Christ ⁹and be found in him, not having a righteousness of my own that comes from the law, but that which is through faith in Christ—the righteousness that comes from God and is by faith. ¹⁰I want to know Christ and the power of his resurrection and the fellowship of sharing in his sufferings, becoming like him in his death, ¹¹and so, somehow, to attain to the resurrection from the dead.

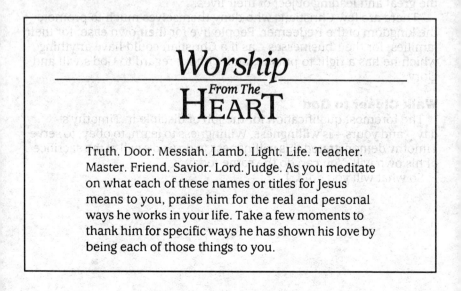

Worship
From The
HEART

Truth. Door. Messiah. Lamb. Light. Life. Teacher. Master. Friend. Savior. Lord. Judge. As you meditate on what each of these names or titles for Jesus means to you, praise him for the real and personal ways he works in your life. Take a few moments to thank him for specific ways he has shown his love by being each of those things to you.

The Choice That Shapes Your Destiny

What is more, I consider everything a loss compared to the surpassing greatness of knowing Christ Jesus my Lord, for whose sake I have lost all things (Philippians 3:8).

When Jesus Christ confronts an individual, choices are inevitable. The rich young man (Mark 10:17–23) chose to keep his possessions rather than follow Jesus. Centuries later, another rich young man made a far different choice. Francis of Assisi set aside the inheritance that awaited him to spend his life serving Christ.

The rich young man of Jesus' day was never heard from again. Francis of Assisi is still remembered for his devotion to Christ. The choice of each man helped shape his destiny. Let this old Irish hymn guide you into the choice of a lifetime.

Walk With an Irish Hymnwriter

Be Thou my Vision,/ O Lord of my heart;
Nought be all else to me,/ Save that Thou art—
Thou my best thought,/ By day or by night,
Waking or sleeping,/ Thy presence my light.

Be Thou my Wisdom,/ And Thou my true Word;
I ever with Thee/ And Thou with me, Lord;
Thou my great Father,/ I Thy true son;
Thou in me dwelling,/ And I with Thee one.

Riches I heed not,/ Nor man's empty praise,
Thou mine inheritance,/ Now and always:
Thou and Thou only,/ First in my heart,
High King of heaven,/ My treasure Thou art.

High King of heaven,/ My victory won,
May I reach heaven's joys,/ O bright heaven's Sun!
Heart of my own heart,/ Whatever befall,
Still be my Vision,/ O Ruler of all.

Walk Closer to God

Two rich young rulers wrestled with life-changing decisions. One concluded, "I will follow my gold." The other, "I will follow my God."

One thought he had gained the world, yet lost his own soul. The other knew he had lost much from the world's perspective, yet gained far more.

What will be the end result of your decision? ◖

AUGUST 25

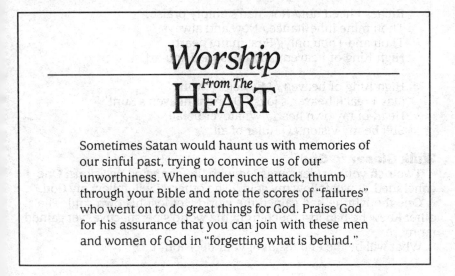 Walk in the Word
Philippians 3:12—4:1

Paul encourages the Christians in Philippi to press on to maturity in their faith as they wait for the final return of the Lord Jesus Christ.

Pressing on Toward the Goal

¹²Not that I have already obtained all this, or have already been made perfect, but I press on to take hold of that for which Christ Jesus took hold of me. ¹³Brothers, I do not consider myself yet to have taken hold of it. But one thing I do: Forgetting what is behind and straining toward what is ahead, ¹⁴I press on toward the goal to win the prize for which God has called me heavenward in Christ Jesus.

¹⁵All of us who are mature should take such a view of things. And if on some point you think differently, that too God will make clear to you. ¹⁶Only let us live up to what we have already attained.

¹⁷Join with others in following my example, brothers, and take note of those who live according to the pattern we gave you. ¹⁸For, as I have often told you before and now say again even with tears, many live as enemies of the cross of Christ. ¹⁹Their destiny is destruction, their god is their stomach, and their glory is in their shame. Their mind is on earthly things. ²⁰But our citizenship is in heaven. And we eagerly await a Savior from there, the Lord Jesus Christ, ²¹who, by the power that enables him to bring everything under his control, will transform our lowly bodies so that they will be like his glorious body.

4 Therefore, my brothers, you whom I love and long for, my joy and crown, that is how you should stand firm in the Lord, dear friends!

Worship From The HEART

Sometimes Satan would haunt us with memories of our sinful past, trying to convince us of our unworthiness. When under such attack, thumb through your Bible and note the scores of "failures" who went on to do great things for God. Praise God for his assurance that you can join with these men and women of God in "forgetting what is behind."

Putting the Past Behind

One thing I do: Forgetting what is behind and straining toward what is ahead (Philippians 3:13).

Paul's past as a persecutor of the faith could have paralyzed him as an apostle of the faith. But knowing the power of God's grace to forgive and forget, Paul was able to put away his sordid past and reach for "what is ahead."

F.B. Meyer shows how you can make the same freeing discovery.

Walk With F.B. Meyer

"We ought not to dwell upon our past sins as though they were ever present to the eye of God, so we will not be incapacitated for high and holy service.

"What would Peter have done on the day of Pentecost if he had persisted in pensively dwelling on the scenes of the denial, and had not dared to believe that all was forgiven and forgotten?

"What would have been the effect on the apostle Paul if he had allowed the memory of his share in the harrying of the saints to overcast his spirit when summoned to found churches, write epistles, and traverse continents?

"When once we confess it, sin is immediately put away. God will never mention it again. It need not be a barrier on our service; it should not hinder us from aspiring to and enjoying the most intimate fellowship which is within the reach of mortals."

Walk Closer to God

The choice is yours. Either brood over your past, or "press on toward the goal to win the prize for which God has called me heavenward in Christ Jesus" (Philippians 3:14).

Nothing compares with the excellency of knowing and serving Jesus Christ. So don't allow the haunting reminder of past sin to deflect you from pursuing your present goal. Concentrate instead on developing your relationship with him, and your mind and heart will be filled with dreams, goals, projects and prayers for the days ahead.

Press toward the goal of knowing Jesus and of making him known. It's the best way to move toward the mark in your Christian life.

AUGUST 26

Walk in the Word
Philippians 4:2–23

After giving some final exhortations on how to live for God, Paul thanks the Philippians for all that they have done for him, especially for the gift of money that they sent to him.

Exhortations

[2]I plead with Euodia and I plead with Syntyche to agree with each other in the Lord. [3]Yes, and I ask you, loyal yokefellow,[a] help these women who have contended at my side in the cause of the gospel, along with Clement and the rest of my fellow workers, whose names are in the book of life.

[4]Rejoice in the Lord always. I will say it again: Rejoice! [5]Let your gentleness be evident to all. The Lord is near. [6]Do not be anxious about anything, but in everything, by prayer and petition, with thanksgiving, present your requests to God. [7]And the peace of God, which transcends all understanding, will guard your hearts and your minds in Christ Jesus.

[8]Finally, brothers, whatever is true, whatever is noble, whatever is right, whatever is pure, whatever is lovely, whatever is admirable — if anything is excellent or praiseworthy — think about such things. [9]Whatever you have learned or received or heard from me, or seen in me — put it into practice. And the God of peace will be with you.

Thanks for Their Gifts

[10]I rejoice greatly in the Lord that at last you have renewed your concern for me. Indeed, you have been concerned, but you had no opportunity to show it. [11]I am not saying this because I am in need, for I have learned to be content whatever the circumstances. [12]I know what it is to be in need, and I know what it is to have plenty. I have learned the secret of being content in any and every situation, whether well fed or hungry, whether living in plenty or in want. [13]I can do everything through him who gives me strength.

[14]Yet it was good of you to share in my troubles. [15]Moreover, as you Philippians know, in the early days of your acquaintance with the gospel, when I set out from Macedonia, not one church shared with me in the matter of giving and receiving, except you only; [16]for even when I was in Thessalonica, you sent me aid again and again when I was in need. [17]Not that I am looking for a gift, but I am looking for what may be credited to your account. [18]I have received full payment and even more; I am amply supplied, now that I have received from Epaphroditus the gifts you sent. They are a fragrant offering, an acceptable sacrifice, pleasing to God. [19]And my God will meet all your needs according to his glorious riches in Christ Jesus.

[20]To our God and Father be glory for ever and ever. Amen.

Final Greetings

²¹Greet all the saints in Christ Jesus. The brothers who are with me send greetings. ²²All the saints send you greetings, especially those who belong to Caesar's household.

²³The grace of the Lord Jesus Christ be with your spirit. Amen.ᵇ

ᵃ3 Or loyal Syzygus   ᵇ23 Some manuscripts do not have Amen.

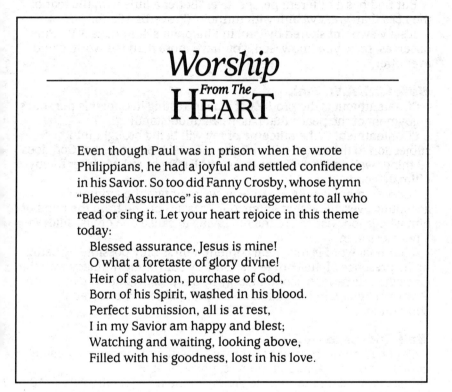

Worship
HEART *From The*

Even though Paul was in prison when he wrote Philippians, he had a joyful and settled confidence in his Savior. So too did Fanny Crosby, whose hymn "Blessed Assurance" is an encouragement to all who read or sing it. Let your heart rejoice in this theme today:

Blessed assurance, Jesus is mine!
O what a foretaste of glory divine!
Heir of salvation, purchase of God,
Born of his Spirit, washed in his blood.
Perfect submission, all is at rest,
I in my Savior am happy and blest;
Watching and waiting, looking above,
Filled with his goodness, lost in his love.

AUGUST 26

Learning the Secret of Contentment

I am not saying this because I am in need, for I have learned to be content whatever the circumstances (Philippians 4:11).

Contentment. It's rare in a world searching for more money, more power, more status.

But God has a different perspective: "Better a little with the fear of the LORD than great wealth with turmoil" (Proverbs 15:16).

It's a viewpoint shared by Paul in Philippians 4. And, as A.W. Pink observes, once you know God, you have more than the world could ever offer.

Walk With A.W. Pink

"Contentment is the product of a heart resting in God. It is the soul's enjoyment of the peace that passes all understanding.

"Contentment is the outcome of my will being brought into subjection to the divine will. It is the blessed assurance that God does all things well and is even now making all things work together for my ultimate good.

"Contentment is only possible as we maintain the attitude of accepting everything that enters our lives as coming from the hand of him who is too wise to err and too loving to cause one of his children a needless tear.

"Our final word is this: Real contentment is only possible by being in the presence of the Lord Jesus. Only by cultivating intimacy with the One who was never discontent, only by daily fellowship with him who always delighted in the Father's will, will we learn the secret of contentment."

Walk Closer to God

Paul had ample reason to complain about circumstances: hostile audiences, misunderstood motives, physical abuse.

Instead, he chose to "rejoice greatly in the Lord" (Philippians 4:10). His life radiated the very words he wrote to the Philippians: "Whatever is true . . . noble . . . right . . . pure . . . lovely . . . admirable . . . think about such things" (Philippians 4:8).

Like Paul, don't be content to settle for less than God's best. And that "best" includes contentment found only in him!

AUGUST 27

Walk in the Word
Colossians 1:1-14

Paul greets the Christian church in Colosse, thanks God for members, and assures them of his daily prayers for them.

1 Paul, an apostle of Christ Jesus by the will of God, and Timothy our brother,

²To the holy and faithful*ᵃ* brothers in Christ at Colosse:

Grace and peace to you from God our Father.*ᵇ*

Thanksgiving and Prayer

³We always thank God, the Father of our Lord Jesus Christ, when we pray for you, ⁴because we have heard of your faith in Christ Jesus and of the love you have for all the saints — ⁵the faith and love that spring from the hope that is stored up for you in heaven and that you have already heard about in the word of truth, the gospel ⁶that has come to you. All over the world this gospel is bearing fruit and growing, just as it has been doing among you since the day you heard it and understood God's grace in all its truth. ⁷You learned it from Epaphras, our dear fellow servant, who is a faithful minister of Christ on our*ᶜ* behalf, ⁸and who also told us of your love in the Spirit.

⁹For this reason, since the day we heard about you, we have not stopped praying for you and asking God to fill you with the knowledge of his will through all spiritual wisdom and understanding. ¹⁰And we pray this in order that you may live a life worthy of the Lord and may please him in every way: bearing fruit in every good work, growing in the knowledge of God, ¹¹being strengthened with all power according to his glorious might so that you may have great endurance and patience, and joyfully ¹²giving thanks to the Father, who has qualified you*ᵈ* to share in the inheritance of the saints in the kingdom of light. ¹³For he has rescued us from the dominion of darkness and brought us into the kingdom of the Son he loves, ¹⁴in whom we have redemption,*ᵉ* the forgiveness of sins.

ᵃ2 Or believing manuscripts *your* *ᵇ2 Some manuscripts Father and the Lord Jesus Christ* *ᶜ7 Some* *ᵈ12 Some manuscripts us* *ᵉ14 A few late manuscripts redemption through his blood*

AUGUST 27

The Words Your Father Loves to Hear

Giving thanks to the Father, who has qualified you to share in the inheritance of the saints in the kingdom of light (Colossians 1:12).

In the opening lines of his letter to the Colossians, Paul echoes the psalmist's thought that "it is fitting for the upright to praise him" (Psalm 33:1).

Listen as R.A. Torrey explains that prayer is more than bringing a "grocery list" of needs and wants to God. It is an opportunity to express gratitude for God's good gifts to us.

Walk With R.A. Torrey

"If any one of us would stop and think how many of the prayers we have offered to God have been answered, and how seldom we have thanked God for the answers thus given, I am sure we would be overwhelmed with conviction.

"We should be just as definite in returning thanks as we are in prayer. We come to God with specific petitions, but when we return thanks to him our thanksgiving is vague.

"Doubtless one reason why so many of our prayers lack power is because we have neglected to return thanks for blessings already received. If anyone were constantly to come to us asking help from us, and should never say 'thank you' for the help thus given, we would soon tire of helping one so ungrateful.

"Doubtless our heavenly Father, out of a wise regard for our highest welfare, oftentimes refuses to answer petitions that we send up to him in order that we may be brought to a sense of our ingratitude and be taught to be thankful."

Walk Closer to God

No doubt you are learning to be specific in your requests to God. But have you learned yet to be specific in your thanks as well?

After all, if you aren't thankful for what you have as a "share in the inheritance," you aren't likely to be thankful for what God holds in store for you!

"Father, thank you."

Those are words any father loves to hear—even your heavenly one.

AUGUST 28

Walk in the Word
Colossians 1:15—2:5

Paul wants the Colossian Christians to know how glorious Jesus Christ is and how much of a privilege it was for him to suffer on behalf of his Lord.

The Supremacy of Christ

¹⁵He is the image of the invisible God, the firstborn over all creation. ¹⁶For by him all things were created: things in heaven and on earth, visible and invisible, whether thrones or powers or rulers or authorities; all things were created by him and for him. ¹⁷He is before all things, and in him all things hold together. ¹⁸And he is the head of the body, the church; he is the beginning and the firstborn from among the dead, so that in everything he might have the supremacy. ¹⁹For God was pleased to have all his fullness dwell in him, ²⁰and through him to reconcile to himself all things, whether things on earth or things in heaven, by making peace through his blood, shed on the cross.

²¹Once you were alienated from God and were enemies in your minds because of*ᵃ* your evil behavior. ²²But now he has reconciled you by Christ's physical body through death to present you holy in his sight, without blemish and free from accusation— ²³if you continue in your faith, established and firm, not moved from the hope held out in the gospel. This is the gospel that you heard and that has been proclaimed to every creature under heaven, and of which I, Paul, have become a servant.

Paul's Labor for the Church

²⁴Now I rejoice in what was suffered for you, and I fill up in my flesh what is still lacking in regard to Christ's afflictions, for the sake of his body, which is the church. ²⁵I have become its servant by the commission God gave me to present to you the word of God in its fullness— ²⁶the mystery that has been kept hidden for ages and generations, but is now disclosed to the saints. ²⁷To them God has chosen to make known among the Gentiles the glorious riches of this mystery, which is Christ in you, the hope of glory.

²⁸We proclaim him, admonishing and teaching everyone with all wisdom, so that we may present everyone perfect in Christ. ²⁹To this end I labor, struggling with all his energy, which so powerfully works in me. 2 I want you to know how much I am struggling for you and for those at Laodicea, and for all who have not met me personally. ²My purpose is that they may be encouraged in heart and united in love, so that they may have the full riches of complete understanding, in order that they may know the mystery of God, namely, Christ, ³in whom are hidden all the treasures of wisdom and knowledge. ⁴I tell you this so that no one may deceive you by fine-sounding arguments. ⁵For though I am absent from you in body, I am present with you in spirit and delight to see how orderly you are and how firm your faith in Christ is.

ᵃ21 Or minds, as shown by

AUGUST 28

Joined to the Father Through the Son

For God was pleased to have all his fullness dwell in him (Colossians 1:19).

Mention the name Jesus Christ, and many images come to mind.

A babe in a manger . . . a rugged carpenter . . . an authoritative teacher . . . a crucified Savior.

But in speaking of Christ in Colossians 1, Paul mentions none of these.

Instead, he focuses on the Christ who has existed through eternity. The Creator. The image of God himself.

It's a big picture of Christ, a full picture. John Calvin speaks of the significance of this larger-than-life Christ for the Christian.

Walk With John Calvin

"Whatever God has, he has conferred upon his Son, that he may be glorified in him.

"He shows us that we must draw from the fullness of Christ everything good that we desire for our salvation, because God will not communicate himself or his gifts to people, except by his Son.

"So it follows that whatever detracts from Christ, or takes away a drop from his fullness, stands in opposition to God's eternal counsel.

"It is a magnificent commendation of Christ that we cannot be joined to God except through him.

"Our happiness consists in our cleaving to God.

"Christ is the bond of our connection with God, and apart from him we are most miserable because we are shut out from God.

"What God ascribes to Christ belongs solely to him, that no portion of this praise may be transferred to any other."

Walk Closer to God

What is the most important question confronting the human race today?

Is it the threat of nuclear war? The economy? Respect for human life? Poverty? Race relations?

Important issues, to be sure. But the most important question is: "What do you think about the Christ?"

It's a question thinking people cannot avoid. What do you think?

AUGUST 29

Walk in the Word
Colossians 2:6–23

Since Christ has set Christians free from sin and the law, Paul insists that they should free themselves from all man-made rules and regulations.

Freedom From Human Regulations Through Life With Christ

⁶So then, just as you received Christ Jesus as Lord, continue to live in him, ⁷rooted and built up in him, strengthened in the faith as you were taught, and overflowing with thankfulness.

⁸See to it that no one takes you captive through hollow and deceptive philosophy, which depends on human tradition and the basic principles of this world rather than on Christ.

⁹For in Christ all the fullness of the Deity lives in bodily form, ¹⁰and you have been given fullness in Christ, who is the head over every power and authority. ¹¹In him you were also circumcised, in the putting off of the sinful nature, *ᵃ* not with a circumcision done by the hands of men but with the circumcision done by Christ, ¹²having been buried with him in baptism and raised with him through your faith in the power of God, who raised him from the dead.

¹³When you were dead in your sins and in the uncircumcision of your sinful nature, *ᵇ* God made you *ᶜ* alive with Christ. He forgave us all our sins, ¹⁴having canceled the written code, with its regulations, that was against us and that stood opposed to us; he took it away, nailing it to the cross. ¹⁵And having disarmed the powers and authorities, he made a public spectacle of them, triumphing over them by the cross. *ᵈ*

¹⁶Therefore do not let anyone judge you by what you eat or drink, or with regard to a religious festival, a New Moon celebration or a Sabbath day. ¹⁷These are a shadow of the things that were to come; the reality, however, is found in Christ. ¹⁸Do not let anyone who delights in false humility and the worship of angels disqualify you for the prize. Such a person goes into great detail about what he has seen, and his unspiritual mind puffs him up with idle notions. ¹⁹He has lost connection with the Head, from whom the whole body, supported and held together by its ligaments and sinews, grows as God causes it to grow.

²⁰Since you died with Christ to the basic principles of this world, why, as though you still belonged to it, do you submit to its rules: ²¹"Do not handle! Do not taste! Do not touch!"? ²²These are all destined to perish with use, because they are based on human commands and teachings. ²³Such regulations indeed have an appearance of wisdom, with their self-imposed worship, their false humility and their harsh treatment of the body, but they lack any value in restraining sensual indulgence.

ᵃ11 Or *the flesh*   *ᵇ13* Or *your flesh*   *ᶜ13* Some manuscripts *us*   *ᵈ15* Or *them in him*

675

AUGUST 29

God's Perspective on Life's Priorities

Do not let anyone judge you . . . with regard to a religious festival, a New Moon celebration or a Sabbath day. These are a shadow of the things that were to come; the reality, however, is found in Christ (Colossians 2:16–17).

Is Christianity a segment of your schedule or the focus of your existence?

If God asks for the first day of your week, does that mean he doesn't care about the other six?

Abraham Kuyper points out God's perspective on right priorities.

Walk With Abraham Kuyper

"In his Word God absolutely forbids every inclination and every attempt to divide your life into two parts, one part for you and the other for him.

"There must be no division. Not six days for you and Sunday for God. Not a secular life sprinkled with godliness.

"No, on this point the claim of Scripture is as inclusive as possible; and though it may sound strange to your ears, the obligation is imposed upon you that whatsoever you do, you shall do it as unto the Lord.

"He who as child of God, as servant of Christ, lives his life in this world must in everything be led and carried by his faith. He who divides and makes distinctions robs God of a part that belongs to him alone.

"If you are to love your God with all your heart, all your soul, and your mind and powers, every avenue of escape is closed against you."

Walk Closer to God

You have only one life to live for God—and he is vitally interested in all of it.

Viewing one day as more holy—or one dollar as more heavenly—can only cause you to "rob God of a part that belongs to him alone."

By contrast, agreeing that you and all you have are wholly his is one of the best ways of saying with your life—as well as your lips—"All that God wants is all of me, and that's all he gets!"

AUGUST 30

Walk in the Word
Colossians 3:1—4:1

Paul gives the Colossians some general principles on how to live a Christian life and then focuses on how to build a Christian home.

Rules for Holy Living

3 Since, then, you have been raised with Christ, set your hearts on things above, where Christ is seated at the right hand of God. ²Set your minds on things above, not on earthly things. ³For you died, and your life is now hidden with Christ in God. ⁴When Christ, who is your*ᵃ* life, appears, then you also will appear with him in glory.

⁵Put to death, therefore, whatever belongs to your earthly nature: sexual immorality, impurity, lust, evil desires and greed, which is idolatry. ⁶Because of these, the wrath of God is coming.*ᵇ* ⁷You used to walk in these ways, in the life you once lived. ⁸But now you must rid yourselves of all such things as these: anger, rage, malice, slander, and filthy language from your lips. ⁹Do not lie to each other, since you have taken off your old self with its practices ¹⁰and have put on the new self, which is being renewed in knowledge in the image of its Creator. ¹¹Here there is no Greek or Jew, circumcised or uncircumcised, barbarian, Scythian, slave or free, but Christ is all, and is in all.

¹²Therefore, as God's chosen people, holy and dearly loved, clothe yourselves with compassion, kindness, humility, gentleness and patience. ¹³Bear with each other and forgive whatever grievances you may have against one another. Forgive as the Lord forgave you. ¹⁴And over all these virtues put on love, which binds them all together in perfect unity.

¹⁵Let the peace of Christ rule in your hearts, since as members of one body you were called to peace. And be thankful. ¹⁶Let the word of Christ dwell in you richly as you teach and admonish one another with all wisdom, and as you sing psalms, hymns and spiritual songs with gratitude in your hearts to God. ¹⁷And whatever you do, whether in word or deed, do it all in the name of the Lord Jesus, giving thanks to God the Father through him.

Rules for Christian Households

¹⁸Wives, submit to your husbands, as is fitting in the Lord.

¹⁹Husbands, love your wives and do not be harsh with them.

²⁰Children, obey your parents in everything, for this pleases the Lord.

²¹Fathers, do not embitter your children, or they will become discouraged.

²²Slaves, obey your earthly masters in everything; and do it, not only when their eye is on you and to win their favor, but with sincerity of heart and reverence for the Lord. ²³Whatever you do, work at it with all your heart, as working for the Lord, not for men, ²⁴since you know that you will

AUGUST 30

receive an inheritance from the Lord as a reward. It is the Lord Christ you are serving. 25Anyone who does wrong will be repaid for his wrong, and there is no favoritism.

4 Masters, provide your slaves with what is right and fair, because you know that you also have a Master in heaven.

a4 Some manuscripts *our*   b6 Some early manuscripts *coming on those who are disobedient*

PSALM 15

A psalm of David.

Lᴏʀᴅ, who may dwell in your sanctuary?
  Who may live on your holy hill?

2He whose walk is blameless
  and who does what is righteous,
who speaks the truth from his heart
3 and has no slander on his tongue,
who does his neighbor no wrong
  and casts no slur on his fellowman,
4who despises a vile man
  but honors those who fear the Lᴏʀᴅ,
who keeps his oath
  even when it hurts,
5who lends his money without usury
  and does not accept a bribe against the innocent.

He who does these things
  will never be shaken.

AUGUST 30

Coming to Love the Things That Endure

Since, then, you have been raised with Christ, set your hearts on things above, where Christ is seated at the right hand of God (Colossians 3:1).

In Colossians 3 Paul introduces the subject of practical Christian living by telling his readers to look to Christ.

Later in the same chapter, he sums up the Christian's earthly life this way: "Whatever you do, whether in word or deed, do it all in the name of the Lord Jesus" (Colossians 3:17).

Peter Marshall, former chaplain of the United States Senate, prayed this prayer for heavenly perspective in the midst of earthly pursuits.

Walk With Peter Marshall

"There awaits just behind the curtain a life that will never end, a life of beauty and peace and love, a life of reunion with loved ones, a life to be lived in the very presence of God.

"There will be no more pain, no more sorrow, nor tears, nor crying, nor parting, nor death after death. Age shall not weary them, nor the years erode. We shall enter into that for which we were created. It shall be the journey's end for the heart and all its hopes.

"And yet there are those among us whose actions—let us eat, drink, and be merry, for tomorrow we die—suggest that they believe in no better hereafter.

"There never was a time when the conviction of immortality was more needed than in this day when materialism has so exalted present life as to make it all-important."

Walk Closer to God

The Christian life, as Paul describes it, is an "off and on" experience.

We put off the deeds of anger, lying and idolatry—behavior unbecoming a child of God—and put on the qualities of kindness, patience and love.

Like a change of clothing, this involves exchanging the soiled conduct of the world for the holy garments of heavenly living.

Putting on Christ. It's a wardrobe that will never go out of style. ◖

AUGUST 31

📖 Walk in the Word
Colossians 4:2–18

After asking the church in Colosse to pray for him, Paul sends final greetings from himself and his fellow workers.

Further Instructions

2Devote yourselves to prayer, being watchful and thankful. 3And pray for us, too, that God may open a door for our message, so that we may proclaim the mystery of Christ, for which I am in chains. 4Pray that I may proclaim it clearly, as I should. 5Be wise in the way you act toward outsiders; make the most of every opportunity. 6Let your conversation be always full of grace, seasoned with salt, so that you may know how to answer everyone.

Final Greetings

7Tychicus will tell you all the news about me. He is a dear brother, a faithful minister and fellow servant in the Lord. 8I am sending him to you for the express purpose that you may know about our*a* circumstances and that he may encourage your hearts. 9He is coming with Onesimus, our faithful and dear brother, who is one of you. They will tell you everything that is happening here.

10My fellow prisoner Aristarchus sends you his greetings, as does Mark, the cousin of Barnabas. (You have received instructions about him; if he comes to you, welcome him.) 11Jesus, who is called Justus, also sends greetings. These are the only Jews among my fellow workers for the kingdom of God, and they have proved a comfort to me. 12Epaphras, who is one of you and a servant of Christ Jesus, sends greetings. He is always wrestling in prayer for you, that you may stand firm in all the will of God, mature and fully assured. 13I vouch for him that he is working hard for you and for those at Laodicea and Hierapolis. 14Our dear friend Luke, the doctor, and Demas send greetings. 15Give my greetings to the brothers at Laodicea, and to Nympha and the church in her house.

16After this letter has been read to you, see that it is also read in the church of the Laodiceans and that you in turn read the letter from Laodicea.

17Tell Archippus: "See to it that you complete the work you have received in the Lord."

18I, Paul, write this greeting in my own hand. Remember my chains. Grace be with you.

a8 Some manuscripts *that he may know about your*

Touch the World—Through Prayer

Epaphras, who is one of you and a servant of Christ Jesus, sends greetings. He is always wrestling in prayer for you (Colossians 4:12).

Contrary to what you may have heard, long distance is not the next best thing to being there. Prayer is!

Epaphras was far away from those to whom he had ministered. But his absence from them made his heart grow fonder in prayer for them.

His example of zealous prayer provides F.B. Meyer with these thoughts for present-day prayer warriors.

Walk With F.B. Meyer

"Epaphras had come from Colossae with tidings for the apostle Paul; but amid all the crowding interests of his visit to Rome, his heart was with his friends, and he sought to help them, as we may all help dear ones far away.

"He strove for them in prayer. It was not hastily mumbled prayer that he gave; no light breathing of desire; no formal mention of their names; but it seemed as though he were a wrestler whose muscles stood out like whipcord as he agonized and labored for the prize.

"We shall never know, till we stand in heaven, how much has been done by prayer. Probably the work of which we are prone to pride ourselves is due far less to us than we suppose, and far more to unrecognized fellow workers who labor in prayer for us."

Walk Closer to God

A close friend or relative comes to Christ. A tense conflict at work or home is resolved. A troubling deadline passes with no problem.

Later you tell a Christian friend what happened, and he replies, "I prayed for you that day."

Coincidence? Or your sovereign God at work through long-distance prayer?

It isn't always possible to be with the one you love. But you can always pray.

Take a moment to lift up a long-distance message on someone's behalf. You may be calling at just the right time! ◖◗

CHARLES SPURGEON

(1834–1892) AMBASSADOR OF GOD'S TRUTH

A Master of the Spoken Word

For nearly thirty-five years, Charles Spurgeon, an English-born preacher, attained unequaled popularity and prominence as an ambassador of God's truth. He became the dominant figure in nineteenth-century British Christianity until his death in 1892 at the age of fifty-eight, and his popularity has not noticeably diminished since his death.

Born in 1834, Charles always excelled in school, even becoming an assistant teacher as a teenager. During this time he committed his life to Christ and preached his first sermon at the age of sixteen. Instead of going on to college, Spurgeon became the pastor of a small church. Three years later, at age twenty, the New Park Street Church in London asked him to become its pastor. The young preacher accepted, and in a few short years saw his congregation grow from one thousand to several thousand members.

An unquestioned master of the spoken word, Spurgeon never missed an opportunity to declare God's truth fearlessly. Heard and read by millions on both sides of the Atlantic, Spurgeon stood tall as a preacher of God's Word. But his ministry was not limited to the pulpit. He also established an orphanage, trained young men for the ministry, wrote devotional and theological books and pamphlets, and edited his sermons for publication.

Charles Spurgeon willingly placed his gifts and abilities entirely at the disposal of his Lord. You too have talents that God has given you, such as the ability to speak, to write, to serve or to encourage. Perhaps you have a gift that is as yet undiscovered or undeveloped. Whatever it may be, the best place to use your gifts is in the service of the Lord. God is not as concerned about how many people you stand before as he is about what you stand for!

A LESSON FROM THE LIFE OF CHARLES SPURGEON

When I place my gifts and talents at the Lord's disposal, other lives will be blessed.

Your Manual for Growing Relationships

1 AND 2 THESSALONIANS 1 AND 2 TIMOTHY TITUS / PHILEMON

Letters are probably the most intimate form of written communication. They can present information, communicate emotion and provide inspiration. Paul's letters portray the depth of the relationships he enjoyed with his readers. Far from being mere "people in the pews," Paul addresses them as "brothers," "fellow workers," "son in the faith," "dear friend" and "those who love us in the faith"—all terms of endearment and affection.

Paul's two letters to the church in Thessalonica demonstrate a parent's love and concern; he compares himself both to a caring mother and an encouraging father (1 Thessalonians 2:7,11). The church was Paul's spiritual family, and like any family it required nurture, discipline, instruction and exhortation.

In his letters to Timothy and Titus, Paul shows the depth of his relationship with two of his co-workers. These young men were pastoral trainees of the apostle. The two letters to Timothy contain personal advice on the conduct of the minister and provide guidelines by which the young pastor could evaluate faithful men for church leadership. Titus emphasizes "our great God and Savior, Jesus Christ" (Titus 2:13), as the one who enables us to live a God-pleasing life, redeemed by God's grace and zealous to serve.

Philemon, Paul's postcard-size letter, deals with the specific case of a runaway slave named Onesimus. After escaping from his Christian master, Onesimus encountered Paul and found a new master—Jesus Christ. Paul, sensing the need to reconcile the slave with his human master, writes a brief letter to accompany Onesimus as he returns to Philemon.

One thing is certain as you begin your journey through these letters: You will encounter people. That's why Paul's letters remain so timely! Let him share with you each day this month how you can better relate to others. At the same time, you'll find your own relationship with the Lord deepening, for as you get to know other Christians, you get to know the Lord who lives in them.

SEPTEMBER 1

Walk in the Word
1 Thessalonians 1

Paul greets the Christians in Thessalonica and gives thanks to God for their steadfastness in the faith in spite of persecution.

1 Paul, Silas[a] and Timothy,

To the church of the Thessalonians in God the Father and the Lord Jesus Christ:

Grace and peace to you.[b]

Thanksgiving for the Thessalonians' Faith

[2]We always thank God for all of you, mentioning you in our prayers. [3]We continually remember before our God and Father your work produced by faith, your labor prompted by love, and your endurance inspired by hope in our Lord Jesus Christ.

[4]For we know, brothers loved by God, that he has chosen you, [5]because our gospel came to you not simply with words, but also with power, with the Holy Spirit and with deep conviction. You know how we lived among you for your sake. [6]You became imitators of us and of the Lord; in spite of severe suffering, you welcomed the message with the joy given by the Holy Spirit. [7]And so you became a model to all the believers in Macedonia and Achaia. [8]The Lord's message rang out from you not only in Macedonia and Achaia—your faith in God has become known everywhere. Therefore we do not need to say anything about it, [9]for they themselves report what kind of reception you gave us. They tell how you turned to God from idols to serve the living and true God, [10]and to wait for his Son from heaven, whom he raised from the dead—Jesus, who rescues us from the coming wrath.

[a]1 Greek *Silvanus*, a variant of *Silas*   [b]1 Some early manuscripts *you from God our Father and the Lord Jesus Christ*

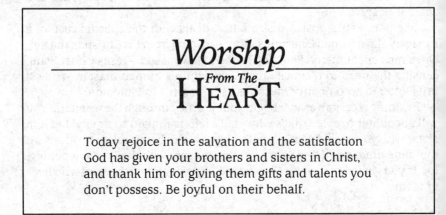

Worship
From The
HEART

Today rejoice in the salvation and the satisfaction
God has given your brothers and sisters in Christ,
and thank him for giving them gifts and talents you
don't possess. Be joyful on their behalf.

A Grateful Sense of God's Goodness to Others

We always thank God for all of you, mentioning you in our prayers. We continually remember before our God and Father your work produced by faith (1 Thessalonians 1:2–3).

Paul's customary greeting in his letters included gratitude for God's goodness. And the Thessalonians provided plenty of reasons for thanksgiving.

For instance, they "became a model to all the believers in Macedonia and Achaia" (1 Thessalonians 1:7). Their reputation sparked the spread of the gospel and Paul's gratitude to God. Matthew Henry has this to say about Paul's thankfulness.

Walk With Matthew Henry

"Since the apostle is about to mention the things that were a matter of joy to him and highly praiseworthy in them, he chooses to do this by way of thanksgiving to God who is the Author of all good that comes to us, or is done by us, at any time.

"God is the object of all worship by prayer and praise. And thanksgiving to God is a great duty, to be performed constantly. Even when we do not actually give thanks to God by our words, we should have a grateful sense of God's goodness on our minds.

"Thanksgiving should be repeated often; and not only should we be thankful for the favors we receive ourselves, but also for the benefits bestowed on others."

Walk Closer to God

"What God Has Done in My Life." Chances are good you could construct a long list in a short time on that subject. But could you make a list entitled, "What God Has Done in the Life of My Brother or Sister in Christ"?

You could—if you have been "mentioning [them] in [your] prayers," if their problems were your cause for intercession; their joys, your cause for celebration.

Where your time and energy are invested, "there your heart will be also" (Luke 12:34).

Getting involved in the lives of others. It's something they—and you—will both be thankful for! ◖

SEPTEMBER 2

Walk in the Word
1 Thessalonians 2:1–16

Paul reminds the Thessalonians how dedicated his ministry among them was, and he assures them of his continued love.

Paul's Ministry in Thessalonica

2 You know, brothers, that our visit to you was not a failure. [2]We had previously suffered and been insulted in Philippi, as you know, but with the help of our God we dared to tell you his gospel in spite of strong opposition. [3]For the appeal we make does not spring from error or impure motives, nor are we trying to trick you. [4]On the contrary, we speak as men approved by God to be entrusted with the gospel. We are not trying to please men but God, who tests our hearts. [5]You know we never used flattery, nor did we put on a mask to cover up greed — God is our witness. [6]We were not looking for praise from men, not from you or anyone else.

As apostles of Christ we could have been a burden to you, [7]but we were gentle among you, like a mother caring for her little children. [8]We loved you so much that we were delighted to share with you not only the gospel of God but our lives as well, because you had become so dear to us. [9]Surely you remember, brothers, our toil and hardship; we worked night and day in order not to be a burden to anyone while we preached the gospel of God to you.

[10]You are witnesses, and so is God, of how holy, righteous and blameless we were among you who believed. [11]For you know that we dealt with each of you as a father deals with his own children, [12]encouraging, comforting and urging you to live lives worthy of God, who calls you into his kingdom and glory.

[13]And we also thank God continually because, when you received the word of God, which you heard from us, you accepted it not as the word of men, but as it actually is, the word of God, which is at work in you who believe. [14]For you, brothers, became imitators of God's churches in Judea, which are in Christ Jesus: You suffered from your own countrymen the same things those churches suffered from the Jews, [15]who killed the Lord Jesus and the prophets and also drove us out. They displease God and are hostile to all men [16]in their effort to keep us from speaking to the Gentiles so that they may be saved. In this way they always heap up their sins to the limit. The wrath of God has come upon them at last.[a]

[a]16 Or *them fully*

The Benefits of Truth Clothed in Tenderness

We were gentle among you, like a mother caring for her little children . . . . We dealt with each of you as a father deals with his own children (1 Thessalonians 2:7,11).

Parenting a child. Nurturing a church. It's no accident Paul uses the first to illustrate the second. And in each case, the key is love.

Love begets love. It's a principle Paul embodies in his parent-like care for the Thessalonians. Albert Barnes gleans this lesson for today.

Walk With Albert Barnes

"Those who minister the gospel should be gentle, tender, and affectionate.

"Nothing is ever gained by a sour, harsh, crabby, dissatisfied manner. Sinners are never scolded into either duty or heaven. No man is a better or more faithful preacher because he is rough in manner, coarse or harsh in his expressions, or sour in his speech. Not thus was either the Master or Paul.

"There is no crime in being polite and courteous; and there is no piety in outraging all the laws which promote happy communication.

"What is wrong we should indeed oppose—but it should be in the kindest manner towards those who do wrong. What is true and right we should maintain and defend—and we shall always do it more effectively if we do it kindly."

Walk Closer to God

To summarize Mr. Barnes' last paragraph: Hate the sin, love the sinner. It sounds so simple—until you try it with a child . . . or a Christian . . . or a church exhibiting immature attitudes and actions.

C.S. Lewis struggled with the same principle. He wrote, "For a long time I used to think this a silly, straw-splitting distinction—how could you hate what a man did and not hate the man? But later it occurred to me that there was a man to whom I had been doing this all my life—namely myself."

Take that attitude, which you so naturally show to yourself, and try it on someone else. Then discover how truth clothed in tenderness can mark the lives of those you are called to "parent." ❏

September 3

📖 Walk in the Word
1 Thessalonians 2:17 — 3:13

Because Paul had been chased out of Thessalonica so suddenly, he sent Timothy back to them to find out how they were doing; he is pleased with the report that Timothy brought back.

Paul's Longing to See the Thessalonians

¹⁷But, brothers, when we were torn away from you for a short time (in person, not in thought), out of our intense longing we made every effort to see you. ¹⁸For we wanted to come to you—certainly I, Paul, did, again and again—but Satan stopped us. ¹⁹For what is our hope, our joy, or the crown in which we will glory in the presence of our Lord Jesus when he comes? Is it not you? ²⁰Indeed, you are our glory and joy.

3 So when we could stand it no longer, we thought it best to be left by ourselves in Athens. ²We sent Timothy, who is our brother and God's fellow worker*a* in spreading the gospel of Christ, to strengthen and encourage you in your faith, ³so that no one would be unsettled by these trials. You know quite well that we were destined for them. ⁴In fact, when we were with you, we kept telling you that we would be persecuted. And it turned out that way, as you well know. ⁵For this reason, when I could stand it no longer, I sent to find out about your faith. I was afraid that in some way the tempter might have tempted you and our efforts might have been useless.

Timothy's Encouraging Report

⁶But Timothy has just now come to us from you and has brought good news about your faith and love. He has told us that you always have pleasant memories of us and that you long to see us, just as we also long to see you. ⁷Therefore, brothers, in all our distress and persecution we were encouraged about you because of your faith. ⁸For now we really live, since you are standing firm in the Lord. ⁹How can we thank God enough for you in return for all the joy we have in the presence of our God because of you? ¹⁰Night and day we pray most earnestly that we may see you again and supply what is lacking in your faith.

¹¹Now may our God and Father himself and our Lord Jesus clear the way for us to come to you. ¹²May the Lord make your love increase and overflow for each other and for everyone else, just as ours does for you. ¹³May he strengthen your hearts so that you will be blameless and holy in the presence of our God and Father when our Lord Jesus comes with all his holy ones.

a2 Some manuscripts brother and fellow worker; other manuscripts brother and God's servant

The Spiritual Gold of a Godly Life

No one would be unsettled by these trials. You know quite well that we were destined for them (1 Thessalonians 3:3).

Mining for gold requires a willingness to work long hours in uncomfortable surroundings. But once a strike is made, the toil and tears seem a small price to pay.

The spiritual gold of a godly life is no different. Holiness and hardship are inseparable parts of the same endeavor. F.B. Meyer examines the purpose behind God-appointed trials in the Christian life.

Walk With F.B. Meyer

"We all love the sunshine, but the Arabs have a proverb that 'all sunshine makes the desert.'

"And we commonly observe how the graces of Christian living are more often apparent in the case of those individuals who have passed through great tribulation.

"God desires to get as rich a crop as possible from the soil of our natures. There are certain plants of the Christian life, such as meekness, gentleness, kindness, humility, which cannot come to perfection if the sun of prosperity always shines.

"As the weights of the clock or the ballast in the vessel are necessary for their right ordering, so is trouble in the soul-life. The sweetest scents are only obtained by tremendous pressure; the fairest flowers grow amid Alpine snow-solitudes; the rarest gems have suffered longest from the cutter's wheel; the noblest statues have borne the most blows of the chisel.

"All, however, is under God's supervision. Nothing happens that has not been appointed with consummate care and foresight."

Walk Closer to God

Just as the sculptor's chisel reveals the hidden beauty in a chunk of marble, so difficulties pare away the rough edges in your life. Even as the gardener's shears prune bushes for greater beauty and productivity, so the difficulties in your life prepare you for fruit-bearing in God's kingdom.

And when they do, you have the "consummate care and foresight" of God to thank.

September 4

Walk in the Word
1 Thessalonians 4:1–12

Paul gives some general principles on how the Thessalonian Christians should live in their society to the glory of God.

Living to Please God

4 Finally, brothers, we instructed you how to live in order to please God, as in fact you are living. Now we ask you and urge you in the Lord Jesus to do this more and more. ²For you know what instructions we gave you by the authority of the Lord Jesus.

³It is God's will that you should be sanctified: that you should avoid sexual immorality; ⁴that each of you should learn to control his own body*a* in a way that is holy and honorable, ⁵not in passionate lust like the heathen, who do not know God; ⁶and that in this matter no one should wrong his brother or take advantage of him. The Lord will punish men for all such sins, as we have already told you and warned you. ⁷For God did not call us to be impure, but to live a holy life. ⁸Therefore, he who rejects this instruction does not reject man but God, who gives you his Holy Spirit.

⁹Now about brotherly love we do not need to write to you, for you yourselves have been taught by God to love each other. ¹⁰And in fact, you do love all the brothers throughout Macedonia. Yet we urge you, brothers, to do so more and more.

¹¹Make it your ambition to lead a quiet life, to mind your own business and to work with your hands, just as we told you, ¹²so that your daily life may win the respect of outsiders and so that you will not be dependent on anybody.

a4 Or learn to live with his own wife; or learn to acquire a wife

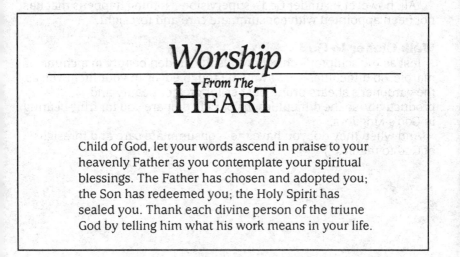

Worship
From The
Heart

Child of God, let your words ascend in praise to your
heavenly Father as you contemplate your spiritual
blessings. The Father has chosen and adopted you;
the Son has redeemed you; the Holy Spirit has
sealed you. Thank each divine person of the triune
God by telling him what his work means in your life.

The Deep Roots That Yield Delightful Fruit

It is God's will that you should be sanctified (1 Thessalonians 4:3).

One teenage boy straightens his room every day without being asked. Another straightens his only after endless appeals from his parents.

Either way the result is a clean room. But only one is the result of a right attitude.

Abraham Kuyper points out the proper balance between a heart that wills and hands that work in the Christian life.

Walk With Abraham Kuyper

"The difference between sanctification and good works should be well understood.

"Many confuse the two and believe that sanctification means to lead an honorable and virtuous life; and, since this is equal to good works, sanctification—without which no one shall see God—is made to consist in the diligent effort to do good works.

"Instead, sanctification is God's work in us in which he gives us a holy disposition, inwardly filling us with delight in his law and repugnance to sin. But good works are acts of mankind, which spring from this holy disposition. Hence sanctification is the source of good works.

"Sanctification is a work of God. It works internally, imparts something to the believer, and roots him like a tree. Good works are of men, are external, and are the fruit produced by a tree that is rooted. To confuse the two leads people astray."

Walk Closer to God

It's impossible for a tree to produce fruit without first being planted and nurtured. Only then can the nourishment rise to bring forth fruit.

Sanctification and good works have a cause-effect relationship. God, in sanctifying you, gives you the capacity to bear spiritual fruit that is pleasing to him. Fruit in abundance. Fruit in season and out. Fruit that is rooted in trusting him.

Read about it; thank God for it; then let your roots go down deep into the one who can make your life a source of fruit to his glory. ◻

SEPTEMBER 5

Walk in the Word
1 Thessalonians 4:13–18

Because some in Thessalonica had questions about the doctrine of Christ's coming again, Paul gives a brief timetable of what will happen when Christ returns.

The Coming of the Lord

¹³Brothers, we do not want you to be ignorant about those who fall asleep, or to grieve like the rest of men, who have no hope. ¹⁴We believe that Jesus died and rose again and so we believe that God will bring with Jesus those who have fallen asleep in him. ¹⁵According to the Lord's own word, we tell you that we who are still alive, who are left till the coming of the Lord, will certainly not precede those who have fallen asleep. ¹⁶For the Lord himself will come down from heaven, with a loud command, with the voice of the archangel and with the trumpet call of God, and the dead in Christ will rise first. ¹⁷After that, we who are still alive and are left will be caught up together with them in the clouds to meet the Lord in the air. And so we will be with the Lord forever. ¹⁸Therefore encourage each other with these words.

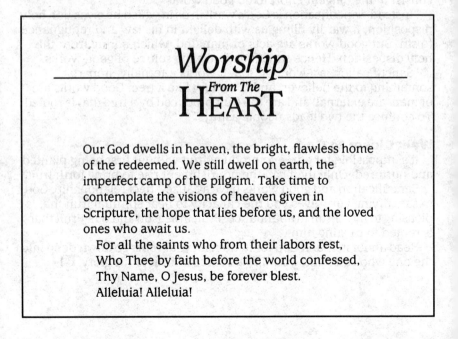

Worship
From The HEART

Our God dwells in heaven, the bright, flawless home of the redeemed. We still dwell on earth, the imperfect camp of the pilgrim. Take time to contemplate the visions of heaven given in Scripture, the hope that lies before us, and the loved ones who await us.

For all the saints who from their labors rest,
Who Thee by faith before the world confessed,
Thy Name, O Jesus, be forever blest.
Alleluia! Alleluia!

The Mortal Enemy All Must Face

Brothers, we do not want you to be ignorant about those who fall asleep, or to grieve like the rest of men, who have no hope (1 Thessalonians 4:13).

Death. It's a reality every mortal must face. Some view it with horror; others see it as a homecoming.

What is it that can transform a funeral into a praise gathering? Listen as Elizabeth Rowe presents the ringing note of hope that can—and should—accompany the passing of a child of God.

Walk With Elizabeth Rowe

"What unutterable ecstasies I shall feel when I meet those smiles which enlighten heaven and exhilarate all the celestial regions . . . when I shall view his glory without one interposing cloud . . . when I shall drink my fill at the fountain of joy that flows from his right hand forever.

"How dazzling is your prospect, O city of God, of whom such glorious things are spoken. There holy souls keep perpetual sabbaths; there newly-arrived saints are crowned with wreaths of light, while ivory harps and silver trumpets sound; there flaming seraphs sacred hymns begin, and cherubs loud responses sing."

Walk Closer to God

For the Christian, the loss of a loved one in the Lord is only for a time. Death is rest, not regret, for reunion is certain.

As Paul proclaims, " 'Where, O death, is your victory? Where, O death, is your sting? ' . . . But thanks be to God! He gives us the victory through our Lord Jesus Christ" (1 Corinthians 15:55,57).

Many refrains have been written capturing the essence of that victory. Here is one to reflect on:

Brief life is here our portion,
    Brief life, short-lived care.
The life that knows no ending,
    The tearless life, is there.
O happy retribution!
    Short toil, eternal rest;
For mortals and for sinners
    A mansion with the blest!

SEPTEMBER 6

Walk in the Word
1 Thessalonians 5:1–11

Paul emphasizes that Christians should live in continual expectation of Christ's second coming.

5 Now, brothers, about times and dates we do not need to write to you, ²for you know very well that the day of the Lord will come like a thief in the night. ³While people are saying, "Peace and safety," destruction will come on them suddenly, as labor pains on a pregnant woman, and they will not escape.

⁴But you, brothers, are not in darkness so that this day should surprise you like a thief. ⁵You are all sons of the light and sons of the day. We do not belong to the night or to the darkness. ⁶So then, let us not be like others, who are asleep, but let us be alert and self-controlled. ⁷For those who sleep, sleep at night, and those who get drunk, get drunk at night. ⁸But since we belong to the day, let us be self-controlled, putting on faith and love as a breastplate, and the hope of salvation as a helmet. ⁹For God did not appoint us to suffer wrath but to receive salvation through our Lord Jesus Christ. ¹⁰He died for us so that, whether we are awake or asleep, we may live together with him. ¹¹Therefore encourage one another and build each other up, just as in fact you are doing.

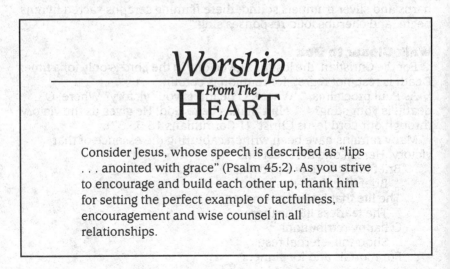

Worship
From The HEART

Consider Jesus, whose speech is described as "lips . . . anointed with grace" (Psalm 45:2). As you strive to encourage and build each other up, thank him for setting the perfect example of tactfulness, encouragement and wise counsel in all relationships.

When His Life Lights My Life

You are all sons of the light and sons of the day. We do not belong to the night or to the darkness (1 Thessalonians 5:5).

For the Christian, light and darkness represent the conflict between the ways of God and the ways of the world.

As John describes it in his Gospel: "In him [Christ] was life, and that life was the light of men. The light shines in the darkness, but the darkness has not understood it" (John 1:4–5). You will learn more about living in the light by reading Charles Hodge's helpful description.

Walk With Charles Hodge

"Christians should live as children of the light. Light stands for knowledge, holiness, and happiness. Darkness stands for ignorance, sin, and misery.

"The exhortation therefore is, in its negative form, not to sink back into the world, which belongs to the kingdom of darkness. That is, not to give yourself up to the opinions and practice of the world, and thus inevitably involve yourself in the ruin in which the kingdom of darkness must ultimately issue.

"It is an exhortation to act as becomes those who are members of the kingdom of Christ. An exhortation to exhibit the knowledge and holiness, especially in faith, hope, and charity, which characterize those who belong to that kingdom.

"The motive by which this exhortation is enforced is that we are destined not to wrath but to salvation (1 Thessalonians 5:9). And this salvation is secured by Christ who died, that whether we live or die, we should live together with him."

Walk Closer to God

As a Christian, you no longer live in the darkness. Christ has become your light. And because of that light, you can see where you are going. You can avoid life's pitfalls; you can follow the paths of holiness.

Jesus said it best: "I am the light of the world. Whoever follows me will never walk in darkness, but will have the light of life" (John 8:12). Invite him to do what light does best in your life . . . right now. ⟂

SEPTEMBER 7

📖 Walk in the Word
1 Thessalonians 5:12–28

Paul concludes this first letter to the Thessalonians by giving them some brief, practical instructions on the Christian life.

Final Instructions

¹²Now we ask you, brothers, to respect those who work hard among you, who are over you in the Lord and who admonish you. ¹³Hold them in the highest regard in love because of their work. Live in peace with each other. ¹⁴And we urge you, brothers, warn those who are idle, encourage the timid, help the weak, be patient with everyone. ¹⁵Make sure that nobody pays back wrong for wrong, but always try to be kind to each other and to everyone else.

¹⁶Be joyful always; ¹⁷pray continually; ¹⁸give thanks in all circumstances, for this is God's will for you in Christ Jesus.

¹⁹Do not put out the Spirit's fire; ²⁰do not treat prophecies with contempt. ²¹Test everything. Hold on to the good. ²²Avoid every kind of evil.

²³May God himself, the God of peace, sanctify you through and through. May your whole spirit, soul and body be kept blameless at the coming of our Lord Jesus Christ. ²⁴The one who calls you is faithful and he will do it.

²⁵Brothers, pray for us. ²⁶Greet all the brothers with a holy kiss. ²⁷I charge you before the Lord to have this letter read to all the brothers.
²⁸The grace of our Lord Jesus Christ be with you.

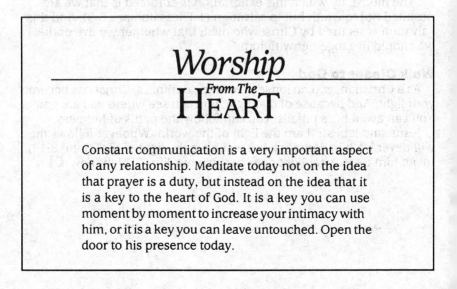

Worship
From The
HEART

Constant communication is a very important aspect of any relationship. Meditate today not on the idea that prayer is a duty, but instead on the idea that it is a key to the heart of God. It is a key you can use moment by moment to increase your intimacy with him, or it is a key you can leave untouched. Open the door to his presence today.

Developing a Heart of Ceaseless Prayer

Pray continually (1 Thessalonians 5:17).

Continual prayer in a nonstop world—that's your assignment. It's hard enough to "pray continually" while kneeling! But how do you "pray continually" while driving? Eating?

Paul was concerned with more than the posture of prayer. He knew as well that the attitude of prayer was all important. And there's plenty of challenge in developing a heart for continual prayer, as Alexander Maclaren explains.

Walk With Alexander Maclaren

"Can I pray continually? Not if prayer means only words of supplication and petition. But if prayer also means a mental attitude of devotion and a subconscious reference to God in all that we do, unceasing prayer is possible.

"Do not let us blunt the edge of this commandment by discussing whether the ideal of unbroken communion with God is possible in this life. At all events it is possible for us to approximate that ideal more closely than we have ever done.

"If we are trying to keep our hearts in contact with God in the midst of daily duty, and if during the press of our work we cast a thought towards him and a prayer, then joy and hope and patience will come to us in a degree that we do not know much about yet, but might have known all about long, long ago."

Walk Closer to God

The effectiveness of prayer does not rest on the volume of words spoken or the time spent.

Consider these examples of to-the-point prayers:

Peter: "Lord, save me!" (Matthew 14:30).

The publican: "God, have mercy on me, a sinner" (Luke 18:13).

Nehemiah: "Then I prayed to the God of heaven, and I answered the king . . . " (Nehemiah 2:4–5).

Short. To the point. Fervent. Offered with the attitude of going to God in every situation, of keeping the lines of communication open, of having fellowship with the one who is your very life. Such is the privilege to excite the heart of every believer! ◖◗

SEPTEMBER 8

Walk in the Word
2 Thessalonians 1

In view of Christ's return as judge, Paul prays that the Thessalonian Christians will be worthy of God's calling.

1 Paul, Silas[a] and Timothy,

To the church of the Thessalonians in God our Father and the Lord Jesus Christ:

²Grace and peace to you from God the Father and the Lord Jesus Christ.

Thanksgiving and Prayer

³We ought always to thank God for you, brothers, and rightly so, because your faith is growing more and more, and the love every one of you has for each other is increasing. ⁴Therefore, among God's churches we boast about your perseverance and faith in all the persecutions and trials you are enduring.

⁵All this is evidence that God's judgment is right, and as a result you will be counted worthy of the kingdom of God, for which you are suffering. ⁶God is just: He will pay back trouble to those who trouble you ⁷and give relief to you who are troubled, and to us as well. This will happen when the Lord Jesus is revealed from heaven in blazing fire with his powerful angels. ⁸He will punish those who do not know God and do not obey the gospel of our Lord Jesus. ⁹They will be punished with everlasting destruction and shut out from the presence of the Lord and from the majesty of his power ¹⁰on the day he comes to be glorified in his holy people and to be marveled at among all those who have believed. This includes you, because you believed our testimony to you.

¹¹With this in mind, we constantly pray for you, that our God may count you worthy of his calling, and that by his power he may fulfill every good purpose of yours and every act prompted by your faith. ¹²We pray this so that the name of our Lord Jesus may be glorified in you, and you in him, according to the grace of our God and the Lord Jesus Christ.[b]

---

a1 Greek *Silvanus*, a variant of *Silas*   *b12* Or *God and Lord, Jesus Christ*

The Fragrant Flower of a Renewed Heart

We ought always to thank God for you, brothers . . . because your faith is growing more and more (2 Thessalonians 1:3).

A farmer plows, enriches the soil with fertilizer, and then waters throughout the dry months. And come harvest-time, what does he have to show for his labors? Nothing unless he has also planted the seed, for no amount of cultivation can make up for a lack of life.

And until you have the life of Christ within, there can be no Christ-honoring fruit without—a principle Charles Spurgeon probes from the example of the Thessalonians.

Walk With Charles Spurgeon

"The holiness which will honor Christ at last is a holiness based on faith in him, a holiness of which this was the root—that the Thessalonians trusted in Christ, and then, being saved, they loved their Lord and obeyed him. Holiness is an inner as well as an outer purity, arising out of the living and operative principle of faith.

"If any think they can achieve holiness apart from faith in Christ, they are as much mistaken as one who would hope to reap a harvest without casting seed into the furrows. Faith is the bulb, and holiness is the fragrant flower that comes of it when planted in the soil of a renewed heart.

"Beware of any pretense to a holiness arising out of yourselves and maintained by the energy of your own unaided will. True holiness must spring from confidence in the Savior of sinners."

Walk Closer to God

Faith in Christ. Without it, holiness is all labor and no fruit. But once the seed of new life in Christ has been planted in your life, barrenness gives way to . . . growing faith (2 Thessalonians 1:3) . . . growing perseverance (2 Thessalonians 1:4) . . . growing glory to God (2 Thessalonians 1:10).

Are you trying to cultivate a godly walk without first having received the "word planted in you, which can save you" (James 1:21)?

Only the seed of life in Christ can lead to a harvest that will last for eternity. ⚬

SEPTEMBER 9

📖 Walk in the Word
2 Thessalonians 2:1–12

Some intruders into the church at Thessalonica were confusing them by saying that the day of the Lord had already come. Consequently Paul informs them of some events that had to happen before that day came.

The Man of Lawlessness

2 Concerning the coming of our Lord Jesus Christ and our being gathered to him, we ask you, brothers, ²not to become easily unsettled or alarmed by some prophecy, report or letter supposed to have come from us, saying that the day of the Lord has already come. ³Don't let anyone deceive you in any way, for ‚that day will not come‚ until the rebellion occurs and the man of lawlessness*a* is revealed, the man doomed to destruction. ⁴He will oppose and will exalt himself over everything that is called God or is worshiped, so that he sets himself up in God's temple, proclaiming himself to be God.

⁵Don't you remember that when I was with you I used to tell you these things? ⁶And now you know what is holding him back, so that he may be revealed at the proper time. ⁷For the secret power of lawlessness is already at work; but the one who now holds it back will continue to do so till he is taken out of the way. ⁸And then the lawless one will be revealed, whom the Lord Jesus will overthrow with the breath of his mouth and destroy by the splendor of his coming. ⁹The coming of the lawless one will be in accordance with the work of Satan displayed in all kinds of counterfeit miracles, signs and wonders, ¹⁰and in every sort of evil that deceives those who are perishing. They perish because they refused to love the truth and so be saved. ¹¹For this reason God sends them a powerful delusion so that they will believe the lie ¹²and so that all will be condemned who have not believed the truth but have delighted in wickedness.

a3 Some manuscripts *sin*

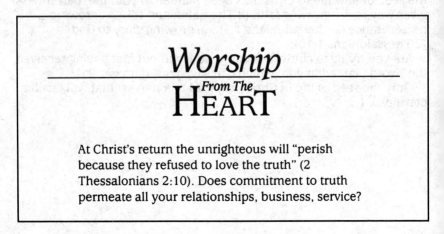

Worship
From The
HEART

At Christ's return the unrighteous will "perish because they refused to love the truth" (2 Thessalonians 2:10). Does commitment to truth permeate all your relationships, business, service?

SEPTEMBER 9

Living in the Light of Christ's Return

Concerning the coming of our Lord Jesus Christ . . . we ask you, brothers, not to become easily unsettled or alarmed (2 Thessalonians 2:1–2).

Setting dates for the events related to Christ's return is a popular pastime. Preoccupation with the when often obscures the what and why of that "blessed hope." It's more exciting to speculate on the unknown than to live in the purifying light of what is known about Christ's return.

The thought of that future prompted poet John Milton to compose this psalm of meditation.

Walk With John Milton

The Lord will come and not be slow,
   His footsteps cannot err;
Before him righteousness shall go,
   His royal harbinger.
Truth from the earth, like to a flower,
   Shall bud and blossom then;
And justice, from her heavenly bower,
   Look down on mortal man.
Rise, God, judge thou the earth in might,
   This wicked earth redress;
And Thou art he who shall by right
   The nations all possess.
For great thou art, and wonders great
   By thy strong hand are done;
Thou in thy everlasting seat
   Remainest God alone.

Walk Closer to God

You may not know when Christ is coming back, but Scripture sheds plenty of light on what will happen when he does. Milton's poem is a helpful summary: righteousness, truth, justice, judgment, retribution.

Christ will come to set things right. How should you live in light of that knowledge?

Be prepared (Matthew 24:44).
Be faithful (Luke 19:13).
Be blameless (1 Thessalonians 5:23).
Be obedient (1 Timothy 6:14).
Be expectant (Titus 2:13).
That's enough to keep you busy until he returns!

SEPTEMBER 10

Walk in the Word
2 Thessalonians 2:13 – 3:5

Paul encourages the Christians in Thessalonica to stand firm in the faith and then asks them to pray for him, since he was facing a time of danger.

Stand Firm

¹³But we ought always to thank God for you, brothers loved by the Lord, because from the beginning God chose you*a* to be saved through the sanctifying work of the Spirit and through belief in the truth. ¹⁴He called you to this through our gospel, that you might share in the glory of our Lord Jesus Christ. ¹⁵So then, brothers, stand firm and hold to the teachings*b* we passed on to you, whether by word of mouth or by letter.

¹⁶May our Lord Jesus Christ himself and God our Father, who loved us and by his grace gave us eternal encouragement and good hope, ¹⁷encourage your hearts and strengthen you in every good deed and word.

Request for Prayer

3 Finally, brothers, pray for us that the message of the Lord may spread rapidly and be honored, just as it was with you. ²And pray that we may be delivered from wicked and evil men, for not everyone has faith. ³But the Lord is faithful, and he will strengthen and protect you from the evil one. ⁴We have confidence in the Lord that you are doing and will continue to do the things we command. ⁵May the Lord direct your hearts into God's love and Christ's perseverance.

a13 Some manuscripts because God chose you as his firstfruits   *b15 Or traditions*

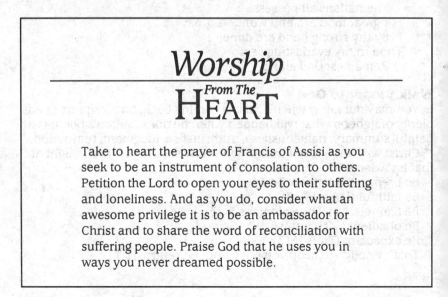

Worship
From The
HEART

Take to heart the prayer of Francis of Assisi as you seek to be an instrument of consolation to others. Petition the Lord to open your eyes to their suffering and loneliness. And as you do, consider what an awesome privilege it is to be an ambassador for Christ and to share the word of reconciliation with suffering people. Praise God that he uses you in ways you never dreamed possible.

SEPTEMBER 10

Becoming Instruments of God's Peace

May our Lord Jesus Christ himself and God our Father, . . . encourage your hearts and strengthen you in every good deed and word (2 Thessalonians 2:16–17).

Stories abound of men and women who, during their final hours on earth, became the givers rather than the recipients of consolation. Even the apostle Paul, imprisoned and on trial for his life, could offer words of encouragement in his letters to the churches. His secret? The "living love of God." Charles Spurgeon explains.

Walk With Charles Spurgeon

"Union with the risen Lord is a consolation of the most abiding order: it is, in fact, everlasting. Let sickness prostrate us; have we not seen hundreds of believers as happy in the weakness of disease as they would have been in the strength of hale and blooming health? Let death's arrows pierce us to the heart; our comfort dies not, for have not our ears often heard the songs of saints as they have rejoiced because the living love of God was shed abroad in their hearts in dying moments?

"Yes, a sense of acceptance in the Beloved is an everlasting consolation. Moreover, the Christian has a conviction of this security.

"Whatever may occur in providence, whatever onslaughts there may be of inward corruption or outward temptation, he is safely bound up with the person and work of Jesus. Is not this a source of consolation, overflowing and delightful?"

Walk Closer to God

Francis of Assisi, thirteenth-century saint, perhaps said it best:

"Lord, make me an instrument of thy peace. Where there is hatred, let me sow love; where there is injury, pardon; where there is doubt, faith; where there is despair, hope; where there is darkness, light; where there is sadness, joy."

"O divine Master, grant that I may not so much seek to be consoled as to console, to be understood as to understand, to be loved as to love; for it is in giving that we receive, it is in pardoning that we are pardoned, and it is in dying that we are born to eternal life."

703

SEPTEMBER 11

📖 Walk in the Word
2 Thessalonians 3:6–18

Paul instructs the Thessalonians to keep on serving God in their daily work until the time of Christ's return.

Warning Against Idleness

⁶In the name of the Lord Jesus Christ, we command you, brothers, to keep away from every brother who is idle and does not live according to the teaching*ᵃ* you received from us. ⁷For you yourselves know how you ought to follow our example. We were not idle when we were with you, ⁸nor did we eat anyone's food without paying for it. On the contrary, we worked night and day, laboring and toiling so that we would not be a burden to any of you. ⁹We did this, not because we do not have the right to such help, but in order to make ourselves a model for you to follow. ¹⁰For even when we were with you, we gave you this rule: "If a man will not work, he shall not eat."

¹¹We hear that some among you are idle. They are not busy; they are busybodies. ¹²Such people we command and urge in the Lord Jesus Christ to settle down and earn the bread they eat. ¹³And as for you, brothers, never tire of doing what is right.

¹⁴If anyone does not obey our instruction in this letter, take special note of him. Do not associate with him, in order that he may feel ashamed. ¹⁵Yet do not regard him as an enemy, but warn him as a brother.

Final Greetings

¹⁶Now may the Lord of peace himself give you peace at all times and in every way. The Lord be with all of you.

¹⁷I, Paul, write this greeting in my own hand, which is the distinguishing mark in all my letters. This is how I write.

¹⁸The grace of our Lord Jesus Christ be with you all.

ᵃ6 Or tradition

SEPTEMBER 11

God Feeds the Sparrows, but He Doesn't Throw the Worms

We hear that some among you are idle . . . . Such people we command . . . to settle down and earn the bread they eat (2 Thessalonians 3:11–12).

Eat, drink and be merry, "for tomorrow we die," was the misguided notion of God's people in Isaiah's day (Isaiah 22:13).

"Eat, drink and be merry, for tomorrow the Lord returns," was the equally misguided notion of God's people in Paul's day. But Paul had a word of advice for the Thessalonians: "If a man will not work, he shall not eat" (2 Thessalonians 3:10). Martin Luther underscores this point.

Walk With Martin Luther

"To put it briefly, God wants people to work. It is true that God could support you without work, could let food and drink grow on the table for you. But he will not do this. He wants you to work and to use your reason in this matter.

"In everything God acts in such a way that he will provide, but we should work. If God did not bless, not one hair, not a solitary wisp of straw, would grow.

"At the same time God wants me to take this stand: I would have nothing whatever if I did not plow and sow. God does not want to have success come without work, and yet I am not to achieve it by my work.

"He does not want me to sit at home, to loaf and wait till a fried chicken flies into my mouth. That would be tempting God."

Walk Closer to God

God has promised to meet your needs; but as Martin Luther points out, he never promised to deliver your meals!

His responsibility, rather, is to "meet all your needs according to his glorious riches in Christ Jesus" (Philippians 4:19).

Your responsibility is this: "So whether you eat or drink or whatever you do, do it all for the glory of God" (1 Corinthians 10:31).

And the best place for you to be when Christ returns: somewhere hard at work! ◯

SEPTEMBER 12

📖 Walk in the Word
1 Timothy 1:1–11

False teachers were beginning to infiltrate the church in the latter years of Paul's life as a missionary; consequently, he warns Timothy to be careful of them.

1 Paul, an apostle of Christ Jesus by the command of God our Savior and of Christ Jesus our hope,

²To Timothy my true son in the faith:

Grace, mercy and peace from God the Father and Christ Jesus our Lord.

Warning Against False Teachers of the Law

³As I urged you when I went into Macedonia, stay there in Ephesus so that you may command certain men not to teach false doctrines any longer ⁴nor to devote themselves to myths and endless genealogies. These promote controversies rather than God's work — which is by faith. ⁵The goal of this command is love, which comes from a pure heart and a good conscience and a sincere faith. ⁶Some have wandered away from these and turned to meaningless talk. ⁷They want to be teachers of the law, but they do not know what they are talking about or what they so confidently affirm.

⁸We know that the law is good if one uses it properly. ⁹We also know that law*ᵃ* is made not for the righteous but for lawbreakers and rebels, the ungodly and sinful, the unholy and irreligious; for those who kill their fathers or mothers, for murderers, ¹⁰for adulterers and perverts, for slave traders and liars and perjurers — and for whatever else is contrary to the sound doctrine ¹¹that conforms to the glorious gospel of the blessed God, which he entrusted to me.

ᵃ9 Or that the law

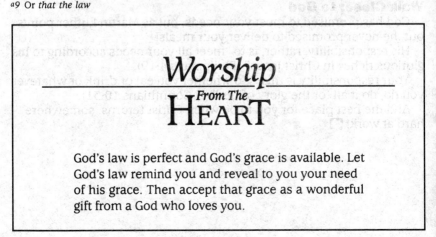

Worship
From The
HEART

God's law is perfect and God's grace is available. Let God's law remind you and reveal to you your need of his grace. Then accept that grace as a wonderful gift from a God who loves you.

The Grace of Law

We know that the law is good if one uses it properly (1 Timothy 1:8).

"Dear Paul, I have a question. In some places the Scripture says things like I have been released from the law, and that I am not under the law, but under grace.

"In other places it says that the perfect law gives freedom.

"Is this a contradiction?"

Have you ever wished you could write a similar letter to the apostle? How do we reconcile these apparently contradictory statements about God's law? R.L. Dabney explains that the word *law* has different meanings in Scripture.

Walk With R.L. Dabney

"First, the law is the authoritative declaration of God's character. It is the unchanging expression of how God distinguishes right from wrong.

"Second, the law was 'put in charge to lead us to Christ' (Galatians 3:24). By showing us our sinfulness it prepares us to submit to the Redeemer.

"Third, the believer has been chosen to be holy and blameless; he has been redeemed from all wickedness to be one of Christ's very own people, eager to do what is good. This great end, the believer's sanctification, can only be attained through a holy rule of conduct. Such a rule is the law. It is to be diligently observed as the guide to holiness.

"Fourth, its precepts restrain the aboundings of sin. They partially instruct the consciences even of the unrenewed. They guide secular laws, and thus lay a foundation for a wholesome civil society.

"And last, the publication of the law convicts God's enemies on earth in a way that foreshadows their conviction on judgment day.

"For these reasons, the preaching and expounding of the law is to be kept up diligently in every gospel church."

Walk Closer to God

John saw God's law as the standard that distinguishes love (1 John 5:3) from sin (1 John 3:4).

James expressed the same thought when he wrote of the law as a mirror that shows us where our spiritual complexion is blemished and where it is clear (James 1:22–25).

Paul shows us that God's law defines and restrains civil criminals (1 Timothy 1:8–11).

Have you been quick to use God's grace as an excuse for ignoring his commands? Meditate on Psalm 119 for a different perspective.

SEPTEMBER 13

Walk in the Word
1 Timothy 1:12–20

Paul reminds Timothy of the marvellous saving grace of God in Jesus Christ, the grace that he himself experienced when he had been persecuting the church.

The Lord's Grace to Paul

[12]I thank Christ Jesus our Lord, who has given me strength, that he considered me faithful, appointing me to his service. [13]Even though I was once a blasphemer and a persecutor and a violent man, I was shown mercy because I acted in ignorance and unbelief. [14]The grace of our Lord was poured out on me abundantly, along with the faith and love that are in Christ Jesus.

[15]Here is a trustworthy saying that deserves full acceptance: Christ Jesus came into the world to save sinners — of whom I am the worst. [16]But for that very reason I was shown mercy so that in me, the worst of sinners, Christ Jesus might display his unlimited patience as an example for those who would believe on him and receive eternal life. [17]Now to the King eternal, immortal, invisible, the only God, be honor and glory for ever and ever. Amen.

[18]Timothy, my son, I give you this instruction in keeping with the prophecies once made about you, so that by following them you may fight the good fight, [19]holding on to faith and a good conscience. Some have rejected these and so have shipwrecked their faith. [20]Among them are Hymenaeus and Alexander, whom I have handed over to Satan to be taught not to blaspheme.

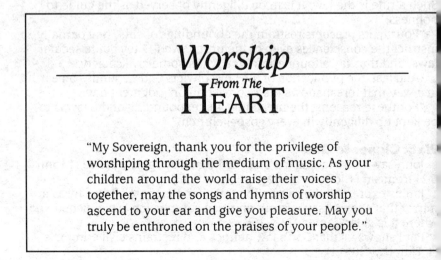

Worship
From The
HEART

"My Sovereign, thank you for the privilege of worshiping through the medium of music. As your children around the world raise their voices together, may the songs and hymns of worship ascend to your ear and give you pleasure. May you truly be enthroned on the praises of your people."

Immortal Invisible, God Only Wise

Now to the King eternal, immortal, invisible, the only God, be honor and glory for ever and ever (1 Timothy 1:17).

"Due to circumstances beyond our control . . . " are usually words that generate frustration. But the apostle Paul owed his very salvation to "circumstances beyond his control" (1 Timothy 1:12–16), and he wouldn't have had it any other way!

Intercepted by Christ on the road to Damascus, Paul's plans underwent a dramatic change. The "worst" of sinners found mercy in Christ.

And the result? Patrick Fairbairn, in commenting on Paul's expression of praise, probes the motive behind his spontaneous doxology (1 Timothy 1:17).

Walk With Patrick Fairbairn

"The train of reflection into which Paul had been led naturally brought the thought of God very prominently before him.

"Penetrated with a sense of the infinite greatness and overruling wisdom, power, and goodness of God, Paul winds up his personal discourse by a devout acknowledgment of God as the Lord of the universe, and glorifies him as such.

"When God is spoken of as King of the ages, he is presented to our view as supreme Lord and Director—the Sovereign Epochmaker, who arranges everything pertaining to the affairs of this world beforehand, according to the counsel of his own will, and controls whatever takes place, so as to subordinate it to his own design."

Walk Closer to God

Meditate for a few moments on Walter Chalmers Smith's hymn:
Immortal, invisible, God only wise,
  In light inaccessible, hid from our eyes,
Most blessed, most glorious, the Ancient of days,
  Almighty, victorious, Thy great name we praise.
To all, life Thou givest—to both great and small
  In all life Thou livest, the true life of all.
We blossom and flourish as leaves on the tree,
  And wither and perish—but naught changeth Thee.

SEPTEMBER 14

Walk in the Word
1 Timothy 2

Since Timothy was responsible for leading the church in Ephesus, Paul gives various instructions on how worship services should be conducted.

Instructions on Worship

2 I urge, then, first of all, that requests, prayers, intercession and thanksgiving be made for everyone— ²for kings and all those in authority, that we may live peaceful and quiet lives in all godliness and holiness. ³This is good, and pleases God our Savior, ⁴who wants all men to be saved and to come to a knowledge of the truth. ⁵For there is one God and one mediator between God and men, the man Christ Jesus, ⁶who gave himself as a ransom for all men—the testimony given in its proper time. ⁷And for this purpose I was appointed a herald and an apostle—I am telling the truth, I am not lying—and a teacher of the true faith to the Gentiles.

⁸I want men everywhere to lift up holy hands in prayer, without anger or disputing.

⁹I also want women to dress modestly, with decency and propriety, not with braided hair or gold or pearls or expensive clothes, ¹⁰but with good deeds, appropriate for women who profess to worship God.

¹¹A woman should learn in quietness and full submission. ¹²I do not permit a woman to teach or to have authority over a man; she must be silent. ¹³For Adam was formed first, then Eve. ¹⁴And Adam was not the one deceived; it was the woman who was deceived and became a sinner. ¹⁵But women*ᵃ* will be saved*ᵇ* through childbearing—if they continue in faith, love and holiness with propriety.

ᵃ15 Greek *she*   *ᵇ15* Or *restored*

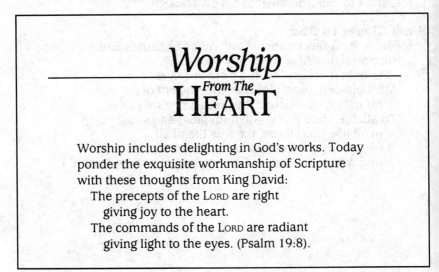

Worship
From The HEART

Worship includes delighting in God's works. Today ponder the exquisite workmanship of Scripture with these thoughts from King David:

The precepts of the LORD are right
giving joy to the heart.
The commands of the LORD are radiant
giving light to the eyes. (Psalm 19:8).

Guidebook for Godly Living

And for this purpose I was appointed a herald and an apostle . . . a teacher of the true faith to the Gentiles (1 Timothy 2:7).

You can find support for almost anything in the Bible: Stealing: "He who has been stealing must steal" (Ephesians 4:28).

Atheism: "There is no God" (Psalm 14:1; 53:1).

Of course, none of these verses means what it appears to say when taken out of its context.

That's why the task of a teacher and preacher is so important. They are charged with correctly handling "the word of truth" (2 Timothy 2:15).

Charles Simeon expresses his high regard for God's Word—and explains how it should be handled.

Walk With Charles Simeon

"I love the simplicity of the Scriptures; and I wish to receive and communicate every truth precisely in the way, and to the extent, that it is set forth in the inspired volume.

"My endeavor is to bring out of Scripture what is there, and not to thrust in what I think might be there. I have a great conviction on this point; never to speak more or less than what I believe to be the mind of the Spirit in the passage I am expounding.

"It is an invariable rule with me to give to every portion of the Word of God its full and proper force. Where the inspired writers speak in unqualified terms, I think myself at liberty to do the same, judging that they need no instruction from me as to how to propagate the truth."

Walk Closer to God

In order to be a teacher of the Scripture, you must first be a learner.

The assignment will not always be simple. Even Peter admitted some of Paul's letters were weighty and difficult (2 Peter 3:16).

Yet Peter never used that excuse to twist Paul's words into something more palatable—but false!

Whether you are called on to teach others or merely to teach yourself, the need is the same: to come to the Bible as God's trustworthy guidebook for your life.

It's always safe to say, "I will do nothing else."

SEPTEMBER 15

📖 Walk in the Word
1 Timothy 3

Paul describes the type of people who should be chosen as elders and deacons in the church.

Overseers and Deacons

3 Here is a trustworthy saying: If anyone sets his heart on being an overseer,[a] he desires a noble task. ²Now the overseer must be above reproach, the husband of but one wife, temperate, self-controlled, respectable, hospitable, able to teach, ³not given to drunkenness, not violent but gentle, not quarrelsome, not a lover of money. ⁴He must manage his own family well and see that his children obey him with proper respect. ⁵(If anyone does not know how to manage his own family, how can he take care of God's church?) ⁶He must not be a recent convert, or he may become conceited and fall under the same judgment as the devil. ⁷He must also have a good reputation with outsiders, so that he will not fall into disgrace and into the devil's trap.

⁸Deacons, likewise, are to be men worthy of respect, sincere, not indulging in much wine, and not pursuing dishonest gain. ⁹They must keep hold of the deep truths of the faith with a clear conscience. ¹⁰They must first be tested; and then if there is nothing against them, let them serve as deacons.

¹¹In the same way, their wives[b] are to be women worthy of respect, not malicious talkers but temperate and trustworthy in everything.

¹²A deacon must be the husband of but one wife and must manage his children and his household well. ¹³Those who have served well gain an excellent standing and great assurance in their faith in Christ Jesus.

¹⁴Although I hope to come to you soon, I am writing you these instructions so that, ¹⁵if I am delayed, you will know how people ought to conduct themselves in God's household, which is the church of the living God, the pillar and foundation of the truth. ¹⁶Beyond all question, the mystery of godliness is great:

> He[c] appeared in a body,[d]
> was vindicated by the Spirit,
> was seen by angels,
> was preached among the nations,
> was believed on in the world,
> was taken up in glory.

---

a1 Traditionally *bishop*; also in verse 2   *b11* Or *way, deaconesses*   *c16* Some manuscripts *God*   *d16* Or *in the flesh*

The Right Person in the Right Job

> Here is a trustworthy saying: If anyone sets his heart on being an overseer, he desires a noble task (1 Timothy 3:1).

Prospective employers often seem more concerned with outward achievement than with inward character. In the business world, quality of life often takes a back seat to accomplishments.

Not so in the family of God! There, what you are counts for more than what you have achieved. The work of the ministry demands more than good businessmen, good civic leaders, good politicians. It demands good people.

Patrick Fairbairn discusses the importance of good character in the selection of godly leaders in the church.

Walk With Patrick Fairbairn

"The apostle's list of qualifications is predominantly moral and consists of attributes of character rather than gifts and endowments of mind. The latter are included only as they might be required to form clear perceptions of truth and duty, to distinguish between things that differ, and in difficult or perplexing circumstances to discern the right and know how to maintain and vindicate it.

"Yet it is the characteristics which go to constitute the living, practical Christian, the man or woman of God, that are here brought into view.

"And whatever the church finds necessary to add to the number, in order to render her leaders fit for the varied work and service to which they are called, the grand moral characteristics specified here must still be regarded as the primary and more essential elements in the qualifications of a true spiritual overseer."

Walk Closer to God

"Father, as I seek to minister to others in your name, make me conscious that serving you is more than doing the right things; it is being the right person—your Christlike child.

"Build into my life those qualities that make serving you not simply a job but rather a lifestyle. In the name of him whose hands and heart were never in conflict. Amen." ❍

September 16

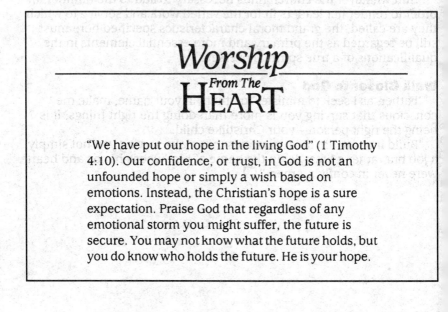

Walk in the Word
1 Timothy 4:1–10

Because some were beginning to fall away from the Christian faith, Paul encourages Timothy to stand firm in the truth.

Instructions to Timothy

4 The Spirit clearly says that in later times some will abandon the faith and follow deceiving spirits and things taught by demons. ²Such teachings come through hypocritical liars, whose consciences have been seared as with a hot iron. ³They forbid people to marry and order them to abstain from certain foods, which God created to be received with thanksgiving by those who believe and who know the truth. ⁴For everything God created is good, and nothing is to be rejected if it is received with thanksgiving, ⁵because it is consecrated by the word of God and prayer.

⁶If you point these things out to the brothers, you will be a good minister of Christ Jesus, brought up in the truths of the faith and of the good teaching that you have followed. ⁷Have nothing to do with godless myths and old wives' tales; rather, train yourself to be godly. ⁸For physical training is of some value, but godliness has value for all things, holding promise for both the present life and the life to come.

⁹This is a trustworthy saying that deserves full acceptance ¹⁰(and for this we labor and strive), that we have put our hope in the living God, who is the Savior of all men, and especially of those who believe.

Worship
From The HEART

"We have put our hope in the living God" (1 Timothy 4:10). Our confidence, or trust, in God is not an unfounded hope or simply a wish based on emotions. Instead, the Christian's hope is a sure expectation. Praise God that regardless of any emotional storm you might suffer, the future is secure. You may not know what the future holds, but you do know who holds the future. He is your hope.

The Most Profitable Thing in the World

Train yourself to be godly. For . . . godliness has value for all things, holding promise for both the present life and the life to come (1 Timothy 4:7–8).

Godliness is often associated with individuals past the age of sixty-five. But it may surprise you to learn that Paul talks more about godliness in his letters to two young disciples (Timothy and Titus) than in any of his other correspondence.

Johann Peter Lange comments on the practical importance of making godliness your goal.

Walk With Johann Peter Lange

"That godliness is profitable for all things, and thus the most profitable thing in the world, cannot be too strongly enforced against an abstract idealism on one side, and an irreligious materialism on the other.

"There are many who know that godliness is good for a peaceful death but do not hold it necessary for a happy life. Many others think faith very beautiful for the poor, the weak, the suffering, and the dying, but not for real, able, practical people.

"It must always be remembered that the gospel is a power which grasps the whole person. The true Christian is not only the happiest person, but the bravest citizen, the best patriot, the greatest leader. In a word, the Christian is, in all relations, a co-worker with God and an honor to Christ."

Walk Closer to God

"Godliness . . . is great gain" (1 Timothy 6:6). It is also a great challenge—a balance between two equally ungodly extremes.

On the one hand is "abstract idealism," as characterized by Simeon Stylites, a fifth-century ascetic who lived atop a pillar most of his life in an attempt to become "saintly." On the other is "irreligious materialism" leading to a preoccupation with wealth.

Genuine godliness makes "real, able, practical" Christians—men and women who respond to God and government, family and society, as he intended—regardless of their age. ❒

SEPTEMBER 17

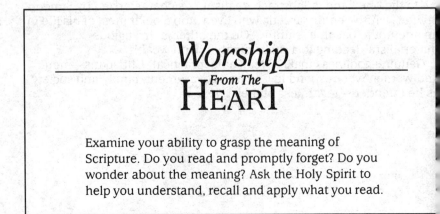 Walk in the Word
1 Timothy 4:11 — 5:8

Paul stresses how important it is that Timothy diligently fulfill the duties he has as a young pastor, giving him concrete advice on how to deal with the large number of widows in his church.

¹¹Command and teach these things. ¹²Don't let anyone look down on you because you are young, but set an example for the believers in speech, in life, in love, in faith and in purity. ¹³Until I come, devote yourself to the public reading of Scripture, to preaching and to teaching. ¹⁴Do not neglect your gift, which was given you through a prophetic message when the body of elders laid their hands on you.

¹⁵Be diligent in these matters; give yourself wholly to them, so that everyone may see your progress. ¹⁶Watch your life and doctrine closely. Persevere in them, because if you do, you will save both yourself and your hearers.

Advice About Widows, Elders and Slaves

5 Do not rebuke an older man harshly, but exhort him as if he were your father. Treat younger men as brothers, ²older women as mothers, and younger women as sisters, with absolute purity.

³Give proper recognition to those widows who are really in need. ⁴But if a widow has children or grandchildren, these should learn first of all to put their religion into practice by caring for their own family and so repaying their parents and grandparents, for this is pleasing to God. ⁵The widow who is really in need and left all alone puts her hope in God and continues night and day to pray and to ask God for help. ⁶But the widow who lives for pleasure is dead even while she lives. ⁷Give the people these instructions, too, so that no one may be open to blame. ⁸If anyone does not provide for his relatives, and especially for his immediate family, he has denied the faith and is worse than an unbeliever.

Worship
From The HEART

Examine your ability to grasp the meaning of Scripture. Do you read and promptly forget? Do you wonder about the meaning? Ask the Holy Spirit to help you understand, recall and apply what you read.

SEPTEMBER 17

Filling the Mind With Timeless Truth

Devote yourself to the public reading of Scripture, to preaching and to teaching. . . . Be diligent in these matters (1 Timothy 4:13,15).

"Garbage in, garbage out."

It's a principle of computer programming, which states that a computer can only respond to a question on the basis of information it has been supplied. If all you put in is "garbage," that's all you will get back in return.

What you feed your mind becomes the basis for the lifestyle you lead. Charles Hodge discusses the significance of good "input" in the Christian life.

Walk With Charles Hodge

"It is unreasonable to expect to be conformed to the image of God unless the truth concerning God operates continuously upon the mind.

"How can the love of Christ increase in those who hardly ever think of him or of his work? We cannot make progress in holiness unless we devote much time to reading, hearing, and meditating upon the Word of God, which is the truth whereby we are sanctified.

"The more this truth is brought before the mind—the more we commune with it, entering into its concerns, applying it to our own case, appropriating its principles, rejoicing in its promises—the more we may expect to be transformed by the renewing of our minds.

"Those distinguished for their godliness have been those accustomed to withdraw the mind from the influence of the world and to bring it under the influence of the Word of God."

Walk Closer to God

Here is a helpful "five-finger" method for getting a grasp on a passage of Scripture:

1. Read it.
2. Hear it.
3. Study it.
4. Memorize it.
5. Meditate on it.

The grasp will be weaker or stronger depending on the number of fingers you use and how often you exercise that grasp. ✿

SEPTEMBER 18

📖 Walk in the Word
1 Timothy 5:9 — 6:2

Paul concludes his counsel to Timothy on widows in the church and goes on to give advice on how to deal with problems concerning elders and slaves.

---

⁹No widow may be put on the list of widows unless she is over sixty, has been faithful to her husband,ᵃ ¹⁰and is well known for her good deeds, such as bringing up children, showing hospitality, washing the feet of the saints, helping those in trouble and devoting herself to all kinds of good deeds.

¹¹As for younger widows, do not put them on such a list. For when their sensual desires overcome their dedication to Christ, they want to marry. ¹²Thus they bring judgment on themselves, because they have broken their first pledge. ¹³Besides, they get into the habit of being idle and going about from house to house. And not only do they become idlers, but also gossips and busybodies, saying things they ought not to. ¹⁴So I counsel younger widows to marry, to have children, to manage their homes and to give the enemy no opportunity for slander. ¹⁵Some have in fact already turned away to follow Satan.

¹⁶If any woman who is a believer has widows in her family, she should help them and not let the church be burdened with them, so that the church can help those widows who are really in need.

¹⁷The elders who direct the affairs of the church well are worthy of double honor, especially those whose work is preaching and teaching. ¹⁸For the Scripture says, "Do not muzzle the ox while it is treading out the grain,"ᵇ and "The worker deserves his wages."ᶜ ¹⁹Do not entertain an accusation against an elder unless it is brought by two or three witnesses. ²⁰Those who sin are to be rebuked publicly, so that the others may take warning.

²¹I charge you, in the sight of God and Christ Jesus and the elect angels, to keep these instructions without partiality, and to do nothing out of favoritism.

²²Do not be hasty in the laying on of hands, and do not share in the sins of others. Keep yourself pure.

²³Stop drinking only water, and use a little wine because of your stomach and your frequent illnesses.

²⁴The sins of some men are obvious, reaching the place of judgment ahead of them; the sins of others trail behind them. ²⁵In the same way, good deeds are obvious, and even those that are not cannot be hidden.

6 All who are under the yoke of slavery should consider their masters worthy of full respect, so that God's name and our teaching may not be slandered. ²Those who have believing masters are not to show less respect for them because they are brothers. Instead, they are to serve them even better, because those who benefit from their service are believers, and dear to them. These are the things you are to teach and urge on them.

ᵃ9 Or *has had but one husband*   ᵇ18 Deut. 25:4   ᶜ18 Luke 10:7

Real Needs and Real Responsibilities

If any woman who is a believer has widows in her family, she should help them and not let the church be burdened with them, so that the church can help those widows who are really in need (1 Timothy 5:16).

From its earliest days, the church has sought to meet the needs of those who need help. The widows (Acts 6:1–3) . . . the hungry brothers in Judea (Acts 11:29) . . . any who had need (Acts 4:35).

But how do you discover who is truly needy? Alfred Plummer elaborates on Paul's guidelines to Timothy.

Walk With Alfred Plummer

"The church accepts the duty which it teaches of 'providing for its own.'

"But it ought not to be burdened with the support of any but those who are truly in need.

"The near relations of those in need must be taught to leave the church free to relieve those who have no near relations to support them.

"Paul has no intention of creating a welfare class. So long as they can, the needy must maintain themselves. When they have ceased to be able to do this, they must be supported by their family. If they have no one to support them, the church must undertake their support.

"Widows as a rule ought to be supported by their own relations. Only in exceptional cases where there are no relations who can help ought the church to have to undertake this duty."

Walk Closer to God

Paul's guidelines to Timothy are detailed and time-consuming—both to read and to implement.

It's much easier to tell someone in need, "I'll pray for you," than to say, "I'll prepare a meal for you." It's much cheaper to rely on welfare than to be responsible for the welfare of someone you love.

Once a need has been clearly established in the life of another, God's will is clear.

Commenting on a previous generation of Christians, one pagan emperor remarked, "They feed not only their poor but ours also."

Might that be said of your generation as well?

SEPTEMBER 19

Walk in the Word
1 Timothy 6:3–10

Since some false teachers were using Christianity as a means of bilking church members out of their money, Paul emphasizes that no one should live a life of scrambling after money and possessions.

Love of Money

³If anyone teaches false doctrines and does not agree to the sound instruction of our Lord Jesus Christ and to godly teaching, ⁴he is conceited and understands nothing. He has an unhealthy interest in controversies and quarrels about words that result in envy, strife, malicious talk, evil suspicions ⁵and constant friction between men of corrupt mind, who have been robbed of the truth and who think that godliness is a means to financial gain.

⁶But godliness with contentment is great gain. ⁷For we brought nothing into the world, and we can take nothing out of it. ⁸But if we have food and clothing, we will be content with that. ⁹People who want to get rich fall into temptation and a trap and into many foolish and harmful desires that plunge men into ruin and destruction. ¹⁰For the love of money is a root of all kinds of evil. Some people, eager for money, have wandered from the faith and pierced themselves with many griefs.

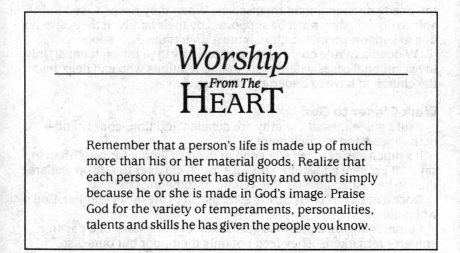

Worship From The HEART

Remember that a person's life is made up of much more than his or her material goods. Realize that each person you meet has dignity and worth simply because he or she is made in God's image. Praise God for the variety of temperaments, personalities, talents and skills he has given the people you know.

Hoarding, Holding, and Letting Go

For the love of money is a root of all kinds of evil (1 Timothy 6:10).

First Timothy 6:10 certainly would sound more appealing if it read, "The lack of money is the root of all evil." Or "Money is the root of all evil."

But notice the correct rendering of the verse. The problem does not rest in having money but in the attitude you have toward money.

The proper use of your assets begins with the proper attitude, as G. Campbell Morgan explains.

Walk With G. Campbell Morgan

"Love of money. Perhaps the word which best conveys the thought is the word avarice.

" 'Love of money' hoards and holds.

"It is indeed a root of all evil. It dries up the springs of compassion in the soul. It lowers the whole standard of morality. It is the inspiration of all the basest things, even covetousness; for if there may be covetousness without love of money, there is never love of money without covetousness.

"Avarice is often created by prosperity and the consequent possession of money. It is often powerfully present in the lives of those who are devoid of wealth.

"It is wholly material, the result of a wrong conception of life, due to forgetfulness of the fact that 'a man's life does not consist in the abundance of his possessions' (Luke 12:15)."

Walk Closer to God

There is good news for those with humble means. Regardless of your net worth, God wants you to be rich.

Ah, but rich in assets that time cannot tarnish and inflation cannot destroy. Rich in the assets of "righteousness, godliness, faith, love, endurance and gentleness" (1 Timothy 6:11).

You may possess vast earthly treasures yet live like a pauper by the one standard that counts for eternity—God's standard.

Loving God versus loving gold.

There's a wealth of difference between the two. And you can't afford to make the wrong choice. ◖◗

SEPTEMBER 20

📖 Walk in the Word
1 Timothy 6:11–21

Paul gives his final instructions to Timothy as pastor of the church in Ephesus: he must keep himself morally clean and take special care to admonish the rich in his congregation.

Paul's Charge to Timothy

[11]But you, man of God, flee from all this, and pursue righteousness, godliness, faith, love, endurance and gentleness. [12]Fight the good fight of the faith. Take hold of the eternal life to which you were called when you made your good confession in the presence of many witnesses. [13]In the sight of God, who gives life to everything, and of Christ Jesus, who while testifying before Pontius Pilate made the good confession, I charge you [14]to keep this command without spot or blame until the appearing of our Lord Jesus Christ, [15]which God will bring about in his own time — God, the blessed and only Ruler, the King of kings and Lord of lords, [16]who alone is immortal and who lives in unapproachable light, whom no one has seen or can see. To him be honor and might forever. Amen.

[17]Command those who are rich in this present world not to be arrogant nor to put their hope in wealth, which is so uncertain, but to put their hope in God, who richly provides us with everything for our enjoyment. [18]Command them to do good, to be rich in good deeds, and to be generous and willing to share. [19]In this way they will lay up treasure for themselves as a firm foundation for the coming age, so that they may take hold of the life that is truly life.

[20]Timothy, guard what has been entrusted to your care. Turn away from godless chatter and the opposing ideas of what is falsely called knowledge, [21]which some have professed and in so doing have wandered from the faith.

Grace be with you.

Battling in the Trenches of Everyday Experience

Fight the good fight of the faith. Take hold of the eternal life to which you were called when you made your good confession in the presence of many witnesses (1 Timothy 6:12).

The Christian life is not something lived out from the comfort of an overstuffed armchair. Rather, it is daily battles fought and won in the trenches of everyday experience as the Spirit triumphs over the flesh.

Charles Spurgeon draws a strategic lesson from the pages of military history and challenges today's Christians.

Walk With Charles Spurgeon

"When the Spartans marched into battle, they advanced with cheerful songs, willing to fight. But when the Persians entered the conflict, you could hear as the regiments came on the crack of whips by which the officers drove the cowards into the thick of the battle. You need not wonder that a few Spartans were more than a match for thousands of Persians, that in fact they were like lions in the midst of sheep.

"So let it be with the church; never should she need to be forced to reluctant action. Full of irrepressible life, she should long for conflict against everything which is contrary to God.

"Were we enthusiastic soldiers of the cross, we should be like lions in the midst of herds and enemies, and through God's help nothing would be able to stand against us."

Walk Closer to God

What more appropriate response to Paul's words could there be than the "call to arms" of the hymn "Onward, Christian Soldiers"?

Onward, Christian soldiers,
   Marching as to war,
With the cross of Jesus
   Going on before:
Christ the royal Master
   Leads against the foe;
Forward into battle,
   See his banners go. ⟡

SEPTEMBER 21

📖 Walk in the Word
2 Timothy 1:1–14

Because Christians were entering a time in which they might be persecuted for their faith, Paul encourages Timothy to remain faithful to the Lord and to his Word.

---

1 Paul, an apostle of Christ Jesus by the will of God, according to the promise of life that is in Christ Jesus,

²To Timothy, my dear son:

Grace, mercy and peace from God the Father and Christ Jesus our Lord.

Encouragement to Be Faithful

³I thank God, whom I serve, as my forefathers did, with a clear conscience, as night and day I constantly remember you in my prayers. ⁴Recalling your tears, I long to see you, so that I may be filled with joy. ⁵I have been reminded of your sincere faith, which first lived in your grandmother Lois and in your mother Eunice and, I am persuaded, now lives in you also. ⁶For this reason I remind you to fan into flame the gift of God, which is in you through the laying on of my hands. ⁷For God did not give us a spirit of timidity, but a spirit of power, of love and of self-discipline.

⁸So do not be ashamed to testify about our Lord, or ashamed of me his prisoner. But join with me in suffering for the gospel, by the power of God, ⁹who has saved us and called us to a holy life—not because of anything we have done but because of his own purpose and grace. This grace was given us in Christ Jesus before the beginning of time, ¹⁰but it has now been revealed through the appearing of our Savior, Christ Jesus, who has destroyed death and has brought life and immortality to light through the gospel. ¹¹And of this gospel I was appointed a herald and an apostle and a teacher. ¹²That is why I am suffering as I am. Yet I am not ashamed, because I know whom I have believed, and am convinced that he is able to guard what I have entrusted to him for that day.

¹³What you heard from me, keep as the pattern of sound teaching, with faith and love in Christ Jesus. ¹⁴Guard the good deposit that was entrusted to you—guard it with the help of the Holy Spirit who lives in us.

The Invisible, Invincible Inside Helper

Guard the good deposit that was entrusted to you—guard it with the help of the Holy Spirit who lives in us (2 Timothy 1:14).

Some decisions in life are clear choices between right and wrong. Others require discernment to know what is right and what is wrong.

When confronted with the second—and more difficult—kind of choice, how do you respond?

According to what you think . . . what you were taught . . . what the law says . . . what the public believes? Here's a fifth option you might not have considered: Ask an "insider" who knows.

That "insider," of course, is the Holy Spirit. A.B. Simpson provides this helpful description of the Spirit's ministry which helps believers discern right from wrong.

Walk With A.B. Simpson

"God gives to us a power within, which will hold our hearts in purity and victory.

"It—or rather he—is the Holy Spirit. When any thought or suggestion of evil arises in our mind, the conscience can instantly call upon the Holy Spirit to drive it out, and he will expel it at the command of faith or prayer, and keep us as pure as we are willing to be kept.

"God requires us to stand in holy vigilance, and he will do exceedingly abundantly for us as we hold fast to that which is good. He will also show us the evil and enable us to detect it, and to bring it to him for expulsion and destruction."

Walk Closer to God

Being alert to the attacks of Satan means being sensitive to the guidance of the Spirit, for his role is crucial if you are to "take your stand against the devil's schemes" (Ephesians 6:10–18).

Satan's power is strong; that's why you need the "sword of the Spirit" (Ephesians 6:17). Satan's attacks are persistent; that's why you need to "pray in the Spirit on all occasions with all kinds of prayers" (Ephesians 6:18).

The Holy Spirit is within you, providing wisdom and protection against invisible forces from without. Wouldn't you agree that's a truth worth thinking about? ◖◗

SEPTEMBER 22

Walk in the Word
2 Timothy 1:15—2:13

Paul assures Timothy that all of those who faithfully endure hardship in difficult times will be rewarded by the Lord.

¹⁵You know that everyone in the province of Asia has deserted me, including Phygelus and Hermogenes.

¹⁶May the Lord show mercy to the household of Onesiphorus, because he often refreshed me and was not ashamed of my chains. ¹⁷On the contrary, when he was in Rome, he searched hard for me until he found me. ¹⁸May the Lord grant that he will find mercy from the Lord on that day! You know very well in how many ways he helped me in Ephesus.

2 You then, my son, be strong in the grace that is in Christ Jesus. ²And the things you have heard me say in the presence of many witnesses entrust to reliable men who will also be qualified to teach others. ³Endure hardship with us like a good soldier of Christ Jesus. ⁴No one serving as a soldier gets involved in civilian affairs—he wants to please his commanding officer. ⁵Similarly, if anyone competes as an athlete, he does not receive the victor's crown unless he competes according to the rules. ⁶The hardworking farmer should be the first to receive a share of the crops. ⁷Reflect on what I am saying, for the Lord will give you insight into all this.

⁸Remember Jesus Christ, raised from the dead, descended from David. This is my gospel, ⁹for which I am suffering even to the point of being chained like a criminal. But God's word is not chained. ¹⁰Therefore I endure everything for the sake of the elect, that they too may obtain the salvation that is in Christ Jesus, with eternal glory.

¹¹Here is a trustworthy saying:

> If we died with him,
> we will also live with him;
> ¹²if we endure,
> we will also reign with him.
> If we disown him,
> he will also disown us;
> ¹³if we are faithless,
> he will remain faithful,
> for he cannot disown himself.

Greatness That Begins in the Heart

You then, my son, be strong in the grace that is in Christ Jesus (2 Timothy 2:1).

There is something remarkable—and unexpected—about many who receive that cherished accolade "tower of strength." They are neither towering physically nor strong emotionally.

David Brainerd was one such individual. Though physically weak and given to periods of depression, Brainerd was greatly used by God among the American Indians.

Read carefully as Jonathan Edwards, who cared for the dying young missionary, probes the inward strength behind this quiet giant.

Walk With Jonathan Edwards

"That Brainerd's temper or constitution inclined him to despondency is no reason to suppose that his extraordinary devotion was simply the fruit of his imagination.

"Certainly his natural disposition had some influence in his religious exercises, as it did in the lives of King David, and the apostles Peter, John, and Paul. There was undoubtedly some mixture of melancholy with true godly sorrow and real Christian humility: some mixture of the natural fire of youth with his holy zeal for God.

"In spite of these imperfections, every careful reader will readily acknowledge that what is here set before him is a remarkable instance of true piety in heart and practice, and that it is most worthy of imitation."

Walk Closer to God

Edwards's words are from the introduction to *The Life and Diary of David Brainerd*, a remarkable account of one man's walk with God.

No matter what your age or personality, you can walk with God as David Brainerd did. You may not look like a tower of spiritual strength, but you can be one—by cultivating your relationship with God.

Your appearance may be unassuming, your manner quiet and reserved, but remember—greatness in God's sight begins in your heart. ⬚

SEPTEMBER 23

📖 Walk in the Word
2 Timothy 2:14–26

Paul reminds Timothy that not only should he himself live a life pleasing to the Lord, but as a pastor he should also warn those under his care to live a holy life.

A Workman Approved by God

14Keep reminding them of these things. Warn them before God against quarreling about words; it is of no value, and only ruins those who listen. 15Do your best to present yourself to God as one approved, a workman who does not need to be ashamed and who correctly handles the word of truth. 16Avoid godless chatter, because those who indulge in it will become more and more ungodly. 17Their teaching will spread like gangrene. Among them are Hymenaeus and Philetus, 18who have wandered away from the truth. They say that the resurrection has already taken place, and they destroy the faith of some. 19Nevertheless, God's solid foundation stands firm, sealed with this inscription: "The Lord knows those who are his,"*a* and, "Everyone who confesses the name of the Lord must turn away from wickedness."

20In a large house there are articles not only of gold and silver, but also of wood and clay; some are for noble purposes and some for ignoble. 21If a man cleanses himself from the latter, he will be an instrument for noble purposes, made holy, useful to the Master and prepared to do any good work.

22Flee the evil desires of youth, and pursue righteousness, faith, love and peace, along with those who call on the Lord out of a pure heart. 23Don't have anything to do with foolish and stupid arguments, because you know they produce quarrels. 24And the Lord's servant must not quarrel; instead, he must be kind to everyone, able to teach, not resentful. 25Those who oppose him he must gently instruct, in the hope that God will grant them repentance leading them to a knowledge of the truth, 26and that they will come to their senses and escape from the trap of the devil, who has taken them captive to do his will.

a19 Num. 16:5 (see Septuagint)

Your Life: God's Project

If a man cleanses himself from the latter, he will be an instrument for noble purposes, made holy, useful to the Master and prepared to do any good work (2 Timothy 2:21).

"Stir up."
"Hold fast."
"Be strong."
"Endure hardness."
"Study . . . shun . . . flee . . . ."
At first glance the Christian life might appear to be a "do-it-yourself" project—until you try it and discover how inadequate your own strength is.

But God never asks of you what he has not first empowered you to do—a truth John Calvin understood.

Walk With John Calvin

"It is clear beyond contradiction that we are called to holiness. But the calling and duty of Christians is one thing, and it is another to have the power to make it happen.

"We do not deny that the faithful are required to purify themselves; but that this is a matter which belongs to the Lord he declares himself, when through the prophet Ezekiel he promises to send forth the Holy Spirit that we may be cleansed (Ezekiel 36:25–26).

"Therefore, we should beseech the Lord to purge us rather than vainly attempt such a matter in our own strength without his aid."

Walk Closer to God

It is one thing to read the Word of God; it is another to live it.

Enthusiasm is easier than obedience. But it takes more than zeal and grim determination to become an "instrument . . . useful to the Master."

For that you need strength which only the Master can supply. Strength to stay morally clean and spiritually sensitive.

The world would label such a lifestyle "narrow." God calls it "holy." And he is calling you to it—today! ❍

SEPTEMBER 24

📖 Walk in the Word
2 Timothy 3:1–9

Paul informs Timothy of the type of people who will characterize society in the last days. Timothy should have nothing to do with such people.

Godlessness in the Last Days

3 But mark this: There will be terrible times in the last days. ²People will be lovers of themselves, lovers of money, boastful, proud, abusive, disobedient to their parents, ungrateful, unholy, ³without love, unforgiving, slanderous, without self-control, brutal, not lovers of the good, ⁴treacherous, rash, conceited, lovers of pleasure rather than lovers of God— ⁵having a form of godliness but denying its power. Have nothing to do with them.

⁶They are the kind who worm their way into homes and gain control over weak-willed women, who are loaded down with sins and are swayed by all kinds of evil desires, ⁷always learning but never able to acknowledge the truth. ⁸Just as Jannes and Jambres opposed Moses, so also these men oppose the truth—men of depraved minds, who, as far as the faith is concerned, are rejected. ⁹But they will not get very far because, as in the case of those men, their folly will be clear to everyone.

Worship
From The
HEART

One of the reasons the children of Israel were scattered and taken captive in judgment was the covetousness that ran rampant through the tribes. Greed was so ingrained that the pleas of God's prophets fell on deaf ears. Ask the Lord to help you loosen your grip on material things. In the tradition of Joseph of Arimathea (Matthew 27:57–60) use your gain for Christ's glory.

Lover of God or Lover of Gold?

There will be terrible times in the last days. People will be . . . lovers of money (2 Timothy 3:1–2).

Loving God. Loving gold. Only one letter separates the two, but the outlooks are worlds apart. And the love of one will overpower the love of the other. As Jesus said, "No servant can serve two masters . . . . You cannot serve both God and Money" (Luke 16:13).

Paul accurately describes the perilous times when men shall be "lovers of themselves," "lovers of pleasure,"—the result of embracing the world's system of values.

John Wesley has been described as a man who died leaving behind nothing but his Bible, his horse and the Methodist church. Listen as he echoes Paul's admonition about the deceitfulness of riches.

Walk With John Wesley

"Let us but open our eyes, and we may daily see the melancholy proofs of this—those who, resolving to be rich, coveting after money, the root of all evil, have already pierced themselves through with many sorrows. The cautiousness with which the apostle here speaks is highly observable. For one may possibly be rich, without any fault of his, by an overruling Providence, preventing his own choice.

"Riches, dangerous as they are, do not always 'drown men in destruction and perdition,' but the desire for riches does. Those who calmly desire and deliberately seek to attain them, whether they do in fact gain the world or not, do invariably lose their own souls.

"These are they that sell him, who bought them with his blood, for a few pieces of gold or silver."

Walk Closer to God

Worldly voices and values clamor for your attention every day. And given the chance, they will dictate your priorities. Paul's advice has never been more timely: Focus on "the Holy Scriptures, which are able to make you wise for salvation" (2 Timothy 3:15). God's Word—a "gold mine" for the one who loves God.

SEPTEMBER 25

Walk in the Word
2 Timothy 3:10 — 4:8

Although Paul knows he is soon to become a martyr for being a Christian, he exhorts Timothy to remain faithful to the Scriptures and to keep preaching the Word of God.

Paul's Charge to Timothy

[10]You, however, know all about my teaching, my way of life, my purpose, faith, patience, love, endurance, [11]persecutions, sufferings — what kinds of things happened to me in Antioch, Iconium and Lystra, the persecutions I endured. Yet the Lord rescued me from all of them. [12]In fact, everyone who wants to live a godly life in Christ Jesus will be persecuted, [13]while evil men and impostors will go from bad to worse, deceiving and being deceived. [14]But as for you, continue in what you have learned and have become convinced of, because you know those from whom you learned it, [15]and how from infancy you have known the holy Scriptures, which are able to make you wise for salvation through faith in Christ Jesus. [16]All Scripture is God-breathed and is useful for teaching, rebuking, correcting and training in righteousness, [17]so that the man of God may be thoroughly equipped for every good work.

4 In the presence of God and of Christ Jesus, who will judge the living and the dead, and in view of his appearing and his kingdom, I give you this charge: [2]Preach the Word; be prepared in season and out of season; correct, rebuke and encourage — with great patience and careful instruction. [3]For the time will come when men will not put up with sound doctrine. Instead, to suit their own desires, they will gather around them a great number of teachers to say what their itching ears want to hear. [4]They will turn their ears away from the truth and turn aside to myths. [5]But you, keep your head in all situations, endure hardship, do the work of an evangelist, discharge all the duties of your ministry.

[6]For I am already being poured out like a drink offering, and the time has come for my departure. [7]I have fought the good fight, I have finished the race, I have kept the faith. [8]Now there is in store for me the crown of righteousness, which the Lord, the righteous Judge, will award to me on that day — and not only to me, but also to all who have longed for his appearing.

The Revelation That's Forever Relevant

All Scripture is God-breathed and is useful for teaching, rebuking, correcting and training in righteousness (2 Timothy 3:16).

God's Word, the Bible, has been translated into more languages, printed in more sizes, and published in more editions than any other volume in history. Yet its content has never changed or become irrelevant. Its truth is as needed today as when it was first given centuries ago.

W. Graham Scroggie offers this insight into the enduring character of God's Word.

Walk With W. Graham Scroggie

"This truly is the Word of God which lives and abides forever. It does not need our apologies and our special pleading. Give it a chance, and it will demonstrate its own character and its own power.

"This is the light by which millions have found their way to the shining home among the delectable mountains. This is the star which has guided mariners on stormy seas throughout the ages.

"This is the weapon with which the Christian soldier has fought his battles to glorious victory. This is the compass which has guided men in darkness and distress. This is the Book on which many a saintly Christian has laid down his head as on a pillow in the last moments of life, whispering some psalm of Scripture.

"There need be no panic. This is the rock of all ages, and those built on it are as eternal as God."

Walk Closer to God

Timothy's education in the Scriptures began when he was only a child (2 Timothy 3:15), literally at the knee of his mother and grandmother (2 Timothy 1:5).

What can even young children learn from such an exposure? They can learn "teaching" (truth about God) . . . "rebuking" (truth about error) . . . "correcting" (getting back on the right track) . . . "training in righteousness" (continuing education in the faith).

Build your life on the Word of God, and you—like Timothy—will find an unshakable foundation for this life and the next. ◖◗

SEPTEMBER 26

📖 Walk in the Word
2 Timothy 4:9–22

Paul, sitting in prison, writes his closing remarks to Timothy, asking him to greet his Christian friends and to come to visit him one more time before he dies.

Personal Remarks

[9]Do your best to come to me quickly, [10]for Demas, because he loved this world, has deserted me and has gone to Thessalonica. Crescens has gone to Galatia, and Titus to Dalmatia. [11]Only Luke is with me. Get Mark and bring him with you, because he is helpful to me in my ministry. [12]I sent Tychicus to Ephesus. [13]When you come, bring the cloak that I left with Carpus at Troas, and my scrolls, especially the parchments.

[14]Alexander the metalworker did me a great deal of harm. The Lord will repay him for what he has done. [15]You too should be on your guard against him, because he strongly opposed our message.

[16]At my first defense, no one came to my support, but everyone deserted me. May it not be held against them. [17]But the Lord stood at my side and gave me strength, so that through me the message might be fully proclaimed and all the Gentiles might hear it. And I was delivered from the lion's mouth. [18]The Lord will rescue me from every evil attack and will bring me safely to his heavenly kingdom. To him be glory for ever and ever. Amen.

Final Greetings

[19]Greet Priscilla[a] and Aquila and the household of Onesiphorus. [20]Erastus stayed in Corinth, and I left Trophimus sick in Miletus. [21]Do your best to get here before winter. Eubulus greets you, and so do Pudens, Linus, Claudia and all the brothers.

[22]The Lord be with your spirit. Grace be with you.

a19 Greek *Prisca*, a variant of *Priscilla*

Fellowship in the Family of God

Do your best to come to me quickly, for Demas, because he loved this world, has deserted me (2 Timothy 4:9–10).

In the world of athletics, there are two kinds of sports: individual and team. And woe to the person who joins a team but continues to play only as an individual!

Though Paul's life was characterized by personal achievement, he rarely traveled alone; he constantly spoke of the "one another" responsibilities in the body of Christ and he established churches for mutual encouragement and fellowship.

Fellowship is not an option, but an imperative in the Christian life, as William Biederwolf explains.

Walk With William Biederwolf

"I do not believe it is possible to be a good Christian without having godly friends.

"If I could find a man who was filled with the Spirit of Jesus, I would rather know him and get into the secret of his heart, and have the benediction and blessing that necessarily come from fellowship with him, than to have all that ever came to Demas through the decision he made when he quit the fight, quit the faith, quit the race, said 'goodbye' to Paul, and went off to Thessalonica.

"Better to have one Christian friend than anything the world might offer me. And this, in the first place, is what Demas lost.

"He lost Paul."

Walk Closer to God

Paul knew that Christians need each other, so he gave instructions on how to treat one another:

"Carry each other's burdens" (Galatians 6:2).

"Be kind and compassionate to one another, forgiving each other" (Ephesians 4:32).

"Love one another" (Romans 13:8).

As part of God's family, you have the Lord. But you have something more: an entire family of brothers and sisters in Christ. Trying to live for him while ignoring them is a losing proposition.

And the loser is you! ◖◗

SEPTEMBER 27

📖 Walk in the Word
Titus 1

Paul gives Titus some instructions on how he should organize the churches on the island of Crete.

1 Paul, a servant of God and an apostle of Jesus Christ for the faith of God's elect and the knowledge of the truth that leads to godliness — [2]a faith and knowledge resting on the hope of eternal life, which God, who does not lie, promised before the beginning of time, [3]and at his appointed season he brought his word to light through the preaching entrusted to me by the command of God our Savior,

[4]To Titus, my true son in our common faith:

Grace and peace from God the Father and Christ Jesus our Savior.

Titus' Task on Crete

[5]The reason I left you in Crete was that you might straighten out what was left unfinished and appoint[a] elders in every town, as I directed you. [6]An elder must be blameless, the husband of but one wife, a man whose children believe and are not open to the charge of being wild and disobedient. [7]Since an overseer[b] is entrusted with God's work, he must be blameless — not overbearing, not quick-tempered, not given to drunkenness, not violent, not pursuing dishonest gain. [8]Rather he must be hospitable, one who loves what is good, who is self-controlled, upright, holy and disciplined. [9]He must hold firmly to the trustworthy message as it has been taught, so that he can encourage others by sound doctrine and refute those who oppose it.

[10]For there are many rebellious people, mere talkers and deceivers, especially those of the circumcision group. [11]They must be silenced, because they are ruining whole households by teaching things they ought not to teach — and that for the sake of dishonest gain. [12]Even one of their own prophets has said, "Cretans are always liars, evil brutes, lazy gluttons." [13]This testimony is true. Therefore, rebuke them sharply, so that they will be sound in the faith [14]and will pay no attention to Jewish myths or to the commands of those who reject the truth. [15]To the pure, all things are pure, but to those who are corrupted and do not believe, nothing is pure. In fact, both their minds and consciences are corrupted. [16]They claim to know God, but by their actions they deny him. They are detestable, disobedient and unfit for doing anything good.

a5 Or *ordain*   *b7* Traditionally *bishop*

Actions Reflecting Your Knowledge of God

> They claim to know God, but by their actions they deny him. They are detestable, disobedient (Titus 1:16).

Good works cannot save you (Titus 3:5), but the absence of good works can effectively deny what you claim to possess (Titus 1:16).

God saved you not by good works but for good works. John Calvin explores this as he explains why true knowledge produces correct actions.

Walk With John Calvin

"If we want to know how our life should be regulated, let us examine the Word of God; for we cannot be sanctified by outward show and pomp, although they are highly esteemed among men.

"We must call upon God in sincerity and put our whole trust in him; we must give up pride and presumption and turn to him with true lowliness of mind so that we will not be given to fleshly affections.

"We must hold ourselves under subjection to God, and flee from gluttony, excess, robbery, blasphemy, and other evils. Thus we see what God would have us to do, in order to have our lives well regulated.

"When people try to justify themselves by outward works, it is like covering a heap of filth with a clean linen cloth. Therefore, let us put away the filthiness that is hidden in our hearts. Thus we may see wherein consists the true knowledge of God! When we understand this correctly, it will lead us to live in obedience to his will."

Walk Closer to God

Actions are no substitute for knowledge, as John Calvin suggests. Rather, they are a reflection of knowledge—or lack of it.

People may be fooled for a time by your profession, but God is never fooled. Without the proper knowledge of him, "all our righteous acts are like filthy rags" (Isaiah 64:6).

First things first. In the matter of becoming a Christian, it's not what you do but whom you know. Take God at his word and you won't be fooling anyone—least of all yourself. ❍

September 28

📖 Walk in the Word
Titus 2

In view of the growing danger of worldliness, Paul lists for Titus some of the important teachings he must give to various groups within the church.

What Must Be Taught to Various Groups

2 You must teach what is in accord with sound doctrine. ²Teach the older men to be temperate, worthy of respect, self-controlled, and sound in faith, in love and in endurance.

³Likewise, teach the older women to be reverent in the way they live, not to be slanderers or addicted to much wine, but to teach what is good. ⁴Then they can train the younger women to love their husbands and children, ⁵to be self-controlled and pure, to be busy at home, to be kind, and to be subject to their husbands, so that no one will malign the word of God.

⁶Similarly, encourage the young men to be self-controlled. ⁷In everything set them an example by doing what is good. In your teaching show integrity, seriousness ⁸and soundness of speech that cannot be condemned, so that those who oppose you may be ashamed because they have nothing bad to say about us.

⁹Teach slaves to be subject to their masters in everything, to try to please them, not to talk back to them, ¹⁰and not to steal from them, but to show that they can be fully trusted, so that in every way they will make the teaching about God our Savior attractive.

¹¹For the grace of God that brings salvation has appeared to all men. ¹²It teaches us to say "No" to ungodliness and worldly passions, and to live self-controlled, upright and godly lives in this present age, ¹³while we wait for the blessed hope — the glorious appearing of our great God and Savior, Jesus Christ, ¹⁴who gave himself for us to redeem us from all wickedness and to purify for himself a people that are his very own, eager to do what is good.

¹⁵These, then, are the things you should teach. Encourage and rebuke with all authority. Do not let anyone despise you.

To Display the Loveliness of Christ

In everything set them an example by doing what is good . . . so that in every way [you] will make the teaching about God our Savior attractive (Titus 2:7,10).

A picture frame—seemingly an after-thought to the picture itself—can either help or hinder the viewer's appreciation of the picture.

The same could be said of the Christian life.

The masterpiece of the gospel is breathtaking, but its beauty is either tarnished or enhanced by the Christian life that frames it.

F.B. Meyer has these thoughts on adorning the gospel with the right words and deeds.

Walk With F.B. Meyer

"Even the lowliest worker might 'make attractive' the gospel as jewels make attractive the brow of beauty. Holy lives can display its loveliness.

"To please one's superiors in all things, so far as our loyalty to Christ permits, is to commend Christ to our households and win his approval.

"The grace of God has ever offered salvation, but in Jesus it was brought to our doors.

"Have we sat sufficiently long in the school of grace that our gentle Teacher may instruct us how to live? It must be 'soberly' in regard to ourselves, 'righteously' toward others, and 'godly' toward God. We cannot realize any one of these unless we resolutely deny ungodliness and worldly lusts.

"This was the aim and purpose of Jesus coming to die for us. He wanted to redeem us from all iniquity, purify us as his own, and use us in all manner of good works. It is a solemn question whether that supreme purpose has been realized in our own experience. If not, why not?"

Walk Closer to God

A bad frame draws attention to itself; a good frame highlights that which it displays. In a similar way, certain qualities of life make the gospel attractive: "integrity, seriousness and soundness of speech" (Titus 2:7–8).

Surrounding your witness with these is one way to help others realize that "the grace of God that brings salvation has appeared to all men" (Titus 2:11). ☐

September 29

Walk in the Word
Titus 3

Paul reminds Titus of the basic gospel message of how we can be saved by God's grace revealed in Christ, concluding this letter with several parting admonitions.

Doing What Is Good

3 Remind the people to be subject to rulers and authorities, to be obedient, to be ready to do whatever is good, ²to slander no one, to be peaceable and considerate, and to show true humility toward all men.

³At one time we too were foolish, disobedient, deceived and enslaved by all kinds of passions and pleasures. We lived in malice and envy, being hated and hating one another. ⁴But when the kindness and love of God our Savior appeared, ⁵he saved us, not because of righteous things we had done, but because of his mercy. He saved us through the washing of rebirth and renewal by the Holy Spirit, ⁶whom he poured out on us generously through Jesus Christ our Savior, ⁷so that, having been justified by his grace, we might become heirs having the hope of eternal life. ⁸This is a trustworthy saying. And I want you to stress these things, so that those who have trusted in God may be careful to devote themselves to doing what is good. These things are excellent and profitable for everyone.

⁹But avoid foolish controversies and genealogies and arguments and quarrels about the law, because these are unprofitable and useless. ¹⁰Warn a divisive person once, and then warn him a second time. After that, have nothing to do with him. ¹¹You may be sure that such a man is warped and sinful; he is self-condemned.

Final Remarks

¹²As soon as I send Artemas or Tychicus to you, do your best to come to me at Nicopolis, because I have decided to winter there. ¹³Do everything you can to help Zenas the lawyer and Apollos on their way and see that they have everything they need. ¹⁴Our people must learn to devote themselves to doing what is good, in order that they may provide for daily necessities and not live unproductive lives.

¹⁵Everyone with me sends you greetings. Greet those who love us in the faith.

Grace be with you all.

Asking the Questions God Delights to Answer

But avoid foolish controversies and genealogies and arguments and quarrels about the law, because these are unprofitable and useless (Titus 3:9).

How many angels can dance on the head of a pin? Can God make a rock so big that he cannot move it? Where did Cain get his wife?

Such questions produce only endless speculation—and far more heat than light!

Paul admonishes both Timothy and Titus to avoid the kind of questions that serve no useful purpose but only detract from the weightier questions and pursuits of the Christian life.

Charles Spurgeon points the way to another set of questions for the child of God to consider.

Walk With Charles Spurgeon

"Our business is neither to ask nor answer foolish questions, but to avoid them altogether. And if we observe the apostle's precept to be careful to maintain good works, we shall find ourselves far too occupied with profitable business to take interest in unworthy and needless quarrels.

"There are, however, some questions which are the reverse of foolish, which we must not avoid, but fairly and honestly meet, such as these: Do I believe in the Lord Jesus Christ? Am I renewed in the spirit of my mind? Am I walking, not after the flesh, but after the Spirit? Am I growing in grace? Am I looking for the coming of the Lord?

"Such inquiries as these urgently demand our attention; and if we have all been given to making excuses, let us now turn our attention to a service much more profitable. Let us be peacemakers and endeavor to lead others both by our precept and example, to avoid foolish questions."

Walk Closer to God

Every Christian has a growing list of questions that yearn for answers this side of heaven. Good questions. Questions God may see fit to answer . . . someday. But in the meantime, you might want to ask yourself one question:

"When I meet God face to face, what will be my answers to the questions he will have for me?" ❐

DWIGHT L. MOODY

(1837–1899) GIVER OF THE GOSPEL

Preacher and Evangelist

The success of revivals in the late nineteenth century can be attributed to a former shoe salesman, Dwight L. Moody, whose formal education ended at age thirteen. Born in 1837 in Northfield, Massachusetts, Moody's early years were marked by hardship. His father died suddenly when he was only four years old, leaving his mother to raise nine children. In his late teens, he left home to work for his uncle in Boston as a shoe salesman.

But Moody demonstrated one remarkable quality: an abundance of energy. Whatever he did, he threw himself into with full enthusiasm. In Boston he became involved in a church where he came to a saving knowledge of Christ. Moving to Chicago, he began devoting more and more time to church activities, especially a Sunday school class with over 1,500 children attending. At age twenty-three he decided to go fulltime into soul-winning.

Though he was never ordained, he was widely sought as a preacher and evangelist. A trip to England in 1873 marked the beginning of several highly visible and successful evangelistic speaking tours in England and America. His sermons were always filled with vivid illustrations and fast-paced stories that helped clarify and apply spiritual truths. During his lifetime he preached to and counseled millions of people. In addition to the campaigns, Moody began several schools to provide for others the education he never received—the best-known being Moody Bible Institute. He started a book service to provide low-cost Christian literature.

Moody's enthusiasm touched two continents for God. Let his life encourage you to seek ways you can spread the good news of God's redeeming love.

A LESSON FROM THE LIFE OF DWIGHT L. MOODY

By sharing the gospel in an enthusiastic and loving way, I can touch others for Jesus Christ.

SEPTEMBER 30

📖 Walk in the Word
Philemon

Paul appeals to Philemon to forgive and receive back his runaway slave Onesimus, whom Paul had led to the Lord Jesus Christ and who had been helping Paul while in prison.

[1]Paul, a prisoner of Christ Jesus, and Timothy our brother,

To Philemon our dear friend and fellow worker, [2]to Apphia our sister, to Archippus our fellow soldier and to the church that meets in your home:

[3]Grace to you and peace from God our Father and the Lord Jesus Christ.

Thanksgiving and Prayer

[4]I always thank my God as I remember you in my prayers, [5]because I hear about your faith in the Lord Jesus and your love for all the saints. [6]I pray that you may be active in sharing your faith, so that you will have a full understanding of every good thing we have in Christ. [7]Your love has given me great joy and encouragement, because you, brother, have refreshed the hearts of the saints.

Paul's Plea for Onesimus

[8]Therefore, although in Christ I could be bold and order you to do what you ought to do, [9]yet I appeal to you on the basis of love. I then, as Paul — an old man and now also a prisoner of Christ Jesus — [10]I appeal to you for my son Onesimus,[a] who became my son while I was in chains. [11]Formerly he was useless to you, but now he has become useful both to you and to me.

[12]I am sending him — who is my very heart — back to you. [13]I would have liked to keep him with me so that he could take your place in helping me while I am in chains for the gospel. [14]But I did not want to do anything without your consent, so that any favor you do will be spontaneous and not forced. [15]Perhaps the reason he was separated from you for a little while was that you might have him back for good — [16]no longer as a slave, but better than a slave, as a dear brother. He is very dear to me but even dearer to you, both as a man and as a brother in the Lord.

[17]So if you consider me a partner, welcome him as you would welcome me. [18]If he has done you any wrong or owes you anything, charge it to me. [19]I, Paul, am writing this with my own hand. I will pay it back — not to mention that you owe me your very self. [20]I do wish, brother, that I may have some benefit from you in the Lord; refresh my heart in Christ. [21]Confident of your obedience, I write to you, knowing that you will do even more than I ask.

[22]And one thing more: Prepare a guest room for me, because I hope to be restored to you in answer to your prayers.

SEPTEMBER 30

²³Epaphras, my fellow prisoner in Christ Jesus, sends you greetings. ²⁴And so do Mark, Aristarchus, Demas and Luke, my fellow workers. ²⁵The grace of the Lord Jesus Christ be with your spirit.

ᵃ10 Onesimus means *useful*.

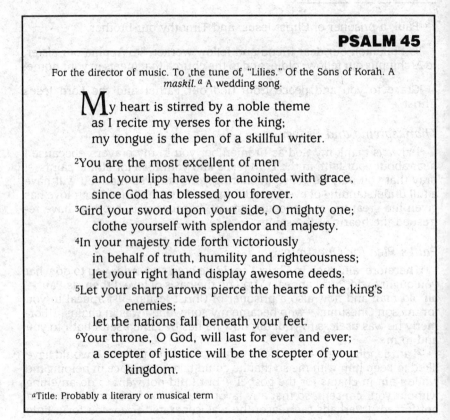

PSALM 45

For the director of music. To the tune of, "Lilies." Of the Sons of Korah. A *maskil.* ᵃ A wedding song.

My heart is stirred by a noble theme
   as I recite my verses for the king;
   my tongue is the pen of a skillful writer.

²You are the most excellent of men
   and your lips have been anointed with grace,
   since God has blessed you forever.
³Gird your sword upon your side, O mighty one;
   clothe yourself with splendor and majesty.
⁴In your majesty ride forth victoriously
   in behalf of truth, humility and righteousness;
   let your right hand display awesome deeds.
⁵Let your sharp arrows pierce the hearts of the king's
      enemies;
   let the nations fall beneath your feet.
⁶Your throne, O God, will last for ever and ever;
   a scepter of justice will be the scepter of your
      kingdom.

ᵃTitle: Probably a literary or musical term

Tactful Words to Touch the Heart

> I appeal to you on the basis of love . . . for my son Onesimus, who became my son while I was in chains (Philemon 9–10).

Tact has been called the ability to organize awkward truth attractively.

The case of the runaway slave Onesimus provided Paul with a supreme test of his tactfulness, for his letter to Philemon would be the basis for the reconciliation of master and slave.

Albert Barnes highlights the tender tone of Paul's brief message.

Walk With Albert Barnes

"The address and tact of Paul here are worthy of particular observation. If Paul had simply said, 'I beseech you for Onesimus'; or 'I appeal to you for your servant Onesimus,' he would at once have reminded Philemon of his slave's former conduct, his ingratitude and disobedience.

"But the phrase 'my son' makes the way easy for the mention of his name, for Paul had already found the way to Philemon's heart before his eye lighted on the name. Who could refuse Paul—a servant of Christ—the request which he made for one he regarded as his son?

"The name Onesimus is not suggested until Paul had mentioned that Onesimus has sustained to him the relation of a 'son'—the fruit of his labors while he was a prisoner.

"Then, when the name of Onesimus is mentioned, it would occur to Philemon not primarily as the name of a disobedient servant, but as one converted by labors of his own friend in prison.

"Was ever more delicacy shown in disarming one of prejudice and carrying an appeal to the heart?"

Walk Closer to God

Cultivating tact will help you minimize friction and maximize communication.

Let these admonitions point the way: "A gentle answer turns away wrath, but a harsh word stirs up anger" (Proverbs 15:1). "Let your conversation be always full of grace" (Colossians 4:6).

OCTOBER

Knowing and Doing: The Balanced Christian Life

HEBREWS / JAMES

Tightrope walking and juggling are skills requiring intense concentration, especially when the performer attempts both skills at the same time! Christians often find themselves in a similar tension. On the one hand, they are called on to learn more about their faith in God: "Be still, and know that I am God" (Psalm 46:10). On the other hand, they are commanded to exercise their faith in God: "Do what [the word] says" (James 1:22). Accomplishing both assignments simultaneously requires careful attention and daily diligence. The two books you read this month will help you understand how to achieve that delicate balance. The letter to the Hebrews informs you about the Christian faith; the letter of James instructs you in proper Christian conduct.

Knowing what you must believe is the thrust of the letter to the Hebrews. In his well-crafted explanation, the anonymous author demonstrates the superiority of Christ and his finished work on the cross to any other supposed "plan of salvation." Over and over he stresses that Christ came not to annul the Old Testament, but to fulfill it. Understanding how the Old Testament patterns are fulfilled in the New Testament person of Christ can't help but deepen your faith in him!

Living what you believe becomes the focus of the book of James. It is inconsistent to say you believe as you should when you behave as you shouldn't! In pithy, practical statements—similar to Proverbs—James sets forth guidelines regarding how to avoid temptation and favoritism, how to use wealth and the tongue, how to respond to widows and orphans. In short, he gives words of wisdom for your daily walk of faith.

After spending a month in the pages of Hebrews and James, you will find that you are better able to maintain a proper balance between doctrinal input and practical output in the Christian life. Knowing what to do and doing what you know—both are essential to growing in Christ.

OCTOBER 1

📖 Walk in the Word
Hebrews 1

After extolling Jesus as the eternal Son of God, the writer to the Hebrews proves from the Old Testament how much greater Christ is than the angels.

The Son Superior to Angels

1 In the past God spoke to our forefathers through the prophets at many times and in various ways, ²but in these last days he has spoken to us by his Son, whom he appointed heir of all things, and through whom he made the universe. ³The Son is the radiance of God's glory and the exact representation of his being, sustaining all things by his powerful word. After he had provided purification for sins, he sat down at the right hand of the Majesty in heaven. ⁴So he became as much superior to the angels as the name he has inherited is superior to theirs.

⁵For to which of the angels did God ever say,

> "You are my Son;
>   today I have become your Father*ª*"*ᵇ*?

Or again,

> "I will be his Father,
>   and he will be my Son"*ᶜ*?

⁶And again, when God brings his firstborn into the world, he says,

> "Let all God's angels worship him."*ᵈ*

⁷In speaking of the angels he says,

> "He makes his angels winds,
>   his servants flames of fire."*ᵉ*

⁸But about the Son he says,

> "Your throne, O God, will last for ever and ever,
>   and righteousness will be the scepter of your kingdom.
> ⁹You have loved righteousness and hated wickedness;
>   therefore God, your God, has set you above your
>   companions
>   by anointing you with the oil of joy."*ᶠ*

¹⁰He also says,

> "In the beginning, O Lord, you laid the foundations of the
>   earth,
>   and the heavens are the work of your hands.
> ¹¹They will perish, but you remain;
>   they will all wear out like a garment.
> ¹²You will roll them up like a robe;
>   like a garment they will be changed.
> But you remain the same,
>   and your years will never end."*ᵍ*

October 1

¹³To which of the angels did God ever say,

> "Sit at my right hand
> until I make your enemies
> a footstool for your feet"ʰ?

¹⁴Are not all angels ministering spirits sent to serve those who will inherit salvation?

ᵃ5 Or *have begotten you*   ᵇ5 Psalm 2:7   ᶜ5 2 Samuel 7:14; 1 Chron. 17:13
ᵈ6 Deut. 32:43 (see Dead Sea Scrolls and Septuagint)   ᵉ7 Psalm 104:4   ᶠ9 Psalm 45:6,7
ᵍ12 Psalm 102:25-27   ʰ13 Psalm 110:1

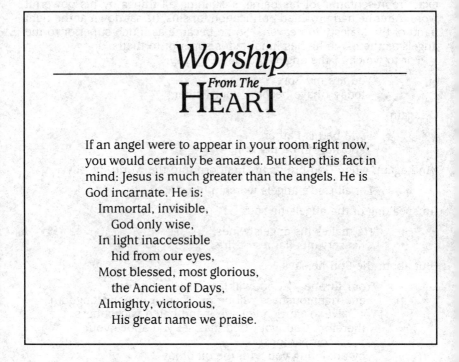

Worship
H*From The*EART

If an angel were to appear in your room right now, you would certainly be amazed. But keep this fact in mind: Jesus is much greater than the angels. He is God incarnate. He is:

> Immortal, invisible,
>   God only wise,
> In light inaccessible
>   hid from our eyes,
> Most blessed, most glorious,
>   the Ancient of Days,
> Almighty, victorious,
>   His great name we praise.

The Majesty of the Father Shining Through His Son

The Son is the radiance of God's glory and the exact representation of his being . . . he sat down at the right hand of the Majesty in heaven (Hebrews 1:3).

Painters have tried. Sculptors have tried. Poets have tried. Yet all have failed, for only one picture of God has ever been accurately rendered.

Jesus Christ alone is the exact representation of God's nature. In Jesus, God became a man so that all the human race might see God.

If your picture of God is a bit fuzzy, the opening verses of Hebrews will sharpen your focus, and John Calvin's words will help you better appreciate the picture.

Walk With John Calvin

"The Son is said to be 'the radiance of God's glory' and the 'exact representation of his being'; these are words which borrow from created things to describe the hidden majesty of God. But the things which are evident to our senses are fitly applied to God, that we may know what is to be found in Christ and what benefits he brings to us.

"When you hear that the Son is the brightness of the Father's glory, think that the glory of the Father is invisible until it shines forth in Christ, and that he is called the 'exact representation of his being' because the Father's majesty is hidden until it shows itself impressed on the Son's image.

"The writer's purpose is to build up our faith so that we may learn that God is made known to us in no other way than in Christ. Thus it follows that we are blind to the light of God until in Christ it shines on us."

Walk Closer to God

God is light. So is Jesus: "I am the light of the world" (John 8:12).

God is truth. So is Jesus: "I am . . . the truth" (John 14:6).

God is God alone. So is Jesus: "I am" (John 8:58).

"God . . . in these last days . . . has spoken to us by his Son" (Hebrews 1:1–2).

Therefore, you are no longer "in the dark" about God when you have met the Savior.

And that's a thought to brighten any day!

OCTOBER 2

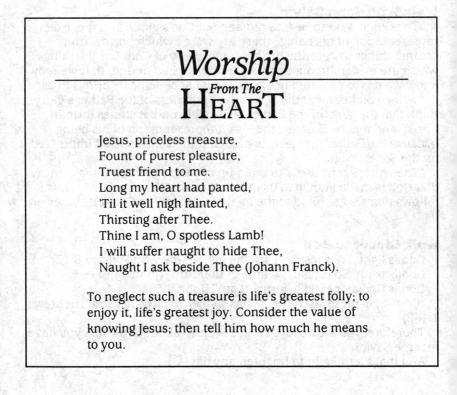

Walk in the Word
Hebrews 2:1–4

The writer to the Hebrews warns us to pay careful attention to the Word of God so that we do not drift away from God's great salvation.

Warning to Pay Attention

2 We must pay more careful attention, therefore, to what we have heard, so that we do not drift away. ²For if the message spoken by angels was binding, and every violation and disobedience received its just punishment, ³how shall we escape if we ignore such a great salvation? This salvation, which was first announced by the Lord, was confirmed to us by those who heard him. ⁴God also testified to it by signs, wonders and various miracles, and gifts of the Holy Spirit distributed according to his will.

Worship
From The HEART

Jesus, priceless treasure,
Fount of purest pleasure,
Truest friend to me.
Long my heart had panted,
'Til it well nigh fainted,
Thirsting after Thee.
Thine I am, O spotless Lamb!
I will suffer naught to hide Thee,
Naught I ask beside Thee (Johann Franck).

To neglect such a treasure is life's greatest folly; to enjoy it, life's greatest joy. Consider the value of knowing Jesus; then tell him how much he means to you.

The Greatest Treasure Ever Offered to the World

How shall we escape if we ignore such a great salvation? (Hebrews 2:3).

Jesus declared, "The kingdom of heaven is like a merchant looking for fine pearls. When he found one of great value, he went away and sold everything he had (Matthew 13:45–46).

That man knew that salvation is worth far more than anything the world has to offer.

Being reminded of the surpassing value of "such a great salvation" gives believers the right perspective when confronted with the concerns of this world, as Martin Luther explains.

Walk With Martin Luther

"The supreme blessing in which one can truly know the goodness of God is not temporal possessions, but the eternal blessing that God has called us to—his holy gospel.

"In this gospel we hear that God will be gracious to us for the sake of his Son, will forgive and eternally save us, and will protect us in this life against the tyranny of the devil and the world.

"To someone who properly appreciates this blessing, everything else is a trifle. Though he is poor, sick, despised, and burdened with adversities, he sees that he keeps more than he has lost. If he has no money and goods, he knows nevertheless that he has a gracious God; if his body is sick, he knows that he is called to eternal life.

"His heart has this constant consolation: Only a short time, and everything will be better."

Walk Closer to God

Your "great salvation" carries great benefits:

> Eternal life (John 3:16)
> Forgiveness (Ephesians 1:7)
> Deliverance (Colossians 1:13)
> Adoption (Galatians 4:4–7)

Salvation is not simply good news; it's great news! So when you have seen enough of this world, do as one hymnwriter has suggested:

> Turn your eyes upon Jesus,
>   Look full in his wonderful face;
> And the things of earth will grow strangely dim
>   In the light of his glory and grace.

OCTOBER 3

Walk in the Word
Hebrews 2:5–18

The writer emphasizes how Jesus shared our humanity, thereby enabling him to free us as humans from Satan's power.

Jesus Made Like His Brothers

⁵It is not to angels that he has subjected the world to come, about which we are speaking. ⁶But there is a place where someone has testified:

> "What is man that you are mindful of him,
>> the son of man that you care for him?
> ⁷You made him a little*ᵃ* lower than the angels;
>> you crowned him with glory and honor
> ⁸ and put everything under his feet."*ᵇ*

In putting everything under him, God left nothing that is not subject to him. Yet at present we do not see everything subject to him. ⁹But we see Jesus, who was made a little lower than the angels, now crowned with glory and honor because he suffered death, so that by the grace of God he might taste death for everyone.

¹⁰In bringing many sons to glory, it was fitting that God, for whom and through whom everything exists, should make the author of their salvation perfect through suffering. ¹¹Both the one who makes men holy and those who are made holy are of the same family. So Jesus is not ashamed to call them brothers. ¹²He says,

> "I will declare your name to my brothers;
>> in the presence of the congregation I will sing your
>>> praises."*ᶜ*

¹³And again,

> "I will put my trust in him."*ᵈ*

And again he says,

> "Here am I, and the children God has given me."*ᵉ*

¹⁴Since the children have flesh and blood, he too shared in their humanity so that by his death he might destroy him who holds the power of death—that is, the devil— ¹⁵and free those who all their lives were held in slavery by their fear of death. ¹⁶For surely it is not angels he helps, but Abraham's descendants. ¹⁷For this reason he had to be made like his brothers in every way, in order that he might become a merciful and faithful high priest in service to God, and that he might make atonement for*ᶠ* the sins of the people. ¹⁸Because he himself suffered when he was tempted, he is able to help those who are being tempted.

*ᵃ7 Or him for a little while; also in verse 9   ᵇ8 Psalm 8:4-6   ᶜ12 Psalm 22:22
ᵈ13 Isaiah 8:17   ᵉ13 Isaiah 8:18   ᶠ17 Or and that he might turn aside God's wrath, taking away*

OCTOBER 3

Learning to Walk as Jesus Walked

For this reason he had to be made like his brothers in every way, in order that he might become a merciful and faithful high priest in service to God (Hebrews 2:17).

Soon after he arrived in inland China, Hudson Taylor spoke Chinese, wore Chinese clothes, ate Chinese food and observed Chinese customs. As a pioneer missionary to the masses of people in the interior of China, Taylor knew the importance of identifying with those he wanted to reach.

When God became man in the person of Christ, he secured our salvation by living and dying as God incarnate, in the flesh. J. Hudson Taylor explains why identification with the lost is a powerful testimony of Christ's incarnation.

Walk With J. Hudson Taylor

"Consider the Apostle and High Priest of our profession, Christ Jesus, who was faithful to the One who appointed him, and left us an example that we should follow.

"To save man he became Man—not merely like man, but very man. In language, in costume, in everything unsinful, he made himself one with those he sought to benefit.

"Had he been born a noble Roman rather than a Jew, he would perhaps have commanded more of a certain kind of respect; and he would assuredly have been spared much indignity. This, however, was not his aim; he emptied himself.

"Surely no follower of the meek and lowly Jesus will be likely to conclude that it is beneath the dignity of a Christian to seek identification with poor people, in the hope that he may see them washed, sanctified, and justified in the name of the Lord Jesus, and by the Spirit of our God!

"Let us be followers of him."

Walk Closer to God

Hudson Taylor's strategy for reaching the teeming millions of China was simple: When in China, do as the Chinese do. Those with a genuine concern for the lost will do everything they can to "free those who all their lives were held in slavery by their fear of death" (Hebrews 2:15).

Jesus did; Hudson Taylor did. What about you? ❍

OCTOBER 4

Walk in the Word
Hebrews 3:1–6

Just as the first chapter of Hebrews describes how much greater Jesus is than the angels, this chapter records how much greater Jesus is than Moses.

Jesus Greater Than Moses

3 Therefore, holy brothers, who share in the heavenly calling, fix your thoughts on Jesus, the apostle and high priest whom we confess. ²He was faithful to the one who appointed him, just as Moses was faithful in all God's house. ³Jesus has been found worthy of greater honor than Moses, just as the builder of a house has greater honor than the house itself. ⁴For every house is built by someone, but God is the builder of everything. ⁵Moses was faithful as a servant in all God's house, testifying to what would be said in the future. ⁶But Christ is faithful as a son over God's house. And we are his house, if we hold on to our courage and the hope of which we boast.

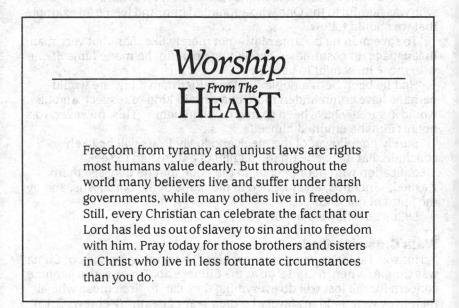

Worship
From The
HEART

Freedom from tyranny and unjust laws are rights most humans value dearly. But throughout the world many believers live and suffer under harsh governments, while many others live in freedom. Still, every Christian can celebrate the fact that our Lord has led us out of slavery to sin and into freedom with him. Pray today for those brothers and sisters in Christ who live in less fortunate circumstances than you do.

Consider Jesus and Rejoice

Therefore, holy brothers, who share in the heavenly calling, fix your thoughts on Jesus, the apostle and high priest whom we confess (Hebrews 3:1).

Take away the heart, and the body ceases to have life. Take away Christ, and whatever you have left is not the Christian life.

Hebrews 3 calls you to "fix your thoughts on Jesus." F.B. Meyer analyzes the who, why and how of that calling.

Walk With F.B. Meyer

"We should emulate the saints of all ages in the gaze at Christ. We must possess the holiness without which none can see the Lord, and we must live in holy love with all those who bear the name of Christ.

"What right have we to fix our thoughts on him? Because we are 'sharers in the heavenly calling.' Those who have turned from the world, from the fascinations of sin and the flesh, who are seeking the heavenly city, the new Jerusalem. Surely such have a right—given them by grace—to live in daily, personal vision of their King!

"In what aspects should they fix their thoughts on him?

"As Apostle, whom God has sent out of his bosom to mankind.

"As Priest, who was in all points tempted as we are, yet without sin, who bears our needs and sins and sorrows on his heart.

"As the Son, compared with whom Moses was but a servant.

"As Creator, by whom all things were made, and without whom not any thing was made.

"As the Head of the household of those who believe.

"As the All-faithful One, who will never resign his charge.

"Consider Jesus in each of these aspects, and rejoice in him."

Walk Closer to God

Spend a few quiet moments reflecting on your Apostle . . . Priest . . . Creator . . . All-faithful One . . . until his greatness overwhelms you with gratitude that he is your Savior and Lord. ❍

OCTOBER 5

📖 Walk in the Word
Hebrews 3:7–19

Using Psalm 95:7–11, the writer to the Hebrews warns his readers against the same sort of unbelief as the Israelites of old manifested.

Warning Against Unbelief

⁷So, as the Holy Spirit says:

"Today, if you hear his voice,
⁸   do not harden your hearts
as you did in the rebellion,
      during the time of testing in the desert,
⁹where your fathers tested and tried me
      and for forty years saw what I did.
¹⁰That is why I was angry with that generation,
      and I said, 'Their hearts are always going astray,
      and they have not known my ways.'
¹¹So I declared on oath in my anger,
      'They shall never enter my rest.' "ᵃ

¹²See to it, brothers, that none of you has a sinful, unbelieving heart that turns away from the living God. ¹³But encourage one another daily, as long as it is called Today, so that none of you may be hardened by sin's deceitfulness. ¹⁴We have come to share in Christ if we hold firmly till the end the confidence we had at first. ¹⁵As has just been said:

"Today, if you hear his voice,
      do not harden your hearts
as you did in the rebellion."ᵇ

¹⁶Who were they who heard and rebelled? Were they not all those Moses led out of Egypt? ¹⁷And with whom was he angry for forty years? Was it not with those who sinned, whose bodies fell in the desert? ¹⁸And to whom did God swear that they would never enter his rest if not to those who disobeyedᶜ? ¹⁹So we see that they were not able to enter, because of their unbelief.

ᵃ11 Psalm 95:7-11   ᵇ15 Psalm 95:7,8   ᶜ18 Or *disbelieved*

OCTOBER 5

A Heart Focused on Pleasing God

But encourage one another daily, as long as it is called Today, so that none of you may be hardened by sin's deceitfulness (Hebrews 3:13).

Each day has its own challenges, responsibilities, and problems. Each can be faced only one at a time. The author of Hebrews suggests three daily disciplines to help you remain faithful, no matter what day it is.

Today, hear God's voice (Hebrews 3:7).

Today, encourage one another (Hebrews 3:13).

Today, do not harden your hearts (Hebrews 3:8,15).

Listening to God's voice, encouraging your brothers and sisters in Christ, and refusing to harden your heart—three essentials for enjoying daily victory in Christ.

Today, Alexander Maclaren challenges you to examine and avoid that which tempts you to be unfaithful to God.

Walk With Alexander Maclaren

"We may get the things which tempt our desires; and there will be no illusion at all about the reality of the pleasure. But another question must be asked.

"You have received the thing you wanted; what then? Are you much the better for it? Are you satisfied with it? Is it as good as it looked when it was not yours?

"Is it as blessed now that you have stretched your hand and made it your own as it seemed when it danced there on the other side?

"Having attained the desire, do we not find that it fails to satisfy us fully?"

Walk Closer to God

"Father, thank you for your Word, which teaches me how to avoid sin. Help me to listen carefully whenever you speak to me through its pages. Cause me to encourage my brothers and sisters in Christ and to draw strength from their example and fellowship.

"Above all, Lord, grant me a soft, pliable, teachable heart, one that beats strongly for you. In the name of the one who wants to keep my heart focused on pleasing you. Amen." ◖◗

OCTOBER 6

📖 Walk in the Word
Hebrews 4:1–13

Believers are encouraged to strive to enter into God's eternal rest through persistent faith and obedience.

A Sabbath-Rest for the People of God

4 Therefore, since the promise of entering his rest still stands, let us be careful that none of you be found to have fallen short of it. ²For we also have had the gospel preached to us, just as they did; but the message they heard was of no value to them, because those who heard did not combine it with faith.ᵃ ³Now we who have believed enter that rest, just as God has said,

> "So I declared on oath in my anger,
> 'They shall never enter my rest.'"ᵇ

And yet his work has been finished since the creation of the world. ⁴For somewhere he has spoken about the seventh day in these words: "And on the seventh day God rested from all his work."ᶜ ⁵And again in the passage above he says, "They shall never enter my rest."

⁶It still remains that some will enter that rest, and those who formerly had the gospel preached to them did not go in, because of their disobedience. ⁷Therefore God again set a certain day, calling it Today, when a long time later he spoke through David, as was said before:

> "Today, if you hear his voice,
> do not harden your hearts."ᵈ

⁸For if Joshua had given them rest, God would not have spoken later about another day. ⁹There remains, then, a Sabbath-rest for the people of God; ¹⁰for anyone who enters God's rest also rests from his own work, just as God did from his. ¹¹Let us, therefore, make every effort to enter that rest, so that no one will fall by following their example of disobedience.

¹²For the word of God is living and active. Sharper than any double-edged sword, it penetrates even to dividing soul and spirit, joints and marrow; it judges the thoughts and attitudes of the heart. ¹³Nothing in all creation is hidden from God's sight. Everything is uncovered and laid bare before the eyes of him to whom we must give account.

ᵃ2 Many manuscripts *because they did not share in the faith of those who obeyed*
ᵇ3 Psalm 95:11; also in verse 5   ᶜ4 Gen. 2:2   ᵈ7 Psalm 95:7,8

October 6

Hearing the Heartthrobs of God

For the word of God is living and active. Sharper than any double-edged sword, it penetrates even to dividing soul and spirit, joints and marrow; it judges the thoughts and attitudes of the heart (Hebrews 4:12).

Penetrating sirens . . . penetrating screams . . . penetrating stares . . . penetrating words.

In each case, your body reacts with quick determination. Adrenalin sends a message to your heart. "Action needed—now!"

The same could be said of the Word of God: It penetrates the heart with truth too important to ignore.

A.T. Pierson explores the power of God's forceful and piercing Word.

Walk With A.T. Pierson

"The life of God is in his Word. The Word is quick, living.

"Is it a mirror? Yes, but such a mirror as the living eye. Is it a seed? Yes, but a seed hiding the vitality of God. Is it a sword? Yes, but a sword that omnisciently discerns and pierces the human heart.

"Hold it reverently, for it is a living Book. Speak to it, and it will answer you. Bend to listen, and you will hear in it the heartthrobs of God.

"This Book we are to hold forth as the Word of life and the Light of God in the midst of a crooked and perverse generation.

"Like the birds that beat themselves senseless against the light of the Statue of Liberty in New York Harbor, the creatures of darkness will assault this Word and vainly seek to put out its base, while it still rises from its rock pedestal, immovable and serene!"

Walk Closer to God

Perhaps you find it a bit unnerving to know there is something that can penetrate all your defenses and pierce your heart with convicting truth.

You can't change the truth—but you can allow it to change you. And that is its purpose: to penetrate, divide, judge and transform your life.

Hold it reverently . . . and often. ❏

OCTOBER 7

📖 Walk in the Word
Hebrews 4:14—5:10

Jesus, as God's chosen high priest, is shown to be the source of our eternal salvation.

Jesus the Great High Priest

[14]Therefore, since we have a great high priest who has gone through the heavens,[a] Jesus the Son of God, let us hold firmly to the faith we profess. [15]For we do not have a high priest who is unable to sympathize with our weaknesses, but we have one who has been tempted in every way, just as we are—yet was without sin. [16]Let us then approach the throne of grace with confidence, so that we may receive mercy and find grace to help us in our time of need.

5 Every high priest is selected from among men and is appointed to represent them in matters related to God, to offer gifts and sacrifices for sins. [2]He is able to deal gently with those who are ignorant and are going astray, since he himself is subject to weakness. [3]This is why he has to offer sacrifices for his own sins, as well as for the sins of the people.

[4]No one takes this honor upon himself; he must be called by God, just as Aaron was. [5]So Christ also did not take upon himself the glory of becoming a high priest. But God said to him,

"You are my Son;
today I have become your Father.[b]"[c]

[6]And he says in another place,

"You are a priest forever,
in the order of Melchizedek."[d]

[7]During the days of Jesus' life on earth, he offered up prayers and petitions with loud cries and tears to the one who could save him from death, and he was heard because of his reverent submission. [8]Although he was a son, he learned obedience from what he suffered [9]and, once made perfect, he became the source of eternal salvation for all who obey him [10]and was designated by God to be high priest in the order of Melchizedek.

---

[a]14 Or *gone into heaven*   [b]5 Or *have begotten you*   [c]5 Psalm 2:7   [d]6 Psalm 110:4

The Priest Who Passed Through the Heavens

We have a great high priest who has gone through the heavens, Jesus the Son of God (Hebrews 4:14).

The book of Leviticus clearly shows that the priesthood lived with many restrictions—and enjoyed many privileges—that were not true of the nation of Israel as a whole. But priest and people alike shared a common problem: sin.

Now the writer to the Hebrews points to a better solution: a great high priest of heavenly origin. G. Campbell Morgan extols the virtues of this perfect go-between.

Walk With G. Campbell Morgan

"To the Hebrew mind the phrase *High Priest* expressed the highest form of priestly service; it was the ultimate word. The phrase is still further strengthened by the word great. Jesus is not merely a priest; he is the High Priest, and in that he is great. His priestly work and position are characterized by the utmost finality.

"He has 'gone *through* [into] the heavens.' The statement is far stronger than it would be if it read 'passed unto the heavens.' It helps us to think of him as entering into the place of closest nearness to God in his priestly position.

"No lower heaven is the place of his work. He passed through all heavens to the very place and being of God himself. He passed through the heavens to come to mankind, into closest identification; and having accomplished his purposes there, he passed back through the heavens to go to God."

Walk Closer to God

Just think: Your representative before the king of creation is none other than the king's own Son! The one with whom he is well pleased. The great high priest.

"For we do not have a high priest who is unable to sympathize with our weaknesses, but we have one who has been tempted in every way, just as we are—yet was without sin. Let us then approach the throne of grace with confidence, so that we may receive mercy and find grace to help us in our time of need" (Hebrews 4:15–16).

What are you waiting for? Come boldly to God today, for the way has already been spanned. ◖◗

OCTOBER 8

📖 Walk in the Word
Hebrews 5:11 — 6:12

In one of the strongest passages of the New Testament, the writer to the Hebrews warns believers against falling away from faith in Christ; rather, we should continue to grow and mature in our faith.

Warning Against Falling Away

¹¹We have much to say about this, but it is hard to explain because you are slow to learn. ¹²In fact, though by this time you ought to be teachers, you need someone to teach you the elementary truths of God's word all over again. You need milk, not solid food! ¹³Anyone who lives on milk, being still an infant, is not acquainted with the teaching about righteousness. ¹⁴But solid food is for the mature, who by constant use have trained themselves to distinguish good from evil.

6 Therefore let us leave the elementary teachings about Christ and go on to maturity, not laying again the foundation of repentance from acts that lead to death, *a* and of faith in God, ²instruction about baptisms, the laying on of hands, the resurrection of the dead, and eternal judgment. ³And God permitting, we will do so.

⁴It is impossible for those who have once been enlightened, who have tasted the heavenly gift, who have shared in the Holy Spirit, ⁵who have tasted the goodness of the word of God and the powers of the coming age, ⁶if they fall away, to be brought back to repentance, because *b* to their loss they are crucifying the Son of God all over again and subjecting him to public disgrace.

⁷Land that drinks in the rain often falling on it and that produces a crop useful to those for whom it is farmed receives the blessing of God. ⁸But land that produces thorns and thistles is worthless and is in danger of being cursed. In the end it will be burned.

⁹Even though we speak like this, dear friends, we are confident of better things in your case — things that accompany salvation. ¹⁰God is not unjust; he will not forget your work and the love you have shown him as you have helped his people and continue to help them. ¹¹We want each of you to show this same diligence to the very end, in order to make your hope sure. ¹²We do not want you to become lazy, but to imitate those who through faith and patience inherit what has been promised.

a1 Or from useless rituals   b6 Or repentance while

OCTOBER 8

Growing Beyond the Basics

You need someone to teach you the elementary truths of God's word all over again (Hebrews 5:12).

After a certain age people are expected to master the basics of life. But the Hebrews had never gotten beyond the kindergarten stage of the Christian life. Instead of becoming teachers, they were still toddlers in the faith. Growth in grace was long overdue.

It's a phenomenon not unique to the first century A.D., as Albert Barnes points out.

Walk With Albert Barnes

"It often occurs that people are true Christians, yet they are ignorant of some of the elementary principles of religion.

"This is a result of such things as a lack of early religious instruction; the faults of preachers who fail to teach their people; a lack of proper interest in the subject of religion; and a greater interest in other things than in religion.

"It is often surprising what vague and unsettled opinions Christians have on some of the most important points of Christianity, and how little qualified they are to defend their beliefs.

"To some of the elementary doctrines of Christianity—about deadness to the world, about self-denial, about prayer, about doing good, and about spirituality—they are utter strangers. So also of forgiveness, and charity, and love for a dying world.

"These are the elements of Christianity—rudiments which children in righteousness should learn."

Walk Closer to God

Perhaps you can identify with the person who said, "My favorite grade in school was the second grade, because three of the happiest years of my life were spent there!"

The problem? Lack of visible, definable, reasonable progress in the basics of education.

Maturity is the by-product of applying what you know—putting it to good use. Then you will make progress in the school of faith.

The basics. That's the best place to start—and the worst place to stop! 🗘

OCTOBER 9

📖 Walk in the Word
Hebrews 6:13–20

The writer to the Hebrews assures us that God's promises, contained in the Scriptures, are sure and certain and serve as an anchor for our souls.

The Certainty of God's Promise

¹³When God made his promise to Abraham, since there was no one greater for him to swear by, he swore by himself, ¹⁴saying, "I will surely bless you and give you many descendants."ᵃ ¹⁵And so after waiting patiently, Abraham received what was promised.

¹⁶Men swear by someone greater than themselves, and the oath confirms what is said and puts an end to all argument. ¹⁷Because God wanted to make the unchanging nature of his purpose very clear to the heirs of what was promised, he confirmed it with an oath. ¹⁸God did this so that, by two unchangeable things in which it is impossible for God to lie, we who have fled to take hold of the hope offered to us may be greatly encouraged. ¹⁹We have this hope as an anchor for the soul, firm and secure. It enters the inner sanctuary behind the curtain, ²⁰where Jesus, who went before us, has entered on our behalf. He has become a high priest forever, in the order of Melchizedek.

ᵃ14 Gen. 22:17

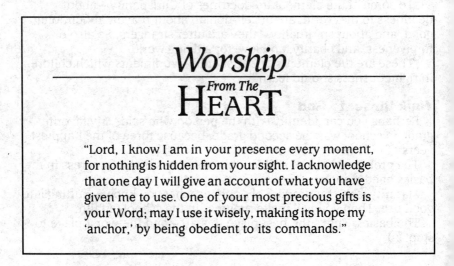

Worship
From The
HEART

"Lord, I know I am in your presence every moment, for nothing is hidden from your sight. I acknowledge that one day I will give an account of what you have given me to use. One of your most precious gifts is your Word; may I use it wisely, making its hope my 'anchor,' by being obedient to its commands."

OCTOBER 9

Doing What He Says He Will Do

Because God wanted to make the unchanging nature of his purpose very clear to the heirs of what was promised, he confirmed it with an oath (Hebrews 6:17).

"Promises are like pie crusts, made to be broken." It's a thought that's too often true—at least in human circles. But don't view God's promises that way. When he speaks, a promise made is as good as a promise *kept*.

The Old Testament is filled with examples of God's keeping his word when others broke theirs. And Hebrews 6 will reassure you of God's faithfulness to his covenants. They are as sure as the ground you walk on. Charles Spurgeon calls attention to the stability of God's promises.

Walk With Charles Spurgeon

"It is a cause of much weakness to many that they do not treat the promises of God as realities. If a friend makes a promise, they regard it as a substantial thing, and look for that which it secures; but the declarations of God are often viewed as words which mean very little.

"This is most dishonoring to the Lord and very injurious to us. Rest assured that the Lord never trifles with words. 'Has he said, and will he not do it?' His engagements are always kept.

"God speaks deliberately, in due order and determination, and we may depend upon it that his words are sure and will be fulfilled as certainly as they are uttered. Can an instance be found in which our God has been false to his Word? The ages cannot produce a single proof that the promise-making Jehovah has run back from that which he has spoken."

Walk Closer to God

Let these verses, one from the Old Testament and one from the New, testify regarding how well God keeps his word:

"God is not a man, that he should lie . . ." (Numbers 23:19). "For no matter how many promises God has made, they are 'Yes' in Christ. And so through him the 'Amen' is spoken by us to the glory of God" (2 Corinthians 1:20).

God's promises. Not made to be broken, but made to be kept. ◖

OCTOBER 10

Walk in the Word
Hebrews 7:1–10

The writer of the book of Hebrews shows how Melchizedek was far greater than Israel's priestly tribe of Levi.

Melchizedek the Priest

7 This Melchizedek was king of Salem and priest of God Most High. He met Abraham returning from the defeat of the kings and blessed him, ²and Abraham gave him a tenth of everything. First, his name means "king of righteousness"; then also, "king of Salem" means "king of peace." ³Without father or mother, without genealogy, without beginning of days or end of life, like the Son of God he remains a priest forever.

⁴Just think how great he was: Even the patriarch Abraham gave him a tenth of the plunder! ⁵Now the law requires the descendants of Levi who become priests to collect a tenth from the people — that is, their brothers — even though their brothers are descended from Abraham. ⁶This man, however, did not trace his descent from Levi, yet he collected a tenth from Abraham and blessed him who had the promises. ⁷And without doubt the lesser person is blessed by the greater. ⁸In the one case, the tenth is collected by men who die; but in the other case, by him who is declared to be living. ⁹One might even say that Levi, who collects the tenth, paid the tenth through Abraham, ¹⁰because when Melchizedek met Abraham, Levi was still in the body of his ancestor.

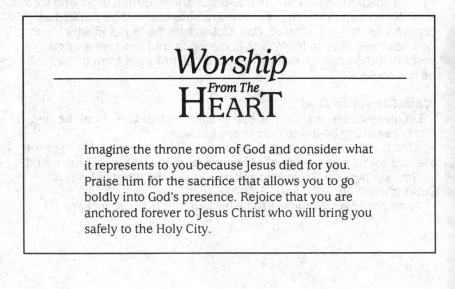

Worship
From The
HEART

Imagine the throne room of God and consider what it represents to you because Jesus died for you. Praise him for the sacrifice that allows you to go boldly into God's presence. Rejoice that you are anchored forever to Jesus Christ who will bring you safely to the Holy City.

Made New in Righteousness and True Holiness

This Melchizedek was king of Salem and priest of God Most High (Hebrews 7:1).

Scripture records that Melchizedek was "without father or mother, without genealogy, without beginning of days or end of life, like the Son of God" (Hebrews 7:3).

And, like Melchizedek, Christ is "king of righteousness" and "king of peace" (Hebrews 7:2).

But what does all this mean for the believer? Alexander Maclaren explains Jesus' role as the righteous King.

Walk With Alexander Maclaren

"The very heart of the Christian doctrine is this: As soon as a person puts his trembling trust in Jesus Christ as his Savior, then he receives not merely pardon and the uninterrupted flow of the divine love in spite of his sin, but an imparting to him of that new life, which, after God, is created in righteousness and true holiness.

"Do not suppose that the great message of the gospel is merely forgiveness. Do not suppose that its blessed gift is only that one is acquitted because Christ died.

"All that is true. But there is something more. By faith in Jesus Christ, I am so knit to him that there passes into me, by his gift, a life which is created after his life, and is in fact kindred with it.

"He is first of all King of righteousness. Let that which is first in all his gifts be first in all your efforts too; and do not seek so much for comfort as for grace to know and to do your duty, and strength to 'put aside the deeds of darkness and put on the armor of light' (Romans 13:12)"

Walk Closer to God

Because Jesus is righteous, you are forgiven, and God sees you as righteous. Because Jesus is righteous, you can live a righteous life—through the power of his life in you.

Abraham gave to Melchizedek a tenth part of all the spoil as a sign of his subjection to one greater than he. Is it too much to ask that you, being made righteous by the King of righteousness, give him your life in return?

OCTOBER 11

📖 Walk in the Word
Hebrews 7:11-28

According to the writer to the Hebrews, Jesus Christ corresponds more closely to the priestly line of Melchizedek than that of Levi; in fact, Jesus is the greatest high priest who ever lived, and continues to live on our behalf.

Jesus Like Melchizedek

¹¹If perfection could have been attained through the Levitical priesthood (for on the basis of it the law was given to the people), why was there still need for another priest to come—one in the order of Melchizedek, not in the order of Aaron? ¹²For when there is a change of the priesthood, there must also be a change of the law. ¹³He of whom these things are said belonged to a different tribe, and no one from that tribe has ever served at the altar. ¹⁴For it is clear that our Lord descended from Judah, and in regard to that tribe Moses said nothing about priests. ¹⁵And what we have said is even more clear if another priest like Melchizedek appears, ¹⁶one who has become a priest not on the basis of a regulation as to his ancestry but on the basis of the power of an indestructible life. ¹⁷For it is declared:

> "You are a priest forever,
> in the order of Melchizedek."[a]

¹⁸The former regulation is set aside because it was weak and useless ¹⁹(for the law made nothing perfect), and a better hope is introduced, by which we draw near to God.

²⁰And it was not without an oath! Others became priests without any oath, ²¹but he became a priest with an oath when God said to him:

> "The Lord has sworn
> and will not change his mind:
> 'You are a priest forever.' "[a]

²²Because of this oath, Jesus has become the guarantee of a better covenant.

²³Now there have been many of those priests, since death prevented them from continuing in office; ²⁴but because Jesus lives forever, he has a permanent priesthood. ²⁵Therefore he is able to save completely[b] those who come to God through him, because he always lives to intercede for them.

²⁶Such a high priest meets our need—one who is holy, blameless, pure, set apart from sinners, exalted above the heavens. ²⁷Unlike the other high priests, he does not need to offer sacrifices day after day, first for his own sins, and then for the sins of the people. He sacrificed for their sins once for all when he offered himself. ²⁸For the law appoints as high priests men who are weak; but the oath, which came after the law, appointed the Son, who has been made perfect forever.

[a]17,21 Psalm 110:4   [b]25 Or *forever*

OCTOBER 11

The One Who Is Both Purchaser and Price

Therefore he is able to save completely those who come to God through him, because he always lives to intercede for them (Hebrews 7:25).

Umpires. Referees. Arbitrators. Judges. Without them, disputes could never be settled.

But a dispute of eternal dimensions between a sinful human race and the holy God required a Mediator who could go between heaven and earth.

God acted to send the only one fully qualified to represent his need for justice and our need for mercy—the God-man Jesus Christ.

Jonathan Edwards discusses God's unilateral action on behalf of humanity.

Walk With Jonathan Edwards

"The redeemed are dependent on God for all.

"All that we have—wisdom, the pardon of sin, deliverance, acceptance in God's favor, grace, holiness, true comfort and happiness, eternal life and glory—we have from God by a mediator; and this mediator is God.

"God not only gives us the Mediator, and accepts his mediation, and of his power and grace bestows the things purchased by the Mediator, but he is the mediator.

"Our blessings are what we have by purchase; and the purchase is made of God; the blessings are purchased of him; and not only so, but God is the purchaser.

"Yes, God is both the purchaser and the price; for Christ, who is God, purchased these blessings by offering himself as the price of our salvation."

Walk Closer to God

As God incarnate, Jesus was the perfect go-between. Paul describes his unique role this way: "For there is one God and one mediator between God and men, the man Christ Jesus, who gave himself as a ransom for all" (1 Timothy 2:5–6).

The price for man's rebellion was high, demanding nothing less than the death of the Mediator.

The response of the Mediator was love personified: "He offered himself" (Hebrews 7:27).

And you have God to thank that he did all that for you! ◖

OCTOBER 12

📖 Walk in the Word
Hebrews 8

Here we are introduced to the main idea of the next three chapters: that the new covenant Jesus instituted is far superior to the old covenant, the one God made with his people at Mount Sinai.

The High Priest of a New Covenant

8 The point of what we are saying is this: We do have such a high priest, who sat down at the right hand of the throne of the Majesty in heaven, ²and who serves in the sanctuary, the true tabernacle set up by the Lord, not by man.

³Every high priest is appointed to offer both gifts and sacrifices, and so it was necessary for this one also to have something to offer. ⁴If he were on earth, he would not be a priest, for there are already men who offer the gifts prescribed by the law. ⁵They serve at a sanctuary that is a copy and shadow of what is in heaven. This is why Moses was warned when he was about to build the tabernacle: "See to it that you make everything according to the pattern shown you on the mountain."[a] ⁶But the ministry Jesus has received is as superior to theirs as the covenant of which he is mediator is superior to the old one, and it is founded on better promises.

⁷For if there had been nothing wrong with that first covenant, no place would have been sought for another. ⁸But God found fault with the people and said[b]:

> "The time is coming, declares the Lord,
>   when I will make a new covenant
> with the house of Israel
>   and with the house of Judah.
> ⁹It will not be like the covenant
>   I made with their forefathers
> when I took them by the hand
>   to lead them out of Egypt,
> because they did not remain faithful to my covenant,
>   and I turned away from them,
>   declares the Lord.
> ¹⁰This is the covenant I will make with the house of Israel
>   after that time, declares the Lord.
> I will put my laws in their minds
>   and write them on their hearts.
> I will be their God,
>   and they will be my people.
> ¹¹No longer will a man teach his neighbor,
>   or a man his brother, saying, 'Know the Lord,'
> because they will all know me,
>   from the least of them to the greatest.
> ¹²For I will forgive their wickedness
>   and will remember their sins no more."[c]

OCTOBER 12

¹³By calling this covenant "new," he has made the first one obsolete; and what is obsolete and aging will soon disappear.

a5 Exodus 25:40   *b8* Some manuscripts may be translated *fault and said to the people.*
c12 Jer. 31:31-34

PSALM 53

For the director of music. According to *mahalath.* ᵃ A *maskil* ᵇ of David.

T he fool says in his heart,
    "There is no God."
They are corrupt, and their ways are vile;
    there is no one who does good.

²God looks down from heaven
    on the sons of men
to see if there are any who understand,
    any who seek God.
³Everyone has turned away,
    they have together become corrupt;
there is no one who does good,
    not even one.

⁴Will the evildoers never learn—
    those who devour my people as men eat bread
    and who do not call on God?
⁵There they were, overwhelmed with dread,
    where there was nothing to dread.
God scattered the bones of those who attacked you;
    you put them to shame, for God despised them.

⁶Oh, that salvation for Israel would come out of Zion!
    When God restores the fortunes of his people,
    let Jacob rejoice and Israel be glad!

ᵃTitle: Probably a musical term   ᵇTitle: Probably a literary or musical term

OCTOBER 12

The Grace That Is Suitable and Sufficient

"This is the covenant I will make . . . declares the Lord. . . . I will be their God, and they will be my people" (Hebrews 8:10).

In the case of God and man, once the price was paid by the perfect Mediator, the foundation was laid for a lasting reconciliation.

Salvation thus involves more than forgiveness of sins; it also brings the sinner into a privileged relationship with God.

It's a remarkable relationship all believers in Christ enjoy, as Matthew Henry explains.

Walk With Matthew Henry

"God covenants with them [believers] to take them into a near and very honorable relation to himself. He will be to them a God: that is, he will be all to them, and do all for them, that God can be and do. Nothing more can be said in a thousand volumes than is comprehended in these few words: 'I will be their God.'

"They shall be to him a people, to love, honor, and obey him; complying with his cautions, conforming to his commands, copying his example.

"Those who have the true God for their God must and will do this, for they are bound to do so as their part of the contract. And God will enable them to do it, as an evidence that he is their God and that they are his people.

"It is God himself who first establishes the relationship, and then fills it up with grace suitable and sufficient, and helps them in their measure to fill it up with love and duty."

Walk Closer to God

"Anyone who comes to him [God] must believe that he exists" (Hebrews 11:6). But more than that, the God who exists is your God— filling up your life with "grace suitable and sufficient."

In exchange he offers you the matchless privilege of being called his people . . . called to love him, honor him, obey him. Called to fill up your life with love and duty.

Put it all together, and who but a Christian could declare, "I belong to him, and he belongs to me!"

OCTOBER 13

📖 Walk in the Word
Hebrews 9:1–10

After briefly describing the function of the priests in the Old Testament, the writer insists that they were only provisional, paving the way for the coming of Jesus Christ in the new covenant.

Worship in the Earthly Tabernacle

9 Now the first covenant had regulations for worship and also an earthly sanctuary. ²A tabernacle was set up. In its first room were the lampstand, the table and the consecrated bread; this was called the Holy Place. ³Behind the second curtain was a room called the Most Holy Place, ⁴which had the golden altar of incense and the gold-covered ark of the covenant. This ark contained the gold jar of manna, Aaron's staff that had budded, and the stone tablets of the covenant. ⁵Above the ark were the cherubim of the Glory, overshadowing the atonement cover.ᵃ But we cannot discuss these things in detail now.

⁶When everything had been arranged like this, the priests entered regularly into the outer room to carry on their ministry. ⁷But only the high priest entered the inner room, and that only once a year, and never without blood, which he offered for himself and for the sins the people had committed in ignorance. ⁸The Holy Spirit was showing by this that the way into the Most Holy Place had not yet been disclosed as long as the first tabernacle was still standing. ⁹This is an illustration for the present time, indicating that the gifts and sacrifices being offered were not able to clear the conscience of the worshiper. ¹⁰They are only a matter of food and drink and various ceremonial washings—external regulations applying until the time of the new order.

ᵃ5 Traditionally *the mercy seat*

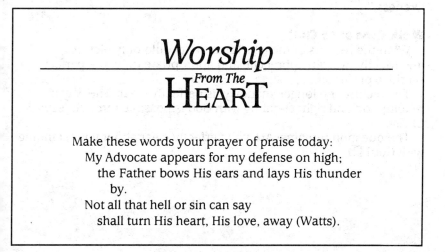

Worship From The HEART

Make these words your prayer of praise today:
My Advocate appears for my defense on high;
    the Father bows His ears and lays His thunder
    by.
Not all that hell or sin can say
    shall turn His heart, His love, away (Watts).

OCTOBER 13

When That Which Is Perfect Is Come . . .

When Christ came as high priest of the good things that are already here, he . . . entered the Most Holy Place once for all by his own blood, having obtained eternal redemption (Hebrews 9:11–12).

Which would you prefer: Seeing the shadow of the Eiffel Tower or the Tower itself?

Seeing a famous person's picture or meeting that celebrity in person? In each case, the former hints at what only the latter can reveal.

The Old Testament system of sacrifices was an imperfect forerunner of the perfect New Testament sacrifice to come.

B.F. Westcott probes the meaning behind both the old and new sacrifices.

Walk With B.F. Westcott

"The levitical sacrifices expressed the ideas of atonement and fellowship resting upon the idea of a covenant.

"In vivid symbols and outward forms they showed how human beings might yet reach the destiny for which they were created.

"The self-sacrifice of Christ upon the cross fulfilled absolutely all that was thus shadowed forth. That sacrifice had a spiritual, eternal, and universal validity, where the 'shadow' had been necessarily external and confined.

"And when we look back over the facts of Christ's sacrifice brought forward in the epistle, we notice two series of blessings gained for mankind by him: the one being the restoration of man's right relation to God which has been violated by sin, and the other fulfilling the purpose of creation, which is the attainment by mankind of the divine likeness."

Walk Closer to God

What the readers of the Old Testament could only picture imperfectly, we can appreciate and appropriate fully: the perfect sacrifice of Christ.

The picture, no longer shadowy, is perfectly clear. The way of redemption and right standing with God is possible through Jesus Christ.

The question remains: Are you perfectly clear about your standing with God? ◖◗

October 14

Walk in the Word
Hebrews 9:11–28

Since Christ shed his own blood and brought it before his Father in heaven, the writer to the Hebrews assures us that our salvation has been taken care of once and for all.

The Blood of Christ

[11]When Christ came as high priest of the good things that are already here,[a] he went through the greater and more perfect tabernacle that is not man-made, that is to say, not a part of this creation. [12]He did not enter by means of the blood of goats and calves; but he entered the Most Holy Place once for all by his own blood, having obtained eternal redemption. [13]The blood of goats and bulls and the ashes of a heifer sprinkled on those who are ceremonially unclean sanctify them so that they are outwardly clean. [14]How much more, then, will the blood of Christ, who through the eternal Spirit offered himself unblemished to God, cleanse our consciences from acts that lead to death,[b] so that we may serve the living God!

[15]For this reason Christ is the mediator of a new covenant, that those who are called may receive the promised eternal inheritance — now that he has died as a ransom to set them free from the sins committed under the first covenant.

[16]In the case of a will,[c] it is necessary to prove the death of the one who made it, [17]because a will is in force only when somebody has died; it never takes effect while the one who made it is living. [18]This is why even the first covenant was not put into effect without blood. [19]When Moses had proclaimed every commandment of the law to all the people, he took the blood of calves, together with water, scarlet wool and branches of hyssop, and sprinkled the scroll and all the people. [20]He said, "This is the blood of the covenant, which God has commanded you to keep."[d] [21]In the same way, he sprinkled with the blood both the tabernacle and everything used in its ceremonies. [22]In fact, the law requires that nearly everything be cleansed with blood, and without the shedding of blood there is no forgiveness.

[23]It was necessary, then, for the copies of the heavenly things to be purified with these sacrifices, but the heavenly things themselves with better sacrifices than these. [24]For Christ did not enter a man-made sanctuary that was only a copy of the true one; he entered heaven itself, now to appear for us in God's presence. [25]Nor did he enter heaven to offer himself again and again, the way the high priest enters the Most Holy Place every year with blood that is not his own. [26]Then Christ would have had to suffer many times since the creation of the world. But now he has appeared once for all at the end of the ages to do away with sin by the sacrifice of himself. [27]Just as man is destined to die once, and after that

775

OCTOBER 14

to face judgment, ²⁸so Christ was sacrificed once to take away the sins of many people; and he will appear a second time, not to bear sin, but to bring salvation to those who are waiting for him.

a11 Some early manuscripts *are to come*   *b14* Or *from useless rituals*   *c16* Same Greek word as *covenant*; also in verse 17   *d20* Exodus 24:8

PSALM 98

A psalm.

Sing to the LORD a new song,
  for he has done marvelous things;
his right hand and his holy arm
  have worked salvation for him.
²The LORD has made his salvation known
  and revealed his righteousness to the nations.
³He has remembered his love
  and his faithfulness to the house of Israel;
all the ends of the earth have seen
  the salvation of our God.

⁴Shout for joy to the LORD, all the earth,
  burst into jubilant song with music;
⁵make music to the LORD with the harp,
  with the harp and the sound of singing,
⁶with trumpets and the blast of the ram's horn—
  shout for joy before the LORD, the King.

⁷Let the sea resound, and everything in it,
  the world, and all who live in it.
⁸Let the rivers clap their hands,
  let the mountains sing together for joy;
⁹let them sing before the LORD,
  for he comes to judge the earth.
He will judge the world in righteousness
  and the peoples with equity.

No Atonement Apart From the Blood

And without the shedding of blood there is no forgiveness (Hebrews 9:22).

Many a person with oxygen to breathe and food to consume has died nonetheless. The problem: insufficient blood to transport oxygen and nutrients to the rest of the body. In short: no blood, no life.

Do you see a spiritual analogy in that?

Take away the blood of Christ, and there can be no spiritual life. For sins to be covered, blood must be spilled . . . and that requirement was met by Jesus on the cross.

Charles Spurgeon paints a picture in words of that life-giving sacrifice.

Walk With Charles Spurgeon

"By no means can sin be pardoned without atonement. Clearly, there is no hope for me outside of Christ; for there is no other blood-shedding which is worth a thought as an atonement for sin.

"All people are on a level as to their need of him. Even if we are moral, generous, amiable, or patriotic, the rule will not be altered to make an exception for us. It will yield to nothing less potent than the blood of him whom God has set forth as a satisfaction for sin.

"Persons of merely formal religion cannot understand how we can rejoice that all our sins are forgiven for Christ's sake. Their works, prayers, and ceremonies give them very poor comfort.

"And well may they be uneasy, for they are neglecting the one great salvation, and are endeavoring to get forgiveness without blood."

Walk Closer to God

Make these words of hymnist William Cowper the basis for your prayer of praise today:

There is a fountain filled with blood,
    Drawn from Immanuel's veins;
And sinners, plunged beneath that flood,
    Lose all their guilty stains.
Dear dying Lamb, Thy precious blood
    Shall never lose its power,
Till all the ransomed church of God
    Be saved, to sin no more.

OCTOBER 15

📖 Walk in the Word
Hebrews 10:1–18

The section on the relationship of the old covenant to the new covenant closes by showing how much greater the sacrifice of Christ is than the sacrifices commanded in the Old Testament.

Christ's Sacrifice Once for All

10 The law is only a shadow of the good things that are coming — not the realities themselves. For this reason it can never, by the same sacrifices repeated endlessly year after year, make perfect those who draw near to worship. ²If it could, would they not have stopped being offered? For the worshipers would have been cleansed once for all, and would no longer have felt guilty for their sins. ³But those sacrifices are an annual reminder of sins, ⁴because it is impossible for the blood of bulls and goats to take away sins.

⁵Therefore, when Christ came into the world, he said:

> "Sacrifice and offering you did not desire,
>   but a body you prepared for me;
> ⁶with burnt offerings and sin offerings
>   you were not pleased.
> ⁷Then I said, 'Here I am — it is written about me in the
>   scroll —
>   I have come to do your will, O God.' "ᵃ

⁸First he said, "Sacrifices and offerings, burnt offerings and sin offerings you did not desire, nor were you pleased with them" (although the law required them to be made). ⁹Then he said, "Here I am, I have come to do your will." He sets aside the first to establish the second. ¹⁰And by that will, we have been made holy through the sacrifice of the body of Jesus Christ once for all.

¹¹Day after day every priest stands and performs his religious duties; again and again he offers the same sacrifices, which can never take away sins. ¹²But when this priest had offered for all time one sacrifice for sins, he sat down at the right hand of God. ¹³Since that time he waits for his enemies to be made his footstool, ¹⁴because by one sacrifice he has made perfect forever those who are being made holy.

¹⁵The Holy Spirit also testifies to us about this. First he says:

> ¹⁶"This is the covenant I will make with them
>   after that time, says the Lord.
> I will put my laws in their hearts,
>   and I will write them on their minds."ᵇ

¹⁷Then he adds:

OCTOBER 15

> "Their sins and lawless acts
>   I will remember no more."[c]

[18]And where these have been forgiven, there is no longer any sacrifice for sin.

[a]7 Psalm 40:6-8 (see Septuagint)   [b]16 Jer. 31:33   [c]17 Jer. 31:34

PSALM 119

ה He

Teach me, O LORD, to follow your decrees;
  then I will keep them to the end.
[34]Give me understanding, and I will keep your law
  and obey it with all my heart.
[35]Direct me in the path of your commands,
  for there I find delight.
[36]Turn my heart toward your statutes
  and not toward selfish gain.
[37]Turn my eyes away from worthless things;
  preserve my life according to your word.[a]
[38]Fulfill your promise to your servant,
  so that you may be feared.
[39]Take away the disgrace I dread,
  for your laws are good.
[40]How I long for your precepts!
  Preserve my life in your righteousness.

[a]37 Two manuscripts of the Masoretic Text and Dead Sea Scrolls; most manuscripts of the Masoretic Text *life in your way*

OCTOBER 15

The Daily Delight of Obedience

"I will put my laws in their hearts, and I will write them on their minds" (Hebrews 10:16).

Which motivates you more: what you are commanded to do or what you desire to do?

Often the two are in conflict. But in Christ, God changes all that. Obeying God's laws is no longer a chore to be endured; rather, it becomes your daily delight.

Ambitions and appetites change when the king rules the human heart, as John Henry Jowett explains.

Walk With John Henry Jowett

"Everything depends on where we carry the law of the Lord. If it rests only in the memory, any little care may snatch it away. A thought is never secure until it has passed from the mind into the heart, and has become a desire, an aspiration, a passion.

"When God's law is taken into the heart, it is no longer merely remembered; it is loved. The strength of the heart is wrapped about it, and no passing bother can carry it away. And this is where the Lord is willing to put his laws. He wants to put them among our loves.

"And the wonderful thing is this: When laws are put among loves, they change their form, and his statutes become our songs. Laws that are loved are no longer dreadful policemen, but compassionate friends. And so shall it be unto all of us when we love the law of the Lord."

Walk Closer to God

Here are some words to "sweeten" your taste for God's Word:
The law of the LORD is perfect,
reviving the soul.
The statutes of the LORD are trustworthy,
making wise the simple.
The precepts of the LORD are right,
giving joy to the heart.
The commands of the LORD are radiant,
giving light to the eyes . . .
The ordinances of the LORD are sure
and altogether righteous . . .
. . . sweeter than honey,
than honey from the comb (Psalm 19:7–10).
God's Word: It tastes good. And it is good . . . for you!

OCTOBER 16

📖 Walk in the Word
Hebrews 10:19–39

The Hebrew Christians had been facing a time of intense persecution; consequently, the writer of this letter strongly urges them to persevere.

A Call to Persevere

¹⁹Therefore, brothers, since we have confidence to enter the Most Holy Place by the blood of Jesus, ²⁰by a new and living way opened for us through the curtain, that is, his body, ²¹and since we have a great priest over the house of God, ²²let us draw near to God with a sincere heart in full assurance of faith, having our hearts sprinkled to cleanse us from a guilty conscience and having our bodies washed with pure water. ²³Let us hold unswervingly to the hope we profess, for he who promised is faithful. ²⁴And let us consider how we may spur one another on toward love and good deeds. ²⁵Let us not give up meeting together, as some are in the habit of doing, but let us encourage one another—and all the more as you see the Day approaching.

²⁶If we deliberately keep on sinning after we have received the knowledge of the truth, no sacrifice for sins is left, ²⁷but only a fearful expectation of judgment and of raging fire that will consume the enemies of God. ²⁸Anyone who rejected the law of Moses died without mercy on the testimony of two or three witnesses. ²⁹How much more severely do you think a man deserves to be punished who has trampled the Son of God under foot, who has treated as an unholy thing the blood of the covenant that sanctified him, and who has insulted the Spirit of grace? ³⁰For we know him who said, "It is mine to avenge; I will repay,"ᵃ and again, "The Lord will judge his people."ᵇ ³¹It is a dreadful thing to fall into the hands of the living God.

³²Remember those earlier days after you had received the light, when you stood your ground in a great contest in the face of suffering. ³³Sometimes you were publicly exposed to insult and persecution; at other times you stood side by side with those who were so treated. ³⁴You sympathized with those in prison and joyfully accepted the confiscation of your property, because you knew that you yourselves had better and lasting possessions.

³⁵So do not throw away your confidence; it will be richly rewarded. ³⁶You need to persevere so that when you have done the will of God, you will receive what he has promised. ³⁷For in just a very little while,

"He who is coming will come and will not delay.
³⁸ But my righteous oneᶜ will live by faith.
And if he shrinks back,
I will not be pleased with him."ᵈ

³⁹But we are not of those who shrink back and are destroyed, but of those who believe and are saved.

ᵃ30 Deut. 32:35   ᵇ30 Deut. 32:36; Psalm 135:14   ᶜ38 One early manuscript *But the righteous*   ᵈ38 Hab. 2:3,4

OCTOBER 16

Warning Signs of Danger

So do not throw away your confidence; it will be richly rewarded (Hebrews 10:35).

The altitude, unpredictable weather and rugged terrain all combine to make mountain climbing a harrowing adventure. If an unsuspecting, poorly equipped hiker gets caught by a sudden storm, he or she may be in serious danger.

In life, as in mountain climbing, signposts guide the inexperienced. And it's often the hidden, unexpected dangers that pose the greatest threat to your soul's survival. Charles Hodge points to the signs that warn you of spiritual danger.

Walk With Charles Hodge

"One great and fatal offense under the Old Testament was apostasy from the worship of Jehovah. This was punishable by death. It admitted of no repentance.

"The author strives to impress upon his readers that their danger was the same, their crime if they forsook Christ would be greater, and their punishment far more severe. It was greater, as much as Christ was greater than Moses, and his blood more sacred than that of bulls and goats.

"We still need this caution and exhortation. Our danger from within is an evil heart, not to be despised, not to be neglected, but strenuously watched. Our danger also comes from the influence of the world, its avocations, its amusements, its spirit, its opinions leading to indifference, tolerance of unbelief, and unfaithfulness."

Walk Closer to God

Affluence . . . deceptive teaching . . . improper thought life . . . worldly pleasures . . . immorality . . . just plain laziness—each can tempt you to "throw away your confidence" by chipping away at your faith. The pathway to destruction isn't necessarily taken with giant steps. More often than not, it's little shuffles.

But God delights in those who diligently guard their faith, standing firmly in the confidence of his Word and pressing on toward the goal of Christlikeness—regardless of their earthly circumstances or tribulations. ◖◗

OCTOBER 17

📖 Walk in the Word
Hebrews 11:1–16

In order to encourage the Hebrew Christians to persevere in their faith, the writer of this letter recalls for them some of the great heroes in the Old Testament who remained steadfast in their faith in spite of difficult circumstances.

By Faith

11 Now faith is being sure of what we hope for and certain of what we do not see. ²This is what the ancients were commended for.

³By faith we understand that the universe was formed at God's command, so that what is seen was not made out of what was visible.

⁴By faith Abel offered God a better sacrifice than Cain did. By faith he was commended as a righteous man, when God spoke well of his offerings. And by faith he still speaks, even though he is dead.

⁵By faith Enoch was taken from this life, so that he did not experience death; he could not be found, because God had taken him away. For before he was taken, he was commended as one who pleased God. ⁶And without faith it is impossible to please God, because anyone who comes to him must believe that he exists and that he rewards those who earnestly seek him.

⁷By faith Noah, when warned about things not yet seen, in holy fear built an ark to save his family. By his faith he condemned the world and became heir of the righteousness that comes by faith.

⁸By faith Abraham, when called to go to a place he would later receive as his inheritance, obeyed and went, even though he did not know where he was going. ⁹By faith he made his home in the promised land like a stranger in a foreign country; he lived in tents, as did Isaac and Jacob, who were heirs with him of the same promise. ¹⁰For he was looking forward to the city with foundations, whose architect and builder is God.

¹¹By faith Abraham, even though he was past age — and Sarah herself was barren — was enabled to become a father because he*ᵃ* considered him faithful who had made the promise. ¹²And so from this one man, and he as good as dead, came descendants as numerous as the stars in the sky and as countless as the sand on the seashore.

¹³All these people were still living by faith when they died. They did not receive the things promised; they only saw them and welcomed them from a distance. And they admitted that they were aliens and strangers on earth. ¹⁴People who say such things show that they are looking for a country of their own. ¹⁵If they had been thinking of the country they had left, they would have had opportunity to return. ¹⁶Instead, they were longing for a better country — a heavenly one. Therefore God is not ashamed to be called their God, for he has prepared a city for them.

ᵃ11 Or By faith even Sarah, who was past age, was enabled to bear children because she

OCTOBER 17

Faith: Seeing With the Eyes of the Soul

Now faith is being sure of what we hope for and certain of what we do not see (Hebrews 11:1).

Contrary to popular belief, faith is not . . . a blind leap in the dark . . . an attempt to believe something regardless of the evidence . . . a hope and a prayer.

Faith. How could something that appears so uncertain be the basis for something the Scripture communicates as certain? Either the world is wrong, or the Bible is wrong. Matthew Henry explores the Biblical definition of faith.

Walk with Matthew Henry

"Here we have a twofold definition of faith. First, it 'is being sure of what we hope for.'

"Faith and hope go together. Faith is a firm persuasion and expectation that God will perform all that he has promised to us in Christ. And this persuasion is so strong that it gives the soul a kind of possession and present fruition of those things, gives them a subsistence in the soul by the firstfruits and foretastes of them, so that believers in the exercise of faith are filled with joy unspeakable and full of glory.

"Second, it is being 'certain of what we do not see.' Faith demonstrates to the eye of the mind the reality of those things that cannot be discerned by the eye of the body. It is the firm assent of the soul to the divine revelation and every part of it, and sets to its seal that God is true. It is a full approval of all that God has revealed as holy, just, and good; and so it is designed to serve the believer instead of sight, and to be to the soul all that the senses are to the body."

Walk Closer to God

In the physical realm, one can say, "I'll believe it when I see it!"

But on the spiritual level, one must turn that idea around and say, "I'll see it when I believe it!"

For example, Noah and Abraham—along with many others—are enshrined in God's "Hall of Faith"—Hebrews 11. They saw God at work in their lives—when they believed.

Their spiritual vision was 20/20. How's yours? ❏

OCTOBER 18

📖 Walk in the Word
Hebrews 11:17–40

The writer continues his description of famous people in the Old Testament who exercised victorious faith.

---

¹⁷By faith Abraham, when God tested him, offered Isaac as a sacrifice. He who had received the promises was about to sacrifice his one and only son, ¹⁸even though God had said to him, "It is through Isaac that your offspring*a* will be reckoned."*b* ¹⁹Abraham reasoned that God could raise the dead, and figuratively speaking, he did receive Isaac back from death.

²⁰By faith Isaac blessed Jacob and Esau in regard to their future.

²¹By faith Jacob, when he was dying, blessed each of Joseph's sons, and worshiped as he leaned on the top of his staff.

²²By faith Joseph, when his end was near, spoke about the exodus of the Israelites from Egypt and gave instructions about his bones.

²³By faith Moses' parents hid him for three months after he was born, because they saw he was no ordinary child, and they were not afraid of the king's edict.

²⁴By faith Moses, when he had grown up, refused to be known as the son of Pharaoh's daughter. ²⁵He chose to be mistreated along with the people of God rather than to enjoy the pleasures of sin for a short time. ²⁶He regarded disgrace for the sake of Christ as of greater value than the treasures of Egypt, because he was looking ahead to his reward. ²⁷By faith he left Egypt, not fearing the king's anger; he persevered because he saw him who is invisible. ²⁸By faith he kept the Passover and the sprinkling of blood, so that the destroyer of the firstborn would not touch the firstborn of Israel.

²⁹By faith the people passed through the Red Sea*c* as on dry land; but when the Egyptians tried to do so, they were drowned.

³⁰By faith the walls of Jericho fell, after the people had marched around them for seven days.

³¹By faith the prostitute Rahab, because she welcomed the spies, was not killed with those who were disobedient.*d*

³²And what more shall I say? I do not have time to tell about Gideon, Barak, Samson, Jephthah, David, Samuel and the prophets, ³³who through faith conquered kingdoms, administered justice, and gained what was promised; who shut the mouths of lions, ³⁴quenched the fury of the flames, and escaped the edge of the sword; whose weakness was turned to strength; and who became powerful in battle and routed foreign armies. ³⁵Women received back their dead, raised to life again. Others were tortured and refused to be released, so that they might gain a better resurrection. ³⁶Some faced jeers and flogging, while still others were chained and put in prison. ³⁷They were stoned*e*; they were sawed in two; they were put to death by the sword. They went about in sheepskins and goatskins, destitute, persecuted and mistreated— ³⁸the world was not worthy of them. They wandered in deserts and mountains, and in caves and holes in the ground.

OCTOBER 18

³⁹These were all commended for their faith, yet none of them received what had been promised. ⁴⁰God had planned something better for us so that only together with us would they be made perfect.

a18 Greek *seed*   *b18* Gen. 21:12   *c29* That is, Sea of Reeds   *d31* Or *unbelieving*
e37 Some early manuscripts *stoned; they were put to the test;*

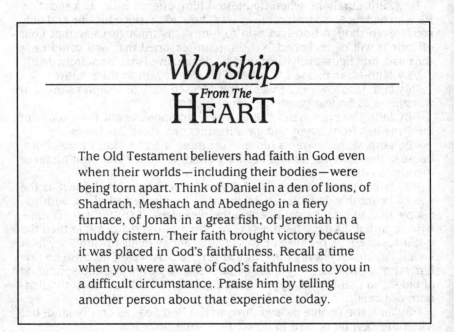

Worship
From The
HEART

The Old Testament believers had faith in God even when their worlds—including their bodies—were being torn apart. Think of Daniel in a den of lions, of Shadrach, Meshach and Abednego in a fiery furnace, of Jonah in a great fish, of Jeremiah in a muddy cistern. Their faith brought victory because it was placed in God's faithfulness. Recall a time when you were aware of God's faithfulness to you in a difficult circumstance. Praise him by telling another person about that experience today.

The Persecution That Reveals the Power of God

They were stoned . . . put to death by the sword . . . destitute, persecuted and mistreated—the world was not worthy of them. . . . These were all commended for their faith (Hebrews 11:37–39).

Through the centuries, heroes of the church have announced allegiance to Christ and have refused to be moved—even in the face of death. One such hero is Polycarp, a disciple of the apostle John and an early church leader whose life ended when he refused to betray his Lord.

Asked one last time to disavow his Christ, the old man replied: "Eighty and six years have I served him, and he has done me no wrong. How can I speak evil of my King who saved me?"

Here is his martyr's prayer, as recorded by the historian Eusebius.

Walk With Polycarp

"Father of your beloved and blessed Son Jesus Christ, through whom we have received the knowledge of you, I bless you that you have counted me worthy of this day and hour, that I might be in the number of the martyrs.

"Among these may I be received before you today in a rich and acceptable sacrifice, as you have beforehand prepared and revealed.

"Wherefore I also praise you also for everything; I bless you; I glorify you, through the eternal High Priest Jesus Christ, your beloved Son, through whom, with him, in the Holy Spirit, be glory unto you both now and for the ages to come. Amen."

Eusebius adds: "When he had offered up his amen and had finished his prayer, the firemen lighted the fire."

Walk Closer to God

Killing believers has never been an effective way to kill the church. Instead, others see that a faith worth dying for must also be a faith worth having. Persecution merely reveals salvation at work, causing heroes of the faith to rise to the occasion.

Faith in God may not give you a long life—on this earth. But it will give you a powerful life . . . a persuasive life . . . a heroic life—in a day when heroes are in short supply. ◖

OCTOBER 19

📖 Walk in the Word
Hebrews 12:1–13

In order to help Christians persevere in the faith, the writer to the Hebrews urges us to look to the example of Jesus and to remember that God our Father loves us as his children.

God Disciplines His Sons

12 Therefore, since we are surrounded by such a great cloud of witnesses, let us throw off everything that hinders and the sin that so easily entangles, and let us run with perseverance the race marked out for us. ²Let us fix our eyes on Jesus, the author and perfecter of our faith, who for the joy set before him endured the cross, scorning its shame, and sat down at the right hand of the throne of God. ³Consider him who endured such opposition from sinful men, so that you will not grow weary and lose heart.

⁴In your struggle against sin, you have not yet resisted to the point of shedding your blood. ⁵And you have forgotten that word of encouragement that addresses you as sons:

"My son, do not make light of the Lord's discipline,
and do not lose heart when he rebukes you,
⁶because the Lord disciplines those he loves,
and he punishes everyone he accepts as a son."[a]

⁷Endure hardship as discipline; God is treating you as sons. For what son is not disciplined by his father? ⁸If you are not disciplined (and everyone undergoes discipline), then you are illegitimate children and not true sons. ⁹Moreover, we have all had human fathers who disciplined us and we respected them for it. How much more should we submit to the Father of our spirits and live! ¹⁰Our fathers disciplined us for a little while as they thought best; but God disciplines us for our good, that we may share in his holiness. ¹¹No discipline seems pleasant at the time, but painful. Later on, however, it produces a harvest of righteousness and peace for those who have been trained by it.

¹²Therefore, strengthen your feeble arms and weak knees. ¹³"Make level paths for your feet,"[b] so that the lame may not be disabled, but rather healed.

[a]6 Prov. 3:11,12   [b]13 Prov. 4:26

God's Opinion Is the Only One That Really Matters

In your struggle against sin, you have not yet resisted to the point of shedding your blood (Hebrews 12:4).

You are in a strange city, far from home, friends and family, when suddenly you're tempted to do something wrong. Is your first thought, "What would others think?" Or is it, "What would God think?"

God's opinion is the one that really matters, and it's never right to do wrong. But have you ever considered why you do what you do when faced with temptation?

It may not be for the best of reasons, as Abraham Kuyper makes painfully clear.

Walk With Abraham Kuyper

"Not every resistance against sin can be called 'struggle against sin.' Everything here hinges upon what it is that moves you to oppose this or that sin.

"One person will avoid a sin from concern for his health. Another is on his guard lest, if his sin became known, it would injure his good name. A third resists a temptation because yielding to it would ruin him financially. A fourth puts a mark against a particular sin because in his narrow circle of life it is sharply condemned.

"And in this way and by all sorts of persons this or that sin is put under the ban for reasons that have nothing to do with real striving against sin.

"With not a few there is even no mention of a conscious motive, and all their opposition to this or that sin springs from a certain moral instinct, from the judgment of public opinion, or from a certain impulse to be decent.

"A certain sin may decrease, but far more because it is now looked upon as coarse and impolite than from fear of the Holy God!"

Walk Closer to God

Fear of people may keep you from certain sins; but fear of God will make you wary of all sin.

The fear of God is more than an emotional response; it is an attitude of life that seeks to please him in every action—both public and private.

Which is only fitting when you consider your calling: "Be holy, because I am holy" (1 Peter 1:16). ⟨⟩

OCTOBER 20

📖 Walk in the Word
Hebrews 12:14–29

Since Christians have such a wonderful heavenly inheritance awaiting us, the writer to the Hebrews strongly urges us to persevere faithfully, at the same time warning us about the awesome power of God.

Warning Against Refusing God

¹⁴Make every effort to live in peace with all men and to be holy; without holiness no one will see the Lord. ¹⁵See to it that no one misses the grace of God and that no bitter root grows up to cause trouble and defile many. ¹⁶See that no one is sexually immoral, or is godless like Esau, who for a single meal sold his inheritance rights as the oldest son. ¹⁷Afterward, as you know, when he wanted to inherit this blessing, he was rejected. He could bring about no change of mind, though he sought the blessing with tears.

¹⁸You have not come to a mountain that can be touched and that is burning with fire; to darkness, gloom and storm; ¹⁹to a trumpet blast or to such a voice speaking words that those who heard it begged that no further word be spoken to them, ²⁰because they could not bear what was commanded: "If even an animal touches the mountain, it must be stoned."ᵃ ²¹The sight was so terrifying that Moses said, "I am trembling with fear."ᵇ

²²But you have come to Mount Zion, to the heavenly Jerusalem, the city of the living God. You have come to thousands upon thousands of angels in joyful assembly, ²³to the church of the firstborn, whose names are written in heaven. You have come to God, the judge of all men, to the spirits of righteous men made perfect, ²⁴to Jesus the mediator of a new covenant, and to the sprinkled blood that speaks a better word than the blood of Abel.

²⁵See to it that you do not refuse him who speaks. If they did not escape when they refused him who warned them on earth, how much less will we, if we turn away from him who warns us from heaven? ²⁶At that time his voice shook the earth, but now he has promised, "Once more I will shake not only the earth but also the heavens."ᶜ ²⁷The words "once more" indicate the removing of what can be shaken — that is, created things — so that what cannot be shaken may remain.

²⁸Therefore, since we are receiving a kingdom that cannot be shaken, let us be thankful, and so worship God acceptably with reverence and awe, ²⁹for our "God is a consuming fire."ᵈ

---

a20 Exodus 19:12,13   *b21* Deut. 9:19   *c26* Haggai 2:6   *d29* Deut. 4:24

Seeing Sin From God's Perspective

Worship God . . . with reverence and awe, for our "God is a consuming fire" (Hebrews 12:28–29).

Sinful humans usually get angry for all the wrong reasons. The holy God is angry for all the right reasons.

"The wrath of God is being revealed from heaven against all the godlessness and wickedness of men" (Romans 1:18).

God hates sin and is intolerant of anyone or anything that would compete for the glory that rightly belongs to him.

A.W. Pink offers these reasons why. Remembering God's righteous wrath will aid you in your own struggle against sin.

Walk With A.W. Pink

"The wrath of God is a perfection of the divine character on which we need to meditate frequently.

"First, that our hearts may be impressed by God's hatred of sin. We are ever prone to regard sin lightly, to gloss over its hideousness, to make excuses for it. But the more we study and ponder God's abhorrence of sin and his frightful vengeance upon it, the more likely we are to realize its heinousness.

"Second, to beget a true fear in our souls for God. We cannot serve him acceptably unless there is deep reverence for his majesty and godly fear of his righteous anger. These are best promoted by frequently calling to mind that our God is a consuming fire.

"Third, to draw out our soul in fervent praise to Jesus Christ for having delivered us from the wrath to come. In truth, our readiness or our reluctance to meditate upon the wrath of God becomes a test of how our hearts stand toward him."

Walk Closer to God

"Father, I confess that I often fail to remember your consuming hatred of sin and too often forget the one on whom your wrath was poured.

"Teach me to be angry at the things that anger you. Then will I sense the burning light of your holiness and the true depth of your love for me. Amen." 〇

FREDERICK B. MEYER

(1847–1929) HE PRACTICED WHAT HE PREACHED

A Redirected Ministry

Anyone familiar with the life of F. B. Meyer may wonder how he ever found time to write. Preacher, pastor, social reformer, commentator, writer of more than fifty volumes— Meyer wore many hats during his eighty-two years of service to God.

Born in 1847 to a prosperous London family, Frederick B. Meyer grew up in a home where both spiritual and physical needs were amply met. He began to learn the Bible at an early age and practiced "preaching" before the appreciative audience of his brothers and sisters. It is not surprising that he decided to enter the ministry. Before he did so, however, he followed the advice of his pastor by working two years in the business world. That experience proved a base for reaching businesssmen in his later years.

Upon graduation, Meyer entered the pastorate. In 1874 Dwight L. Moody, the prominent American evangelist, preached a series of messages in Meyer's church. That event transformed the young preacher's life and redirected the course of his ministry to include starting a prison ministry to thousands of inmates, beginning job brigades for those out of work, organizing opposition to prostitution, and forming groups to help unwed mothers, to improve working conditions, and to aid the poor. All this came from a man who never experienced personally the type of hardships he sought to alleviate.

He could accomplish so much because he involved others in these many ministries, freeing him up to pursue other unmet needs. In all his activites he knew that Jesus Christ was the source of all help and strength—a source adequate to meet the needs of every hurting individual, both physically and spiritually. This source is adequate for your own personal needs too.

A LESSON FROM THE LIFE OF FREDERICK B. MEYER

Even though I am busy, my relationship with God deserves top priority above all other demands on my time.

OCTOBER 21

📖 Walk in the Word
Hebrews 13

The writer to the Hebrews concludes his lengthy letter with some practical exhortations about living as Christians in the world, reminding believers that God promises never to forsake those who are faithful to him.

Concluding Exhortations

13 Keep on loving each other as brothers. ²Do not forget to entertain strangers, for by so doing some people have entertained angels without knowing it. ³Remember those in prison as if you were their fellow prisoners, and those who are mistreated as if you yourselves were suffering.

⁴Marriage should be honored by all, and the marriage bed kept pure, for God will judge the adulterer and all the sexually immoral. ⁵Keep your lives free from the love of money and be content with what you have, because God has said,

> "Never will I leave you;
> never will I forsake you."[a]

⁶So we say with confidence,

> "The Lord is my helper; I will not be afraid.
> What can man do to me?"[b]

⁷Remember your leaders, who spoke the word of God to you. Consider the outcome of their way of life and imitate their faith. ⁸Jesus Christ is the same yesterday and today and forever.

⁹Do not be carried away by all kinds of strange teachings. It is good for our hearts to be strengthened by grace, not by ceremonial foods, which are of no value to those who eat them. ¹⁰We have an altar from which those who minister at the tabernacle have no right to eat.

¹¹The high priest carries the blood of animals into the Most Holy Place as a sin offering, but the bodies are burned outside the camp. ¹²And so Jesus also suffered outside the city gate to make the people holy through his own blood. ¹³Let us, then, go to him outside the camp, bearing the disgrace he bore. ¹⁴For here we do not have an enduring city, but we are looking for the city that is to come.

¹⁵Through Jesus, therefore, let us continually offer to God a sacrifice of praise—the fruit of lips that confess his name. ¹⁶And do not forget to do good and to share with others, for with such sacrifices God is pleased.

¹⁷Obey your leaders and submit to their authority. They keep watch over you as men who must give an account. Obey them so that their work will be a joy, not a burden, for that would be of no advantage to you.

¹⁸Pray for us. We are sure that we have a clear conscience and desire to live honorably in every way. ¹⁹I particularly urge you to pray so that I may be restored to you soon.

²⁰May the God of peace, who through the blood of the eternal covenant brought back from the dead our Lord Jesus, that great Shepherd of the

OCTOBER 21

sheep, [21]equip you with everything good for doing his will, and may he work in us what is pleasing to him, through Jesus Christ, to whom be glory for ever and ever. Amen.

[22]Brothers, I urge you to bear with my word of exhortation, for I have written you only a short letter.

[23]I want you to know that our brother Timothy has been released. If he arrives soon, I will come with him to see you.

[24]Greet all your leaders and all God's people. Those from Italy send you their greetings.

[25]Grace be with you all.

[a]5 Deut. 31:6   [b]6 Psalm 118:6,7

PSALM 23

A psalm of David.

The LORD is my shepherd, I shall not be in want.
[2] He makes me lie down in green pastures,
he leads me beside quiet waters,
[3] he restores my soul.
He guides me in paths of righteousness
for his name's sake.
[4]Even though I walk
through the valley of the shadow of death,[a]
I will fear no evil,
for you are with me;
your rod and your staff,
they comfort me.

[5]You prepare a table before me
in the presence of my enemies.
You anoint my head with oil;
my cup overflows.
[6]Surely goodness and love will follow me
all the days of my life,
and I will dwell in the house of the LORD
forever.

[a]4 Or through the darkest valley

The Shepherd Who Has Promised to See Us Through

Our Lord Jesus, that great Shepherd of the sheep (Hebrews 13:20).

Sheep have never been noted for their ability to fend for themselves. They are prone to wander . . . defenseless in the face of danger . . . easily "fleeced." What the sheep lack, their shepherd must supply. This is no less true when the sheep are Christians.

The image of Christ as Shepherd is a consistent—and comforting—picture from the pages of Scripture: Psalm 23 . . . John 10 . . . Ezekiel 34.

H.A. Ironside offers these encouraging reminders about Jesus, your great Shepherd.

Walk With H.A. Ironside

"The shepherd character of our Lord Jesus suggests loving care for his own. He has given us many pictures of his Shepherd-service.

"As the *Good Shepherd* he died for us. As the *Great Shepherd* he is ever watching over us. As the *Chief Shepherd* he will gather us all about himself when he comes again.

"His promises are sufficient for every difficulty. Yet in times of stress we forget them all, and worry and fret as though we had to meet all our problems ourselves, instead of trusting in his love and wisdom to undertake for us. He has promised to see us through.

"The One to whom we have committed our souls is more than a match for all that may rise against us. He is the *unfailing shepherd*, having our best interests in view. His glory and our blessing are indissolubly linked together."

Walk Closer to God

In Ezekiel 34, God harshly rebukes Israel's shepherds for failing to do their job, and gives his own description of the Good Shepherd:

"I will tend them in a good pasture . . . I . . . will . . . have them lie down . . . I will search for the lost and bring back the strays. I will bind up the injured and strengthen the weak" (Ezekiel 34:14–16).

That's good news for sheep who are prone to wander!

OCTOBER 22

📖 Walk in the Word
James 1:1–18

James encourages his readers about living as Christians in the midst of trials and temptations.

1 James, a servant of God and of the Lord Jesus Christ,

To the twelve tribes scattered among the nations:

Greetings.

Trials and Temptations

²Consider it pure joy, my brothers, whenever you face trials of many kinds, ³because you know that the testing of your faith develops perseverance. ⁴Perseverance must finish its work so that you may be mature and complete, not lacking anything. ⁵If any of you lacks wisdom, he should ask God, who gives generously to all without finding fault, and it will be given to him. ⁶But when he asks, he must believe and not doubt, because he who doubts is like a wave of the sea, blown and tossed by the wind. ⁷That man should not think he will receive anything from the Lord; ⁸he is a double-minded man, unstable in all he does.

⁹The brother in humble circumstances ought to take pride in his high position. ¹⁰But the one who is rich should take pride in his low position, because he will pass away like a wild flower. ¹¹For the sun rises with scorching heat and withers the plant; its blossom falls and its beauty is destroyed. In the same way, the rich man will fade away even while he goes about his business.

¹²Blessed is the man who perseveres under trial, because when he has stood the test, he will receive the crown of life that God has promised to those who love him.

¹³When tempted, no one should say, "God is tempting me." For God cannot be tempted by evil, nor does he tempt anyone; ¹⁴but each one is tempted when, by his own evil desire, he is dragged away and enticed. ¹⁵Then, after desire has conceived, it gives birth to sin; and sin, when it is full-grown, gives birth to death.

¹⁶Don't be deceived, my dear brothers. ¹⁷Every good and perfect gift is from above, coming down from the Father of the heavenly lights, who does not change like shifting shadows. ¹⁸He chose to give us birth through the word of truth, that we might be a kind of firstfruits of all he created.

Learning in the Crucible of Life

Consider it pure joy, my brothers, whenever you face trials of many kinds, because you know that the testing of your faith develops perseverance (James 1:2–3).

Character qualities such as perseverance develop with use and are learned not in the classroom but in the crucible of life. As Paul said in Romans, "We also rejoice in our sufferings, because we know that suffering produces perseverance" (Romans 5:3).

God knows the best way to build character, and he has his reasons for letting experience be the best teacher, as H.A. Ironside makes clear.

Walk With H.A. Ironside

"It is no evidence of God's displeasure when his people are called upon to pass through great trials.

"If someone professes to have faith in the Lord, that person can be sure that his or her profession will be put to the test sooner or later.

"Alas, that we so frequently lose courage and become despondent in the hour of temptation, instead of realizing that it is the very time when we should look up into the Father's face with confidence, knowing that he is working out some purpose in us which could not be accomplished in any other way.

"We are called to consider it pure joy when we face trials. The trials of many kinds do not refer to our being tempted to sin, but rather as when God tempted Abraham, to the testing of our faith.

"The man or woman who learns to be submissive to whatever God permits glorifies him who orders all things according to the counsel of his own will."

Walk Closer to God

Gold subjected to high temperatures emerges much the same . . . yet different. It is still gold, but it's a gold of a brighter, purer character.

Faith in the furnace is like gold in the fire. The heat only serves to refine it, purify it, strengthen it, deepen it. It emerges with a brighter, purer quality.

As the fire grows hotter, thank God that he values your faith in him and that this test will result in "praise, glory and honor"—to him! (1 Peter 1:7).

October 23

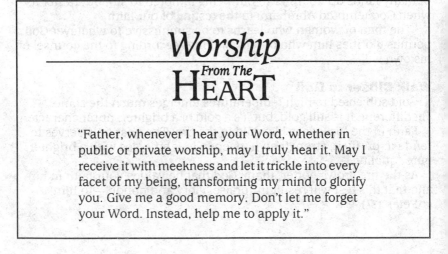 Walk in the Word
James 1:19–27

James reminds his readers that listening to the Word of God is not enough; what pleases God is that we be doers of the Word.

Listening and Doing

¹⁹My dear brothers, take note of this: Everyone should be quick to listen, slow to speak and slow to become angry, ²⁰for man's anger does not bring about the righteous life that God desires. ²¹Therefore, get rid of all moral filth and the evil that is so prevalent and humbly accept the word planted in you, which can save you.

²²Do not merely listen to the word, and so deceive yourselves. Do what it says. ²³Anyone who listens to the word but does not do what it says is like a man who looks at his face in a mirror ²⁴and, after looking at himself, goes away and immediately forgets what he looks like. ²⁵But the man who looks intently into the perfect law that gives freedom, and continues to do this, not forgetting what he has heard, but doing it—he will be blessed in what he does.

²⁶If anyone considers himself religious and yet does not keep a tight rein on his tongue, he deceives himself and his religion is worthless. ²⁷Religion that God our Father accepts as pure and faultless is this: to look after orphans and widows in their distress and to keep oneself from being polluted by the world.

Worship
From The
Heart

"Father, whenever I hear your Word, whether in public or private worship, may I truly hear it. May I receive it with meekness and let it trickle into every facet of my being, transforming my mind to glorify you. Give me a good memory. Don't let me forget your Word. Instead, help me to apply it."

The Blessing That Comes on the Path of Obedience

Do not merely listen to the word, and so deceive yourselves. Do what it says (James 1:22).

The casual reader of *The Adventures of Tom Sawyer* might conclude that the boy had a severe hearing problem, for if he had heard Aunt Polly calling, surely he would have responded . . . wouldn't he?

But the problem is that Tom did hear and respond—though not in the way his Aunt Polly would have liked!

John Henry Jowett explores James's teaching that to *hear* and not to *do* is simply not to *hear*.

Walk With John Henry Jowett

"When we hear the Word but do not do it, there has been a defect in our hearing. We may listen to the Word for mere entertainment. Or we may attach a virtue to the mere act of listening to the Word. We may assume that some magical power belongs to the mere reading of the Word. All this is perverse and delusive, for no listening is healthy which is not mentally referred to obedience.

"We are to listen with a view to obedience, with our eyes upon the very road where the obedient feet will travel. That is to say, we are to listen with purpose, as though we were ambassadors receiving instructions from the king concerning some momentous mission.

" 'Doing' makes a new thing of 'hearing.' The statute obeyed becomes a song. The commandment is found to be a beatitude. The decree discloses riches of grace. The hidden things of God are not discovered until we are treading the path of obedience."

Walk Closer to God

Someone can offer many excuses for hearing but not obeying the King's command:

"I didn't pay attention to it."

"I heard it . . . but I didn't believe it."

"I forgot."

In each case, that person lost sight of his marching orders: to represent the King by responding to his commands. Will you tune your ears—and actions—to the one who speaks words of life?

OCTOBER 24

Walk in the Word
James 2:1–13

Because of a tendency to show favoritism to the rich, James insists that we act impartially and show love to everyone alike.

Favoritism Forbidden

2 My brothers, as believers in our glorious Lord Jesus Christ, don't show favoritism. ²Suppose a man comes into your meeting wearing a gold ring and fine clothes, and a poor man in shabby clothes also comes in. ³If you show special attention to the man wearing fine clothes and say, "Here's a good seat for you," but say to the poor man, "You stand there" or "Sit on the floor by my feet," ⁴have you not discriminated among yourselves and become judges with evil thoughts?

⁵Listen, my dear brothers: Has not God chosen those who are poor in the eyes of the world to be rich in faith and to inherit the kingdom he promised those who love him? ⁶But you have insulted the poor. Is it not the rich who are exploiting you? Are they not the ones who are dragging you into court? ⁷Are they not the ones who are slandering the noble name of him to whom you belong?

⁸If you really keep the royal law found in Scripture, "Love your neighbor as yourself,"ᵃ you are doing right. ⁹But if you show favoritism, you sin and are convicted by the law as lawbreakers. ¹⁰For whoever keeps the whole law and yet stumbles at just one point is guilty of breaking all of it. ¹¹For he who said, "Do not commit adultery,"ᵇ also said, "Do not murder."ᶜ If you do not commit adultery but do commit murder, you have become a lawbreaker.

¹²Speak and act as those who are going to be judged by the law that gives freedom, ¹³because judgment without mercy will be shown to anyone who has not been merciful. Mercy triumphs over judgment!

ᵃ8 Lev. 19:18 ᵇ11 Exodus 20:14; Deut. 5:18 ᶜ11 Exodus 20:13; Deut. 5:17

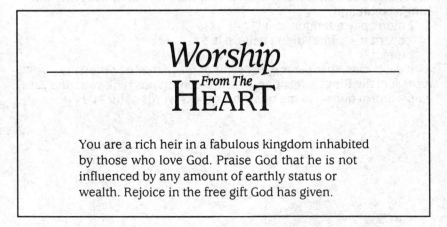

Worship
From The
HEART

You are a rich heir in a fabulous kingdom inhabited by those who love God. Praise God that he is not influenced by any amount of earthly status or wealth. Rejoice in the free gift God has given.

OCTOBER 24

Checking Good Intentions Against God's Intention

> For whoever keeps the whole law and yet stumbles at just one point is guilty of breaking all of it (James 2:10).

Obedience to God's will is not always convenient (Genesis 6:13–22). Nor is it always logical (Judges 6:1–5; 7:2). But the consequences of twisting one of God's commandments into something more appealing can be deadly.

For example, Saul responded in a way that some might describe as logical or prudent: He and his followers "spared . . . everything that was good. These they were unwilling to destroy completely . . . . to sacrifice to the LORD" (1 Samuel 15:9,15).

Good intentions. But not God's intentions. John Calvin explores this perspective on obedience.

Walk With John Calvin

"God will not be honored with exceptions, nor will he allow us to cut off from his law what is less pleasing to us. It is no obedience to God when obedience is rendered according to personal preference rather than all the time. Let there be, therefore, a consistency if we desire rightly to obey God.

"We then understand with James that if we cut off from God's law what is less agreeable to us, though in other parts we may be obedient, yet we become guilty of all, because in one particular thing we violate the whole law.

"It is a general principle: God has prescribed to us a rule of life, which it is not lawful for us to mutilate."

Walk Closer to God

Sheep in the closet are always a sign that you've substituted what is convenient for what is obedient.

Saul's presumption came to light with Samuel's probing question: "What then is this bleating of sheep in my ears?" (1 Samuel 15:14).

Regardless of whether you can explain it fully, God's will is always "good, pleasing and perfect" (Romans 12:2).

And before you conclude that you have a better idea than obeying God's commandments, let Samuel's words burn their way deeply into your heart: "To obey is better than sacrifice" (1 Samuel 15:22).

OCTOBER 25

Walk in the Word
James 2:14–26

By using the example of Abraham, James shows that what saves a person is a faith that manifests itself in actions that please God.

Faith and Deeds

14What good is it, my brothers, if a man claims to have faith but has no deeds? Can such faith save him? 15Suppose a brother or sister is without clothes and daily food. 16If one of you says to him, "Go, I wish you well; keep warm and well fed," but does nothing about his physical needs, what good is it? 17In the same way, faith by itself, if it is not accompanied by action, is dead.

18But someone will say, "You have faith; I have deeds."

Show me your faith without deeds, and I will show you my faith by what I do. 19You believe that there is one God. Good! Even the demons believe that — and shudder.

20You foolish man, do you want evidence that faith without deeds is useless*a*? 21Was not our ancestor Abraham considered righteous for what he did when he offered his son Isaac on the altar? 22You see that his faith and his actions were working together, and his faith was made complete by what he did. 23And the scripture was fulfilled that says, "Abraham believed God, and it was credited to him as righteousness,"*b* and he was called God's friend. 24You see that a person is justified by what he does and not by faith alone.

25In the same way, was not even Rahab the prostitute considered righteous for what she did when she gave lodging to the spies and sent them off in a different direction? 26As the body without the spirit is dead, so faith without deeds is dead.

a20 Some early manuscripts *dead*   *b23* Gen. 15:6

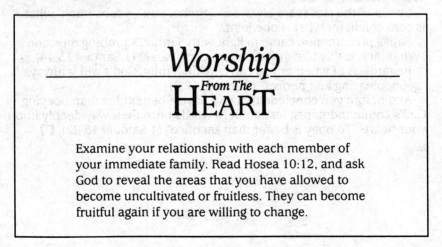

Worship
From The HEART

Examine your relationship with each member of your immediate family. Read Hosea 10:12, and ask God to reveal the areas that you have allowed to become uncultivated or fruitless. They can become fruitful again if you are willing to change.

OCTOBER 25

Translating the Promises of God Into Powerful Deeds for God

In the same way, faith by itself, if it is not accompanied by action, is dead (James 2:17).

No one can live for long by inhaling but never exhaling. No one can stay healthy for long by eating but never exercising.

All input and no output makes for a Dead Sea—and a dead faith. In the Christian life, the outlet of faith is good works.

Charles Hodge discusses the important balance needed to maintain a healthy walk with God.

Walk With Charles Hodge

"Although religion does not consist in outward acts, it always produces them.

"The love of God can no more fail to produce obedience to his commands than a mother's love can fail to produce watchfulness and care for her infant. A person's religion, therefore, is vain which expends itself in exercises that relate exclusively to his own salvation.

"And doubtless many Christians go limping all their days because they confine their attention too much to themselves.

"True religion as we find it in the Bible is a permanent, spontaneous, and progressive principle of spiritual life, influencing the whole man and producing all the fruits of righteousness. It is the root and spring of all right feelings and actions, manifesting itself in love and obedience toward God, in justice and benevolence toward others, and in the proper government of ourselves."

Walk Closer to God

You needn't wonder if a tree is alive. Its fruitful—or fruitless—condition will tell you all you need to know. In the same way, a living faith produces the evidences of faith: good works.

Hebrews 11 describes faith that "conquered kingdoms, administered justice, and gained what was promised; who shut the mouths of lions, . . . escaped the edge of the sword; . . . became powerful in battle and routed foreign armies" (Hebrews 11:33–34).

Do you have a faith like that? Does your faith translate the promises of God into powerful deeds for God? ❐

OCTOBER 26

📖 **Walk in the Word**
James 3:1–12

James shows how one of the most difficult aspects of Christian living is the ability to control one's tongue.

Taming the Tongue

3 Not many of you should presume to be teachers, my brothers, because you know that we who teach will be judged more strictly. ²We all stumble in many ways. If anyone is never at fault in what he says, he is a perfect man, able to keep his whole body in check.

³When we put bits into the mouths of horses to make them obey us, we can turn the whole animal. ⁴Or take ships as an example. Although they are so large and are driven by strong winds, they are steered by a very small rudder wherever the pilot wants to go. ⁵Likewise the tongue is a small part of the body, but it makes great boasts. Consider what a great forest is set on fire by a small spark. ⁶The tongue also is a fire, a world of evil among the parts of the body. It corrupts the whole person, sets the whole course of his life on fire, and is itself set on fire by hell.

⁷All kinds of animals, birds, reptiles and creatures of the sea are being tamed and have been tamed by man, ⁸but no man can tame the tongue. It is a restless evil, full of deadly poison.

⁹With the tongue we praise our Lord and Father, and with it we curse men, who have been made in God's likeness. ¹⁰Out of the same mouth come praise and cursing. My brothers, this should not be. ¹¹Can both fresh water and salt*ᵃ* water flow from the same spring? ¹²My brothers, can a fig tree bear olives, or a grapevine bear figs? Neither can a salt spring produce fresh water.

ᵃ11 Greek *bitter* (see also verse 14)

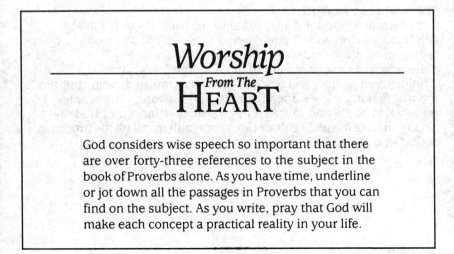

Worship
From The
HEART

God considers wise speech so important that there are over forty-three references to the subject in the book of Proverbs alone. As you have time, underline or jot down all the passages in Proverbs that you can find on the subject. As you write, pray that God will make each concept a practical reality in your life.

Engaging the Mind Before Starting the Tongue

If anyone is never at fault in what he says, he is a perfect man, able to keep his whole body in check (James 3:2).

Be careful when you open your mouth. According to James, the unleashed tongue is an untamable beast. But don't give up, for with God's help you can "be quick to listen, slow to speak and slow to become angry" (James 1:19). Wise words for those convinced it is impossible to speak and not sin.

As F.B. Meyer points out, James's words provide insight by which you can examine your own speech patterns and the various ways the tongue can trip you up.

Walk With F.B. Meyer

"The tongue boasts great things. We are all apt to be vain, boastful, exaggerated. We contrive to focus attention on our own words and deeds; even in delivering God's message we manage to let it be seen that we have a clearer insight into truth or a closer familiarity with God than our fellows.

"We break the law of courtesy, and become harsh, insolent, and uncivil; or the law of purity, and repeat stories that leave a stain; or the law of truth, and practice insincerity; or the law of kindness, and are harsh toward those who are beneath us in station. Or in our desire to stand well with others we are guilty of flattery or servility.

"We disparage other workers; compliment them to their faces and disparage them behind their backs. Alas for us! How greatly we need to offer the prayer of the psalmist: 'Set guard over my mouth, O LORD!' "

Walk Closer to God

The antidote for misguided speech is carefully guarded silence. The Scriptures are filled with examples of periods of silence that refreshed God's men and women. Silence for worship, silence for thought, silence for prayer. "Be still, and know that I am God" (Psalm 46:10).

"Silence," one teacher has observed, "first makes us pilgrims. Secondly, silence guards the fire within. Thirdly, silence teaches us how to speak."

Do you want to speak well? Learn first to speak not at all as you listen to the voice of your Lord. ◯

OCTOBER 27

📖 Walk in the Word
James 3:13–18

James outlines the basic difference between so-called earthly wisdom and true, heavenly wisdom.

Two Kinds of Wisdom

¹³Who is wise and understanding among you? Let him show it by his good life, by deeds done in the humility that comes from wisdom. ¹⁴But if you harbor bitter envy and selfish ambition in your hearts, do not boast about it or deny the truth. ¹⁵Such "wisdom" does not come down from heaven but is earthly, unspiritual, of the devil. ¹⁶For where you have envy and selfish ambition, there you find disorder and every evil practice.

¹⁷But the wisdom that comes from heaven is first of all pure; then peace-loving, considerate, submissive, full of mercy and good fruit, impartial and sincere. ¹⁸Peacemakers who sow in peace raise a harvest of righteousness.

PSALM 119

ם   Mem

Oh, how I love your law!
  I meditate on it all day long.
⁹⁸Your commands make me wiser than my enemies,
  for they are ever with me.
⁹⁹I have more insight than all my teachers,
  for I meditate on your statutes.
¹⁰⁰I have more understanding than the elders,
  for I obey your precepts.
¹⁰¹I have kept my feet from every evil path
  so that I might obey your word.
¹⁰²I have not departed from your laws,
  for you yourself have taught me.
¹⁰³How sweet are your words to my taste,
  sweeter than honey to my mouth!
¹⁰⁴I gain understanding from your precepts;
  therefore I hate every wrong path.

Truth: To Be Lived, Not Debated

Who is wise and understanding among you? Let him show it by his good life, by deeds done in the humility that comes from wisdom (James 3:13).

The clamor of raised voices turns the heads of everyone in the room. Two men in the corner are arguing over the merits of respective candidates in a political campaign.

Arguments tend to bring out the worst in people. Sooner or later, accusations are made that go beyond the search for right and wrong. Anger and bitterness result.

How do you react when confronted with a volatile situation? Conventional wisdom says, "Win at all cost"; godly wisdom suggests otherwise, as the helpful nineteenth-century commentary *An Exposition on the Bible* describes.

Walk With Exposition of the Bible

"This test is a very practical one, and we can apply it to ourselves as well as to others.

"How do we bear ourselves in argument and in controversy? Are we serene about the result, in full confidence that truth and right should prevail? Are we desirous that truth should prevail, even if that should involve our being proved to be in the wrong? Are we meek and gentle toward those who differ from us? Or are we apt to lose our tempers and become heated against our opponents?

"If the last is the case, we have reason to doubt whether our wisdom is of the best sort. He who loses his temper in an argument has begun to care more about himself, and less about the truth.

"He has become like the many would-be teachers rebuked by James: slow to hear, swift to speak; unwilling to learn, eager to dogmatize; less ready to know the truth than to be able to say something, whether true or false."

Walk Closer to God

When Christ admitted to his accusers that he was the Son of God, they violently disagreed. In order to silence the truth, they crucified him. But notice that Christ did not argue; he didn't need to. After all, truth was on his side—indeed, he was the very embodiment of truth. His enemies may have seemingly won the battle, but he triumphed in the end.

Truth has not been entrusted to you just to be debated. Indeed, the whole world waits for a convincing demonstration of the life-changing power of God's truth.

As Christ showed, the application of truth to life is the most powerful argument of all.

OCTOBER 28

📖 Walk in the Word
James 4:1-12

James instructs Christians to avoid friendship with the world and in its place to submit ourselves humbly to God as Lord.

Submit Yourselves to God

4 What causes fights and quarrels among you? Don't they come from your desires that battle within you? ²You want something but don't get it. You kill and covet, but you cannot have what you want. You quarrel and fight. You do not have, because you do not ask God. ³When you ask, you do not receive, because you ask with wrong motives, that you may spend what you get on your pleasures.

⁴You adulterous people, don't you know that friendship with the world is hatred toward God? Anyone who chooses to be a friend of the world becomes an enemy of God. ⁵Or do you think Scripture says without reason that the spirit he caused to live in us envies intensely?ᵃ ⁶But he gives us more grace. That is why Scripture says:

> "God opposes the proud
>   but gives grace to the humble."ᵇ

⁷Submit yourselves, then, to God. Resist the devil, and he will flee from you. ⁸Come near to God and he will come near to you. Wash your hands, you sinners, and purify your hearts, you double-minded. ⁹Grieve, mourn and wail. Change your laughter to mourning and your joy to gloom. ¹⁰Humble yourselves before the Lord, and he will lift you up.

¹¹Brothers, do not slander one another. Anyone who speaks against his brother or judges him speaks against the law and judges it. When you judge the law, you are not keeping it, but sitting in judgment on it. ¹²There is only one Lawgiver and Judge, the one who is able to save and destroy. But you—who are you to judge your neighbor?

ᵃ5 Or *that God jealously longs for the spirit that he made to live in us*; or *that the Spirit he caused to live in us longs jealously*   ᵇ6 Prov. 3:34

Why Wave the White Flag?

Resist the devil, and he will flee from you (James 4:7).

The enemy advances against overwhelming odds. He is out-numbered and outmanned—a clearly beaten foe. And suddenly the "victors" jump up and run away! The war is lost without the enemy even being engaged.

Often, that's how Christians respond to Satan's onslaughts. Instead of standing in the strength which God supplies, they turn and run. No wonder Satan—the defeated adversary—rules nonetheless in so many hearts and homes.

But it doesn't have to be that way! Listen to A.B. Simpson's encouraging commentary on one of James's sentence sermons.

Walk With A.B. Simpson

" 'Resist the devil, and he will flee from you.' This is a promise and God will keep it. If we resist our adversary, God will compel him to flee and will give us the victory. We can, at all times, fearlessly stand up in resistance to the enemy, and claim the protection of our heavenly King, just as a citizen would claim the protection of the government against a violent man.

"At the same time, we are not to stand on the adversary's ground anywhere by any attitude of disobedience, or we give him a terrific power over us, which, while God will restrain in great mercy and kindness, he will not fully remove until we get fully on holy ground.

"Therefore, we must be armed with the breastplate of righteousness, as well as the shield of faith, if we would successfully resist the prince of darkness and the principalities in heavenly places."

Walk Closer to God

Christian, stand your ground!

When Satan attacks you today, don't run. Resist. Claim the promise of James 4:7 to put him on the run. Exercise both humility and courage in your fight against Satan. With those ingredients, plus the assurance of God's assistance to help you win the battle, victory is inevitable!

After all, why lose a single battle to Satan when Christ has already won the war?

OCTOBER 29

📖 Walk in the Word
Walk in the Word
James 4:13 — 5:6

James has some rather harsh words for those who are materialistic and base their lives on the things of this world.

Boasting About Tomorrow

¹³Now listen, you who say, "Today or tomorrow we will go to this or that city, spend a year there, carry on business and make money." ¹⁴Why, you do not even know what will happen tomorrow. What is your life? You are a mist that appears for a little while and then vanishes. ¹⁵Instead, you ought to say, "If it is the Lord's will, we will live and do this or that." ¹⁶As it is, you boast and brag. All such boasting is evil. ¹⁷Anyone, then, who knows the good he ought to do and doesn't do it, sins.

Warning to Rich Oppressors

5 Now listen, you rich people, weep and wail because of the misery that is coming upon you. ²Your wealth has rotted, and moths have eaten your clothes. ³Your gold and silver are corroded. Their corrosion will testify against you and eat your flesh like fire. You have hoarded wealth in the last days. ⁴Look! The wages you failed to pay the workmen who mowed your fields are crying out against you. The cries of the harvesters have reached the ears of the Lord Almighty. ⁵You have lived on earth in luxury and self-indulgence. You have fattened yourselves in the day of slaughter.*ᵃ* ⁶You have condemned and murdered innocent men, who were not opposing you.

ᵃ5 Or yourselves as in a day of feasting

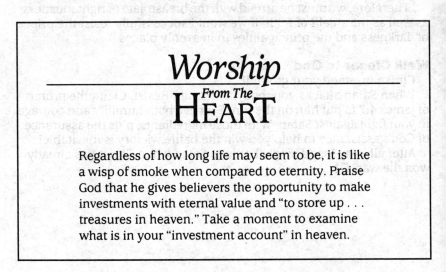

Worship
From The
HEART

Regardless of how long life may seem to be, it is like
a wisp of smoke when compared to eternity. Praise
God that he gives believers the opportunity to make
investments with eternal value and "to store up . . .
treasures in heaven." Take a moment to examine
what is in your "investment account" in heaven.

OCTOBER 29

Doing Good by Getting Involved

Anyone, then, who knows the good he ought to do and doesn't do it, sins (James 4:17).

A pedestrian is mugged in broad daylight while a dozen spectators look on in detached curiosity. When questioned, the onlookers might justify their behavior by claiming, "I didn't do anything wrong." And they would be right.

But not doing a right action is as wrong as doing a wrong one—a truth James declares and one that Albert Barnes explains.

Walk With Albert Barnes

"It is universally true that if a person knows what is right and does not do it, he is guilty of sin.

"If he understands what his duty is; if he has the means of doing good to others; if by his name, his influence, or his wealth, he can promote a good cause; if he can, consistently with other duties, relieve the distressed, the poor, the prisoner, and the oppressed; if he can send the gospel to other lands, or can wipe away the tear of the mourner; and if, by indolence, or avarice, or selfishness, he does not do it, he is guilty of sin before God.

"No man can be released from the obligation to do good in his world to the extent of his ability. No one should desire to be so released.

"The highest privilege conferred on a mortal—besides that of securing salvation—is doing good to others: alleviating sorrow, instructing ignorance, raising up the bowed down, comforting those that mourn, delivering the wronged and oppressed, supplying the wants of the needy, guiding inquirers into the way of truth, and sending liberty, knowledge, and salvation around the world."

Walk Closer to God

Meeting needs is costly . . . inconvenient. It takes time and energy. It may earn no thanks or appreciation. But it is simply the right thing to do.

Aren't you thankful that when the Father asked his Son to bear the burden of humanity's sin, Jesus didn't say, "No—I don't want to get involved"?

What answer will you give to God's call asking you to follow in his footsteps today? ☐

OCTOBER 30

■ Walk in the Word
James 5:7–12

In the midst of whatever sufferings we may have in this life, James encourages us to remain patient and steadfast, remembering that God is a God of compassion.

Patience in Suffering

⁷Be patient, then, brothers, until the Lord's coming. See how the farmer waits for the land to yield its valuable crop and how patient he is for the autumn and spring rains. ⁸You too, be patient and stand firm, because the Lord's coming is near. ⁹Don't grumble against each other, brothers, or you will be judged. The Judge is standing at the door!

¹⁰Brothers, as an example of patience in the face of suffering, take the prophets who spoke in the name of the Lord. ¹¹As you know, we consider blessed those who have persevered. You have heard of Job's perseverance and have seen what the Lord finally brought about. The Lord is full of compassion and mercy.

¹²Above all, my brothers, do not swear—not by heaven or by earth or by anything else. Let your "Yes" be yes, and your "No," no, or you will be condemned.

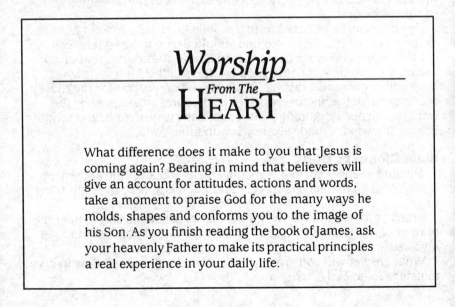

Worship
From The
HEART

What difference does it make to you that Jesus is coming again? Bearing in mind that believers will give an account for attitudes, actions and words, take a moment to praise God for the many ways he molds, shapes and conforms you to the image of his Son. As you finish reading the book of James, ask your heavenly Father to make its practical principles a real experience in your daily life.

OCTOBER 30

Keeping Your Word Sets Your Light on a Hill

Let your "Yes" be yes, and your "No," no, or you will be condemned (James 5:12).

A mortgage is a promise to pay. Break it, and you may lose a house.

A treaty is a promise to protect. Break it, and you may lose an ally.

A wedding vow is a promise to "love, honor and cherish till death do us part." Break it, and you may lose a partner.

But one thing is often lost when promises are broken: the reputation of the promise-maker.

George Müller laments the fact that even Christians are not immune to broken promises and the damage that accompanies them.

Walk With George Müller

"It has often been mentioned to me in various places that fellow believers in business do not attend to the keeping of promises.

"I cannot but entreat all who love our Lord Jesus, and who are engaged in a trade or business, to seek for his sake not to make any promises except those which they absolutely believe they will be able to fulfill.

"They should carefully weigh all the circumstances before making any engagement, for it is even in these little ordinary affairs of life that we may either bring much honor or dishonor to the Lord. And these are the things which every unbeliever takes notice of.

"Surely it ought not to be true that we, who have power with God to obtain by prayer and faith all needful grace, wisdom, and skill, should be bad servants, bad tradesmen, bad masters."

Walk Closer to God

In the pursuit of Christlikeness, don't overlook the importance of letting your word be your honor.

God's word "cannot be broken" (John 10:35). Jesus Christ is "the same yesterday and today and forever" (Hebrews 13:8). "No matter how many promises God has made, they are 'Yes' in Christ" (2 Corinthians 1:20).

Remember, you may have trouble remembering the promises you made. But others will have little trouble remembering the promises you broke. ⬠

OCTOBER 31

Walk in the Word
James 5:13–20

James stresses the importance of prayer in the lives of God's people. The prayers of the righteous are powerful and effective.

The Prayer of Faith

¹³Is any one of you in trouble? He should pray. Is anyone happy? Let him sing songs of praise. ¹⁴Is any one of you sick? He should call the elders of the church to pray over him and anoint him with oil in the name of the Lord. ¹⁵And the prayer offered in faith will make the sick person well; the Lord will raise him up. If he has sinned, he will be forgiven. ¹⁶Therefore confess your sins to each other and pray for each other so that you may be healed. The prayer of a righteous man is powerful and effective.

¹⁷Elijah was a man just like us. He prayed earnestly that it would not rain, and it did not rain on the land for three and a half years. ¹⁸Again he prayed, and the heavens gave rain, and the earth produced its crops.

¹⁹My brothers, if one of you should wander from the truth and someone should bring him back, ²⁰remember this: Whoever turns a sinner from the error of his way will save him from death and cover over a multitude of sins.

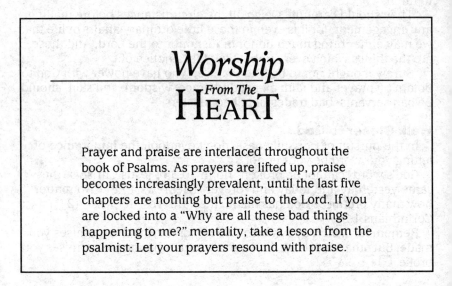

Worship
From The
HEART

Prayer and praise are interlaced throughout the book of Psalms. As prayers are lifted up, praise becomes increasingly prevalent, until the last five chapters are nothing but praise to the Lord. If you are locked into a "Why are all these bad things happening to me?" mentality, take a lesson from the psalmist: Let your prayers resound with praise.

OCTOBER 31

Prayer and Praise: Legs for a Balanced Walk

Is any one of you in trouble? He should pray. Is anyone happy? Let him sing songs of praise (James 5:13).

James was a man of prayer. He even received the nickname "Camel Knees" because of his hard, calloused knees—the result of long hours in prayer.

According to James, the Christian should pray, whatever his needs, whatever his circumstances, both privately and publicly. Pray for wisdom (James 1:5); pray for those who are afflicted or sick (James 5:14–15). Why? Because "the prayer of a righteous man is powerful and effective" (James 5:16).

Real prayer penetrates every sphere of life and invokes God to answer on your behalf, as Alfred Plummer observes.

Walk With Alfred Plummer

"It is hard enough to win converts from heathenism; but it is still harder to teach the newly converted that worshiping God has any bearing on their conduct. This idea is utterly alien to their whole mode of thought.

"They have been accustomed to regard worship as a series of acts which must be religiously performed. It has never occurred to them that they must live in accordance with their worship, or that the one has any connection with the other.

"From this it follows that when the idolater has been induced to substitute the worship of God for the worship of idols, there still remains an immense amount to be done. Prayer and praise must go hand in hand with work and life."

Walk Closer to God

Prayer and praise. Two equally important legs for a balanced walk with God. You pray, God answers, you praise.

How will you link these essentials for a harmonious walk with God? Are you in the midst of a testing situation or on a bed of sickness or low on finances or discouraged? Pray! Has God answered your prayers by blessing you with health, strength, extra finances, joy or guidance? Praise!

You'll discover how much can be accomplished as you walk with God on the sturdy legs of prayer and praise. ❐

Discovering the Truth of the Word

Faced with increasing doubts about Scripture through reading modern views of the Bible, a searching twenty-one-year-old minister took all his books about the Bible, locked them in the cupboard, and sat down with only the Bible, in order to discover for himself what it had to say. His own study convinced him of the truth of Scripture, and for the next sixty years, George Campbell Morgan taught the Bible to all who would listen.

Born in a small English village on December 9, 1863, Morgan grew up in a preacher's family. As a young boy he emulated his father by preaching to a mock congregation of his sister's dolls. At age thirteen he preached his first "real" sermon, and by age fifteen he was preaching on a regular basis.

After his ordination in 1890, he began a busy life of traveling and speaking—crossing the Atlantic fifty-four times to teach God's Word in England and America. He never tired of explaining and applying the Bible to hungry hearts. More than sixty books resulted from his teaching. His career culminated at Westminster Chapel in London during the difficult days of World War II.

The arrival of many new converts into the churches through evangelists such as Dwight L. Moody and Billy Sunday signaled the need for preachers who could explain the Scriptures. Morgan's life stands as an eloquent reminder that after the milk of the gospel must come the meat of the Word.

If spiritual nourishment is your goal when you read the Word of God, then servants of God such as G. Campbell Morgan can teach you much about feeding on the truths of Scripture. Thank God for the privilege of coming to his Word for strength and direction.

A LESSON FROM THE LIFE OF G. CAMPBELL MORGAN

I can have confidence in God's Word and can be assured that he will reveal himself to me as I study it.

Light in the Darkness

**1 AND 2 PETER
1, 2 AND 3 JOHN
JUDE**

A room devoid of light is a good place to stub your toe; a mountainside cloaked in darkness is a likely place to fall off the edge of a cliff. But turn on a light in the room or use a flashlight on the mountain, and the chances of hurting yourself diminish. For the Christian, God's Word is a light to guide you through life (Psalm 119:105), for in it God tells you how to live in the world in which he has called you to serve. But other voices—those of false teachers—contradict what God has said. Their words confuse rather than comfort, and they lead people astray. God has much to say about how to avoid being ambushed by these "wolves in sheep's clothing" (cf. Matthew 7:15). The letters of Peter, John and Jude can help you unmask error and guard the truth.

Peter's two letters contain practical admonitions for those called to be representatives of God's truth. His first letter reminds Christians that suffering for doing what is right is not a sign that things have gone wrong. Instead, God is being glorified, for Christ himself suffered for doing good. In his second letter, Peter first calls his readers to consider the virtues of truth as it is proclaimed in Jesus Christ; then he turns his attention to false teachers and their rightful condemnation.

John's three letters are masterpieces of profound truth expressed in simple terms. His overriding concern emerges in his third letter: "I have no greater joy than to hear that my children are walking in the truth" (3 John 4). His first letter centers on the true characteristics of one who trusts in Christ—fellowship, forgiveness, righteousness, faith. The other two letters contain guidelines for dealing with people who do not live according to truth.

The short letter of Jude is a succinct, yet passionate exhortation to defend the faith against ungodly men who would subvert the truth.

After reading these six letters, you will see that God's truth is worth defending and applying to your life. Turn the light of God's Word on your life this month and discover that it is indeed truth to live by, truth to die for.

NOVEMBER 1

📖 Walk in the Word
1 Peter 1:1–12

Because Peter knows his readers are suffering various kinds of trials, he points them to the resurrected Christ and the glorious salvation that is offered to us.

1 Peter, an apostle of Jesus Christ,

To God's elect, strangers in the world, scattered throughout Pontus, Galatia, Cappadocia, Asia and Bithynia, ²who have been chosen according to the foreknowledge of God the Father, through the sanctifying work of the Spirit, for obedience to Jesus Christ and sprinkling by his blood:

Grace and peace be yours in abundance.

Praise to God for a Living Hope

³Praise be to the God and Father of our Lord Jesus Christ! In his great mercy he has given us new birth into a living hope through the resurrection of Jesus Christ from the dead, ⁴and into an inheritance that can never perish, spoil or fade—kept in heaven for you, ⁵who through faith are shielded by God's power until the coming of the salvation that is ready to be revealed in the last time. ⁶In this you greatly rejoice, though now for a little while you may have had to suffer grief in all kinds of trials. ⁷These have come so that your faith—of greater worth than gold, which perishes even though refined by fire—may be proved genuine and may result in praise, glory and honor when Jesus Christ is revealed. ⁸Though you have not seen him, you love him; and even though you do not see him now, you believe in him and are filled with an inexpressible and glorious joy, ⁹for you are receiving the goal of your faith, the salvation of your souls.

¹⁰Concerning this salvation, the prophets, who spoke of the grace that was to come to you, searched intently and with the greatest care, ¹¹trying to find out the time and circumstances to which the Spirit of Christ in them was pointing when he predicted the sufferings of Christ and the glories that would follow. ¹²It was revealed to them that they were not serving themselves but you, when they spoke of the things that have now been told you by those who have preached the gospel to you by the Holy Spirit sent from heaven. Even angels long to look into these things.

Regarding God With Total Esteem and Complete Admiration

Praise be to the God and Father of our Lord Jesus Christ!
(1 Peter 1:3).

The "worshiper" attends faithfully every Sunday, concentrating intently on the object of his worship. All week he has prepared for this day, his thoughts turning frequently to the object of his adoration. When he leaves hours later, his gratitude is profound. His team won, 14–10.

Football fans often reflect a truer attitude of worship than the average Christian. A.W. Tozer diagnoses this problem and suggests a helpful remedy.

Walk With A.W. Tozer

"The quality of our worship is enhanced as we move away from the thought of what God has done for us, and move nearer the thought of the excellence of his holy nature.

"This leads us to admire God. The dictionary defines admire as 'to regard with wondering esteem, accompanied by pleasure and delight; to look at or upon with an elevated feeling of pleasure.'

"According to this definition, God has few admirers among Christians today. Many are simply grateful for his goodness in providing salvation, or answering their prayer in troublesome situations. But the simple truth is that worship is still in infancy until it begins to take on the quality of admiration.

"Just as long as the worshiper is engrossed with himself and his own concerns, he is a babe. We begin to grow up when our worship passes from thanksgiving to admiration."

Walk Closer to God

One quality that binds a fan to his favorite team is his admiration for the players' abilities. To consider the attributes of God should cause no less wonder.

He is good. Just. Merciful.

Loving. Omniscient. Omnipotent.

Majestic. Infinite. Perfect.

Before your next visit to a house of worship, stop to recall who made it all possible.

Then "ascribe to the Lord the glory due his name" (1 Chronicles 16:29).

NOVEMBER 2

📖 Walk in the Word
1 Peter 1:13—2:3

More than anything else, Peter emphasizes that Christians must live holy lives, purified by the Word of God.

Be Holy

¹³Therefore, prepare your minds for action; be self-controlled; set your hope fully on the grace to be given you when Jesus Christ is revealed. ¹⁴As obedient children, do not conform to the evil desires you had when you lived in ignorance. ¹⁵But just as he who called you is holy, so be holy in all you do; ¹⁶for it is written: "Be holy, because I am holy."[a]

¹⁷Since you call on a Father who judges each man's work impartially, live your lives as strangers here in reverent fear. ¹⁸For you know that it was not with perishable things such as silver or gold that you were redeemed from the empty way of life handed down to you from your forefathers, ¹⁹but with the precious blood of Christ, a lamb without blemish or defect. ²⁰He was chosen before the creation of the world, but was revealed in these last times for your sake. ²¹Through him you believe in God, who raised him from the dead and glorified him, and so your faith and hope are in God.

²²Now that you have purified yourselves by obeying the truth so that you have sincere love for your brothers, love one another deeply, from the heart.[b] ²³For you have been born again, not of perishable seed, but of imperishable, through the living and enduring word of God. ²⁴For,

> "All men are like grass,
>   and all their glory is like the flowers of the field;
>   the grass withers and the flowers fall,
> ²⁵   but the word of the Lord stands forever."[c]

And this is the word that was preached to you.

2 Therefore, rid yourselves of all malice and all deceit, hypocrisy, envy, and slander of every kind. ²Like newborn babies, crave pure spiritual milk, so that by it you may grow up in your salvation, ³now that you have tasted that the Lord is good.

a16 Lev. 11:44,45; 19:2; 20:7   b22 Some early manuscripts *from a pure heart*
c25 Isaiah 40:6-8

Designed and Destined for Holiness

But just as he who called you is holy, so be holy in all you do; for it is written: "Be holy, because I am holy" (1 Peter 1:15–16).

A child complains because he got clothes for Christmas instead of toys. A teenager is disappointed because he received a savings bond rather than the car he had requested. In each case, the gifts were wise while the requests were shortsighted.

Even in the Christian life desires often get in the way of deeper joys. Holiness may not be high on your list of "most wanted gifts," but it does bring joy to God and to his children because it fulfills the purpose for which God created you.

Oswald Chambers challenges you to remember your calling.

Walk With Oswald Chambers

"Continually restate to yourself what the purpose of your life is. The destined end of an individual is not happiness, not health, but *holiness*.

"The one thing that matters most is whether a person will accept the God who will make him holy. At all costs one must be rightly related to God.

"Do I believe I need to be holy? Do I believe God can come into me and make me holy?

"God has one destined end for humans—holiness. He is not an eternal 'blessing machine' for people. He did not come to save people out of pity; he came to save people because he had created them to be holy."

Walk Closer to God

Those who attain power, fame or wealth are applauded and emulated by the world.

But God says you were created for a different purpose altogether. He made you to be like him, "conformed to the likeness of his Son" (Romans 8:29), fitted to enjoy all the blessings and privileges that come with being a "saint"—a holy one of God.

Holiness deserves to become the priority of your life because it is God's purpose for your life.

Fulfill that purpose and you will experience a joy that will last forever! ◖◗

November 3

Walk in the Word
1 Peter 2:4–12

Peter encourages believers to abstain from the pleasures of the world and instead to become a part of God's holy building, the church.

The Living Stone and a Chosen People

⁴As you come to him, the living Stone—rejected by men but chosen by God and precious to him— ⁵you also, like living stones, are being built into a spiritual house to be a holy priesthood, offering spiritual sacrifices acceptable to God through Jesus Christ. ⁶For in Scripture it says:

> "See, I lay a stone in Zion,
>   a chosen and precious cornerstone,
> and the one who trusts in him
>   will never be put to shame."[a]

⁷Now to you who believe, this stone is precious. But to those who do not believe,

> "The stone the builders rejected
>   has become the capstone,[b]"[c]

⁸and,

> "A stone that causes men to stumble
>   and a rock that makes them fall."[d]

They stumble because they disobey the message—which is also what they were destined for.

⁹But you are a chosen people, a royal priesthood, a holy nation, a people belonging to God, that you may declare the praises of him who called you out of darkness into his wonderful light. ¹⁰Once you were not a people, but now you are the people of God; once you had not received mercy, but now you have received mercy.

¹¹Dear friends, I urge you, as aliens and strangers in the world, to abstain from sinful desires, which war against your soul. ¹²Live such good lives among the pagans that, though they accuse you of doing wrong, they may see your good deeds and glorify God on the day he visits us.

---

[a]6 Isaiah 28:16   [b]7 Or *cornerstone*   [c]7 Psalm 118:22   [d]8 Isaiah 8:14

Christ Is Made the Sure Foundation

"See, I lay a stone in Zion, a chosen and precious cornerstone, and the one who trusts in him will never be put to shame" (1 Peter 2:6).

Houses without foundations are unstable, are susceptible to weakening at the worst possible moment, and never stand up to storms. As Jesus said in his Sermon on the Mount, a house built to stand must be built on something solid.

The imagery of Jesus as the chief cornerstone is captured in this anonymous seventh-century hymn.

Walk With a Seventh-Century Poet

> Christ is made the sure foundation,
> Christ the Head and Cornerstone,
> Chosen of the Lord and precious,
> Binding all the church in one;
> Holy Zion's help forever,
> And her confidence alone.
>
> To this temple, where we call Thee,
> Come, O Lord of hosts, today;
> With accustomed loving-kindness
> Hear Thy people as they pray,
> And Thy fullest benediction
> Shed within its walls alway.
>
> Here vouchsafe to all Thy servants
> What they ask of Thee to gain,
> What they gain from Thee forever
> With the blessed to retain,
> And hereafter in Thy glory
> Evermore with Thee to reign.

Walk Closer to God

Steady. Indestructible. Immovable. Jesus was all that. And now he calls you to be the same.

Steady when the winds of false doctrine swirl around you. Indestructible when temptations seek to weaken you. Immovable when Satan tries to overwhelm you.

Peter—whose name means "rock"—lived up to his name with God's help. Today, you can build on that same foundation, "so that when the day of evil comes, you may be able to stand your ground, and after you have done everything, to stand" (Ephesians 6:13).

NOVEMBER 4

📖 Walk in the Word
1 Peter 2:13–25

Peter admonishes us to submit ourselves to the Lord in all areas of life, even if it means that we may have to suffer for our faith.

Submission to Rulers and Masters

¹³Submit yourselves for the Lord's sake to every authority instituted among men: whether to the king, as the supreme authority, ¹⁴or to governors, who are sent by him to punish those who do wrong and to commend those who do right. ¹⁵For it is God's will that by doing good you should silence the ignorant talk of foolish men. ¹⁶Live as free men, but do not use your freedom as a cover-up for evil; live as servants of God. ¹⁷Show proper respect to everyone: Love the brotherhood of believers, fear God, honor the king.

¹⁸Slaves, submit yourselves to your masters with all respect, not only to those who are good and considerate, but also to those who are harsh. ¹⁹For it is commendable if a man bears up under the pain of unjust suffering because he is conscious of God. ²⁰But how is it to your credit if you receive a beating for doing wrong and endure it? But if you suffer for doing good and you endure it, this is commendable before God. ²¹To this you were called, because Christ suffered for you, leaving you an example, that you should follow in his steps.

> ²²"He committed no sin,
> and no deceit was found in his mouth."[a]

²³When they hurled their insults at him, he did not retaliate; when he suffered, he made no threats. Instead, he entrusted himself to him who judges justly. ²⁴He himself bore our sins in his body on the tree, so that we might die to sins and live for righteousness; by his wounds you have been healed. ²⁵For you were like sheep going astray, but now you have returned to the Shepherd and Overseer of your souls.

[a]22 Isaiah 53:9

Seeing the Rainbow Through the Rain

But if you suffer for doing good and you endure it, this is
commendable before God. To this you were called (1 Peter
2:20–21).

Anyone can attend a concert and enjoy a violinist's skill. But only
another violinist can fully understand a violinist's suffering: the years
of practice, self-denial and financial hardship it takes to achieve the
expertise that others will travel miles to hear. But through the
musician's suffering, others are richly blessed.

Peter and the early Christians understood that suffering has a place
in life, and today's insight from J. Hudson Taylor will help you to do the
same.

Walk with J. Hudson Taylor

"It is possible to receive salvation through Christ but still have an
imperfect appreciation of the nature and responsibilities of our calling.

"To what are we called? To do good, to suffer for it, and to take it
patiently.

"Now none of the proceedings of God are arbitrary: All the acts and
all the requirements of perfect wisdom and perfect goodness must of
necessity be wise and good.

"We are called when we so suffer to take it patiently, thankfully, and
joyfully because—seen from a right point of view—there is neither
ground nor excuse for impatience. On the contrary, there is abundant
cause for overflowing thanks and joy.

"To make the message intelligible, it must be lived. Be glad that you
have the opportunity to make the grace of God intelligible to
unbelievers. The greater the persecutions are, the greater the power
of your testimony."

Walk Closer to God

As Hudson Taylor makes clear, God has his own purposes in mind
when Christians suffer—reasons that will glorify him, even if no one
else understands.

Your calling is to trust and obey, in order that the overflow of your
suffering might be sweet music to God. It may be just the melody a
fellow sufferer needs to hear!

NOVEMBER 5

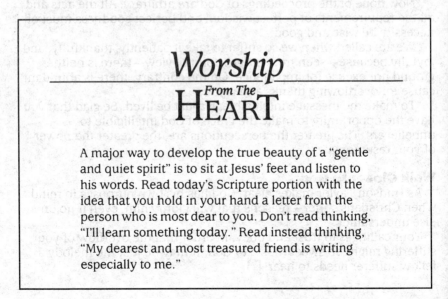 Walk in the Word
1 Peter 3:1–7

Peter uses this brief section to instruct husbands and wives in their mutual responsibilities, especially to treat each other kindly.

Wives and Husbands

3 Wives, in the same way be submissive to your husbands so that, if any of them do not believe the word, they may be won over without words by the behavior of their wives, ²when they see the purity and reverence of your lives. ³Your beauty should not come from outward adornment, such as braided hair and the wearing of gold jewelry and fine clothes. ⁴Instead, it should be that of your inner self, the unfading beauty of a gentle and quiet spirit, which is of great worth in God's sight. ⁵For this is the way the holy women of the past who put their hope in God used to make themselves beautiful. They were submissive to their own husbands, ⁶like Sarah, who obeyed Abraham and called him her master. You are her daughters if you do what is right and do not give way to fear.

⁷Husbands, in the same way be considerate as you live with your wives, and treat them with respect as the weaker partner and as heirs with you of the gracious gift of life, so that nothing will hinder your prayers.

Worship
From The
HEART

A major way to develop the true beauty of a "gentle and quiet spirit" is to sit at Jesus' feet and listen to his words. Read today's Scripture portion with the idea that you hold in your hand a letter from the person who is most dear to you. Don't read thinking, "I'll learn something today." Read instead thinking, "My dearest and most treasured friend is writing especially to me."

Looking Your Best for Your Heavenly Bridegroom

Your beauty should not come from outward adornment. . . . Instead, it should be that of your inner self, the unfading beauty of a gentle and quiet spirit, which is of great worth in God's sight (1 Peter 3:3–4).

God could have created a very functional, very bland, black-and-white world. Instead, he made a universe abounding in luxuriant variety, rich color and amazing textures. He created a world for all his creatures to enjoy.

The adorning of creation provides a lesson on which Peter draws in chapter three, and which poet Anne Bradstreet underscores in this insight.

Walk With Anne Bradstreet

If so much excellence abides below,
    How excellent is He that dwells on high,
Whose power and beauty by His works we know?
    Sure He is goodness, wisdom, glory, light,
That hath this under world so richly dight* . . .

    My great Creator I would magnify,
That nature had thus decked liberally:
    But ah, and ah, again, my imbecility!
O Time, the fatal wrack of mortal things,
    That draws oblivion's curtains over kings,
Their sumptuous monuments, men know not,
    Their names without a record are forgot,
Their parts, their ports, their pomp's all laid in th' dust,
    Nor wit, nor gold, nor buildings 'scape time's rust;
But He whose name is graved in the white stone
    Shall last and shine when all of these are gone.

*Obsolete word meaning "adorned" or "arrayed."

Walk Closer to God

Outward adornment is nice—but not necessary.

By contrast, inward adornment is more than a good idea—it is a command!

God has called his bride to develop a beautiful inner life . . . a life adorned with the fruit of his Spirit . . . a life colored by the character of Christ.

And, as Peter suggests, a meek and quiet spirit is a good place to start "looking your best" for God.

NOVEMBER 6

Walk in the Word
1 Peter 3:8–22

Peter encourages those who are going through difficult times as Christians to be willing to suffer for doing good, for this is what Christ himself did.

Suffering for Doing Good

8Finally, all of you, live in harmony with one another; be sympathetic, love as brothers, be compassionate and humble. 9Do not repay evil with evil or insult with insult, but with blessing, because to this you were called so that you may inherit a blessing. 10For,

> "Whoever would love life
>   and see good days
> must keep his tongue from evil
>   and his lips from deceitful speech.
> 11He must turn from evil and do good;
>   he must seek peace and pursue it.
> 12For the eyes of the Lord are on the righteous
>   and his ears are attentive to their prayer,
> but the face of the Lord is against those who do evil."*a*

13Who is going to harm you if you are eager to do good? 14But even if you should suffer for what is right, you are blessed. "Do not fear what they fear*b*; do not be frightened."*c* 15But in your hearts set apart Christ as Lord. Always be prepared to give an answer to everyone who asks you to give the reason for the hope that you have. But do this with gentleness and respect, 16keeping a clear conscience, so that those who speak maliciously against your good behavior in Christ may be ashamed of their slander. 17It is better, if it is God's will, to suffer for doing good than for doing evil. 18For Christ died for sins once for all, the righteous for the unrighteous, to bring you to God. He was put to death in the body but made alive by the Spirit, 19through whom*d* also he went and preached to the spirits in prison 20who disobeyed long ago when God waited patiently in the days of Noah while the ark was being built. In it only a few people, eight in all, were saved through water, 21and this water symbolizes baptism that now saves you also—not the removal of dirt from the body but the pledge*e* of a good conscience toward God. It saves you by the resurrection of Jesus Christ, 22who has gone into heaven and is at God's right hand—with angels, authorities and powers in submission to him.

---

a12 Psalm 34:12-16   *b14* Or *not fear their threats*   *c14* Isaiah 8:12   *d18,19* Or *alive in the spirit,* 19*through which*   *e21* Or *response*

Freedom From Everything That Is Unlike Jesus

> But in your hearts set apart Christ as Lord (1 Peter 3:15).

Sanctification is a term that summarizes a profound transaction: becoming like Jesus Christ. The Bible often speaks of sanctification in terms of putting off and putting on . . . "setting apart Christ as Lord" of your life and setting aside the things of the world.

Oswald Chambers shares these thoughts about the truth behind the term.

Walk With Oswald Chambers

"Sanctification means intense concentration on God's point of view. It means every power of body, soul, and spirit is chained and kept for God's purpose only. It will cause an intense narrowing of all our interests on earth, and an immense broadening of all our interests in God.

"Are we prepared for God to do all in us that he separated us for? The reason some of us have not entered into the experience of sanctification is that we have not realized its meaning from God's standpoint. Sanctification means being made one with Jesus so that the disposition that ruled him will rule us.

"Jesus has prayed that we might be one with him as he is one with the Father. The one and only characteristic of the Holy Spirit in a person is a strong family likeness to Jesus Christ and freedom from everything that is unlike him."

Walk Closer to God

Do you want to be like Christ?

The question may sound too basic, but before you set it aside, make sure you consider its implications:

Are you prepared for what sanctification will cost?

Are you prepared for God to do in you all for which he separated you?

Are you prepared to let God shape your life so that it bears a strong likeness to his Son?

From God's point of view, there's no higher purpose in life. But the extent that this purpose is realized in your life depends on your point of view. ❍

NOVEMBER 7

Walk in the Word
1 Peter 4:1–11

The basic goal of the Christian life, as far as Peter is concerned, is to live for the glory and praise of God, which means loving each other deeply.

Living for God

4 Therefore, since Christ suffered in his body, arm yourselves also with the same attitude, because he who has suffered in his body is done with sin. ²As a result, he does not live the rest of his earthly life for evil human desires, but rather for the will of God. ³For you have spent enough time in the past doing what pagans choose to do—living in debauchery, lust, drunkenness, orgies, carousing and detestable idolatry. ⁴They think it strange that you do not plunge with them into the same flood of dissipation, and they heap abuse on you. ⁵But they will have to give account to him who is ready to judge the living and the dead. ⁶For this is the reason the gospel was preached even to those who are now dead, so that they might be judged according to men in regard to the body, but live according to God in regard to the spirit.

⁷The end of all things is near. Therefore be clear minded and self-controlled so that you can pray. ⁸Above all, love each other deeply, because love covers over a multitude of sins. ⁹Offer hospitality to one another without grumbling. ¹⁰Each one should use whatever gift he has received to serve others, faithfully administering God's grace in its various forms. ¹¹If anyone speaks, he should do it as one speaking the very words of God. If anyone serves, he should do it with the strength God provides, so that in all things God may be praised through Jesus Christ. To him be the glory and the power for ever and ever. Amen.

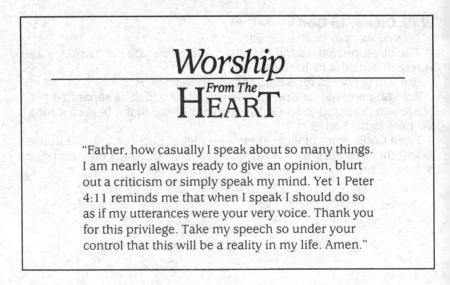

Worship
From The
HEART

"Father, how casually I speak about so many things.
I am nearly always ready to give an opinion, blurt
out a criticism or simply speak my mind. Yet 1 Peter
4:11 reminds me that when I speak I should do so
as if my utterances were your very voice. Thank you
for this privilege. Take my speech so under your
control that this will be a reality in my life. Amen."

Reigning With Christ Requires Submission to His Cross

Therefore, since Christ suffered in his body, arm yourselves also with the same attitude, because he who has suffered in his body is done with sin (1 Peter 4:1).

When one criminal testifies against another criminal, he is often given a fresh start in exchange for his help—a new name, a new home, a new life. No one knows of the past, and he can either "go straight" or revert to his old ways.

The Christian has a new life given him by God. In God's eyes, the old life of sin is done away with. The statute of limitations has run out.

F.B. Meyer suggests the following course of action for Christians in their "new life."

Walk With F.B. Meyer

"The apostle Peter urges the disciples to make a clean break with sin.

"As our Lord's grave lay between him and his earlier life, so should there be a clean break between our life as believers and our earthbound life which was dominated by lawless passions.

"Sometimes God employs the acid of persecution or suffering to eat away the bonds that bind us to our past. Let us accept these with a willing mind. The one condition of reigning with Christ is to submit to his cross.

"Of course, we must die to the allure of the world, and to the temptations of the evil one, but it is quite as important to die to our self-life.

"Let us cultivate the unchanging habit of looking up from our service, of whatever kind, to claim the ability to do it for the glory of God."

Walk Closer to God

Leaving behind a life of crime, most respond with gratitude to the offer of a fresh start: offenses forgiven, new opportunities provided. The one requirement: Keep out of trouble!

It's a tough assignment . . . especially if you keep going back and trying to mix the old with the new.

Looking back won't help you make progress in your Christian life either. Rather, look up to draw from the source of strength that God has given you to live the new life God has set before you.

NOVEMBER 8

Walk in the Word
1 Peter 4:12–19

Peter again encourages those who read his letter to be willing to suffer for the name of Jesus.

Suffering for Being a Christian

[12]Dear friends, do not be surprised at the painful trial you are suffering, as though something strange were happening to you. [13]But rejoice that you participate in the sufferings of Christ, so that you may be overjoyed when his glory is revealed. [14]If you are insulted because of the name of Christ, you are blessed, for the Spirit of glory and of God rests on you. [15]If you suffer, it should not be as a murderer or thief or any other kind of criminal, or even as a meddler. [16]However, if you suffer as a Christian, do not be ashamed, but praise God that you bear that name. [17]For it is time for judgment to begin with the family of God; and if it begins with us, what will the outcome be for those who do not obey the gospel of God? [18]And,

> "If it is hard for the righteous to be saved,
>   what will become of the ungodly and the sinner?"[a]

[19]So then, those who suffer according to God's will should commit themselves to their faithful Creator and continue to do good.

[a]18 Prov. 11:31

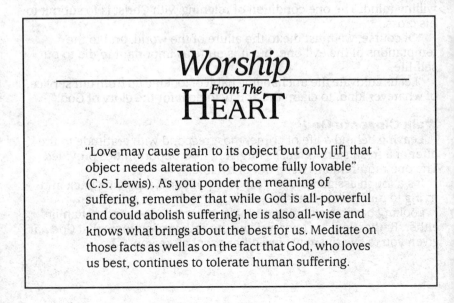

Worship
From The
HEART

"Love may cause pain to its object but only [if] that object needs alteration to become fully lovable" (C.S. Lewis). As you ponder the meaning of suffering, remember that while God is all-powerful and could abolish suffering, he is also all-wise and knows what brings about the best for us. Meditate on those facts as well as on the fact that God, who loves us best, continues to tolerate human suffering.

Putting Our Pain in His Perspective

Dear friends, do not be surprised at the painful trial you are suffering. . . . But rejoice that you participate in the sufferings of Christ (1 Peter 4:12–13).

"Misery loves company." That maxim is often invoked but seldom enjoyed. Yet when the "company" happens to be Jesus Christ, your suffering need not be burdensome. His own suffering and death will help you put your pain in perspective.

Peter's original audience had already learned this firsthand. Now John Calvin tells how to prepare for similar times of trouble today. Read his words slowly, aloud, looking for the focus that provides hope in the midst of painful trials.

Walk With John Calvin

"In order that we may be prepared when we encounter persecutions, we should accustom ourselves to such situations by meditating continually on the cross.

"Peter proves to us that the cross is useful to us by two arguments: that God thus tries our faith, and that we become thus partakers with Christ.

"In the first place, let us remember that the trial of our faith is most necessary, and that we ought thus to obey God willingly who provides for our salvation.

"However, the chief consolation is to be derived from a fellowship with Christ.

"It is a twofold joy, one part which we now enjoy in hope, and the other being the full fruition of which the coming of Christ shall bring to us. The first is mingled with grief and sorrow; the second is connected with exultation."

Walk Closer to God

In difficult times, the cross of Christ becomes a haven of consolation. Why?

Because there you realize your own suffering is small by comparison . . . there you discover joy to come when the troubles are over . . . there you find that the glory of heaven will one day replace the gloom of earth.

So take heart! "Do not be surprised . . . but rejoice"! The best is yet to come. ❍

NOVEMBER 9

📖 Walk in the Word
1 Peter 5

Peter gives some parting instructions to the church, especially to its leaders, warning them to stand firm against the onslaughts of the devil.

To Elders and Young Men

5 To the elders among you, I appeal as a fellow elder, a witness of Christ's sufferings and one who also will share in the glory to be revealed: ²Be shepherds of God's flock that is under your care, serving as overseers—not because you must, but because you are willing, as God wants you to be; not greedy for money, but eager to serve; ³not lording it over those entrusted to you, but being examples to the flock. ⁴And when the Chief Shepherd appears, you will receive the crown of glory that will never fade away.

⁵Young men, in the same way be submissive to those who are older. All of you, clothe yourselves with humility toward one another, because,

> "God opposes the proud
> but gives grace to the humble."ᵃ

⁶Humble yourselves, therefore, under God's mighty hand, that he may lift you up in due time. ⁷Cast all your anxiety on him because he cares for you.

⁸Be self-controlled and alert. Your enemy the devil prowls around like a roaring lion looking for someone to devour. ⁹Resist him, standing firm in the faith, because you know that your brothers throughout the world are undergoing the same kind of sufferings.

¹⁰And the God of all grace, who called you to his eternal glory in Christ, after you have suffered a little while, will himself restore you and make you strong, firm and steadfast. ¹¹To him be the power for ever and ever. Amen.

Final Greetings

¹²With the help of Silas,ᵇ whom I regard as a faithful brother, I have written to you briefly, encouraging you and testifying that this is the true grace of God. Stand fast in it.

¹³She who is in Babylon, chosen together with you, sends you her greetings, and so does my son Mark. ¹⁴Greet one another with a kiss of love.

Peace to all of you who are in Christ.

ᵃ5 Prov. 3:34   ᵇ12 Greek *Silvanus*, a variant of *Silas*

NOVEMBER 9

A Humble Work Outlasting the Stars

Be shepherds of God's flock that is under your care, serving as overseers—not because you must, but because you are willing (1 Peter 5:2).

The similarities between a shepherd of sheep and a shepherd of the flock of God are many:

Both provide a healthy diet for the sheep.

Both protect the flock from predators.

Both lead the sheep in paths that are safe.

Both have a thankless job!

Charles E. Jefferson, a pastor himself at the turn of the century, provides this portrait of a pastor and shepherd.

Walk With Charles E. Jefferson

"The shepherd's work must be done in obscurity. The things which he does do not make interesting copy.

"It is a form of service which eats up a man's life. It makes a man old before his time. Every good shepherd lays down his life for the sheep.

"The finest things a minister does are done out of sight and never get reported. His joy is not that his success is being talked about on earth, but that his name is written in heaven.

"The shepherd in Bible lands had no crowd to admire him. He lived alone with the sheep and the stars.

"The messengers of Christ must not expect brass bands to attend them on their way. Theirs is humble, unpretentious, and oftentimes unnoticed labor. But if it builds souls in righteousness, it is more lasting than the stars."

Walk Closer to God

In the pages of this devotional guide you have met many renowned shepherds of the flock of God—men and women whose ministries have continued long after their passing.

But there are countless other such shepherds who have labored—and are laboring—to nourish the flocks entrusted to them.

How about your own spiritual leaders? Does their labor go unnoticed by their own flock?

Thank God that you have a shepherd—and a Shepherd—who cares for you! ❍

November 10

Walk in the Word
2 Peter 1:1–11

One of the most important aspects of the Christian life, according to Peter, is to grow in godly conduct, because as we do so, we become sure of our salvation.

1 Simon Peter, a servant and apostle of Jesus Christ,

To those who through the righteousness of our God and Savior Jesus Christ have received a faith as precious as ours:

²Grace and peace be yours in abundance through the knowledge of God and of Jesus our Lord.

Making One's Calling and Election Sure

³His divine power has given us everything we need for life and godliness through our knowledge of him who called us by his own glory and goodness. ⁴Through these he has given us his very great and precious promises, so that through them you may participate in the divine nature and escape the corruption in the world caused by evil desires.

⁵For this very reason, make every effort to add to your faith goodness; and to goodness, knowledge; ⁶and to knowledge, self-control; and to self-control, perseverance; and to perseverance, godliness; ⁷and to godliness, brotherly kindness; and to brotherly kindness, love. ⁸For if you possess these qualities in increasing measure, they will keep you from being ineffective and unproductive in your knowledge of our Lord Jesus Christ. ⁹But if anyone does not have them, he is nearsighted and blind, and has forgotten that he has been cleansed from his past sins.

¹⁰Therefore, my brothers, be all the more eager to make your calling and election sure. For if you do these things, you will never fall, ¹¹and you will receive a rich welcome into the eternal kingdom of our Lord and Savior Jesus Christ.

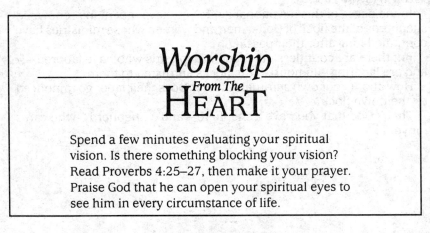

Worship From The HEART

Spend a few minutes evaluating your spiritual vision. Is there something blocking your vision? Read Proverbs 4:25–27, then make it your prayer. Praise God that he can open your spiritual eyes to see him in every circumstance of life.

Farsighted Vision That Looks to Heaven

But if anyone does not have [these qualities], he is nearsighted and blind, and has forgotten that he has been cleansed from his past sins (2 Peter 1:9).

Try to focus on two different objects at the same time, and you'll succeed in seeing neither clearly. It's like having one eye nearsighted and the other farsighted.

The result? Frustration and double vision—the same diagnosis provided by James for the double-minded person who is "unstable in all he does" (James 1:8).

The only cure is single-minded focus: picking one path and sticking to it. Dwight L. Moody explains the pitfalls of trying to follow both forks in a road.

Walk With Dwight L. Moody

"The church is full of people who want one eye for the world and the other for the kingdom of God. Therefore, everything is blurred; one eye is long and the other is short; all is confusion.

"Abraham was longsighted; he had glimpses of the celestial city.

"Stephen was longsighted; he looked clear into heaven. The world had no temptation for him. He had put the world under his feet.

"Paul also had longsighted vision; he had been caught up and had seen things unlawful for him to utter, things grand and glorious.

"When the Spirit of God is on us, the world looks very empty; the world has a very small hold on us, and we begin to let go our hold of it and lay hold of things eternal.

"This is the church's need today. Oh, that the Spirit might come in mighty power and consume all the vile dross there is in us."

Walk Closer to God

Abraham, Stephen, Paul and others saw better things ahead than the things of this world. The Spirit of God controlled the focus of their lives.

How's your spiritual vision? Are you—like Abraham—looking "forward to the city . . . whose architect and builder is God" (Hebrews 11:10)?

That's the only path worth focusing on and following eternally.

NOVEMBER 11

Walk in the Word
2 Peter 1:12–21

Peter insists that no Christian can grow in faith unless he or she is firmly committed to the Word of God, the holy Scriptures.

Prophecy of Scripture

12So I will always remind you of these things, even though you know them and are firmly established in the truth you now have. 13I think it is right to refresh your memory as long as I live in the tent of this body, 14because I know that I will soon put it aside, as our Lord Jesus Christ has made clear to me. 15And I will make every effort to see that after my departure you will always be able to remember these things.

16We did not follow cleverly invented stories when we told you about the power and coming of our Lord Jesus Christ, but we were eyewitnesses of his majesty. 17For he received honor and glory from God the Father when the voice came to him from the Majestic Glory, saying, "This is my Son, whom I love; with him I am well pleased."*a* 18We ourselves heard this voice that came from heaven when we were with him on the sacred mountain.

19And we have the word of the prophets made more certain, and you will do well to pay attention to it, as to a light shining in a dark place, until the day dawns and the morning star rises in your hearts. 20Above all, you must understand that no prophecy of Scripture came about by the prophet's own interpretation. 21For prophecy never had its origin in the will of man, but men spoke from God as they were carried along by the Holy Spirit.

a17 Matt. 17:5; Mark 9:7; Luke 9:35

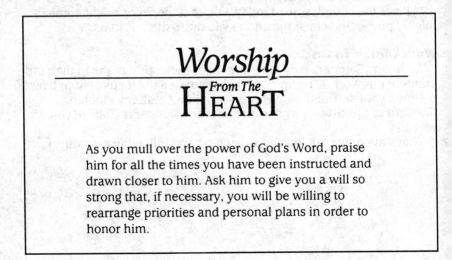

Worship
From The
HEART

As you mull over the power of God's Word, praise him for all the times you have been instructed and drawn closer to him. Ask him to give you a will so strong that, if necessary, you will be willing to rearrange priorities and personal plans in order to honor him.

NOVEMBER 11

A Conscience Captive to the Word of God

No prophecy of Scripture came about by the prophet's own interpretation. For prophecy never had its origin in the will of man, but men spoke from God as they were carried along by the Holy Spirit (2 Peter 1:20–21).

Times have changed. But one book hasn't. With no additions or deletions, the Bible remains a foundation of truth for the Christian.

More than the product of God speaking *to* men, the Bible is the result of God speaking *through* men—moving them by the Spirit to pen "the very words of God" (Romans 3:2).

And what God has said with authority remains a source of comfort and guidance today, as Martin Luther proclaims.

Walk With Martin Luther

"Oh! How great and glorious a thing it is to have before one the Word of God!

"With that we may at all times feel joyous and secure; we need never be in want of consolation, for we see before us, in all its brightness, the pure and right way.

"He who loses sight of the Word of God falls into despair; he follows only the disorderly tendency of his heart and of the world's vanity, which lead him on to destruction.

"A fiery shield is God's Word; of more substance and purer than gold which, tried in the fire, loses none of its substance, but resists and overcomes all the fury of the fiery heat. Even so, he that believes God's Word overcomes all.

"The Holy Scripture is certain and true: God grant me grace to catch hold of its just use."

Walk Closer to God

When challenged by men to renounce the teaching of Scripture, Luther replied, "Unless I am convicted by Scripture and plain reason . . . my conscience is captive to the Word of God."

The Word of God comforted him, strengthened him and guided him. Truth transformed Martin Luther and, through him, his world. The same can happen to you when you "catch hold of its just use" in your life and, like Luther, obey that Word unquestioningly.

NOVEMBER 12

📖 Walk in the Word
2 Peter 2:1–12

According to Peter, the church will always have to face the danger of false teachers, who reject God's truth and try to lead people into all kinds of immorality.

False Teachers and Their Destruction

2 But there were also false prophets among the people, just as there will be false teachers among you. They will secretly introduce destructive heresies, even denying the sovereign Lord who bought them—bringing swift destruction on themselves. ²Many will follow their shameful ways and will bring the way of truth into disrepute. ³In their greed these teachers will exploit you with stories they have made up. Their condemnation has long been hanging over them, and their destruction has not been sleeping.

⁴For if God did not spare angels when they sinned, but sent them to hell,ᵃ putting them into gloomy dungeonsᵇ to be held for judgment; ⁵if he did not spare the ancient world when he brought the flood on its ungodly people, but protected Noah, a preacher of righteousness, and seven others; ⁶if he condemned the cities of Sodom and Gomorrah by burning them to ashes, and made them an example of what is going to happen to the ungodly; ⁷and if he rescued Lot, a righteous man, who was distressed by the filthy lives of lawless men ⁸(for that righteous man, living among them day after day, was tormented in his righteous soul by the lawless deeds he saw and heard) — ⁹if this is so, then the Lord knows how to rescue godly men from trials and to hold the unrighteous for the day of judgment, while continuing their punishment.ᶜ ¹⁰This is especially true of those who follow the corrupt desire of the sinful natureᵈ and despise authority.

Bold and arrogant, these men are not afraid to slander celestial beings; ¹¹yet even angels, although they are stronger and more powerful, do not bring slanderous accusations against such beings in the presence of the Lord. ¹²But these men blaspheme in matters they do not understand. They are like brute beasts, creatures of instinct, born only to be caught and destroyed, and like beasts they too will perish.

ᵃ4 Greek *Tartarus*   ᵇ4 Some manuscripts *into chains of darkness*   ᶜ9 Or *unrighteous for punishment until the day of judgment*   ᵈ10 Or *the flesh*

NOVEMBER 12

Knowing and Loving the Truth

But these men blaspheme in matters they do not understand (2 Peter 2:12).

Contrary to the popular notion, ignorance isn't bliss. Ignoring what you know to be true is dangerous; ridiculing what you choose to ignore can be deadly.

Peter speaks of the consequences for those who ignore the truth about God. And Thomas Manton examines some of the reasons men "blaspheme in matters they do not understand."

Walk With Thomas Manton

"I observe that truth is usually slandered out of ignorance.

"In the apostles' days, the doctrine of the cross was thought to be foolish by those who knew the least about it. Later, the Christian religion was condemned without having been heard.

"It is the devil's cunning to keep us at a distance from truth, and burden it with prejudices, so that we may suspect rather than search, and condemn out of ignorance what upon knowledge we can only love.

"When we speak out against things, we should speak out of advised knowledge, not rash zeal.

"It is a vain thing to begin with the emotions, and to hate before we know. Rash prejudices engage men in opposition, and they will not admit the truth when presented to them.

"Having hated it without knowledge, they hate it against knowledge, and so are hardened against the ways of God."

Walk Closer to God

Ignoring the facts will never change the facts. But it will change the way the facts impact your life.

When confronted with the Word of God, many have staked their lives on it; others have ridiculed it. The former have found everlasting life; the latter stand "condemned already" (John 3:18).

When confronted with God's truth, do you respond, "I don't know" . . . "I don't understand" . . . "I don't care" . . . or "I don't dare say no"? That's a question you cannot ignore. ❏

NOVEMBER 13

📖 Walk in the Word
2 Peter 2:13–22

In his continuing discussion of false teachers, Peter points out their greed and their condemnation by God.

---

[13]They will be paid back with harm for the harm they have done. Their idea of pleasure is to carouse in broad daylight. They are blots and blemishes, reveling in their pleasures while they feast with you.[a] [14]With eyes full of adultery, they never stop sinning; they seduce the unstable; they are experts in greed — an accursed brood! [15]They have left the straight way and wandered off to follow the way of Balaam son of Beor, who loved the wages of wickedness. [16]But he was rebuked for his wrongdoing by a donkey — a beast without speech — who spoke with a man's voice and restrained the prophet's madness.

[17]These men are springs without water and mists driven by a storm. Blackest darkness is reserved for them. [18]For they mouth empty, boastful words and, by appealing to the lustful desires of sinful human nature, they entice people who are just escaping from those who live in error. [19]They promise them freedom, while they themselves are slaves of depravity — for a man is a slave to whatever has mastered him. [20]If they have escaped the corruption of the world by knowing our Lord and Savior Jesus Christ and are again entangled in it and overcome, they are worse off at the end than they were at the beginning. [21]It would have been better for them not to have known the way of righteousness, than to have known it and then to turn their backs on the sacred command that was passed on to them. [22]Of them the proverbs are true: "A dog returns to its vomit,"[b] and, "A sow that is washed goes back to her wallowing in the mud."

---

[a]13 Some manuscripts *in their love feasts*   [b]22 Prov. 26:11

Worship
From The HEART

The donkey that opened its mouth to rebuke its master was God's instrument for getting Balaam's attention. Recall the three most unusual ways God has used to get your attention. Rejoice that he is a God who guides your steps. Thank him for preserving you, his child, from error and danger.

Startling Situations and Strange Rebukes

They have left the straight way and wandered off to follow the way of Balaam . . . who loved the wages of wickedness. But he was rebuked for his wrongdoing by a donkey (2 Peter 2:15–16).

Listening to a talking animal may seem very curious. But in Balaam's case, God used the donkey to show how Balaam's rebelliousness had blinded his eyes and stopped his ears to the angel of the Lord.

But though talking animals are seldom encountered, the reason for Balaam's rebellion is as common now as it was then, as Matthew Henry's insight reveals.

Walk With Matthew Henry

"The inordinate love of this world turns people out of the way which leads to the unspeakably better things of another life. The love of riches and honor turned Balaam away from duty, although he knew the way that he took displeased the Lord.

"Hardened sinners sometimes meet with rebukes for their iniquity. God stops them in their way and opens the mouth of conscience, or by some startling circumstance confronts them.

"Though some extraordinary rebuke may for a little while cool men's courage and hinder their violent progress in the way of sin, it will not make them forsake the way of iniquity and go over into the way of holiness.

"Those who will not yield to usual methods of reproof will be but little influenced by miraculous appearances to turn from their sinful course."

Walk Closer to God

If you're not listening to God's Word, don't be surprised if his "still small voice" becomes loud and painfully clear through some out-of-the-ordinary circumstance. But even then, there's no guarantee you'll get the message.

As Abraham warned the rich man in Luke 16:31, "They will not be convinced even if someone rises from the dead."

It's dangerous to grow "hard of hearing" toward the things of God. What does it take for you to hear—and heed—God's Word? ⟨⟩

NOVEMBER 14

Walk in the Word
2 Peter 3:1–10

Peter assures his readers that if they remain patient just a little longer, the day of the Lord will indeed arrive and the wicked will be destroyed.

The Day of the Lord

3 Dear friends, this is now my second letter to you. I have written both of them as reminders to stimulate you to wholesome thinking. ²I want you to recall the words spoken in the past by the holy prophets and the command given by our Lord and Savior through your apostles.

³First of all, you must understand that in the last days scoffers will come, scoffing and following their own evil desires. ⁴They will say, "Where is this 'coming' he promised? Ever since our fathers died, everything goes on as it has since the beginning of creation." ⁵But they deliberately forget that long ago by God's word the heavens existed and the earth was formed out of water and by water. ⁶By these waters also the world of that time was deluged and destroyed. ⁷By the same word the present heavens and earth are reserved for fire, being kept for the day of judgment and destruction of ungodly men.

⁸But do not forget this one thing, dear friends: With the Lord a day is like a thousand years, and a thousand years are like a day. ⁹The Lord is not slow in keeping his promise, as some understand slowness. He is patient with you, not wanting anyone to perish, but everyone to come to repentance.

¹⁰But the day of the Lord will come like a thief. The heavens will disappear with a roar; the elements will be destroyed by fire, and the earth and everything in it will be laid bare. ᵃ

ᵃ10 Some manuscripts *be burned up*

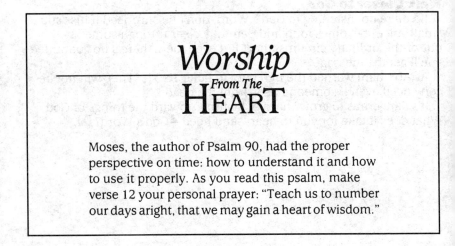

Worship
From The HEART

Moses, the author of Psalm 90, had the proper perspective on time: how to understand it and how to use it properly. As you read this psalm, make verse 12 your personal prayer: "Teach us to number our days aright, that we may gain a heart of wisdom."

Minutes in the Mind of God

But do not forget this one thing, dear friends: With the Lord a day is like a thousand years, and a thousand years are like a day (2 Peter 3:8).

For God, it is never too early or too late. He controls time. When the need arises, he can even stop a day in its tracks (Joshua 10:12–14)!

God's timing is always perfect, a lesson his children need to learn repeatedly. When circumstances appear overwhelming and time seems to have run out, God is right on schedule, as F.B. Meyer explains.

Walk With F.B. Meyer

"There is no succession of time with God; no past, no future. He dwells in the eternal present, as I AM. One day is as a thousand years. He could do in a single day, if he chose, what he has at other times taken a thousand years to accomplish.

"Do not say that he must have as long to make the second heaven and earth as the first.

"All this could be changed in a moment, in the twinkling of an eye; and between sunrise and sunset God could accomplish the work of a thousand ordinary years. Periods that seem so long to our finite minds are not so to God. A thousand years in our reckoning is but a day in his.

"You say it is nearly two thousand years ago since Jesus died, or at least that we are in the evening of the second thousand. But in God's reckoning, the cross, the grave, the resurrection, took place in the morning of yesterday.

"Take wider views of God's horizon; believe in his mighty march throughout the centuries. And the centuries are the beats of the minutehand to God."

Walk Closer to God

Time is too important to squander. Take a look at your daily schedule. How do you spend your time? How do you waste time? How can you better use the time given you?

You cannot learn too early who is best able to manage your schedule. Following him a day . . . an hour . . . a minute at a time is one sure way of redeeming the time. ❒

NOVEMBER 15

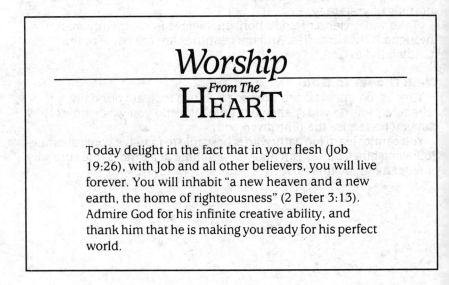 Walk in the Word
2 Peter 3:11–18

Peter encourages Christians to persevere in a blameless lifestyle until the day of the Lord arrives and concludes with a warning against the false teachers.

---

¹¹Since everything will be destroyed in this way, what kind of people ought you to be? You ought to live holy and godly lives ¹²as you look forward to the day of God and speed its coming.ᵃ That day will bring about the destruction of the heavens by fire, and the elements will melt in the heat. ¹³But in keeping with his promise we are looking forward to a new heaven and a new earth, the home of righteousness.

¹⁴So then, dear friends, since you are looking forward to this, make every effort to be found spotless, blameless and at peace with him. ¹⁵Bear in mind that our Lord's patience means salvation, just as our dear brother Paul also wrote you with the wisdom that God gave him. ¹⁶He writes the same way in all his letters, speaking in them of these matters. His letters contain some things that are hard to understand, which ignorant and unstable people distort, as they do the other Scriptures, to their own destruction.

¹⁷Therefore, dear friends, since you already know this, be on your guard so that you may not be carried away by the error of lawless men and fall from your secure position. ¹⁸But grow in the grace and knowledge of our Lord and Savior Jesus Christ. To him be glory both now and forever! Amen.

ᵃ12 Or as you wait eagerly for the day of God to come

Worship
From The HEART

Today delight in the fact that in your flesh (Job 19:26), with Job and all other believers, you will live forever. You will inhabit "a new heaven and a new earth, the home of righteousness" (2 Peter 3:13). Admire God for his infinite creative ability, and thank him that he is making you ready for his perfect world.

Nestling Nearer to the Heart of God

> But grow in the grace and knowledge of our Lord and Savior Jesus Christ (2 Peter 3:18).

Making notches in a door frame is one way to measure the physical growth of a child. But how do you measure the spiritual growth of a child of God?

Maturity in the faith cannot be tallied in inches or pounds. Instead, growth in the Christian life takes place in the inner man—"in the grace and knowledge of our Lord and Savior Jesus Christ."

Alexander Maclaren provides several "yardsticks" for Christian growth.

Walk With Alexander Maclaren

"If you are a Christian, you ought to be realizing continually a deeper consciousness of Christ's love and favor as yours. You ought to be nestling every day nearer to his heart, and getting more and more sure of his mercy and love for you.

"And you ought not only to be realizing the fact of his love with increasing certitude, but you ought to be drinking in the consequences of that love and every day deriving more and more of the spiritual gifts of which his hands are full. In him is an inexhaustible store of abundance for each of us.

"There is nothing mystical or removed from the experience of daily life in this exhortation: 'Grow in grace.' It is not growth in some strange experience, but a very plain, practical thing—a daily transformation, with growing completeness, into the likeness of Jesus Christ."

Walk Closer to God

A young boy looks in the mirror and knows he is growing up. He is growing taller, stronger, wiser. He is developing a striking family resemblance to the one who calls him "son."

As Jesus grew up, he "grew in wisdom and stature, and in favor with God and men" (Luke 2:52).

Four essential areas of growth: Mental. Physical. Spiritual. Social. Every day as you look intently into the mirror of God's Word, ask yourself what you can do to promote healthy growth in each of those areas of your life. ❍

NOVEMBER 16

📖 Walk in the Word
1 John 1:1–4

John begins his first letter by proclaiming Jesus Christ as the Word of life, in whom we have eternal life.

The Word of Life

1 That which was from the beginning, which we have heard, which we have seen with our eyes, which we have looked at and our hands have touched—this we proclaim concerning the Word of life. ²The life appeared; we have seen it and testify to it, and we proclaim to you the eternal life, which was with the Father and has appeared to us. ³We proclaim to you what we have seen and heard, so that you also may have fellowship with us. And our fellowship is with the Father and with his Son, Jesus Christ. ⁴We write this to make our*a* joy complete.

a4 Some manuscripts your

PSALM 25*a*

Of David.

To you, O LORD, I lift up my soul;
2   in you I trust, O my God.
Do not let me be put to shame,
    nor let my enemies triumph over me.
³No one whose hope is in you
    will ever be put to shame,
but they will be put to shame
    who are treacherous without excuse.

⁴Show me your ways, O LORD,
    teach me your paths;
⁵guide me in your truth and teach me,
    for you are God my Savior,
    and my hope is in you all day long.
⁶Remember, O LORD, your great mercy and love,
    for they are from of old.
⁷Remember not the sins of my youth
    and my rebellious ways;
according to your love remember me,
    for you are good, O LORD.

aThis psalm is an acrostic poem, the verses of which begin with the successive letters of the Hebrew alphabet.

I Know That My Redeemer Lives

> That which was from the beginning, which we have heard, which we have seen with our eyes, which we have looked at and our hands have touched—this we proclaim concerning the Word of life (1 John 1:1).

John's proclamation is a triumphant statement of faith.

Some Christians were stumbling over the Gnostic teaching that Jesus did not really have a body. This heresy borrowed much from contemporary philosophy but contradicted the gospel. Gnosticism had weakened the faith of some, so John wrote to remind the church of the truth of the incarnation.

How like John's audience we are! The foolish philosophies of this world easily take us captive. Robert Murray McCheyne urges us to fix our eyes on Jesus and throw doubt to the wind.

Walk With Robert Murray McCheyne

"Oh, brethren, could you and I pass this day through these heavens and see what is now going on in the sanctuary above—could you see what the child of God now sees who died last night—could you see the Lamb with the scars of his five deep wounds sitting in the very midst of the throne—could you see the thousands, all singing, 'Worthy is the Lamb that was slain'—and were one of these angels to tell you, 'This is he that undertook the cause of lost sinners; there he is upon the throne of heaven; consider him; look long and earnestly upon his wounds and glory'—could you see all these things, do you think it would be safe to trust him?

" 'Yes, yes,' every soul exclaims. 'Lord, it is enough! Let me ever stand and gaze upon the almighty, all-worthy, all-divine Savior! Yes, though the sins of all the world were on my wicked head, still I could not doubt that his work is complete, and that I am quite safe when I believe in him.' "

Walk Closer to God

John had enough faith to publicly proclaim his Christianity at a time when it brought imprisonment or death. Do you have enough faith to "salt" your conversation with Christ at a time when it might bring scorn?

If you're like most of us, you answered, "Well, maybe." Fortunately, we have a Savior who hears us when we cry, "I do believe; help me overcome my unbelief!" Be encouraged. That is a prayer he will answer. ○

November 17

Walk in the Word
1 John 1:5 — 2:2

John emphasizes that everything we need for salvation can be found in Jesus Christ — fellowship with God, forgiveness of sin and someone to speak to God.

Walking in the Light

⁵This is the message we have heard from him and declare to you: God is light; in him there is no darkness at all. ⁶If we claim to have fellowship with him yet walk in the darkness, we lie and do not live by the truth. ⁷But if we walk in the light, as he is in the light, we have fellowship with one another, and the blood of Jesus, his Son, purifies us from all*a* sin.

⁸If we claim to be without sin, we deceive ourselves and the truth is not in us. ⁹If we confess our sins, he is faithful and just and will forgive us our sins and purify us from all unrighteousness. ¹⁰If we claim we have not sinned, we make him out to be a liar and his word has no place in our lives.

2 My dear children, I write this to you so that you will not sin. But if anybody does sin, we have one who speaks to the Father in our defense — Jesus Christ, the Righteous One. ²He is the atoning sacrifice for our sins, and not only for ours but also for*b* the sins of the whole world.

a7 Or every   b2 Or He is the one who turns aside God's wrath, taking away our sins, and not only ours but also

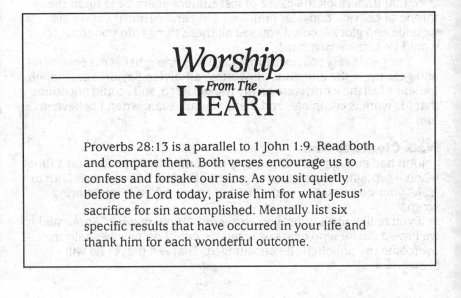

Worship
From The HEART

Proverbs 28:13 is a parallel to 1 John 1:9. Read both and compare them. Both verses encourage us to confess and forsake our sins. As you sit quietly before the Lord today, praise him for what Jesus' sacrifice for sin accomplished. Mentally list six specific results that have occurred in your life and thank him for each wonderful outcome.

Sins Removed for Time and Eternity

If we confess our sins, he is faithful and just and will forgive us our sins and purify us from all unrighteousness (1 John 1:9).

What happens when you incur a debt so large that you can never repay it? Then it is up to someone else to forgive you . . . or else!

That's precisely what happened when you became a Christian. Your insurmountable debt of sin was forgiven by the payment of an infinite price: the blood of Jesus Christ.

Dwight L. Moody offers this illustration to help you comprehend the magnitude of forgiveness.

Walk With Dwight L. Moody

"We greatly dishonor God by bringing up our sins after he has forgiven them. Hundreds of Christians are doing this all the time.

"Suppose my little child has disobeyed me, and comes to me and says, 'Papa, I did what you told me not to do; I want to be forgiven.' She has deep and genuine repentance. I kiss away her tears and forgive her.

"She then comes to me the next day and wants to talk about it. 'No,' I say, 'it is all forgiven.'

"The next day she says, 'Papa, won't you forgive me for that sin I did two days ago?' I think that would grieve me! Suppose she came to me every morning for six months: Would it not grieve and dishonor me?

"God has not only forgiven our sins, but has removed them for time and eternity. Ought one to grieve and dishonor him by bringing them up before him every day?"

Walk Closer to God

God's forgiveness is like a canceled note—torn apart and burned, never to be shown to you again.

Let the words of this simple chorus reflect your response to God for his forgiveness to you:

He paid a debt he did not owe,
    I owed a debt I could not pay,
I needed someone to wash my sins away.
    And now I sing a brand new song—
Amazing grace—
    Christ Jesus paid a debt that I could never pay. ❒

NOVEMBER 18

Walk in the Word
1 John 2:3–11

John stresses that the most important command for Christians to obey is to love one another, since refusing to do so means that we are still in the darkness of sin.

³We know that we have come to know him if we obey his commands. ⁴The man who says, "I know him," but does not do what he commands is a liar, and the truth is not in him. ⁵But if anyone obeys his word, God's love*a* is truly made complete in him. This is how we know we are in him: ⁶Whoever claims to live in him must walk as Jesus did.

⁷Dear friends, I am not writing you a new command but an old one, which you have had since the beginning. This old command is the message you have heard. ⁸Yet I am writing you a new command; its truth is seen in him and you, because the darkness is passing and the true light is already shining.

⁹Anyone who claims to be in the light but hates his brother is still in the darkness. ¹⁰Whoever loves his brother lives in the light, and there is nothing in him*b* to make him stumble. ¹¹But whoever hates his brother is in the darkness and walks around in the darkness; he does not know where he is going, because the darkness has blinded him.

a5 Or *word, love for God*   *b10* Or *it*

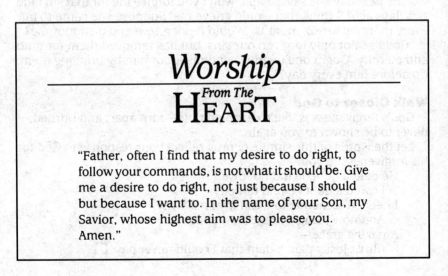

Worship From The HEART

"Father, often I find that my desire to do right, to follow your commands, is not what it should be. Give me a desire to do right, not just because I should but because I want to. In the name of your Son, my Savior, whose highest aim was to please you. Amen."

Work Out Your Salvation

We know that we have come to know him if we obey his commands. The man who says, "I know him," but does not do what he commands is a liar, and the truth is not in him (1 John 2:3–4).

Just mention the word *commands* in our society and watch what happens. Some people bristle and the rest squirm. Sadly, that attitude not only permeates the world, but also the church. But the apostle John regards obedience to God's commands as a good way to judge whether we know Christ.

In the first chapter we saw that John wrote to refute the Gnostic heresy that matter was evil and thus Jesus could not have come in the flesh. John also wrote to correct another Gnostic error: licentiousness. Their reasoning went like this: If evil is in matter, rather than in breaking God's law, then breaking God's law is not evil. You can imagine what kind of wickedness followed.

Shouldn't the Christian want to obey God? Listen to Bishop Ryle.

Walk With J.C. Ryle

"Believers are eminently and peculiarly under a special obligation to live holy lives. They are not dead, blind and unrenewed; they are alive unto God, enlightened, and have a new principle within them. Whose fault is it if they are not holy? On whom can they throw the blame if they are not sanctified? God, who has given them a new heart and a new nature, has deprived them of all excuse if they do not live for his praise.

"This is a point which is far too much forgotten. A man who professes to sanctification (if indeed any at all), and coolly tells you he 'can do nothing,' is a very pitiable sight and a very ignorant man. Against this delusion let us be on our guard. If the Savior of sinners gives us renewing grace, and calls us by his Spirit, we may be sure that he expects us not to go to sleep."

Walk Closer to God

John says God's commands distinguish love from sin and are not burdensome (1 John 3:4; 5:3). The world says God's commands are chains to be broken and fetters to be thrown off (Psalm 2:3). Which attitude characterizes you? ❍

November 19

Walk in the Word
1 John 2:12–17

John points out how important it is for us to fight against and overcome the devil and the world.

> [12]I write to you, dear children,
>   because your sins have been forgiven on account of his
>   name.
> [13]I write to you, fathers,
>   because you have known him who is from the beginning.
> I write to you, young men,
>   because you have overcome the evil one.
> I write to you, dear children,
>   because you have known the Father.
> [14]I write to you, fathers,
>   because you have known him who is from the beginning.
> I write to you, young men,
>   because you are strong,
>   and the word of God lives in you,
>   and you have overcome the evil one.

Do Not Love the World

[15]Do not love the world or anything in the world. If anyone loves the world, the love of the Father is not in him. [16]For everything in the world—the cravings of sinful man, the lust of his eyes and the boasting of what he has and does—comes not from the Father but from the world. [17]The world and its desires pass away, but the man who does the will of God lives forever.

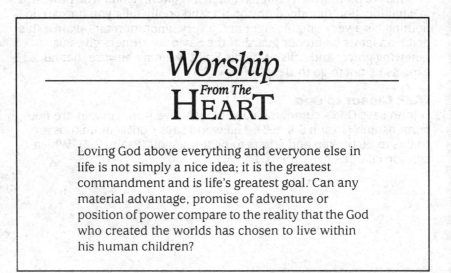

Worship
From The
HEART

Loving God above everything and everyone else in life is not simply a nice idea; it is the greatest commandment and is life's greatest goal. Can any material advantage, promise of adventure or position of power compare to the reality that the God who created the worlds has chosen to live within his human children?

Love and Loyalty in a Dangerous World

Do not love the world. . . . For everything in the world—the cravings of sinful man, the lust of his eyes and the boasting of what he has and does—comes not from the Father but from the world (1 John 2:15–16).

It's easier to worship what is seen than what is unseen—which helps explain why many love the creation and neglect the Creator.

But as Paul points out in Romans 1, love for the world, when set above love for its maker, opens the door for a downward spiral of degradation—a theme John explores in chapter two of his letter, and Andrew Murray probes in this insight.

Walk With Andrew Murray

"The world is the power that mankind has fallen under through sin. And the god of this world, in order to deceive mankind, conceals himself under the form of what God has created. The world surrounds the Christian with temptations, as was the case in the Garden of Eden. We find in Genesis 3 the three characteristics which John mentions:

"1. The lust of the flesh—'The woman saw that the fruit of the tree was good for food.'

"2. The lust of the eyes—'. . . pleasing to the eyes.'

"3. The pride of life—'. . . desirable for gaining wisdom.'

"And the world still offers us desirable food and much to please the fleshly appetites.

"Christian, you live in a dangerous world! Cleave fast to the Lord Jesus. But remember: There must be daily fellowship with Jesus. His love alone can expel the love of the world. Take time to be alone with your Lord."

Walk Closer to God

Food. Wealth. Beauty. Knowledge. None of these is, of itself, evil.

The problem comes when you—like Eve—shift your love and loyalty from the one who made you to the things he made for you.

As Andrew Murray suggests, the cure for a misplaced love for the world is deeper love for the Lord, a passion that grows with every hour you spend in his presence.

855

NOVEMBER 20

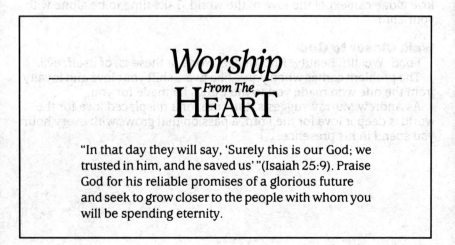 Walk in the Word
1 John 2:18–27

Because false teachers are trying to lead the church astray, John instructs his readers to remain firm in the truths they have been taught.

Warning Against Antichrists

¹⁸Dear children, this is the last hour; and as you have heard that the antichrist is coming, even now many antichrists have come. This is how we know it is the last hour. ¹⁹They went out from us, but they did not really belong to us. For if they had belonged to us, they would have remained with us; but their going showed that none of them belonged to us.

²⁰But you have an anointing from the Holy One, and all of you know the truth.[a] ²¹I do not write to you because you do not know the truth, but because you do know it and because no lie comes from the truth. ²²Who is the liar? It is the man who denies that Jesus is the Christ. Such a man is the antichrist—he denies the Father and the Son. ²³No one who denies the Son has the Father; whoever acknowledges the Son has the Father also.

²⁴See that what you have heard from the beginning remains in you. If it does, you also will remain in the Son and in the Father. ²⁵And this is what he promised us—even eternal life.

²⁶I am writing these things to you about those who are trying to lead you astray. ²⁷As for you, the anointing you received from him remains in you, and you do not need anyone to teach you. But as his anointing teaches you about all things and as that anointing is real, not counterfeit—just as it has taught you, remain in him.

a20 Some manuscripts *and you know all things*

Worship
From The
HEART

"In that day they will say, 'Surely this is our God; we trusted in him, and he saved us' "(Isaiah 25:9). Praise God for his reliable promises of a glorious future and seek to grow closer to the people with whom you will be spending eternity.

Worth the Wait and Worth the Conflict

And this is what he promised us—even eternal life (1 John 2:25).

Studies show that all work and no rest make for a poor worker. And the promise of future rest for the Christian makes the struggle of this world easier to bear.

Sin and sorrow, death and tears will all be left behind when the child of God goes to be with his heavenly Father.

Thomas à Kempis shares this comforting glimpse of God's perspective on life—a view only visible from the standpoint of eternity.

Walk With Thomas à Kempis

"Do not be worn out by the labors which you have undertaken for my sake, and do not let tribulations ever cast you down. Instead, let my promise strengthen and comfort you under every circumstance.

"I am well able to reward you above all measure and degree. You shall not toil here long, nor always be oppressed with griefs. A time will come when all labor and trouble will cease.

"Labor faithfully in my vineyard; I will be thy recompense. Life everlasting is worth all these conflicts, and greater than these. Are not all plentiful labors to be endured for the sake of life eternal?

"Lift your face therefore unto heaven; behold, I and all my saints with me—who in this world had great conflicts—are now comforted, now rejoicing, now secure, now at rest, and shall remain with me everlastingly in the kingdom of my Father."

Walk Closer to God

Two verses speak volumes about the benefits of eternal life:

"For God so loved the world that he gave his one and only Son, that whoever believes in him shall not perish but have eternal life" (John 3:16).

"Now this is eternal life: that they may know you, the only true God, and Jesus Christ, whom you have sent" (John 17:3).

Get to know Jesus Christ, and you will spend an eternity getting to know God.

NOVEMBER 21

📖 Walk in the Word
1 John 2:28 — 3:10

According to John, true children of God continue in Christ, purify themselves, fight against sin and gain victory over the devil.

Children of God

28And now, dear children, continue in him, so that when he appears we may be confident and unashamed before him at his coming.

29If you know that he is righteous, you know that everyone who does what is right has been born of him.

3 How great is the love the Father has lavished on us, that we should be called children of God! And that is what we are! The reason the world does not know us is that it did not know him. 2Dear friends, now we are children of God, and what we will be has not yet been made known. But we know that when he appears,*a* we shall be like him, for we shall see him as he is. 3Everyone who has this hope in him purifies himself, just as he is pure.

4Everyone who sins breaks the law; in fact, sin is lawlessness. 5But you know that he appeared so that he might take away our sins. And in him is no sin. 6No one who lives in him keeps on sinning. No one who continues to sin has either seen him or known him.

7Dear children, do not let anyone lead you astray. He who does what is right is righteous, just as he is righteous. 8He who does what is sinful is of the devil, because the devil has been sinning from the beginning. The reason the Son of God appeared was to destroy the devil's work. 9No one who is born of God will continue to sin, because God's seed remains in him; he cannot go on sinning, because he has been born of God. 10This is how we know who the children of God are and who the children of the devil are: Anyone who does not do what is right is not a child of God; nor is anyone who does not love his brother.

a2 Or when it is made known

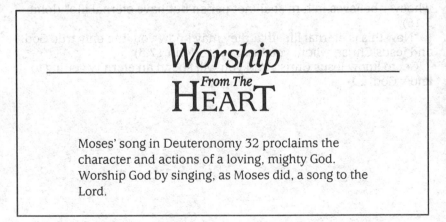

Worship
From The HEART

Moses' song in Deuteronomy 32 proclaims the character and actions of a loving, mighty God. Worship God by singing, as Moses did, a song to the Lord.

Souls That Bear His Image Bright

Dear friends, now we are children of God, and what we will be has not yet been made known. But we know that when he appears, we shall be like him (1 John 3:2).

Adopting a son is one way to ensure that the family name will be passed on. The family likeness, however, is not so easily transmitted!

Adoption into the family of God is different. There you receive both a new name and a new nature—the nature of God's Son. The nature of purity, holiness, godliness.

Being loved by him would be reason enough to rejoice. But now John adds that "we shall be like him" when we see him face to face. Isaac Watts offers praise for that fact in these majestic stanzas.

Walk With Isaac Watts

Behold, the amazing gift of love
　　The Father hath bestowed
On us, the sinful sons of men,
　　To call us sons of God!

Concealed as yet this honor lies
　　By this dark world unknown,
A world that knew not when He came,
　　Even God's eternal Son.

Our souls, we know, when He appears
　　Shall bear His image bright:
For all His glory, full disclosed,
　　Shall open to His sight.

A hope so great, and so divine,
　　May trials well endure;
And purge the soul from carnal sin,
　　As Christ Himself is pure.

Walk Closer to God

When you've received so much from the Father—life eternal in the family of God and all its accompanying blessings—the challenge to "well endure" trials doesn't sound so unreasonable.

Not when you have a Father to whom you can cry "Abba"... one who cares for his own like a tender shepherd.... one who knows all his children by name. Now would be a good time to bow in gratitude for such an "amazing gift of love." ❍

November 22

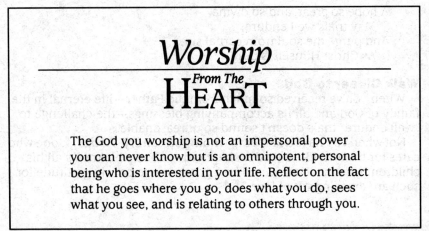 Walk in the Word
1 John 3:11–24

John instructs us to love one another not just with words but especially with deeds; that is how Jesus loved us and that is how his love is made perfect in us.

Love One Another

¹¹This is the message you heard from the beginning: We should love one another. ¹²Do not be like Cain, who belonged to the evil one and murdered his brother. And why did he murder him? Because his own actions were evil and his brother's were righteous. ¹³Do not be surprised, my brothers, if the world hates you. ¹⁴We know that we have passed from death to life, because we love our brothers. Anyone who does not love remains in death. ¹⁵Anyone who hates his brother is a murderer, and you know that no murderer has eternal life in him.

¹⁶This is how we know what love is: Jesus Christ laid down his life for us. And we ought to lay down our lives for our brothers. ¹⁷If anyone has material possessions and sees his brother in need but has no pity on him, how can the love of God be in him? ¹⁸Dear children, let us not love with words or tongue but with actions and in truth. ¹⁹This then is how we know that we belong to the truth, and how we set our hearts at rest in his presence ²⁰whenever our hearts condemn us. For God is greater than our hearts, and he knows everything.

²¹Dear friends, if our hearts do not condemn us, we have confidence before God ²²and receive from him anything we ask, because we obey his commands and do what pleases him. ²³And this is his command: to believe in the name of his Son, Jesus Christ, and to love one another as he commanded us. ²⁴Those who obey his commands live in him, and he in them. And this is how we know that he lives in us: We know it by the Spirit he gave us.

Worship
From The
HEART

The God you worship is not an impersonal power
you can never know but is an omnipotent, personal
being who is interested in your life. Reflect on the fact
that he goes where you go, does what you do, sees
what you see, and is relating to others through you.

Lighten the Burdens of Another Along the Way

If anyone has material possessions and sees his brother in need but has no pity on him, how can the love of God be in him? (1 John 3:17).

Jesus, who walked the earth as love personified, is rarely pictured in the gospels telling another individual, "I love you."

He didn't have to; his actions spoke volumes. To the poor . . . the lepers . . . the blind . . . the lame . . . the socially shunned.

By dealing with their physical need, Jesus set the stage for speaking to their spiritual need as well.

The world's calamity thus becomes the Christian's opportunity, a situation Jonathan Edwards addresses.

Walk With Jonathan Edwards

"There are innumerable kinds of temporal calamities in which men and women need help. Many are hungry, or thirsty, or strangers, or naked, or sick, or in prison, or in suffering of some other kind; and to all such we may minister.

"By thus endeavoring to do good to them externally, we have a greater opportunity to do good to their souls. For when our preachings are accompanied with such outward kindness, it opens the way to give the preachings their full force.

"And we may thus contribute to the good of others in three ways: By giving to them those things that they need and which we possess; by doing for them and helping promote their welfare; and by suffering for them, aiding them to bear their burdens, and doing all in our power to make those burdens lighter."

Walk Closer to God

In the final analysis, what every person needs is Jesus Christ. But if an empty stomach . . . or a burdened heart . . . or some other pressing need is clouding the message, perhaps it's time for sympathy rather than a sermon.

You can give that others might listen. You can help that others might hear. You can lift a burden that others might learn firsthand of your burden-bearer.

That kind of love is hard to resist. ⟨⟩

November 23

Walk in the Word

1 John 4:1–6

In view of false prophets and antichrists, says John, Christians must be able to distinguish between the spirit of truth and the spirit of falsehood.

Test the Spirits

4 Dear friends, do not believe every spirit, but test the spirits to see whether they are from God, because many false prophets have gone out into the world. ²This is how you can recognize the Spirit of God: Every spirit that acknowledges that Jesus Christ has come in the flesh is from God, ³but every spirit that does not acknowledge Jesus is not from God. This is the spirit of the antichrist, which you have heard is coming and even now is already in the world.

⁴You, dear children, are from God and have overcome them, because the one who is in you is greater than the one who is in the world. ⁵They are from the world and therefore speak from the viewpoint of the world, and the world listens to them. ⁶We are from God, and whoever knows God listens to us; but whoever is not from God does not listen to us. This is how we recognize the Spirit*a* of truth and the spirit of falsehood.

*a*6 Or *spirit*

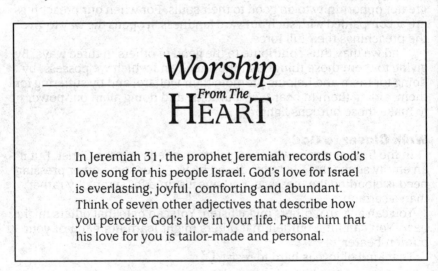

Worship
From The
Heart

In Jeremiah 31, the prophet Jeremiah records God's
love song for his people Israel. God's love for Israel
is everlasting, joyful, comforting and abundant.
Think of seven other adjectives that describe how
you perceive God's love in your life. Praise him that
his love for you is tailor-made and personal.

Time for a Test

> Dear friends, do not believe every spirit, but test the spirits to see whether they are from God (1 John 4:1).

"It's time for a test." These words periodically send shock waves through countless classrooms; but without the test, there's no assurance that you've learned the lesson. In chapter four, John gives his readers a series of tests to help them distinguish between false spirits, evil spirits and God's Spirit.

Testing your spiritual experiences against the timeless standard of God's Word is another "exam" you can't afford to miss, as A.W. Tozer comments.

Walk With A.W. Tozer

"The seeker after God's best is always eager to hear from anyone who offers a way by which he can obtain it. He longs for some new experience, some elevated view of truth, some operation of the Spirit that will raise him above the religious mediocrity he sees all around him.

"Our Lord has made it plain not only that there shall be false spirits abroad, endangering our Christian lives, but that they may be identified and known for what they are!

"The first test must be: 'What has this done to my relationship with and my attitude toward the Lord Jesus Christ?' Do I love God more? Is Jesus Christ still to me the center of all true doctrine?

"Again: 'How does it affect my attitude toward the Scriptures?' Did this new view of truth spring from the Word of God itself or was it the result of some stimulus that lay outside the Bible? Be assured that anything that comes to us from the God of the Word will deepen our love for the Word of God!"

Walk Closer to God

"Father, now is a good time to test myself and see if I am growing in my walk with you.

"When seeking the truth, may I be quick to ask these two questions: 'What will this do to my relationship with and attitude toward Jesus Christ?' and 'How does this affect my attitude toward your Word?'

"May my answers reflect my deep love for you, Father. Amen." ❍

November 24

📖 Walk in the Word
1 John 4:7–21

In one of the Bible's most beautiful passages, John says, "God is love," then goes on to stress that Christ's sacrificial love for us should influence our treatment of others.

God's Love and Ours

⁷Dear friends, let us love one another, for love comes from God. Everyone who loves has been born of God and knows God. ⁸Whoever does not love does not know God, because God is love. ⁹This is how God showed his love among us: He sent his one and only Son*ᵃ* into the world that we might live through him. ¹⁰This is love: not that we loved God, but that he loved us and sent his Son as an atoning sacrifice for*ᵇ* our sins. ¹¹Dear friends, since God so loved us, we also ought to love one another. ¹²No one has ever seen God; but if we love one another, God lives in us and his love is made complete in us.

¹³We know that we live in him and he in us, because he has given us of his Spirit. ¹⁴And we have seen and testify that the Father has sent his Son to be the Savior of the world. ¹⁵If anyone acknowledges that Jesus is the Son of God, God lives in him and he in God. ¹⁶And so we know and rely on the love God has for us.

God is love. Whoever lives in love lives in God, and God in him. ¹⁷In this way, love is made complete among us so that we will have confidence on the day of judgment, because in this world we are like him. ¹⁸There is no fear in love. But perfect love drives out fear, because fear has to do with punishment. The one who fears is not made perfect in love.

¹⁹We love because he first loved us. ²⁰If anyone says, "I love God," yet hates his brother, he is a liar. For anyone who does not love his brother, whom he has seen, cannot love God, whom he has not seen. ²¹And he has given us this command: Whoever loves God must also love his brother.

ᵃ9 Or *his only begotten Son*   *ᵇ10* Or *as the one who would turn aside his wrath, taking away*

Hearts Aglow With Responsive Love

> And so we know and rely on the love God has for us. God is love. Whoever lives in love lives in God, and God in him (1 John 4:16).

What does love look like?

Augustine pictured love this way: "It has the hands to help others. It has the feet to hasten to the poor and needy. It has eyes to see misery and want. It has the ears to hear the sighs of men."

In a word: Love looks like Jesus!

Love talked about is easily turned aside. Love demonstrated is irresistible. And love modeled is the best way to learn how to love in return. "We love because he first loved us" (1 John 4:19). That's why John used the word love more than thirty times in his letter . . . and why this thought from A.B. Simpson is both appropriate and timely.

Walk With A.B. Simpson

"The secret of walking closely with Christ, and working successfully for him, is to fully realize that we are his beloved.

"Let us but feel that he has his heart set upon us, that he is watching us from those heavens with tender interest, that he is following us day by day as a mother follows her babe in his first attempt to walk alone, that he has set his love upon us, and in spite of ourselves is working out for us his highest will and blessing, as far as we will let him—and then nothing can discourage us.

"Our hearts will glow with responsive love. Our faith will spring to meet his mighty promises, and our sacrifices shall become the very luxuries of love for one so dear.

"This was the secret of John's spirit. 'And so we know and rely on the love God has for us.' The heart that has fully learned this has found the secret of unbounded faith and enthusiastic service."

Walk Closer to God

How much does God love you? The telltale evidences are not hard to find. Calvary's cross . . . the empty tomb . . . the indwelling Comforter.

How much do you love God? The evidences should also be obvious. Count them with gratitude for God's goodness to you. ◖◗

NOVEMBER 25

Walk in the Word
1 John 5:1–12

To John, the most important decision a person can make is to believe in the name of the Son of God, for by doing so we receive the gift of eternal life.

Faith in the Son of God

5 Everyone who believes that Jesus is the Christ is born of God, and everyone who loves the father loves his child as well. ²This is how we know that we love the children of God: by loving God and carrying out his commands. ³This is love for God: to obey his commands. And his commands are not burdensome, ⁴for everyone born of God overcomes the world. This is the victory that has overcome the world, even our faith. ⁵Who is it that overcomes the world? Only he who believes that Jesus is the Son of God.

⁶This is the one who came by water and blood—Jesus Christ. He did not come by water only, but by water and blood. And it is the Spirit who testifies, because the Spirit is the truth. ⁷For there are three that testify: ⁸the*ᵃ* Spirit, the water and the blood; and the three are in agreement. ⁹We accept man's testimony, but God's testimony is greater because it is the testimony of God, which he has given about his Son. ¹⁰Anyone who believes in the Son of God has this testimony in his heart. Anyone who does not believe God has made him out to be a liar, because he has not believed the testimony God has given about his Son. ¹¹And this is the testimony: God has given us eternal life, and this life is in his Son. ¹²He who has the Son has life; he who does not have the Son of God does not have life.

ᵃ7,8 Late manuscripts of the Vulgate testify in heaven: the Father, the Word and the Holy Spirit, and these three are one. 8And there are three that testify on earth: the (not found in any Greek manuscript before the sixteenth century)

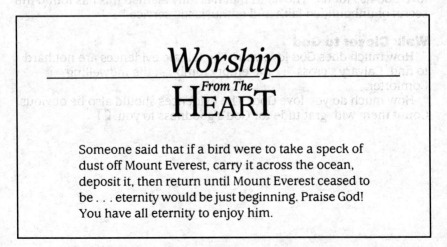

Worship
From The
HEART

Someone said that if a bird were to take a speck of dust off Mount Everest, carry it across the ocean, deposit it, then return until Mount Everest ceased to be . . . eternity would be just beginning. Praise God! You have all eternity to enjoy him.

Certain Beyond All Doubt

And this is the testimony: God has given us eternal life, and this life is in his Son (1 John 5:11).

Saying "I know" can either be a sign of bored resistance or enthusiastic affirmation. It all depends on your attitude.

The child who responds "I know, I know," to a parent's commands, probably doesn't. The believer who responds to his Lord's promises with a confident, "I know, I know," hopefully does.

A careful reading of 1 John will uncover many things God wants you to know (1 John 2:20–21,29; 3:2,5,14–15; 5:13,15,18–20).

Because of what God has done or said, you can know, without doubt, that you belong to him. When God makes a promise, you can stand upon it with confidence. Charles Spurgeon examines the promise of eternal life in Jesus Christ.

Walk With Charles Spurgeon

"Let us regard the promise as a thing so sure and certain that we act upon it and make it a chief figure in all our calculations.

"The Lord promises eternal life to those who believe in Jesus; therefore, if we really believe in Jesus, let us conclude that we have eternal life, and rejoice in this great privilege. The promise of God is our best ground of assurance; it is far more sure than dreams or visions, and fancied revelations; and it is far more to be trusted than feelings, either joy or sorrow.

"Nothing can be more certain than that which is declared by God himself; nothing more sure to happen than that which he has guaranteed by his own hand and seal."

Walk Closer to God

John proclaims a powerful message: "God has given us eternal life, and this life is in his Son" (1 John 5:11). If you have the Son, you have life. And whether you need to invite him into your life for the first time, or simply need to invite him into the complexities of your life today, you can act upon that verse right now.

Nothing can be more certain than what the Son himself declares. ⬭

NOVEMBER 26

Walk in the Word
1 John 5:13–21

John concludes his first letter with some comments on how those who are in Christ can be victorious over sin and the devil.

Concluding Remarks

¹³I write these things to you who believe in the name of the Son of God so that you may know that you have eternal life. ¹⁴This is the confidence we have in approaching God: that if we ask anything according to his will, he hears us. ¹⁵And if we know that he hears us—whatever we ask—we know that we have what we asked of him.

¹⁶If anyone sees his brother commit a sin that does not lead to death, he should pray and God will give him life. I refer to those whose sin does not lead to death. There is a sin that leads to death. I am not saying that he should pray about that. ¹⁷All wrongdoing is sin, and there is sin that does not lead to death.

¹⁸We know that anyone born of God does not continue to sin; the one who was born of God keeps him safe, and the evil one cannot harm him. ¹⁹We know that we are children of God, and that the whole world is under the control of the evil one. ²⁰We know also that the Son of God has come and has given us understanding, so that we may know him who is true. And we are in him who is true—even in his Son Jesus Christ. He is the true God and eternal life.

²¹Dear children, keep yourselves from idols.

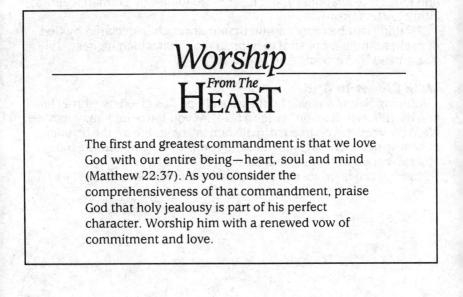

Worship
From The
HEART

The first and greatest commandment is that we love God with our entire being—heart, soul and mind (Matthew 22:37). As you consider the comprehensiveness of that commandment, praise God that holy jealousy is part of his perfect character. Worship him with a renewed vow of commitment and love.

NOVEMBER 26

The Supreme Place in Our Affections

Dear children, keep yourselves from idols (1 John 5:21).

While few people bow before tree stumps or stone pillars today, that doesn't mean idolatry is a thing of the past. As one commentator stated, "Most of the gods of this world are composed of tinted glass, baked-on enamel, chrome, dacron, wool, silk, or alligator leather."

Albert Barnes examines some of the subtle ways in which devotion for God can be misdirected—with disastrous consequences.

Walk With Albert Barnes

"We are not in danger, indeed, of bowing down to idols. But we may be in danger of substituting other things in our affections in the place of God, and of devoting to them the time and the affection which are due to him. It is possible to love even our children with an attachment as shall effectually exclude the true God from the heart. And we may love the world with an attachment such as an idolator would his idol-gods.

"There is practical idolatry all over the world.

"God should have the supreme place in our affections. The love of everything else should be held in subordination to the love of him.

"He should reign in our hearts; be acknowledged in our families; be submitted to at all times as having a right to command and control us; be obeyed in all expressions of his will; and be so loved that we shall be willing to part without a murmur with the dearest object of affection when he takes it from us."

Walk Closer to God

"God or _____."

Is there anything you might put in that blank that would cause you to think twice about the choice?

If so, now is the time to call it what it is—an idol—and to deal with it accordingly.

If not, ask God for an undivided and undiminishing love for him.

There's no better way to "keep yourself from idols" than to keep yourself wholly his. ◖

NOVEMBER 27

Walk in the Word
2 John

In this brief letter, John urges some friends to walk in the truth and to discern properly who are false teachers in the church.

---

¹The elder,

To the chosen lady and her children, whom I love in the truth — and not I only, but also all who know the truth — ²because of the truth, which lives in us and will be with us forever:

³Grace, mercy and peace from God the Father and from Jesus Christ, the Father's Son, will be with us in truth and love.

⁴It has given me great joy to find some of your children walking in the truth, just as the Father commanded us. ⁵And now, dear lady, I am not writing you a new command but one we have had from the beginning. I ask that we love one another. ⁶And this is love: that we walk in obedience to his commands. As you have heard from the beginning, his command is that you walk in love.

⁷Many deceivers, who do not acknowledge Jesus Christ as coming in the flesh, have gone out into the world. Any such person is the deceiver and the antichrist. ⁸Watch out that you do not lose what you have worked for, but that you may be rewarded fully. ⁹Anyone who runs ahead and does not continue in the teaching of Christ does not have God; whoever continues in the teaching has both the Father and the Son. ¹⁰If anyone comes to you and does not bring this teaching, do not take him into your house or welcome him. ¹¹Anyone who welcomes him shares in his wicked work.

¹²I have much to write to you, but I do not want to use paper and ink. Instead, I hope to visit you and talk with you face to face, so that our joy may be complete.

¹³The children of your chosen sister send their greetings.

A Life That Will Leave No Regrets

Watch out that you do not lose what you have worked for, but that you may be rewarded fully (2 John 8).

Salvation in Christ is not a "paycheck" for good works but is instead the unmerited gift of God's love. As with any gift, a heartfelt "thank you" is appropriate.

And as H.A. Ironside points out, thankful service is a reasonable response when you have experienced the mercies of God and received by grace a gift you don't deserve.

Walk With H.A. Ironside

"All who trust in the Lord Jesus are saved, and this totally apart from human merit.

"But all who profess to believe in him are responsible to serve him and to use whatever gift, ability, or means they have for his glory, and to further his interests in this world.

"There are those who profess to be servants who are not even born of the Spirit. But God holds people accountable for what they know and profess. It is incumbent on those who believe his Word to serve wholeheartedly in view of the day when every one of us shall give an account.

"In that solemn hour no one will regret having been too much concerned about living for him. But many will regret the hours spent in selfishness and folly which might have been used for his glory, and talents wasted or hidden away that if properly invested in the light of eternity would have earned Christ's 'well done.'

"He will reward all that is done in accordance with his Word."

Walk Closer to God

Jesus Christ bore the cost of your salvation that you might reap the riches of his grace.

Because he willingly paid the price of sin, you are now free to serve him in "a new life" (Romans 6:4).

Riches in Christ now.

Rewards for faithful service to Christ later.

What greater motivation could there be to turn your gratitude into good works—for his glory?

NOVEMBER 28

📖 Walk in the Word
3 John

John compliments Gaius, a Christian friend, for the hospitality he has shown to some traveling teachers sent out by John, at the same time criticizing Diotrephes who refused to cooperate with these teachers.

¹The elder,

To my dear friend Gaius, whom I love in the truth.

²Dear friend, I pray that you may enjoy good health and that all may go well with you, even as your soul is getting along well. ³It gave me great joy to have some brothers come and tell about your faithfulness to the truth and how you continue to walk in the truth. ⁴I have no greater joy than to hear that my children are walking in the truth.

⁵Dear friend, you are faithful in what you are doing for the brothers, even though they are strangers to you. ⁶They have told the church about your love. You will do well to send them on their way in a manner worthy of God. ⁷It was for the sake of the Name that they went out, receiving no help from the pagans. ⁸We ought therefore to show hospitality to such men so that we may work together for the truth.

⁹I wrote to the church, but Diotrephes, who loves to be first, will have nothing to do with us. ¹⁰So if I come, I will call attention to what he is doing, gossiping maliciously about us. Not satisfied with that, he refuses to welcome the brothers. He also stops those who want to do so and puts them out of the church.

¹¹Dear friend, do not imitate what is evil but what is good. Anyone who does what is good is from God. Anyone who does what is evil has not seen God. ¹²Demetrius is well spoken of by everyone—and even by the truth itself. We also speak well of him, and you know that our testimony is true.

¹³I have much to write you, but I do not want to do so with pen and ink. ¹⁴I hope to see you soon, and we will talk face to face.

Peace to you. The friends here send their greetings. Greet the friends there by name.

Having a Soul That is Saturated With the Truth

It gave me great joy to have some brothers come and tell about your faithfulness to the truth and how you continue to walk in the truth (3 John 3).

Being in close proximity to truth is not enough; truth must be digested before it is of any real benefit in a life.

The apostle John had a deep concern for the role of truth in the lives of his readers. And he had a burden to protect them from destructive error.

The attitude he expresses toward truth in his third letter is explored by Charles Spurgeon.

Walk With Charles Spurgeon

"Truth must enter into the soul, penetrate and saturate it, or else it is of no value.

"Doctrines held as a matter of creed are like bread in the hand, which gives no nourishment to the frame; but doctrine accepted by the heart is as food digested, which by assimilation sustains and builds up the body.

"In us truth must be a living force, an active energy, an indwelling reality, a part of the woof and warp of our being.

"It is a rule of nature that the inward affects the outward as light shines from the center of the lantern through the glass. When therefore the truth is kindled within, its brightness soon beams forth in the outward life and conversation.

"To walk in the truth imparts a life of integrity, holiness, faithfulness, and simplicity—the natural products of those principles of truth which the gospel teaches, and which the Spirit of God enables us to receive."

Walk Closer to God

Without food, it is impossible to sustain physical life.

Without truth, it is impossible to sustain spiritual life.

The nourishing truth of God's Word will help you grow daily into the likeness of the one who is "the truth"—Jesus Christ (John 14:6).

The cleansing, strengthening truth of God: Feed on it daily . . . and watch how life-giving it can be for you! ⟨⟩

NOVEMBER 29

📖 Walk in the Word
Jude 1–16

Although Jude wants to write a letter to build up Christians in the faith, he finds it necessary to warn them severely about the danger of false teachers who are trying to lead people down the pathway of immorality.

¹Jude, a servant of Jesus Christ and a brother of James,

To those who have been called, who are loved by God the Father and kept by*ᵃ* Jesus Christ:

²Mercy, peace and love be yours in abundance.

The Sin and Doom of Godless Men

³Dear friends, although I was very eager to write to you about the salvation we share, I felt I had to write and urge you to contend for the faith that was once for all entrusted to the saints. ⁴For certain men whose condemnation was written about*ᵇ* long ago have secretly slipped in among you. They are godless men, who change the grace of our God into a license for immorality and deny Jesus Christ our only Sovereign and Lord.

⁵Though you already know all this, I want to remind you that the Lord*ᶜ* delivered his people out of Egypt, but later destroyed those who did not believe. ⁶And the angels who did not keep their positions of authority but abandoned their own home—these he has kept in darkness, bound with everlasting chains for judgment on the great Day. ⁷In a similar way, Sodom and Gomorrah and the surrounding towns gave themselves up to sexual immorality and perversion. They serve as an example of those who suffer the punishment of eternal fire.

⁸In the very same way, these dreamers pollute their own bodies, reject authority and slander celestial beings. ⁹But even the archangel Michael, when he was disputing with the devil about the body of Moses, did not dare to bring a slanderous accusation against him, but said, "The Lord rebuke you!" ¹⁰Yet these men speak abusively against whatever they do not understand; and what things they do understand by instinct, like unreasoning animals—these are the very things that destroy them.

¹¹Woe to them! They have taken the way of Cain; they have rushed for profit into Balaam's error; they have been destroyed in Korah's rebellion.

¹²These men are blemishes at your love feasts, eating with you without the slightest qualm—shepherds who feed only themselves. They are clouds without rain, blown along by the wind; autumn trees, without fruit and uprooted—twice dead. ¹³They are wild waves of the sea, foaming up their shame; wandering stars, for whom blackest darkness has been reserved forever.

¹⁴Enoch, the seventh from Adam, prophesied about these men: "See, the Lord is coming with thousands upon thousands of his holy ones ¹⁵to

judge everyone, and to convict all the ungodly of all the ungodly acts they have done in the ungodly way, and of all the harsh words ungodly sinners have spoken against him." ¹⁶These men are grumblers and faultfinders; they follow their own evil desires; they boast about themselves and flatter others for their own advantage.

ᵃ1 Or for; or in   ᵇ4 Or men who were marked out for condemnation   ᶜ5 Some early manuscripts *Jesus*

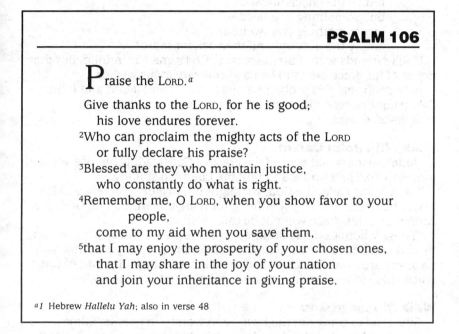

PSALM 106

Praise the Lᴏʀᴅ.ᵃ

Give thanks to the Lᴏʀᴅ, for he is good;
  his love endures forever.
²Who can proclaim the mighty acts of the Lᴏʀᴅ
  or fully declare his praise?
³Blessed are they who maintain justice,
  who constantly do what is right.
⁴Remember me, O Lᴏʀᴅ, when you show favor to your
      people,
  come to my aid when you save them,
⁵that I may enjoy the prosperity of your chosen ones,
  that I may share in the joy of your nation
  and join your inheritance in giving praise.

ᵃ1 Hebrew Hallelu Yah; also in verse 48

NOVEMBER 29

Abusing the Valuable Treasure of Grace

Contend for the faith. . . . For certain men . . . have secretly slipped in among you. They are godless men, who change the grace of our God into a license for immorality and deny Jesus Christ (Jude 3–4).

If a rich friend gave you a blank check, would you:
 . . . return the check unused?
 . . . buy something you needed?
 . . . buy something you wanted?
 . . . empty the account and then ask for more?

Unlike friends with finite resources, God's grace is infinite. But the riches of his grace aren't to be used contrary to his wishes.

Jude confronts this problem in his short, potent letter, and John Calvin comments on the author's admonition concerning the recipients' abuses.

Walk With John Calvin

"Jude's readers had abused the grace of God, leading themselves and others to take an impure and profane liberty in sinning.

"After being called by God, we ought not to glory carelessly in his grace, but instead walk watchfully; for if anyone trifles with God, the contempt of his grace will not be unpunished.

"Those whom God has honored with the greatest blessings, whom he had extolled to the same degree of honor as we enjoy at this day, he afterwards severely punished. In vain were they all proud of God's grace who did not live in a manner suitable to their calling."

Walk Closer to God

Gifts tend to bring out the best—and worst—in people. Some respond with pride, as if they deserved what they received all along. Others respond with humility, acknowledging the goodness of the giver and the unworthiness of the recipient.

God's gift of grace shines brightly when you recall that you didn't deserve what you received—forgiveness and pardon. Nor did you receive what you deserved—condemnation and judgment.

Don't hesitate to receive God's grace with gladness. But be careful how you handle it—as befitting a treasure too valuable to trifle with. ◖◗

November 30

Walk in the Word
Jude 17–25

In view of the danger of false teachers, Jude calls upon Christians to build themselves up in the faith, to pray, and to show compassion to one another.

A Call to Persevere

17But, dear friends, remember what the apostles of our Lord Jesus Christ foretold. 18They said to you, "In the last times there will be scoffers who will follow their own ungodly desires." 19These are the men who divide you, who follow mere natural instincts and do not have the Spirit.

20But you, dear friends, build yourselves up in your most holy faith and pray in the Holy Spirit. 21Keep yourselves in God's love as you wait for the mercy of our Lord Jesus Christ to bring you to eternal life.

22Be merciful to those who doubt; 23snatch others from the fire and save them; to others show mercy, mixed with fear — hating even the clothing stained by corrupted flesh.

Doxology

24To him who is able to keep you from falling and to present you before his glorious presence without fault and with great joy — 25to the only God our Savior be glory, majesty, power and authority, through Jesus Christ our Lord, before all ages, now and forevermore! Amen.

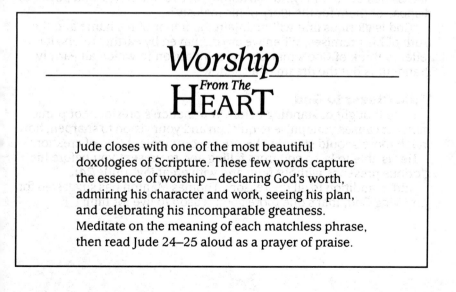

Worship
H*From The*EART

Jude closes with one of the most beautiful doxologies of Scripture. These few words capture the essence of worship—declaring God's worth, admiring his character and work, seeing his plan, and celebrating his incomparable greatness. Meditate on the meaning of each matchless phrase, then read Jude 24–25 aloud as a prayer of praise.

November 30

O Worship the King, All Glorious Above

To the only God our Savior be glory, majesty, power and authority, through Jesus Christ our Lord, before all ages, now and forevermore! Amen (Jude 25).

If you received an invitation requesting your presence at the White House, chances are high that your initial excitement would soon dissolve into a mixture of fear, wonder and curiosity.

Fear at the power of the officeholder. Wonder over the grandeur of his office. Curiosity about why you were invited!

Attitudes change when God is in view. Thomas Manton describes the attitude of a Christian confronted with the greatness of God.

Walk With Thomas Manton

"It is a comfort to the soul to consider God's glory, majesty, dominion, and power; for this is the ground of our respect to him and that which encourages us in our service. We need not be ashamed to serve him to whom glory, and power, and majesty, and dominion belong.

"It heartens us against dangers. Surely the great and glorious God will bear us out in his work.

"It increases our awe and reverence. To whom should we go in our necessities but to him who has dominion over all things, and power to dispose of them for the glory of his majesty?

"God is glorious and will maintain the honor of his name and the truth of his promises. When we are dismayed by earthly rulers, it is a relief to think of God's majesty, in comparison to which all earthly grandeur is but the dream of a shadow."

Walk Closer to God

If the thought of standing before your nation's president or prime minister causes your pulse to quicken and your vision to sharpen, how much more should standing before the omnipotent God of creation!

He "is able to keep you from falling and to present you before his glorious presence without fault and with great joy" (Jude 24).

And in addition to all the reasons Thomas Manton has suggested for glorifying God, that's one more good reason to live for him! ◯

DECEMBER

Worship Him and Crown Him King of Kings

REVELATION

Casually mention to a friend that you are reading the book of Revelation and the odds are good you will receive one of two reactions: either a skeptical look and a raised eyebrow, as if to say, "What's the use of inquiring into such mysteries?" or an admiring look of fascination, as if to say, "What secrets are you discovering between the lines?" You may finish the last chapter with more questions than when you began! And if you turn to the commentators for help, you will quickly discover there are about as many interpretations of the book as there are visions in it! But don't allow this to keep you from reading—and responding to—God's final words in Scripture.

The apostle John, who received this revelation from God, introduces the book by saying, "Blessed is the one who reads the words of this prophecy, and blessed are those who hear it and take to heart what is written in it" (Revelation 1:3). That's your challenge: to read it, to understand it, and to live it. Though interpreting this book has always been difficult, certain themes emerge clearly and insistently, regardless of the precise method you use. (1) Faith triumphs over might; all the gathering powers of antagonistic forces are laid low at the end. (2) Divine judgment is inevitable. (3) History will reach a final satisfactory consummation when Jesus Christ returns as King of kings.

The book is, therefore, a book of encouragement and exhortation. To those who combat the great forces of evil with apparently little success, the book brings particular inspiration. To those tempted to forsake their faith because the odds against them seem too great, the book issues an insistent warning and a powerful challenge to endure. The end is coming. Jesus will return. Inequities will be set right. The victory is yours in Christ.

Your own worship of God, both private and corporate, will be enriched by the grandeur and finality of his ultimate triumph. Your opportunity to broaden your horizon is as near as the first chapter of this powerful book.

DECEMBER 1

Walk in the Word
Revelation 1:1-8

*After John sends greetings to the seven churches in the province of Asia,
he praises God and his Son Jesus.*

Prologue

1 The revelation of Jesus Christ, which God gave him to show his servants what must soon take place. He made it known by sending his
angel to his servant John, [2]who testifies to everything he saw — that is, the
word of God and the testimony of Jesus Christ. [3]Blessed is the one who
reads the words of this prophecy, and blessed are those who hear it and
take to heart what is written in it, because the time is near.

Greetings and Doxology

[4]John,

To the seven churches in the province of Asia:

Grace and peace to you from him who is, and who was, and who is to
come, and from the seven spirits[a] before his throne, [5]and from Jesus
Christ, who is the faithful witness, the firstborn from the dead, and the
ruler of the kings of the earth.

To him who loves us and has freed us from our sins by his blood, [6]and
has made us to be a kingdom and priests to serve his God and Father — to
him be glory and power for ever and ever! Amen.

[7]Look, he is coming with the clouds,
    and every eye will see him,
    even those who pierced him;
        and all the peoples of the earth will mourn because of
        him.
                                                    So shall it be! Amen.

[8]"I am the Alpha and the Omega," says the Lord God, "who is, and who
was, and who is to come, the Almighty."

a4 Or *the sevenfold Spirit*

Worth Praising With Exuberance

To him who loves us and has freed us from our sins by his blood, and has made us to be a kingdom and priests to serve his God and Father—to him be glory and power for ever and ever! Amen (Revelation 1:5–6).

If there is anything the book of Revelation reveals, it is that God is worthy to be praised. Amidst the imagery and action as God's plan is fulfilled, the language of praise and worship bursts forth with exuberance.

Even in his greetings to the churches, John cannot help but add a note of praise. H.A. Ironside explains the reason why.

Walk With H.A. Ironside

"John's heart was full and could hold back no longer. Adoration and praise were the spontaneous result of Christ's person and offices as Prophet, Priest, and King.

"Then John heralds the glad news of his coming again. He is going to return—not as a babe, born of woman, but as the glorified one descending from heaven. John speaks for all the church when he cries with rapture, 'So shall it be! Amen.'

"He is the Alpha and the Omega—the beginning and the ending; he created all things; he will wind up all things and will bring in the new heavens and the new earth. He is, and was, and is the coming one. May our hearts be occupied with him, and his return be ever for us 'the blessed hope'!"

Walk Closer to God

What better way to begin a month of praise than to sing Charles Wesley's great hymn:

O for a thousand tongues to sing
    My great Redeemer's praise,
The glories of my God and King,
    The triumphs of His grace!
My gracious Master and my God,
    Assist me to proclaim,
To spread through all the earth abroad
    The honors of Thy Name.
Glory to God, and praise, and love
    Be now and ever given
By saints below and saints above,
    The Church in earth and heaven.

December 2

Walk in the Word
Revelation 1:9–20

John receives a vision of Jesus Christ walking among the seven churches, giving his assurance that he is in charge of everything that is happening in the church and the world.

One Like a Son of Man

⁹I, John, your brother and companion in the suffering and kingdom and patient endurance that are ours in Jesus, was on the island of Patmos because of the word of God and the testimony of Jesus. ¹⁰On the Lord's Day I was in the Spirit, and I heard behind me a loud voice like a trumpet, ¹¹which said: "Write on a scroll what you see and send it to the seven churches: to Ephesus, Smyrna, Pergamum, Thyatira, Sardis, Philadelphia and Laodicea."

¹²I turned around to see the voice that was speaking to me. And when I turned I saw seven golden lampstands, ¹³and among the lampstands was someone "like a son of man,"ᵃ dressed in a robe reaching down to his feet and with a golden sash around his chest. ¹⁴His head and hair were white like wool, as white as snow, and his eyes were like blazing fire. ¹⁵His feet were like bronze glowing in a furnace, and his voice was like the sound of rushing waters. ¹⁶In his right hand he held seven stars, and out of his mouth came a sharp double-edged sword. His face was like the sun shining in all its brilliance.

¹⁷When I saw him, I fell at his feet as though dead. Then he placed his right hand on me and said: "Do not be afraid. I am the First and the Last. ¹⁸I am the Living One; I was dead, and behold I am alive for ever and ever! And I hold the keys of death and Hades.

¹⁹"Write, therefore, what you have seen, what is now and what will take place later. ²⁰The mystery of the seven stars that you saw in my right hand and of the seven golden lampstands is this: The seven stars are the angelsᵇ of the seven churches, and the seven lampstands are the seven churches.

ᵃ13 Daniel 7:13   ᵇ20 Or *messengers*

December 2

Fall Before Him and Adore Him

Among the lampstands was someone "like a son of man" . . . When I saw him, I fell at his feet as though dead (Revelation 1:13,17).

It is difficult to imagine a congregation of modern worshipers falling down on the ground in their Sunday best. But read John's description of what he saw in Revelation 1, and it's even harder to imagine anyone *not* falling down before the glorified Christ!

Humble worship is the only appropriate response when the King is in view. Charles Spurgeon explores the significance of John's action.

Walk With Charles Spurgeon

"Does death alarm you?

"We are never so much alive as when we are dead at his feet. We are never so truly living as when the creature dies away in the presence of the all-glorious, reigning King.

"I know this, that the death of all that is sinful in me is my soul's highest ambition, yes, and the death of all that is carnal. And all that savors of the old Adam. Oh, that it would die.

"And where can it die but at the feet of him who has the new life, and who by manifesting himself in all his glory is to purge away our dross and sin?

"I only desire that I had enough of the Spirit's might so to set forth my Master that I might contribute even in a humble measure to make you fall at his feet as dead, that he might be in us our All in All."

Walk Closer to God

Put yourself in John's trembling sandals . . . listen to the thundering voice of the Alpha and Omega . . . fall before him as your Lord of hosts . . . then rise to serve him in holy consecration.

When Isaiah was confronted by the Lord of hosts, he responded in a way similar to John: "Woe to me! . . . I am ruined!" (Isaiah 6:5).

Confronted by the God of holiness and glory, Isaiah and John saw themselves worthy only of death. But God touched them and made them alive to serve him. He can touch you that way, too. ◖

December 3

📖 Walk in the Word
Revelation 2:1–11

Jesus instructs John what to say to the churches in Ephesus and Smyrna; he chides the former for forsaking their initial love for Jesus and encourages the latter to stand firm in the midst of persecution.

To the Church in Ephesus

2 "To the angel[a] of the church in Ephesus write:

These are the words of him who holds the seven stars in his right hand and walks among the seven golden lampstands: ²I know your deeds, your hard work and your perseverance. I know that you cannot tolerate wicked men, that you have tested those who claim to be apostles but are not, and have found them false. ³You have persevered and have endured hardships for my name, and have not grown weary.

⁴Yet I hold this against you: You have forsaken your first love. ⁵Remember the height from which you have fallen! Repent and do the things you did at first. If you do not repent, I will come to you and remove your lampstand from its place. ⁶But you have this in your favor: You hate the practices of the Nicolaitans, which I also hate.

⁷He who has an ear, let him hear what the Spirit says to the churches. To him who overcomes, I will give the right to eat from the tree of life, which is in the paradise of God.

To the Church in Smyrna

⁸"To the angel of the church in Smyrna write:

These are the words of him who is the First and the Last, who died and came to life again. ⁹I know your afflictions and your poverty—yet you are rich! I know the slander of those who say they are Jews and are not, but are a synagogue of Satan. ¹⁰Do not be afraid of what you are about to suffer. I tell you, the devil will put some of you in prison to test you, and you will suffer persecution for ten days. Be faithful, even to the point of death, and I will give you the crown of life.

¹¹He who has an ear, let him hear what the Spirit says to the churches. He who overcomes will not be hurt at all by the second death.

---

a1 Or messenger; also in verses 8, 12 and 18

The Excitement of Your First Love

Yet I hold this against you: You have forsaken your first love (Revelation 2:4).

Love is more than a feeling of exhilaration in the presence of another. Rather, love is a commitment that grows deeper with the years.

In the case of the Ephesian church, the excitement of first love for God had faded into meaningless ritual. Motions without enthusiasm. Works without warmth.

G. Campbell Morgan illustrates the problem of losing your "first love" for God with this story.

Walk With G. Campbell Morgan

"A friend of mine had a daughter whom he dearly loved. They were great friends. One day his birthday came; and in the morning of that day she came into his room with her face wreathed in smiles and said, 'Father, I have brought you a present.' She handed him a box in which he found an exquisitely decorated pair of slippers.

"He said, 'Darling, it was very good of you to buy these for me.'

" 'O Father,' she said, 'I did not buy them. I have made them for you.'

"Then looking at her he said, 'Oh, now I understand. Is this what you have been doing for the last three months?'

"She replied, 'Yes, Father. But how did you know how long I had been at work on them?'

"He said, 'Because for three months I have not had your company. You have been too busy. My darling, I like these slippers very much. But next time, buy the slippers, and let me have your company. I would rather have my child than anything she can make for me.' "

Walk Closer to God

"Father, I find it so much easier today to *work* for you than to *walk* with you.

"Restore to me the freshness and vitality of 'first love.' Let me sense again your touch in my life.

"In place of my meager labors I offer you the one thing you desire most—myself.

"In the name of the one who gave himself in love. Amen."

A.W. TOZER

(1897–1963) MAN IN PURSUIT OF GOD

A Powerful and Challenging Preacher

In contrast to a disturbing contemporary trend among pastors to neglect adequate time for study and reflection on God's Word, there stands a man whose sermons and books still stir many to a deeper knowledge of God and his Word. This man, Aiden Wilson Tozer, born on a Pennsylvania farm in 1897, demonstrated at an early age a keen mind and inquisitive spirit. He was encouraged to read good books and to settle for nothing but the best.

Though his formal education ended with grammar school, Tozer continued to read widely and enthusiastically. At age fifteen he took a job in a factory in Akron, Ohio. There the family began attending church for the first time, and at age seventeen he became a Christian through the ministry of a street preacher. Soon after, he himself began to preach on the streets of Akron, leading his parents and two sisters to Christ.

Tozer accepted a pastorate in West Virginia in 1919. From there he moved to the Southside Alliance Church in Chicago, where he remained for thirty-one years. He concentrated on his preaching, while others assisted with pastoral chores. Tozer fostered growth in his church by preaching powerful and challenging sermons, marked by quality, not quantity. He was articulate and well-informed on the issues of his day.

In 1959 Tozer moved to a church in Toronto, Canada, and four years later, suddenly died. His tombstone reads simply: "A. W. Tozer, A Man of God." His entire life had been spent preaching to sinful people about the way to fellowship with their God—a path Tozer himself had faithfully followed.

What about you? Are you growing in your love and knowledge of God? Is your ministry in the lives of others the overflow of a life of devotion to the Lord?

A LESSON FROM THE LIFE OF A.W. TOZER

Diligent study of God's Word leads to an ever-increasing love for God and builds a deep spiritual strength.

DECEMBER 4

Walk in the Word
Revelation 2:12–29

Jesus instructs John what to say to the churches in Pergamum and Thyatira; he rebukes the former for tolerating sinful teachings and the latter for tolerating immorality.

To the Church in Pergamum

¹²"To the angel of the church in Pergamum write:

These are the words of him who has the sharp, double-edged sword. ¹³I know where you live — where Satan has his throne. Yet you remain true to my name. You did not renounce your faith in me, even in the days of Antipas, my faithful witness, who was put to death in your city — where Satan lives.

¹⁴Nevertheless, I have a few things against you: You have people there who hold to the teaching of Balaam, who taught Balak to entice the Israelites to sin by eating food sacrificed to idols and by committing sexual immorality. ¹⁵Likewise you also have those who hold to the teaching of the Nicolaitans. ¹⁶Repent therefore! Otherwise, I will soon come to you and will fight against them with the sword of my mouth.

¹⁷He who has an ear, let him hear what the Spirit says to the churches. To him who overcomes, I will give some of the hidden manna. I will also give him a white stone with a new name written on it, known only to him who receives it.

To the Church in Thyatira

¹⁸"To the angel of the church in Thyatira write:

These are the words of the Son of God, whose eyes are like blazing fire and whose feet are like burnished bronze. ¹⁹I know your deeds, your love and faith, your service and perseverance, and that you are now doing more than you did at first.

²⁰Nevertheless, I have this against you: You tolerate that woman Jezebel, who calls herself a prophetess. By her teaching she misleads my servants into sexual immorality and the eating of food sacrificed to idols. ²¹I have given her time to repent of her immorality, but she is unwilling. ²²So I will cast her on a bed of suffering, and I will make those who commit adultery with her suffer intensely, unless they repent of her ways. ²³I will strike her children dead. Then all the churches will know that I am he who searches hearts and minds, and I will repay each of you according to your deeds. ²⁴Now I say to the rest of you in Thyatira, to you who do not hold to her teaching and have not learned Satan's so-called deep secrets (I will not impose any other burden on you): ²⁵Only hold on to what you have until I come.

²⁶To him who overcomes and does my will to the end, I will give authority over the nations —

December 4

> 27"He will rule them with an iron scepter;
>   he will dash them to pieces like pottery'*a*—

just as I have received authority from my Father. 28I will also give him the morning star. 29He who has an ear, let him hear what the Spirit says to the churches.

*a*27 Psalm 2:9

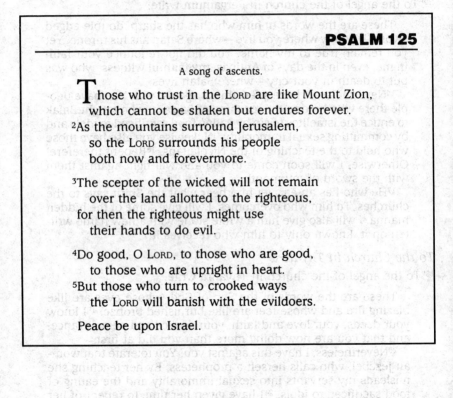

PSALM 125

A song of ascents.

Those who trust in the LORD are like Mount Zion,
    which cannot be shaken but endures forever.
2As the mountains surround Jerusalem,
    so the LORD surrounds his people
    both now and forevermore.

3The scepter of the wicked will not remain
    over the land allotted to the righteous,
  for then the righteous might use
    their hands to do evil.

4Do good, O LORD, to those who are good,
    to those who are upright in heart.
5But those who turn to crooked ways
    the LORD will banish with the evildoers.

  Peace be upon Israel.

DECEMBER 4

Stepping Ahead in the Walk of Faith

I know your deeds, your love and faith, your service and perseverance, and that you are now doing more than you did at first (Revelation 2:19).

Maintaining the status quo. That may sound like a commendable, if somewhat conservative, goal for life. But the Christian life calls for more than a "status quo" mentality. Rather, it calls for growth, maturity, fruit-bearing.

The believers at Thyatira belonged to a growing, pace-setting church. Albert Barnes uses their example to emphasize the importance of moving ahead in the walk of faith.

Walk With Albert Barnes

"The works which had been recently done at Thyatira were more commendable than those which had been done previously.

"They were making progress; they had been acting more and more in accordance with the nature and claims of the Christian profession.

"Religion of the soul, and in a community, is designed to be progressive. We always should seek to live so that we will have the commendation of the Savior; and we should regard it as something to be greatly desired if we are approved as making advances in knowledge and holiness; that as we grow in years we may grow alike in the disposition to do good, and in the ability to do it; that as we gain in experience, we may also gain in a readiness to apply the results of our experience in promoting the cause of religion."

Walk Closer to God

The Christian life is rarely composed of giant steps of progress. "Three steps forward, two steps backward" might even be a more accurate description.

Keeping "in step" with the Father requires that you make small but significant decisions in concert with him every day. Decisions in matters of love, faith, service and perseverance.

It's important to know where you are—and where you are headed. But don't overlook the equally important question: How fast are you headed there? ⟡

DECEMBER 5

 Walk in the Word
Revelation 3:1-6

Jesus instructs John what to say to the church in Sardis; he wants them to wake up and repent before it is too late.

To the Church in Sardis

3 "To the angel*a* of the church in Sardis write:

These are the words of him who holds the seven spirits*b* of God and the seven stars. I know your deeds; you have a reputation of being alive, but you are dead. ²Wake up! Strengthen what remains and is about to die, for I have not found your deeds complete in the sight of my God. ³Remember, therefore, what you have received and heard; obey it, and repent. But if you do not wake up, I will come like a thief, and you will not know at what time I will come to you.

⁴Yet you have a few people in Sardis who have not soiled their clothes. They will walk with me, dressed in white, for they are worthy. ⁵He who overcomes will, like them, be dressed in white. I will never blot out his name from the book of life, but will acknowledge his name before my Father and his angels. ⁶He who has an ear, let him hear what the Spirit says to the churches.

a1 Or *messenger*; also in verses 7 and 14   *b1* Or *the sevenfold Spirit*

Worship
From The
HEART

During the first century, believers in Christ were often considered traitors and were stripped of their citizenship. As you try to imagine what it would be like to be in a godless nation without any legal rights or protections, praise God for the assurance that your citizenship in heaven is secure. God will not blot out the names of his own children from the book of life.

Splendor That Suits the Dress Code of Heaven

Yet you have a few people in Sardis who have not soiled their clothes. They will walk with me, dressed in white, for they are worthy (Revelation 3:4).

"How little people know who think that holiness is dull."

C.S. Lewis wrote those words to counteract the notion that holiness is somehow drab and boring.

If that idea were true, then the saints of Revelation 3 ought to be wearing drab gray or dull black. Instead, they are adorned in dazzling white.

Matthew Henry shares this insight into what the faithful servant of God can expect to wear.

Walk With Matthew Henry

"The small faithful remnant in Sardis had not given in to the prevailing corruptions of the day and place in which they lived.

"God notices the smallest number of those who abide with him and makes a very gracious promise to them: 'They will walk with me dressed in white, for they are worthy'—in the white robes of justification, and adoption, and comfort, in the white robes of honor and glory in the next world.

"Their fidelity has prepared them for it.

"Those who walk with Christ in the clean garments of real, practical holiness here, and keep themselves unspotted from the world, shall walk with Christ in the white robes of honor and glory in the life to come: This is a suitable reward.

"The purity of grace shall be rewarded with the perfect purity of glory. Holiness, when perfected, shall be its own reward."

Walk Closer to God

In heaven God's children will wear the reward of holiness. But for now, those around you may be wearing clothes more "in style" with the world. That's a style that will change and be discarded.

By contrast, God's "style" never varies: integrity . . . fidelity . . . purity. They are timeless as God himself.

Holiness. Wear it well, as befitting the beautiful bride of Christ of which you are a part. You needn't wait till heaven to begin to walk with him in white. ◖

DECEMBER 6

Walk in the Word
Revelation 3:7–13

Jesus instructs John what to say to the church in Philadelphia; because of their faithfulness, he promises to keep them safe in the coming hour of trial.

To the Church in Philadelphia

7"To the angel of the church in Philadelphia write:

These are the words of him who is holy and true, who holds the key of David. What he opens no one can shut, and what he shuts no one can open. 8I know your deeds. See, I have placed before you an open door that no one can shut. I know that you have little strength, yet you have kept my word and have not denied my name. 9I will make those who are of the synagogue of Satan, who claim to be Jews though they are not, but are liars—I will make them come and fall down at your feet and acknowledge that I have loved you. 10Since you have kept my command to endure patiently, I will also keep you from the hour of trial that is going to come upon the whole world to test those who live on the earth.

11I am coming soon. Hold on to what you have, so that no one will take your crown. 12Him who overcomes I will make a pillar in the temple of my God. Never again will he leave it. I will write on him the name of my God and the name of the city of my God, the new Jerusalem, which is coming down out of heaven from my God; and I will also write on him my new name. 13He who has an ear, let him hear what the Spirit says to the churches.

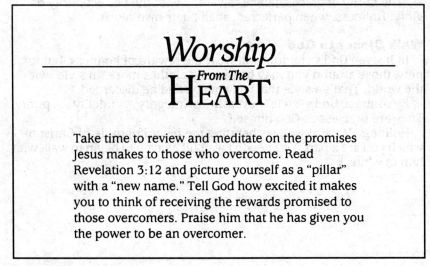

Worship
From The
HEART

Take time to review and meditate on the promises Jesus makes to those who overcome. Read Revelation 3:12 and picture yourself as a "pillar" with a "new name." Tell God how excited it makes you to think of receiving the rewards promised to those overcomers. Praise him that he has given you the power to be an overcomer.

DECEMBER 6

Faith: Courageous Confidence in God

Since you have kept my command to endure patiently, I will also keep you from the hour of trial (Revelation 3:10).

Near the end of a long run, the weary but determined jogger is sorely tempted to ease up, to quit a few steps early.

But the mind has ways of overcoming the muscles, and ten telephone poles later he reaches the finish line. He has done what his body told him it was impossible to do.

In Revelation 3, John speaks of the goal of patience that seems unreachable to many believers. And yet it is a goal that God is committed to developing in the lives of his children.

Oswald Chambers has insight into the relationships between patience, confidence and faith.

Walk With Oswald Chambers

"Patience is more than endurance. God is aiming at something the saint cannot see, and he stretches and strains, and every now and again the saint says, 'I can't stand anymore.'

"But trust yourself in God's hands. Maintain your confidence in Jesus Christ by the patience of faith. You cannot see him just now; you cannot understand all he is doing, but you know him.

"Shipwreck occurs where there is not that mental poise which comes from being established on the eternal truth that God is holy love. Faith is the heroic effort of your life, as you fling yourself in reckless confidence on God.

"God has ventured all in Jesus Christ to save us; now he wants us to venture our all in abandoned confidence in him."

Walk Closer to God

God calls you to trust him even as you are being stretched to the limit—and beyond. Patience comes when you look ahead and see God waiting at the finish line of life. He is the one who controls all the circumstances, knows the limits of your endurance and will reward you at the end.

You can be confident he'll finish the good work he has begun in you. ◘

DECEMBER 7

Walk in the Word
Revelation 3:14–22

Jesus instructs John what to say to the church in Laodicea; he strongly rebukes them because they are lukewarm in the faith.

To the Church in Laodicea

14"To the angel of the church in Laodicea write:

These are the words of the Amen, the faithful and true witness, the ruler of God's creation. 15I know your deeds, that you are neither cold nor hot. I wish you were either one or the other! 16So, because you are lukewarm—neither hot nor cold—I am about to spit you out of my mouth. 17You say, 'I am rich; I have acquired wealth and do not need a thing.' But you do not realize that you are wretched, pitiful, poor, blind and naked. 18I counsel you to buy from me gold refined in the fire, so you can become rich; and white clothes to wear, so you can cover your shameful nakedness; and salve to put on your eyes, so you can see.

19Those whom I love I rebuke and discipline. So be earnest, and repent. 20Here I am! I stand at the door and knock. If anyone hears my voice and opens the door, I will come in and eat with him, and he with me.

21To him who overcomes, I will give the right to sit with me on my throne, just as I overcame and sat down with my Father on his throne. 22He who has an ear, let him hear what the Spirit says to the churches."

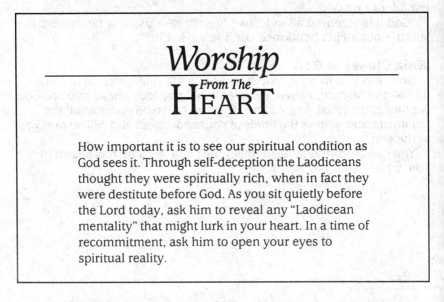

Worship
From The HEART

How important it is to see our spiritual condition as God sees it. Through self-deception the Laodiceans thought they were spiritually rich, when in fact they were destitute before God. As you sit quietly before the Lord today, ask him to reveal any "Laodicean mentality" that might lurk in your heart. In a time of recommitment, ask him to open your eyes to spiritual reality.

894

DECEMBER 7

The Weakness That Kills Repentance

Those whom I love I rebuke and discipline. So be earnest, and repent. He who has an ear, let him hear what the Spirit says to the churches (Revelation 3:19,22).

The church at Laodicea suffered from a bad case of "the emperor's new clothes." Like that fabled emperor, their true condition was obvious to all but them.

A church in the same condition is no laughing matter. Appearances can't mask reality . . . especially from God.

But how do you correct such a situation?

Charles Spurgeon offers the following suggestions for a well-dressed church.

Walk With Charles Spurgeon

"You may know of the faults of other people; and in watching a church, you may have observed weak points in many places. But have you wept or prayed over them?

"If not, you have not watched as you should for the good of your brothers and sisters, and perhaps have allowed evils to grow which ought to have been uprooted. You have been silent when you should have kindly and earnestly spoken to the offenders, or made your own example a warning.

"Do not judge your brother, but judge yourself; if you have any severity, use it on your own conduct and heart. We must pray the Lord to use this remedy, and make us know just where we are.

"We shall never get right as long as we are confident that we are so already. Self-complacency is the death of repentance."

Walk Closer to God

In the first three chapters of Revelation, seven churches received personal messages from the Lord of the church. And within a few hundred years, all seven had disappeared. Perhaps, in Spurgeon's words, they were "confident" and "self-complacent," believing that they were well dressed already.

How about you? Are you satisfied with your walk with God? More importantly, is he satisfied with your walk with him?

December 8

▟▌ Walk in the Word
Revelation 4

John is carried in the Spirit into heaven and receives a vision of the throne of God and of the heavenly creatures praising God.

The Throne in Heaven

4 After this I looked, and there before me was a door standing open in heaven. And the voice I had first heard speaking to me like a trumpet said, "Come up here, and I will show you what must take place after this." ²At once I was in the Spirit, and there before me was a throne in heaven with someone sitting on it. ³And the one who sat there had the appearance of jasper and carnelian. A rainbow, resembling an emerald, encircled the throne. ⁴Surrounding the throne were twenty-four other thrones, and seated on them were twenty-four elders. They were dressed in white and had crowns of gold on their heads. ⁵From the throne came flashes of lightning, rumblings and peals of thunder. Before the throne, seven lamps were blazing. These are the seven spirits *a* of God. ⁶Also before the throne there was what looked like a sea of glass, clear as crystal.

In the center, around the throne, were four living creatures, and they were covered with eyes, in front and in back. ⁷The first living creature was like a lion, the second was like an ox, the third had a face like a man, the fourth was like a flying eagle. ⁸Each of the four living creatures had six wings and was covered with eyes all around, even under his wings. Day and night they never stop saying:

> "Holy, holy, holy
> is the Lord God Almighty,
> who was, and is, and is to come."

⁹Whenever the living creatures give glory, honor and thanks to him who sits on the throne and who lives for ever and ever, ¹⁰the twenty-four elders fall down before him who sits on the throne, and worship him who lives for ever and ever. They lay their crowns before the throne and say:

> ¹¹"You are worthy, our Lord and God,
> to receive glory and honor and power,
> for you created all things,
> and by your will they were created
> and have their being."

a5 Or *the sevenfold Spirit*

Letting God Be All in All

You are worthy, our Lord and God, to receive glory and honor and power, for you created all things, and by your will they were created and have their being (Revelation 4:11).

Humility has been called "the ability to withhold from others the high opinion you hold of yourself" and "the art of wearing greatness gently."

More accurately, it is the result of a correct estimation of oneself.

The incomparable example of humility is, of course, Jesus. The Creator became the creature in order that "every tongue confess that Jesus Christ is Lord" (Philippians 2:11). Andrew Murray shares this insight into the practice of humility.

Walk With Andrew Murray

"The call to humility has been too little regarded in the church, because its true nature and importance have not been understood.

"It is not something we bring to God, or he bestows. It is simply the sense of entire nothingness, which comes when we see how truly God is all, and in which we make way for God to be all.

"When the creature realizes that this is the true nobility, and consents with his will, his mind, and his affections to be the form, the vessel in which the life and glory of God are to work and manifest themselves, then he sees that humility is simply acknowledging the truth of his position as creature, and yielding to God his rightful place."

Walk Closer to God

The bigger your God becomes, the smaller will seem his creatures—including you!

Drawing near to God is the best way to gain a fresh view of his greatness and grandeur.

In C.S. Lewis's popular fantasy *The Chronicles of Narnia*, one of the characters provides this concise definition of what it meant for God to become a man: "A stable once held something inside that was bigger than our whole world."

Think of it: God residing in the lives of his believing creatures!

The question remains: How much room does he occupy in your life? ⬤

DECEMBER 9

Walk in the Word
Revelation 5

When the heavenly throngs realize that Jesus, the Lamb of God, is in control of all history, they burst forth into praise of him.

The Scroll and the Lamb

5 Then I saw in the right hand of him who sat on the throne a scroll with writing on both sides and sealed with seven seals. ²And I saw a mighty angel proclaiming in a loud voice, "Who is worthy to break the seals and open the scroll?" ³But no one in heaven or on earth or under the earth could open the scroll or even look inside it. ⁴I wept and wept because no one was found who was worthy to open the scroll or look inside. ⁵Then one of the elders said to me, "Do not weep! See, the Lion of the tribe of Judah, the Root of David, has triumphed. He is able to open the scroll and its seven seals."

⁶Then I saw a Lamb, looking as if it had been slain, standing in the center of the throne, encircled by the four living creatures and the elders. He had seven horns and seven eyes, which are the seven spirits* of God sent out into all the earth. ⁷He came and took the scroll from the right hand of him who sat on the throne. ⁸And when he had taken it, the four living creatures and the twenty-four elders fell down before the Lamb. Each one had a harp and they were holding golden bowls full of incense, which are the prayers of the saints. ⁹And they sang a new song:

> "You are worthy to take the scroll
>   and to open its seals,
> because you were slain,
>   and with your blood you purchased men for
>   God
>   from every tribe and language and people and
>   nation.
> ¹⁰You have made them to be a kingdom and priests to
>   serve our God,
>   and they will reign on the earth."

¹¹Then I looked and heard the voice of many angels, numbering thousands upon thousands, and ten thousand times ten thousand. They encircled the throne and the living creatures and the elders. ¹²In a loud voice they sang:

> "Worthy is the Lamb, who was slain,
>   to receive power and wealth and wisdom and
>   strength
>   and honor and glory and praise!"

¹³Then I heard every creature in heaven and on earth and under the earth and on the sea, and all that is in them, singing:

898

DECEMBER 9

"To him who sits on the throne and to the Lamb
be praise and honor and glory and power,
for ever and ever!"

¹⁴The four living creatures said, "Amen," and the elders fell down and worshiped.

a6 Or the sevenfold Spirit

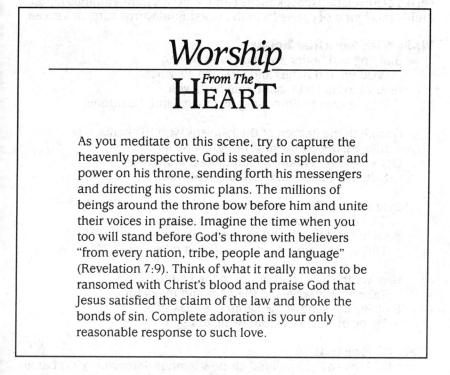

Worship
From The
HEART

As you meditate on this scene, try to capture the heavenly perspective. God is seated in splendor and power on his throne, sending forth his messengers and directing his cosmic plans. The millions of beings around the throne bow before him and unite their voices in praise. Imagine the time when you too will stand before God's throne with believers "from every nation, tribe, people and language" (Revelation 7:9). Think of what it really means to be ransomed with Christ's blood and praise God that Jesus satisfied the claim of the law and broke the bonds of sin. Complete adoration is your only reasonable response to such love.

DECEMBER 9

Singing the Wonderful Song of the Lamb

Then I heard every creature . . . singing: "To him who sits on the throne and to the Lamb be praise and honor and glory and power, for ever and ever!" (Revelation 5:13).

The Lamb of God has inspired more songs than all other creatures combined, and many hymns owe their inspiration to the praise-filled verses of Revelation that extol the Lamb that was slain. Horatius Bonar builds this hymn of praise from the worshipful words sung in heaven.

Walk With Horatius Bonar

Blessing and honor and glory and power,
   Wisdom and riches and strength evermore,
Give ye to Him who our battle hath won,
   Whose are the Kingdom, the crown, and the throne.

Soundeth the heaven of the heavens with His name;
   Ringeth the earth with His glory and fame;
Ocean and mountain, stream, forest and flower
   Echo His praises and tell of His power.

Ever ascendeth the song and the joy;
   Ever descendeth the love from on high;
Blessing and honor and glory and praise—
   This is the theme of the hymns we raise.

Give we the glory and praise to the Lamb;
   Take we the robe and the harp and the palm;
Sing we the song of the Lamb that was slain,
   Dying in weakness, but rising to reign.

Walk Closer to God

In 1432 Jan van Eyck painted his now famous *Adoration of the Lamb*. In the center of that painting Christ stands as the Lamb of God, blood pouring from his sacrificial wounds. All around are gathered worshipers of the Lamb.

Yet the Lamb is not lying on the altar near death. Instead he stands tall and straight, in triumph and splendor. Death has been defeated. It is no wonder he is worthy of praise. This Lamb is your Lord. ☖

DECEMBER 10

📖 Walk in the Word
Revelation 6

John sees the Lamb opening the first six seals of the scroll of history, which unleash destruction on the earth.

The Seals

6 I watched as the Lamb opened the first of the seven seals. Then I heard one of the four living creatures say in a voice like thunder, "Come!" ²I looked, and there before me was a white horse! Its rider held a bow, and he was given a crown, and he rode out as a conqueror bent on conquest.

³When the Lamb opened the second seal, I heard the second living creature say, "Come!" ⁴Then another horse came out, a fiery red one. Its rider was given power to take peace from the earth and to make men slay each other. To him was given a large sword.

⁵When the Lamb opened the third seal, I heard the third living creature say, "Come!" I looked, and there before me was a black horse! Its rider was holding a pair of scales in his hand. ⁶Then I heard what sounded like a voice among the four living creatures, saying, "A quart*ᵃ* of wheat for a day's wages,*ᵇ* and three quarts of barley for a day's wages,*ᵇ* and do not damage the oil and the wine!"

⁷When the Lamb opened the fourth seal, I heard the voice of the fourth living creature say, "Come!" ⁸I looked, and there before me was a pale horse! Its rider was named Death, and Hades was following close behind him. They were given power over a fourth of the earth to kill by sword, famine and plague, and by the wild beasts of the earth.

⁹When he opened the fifth seal, I saw under the altar the souls of those who had been slain because of the word of God and the testimony they had maintained. ¹⁰They called out in a loud voice, "How long, Sovereign Lord, holy and true, until you judge the inhabitants of the earth and avenge our blood?" ¹¹Then each of them was given a white robe, and they were told to wait a little longer, until the number of their fellow servants and brothers who were to be killed as they had been was completed.

¹²I watched as he opened the sixth seal. There was a great earthquake. The sun turned black like sackcloth made of goat hair, the whole moon turned blood red, ¹³and the stars in the sky fell to earth, as late figs drop from a fig tree when shaken by a strong wind. ¹⁴The sky receded like a scroll, rolling up, and every mountain and island was removed from its place.

¹⁵Then the kings of the earth, the princes, the generals, the rich, the mighty, and every slave and every free man hid in caves and among the rocks of the mountains. ¹⁶They called to the mountains and the rocks, "Fall on us and hide us from the face of him who sits on the throne and from the wrath of the Lamb! ¹⁷For the great day of their wrath has come, and who can stand?"

---

*ᵃ*6 Greek *a choinix* (probably about a liter)   *ᵇ*6 Greek *a denarius*

DECEMBER 10

Choosing the Lamb's Wrath or the Lamb's Love

Fall on us and hide us from the face of him who sits on the throne and from the wrath of the Lamb! For the great day of their wrath has come, and who can stand? (Revelation 6:16–17).

By nature lambs are among the gentlest of creatures. How then is it possible that men and women flee in terror from the wrath of the Lamb?

It's not a pleasant picture. But as H.A. Ironside explains, the imagery is painfully appropriate.

Walk With H.A. Ironside

"In that day there shall dawn upon multitudes the realization that the Lamb of God whom they had rejected and whose gentle rule they had spurned has visited their sins upon their own heads.

"Yet we read of no repentance, no true turning to God or trusting his Christ—just an awful realization that it is the rejected Lamb whom they must face, and whose wrath they cannot escape.

"Notice the solemnity of the expression 'the wrath of the Lamb.' We are not accustomed to linking the thought of wrath with the Lamb, which has always been the symbol of gentleness.

"But there is a terrible truth involved in this nevertheless. For if the grace of the Lamb of God is rejected, his indignation and wrath must be faced. It cannot be otherwise.

"But now grace is still reigning through righteousness, and a just God waits in lovingkindness to be the Justifier of everyone who believes in Jesus."

Walk Closer to God

When confronted with your own sinfulness, you can respond in one of two ways:

1. Seek to remove the symptoms (even in such radical ways as asking mountains to fall on you).
2. Appropriate God's solution.

The blood of the Lamb will either be the covering or the condemnation for your sins.

Choose carefully your way of escape. And choose quickly. "Now is the time of God's favor, now is the day of salvation" (2 Corinthians 6:2).

DECEMBER 11

📖 Walk in the Word
Revelation 7

John sees both the 144,000 who have God's seal and the numberless multitude standing before the Lamb and singing his praises.

144,000 Sealed

7 After this I saw four angels standing at the four corners of the earth, holding back the four winds of the earth to prevent any wind from blowing on the land or on the sea or on any tree. ²Then I saw another angel coming up from the east, having the seal of the living God. He called out in a loud voice to the four angels who had been given power to harm the land and the sea: ³"Do not harm the land or the sea or the trees until we put a seal on the foreheads of the servants of our God." ⁴Then I heard the number of those who were sealed: 144,000 from all the tribes of Israel.

⁵From the tribe of Judah 12,000 were sealed,
  from the tribe of Reuben 12,000,
  from the tribe of Gad 12,000,
  ⁶from the tribe of Asher 12,000,
  from the tribe of Naphtali 12,000,
  from the tribe of Manasseh 12,000,
  ⁷from the tribe of Simeon 12,000,
  from the tribe of Levi 12,000,
  from the tribe of Issachar 12,000,
  ⁸from the tribe of Zebulun 12,000,
  from the tribe of Joseph 12,000,
  from the tribe of Benjamin 12,000.

The Great Multitude in White Robes

⁹After this I looked and there before me was a great multitude that no one could count, from every nation, tribe, people and language, standing before the throne and in front of the Lamb. They were wearing white robes and were holding palm branches in their hands. ¹⁰And they cried out in a loud voice:

> "Salvation belongs to our God,
> who sits on the throne,
> and to the Lamb."

¹¹All the angels were standing around the throne and around the elders and the four living creatures. They fell down on their faces before the throne and worshiped God, ¹²saying:

> "Amen!
> Praise and glory
> and wisdom and thanks and honor
> and power and strength
> be to our God for ever and ever.
> Amen!"

December 11

¹³Then one of the elders asked me, "These in white robes—who are they, and where did they come from?"

¹⁴I answered, "Sir, you know."

And he said, "These are they who have come out of the great tribulation; they have washed their robes and made them white in the blood of the Lamb. ¹⁵Therefore,

> "they are before the throne of God
>   and serve him day and night in his temple;
> and he who sits on the throne will spread his tent over
>   them.
> ¹⁶Never again will they hunger;
>   never again will they thirst.
> The sun will not beat upon them,
>   nor any scorching heat.
> ¹⁷For the Lamb at the center of the throne will be their
>   shepherd;
>   he will lead them to springs of living water.
> And God will wipe away every tear from their eyes."

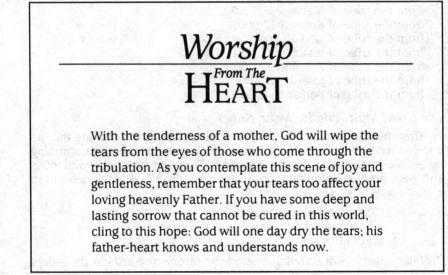

Worship From The HEART

With the tenderness of a mother, God will wipe the tears from the eyes of those who come through the tribulation. As you contemplate this scene of joy and gentleness, remember that your tears too affect your loving heavenly Father. If you have some deep and lasting sorrow that cannot be cured in this world, cling to this hope: God will one day dry the tears; his father-heart knows and understands now.

The Way God Leads Those He Loves

These are they who have come out of the great tribulation; they have washed their robes and made them white in the blood of the Lamb (Revelation 7:14).

"Everyone who wants to live a godly life in Christ Jesus will be persecuted" (2 Timothy 3:12).

"Do not be surprised at the painful trial you are suffering" (1 Peter 4:12).

Jesus warned His disciples, "If the world hates you, keep in mind that it hated me first" (John 15:18).

Robert Murray McCheyne, who himself suffered an early death, has this to say about the purpose behind the pain of suffering for the Savior.

Walk With Robert Murray McCheyne

"Some believers are very surprised when they are called to suffer. They thought they would do some great thing for God, but all God permits them to do is to suffer.

"Just suppose you could speak with those who have gone to be with the Lord; everyone has a different story, yet everyone has a tale of suffering.

"One was persecuted by family and friends . . . another was inflicted with pain and disease, neglected by the world . . . another was bereaved of children . . . another had all these afflictions.

"But you will notice that though the water was deep, they all have reached the other side. Not one of them blames God for the road he led them; 'Salvation' is their only cry.

"Are there any of you, dear children, murmuring at your lot? Do not sin against God. This is the way God leads all his redeemed ones."

Walk Closer to God

This hymn expresses the hope of every heart that has suffered for Jesus:

My soul, be on thy guard,
    Ten thousand foes arise;
The hosts of sin are pressing hard
    To draw thee from the skies.
Fight on, my soul, till death
    Shall bring thee to thy God;
He'll take thee at thy parting breath,
    Up to His blest abode. ⬭

DECEMBER 12

📖 Walk in the Word
Revelation 8

When the Lamb opens the seventh seal, John sees seven angels ready to blow their trumpets; as the first four blow their trumpets, destruction comes on the earth.

The Seventh Seal and the Golden Censer

8 When he opened the seventh seal, there was silence in heaven for about half an hour.

²And I saw the seven angels who stand before God, and to them were given seven trumpets.

³Another angel, who had a golden censer, came and stood at the altar. He was given much incense to offer, with the prayers of all the saints, on the golden altar before the throne. ⁴The smoke of the incense, together with the prayers of the saints, went up before God from the angel's hand. ⁵Then the angel took the censer, filled it with fire from the altar, and hurled it on the earth; and there came peals of thunder, rumblings, flashes of lightning and an earthquake.

The Trumpets

⁶Then the seven angels who had the seven trumpets prepared to sound them.

⁷The first angel sounded his trumpet, and there came hail and fire mixed with blood, and it was hurled down upon the earth. A third of the earth was burned up, a third of the trees were burned up, and all the green grass was burned up.

⁸The second angel sounded his trumpet, and something like a huge mountain, all ablaze, was thrown into the sea. A third of the sea turned into blood, ⁹a third of the living creatures in the sea died, and a third of the ships were destroyed.

¹⁰The third angel sounded his trumpet, and a great star, blazing like a torch, fell from the sky on a third of the rivers and on the springs of water— ¹¹the name of the star is Wormwood.ᵃ A third of the waters turned bitter, and many people died from the waters that had become bitter.

¹²The fourth angel sounded his trumpet, and a third of the sun was struck, a third of the moon, and a third of the stars, so that a third of them turned dark. A third of the day was without light, and also a third of the night.

¹³As I watched, I heard an eagle that was flying in midair call out in a loud voice: "Woe! Woe! Woe to the inhabitants of the earth, because of the trumpet blasts about to be sounded by the other three angels!"

ᵃ11 That is, Bitterness

DECEMBER 12

The Fragrant Aroma of the Saints' Prayers

He [the angel] was given much incense to offer, with the prayers of all the saints, on the golden altar before the throne (Revelation 8:3).

A young child, enamored with his teacher, gave her three daisies with this note attached:

These flowers will fade and die,
But you will smell forever.

In your prayer life, as in poetry, it's the thought—and the fragrance—that counts. John refers to the "golden bowls full of incense, which are the prayers of the saints" (Revelation 5:8).

And the angel in Revelation 8 is seen bringing those sweet offerings of adoration before the Father, as William R. Newell explains.

Walk With William R. Newell

"This angel is publicly to bring before heaven three things:

"First, that the prayers of the saints are ever before God: a most blessed and solemn truth!

"Second, that the incense (ever in Scripture setting forth the power of Christ's atonement acting upon God), representing our Lord's person and work at Calvary, added in due time to the prayers of all the saints, makes them effectual before God.

"Third, that God's judgment is in a sense the answer to 'Your kingdom come,' which the saints of all ages have prayed. No other answer could be given, since earth has rejected the rightful King!"

Walk Closer to God

"Father, all too often I neglect my times of prayer, not realizing the eternal impact of those heavenly conversations.

"To know that my prayers ascend to you as a fragrant aroma causes me to think more of what I pray and how I pray.

"To know that you hear and answer causes me to wonder at the relationship I enjoy with you.

"To know that my prayers help to usher in your kingdom makes me bolder to pray according to your will. May your kingdom come!

"In the name of him who taught me to pray. Amen."

DECEMBER 13

📖 Walk in the Word
Revelation 9

The fifth and sixth angels blow their trumpets, and death and destruction on the earth intensifies.

9 The fifth angel sounded his trumpet, and I saw a star that had fallen from the sky to the earth. The star was given the key to the shaft of the Abyss. ²When he opened the Abyss, smoke rose from it like the smoke from a gigantic furnace. The sun and sky were darkened by the smoke from the Abyss. ³And out of the smoke locusts came down upon the earth and were given power like that of scorpions of the earth. ⁴They were told not to harm the grass of the earth or any plant or tree, but only those people who did not have the seal of God on their foreheads. ⁵They were not given power to kill them, but only to torture them for five months. And the agony they suffered was like that of the sting of a scorpion when it strikes a man. ⁶During those days men will seek death, but will not find it; they will long to die, but death will elude them.

⁷The locusts looked like horses prepared for battle. On their heads they wore something like crowns of gold, and their faces resembled human faces. ⁸Their hair was like women's hair, and their teeth were like lions' teeth. ⁹They had breastplates like breastplates of iron, and the sound of their wings was like the thundering of many horses and chariots rushing into battle. ¹⁰They had tails and stings like scorpions, and in their tails they had power to torment people for five months. ¹¹They had as king over them the angel of the Abyss, whose name in Hebrew is Abaddon, and in Greek, Apollyon.[a]

¹²The first woe is past; two other woes are yet to come.

¹³The sixth angel sounded his trumpet, and I heard a voice coming from the horns[b] of the golden altar that is before God. ¹⁴It said to the sixth angel who had the trumpet, "Release the four angels who are bound at the great river Euphrates." ¹⁵And the four angels who had been kept ready for this very hour and day and month and year were released to kill a third of mankind. ¹⁶The number of the mounted troops was two hundred million. I heard their number.

¹⁷The horses and riders I saw in my vision looked like this: Their breastplates were fiery red, dark blue, and yellow as sulfur. The heads of the horses resembled the heads of lions, and out of their mouths came fire, smoke and sulfur. ¹⁸A third of mankind was killed by the three plagues of fire, smoke and sulfur that came out of their mouths. ¹⁹The power of the horses was in their mouths and in their tails; for their tails were like snakes, having heads with which they inflict injury.

²⁰The rest of mankind that were not killed by these plagues still did not repent of the work of their hands; they did not stop worshiping demons,

DECEMBER 13

and idols of gold, silver, bronze, stone and wood—idols that cannot see or hear or walk. [21]Nor did they repent of their murders, their magic arts, their sexual immorality or their thefts.

a11 Abaddon and *Apollyon* mean *Destroyer.*   *b13* That is, projections

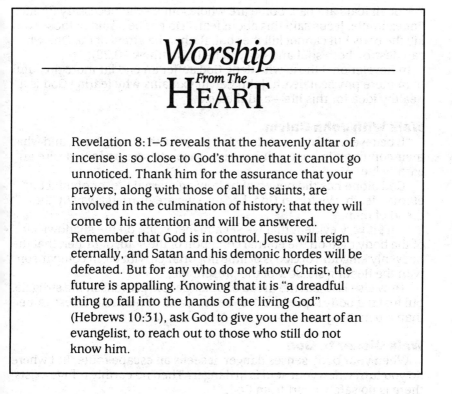

Worship From The HEART

Revelation 8:1–5 reveals that the heavenly altar of incense is so close to God's throne that it cannot go unnoticed. Thank him for the assurance that your prayers, along with those of all the saints, are involved in the culmination of history; that they will come to his attention and will be answered. Remember that God is in control. Jesus will reign eternally, and Satan and his demonic hordes will be defeated. But for any who do not know Christ, the future is appalling. Knowing that it is "a dreadful thing to fall into the hands of the living God" (Hebrews 10:31), ask God to give you the heart of an evangelist, to reach out to those who still do not know him.

DECEMBER 13

Created for Immortality

> They were told not to harm the grass of the earth or any plant or tree, but only those people who did not have the seal of God on their foreheads (Revelation 9:4).

Not all fears are bad. Some are wholesome, even necessary for life. For example, Jesus said this about fear: "Do not be afraid of those who kill the body but cannot kill the soul. Rather, be afraid of the One who can destroy both soul and body in hell" (Matthew 10:28).

In Revelation 9 those who deny God suffer an end far more dreadful than mere physical death. John Calvin explains why fearing God is a healthy idea for this life—and the next.

Walk With John Calvin

"If believers will consider for what purpose they were born, and what their condition is, they will have no reason to so earnestly desire an earthly life.

"God alone has the power of bestowing eternal life, or of inflicting eternal death. We forget God, because we are hurried away by the dread of men.

"Isn't it very evident that we set a higher value on the shadowy life of the body than on the eternal condition of the soul; or rather, that the heavenly kingdom of God is of little importance with us, in comparison with the fleeting shadow of the present life?

"How else is it that the dread of other people prevails in the struggle, but that the body is preferred to the soul, and immortality is less valued than a perishing life?"

Walk Closer to God

When your body senses danger, it seeks an escape route. But where do you turn when your soul is in danger? Then no earthly refuge exists; there is no safety apart from God.

Seventy years in the body cannot compare with an eternity in heaven. But which takes priority in your decisions . . . your investments . . . your plans . . . your commitments?

Loving and serving God with your whole body and soul. There's no greater command, no higher calling in this life or the next! ◖◗

DECEMBER 14

Walk in the Word
Revelation 10

John sees another mighty angel with a little scroll; this angel instructs him to eat the scroll and to prophesy.

The Angel and the Little Scroll

10 Then I saw another mighty angel coming down from heaven. He was robed in a cloud, with a rainbow above his head; his face was like the sun, and his legs were like fiery pillars. ²He was holding a little scroll, which lay open in his hand. He planted his right foot on the sea and his left foot on the land, ³and he gave a loud shout like the roar of a lion. When he shouted, the voices of the seven thunders spoke. ⁴And when the seven thunders spoke, I was about to write; but I heard a voice from heaven say, "Seal up what the seven thunders have said and do not write it down."

⁵Then the angel I had seen standing on the sea and on the land raised his right hand to heaven. ⁶And he swore by him who lives for ever and ever, who created the heavens and all that is in them, the earth and all that is in it, and the sea and all that is in it, and said, "There will be no more delay! ⁷But in the days when the seventh angel is about to sound his trumpet, the mystery of God will be accomplished, just as he announced to his servants the prophets."

⁸Then the voice that I had heard from heaven spoke to me once more: "Go, take the scroll that lies open in the hand of the angel who is standing on the sea and on the land."

⁹So I went to the angel and asked him to give me the little scroll. He said to me, "Take it and eat it. It will turn your stomach sour, but in your mouth it will be as sweet as honey." ¹⁰I took the little scroll from the angel's hand and ate it. It tasted as sweet as honey in my mouth, but when I had eaten it, my stomach turned sour. ¹¹Then I was told, "You must prophesy again about many peoples, nations, languages and kings."

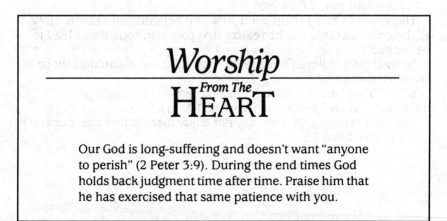

Worship From The HEART

Our God is long-suffering and doesn't want "anyone to perish" (2 Peter 3:9). During the end times God holds back judgment time after time. Praise him that he has exercised that same patience with you.

December 14

The Bittersweet Blessing of Pain

I took the little scroll . . . and ate it. It tasted as sweet as honey in my mouth, but when I had eaten it, my stomach turned sour (Revelation 10:10).

What surgeon hasn't consoled a patient with the thought that the pain of the scalpel will promote healing and health? It's good news and bad news both at the same time . . . much like the bittersweet news of the cross.

So often it's the same in our lives. We achieve maturity through the bitterness of suffering. Susannah Spurgeon, who suffered for over twenty-five years, understood the reward suffering brings.

Walk With Susannah Spurgeon

"At the close of a gloomy day, I lay resting on my couch. Though all was bright within my cozy room, some of the external darkness seemed to have entered my soul and obscured its spiritual vision. In sorrow I asked, 'Why does my Lord so often send sharp and bitter pain to visit me?'

"Suddenly I heard a sweet, soft sound, a clear, musical note. It came from the oak log crackling on the fire! The fire was letting loose the imprisoned music from the old oak's inmost heart!

" 'Ah,' I thought, 'when the fire of affliction draws songs of praise from us, then indeed we are purified, and our God is glorified!'

"Perhaps some of us are like this old oak log, cold, hard, insensible; we should give forth no melodious sounds were it not for the fire which kindles around us, and releases notes of trust in him and cheerful compliance with his will."

Walk Closer to God

"This might hurt a little bit!"

Those words bring scant comfort at the pediatrician's office. Only as the child matures will he realize that pain can sometimes lead to better health.

So too God's children must learn that "the Lord disciplines those he loves" (Hebrews 12:6).

Why? "That we may share in his holiness . . . a harvest of righteousness and peace (Hebrews 12:10–11).

Bittersweet blessings. You may not enjoy them at first bite, but you'll love the aftertaste. 〔〕

DECEMBER 15

Walk in the Word
Revelation 11:1–14

The two witnesses prophesy on the earth and are killed by the beast from the Abyss; God then raises them back to life and calls them to heaven.

The Two Witnesses

11 I was given a reed like a measuring rod and was told, "Go and measure the temple of God and the altar, and count the worshipers there. ²But exclude the outer court; do not measure it, because it has been given to the Gentiles. They will trample on the holy city for 42 months. ³And I will give power to my two witnesses, and they will prophesy for 1,260 days, clothed in sackcloth." ⁴These are the two olive trees and the two lampstands that stand before the Lord of the earth. ⁵If anyone tries to harm them, fire comes from their mouths and devours their enemies. This is how anyone who wants to harm them must die. ⁶These men have power to shut up the sky so that it will not rain during the time they are prophesying; and they have power to turn the waters into blood and to strike the earth with every kind of plague as often as they want.

⁷Now when they have finished their testimony, the beast that comes up from the Abyss will attack them, and overpower and kill them. ⁸Their bodies will lie in the street of the great city, which is figuratively called Sodom and Egypt, where also their Lord was crucified. ⁹For three and a half days men from every people, tribe, language and nation will gaze on their bodies and refuse them burial. ¹⁰The inhabitants of the earth will gloat over them and will celebrate by sending each other gifts, because these two prophets had tormented those who live on the earth.

¹¹But after the three and a half days a breath of life from God entered them, and they stood on their feet, and terror struck those who saw them. ¹²Then they heard a loud voice from heaven saying to them, "Come up here." And they went up to heaven in a cloud, while their enemies looked on.

¹³At that very hour there was a severe earthquake and a tenth of the city collapsed. Seven thousand people were killed in the earthquake, and the survivors were terrified and gave glory to the God of heaven.

¹⁴The second woe has passed; the third woe is coming soon.

DECEMBER 15

Taking the Measure of a Christlike Character

I was given a reed . . . and was told, "Go and measure the temple of God and the altar, and count the worshipers there" (Revelation 11:1).

Trying to measure up to another's expectations can be nerve-racking. But when God is the evaluator, then you'd better have help—the kind only to be found in a divine helper!

In Revelation 11 John is told to evaluate the place of worship and the people of worship to see if they "measure up." Therein is a lesson for every true worshiper of God, as Albert Barnes explains.

Walk With Albert Barnes

"John is commanded to 'Go and measure the temple of God.' That is, ascertain its true dimensions.

"If the direction had been literally to measure the temple at Jerusalem, John would measure its length, and breadth, and height; he would measure its rooms, its doorways, its porticoes.

"If the direction is understood figuratively, as applicable to the Christian church, John's work would be to obtain an exact estimate or measurement of what the true church was.

"John has not preserved the measurement; for the idea here is not that he was to preserve such a model, but that its true character might be known.

"The obvious meaning is that he was to take a correct estimate of their character; of what they professed; of the reality of their piety; of their lives; and of the general state of the church professing to worship God."

Walk Closer to God

When the yardstick of Christ's life is laid alongside your life, what does it reveal about the

. . . intensity of your worship?
. . . level of your commitment?
. . . purity of your attitudes and actions?
. . . degree of your Christlikeness?

The measure of a person without Christ always comes up short. Only in Christ can you truly measure up, for there "you have been given fullness in Christ, who is the head over every power and authority (Colossians 2:10).

DECEMBER 16

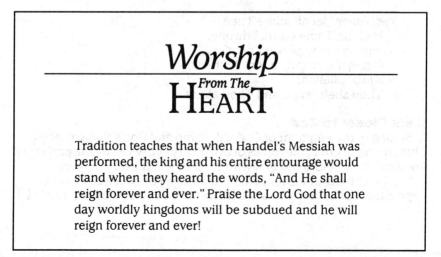 Walk in the Word
Revelation 11:15–19

When the seventh angel blows his trumpet, loud voices proclaim the victory of the kingdom of Christ.

The Seventh Trumpet

¹⁵The seventh angel sounded his trumpet, and there were loud voices in heaven, which said:

> "The kingdom of the world has become the kingdom of our
>   Lord and of his Christ,
>   and he will reign for ever and ever."

¹⁶And the twenty-four elders, who were seated on their thrones before God, fell on their faces and worshiped God, ¹⁷saying:

> "We give thanks to you, Lord God Almighty,
>   the One who is and who was,
> because you have taken your great power
>   and have begun to reign.
> ¹⁸The nations were angry;
>   and your wrath has come.
> The time has come for judging the dead,
>   and for rewarding your servants the prophets
> and your saints and those who reverence your name,
>   both small and great—
> and for destroying those who destroy the earth."

¹⁹Then God's temple in heaven was opened, and within his temple was seen the ark of his covenant. And there came flashes of lightning, rumblings, peals of thunder, an earthquake and a great hailstorm.

Worship
From The
HEART

Tradition teaches that when Handel's Messiah was performed, the king and his entire entourage would stand when they heard the words, "And He shall reign forever and ever." Praise the Lord God that one day worldly kingdoms will be subdued and he will reign forever and ever!

DECEMBER 16

The Blessed Hope of Christ's Return

The kingdom of the world has become the kingdom of our Lord and of his Christ, and he will reign for ever and ever (Revelation 11:15).

Christians today, like those of old, are prompted to ask, "Where is the promise of his coming?"

Patience, Christian. God is working out his purposes. Sometimes visibly, sometimes invisibly, he is patiently gathering the sons and daughters of the kingdom from every tongue, tribe and nation.

Hymnwriter Charles Wesley knew this truth well. In one of his inspiring compositions he proclaims the hope of every Christian—"Christ the Lord Returns to Reign."

Walk With Charles Wesley

Lo! He comes, with clouds descending,
    Once for our salvation slain;
Thousand thousand saints attending
    Swell the triumph of His train:
Alleluia, alleluia!
    Christ the Lord returns to reign.

Every eye shall now behold Him,
    Robed in dreadful majesty;
Those who set at naught and sold Him,
    Pierced and nailed Him to the tree,
Deeply wailing, deeply wailing,
    Shall the true Messiah see.

Yes, Amen! let all adore Thee,
    High on Thine eternal throne:
Savior, take the power and glory;
    Claim the kingdom for Thine own:
Alleluia, alleluia!
    Thou shalt reign, and Thou alone.

Walk Closer to God

Someday the kingdom of God will come and God's Son will enjoy ultimate victory over the forces of evil. Every eye will see him, and every knee will bow before the one who shall reign for ever and ever.

Let the coming of his kingdom encourage you to readiness and expectancy. Someday you too will "swell the triumph of His train."

DECEMBER 17

📖 Walk in the Word
Revelation 12:1 — 13:1a

John sees three periods of the conflict between Christ and Satan: on earth at the time of Christ's birth, in heaven at the time of his ascension, and on earth against the church. The final victory, however, belongs to Christ.

The Woman and the Dragon

12 A great and wondrous sign appeared in heaven: a woman clothed with the sun, with the moon under her feet and a crown of twelve stars on her head. ²She was pregnant and cried out in pain as she was about to give birth. ³Then another sign appeared in heaven: an enormous red dragon with seven heads and ten horns and seven crowns on his heads. ⁴His tail swept a third of the stars out of the sky and flung them to the earth. The dragon stood in front of the woman who was about to give birth, so that he might devour her child the moment it was born. ⁵She gave birth to a son, a male child, who will rule all the nations with an iron scepter. And her child was snatched up to God and to his throne. ⁶The woman fled into the desert to a place prepared for her by God, where she might be taken care of for 1,260 days.

⁷And there was war in heaven. Michael and his angels fought against the dragon, and the dragon and his angels fought back. ⁸But he was not strong enough, and they lost their place in heaven. ⁹The great dragon was hurled down — that ancient serpent called the devil, or Satan, who leads the whole world astray. He was hurled to the earth, and his angels with him.

¹⁰Then I heard a loud voice in heaven say:

> "Now have come the salvation and the power and the
>   kingdom of our God,
>   and the authority of his Christ.
> For the accuser of our brothers,
>   who accuses them before our God day and night,
>   has been hurled down.
> ¹¹They overcame him
>   by the blood of the Lamb
>   and by the word of their testimony;
> they did not love their lives so much
>   as to shrink from death.
> ¹²Therefore rejoice, you heavens
>   and you who dwell in them!
> But woe to the earth and the sea,
>   because the devil has gone down to you!
> He is filled with fury,
>   because he knows that his time is short."

¹³When the dragon saw that he had been hurled to the earth, he pursued the woman who had given birth to the male child. ¹⁴The woman was given the two wings of a great eagle, so that she might fly to the place prepared

DECEMBER 17

for her in the desert, where she would be taken care of for a time, times and half a time, out of the serpent's reach. [15]Then from his mouth the serpent spewed water like a river, to overtake the woman and sweep her away with the torrent. [16]But the earth helped the woman by opening its mouth and swallowing the river that the dragon had spewed out of his mouth. [17]Then the dragon was enraged at the woman and went off to make war against the rest of her offspring—those who obey God's com-

13 mandments and hold to the testimony of Jesus. [1]And the dragon[a] stood on the shore of the sea.

[a]1 Some late manuscripts *And I*

Worship
From The
HEART

Satan loves to accuse you before the Lord, enumerating your sins and shortcomings. On the other hand, he will also whisper accusations against God into the ears of believers. Guard your heart and mind against Satan's deception, and rejoice now that you have "one who speaks to the Father in [your] defense—Jesus Christ, the Righteous One" (1 John 2:1).

December 17

Respond With Praise to the Perfection of God

Now have come the salvation and the power and the kingdom of our God, and the authority of his Christ. . . . Therefore rejoice, you heavens and you who dwell in them! (Revelation 12:10,12).

Clapping. Cheering. Cries of "Bravo!" All are appropriate responses when an audience enjoys talent displayed at the peak of perfection.

C.S. Lewis offers this intriguing suggestion why an eternal chorus of praise for a "performance" that is perfect in every way is such a satisfying activity for the Christian.

Walk With C.S. Lewis

"I think we delight to praise what we enjoy because the praise not merely expresses but completes the enjoyment; it is its appointed consummation.

"If it were possible for a created soul fully to 'appreciate,' that is, to love and delight in, the worthiest object of all, and simultaneously at every moment to give this delight perfect expression, then that soul would be in supreme blessedness.

"To praise God fully we must suppose ourselves to be in perfect love with God, drowned in, dissolved by that delight which, far from remaining pent up within ourselves as incommunicable bliss, flows out from us incessantly again in effortless and perfect expression.

"Our joy is no more separable from the praise in which it liberates and utters itself than the brightness a mirror receives is separable from the brightness it sheds."

Walk Closer to God

The quest for perfection. It's a worthy endeavor for any performer or musician.

And as C.S. Lewis has suggested, the Christian has his own quest: to love God perfectly. To respond with perfect praise to the one who perfectly deserves it—the one who perfectly loves you.

The more you behold him, the more appropriate—and enthusiastic—will be your response, until finally "we shall be like him, for we shall see him as he is" (1 John 3:2).

That's one performance you won't want to miss! ◖

DECEMBER 18

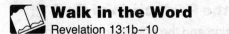

Walk in the Word
Revelation 13:1b–10

John sees the beast, who rules the earth with great power and authority, making life intolerable for the faithful saints.

The Beast out of the Sea

And I saw a beast coming out of the sea. He had ten horns and seven heads, with ten crowns on his horns, and on each head a blasphemous name. ²The beast I saw resembled a leopard, but had feet like those of a bear and a mouth like that of a lion. The dragon gave the beast his power and his throne and great authority. ³One of the heads of the beast seemed to have had a fatal wound, but the fatal wound had been healed. The whole world was astonished and followed the beast. ⁴Men worshiped the dragon because he had given authority to the beast, and they also worshiped the beast and asked, "Who is like the beast? Who can make war against him?"

⁵The beast was given a mouth to utter proud words and blasphemies and to exercise his authority for forty-two months. ⁶He opened his mouth to blaspheme God, and to slander his name and his dwelling place and those who live in heaven. ⁷He was given power to make war against the saints and to conquer them. And he was given authority over every tribe, people, language and nation. ⁸All inhabitants of the earth will worship the beast—all whose names have not been written in the book of life belonging to the Lamb that was slain from the creation of the world. *a*

⁹He who has an ear, let him hear.

> ¹⁰If anyone is to go into captivity,
>   into captivity he will go.
> If anyone is to be killed *b* with the sword,
>   with the sword he will be killed.

This calls for patient endurance and faithfulness on the part of the saints.

a8 Or written from the creation of the world in the book of life belonging to the Lamb that was slain   *b10 Some manuscripts anyone kills*

Hiding With Christ Is the Safest Place to Be

If anyone is to go into captivity, into captivity he will go. If anyone is to be killed with the sword, with the sword he will be killed. This calls for patient endurance and faithfulness on the part of the saints (Revelation 13:10).

To say that something "boomeranged" means that what you intended to send somewhere else has instead come back to haunt you.

In the case of the enemies of God and his people, all the enmity that they can muster against the forces of righteousness will "boomerang." They will suffer at the hands of their own weapons.

William Milligan offers these words of comfort for Christians threatened by suffering and opposition.

Walk With William Milligan

"Nothing can harm the life that is hidden with Christ in God. But the saints may still be troubled, persecuted and killed—as were the witnesses of chapter eleven—by the beast that was given power to make war and to conquer them.

"Such is the thought that leads to the words which we now consider: 'If anyone is to go into captivity, into captivity he will go. If anyone is to be killed with the sword, with the sword he will be killed.'

"In the great law of God, consolation is given to the persecuted. Their enemies would lead them into captivity, but a worse captivity awaits themselves. They would kill with the sword, but with a sharper sword than that of human power they shall themselves be killed. Is there not enough in that to inspire the saints with faith and patience?

"Well may they endure with unfailing hearts when they remember who is on their side, for 'God is just: He will pay back trouble to those who trouble you' " (2 Thessalonians 1:6).

Walk Closer to God

"If God is for us"—and he is—"who can be against us?" (Romans 8:31).

The enemy's attempts at sabotage will boomerang to his own destruction; the believer in Christ will enjoy a well-deserved rest. So take heart!

"Hiding with Christ in God" is the safest place to be. ⟨⟩

DECEMBER 19

Walk in the Word
Revelation 13:11–18

John sees another beast, with the number 666, coming out of the earth and forcing everyone to worship the first beast.

The Beast out of the Earth

¹¹Then I saw another beast, coming out of the earth. He had two horns like a lamb, but he spoke like a dragon. ¹²He exercised all the authority of the first beast on his behalf, and made the earth and its inhabitants worship the first beast, whose fatal wound had been healed. ¹³And he performed great and miraculous signs, even causing fire to come down from heaven to earth in full view of men. ¹⁴Because of the signs he was given power to do on behalf of the first beast, he deceived the inhabitants of the earth. He ordered them to set up an image in honor of the beast who was wounded by the sword and yet lived. ¹⁵He was given power to give breath to the image of the first beast, so that it could speak and cause all who refused to worship the image to be killed. ¹⁶He also forced everyone, small and great, rich and poor, free and slave, to receive a mark on his right hand or on his forehead, ¹⁷so that no one could buy or sell unless he had the mark, which is the name of the beast or the number of his name.

¹⁸This calls for wisdom. If anyone has insight, let him calculate the number of the beast, for it is man's number. His number is 666.

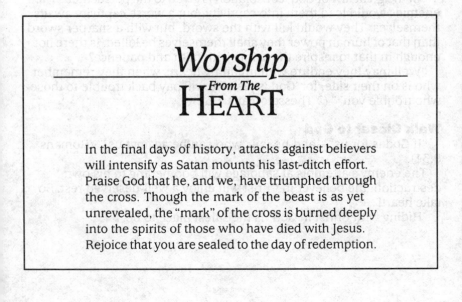

Worship
From The
HEART

In the final days of history, attacks against believers will intensify as Satan mounts his last-ditch effort. Praise God that he, and we, have triumphed through the cross. Though the mark of the beast is as yet unrevealed, the "mark" of the cross is burned deeply into the spirits of those who have died with Jesus. Rejoice that you are sealed to the day of redemption.

Suffering for What You Value

No one could buy or sell unless he had the mark, which is the name of the beast or the number of his name (Revelation 13:17).

A world that ignores God is a world that rejects Christians. In the eyes of the world, the only thing worse than a Christian who lives like Christ is a Christian who doesn't live like Christ.

When John writes of the mark of the beast, he speaks of the unholy fraternity that confronts Christians. F.B. Meyer shares two resolutions for you to consider as a person devoted to Christ.

Walk With F.B. Meyer

"Christians are finding it increasingly difficult to carry on their businesses without adopting a lower standard than that of the sanctuary.

"Yet Christians must resolve that they will not trifle with their consciences, but will obey the law of Christ in all respects. For everyone there is an inevitable choice to be made and maintained, whether a clear conscience or a fortune is to hold first place in their business careers.

"Second, they must be content to bear poverty as part of the cross of Christ. We admire and canonize martyrs, but are strangely unwilling to face the disgrace of poverty, the dens and caves of the earth, which they endured for principle. Our religion will cost us something, or we may fairly question its vitality and worth. What one will not suffer for, one does not value."

Walk Closer to God

If it might cost you your livelihood to take a stand for your living Lord, would you sway in your commitment? Consider:

"If anyone would come after me, he must deny himself and take up his cross daily and follow me" (Luke 9:23).

"Anyone who does not carry his cross and follow me cannot be my disciple" (Luke 14:27).

"Any of you who does not give up everything he has cannot be my disciple" (Luke 14:33).

Dare to obey Christ—regardless of the cost—and he will give you a contentment and confidence no earthly profession can supply.

DECEMBER 20

📖 Walk in the Word
Revelation 14

John receives a vision of the victorious Lamb of God with his 144,000 singing his praises, followed by several angels who come to bring God's judgment on the earth.

The Lamb and the 144,000

14 Then I looked, and there before me was the Lamb, standing on Mount Zion, and with him 144,000 who had his name and his Father's name written on their foreheads. 2And I heard a sound from heaven like the roar of rushing waters and like a loud peal of thunder. The sound I heard was like that of harpists playing their harps. 3And they sang a new song before the throne and before the four living creatures and the elders. No one could learn the song except the 144,000 who had been redeemed from the earth. 4These are those who did not defile themselves with women, for they kept themselves pure. They follow the Lamb wherever he goes. They were purchased from among men and offered as firstfruits to God and the Lamb. 5No lie was found in their mouths; they are blameless.

The Three Angels

6Then I saw another angel flying in midair, and he had the eternal gospel to proclaim to those who live on the earth—to every nation, tribe, language and people. 7He said in a loud voice, "Fear God and give him glory, because the hour of his judgment has come. Worship him who made the heavens, the earth, the sea and the springs of water."

8A second angel followed and said, "Fallen! Fallen is Babylon the Great, which made all the nations drink the maddening wine of her adulteries."

9A third angel followed them and said in a loud voice: "If anyone worships the beast and his image and receives his mark on the forehead or on the hand, 10he, too, will drink of the wine of God's fury, which has been poured full strength into the cup of his wrath. He will be tormented with burning sulfur in the presence of the holy angels and of the Lamb. 11And the smoke of their torment rises for ever and ever. There is no rest day or night for those who worship the beast and his image, or for anyone who receives the mark of his name." 12This calls for patient endurance on the part of the saints who obey God's commandments and remain faithful to Jesus.

13Then I heard a voice from heaven say, "Write: Blessed are the dead who die in the Lord from now on."

"Yes," says the Spirit, "they will rest from their labor, for their deeds will follow them."

The Harvest of the Earth

14I looked, and there before me was a white cloud, and seated on the cloud was one "like a son of man"*a* with a crown of gold on his head and a sharp sickle in his hand. 15Then another angel came out of the temple and called in a loud voice to him who was sitting on the cloud, "Take your

DECEMBER 20

sickle and reap, because the time to reap has come, for the harvest of the earth is ripe." ¹⁶So he who was seated on the cloud swung his sickle over the earth, and the earth was harvested.

¹⁷Another angel came out of the temple in heaven, and he too had a sharp sickle. ¹⁸Still another angel, who had charge of the fire, came from the altar and called in a loud voice to him who had the sharp sickle, "Take your sharp sickle and gather the clusters of grapes from the earth's vine, because its grapes are ripe." ¹⁹The angel swung his sickle on the earth, gathered its grapes and threw them into the great winepress of God's wrath. ²⁰They were trampled in the winepress outside the city, and blood flowed out of the press, rising as high as the horses' bridles for a distance of 1,600 stadia.ᵇ

ᵃ14 Daniel 7:13   ᵇ20 That is, about 180 miles (about 300 kilometers)

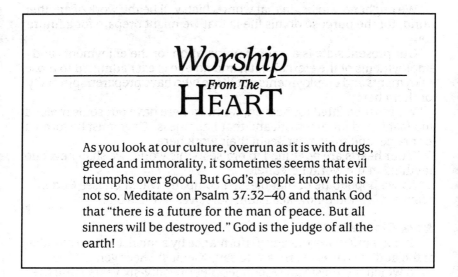

Worship
From The
HEART

As you look at our culture, overrun as it is with drugs, greed and immorality, it sometimes seems that evil triumphs over good. But God's people know this is not so. Meditate on Psalm 37:32–40 and thank God that "there is a future for the man of peace. But all sinners will be destroyed." God is the judge of all the earth!

DECEMBER 20

Souls That Are Shaped for Life in Heaven

And I heard a sound from heaven. . . . The sound I heard was like that of harpists playing their harps. And they sang a new song before the throne (Revelation 14:2–3).

Think of your life on earth as an opportunity to practice what you will be spending an eternity in heaven "performing": praising God.

Vocalists and violinists, actors and conductors, all strive for perfection in their respective disciplines. Jonathan Edwards exhorts you to practice your grand chorus of praise with the same enthusiasm and commitment to excellence.

Walk With Jonathan Edwards

"We ought now to begin that work which will be the work of another world; for the purpose of this life is that we might prepare for a future life.

"Our present state is a state of preparation for the enjoyments and employments of the eternal state; and no one is ever admitted to those enjoyments and employments but those who have prepared spiritually for them here.

"We must be fitted for heaven; we must here have our souls molded and fashioned for that work and that happiness. They must be formed for praise, and they must begin their work here.

"If our hearts are not tuned to praise in this world, we shall never do anything in the world hereafter.

"As we hope to be of that blessed company which praises God in heaven, we should now accustom ourselves to the work."

Walk Closer to God

After a particularly moving performance by a musician, one member of the audience was overheard to say, "Genius! Sheer genius!"

To which the musician responded, "For twenty-six years I practice ten hours a day . . . and now they call me a genius!"

You have only a handful of years to practice what will be your eternal preoccupation.

So if you know you're going to be singing a "new song" of praise before the throne, now would be a good time to start. ◖

DECEMBER 21

📖 Walk in the Word
Revelation 15

John sees the seven angels ready to pour forth the seven last plagues of the wrath of God.

Seven Angels With Seven Plagues

15 I saw in heaven another great and marvelous sign: seven angels with the seven last plagues—last, because with them God's wrath is completed. ²And I saw what looked like a sea of glass mixed with fire and, standing beside the sea, those who had been victorious over the beast and his image and over the number of his name. They held harps given them by God ³and sang the song of Moses the servant of God and the song of the Lamb:

> "Great and marvelous are your deeds,
>   Lord God Almighty.
> Just and true are your ways,
>   King of the ages.
> ⁴Who will not fear you, O Lord,
>   and bring glory to your name?
> For you alone are holy.
> All nations will come
>   and worship before you,
> for your righteous acts have been revealed."

⁵After this I looked and in heaven the temple, that is, the tabernacle of the Testimony, was opened. ⁶Out of the temple came the seven angels with the seven plagues. They were dressed in clean, shining linen and wore golden sashes around their chests. ⁷Then one of the four living creatures gave to the seven angels seven golden bowls filled with the wrath of God, who lives for ever and ever. ⁸And the temple was filled with smoke from the glory of God and from his power, and no one could enter the temple until the seven plagues of the seven angels were completed.

December 21

Outward Energy Regulated by Inward Peace

I saw what looked like a sea of glass mixed with fire
(Revelation 15:2).

Before the seven last bowls of judgment are poured, John pictures an unusual scene: a "sea of glass mixed with fire." Contradictory images evoking both peace and judgment. In the same way, Jesus is called both Lion and Lamb (Revelation 5:5–6).

Contradictions? No—balance.

Out of John's description of peace and judgment, W. Graham Scroggie gleans a lesson on the powerful possibilities of a balanced life.

Walk With W. Graham Scroggie

"Peace and energy do not always go together, though they should. Peace without energy may be only stagnation; and energy without peace may be but a form of panic.

"What we need is that our glassy sea be mixed with fire, and that our fire shall have for its home a glassy sea.

"Why should peace exclude passion, and why should passion destroy peace? Why should one moral quality triumph at the expense of another?

"Yet too often it is so. Sometimes our sea is not glass, but tempest-tossed, and sometimes our fire burns low. Sometimes it is all calm and no energy, and sometimes it is all energy and no calm.

"But what is possible and right is that the glassy sea be mixed with fire, that our outward energy be regulated by inward peace, and that our inward peace find expression in outward energy. Then shall there be power in balance."

Walk Closer to God

Power out of control (such as an earthquake or volcanic eruption) can endanger many.

Power under control (an internal combustion engine or a hydroelectric plant) can benefit many.

And a power outage accomplishes nothing for anyone!

Which of the three power levels best characterizes your life?

If the answer is unsettling, look to the one who can help you catch—and keep—the balanced walk of a child of God. ⟪⟫

DECEMBER 22

📖 Walk in the Word
Revelation 16

The seven angels pour out their bowls, filled with the wrath of God, on the earth.

The Seven Bowls of God's Wrath

16 Then I heard a loud voice from the temple saying to the seven angels, "Go, pour out the seven bowls of God's wrath on the earth."

²The first angel went and poured out his bowl on the land, and ugly and painful sores broke out on the people who had the mark of the beast and worshiped his image.

³The second angel poured out his bowl on the sea, and it turned into blood like that of a dead man, and every living thing in the sea died.

⁴The third angel poured out his bowl on the rivers and springs of water, and they became blood. ⁵Then I heard the angel in charge of the waters say:

> "You are just in these judgments,
> you who are and who were, the Holy One,
> because you have so judged;
> ⁶for they have shed the blood of your saints and prophets,
> and you have given them blood to drink as they deserve."

⁷And I heard the altar respond:

> "Yes, Lord God Almighty,
> true and just are your judgments."

⁸The fourth angel poured out his bowl on the sun, and the sun was given power to scorch people with fire. ⁹They were seared by the intense heat and they cursed the name of God, who had control over these plagues, but they refused to repent and glorify him.

¹⁰The fifth angel poured out his bowl on the throne of the beast, and his kingdom was plunged into darkness. Men gnawed their tongues in agony ¹¹and cursed the God of heaven because of their pains and their sores, but they refused to repent of what they had done.

¹²The sixth angel poured out his bowl on the great river Euphrates, and its water was dried up to prepare the way for the kings from the East. ¹³Then I saw three evil*ᵃ* spirits that looked like frogs; they came out of the mouth of the dragon, out of the mouth of the beast and out of the mouth of the false prophet. ¹⁴They are spirits of demons performing miraculous signs, and they go out to the kings of the whole world, to gather them for the battle on the great day of God Almighty.

¹⁵"Behold, I come like a thief! Blessed is he who stays awake and keeps his clothes with him, so that he may not go naked and be shamefully exposed."

¹⁶Then they gathered the kings together to the place that in Hebrew is called Armageddon.

¹⁷The seventh angel poured out his bowl into the air, and out of the

DECEMBER 22

temple came a loud voice from the throne, saying, "It is done!" ¹⁸Then
there came flashes of lightning, rumblings, peals of thunder and a severe
earthquake. No earthquake like it has ever occurred since man has been
on earth, so tremendous was the quake. ¹⁹The great city split into three
parts, and the cities of the nations collapsed. God remembered Babylon
the Great and gave her the cup filled with the wine of the fury of his wrath.
²⁰Every island fled away and the mountains could not be found. ²¹From
the sky huge hailstones of about a hundred pounds each fell upon men.
And they cursed God on account of the plague of hail, because the plague
was so terrible.

ᵃ13 Greek *unclean*

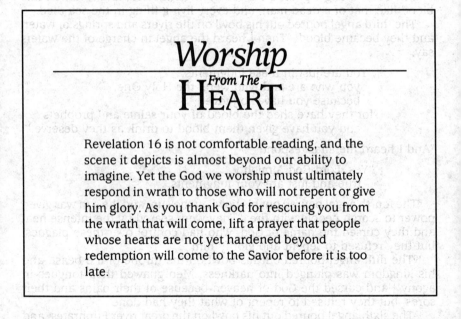

Worship
From The
HEART

Revelation 16 is not comfortable reading, and the
scene it depicts is almost beyond our ability to
imagine. Yet the God we worship must ultimately
respond in wrath to those who will not repent or give
him glory. As you thank God for rescuing you from
the wrath that will come, lift a prayer that people
whose hearts are not yet hardened beyond
redemption will come to the Savior before it is too
late.

DECEMBER 22

Your Chance to Choose the Right Side

Then I heard the angel in charge of the waters say: "You are just in these judgments, you who are and who were, the Holy One, because you have so judged" (Revelation 16:5).

Someone facing an unpleasant task often goes through three phases: contemplating how to do it; contemplating when to do it; and contemplating.

That formula may be humorous for mundane chores. But in eternal matters, procrastination can be lethal. When God's judgment comes, it will come with finality. No postponements. No excuses.

C.S. Lewis paints this picture in words of what that day will be like.

Walk With C.S. Lewis

"When the author walks onto the stage, the play is over. God is going to invade, all right; but what is the good of saying you are on his side then, when you see the whole natural universe melting away like a dream and something else comes crashing in?

"This time it will be God without disguise; something so overwhelming that it will strike either irresistible love or irresistible horror into every creature.

"It will be too late then to choose your side. That will not be the time for choosing: It will be the time when we discover which side we really have chosen, whether we realized it before or not.

"Now, today, this moment, is our chance to choose the right side."

Walk Closer to God

Today you face a choice; tomorrow you will face the consequences of the choice you made.

Today you may choose your path; tomorrow you will discover just where the path has led you.

"Then the King will say to those on his right, 'Come, you who are blessed by my Father; take your inheritance, the kingdom prepared for you.' . . . Then he will say to those on his left, 'Depart from me, you who are cursed, into the eternal fire prepared for the devil and his angels' " (Matthew 25:34,41).

Which will it be: getting right with God . . . or getting left?

DECEMBER 23

📖 Walk in the Word
Revelation 17

John sees the blasphemous prostitute—Babylon the Great, she who had been persecuting the saints—being prepared for her destruction.

The Woman on the Beast

17 One of the seven angels who had the seven bowls came and said to me, "Come, I will show you the punishment of the great prostitute, who sits on many waters. ²With her the kings of the earth committed adultery and the inhabitants of the earth were intoxicated with the wine of her adulteries."

³Then the angel carried me away in the Spirit into a desert. There I saw a woman sitting on a scarlet beast that was covered with blasphemous names and had seven heads and ten horns. ⁴The woman was dressed in purple and scarlet, and was glittering with gold, precious stones and pearls. She held a golden cup in her hand, filled with abominable things and the filth of her adulteries. ⁵This title was written on her forehead:

MYSTERY

BABYLON THE GREAT

THE MOTHER OF PROSTITUTES

AND OF THE ABOMINATIONS OF THE EARTH.

⁶I saw that the woman was drunk with the blood of the saints, the blood of those who bore testimony to Jesus.

When I saw her, I was greatly astonished. ⁷Then the angel said to me: "Why are you astonished? I will explain to you the mystery of the woman and of the beast she rides, which has the seven heads and ten horns. ⁸The beast, which you saw, once was, now is not, and will come up out of the Abyss and go to his destruction. The inhabitants of the earth whose names have not been written in the book of life from the creation of the world will be astonished when they see the beast, because he once was, now is not, and yet will come.

⁹"This calls for a mind with wisdom. The seven heads are seven hills on which the woman sits. ¹⁰They are also seven kings. Five have fallen, one is, the other has not yet come; but when he does come, he must remain for a little while. ¹¹The beast who once was, and now is not, is an eighth king. He belongs to the seven and is going to his destruction.

¹²"The ten horns you saw are ten kings who have not yet received a kingdom, but who for one hour will receive authority as kings along with the beast. ¹³They have one purpose and will give their power and authority to the beast. ¹⁴They will make war against the Lamb, but the Lamb will overcome them because he is Lord of lords and King of kings—and with him will be his called, chosen and faithful followers."

¹⁵Then the angel said to me, "The waters you saw, where the prostitute sits, are peoples, multitudes, nations and languages. ¹⁶The beast and the ten horns you saw will hate the prostitute. They will bring her to ruin and leave her naked; they will eat her flesh and burn her with fire. ¹⁷For God

DECEMBER 23

has put it into their hearts to accomplish his purpose by agreeing to give the beast their power to rule, until God's words are fulfilled. ¹⁸The woman you saw is the great city that rules over the kings of the earth."

PSALM 8

For the director of music. According to *gittith.* ᵃ A psalm of David.

O LORD, our Lord,
how majestic is your name in all the earth!

You have set your glory
above the heavens.
²From the lips of children and infants
you have ordained praise ᵇ
because of your enemies,
to silence the foe and the avenger.

³When I consider your heavens,
the work of your fingers,
the moon and the stars,
which you have set in place,
⁴what is man that you are mindful of him,
the son of man that you care for him?
⁵You made him a little lower than the heavenly beings ᶜ
and crowned him with glory and honor.

⁶You made him ruler over the works of your hands;
you put everything under his feet:
⁷all flocks and herds,
and the beasts of the field,
⁸the birds of the air,
and the fish of the sea,
all that swim the paths of the seas.

⁹O LORD, our Lord,
how majestic is your name in all the earth!

ᵃTitle: Probably a musical term   ᵇ2 Or *strength*   ᶜ5 Or *than God*

December 23

Crown Him With Many Crowns!

They will make war against the Lamb, but the Lamb will overcome them because he is Lord of lords and King of kings (Revelation 17:14).

In Revelation the Lamb of God overcomes his enemies as King of kings (Revelation 17:14).

Perhaps you find it easy to envision Jesus as the "Lamb of God, who takes away the sin of the world" (John 1:29) — but harder to view him as the Lord of lords vanquishing the forces of evil.

If so, Abraham Kuyper will help you with this timely description of Christ as both victim and victor.

Walk With Abraham Kuyper

"Christ is your King! Does this title of honor tend merely to have you think of Christ as in a distant hamlet the man behind his plow thinks of his sovereign in the royal residence?

"Is the kingly image of the earthly prince, applied to your Savior purely by way of comparison, a way to express his power and honor?

"The Lamb, so it is proclaimed unto you in Revelation, is not merely your Reconciliation and your Surety, not alone your Redeemer and Savior, nor yet alone your Shepherd and your Guide.

"No, the Lamb of God—and in this contrast you feel what amazes and inspires—the Lamb of God is at the same time the Lord of lords and King of kings.

"The Lamb with the crown, the high, the holy union of self-effacement and dominion—your King!"

Walk Closer to God

Lamb and Lord. Shepherd and Savior.

It's a twin theme echoed in this familiar hymn. Use it right now to exalt your God and Guide:

Crown Him the Lord of years,
    The Potentate of time;
Creator of the rolling spheres,
    Ineffably sublime:
All hail, Redeemer, hail!
    For Thou hast died for me:
Thy praise shall never, never fail
    Throughout eternity. ◖◗

DECEMBER 24

📖 Walk in the Word
Revelation 18

Babylon the Great falls amidst great violence; all those who had depended on her for their livelihood mourn, but heaven rejoices.

The Fall of Babylon

18 After this I saw another angel coming down from heaven. He had great authority, and the earth was illuminated by his splendor. ²With a mighty voice he shouted:

> "Fallen! Fallen is Babylon the Great!
> She has become a home for demons
> and a haunt for every evil*ᵃ* spirit,
> a haunt for every unclean and detestable bird.
> ³For all the nations have drunk
> the maddening wine of her adulteries.
> The kings of the earth committed adultery with her,
> and the merchants of the earth grew rich from her
> excessive luxuries."

⁴Then I heard another voice from heaven say:

> "Come out of her, my people,
> so that you will not share in her sins,
> so that you will not receive any of her plagues;
> ⁵for her sins are piled up to heaven,
> and God has remembered her crimes.
> ⁶Give back to her as she has given;
> pay her back double for what she has done.
> Mix her a double portion from her own cup.
> ⁷Give her as much torture and grief
> as the glory and luxury she gave herself.
> In her heart she boasts,
> 'I sit as queen; I am not a widow,
> and I will never mourn.'
> ⁸Therefore in one day her plagues will overtake her:
> death, mourning and famine.
> She will be consumed by fire,
> for mighty is the Lord God who judges her.

⁹"When the kings of the earth who committed adultery with her and shared her luxury see the smoke of her burning, they will weep and mourn over her. ¹⁰Terrified at her torment, they will stand far off and cry:

> "'Woe! Woe, O great city,
> O Babylon, city of power!
> In one hour your doom has come!'

935

DECEMBER 24

11"The merchants of the earth will weep and mourn over her because no one buys their cargoes any more— 12cargoes of gold, silver, precious stones and pearls; fine linen, purple, silk and scarlet cloth; every sort of citron wood, and articles of every kind made of ivory, costly wood, bronze, iron and marble; 13cargoes of cinnamon and spice, of incense, myrrh and frankincense, of wine and olive oil, of fine flour and wheat; cattle and sheep; horses and carriages; and bodies and souls of men.

14"They will say, 'The fruit you longed for is gone from you. All your riches and splendor have vanished, never to be recovered.' 15The merchants who sold these things and gained their wealth from her will stand far off, terrified at her torment. They will weep and mourn 16and cry out:

> " 'Woe! Woe, O great city,
>> dressed in fine linen, purple and scarlet,
>> and glittering with gold, precious stones and pearls!
> 17In one hour such great wealth has been brought to ruin!'

"Every sea captain, and all who travel by ship, the sailors, and all who earn their living from the sea, will stand far off. 18When they see the smoke of her burning, they will exclaim, 'Was there ever a city like this great city?' 19They will throw dust on their heads, and with weeping and mourning cry out:

> " 'Woe! Woe, O great city,
>> where all who had ships on the sea
>> became rich through her wealth!
> In one hour she has been brought to ruin!
> 20Rejoice over her, O heaven!
>> Rejoice, saints and apostles and prophets!
> God has judged her for the way she treated you.' "

21Then a mighty angel picked up a boulder the size of a large millstone and threw it into the sea, and said:

> "With such violence
>> the great city of Babylon will be thrown down,
>> never to be found again.
> 22The music of harpists and musicians, flute players and
>> trumpeters,
>> will never be heard in you again.
> No workman of any trade
>> will ever be found in you again.
> The sound of a millstone
>> will never be heard in you again.
> 23The light of a lamp
>> will never shine in you again.
> The voice of bridegroom and bride
>> will never be heard in you again.
> Your merchants were the world's great men.

DECEMBER 24

By your magic spell all the nations were led astray.
24In her was found the blood of prophets and of the saints,
and of all who have been killed on the earth."

a2 Greek *unclean*

PSALM 26

Of David.

Vindicate me, O LORD,
for I have led a blameless life;
I have trusted in the LORD
without wavering.
2Test me, O LORD, and try me,
examine my heart and my mind;
3for your love is ever before me,
and I walk continually in your truth.
4I do not sit with deceitful men,
nor do I consort with hypocrites;
5I abhor the assembly of evildoers
and refuse to sit with the wicked.
6I wash my hands in innocence,
and go about your altar, O LORD,
7proclaiming aloud your praise
and telling of all your wonderful deeds.
8I love the house where you live, O LORD,
the place where your glory dwells.

9Do not take away my soul along with sinners,
my life with bloodthirsty men,
10in whose hands are wicked schemes,
whose right hands are full of bribes.
11But I lead a blameless life;
redeem me and be merciful to me.

12My feet stand on level ground;
in the great assembly I will praise the LORD.

DECEMBER 24

Leaving Behind the Fortress of Darkness

Then I heard another voice from heaven say: "Come out of her, my people, so that you will not share in her sins" (Revelation 18:4).

There is a time to take a stand, and a time to take your leave. And woe to the believer who fails to discern which time is which.

Paul's question is timely: "What do righteousness and wickedness have in common? Or what fellowship can light have with darkness?" (2 Corinthians 6:14).

Even the prophet Isaiah—certainly no stranger to the evils of his day—urged his readers, "Come out . . . and be pure" (Isaiah 52:11).

F.B. Meyer uses Old Testament examples to show when and how to separate from the fortresses of darkness.

Walk With F.B. Meyer

"It is often argued that we should stay in the midst of churches and bodies whose sins and follies we deplore, in the hope of saving them for God and mankind. Such reasoning has a good deal of force in the first stages of decline. A strong protest may arrest error and stop the gangrene.

"But as time advances, and the whole body becomes diseased; when the protests have been disregarded, and the arguments trampled underfoot; when the majority have clearly taken up their position against the truth—we have no alternative but to come out and be pure.

"The place from which we can exert the strongest influence for good is not from within, but from without.

"Lot lost all influence in his life in Sodom; but Abraham, from the heights of Mamre, was able to exert a mighty influence on its history."

Walk Closer to God

You may find yourself resembling a "speck of saintliness" in a sea of sin. If so, the question to ask may not be, "What sort of impact can I make?" but, "How long can I maintain an effective witness here?"

Answer carefully; your spiritual health may well be at stake.

DECEMBER 25

Walk in the Word
Revelation 19:1–10

John receives a vision of the heavenly multitude singing the praises of God, for God had brought just judgment on the great prostitute and avenged the blood of the saints.

Hallelujah!

19 After this I heard what sounded like the roar of a great multitude in heaven shouting:

> "Hallelujah!
> Salvation and glory and power belong to our God,
> 2 for true and just are his judgments.
> He has condemned the great prostitute
> who corrupted the earth by her adulteries.
> He has avenged on her the blood of his servants."

³And again they shouted:

> "Hallelujah!
> The smoke from her goes up for ever and ever."

⁴The twenty-four elders and the four living creatures fell down and worshiped God, who was seated on the throne. And they cried:

> "Amen, Hallelujah!"

⁵Then a voice came from the throne, saying:

> "Praise our God,
> all you his servants,
> you who fear him,
> both small and great!"

⁶Then I heard what sounded like a great multitude, like the roar of rushing waters and like loud peals of thunder, shouting:

> "Hallelujah!
> For our Lord God Almighty reigns.
> ⁷Let us rejoice and be glad
> and give him glory!
> For the wedding of the Lamb has come,
> and his bride has made herself ready.
> ⁸Fine linen, bright and clean,
> was given her to wear."

(Fine linen stands for the righteous acts of the saints.)

⁹Then the angel said to me, "Write: 'Blessed are those who are invited to the wedding supper of the Lamb!' " And he added, "These are the true words of God."

December 25

¹⁰At this I fell at his feet to worship him. But he said to me, "Do not do it! I am a fellow servant with you and with your brothers who hold to the testimony of Jesus. Worship God! For the testimony of Jesus is the spirit of prophecy."

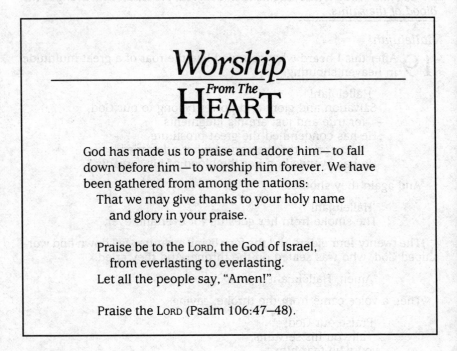

Worship
From The
HEART

God has made us to praise and adore him—to fall
down before him—to worship him forever. We have
been gathered from among the nations:
  That we may give thanks to your holy name
    and glory in your praise.

Praise be to the Lord, the God of Israel,
  from everlasting to everlasting.
Let all the people say, "Amen!"

Praise the Lord (Psalm 106:47–48).

DECEMBER 25

The Marriage Supper of the Lamb

Let us rejoice and be glad and give him glory! For the wedding of the Lamb has come, and his bride has made herself ready (Revelation 19:7).

In Revelation 19, John describes the marriage supper of the Lamb—and you're invited! In preparation for that gala event, says John, your deeds, your conduct, your life of service on earth—all help to weave the fine linen for the wedding dress Christ's bride will wear.

While you're waiting, don't lose heart wondering why God waits to deal with evil and the enemies who oppose him. Take careful note of Clarence Macartney's wise observations.

Walk With Clarence Macartney

"We find comfort in the thought that God is able to bring good out of evil, but still we ask: Is God not omnipotent? Is not God all good? If so, why did He permit evil? Why doesn't He destroy it now?

"The great answer that the Bible gives us, and the answer of this vision, is the certainty of the overthrow of evil. When Robinson Crusoe's man Friday wanted to know why God did not destroy the devil, the answer that Crusoe finally gave him was the right answer, and the only answer, and the great answer: 'God *will* destroy him.'

"We see the unfolding of the long and bloody panorama of history, humanity's aspiration of the best and its doing of the worst. We also see the church in ceaseless battle with the beast. But that is not all we see. 'Then cometh the end.' We see the Lamb of God standing upon Mount Zion."

Walk Closer to God

The wonderful marriage celebration John describes will take place. God has promised. And you'll be there to join in the festivities!

But it's not an event to be taken lightly. "And his bride has made herself ready. Fine linen, bright and clean, was given her to wear." (Fine linen stands for the righteous acts of the saints) (Revelation 19:7–8).

Only those properly attired in righteousness will be ready to meet the bridegroom, the Lamb of God. Is your wardrobe "pressed and prepared"?

DECEMBER 26

📖 Walk in the Word
Revelation 19:11–21

John sees the conquering Christ as King of kings and Lord of lords; he is gathering the armies of heaven to bring final defeat to the beast and to the kings of the earth.

The Rider on the White Horse

[11]I saw heaven standing open and there before me was a white horse, whose rider is called Faithful and True. With justice he judges and makes war. [12]His eyes are like blazing fire, and on his head are many crowns. He has a name written on him that no one knows but he himself. [13]He is dressed in a robe dipped in blood, and his name is the Word of God. [14]The armies of heaven were following him, riding on white horses and dressed in fine linen, white and clean. [15]Out of his mouth comes a sharp sword with which to strike down the nations. "He will rule them with an iron scepter."[a] He treads the winepress of the fury of the wrath of God Almighty. [16]On his robe and on his thigh he has this name written:

KING OF KINGS AND LORD OF LORDS.

[17]And I saw an angel standing in the sun, who cried in a loud voice to all the birds flying in midair, "Come, gather together for the great supper of God, [18]so that you may eat the flesh of kings, generals, and mighty men, of horses and their riders, and the flesh of all people, free and slave, small and great."

[19]Then I saw the beast and the kings of the earth and their armies gathered together to make war against the rider on the horse and his army. [20]But the beast was captured, and with him the false prophet who had performed the miraculous signs on his behalf. With these signs he had deluded those who had received the mark of the beast and worshiped his image. The two of them were thrown alive into the fiery lake of burning sulfur. [21]The rest of them were killed with the sword that came out of the mouth of the rider on the horse, and all the birds gorged themselves on their flesh.

[a]15 Psalm 2:9

The Thrill of Victory

> On his robe and on his thigh he has this name written: KING OF KINGS AND LORD OF LORDS (Revelation 19:16).

"Oh, the times, they are a-changin'." The successes of atheistic humanism read like a devil's litany: God has been expelled from the public schools; abortion is still a legal "choice"; pornography is viewed as harmless; homosexuality as healthy. Christianity is grossly misrepresented and ridiculed in the media.

In times like these, the temptation is to withdraw in silence—become a "secret agent" for Jesus. But do you know how God reacts to those who conspire against him? He laughs (Psalm 2:4). We can laugh, too, even when God's enemies laugh at us, for we know the one who is going to laugh last. B.B. Warfield encourages us to take comfort in this: Christ is going to win.

Walk With B.B. Warfield

"The section opens with a vision of the victory of the Word of God, the King of kings and Lord of lords over all his enemies. We see him come forth from heaven girded for war, followed by the armies of heaven. The birds of the air are summoned to the feast of corpses that shall be prepared for them. The armies of the enemy—the beasts and the kings of the earth—are gathered against him and are totally destroyed.

"It is a vivid picture of a complete victory, an entire conquest, that we have here; and all the imagery of war and battle is employed to give it life. This is the symbol. The thing symbolized obviously is the complete victory of the Son of God over all the hosts of wickedness. Christ is to conquer the earth: He is to overcome all his enemies."

Walk Closer to God

These times are not unique. God's people have often been surrounded by wickedness. The Psalmist asked, "Why, O LORD, do you stand far off?"(Psalm 10:1). He took courage in God's coming victory: "The LORD is King for ever and ever; the nations will perish from his land" (Psalm 10:16).

Likewise, the apostle Paul wrote: "God is just: He will pay back trouble to those who trouble you . . . when the Lord Jesus is revealed from heaven in blazing fire" (2 Thessalonians 1:6–7).

Do you have this same confidence? Make a habit of meditating on Christ's victory, and you will be thrilled!

DECEMBER 27

Walk in the Word
Revelation 20:1–6

When the devil is cast into the Abyss and locked there for a thousand years, the martyred saints come to life and reign with Christ during that millennium.

The Thousand Years

20 And I saw an angel coming down out of heaven, having the key to the Abyss and holding in his hand a great chain. ²He seized the dragon, that ancient serpent, who is the devil, or Satan, and bound him for a thousand years. ³He threw him into the Abyss, and locked and sealed it over him, to keep him from deceiving the nations anymore until the thousand years were ended. After that, he must be set free for a short time.

⁴I saw thrones on which were seated those who had been given authority to judge. And I saw the souls of those who had been beheaded because of their testimony for Jesus and because of the word of God. They had not worshiped the beast or his image and had not received his mark on their foreheads or their hands. They came to life and reigned with Christ a thousand years. ⁵(The rest of the dead did not come to life until the thousand years were ended.) This is the first resurrection. ⁶Blessed and holy are those who have part in the first resurrection. The second death has no power over them, but they will be priests of God and of Christ and will reign with him for a thousand years.

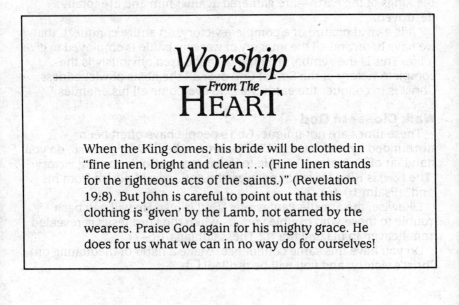

Worship
From The
HEART

When the King comes, his bride will be clothed in "fine linen, bright and clean . . . (Fine linen stands for the righteous acts of the saints.)" (Revelation 19:8). But John is careful to point out that this clothing is 'given' by the Lamb, not earned by the wearers. Praise God again for his mighty grace. He does for us what we can in no way do for ourselves!

The Glory That Makes Burdens Bearable

They came to life and reigned with Christ a thousand years (Revelation 20:4).

Although some passages of the book of Revelation are difficult to understand, many verses—like small diamonds of encouragement—shine brightly with comfort.

As John switches his focus from the present to the future, from this world to the next, he discovers encouragement to face each fresh challenge to his faith. Martin Luther also has these encouraging observations for those facing unjust suffering.

Walk With Martin Luther

"If we consider the great glory of the future life, it would not be at all difficult for us to bear the vexations of this world. But when Christ comes to judge the living and the dead and we experience these blessings, everyone will have to say for himself: 'Shame on me!'

"If I believe the Word, I shall on the last day not only gladly have suffered ordinary temptations, insults, imprisonment, but I shall also say: 'Oh, if I had only thrown myself under the feet of all the godless for the sake of the great glory which I now see revealed and which has come to me through the merit of Christ.'

"Paul well says, 'I consider that our present sufferings are not worth comparing with the glory that will be revealed in us' (Romans 8:18)."

Walk Closer to God

Remember Stephen, perhaps the first martyr of the New Testament church. Even as the rocks were hurtling toward him, Stephen looked up to heaven and saw Jesus at God's right hand. Then, like his Lord, he died praying for those who were taking his life.

Chances are you won't be stoned for your faith, but don't be surprised if you feel the heat as you live out your faith.

One message permeates nearly every chapter of John's book: Victory is assured. So take heart . . . look up . . . wait patiently. The glory to be revealed in us makes any burden bearable. ♡

DECEMBER 28

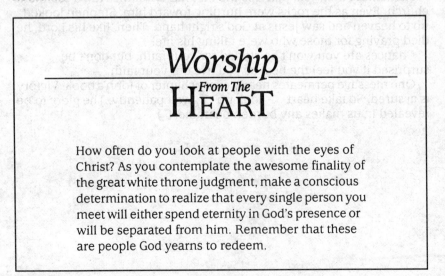 Walk in the Word
Revelation 20:7–15

After the thousand years, Satan is given one final chance to deceive the nations but to no avail; then, in the great white throne judgment, all those whose names are not in the book of life are thrown into the lake of fire.

Satan's Doom

⁷When the thousand years are over, Satan will be released from his prison ⁸and will go out to deceive the nations in the four corners of the earth—Gog and Magog—to gather them for battle. In number they are like the sand on the seashore. ⁹They marched across the breadth of the earth and surrounded the camp of God's people, the city he loves. But fire came down from heaven and devoured them. ¹⁰And the devil, who deceived them, was thrown into the lake of burning sulfur, where the beast and the false prophet had been thrown. They will be tormented day and night for ever and ever.

The Dead Are Judged

¹¹Then I saw a great white throne and him who was seated on it. Earth and sky fled from his presence, and there was no place for them. ¹²And I saw the dead, great and small, standing before the throne, and books were opened. Another book was opened, which is the book of life. The dead were judged according to what they had done as recorded in the books. ¹³The sea gave up the dead that were in it, and death and Hades gave up the dead that were in them, and each person was judged according to what he had done. ¹⁴Then death and Hades were thrown into the lake of fire. The lake of fire is the second death. ¹⁵If anyone's name was not found written in the book of life, he was thrown into the lake of fire.

Worship From The HEART

How often do you look at people with the eyes of Christ? As you contemplate the awesome finality of the great white throne judgment, make a conscious determination to realize that every single person you meet will either spend eternity in God's presence or will be separated from him. Remember that these are people God yearns to redeem.

Admitted to the Realm of Hidden Treasure

> And books were opened. Another book was opened, which is the book of life (Revelation 20:12).

You heard the Good News; you believed the Good News; but you have yet to see all that the Good News holds in store.

Hoped for, yet not seen. John Calvin explores some of the reasons why you still have some surprises to come.

Walk With John Calvin

"Until the last day when the books will be opened, there is no possible way in which the things pertaining to our salvation can be possessed by us, unless we can transcend the reach of our own intellect and raise our eye above all worldly objects; in short, unless we surpass ourselves.

"Such mysteries of God cannot be discerned in themselves, but we behold them only in his Word. But how can the mind rise to such a perception of the divine goodness without at the same time being wholly inflamed with love to God?

"The abundance of joy which God has treasured up for those who fear him cannot be truly known without making a most powerful impression.

"Hence it is not strange that no sinister, perverse heart ever experiences this feeling—a feeling by which we are admitted to the most hidden treasures of God and the holiest recesses of his kingdom, which must not be profaned by the entrance of a heart that is impure."

Walk Closer to God

To realize fully the wonders of salvation would be more than your finite mind could comprehend. Now you experience only a taste of the banquet you'll enjoy forever.

Peter describes it this way: "Praise be to the God and Father of our Lord Jesus Christ! In his great mercy he has given us new birth into a living hope . . . an inheritance . . . kept in heaven for you, who through faith are shielded by God's power until the coming of the salvation that is ready to be revealed in the last time" (1 Peter 1:3–5).

God will one day reveal the full scope and grandeur of salvation. And you can rest assured it will be well worth the wait. ◯

December 29

Walk in the Word
Revelation 21:1–8

John sees the New Jerusalem coming down out of heaven, prepared as a bride; and Jesus promises his inheritance to all those who have come to him.

The New Jerusalem

21 Then I saw a new heaven and a new earth, for the first heaven and the first earth had passed away, and there was no longer any sea. ²I saw the Holy City, the new Jerusalem, coming down out of heaven from God, prepared as a bride beautifully dressed for her husband. ³And I heard a loud voice from the throne saying, "Now the dwelling of God is with men, and he will live with them. They will be his people, and God himself will be with them and be their God. ⁴He will wipe every tear from their eyes. There will be no more death or mourning or crying or pain, for the old order of things has passed away."

⁵He who was seated on the throne said, "I am making everything new!" Then he said, "Write this down, for these words are trustworthy and true."

⁶He said to me: "It is done. I am the Alpha and the Omega, the Beginning and the End. To him who is thirsty I will give to drink without cost from the spring of the water of life. ⁷He who overcomes will inherit all this, and I will be his God and he will be my son. ⁸But the cowardly, the unbelieving, the vile, the murderers, the sexually immoral, those who practice magic arts, the idolaters and all liars—their place will be in the fiery lake of burning sulfur. This is the second death."

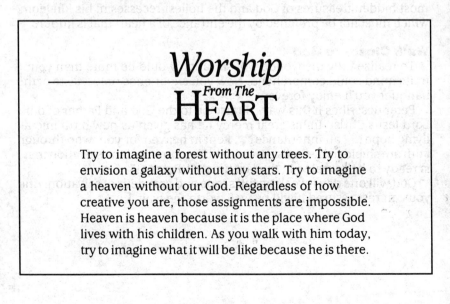

Worship
From The
Heart

Try to imagine a forest without any trees. Try to envision a galaxy without any stars. Try to imagine a heaven without our God. Regardless of how creative you are, those assignments are impossible. Heaven is heaven because it is the place where God lives with his children. As you walk with him today, try to imagine what it will be like because he is there.

He Who Is Worthy of First Place in Your Heart

He said to me: "It is done. I am the Alpha and Omega, the Beginning and the End" (Revelation 21:6).

God at the beginning. God at the end. And God at work in between.

The Bible speaks clearly of the Creator intimately involved in his world—preserving it, redeeming it. It also speaks of a Father who cares for each of his children, looking after their concerns from A to Z.

Clarence Macartney calls you to consider your commitment to the one who is your all in all.

Walk With Clarence Macartney

"Christ is the Alpha and Omega of the believer. He is the Author and Finisher of our faith.

"His Word is our rule and law, his life our example and pattern, his death on the cross our salvation, his presence our joy, his smile our reward, and to be with him in glory is our eternal hope.

"What place does Christ take in your life? To what degree can you say, 'He is for me the Alpha and the Omega, the First and the Last, the Beginning and the End'?

"He who is the Lord of the ages, the King of time, and the Adored of the angels, is worthy of the first place in your life. Will you give that place to him?

"No one ever did that and lived to regret it. On the contrary, you will be able to say, as John Bunyan did: 'His love to me has been most sweet, and his countenance I have more desired than they that have most desired the light of the sun.'"

Walk Closer to God

Ask a real estate agent for the three keys to good investments, and you'll hear this response: "Location, location, location."

Ask a coach three reasons for his winning season, and he'll tell you, "Practice, practice, practice."

Ask a Christian for the top three priorities in his life, and you should hear, "Jesus, Jesus, Jesus!"

Christ is Lord over birth; he is Lord over death. And he is Lord over everything in between. He wants to do more than fit among your priorities; he wants to set your priorities.

DECEMBER 30

◤ Walk in the Word
Revelation 21:9–27

As an angel shows John the bride, the wife of the Lamb, he sees the layout of the New Jerusalem, a city whose lights are God and the Lamb.

⁹One of the seven angels who had the seven bowls full of the seven last plagues came and said to me, "Come, I will show you the bride, the wife of the Lamb." ¹⁰And he carried me away in the Spirit to a mountain great and high, and showed me the Holy City, Jerusalem, coming down out of heaven from God. ¹¹It shone with the glory of God, and its brilliance was like that of a very precious jewel, like a jasper, clear as crystal. ¹²It had a great, high wall with twelve gates, and with twelve angels at the gates. On the gates were written the names of the twelve tribes of Israel. ¹³There were three gates on the east, three on the north, three on the south and three on the west. ¹⁴The wall of the city had twelve foundations, and on them were the names of the twelve apostles of the Lamb.

¹⁵The angel who talked with me had a measuring rod of gold to measure the city, its gates and its walls. ¹⁶The city was laid out like a square, as long as it was wide. He measured the city with the rod and found it to be 12,000 stadia*ᵃ* in length, and as wide and high as it is long. ¹⁷He measured its wall and it was 144 cubits*ᵇ* thick,*ᶜ* by man's measurement, which the angel was using. ¹⁸The wall was made of jasper, and the city of pure gold, as pure as glass. ¹⁹The foundations of the city walls were decorated with every kind of precious stone. The first foundation was jasper, the second sapphire, the third chalcedony, the fourth emerald, ²⁰the fifth sardonyx, the sixth carnelian, the seventh chrysolite, the eighth beryl, the ninth topaz, the tenth chrysoprase, the eleventh jacinth, and the twelfth amethyst.*ᵈ* ²¹The twelve gates were twelve pearls, each gate made of a single pearl. The great street of the city was of pure gold, like transparent glass.

²²I did not see a temple in the city, because the Lord God Almighty and the Lamb are its temple. ²³The city does not need the sun or the moon to shine on it, for the glory of God gives it light, and the Lamb is its lamp. ²⁴The nations will walk by its light, and the kings of the earth will bring their splendor into it. ²⁵On no day will its gates ever be shut, for there will be no night there. ²⁶The glory and honor of the nations will be brought into it. ²⁷Nothing impure will ever enter it, nor will anyone who does what is shameful or deceitful, but only those whose names are written in the Lamb's book of life.

ᵃ16 That is, about 1,400 miles (about 2,200 kilometers)   *ᵇ17* That is, about 200 feet (about 65 meters)   *ᶜ17* Or *high*   *ᵈ20* The precise identification of some of these precious stones is uncertain.

Citizens of the Holy City

I did not see a temple in the city, because the Lord God Almighty and the Lamb are its temple (Revelation 21:22).

For some, city life evokes the excitement and challenge of being in a fast-paced beehive of business and opportunity. For others, it represents crime, squalor, poverty, unfulfilled dreams, dashed hopes, terrible loneliness. But one city will change all that—the holy Jerusalem—the great city of God that John describes in Revelation 21.

To understand the uniqueness of this city, says Alexander Maclaren, you must reverse the miseries of earth.

Walk With Alexander Maclaren

"All turns on two great thoughts—the blessed closeness of perfect and eternal union between God and men, and the consequent dawning of a new day in which all human ills shall be swept away.

"When the church was on the old earth, God dwelt with his people in reality, but, alas, with many breaks in their relationship caused by his people defiling the temple. But in the future everything that was symbolic shall be spiritual reality, and there will be no separation between the God who tabernacles among his people and the people in whom he dwells.

"His presence drives away all evils, as the risen moon clears the sky of clouds. How can sorrow, or crying, or pain, or death live where he is?

"Reverse the miseries of earth, and you know something of the joys of heaven. But begin with God's presence, or you will know nothing of its most joyful joy."

Walk Closer to God

Think of John's description as a travelogue of the heavenly Jerusalem:

A city in which there is no temple, for the Lamb is personally present.

No sun or moon, for the Lamb is its light.

No night, for the Son always shines there.

No defilement, for holiness is its hallmark.

Best of all, there is no waiting list to become one of its citizens. Now, wouldn't you agree that's a city you'll enjoy living in—forever?

DECEMBER 31

📖 Walk in the Word
Revelation 22

After John concludes his description of the new Jerusalem, Jesus himself speaks directly, assuring his people of his imminent return, for which the church hopes.

The River of Life

22 Then the angel showed me the river of the water of life, as clear as crystal, flowing from the throne of God and of the Lamb [2]down the middle of the great street of the city. On each side of the river stood the tree of life, bearing twelve crops of fruit, yielding its fruit every month. And the leaves of the tree are for the healing of the nations. [3]No longer will there be any curse. The throne of God and of the Lamb will be in the city, and his servants will serve him. [4]They will see his face, and his name will be on their foreheads. [5]There will be no more night. They will not need the light of a lamp or the light of the sun, for the Lord God will give them light. And they will reign for ever and ever.

[6]The angel said to me, "These words are trustworthy and true. The Lord, the God of the spirits of the prophets, sent his angel to show his servants the things that must soon take place."

Jesus Is Coming

[7]"Behold, I am coming soon! Blessed is he who keeps the words of the prophecy in this book."

[8]I, John, am the one who heard and saw these things. And when I had heard and seen them, I fell down to worship at the feet of the angel who had been showing them to me. [9]But he said to me, "Do not do it! I am a fellow servant with you and with your brothers the prophets and of all who keep the words of this book. Worship God!"

[10]Then he told me, "Do not seal up the words of the prophecy of this book, because the time is near. [11]Let him who does wrong continue to do wrong; let him who is vile continue to be vile; let him who does right continue to do right; and let him who is holy continue to be holy."

[12]"Behold, I am coming soon! My reward is with me, and I will give to everyone according to what he has done. [13]I am the Alpha and the Omega, the First and the Last, the Beginning and the End.

[14]"Blessed are those who wash their robes, that they may have the right to the tree of life and may go through the gates into the city. [15]Outside are the dogs, those who practice magic arts, the sexually immoral, the murderers, the idolaters and everyone who loves and practices falsehood.

[16]"I, Jesus, have sent my angel to give you[a] this testimony for the churches. I am the Root and the Offspring of David, and the bright Morning Star."

DECEMBER 31

¹⁷The Spirit and the bride say, "Come!" And let him who hears say, "Come!" Whoever is thirsty, let him come; and whoever wishes, let him take the free gift of the water of life.

¹⁸I warn everyone who hears the words of the prophecy of this book: If anyone adds anything to them, God will add to him the plagues described in this book. ¹⁹And if anyone takes words away from this book of prophecy, God will take away from him his share in the tree of life and in the holy city, which are described in this book.

²⁰He who testifies to these things says, "Yes, I am coming soon." Amen. Come, Lord Jesus.

²¹The grace of the Lord Jesus be with God's people. Amen.

a16 The Greek is plural.

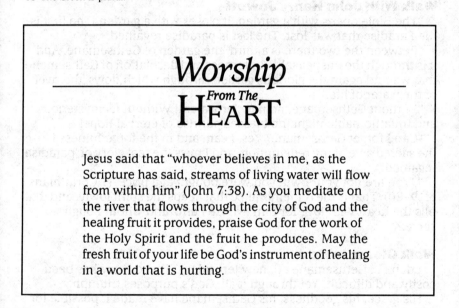

Worship

From The
HEART

Jesus said that "whoever believes in me, as the Scripture has said, streams of living water will flow from within him" (John 7:38). As you meditate on the river that flows through the city of God and the healing fruit it provides, praise God for the work of the Holy Spirit and the fruit he produces. May the fresh fruit of your life be God's instrument of healing in a world that is hurting.

DECEMBER 31

Home at Last in God's Beautiful Garden

Then the angel showed me the river of the water of life, as clear as crystal, flowing from the throne of God and of the Lamb (Revelation 22:1).

Throughout history the garden has been the scene of significant life-and-death struggles. In a garden Eve made a decision that bore the fruit of death. In a garden the Savior agonized over a decision that would mean life eternal for all who believed.

John Henry Jowett probes the significance of that fateful night in a garden called Gethsemane.

Walk With John Henry Jowett

"The Bible opens with a garden. It closes with a garden. The first is the Paradise that was lost. The last is paradise regained.

"Between the two there is a third, the garden of Gethsemane. And it is through the unspeakable bitterness and desolation of Gethsemane that we find again the glorious garden through which flows 'the river of the water of life.'

"Without Gethsemane, no new Jerusalem! Without its mysterious and unfathomable night, no blessed sunrise of eternal hope!

"Can I forget Gethsemane? Yes, I can; and in the forgetfulness I lose the sacred awe of my redemption, and I miss the real glory of 'paradise regained.'

" 'You are not your own; you were bought at a price' (1 Corinthians 6:19–20). That is the remembrance that keeps the spirit lowly, and that fills the heart with love for him 'whose I am,' and whom I ought to serve."

Walk Closer to God

Eden . . . Gethsemane . . . new Jerusalem. The journey has been costly and difficult. Yet through it all, God's purposes triumph.

His grace, his goodness, his Gethsemane have made it possible for you to dwell in the garden of God—forever.

A garden in which there is no curse or darkness, only face-to-face fellowship with the Creator.

To forget such a gift might seem unthinkable. To understand fully such a gift—unfathomable. To spend this day thanking him for it— unbeatable! ◖

ACKNOWLEDGMENTS
INDEXES

Acknowledgments

The editors wish to express appreciation for permission to reprint excerpts from:

The Greatest Texts of the Bible, by Clarence E. MacCartney, published by Abingdon Press, Nashville, TN.

Prayer, by O. Hallesby, published by Augsburg Fortress Publishers, Minneapolis, MN.

A Treasury of W. Graham Scroggie, published by Baker Book House.

Daily Devotions from Spiritual Giants of the Past, published by Baker Book House.

Comfort for Christians, by A. W. Pink, published by Baker Book House.

Renewed Day by Day, by A. W. Tozer. Used by permission of Christian Publications, 3825 Hartzdale Drive, Camp Hill, PA 17011, 1 (800) 233-4443.

John Doe: Disciple, by Peter Marshall, published by Chosen Books, Lincoln, VA.

Specified excerpts from the works of C. S. Lewis reprinted by permission of Collins Publishers, London.

God's Covenants, God's Discipline, God's Glory Vol. 4, by Donald Grey Barnhouse, published by Wm. B. Eerdmans Publishing Co., Grand Rapids, MI.

Awake O America, by W. Biederwolf, published by Wm. B. Eerdmans Publishing Co., Grand Rapids, MI.

The Continual Burnt Offering, Lectures on the Book of Acts, Lectures on the Revelation, Notes on James and Peter, Second Epistle to the Corinthians, by H. A. Ironside. Used by permission of Loizeaux Brothers, Inc., Neptune, New Jersey.

The Book of Revelation, by Wm. R. Newell. Used by permission of Moody Press.

An Exposition of the Whole Bible, by G. Campbell Morgan, copyright 1959, renewed 1987. Used by permission of Fleming H. Revell Company.

The Gospel According to Matthew, by G. Campbell Morgan, copyright 1929. Used by permission of Fleming H. Revell Company.

Searchlights From the Word, and *Studies In the Four Gospels,* by G. Campbell Morgan. Used by permission of Fleming H. Revell Company.

Index of Authors

This index of authors will give you some information about each Christian leader who is quoted in the Closer Walk devotions and will give you the page numbers where their quotations can be found.

James Stalker (1848–1927)
Scottish preacher and scholar who wrote about the life of Christ.
Page 307

J. Hudson Taylor (1832–1905)
English founder of the China Inland Mission.
Pages 35, 49, 153, 344, 462, 501, 607, 659, 753, 825

W. H. Griffith Thomas (1861–1924)
English-born preacher and theologian.
Pages 264, 471, 507, 517

Thomas à Kempis (1380–1471)
Little-known author of the classic *The Imitation of Christ*.
Pages 71, 446, 493, 554, 857

R. A. Torrey (1856–1928)
American evangelist and associate of Dwight L. Moody.
Pages 347, 672

A. W. Tozer (1897–1963)
American preacher and prolific author on spiritual themes.
Pages 173, 224, 238, 374, 633, 819, 863

B. B. Warfield (1851–1921)
Beloved professor of Systematic Theology at Princeton Theological Seminary.
Page 943

Isaac Watts (1674–1748)
Author of some six hundred hymns, many of which are still popular today.
Page 859

Charles Wesley (1707–1788)
One of the most prolific hymnists of the Christian faith.
Page 916

John Wesley (1703–1791)
Englishman who founded the Methodist Church.
Pages 20, 469, 731

Susannah Wesley (1669–1742)
Textbook author and teacher, but best remembered as the mother of John and Charles Wesley.
Page 651

B. F. Westcott (1825–1901)
English scholar and missionary advocate.
Page 774

George Whitefield (1716–1778)
English evangelist who popularized open-air preaching and was renowned for his speaking ability.
Page 209

Alexander Whyte (1837–1921)
Scottish pastor, professor, church leader.
Pages 52, 635

More complete biographies can be found about the following authors on the page listed with their name:

Subject Index

This subject index will direct you to Closer Walk devotions covering a wide range of issues, concerns and topics facing you in your daily walk with God.